Who Built America?

American Social History Project
The City University of New York

Who Built America?

WORKING PEOPLE AND THE NATION'S ECONOMY, POLITICS, CULTURE, AND SOCIETY

VOLUME TWO SINCE 1877

Nelson Lichtenstein, University of Virginia
Susan Strasser, University of Delaware
Roy Rosenzweig, George Mason University

Executive Editor: **Stephen Brier**, The Graduate Center, City University of New York

Visual Editor: **Joshua Brown**, The Graduate Center, City University of New York

Based on the original edition authored by:
Joshua Freeman, Nelson Lichtenstein, Stephen Brier, David Bensman, Susan Porter Benson, David Brundage, Bret Eynon, Bruce Levine, and Bryan Palmer

Bedford / St. Martin's
Boston ◆ New York

Who Built America?
Volume 2: Since 1877

Printed in the United States of America.
ISBN: 1-57259-303-2
Printing: 9 8 7 6
Year: 07 06

Publisher: Catherine Woods
Sponsoring editor: Laura Edwards
Development editor: Judith Kromm
Marketing manager: Jenna Bookin Barry
Production editors: Margaret Comaskey, Tracey Kuehn
Production manager: Barbara Anne Seixas
Design director: Barbara Rusin
Production: Progressive Publishing Alternatives
Composition: Progressive Information Technologies
Printing and binding: R. R. Donnelley and Sons

Cover credits (left to right):
Row 1: Pare Lorentz, *The Roosevelt Year: A Photographic Record* (1934)—American Social History Project; *1199 News,* Local 1199, Health Care Employees Union, New York City; Lewis Hine, January 1911—International Museum of Photography at George Eastman House, Rochester, New York.
Row 2: War Relocation Authority Photo 210-GID-B3, from Edward H. Spicer, Asael T. Hansen, Katherine Luomala, and Marvin R. Opler, *Impounded People* (1969)—Used by permission of Rosamond B. Spicer; Sophia Smith Collection, Smith College; The Bancroft Library, University of California, Berkeley.
Row 3: Dorothea Lange—Prints and Photographs Division, Library of Congress; Ashfield Historical Society, Ashfield, Massachusetts; Solomon d. Butcher, 1885—Butcher Collection, Nebraska Historical Society.
Row 4: State Historical Society of Wisconsin; Walker Evans, 1936—Prints and Photographs Division, Library of Congress; Schomburg Center for Research in Black Culture, New York Public Library, Astor, Lenox, and Tilden Foundations.
Background: *Photo-History* (July 1937)—Prints and Photographs Division, Library of Congress.

For information, contact: Bedford/St. Martin's, 75 Arlington Street, Boston, MA 02116
617-399-4000
www.bedfordstmartins.com

To the late Joe Murphy, former chancellor of the City University of New York, who was a passionate believer in educating working people and a stalwart supporter of the American Social History Project and *Who Built America?*

Contents

1 Prologue

16 **part one:** Monopoly and Upheaval (1877-1914)

20 **chapter 1:** Progress and Poverty: Economy, Society, and Politics in the Gilded Age (1877 – 1893)

22 Building a Railroad System
25 Explosive and Unstable Development
27 The Emergence of Urban-Industrial Life
32 The Remaking of the American Working Class
35 Working Conditions
37 Businessmen Seek Control
41 New Management Systems
43 Businessmen Look To Politics
47 The New South
50 Crop Liens, Debt, and Sharecropping
54 Conflict on the Plains
60 Western Farming and Ranching
64 Extractive Industries and Exploited Workers
68 Capitalism and the Meaning of Democracy
70 The Years in Review
72 Suggested Readings
73 And on the World Wide Web

74 **chapter 2:** Community and Conflict: Working People Respond to Industrial Capitalism (1877 – 1893)

76 Neighborhood Cultures
80 Working Women at Home
82 Religion and Community
85 The Workingman's Club
88 The Labor Community
90 "Union for All": The Knights of Labor
97 1886: The Eight-Hour Movement and Haymarket Square
101 The Decline of the Knights
103 Politics and the Workingman
106 The Rise of the AFL

Contents

109 Class Conflict in the Country
112 Bloody Battles at Homestead
115 The Years in Review
117 Suggested Readings
119 And on the World Wide Web

120 chapter 3: The Producing Classes and the Money Power: A Decade of Hard Times, Struggles, and Defeat (1893–1904)

122 The Depression of the 1890s
124 Workers on the March
125 Pullman: Solidarity and Defeat
129 The Farmers' Alliance and the People's Party
135 The Cross of Gold
139 Jim Crow
144 The New Immigrants
146 Nativism and Immigration Restriction
149 A Splendid Little War
152 An Overseas Empire
156 Business on the Rebound
158 Organized Labor in a Time of Recovery
161 End of a Century; End of an Era
161 The Years in Review
164 Suggested Readings
165 And on the World Wide Web

166 chapter 4: Change and Continuity in Daily Life (1900–1914)

169 Mass Production
170 Scientific Management
172 Welfare Capitalism
175 New Standards of Living
177 Wiring a Nation
179 Marketing to the Masses
182 Leisure Time and Public Recreation
185 Entertainment for the Masses
188 Uplifting the Masses
192 White Collars and Middle-Class Values
194 Women Making Money
197 Fordism
199 Change and Continuity

201 The Years in Review
204 Suggested Readings
205 And on the World Wide Web

206 **chapter 5: Radicals and Reformers in the Progressive Era (1900–1914)**

209 Andru Karnegi and Mr. Rucevelt: Simplified Spelling and the Contours of Progressivism
213 Social Settlements and Municipal Housekeeping
216 Women's Political Culture
219 Woman Suffrage
221 Factory Reform and the Conditions of Labor
224 The Garment Industry and Working Women's Activism
227 Socialists, Marxists, and Anarchists
229 Militant Communities
234 Local and State Reform Politics
237 Progressivism and Participation
239 Reform Comes to National Politics
243 The Highpoint—and the Limits—of Progressivism
247 Toward the Modern State
249 The Years in Review
251 Suggested Readings
253 And on the World Wide Web

254 **part two: War, Depression, and Industrial Unionism (1914–1945)**

258 **chapter 6: Wars for Democracy (1914–1919)**

260 From Assassination in the Balkans to War in Europe
263 Total War in Europe
264 American Neutrality and American Business
266 The Debate over American Involvement
269 Toward Intervention
271 Mobilizing the Home Front
274 Wartime Labor Gains
276 The Great Migration
282 Tension on the Southern Border
286 Women Workers and Woman Suffrage
288 Working-Class Protest and Political Radicalism
292 Repression and Nativism

295 American Troops and the Battles They Fought
298 Wilson and the Shape of the Peace
301 Postwar Strikes and Race Riots
305 The Red Scare
308 Toward a Postwar Society
309 The Years in Review
311 Suggested Readings
313 And on the World Wide Web

314 **chapter 7: A New Era (1920–1929)**

316 Conservatism and Corruption in Political Life
318 The Business of America Is Business
319 The United States and the World
323 Shifts in Manufacturing
324 Economic Growth and Instability
327 Daily Life in the New Consumer Culture
329 Autos for the Masses
333 The Creation of Customers
334 Mass Culture: Radio, Music, and the Movies
338 Women as Workers and Consumers
342 Agriculture in Crisis
345 Organized Labor in Decline
347 African-American Life in the 1920s
353 Cultural Conflicts
360 Hoover and the Crash
362 The Years in Review
364 Suggested Readings
365 And on the World Wide Web

366 **chapter 8: The Great Depression and the First New Deal (1929–1935)**

368 The Onset of the Great Depression
371 Hard Times
376 Depression and Drought in the Farm Belt
380 Hoover's Response to the Crisis
385 Self-Help and Its Limits
387 Poor People's Movements
392 Roosevelt's Promise of a New Deal
396 Financial Rescue and Emergency
398 Agricultural Supports and Industrial Codes
402 The New Deal in the South and West

404 Section 7a and the Revival of Organized Labor
407 The New Union Leaders
408 A Wave of Strikes
415 The Collapse of the First New Deal
416 Populist Critics of the New Deal
419 The Years in Review
421 Suggested Readings
423 And on the World Wide Web

424 chapter 9: Labor Democratizes America (1935–1939)

425 An Expanded Jobs Program
427 The Social Security Act
431 The Wagner Act
432 The Committee for Industrial Organizations
434 The Roosevelt Landslide
439 The Flint Sit-Down Strike
443 Industrial Unionism at High Tide
448 Women's Place in the New Unions and the New Deal
452 The New Deal and Popular Culture
459 The African-American Struggle for Equal Rights
463 Backlash Against Labor and the New Deal
467 Defeat of the New Deal in the South
471 Labor Divided and Besieged
473 The "Roosevelt Recession"
476 The Legacies of the New Deal and the CIO
477 The Years in Review
479 Suggested Readings
481 And on the World Wide Web

482 chapter 10: A Nation Transformed: The United States in World War II (1939–1946)

483 Militarism and Fascism Abroad
486 From Isolationism to Internationalism
490 The End of the New Deal
493 War in the Pacific and in Europe
496 Life in the Armed Forces
503 Mobilizing the Home Front
505 The Wartime Industrial Boom
507 Women in the Workforce
511 The Limits of Pluralism
515 Origins of the Modern Civil Rights Movement
520 Labor's War at Home
522 Victory in Europe

525 Japan's Surrender
528 Conversion to a Peacetime Economy
535 The Years in Review
537 Suggested Readings
539 And on the World Wide Web

540 **part three: Cold War America—and After (1945–1999)**

544 **chapter 11: The Cold War Boom (1946–1960)**

545 Origins of the Cold War
548 The Division of Europe
551 The Cold War in Asia
555 Labor Loses Ground
559 The 1948 Election
562 The Weapon of Anti-Communism
568 I Like Ike
570 The Postwar Economic Boom
575 A Classless Society?
576 The Labor–Management Accord
581 Flight from the Farms
586 The Growth of the Service Sector
590 The Decline of Ethnicity
591 Suburban America
596 The Splintering of the Working Class
597 The World of *Father Knows Best*
601 The Years in Review
604 Suggested Readings
605 And on the World Wide Web

606 **chapter 12: The Rights Conscious 1960s**

608 Birth of the Civil Rights Movement
612 Freedom Now!
617 The Kennedy Administration
618 The Liberal Hour
622 The War on Poverty
626 The Riots and Black Power
630 Rights Consciousness in the Workplace
633 The Road to Vietnam
636 Escalation of the Vietnam War
640 The Antiwar Movement and the New Left
645 Rise of the Counterculture

649 1968: A Watershed Year
654 The Nixon Administration
657 The Environmental Movement
660 Pluralism in American Life
662 The Women's Movement
667 Militancy and Dissension in the Labor Movement
671 Political Polarization
674 The Watergate Crisis
677 The Years in Review
679 Suggested Readings
681 And on the World Wide Web

682 **chapter 13: Economic Adversity Transforms the Nation (1973–1989)**

683 End of the Postwar Boom
688 The New Shape of American Business
690 Stagflation Politics: From Nixon to Carter
695 The Collapse of Détente
698 Rise of the New Right
700 Revolt Against Taxes and Busing
703 Gender Politics
708 Ronald Reagan: Enter Stage Right
711 The Reagan Boom
715 The New Immigration
720 The Ranks of the Poor
724 The Labor Movement Under Fire
728 Reaganism in Triumph and at an Impasse
732 Culture Wars
734 The Reagan Legacy
735 The Years in Review
738 Suggested Readings
739 And on the World Wide Web

740 **chapter 14: The American People in an Age of Global Capitalism (1989–2000)**

742 End of the Cold War
745 George Bush's "New World Order"
749 A New Economy
756 The 1992 Election
759 The Clinton Administration
763 Health Care Reform
767 Challenge from the Right
770 New Leadership and New Ideas for the Labor Movement
774 On Trial: Gender, Race, and National Identity
778 The Impeachment and Trial of a President

781 At the Dawn of a New Century
783 The Years in Review
785 Suggested Readings
786 And on the World Wide Web

A-1 appendix

I-1 index

Preface

Who built the seven towers of Thebes?
The books are filled with the names of kings.
Was it kings who hauled the craggy blocks of stone? . . .
In the evening when the Chinese wall was finished,
Where did the masons go?

–Bertolt Brecht,

"Questions from a Worker Who Reads" (1935)

WHO BUILT AMERICA? surveys the nation's past from an important but often neglected perspective—the experiences of ordinary men and women and the role they have played in the making of modern America. It is not merely a documentation of the country's past presidents, politics, wars, and the life and values of the nation's elite, but focuses more on the fundamental social and economic conflicts in our history. *Who Built America?* challenges the notion that the vast majority of its citizens have always been united in a broad consensus about the nation's basic values and shared in its extraordinary prosperity.

In the past three decades or so, historians have made dramatic discoveries about the behavior and beliefs of groups traditionally slighted by their discipline: women; African Americans, enslaved and free; American Indians; factory and white-collar workers; and myriad immigrant groups. They have also unearthed a long and sustained history of conflict among Americans of different classes, races, national origins, and genders over the meaning of the American ideals of liberty and equality and over the distribution of the nation's enormous material wealth. Their findings have enabled historians to think and write differently about familiar topics, including the rise of industrial capitalism, U.S. overseas expansion, successive waves of internal migration and foreign immigration to the nation's cities, depression and war, the rise of industrial unionism, and the widening struggle for civil rights. With this new information, historians have been able to incorporate into the broader narrative of U.S. history the stories of those whose voices had been left out of traditional accounts.

This book grew out of the effort to reinterpret American history from "the bottom up." Its authors and editors are among those whose studies of workers, women, consumers, farmers, African Americans, and immigrants have helped to transform our understanding of the past. The first edition of the book was the work of the American Social History Project (ASHP), which was founded in 1981 by Herbert Gutman (a pioneer of "the new social history") and Stephen Brier to bring this research to the broadest possible audience. In addition to this book, ASHP has produced a wide range of accessible educational materials, in print, video, and digital media, and worked closely with college, high-school, and adult- and labor-education teachers to help them use these resources effectively in their classrooms.

THEMES

Who Built America? thus offers a uniquely wrought history of the United States. Its central focus and organizing themes are the changing nature of the work that built, sustained, and transformed American society over the course of four centuries and the changing conditions, experiences, outlooks, and conduct of the workers themselves. This focus permits the integration of the history of community, family, gender roles, race, and ethnicity into the more familiar history of politics and economic development. Exploring the history of the nation's laboring majority, moreover, also renders more intelligible the beliefs and actions of the nation's economic, political, and intellectual elite.

For the purposes of this book, we have defined the category of "working people" broadly. Throughout much of its history, the nation's actual workforce embraced a wide spectrum of people laboring in very different conditions and settings—free and unfree, small proprietor and propertyless wage earner, agricultural and domestic laborers, as well as industrial, commercial, clerical, service, and technical workers. Answering the question "who built America?" therefore requires attention not only to wage-earning industrial employees but also to indentured servants, slaves, tenants, sharecroppers, independent farm families, artisans, day laborers, clerks, domestic workers, outworkers, fast food workers and women and children performing unpaid family labor—in short, the great majority of the American population at every phase of the country's development.

Who Built America? departs from convention in other respects as well. Rather than avoiding controversy or strong intepretation, we have not shied away from controversial issues and have offered opinions that are sometimes critical of celebrated figures or dominant beliefs. Our view is that readers would rather encounter a clearly stated perspective, even if they disagree with it, instead of bland platitudes about the past.

STRUCTURE

This study is divided into two volumes. The principal theme of the first volume is the rise and subsequent decline of various precapitalist labor systems, especially racial slavery, and the parallel development and ultimate dominance of capitalism and its system of wage labor. The second volume carries the narrative and analysis to the present day. It considers the increasing significance of industrial capitalism and wage labor for the country's economy, social relations, domestic politics, foreign policy, and intellectual life during the nation's second century and focuses on the corresponding growth and recomposition of the American working class. A prologue sets the stage for this story by recapitulating the story of Reconstruction and the 1877 railroad strikes, which are also covered in the first volume. This volume's fourteen chapters are divided into three parts:

- Part One considers the years between the great railroad strikes of 1877 and the outbreak of war in Europe in 1914, exploring industrial capitalism's Gilded Age growth and the resulting rise of mass movements of protest, including the labor movement, Populism, and socialism. It also considers U.S. overseas expansion and the increasing racism and segregationist legislation that rolled back the gains won by African Americans in the Reconstruction era, the massive wave of immigration from eastern and southern Europe that transformed the nation's cities after 1900, the dramatic changes in popular culture and everyday life in the early part of the century, and the progressive movement that emerged in response to the nation's growing political and economic crises.
- Part Two surveys the turbulent decades between the two world wars, examining the unparalleled growth and power of U.S. political and economic institutions, and the continued recomposition of the American working class through a vast internal migration of Americans, black and white, from the rural South. Tracing the dramatic impact of the Great Depression, it details working people's unprecedented mobilization that gave birth to the industrial union movement and helped sustain the partial welfare state created by Franklin Roosevelt's New Deal and America's entry and ultimate victory in World War II.
- Part Three examines life in post-World War II America, as U.S. military and economic ascendancy and tensions with the Soviet Union defined the Cold War era. It explores the triumph, decline, and partial revival of the labor movement and the changing working-class experience. Highlighting the birth of the civil rights movement that transformed America's political culture and moral values it also ex-

plores U.S. involvement in Vietnam and the rise of new social movements, such as the women's movement and gay liberation, in the 1960s and 1970s. Examining events of the 1980s and 1990s, it considers the influx of new immigrants from Asia and Latin America, the rise of the New Right and the undermining of the New Deal-era commitment to insuring the economic well being of all Americans, the collapse of the Cold War, the triumph of capitalism as a global system, the continuing conflicts over gender and race, and President Bill Clinton's narrow brush with impeachment.

FEATURES

What distinguishes *Who Built America?* from other U.S. history texts is, of course, its point of view. By emphasizing the experiences of the people whose labor shaped the nation and made it prosper, this text gives life to a story that all too often is perceived as having little to do with life in contemporary America. To further counteract the impression that history is little more than names and dates, we have enriched the narrative with excerpts from letters, diaries, autobiographies, poems, songs, journalism, fiction, official testimony, oral histories, and other historical documents. These sidebars convey the experience and often the voices of working people who lived through the events recounted in the text. In the interest of clarity, we have modernized some of the spelling, punctuation, and (especially in the case of the earliest documents) language in these records. To ensure that key events are not lost in the narrative flow and to facilitate review, we have provided timelines at the end of each chapter. These "years in review" reprise the important events covered in the chapter, particularly milestones in political and diplomatic history. Because we believe that history should also be fun, we have included in these chronologies some of the quirkier landmarks in our history—from why the "discovery" of the New World led to the invention of lemonade to why World War II resulted in the popularity of M&Ms.

Each chapter also contains drawings, paintings, prints, and photographs that derive from the era under discussion. Most of the illustrations in this book are images that were reproduced in contemporary books, pamphlets, newspapers, and magazines, individually published broadsides and lithographs, paired photographs sold as "stereoscopic views," and other media. Interpreting the visual record of the past—particularly images of working men and women, immigrants, and people of color—requires great care, and our captions alert readers to distortions and gaps that might not be obvious.

CHANGES IN THE NEW EDITION

The first edition of *Who Built America?* appeared in 1990 and 1992 as a work for a general audience as well as students. For this major revision we began with three main goals in mind. First, we wanted to take account of the vast outpouring of scholarship in the past decade. Where new historical evidence has come to light, we have altered or modified our interpretation. Second, we have sought to increase our coverage of several topics and areas of history—in particular, Spanish America, American Indians, women's history, U.S. foreign policy, electoral politics, consumer culture, and sexuality. To create space for the additional material, we have reduced the coverage of trade union history somewhat. Third, to increase the accessibility of the book we needed to give it a stronger chronological focus. Consequently, we have reorganized a number of chapters to clarify the sequence of events and given more attention to the political context of U.S. history. Fourth, to aid students in understanding the geographical and statistical patterns in American history, we have added charts and maps.

ACKNOWLEDGMENTS

Despite the major changes implemented by the authors of this edition, the narrative of *Who Built America?* rests heavily on the labors of the authors of the original edition, whose names appear on the title page and to whom we are deeply indebted.

We also want to thank the many people who helped bring forth this new edition, especially our friends at Worth Publishers, Susan Driscoll, Judith Kromm and Catherine Woods, who loyally supported and nurtured this project over the past few years. Developmental editors Nancy Fleming, Ann Grogg, Mary Marshall, Mimi Melek, and Betty Morgan provided invaluable feedback through several drafts of the manuscript. Tracey Kuehn, Margaret Comasky, and Barbara Seixas ably guided the book through the editing and production stages. Worth art director Barbara Rusin's appreciation of the unique character of *Who Built America?* is reflected in the book's cover and interior. We also benefited from the collaborative efforts of Charles Cavaliere and Todd Elder on marketing and promotion.

We thank Pennee Bender, Daniel Brown, George Chauncey, Jessica Finnefrock, Gerald Markowitz, Lauren Mucciolo, Ellen Noonan, Linda Shopes, John Summers, Andrea Ades Vásquez, Linda Zeidman, and in particular, Mario Frieson and Gideon Brown, for research assistance and help in locating and captioning illustrations. Dan Geary also provided research assistance. And we reiterate our sincere thanks to the many people who helped on the first edition (and are acknowledged in those volumes).

To the following colleagues who gave us encouragement and valuable feedback at various stages during the preparation of this edition, we are most grateful:

Laura Anker, SUNY—Old Westbury
William Blair, University of North Carolina, Greensboro
Kathy Brown, University of Pennsylvania
Richard Burg, Arizona State University
Victoria Bynum, Southwest Texas State University
Kathleen S. Carter, High Point University
Judith L. DeMark, Northern Michigan University
David Engerman, Brandeis University
E. J. Fabyan, Vincennes University
Bradley T. Gericke, U.S. Military Academy, West Point
Gary L. Gerstle, University of Maryland
Julia Greene, University of Colorado, Boulder
Cindy Hahamovitch, The College of William and Mary
David M. Head, John Tyler Community College
Lybeth Hodges, Texas Women's University
Reeve Huston, University of Arizona
Robert P. Ingalls, University of South Florida
Maurice J. Isserman, Hamilton College
Wilma King, Michigan State University
Stephen Kneeshaw, College of the Ozarks
Thomas J. Knock, Southern Methodist University
Nancy Koppelman, Evergreen State College
Gary Kornblith, Oberlin College
Kurt E. Leichtle, University of Wisconsin, River Falls
Molly McGarry, Sarah Lawrence College
John Mayfield, Samford University
Joanne Meyerowitz, University of Cincinnati
Betty Mitchell, University of Massachusetts—Dartmouth
Tiffany Patterson, SUNY—Binghamton
Dolores Peterson, Foothill College
Joseph P. Reidy, Howard University
Bruce J. Schulman, Boston University
Ronald Schultz
Janann Sherman, University of Memphis
Martin J. Sherwin, Tufts University
Rebecca Shoemaker, Indiana State University
Manfred Silva, El Paso Community College

Victor Silverman, University of California, Berkeley
Katherine Sklar, SUNY—Binghamton
David Sloan, University of Arkansas
Herbert Sloan, Barnard College
Michael L. Topp, University of Texas at El Paso
David Waldstreicher, University of Notre Dame
Peter Wood, Duke University
Sherri Yeager, Chabot College
William Young, Johnson County Community College

Finally, we would be remiss if we ended our acknowledgments without noting the role of the late Herbert Gutman in creating the American Social History Project, which gave birth to this book, and in shaping the generation of historical scholarship on which it is based. Our collective and individual debts to Herb are immeasurable. We hope that this new edition of *Who Built America?* meets the high standards he set for himself throughout his rich but too brief career.

Stephen Brier
Joshua Brown
Roy Rosenzweig

ABOUT THE EDITORS AND AUTHORS

Stephen Brier, Executive Editor, cofounded the American Social History Project in 1981 with the late Herbert G. Gutman and served as its Executive Director until 1998. He was the supervising editor and co-author of the first edition of the *Who Built America* textbook. He also co-authored the *Who Built America?* CD-ROMs and was the executive producer of the ASHP's award-winning *Who Built America?* video series. Dr. Brier is the Associate Provost for Instructional Technology and External Programs and the co-director of the New Media Lab at the Graduate Center of the City University of New York. He co-edits the "Critical Perspectives on the Past" book series at Temple University Press. Brier has written numerous scholarly and popular articles on race, class and ethnicity in U.S. labor history and on the educational impact of instructional media.

Joshua Brown, Visual Editor, is the Acting Executive Director and Creative Director of the American Social History Project at the Center for Media and Learning at the Graduate School and University Center of the City University of New York. He also co-directs the new media lab at the Graduate School of the Univeristy Center at CUNY. The author of many publications, Professor Brown has also written, produced, and directed a number of video, film, television, and interactive/multimedia projects. His publications include *A Spectator of Life—A Reverential, Enthusiastic, Emotional Spectator* (1997) and *Reconstructing Representation: Social Types, Readers, and the Pictorial Press, 1865–1877* (1996). Among his works for visual media are *Up South* (1996) and *Heaven Will Protect the Working Girl* (1993). In addition, he was the creative director of *History Matters: The U.S. History Survey on the Web* (1998). Current projects include *Exploring The French Revolution; The Secret; The Lost Museum; Gay New York; Everything in Its Place: The World of an Urban Commercial Photographer, William F. Cone, 1895–1966;* and *Rough Sketched, A Novel About Nineteenth Century New York.*

Nelson Lichtenstein, a professor of history at the University of Virginia, is the author of *The "Labor Question," a Twentieth Century History* (2001), *Walter Reuther: The Most Dangerous Man in Detroit* (1997), and *Labor's War at Home: The CIO in World War II* (1982). He has held fellowships from the Guggenheim and Rockefeller Foundations and served as a Fulbright Scholar in Helsinki. He sits on the editorial board of Labor History and writes frequently for *Dissent*, *New Labor Forum*, *The Los Angeles Times*, and *The New York Times Book Review.* Professor Lichtenstein has also co-edited three books: *On the Line: Essays in the History of Auto Work* (1989), *Major Problems in the History of American Workers* (1991), and *Industrial Democracy in America: the Ambiguous Promise* (1993).

Roy Rosenzweig is College of Arts and Sciences Distinguished Professor of History at George Mason University, where he founded and directs the Center for History and New Media (CHNM). A Guggenheim scholar, Professor Rosenzweig is the author and editor of a number of books including *Eight Hours for What We Will: Workers and Leisure in an Industrial City, 1870–1920* (1983), *The Park and the People: A History of Central Park* (1992), co-authored with Elizabeth Blackmar, and *The Presence of the Past: Popular Uses of History in American Life* (1998), co-authored with David Thelen. With Stephen Brier and Joshua Brown, he wrote the award-winning CD-ROM *Who Built America? From the Centennial Celebration of 1876 to the Great War of 1914* (1993) and the sequel, *Who Built America? From the Great War of 1914 to the Dawn of the Atomic Age* (2000).

Susan Strasser is professor of history at the University of Delaware and a Senior Resident Scholar at the Center for the History of Business, Technology, and Society at the Hagley Museum and Library. Professor Strasser has also been a Guggenheim Fellow and a resident in the Rockefeller Study and Conference Center, Bellagio, Italy. Some of her publications are *Waste and Want: A Social History of Trash* (1999); *Getting and Spending* (1998); *Social Justice Feminists in the United States and Germany: A Dialogue in Documents* (1998); *Satisfaction Guaranteed: The Making of the American Mass Market* (1996); *Washington: Images of a State's Heritage* (1988); and *Never Done: A History of American Housework* (1982). She is currently on the Editorial Advisory Board for *Business History Review.*

prologue

From the Civil War to the Great Uprising of Labor

Reconstructing the Nation

1865–1877

Shortly after the Confederate capital of Richmond, Virginia, fell to Union troops in April 1865, an ex-slave, whose name is recorded only as "Cyrus," decided he would no longer work in the fields. Emma Mordecai, the mistress of Rosewood plantation where Cyrus lived, questioned him about his refusal. Cyrus responded with a radically new interpretation of the relationship between former slaves and their former masters. He rejected a regime under which " it seems like we 'uns do all the work and [only] gets a part." Now, he continued, "there ain't going to be no more Master and Mistress, Miss Emma. All is equal. I done hear it from the courthouse steps. . . . All the land belongs to the Yankees now, and they gonna divide it among the colored people. Besides, the kitchen of the big house is my share. I help build it."

Cyrus's eloquent response to Miss Emma raised a fundamental question—whether those who had "built" America would share in the fruits of their labor. Such questions would echo through not only the dozen years that followed the end of the Civil War but also the century and a quarter after that, from Reconstruction's end to the new millennium—the period covered in this volume of *Who Built America?* For those who begin the story in Volume 2, this prologue briefly summarizes some of the key developments in the dozen years following the end of the Civil War. It focuses particularly on matters of labor and politics and especially on three key events—Reconstruction, the Centennial celebration of 1876, and the great railroad strikes of 1877.

"The First Vote." An 1867 *Harper's Weekly* illustration featured three figures symbolizing black political leadership: a skilled craftsman, a sophisticated city dweller, and a Union army veteran.

Source: Alfred R. Waud, *Harper's Weekly,* November 16, 1867—American Social History Project.

Reconstruction: The Second American Revolution

The South's defeat in 1865 settled two major debates—the nation was preserved and slavery was dead. But everything else was in doubt. Who would hold economic and political power in the South in the war's aftermath? How would the land be worked and how would labor be organized? What would freedom mean for the four million former slaves? The answers to these momentous questions would define the era known as Reconstruction.

African Americans' unceasing efforts to secure economic, political, and familial rights made them central players in the Reconstruction drama. Ex-slaves expressed their newfound freedom in diverse ways. For some, it was as specific and personal as the decision to take a new name; for others, as fundamental as uniting their family in a single household. Freedom was dressing as one pleased, perhaps wearing a colorful shirt or hat. And it was also refusing to be deferential to one's former owner. Soon after the Confederacy's final defeat freedpeople in Richmond, Virginia, for example, held meetings without securing white permission, and they walked in Capitol Square, an area previously restricted to white residents, refusing to yield the sidewalks to approaching white men and women. Freedom also meant that thousands of freed slaves could travel unrestricted and search for loved ones sold away or displaced during the war's upheavals. Emancipation enabled these and other black Americans to formalize longstanding relationships, officially registering and solemnizing their marriages.

The first years after emancipation also saw a tremendous upsurge in African-American demands for education and control over their churches. Freedpeople built schools and hired black teachers. They also challenged white domination of biracial congregations and founded their own churches, such as the African Methodist Episcopal (AME) Church. These independent churches became the moral and cultural center of African-American life, and their preachers—along with schoolteachers and ex-soldiers—emerged as community leaders. The churches often hosted black political meetings, including dozens of conventions, meetings, and rallies where freedmen raised demands for full civil equality.

The newly free Americans saw land ownership as the key to realizing their independence and ensuring their freedom. "Every colored man will be a slave, and feel himself a slave," one soldier argued, "until he can raise his own bale of cotton and put his own mark upon it and say this is mine." Many believed they were entitled to land in return for their years of unpaid labor, which had created the wealth of the cotton South and the industrialized North. They knew all too well that without land, they would remain fundamentally subservient to the economic power of their former owners.

Many southern blacks trusted the federal government, acting through the Freedmen's Bureau (which Congress had set up just before the end of the war), to help them achieve economic self-sufficiency. The bureau's nine hundred agents and officials, many of them idealistic Union army officers, did much to aid the freedpeople with education and medical care in the war's aftermath. And though the Freedmen's Bureau adopted extremely coercive labor policies throughout the South, the freedpeople continued to turn to bureau agents to protest brutality, harsh working conditions, and the hostility and inattention of local courts and police.

"The Great Labor Question from a Southern Point of View." An 1865 *Harper's Weekly* cartoon contrasted the idle planter with the industrious former slave. "My boy," the planter says hypocritically, "we've toiled and taken care of you long enough—now you've got to work!"

Source: *Harper's Weekly,* July 29, 1865—American Social History Project.

The struggles over the meaning of emancipation generated constant conflicts between black and white southerners. The realities of daily life and the enduring power of white southerners set boundaries on black freedom. These boundaries were especially narrow in rural areas still dominated by whites, who reacted badly to any assertion of personal freedom by former slaves. During the first year of freedom, countless incidents of violence were directed against freed slaves for simply expressing their personal independence.

Plantation owners especially opposed black southerners' efforts to secure land. Planters and freedpeople alike understood that black landownership would destroy white control of labor in the South and would lead to the collapse of the plantation economy. If even a few independent black farmers succeeded, concluded one Mississippi planter, "all the others will be dissatisfied with their wages no matter how good they may be and thus our whole labor system is bound to be upset." To maintain control, planters looked to their state governments. The struggle over the meaning and extent of freedom for African Americans would now shift to the political arena.

Presidential Reconstruction and Its Critics

By the end of 1865, state governments would once again be under the control of former supporters and leaders of the Confederacy. These men were able to reassert their dominance largely because of the lenient pardoning policies of President Andrew Johnson. Johnson, a tailor from Tennessee, had been the only southerner who chose to remain in his seat in the U.S. Senate after his home state seceded from the Union. His reward for that decision was selection as Lincoln's running mate in 1864, and he became president when Lincoln was assassinated in April 1865. As president, Johnson believed that only the planters possessed the experience, prestige, and power to "control" the volatile black population and that they were therefore the best hope for the South's future. In May 1865, he offered total amnesty to white southerners who would swear basic loyalty to the Union. He allowed the Confederate states to be rapidly readmitted to the Union, encouraging them to organize state elections and reestablish governments, a process completed in nearly all southern states by the fall of 1865. For Johnson, Reconstruction was now complete.

Many ex-Confederates were returned to office in the fall elections, and the new state governments immediately passed legislation favoring the interests of planters. Among them were the Black Codes, a series of rigid labor-control laws defining the status of newly freed African Americans as landless agricultural laborers with no bargaining power and restricted mobility. A freedman found without "lawful employment," for example, could be arrested. The laws were an attempt to ensure that planters would have an ongoing immobile and dependent supply of cheap labor.

The Black Codes were never fully enforced, largely because labor was scarce throughout the South and African-American workers and Freedmen's Bureau agents opposed the laws. Nonetheless, their passage enraged Radical Republicans, a group of congressmen whose political roots lay in the antebellum antislavery movement. Led by Representative Thaddeus Stevens of Pennsylvania and Senator Charles Sumner of Massachusetts, the Radicals sought a vast increase in federal power to obtain new rights for the freedpeople and to revolutionize social conditions in the South. Although Republicans held a three-to-one majority in Congress, most were moderates. But even they were profoundly disturbed by the Black Codes and by the restored power and influence of the ex-Confederate leaders who had passed these laws. In December 1865, moderates joined Radicals in refusing to seat the newly elected southern congressional representatives. This action initiated a confrontation with President Johnson and, in the process, transformed the meaning and nature of Reconstruction.

One of the first steps in this transformation occurred in early 1866, when Congress passed a civil rights bill that conferred U.S. citizenship on the freedpeople. This bill marked a dramatic break from the deeply rooted American tradition of states' rights and placed the federal government squarely on the side of extending citizenship and defending individual rights. President Johnson was outraged and vetoed the legislation as an unconstitutional infringement of states' rights. But the Republican Congress overrode Johnson's veto in April 1866, the first time in U.S. history that a major piece of legislation was passed over a president's objection. Three months later, Congress also overrode Johnson's veto of a bill to extend the life and power of the Freedmen's Bureau.

The Radicals in Congress sought an even more sweeping approach. Stevens and Sumner en-

Pardoned. A cartoon in the news weekly, *Frank Leslie's Illustrated Newspaper,* portrayed Andrew Johnson with a basket overflowing with pardons to be distributed to former Confederate officials. "Look here, Andy," says a recently reinstated southerner, "if you want Reconstruction, you had better set me over the whole thing down in our state."

Source: *Frank Leslie's Illustrated Newspaper,* August 1865—American Social History Project.

visioned not just civil rights for African Americans but a total transformation of southern society. Echoing the demands of freedpeople, Stevens called in 1866 for confiscating the land of the planters and distributing it among the ex-slaves. "The whole fabric of southern society must be changed," he proclaimed, "and never can it be done if this opportunity is lost." The best the Radicals could achieve, however, was the Fourteenth Amendment, which passed both houses of Congress in June 1866 and was then sent to the states for ratification. When finally approved in 1868, the Fourteenth Amendment granted full citizenship to African Americans and prohibited states from denying them "equal protection of the laws." This was a stunning transformation of the constitutional balance of power.

President Johnson issued an appeal to southern legislatures to reject the new amendment. Encouraged by Johnson's position, all southern states but one (ironically, Tennessee) refused to ratify the Fourteenth Amendment. The Union had won the war but now appeared to be losing the peace. The fall 1866 congressional elections thus became a referendum on the Fourteenth Amendment and on Johnson's opposition to extending Reconstruction. As voters considered the issues, increasing anti-black violence was reported throughout the South. In Memphis in May and in New Orleans in July, local authorities stood by or actively participated as white southerners slaughtered African Americans. In the wake of this racist brutality, Republicans scored a landslide victory in the November 1866 elections, and the biggest winners among them were the Radicals.

Radical Reconstruction

The Republican mandate encouraged the Radicals to present an even bolder agenda, which became known as Radical Reconstruction. The centerpiece of this agenda, the Reconstruction Act of March 1867, passed over President Johnson's veto, and it divided the former confederate states into five military districts. Each state was required to hold a constitutional convention and to draft a new state constitution. African Americans, protected by federal troops, would participate in the conventions, and the new constitutions would include provisions for black suffrage. The act also required newly elected state legislatures to ratify the Fourteenth Amendment as a condition for their readmission to the Union. The guarantee of black voting rights seemed to many Americans to represent the final stage of sweeping political revolution.

Passage of the Reconstruction Act in March 1867 undercut the political and economic power of the planter class and fostered political activity among freedpeople. A massive and unprecedented movement of freedpeople into the political arena soon followed. Black southerners created Union (or Loyal) Leagues, which helped build schools and churches. The leagues also organized militia companies to defend communities from white violence and called strikes and boycotts for better wages and fairer labor contracts. A number of local chapters were even organized on an interracial basis.

In the fall of 1867, southerners began electing delegates to the state constitutional conventions. The participation of freedpeople was truly astonishing. Women joined in local meetings to select candidates. Between 70 and 90 percent of eligible black males voted in every state in the South, and they elected a total of 265 African Americans as delegates. For the first time in American history, blacks and whites met together to prepare constitutions under which they would be governed. The constitutions they produced were among the most progressive in the nation. They created social-welfare agencies, reformed the criminal law, and more equitably distributed the burden of taxation. Most important, the constitutions guaranteed civil and political rights to both black and white Americans.

The intensity and extent of black political participation transformed southern politics. After 1867 the southern Republican party, with heavy support from African Americans, dominated all the new state governments. Although they represented an actual majority only in South Carolina's legislature, black Americans captured a total of six hundred legislative seats in southern states. Between 1868 and 1876, southern states elected fourteen black representatives to the U.S. Congress, two black U.S. senators, and six black lieutenant governors. In addition, thousands of African Americans served local southern communities as supervisors, voter registrars, aldermen, mayors, magistrates, sheriffs and deputies, postal clerks, members of local school boards, and justices of the peace.

White allies were essential to black political success. With African Americans in a majority only in South Carolina and Mississippi, the Republican party needed to develop a coalition that included some white support. White "carpetbaggers"—northerners who traveled to the South to participate in Reconstruction—were perhaps most visible, but the "scalawags", the native white southerners who supported the Republican party, were most critical to Republican successes in the South. Most scalawags were poor yeoman farmers from the southern mountains who had long resented the large planters' monopoly on land, labor, and political power. Most of the Republican party's southern adherents, then, were poor people, black and white, with a strong hostility to the planter aristocracy.

During their period in power—from two years in Tennessee to eight in South Carolina—the Republican

Hiram Revels. In 1870, the Boston firm of Louis Prang and Company published a chromolithograph (an inexpensive type of color print) portrait of the first African-American U.S. senator. One prominent admirer of the portrait, Frederick Douglass, wrote to Prang, "Whatever may be the prejudices of those who may look upon it, they will be compelled to admit that the Mississippi senator is a man, and one who will easily pass for a man among men. We colored men so often see ourselves described and painted as monkeys, that we think it a great piece of good fortune to find an exception to this general rule."

Source: L. Prang and Company (after a painting by Theodore Kaufmann), 1870, chromolithograph, 14 by $11\frac{3}{4}$ inches—Prints and Photographs Division, Library of Congress.

governments made important economic and legal gains for black and white working people. They created a public school system where none had existed before. These schools—although segregated by race and better in the cities than in the countryside—were nonetheless a symbol of real progress. By 1876, about half of all southern children were enrolled in school. Several Radical governments also passed laws banning racial discrimination in public accommodations, notably streetcars, restaurants, and hotels.

New laws helped landless agricultural laborers, both black and white. Radical Republicans passed lien laws that gave farm laborers a first claim on crops if their employers went bankrupt. And the repeal of the notorious Black Codes enabled some people to achieve their dream of land ownership. By 1876, fourteen thousand African-American families in South Carolina (about one-seventh of the state's black population) had acquired homesteads, as had a handful of white families.

Freedpeople were now able to negotiate a new kind of compromise with planters on how the land would be worked and who would reap its bounty. Rather than working in gangs for wages, individual families now tended small plots independently, renting land from planters for cash or, more commonly, for a fixed share of the year's crop. By 1870, "sharecropping" had become the dominant form of black agricultural labor, especially in the vast cotton lands. The system was a far cry from the freedpeople's first objective, which was to own land, and it became connected to a credit system that drastically reduced workers' economic freedom later in the century. But in the short run, sharecropping freed black workers from the highly regimented gang-labor system, allowing them a good deal of control and autonomy over their work, their time, and their family arrangements.

These very real economic and legal gains did not occur without cost. The southern Republican party experienced constant tensions within the fragile coalition that was its base. Large increases in state spending on schools and social programs, combined with the ongoing promotion of transportation and industry, led to tremendous hikes in taxes. This tax burden fell increasingly not only on wealthy planters but also on poor whites who owned little property. Revelations of political corruption among Republican officials compounded the growing disaffection of white voters.

The End of Reconstruction

The Republican party's loss of political power and influence among its white constituents was clear in 1869, when Tennessee and Virginia became the first states to return to conservative Democratic control. This political retreat—a process conservatives called "redemption"—could not have happened without a sharp change in northern public opinion and the movement of the northern Republican party away from the original goals of Radical Reconstruction.

The commitment of ordinary northerners to the political and civil rights of African Americans was limited, and after 1867 Republicans were defeated in a number of states in the North. Many northerners claimed they were simply worn out by the long military battles of the Civil War and the political battles that followed. With the removal of the most overt signs of southern intransigence, their support for further change weakened. Waning enthusiasm for Reconstruction was evident in the failure to drive Andrew Johnson from office after his impeachment by the House of Representatives in 1868; the U.S. Senate failed by one vote to remove Johnson from office for his efforts to undermine Reconstruction.

Moderate Republican leaders who came to power in the late 1860s were willing to abandon southern blacks in order to cultivate northern business support. That support depended on revitalizing the southern economy and retreating from the social and political experimentation that had defined Reconstruction's early years. Northern politicians were now prepared to leave the fate of the South, economically if not yet politically, in the hands of the former slaveowners. Northern Republicans thus began removing federal troops from the region, leaving large planters free to "redeem" the South as they saw fit.

The presence of black voters stood as the remaining major obstacle to the return of conservative rule. The large planters first tried to limit freedpeople's political activities by using economic power to threaten them with loss of employment. When economic pressure proved unsuccessful, the planters turned to more violent methods of intimidation. The Ku Klux Klan provided their most effective weapon. Founded by Confederate veterans in Tennessee in 1866, the Klan grew rapidly after the advent of Radical Reconstruction. Many of its rank-and-file members were poor men, but its leaders tended to be prominent planters and their sons. The Klan was in essence the paramilitary arm of the southern Democratic party, systematically employing violence against freedpeople and their organizations. Klan nightriders terrorized individual freedmen who refused to work for their employers or complained about low wages. They targeted black Civil War veterans and freedpeople who had succeeded in breaking out of the plantation system. Hooded Klansmen broke up meetings, threatened, shot, and lynched Radical and Union League leaders, and drove black voters away from the polls all across the South. Such targeted violence profoundly affected postwar politics in the South. Even though African Americans fought back valiantly, the Klan succeeded in destroying Republican organizations and demoralizing entire communities of freedpeople.

"A Prospective Scene in the 'City of Oaks,' 4th of March, 1869." A September 1868 edition of the Tuscaloosa, Alabama, *Independent Monitor* proposed the treatment its Republican opponents should receive if they lost the upcoming presidential election. The editor of the Democratic newspaper was the Grand Cyclops of the Tuscaloosa Ku Klux Klan. **Source:** Tuscaloosa *Independent Monitor,* September 1, 1868—Alabama Department of Archives and History, Montgomery, Alabama.

In the face of such incredible violence, Congress finally acted. In 1869 it approved the Fifteenth Amendment to the U.S. Constitution. The amendment (which was ratified in 1870), stated that the states could not deny or abridge the right to vote "on account of race, color, or previous condition of servitude." It did allow numerous "nonracial" means of limiting suffrage: southern states would later introduce poll (voting) taxes and literacy tests to restrict black voting. Nevertheless, the Fifteenth Amendment demonstrated that moderate Republicans were not yet willing to stand by and allow their party in the South to be terrorized and destroyed by violence.

In March 1871, a series of grisly events shook the nation and galvanized Congress to take further action. In the small town of Meridian, Mississippi, Klansmen and their supporters had brutally murdered thirty African Americans. Congress appointed a committee to investigate. Aghast at the tales of carnage they heard, members of Congress passed a series of enforcement acts imposing harsh penalties on those who used organized terrorism for political purposes. The Ku Klux Klan Act, for example, made certain crimes against a citizen's rights punishable under federal, not state, law. President Ulysses S. Grant, who had been a victorious Union army general before being elected president in 1868, declared martial law in parts of South Carolina and dispatched U.S. Army troops to the area in 1871. Hundreds of Klansmen were indicted and tried by the U.S. attorney general in South Carolina, North Carolina, and Mississippi. The federal government had broken the Klan's back, at least temporarily.

But 1872 marked the beginning of the end of the federal presence in the South. Groups similar to the Klan multiplied, using violence and intimidation to achieve Democratic victories. The Democrats assumed, correctly as it turned out, that neither Congress nor the president would again act decisively to prevent political violence and fraud in the South.

The political retreat was made worse by the economic panic of 1873, which launched a severe nationwide depression that would last more than five years. Across the South, the depression drove many black landowners and renters back into the ranks of laborers, sharply reduced wage levels, and eventually helped transform sharecropping into a system of peonage. In the North, the depression encouraged businessmen to abandon the last remnants of Reconstruction. White working people, focusing their attention on immediate problems in their own workplaces and communities and still unconvinced by arguments for racial equality, also turned away from the biracial promise of Reconstruction.

Only federal intervention could have prevented the renewed violence that reinstalled white Democratic regimes throughout the South. But President Grant's administration, which had acted forcefully against the Klan in 1871, turned down requests for federal troops in 1875. The North no longer seemed outraged by political violence directed against freedpeople. Most white Americans wanted to turn their attention elsewhere.

The Centennial and the Other America

In 1876, the United States reached a venerable anniversary that provided an opportunity for celebration. The republic had survived for a century since declaring its independence from England. Although only a decade had passed since the end of the bloody Civil War, Americans believed their country deserved a spectacular birthday party—a centennial celebration that would display the nation's achievements in industry, science, agriculture, and the arts. Designed to meet these heady expectations, the Centennial Exposition opened on 450 expansive acres in Philadelphia's Fairmount Park on May 10, 1876. Ten million people, from every state and more than thirty countries, flocked to the party over the next six months.

The major exhibition buildings were gigantic. In this still largely rural nation, Agricultural Hall covered more than ten acres. Inside, visitors marveled at the latest mowing and reaping machines. But the centerpiece of the Exposition was the 700-ton, 40-foot-high Corliss Double Walking-Beam Engine, which generated 1,400 horsepower, enough to drive all the other machines in the enormous hall. Powered by a steam boiler in an adjacent building and running almost silently, the engine was an awesome creation, representing in the beauty of its motion, design, and power the very essence of the new industrial age.

"The Stride of a Century." Uncle Sam triumphantly, if uncomfortably, straddled a united and prospering nation on its hundredth birthday in this 1876 Currier and Ives lithograph commemorating the Philadelphia Centennial Exposition.

Source: Currier and Ives, 1876, lithograph—Prints and Photographs Division, Library of Congress.

Some Americans, however, were less enthralled by the sights, grandeur, pomp, and sense of marvel of the Centennial Exposition. They viewed it less as a celebration of the nation's achievements than as a diversion from hard and bitter daily reality. Neglected and sometimes stifled by the lavish festivities, these "other Americans"—women, African Americans, American Indians, and workers—raised issues that would resonate through the next century and a quarter.

The Centennial's Women's Pavilion, for example, was fraught with division. Paid for with contributions from across the country, the pavilion presented visitors with crafts, inventions, and institutions established and conducted by women. But to many observers, the displays seemed no more than curiosities, a glimpse of a quaint and separate world. The National Woman's Suffrage Association—as if announcing the division between the pavilion planners who espoused the private, "domestic" sphere and the advocates who demanded a wider role for women in American society—held its founding meeting in New York City on the same day that the Women's Pavilion opened in Philadelphia. And at the Centennial's July Fourth ceremonies, feminists Elizabeth Cady Stanton and Susan B. Anthony disrupted the proceedings to read a Woman's Declaration of Independence.

But if women's role was limited, African Americans' role was to be invisible. African-American women, who had helped raise funds for the Centennial, found no place in the Women's Pavilion. No black men were hired on the crews that constructed the Centennial buildings, and visitors saw African Americans doing only menial tasks, or performing in the Southern Restaurant, where (as a guidebook described it) "a band of old-time plantation 'darkies' . . . sing their quaint melodies and strum the banjo." This pervasive racism manifested itself again during the Centennial's opening ceremonies. Frederick Douglass—escaped slave, militant abolitionist, and acknowledged leader of the nation's African Americans—had been invited to sit on the opening-day speakers' platform, although he was not given an opportunity to speak. A policeman, convinced that no black man belonged among the invited dignitaries, barred Douglass's way until a U.S. senator finally intervened on his behalf.

"The Freed Slave." African Americans were generally unwelcome at the 1876 Centennial Exposition. But one exhibit attracted black visitors to the Philadelphia fairgrounds, a statue by an Austrian sculptor commemorating emancipation.
Source: Fernando Miranda, *Frank Leslie's Illustrated Newspaper,* August 5, 1876—American Social History Project.

Even America's Indian population played a more pronounced—if not more popular—role than that of African Americans. The Smithsonian Institution had mounted a massive Centennial exhibit of Indian artifacts, replete with pottery, tepees, totem poles, and life-size costumed mannequins. In July 1876, news reached the Centennial of the victory of Sioux and Cheyenne warriors at the Battle of Little Big Horn in Dakota Territory, where General George Custer and more than two hundred U.S. Army soldiers perished. Many white visitors viewing the material artifacts of destroyed Indian cultures shared the feelings of William Dean Howells, who wrote, "The red man, as he appears in effigy and in photograph in this collection, is a hideous demon, whose malign traits can hardly inspire any emotion softer than abhorrence."

Some employers arranged excursions to the Centennial as a way of easing workers' growing discontent with the ravages of industrial capitalism. Railroad and coal-mining firms were particularly enthusiastic about such trips, hoping that they would soothe the bitterness Irish mining families felt over the suppression of the recent "Long Strike" in eastern Pennsylvania and the destruction of their union. The Philadelphia and Reading Coal and Iron Company sent eleven hundred men, women, and children from the Pennsylvania mines on an all-expense-paid trip to the Centennial. As the travelers visited the exposition, twenty miners were being tried in a Schuylkill County courtroom as alleged members of a secret society called the Molly Maguires; they were ultimately convicted of murder and hanged in June 1877.

The Great Uprising of Labor

The vision of industrial progress hallowed by the Centennial and seemingly ushered in by the formal end of Reconstruction, which came in 1877, would meet its greatest challenge just a few short months later. A massive railroad strike, the first truly national strike in the country's history, became a turning point in U.S. history. Although the strike failed in the short run, it marked the birth of a working-class movement far broader and more powerful than anything seen before.

The Great Uprising of 1877 was brought on by the hard times of the 1873 depression, then in its fourth year. Railroad workers had suffered one wage reduction after another since the onset of the depression. On July 16, 1877, Baltimore and Ohio (B&O) workers in Martinsburg, West Virginia, staged a spontaneous strike in response to yet another wage cut. Three days later, as the strike intensified, President Rutherford B. Hayes ordered federal troops into West Virginia to protect the B&O and the nation from "insurrection."

The use of federal troops in a domestic labor dispute incited popular anger across the country. In Baltimore, the Maryland state militia fired on huge crowds of workers, leaving eleven dead and forty wounded. Work stoppages rapidly spread north and west along the railroad lines to Pennsylvania, where in Pittsburgh the strike reached its most dramatic climax. Because many Pittsburgh citizens sympathized with the railroad workers, the Pennsylvania Railroad sought help from the state militia. But when the Philadelphia-based troops reached Pittsburgh on July 21, 1877, they

The Spark. *Frank Leslie's Illustrated Newspaper* depicted striking railroad workers stopping trains in Martinsburg, West Virginia, on Tuesday, July 17, 1877.

Source: Fernando Miranda, *Frank Leslie's Illustrated Newspaper,* August 4, 1877—American Social History Project.

were met by a large and angry crowd of strikers and sympathizers. Unnerved by the reception, the soldiers suddenly thrust their bayonets at members of the crowd. Rocks were thrown, and the troops answered with a volley of rifle fire, killing twenty Pittsburgh citizens, including a woman and three small children.

News of the deaths spread quickly. Pittsburgh residents, including thousands of workers from nearby mills, mines, and factories, converged on the Pennsylvania Railroad yards. By dawn they had set fire to the railroad roundhouse where the militiamen had retreated. Twenty more Pittsburgh residents and five soldiers lay dead at the end of the ensuing gun battle.

In the next few days the strike spread across the Midwest. Workers took over entire towns, shutting down work until employers met their demands. The same railroad and telegraph lines that had unified the nation and laid the groundwork for the full emergence of industrial capitalism now linked and unified workers' protests. Without any central organization (most national unions were defunct as a result of the depression), the conflict spawned local committees, many led by anarchists and socialists, that provided unity and direction to the strike. In Chicago, for example, the conflict quickly became a citywide general strike that touched off open class warfare. In St. Louis, thousands of workers participated in a general strike that, although largely peaceful, shut down virtually all of the city's industries while government officials fled. Black workers took an active role in that strike, closing down canneries and docks. When an African-American steamboat worker, addressing a crowd of white workers, asked, "Will you stand to us regardless of color?" the crowd responded, "We will! We will! We will!" Racism prevailed in other strikes, however, particularly in the Far West. In San Francisco a crowd that had gathered to discuss strike action ended up rampaging through the city's Chinese neighborhoods, killing several residents and burning buildings.

The Scene of Battle. The interior of the Pennsylvania Railroad upper roundhouse on July 22, 1877, the day after the battle between Philadelphia militia and Pittsburgh strikers.

Source: S. V. Albee, "The Railroad War"—Paul Dickson Collection.

The Great Uprising of 1877 was directed mainly against the railroads and the unchecked corporate power they typified, not against capitalism as a whole. Working people in 1877 were seeking to set limits on the system's unbridled economic power and (like the former slave Cyrus in 1865) to assert workers' right to an equitable share of the economic bounty they helped produce. Despite the nationwide mobilization of workers in the first truly national strike in U.S. history, the strikers failed in the face of the massive power of the railroads and their allies in state and national government. But no matter which side Americans had supported in the strike, few who surveyed the death and destruction left in its wake could find solace—let alone take pride—in the memory of the unmitigated industrial progress that had been celebrated at the Centennial a short year before.

The Great Uprising demonstrated that the United States was not immune to the class-based conflict that had plagued Europe since the birth of industrial capitalism. That conflict would intensify at critical moments over the coming years, but it would never recur in quite the way it had in the summer of 1877. The chapters that follow detail the changing form and substance of the divisions that dominated American life in the century and a quarter that followed the end of Reconstruction and the great railroad strike. First and foremost among these divisions was the conflict between capital and labor. But the chapters also chronicle the struggles of women, African Americans, American Indians, and European, Latino, Asian, and Caribbean immigrants as they attempted to achieve greater rights and inclusion in American society. As you will see, these struggles were played out in an international arena increasingly dominated by the United States but also fundamentally shaped by the American people's experience of war, economic dislocation, and ideological conflict. In the process, working people like Cyrus who "helped build" America would repeatedly ask whether they would receive an equal share of its bounty.

part one

The great railroad strikes of the summer of 1877, as the young labor leader Samuel Gompers noted, sounded an alarm heralding a new era of conflict and division in the nation. The previous era, which had been defined by questions relating to slavery and the status of the newly emancipated former slaves, had ended more with a whimper than a bang a few months before. In the early months of 1877, the newly installed administration of Republican president Rutherford B. Hayes had agreed to withdraw the few remaining federal troops from the southern states in exchange for Democratic party support for Hayes's contested election. That agreement brought down the final curtain on the dozen-year drama that had been Reconstruction—a time when the freedpeople in the post–Civil War South not only gained their emancipation but also secured U.S. citizenship, the right to vote and hold elective office, access to education, and some modest measure of economic and religious independence. Such issues would now be pushed off center stage, as Americans entered a new arena of national conflict and division. Over the next four decades, the battles fought by working men and women would be staged against a backdrop of extraordinary economic, political, and social changes wrought by industrial capitalism.

The United States became the world's most powerful industrial nation during these years, giving rise to manufacturing enterprises of breathtaking and unprecedented size and output. In this same period, the nation launched a war with Spain that resulted in U.S. domination of Puerto Rico, the Philippines, Cuba, and Hawaii. The face of America also changed, as millions of immigrants from Europe, Asia, and Latin America

Monopoly and Upheaval

1877–1914

poured into the United States after 1900, feeding industrial capitalism's seemingly insatiable appetite for new workers. Urban America took modern form and shape, as the populations of New York and Chicago swelled beyond a million residents each and contemporary transportation, sanitation, and safety systems came into being. New consumer products, new means of mass distribution, and new forms of recreation reshaped everyday life in the city and the countryside.

Few Americans were able to avoid being drawn into new forms of dependency—on wages or on market relations—that U.S. capitalism imposed on their lives. Nor were millions of other individuals who lived and worked under U.S. control in the Caribbean, Latin America, and the islands in the Pacific Ocean immune from this dependency. As you will see in the chapters that follow, working men and women—African Americans, native-born white Americans, and European, Latin American, Caribbean, and Asian immigrants—struggled repeatedly to find a place for themselves as their communities were transformed by the growth of economic monopoly, unimaginable individual wealth, and unbridled political power that characterized industrial America during the forty years that began with the 1877 strikes and ended with U.S. entry into World War I.

Americans were sharply divided on the meaning of the changes in their nation. On one side stood industrial capitalists and their political and intellectual supporters: they justified capitalists' newly won wealth and power with an ideology that celebrated acquisitive individualism, free markets, and the "survival of the fittest." On the other side, working men and women embraced the ideal of collectivity and the power of mutual, rather than individual, action to blunt the devastating impact of industrial capitalism on their work and family life and their communities. Of course, many Americans—small business owners, machine politicians, white-collar workers—did not entirely agree with either position, siding with industrial capitalists in some circumstances and with working people in others. And working people themselves were often divided along lines of race, gender, ethnicity, religion, and region.

As people and communities were transformed by the dizzying growth of industrial capitalism, cultures of collectivity arose, and from those bases working people launched a series of violent class wars unprecedented in the nation's history. The names and dates of individual battles—Haymarket (1886), Homestead and Coeur D'Alene (1892), Pullman (1894), Lawrence (1912), Paterson (1913), and Ludlow (1914)—became signposts along the tortuous road of industrial and political conflict that defined the era. Radical ideas—including Populism, feminism, anarchism, and socialism—animated many of these conflicts.

By 1900, however, many of the most fundamental challenges to industrial capitalism—the Knights of Labor and the Populists, in particular—had been beaten back. At the same time, this heady brew of labor struggle, political unrest, and a spate of tragic factory fires and coal mine explosions fostered a belief, shared by workers, middle-class professionals, and even some business leaders, that the Gilded Age excesses of industrial capitalism plaguing America at the turn of the century required reform. This movement (really a series of reform movements) came to be known as progressivism. Spearheaded particularly by women, progressivism articulated a modern notion that government should play a central role in regulating the nation's social, economic, and political ills.

Some of the issues facing the nation—child labor, factory safety, tainted food and drugs, political corruption, unchecked economic monopoly—proved amenable to the efforts of this diverse reform coalition to improve conditions of work and life in post–1900 America. But reformers did little for African Americans; for them, the four decades following 1877 were most remarkable for the regression from the gains they had won during Reconstruction.

As war loomed over Europe, the particular conflicts that gave rise to progressivism would increasingly take a back seat to concern over the spreading international crisis. Nonetheless, progressive reform inaugurated a new era in U.S. politics, one in which the federal government took some small steps toward its now familiar role as guarantor of economic stability and the minimal safety and health of its citizenry.

"1876—On Guard." Even as Americans celebrated the Centennial, they remained uneasy about the nation's future. In 1876 few could ignore the effects of three years of economic depression. But as this Currier and Ives print indicated, many Americans blamed the nation's problems on agitators and ideas from abroad.
Source: Currier and Ives, 1876, lithograph—Prints and Photographs Division, Library of Congress.

chapter 1

Progress and Poverty: Economy, Society, and Politics in the Gilded Age

1877–1893

The North's victory in the Civil War inaugurated a period of extraordinary growth and consolidation for the American economy. With the nation's political boundaries restored, northern manufacturers again had access to southern markets, and dramatic industrial development brought the United States into a new era. Within fifteen years of the war's end, Andrew Carnegie built his first steel plant, John D. Rockefeller organized Standard Oil, and Alexander Graham Bell began manufacturing telephones. By 1894 the United States was the world's leading industrial power, producing more than the combined total of its three largest competitors—England, France, and Germany. Leading entrepreneurs like Carnegie and Rockefeller became unimaginably wealthy.

The nation's postwar economic growth owed much to its abundant natural resources: rich farmland provided food for a growing urban workforce, and extensive coal, iron, and mineral deposits supplied raw materials to mills and factories. During and immediately after the war, Republicans—backed by powerful iron manufacturers and coal-mine owners—had passed laws to stimulate industrial growth, enabling wealthy investors and industrialists to exploit the nation's resources. High import tariffs protected American industry from foreign competition, and federal loans and huge land grants encouraged railroad expansion. Although their legislation served the wealthy, Republicans paid lip service to the key role of labor in the expanding economy. That ideology helped ensure the party's political dominance in the postwar decades.

Wartime legal and financial innovations also regularized and enabled the movement of capital—money invested in businesses to generate additional wealth. In 1862, Congress had authorized the printing of $150 million in U.S. Treasury notes (dubbed "greenbacks" because of their color). One year later, the first of the National Banking acts had created a national banking system. In borrowing money to pay for the war, the government had relied on the services of investment bankers, especially Jay Cooke & Co., founded in 1861, which organized the sale of bonds. Cooke and his fellow bankers soon developed new techniques to bring together investors and entrepreneurs seeking capital. When the federal govern-

"The Ironworkers' Noontime." Few painters chose industrial work as a subject in the late nineteenth century, its conditions seeming inappropriate for a medium that tended to highlight noble and aesthetic themes. Thomas Anshutz's painting, completed around 1880, is therefore an unusual work, realistically portraying the weariness of skilled ironworkers at a nail factory in Wheeling, West Virginia, while also celebrating the workers' strength and pride in their craft.

Source: Thomas Pollock Anshutz, 1880, oil on canvas, 17-1/8 × 24 inches—The Fine Arts Museums of San Francisco, Gift of Mr. and Mrs. John D. Rockefeller 3rd.

ment paid its debts after the war, it further stimulated the economy, increasing the supply of funds available for long-term investment.

The phenomenal growth of the American economy in the nineteenth century also had a dark underside, however, and a short, red-haired newspaperman named Henry George experienced it firsthand. George had started as a printer but lost that job in the depression of 1857. He went on to launch a successful, crusading San Francisco newspaper, which was wiped out in the panic of 1873. In the aftermath of the epochal railroad strikes of 1877, George redirected his crusading spirit toward writing a book that would expose what he saw as the fundamental paradox of his day—the persistence of horrifying poverty amid stunning economic progress. "The 'tramp' comes with the locomotive," he wrote in burning indignation, "and the almshouse and prisons are as surely the makers of 'material progress' as are costly dwellings, rich warehouses, and magnificent churches." The men and women who built America in the late nineteenth century—railroad magnates, Chinese track layers, Yankee stenographers, Welsh coal miners, New York society matrons, Irish maids, southern black sharecroppers, Basque sheep herders, and many others—might differ on many things, but they would likely agree that the title of George's famous book, *Poverty and Progress,* offered an apt description of their era.

Building a Railroad System

The explosion of industrial growth depended on the dramatic expansion of the railroads and their alliance in creating a unified railroad system. In 1869, the transcontinental link was completed. The 125,000 miles of track that would be laid in the next twenty-five years would give the United States the most extensive transportation system in the world, promoting economic development across the continent. The transcontinental lines sponsored and controlled the building of feeder lines, such as the Spokane and Palouse Railroad, which linked the Northern Pacific to the wheat fields of eastern Washington.

Laying those thousands of miles of track was hard, dirty work. All over the country, bosses recruited workers, oversaw their work, and organized the camps where they lived. Chinese work gangs predominated in western railroad work during the 1860s and 1870s. Japanese firms provided laborers to northwestern railroads. In the Southwest, agents recruited laborers in Mexican border towns and turned them over to railroad contractors. In West Virginia and Virginia, the work was done by Italians brought in by *padrones* from New York; farther south, bosses patrolled as young unmarried African Americans laid track.

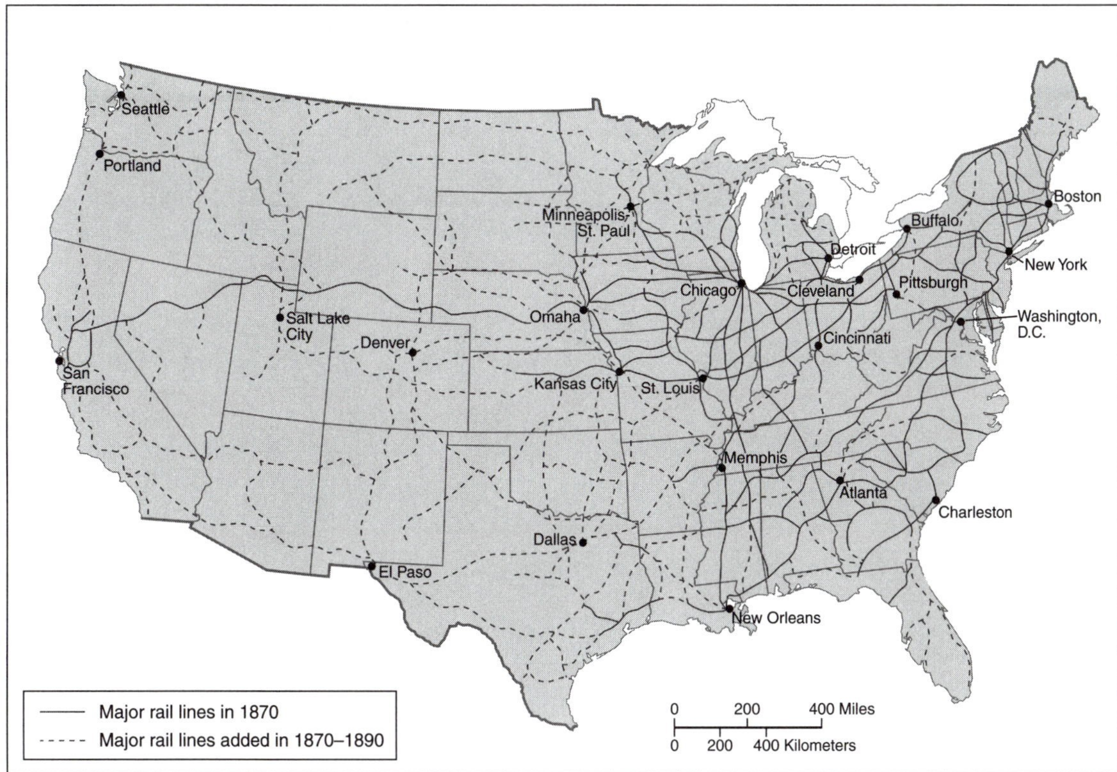

Railroads Span the Nation, 1870–1890 The completion of the transcontinental railroad in 1869 marked the start rather than the finish of the railroad construction boom. In the next two decades, the nation's railroad network almost tripled in size. By 1890, the United States had 164,000 miles of railroad track and the most extensive transportation network in the world. But the system continued to grow, and it reached a peak of 254,000 miles in 1964. Today—with a vastly larger population—the railroad system is about the size it was in 1890.

But laying track was only one part of the evolution of the rail network and the national market. To provide dependable transportation for shippers' goods, railroad systems required new kinds of organization and coordination. Railroad executives were the first modern salaried business managers, employees with little or no financial interest in the companies they served. Even before the Civil War, these people had developed entirely new kinds of accounting procedures, reporting practices, and channels of authority that enabled their organizations to operate across broad geographic expanses. In the 1870s and 1880s, they faced a new challenge: cooperating to ensure that cars loaded with manufactured products could move freely from one rail line to another. Meeting this challenge would require the railroads to agree on uniform standards and codes.

An immediate problem was that early trains ran on tracks of various gauges. The gauge is the distance between the two parallel rails, and cars built for one gauge could not run on track of other gauges. Over a period of about fifteen years, the railroads agreed to a standard distance of 4 feet, 8.5 inches. On the night of May 31–June 1, 1886, the last remaining lines outside the network adopted the standard gauge.

Timetables also had to be standardized. Although the telegraph enabled the instantaneous transmission of time signals and thus reduced the potential for collisions, railroads operated on a chaotic system of local and regional times, each set by the sun. Railroad men and travelers used guidebooks full of timetables. Under this system, a passenger might arrive in New York at 1:30 Pittsburgh time and still catch a train leaving that city at 1:15 New York time. To bring order out of this chaos, the railroads adopted the four standard time zones in use today, and on Sunday, November 18, 1883, the country set its clocks to the new uniform standard time. "The sun is no longer boss of the job," an Indianapolis newspaper complained. "People . . . must eat, sleep, and work as well as travel by railroad time."

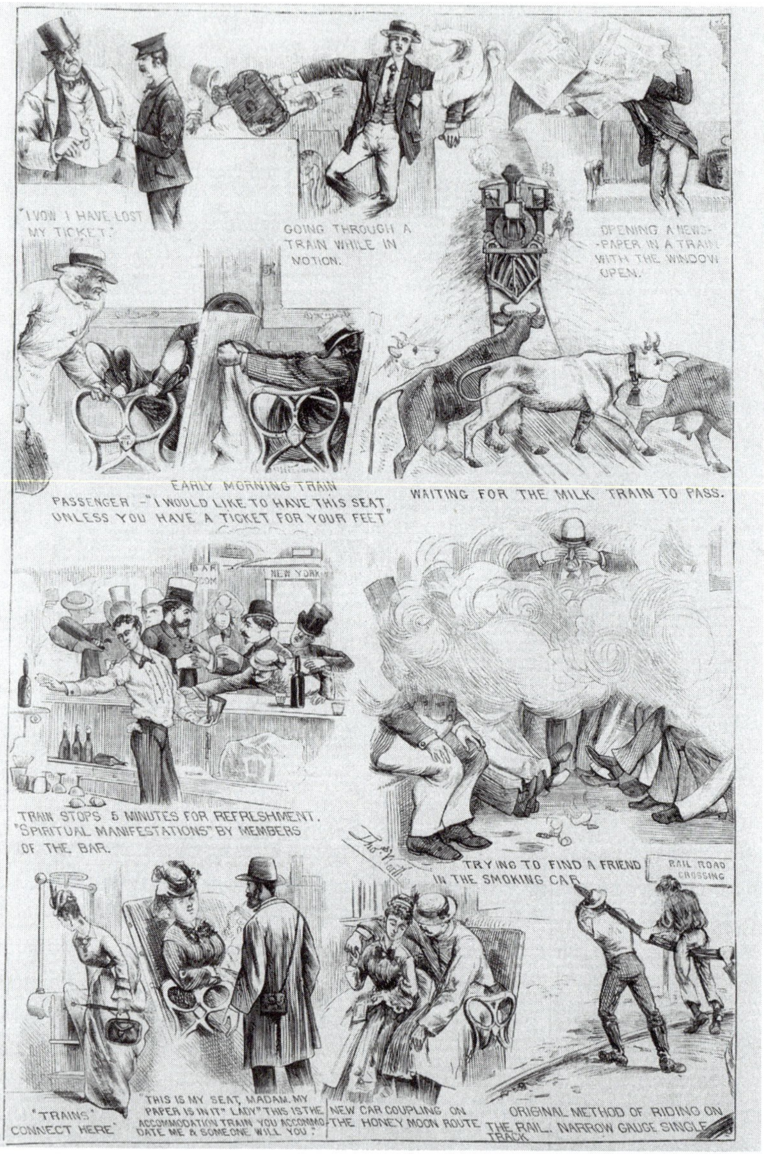

Life with the Railroad. Vignettes showing the hazards of train travel in the 1870s.

Source: Thomas Worth, *Harper's Weekly,* September 20, 1873—American Social History Project (ASHP).

Railroads had to work out accounting procedures so that shippers could use different lines without transferring their products from one railroad's cars to another. The Interstate Commerce Act of 1887, which the biggest railroads helped to shape, codified accounting methods so that goods could move unhindered across the country.

The effects of the railroads' expansion rippled throughout the nation. Small producers who had once dominated local markets—for example, a

Cincinnati maker of iron stoves—faced more distant competition. Industries feeding the railroads' enormous demands for iron, steel, stone, and lumber also expanded. In 1882, nine-tenths of the steel the nation produced went into rails, and about a quarter of the country's annual timber production went into crossties. And because railroads enabled producers to sell to consumers across the continent, manufacturers produced larger quantities and experimented with new, large-scale production processes. The Bessemer converter, which transformed pig iron into steel at a relatively low cost, helped increase steel output, which was ten times greater in 1892 than 1877. Other basic industries grew, too: the output of copper multiplied by seven, and that of crude oil by four during the same years.

Explosive and Unstable Development

Despite an expanding market, America's late–nineteenth-century economy was profoundly unstable. The cost of building the railroads was unprecedented. Pursuing huge commissions and profits from every aspect of the business, investment bankers acted as agents for railroads seeking capital, as brokers for investors, as members of the railroads' boards of directors, and as investors of their own firms' money. Jay Cooke, who had organized the financing of the Civil War, entered into such an agreement with the Northern Pacific (NP), a proposed new transcontinental line. Cooke agreed to market NP's bonds in exchange for a majority interest in the railroad, and—although NP did not have title to its huge land grant because the tracks were not yet built—he convinced Congress to allow him to mortgage the land. His firm then lent enormous sums to the railroad to finance construction. But Jay Cooke & Co. failed to sell the bonds, and in September 1873 the firm collapsed. It was so large, so central to railroad financing, and so tied to prominent politicians that its failure triggered a financial panic. The New York Stock Exchange closed for a week; across the country banks failed as people tried to get their money out.

Then followed five years of the most severe depression America had seen. One million workers lost their jobs; many faced starvation, and others tramped the land seeking relief and employment. Railroad building virtually stopped. Nearly 50,000 firms closed their doors. An upswing in the late 1870s brought a brief return to prosperity, but industrial expansion was again undercut by another depression lasting from 1882 to 1885. This downturn was moderate compared with the longer and deeper slump that preceded it, but many industrial towns and working-class communities were hit hard.

"Tramps' Terror." To some Americans, the unemployed who wandered the country in search of work during the 1870s posed a threat to order and safety. The "tramp menace," many argued, required a repressive response—and advertisements like this exploited the pervasive fear.

Source: *Frank Leslie's Illustrated Newspaper,* April, 7, 1877—American Social History Project.

The "business cycle," this boom-and-bust pattern of alternating rapid growth and sharp depression, was a characteristic feature of rapidly developing industrial capitalism that haunted both workers and capitalists, the entrepreneurs and financiers who organized capital investment. Security was fleeting. Even during an economic boom, few wage-workers—even the highly skilled—could count on full-time, year-round work. Businessmen faced similar uncertainty. Those who avoided outright failure grappled with a long-term decline in the prices of manufactured goods: from 1866 to 1890, average prices for products dropped by over half. This decline affected nearly every sector of the economy, slashing both profits and the wages businessmen were willing or able to pay.

Rapid growth, competition, and plummeting prices went hand in hand, as illustrated in the case of the railroads. Railroad companies had to pay high fixed costs to maintain equipment and track as well as substantial interest on the bonds that had financed their construction. Given these

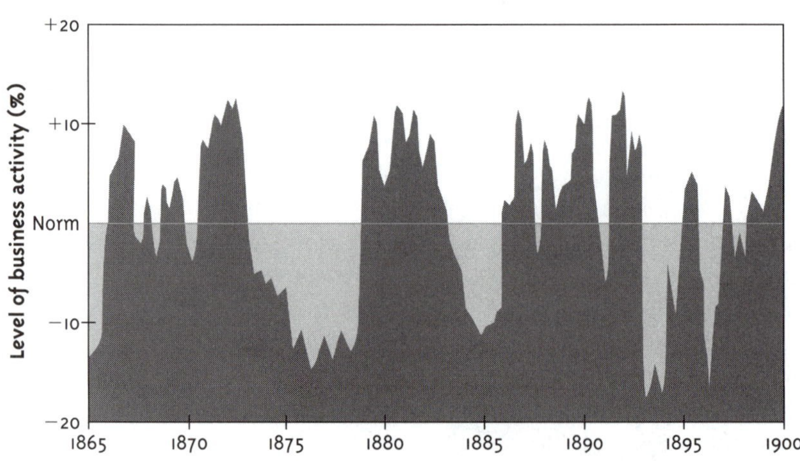

An Unstable Economy The late nineteenth century was an era of explosive growth and also devastating depression. Three major depressions—in the 1870s, 1880s, and 1890s—shrouded the so-called "Gilded Age."

strong incentives to continue operations, managers dropped rates to rock bottom. Low revenues were preferable to no revenues, and hauling empty cars was nearly as expensive as hauling cars loaded with freight. Over the last thirty years of the nineteenth century, freight prices fell by 70 percent, severely squeezing railroad profits. And as railroad rates plummeted, so did wholesale prices because transportation costs made up such a large share of the final cost of manufactured goods.

Industrial overproduction and intense competition among manufacturers also caused prices to fall. Like railroads, manufacturers who installed expensive machinery faced the problem of high fixed costs: they had to pay for equipment even if it lay idle, so they kept producing. Bessemer converters, for example, produced more steel than the market could absorb. Production outstripped demand, corporations aggressively cut prices, and profit margins disappeared.

America's extraordinary post–Civil War economic expansion was volatile, as unstable as it was explosive. The industrial system held out the hope of material plenty, but it was anything but predictable.

The Emergence of Urban-Industrial Life

As railroads and industries developed, citizens from all walks of life became increasingly dependent on the financial ups and downs of companies representing huge concentrations of money and power. Americans found their accustomed ways of living and working overturned. In just over thirty years of industrial growth, a modern working class and a new business elite had emerged in a nation once dominated by farmers, merchants, and small-town artisans. Wide-scale poverty emerged at the same time; the human misery that had horrified American observers of English industrialization now scarred the United States. "We are fast drifting to that condition of society which preceded the downfall of [ancient] Sparta, Macedonia, Athens, and Rome," wrote a railroad carpenter in the late 1870s, "where a few were very rich, and the many very poor." But this neat division oversimplified the situation. Many Americans lived between these two dramatic extremes.

With industrialization came a transition from household and artisan to factory production, a change that affected the daily lives of most Americans. By the eve of the Civil War, most people were buying and wearing manufactured textiles instead of weaving homespun. By the 1890s, many other consumer goods were factory-made—not only longstanding craft products like soap and furniture but also items nobody had ever made by hand, such as kerosene lamps and sewing machines.

"Bandit's Roost." New Yorker Jacob Riis's photographs starkly portrayed "how the other half lives" to the audiences who attended his lantern-slide shows or saw engraved versions in newspapers. But, as is evident in this photograph of an alley on the Lower East Side, Riis often posed and framed his subjects in ways that were meant to arouse not only sympathy but also fear and distaste among viewers.

Source: Dr. Henry Piffard or Richard Hoe Lawrence (for Jacob Riis), 1888—Jacob A. Riis Collection, Museum of the City of New York.

The change from home to factory production was tied to a fundamental shift from agriculture to industry. Before the Civil War, the United States was still overwhelmingly an agricultural nation. Eight out of ten Americans lived in rural areas. About 52 percent of those who worked for wages cultivated the soil, with only 14 percent employed in manufacturing. But the balance shifted over the next decades, as farm machinery dramatically increased productivity. Fewer farmers could feed more workers in other industries. Manufacturing grew dramatically; the number of factor laborers almost tripled between 1860 and 1890, and nearly doubled again by 1910.

Intertwined with the shift from agriculture to industry was the eclipse of self-employment and the emergence of wage work. In 1860, half of American workers were self-employed, and the other half earned wages. Many still believed that hard work and individual sacrifice would pave the way from wage labor to economic independence. Industrial growth after the Civil War frustrated these hopes, and by 1900 two-thirds of the American workers were wage dependents. Writing in the 1880s, Joseph Buchanan, a Colorado printer and labor leader, recalled that an industrious and economical worker could have bought a little business in the 1860s. "Today the opportunity to start in his business for himself has been thrust from him by the greedy hand of the great manufacturers. . . . The man who can rise from the wage condition in these days must catch a windfall from his uncle or [find] a bank unlocked."

Industrialization after the Civil War involved another profound transformation, from water power and animal power to fossil fuels. Coal had been used extensively since the 1840s, but its use expanded exponentially during the decades after the war, as did that of the newer fuels, oil and gas. No longer was energy locally produced by rushing streams powering water mills or by oxen and mules. Now it was extracted from the earth using expensive technologies and shipped long distances by rail. Mining companies ravaged the land they exploited, and fossil fuels polluted the air as they burned.

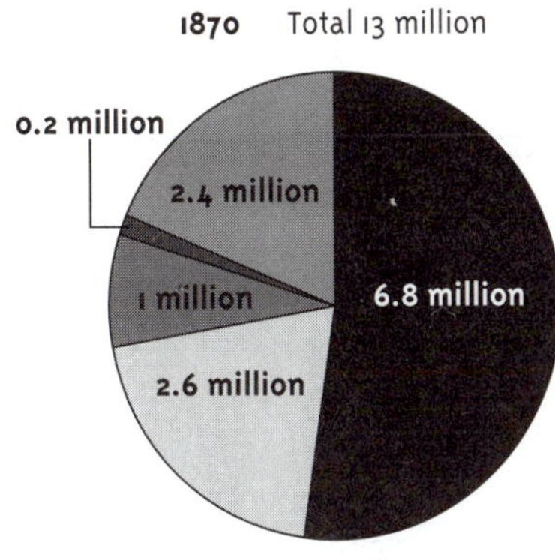

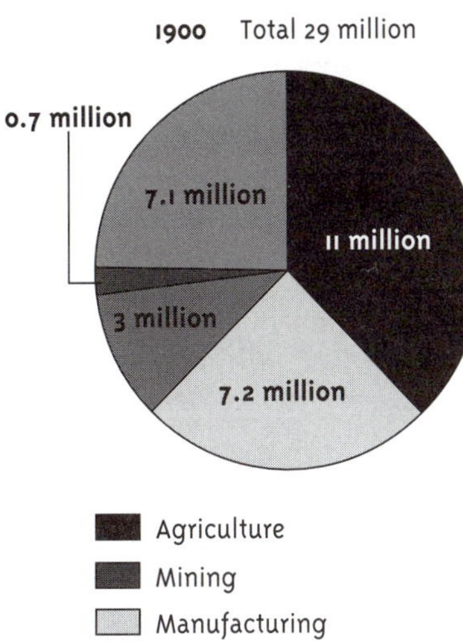

From Agriculture to Industry: A Changing Workforce Between 1870 and 1900, the labor force more than doubled. But the biggest increases came in manufacturing, which almost tripled, and trade, which quadrupled.

Manufacturers using coal and steam no longer had to locate factories alongside rivers and could instead choose sites for their access to railroads, raw materials, consumer markets, and ready supply of workers. Industrial growth therefore centered in cities, which grew twice as fast as the nation's population as a whole. In 1860, only New York, Philadelphia, and Brooklyn had more than 250,000 inhabitants. Thirty years later, eleven cities surpassed that size, and Philadelphia, Chicago, and New York each topped one million. "We cannot all live in cities," newspaper editor Horace Greeley mused, "yet nearly all seem determined to do so." The modern American city that emerged during these decades offered such essential urban services as professional fire and police forces, sewers and garbage disposal, large hospitals, and public transportation systems.

Chicago grew most spectacularly of all, from 100,000 on the eve of the Civil War to more than one million in 1890. Like other cities, it was home both to great wealth and to the foulest slums. Rapid expansion bred overcrowding and squalor: investors put too little money into new housing, and the city was unable to expand its delivery of services fast enough to meet demands. Outdoor privies overflowed into the courtyards where children played in the tenements of the North Side. Not far away, businessman Potter Palmer's Lake Shore Drive mansion boasted marble floors and mother-of-pearl washbasins.

Between the extremes of great wealth and poverty were skilled workers and members of a distinctive new middle socioeconomic stratum. These people were primarily descendants of old American stock and immigrants from the British Isles; they worked as self-employed businessmen, as professionals, or in the office jobs created by expanding corporations. They lived in growing suburban neighborhoods, joined there by the best-paid skilled workers and their families, who moved to escape the noise and dirt of downtown industrial districts.

Most of the new office jobs were products of the rise of large organizations in business and government. Before 1880, only a handful of large firms, such as Western Union and Montgomery Ward, operated on a national scale. By 1890, a number of industrial enterprises were beginning to do so, selling such products as cigarettes, soap, matches, oatmeal, and other processed foods. To serve national markets and handle the increased paperwork, these businesses had to expand not only their productive capacity but also their office staffs. Similarly, bureaucracies developed in national government. The Patent Office demanded and generated vast amounts of paperwork to deal with the explosion of patent applications that went along with rapid economic development. Another new bureaucracy processed the claims of Civil War veterans and their widows and children.

Both national companies and government bureaucracies created new kinds of work, mechanized during the 1880s by the typewriter, which produced letters and memoranda three times faster than writing by hand with pen and ink. "Five years ago the type writer was simply a mechanical curiosity," one observer commented in 1887. "Today its monotonous click can be heard in almost every well regulated business establishment in the country." The typewriter, combined with the demand for clerical labor in the growing bureaucracies, facilitated the entrance of women into these workplaces, transforming the office from an all-male preserve to a gendered hierarchy in which men dictated and women served. By 1890, some 28 percent of students in commercial schools were women, mostly enrolled in stenography and typing courses.

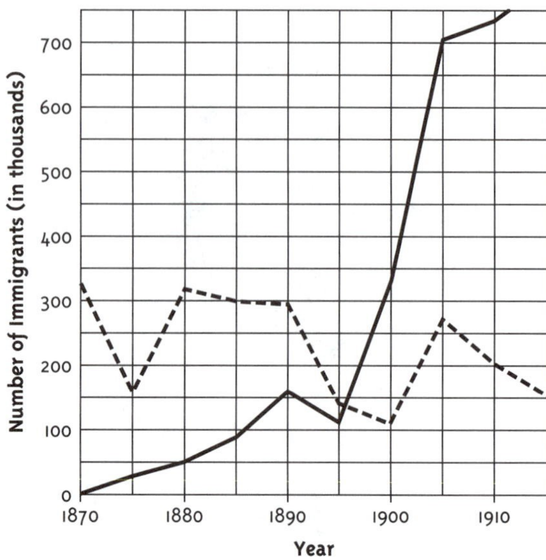

The Transformation of Immigration, 1870–1914 Before the end of the nineteenth century, European immigrants came primarily from Northern and Western parts of Europe—especially Great Britain, Ireland, and Germany. These "old" immigrants continued to arrive in significant numbers at the turn of the century. But the predominant streams of "new" immigrants after 1895 were from the Southern and Eastern areas of Europe, including Russia and Italy.

A great wave of immigration was the final process shaping American society during the late nineteenth century. The largest worldwide population movement in human history brought 10 million immigrants to the United States between 1860 and 1890. In the 1880s alone, 5.25 million entered, as many as had arrived during the first six decades of the century. They came primarily from Ireland, Germany, and Britain, as they had before the Civil War, but smaller streams from all points of the compass now joined them. Scandinavia, Italy, China, and the Austro-Hungarian Empire sent hundreds of thousands of men to work on American farms, railroads, and factories. Increasingly, in the 1880s and 1890s, immigrants came from eastern and southern Europe.

Immigrants and their second-generation sons and daughters constituted most of the population in the large cities. By 1880, nearly nine of every ten Chicagoans were first- or second-generation immigrants. These new Americans especially dominated the urban industrial workforce: approximately one of every three industrial workers in late–nineteenth-century America was an immigrant. As a clergyman observed of Chicago,

"Not every foreigner is a workingman, but in the cities, at least, it may almost be said that every workingman is a foreigner."

They came as part of a global labor market, sensitive to the potential for employment in both their native lands and their adopted one. Matthias Dorgathen, for example, was one of 1,700 miners who emigrated to North America from the Ruhr district of Germany in 1881, when mines there cut wages and laid off workers. Those leaving their homelands adjusted their plans according to the ups and downs of the U.S. business cycle: immigration fell sharply during the American depressions of 1873–1878 and 1882–1885, and it rose during the boom period of the late 1880s. The catalysts that sent people to America varied from group to group. Chinese immigration was part of a pattern of Asian migration that sent Chinese workers all over the world. Most of the 1.5 million Irish men and women who left for America between the Civil War and 1890 had been forced off the land by rapid population growth and a major agricultural depression. Emigrants from more developed economies such as Great Britain and Germany were fleeing a long European industrial depression that had been triggered in part by competition from the United States and that was impoverishing many European artisans and factory hands.

As American demand for industrial labor took off, railroad and steamship companies made open attempts to attract this much-needed labor force, advertising the glories of American life throughout Europe and China. But even more convincing were the stories told by friends and family already at home in America. Pioneering immigrants kept in touch with their Old World families and communities and sponsored those who chose to follow. The success of Francesco Barone, a prosperous Buffalo saloon keeper, inspired eight thousand people to move from his home village in Sicily to his adopted city; he assisted many of them directly.

These movements—from agriculture to industry, from household and artisan to factory production, from water and animal power to fossil fuels, from country to city, from economic independence to wage dependency, from the homeland of one's ancestors to a strange new land—transformed American life. All of these intertwined processes had begun before the Civil War, but they accelerated sharply in the 1870s and 1880s. A genuinely new urban-industrial society was characterized by class transformations—extremes of wealth and poverty and a new middle class—and by new bureaucratic organizations in industry and government. The tentacles of urban-industrial life reached far into the countryside, drawing everybody into a market economy no longer local or face-to-face. A family who lived in a Nebraska sod hut and ordered a dishpan from a Montgomery Ward catalog paid for it with money from the sale of their grain. How much they got for the grain depended on decisions made in eastern corporate headquarters and on the weather in other grain-growing areas around the globe.

The Remaking of the American Working Class

A diverse and stratified working class emerged as part of industrial capitalism's post–Civil War growth. Race and ethnicity, skill levels, gender, and age separated working people. Even in the same family, men and women, adults and children encountered very different employment opportunities, and those identities framed their lives. Skilled workers made up one-sixth of the workforce. They were typically white men of old American stock, but some were immigrants and children of immigrants from England, Ireland, and Germany. Dominating trades such as carpentry and steelmaking, these skilled craftsmen were sometimes called a "labor aristocracy." They were proud of their respectability and their ability to support their families comfortably.

Because workers usually secured jobs through family and friends, many trades took on a decidedly ethnic character. The sons of Irish immigrants tended to work as plumbers, carpenters, and bricklayers. Germans dominated furniture making, brewing, and baking. The English, Welsh, and Scots—who had emigrated from the center of the world's first industrial revolution—filled the ranks of skilled machinists, metalworkers, and miners.

Skilled workers enjoyed high wages because employers relied on their knowledge and were prepared to pay a premium for it. Few late–nineteenth-century entrepreneurs were master craftsmen who understood the details of production. They excelled at amassing the wherewithal to build factories, but they depended on skilled workers to run them. Craft skills therefore offered workers some measure of power and control over daily conditions on the job. Craft workers who took collective action could demand respect from the boss and might refuse to work in unsatisfactory circumstances.

The ideals of craft unity and collective action were as central to the world view of late–nineteenth-century skilled workers as individualism and profitability were to capitalists. Some skilled workers unionized, and some joined radical groups to fulfill collective ideals. But no more than one-third of the workers in any nineteenth-century trade were union members, and skilled craftsmen were not usually central to radical movements. As long as they could earn a good living and keep their employers' respect, most craft workers wanted neither trouble on the job nor social upheaval. Their power rested as much on their skills, knowledge, and workplace relationships as on the strength of their formal

Cigars and the News. While his fellow workers make cigars, one craftsman reads aloud from a newspaper. This arrangement, where cigar makers pooled their wages to cover the pay of the designated reader, indicates how some skilled trades maintained preindustrial customs even as their work became subdivided and mechanized.

Source: Lewis Hine, 1909—International Museum of Photography at George Eastman House.

organizations or any larger social vision.

Unskilled laborers were less able to control their working conditions. Most were new immigrants, African Americans, and impoverished women and children of all races and nationalities who were compelled by financial circumstances to take any available work. First-generation Irish women usually worked as live-in domestic servants. Theirs was a life of drudgery and isolation; it was hard, one Irish maid said, "to give up your whole life to somebody else's orders." African-American men did menial labor for wages, serving as gardeners, coach drivers, and doormen. African-American women took in laundry and worked as domestic servants. Mexican-American men labored on the railroads and in the expanding mining industries of Colorado, New Mexico, and Arizona; their wives and children worked southwestern farmlands that their ancestors had occupied for generations. Chinese-American men found work in laundries and restaurants in the Far West; few Chinese women emigrated.

As a rule, wages varied directly with an occupational group's power and social status. Men's wages were typically at least 50 percent higher than women's. White workers commanded wages significantly higher than those paid to African Americans, Mexican Americans, and Chinese Americans. Skilled craftsmen earned much more than the unskilled. The best-paid craftsman (a locomotive engineer or a glassblower, for example) could bring home more than $800 a year in the 1880s, whereas an unskilled textile worker's family had to survive on $350.

Even skilled workers had reason to worry. The proportion of skilled jobs in the labor market was declining rapidly as industry mechanized. Workers frequently lost time because of injury or illness. And all workers faced the burden of unemployment during the troughs of the business cycle. In 1878, at the end of the five-year depression, well over half a million working people remained unemployed. Employment picked up, but by the mid-1880s as many as 2 million were again out of work.

From 1870 until the end of the century, wages remained fairly steady, and virtually everything became less expensive. The food that cost $1.00 in 1870 sold for just 78 cents a decade later—an enormous benefit to working-class families, who generally spent half their income on food. Thus "real" wages, adjusted for changes in the cost of living, actually rose slowly. Nevertheless, most unskilled workers remained in poverty during this period, and many families had to send more than one family member out to work. The number of women and children in the labor force more than doubled between 1870 and 1890. In 1890, 4 million women and 1.5 million children, ten to fifteen years old, were working for wages.

In the 1870s and 1880s, one in every six or seven paid workers was a woman. English-speaking women could take advantage of two rapidly growing white-collar occupations: retail selling and office work. But in general, the women who most often worked outside their homes were the ones with the worst economic prospects. African-American women were more likely to be wage-earners than white women were, immigrant women more than native-born women, immigrant daughters more than the daughters of the native-born. Except for African-American women, who worked for wages throughout their lives, these female workers were almost all young and unmarried. Still, by 1890, a small but growing minority—almost one in every seven female wage-earners—was married.

Women's employment outside the home aroused controversy. Some wondered if a woman who worked could be truly respectable. Others contended that women worked just for "pin money," in order "to decorate themselves beyond their needs and station." Employers often used this argument to justify paying women less than men and laying them off first during hard times. Persistent questions about the legitimacy of women's paid work dragged down female workers' self-esteem and earnings. As one Iowa shoe saleswoman complained in 1886, "I don't get the salary the men clerks do, although this day I am six hundred sales ahead! Call this justice? But I have to grin and bear it, because I am so unfortunate as to be a woman."

Most of those who could afford to stay at home did so. Employment was hazardous to women's health: the death rate of women wage-earners was twice that of other women. Many predominantly female occupations, such as domestic service and "home work"—piecework done in tenement residences—demanded extraordinarily long hours, and sexual exploitation and abuse by male bosses and coworkers were not uncommon. At best, wage-earning women suffered the same hardships as men—periodic unemployment, long hours, and dangerous conditions—with even lower pay. And at the end of a day of toil in the factory, they faced an evening of household work in homes not equipped with running water or electricity.

Children's labor helped sustain millions of working-class families. During the last thirty years of the nineteenth century, about one in six children between the ages of ten and fifteen held jobs. They toiled in textile

"The Slaves of the Sweaters." A New York immigrant tailor's family returns from a contractor, carrying material to be sewn into garments back home. Scenes of urban poverty, such as this one depicted in an 1890 engraving, were featured in illustrated newspapers. Photography and individual "art" prints, however, tended to celebrate the city, with depopulated images focusing on the "grand style" architecture of new buildings or constructing distant bird's-eye views of ideal urban landscapes.

Source: William A. Rogers, *Harper's Weekly,* April 26, 1890—American Social History Project.

mills, tobacco-processing plants, and print shops. They roamed the streets as newsboys, bootblacks, and scrap collectors. Their employers worked them hard. In one Chicago candy factory, children worked 82-hour weeks during the Christmas season. In southern cotton mills, their year-round workdays lasted twelve hours, and they sometimes worked the night shift. A few states prohibited child labor and required school attendance, but the laws were loosely enforced and easily ignored by desperate parents and greedy employers. Children's wages ranged from a few pennies to about 75 cents a day, half the amount paid to an unskilled adult laborer.

At the very bottom of the wage-earning class were the families who labored for long hours in cramped tenement apartments—rolling cigars, making artificial flowers, cracking nuts, and sewing clothing. In 1892, nearly 11,000 people toiled in 600 tenement workshops in Chicago. One typical family of eight lived and labored in a three-room flat. "The father, mother, two daughters and a cousin work together making trousers at 65 cents a dozen pairs," reported an investigator. "They work 7 days a week. . . . Their destitution is very great."

Working Conditions

Although divided by skill, ethnicity, race, gender, and age, working people in the late nineteenth century had much in common. They worked long hours—typically ten-hour days, six days a week. "I get so exhausted that I can scarcely drag myself home when night comes," a Massachusetts textile worker remarked in 1881. More and more workers encountered the impersonality of the large factory, the sense of being an anonymous cog in a big wheel. Between 1870 and 1900, the average workforce in cotton mills and tobacco factories doubled.

Many employers sought ways to raise profits by reducing workers' already meager wages. Some cut wages; others required workers to bear part of the cost of working. Clothing manufacturers required workers to buy sewing machines, needles, and thread. Some employers shifted the costs of rent, heat, and light onto the workers by hiring them to manufacture clothing, artificial flowers, and other small items in their tenement apartments. And mining companies and others often paid in "scrip," or company-issued paper money. This money could be used only at company-owned stores, which charged highly inflated prices. One mining company made $1,000 a month by selling gunpowder—which miners were required to buy to extract coal or ore—at

$3.25 a keg, more than $1.25 above the going rate. Miners, one observer commented, became "virtually the slaves" of the scrip and company-store system.

Most late–nineteenth-century businessmen ignored hazardous working conditions, largely because they had little financial incentive to make the workplace safer. Railroads provide a classic example. Workers risked being maimed as they ran along the tops of trains to set the brakes for each car or stood on the tracks to drop a coupling pin as the cars crashed together. In 1881 alone, long after safety devices such as automatic coupler systems and the Westinghouse air brake had become widely available, 30,000 railroad workers were killed or injured on the job. "So long as brakes cost more than trainmen," the prominent minister Lyman Abbott predicted, "we may expect the present sacrificial method of car coupling to continue." The courts repeatedly denied damages to injured workers, maintaining that they shared the blame for accidents and that by going to work they accepted the risks of the job. In 1893, the federal Railroad Safety Appliance Act finally made it illegal for trains to operate without automatic couplers and air brakes.

The harsh conditions of life and labor in the emerging industrial capitalist economy—long hours, child labor, payment in scrip, and unsafe workplaces—all enhanced corporate profits. Deteriorating working conditions and growing powerlessness engendered bitterness among working people. Workers sought ways to improve their circumstances under the

The Ironworkers Sell Soap. After Thomas Anshutz's painting "The Ironworkers' Noontime" (see chapter-opening illustration) was reproduced as a *Harper's Weekly* engraving in 1884, the popularity of the print prompted Procter and Gamble to exploit its theme to sell the company's Ivory Soap. Publishing a series of lithographs "suitable for framing," Procter and Gamble transformed the nobility of skilled labor articulated by Anshutz into a picture of grimy industrial work relieved by its "99 and 44/100% pure" product.

Source: Chicago Historical Society.

"Caught in the Shafting." The *National Police Gazette* portrayed, in a characteristically lurid fashion, an industrial accident in a North Grosvenor, Connecticut, cotton mill. The *Police Gazette* enthusiastically violated the mores of a genteel culture by focusing on legal and illegal sports, violent crimes and accidents, and sex. Often women were depicted as perpetrators or victims of violence, providing titillation to the male readership.

Source: *National Police Gazette,* May 28, 1892—Prints and Photographs Division, Library of Congress.

new industrial order, while employers tried to make the system even more productive and profitable.

Businessmen Seek Control

Chaotic economic and political forces appeared to hinder the best efforts of businessmen to dominate their industries and even their firms in the late nineteenth century. A legal tradition against monopolies further limited successful capitalists from simply buying out or merging with their competitors. *Control* became their watchword: control of the markets for their raw materials and their products, control of production within their firms, control of the workers who toiled for them, and control of their political environment. To achieve these ends, businessmen, especially those in large-scale production industries such as iron and steel, continually expanded their firms. They hoped to wipe out competitors, guarantee supplies of raw materials, and market their products more effectively.

Railroad executives pioneered the effort to control markets. In the 1870s they had organized themselves into pools to divide up traffic and set freight rates, an approach that seemed preferable to cutthroat competition. But the pools collapsed when railroad executives reneged on their agreements. In hard times, they slashed freight rates to win customers. When a pool member broke ranks, rivals had no recourse but to follow suit; their agreements were not enforceable legal contracts.

Railroad managers were also undermined by a new breed of financial speculators, men who had little interest in running railroads but great interest in profiting from them. Financiers led by Jay Gould, Jim Fisk, and Cornelius Vanderbilt rigged the stock market, issuing thousands of shares of new, "watered" stock without increasing the assets they represented. They also launched rate wars to drive down the price of railroad stocks and bonds temporarily so they could buy distressed railroads at bargain prices.

When the pools collapsed in the 1880s, railroad managers turned to a new method of controlling competition: they built huge rail networks to drive smaller lines out of business. Between 1880 and 1893, the big railroads leased more land, bought more equipment, and laid more track, enormously increasing the scale of their operations. Constructed from inferior materials, and laid along badly prepared routes, much of this new track had to be rebuilt, at significant expense, within fifteen years. During the depression of 1893–1898, scores of railroad lines went bankrupt.

Large-scale manufacturing enterprises experienced similar boom-and-bust patterns of expansion, competition, and bankruptcy. Industrialists rushed into new markets, overbuilding capacity until initially high prices and profits gave way to sharp competition, falling prices, and declining profits. To protect themselves, manufacturers organized cartels, organizations dedicated to eliminating competition by limiting production and maintaining high prices. In the hardware industry alone, more than sixty cartels appeared in the 1870s and 1880s. But industrial cartels worked no better than railroad pools: individual firms cut prices to steal customers when it suited them.

Many manufacturers attempted to compete through new technology. By installing a new production process, a firm might cut expenses, lower prices, drive competitors out of business, and then raise prices again. But technology often worsened manufacturers' financial problems, for as soon as one producer achieved a slight cost advantage, rival firms would match the technological improvement and add new ones of their own. Moreover, industrialists had to borrow massive amounts of capital to stay in the technology game. With prices falling, they couldn't easily repay their loans with interest and still show the profits needed to attract new investors.

Again like the railroads, manufacturers used size as a competitive weapon. One means of growth was horizontal integration, in which several companies producing the same product merged to form a single larger unit that could gain control of prices and markets, both in purchasing raw materials and selling manufactured goods. Other manufacturers focused on vertical integration, in which one firm coordinated all aspects of production and distribution, rather than buying materials from and selling products to other companies. This strategy insulated firms from competition by enabling them to control their costs of manufacturing.

The most successful firms combined these approaches, as demonstrated by the activities of the two leading industrialists of the period, John D. Rockefeller and Andrew Carnegie. Rockefeller, the son of an itinerant patent-medicine salesman, started as a bookkeeper, earning enough to become a partner in a successful wholesaling firm. In 1863, he invested his money in the fledgling petroleum industry, which primarily produced kerosene for lighting.

Seven years later, Rockefeller and his partners incorporated Standard Oil, a centrally organized combination of oil corporations. Thanks to its close ties with the railroads, which granted discounts or rebates to major shippers, Standard Oil could price its products much lower than its competitors and drive them out of business. Dismissing rival cartels as "ropes of sand," Rockefeller merged competing firms with Standard Oil, pledging willing competitors to secrecy and ruthlessly coercing the unwilling. By 1880, the Standard Oil Trust controlled about 90 percent of the na-

Andrew Carnegie. A less than flattering view of the industrialist's philanthropic philosophy, published in an April 1905 edition of the satirical weekly *Life*.
Source: Albert Levering, *Life*, April 13, 1905—American Social History Project.

tion's oil-refining capacity; Rockefeller could set the price and virtually control the output of oil. During the next decade, Standard Oil moved to vertical integration, purchasing oil fields, constructing pipelines, establishing a nationwide system of licensed dealers, and building fleets of tankers to serve newly created foreign marketing subsidiaries.

Andrew Carnegie—the wealthiest American capitalist of the period—was an even more potent symbol of individual advancement, although his rags-to-riches rise was actually quite unusual for his day. Carnegie's Scottish father, a linen weaver, had lost his job when the power loom was introduced. Like many other European skilled workers displaced by technological advances, the elder Carnegie moved his family to the United States. He and his wife eked out a living in an immigrant neighborhood in Pittsburgh, weaving and taking in laundry. Young Andrew began his working life in factories and eventually became a telegrapher and personal secretary for Thomas A. Scott, the superintendent of the Pennsylvania Railroad's Western Division. When Scott was promoted in 1859, Carnegie, at age twenty-four, was given Scott's job.

Six years later, Carnegie left the railroad—probably the most complex enterprise in the world and the best possible training ground for a future industrialist. He soon focused his energies on steel production, and he spent the next quarter-century using new technology and techniques of vertical and horizontal integration to ensure his absolute domination over that industry. He built up-to-date mills, acquired companies from competitors, forged alliances with the railroads that both used and hauled his steel, and adapted the management and marketing techniques he had learned at the Pennsylvania Railroad.

Carnegie carried the techniques of vertical integration further than had any of his contemporaries. Annoyed by fluctuations in the price and supply of the pig iron basic to steel making, he began to integrate backward, producing the supplies he needed. With his partner Henry Clay Frick, he acquired sources of iron ore, coke, and coal, expanded his ironmaking operations, and developed a fleet of steamships and a railroad to transport materials directly to his steel mills. "From the moment these crude stuffs were dug out of the earth until they flowed in a stream of liquid steel in the ladles," trumpeted one admiring observer, "there was never a price, profit, or royalty paid to an outsider." Carnegie also integrated forward, establishing sales offices across the country and doing his own wholesaling.

" . . . The Duty of the Man of Wealth"

In *The Gospel of Wealth and Other Timely Essays,* published in 1889, the industrialist Andrew Carnegie argued that individual capitalists were duty bound to play a broader cultural and social role and thus improve the world.

This then, is held to be the duty of the man of wealth: To set an example of modest, unostentatious living, shunning display or extravagance; to provide moderately for the legitimate wants of those dependent upon him; and, after doing so, to consider all surplus revenues which came to him simply as trust funds, which he is called upon to administer, and strictly bound as a matter of duty to administer in the manner which, in his judgment, is best calculated to produce the most beneficial results for the community—the man of wealth thus becoming the mere trustee and agent for his poorer brethren, bringing to their service his superior wisdom, experience, and ability to administer, doing for them better than they would or could do for themselves. . . .

"A Workingman's Prayer"

Carnegie's point of view contrasts sharply with those of "A Workman," who published a satirical response to Carnegie's book in an 1894 issue of a Pittsburgh labor newspaper.

Oh, almighty Andrew Philanthropist Library Carnegie, who art in America when not in Europe spending the money of your slaves and serfs, thou art a good father to the people of Pittsburgh, Homestead and Beaver Falls. We bow before thee in humble obedience of slavery. . . . We have no desire but to serve thee. If you sayest black was white we believe you, and are willing, with the assistance of . . . the Pinkerton's agency, to knock the stuffin[g] out of anyone who thinks different, or to shoot down and imprison serfs who dare say you have been unjust in reducing the wages of your slaves, who call themselves citizens of the land of the free and the home of the brave. . . .

Oh, lord and master, we love thee because you and other great masters of slaves favor combines and trusts to enslave and make paupers of us all. We love thee though our children are clothed in rags. We love thee though our wives . . . are so scantily dressed and look so shabby. But, oh master, thou hast given us one great enjoyment which man has never dreamed of before—a free church organ, so that we can take our shabby families to church to hear your great organ pour forth its melodious strains. . . .

Oh, master, we thank thee for all the free gifts you have given the public at the expense of your slaves. . . . Oh, master, we need no protection, we need no liberty so long as we are under thy care. So we commend ourselves to thy mercy and forevermore sing thy praise.

Amen!

Sources: Andrew Carnegie, *The Gospel of Wealth and Other Timely Essays* (1889); "A Workingman's Prayer": *The Coming Nation,* February 10, 1894.

By the end of the century, Carnegie's companies produced a quarter of the nation's steel, and he personally pocketed $25 million a year. But by the time he died in 1919, he was as well known for giving money away as he had been for making it. In two essays published in 1889, Carnegie described his "gospel of wealth," declaring that the rich should administer their money for the public good. Rather than paying higher wages, however, the wealthy man should become "the sole agent and trustee for his poorer brethren, bringing to their service his superior wisdom, experience, and ability to administer." During the next thirty years, Carnegie endowed 2,800 libraries around the world, as well as other cultural institutions. Although he declared that the wealthy should "set an example of modest, unostentatious living, shunning display or extravagance," Carnegie himself lived in mansions in Pittsburgh and New York and on a 40,000-acre estate in Scotland.

New Management Systems

Not every businessman tried to dominate his industry as Carnegie and Rockefeller did, but virtually all were driven during the last decades of the nineteenth century to trim costs by restructuring their firms and streamlining work processes. Managers of small and large firms alike faced internal and external imperatives to minimize waste and inefficiency. But smaller companies responded more cautiously to the management innovations and production methods that were sweeping corporate America. Most woodworking and metalworking firms, for example, employed fewer than one hundred employees, who turned out relatively small batches of customized products. Such companies opted for limited measures to increase workers' productivity, enhance management control, and increase profits. They might purchase a single new machine, identify a new local or regional market for their products, or modestly (rather than completely) reorganize the work process.

The leaders of gigantic industrial firms, on the other hand, chose a wholly new form of corporate direction. After 1880, big businessmen turned to systematic management, a loose label for various efforts to speed and streamline industrial operations. Their intent was to subject workers, machines, and the final product to management goals. Initially these efforts were handicapped by unsystematic and decentralized labor-control systems. In most nineteenth-century factories, a foreman responsible for achieving production goals supervised each department. Although foremen attempted to drive their crews toward goals, they in fact often cajoled them to get the job done and even negotiated output, pay, and other issues. Industrial workers resisted working ceaselessly at peak efficiency, trying instead to set their own pace and give the boss what *they* considered a fair day of work. Manufacturers complained bitterly about time wasted by workers who stopped to rest, discuss the progress of the work, or wait for machines to be repaired or materials to be delivered.

To increase workers' output, employers strictly enforced formal work rules. Fines for minor infractions became common. Foremen shaved time off lunch periods and kept factories running after the official closing time. Quoting Benjamin Franklin, a New Hampshire factory headed its list of work rules with "NOTICE! TIME IS MONEY!" One rule stated that washing up "must be done outside of working hours, and not at our expense."

Some manufacturers introduced machinery as part of their campaign to exert control over employees. Fuming at his workers' victory in an

THE LABOR DESPOT.

THE supreme tyrant of the labor organizations is the walking delegate, the well-fed, well-paid official who performs the functions of a general overseer, and whose fiat is expected to be obeyed without protest or murmur. Not a few of the disastrous strikes of recent years were prolonged, if they were not instigated, by these representatives of the worst elements of discontent. Happily American workingmen seem now to be losing their respect for this class of petty despots, and it is hardly probable that they will be able in future to exercise any such autocratic power as they have so injuriously employed in the past.

It was the peculiarity of the recent great strike in London that it was spontaneous, that it was based upon a real grievance, was entirely free from coercive excesses on the part of would-be bosses and that it had, from first to last, the genuine sympathy of the great body of the people. The sole obstacle to a settlement was the obstinacy of the dock companies, upon whom the demand for slightly increased compensation was made by the striking laborers. Against these stubborn dock directors were arrayed the merchants, the ship-owners, and all the high officials in church and state, such men as Cardinal Manning, the Lord Mayor, the Bishop of London, and Sir John Lubbock interfering actively in behalf of the strikers, while Lord Randolph Churchill and other men in official life ably championed their cause in public addresses. It was inevitable that, thus sustained, the men on strike should ultimately gain a substantial victory. It will be well if American workingmen shall learn the lesson that, with a just cause, and abstaining from all disorderly and offensive methods, they, too, can depend upon public sympathy, and will be much more likely to win their way than when pursuing an opposite course.

"The Tyranny of the Walking Delegate." The popular image of the trade union official changed as manufacturers attempted to exert greater control over the workplace. In this 1889 engraving, a trade-union officer—"the well-fed, well-paid official . . . whose fiat is expected to be obeyed without protest or murmur"—arbitrarily calls a strike. Portrayed as a despotic opponent of business, the official's manner and dress resembled the familiar figure of the corrupt political boss.

Source: J. Durkin, *Frank Leslie's Illustrated Newspaper,* September 21, 1889—American Social History Project.

1885 strike, Cyrus McCormick of Chicago's McCormick Harvesting Machine Company vowed, "I do not think we will be troubled by the same thing again if we take proper steps to weed out the bad element among the men." McCormick installed $500,000 worth of molding machinery so that he could "weed out" the skilled workers who had led the strike, crush their union, and replace them with low-paid, unskilled workers. Similarly, John D. Rockefeller used new barrel-making technology in his Cleveland plant to break the power—and lower the wages—of the company's highly skilled and once-proud barrel makers.

It was Andrew Carnegie who developed the most coherent plan to gain control over the work process, combining bold technological innovation and ruthless employee management. To control costs, Carnegie hired the renowned engineer Alexander Lyman Holley to design his J. Edgar Thompson steelworks in the 1880s. Holley's design moved materials smoothly through the steel-making process. Elevated trains, for example, carried coal overhead throughout the huge mill, eliminating the jobs of hundreds of shovel-wielding laborers. With such technological innovations, Carnegie's steel plants were far and away the most advanced in the world by the late 1880s.

Turning his attention to taming his workforce, Carnegie successfully resisted an 1892 strike by workers at his giant plant in Homestead, Pennsylvania. After a long struggle, he managed to lengthen the working day in all of his plants without raising the daily wage rate. In the mid-1890s, many of his employees were working twelve-hour shifts, seven days a week. "We stop only the time it takes to oil the engines," said one Homestead worker.

Businessmen Look to Politics

Businessmen saw politics as another means of boosting profits and consolidating their control of markets and workers. Business influence pervaded all levels of government in the late nineteenth century, but as enterprises became national in scope, their owners and managers tried to shape the federal government and nationwide policies. Managers much preferred to deal with a uniform set of federal laws or regulations than with a confusing and contradictory assortment of state and local ones. Big businessmen also found they could influence the federal government more easily than state or local governments, which tended to be more responsive to local interests. And as journalists and reformers began demanding that the national government regulate railroads and control monopolies, businessmen were eager to influence legislation in their own behalf.

"The Bosses of the Senate." An 1889 cartoon from the satirical weekly *Puck* decries corporate control of the U.S. Senate. "This is a Senate of the Monopolists, by the Monopolists, and for the Monopolists!" reads the sign over the corpulent corporate spectators as they watch over the obedient legislators (many of whom were millionaires). Meanwhile, the "People's Entrance" to the Senate is barred shut.

Source: Joseph Keppler, *Puck,* January 23, 1889—New-York Historical Society.

Corruption and favor buying in government had increased notably during the Civil War, and they persisted when peace came. So rife was vote selling that one Ohio politician referred to the House of Representatives in 1873 as "an auction room." The spoils system, a term dating back to the 1830s, was still the policy by which public positions were filled: supporters of the winning party were awarded government offices, and they were in turn expected to give kickbacks to their political parties.

Beginning in 1875, Democrats increasingly challenged Republican dominance in Washington, D.C., as they rebuilt their party from the shambles of the war. The revived Democratic party united most of the South, and it attracted a growing number of workingmen in northern industrial areas by attacking the increasing concentration of wealth and corruption in politics. In the 1876 presidential election, the Democrats seemed on the verge of victory. Their candidate, Samuel J. Tilden, captured a majority of the popular vote and appeared to have won in the electoral college as well. But Republicans, backing Rutherford B. Hayes, disputed the returns in Louisiana, South Carolina, and Florida and threw the election into question. Nearly three months of wrangling and intrigue followed, accompanied not only by growing panic in the business community but also by widespread fear of renewed war between North and South.

In late February 1877, only a few weeks before the new president was to be inaugurated, pressure from businessmen and politicians forced a resolution to the conflict. In the Compromise of 1877, the Democrats yielded the presidency to Hayes. In exchange, they received a share of federal appointments (including the appointment of at least one southerner to Hayes's cabinet), federal assistance to southern railroads, and the by then largely symbolic final removal of federal troops from the southern states. The agreement cleared the way for the removal of African Americans from national and local politics and for the collapse of the Republican party in the South. A key figure in securing the compromise was the Democratic iron magnate Abram Hewitt. A journalist described

Hewitt as a man "with one hand upon his heart and the other hand in his pocket." Hewitt, speaking for himself and for other businessmen who were coming to believe they could best achieve their goals by supporting both parties, announced, "I would prefer four years of Hayes's administration to four years of civil war."

The results of the 1876 election fed growing disillusionment with political corruption. A number of businessmen had grown uncertain of their prospects for successfully bribing politicians; others had principles too strong or wallets too slim to join in the game. Against this background, a campaign to clean up politics emerged in the late 1870s and gained momentum in the early 1880s. Some businessmen and reformers had long advocated replacing the spoils system with a civil service system, based on merit and protected against shifts in party power; such systems were already in place in England, Germany, and elsewhere in Europe. That idea acquired new urgency in 1881, when Republican president James A. Garfield was assassinated by Charles Guiteau, a crazed job-seeker and member of an opposing faction of Republicans (called the "Stalwarts"). When Guiteau shot Garfield, he announced the succession: "I am a Stalwart. [Vice President Chester] Arthur is now president." (Actually, Guiteau was premature; Garfield spent almost three months on his death bed. In this era when the president and the federal government were much less central to national life, an incapacitated president did not pose a major problem.) Two years later, the Pendleton Civil Service Act created the Civil Service Commission to hire federal workers on the basis of competitive examinations.

Still, politics remained a dirty business. The 1884 election was particularly grubby. Democrats described the Republican candidate, Senator James G. Blaine as "the continental liar from the State of Maine." This was meant to highlight the personal honesty of their candidate, Grover Cleveland, the governor of New York. But Cleveland had two skeletons in his own closet. One was his war record—or actually his lack of one, since he had hired a substitute to fight for him in the Civil War, as had many better-off northerners. The other was his fathering of a child out of wedlock, which the Republicans exposed with the chant: "Ma, Ma, where's my Pa? Gone to the White House, Ha, Ha, Ha!" But Blaine was hurt with Irish Catholic voters by a Protestant minister who attacked the Democrats as the party of "Rum, Romanism, and Rebellion" and with working-class voters by his presence—in the midst of a depression—at a sumptuous feast hosted by Jay Gould and other robber barons. Cleveland won narrowly; a shift of 600 votes in the crucial state of New York would have made Blaine president. The close contest reflected the even balance between the parties in this period. In 1888, Cleveland lost narrowly in electoral votes to Benjamin Harrison—but actually won the popular vote. (Four years later, however, Cleveland won a resounding victory and became the only man to serve two nonconsecutive terms as president.)

Aiding Harrison in 1888 was a lavish campaign chest systematically raised from businessmen by department-store magnate John Wanamaker—the first time that truly large sums of money had been raised from businessmen for a presidential campaign. Ironically, the 1883 Pendleton Act had freed political parties from financial dependence on their appointees only to place them at the mercy of businessmen. Industrialists' and financiers' contributions to both the Democratic and Republican parties assured them of support from whichever was in power. As a result, journalist William Allen White argued that senators represented not political but economic entities: "Coal and iron owned a coterie from the Middle and Eastern seaport states. Cotton had half a dozen senators. And so it went."

When popular sentiment demanded that the government regulate business by reining in railroads or curbing monopolies, business-oriented members of Congress could ensure that the resulting laws lacked muscle. Thus, businessmen used their influence to shape the two great measures of federal regulation of business during the late nineteenth century, the Interstate Commerce Act (1887) and the Sherman Antitrust Act (1890). One senator described the Interstate Commerce Act, which established a federal system of railroad regulation, as "a delusion and a sham." Powerful railroads made the Interstate Commerce Commission—the regulatory agency set up under the act—their servant instead of their master.

The most important and reliable bulwark of business power in federal circles was the judiciary. Most federal judges had begun their careers in corporation law, and they served their former business associates from the bench. However feeble federal laws regulating business were, court decisions made them even weaker. The Sherman Antitrust Act (1890), for example, was designed to curb the power of business mergers and combinations. Although the courts rarely found corporations guilty of violating the act, they did find it useful in curbing labor unions, by issuing injunctions—cease-and-desist orders—against strikers and their unions.

U.S. businessmen had taken major steps to reshape the world within which they operated, and the scale and influence of capitalist enterprise were without precedent. Yet big business failed to overcome the instability of the American economy, which would surface again in 1893. Nor could businessmen count on controlling government. Despite bribes and influence peddling, their political power was repeatedly challenged by popular insurgencies.

The New South

The Compromise of 1877 cemented the rule of southern conservatives and made the region "safe" for northern business—a condition that had not existed during the social and political upheavals of Reconstruction. Consequently, when the depression of the 1870s lifted, northern businessmen began to invest large amounts of money in the South. They were courted by a new group of leaders who hoped to gain access to northern industrial capital. Men like Henry Grady, the editor of the *Atlanta Constitution,* envisioned a "New South" filled with cities, immigrants, commerce, and industry financed by northern money. But the development of the New South was slow and unsteady, for the growth of industrial capitalism there was shaped by southern dependence on cotton, the domination of northern capital, and the legacy of slavery. The lives of the small farmers, black and white, who constituted the vast majority of

The New South at the End of the Nineteenth Century
Despite the promises of its boosters, the New South, like the Old South, remained overwhelmingly agricultural. Still, some industries—wood products, coal, cigarettes, and even iron and steel—had emerged by the end of the century. The most important was textile manufacturing, which spread through the Piedmont, the region of rolling hills that stretched from central Virginia down to Georgia and Alabama.

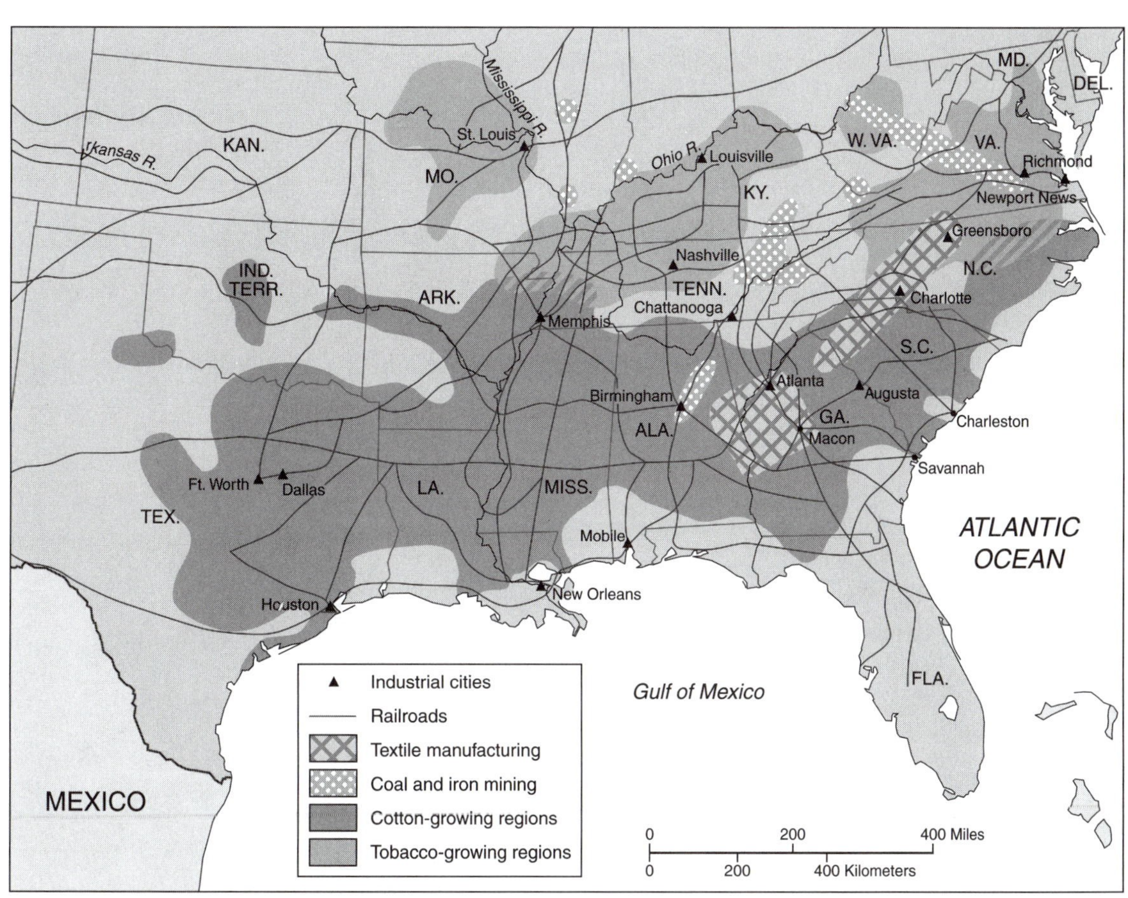

the southern population, were even more insecure and their suffering even more acute than were the lives of northern workers.

Northern business had easily gained control of southern industry and finance after the Civil War. Southern capital invested in slaves had been wiped out by emancipation. Physical destruction from the war caused further losses. Federal action during Reconstruction reinforced the region's dependency. The nation's new financial system was oriented toward promoting industry, and the South was predominantly agricultural. The system also favored creditors, and the South was largely a debtor region. The Republican banking and currency legislation that encouraged northern industry hampered operations of southern banks that had not failed outright.

Industrial development in the South was therefore bankrolled by northern (and to some extent European) investors, who placed their own profits before southern welfare. They set up low-wage operations to extract raw materials or crudely processed products, such as lumber, coal, cotton, turpentine, and seafood. These industries squeezed profits from the region, depleted resources, and left behind destitute people and a dependent economy. The only major southern-controlled industry was tobacco, which came to be dominated by North Carolinians. James B. Duke, who called tobacco "the poor man's luxury," mechanized the industry and played the role that Carnegie and Rockefeller played in steel and oil.

Railroads led the way in southern economic development, as they had in the North. Between 1880 and 1890, laborers laid over 22,000 miles of track, nearly doubling the southern rail network. Large railroad companies swallowed up smaller ones. Twelve large corporations, most of them headquartered in New York City, controlled half of all southern track. The Richmond and West Point Terminal Company, which bought up competing systems across Tennessee, Virginia, and Georgia, emerged as the largest of the southern railroads. In the early 1890s, seventeen of its twenty-man board of directors—including Jay Gould and Abram Hewitt—were New Yorkers.

Aided by state legislators, who provided generous land grants and lenient tax policies to speculators, the railroads helped create new industries that extracted resources. The growth of the iron industry in Tennessee, Virginia, and Alabama was particularly impressive. Birmingham, Alabama, which did not even exist in 1870, became one of the country's largest iron-, steel-, and coal-producing centers. Even so, the South's dependence on northern capital and technical expertise sharply limited southern industrialization.

The most important southern industry, in fact, the key to southern industrialization, was cotton manufacturing. Between 1880 and 1890, the number of spindles—rods holding spools of thread—increased ninefold in the four leading textile states (Georgia, Alabama, and the Carolinas), to just under 4 million. The new southern mills had two unbeatable advantages over their older northern counterparts: the newest, most efficient technology and an impoverished workforce. Southern mills relied heavily on child labor. In 1896, one in four North Carolina cotton-mill workers was a child, as compared with one in twenty in Massachusetts; a North Carolina child also earned less than four cents for every dime a Massachusetts child earned. The difference for adults was narrower: North Carolinians earned from one-half to two-thirds of their Massachusetts counterparts' wages.

Southern textile workers lived in company towns. Describing isolated Georgia mill towns in 1891, social investigator Clare de Graffenreid painted a grim picture of "rows of loosely built, weather-stained frame houses, all of the same ugly pattern and buttressed by clumsy chimneys." A typical interior contained only "a shackling bed, tricked out in gaudy patchwork, a few defunct 'split-bottom' chairs, a rickety table, and a jumble of battered crockery." Mill owners, like slaveholders before the Civil War, thought of themselves as kindly father figures, but in fact they ruled their company-owned towns with iron fists, refusing to allow them to incorporate and establish local governments. Starvation wages, payment in scrip, and price-gouging company stores eclipsed the advantages of low rent and subsidized schools and churches.

In dramatic contrast to the mostly immigrant workforce of the North, virtually all of the southern textile-mill labor force was white and had been born in the United States. Race provided southern employers with a powerful weapon for dividing workers; white workers tolerated exploitation more willingly if black workers were even worse off. Women in an Atlanta mill showed their determination to protect textile work as a white "privilege" in 1898, when 1,400 struck against the employment of two African-American spinners. This pattern of race discrimination was not confined to the textile industry. Cigar factories relied on African Americans: women sorted and stemmed the leaves in filthy, hot, unventilated rooms, and men made cigars or chewing plugs.

Segregation in the Workplace. White workers paused for a photograph in a Richmond, Virginia, cigarette factory.

Source: Valentine Museum, Richmond, Virginia.

African-American Tobacco Workers. In this Richmond, Virginia, factory, women strip stems from leaves. As in most southern industries, black workers labored separately from white workers and were relegated to the lowest-paying and least-skilled jobs. **Source:** Valentine Museum, Richmond, Virginia.

Cigarette factories hired both black and white workers but separated them. The vast majority of urban black women toiled by the day as maids in white people's homes or did laundry for pay in their own homes. They rejected live-in domestic work because its round-the-clock demands and close surveillance smacked of slavery.

As in the North, immigrants made up a disproportionate part of the urban working class, although relatively few foreigners immigrated to the South. In 1880, only one in twenty residents of Richmond, Virginia, was an immigrant, but one in three of the city's unskilled white laborers were foreign-born.

Outside the cities, even southerners employed in factories retained their ties to the soil. In Chatham County, Georgia, black men often stayed on the farms all winter while the women worked in a nearby oyster-processing plant. In Tennessee and Virginia, men of both races labored in sawmills or coal mines while women worked the farms. Many of the South's major employers—tobacco, seafood, and sugar processors—offered only seasonal employment. In the off season, their employees went back to farming.

Crop Liens, Debt, and Sharecropping

For Atlanta's Henry Grady, the railroad was the ultimate symbol of the New South, but for many poor white farmers it symbolized exploitation and greed. This was especially true in the hill country, where most white families had never owned slaves, and poor farmers had produced food for their own consumption or for trade with local artisans. After the war, these farmers shifted from subsistence agriculture to commercial production, but they paid dearly to get their goods to market. With no competition, hill-country railroad owners were free to raise rates, even as freight rates elsewhere were declining. As railroad lines were extended throughout the southern backcountry, farmers were at their mercy.

White farmers' troubles were exacerbated by the crop-lien system. Cash-poor farmers turned for credit to "furnishing merchants," who used funds borrowed from northern banks to buy seed, tools, and other supplies, which they resold to the farmers in exchange for a *lien,* or claim, on their next harvest. The merchants not only charged credit customers significantly higher prices than those paid by cash customers, they also added interest of 25 to 50 percent. In the fall, after the crop had been marketed, the merchants collected their debts.

Merchants usually insisted that borrowers grow cotton because it was readily marketable. Unfortunately, the widespread shift to commercial agriculture coincided with the beginning of a long-term decline in world prices for cotton. A dramatic increase in Brazilian, Egyptian, and Indian cotton production and—more significantly—a leveling off of international demand for cotton led to a ruinous fall in prices. The record-breaking 1894 cotton crop was more than double that of 1873, but farmers suffered because 1894 prices were only one-third of those paid twenty-one years earlier.

Consequently, white small farmers found themselves trapped in a vicious circle: they could get credit only if they grew cotton; cotton prices kept falling, so they had to plant more; the more cotton they planted, the less food they grew; the less food they grew, the more they had to borrow to buy food. More and more often, their debt surpassed the value of their crops. They had no choice but to commit the following year's crop to the merchants as well. "The furnishing man was the boss, pure and simple," wrote a woman who watched the system work in Alabama. "His word was law." In the end, many white farmers lost their land to these merchants.

On the lowest rung of the southern economic ladder were the tenant farmers, or sharecroppers. In large plantation areas across the South, families—most of them African American—rented small plots of land and paid landowners a large share of the crop at the end of the harvest. The landowners retained the ultimate power of ownership, supplying tools, fertilizer, seed, and land and appropriating most of the crop. Sharecroppers were legally free but economically dependent, drawn into the market system like northern wage laborers. But although they raised crops for the market, African-American sharecroppers remained largely outside the money economy. Each family began the agricultural cycle by securing seed, supplies, and food from the landowner; these items were charged to the family and deducted from its share of the crop at harvest time. Even in the best of times, the family's share was small, but as the price of cotton fell in the 1880s and 1890s, sharecroppers descended into a deepening spiral of debt and dependency. And, although legally free, some sharecroppers lived with the ghosts of slavery: many white planters still maintained a system of armed "riders" who monitored and disciplined black workers; one woman told of being whipped until her "back was as raw as a piece of raw beef."

Black families scrambled to make a bit of money because every penny earned brought a degree of freedom from dependency on the landowner. Men worked by the day on nearby farms, and women sold chickens, eggs, milk, cheese, and vegetables. Still, their poverty was remarkable even in this generally poor region: most black sharecropping women kept house with only a straw broom, a laundry tub, a cooking kettle, and a water pail.

Plowing. Too poor to own a mule or other drive animal, some sharecropper families improvised other ways to plow their plots of land.

Source: New-York Historical Society.

Sharecropping or one of its variants occupied the overwhelming majority of black farming families in the late–nineteenth-century South. Since 90 percent of African Americans still lived in the South, and since 80 percent of them lived in rural areas, the system touched the lives of a substantial majority. The story of Browne Cobb, a sharecropper born a slave on an Alabama cotton plantation in 1850, illustrates one man's dependency. After the war, Cobb plowed and chopped cotton on land owned by a white man, Clem Todd. He was "furnished" with seed and equipment, not (as was typical) by Todd, but by another white man, Lloyd Albee. In exchange, Albee held a mortgage on some cattle Cobb had managed to acquire over the years. Wanting to exert greater control over Cobb, Albee continually pressured him to move to Albee's land as a sharecropper.

After Cobb sold one of the cattle, Albee tried again to compel him to move. When Cobb refused, Albee had him thrown in jail for selling property that was not his. Cobb was released through the influence of yet another white man, Jasper Clay, in a deal that Cobb's son Ned later described as "a friendship business amongst the white race." In exchange for securing his release, Clay forced Cobb to join his large gang of black and white sharecroppers. They were supposed to receive "halves," 50 percent of the harvested crop, but Clay was widely known for taking the entire crop for himself. Ned Cobb remembered that his family ate "nothing but sorghum syrup and cornmeal" while they farmed Clay's land.

Working for Clay for almost a year in exchange for only these meager rations, Browne Cobb was desperate to find a way to live and work independently. He proposed a deal: he would use his considerable skill as a basket maker to supply Clay with baskets for storing cotton. In exchange,

"All Must Work Under My Direction"

This 1882 contract spells out the terms and conditions under which African-American tenant farmers could work small plots of land on the Grimes plantation in Pitt County, North Carolina. Although not a return to conditions of slavery, the contract gives the plantation owner extraordinary control over the conditions of field work and the division of the harvested crop. Sharecroppers were forbidden to keep any cotton seed from the harvest, which would have allowed them to plant their own crop without having to be furnished by the plantation owner.

To every one applying to rent land upon shares, the following conditions must be read and *agreed to.*

To every 30 or 35 acres, I agree to furnish the team, plow, and farming implements, except cotton planters, and I *do not* agree to furnish a cart to every cropper. The croppers are to have half of the cotton, corn and fodder (and peas and pumpkins and potatoes if any are planted) if the following conditions are complied with, but—if not—they are to have only two-fifths. Croppers are to have no part or interest in the cotton seed raised from the crop planted and worked by them. No vine crops of any description, that is no watermelons . . . squashes or anything of that kind . . . are to be planted in the cotton or corn. All must work under my direction. All plantation work to be done by the croppers. . . .

All croppers must clean out stables and fill them with straw, and haul straw in front of stables whenever I direct. All the cotton must be manured, and enough fertilizer must be brought to manure each crop highly, the croppers to pay for one half of all manure bought, the quantity to be purchased for each crop must be left to me.

No cropper to work off the plantation when there is any work to be done on the land he has rented, or when his work is needed by me or other croppers. . . .

Every cropper must be responsible for all gear and farming implements placed in his hands, and if not returned must be paid for unless it is worn out by use.

Croppers must sow and plow in oats and haul them to the crib, but *must have no part of them.* Nothing to be sold from their crops, nor fodder, nor corn to be carried out of the fields until my rent is all paid, and all amounts they owe me and for which I am responsible are paid in full. . . .

The sale of every cropper's part of the cotton to be made by me when and where I choose to sell, and after deducting all they may owe me and all sums that I may be responsible for on their accounts, to pay them their half of the net proceeds. Work of every description, particularly the work on fences and ditches, to be done to my satisfaction, and must be done over until I am satisfied that it is done as it should be. . . .

Source: Grimes Family Papers, Southern Historical Collection, University of North Carolina, Chapel Hill.

Clay agreed to let Cobb and his family return to Clem Todd's land. But the cycle of dependency and exploitation started again. A white man named Ruel Akers made Cobb sign a note, taking his whole cotton crop and everything he owned except some household furniture in exchange for cotton seed and equipment. Once again Cobb fled, to yet another white-owned plantation. As his son Ned lamented, "He never did prosper none after that."

Browne Cobb and other black farmers struggled through a lifetime to work and live independently within a system established for the profit and benefit of others. They had much in common with the poorest white southerners. Both tilled the cotton fields laboriously by hand, using simple plows and heavy iron hoes. African Americans were usually in debt to landlords, white hill farmers to merchants, but the yoke of debt bore heavily on both. Black or white, poor southern farmers found themselves trapped in a system that made economic independence ever more remote.

Conflict on the Plains

The decades after 1870 were a time of apparent contradictions: the workforce was shifting from agriculture to industry at the same time that American agriculture was expanding more rapidly than ever before in the nation's history. Within thirty years, the number of farms doubled and more land was brought under cultivation than in the previous two-and-a-half centuries. The contradiction was more apparent than real. Agriculture was industrializing, and fewer workers could produce more food with the help of machinery, irrigation, and drought-resistant grains. The most rapid development occurred on the level, treeless, semi-arid Great Plains (Kansas, Nebraska, the Dakotas, and surrounding areas), once dubbed the Great American Desert and written off as unsuitable for farming. Prairie and grassland were easier to bring into production than forests, which had to be cleared, and the Plains became the heartland of American farming in little more than a generation. White agricultural settlement also extended, although at a slower pace, into California, Nevada, and the huge expanse of land that would become Colorado, Utah, New Mexico, and Arizona.

Until the late 1870s, American Indians had for 250 years so effectively hindered white settlement in the West that white Americans spoke of the "Indian barrier." That barrier was breached when U.S. soldiers suppressed the massive Sioux rebellion of 1876 and then murdered the Sioux leader, Crazy Horse, in 1877. Although few great battles would follow, Army patrols, starvation, disease, and alcohol would continue to take their toll, destroying the Indians' traditional ways of life.

White settlers and officials and Plains Indians were poles apart in their views of land ownership. Unlike Indians in the Northeast and Southwest, those on the Plains hunted over a wide range. Tribes, not individuals, owned the land, and all members shared its fruits. The individualistic ways of white settlers mystified these early Americans; as Sitting Bull of the Sioux remarked, "The white man knows how to make everything, but he does not know how to distribute it." The tradition of communal landholding similarly offended white men, who wanted to carve up the West into private preserves. Even those who saw themselves as humanitarians regarded individualism and private property as the highest expressions of human civilization.

These views, backed by federal power, became part of federal reservation policy, a contradictory strategy designed to segregate Indians, supposedly to prepare them for future integration. Supporters of the policy claimed that reservations would enforce separation, prevent conflict, and protect Indians from white people who refused to acknowledge Indian rights to the land. It did none of these things. Conflict continued as white settlers and Indians fought over land in some places, over livestock in others. Indians shunned reservations across the West. In New Mexico, the reservation established for the Chiricahua Apaches in 1872 included only part of their traditional homeland. They saw it as a prison and continually broke out, resisting government attempts to resettle them until 1886, when their leader Geronimo finally surrendered to the Americans. The U.S. government incarcerated him for more than fourteen years at Fort Sill, Oklahoma. In eastern Oregon, a band of Nez Percé resisted their eviction from nonreservation lands in 1877. The U.S. Army responded by chasing two hundred Nez Percé warriors and their families for 1,700 miles through Idaho, Wyoming, and Montana. When the Nez Percé finally surrendered, they were taken to Fort Leavenworth, Kansas, then moved from place to place over the next several years as many of them grew sick and died. Their leader, Chief Joseph, became a symbol of Indian resistance, though he was a civil chief who did not actually lead in battle.

The government victories cannot be attributed simply to military might. U.S. troops could communicate by telegraph and travel by railroad, and their force was augmented by the cooperation of white ranchers, homesteaders, and prospectors seeking minerals on Indian lands. Over time, the United States won more by attrition than by victory on the battlefield; Indians could not sustain resistance when their traditional ways of life were so disrupted that they could not even get food.

That disruption was perhaps most evident in the destruction of the bison, or buffalo, that had once roamed the plains in huge herds, as many as 25 million animals at their peak. Plains tribes—both nomads like the Blackfeet, Crows, and Comanches, and agricultural groups like the Pawnees and Wichitas—had depended on the bison, not only for meat but also for hides to make tepees and for robes to keep warm. The animal was central to their understanding of the universe; the Pawnee, for example, sacrificed buffalo meat in ceremonies intended to make corn grow.

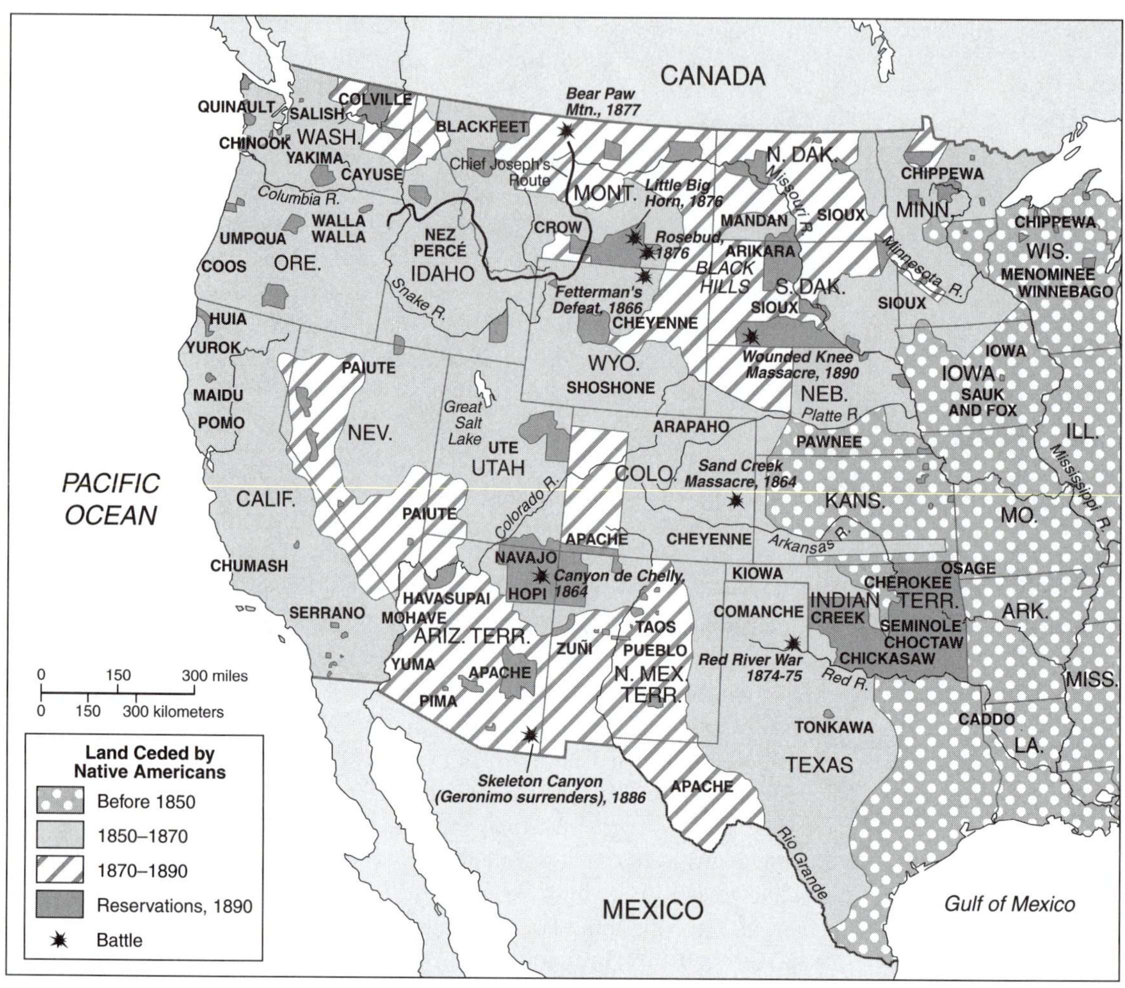

Exiling Indians in their Native Land Indians resisted the white settlement that overran the Great Plains after the Civil War. But by 1890, Indians had been forced to cede vast territories they had once occupied, and they found themselves confined to scattered reservations—almost always on poor quality land.

The herds had been dwindling under the impact of commercial hunting since midcentury, but disaster struck after 1870. Philadelphia tanners perfected a new process for turning buffalo hides into cheap leather; railroads provided a new way to get the hides to market. Hunters took well over 4 million buffalo between 1872 and 1874, leaving much of the meat to rot. Some hunters killed even more than they could skin; for each hide that reached market, three to five bison died. “The buffalo,” wrote one army officer who saw the slaughter, “melted away like snow before a summer's sun.”

The buffalo slaughter devastated the economy of the Plains Indians, while their white Protestant “sympathizers” in the East proposed reforms in government policy that fostered further repression of indigenous cultures. Appalled by decades of atrocity and war, reformers wanted Indians to as-

Ride the Train and Shoot a Buffalo! One of the short-lived attractions of western railroad travel was the opportunity to join a buffalo hunt—often without having to leave the comfort of the railroad carriage. In this 1870 promotional photograph, the official taxidermist displayed his wares outside of the Kansas Pacific Railroad's general offices.

Source: Richard Benecke, *Kansas & Pacific Railroad Album*—DeGolyer Library, Southern Methodist University.

similate. To that end, they supported coercion on three fronts: suppressing Indian religion and undercutting tribal authority; educating Indian children in American Protestant values; and replacing communal landholding with private property.

Persuaded that Indians would adapt to white culture, Congress passed the Dawes, or Indian Allotment, Act of 1887, breaking reservation lands into individually owned plots. The act allowed the president to grant American citizenship to Indians willing to abandon their communal ways. Families who adopted what the law called "habits of civilized life" would be granted ownership of 160 acres. With tribal consent, the government could sell reservation land to white purchasers, holding the proceeds for the "education and civilization" of Indians. The Dawes Act reaffirmed the right of Congress to grant building rights on Indian lands to railroad and telegraph companies. The act pleased settlers, railroad interests, and white "humanitarians."

The Indian Allotment Act led to a massive transfer of land from Indian to white ownership. In 1880, Secretary of the Interior Carl Schurz had predicted that such a bill would "eventually open to settlement by white men the large tracts of land now belonging to the reservations, but not used by the Indians." When the Dawes Act was passed, Native Americans still held 138 million acres. Within thirteen years, they saw their domain shrink to less than 78 million acres, virtually all of it unsuited to the agricultural life the federal government tried to foist on them. Moreover, the Bureau of Indian Affairs destroyed many traditional villages. A few years after allotment, one white observer described the remains of the Hidatsa village at Like-a-fishhook Bend in Minnesota as "rings of dirt where the lodges used to stand, half-filled cache holes all covered with weeds."

Over the next decades, white reformers tried relentlessly to stamp out tribal customs. "Unless the Indians are removed some distance from their village, the tribal organization broken up, and they are deprived of

"You Should Take Allotments . . ."

Americans Indians were not immune from pressures to accommodate to the new industrial order. This selection from the biography of Edward Goodbird, a member of the Hidatsa tribe in Minnesota, describes the period immediately following the passage of the Dawes Act in 1887, when Plains Indians were made to give up communal ways of life for individual family farms. Goodbird's experience was exceptional: he prospered under the new system, ultimately becoming an employee of the Bureau of Indian Affairs.

The time came when we had to forsake our village at Like-a-fish-hook Bend, for the government wanted the Indians to become farmers. "You should take allotments," our [Bureau of Indian Affairs] agent would say. "The big game is being killed off, and you must plant bigger fields or starve. The government will give you plows and cattle."

All knew that the agent's words were true, and little by little our village was broken up. In the summer of my sixteenth year nearly a third of my tribe left to take up allotments. . . .

My father left the village, with my mother and me, in June. He had a wagon, given him by the agent. . . . We camped at Independence in a tepee, while we busied ourselves building a cabin. My father cut the logs; they were notched at the ends, to lock into one another at the corners. . . . The floor was of earth, but we had a stove. We were a month putting up our cabin. . . .

Our agent issued to every Indian family having an allotment a plow, and wheat, flax, and oats for seeding. My father and I broke land near our cabin, and in the Spring seeded it down. We had a fair harvest in the Fall. Threshing was done on the agency machine, and, having sacked our grain, my father and I hauled it, in four trips to Hebron, eighty miles away. Our flax sold for seventy-five cents, our wheat for sixty cents, and our oats for twenty-five cents a bushel. Our four loads brought us about eighty dollars.

I became greatly interested in farming . . . one day the agent sent for me. I went to his office.

"I hear you have become a good farmer," he said, as I came in. "I want to appoint you assistant to our agency farmer. . . . You are to measure off for every able-bodied Indian, ten acres of ground to be plowed and seeded. If an Indian is lazy and will not attend to his plowing, report him to me and I will send a policeman. . . . "

I began my new duties at once. . . .

Source: Edward Goodbird, *Goodbird The Indian: His Story* (1914).

the means, and the opportunities for dances and ceremonies, by scattering them out on farms," one Bureau of Indian Affairs agent declared, "it will in my judgment, be impossible to civilize and render them self-supporting." Communal ceremonies, including all kinds of feasts and rituals, were banned. Indian boys and girls were encouraged to attend boarding schools to learn the language and values of the white majority.

Although they no longer possessed the means to openly resist this systematic destruction of their way of life, Plains Indians did not simply accept their fate. In 1888, Wovoka, a young man of the Nevada Paiutes, began preaching his vision of an Indian messiah who would restore the earth to its primeval glory, return the American continent to the Indians, and bring back the buffalo. The dead would return to life, reunited with their families in peace and eternal youth. To prepare for the great day, followers practiced a five-night mystical dance, which white observers dubbed the "Ghost Dance." The cult spread rapidly throughout the West.

In the Dakotas the cult fed on the extreme misery of the Sioux, weakened by malnutrition after a drought and by epidemics of measles, whooping cough, and influenza. Alarmed as the dance swept through Sioux encampments in the fall of 1890, Indian Bureau agents called for U.S. Army assistance. When the War Department dispatched troops to the area, thousands of Sioux fled to the Dakota Badlands. Their leader, Sitting Bull, remained on the reservation. In mid-December, the army sent U.S.-trained Indian police to arrest him; the encounter ended with the deaths of Sitting Bull, seven of his supporters, and six policemen.

Deprived of their leader and under continuing pressure from the army, the Sioux prepared to surrender. On December 28, the Seventh Cavalry entered the Sioux encampment at Wounded Knee Creek to search for arms. In the ensuing confrontation, army troops massacred at least 146 people, including many women and children; the Sioux set the number closer to 400. Approximately 25 soldiers also died. The Wounded Knee massacre came to signify the violence the white majority was prepared to use to enforce its version of civilization.

Mass Burial. The day after the "battle" of Wounded Knee, the dead Sioux—estimated by the U.S. Army at 84 men, 44 women, and 18 children—were buried in a mass grave at the scene of the massacre on the Pine Ridge Reservation Agency, South Dakota.

Source: George Trager, "Burial of the Dead at the Battle of Wounded Knee, [South Dakota]," 1891, albumen silver print, 4-5/8 × 7-7/16 inches—Amon Carter Museum, Fort Worth, Texas.

"... A Very Sad Sight"

American Horse, a Sioux leader, describes the massacre at Wounded Knee Creek on December 29, 1890.

The men were separated . . . from the women, and they were surrounded by the soldiers. Then came next the village of the Indians and that was entirely surrounded by the soldiers also. When the firing began, of course the people who were standing immediately around the young man who fired the first shot were killed right together, and then they turned their guns, Hotchkiss guns, etc. upon the women who were in the lodges standing there under a flag of truce, and of course as soon as they were fired upon they fled. . . .

[T]he women and children of course were strewn all along the circular village until they were dispatched [killed]. Right near the flag of truce a mother was shot down with her infant; the child not knowing that its mother was dead was still nursing, and that especially was a very sad sight. The women as they were fleeing with their babies were killed together, shot right through, and the women who were very heavy with child were also killed. All the Indians fled . . . and after most all of them had been killed a cry was made that all those who were not killed or wounded should come forth and they would be safe. Little boys who were not wounded came out of their places of refuge, and as soon as they came in sight a number of soldiers surrounded them and butchered them there. . . .

Of course it would have been all right if only the men were killed; we would feel almost grateful for it. But the fact of the killing of the women, and more especially the killing of the young boys and girls who are to go to make up the future strength of the Indian people, is the saddest part of the whole affair and we feel it very sorely.

Source: Robert D. Marcus and David Burner, eds., *America Firsthand* (1989).

Western Farming and Ranching

The suppression of American Indians was not sufficient to quell conflict in the West. Groups with conflicting visions—cattle drivers, sheep herders, farmers, miners, and others—also struggled with one another for domination of the land. Like immigrant factory workers and southern hill farmers, these people found their working lives transformed by the development of industrial capitalism, the expansion of market relationships, and decisions made in eastern boardrooms.

The national railroad network gave a tremendous boost to western settlement and tied the region's farmers into distant markets. Anglo settlers entered New Mexico and Colorado in the 1870s, for example, as the railroad was being completed. The region's economy had been defined for generations by Mexican farm families engaged in subsistence and communal farming and in herding on community-regulated common lands. This system now gave way to commercial farming on private homesteads and to cattle and sheep ranching financed by eastern capital and linked by rail to distant slaughterhouses. By 1889, nearly 72,000 miles of track connected farms west of the Mississippi River to the national and international economies.

Agricultural productivity grew enormously, especially on the Great Plains. Farmers eagerly bought harvesting and threshing machinery on the installment plan, counting on increased output. The gamble seemed worth taking. A single farmer working by hand could reap about seven acres of wheat during the ten days it was in its prime; under automatic binders that cut and tied bundles of wheat, common by 1890, the same farmer could harvest 135 acres. The resulting vast supply enabled the United States to export one-third of its wheat crop by 1900.

But despite rapid productivity gains, the machinery purchases left Plains farmers—already in debt to mortgage holders in the East and in Europe—even more dependent on credit, in an agricultural area that was extremely unstable. In the early 1880s, unusually heavy rainfall and temporarily rising wheat prices created boom conditions. But later in the decade, rainfall dropped to its normal level and drought threatened. Equally important, the price of wheat dropped on the world market. In actual buying power, farmers suffered from seriously fluctuating prices, especially during times of depression: the early and middle 1870s, the late 1880s, and the early and middle 1890s.

Like backcountry southern farmers, Plains farmers were caught between falling prices and rising production costs. They had to produce more just to stay even and pay for their machinery, but the more they produced, the lower prices fell. Developments outside farmers' control further dragged down the price of their crops. The world market was flooded with wheat and corn, thanks to mechanization and to the opening of new grain-producing land in Argentina, Canada, and Russia.

The railroads were partially responsible for the rising costs of farming. In many areas of the West, as in the South, farmers had access to only one railroad line. Railroads charged as much as the traffic would bear, raising rates to make up for losses from rate cutting on competitive routes elsewhere. Freight rates in the West were often two to three times those in the East. Plains farmers also had to pay high prices to the operators of elevators, the giant grain-storage bins that loomed on western horizons. As with the railroads, large eastern corporations usually owned the elevators. Many a farmer learned that freight charges for a bushel of wheat cost more than it could fetch in the marketplace. Plains families perennially ran short of cash and had to resort to short-term, high-interest loans. Anxiety was constant, over payments on machinery and mortgages, falling crop prices, unpredictable weather conditions, and crop diseases.

While male farmers used expensive machinery for planting, harvesting, and threshing, most Plains farmwomen churned by hand, carried water in pails, and cooked at open fireplaces. The fortunate had treadle sewing machines to ease the task of making clothing for entire families. Many families set up housekeeping in huts made from large bricks of prairie sod. Though sturdy and warm, many sod houses were dark, dirty, and leaky. Less fortunate Plains families huddled in tarpaper shacks or dugouts, caves with covered openings.

A Sod House. The Sommers family in front of their sod house in West Custer County, Nebraska, in 1888.

Source: Solomon D. Butcher, 1888—Butcher Collection, Nebraska State Historical Society.

Men usually made the decision to move west, drawn by the prospect of available fertile land. A few single women thrived as independent homesteaders, and newlyweds often regarded the journey as the beginning of their lives together. But most married women—who could not file homesteading claims on their own—went reluctantly. "I stood alone on that wild prairie," Lavinia Porter remembered. "Looking westward I saw my husband driving slowly over the plain; turning my face once more to the East, my dear sister's footsteps were fast widening the distance between us. For the time I knew not which way to go, nor whom to follow . . . in spite of my brave resolve to be the courageous and valiant frontierswoman." Porter chose her husband.

In northeastern Colorado, homesteading husbands and wives both hauled water, milked cows, and gathered cow chips for fuel. Churning butter and collecting eggs were women's work, and they made money selling them locally or shipping them to Denver and points east. Some also sold garden vegetables, sausages, and bread; others took in teachers and railroad workers as boarders, or earned money washing, ironing, and sewing for local bachelors.

Women were cut off from the connections to church, kin, and friends that had sustained them in the more densely populated regions from which they had come. "As soon as the storms let up, the men could get away from the isolation," wrote Mari Sandoz, the daughter of a Nebraska homesteader. "But not their women. They had only the wind and the cold and the problems of clothing, shelter, food, and fuel."

Although more than 1 million family farms sprang up in the West during the last forty years of the nineteenth century, many agricultural products came from operations that bore little resemblance to the idealized small family farm. In the Red River Valley of North Dakota and

Minnesota, and in the Central Valley of California, absentee-owned "bonanza farms" of the 1870s and 1880s relied on heavy mechanization and seasonal migrant laborers for large-scale production. By 1880, one 66,000-acre farm along the Sacramento River yielded more than 1 million bushels of wheat a year. The very largest farms were eventually broken up because they proved too inflexible in bad times, but by 1900, the average farm in the Dakotas measured 7,000 acres.

The cattle boom of the early 1880s and rumors of huge profits brought eastern and British investors into ranching. Large corporations dominated the industry, such as the Chicago-owned, 3-million-acre XIT Ranch in Texas and the Sparks-Harrell Company in Idaho and Nevada, which grazed 150,000 cattle on an equally large expanse of public land. Railroads opened even more land for cattle grazing by creating new shipping centers. Kansas towns like Abilene and Dodge City originated as centers of the cattle trade.

Few ranchers bought the land their cattle grazed. They cared little about the capacity of the public lands they used until 1885 through 1887, when they faced economic and ecological disaster. The pressure of grazing had led to a decline in grasses and to undernourished cattle. Where it once took five acres to raise a steer, it now took fifty or even more. Bad winters in 1885 and 1886 left hundreds of thousands of cattle dead. Years later one rancher wrote, "A business that had been fascinating to me before, suddenly became distasteful. I never wanted to own again an animal that I could not feed and shelter." Sheep herders moved into many of the grazing lands after that, because sheep could thrive on nongrass plants that cattle would not eat.

Although westerners who farmed the land, herded animals, and worked in towns were economically interdependent, some clashed fiercely over their different ways of life. Large ranchers fenced public lands; small ones cut the fences. Farmers saw themselves as guardians of settled and sober living in a region rife with lawlessness. They complained that herds trampled crops and that the freewheeling behavior of the cowboys who tended the herds defied law and order. In Kansas, farmers crusaded against saloons, dance halls, and prostitution. Cattle and sheep ranchers feuded with each other, too, although their conflicts were essentially ethnic and religious in origin. In New Mexico, sheep owners were mostly Mexican Americans; in Nevada and southern Idaho they were Mormons and Basques.

The experience of the López family of southern Colorado suggests that cattle herding, farming, and industrial work were in fact combined in individual lives. The economic boom that followed the completion of the transcontinental railroad in 1869 encouraged Damacio López and eleven other Mexican-American farmers to give up traditional communal farming and risk private homesteading. In 1871, these longtime residents of Colorado filed separate claims for 160-acre homesteads under the federal homesteading law. Only six of the twelve had enough cash to buy shovels for digging irrigation ditches, so they shared tools and other resources. Within the year López and his compatriots had planted three or four acres of wheat on each of their individual homesteads, but they harvested crops communally, a longstanding Mexican custom. Although López managed to acquire a small herd of cattle, he was unable to support his family and in 1876 left his homestead to enter the region's growing wage economy. With several hundred other men, he traveled to the rail town of Las Animas, Colorado, to work on the railroad. Soon his family moved there with their cattle. After two years, the López family returned to their homestead with a much larger herd and enough cash to open a small store.

On the Trail. Cowboys wash up during a cattle drive in Kansas. **Source:** Kansas State Historical Society.

It was railroad work, not farming, that allowed the López family to achieve a measure of success in the new industrial economy. The railroad brought opportunities and a market economy to the Southwest. The López family prospered because they accepted and even embraced aspects of the new order. But it also brought cultural and social change: López and his friends abandoned their traditional communal ways for more individualized economic strategies.

Extractive Industries and Exploited Workers

Although grain farming and cattle ranching dominated the western economy, each region developed other specialties, mainly extractive industries that produced massive quantities of raw materials for shipment to other parts of the world. In the Pacific Northwest, lumber was the product; in the Rockies, the Southwest, and California, metals and coal were mined. The railroad also brought in finished goods of all kinds from the East. Many workers who powered the extractive economy were immigrants, and most lived and labored under harsh conditions. But some reaped handsome rewards. Skilled workers in western cities commanded higher wages than their counterparts in the East, and even western farmhands probably had more cash in their pockets than unskilled industrial workers. But because most regions of the West relied on a single industry, even a slight downturn could bring widespread misery. Boom-and-bust industrial capitalism hit western workers hard.

Large companies controlled by San Francisco capital had begun shipping lumber to California from the Pacific Northwest in the 1850s and 1860s. Completion of the first railroad linking the Northwest with the East in 1883 created a market for railroad ties and connected the Northwest's small railroads to nationwide systems. As in other industries, technological change increased production in the woods. New saws and axes made it possible to cut trees faster, and the "steam donkey," an engine that pulled logs by cables, took them out of the forest. New devices also enabled mills to offer new cuts of finished lumber rather than green logs. As a result, the Northwest served markets all over the world.

In other areas, prospecting for metals continued. Gold was discovered in the Black Hills of South Dakota in the 1870s and in Idaho during the 1880s. Gold and silver mining became more profitable as copper, lead, and zinc—which could be found in gold and silver deposits—gained importance in industry. European and eastern businessmen poured vast amounts of capital into metal mining and smelting. Many investors ended up with shattered hopes, but others reaped huge profits. After 1879, when Colorado emerged as the nation's leading mining region, eastern capital and western workers unlocked vast stores of mineral wealth, turning families like the Guggenheims into an American aristocracy.

Miners who produced this wealth labored under horrendous conditions. Fifteen hundred Mexican Americans worked at California's New Almaden Quicksilver Mine, which produced half of the world's supply of mercury, a metal essential in the smelting of silver ore. Climbing ladders out of the mine, they hauled 200-pound sacks of ore strapped to their foreheads. High temperatures and poor ventilation were daily facts of life in all kinds of mines. Many miners died in explosions, cave-ins, and fires; others were maimed by machinery. Every year, one of every thirty hardrock miners was disabled, and one of eighty killed. The rest were likely to develop lung diseases.

Western mining towns seemed to mushroom overnight, as Leadville, Colorado, did with the discovery of silver in the Rocky Mountains. From a small cluster of log cabins in 1876, Leadville grew to a sprawling city of 15,000 people four years later. Leadville's experience was repeated across Colorado and Idaho in the 1880s. Creede, Cripple Creek, and Coeur d'Alene became urban outposts in the mountains. These towns owed their existence to the mines, but only a minority of their citizens were miners.

In Cripple Creek, one in four residents worked in the mines; the others provided services ranging from retailing to prostitution. Adult men usually outnumbered adult women in these western towns, and saloons competed with the family as the center of social life. Butte, Montana, had a one-block red-light district. In "parlor houses" with gilt-framed mirrors and brocaded furniture, well-dressed women served men both as companions and as sexual partners, but most brothels offered plain furnishings and plain sex. The overwhelming majority of women wage-earners on the mining frontier served men in other ways: waitressing and making beds at hotels and restaurants, doing laundry, or cooking and cleaning in private homes and boardinghouses.

Gambling Man. The rough image of a Colorado mining camp is emphasized in an 1879 engraving in *Frank Leslie's Illustrated Newspaper,* showing "contrasts of life in the new mining district—the first 'swell' arrival at Leadville."

Source: *Frank Leslie's Illustrated Newspaper,* June 7, 1879—American Social History Project.

Although mining towns developed a reputation for crudity and lawlessness, they also established stable community institutions. Even Deadwood, South Dakota, known as a sinkhole of gambling, prostitution, and violence, boasted schools, churches, and a theater within months of its founding. As two early residents reminisced, "On one hand could be heard the impassioned call of the itinerant minister of the Gospel, . . . In close proximity would be a loud-voiced gambler calling his game."

The working class was extraordinarily diverse in western mining towns. Mexican-American miners, Chinese-American laborers and launderers, Basque sheep herders, and African-American cowboys mixed with European immigrants and white migrants from the East and South, participants in an international labor market that helped to populate the West. Indeed, even more of the population of the West was foreign-born than of the East. Between 1860 and 1890, one-third of California's residents were foreign-born, more than twice the proportion of the country as a whole. In 1890, North Dakota had a higher proportion (45 percent) of immigrants than any other state. Immigrants from Scandinavia settled the Great Plains, and many moved on to the Pacific Northwest. Portland, Oregon, had a German newspaper in 1867 and a German-language school in 1871. Many migrants crossed the unregulated Mexican border for short periods to work as field hands or to lay track in Texas, Arizona, and southern California. Also in California, Japanese immigrants and Mexican migrants performed the stoop labor required for agriculture there. A contract labor system—gangs of workers run by bosses who transported them from abroad and sold their labor—brought

Italian workers to California farms and Greek laborers to Utah mining camps.

Of all the western immigrant groups, the Chinese inspired the most hostility. More than 200,000 Chinese, mostly men, had migrated to the United States by 1890. Many had borrowed passage money from labor brokers, who organized crews to do jobs most white Americans deemed too dangerous and arduous. Railroad laborers, in particular, were recruited in China in the 1870s through this contract labor system, which was much like indentured servitude. When they paid off their contracts, they competed for other jobs. White workingmen claimed that the Chinese were semi-slaves who would drive down wages, lower the standard of living, and send American wealth to their families in China. Californians formed anti-Chinese clubs in the 1860s; in 1879 Chinese immigrants were denied the vote and public employment in California. Three years later, the U.S. Congress passed the Chinese Exclusion Act, which suspended Chinese immigration for ten years and made resident Chinese ineligible for naturalization. The act was renewed in 1892.

Legislation did not stem the tide of anti-Chinese mob violence, which peaked in the mid-1880s throughout the West. An 1885 attempt to boycott Chinese-made cigars crystallized the widespread and growing racism of white San Francisco workingmen. "This is the old irrepressible conflict between slave and white labor," one speaker proclaimed. White mobs attacked Chinese immigrants in Eureka, California, and Tacoma, Washington. The Chinatown near the Union Pacific Railroad coal mine in Rock Springs, Wyoming, was torched and many of its residents gunned down. The bodies of twenty-eight victims were found as the ashes cooled the next day.

Lee Chew, who arrived in California just before the Chinese Exclusion Act, was an ambitious young man seeking wealth "in the country of American wizards." For two years he worked as a domestic servant, learning American ways from his employer, sending money to his family, and saving to open a business. With a partner, he opened a laundry, a typical Chinese-American business because it required little capital and demanded grueling labor that white Americans were happy to leave to others. Lee dressed well and enjoyed theater and dinner parties in San Francisco's Chinatown, but he eventually moved East to escape the anti-Chinese sentiment so prevalent in the Far West. He established laundries in Chicago, Detroit, and Buffalo. When factory-style steam laundries began to eat into his

Working-class Racism. The cover of the *San Francisco Illustrated Wasp,* 1877, expresses in no uncertain terms the attitude of white workers toward Chinese laborers.

Source: *San Francisco Illustrated Wasp,* December 8, 1877—California Section, California State Library.

". . . Indebted to Her Master/Mistress"

Almost all of the Chinese who immigrated to the United States before 1900 were men. The Chinese Exclusion Act of 1882 not only banned additional immigration of Chinese laborers, it also prevented Chinese men who remained in the United States from bringing over wives from China to join them. Of the approximately 100,000 Chinese immigrants resident in the United States between 1880 and 1900, only 5,000 were women. Some found work as laundresses and servants; others arrived as indentured prostitutes. This 1886 contract describes the stringent conditions under which Xin Jin worked as a prostitute in San Francisco in exchange for payment of her fare from China.

The contractee Xin Jin became indebted to her master/mistress for food and passage from China to San Francisco. Since she is without funds, she will voluntarily work as a prostitute at Tan Fu's place for four and one-half years for an advance of 1,205 yuan (U.S. $524) to pay this debt. There shall be no interest on the money and Xin Jin shall receive no wages. At the expiration of the contract, Xin Jin shall be free to do as she pleases. Until then, she shall first secure the master/mistress's permission if a customer asks to take her out. If she has the four loathsome diseases she shall be returned within 100 days; beyond that time the procurer has no responsibility. Menstruation disorder is limited to one month's rest only. If Xin Jin becomes sick at any time for more than 15 days, she shall work one month extra; if she becomes pregnant, she shall work one year extra. Should Xin Jin run away before her term is out, she shall pay whatever expense is incurred in finding and returning her to the brothel. This is a contract to be retained by the master/mistress as evidence of the agreement. Receipt of 1,205 yuan ($524) by Ah Yo. Thumb print of Xin Jin the contractee. Eighth month 11th day of the 12th year of Guang-zu (1886).

Source: Alexander McLeod, *Pigtails and Gold Dust* (1948).

business, he moved to New York and founded a successful firm importing Chinese products.

Lee Chew found financial success in America, but not peace of mind. He resented white Americans' distorted images of his countrymen, the unpunished vandalism and violence that plagued Chinese immigrant communities from coast to coast, and the laws that prevented Chinese men from bringing their wives into the country. Railing about this outrageous treatment, Lee asked, "How can I call this my home, and how can anyone blame me if I take my money and go back to my village in China?"

Capitalism and the Meaning of Democracy

The idea that the frontier was a land of opportunity died hard. "The Golden West has been the Mecca in the dream of the misguided worker in all parts of the country," one western labor activist remembered with some bitterness. "If I can only get West, has been his only thought." But by

"The Street of the Gamblers (by day)." Arnold Genthe's photographs of San Francisco's Chinatown provide information about the Chinese community at the turn of the century. His characterization of his subjects, however, often conveys a distorted and ominous message. Despite its title, the significance of this photograph of Ross Alley, taken some time around New Year's, lies in its depiction of unusual daytime congestion resulting from the seasonal unemployment of many Chinatown workers after the holiday.

Source: Prints and Photographs Division, Library of Congress.

1893, when the next business cycle began, industrial capitalism had transformed the West, like other regions.

The United States was the world's richest nation in 1893. Mechanization in both factory production and agriculture had changed forever the way most Americans worked and lived. The miner in the Far West, the tenant farmer in the South, the steelworker in the Midwest, and the garment worker in New York City were all linked to a vast national and international market.

Individuals and families seeking opportunities in industrializing America made new lives for themselves and for their nation. Rural areas in China and Japan gave up their young men to the lure of the "Golden Mountain." Commercialized agriculture and industrial depression drove millions of young European men and women to the "land of opportunity." Poor Mexican families from agricultural areas were drawn to the expanding economy of the Southwest. And young American-born working-class couples sought their fortunes in the West or set up their own businesses.

Beneath the attractions of individual opportunity and technological progress, however, lay pervasive discontent. As large industrial and financial institutions secured ever-greater economic and political power, ordinary Americans of all ethnic backgrounds found themselves increasingly subject to forces beyond their control. Lifelong wage earning meant dependence and a betrayal of the longstanding American dream of being beholden to no one, once symbolized by the autonomous farmer and the self-employed artisan. Workers' earnings and the prices they paid for goods were subject to the impersonal mechanisms of world trade and to decisions made on behalf of profit in remote corporate boardrooms. Class relations became more stratified. Paupers, multimillionaires, and a new middle class all increased in number, but they had little daily contact with one another.

American working people—men and women, wage earners and farmers, American Indians, African Americans, Mexican Americans, European and Chinese immigrants, and descendents of very early white settlers—struggled to find places for themselves in a society characterized by economic concentration and previously unimaginable wealth. In communities based on shared ethnic and craft traditions, working people's daily interactions and the organizations they formed fostered support and solidarity for individuals. Those communities and organizations also nourished resistance to employers and to capitalism itself, in a wide spectrum of protest and class conflict that marked the era.

The Years in Review

1873

- Collapse of Jay Cooke & Co. sets off nationwide financial panic.

1877

- Compromise of 1877: Special electoral commission grants election victory to Republican candidate Rutherford B. Hayes in return for promises to Southern Democrats.
- Reconstruction ends: last federal troops leave the South.
- "Indian barrier" to white settlement of the West removed after U.S. Army crushes Sioux rebellion and kills Sioux leader Crazy Horse.
- U.S. Army chases Nez Percé for 1,700 miles through Idaho, Wyoming, and Montana until they surrender.

1878

- Five-year depression ends—over half a million working people were unemployed.

1879

- California denies Chinese immigrants the right to vote and public employment.
- Congress grants women lawyers the right to argue before the Supreme Court.
- Henry George's *Progress and Poverty* blames inequality and corruption on the private ownership of land.
- F. W. Woolworth, National Cash Register Co., Scott Paper Co., Paine, Webber, Jackson, Curtis, Bache & Co. (brokers); and Aetna Insurance Co. all have their beginnings.

1880

- Republican James Garfield defeats Civil War General Winfield Scott Hancock for presidency.

1881

- Disappointed job seeker assassinates President Garfield; Chester Arthur becomes president.
- Shootout takes place at the O.K. Corral outside Tombstone, Arizona.

1882

- Congress passes the Chinese Exclusion Act, suspending Chinese immigration for ten years and declaring resident Chinese ineligible for naturalization.
- Electricity illuminates parts of New York City (beginning with J. P. Morgan's offices); introduction of world's first electrical fan, flatiron, and electrically lighted Christmas tree.

1883

- Pendleton Act creates the Civil Service Commission to hire federal workers on the basis of scores on competitive examinations.
- Clocks nationwide are set to a new uniform standard time.
- First Yellow Pages appears in Cheyenne, Wyoming.

1884

- Democrat Grover Cleveland defeats James B. Blaine for presidency in dirty campaign in which Cleveland's sexual life and draft dodging are issues.

1886

- Geronimo surrenders to U.S. forces, ending Apache resistance to federal efforts to resettle them.
- The last remaining nonstandard railroad lines shift to the standard gauge.
- First Tournament of Roses Parade held in Pasadena, California.

1887

- Interstate Commerce Act establishes a weak federal system of railroad regulation.
- Dawes Act (Indian Allotment Act) converts communal Indian lands to individual plots in an effort to "civilize" the Indians.
- Richard Sears moves to Chicago, hires watchmaker Alvah C. Roebuck, and sells mail-order watches.
- L. L. Zemenhof invents Esperanto in hope of establishing a universal language.

1888

- Republican Benjamin Harrison is elected president in the electoral college, even though Cleveland wins the popular vote.

1889

- Number of states in the Union rapidly expands with admission of Nevada (1864); Nebraska (1867); Colorado (1876); North Dakota, South Dakota, Washington, and Montana (1889); and Idaho and Wyoming (1890).
- Electric lights installed at the White House, but President and Mrs. Harrison don't touch them.
- Hartford, Connecticut, becomes home of first pay telephone.

1890

- Congress passes the Sherman Antitrust Act; the act does little to stop the growth of trusts, but is used against labor.
- Federal troops massacre 146 Sioux at Wounded Knee.
- Mormon Church ends official sanction of polygamy; as a result, Utah is finally admitted to union in 1896.
- U.S. engineer Herman Hollerith pioneers punch-card processing, adapting techniques from the player piano of 1876.

1891

- First federal penitentiaries are built.
- American Express introduces its Travelers Cheques.

1892

- Grover Cleveland elected president for a second term.
- George Ferris designs the Ferris wheel for the 1893 World's Columbian Exposition in Chicago.
- "Pledge of Allegiance" introduced as part of the 400-year celebration of Columbus's "discovery" of America.

1893

- Federal Railroad Safety Appliance Act makes it illegal for trains to operate without automatic couplers and air brakes.
- Shredded Wheat, Cream of Wheat, Aunt Jemima Pancake Mix, Postum, and Milton Snavely Hershey's Chocolate Co. have their beginnings.

Suggested Readings

Armitage, Susan, and Elizabeth Jameson, eds., *The Women's West* (1987).

Ayers, Edward L., *The Promise of the New South: Life After Reconstruction* (1992).

Benson, Susan Porter, *Counter Cultures: Saleswomen, Managers, and Customers in American Department Stores, 1890–1940* (1986).

Bodnar, John, *The Transplanted: A History of Immigrants in Urban America* (1985).

Brown, Dee, *Bury My Heart at Wounded Knee: An Indian History of the American West* (1972).

Brownlee, W. Elliot, *Dynamics of Ascent: A History of the American Economy* (1979).

Chandler, Alfred D., *The Visible Hand: The Managerial Revolution in American Business* (1977).

Daniel, Pete, *Breaking the Land: The Transformation of Cotton, Tobacco, and Rice Cultures Since 1880* (1985).

Davies, Margery W., *Woman's Place Is at the Typewriter: Office Work and Office Workers, 1870–1930* (1982).

Deutsch, Sarah, *No Separate Refuge: Culture, Class, and Gender on an Anglo-Hispanic Frontier in the American Southwest, 1880–1940* (1987).

Dubofsky, Melvyn, *Industrialism and the American Worker, 1865–1920, 3 ed* (1996).

Dykstra, Robert, *The Cattle Towns* (1968).

Faragher, John Mack, *Women and Men on the Overland Trail* (1979).

Garraty, John A., *The New Commonwealth, 1877–1890* (1963).

Gutman, Herbert G., *Work, Culture, and Society in Industrializing America: Essays in America's Working Class and Social History* (1977).

Hays, Samuel P., *The Response to Industrialism, 1885–1914* (1957).

Hounshell, David, *From the American System to Mass Production, 1800–1932: The Development of Manufacturing Technology in the United States* (1984).

Jeffrey, Julie Roy, *Frontier Women: The Trans-Mississippi West, 1840–1880* (1979).

Jones, Jacqueline, *Labor of Love, Labor of Sorrow: Black Women, Work, and the Family from Slavery to the Present* (1985).

Kamphoerner, Walter D., Wolfgang Helbich, and Ulrike Sommer, eds., *News from the Land of Freedom: German Immigrants Write Home* (1991).

Keller, Morton, *Affairs of State: Public Life in Nineteenth-Century America* (1977).

Martin, Albro, *Railroads Triumphant: The Growth, Rejection, and Rebirth of a Vital American Force* (1982).

Montejano, David, *Anglos and Mexicans in the Making of Texas, 1836–1986* (1987).

Montgomery, David, *The Fall of the House of Labor: The Workplace, the State, and American Labor Activism, 1865–1925* (1987).

Montgomery, David, *Workers' Control in America: Studies in the History of Work, Technology, and Labor Struggles* (1979).

Myers, Sandra, *Western Women and the Frontier Experience, 1880–1915* (1982).

Nelson, Daniel, *Managers and Workers: Origins of the New Factory System in the United States, 1880–1920* (1975).

O'Malley, Michael, *Keeping Watch: A History of American Time* (1990).

Painter, Nell Irvin, *Standing at Armageddon: The United States, 1877–1919* (1987).

Paul, Rodman Wilson, *Mining Frontiers of the Far West, 1848–1880* (1963).

Porter, Glenn, *The Rise of Big Business, 1860–1910* (1973).

Robbins, William, *Colony and Empire: The Capitalist Transformation of the American West* (1994).

Rothman, David, *Politics and Power: The United States Senate, 1869–1901* (1966).

Thernstrom, Stephan, ed., *Harvard Encyclopedia of American Ethnic Groups* (1980).

Utley, Robert M., *The Indian Frontier of the American West, 1846–1890* (1984).

Weeks, Philip, *Farewell, My Nation: The American Indian and the United States, 1820–1920* (1990).

White, Richard, *"It's Your Misfortune and None of My Own": A New History of the American West* (1991).

Wiebe, Robert H., *The Search for Order, 1877–1920* (1967).

Woodward, C. Vann, *The Origins of the New South, 1877–1913* (1966).

Worster, Donald, *Rivers of Empire: Water, Aridity, and the Growth of the American West* (1985).

Yates, Joanne, *Control Through Communication: The Rise of System in American Management* (1989).

And on the World Wide Web

Institute for Regional Studies, North Dakota State University, *The Northern Great Plains, 1880–1920: Photographs from the Fred Hulstrand and F. A. Pazandak Photograph Collections*
(http://memory.loc.gov/ammem/award97/ndfahtml/ngphome.html)

University of North Carolina, Chapel Hill, Libraries, *First-Person Narratives of the American South, Beginnings to 1920*
(http://metalab.unc.edu/docsouth/fpn/fpn.html)

chapter 2

Community and Conflict: Working People Respond to Industrial Capitalism 1877–1893

As industrial capitalism extended its reach into every corner of the nation's life, Americans differed on the merits of the emerging social order. Among those who deplored the industrial system's callous disregard for human beings was the poet Walt Whitman, who in 1871 had railed against the contemporary "hollowness of heart" and "depravity of the business classes." Humorists Mark Twain and Charles Dudley Warner's novel *The Gilded Age* (1874) satirized the politics and values of the post–Civil War boom years: "Get rich . . . dishonestly if we can, honestly if we must." Historians later adopted their title to describe the materialism and superficiality of the late nineteenth century.

But others worshiped at the altar of capitalist success: "That you have property is proof of industry and foresight on your part or your father's," one writer asserted; "that you have nothing is a judgment on your laziness and vices, or on your improvidence." Many businessmen, politicians, and scholars even attempted to explain capitalist social relations by citing the theory of biological evolution proposed by British scientist Charles Darwin in 1859. According to Darwin, a process of natural selection determines the most adaptable or "fittest" members of a plant or animal species, those best able to survive and reproduce. Social Darwinists distorted this theory to explain "scientifically" the impoverishment of the "unfit" masses, and warned that interference on behalf of the "weak" would doom American society. John D. Rockefeller justified ruthless competition as "a survival of the fittest, the working out of a law of nature and a law of God." Gilded Age America was a society dividing along class lines and spoiling for a fight. Industrial capitalists built luxurious mansions and hired private armies to defend their wealth and power. Soon proponents of the new order came to see all working people, in the words of *Century* magazine, as "the vicious and disorderly classes."

Increasingly powerless and dependent on wage labor, working people shook their collective fist at the growing visibility of unbridled privilege. They joined together in the Knights of Labor, the Eight-Hour Movement, and the craft unions. They struck not only for higher wages but to express solidarity with their fellow workers. They formed independent political parties and debated—and sometimes adopted—radical political ideologies such as socialism and anarchism. And in trying to cope with the impact of industrial capitalism on their daily

New York Streetcar Workers Strike, March 1886. New York City police drive back striking streetcar workers and their sympathizers as a lone horsecar, operated by company personnel, attempts to make its usual journey along Grand Street.

Source: Thure de Thulstrup, *Harper's Weekly,* March 13, 1886—American Social History Project.

lives, they drew on shared cultural values—religious, political, ethnic, and craft traditions. In cities, working-class newspapers and debating societies published workers' grievances. Workers inhabited spaces where employers did not go: ethnic, working-class neighborhood stores, saloons, and churches. In rural areas, quilting bees, barn raisings, and outdoor protest meetings provided forums for radical critiques of capitalism's impact on farm families. Resistance—both moderate and militant—flourished in these vibrant labor-reform environments. But the power of large capital would ultimately be much greater.

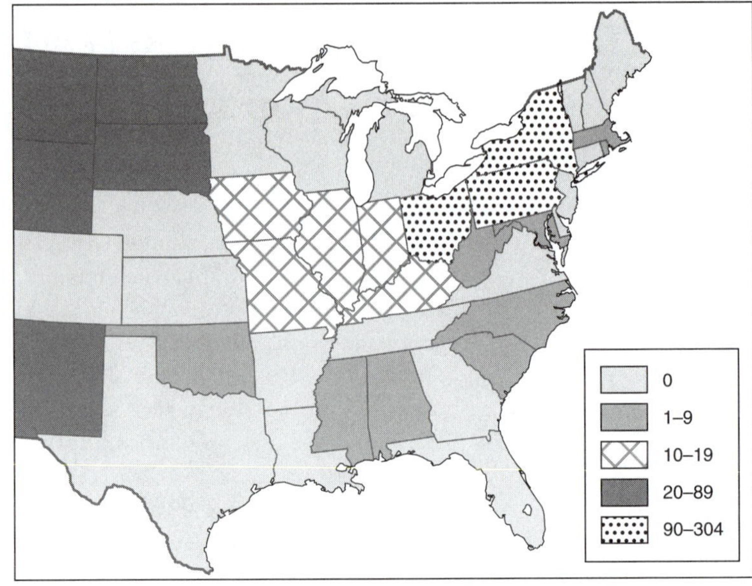

A Striking Map: Work Stoppages in 1880 This map, which shows the number of strikes per state in 1880, indicates that strikes were most common in the industrialized regions of the Northeast and Midwest and were rare in the South.

Neighborhood Cultures

Working-class life was grounded more in group identity than in ideals of individual effort and initiative. Among native-born workers, collective values stemmed from an abiding belief in independence and liberty spawned by the American Revolution, from religious ideals of equality and justice inherent in evangelical Protestantism, and from community institutions. Enriching this mix were the cooperative values and traditions brought by immigrants arriving throughout the nineteenth century. Many veterans of fierce social conflicts in Europe remained fervent advocates of egalitarian principles after their arrival in the United States.

Even immigrants who had not been political activists relied on collective traditions and identities to help ease their entry into urban-industrial America. Neighborhoods with names like German Town, Chinatown, and Little Sweden sprang up across the country, each with its own churches, schools, saloons, and newspapers. In Chicago, for example, German immigrants dominated working-class neighborhoods after the Civil War. By the 1880s, they had established German-language newspapers, athletic and cultural associations, financial institutions, neighborhood militias, and family-oriented beer halls. These institutions helped soften the worst effects of individual isolation in a new land.

African-American neighborhoods, like those of white workers, nurtured solidarity, protest, and resistance. In Washington, Atlanta, and other southern cities, a segregated black culture of mutual aid and self-help eased the afflictions of daily life in a racist society. African Americans fared better—within the severe limitations placed on every aspect of their lives—in large cities, where they could at least secure menial jobs and some small measure of personal freedom.

Working people's neighborhoods nourished collectivity in part because their homes were generally too cramped for socializing. Developers of housing near factories squeezed cheap tenements and wood-frame houses tightly together. In dark apartments, families and boarders shared beds and slept on couches, chairs, and floors. Privacy was nowhere to be found; the streets provided the only escape. There crowds celebrated holi-

". . . This Queer Conglomerate Mass"

Jacob Riis—a journalist and photographer of industrial America, and himself a Danish immigrant—exposed the deplorable conditions of late-nineteenth-century urban life in his widely read book *How the Other Half Lives,* published in 1890. Despite his immigrant background, Riis's attitudes mirrored the prejudices of the dominant culture toward "foreigners," as revealed in this description of an immigrant neighborhood on New York's Lower East Side.

When once I asked the agent of a notorious Fourth Ward alley how many people might be living in it I was told: One hundred and forty families . . . one hundred Irish, thirty-eight Italian, and two that spoke the German tongue. Barring the agent herself, there was not a native-born individual in the court. The answer was characteristic of the cosmopolitan character of lower New York, very nearly so of the whole of it, wherever it runs to alleys and courts. One may find for the asking an Italian, a German, a French, African, Spanish, Bohemian, Russian, Scandinavian, Jewish, colony. Even the Arab, who peddles "holy earth" . . . as a direct importation from Jerusalem, has his exclusive preserves at the end of Washington Street. The one thing you shall vainly ask for in the chief city of America is a distinctively American community. There is none . . . . They [the native-born] are not here. In their place has come this queer conglomerate mass of heterogeneous elements, ever striving and working like whiskey and water in one glass, and with the like result: final union and a prevailing taint of whiskey.

Source: Jacob Riis, *How the Other Half Lives* (1890).

days, neighbors exchanged news and gossip, and activists debated politics, while peddlers sold food and clothing. Mothers socialized on front steps and porches, and children played in streets and alleys.

Immigrant neighborhoods developed an abundant cultural and institutional life. As newcomers arrived, they sought out relatives or people from their villages in the old country. They found housing through the people they worked with and jobs through the people they lived with. Boarding with families from their homelands, they could eat familiar foods, speak their own languages, and discuss their working conditions free from surveillance. Neighborhood grocery stores, butcher shops, boarding houses, churches, and saloons sprang up to meet the needs and tastes of particular ethnic groups, serving as centers of information and communication, connecting neighborhoods with the outside world.

Two Homes. These illustrations in the *Boston Labor Leader* compared the homes of a union workman and a scab workman. In this view, strikebreaking was a logical outgrowth of the general moral and physical degradation of the one-room scab household. The "superiority" of the trade unionist was portrayed in the modest but solidly domestic atmosphere of the family's parlor.

Source: *Boston Labor Leader,* October 6, 1894—State Historical Society of Wisconsin.

In working-class neighborhoods in cities like Pittsburgh, Milwaukee, and St. Louis, immigrants supported ethnic fraternal organizations—the Sons of Italy, the Polish Union, and the Jewish *Landsmanschaft* organizations—to provide mutual assistance and a familiar cultural milieu. They published newspapers and magazines in dozens of languages, filled with news from the old country and advice to newcomers. Immigrants also created cultural activities, sports teams, and clubs. These institutions nourished a sense of sociability and camaraderie and helped community residents who were sick, injured, or unemployed.

Networks based on extended families and Old World village ties met many of the immediate needs of immigrant workers, but some problems demanded a broader sense of identity. If a community of immigrants from the Abruzzi region of Italy wanted a church with a Catholic priest who spoke Italian, for instance, they might enlist the help of Neapolitans in making their request to church officials. Such alliances created a greater sense of Italian (as opposed to Abruzzian) identity, especially because English-speaking Americans tended to ignore regional differences. Ethnic consciousness gradually evolved as regional identities transformed into national ones. "Italians" and "Germans" were in this sense being invented in America during the same decades that they were created in Europe through political unification.

Immigrant entrepreneurs turned their native languages and knowledge of Old World preferences into business assets. Many acted as intermediaries for individuals dealing with the American legal and financial systems, explaining, translating, and writing letters for a fee. Working-class neighborhoods in cities and small towns provided ready customers for groceries, saloons, barber shops, and variety stores. Although most of the men and women who ran such businesses managed only to establish small, struggling enterprises, the lure of "being one's own boss" attracted the hopeful.

Like industrial tycoons, some small business people believed that the individual pursuit of wealth was the highest realization of American freedoms. But even the most ambitious local politicians and shopkeepers found that to succeed they had to collaborate with their families, workmates, and other members of their ethnic and religious groups. Many businessmen and professionals who relied on working-class patrons for their livelihoods supported working people's demands and struggles. Local shopkeepers helped strikers by providing food and other necessities on credit.

Similarly, the proprietors of general stores at rural crossroads saw many a farm community through a bad harvest. And although rural "neighborhoods" were not as densely populated as urban ones, they too fostered collective problem solving and socializing. During the 1870s, for example, locusts and drought prompted Kansas women to mount a relief campaign for "families in the country whose only safety from starvation lies in the charity of the people." Country people gathered for church services, barn raisings, and picnics. Dances brought together young and old, for good food and rollicking music. Hunts, sleigh rides, and other social occasions further relieved the isolation of rural life. A Kansas woman scoffed at "those who have never lived in a new country [and are] inclined to think such a life is full of privations, with no pleasures mixed in."

The life of William Turner, a skilled ironmolder who in 1880 lived in Troy, New York, with his wife and eight children, illustrates the nature of individual success within the extended family networks and the ethnic, religious, and labor organizations of the late–nineteenth-century neighborhood. Turner emigrated from Ireland in 1850, with his parents and three brothers. His father worked as an unskilled laborer at the Albany Iron Works, and by 1860 William and two of his brothers had jobs there as well. The Turners' life revolved around work in the mill—six twelve-hour days per week—and time with the family. William soon became a skilled ironworker. When he married, he found a home in the same row of brick houses where his parents lived.

William Turner supported his family and rose from the ranks of the unskilled to the more secure and comfortable position of a skilled worker. His was the modest success story experienced by millions of Americans. They dreamed not of riches, but of making a decent life for their families. They found security and solidarity in their ethnic communities, performing the rituals and observing the commandments of their churches and fulfilling their obligations to neighbors and fellow workers.

Working Women at Home

All workers' days began and ended at home, but most married women still worked at home, without wages and independent of bosses. Some women did labor outside their homes intermittently, in the years between late adolescence and marriage, or in later years when they needed money because of an impending family crisis or a husband's death, desertion, or disease. Unlike factory workers, women working at home could choose to change tasks, laying aside their sewing to stir the soup or comfort a crying baby. But even running modest households required arduous manual labor and considerable time. For women working at home, labor was intertwined with family-centered entertainment and neighborhood socializing. Women often did certain tasks together, while chatting about community events, politics, friends and relations, recipes, and housework techniques.

A Barn Raising. Jacob Roher and his neighbors took a break from their construction efforts on his farm near Massillon, Ohio, in 1888 to pose for a photographer.

Source: Theodore Teeple, 1888—Massillon Museum, Massillon, Ohio.

Rural women were more isolated. Long distances separated friends, and many women complained of intense loneliness. But rural women's work, too, had a cooperative dimension. Women helped each other to make quilts, as men shared work to get the harvest in and build houses or barns. Groups of women cooked for the parties associated with both of these kinds of cooperative labor, which featured food, music, and dancing after the work was done.

Before the 1890s, most households were equipped with the same technology that had been used for centuries, with two important exceptions: sewing machines and cast-iron stoves. The sewing machine had been patented in 1846. The machines were quite expensive, but they were marketed on the installment plan and became a fixture in both middle-class and poorer households. In many households, men's clothing was purchased, but most women had to produce much of their own clothing and all of their children's, in addition to family linens. In poorer homes, women invested in machines so they could earn money by sewing.

Cast-iron stoves had become common among the middle class in 1870 and spread to people of all classes by 1890. Stoves heated rooms more evenly than did old-fashioned fireplaces. They allowed finer adjustments in cooking temperatures, and cooks no longer had to bend down by open flames to move pots on the hearth. Nevertheless, the stoves were heated by coal and wood, so most women still had to haul fuel and build fires for all of their cooking and heating. Other regular household tasks included hauling pails of water from outside wells and from pumps connected to city water systems, lugging tubs of hot water from the stove for laundry and dishes, and carrying dirty water and bodily wastes back outside.

In some homes, domestic servants did these tasks for pay; this work was the largest source of paid employment for women in the late nineteenth century. In northern cities, most domestic servants were Irish women; in the South, they were African-American women, who rarely had other options and worked for extremely low wages. But domestic servants were not common in workers' homes; most people hired household help only in emergencies.

"Union Against Union." A wry comment on the general refusal of working-class men and the trade union movement to consider women's maintenance of the household as work.

Source: J. S. Pughe, *Puck,* 1900—Scott Molloy Labor Archives.

Many women earned money by adding to their household workloads—caring for boarders or taking in laundry or sewing. All over the United States, married and widowed women rented rooms to single people and sometimes to couples. In immigrant neighborhoods, married women provided lodging for newcomers from their home villages or regions. By boarding these tenants—mostly single men and married ones who had immigrated without their families—women with families could supplement their husbands' meager wages. In western mining towns, women rented or bought large houses and took in workingmen who needed lodgings. One Nevada widow, Mary Mathews, labored until one o'clock every morning supporting herself and her small child during the 1870s—running a school, sewing, and taking in laundry. Eventually she bought a boarding house where she washed clothes for twenty-six boarders.

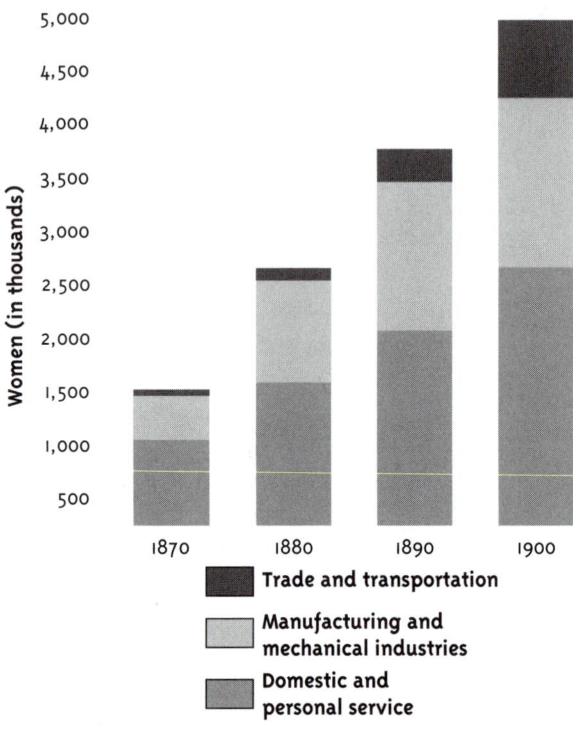

Out of the Household and into the Household: Women and Work, 1870–1900
Between 1870 and 1900, the number of women in the paid labor force more than tripled. But what remained constant was that domestic work continued to be the leading category of women's labor.

Many married African-American women earned money taking in laundry, which offered considerably more independence than domestic service in white people's houses. These workers sometimes fought to maintain their autonomy, especially precious to people with memories of slavery. During the summer of 1881, African-American washerwomen in Atlanta organized a two-week strike, demanding higher fees and recruiting 3,000 supporters by door-to-door canvassing and nightly neighborhood meetings throughout the city. This protest was unusual but not unique. Following the 1877 railroad strike, Galveston household workers had walked off their jobs, and other southern domestics struck from time to time, often led by outspoken washerwomen. More often, however, household workers and independent washerwomen used covert tactics—such as quitting without notice—to resist racism and oppression.

Religion and Community

Of the many institutions that supported community life in working people's neighborhoods, churches were the most important. Most Americans before the Civil War had been Protestants, but many new immigrants were Catholic and Jewish. Still, in 1890, Protestant denominations claimed more than six of every ten church members. All across the country, rural Protestant churches continued to flourish: the vast majority of the nation's farmers, black and white, sustained and were sustained by countless small, often poor, churches.

Churches were the central institutions of the largely rural African-American culture. In Edgefield County, South Carolina—an area renowned for lynchings—black tenant farmers and sharecroppers joined some forty small churches established by Alexander Bettis, a leader who urged African Americans to organize their own institutions. The churches engendered Masonic lodges, benevolent societies, burial organizations, and schools, as well as fairs and other social gatherings. This cultural foundation sustained black Americans in "Bloody Edgefield." Many white southerners viewed the networks of black churches and organizations as a threat. "The meanest negroes in the country are those who are members of the churches," declared a writer in the *North Georgia Citizen* in 1879, "and, as a general thing, the more devout and officious they are, the more closely they need watching."

Saving Souls and Selling Soap. Henry Ward Beecher's testimonial for Pear's Soap in an 1883 advertisement. "If cleanliness is next to Godliness," Beecher declared in this ad, "soap must be considered as a means of Grace."

Source: *Frank Leslie's Illustrated Newspaper,* November 10, 1883—American Social History Project.

Churches created community in mining camps and cattle towns. Although some Kansans claimed in the 1870s that there was "no Sunday west of Junction City and no God west of Salina," that was an exaggeration. Protestants sent missionaries west to preach against Mormons, Catholics, and moral decay. The first community building in western towns was usually a school, and it often served as a place of worship on Sunday, uniting different Protestant sects. Josiah Strong, a well-known reformer who began as a young minister in Wyoming, observed that western church meetings brought strangers together as Christians. His church spawned a library, a park, and voluntary organizations that battled liquor and prostitution.

In eastern cities, middle- and upper-class Protestants had moved to the suburbs and abandoned many downtown churches in neighborhoods now filled with immigrant Catholics and Jews. As a result, white Protestant churches lost touch with urban working people and became more oriented toward the well-to-do. Wealthy congregations produced nationally renowned ministers, such as Brooklyn's Henry Ward Beecher, one of the best-known and most influential of these "princes of the pulpit." Beecher was a tremendously popular orator known for his wit and eloquence, despite much publicity about his alleged extramarital affairs. Although he had supported the antislavery movement, his social philosophy was profoundly conservative, sympathetic to the rich and hostile to the poor. "No man in this land suffers from poverty unless it be more than his fault—unless it be his sin," Beecher proclaimed.

The Young Men's Christian Association (YMCA) and the Salvation Army did try to bring Protestantism to urban working people. The Salvation Army, an evangelical organization run along military lines, held meetings in the worst slums, even in saloons, and offered "degenerate souls" food, shelter, and low-wage work. The YMCA established gymnasiums, lecture halls, and reading rooms in cities to provide a "wholesome" atmosphere where men could exercise and socialize without the drinking and gambling that prevailed at pool halls, bowling alleys, and saloons. Bible study classes were central to the program.

The YMCA was closely linked with the social purity movement, which rejected overt sexual expression and practice. In 1872, Anthony Comstock, a drygoods salesman, YMCA member, and founder of the New York Society for the Suppression of Vice, won passage of an anti-obscenity statute (the so-called Comstock Act), which forbade the mailing of obscene, lewd, lascivious, and indecent writing or advertisements, as well as contraceptive devices. As an unpaid postal inspector, Comstock personally supervised forty-seven arrests and the destruction of more than 29,000 photos, leaflets, and rubber items in 1875 alone. Sustained by Congress, the courts, and the mainstream press, Comstock's crusade throughout the 1880s and 1890s criminalized social and sexual behavior that deviated from an idealized norm of so-

"The Modern News Stand and Its Results." The frontispiece of *Traps for the Young,* an influential 1883 tract by Anthony Comstock, illustrates the threat purportedly posed by the "debased" commercial press. "They open the way for grossest evils," Comstock wrote. "Foul thoughts are the precursors of foul actions."

Source: [A. B. Davis], Anthony Comstock, *Traps for the Young* (1883)—General Research Division, New York Public Library, Astor, Lenox, and Tilden Foundations.

briety, heterosexual monogamy, and piety. Prostitutes, homosexuals, and sexual and political radicals bore the brunt of the public's wrath.

Unlike Protestant churches, many of which backed the social purity movement, the Catholic Church was predominantly urban and working class. It had expanded with the influx of poor Irish and German immigrants in the decades before the Civil War and continued to gain strength as Italians and Poles entered the country after 1880. Parochial schools provided Catholics with educational opportunities that extended through college, and large city parishes offered programs to meet their spiritual, recreational, and charitable needs. The church's hierarchy remained extremely conservative on social issues, as illustrated by the policy of excommunicating members who were active in socialist organizations. But at the local parish level, priests defended the aspirations of their working-class parishioners.

The Workingman's Club

The saloon was another central institution of working-class culture; one writer called it "the one democratic club in American life." From Boston to Cripple Creek, Colorado, saloons served as social centers for working men. Chicago alone supported 3,500 of them in 1884. Plain saloons operated in tents and shacks; fancy ones boasted huge mirrors and carved wooden bars.

Drinking on the job, prevalent early in the nineteenth century, had generally been abolished by the 1870s. With a shorter workday—usually ten hours for skilled workers—men drank during leisure hours, in popular taverns that were usually located across the street from a factory or down the road from a mine. "Watch the 'dinner pail' brigade," a Worcester, Massachusetts, observer noted in 1891, "and see how many men and boys drop into the saloons along the north end of Main Street."

Before the 1870s and 1880s, beer—the drink of the urban masses—was locally produced and sold in informal, unlicensed drinking establishments or at beer gardens and beer halls annexed to small breweries. Once pasteurization and refrigerated railcars enabled long-distance shipping, aggressive midwestern beer barons—Anheuser Busch, Schlitz, and Pabst—created a national market. They backed larger saloons that rented their fixtures and promoted their brands; Pabst actually purchased saloons and rented them to operators.

Saloons filled tangible needs. Saloon owners cashed workers' checks and lent them money. The beer they served was considered full of nutrients and healthier than the water in working-class neighborhoods, which was drawn from wells and pumps near overused outhouses. Many workingmen ate their meals at saloons. "It is cheaper to live at the barroom

Morning Customers. A Chicago saloon, around 1890. **Source:** Chicago Historical Society.

than at the poor beaneries," an unemployed Boston man reported in 1889. At Chicago's Workingmen's Exchange, a dime bought two pork chops, four slices of toast, fried potatoes, and a 25-ounce schooner of beer.

At the saloon, workingmen could experience mutuality and collectivity, sym-bolized by "treating"—buying rounds of drinks. They could read newspapers, pick up job leads, enjoy good fellowship, and escape from overcrowded houses and tenements. Popular entertainments—illegal boxing matches, cockfights, and gambling—enlivened the atmosphere. Trade unions and ethnic organizations that lacked their own facilities met in saloons, and local politicians set up unofficial headquarters at the bar, dispensing favors and buying drinks for "the boys." In Chicago and elsewhere, many saloonkeepers entered local politics.

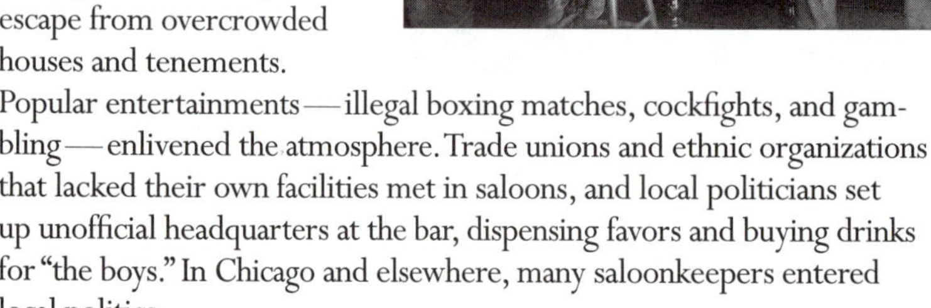

Saloons were conspicuously male preserves. Except for German family establishments that served beer, most saloons catered only to men. Women who drank generally did so at home. In some places, police regulations aimed at curbing prostitution forbade women from entering barrooms. Even when not legally excluded, women who considered themselves respectable did not go to saloons, so they were effectively prohibited from joining organizations that met there.

Saloon culture went outside on the Fourth of July. In industrial cities, contests, boat regattas, and picnics followed annual parades featuring ethnic, neighborhood, and occupational groups. Independence Day celebrations also included brawls, beer, and boxing matches; noisy and unrestrained, immigrant workers cut loose. Until the late 1880s, the patriotic facade of Independence Day celebrations protected the holiday revelers. But people of substance and standing saw the festivities as a breach of decorum and a threat to their property. "Among people of refined tastes and sensitive nerves, 'going out of town to avoid the Fourth' has been a phrase so common in my time that it ceases to awaken attention," social reformer Julia Ward Howe noted in 1893. As the century

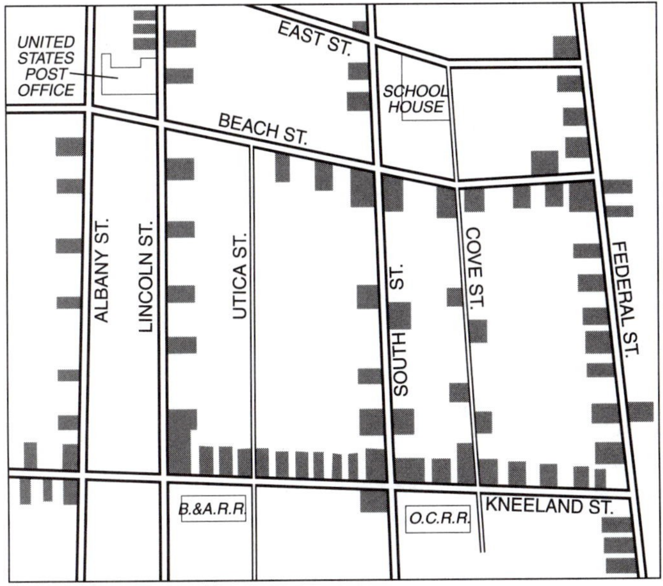

A City of Saloons: Boston Bars in 1884 The saloon was ubiquitous in the late–nineteenth-century city. In the area around Boston's Albany and Old Colony railroad terminals, travelers could find 175 different saloons—eighty of them within just 650 feet of the stations. "Every traveler," complained a temperance advocate, "passes through a gauntlet of rum."

closed, reformers set up committees to impose "safe and sane" behavior on the Fourth.

Similarly, many wealthy people—who did their own drinking at private clubs, expensive hotels, and home—crusaded to close saloons. Some of the hardest fought political battles of the nineteenth century involved efforts to limit drinking. Factory owners led campaigns against licensing individual establishments, in an effort to keep their workmen sober. They contended that temperance increased efficiency: "the men earn better wages, lose less time, do better work . . . while the relations between employers and workmen are most harmonious." Other temperance crusaders were motivated by religious convictions, a fear of the political threat posed by the independent saloon culture, or by a sincere conviction that drinking was the source of working-class poverty.

Indeed, alcohol and alcoholism could create real problems in working-class families. Therefore labor reformers, too, decried the debilitating consequences of drink and argued that workers who criticized wage dependency should also shun alcohol dependency. Some unions actively promoted temperance, although it often seemed a losing cause. Terence V. Powderly, head of the Knights of Labor, the most important labor organization of the Gilded Age, implored workers to "throw strong drink aside as you would an ounce of liquid hell."

Women temperance leaders organized marches on saloons to pray, sing hymns, implore drinkers to pledge abstinence, and shame proprietors. They argued that saloons widened and reinforced the gulf between men's and women's leisure activities, that drinking diverted wages from family support, deprived babies of food, and promoted domestic violence. Individually, women temperance activists told tales of destitution and degradation, describing alcoholic husbands and fathers who were unable to earn wages at all. One such group of women, successful in ending the local liquor trade in an Ohio county, formed the Woman's Christian Temperance Union (WCTU) in 1874. Politicizing farmwomen and women from "respectable" Protestant working-class families, the WCTU recognized the connection between alcoholism and social issues. In the 1890s it

"The Workingman's Club"

This description, taken from an article titled "The Saloon in Chicago," conveys a sense of how the late–nineteenth-century saloon met a range of urban workers' social, economic, and cultural needs. The writer, a sociologist, calls the saloon "the workingman's club," comparing it to such institutions as the eating and political clubs that catered to the urban middle and upper classes.

The term "club" applies; for, though unorganized, each saloon has about the same constituency night after night. Its character is determined by the character of the men who, having something in common, make the saloon their rendezvous . . . The "club-room" is furnished with tables, usually polished and cleaned, with from two to six chairs at each table. As you step in, you find a few men standing at the bar, a few drinking, and farther back men are seated about the tables, reading, playing cards, eating, and discussing, over a glass of beer, subjects varying from the political and sociological problems of the day to the sporting news and the lighter chat of the immediate neighborhood. . . . That general atmosphere of freedom, that spirit of democracy, which men crave, is here realized; that men seek it and that the saloon tries to cultivate it is blazoned forth in such titles as "The Freedom," "The Social," "The Club," etc. Here men "shake out their hearts together." . . .

In many of these discussions, to which I have listened and in which I have joined, there has been revealed a deeper insight into the real causes of present evils than is often manifested from lecture platforms . . . . This is the workingman's school . . . . Here the masses receive their lessons in civil government, learning less of our ideals, but more of the practical workings than the public schools teach. It is the most cosmopolitan institution in the most cosmopolitan of cities . . . Men of all nationalities meet and mingle . . . . It does much to assimilate the heterogeneous crowds that are constantly pouring into our city from foreign shores. But here, too, they learn their lessons in corruption and vice. It is their school for good and evil.

Source: Royal Melendy, "The Saloon in Chicago," *American Journal of Sociology* (November 1900).

took the position that poverty created drinking problems, reversing an earlier stand that excessive drinking caused poverty. The WCTU worked to improve the conditions of the working class, sought power for women inside the home, and endorsed woman suffrage in 1882—decades before any other national group. Its motto, "Do Everything," encouraged women activists to embrace a wide range of social legislation. The WCTU eventually became the largest American women's organization ever.

The Labor Community

As the social and economic gulf separating wage earners and their employers widened, a labor movement of astonishing breadth emerged in the 1880s. Recognizing common interests, workers began to unionize to

"Father, Come Home!" Temperance tracts emphasized the destructive effects of liquor consumption on familial relationships, framing messages in sentimental accounts of little children appealing to drunken parents to forsake the saloon and come home. This Thomas Nast cartoon, "The Bar of Destruction," repeated a motif that dated back to Timothy Shay Arthur's antebellum bestseller, *Ten Nights in a Bar-room*.

Source: *Harper's Weekly*, March 21, 1874—American Social History Project.

contest poor working conditions and assert their rights. With the exception of the Knights of Labor, the national organization that led the early labor movement, most of these unions were local and confined to an individual trade. Cincinnati, an important manufacturing center, boasted thirty-five separate unions in the early 1880s. Here, as elsewhere, most union members were skilled craftsmen in the building trades, foundries, and small consumer-goods industries.

Craft unionists created strong central labor bodies in cities all across the country, from Boston to Chicago, Denver, New Orleans, and San Francisco. In 1882, New York City's Central Labor Union (CLU) brought together a dozen small unions. Within a few years, it functioned as an effective "parliament of labor" for more than two hundred labor organizations. It became a meeting ground for both skilled and unskilled workers and for labor radicals of all stripes. As one printer put it, the CLU constituted an effort to replace the "little-minded, narrow-minded view of the interests of a single occupation" with that of "the general interests of all bodies of wage workers."

The labor movement offered workers good fellowship and activities that reinforced a working-class perspective. Unions and their citywide central organizations sponsored social activities: parades, balls, and picnics. More broadly, labor organizations were part of an alternative culture that belonged unmistakably to the producing classes. Many cities had reading rooms established by the Knights of Labor in the 1870s and 1880s; Atlanta's Union Hall and Library Association drew eight hundred people a week during the mid-1880s to read its collection of over 350 newspapers. In Detroit, the labor movement supported a range of daily activities. Workers gathered to read pro-labor newspapers in English and German, to argue politics, and to participate in theater groups, singing societies, dances, and educational events. Some joined the Detroit Rifles, a militia that drilled and practiced target-shooting on the outskirts of town under cover of darkness. This mixture of the ordinary and the startlingly militant made employers more than a little uneasy.

Besides daily fellowship, the labor community offered a spiritual experience of solidarity, a new form of evangelism based on old ideals—the brotherhood of man, divine retribution against injustice, and indignation at human suffering. The labor movement adapted these religious ideals and used spiritual language to reflect and interpret the growing class division. Labor songs were based on hymns, their words changed but their zealous spirit intact. Unions, the *United Mine Workers' Journal* suggested, had stepped into the space left when the conservative churches abdicated their true mission. "Jesus Christ is with us outside the church," one worker explained, "and we shall prevail with God."

Righteous belief and a context of community provided the foundation for a wave of boycotts in the mid-1880s. The boycott, an effort to win concessions from an employer by persuading other workers to stop patronizing his business, was especially effective in trades serving urban working-class consumers. One business journal reported more than 200 boycotts in 1884 and 1885—against newspapers, street railways, and manufacturers of cigars, hats, carpets, clothing, shoes, and brooms. The movement hit its peak in 1886, when countless campaigns touched the South, Far West, Midwest, and Eastern Seaboard. In New York State alone, 150 boycotts were organized. Denouncing boycotts as "un-American and anti-American," employers turned to the courts for confirmation and support. In the spring of 1886, New York courts prohibited boycotts as a form of criminal conspiracy, handing down indictments against more than 100 organizers. In the most widely publicized of the subsequent trials, five workers who had organized a boycott against a local music hall were sentenced to long prison terms.

"The Great Labor Parade of September 1st." A placard in an 1884 Labor Day march presented the struggle over inequality in the nineteenth century. "Wage-slavery" emerged as an oppressive institution to take the place of racial slavery, defeated in the Civil War.

Source: *Frank Leslie's Illustrated Newspaper,* September 13, 1884—American Social History Project.

"Union for All": The Knights of Labor

At the center of labor activity in the 1880s was the Noble and Holy Order of the Knights of Labor, a group founded by nine Philadelphia tailors in 1869. Its first leader, Uriah Stephens, had studied for the ministry before apprenticing as a tailor. A man of broad moral vision, he called for an organization that would unite all workers, regardless of race, nationality, occupation, or skill level. In the words of a Detroit parade banner, " 'Each for himself' is the bosses' plea; Union for all will make you free."

Like middle-class Masons, the Knights of Labor engaged in elaborate rituals at secret meetings. In 1879, the Knights of Labor chose Terence V. Powderly as their "Grand Master Workman." An Irish Catholic machinist and mayor of Scranton, Pennsylvania, Powderly led the Knights for fifteen years. The Order's programs reflected not only Powderly's beliefs in temperance, education, and land reform but also his conviction that the wage system should be abolished. Under his leadership, the Knights gradually put aside their secrecy, which had hampered their ability to grow, and membership soared.

Drastic wage cuts accompanying the economic downturn of the early 1880s gave the organization its greatest impetus for growth. Victories against two of the country's most powerful railroads—the giant Union Pacific and financier Jay Gould's Southwestern—brought workers across

Boycott Fever. A cartoon in the weekly *Life* satirized the growth of boycotts. "Whereas," reads one boy, representing a committee of disgruntled candy-cart customers, "we find we don't git red color enough in our strawberry cream, nor enough yaller in our wanilla, . . . to say nothin' o' the small measure of peanuts we gits for a cent; therefore, be it resolved . . . that all the stands in the city is boycotted until these things is righted."

Source: *Life,* May 27, 1887—Scott Molloy Labor Archives.

"Labor is Noble and Holy"

The Knights of Labor employed elaborate rituals and symbols in their local assembly meetings. The initiation ceremony for new members, for example, relied heavily on religious imagery and language. The ceremony emphasized that all that was valuable and worthy in society derived from human labor. New Knights agreed to commit themselves to improve the conditions of all working people.

In the beginning, God ordained that man should labor, not as a curse, but as a blessing; not as a punishment, but as means of development, physically, mentally, morally, and has set thereunto his seal of approval in the rich increase and reward. By labor is brought forward the kindly fruits of the earth in rich abundance for our sustenance and comfort; by labor (not exhaustive) is promoted health of the body and strength of mind, labor garners the priceless stores of wisdom and knowledge. It is the "Philosopher's Stone," everything it touches turns to wealth. "Labor is noble and holy." To glorify God in its exercise, to defend it from degradation, to divest it of the evils to body, mind, and estate, which ignorance and greed have imposed; to rescue the toiler from the grasp of the selfish is a work worthy of the noblest and best of our race.

You have been selected from among your associates for that exalted purpose. Are you willing to accept the responsibility, and, trusting in the support of pledged true Knights, labor, with what ability you possess, for the triumph of these principles among men?

Source: Peter J. Rachleff, *Black Labor in the South: Richmond, Virginia, 1865–1900* (1984).

the nation into the Knights. By 1886, the Order boasted 15,000 local assemblies, representing between 700,000 and 1 million members. This was nearly 10 percent of the country's nonagricultural workforce, a much higher proportion than had ever been enrolled in unions. In Milwaukee, where German-American craftsmen had dominated the Order in the early 1880s, less-skilled Polish immigrants streamed into the organization in 1886; nearly a thousand joined on a single day.

The Knights' commitment to equality extended beyond healing the split between skilled and unskilled workers and included women, immigrants, and African Americans, all previously shut out of the labor movement. African Americans were welcomed from the beginning. Most joined all-black assemblies, but some locals had mixed membership, even in the South. Black dockworkers in New Orleans, turpentine workers in Mississippi, tobacco factory workers in Virginia, and coal miners in

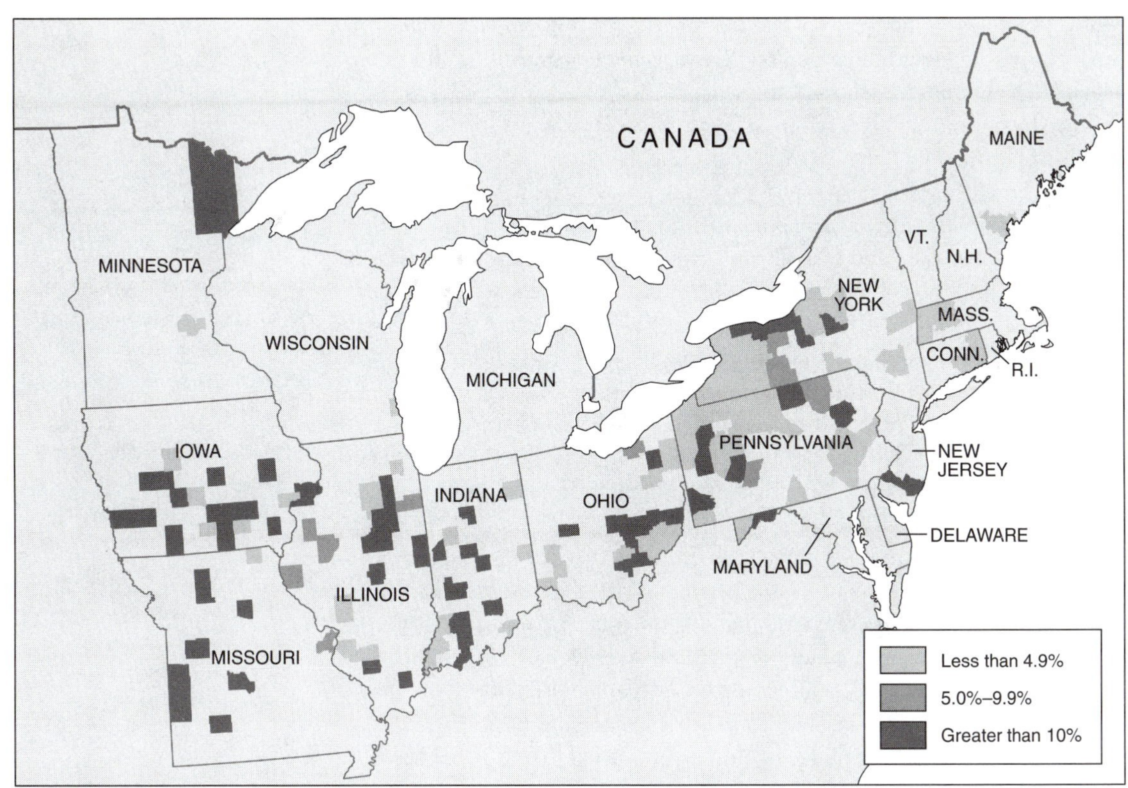

Where the Knights Roamed: Knights of Labor Membership by County, 1883 The Knights of Labor was the nation's largest labor organization in the 1880s, and, as this map shows, their influence was spread widely across the Northeast and Midwest.

Alabama, West Virginia, and Tennessee all joined the Knights in the first half of the 1880s. African-American workers became the mainstays of many fledgling local assemblies. "The colored people of the South are flocking to us," trumpeted one Knights organizer.

In Fort Worth, Texas, the Knights united European- , African- , and Mexican-American workers in the first coalition of its kind in state history. The Central Trades and Labor Assembly in New Orleans represented some 10,000 black and white workers who regularly joined forces in demonstrations and parades. "In view of the prejudice that existed a few years ago against the negro race," a Brooklyn Knight wrote, "who would have thought that negroes could ever be admitted into a labor organization on an equal footing with white men?"

The Order's practice of organizing separate black assemblies provoked controversy among African Americans. Some criticized the labor movement's continuing racism, particularly its exclusion of African Americans from skilled trades. A North Carolina mason complained, "The white Knights of Labor prevent me from getting employment because I am a colored man, although I belong to the same organization." But other black leaders believed that the Order's local and national assemblies represented a significant advance, providing a context in which black and white workers could begin to make common cause.

The emergence of the Knights of Labor also moved Irish immigrants to the center of the American labor movement. Irish activism had begun with support for the Land League, an organization of tenant farmers in Ireland that built an enormous following in the late 1870s. In the early years, Powderly claimed, the American labor movement and the Irish land movement were "almost identical," and secret gatherings of the Knights frequently followed public meetings of the Land League. As Patrick Ford, a New York editor, explained, "The cause of the poor in Donegal [Ireland] is the cause of the factory slave in Fall River [Massachusetts]." Monopoly took the form of rent-gouging in Ireland, of labor exploitation in America.

Unlike African Americans and Irish immigrants, women had to fight their way into the Knights of Labor. Leaders of the Order spoke vaguely about "equal rights" and embraced the idea of equal pay for women, but equal pay meant little in a gender-segregated workforce. The Knights stopped short of granting membership to women, and Powderly refused to implement a resolution calling for women to be admitted until rules "for the governing of assemblies of women" were prepared. Then, Mary

"An Injury to One Is an Injury to All." During the 1886 Knights of Labor convention in Richmond, Virginia, the Order's dedication to racial equality and the prominent role played by African-American delegates in the proceedings impressed reporters and artists covering the event.

Source: Joseph Becker, *Frank Leslie's Illustrated Newspaper,* October 16, 1886—Prints and Photographs Division, Library of Congress.

". . . Women Should Do Anything They Liked That Was Good"

The commitment of the Knights of Labor to equality for women was more than rhetorical, as evidenced by the career of Elizabeth Rodgers, the organization's Master Workman, or head, of the giant Chicago District No. 24.. This 1889 portrait of Rodgers, offered by leading national antiliquor activist Frances Willard, underscores the desire on the part of many Knights, both men and women, to connect the struggle for labor reform with a broader vision that included vehement opposition to liquor.

So I went; in an unfamiliar, but reputable, part of the city where the streetcar patrons are evidently wage-workers. I was welcomed to a small, but comfortable, modern house by a woman who came to the door with sleeves rolled up and babe in arms. She was the presiding officer over all the Knights of Labor in Chicago and the suburbs, except the Stock Yards division . . . including fifty thousand or more working men and women. . . . Probably no parallel instance of leadership in a woman's hands, conferred by such peers, can be cited in this country, if indeed in any other.

Mrs. Rodgers is about forty years of age. . . . She has been the mother of twelve children, ten of whom are still living. The youngest was but twelve days old when her mother started for the [1886] Richmond Convention, where the baby was made "Delegate No. 800," and presented by the Knights with a silver cup and spoon, and the mother with a handsome Knights of Labor gold watch.

"My husband always believed that women should do anything they liked that was good and which they could do well," said Mrs. Rodgers, proudly; "but for him, I never could have got on so well as a Master Workman. I was the first woman in Chicago to join the Knights. They offered us the chance, and I said to myself, 'There must be a first one, and so I'll go forward.'"

. . . Mrs. Rodgers got her training as the chief officer of a local board of the Knights of Labor, which office she held four years, and by the death of the District Master Workman became the chief for our great city.

"We take no saloon-keepers," she said, "not even a saloon-keeper's wife. We will have nothing to do with men who have capital invested in a business which is the greatest curse the poor have ever known; but wage-workers connected with the liquor business are not forbidden to join us." I told her I hoped the pledge of total abstinence might be made a test of membership, and she heartily acquiesced in the plan. . . . She seemed to me a sincere Christian, and warmly seconded my statement that "Mr. Powderly [the Knights' national leader] must have the help of God, or he could not speak and act so wisely."

Source: Frances E. Willard, *Glimpses of Fifty Years: The Autobiography of an American Woman* (1889).

Stirling, who had led a successful strike of "lady shoemakers" in Philadelphia, presented herself as a delegate at the Knights' convention in 1881. Forced to take a stand, Powderly finally declared that "women should be admitted on equality with men." Within a few years, one in ten Knights was a woman.

The Knights of Labor provided an unprecedented opportunity for working-class women to join men in the struggle for better lives. The Knights mobilized support for equal pay for women, equal rights for women within all organizations, and respect for women's work, whether unpaid in the home or for wages in the factory or mill. The Order's eclectic reform vision linked women's industrial and domestic concerns to broad social and political issues, giving rise to a kind of "labor feminism" in the 1880s.

The Knights of Labor, did, however, blatantly discriminate against one group: the Chinese. In the early 1880s, the major focus of the Order's political activity was promoting the Chinese Exclusion Act, which closed the nation's gates to Chinese immigrants. When it was passed in 1882, Knights hailed the law as a step forward for "American" workers. Especially on the West Coast, the union label was as much an expression of antagonism to the Chinese as a symbol of worker's solidarity. Chinese workers served as convenient scapegoats when times were tough.

"The Gospel of the Knights of Labor." "We work not selfishly for ourselves alone," said Terence Powderly at the Richmond convention, "but extend the hand of fellowship to all mankind." In this 1886 cartoon, *Puck* editor/artist Joseph Keppler parodied Powderly's gesture as a hypocritical and aggressive act. Other conservative editors unsettled by increasingly militant and effective union activism shared Keppler's sentiments.

Source: Joseph Keppler, *Puck,* October 13, 1886—General Research Division, New York Public Library, Astor, Lenox, and Tilden Foundations.

Despite this persistent racism, the Knights claimed to represent the last best hope for a republic weakened by the forces of monopoly, political corruption, cutthroat competition, and—most important—wage labor. "We declare an inevitable and irresistible conflict between the wage system of labor and republican system of government," proclaimed the Knights, who sought to eliminate political corruption and industrial degradation and restore independence to American citizens.

With this commitment to republicanism went a deep faith in the "producing classes." If properly mobilized, the Knights believed, this broad social group producing society's wealth—the workers, the farmers, even the honest manufacturers—could rescue America from the hands of monopolists and other social parasites. "Nonproducers," such as bankers, speculators, lawyers, and liquor dealers, were excluded from the ranks of the Knights of Labor. But "fair" employers, who respected the "dignity of labor" by employing union workers and selling union-made goods, could join.

Local Knights of Labor assemblies developed a variety of institutions that reflected the ideals of mutuality and solidarity. Many maintained cooperative stores on the ground floors of their halls and assembly rooms above, where members could hear labor sermons, read reform papers, or debate politics and economics. The balls, picnics, and parades sponsored by the Knights were distinctive forms of recreation and group expression.

There was never total harmony among the groups that comprised the Knights of Labor, but for a time the alliance was sufficiently stable to spark widespread fear among industrialists and their friends. During a Cleveland steel strike, employers called on police to intervene. After violent confrontations at the mill gates, the city's daily newspapers launched a torrent of invective against the "un-American" Polish workers, labeling them "foreign devils," "ignorant and degraded whelps," and "Communistic scoundrels." But to those who joined the Knights, the important fact was that people of diverse backgrounds were marching together. "All I knew then of the principles of the Knights of Labor," the Jewish immigrant Abraham Bisno later remembered, "was that the motto . . . was One for All, and All for One."

1886: The Eight-Hour Movement and Haymarket Square

"The year 1886 will be known as the year of the great uprising of labor," proclaimed George McNeill, a Massachusetts member of the Knights of Labor. "The skilled and the unskilled, the high-paid and the low-paid all joined hands." The Knights' membership drive and the boycott movement peaked that year. Even more important, hundreds of thousands of workers struck, demonstrated, and fought for an eight-hour day.

American workers had been agitating for shorter workdays for decades. In 1884, the demand resurfaced when the Federation of Organized Trades and Labor Unions began a two-year campaign, resolving that "eight hours shall constitute a legal day's work from and after May 1, 1886" and calling for a general strike to begin that day. The federation, an alliance of eighteen national unions, had been formed in 1881 by local unionists who called for national organizing to deal with employers operating in national markets. At its peak in 1886, federation membership totaled as much as 350,000, or 3 percent of the nation's nonagricultural workforce.

From Milwaukee, Chicago, and New York, the eight-hour movement spread to towns and cities throughout the country. "This is the workingman's hour," proclaimed the workers at Boston's Faneuil Hall on the eve of May 1, 1886. Across the nation, about one-third of a million workers demonstrated for the eight-hour day, and 200,000 actually went out on strike. By the end of the year, 400,000 workers had participated in 1,500 strikes, more than in any previous year of American history. Most of the strikers won shorter workdays, and 42,000 won an eight-hour day. These strikes marked an important new phase in the mobilization of unskilled workers, brought many workers into the ranks of the labor movement, and turned thousands of union members into activists.

The national leadership of the Knights of Labor discouraged the demonstrations and strikes for the eight-hour day, but many Knights led local campaigns, working with the unions and with the socialists and anarchists who played a prominent role in the agitation. Although united in their challenge to the concept of private property, socialists and anarchists differed in their views of the role of government. Socialists advocated government ownership of factories and mines, whereas anarchists argued that organized government was by its very nature oppressive.

In Chicago, the eight-hour movement was led by radicals—most notably Albert Parsons, the son of a prominent New England family. Parsons arrived in Chicago after apprenticing as a printer in Waco, Texas, where he had moved before the Civil War. Although he had served in the Confederate Army, Parsons became a Radical Republican during Reconstruction, championing African-American rights, addressing meetings, and mobilizing black voters. He met his wife Lucy when she was sixteen and already a passionate labor and anti-racist activist. Lucy had probably been born a slave in Texas, but she claimed to be the orphaned child of Mexican and Indian parents. Because Texas laws banned interracial marriage, they moved north in 1873, settling in Chicago, where Albert found employment as a typesetter.

Making contacts among Chicago radicals and hosting socialist study groups in their home, Lucy and Albert Parsons were soon at the center of socialist and anarchist agitation. When Albert lost his job because of speeches he gave during the 1877 railroad strike, Lucy set up a dressmaking shop to support them both. By 1885, the Parsons were the most famous radical couple in Chicago and were subjected to regular and vicious attacks in the mainstream press.

On May 1, 1886, Parsons led the 80,000 Chicago marchers in a parade for the eight-hour day. The day passed without incident, but two days later, a clash at the McCormick Reaper Works ended in police beatings and the fatal shooting of two unarmed workmen. August Spies, the editor of a pro-labor German newspaper witnessed the bloodshed and issued a fiery leaflet, calling Chicago's workers to a protest at Haymarket Square the following evening. Attendance was sparse at the hastily called rally. As the small crowd began to drift away, a bomb exploded, killing a police-

"Eight Hours for What We Will!"

This poem, titled "Eight Hours," was written by I. G. Blanchard in 1866. Half a dozen years later Blanchard's poem was set to music by the Reverend Jesse H. Jones, who was closely associated with Boston's Eight-Hour League. The song became a rallying cry during the 1886 strike wave that demanded an eight-hour workday.

We mean to make things over,
We're tired of toil for naught,
With bare enough to live upon,
And never an hour for thought;
We want to feel the sunshine,
And we want to smell the flowers,
We're sure that God has willed it,
And we mean to have Eight Hours.
We're summoning our forces
From shipyard, shop and mill;
Eight hours for work, eight hours for rest,
Eight hours for what we will!

From the factories and workshops,
In long and weary lines,
From all the sweltering forges,
From all the sunless mines;
Wherever Toil is wasting
The force of life to live;
Its bent and battered armies
Come to claim what God doth give.
And the blazon on its banner
Doth with hope the nations fill.
Eight hours for work, eight hours for rest,
Eight hours for what we will!

The voice of God within us
Is calling us to stand
Erect, as is becoming
To the work of His right hand.
Should he, to whom the Maker
His glorious image gave,
The meanest of His creatures crouch,
A bread-and-butter slave?
Let the shout ring down the valleys
And echo from ev'ry hill,
Eight hours for work, eight hours for rest,
Eight hours for what we will!

Source: I. G. Blanchard, *Boston Daily Voice,* August 7, 1886.

man. The police opened fire immediately, killing at least one more person and wounding many more.

The city's anti-radical, anti-immigrant civic leaders quickly sought revenge for the policeman's death. Parsons, Spies, and six other anarchist leaders were arrested, charged with conspiracy to commit murder, tried, convicted, and sentenced to death. No evidence ever connected any of the accused with the bomb. Even so, Powderly refused to support Parsons, a member of the Knights, or to criticize the courts. Despite worldwide protest, Spies, Parsons, and two of their comrades went to the gallows in November 1887. One of the remaining anarchists committed suicide; the three others were pardoned in 1893 by John Peter Altgeld, a German immigrant who had by then become the pro-labor governor of Illinois.

Many lives were changed by the 1886 strikes, including that of Oscar Ameringer. A teenager newly arrived in Cincinnati, Ameringer brought with him cabinetmaking skills he had learned from his father in Germany. But Ameringer's skills meant little in the furniture factories of the United States. "The work was monotonous, the hours of drudgery ten a day, my wages a dollar," he later remembered. When the strikes for the eight-hour day rocked Cincinnati, Ameringer left his job to march with the *Lehr und Wehr-Verein* (Education and Defense League), one of a variety of ethnic community organizations that sustained workers' protests for many decades. Operating in a number of American cities these groups sponsored military training drills, gymnastic exercises, and instruction in American laws. Calling on the republican traditions of an armed citizenry, the *Cincinnati Lehr und Wehr-Verein* mustered a labor militia of 400 men armed with Springfield rifles. They signaled their revolutionary fervor by carrying red flags and the *Arbeiter Zeitung* (Workers' Times), a newspaper printed on red paper.

Thirty-two thousand Cincinnati workers participated in the May strikes. Most later found their way back to their jobs, but Ameringer—who had been blacklisted for assaulting a strikebreaker in front of the furniture factory—was not one of them. He became active in Cincinnati's German socialist community, writing and agitating for several decades, and he made his living playing the cornet in German saloons. For Ameringer, socialism offered a vision of a fu-

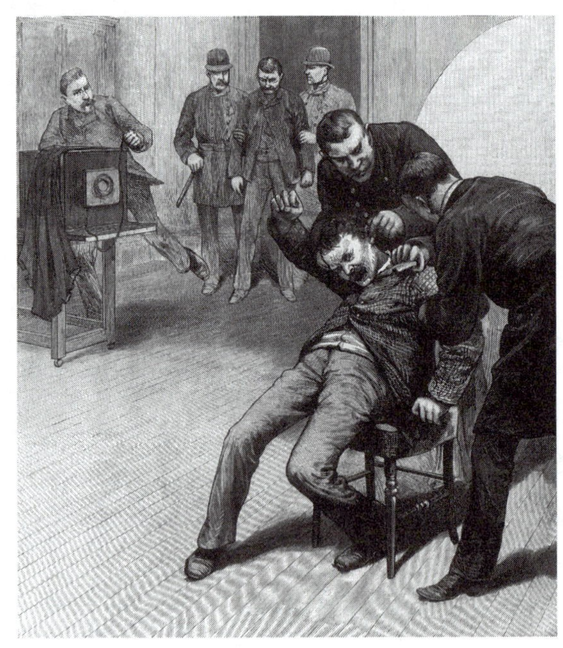

"Photographing Criminals." As part of its coverage of the Haymarket incident, one newspaper displayed this scene in Chicago's police headquarters, showing the construction of a criminal identification system based on photographs. The "Rogues' Gallery" would serve as an archive to identify individual criminals (including political dissenters and labor activists) and to discern, according to contemporary scientific beliefs, what "physiognomic" traits (such as skull shape and facial characteristics) indicated innate criminal tendencies.

Source: Charles Upham, *Frank Leslie's Illustrated Newspaper*, July 31, 1886—American Social History Project.

ture in which wealth would not entitle some to oppress others, and workers would be ensured dignity and the right to a livelihood. As he saw it, the primary problem to be addressed was that of class conflict: the struggle between those who owned the mines and factories, and those who lived by the sweat of their brow.

The Decline of the Knights

Haymarket raised fears among the middle and upper classes—anxiety about aliens, radicals, mobs, and labor organizations, and more broadly about the prospects for anarchism and revolution. Government responded to these fears by strengthening the police, militia, and the U.S. Army, and vigilante groups proliferated. Capitalists mounted a sustained counteroffensive to destroy the insurgency of the eight-hour movement and other organized labor efforts. Some employers attempted to undercut unionization by hiring workers from different ethnic groups who would have difficulty communicating with one another. Trade association members discharged strikers, locked out workers who joined unions, and circulated blacklists of labor activists. Industrial spies, many of them employees of the rapidly growing Pinkerton Detective Agency, infiltrated labor organizations.

Employers also relied increasingly on the coercive power of the government. During the 1880s, legal charges such as "inciting to riot," "obstructing the streets," "intimidation," and "trespass" were first used extensively against strikers, and court injunctions restricting workers' right to picket became commonplace. One judge, handing down an injunction in a labor dispute, proudly called it a "Gatling [machine] gun on paper."

Weakened by internal disputes, faulty decisions, and disunity of purpose, the Knights of Labor proved especially vulnerable. The most dramatic setback occurred on the same rail lines where the Knights had first become prominent. After a successful strike in 1885, Southwestern Railroad workers struck again in March 1886, demanding wage increases and the reinstatement of a discharged comrade. But railroad executives, having discovered that placating workers' organizations fostered militancy and unionization, were intransigent. In the midst of the eight-hour strikes, the Knights capitulated on May 4, 1886 and called off the walkout.

Across the country, employers who had negotiated with labor in 1884 and 1885 refused to do so two years later. The Illinois Bureau of Labor reported that of seventy-six attempts to negotiate differences between labor and employers in 1886, employers rejected any discussion in thirty-two cases. In the second half of 1886, employers locked out some 100,000

The "Typical" Anarchist. Hairy, disheveled, and perched above the deadly tools of his "trade," he stares out from the cover of an 1886 edition of *The New York Detective Library,* one of the many weekly "dime novels" eagerly read by working people in the late nineteenth century.

Source: *The New York Detective Library,* August 7, 1886—General Research Division, New York Public Library, Astor, Lenox, and Tilden Foundations.

workers. Attempts to improve working conditions—by laundry workers in Troy, New York; packinghouse workers in Chicago; and knitters in Cohoes and Amsterdam, New York—ended in harsh defeats.

All these unsuccessful strikes involved the Knights of Labor, which collapsed, no longer able to protect members' workplace rights. The Knights had claimed 40,000 members in Chicago prior to a confrontation in the meatpacking plants; less than a year later their number had fallen to 17,000. Across the nation, the organization that had boasted perhaps three

One of the Crowd: The Rise and Fall of Union Membership, 1870–1900 In a single remarkable year—July 1885 to July 1886—membership in the Knights of Labor multiplied at least seven times, probably the most rapid upsurge in union membership in U.S. history. By mid-1886 American trade unions had a combined membership of a million or more people. But the upsurge did not last; by 1890, union membership had dropped by two-thirds.

Union Membership as Percent of Nonagricultural Workforce, 1870–1900

	1870	1880	1886	1890	1900
Union Members (thousands)	300	50	1,010	325	791
Nonagricultural Workforce (thousands)	6,140	8,470	11,404	13,360	17,390
Percent Organized	4.89%	0.59%	8.86%	2.43%	4.55%

Note: All 1886 figures are estimates.

quarters of a million members at its peak in 1886 shrank to half that size within a year. By 1890, the Knights could claim only 100,000 members.

Politics and the Workingman

For much of the nineteenth century, working-class political thought was permeated by an abiding belief in equality and independence. The revolutionary-era ideology of republicanism placed on an equal and fair footing all white men who participated in American political and social life. In fact, political participation and property ownership were connected, but republicanism rested on the assumption that independent producers had skills or access to farmland and could provide adequately for themselves and their families. Women remained outside the bounds of formal political participation as, in practice, did African Americans, American Indians, and most immigrants. Still, the rhetoric of mainstream American politics promoted the idea that fairness and equal opportunity marked the difference between the United States and the privilege-bound Old World.

By the 1870s, this republican vision of a society of independent citizens was badly tarnished. The railroad strikes of 1877 indicated how far the republic had traveled from the egalitarian promise of the eighteenth century: an ugly chasm divided the broad mass of working people from the wealth and political power of industrial capitalists. To Gilded Age labor reformers, the debasement of politics and society rested in part on the capacity of the rich to corrupt governments in their own self-interest. Labor reform undertook the social and moral regeneration not only of the "commonwealth of toil" but also of the nation's political soul. "We stand as the conservators of society," a Vermont labor leader declared in 1887, suggesting that working people sought to cleanse and revive republican government in the new context of economic growth. Observing this effort, labor editor John Swinton gleefully asserted, "There will soon be but two parties in the field, one composed of honest workingmen, lovers of justice and equality; the other . . . composed of kid-gloved, silk-stockinged, aristocratic capitalists and their contemptible toadies."

The Democratic and Republican parties offered workers tangible benefits for participation in mainstream politics, trading municipal jobs for working-class votes. As cogs in well-oiled "machines"—coalitions of ward organizations that controlled politics and jobs in Gilded Age cities—many urban workers, native-born and immigrant alike, took advantage of these economic opportunities. In the West, political machines had ties to the railroads; the Union Pacific, for example, was deeply involved in the politics of Omaha, its eastern terminus. The multilayered state, county, and municipal machines of the South were central to maintaining the Democratic party's power in that region.

Tammany Hall, New York City's powerful Democratic organization, was the best-known urban machine. Working-class families from parishes and social networks all over the city were indebted to Tammany, which provided a range of vital social and personal services, including bail, emergency relief, and financial support of neighborhood social and cultural activities. Above all, jobs bound urban workers to political machines: Tammany dispensed some 12,000 patronage positions after its victory in the 1888 elections. With help from machine bosses, young Irish women got jobs in the public schools, their brothers found positions on the police force, and immigrants fresh off the boat went to work constructing city streets, bridges, and buildings. Meanwhile, Tammany bosses got wealthy from bribes and from so-called "honest graft"—profiting from knowledge about a new streetcar line by buying nearby land.

Labor reformers rejected Tammany and other political machines. They championed working-class political activism, which linked the economic struggle to truly oppositional contests in the electoral arena. Declaring in the midst of the 1886 boycotts that it was time to "boycott" the Democratic and Republican

"Who Stole the People's Money?" Critics of the urban political machine were handicapped by a foe that possessed both charitable and corrupt attributes. Thomas Nast's *Harper's Weekly* cartoons attacking political "boss" William M. Tweed (the portly figure on the left) and his Tammany Hall associates supplied antimachine forces with a powerful weapon. His caricatures, accessible to everyone, succinctly conveyed a negative portrait of the machine that would influence popular perception of the political "boss" into the late twentieth century.

Source: Thomas Nast, *Harper's Weekly,* August 19, 1871—American Social History Project.

"The Workingman Between Two Fires." During the 1886 New York City mayoral campaign, many workingmen faced a dilemma when the Catholic Church hierarchy attacked Henry George, the United Labor Party (ULP) candidate. As this cartoon from the humor weekly *Judge* indicates, although the ULP lost the election, the sizable turnout for George showed that many Catholic voters had ignored Archbishop Michael A. Corrigan's denunciations.

Source: Grant Hamilton, *Judge,* 1886—General Research Division, New York Public Library, Astor, Lenox, and Tilden Foundations.

parties, New York's Central Labor Union launched an independent labor party to run in the November city election. Their candidate for mayor was reformer and author Henry George, whose *Progress and Poverty* (1879) blamed inequality and corruption on the private ownership of land. George—with the help of the Knights of Labor, the New York Central Labor Union, and Father Edward McGlynn (a Catholic priest who embraced labor reform)—generated tremendous working-class support. He drew equally intense opposition from church hierarchy, employers, and the Tammany machine, the last of which fielded iron magnate Abram Hewitt as the Democratic party's nominee. Although George lost the election, he captured 70,000 votes, a third of the total and far more than the Republican candidate, Theodore Roosevelt.

The George campaign was the most prominent but not the only labor-reform effort. In almost every town and city where Knights of Labor assemblies had been organized, workers discovered their political voice in 1886. Even as the Order itself declined, nearly two hundred Union Labor or Workingmen's parties elected aldermen, mayors, and school board officials. The United Labor ticket won more than a quarter of the votes cast in Chicago, securing seats for five judges and several pro-labor assemblymen. In Rutland, Vermont, the United Labor forces scored a stunning victory, electing a Knights candidate to the state legislature and fifteen justices of the peace. In other places labor managed to take control of one of the two established political parties.

This political activity produced legislative results. City councils and state legislatures passed laws protecting trade units and establishing an eight-hour day for public employees. Sometimes simply the threat of third parties provoked concessions from officials, who passed pro-labor legislation or put "friends of the workingman" on their slates. In Rochester, New Hampshire, the entry of the Knights of Labor into politics forced the Democratic party to endorse the new labor ticket. The Knights claimed in November 1886 that they had elected a dozen U.S. congressmen, almost all of them members of the established parties who had joined with the labor-reform forces.

Badly shaken by labor's political upsurge, Democratic and Republican urban machines attempted to co-opt many of its issues. In New York, Tammany endorsed the establishment of a Bureau of Labor Statistics, called for a legal "Labor Day" holiday, and made a variety of other gestures to regain the following it had lost during the George campaign. But what primarily brought trade unionists, like other working people, into the political system was patronage—the provision of municipal jobs to key supporters. By the late 1880s, for example, more than four hundred Knights of Labor were on Chicago's city payroll.

The Rise of the AFL

Many white male skilled workers left the Knights of Labor during the period of legal repression that followed the Haymarket bombing in 1886. Both the Knights and the local and national trade unions organized by craft unions had agitated for the eight-hour day, mounted mass strikes and boycotts, and supported reform legislation. But in the wake of the Haymarket affair, the craft unions, rejecting the Knights' inclusive social and organizational vision, narrowed their focus to issues relevant to their own members.

The breach between the Knights and the craft unions widened significantly with the creation of the American Federation of Labor (AFL). In May 1886, Samuel Gompers, a leader of the Cigar Makers' International Union, invited all the national unions to meet and formulate a common position with respect to the Knights. During halfhearted negotiations, the craft unions insisted on setting the terms for the Knights' organizing, which the Knights' leaders would not accept. In December, the craft unionists organized a loose alliance of independent national unions. Gompers was elected president, a position he was to hold for most of the next four decades. Local AFL unions and assemblies of the Knights broke each others'

"Two Roads for the Workingman." No admirer of the labor movement, *Puck* depicts the warring trade unions and Knights of Labor as essentially the same, taking workers down the "Road of Lawlessness and Disorder." Meanwhile, in the background, P. M. Arthur of the conservative Brotherhood of Locomotive Engineers chugs forward toward prosperity, progress, and, most important, order.

Source: Joseph Keppler, *Puck,* August 25, 1886—Scott Molloy Labor Archives.

strikes and invaded each others' territory as the AFL gained strength and the Knights declined.

Most of the unionists drawn to the AFL had skills that enabled them to bargain effectively with their employers. These workers could secure concessions from employers as long as they limited their demands to improved wages and working conditions. Disillusioned with the defeats of mass strikes and with broad reform programs that would not win immediate material gains, these skilled craft unionists defined an organizational strategy that they hoped would maximize their power and minimize their vulnerability.

The story of Patrick Henry McCarthy testifies to the extraordinary economic and political power exercised by skilled workers. Born in Ireland on Saint Patrick's Day in 1863, McCarthy arrived in the United States at age seventeen and worked as a carpenter's apprentice. After living briefly in Chicago and St. Louis, he settled in San Francisco in 1886, where he helped found the Brotherhood of Carpenters and Joiners. He organized the city's powerful Building Trades Council in 1898 and ran it with an iron hand for twenty-four years.

San Francisco building tradesmen had been in great demand ever since the days of the Gold Rush. When McCarthy arrived, the city was already a center of trade union power, and the building unions exercised tight control of the labor market. No one worked without a union card, everyone worked under union rules at good wages, and union men informally restricted their output so there would be enough work for all. They were not afraid to strike, and in prosperous times they won more battles than they lost. These privileged workers jealously guarded the gates to their trade: some building unions barred all but their members' sons. A black or Asian man had no chance of being admitted.

McCarthy, the czar of this labor fiefdom, was little interested in unions outside of the building trades and even less concerned with the plight of San Francisco's unorganized workers. Popular at union dances, he fancied fine furniture and diamond rings and punctuated his speech with quotations from the classics. His public persona was that of an honest and upright leader, a "responsible pillar of the community." Pragmatic in his dealings with employers, he supported coalitions of employer groups and labor organizations to achieve political ends.

With Samuel Gompers as their national spokesman, the leaders of individual trade unions like those in McCarthy's Building Trades Council developed the concept of "business unionism." Their national unions were strong organizations of skilled workers; each had exclusive jurisdiction within a specific craft, charged relatively high dues, and maintained ample funds to finance a strike. Business unionism focused on concrete material goals, to be achieved through collective bargaining with the employer.

Willing to use political action if necessary—to fight for protective tariffs or against competition from prison labor—business unionists generally avoided involvement in broad-based political movements.

Although business unionists generally accepted capitalist economic relations and the prevailing social and political order, the AFL and its constituent unions did not lack for militancy, and the rhetoric of the labor movement remained radical. McCarthy's Building Trades Council championed cooperative enterprises and land reform, calling such plans a way to free white workers from wage labor and turn control of the urban-industrial order over to the broad mass of American citizens. The national unions often championed craftsmen's efforts to win an eight-hour day, to defend their organizations, and to protect their traditional control over their jobs.

Strikes became more numerous, better organized, more disciplined, and more successful. Over 60 percent of the strikes waged in 1889 and 1890 were victorious. And the strikes of AFL affiliates were not mere expressions of the wage goals of narrow occupational groups. The organization backed sympathy strikes, in which workers demonstrated their support of another striking union by refusing to work. When New York's cabinetmakers struck to preserve their union in 1892, for example, they were joined by more than eleven other craft groups employed in over one hundred firms. Sympathetic job actions increased nearly fourfold in the early 1890s.

As the AFL gained strength among skilled white workers, the Knights of Labor shifted its sights to rural black workers, western and southern miners, and unskilled immigrants. Although leadership remained in the hands of white English-speaking labor reformers, most new members in the southern countryside were African-American tenants, miners, rural day laborers, and domestic workers. Long known for advocacy of African-American rights, the Knights of Labor increasingly became a black organization in the South.

The United Mine Workers of America (UMWA) also played an important role in organizing black workers. Founded in 1890 with the support of dozens of local Knights assemblies in coal-mining areas, the UMWA embraced the Knights of Labor's broad, inclusive vision and initially affiliated with both the Knights and the AFL. The UMWA struggled from the outset to build an interracial, industrial union for skilled and unskilled mine workers alike.

One UMWA organizer, Richard L. Davis, traveled all over the South to exhort his fellow black miners to join the union. Davis lived in Ohio's Hocking Valley, a coal center that had been torn apart by bitter strikes in the 1870s, when black workers were brought in as strikebreakers. Despite fresh memories of racial conflict, he helped organize an interracial

United in Tragedy. Black and white miners and their families gathered outside a mineshaft in Midlothian, Virginia, after a gas explosion in February 1882. This engraving in *Frank Leslie's Illustrated Newspaper* was unusual in portraying an interracial mining scene.

Source: F. C. Burroughs, *Frank Leslie's Illustrated Newspaper,* February 18, 1882—General Research Division, New York Public Library, Astor, Lenox, and Tilden Foundations.

union local there. During the 1890s he worked as a UMWA organizer throughout Ohio, West Virginia, and Alabama. In 1896 and 1897, he won election to the union's National Executive Board, the only African American to hold a national union office. Repeatedly battling segregation and the distorting influence of "the race question," Davis observed, "I think were we, as workingmen, to turn out attention to fighting monopoly in land and money, we would accomplish a great deal more than we will by fighting among ourselves on account of race, creed, color, or nationality."

Encouraged by the efforts of Davis and other organizers and by the earlier successes of the Knights, the UMWA brought black and white mine workers together in dozens of local unions in the southern West Virginia coalfields. A succession of black miners were elected to the West Virginia district vice presidency between 1891 and 1898, and black miners were the most stalwart supporters of the UMWA in West Virginia during these years.

Unfortunately, the UMWA was unique. Most national unions, reflecting the racism of their members, became narrow organizations of skilled, white male workers. Rejecting the Knights' commitment to interracialism and broad industrial organization and the miners' inclusive approach to organizing, craft unions—notably those in the building trades and the railroad brotherhoods—systematically excluded black workers and the unskilled. The increasingly businesslike and racist policies of AFL craft unionism had overwhelmed the Knights' broader vision of working-class organization.

Class Conflict in the Country

The violence, racial strife, and class conflict that defined industrial life in the 1870s and 1880s found expression not only in industrial towns but also in rural areas, where workers and small farmers opposed powerful economic groups. Here, as in the cities, the power of the wealthy was based on their money, while the power of the poor was grounded in their communities.

Struggling for economic self-sufficiency, the independent white farmers of the South relied on one another for loans of much-needed cash and for assistance with large jobs. Kinship connections reinforced this interdependence, and neighboring farm families "swapped work" and labored together at parties or "bees," much as their western counterparts did. Farmers' independence and mutuality were thus intimately linked, even as expanding rail lines and the tightening noose of credit drew them beyond their communities into national and even world markets.

In the Georgia hills, farmers called on their community ties to protect their common-law rights to graze animals on unfenced land. Merchants and landlords with interests in protecting crops demanded laws requiring farmers to enclose their livestock and defining the boundaries of their land as legal fences. Railroad companies, liable for damages if locomotives struck wandering animals, welcomed this attack on open grazing. But poor people, landless or with only small holdings, needed open grazing to sustain their herds and remain independent of sharecropping and debt peonage.

"We as poor men and Negroes do not need the law," cried one Georgia farmer in 1885, "but we need a democratic government and independence that will do the common people good." As another farmer argued, the law requiring fencing was "ultimately going to be the ruin of people and especially the poor people that have nowhere to keep their stock [and] . . . are entirely dependent on the landowners for pasture." Battles raged over elections called to determine whether land should be fenced. The advocates of fencing won, but they had trouble securing their victory. Outlaws lurking in the Georgia night tore down fences, smashed gates, and threatened proponents of enclosure.

The values expressed in Georgia were mirrored across the country in other conflicts over enclosure. In New Mexico, Juan José Herrerra led a group of Hispanic villagers against powerful cattle ranchers and landowners who had begun fencing the best pasturing and watering lands, which previously had been held in common. Calling themselves *Las Gorras Blancas* (the White Caps), Mexican farmers in 1889 burned fences, cut barbed wire, and generally terrorized cattlemen. At their peak, the White Caps claimed more than 1,500 members; they garnered the support of the entire Mexican-American community and even of some Anglos. They stated their program simply: "Our purpose is to

"Settlers Taking the Law into Their Own Hands." Homesteaders in Custer County, Nebraska, reenacted how they cut down *fifteen* miles of wire *fence* erected by cattlemen in 1885.

Source: Solomon D. Butcher, 1885—Butcher Collection, Nebraska Historical Society.

protect the rights and interest of the people in general and especially those of the helpless classes." Among their opponents they listed "land grabbers," political bosses, and monopolizers of water.

The White Caps also fought against lumber operations and the railroads. During the building of the Santa Fe, they burned track, stopped men hauling railroad ties, and sent threatening letters to foremen denouncing unacceptable wage rates. Because they saw themselves as part of a larger collective movement of resistance against industrial capitalism, they applied for membership as an assembly of the Knights of Labor. In the early 1890s they affiliated with the radical agrarian People's (Populist) Party, which won several elections in New Mexico in the 1890s.

At about the same time, neighborhood bands in the Cross Timbers region of Texas were enforcing a similar belief that ownership of the land did not convey the right to restrict free access to grass and water. Many inhabitants were of Scots-Irish and Irish descent, and their deep-seated, traditional dislike of landlords found an outlet in the cry "Land to the cultivator!" Brash fence cutters left taunting notes: "We understand you have plenty of money to spend to build fences. Please put them up again for us to cut them down again. We want the fence guarded with good men so that their mettle can be tested."

The defense of common rights in Texas was linked to a growing opposition to those who monopolized land and credit. Sam Bass, a former Indiana farmhand, was celebrated in song and story as "the Robin Hood of Cross Timbers," for stealing from the railroads. Bass may not have considered his crimes symbolic of community resistance to capitalist speculation, but others saw him in that light. Bandits like Bass and the more infamous Jesse James won the acclaim of farmers and urban workers across the country by taking on railroads and banks, repositories of corporate capital in the Gilded Age.

Bloody Battles at Homestead

The same community basis for class struggles against capitalists could also be found in industrial cities and towns. Yet one of the era's most famous strikes—at Andrew Carnegie's Homestead, Pennsylvania, steel mill in 1892—demonstrated that locally organized workers were ill-matched against new, nationally organized corporations. For their part, urban craft workers seemed to have the upper hand in the campaign to improve their circumstances. The AFL craft unions had consolidated their influence in the late 1880s and early 1890s. Workers in the building trades were largely successful in achieving the eight-hour day. Skilled iron and steel workers, in particular, had won high wages based on their knowledge and command of the production process and on their unity in dealing with employers.

At Carnegie's Homestead works, one of the most advanced mills in the world, the Amalgamated Association of Iron and Steel Workers had won an important victory in 1889, securing wages one-third higher than those paid to skilled workers at neighboring mills. In addition, the settlement pegged the wages of unorganized unskilled workers to those of the skilled craftsmen. The contract therefore benefited not only skilled unionized workers but their unskilled nonunion helpers as well.

In Homestead, as elsewhere, community ties reinforced relationships formed on the job. Homestead, with twelve mills, was one of the world's largest industrial complexes in the late nineteenth century. Of its 11,000 residents, 3,800 men worked in the mills—virtually one person from every household. Steelworkers headed the city government and police department and owned most of Homestead's modest homes. In their view, unionism was a right of citizenship, a bulwark against dependency, and a protector of workers' positions as homeowners in a community they had made their own. As a state militia officer wonderingly remarked, "They believe the works are theirs quite as much as Carnegie's."

Carnegie and his partner, Henry Clay Frick, believed differently, and they decided to break the union's power. Carnegie wanted a cheap and docile labor force, and the Amalgamated Association stood in his way. In June 1892, as Carnegie vacationed in Scotland, Frick broke off contract-renewal negotiations with union representatives, announcing that the company would in the future bargain only with individual workers. He then prepared for battle, surrounding the mills with three miles of twelve-foot steel fence topped with barbed wire; workers dubbed the complex "Fort Frick." He also hired 300 armed Pinkerton agents to protect the scab replacement workers he planned to bring in by boat on the Monongahela River, which ran along company property. On July 2, Frick locked out the workers, shut down the Homestead works, and announced that they would reopen with nonunion labor. The Amalgamated Association responded by mobilizing virtually the entire town, organizing a paramilitary takeover of the local utilities, monitoring all access to Homestead, and closing the saloons.

On July 6, the heavily armed Pinkertons approached the plant from a barge on the river. Armed with guns, rocks, and a small cannon, an enraged crowd of steelworkers and their wives met the Pinkertons at the river's edge. Nine strikers and seven Pinkertons died during a twelve-hour battle, and many more were wounded. The Pinkertons surrendered to the workers.

"An Awful Battle at Homestead, Pa." The *National Police Gazette* portrayed the July 6, 1892, fight between striking steelworkers and Pinkerton strikebreakers on the Monongahela River. Directed to male readers, many of whom were workers, the *Police Gazette* occasionally covered labor conflict, expressing sympathy toward strikers while also exploiting the more sensational aspects of the events.

Source: *National Police Gazette,* July 23, 1892—Prints and Photographs Division, Library of Congress.

In the days that followed, the confrontation spread beyond Homestead as lockouts and sympathy strikes shut down other Carnegie mills. But the Carnegie Company persuaded the governor of Pennsylvania to send in the militia, which escorted repairmen, mechanics, and strikebreakers (recruited from as far away as Ohio) into Carnegie's plants. Still, the Amalgamated Association hung on for four more months. Frick wrote Carnegie, "The firmness with which these strikers hold on is surprising to everyone."

The workers believed they had right on their side, but Carnegie was mightier. As the company restored production and winter approached, morale faded. On November 20, 1892, the union surrendered; the Amalgamated leaders were fired and blacklisted. Frick cabled Carnegie: "Our victory is now complete and most gratifying. Do not think we will ever have any serious labor trouble again."

The defeat at Homestead dealt the skilled men of the Amalgamated Association—and craft unionism in general—a stunning blow. Their union was shattered, their faith in their powerful craft organization severely compromised. They had learned about the power of capital and had experienced firsthand the role of government in labor-capital conflict. Technological change had eroded skilled workers' central role in the production process and made them increasingly vulnerable. Gone were the days when skilled craftsmen had only to

Martial Law in Coeur d'Alene. The interior of a "bull pen," one of the makeshift prison sheds erected by federal and state troops in 1892 to hold arrested union miners and sympathizers.

Source: T. A. Barnard, 1899—Barnard-Stockbridge Collection, University of Idaho Library, Moscow, Idaho.

withhold their labor to get bosses to agree to their demands.

Days after the Homestead workers returned to the mills, another violent incident pitted strikers against strikebreakers and company guards, this time in the silver-mining region of Coeur d'Alene, Idaho. Here, too, the owners called on state government for help. The governor of Idaho declared martial law and sent in the state militia, and the striking workers capitulated. Other major labor defeats in 1892 included a strike by switchmen in the Buffalo railway yards, a strike by Knights of Labor in Tennessee coal mines, and a general strike by black and white workers in New Orleans.

Faced with this record of crushing setbacks, AFL president Samuel Gompers asked, "Shall we change our methods?" AFL union membership held steady despite the 1892 losses, and Gompers answered in the negative, believing that trade unions' very survival in the face of employers' all-out attacks proved his policies correct. But he missed the larger meaning of the year's events. In the face of overwhelming defeat, the culture of solidarity that had inspired many skilled craft workers for thirty years was in decline. If Haymarket in 1886 represented the destruction of the Knights' broad vision of labor unity among workers of diverse backgrounds and skills, the narrower but sustaining vision of craft unionism met an equivalent defeat at Homestead and other sites in 1892.

Another lesson of the 1892 strikes was that political power was shifting from the local to the state level. Large corporations could exert greater influence over governors than over mayors and aldermen—especially in communities where the political power of working people remained significant. Within this new political context, employers made it clear that they would do everything possible to destroy the labor movement.

The Years in Review

1869

- Nine Philadelphia tailors found the Noble and Holy Order of the Knights of Labor.

1872

- Anthony Comstock founds the New York Society for the Suppression of Vice.

1874

- Women activists found the Woman's Christian Temperance Union.

1877

- Great railroad strikes sweep across the nation.

1878

- Women's Suffrage Amendment to the Constitution is defeated in the Senate by a 34-to-16 vote. (Supporters will reintroduce it in every succeeding Congress until it is finally passed after World War I.)
- Procter & Gamble introduces White Soap; four years later, Harley Procter, inspired by psalm-reading in church, renames the soap Ivory.

1880

- Salvation Army opens its first U.S. mission in New York City, offering food, shelter, and low-wage work to needy people.
- National Farmers' Alliance, predecessor of the Populist Party, is formed in Chicago.
- Gold Medal Flour, Thomas's English Muffins, and Philadelphia Cream Cheese are introduced; R. T. French (spice) Co. forms in New York.

1881

- African-American washerwomen in Atlanta organize a two-week strike to demand higher fees.
- Knights of Labor admit women members.
- Jim Crow law segregating railroad cars passes in Tennessee, setting precedent for other southern states.
- First color photographs are produced.
- Booker T. Washington founds the Normal and Industrial Institute for Negroes (later Tuskegee Institute) and becomes its president.
- Barnum and Bailey Circus is born.

1882

- Congress passes Chinese Exclusion Act.
- Knights of Labor sponsor the first Labor Day parade.
- Hatfield-McCoy feud in West Virginia and Kentucky boils over, lasting to 1888.

1883

- In his $2 million New York City mansion, William K. Vanderbilt stages the most lavish party ($250,000) yet held in America.

1884

- Federation of Organized Trades and Labor Unions begins a two-year campaign for an eight-hour workday.
- New York surgeon William Halsted discovers anesthetic properties of cocaine and becomes addicted to the substance.

1885

- First appendectomy is performed in the United States.
- Morton's salt and Moxie tonic drink are introduced.
- English scientist Francis Galton invents fingerprint-identification system.

1886

- American Federation of Labor forms, with Samuel Gompers as its president.
- Knights of Labor enrolls nearly 1 million members—about 10 percent of the country's nonagricultural workforce, a much higher proportion than ever before enrolled in unions.
- Bomb explodes in Haymarket Square; an anti-radical crusade follows.
- Reformer Henry George loses the election for mayor of New York City but gets one-third of votes.
- Weakened by internal disputes, faulty decisions, and disunity of purpose, the Knights of Labor are defeated in the Southwestern Railroad strike. Labor suffers many defeats in 1886 and 1887.
- Caffeine-free Dr. Pepper is touted as the "King of Beverages"; Maxwell House Coffee is named for the Nashville hotel where the blend was invented.
- Cosmetics salesman David McConnell becomes the first "Avon Lady."
- Griswold Lorrillard attends the Autumn Ball of the Tuxedo Club in Tuxedo, New York, in a tailless dress coat that is soon known as the tuxedo.

1887

- Henry Bowers founds the American Protective Association to stop immigration.
- Grocer P. J. Towle introduces Log Cabin syrup in St. Paul, Minnesota.

1888

- Frank J. Sprague installs the first urban electric streetcar system in Richmond, Virginia.
- Electrocution replaces death by hanging in New York.

1889

- The Organization of Mexican-American farmers, *Las Gorras Blancas,* burns fences and cuts barbed wire in opposition to the practices of white cattlemen.
- Jane Addams founds Hull House, a settlement house for the urban poor in Chicago.

1890

- United Mine Workers of America is founded.
- A St. Louis physician invents peanut butter as a health food.

1891

- James Naismith invents the game of basketball.
- Congress passes the International Copyright Act; before 1891, American publishers routinely pirated works by European authors.

1892

- Workers strike but are defeated at Andrew Carnegie's Homestead Steelworks in Pennsylvania.
- Populist Party is founded.
- Miners are defeated in a violent strike in Coeur d'Alene, Idaho.
- John Muir founds the Sierra Club and begins a crusade to preserve nature from "ravaging commercialism."
- William J. Wrigley starts selling chewing gum; James Hazen introduces Fig Newtons.

1893

- Chicago surgeon Daniel H. Williams performs the first open-heart surgery.

Suggested Readings

Ahlstrom, Sydney E., *A Religious History of the American People* (1972).
Ashbaugh, Carolyn, *Lucy Parsons: American Revolutionary* (1976).
Avrich, Paul, *The Haymarket Tragedy* (1983).
Ayers, Edward L., *Vengeance and Justice: Crime and Punishment in the Nineteenth-Century South* (1984).
Bean, Walter, *Boss Ruef's San Francisco: The Story of Work, Culture, and Society in Industrializing the Union Labor Party, Big Business, and the Graft Prosecution* (1967).
Bensman, David, *The Practice of Solidarity* (1985).
Couvares, Francis G., *The Remaking of Pittsburgh: Class and Culture in an Industrializing City, 1877–1919* (1984).
D'Emilio, John, and Estelle B. Freedman, *Intimate Matters: A History of Sexuality in America* (1988).

Diner, Hasia, *Erin's Daughters in America: Irish Immigrant Women in the Nineteenth Century* (1983).
Duis, Perry R., *The Saloon: Public Drinking in Chicago and Boston, 1880–1920* (1983).
Erie, Steven P., *Rainbow's End: Irish Americans and the Dilemmas of Urban Machine Politics, 1840–1945* (1988).
Fink, Leon, *Workingmen's Democracy: The Knights of Labor and American Politics* (1983).
Glenn, Susan A., *Daughters of the Shtetl: Life and Labor in the Immigrant Generation* (1990).
Hahn, Steven, *The Roots of Southern Populism* (1983).
Hayden, Dolores, *The Grand Domestic Revolution* (1983).
Jeffrey, Julie Roy, *Frontier Women: The Trans-Mississippi West, 1840–1880* (1979).
Kasson, John F., *Rudeness and Civility: Manners in Nineteenth-Century Urban America* (1990).
Kazin, Michael, *Barons of Labor: The San Francisco Building Trades and Union Power in the Progressive Era* (1987).
Lears, Jackson, *No Place of Grace: Antimodernism and the Transformation of American Culture, 1880–1920* (1981).
Levine, Lawrence W., *Highbrow/Lowbrow: The Emergence of Cultural Hierarchy in America* (1988).
Levine, Susan, *Labor's True Woman: Carpet Weavers, Industrialization, and Labor Reform in the Gilded Age* (1984).
Miller, Kerby A., *Emigrants and Exiles: Ireland and the Irish Exodus to North America* (1985).
Montgomery, David, *Workers' Control in America: Studies in the History of Work* (1982).
Nash, Michael, *Conflict and Accommodation: Coal Miners, Steel Workers, and Socialism, 1890–1920* (1980).
Powers, Madelon, *Faces Along the Bar: Lore and Order in the Workingman's Saloon, 1870–1920* (1998).
Roediger, Dave, and Franklin Rosemont, *Haymarket Scrapbook* (1986).
Rosengarten, Theodore, *All God's Dangers: The Autobiography of Nate Shaw* (1974).
Rosenzweig, Roy, *Eight Hours for What We Will: Workers and Leisure in an Industrial City, 1870–1920* (1983).
Smith, Carl, *Urban Disorder and the Shape of Belief: The Great Chicago Fire, the Haymarket Bomb, and the Model Town of Pullman* (1995).
Stratton, Joanna L., *Pioneer Women: Voices from the Kansas Frontier* (1981).
Themstrom, Stephan, *Poverty and Progress: Social Mobility in a Nineteenth-Century City* (1968).
Walkowitz, Daniel J., *Worker City, Company Town: Iron- and Cotton-Worker Protest in Troy and Cohoes, New York, 1855–1884* (1978).
Waller, Altina L., *Reverend Beecher and Mrs. Tilton: Sex and Class in Victorian America* (1982).

And on the World Wide Web

Library of Congress, *The American Variety Stage: Vaudeville and Popular Entertainment, 1870–1920* (http://memory.loc.gov/ammem/vshtml/vshome.html)

Library of Congress, *Touring Turn-of-the-Century America: Photographs from the Detroit Publishing Company, 1880–1920* (http://memory.loc.gov/ammem/detroit/dethome.html)

chapter 3

The Producing Classes and the Money Power

A Decade of Hard Times, Struggle, and Defeat

1893–1904

On May 1, 1893, the World's Columbian Exposition—Chicago's great world's fair commemorating the four-hundredth anniversary of Columbus's arrival in the Americas—opened to the public. Chicago's leading merchants, bankers, and real estate men raised millions to build a dazzling fair that would publicize to the world the cultural and economic achievements of their city and nation. Chicago architect Daniel H. Burnham, who oversaw construction of the exposition's "White City," proclaimed that the fair would constitute the third great event in American history, preceded only by the Revolution and the Civil War. The architects and artists who designed the neoclassical buildings of the White City saw themselves as heirs to the Italian Renaissance, who would remake and purify American culture through their work. "Look here, old fellow," the sculptor Augustus Saint-Gaudens told Burnham at a planning session, "do you realize that this is the greatest meeting of artists since the fifteenth century?"

But the White City's shining marble edifices were a sham—the "marble" was really just plaster covering wood and steel. An even deeper contradiction lay outside the fairgrounds. At almost the same moment that the fair opened for business, thousands of factory gates swung closed, as the nation plunged into one of the worst depressions in its history. "From all the manufacturing and commercial centres," declared the New York City branch of the American Federation of Labor (AFL) just months after the fair's triumphant opening, "there comes the anxious demand for work, soon we fear to be followed by the despairing cry for bread." Alluding directly to the Columbian Exposition, they complained that "a few thousand men and women enjoy the opulence of eastern potentates, while abject millions grovel in the dust begging for work and bread. This is the industrial and social exhibit of our Columbian year."

Industrial workers and activist farmers responded to the hard times with militant action and with radical electoral campaigns, organizing the most successful political movements outside the major parties in American history—campaigns that built upon the solidarity and the cooperative vision of the struggles of the 1880s. But before the century was over, those movements would be sharply defeated. Still worse, immigrants and southern blacks faced a rising tide of nativism and racism. To

"Theater at the Brickyard." The workforce of a Massachusetts brick factory exuberantly posed for the photographer sometime in the late nineteenth century.

Source: Ashfield Historical Society, Ashfield, Massachusetts.

be sure, recovery from the depression—fostered in part by the expansion of U.S. capitalism abroad—improved the material conditions of farmers and working people. Fewer workers could be found "begging for work," but it would be many years before they would regain the political clout they had exerted in the 1880s or 1890s. The triumphant claims of the capitalists who planned the White City would ring much more true in 1900 than they had in 1893.

The Depression of the 1890s

On May 3, 1893, the stock market crashed, and by year's end, about 500 banks and 16,000 businesses were bankrupt. Having led the economy into growth, the railroads now pushed it into depression. By the middle of 1894, more than 150 railroad companies were also bankrupt, stimulating trouble in other industries. Weakness in the agricultural economy suggested the extent to which farming was tied into national and international markets. And when farmers fell on bad times, they in turn dragged down farm machine manufacturers, grain elevator operators, and a variety of rural and small-town businesses.

". . . We Are Starving to Death"

In this 1894 letter to the governor of Kansas, Susan Orcutt describes the devastation experienced by western Kansas farming communities caught in the iron grip of the depression (spelling and punctuation corrected).

I take my pen in hand to let you know that we are Starving to death. It is Pretty hard to do without anything to Eat here in this God forsaken country. We would of had Plenty to Eat if the hail hadn't cut our rye down and ruined our corn and Potatoes. I had the Prettiest Garden that you Ever seen and the hail ruined It and I have nothing to look at. My Husband went away to find work and came home last night and told me that we would have to Starve. He had been in ten countys and did not Get no work. It is Pretty hard for a woman to do without anything to Eat when She doesn't know what minute She will be confined to bed. If I was in Iowa I would be all right. I was born there and raised there. I haven't had nothing to Eat today and It is three o'clock.

Source: Lewelling Papers, Kansas Historical Society (1894).

This was the fourth major depression in American history. Each depression was bigger than the one before, and, because the economy and the population kept growing, more people—and a greater proportion of people—were affected each time. More people worked for wages and paid for goods in cash; fewer bartered their labor and the goods they made or the food they grew. Drawn ever more tightly into a national economy, Americans were increasingly vulnerable to economic forces they could not control. What happened on Wall Street now affected the lives of Massachusetts railroad workers and Mississippi sharecroppers who would never own stocks or bonds.

The five years of depression brought misery on a scale not previously experienced in industrial America. Plant closings threw Americans out of work in staggering numbers. The AFL estimated the number of unemployed to be more than 3 million in 1893. In Chicago alone, more than 100,000 of the city's million residents were jobless. As in previous depressions, the unemployed and the homeless traveled the country, hopping freight trains to distant places in search of work or handouts. By the winter of 1893–1894, Chicago police were guarding railroad stations to prevent tramps from entering the city.

The statistics mask the depression's devastating impact on individual lives. Consider George A. Smith, who in November 1893, was laid off by the Boston and Maine and Fitchburg railroads because of the "dull times." Smith, a twenty-seven-year-old father of two, was known as a "steady, industrious man," but over the next four months he could pick up only two weeks of work. Having exhausted his savings, he and his family had not even enough money to heat their apartment, buy yeast to bake bread, or pay for a doctor for their ailing son. Facing eviction by an unsympathetic landlord, a desperate Smith sought refuge at the local police station. But even so, Smith and his family fared better than some during the hard years of the depression. "R. N.," a jobless Boston man, shot himself in the head in June 1896. The state medical examiner noted that R. N. "left a letter explaining that he killed himself to save others the trouble of caring for him."

Riding the Rails in Search of Work. At a rural station, free soup and bread drew hungry unemployed people from their hiding places in railroad freight cars.

Source: Joseph P. Birren, *The Graphic,* September 9, 1893—Chicago Historical Society.

Organized public and private relief efforts did not come close to meeting the needs of unemployed workers like George Smith or R. N. Many middle- and upper-class whites viewed relief with distaste, believing that "getting something for nothing" was a sin. Some thought that charity was socialistic, others that it encouraged laziness. Moved by the plight of an unemployed man with five hungry children, a Massachusetts overseer of the poor gave the man some money but was careful to cover up his good deed "so that it wouldn't get out." Social Darwinism suggested that such charitable acts were wrongheaded: hard times would weed out the "unfit." Relief efforts were regulated by Charity Organization Societies, local organizations that investigated poor people's lives to determine who was "worth" helping. Overall, public assistance and formal charities provided only marginal assistance to the jobless. They were much more likely to rely on the kindness of family, friends, and neighbors. "The kind that always helps you out," observed one tramp, is "the kind that's in hard luck themselves, and knows what it is."

As millions of families faced starvation, labor organizations demanded government help by creating jobs. In December 1893, declaring that "the right to work is the right to live," the annual convention of the AFL asked the federal government to issue $500 million in paper money to fund public works. To spread the work that was available among a larger number of people, the organization called for an eight-hour day.

Workers on the March

Responding to their own misery and to the contempt of their social "betters," some unemployed workers mounted protests during the spring of 1894. The best publicized protest was a march organized by Ohio businessman Jacob S. Coxey in support of his own job-creation scheme that emphasized federal spending on public works. To publicize the plan, Coxey announced the formation of an "industrial army" of the unemployed, to march on Washington, D.C. "We will send a petition to Washington with boots on," Coxey declared.

Thousands cheered Coxey's band of a few hundred marchers as they moved from one industrial town to another. Thorstein Veblen, a young sociologist, claimed the marchers were more significant than their numbers suggested. Coxey's appeal to the federal government for relief, Veblen argued, was in essence an assertion that government had a basic responsibility for the people's welfare. The federal government was hardly ready for such a role. Although Coxey's band numbered fewer than 500 when they arrived in Washington on the morning of May 1, 1894, worried national officials had massed 1,500 troops to greet them. Police arrested Coxey and two other leaders for carrying

On the Road to Washington, D.C. Members of Coxey's Army marched into Alleghany, Virginia, their progress marked by a Chicago reporter on horseback.

Source: *Frank Leslie's Illustrated Newspaper,* April 19, 1894—American Social History Project.

banners on the Capitol grounds, and the marchers disbanded.

Nevertheless, Coxey's movement inspired dozens of industrial armies to set out for Washington that year. In the Far West their ranks numbered in the thousands; most traveled on foot, but they sometimes seized trains. The federal government moved as forcefully against them as it had against Coxey. U.S. Attorney General Richard C. Olney, a former railroad lawyer, deployed U.S. marshals and federal troops to end the train seizures. Although troops stopped the hijackings and curtailed the eastward movement of the armies, about 1,200 marchers made the cross-country trek all the way to Washington during 1894.

Olney also fought the protestors on another front: the courts, which stifled protests by issuing federal injunctions. Injunctions were a longstanding legal weapon that had been used in the 1880s against the Knights of Labor and the boycott movement. Issued by both federal and state judges, they prohibited strike activity and prevented union locals from communicating with each other, often on the grounds that strikes violated employers' property rights. In some of the key struggles of the 1890s, court injunctions would prove to be a powerful anti-labor weapon.

Pullman: Solidarity and Defeat

The defeat of Coxey's Army did not end the escalating conflict between the haves and the have-nots. As the depression worsened, Olney used federal troops and injunctions to quell a major strike against the Pullman Palace Car Company, but this time the result was a violent confrontation.

The Pullman company, which made railroad sleeping cars, was famous not only for its product but for its "model" company town—

". . . An Ulcer on the Body Politic"

The men and women who labored in George Pullman's "model" town during the 1893 depression endured starvation wages and deplorable living and working conditions. They especially loathed Pullman's paternalistic control over all aspects of their lives. This statement from a Pullman striker, delivered at the June 1894 Chicago convention of the American Railway Union, suggests the depth of the strikers' hatred of their employer and their commitment to the ARU.

We struck at Pullman because we were without hope. We joined the American Railway Union because it gave us a glimmer of hope. Twenty thousand souls, men, women, and little ones, have their eyes turned toward this convention today, straining eagerly through dark despondency for a glimmer of the heaven-sent message you alone can give us on this earth.

In stating to this body our grievances it is hard to tell where to begin. . . . Five reductions in wages, work, and in conditions of employment swept through the shops at Pullman between May and December 1893. The last was the most severe, amounting to nearly 30 percent and our rents had not fallen. . . . No man or woman of us all can ever hope to own one inch of George Pullman's land. Why even the very streets are his. . . .

Pullman, both the man and the town, is an ulcer on the body politic. He owns the houses, the schoolhouses, the churches of God. . . . The revenue he derives from these, the wages he pays out with one hand—the Pullman Palace Car Company, he takes back with the other—the Pullman Land Association. He is able by this to bid under any contract car shop in the country. His competitors in business, to meet this, must reduce the wages of their men. . . . And thus the merry war—the dance of skeletons bathed in human tears—goes on, and it will go on, brothers, forever, unless you, the American Railway Union, stop it; end it; crush it out.

Source: U.S. Strike Commission, *Report on the Chicago Strike of June–July 1894* (1895).

Pullman, Illinois, just south of Chicago. The town was overcrowded. It banned saloons, trade unions, and public gatherings other than church. Rents were 20 to 25 percent higher than for similar housing in Chicago, and the Pullman company made huge profits on utility bills, which, like the rent, were deducted from workers' pay. "We are born in a Pullman house," one employee declared, "fed from the Pullman shop, taught in the Pullman school, catechized in the Pullman church, and when we die we shall be buried in the Pullman cemetery and go to the Pullman hell."

As the depression worsened, George Pullman responded by firing a third of his employees, cutting the wages of the rest by 25 to 40 percent, and refusing to reduce rents or food prices at the company store. Some workers literally took home pennies after rent was deducted from their wages. In May 1894, workers met in secret to propose that a committee discuss these matters with management. When three of its members were fired summarily, Pullman workers walked off the job. "Pullman, both the man and the town," the strikers declared, "is an ulcer on the body politic." A local minister put it even more pungently: "George is a bad egg—handle him with care. Should you crack his shell the odor would depopulate Chicago in an hour."

The strikers appealed to the American Railway Union (ARU) for support. Formed in 1893 by charismatic activist Eugene V. Debs and a group of western railroad workers still in the Knights of Labor, the ARU was the fastest-growing union in the United States. It had over 150,000 members, more than all the other railroad unions combined. The ARU offered a new model of industrial unionism. Dues were low, and all white wage workers employed by railroads were welcome, whatever their skill levels or specific jobs. "Even the laundresses who cleaned the sheets from the sleeping compartments" could join, reported Florence Kelley, the chief factory inspector of Illinois. But despite Debs's attempt to admit them, African Americans were excluded.

The ARU called for a boycott and a strike against all trains hauling Pullman cars. Because nearly every railroad had Pullmans, this would be a national strike, and a far more crippling one than the great railroad strikes of 1877. Thousands of miles of track had been laid since then. Chicago and other western cities that had developed with the railroads depended on trains for survival; it would be impossible to transport enough food to feed those cities by horse and wagon.

Unlike the largely spontaneous revolt of 1877, the "Debs Revolution," as the Pullman strike was called, was highly organized, directed by a

"King Debs." Eugene Debs, president of the American Railway Union, was lambasted by much of the press during the Pullman strike. This *Harper's Weekly* cartoon, like many other published pictures, portrayed Debs as a tyrant paralyzing the country's commerce, but it also made his face familiar to readers across the nation.

Source: William A. Rogers, *Harper's Weekly,* July 14, 1894—Scott Molloy Labor Archives.

steering committee made up of representatives from local unions. Committees across the country coordinated their activities with the strike's headquarters in Chicago. The General Managers' Association, an organization of twenty-six railroads operating in Chicago, coordinated the railroads' side. When the boycott started on June 26, this group ordered the discharge of any workers who refused to handle Pullman cars. In response, ARU members around the country brought most of the nation's rail traffic to a halt. Thus an isolated labor dispute became, in Debs's words, "a contest between the producing classes and the money power of the country." An estimated 260,000 railroad workers joined the battle; half a million more may have been idled by the boycott.

"Chicago Under the Mob." An ardent admirer of the military, artist-reporter Frederic Remington displayed no sympathy for the Pullman strikers in his reports for *Harper's Weekly*. Endorsing suppression, Remington described the strikers as a "malodorous crowd of foreign trash," talking "Hungarian or Polack, or whatever the stuff is."

Source: Frederic Remington, *Harper's Weekly,* July 21, 1894—American Social History Project.

Railroad managers then played their trump card. Seeking the intervention of the federal government, they turned to Attorney General Olney, who still served on the boards of several railroads. Olney obtained a sweeping injunction from the federal courts in early July, effectively outlawing the strike. Federal troops and state militia were then dispatched in six states. In Chicago, the arrival of the U.S. Army on the Fourth of July precipitated a violent confrontation with workers that left thirteen dead, more than fifty wounded, and hundreds of thousands of dollars of damage to railroad property. Federal troops were backed by 2,600 U.S. deputy marshals, asked for and paid for by the railroads. Even the Chicago chief of police later testified that the deputies were nothing more than "thugs, thieves, and ex-convicts."

During the next week, violence erupted in twenty-six states, from Maine to California. In Chicago, the battles between troops and strikers continued for days, killing and injuring more people. Freight cars and other equipment burned in railroad yards, destroying merchandise as well as railroad property. "The strike is now war," screamed a headline in the *Chicago Tribune*. By July 11, an estimated thirty-four people had died. When Debs and other ARU leaders were arrested for disobeying the injunction, the strike began to collapse. By mid-July, the Pullman strike was over. In the bitter aftermath, Debs and other leaders were convicted of civil contempt and sentenced to prison; many strikers were blacklisted. Debs served six months in a federal jail near Chicago. Later he attributed his conversion to socialism to the pamphlets visitors brought to his cell.

Although many prominent citizens criticized the handling of the strike, the courts upheld the use of injunctions against strikes and unions. A notoriously conservative Supreme Court decreed that strikes were a conspiracy in restraint of trade, constituting both a civil and a criminal offense. That decision laid the groundwork for the continued use of state militias, federal troops, and injunctions to defend the interests of capital. It also undercut the strength of the labor movement by preventing communication among striking locals and jailing strike leaders. These new legal tactics would cripple militant unionism for decades.

The Pullman strike sharpened the lines of class struggle. Workers had demonstrated a capacity for organization and coordination and an increasingly national orientation. George Pullman, wrote Florence Kelley, "once and for all did away with the delusion that the workers can expect anything from the philanthropy of the big capitalists. No one has contributed more to the development of class consciousness among American wage workers." Like Homestead two years earlier, Pullman reminded workers of the combined power of capitalists' private armies and the military force of the federal and state governments. Some labor leaders argued that workers' only defense was a labor party that would fight for political power in tandem with the unions' struggle for industrial justice. Democrats and Republicans, they charged, were more interested in party patronage than in the workingman's lot. In part because of the defeat of the Pullman strike, ARU leaders joined other labor activists in uniting with a movement that until that time had been mostly agrarian. Urging labor to seek change at the ballot box, rather than on the picket line, they joined with the rapidly rising People's party, one of the largest and most powerful third parties in American history.

The Farmers' Alliance and the People's Party

The People's party, better known as the Populists, shared with the Knights of Labor a communitarian and collective vision that challenged the acquisitive individualism of the Gilded Age. The party had originated in the cooperative crusade of the Farmers' Alliance, which began in Texas in the late 1870s. This crusade, in turn, built on the efforts of the Grange, or Patrons of Husbandry, which for a decade had been promoting cooperative buying and selling across rural America. At its peak, the Farmers' Alliance claimed hundreds of thousands of members and supporters nationwide. Local chapters, or "suballiances," not only managed the thousands of cooperative enterprises or "exchanges," but also helped members recover stray animals and took vigilante action against thieves and ranchers greedy for grazing land. Headed by Charles Macune, the Alliance promoted a simple message: "The Alliance is the people and the people are together."

Thousands of paid lecturers communicated this theme at local meetings, larger county gatherings, and massive Fourth of July encampments. Some were dynamic orators, as were "Sockless" Jerry Simpson of Kansas and Mary Elizabeth Lease, an activist in farmer, labor, and Irish nationalist circles. Lease and her husband knew firsthand the difficulties of the farmer from a decade of struggling (and failing) to succeed on Kansas and Texas farms. Her "magic," as one historian observes, "was in her voice—deep, resonant, and powerful. Her extemporaneous speaking style, charismatic and hypnotic, carried her into such sustained outbursts of emotion and invective that she sometimes could not remember what she had said until she read about it later in the press." Ironically, she became best known for declaring that farmers should "raise less corn and more hell"—a phrase she apparently never uttered. The use of such profanity by a woman would have upset Victorian audiences. When Lease spoke once of "the gates of hell," she had to explain to a shocked audience that the phrase was a quote from the Bible. But if she was more decorous than history records, Lease was still a fiery speaker who routinely denounced "a system which clothes rascals in robes and honesty in rags."

About one-fourth of Alliance members were women—more in some suballiances. Women gave speeches, wrote for Alliance publications, and ran business affairs. At a spring 1891 meeting, Mrs. Brown, the secretary of the Menola Suballiance in North Carolina, spoke directly to her "Alliance sisters" of her "appreciation of woman's opportunity of being coworkers with the brethren in the movement which is stirring this great nation." Quoting temperance reformer Frances E. Willard, she declared that "Drudgery, fashion and gossip are no longer the bounds of woman's Sphere."

"We Feed the World." Grangers, predecessors of the Farmers' Alliance and Populists, gathered in the woods near Winchester, Scott County, Illinois, in August 1873.

Source: Joseph B. Beale, *Frank Leslie's Illustrated Newspaper,* August 30, 1873—American Social History Project.

Spurred by the depression, the Alliance spread like wildfire in the early 1880s. In 1883, the Texas Alliance was supporting twenty-six lecturers in eleven counties, and by 1886 Texas membership had swelled to more than 100,000. Meeting in Waco in 1887, the Texas Alliance joined with farmers' groups from Louisiana, Arkansas, and Mississippi and resolved to send lecturers throughout the cotton belt. They were enormously successful. Texas Alliance lecturer J. B. Barry went back to his native state of North Carolina to organize. "I met the farmers twenty-seven times and twenty-seven times they organized," he wrote back

". . . Monopoly is the Master"

The Populist leader Mary K. Lease held crowds of midwestern and southern farmers spellbound with her fiery oratory. In this selection from one of her many 1890 speeches to large audiences of Kansas farmers, Lease attacked the eastern moneyed interests, whom she accuses of dominating the lives of southern and western farmers.

This is a nation of inconsistencies. The Puritans fleeing from oppression became oppressors. We fought England for our liberty and put chains on four million of blacks. We wiped out slavery and our tariff laws and national banks began a system of white wage slavery worse than the first.

Wall Street owns the country. It is no longer a government of the people, by the people, and for the people, but a government of Wall Street, by Wall Street, and for Wall Street.

The great common people of this country are slaves, and monopoly is the master. The West and South are bound and prostrate before the manufacturing East.

Money rules, and our Vice-President is a London banker. Our laws are the output of a system which clothes rascals in robes and honesty in rags.

The [political] parties lie to us and the political speakers mislead us. . . . The politicians said we suffered from overproduction. Overproduction, when 10,000 little children, so statistics tell us, starve to death every year in the United States, and over 100,000 shopgirls in New York are forced to sell their virtue for the bread their niggardly wages deny them. . . .

We will stand by our homes and stay by our fireside by force if necessary, and we will not pay our debts to the loan-shark companies until the government pays its debts to us. The people are at bay; let the bloodhounds of money who dogged us thus far beware.

Source: W. E. Connelley, ed., *History of Kansas, State and People* (1928).

excitedly. "The farmers seem like unto ripe fruit—you can gather them by a gentle shake of the bush."

Though the Alliance merged the interests of dirt farmers and large planters, it spoke primarily to those who owned land and marketed crops. It did not address the problems of the dispossessed, however much its rhetoric appealed to wage earners or landless rural people. Tenant farmers had little cash for dues or literature and no produce to market cooperatively; what was more, they had to worry about antagonizing their landlords.

Most southern Alliance members opposed efforts to organize black farmers. Deeply racist and committed to the interests of landholders, they were antagonistic to sharecroppers and rural laborers. The Alliance therefore used its growing power to insist that other farmers' organizations drop black chapters when they joined the Alliance. This pressure caused conflict in Alliance efforts to work with the Knights of Labor, who were not about to adopt a whites-only policy. And it worried African Americans in the southern countryside, who feared that the Alliance would strengthen the most racist elements of their society.

Recognizing the potential of the Farmers' Alliance cooperative programs, however, black farmers organized similar groups. The Colored Farmers' National Alliance, which like the white Alliance emerged in Texas, claimed more than one million members by 1890. Its relationship with the white organization was various and changing, on both the national and local levels. Some white Alliance members accepted the black groups as they did black chapters of religious and fraternal organizations; others feared any organized black group and opposed them violently. In some places, black Alliance members created common cause with white ones by trading at Alliance stores, provoking white merchants to accuse the Alliance of stealing their business or supplying black members with guns.

In 1889, members of the southern Alliance met in St. Louis with the smaller organization from the Great Plains. The groups did not merge, but they agreed on a platform that called for nationalizing the railroads, outlawing large landholding companies, abolishing national banks, and instituting a graduated income tax. Alliance leader Charles Macune introduced a plan that captured the imagination of farmers across the nation over the next few years. He proposed that the federal government create warehouses, or "subtreasuries," where farmers could store crops until prices climbed to acceptable levels. In return they would receive loans, paid in certificates that would serve as money. In other words, the government would issue paper money and lend it to farmers, using their stored crops as collateral. The plan would replace and solidify with government support the Alliance's own cooperative efforts. If enacted, it would have challenged the control of banks and fostered inflation, by helping farmers to pay back debts with cheaper money.

In 1890, the Alliance moved into electoral politics, capturing local Democratic parties in the Southwest. In the Plains states, Alliance members formed independent parties and campaigned extensively. Rural Kansas typically had open-air rallies of 25,000 people. Sixteen hundred wagons pulled up for one meeting near Hastings, Nebraska. Out of such gatherings—in which farmers pulling up in their wagons could look back and see long trains of wagons converging on an encampment—the "movement culture" of populism was forged. And the movement seemed to transcend old sectional animosities, as it did on July 4, 1890, when North Carolina Alliance leader Leonidas Polk, who had fought with the Confederate Army, journeyed to Kansas, once a hotbed of Unionist sympathy. Speaking at an open-air rally of thousands of farmers, Polk declared, "I tell you that from New York to the Golden Gate the farmers have risen up and inaugurated a movement such as the world has never seen."

November's election results were dramatic. In the South, the Alliance won four governorships, eight state legislatures, and more than forty seats in the U.S. House of Representatives. In Kansas, Alliance supporters won four-fifths of the seats in the state House of Representatives. In Nebraska, they allied with the Democrats to win the governorship, and a young Democrat named William Jennings Bryan got himself elected to Congress by courting Populist votes. Buoyed by these successes, Alliance activists began to think seriously about launching a national political party. With a Republican president and Senate nd a Democratic House, the national government seemed mired in stalemate while economic conditions deteriorated.

Going to a Meeting. A rare photograph of a group of Populists near Dickinson City, Kansas, sometime during the 1890s.

Source: Kansas State Historical Society.

Although an agricultural depression weakened the Alliance in the South over the next two years, the movement continued to expand in the Midwest and the West. The People's party held its first convention in July 1892, in Omaha, Nebraska. Thirteen hundred delegates adopted a platform that combined a biting attack on economic and social conditions with a hopeful call to action.

"We meet in the midst of a nation brought to the verge of moral, political, and material ruin," declared the preamble. "The fruits of toil of millions are boldly stolen to build up colossal fortunes for a few, unprecedented in the history of mankind; and the possessors of these, in turn, despise the Republic and endanger liberty."

Some planks in the platform spoke directly to farmers. One was "free" (unrestricted) coinage of silver, a scheme to help cash-poor farmers by increasing the amount of currency in circulation. Another was government ownership of railroads and telegraph lines, and a third was Macune's subtreasury system. Other planks had broader appeal: direct election of U.S. senators (then still elected by state legislatures); restriction of presidents to a single term; a graduated income tax; and the initiative and referendum, which enabled voters to initiate and enact laws, ensuring democratic participation in decision-making on major issues. Calls for an eight-hour day and for immigration restriction appealed to organized labor.

The Populists were more than a reform party. At its height, this was the largest and most powerful movement that had ever attempted to transform the American economic and political system and to curb the power of financiers and capitalists. The Populist platform spelled out a radical alternative to corporate capitalism, offering a vision of popular leadership and a democratic "cooperative commonwealth." This new vision sprang directly from the cooperative movement. The opposition that cooperatives had stimulated from furnishing merchants, wholesalers, cotton buyers, grain elevator companies, and bankers had given Alliance members a new understanding of their relationship with commercial elements of American society, spawning a culture of political revolt.

In the 1892 elections, Populists won more than one million votes and elected governors in Kansas and Colorado. Miners helped put Populist Davis Waite into the Colorado governor's mansion, after which Colorado became one of the most pro-labor states in the nation. Presidential candidate James B. Weaver (a former Union general whose presence on the ticket was balanced by running

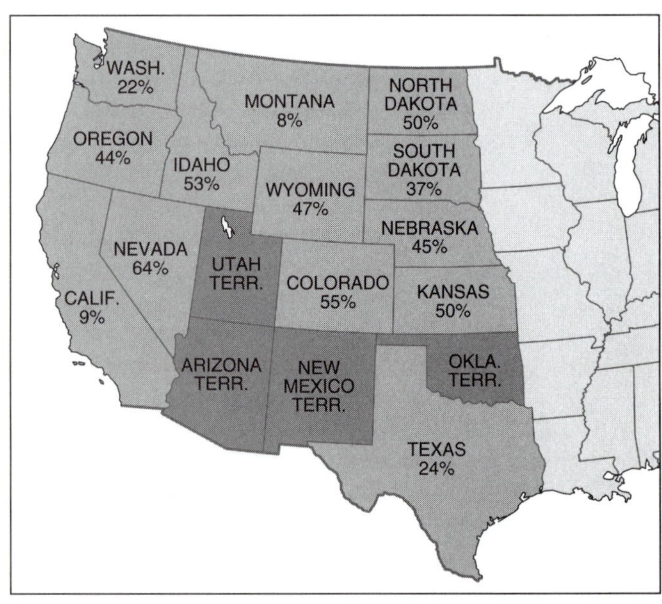

The Winning of the West: Populism in 1892 In the 1892 elections, the Populists became the first third party since the Civil War to capture any electoral votes. This map shows the percentage of the popular vote Populist presidential candidate James Weaver received in the West, where he ran particularly strongly. The same voters elected Populist governors in Kansas and Colorado.

mate James G. Field, a Confederate major who had lost a leg in battle) became the first third-party candidate since the Civil War to win any electoral votes—capturing Kansas, Colorado, Nevada, and Idaho as well as sharing in the electoral votes of North Dakota and Oregon. Still, the more dramatic result of the 1892 elections was the triumph of the Democrats, who had already regained the Congress two years before. Now they defeated incumbent Republican president Benjamin Harrison and returned to that office Grover Cleveland, who had won the presidency in 1884 and then had lost it to Harrison in 1888.

The Cross of Gold

By the time the stock market crashed in 1893, many labor activists were looking to electoral politics for solutions to some of the problems created by the rise of industrial capitalism. Populist successes made such political action look viable, despite a wide spectrum of opinion. And while many working people were too angry and desperate to believe in the electoral process, their support for more militant action had diminished with the defeat of the 1892 Homestead steel strike.

Socialists in the labor movement urged the formation of an independent political movement, modeled on socialist parties in industrialized Europe. Calling trade unions "impotent," unable to "cope with the great power of concentrated wealth," socialists had persuaded the 1892 AFL convention to endorse two planks from the Populist platform: the initiative and referendum, and federal ownership of telegraph and telephone lines. The next year, in the midst of depression, the convention adopted the entire socialist political program, calling for nationalization of railroads and mines, the eight-hour day, abolition of sweatshops, government inspection of mines and factories, and municipal ownership of public utilities.

All over the country, labor activists got into politics during 1894. Two hundred trade unionists ran for political office. Populist leaders, too, had concluded that to grow, the party would have to attract urban workers and create a farmer-labor alliance. Though Samuel Gompers dismissed such an alliance as "unnatural," AFL members had long supported cooperation between poor workers and farmers. That cooperation emerged in Illinois, when Chicago labor leaders and downstate agrarian activists sought to overcome their ideological differences and launch a united Populist movement in the 1894 congressional elections.

On election day many Illinois coal miners and railroad workers did vote Populist. The party also made a strong showing in Milwaukee, the Ohio Valley coal communities, and the Irish Catholic mining regions of the West. But the Republicans were the decisive winners in workingmen's districts, in part because the Populists drew votes away from the Democrats. Appealing to narrow economic interests and ethnic loyalties, Republicans won many workingmen over to the notion that a protective tariff on foreign goods was the key to "a full dinner pail" for all. In the biggest victory in the history of Congress, the Republicans gained 117 seats and became the clear-cut majority party. The 1894 elections had broken through the deadlock of two-party competition and stalemate that had dominated American politics since the Civil War.

Still, the Populists had to be taken seriously. They had gained more than 1.5 million votes in 1894, half again the number they had received in 1892. To win back supporters, Democrats began selectively to endorse parts of the Populist program. In 1896, facing almost certain defeat, the Democratic rank and file moved to adopt one of the planks in the Populist platform: the call for free coinage of silver. This was an attractive issue because it united the interests of miners (and even mine owners) with those of credit-starved farmers.

The free-silver issue had its roots in the years before 1873, when the U.S. Treasury had made both silver and gold into money, at a fixed ratio: 16 ounces of silver equaled one ounce of gold. The system worked until the price of silver rose on world markets. Then, with silver coins worth more than their face value, people melted them down, and they disappeared from circulation. In 1873, the government abandoned silver as a medium of exchange.

After silver was discovered in Nevada and Arizona its price fell dramatically on world markets in the spring of 1893. Hoping to prop up its value, hard-hit western mining interests pressed to resume the coinage of silver at the old 16-to-1 ratio. Bringing silver back into the Treasury would also expand the supply of currency, which was in high demand for industrial and commercial purposes. Farmers joined the campaign to increase the money supply. Strapped with debt and vulnerable to falling cotton and grain prices, they wanted inflation, which would allow them to pay off their debts with cheaper dollars. Their creditors, on the other hand, supported "sound money," by which they meant gold.

"The Supreme Court—as It May Hereafter Be Constituted." *Puck* presented an unabashedly cosmopolitan view of how the Supreme Court might appear if the Populists won the 1896 election. "Gold Bugs and Millionaires" huddle in a "waiting pen," their fate in the hands of nine justices who collectively embody the rustic "old geezer" stereotype: sporting unkempt goatees, their dress severe but informal, their behavior unsophisticated in its lack of ceremony.

Source: Frederick B. Opper, *Puck,* September 9, 1896—New-York Historical Society.

Free silver was only one aspect of the Populists' program. Indeed, some of the most prominent Populist leaders had argued against free silver at the 1892 Omaha convention. Congressman and Farmers' Alliance member Tom Watson of Georgia and urban social democrat Henry Demarest Lloyd both maintained that inflation would alienate wage earners and destroy the farmer-labor alliance. But pro-silver sentiment ran deep in the country at large, especially after the Panic of 1893 and the sharp deflation that followed.

When silver prices plummeted during the spring of 1893, the American West felt the effect immediately. Mines closed, and wages were reduced in the few that remained open. Hundreds of thousands of people were left destitute in Colorado mining towns like Aspen, where mine employment dropped from 2,500 to 150 within a week. Banks shut their doors, and industry ground to a standstill. Some places became ghost towns overnight; discontented idle miners gathered in others.

President Cleveland, a sound-money man, reacted to the crisis by persuading Congress to repeal an 1890 law requiring the government to purchase and coin silver. Meanwhile, gold reserves were being drained, partly by payments for foreign imports and partly because of a rash of redemptions by holders of treasury notes. To replenish the supply, in 1895 the president asked J. P. Morgan and a syndicate of private bankers to finance a purchase of gold. An outraged public saw Cleveland's action as a secret negotiation with Wall Street financiers.

At the 1896 convention, Democrats repudiated Cleveland and instead nominated William Jennings Bryan of Nebraska, the leader of the silver Democrats. The thirty-six-year-old Bryan's brilliant oratory transfixed the convention. Lashing out at Republican hard-money advocates, he declared, "You shall not press down upon the brow of labor this crown of thorns, you shall not crucify mankind on a cross of gold." Meeting soon afterward, the Populists endorsed Bryan, but for vice president they nominated one of their own: Allianceman Tom Watson, who had campaigned for rural free delivery during his term in Congress.

The Republicans nominated William McKinley of Ohio, an advocate of sound money. McKinley appealed to a middle class terrified of violent strikes and gun-toting bankrupt farmers. The campaign, one commentator remarked, "took the form of religious frenzy" as Republicans denounced Bryan as an anarchist and revolutionary. The *New York Times* even wrote a serious editorial declaring Bryan to be of "unsound mind" and endorsing the view of an "alienist" (as psychiatrists were then called) that the candidate was a "madman" and "paranoic reformer." McKinley won with 52 percent of the popular vote and 61 percent of the electoral college, the most lopsided margin in twenty-five years. Bryan ran strong in the South and the West, especially the silver mining states.

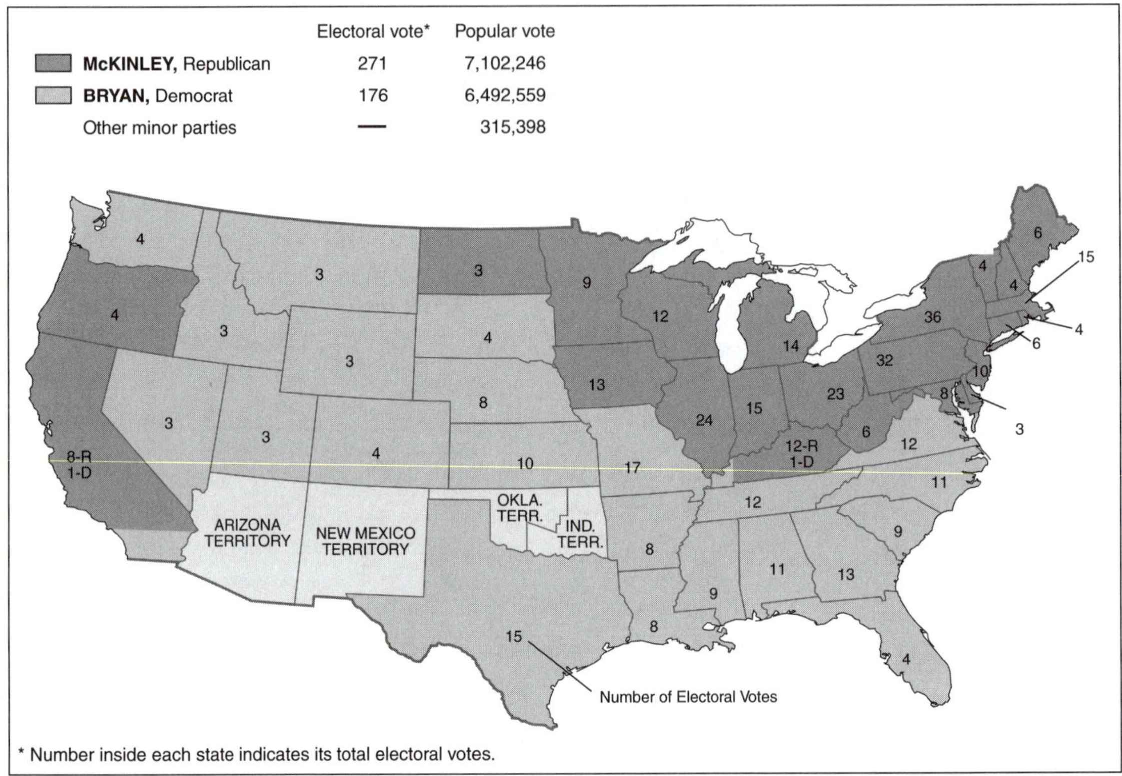

Crucified on a Cross of Gold? The Republican Triumph in 1896 Republican William McKinley won a decisive victory in 1896 by capturing the populous states of the Northeast and Midwest even while Democrat William Jennings Bryan carried the more rural South and West. The Republican victory in 1896 solidified that party's dominance in national politics, which would last until 1932.

Republicans won support from urban working men, especially white Protestant skilled workers in small and medium-size midwestern cities. These men were increasingly alienated by the Democratic party, dominated in the North by immigrants, Catholics, and unskilled workers. Many of them blamed the depression on President Cleveland and the Democrats, the party in power when the depression hit. The Republican program included a high protective tariff intended to protect American business and to ease unemployment.

With the presidential election of 1896 the Republicans gained control of both the executive and legislative branches. Their victory marked the end of Populism. Controversy over the decision to emphasize silver and endorse "fusion" with Bryan and the Democrats soon tore the Populist movement apart. Some leaders vigorously dissented from what they saw as a wholesale desertion of the broad reforms the Populists had once endorsed. Although the People's party would survive for twelve years, Populism and its hope of uniting the producing classes of town and country was dead as a force in American life.

"'Blowing' Himself Around the Country." In September 1896, this *Puck* cartoon derided William Jennings Bryan's candidacy, showing him pumping out political promises from a bellows marked "16 to 1" (the ratio of silver coinage to gold proposed by "soft money" reformers to ease the farm families' economic plight). But the cartoon's major target appears to be rank-and-file Populists, portrayed as gullible, whiskered, and ignorant.

Source: J. S. Pughe, *Puck,* September 16, 1896—New-York Historical Society.

Jim Crow

Following his defeat in the 1896 election, Populist vice-presidential candidate Tom Watson withdrew temporarily from politics. As an Allianceman he had urged white southern farmers to unite with black farmers. But in 1904, when he returned to politics as the People's party presidential candidate, Watson emerged as an outspoken white supremacist, blaming African Americans for the Populists' defeat. In later years he expanded his attacks to include Roman Catholics, Jews, and socialists. As Watson's case suggests, racism became entrenched in American politics and culture as the nineteenth century came to a close.

A generation of African Americans had now been born and raised in freedom, with hopes and expectations appropriate to free people. Nonetheless, de facto segregation (segregation by social custom) was longstanding in the South; schools, poorhouses, cemeteries, trains, and boats were all segregated. In the late 1880s, a coalition of planters, urban elites, and Populists began to pass state and local laws codifying such customs. Thus began de jure segregation (segregation sanctioned by law).

Black people with the financial resources to go to court launched numerous legal challenges. Homer Plessy, who refused to sit in a segregated railroad car, took his case to the U.S. Supreme Court in 1896. In *Plessy v. Ferguson* the justices affirmed segregation, upholding the Louisiana statute that mandated separate railroad cars for white and black passengers. "Legislation is powerless to eradicate racial instincts," the majority declared, enshrining in law the position that "separate but equal" public facilities were constitutional. Only one justice, John Marshall Harlan, dissented. "The thin guise of 'equal' accommodations," Harlan wrote, "will not mislead anyone, or atone for the wrong this day done." The historic decision was not overturned until 1954.

The *Plessy* decision opened the way for even more restrictive racial legislation. It cemented the imposition of "Jim Crow" laws, a system of radical discrimination, segregation of public facilities, and political disfranchisement that was enforced with terror and violence in the 1890s. (The term seems to have originated in a song-and-dance routine first performed by a blackface minstrel in the 1830s.) Industrial employers extended Jim Crow to the job site, where it undercut the possibilities of labor solidarity by segregating black and white workers, while offering privileges to one group and denying them to the other.

Justice of the Peace. After the collapse of Reconstruction, some African Americans in the South continued to hold local elective positions, particularly those of sheriffs and judges. This 1889 engraving shows a black justice of the peace presiding over a Jacksonville, Florida, police court.

Source: Matthew Somerville Morgan, *Frank Leslie's Illustrated Newspaper,* February 23, 1889—Prints and Photographs Division, Library of Congress.

Disfranchising black men helped enact and safeguard segregation. Many social and economic setbacks had followed the end of Reconstruction, but black men still retained their right to participate in politics in much of the South. Some even held elective office. In the 1890s, southern planters, industrialists, and merchants moved decisively to eliminate black men from the political process. To consolidate their power, these southern leaders also disfranchised the poorest whites, who were prone to agrarian radicalism.

Beginning in Mississippi in 1890, southern governments imposed residency requirements, poll taxes, and literacy tests on black voters. (Literacy tests were also used in the North to disfranchise citizens born abroad.) South Carolina adopted Mississippi's formula in 1895; over the next twelve years the remaining southern states followed suit. When someone pointed out that Virginia's constitutional convention was engaged in discrimination, future U.S. senator Carter Glass replied bluntly: "Discrimination! Why, that is precisely what we propose; that, exactly, is what this convention was elected for." Soon little room remained for black men to exercise the rights they had won a generation earlier.

Northern political and business leaders acquiesced in these developments. As late as 1889, Republican leaders such as Henry Cabot Lodge, a leader in the anti-immigrant campaign, had supported African-American voting rights because black votes sustained the southern GOP. But the sweeping Republican victory of 1896 removed that motivation. The Republican party, which had been a channel of political activity for African-American men for three decades, was effectively closed to them.

". . . Our Condition is Precarious in the Extreme"

The intensity of racist violence against African Americans during the 1890s was truly astonishing. In this report printed in Philadelphia's *Christian Recorder* on March 24, 1892, the Reverend E. Malcolm Argyle describes the situation in Arkansas and cries out for help.

There is much uneasiness and unrest all over this State among our people, owing to the fact that [black] people all over the State are being lynched upon the slightest provocation. . . . In the last 30 days there have been not less than eight colored persons lynched in this State. At Texarkana a few days ago, a man was burnt at the stake. In Pine Bluff a few days later two men were strung up and shot. . . . At Varner, George Harris was taken from jail and shot for killing a white man, for poisoning his domestic happiness. At Wilmar, a boy was induced to confess to the commission of an outrage, upon promise of his liberty, and when he had confessed, he was strung up and shot. Over in Toneoke County, a whole family consisting of husband, wife and child were shot down like dogs. Verily the situation is alarming in the extreme.

At this writing 500 people are hovering upon wharves in Pine Bluff, awaiting the steamers to take them up the Arkansas River to Oklahoma. . . . What is the outcome of all this? It is evident that the white people of the South have no further use for the Negro. He is being worse treated now, than at any other time, since the [Confederate] surrender. The white press of the South seems to be subsidized by this lawless element, the white pulpits seem to condone lynching. . . . The Northern press seems to care little about the condition of the Negroes [in the] South. The pulpits of the North are passive. Will not some who are not in danger of their lives, speak out against the tyrannical South . . . speak out against these lynchings and mob violence? For God's sake, say or do something, for our condition is precarious in the extreme.

Source: *Christian Recorder* (Philadelphia) March 24, 1892. Reprinted in Herbert Aptheker, ed., *A Documentary History of the Negro People in the United States,* 2 (1970), 793–794.

With the Populists' electoral defeat and retreat into racism, the limited possibilities of Populism also faded.

Racism enhanced the Democrats' strength in the South. Although the party was in the minority nationally, disfranchisement of black southerners had effectively defused the Republican and the Populist threats, and by 1900, the South was dependably Democratic. Racist ideology played an important role in ensuring this outcome, and violence and brutal terrorism reinforced it. Local officials felt no obligation to protect those who could not vote, hold public office, or serve on juries, and the federal government no longer oversaw black southerners' constitutional rights. White mobs, serving as prosecutor, judge, jury, and executioner, tortured and murdered black men for alleged wrongdoings and even for alleged insults. From 1882 to 1901, more than 100 African Americans were lynched each year in the South for violating the rules of the new order; 161 such deaths occurred in 1892 alone. Lynching was a ritual not only of social control but also of white recreation: families brought their children, and mobs dispensed body parts as souvenirs.

Led by journalist and lecturer Ida B. Wells-Barnett, African Americans formed a national antilynching movement to protest the wave of violence. "Nowhere in the civilized world save the United States of America," she wrote in a petition to President McKinley protesting the lynching of a black South Carolina postmaster, "do men . . . go out in bands of 50 and 5,000 to hunt down, shoot, hang or burn to death a single individual, unarmed and absolutely powerless." Exposing the myth that most lynchings were done to defend white womanhood, she emphasized white men's fear of economic competition from blacks. Local whites had killed the South Carolina postmaster because they were enraged at his recent appointment to the federal post; when his wife, baby in arms, sought to comfort her dying husband, another bullet crashed through the infant's skull.

Antilynching Crusader with the Family of a Lynching Victim. In 1892, Memphis, Tennessee, newspaper editor Ida B. Wells-Barnet revealed the role of local white businessmen in the lynching of three black competitors. She is shown here standing with Betsy Moss and her two children, the widow and orphans of Memphis grocer Tom Moss, one of the murdered black businessmen. A white mob destroyed Wells's office, and she was forced to flee north, where her public lectures and writing brought lynchings to national attention.

Source: W. F. Griffin—Special Collections, University of Chicago Library.

Wells-Barnett was the most visible of the many black women who assumed a growing role in the public sphere after black men lost their rights. When black men could vote, they had served as intermediaries between the black communities and powerful whites, both government officials and political organizations. After they were disfranchised, black women whose political skills had been nurtured in churches, temperance organizations, and Republican party auxiliaries—developed the ideology and organizational structure to carry on.

The single most influential black leader, however, was a man: Booker T. Washington. Born a slave in 1858, Washington had worked as a laborer and domestic servant after the war, eventually fulfilling his dream of attending Virginia's Hampton Institute. In 1881, he founded Tuskegee Institute in Alabama and modeled it on Hampton's industrial education program. The school trained African Americans to work with their hands, on the theory that market economics discriminated between the trained and the untrained, rather than between black and white. Tuskegee eventually attracted support from the richest white people in America, including Andrew Carnegie.

"The Colored Citizens Desire . . . That Some Action Be Taken"

Memphis, Tennessee, newspaper editor Ida Wells-Barnett was the leader in the national effort to get the federal government to stop lynchings of African Americans. Born into slavery in Mississippi in 1862, Wells-Barnett became part owner and editor of the Memphis *Free Speech,* an outspoken advocate for the area's African-American citizens, in the late 1880s. A brutal lynching of three young African-American businessmen in 1892 launched Wells-Barnett's national antilynching crusade. Despite her unstinting efforts, she never succeeded in securing a federal antilynching law before her death in 1931.

In the following 1898 petition to President William McKinley, Wells-Barnett, accompanied by the Chicago delegation of Illinois congressmen, protested the lynching of a South Carolina African-American postmaster. The federal government took no action.

Mr. President, the colored citizens of this country in general, and Chicago in particular, desire to respectfully urge that some action be taken by you as chief magistrate of this great nation, first for the apprehension and punishment of the lynchers of Postmaster Baker, of Lake City, S.C.; second, we ask indemnity for the widow and children, both for the murder of the husband and father, and for injuries sustained by themselves; third, we most earnestly desire that national legislation be enacted for the suppression of the national crime of lynching.

For nearly twenty years lynching crimes, which stand side by side with Armenian and Cuban outrages, have been committed and permitted by this Christian nation. Nowhere in the civilized world save the United States of America do men, possessing all civil and political power, go out in bands of 50 and 5,000 to hunt down, shoot, hang or burn to death a single individual, unarmed and absolutely powerless. Statistics show that nearly 10,000 American citizens have been lynched in the past 20 years. To our appeals for justice the stereotyped reply has been that the government could not interfere in a state matter. Postmaster Baker's case was a federal matter, pure and simple. He died at his post of duty in defense of his country's honor, as truly as did ever a soldier on the field of battle. We refuse to believe this country, so powerful to defend its citizens abroad, is unable to protect its citizens at home. Italy and China have been indemnified by this government for the lynching of their citizens. We ask that the government do as much for its own.

Source: *Cleveland Gazette,* April 9, 1898. Reprinted in Herbert Aptheker, ed., *A Documentary History of the Negro People in the United States,* 2 (1970), 798.

Washington asserted that black people should accommodate themselves to white power. "Cast down your buckets where you are," he urged them in a famous 1895 speech delivered in Atlanta. "In all things that are purely social," he reassured white Americans, "we can be as separate as the fingers, yet one as the hand in all things essential to mutual progress." Washington's accommodationist language appealed to white politicians and businessmen eager to roll back black voting rights and secure a docile labor force. His relationships with the white political and economic elite gave him the opportunity to work behind the scenes and the power to dispense money and patronage jobs to African Americans—power he preserved ruthlessly and sometimes duplicitously.

Washington's most significant black adversary was W. E. B. Du Bois, the preeminent African-American intellectual of the twentieth century. The terms of their debate reflected the inherent tension between capitalism and democracy. In *The Souls of Black Folk* (1903), Du Bois attacked Washington's Atlanta speech, accusing him of accepting segregation and forsaking political rights to obtain economic goals. In 1905 Du Bois and others formed the Niagara Movement, which demanded an end to segregation and racial discrimination. Du Bois later became the first editor of *Crisis,* the journal of the interracial National Association for the Advancement of Colored People (NAACP), founded in 1909–1910. The NAACP adopted many of the Niagara Movement's goals.

The New Immigrants

In the South, segregation and political disfranchisement confined African Americans to the lowest-paying jobs. In the crowded cities of the Northeast and Midwest, newly arrived Slavic and Italian immigrants tended to hold those less-skilled positions. Established immigrants and their American-born children had plenty of opportunity to move into the ranks of foremen and skilled laborers. Because they spoke English, they could also get the new clerical, sales, and managerial jobs. The income of unskilled and semiskilled workers typically was less than half that of these skilled workers. Skilled and less-skilled workers lived differently, fought separately for their rights, and had distinctly different relationships with their employers.

As in the past, the new immigrants were fleeing economic and political turmoil. Rapid population growth had put tremendous pressure on European peasant economies, and sons were inheriting ever-smaller plots of farmland. New technologies had cheapened shipping, which meant that European farmers faced competition from Canada, the United States, and Argentina. To survive, they needed to adopt new techniques, but few could afford to do so. Peasants who lost their farms fell into the ranks of agricultural and urban wage laborers.

Eastern European Jews faced different problems. Living in crowded towns on the western edge of the Russian Empire, they were legally prohibited from owning land; most engaged in trade or artisan labor. Industrialization was undermining their traditional ways of life, and anti-Semitism was making them scapegoats for the region's economic problems.

Detective Bureau

No. 6456

POLICE DEPARTMENT

CITY OF NEW YORK.

Bertillon Measurements.

Height, 1.73.4	Head length, 18.2	L. foot, 25.1+
Outer Arms, 1.74.0	Head width, 14.7+	Mid. f. 11.5
Trunk, 90.5	R. Ear. Length, 5.8+	Lit. f. 9.2
		Fore A. 46.4

Name

Alias

Crime

Age 26 Height 5 Ft. 8¼ In.

Weight 134 Build

Hair Eyes

Complexion Moustache

Born U.S.

Occupation

Date of Arrest Feb. 11. 1903.

Officer

Remarks

Mug Shot. A police department arrest record reflects the faith in data and science espoused by some reformers. The reputedly scientific measurements instituted by French anthropologist Alphonse Bertillon claimed to use physical evidence to detect innate criminality and other character flaws, many associated with particular ethnic and racial groups.

Source: American Social History Project.

As change swept Eastern and Southern Europe, some displaced farmers and workers responded with protests, but millions of other individuals found emigration a more sensible option. Janos Kovacs, a Hungarian peasant who could "earn only enough for bread and water," concluded "there was but one hope, America." Other peasants and workers moved to Canada, Argentina, Australia, and the more prosperous industrial regions of Europe.

The vast majority of emigrants were young. Italian and Slavic men left home without their families, hoping to earn enough money to return to their homelands and marry, buy land, or set up small businesses. Many actually did so, especially Italians. Jews usually came in family groups and seldom returned to their homelands.

Although immigrants' reasons for coming to America in the 1880s and 1890s resembled those of earlier decades, these newcomers faced greater prejudice than had all earlier groups except the Irish and the Chinese. Like the Irish in the 1840s and 1850s, these people were the poorest and least assimilated of the new Americans, and they became targets of nativist, anti-immigrant sentiment. And unlike many earlier immigrants who were Protestant, most of the new immigrants were Catholic or Jewish, and few spoke English. Because they brought agricultural and handcraft skills that were not valued in a rapidly advancing industrial economy, they entered the workforce as unskilled or semiskilled laborers. They also encountered racism. The old elites—white, Protestant, English speaking—regarded the new immigrants as members of an inferior race. Journalists and politicians equated the physical characteristics of different national groups with mental and moral qualities. Phrases like "the Hebrew race" or "the Slavic races" appeared routinely in popular journalism. "You don't call . . . an Italian a white man?" a West Coast construction boss was asked at a congressional hearing. "No, sir," was the reply, "an Italian is a Dago." Like African Americans, although not in such large numbers, Jews, Italians, and other immigrants were lynched in the South.

Nativism and Immigration Restriction

Anti-immigrant sentiment had been prevalent in the United States since at least the 1840s. It had many sources. Nativists played on fears of violence and of the diversity of thought, belief, and custom represented by European radicalism and religion. Reformers blamed immigrants for municipal corruption. Workingmen's organizations claimed that immigrants kept wages low. Militant Protestants called Catholic immigrants pawns of Romanism. The popular press blamed them for political turmoil. Even those who sympathized with immigrants condemned them for their

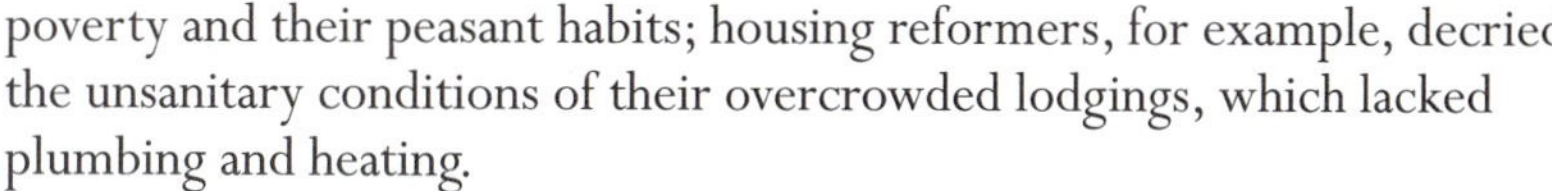

poverty and their peasant habits; housing reformers, for example, decried the unsanitary conditions of their overcrowded lodgings, which lacked plumbing and heating.

In the aftermath of the labor upheavals of the 1880s, nativism fed on fears of foreign-born radicals. Seven of the eight accused conspirators in the Haymarket affair of 1886 were immigrants. In response, the press spouted nativist rhetoric, and anti-immigrant groups formed across the country. Three weeks after Haymarket, a railroad attorney organized the American Party in California, declaring that Americans must exclude "the restless revolutionary horde of foreigners who are now seeking our shores from every part of the world."

"The Last Yankee." An 1888 cartoon predicted the results of "unrestricted immigration. . . . A possible curiosity of the twentieth century."

Source: Matthew Somerville Morgan, *Frank Leslie's Illustrated Newspaper,* September 8, 1888—American Social History Project.

The United States had restricted immigration for the first time in 1882, through the Chinese Exclusion Act and a law denying entrance to paupers and convicts. In 1891 a new immigration law gave the federal government complete authority over immigration and created national administrative mechanisms for its control. The law made it illegal for employers to advertise abroad for workers, and it excluded people with contagious diseases. It created provisions for expelling undesirable aliens, requiring that steamship companies return rejected immigrants to Europe. On January 1, 1892, the Ellis Island immigration depot opened. Medical inspections were performed there, but only for steerage passengers; those who paid for first- or second-class passage received perfunctory inspections in their cabins.

American nativism often took the form of anti-Catholicism. In 1887 the American Protective Association (APA) organized to drive Irish Catholics out of American politics and soon claimed a half-million members, all of whom took an oath never to vote for a Catholic. The APA explicitly blamed the depression on Catholics, asserting that immigrants had taken the jobs of native-born Americans. It endorsed political candidates in 1894, but it broke apart when its members could not agree on establishing a third party or supporting the Republican ticket in 1896.

Immigration restriction was one highlight of the Republican platform of 1896, which called for laws to exclude those who could not pass a literacy test in their native language. Such tests would discriminate against peasants from eastern and southern Europe. Such laws, the platform claimed, would protect the United States by defending American citizenship and "the wages of our workingmen against the fatal competition of low-price labor."

The idea of a literacy test had been advanced by the Immigration Restriction League, a forum for nativism founded in 1893 by a group of Harvard graduates from old Boston families. For them, the flood of foreign poor dramatized and symbolized the problems raised by the expanding urban working class. The League drew a line between "old" and "new" foreigners. Like many other native-born Americans, its members regarded the new immigrants from southern and eastern Europe as racially distinct from old-stock Anglo-Saxons. This distinction became the linchpin of the anti-immigration crusade.

Most advocates of restriction were Republicans, but nativism and nativist racism permeated all corners of American politics. Anti-Semitism was strong among Populists, and labor activists seeking an explanation for the sudden sharp drop in their fortunes embraced anti-immigrant ideas. On the Pacific Coast, where the anti-Chinese movement flourished in the mid-1880s, labor organizations had long been advocates of immigration restriction. Building on white workers' fears of competition from Chinese immigrants, they lobbied actively for extension of the Chinese Exclusion Act when it came up for congressional renewal in 1892.

Employers were divided over immigration restriction. Before the depression many businessmen had supported free immigration, although not necessarily out of tolerance or belief in a free market. New York's *Journal of Commerce* argued nakedly in 1892 that people, like cows, were expensive to produce; immigration represented a gift of a costly commodity. The desire for a cheap and steady labor supply, however, was some-

"At Bay." A newspaper engraving depicting an attack on an Italian strikebreaker during the 1882 New York freight handlers' strike. Although shown as a victim, the Italian's "exotic" dress and earring marked him as an outsider to contemporary readers. **Source:** A. B. Shults, *Frank Leslie's Illustrated Newspaper,* August 5, 1882—American Social History Project.

times counterbalanced by the beliefs that immigrants brought labor strife, violence, and radicalism. The *New York Tribune* called "Huns" (Hungarians and Slavs) the most dangerous of labor unionists and strikers: "They fill up with liquor and cannot be reasoned with."

A Splendid Little War

Strident nationalism and racism intensified into warmongering in the late 1890s, prompting America's entry into overseas adventures. Patriotism, once linked to egalitarian ideas of republican virtue, grew aggressive and jingoistic. New organizations, such as the Daughters of the American Revolution, promoted new forms of patriotism, such as a cult of the American flag, now saluted each morning in schools. Some conservatives championed war as the highest form of patriotism and a way of channeling the unrest of the depression years. According to a Kansas newspaper, war "would clear the atmosphere and stamp out the growth of socialism and anarchy, discontent and sectional prejudices that are gaining a foothold in this nation."

Many business, agricultural, and political leaders argued that to secure the nation's economic interests and absorb its surplus production the United States should expand overseas. "We are raising more than we can consume," avowed Indiana Senator Albert J. Beveridge. "We are making more than we can use. Therefore, we must find new markets for our products, new occupations for our capital, new work for our labor." Recovery from the depression of the 1890s was achieved in part by

The Splendid Little War: The Spanish-American-Cuban War, 1898 In both theatres of the 1898 war against Spain, the United States triumphed quickly, in part because of its naval superiority. In the Philippines, Admiral George Dewey triumphed in a matter of days after the American declaration of war on April 25 and without the loss of a single American life. The Cuban conflict lasted a bit longer, but even there the fighting was over by August. Before the United States entered the fighting, Cuban rebels had already brought Spain close to defeat.

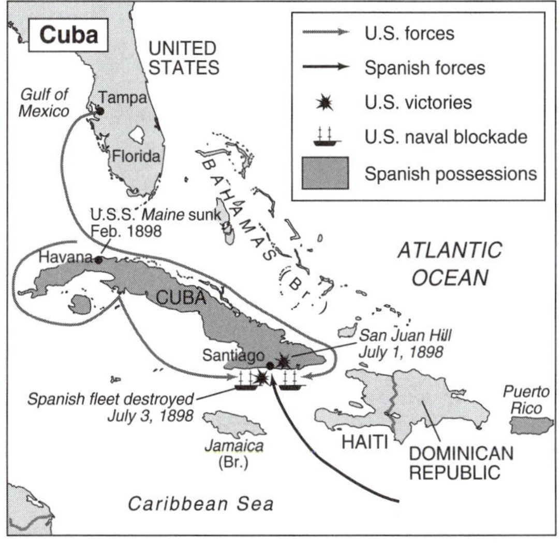

Americans doing business in other countries, and by 1896 the nation's exports had begun to exceed its imports. But American businesses also bought supplies and opened factories abroad. Singer sold sewing machines around the world—machines made in Scotland and Russia as well as New Jersey. International Harvester operated factories in six countries.

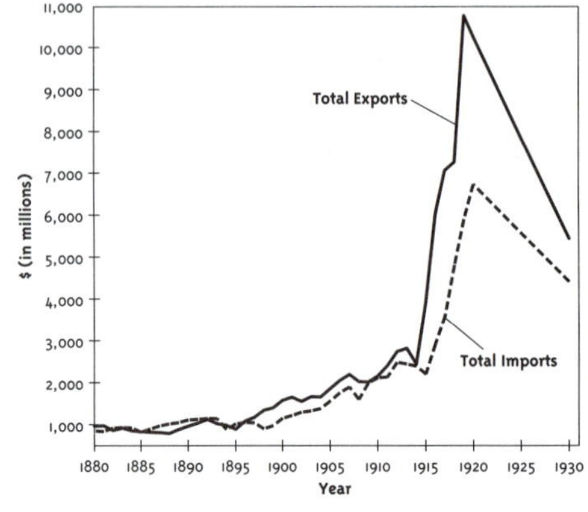

Going Global: U.S. Imports and Exports, 1870–1920 It was only after 1880 that American involvement in the emerging international economy "took off." However, the most rapid growth did not come until the twentieth century.

American companies attempting to expand abroad did not have some of the advantages of their counterparts in Britain, France, and Germany, which were carving out colonial empires in Asia and Africa. Such overseas empires—composed of countries administered by the mother country—extended the colonizers' political and military clout, giving their businesses special investment and marketing opportunities. Some Americans believed that colonies offered the United States the best chance to enter overseas markets. The nation's previous expansion, they noted, had entailed military conflict on the North American continent—with American Indians and, in the 1840s, with Mexico. Now, idealistic and convinced of their own racial superiority, some Americans were willing to risk further military conflict to follow the example of leading European nations.

In 1898, they got their chance when the United States entered the Spanish-American-Cuban war, a "splendid little war," in the words of Secretary of State John Hay. The immediate issue was a revolution that had begun in 1895 in Cuba, ninety miles off the Florida coast. Cuban guerrillas fighting to free their island from Spanish rule had prompted popular sympathy and financial support in the United States. Popular support for U.S. involvement was fed by sensationalized newspaper reports of the brutality of Spanish soldiers toward Cuban civilians. In New York, William Randolph Hearst's *Journal* and Joseph Pulitzer's *World* competed for circulation by detailing Spanish atrocities. These papers and their imitators—called the "yellow press" after cartoonist Richard Outcault's color comic strip "The Yellow Kid"—offered sensationalized foreign coverage with an unprecedented immediacy, thanks to new telegraph cables and fast printing presses. At the height of the war each paper sold more than one million copies a day.

On February 15, 1898, an unexplained explosion aboard the U.S. Navy's battleship *Maine,* which had been sent into Havana Harbor to protect U.S. citizens and property, killed 266 sailors. Congress declared war in April, vowing in the Teller Amendment that the United States would guarantee Cuban independence. The public reaction was enthusiastic. "The newspapers, the theatrical posters, the street conversations for weeks had to do with war and bloodshed," settlement worker Jane Addams wrote of her Chicago neighborhood.

The war with Spain was fought in the Philippine Islands, where since 1896 guerrillas led by Emilio Aguinaldo had been battling Spanish rule. In 1897, Aguinaldo had gone into exile in Hong Kong. Two days after the U.S. Congress declared war, Commodore George Dewey sailed for Manila, with Aguinaldo on board. On May 1, 1898, the U.S. Navy arrived in Manila Bay, securing the harbor while the guerrillas surrounded the capital city. Aguinaldo declared independence June 12.

The war in Cuba was also brief: the U.S. Army and Marines landed in June, and Spanish power was broken in ten weeks. A young assistant secretary of the navy, Theodore Roosevelt, gained fame by quitting his job and leading a group of cavalry volunteers known as the Rough Riders. (The story of their horseback charge up San Juan Hill has often been retold, but the truth was more mundane than the myth. The Rough Riders were not actually on horseback—the horses had been accidentally left behind—and the hill they charged was nearby Kettle Hill. San Juan Hill sounded more exotic and romantic.) Many black soldiers, including the highly decorated "buffalo soldiers" who had served in the West, were mobilized to fight in Cuba. More than 10,000 black men, many of them from the North, answered the call for volunteers.

Competing for Readers. U.S. newspapers headlined stories about Spanish atrocities in Cuba and pressed for U.S. intervention. The papers often reported rumors as facts; the *New York Journal,* for example, distorted an incident involving a search of a Cuban woman by Spanish agents. The illustration showed what amounted to a sexual assault, but the event as pictured never occurred.

Source: Frederic Remington, *New York Journal*—Prints and Photographs Division, Library of Congress.

African-American leaders, like white ones, were divided over the Spanish-American-Cuban war. While Booker T. Washington saw volunteering for the war as an opportunity for black men "to show their loyalty to our land," other black leaders argued that men denied the franchise were not obliged to serve in the army. "In the South today," wrote Richmond editor John Mitchell, "exists a system of oppression as barbarous as that which is alleged to exist in Cuba."

An Overseas Empire

In December 1898 the Treaty of Paris ended the war. Spain relinquished its claim to Cuba, sold the Philippines to the United States for $20 million, and transferred the

Caribbean island of Puerto Rico to the United States without compensation. The United States wanted Puerto Rico as a naval station in the Caribbean and as a market for manufactured goods. U.S. troops had occupied the island in July, meeting little opposition. Not everyone welcomed the terms: Puerto Ricans had little voice in the transfer, and Filipinos were ready to fight for their country's independence.

Although Americans and Filipinos had united to drive the Spanish forces from the islands, their relationship deteriorated after Spanish power was broken. Although Aguinaldo and the insurgents had declared independence and established a republic in June 1898, the United States refused to recognize it. President William McKinley declared that he intended instead to use "every legitimate means for the enlargement of American trade." Filipinos were determined to resist; two days before the Treaty of Paris was ratified by the U.S. Senate in February 1899, Aguinaldo and his forces mounted armed opposition to American occupation.

Nearly 200,000 U.S. troops fought to suppress the independence movement, killing 16,000 to 20,000 Filipino soldiers between 1899 and 1902. Hundreds of thousands of civilians died from war-related famine and disease. Racism heightened the war's brutality. U.S. newspapers portrayed Filipinos as dark-skinned savages; one report declared that "picking off niggers [Filipinos] in the water" was "more fun than a turkey shoot." Though Aguinaldo was captured in 1901 and peace officially restored in 1902, armed conflict continued for another decade.

While the Spanish-American-Cuban war was going on, the United States had also annexed the Hawaiian islands. An American-controlled sugar industry had been developing there for half a century. The sugar interests had established a government favorable to them in 1887, but it was ousted four years later by the new queen, Liliuokalani. In 1893, with the support of the U.S. Marines, a group of planters led by Sanford B. Dole overthrew the queen, and the American ambassador, John L. Stevens, acting on his own authority, proclaimed Hawaii an American protectorate. Dole asked Congress to annex the islands, but an investigation revealed that most Hawaiians opposed it. When the United States sent a special commissioner to restore the queen to her throne under a liberal constitution, Dole refused to step aside. In 1894, he proclaimed Hawaii a republic. After several years of political wrangling, the outbreak of war with Spain demonstrated the U.S. Navy's need for a coaling station in the Pacific. Congress approved Hawaii's annexation in July 1898, and it became a territory, with Dole as governor, in 1900.

"The Spanish Brute Adds Mutilation to Murder." Grant Hamilton's bestial Spaniard, bespattered in American blood, typifies how the U.S. press sensationalized news coverage and exploited patriotic sentiments to support U.S. intervention in Cuba.

Source: Grant Hamilton, *Judge,* July 9, 1898—General Research Division, New York Public Library, Astor, Lenox, and Tilden Foundations.

"Benevolent Assimilation." U.S. troops guard Filipino nationalist prisoners captured in Pasay and Paranque during the Filipino-American War. **Source:** Prints and Photographs Division, Library of Congress.

Not all Americans approved of the nation's overseas expansion. In November 1898, a group of prominent citizens founded the Anti-Imperialist League. The writer Mark Twain, former president Grover Cleveland, steel tycoon Andrew Carnegie, activist Jane Addams, and the AFL's Samuel Gompers became national officers or supporters. Addams hated imperialism because she was a pacifist and an internationalist. Carnegie argued as a capitalist: "Possession of colonies or dependencies is not necessary for trade reasons," he reasoned, pointing out that the United States was leading the world in exports without foreign possessions. Gompers employed the racist language he had long used against Chinese immigration. "If the Philippines are annexed," he asked, "how can we prevent the Chinese coolies from going to the Philippines and from there swarm into the United States and engulf our people and our civilization?"

However prominent, the anti-imperialists did not represent the majority opinion. Most businessmen, farmers, and urban working people believed that the United States had the right and duty to extend its influence. Presidential adviser Mark Hanna explained that the Philippine annexation would allow the United States to "take a large slice of the commerce of Asia. . . . We are bound to share in the commerce of the Far East and it is better to strike for it while the iron is hot." Senator Albert Beveridge of Indiana equated the drive for empire with the near-religious theme of "Manifest Destiny": "Shall the American people continue their march toward commercial supremacy of the world? Shall free institutions broaden their blessed reign. . . until the empire of our principles is established over the hearts of all mankind?"

Politicians and businessmen decided against a policy of European-style colonization; for the most part, the United States would not own territories or administer governments. Instead American policymakers advocated aggressive economic expansion, which was carried out with a heavy hand in Latin America. Theodore Roosevelt, who became president in 1901 following McKinley's assassination, argued that the U.S. government should exercise "international police power" in the Western

Hemisphere, a policy that became known as the Roosevelt Corollary to the Monroe Doctrine. Thus, the United States refused to withdraw its troops from Cuba after the war, reserving the right to intervene whenever order seemed to be threatened. The Platt Amendment of 1901, which granted the United States the right to intervene and build naval bases in Cuba, codified this policy. To end U.S. occupation, Cuban legislators meeting to draft a constitution ratified the amendment. Although troops withdrew in 1902, they returned from 1906 to 1909 and again in 1912 and 1917 to prop up governments sympathetic to U.S. business interests.

With bases in Cuba and Puerto Rico, American businessmen now focused on building a canal across the Isthmus of Panama, a province of Colombia. In 1902 Colombia rejected a proposed treaty granting the United States the right to build the canal. The next year, a group of Colombian businessmen and politicians, operating with U.S. naval support, declared northern Colombia an independent country and named it Panama. Canal rights and construction quickly followed, and the U.S.-built Panama Canal opened in 1914.

The Age of Imperialism: The World in 1900 In 1898, the United States belatedly entered the imperialist race to carve up the globe by acquiring farflung possessions in the Caribbean and the Pacific. But, as this map shows, it lagged behind the established imperial powers like Britain and France.

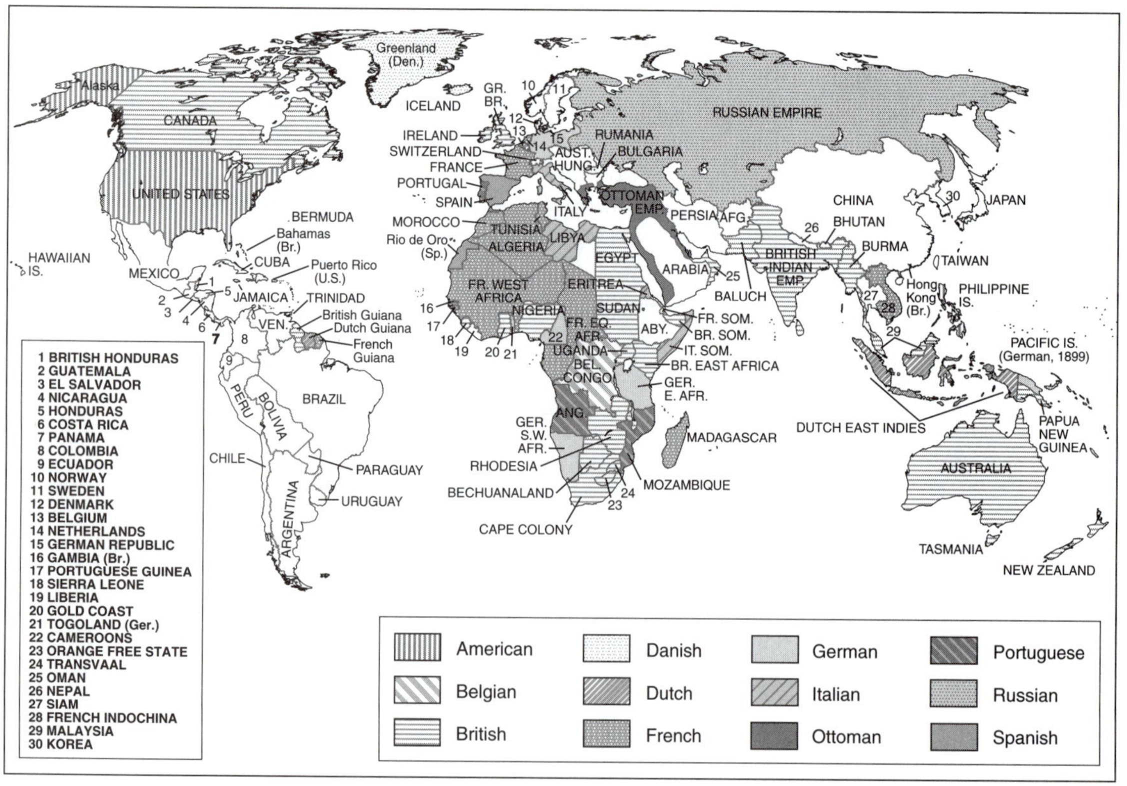

In the 1910s and 1920s, the United States placed troops throughout the Caribbean and Central America. It intervened in revolts in Nicaragua in 1910 and 1912, occupied Haiti from 1915 to 1934, and used military power to support economic interests and protect sea routes in Colombia, Honduras, Panama, and the Dominican Republic. This government muscle protected an increased U.S. corporate presence in South and Central America. Exports to Latin America had more than doubled between 1900 and 1914. U.S. corporations treated Latin America as their private preserve and sought to limit competition from European capitalists.

The United States could not pursue such a bold policy in Asia. European powers already had extensive economic interests there, backed by formal colonies or strong ties with local governments. The United States therefore advocated an "Open Door" policy, hoping to gain new markets and access to raw materials in areas where other nations already dominated. In 1899 Secretary of State John Hay sent notes presenting the new policy to the major occupying powers in China by arguing that all industrialized nations should be given equal access to Chinese trade. The European nations and Japan responded evasively, but Hay brashly insisted that they had given "final and definitive" assent.

Almost at the same time, the Chinese launched a rebellion against foreign exploitation. The "Boxers," a secret nationalist organization, attacked foreigners and foreign influences throughout China. Five thousand U.S. troops joined an expeditionary force to relieve the siege of the British embassy in Beijing, where the foreign diplomatic corps had taken refuge. The U.S. troops help to break the siege in August 1900 and end the Boxer Rebellion. Hay then successfully used the rebellion to persuade the foreign powers to respond more favorably to a second round of Open Door notes. To be sure, Hay's Open Door policy did not end foreign (especially Japanese) control of Chinese soil, but it did become the centerpiece of U.S. foreign policy in the new century. American policymakers embraced the dual beliefs that U.S. economic well-being

"Civilization Begins at Home." A cartoon in the *New York World* derided President McKinley's claim to "uplift and Christianize" the Philippines, graphically portraying the racial terrorism occurring in America's own backyard.

Source: C. G. Bush, *New York World*—American Social History Project.

required global expansion and that this expansion would be accomplished by open markets rather than direct imperial conquest.

As business and political leaders had predicted, global expansion and military expenditures increased the nation's wealth and helped to pull it out of depression. For the first time, the United States had an overseas empire, backed by a standing army that had nearly quadrupled in size between 1898 and 1901. U.S. political and military involvement in the internal affairs of other countries would profoundly shape twentieth-century experience.

By 1914, American businessmen had more than $3.5 billion invested abroad, making the United States one of the world's four largest investor nations. Dozens of American companies—Coca Cola, Du Pont, Standard Oil, Ford, General Electric, and Gillette—operated two or more facilities abroad. The United Fruit Company grew bananas for the U.S. market on more than a million acres it owned in Central America; it also owned or controlled Central American railroads, docks, and communications networks. Direct foreign investment in 1914 was 7 percent of gross national product—the same proportion it would be in 1966. U.S. capitalism had truly become international. Although American foreign investments were still dwarfed by those of England, France, and Germany, they were twice those of the Netherlands.

Business on the Rebound

Supported by global expansion, the U.S. industrial economy began to boom again, growing to astonishing size and strength in the first decade of the new century. The long depression had begun to lift in 1896. The discovery of gold on the Klondike River in the Yukon Territory the next year (and new goldfields in South Africa) suddenly ended both the contentious issue of the gold standard and the deflationary trend that had dominated the economy for the past three decades. The flow of money into the world economy relieved debt-burdened farmers and brought renewed prosperity to industrial workers. With recovery came new talk of cooperation between labor and industry.

Big business was the order of the day, and it was carried on in enormous factories. In 1870 only a handful of plants had employed more than 500 workers. By 1900, nearly 1,500 factories had reached that size, and some became truly gigantic. The Cambria Steel factory in Johnstown, Pennsylvania, employed nearly 20,000 people in 1909. General Electric employed 15,000 at its factory in Schenectady, New York, and 11,000 at another plant in Lynn, Massachusetts.

As the economy gained strength, businessmen resumed their efforts to reduce competition. Some founded trade associations, organizations that brought competitors together to establish standards or lobby politicians in an industry's interests. Others combined forces more directly; beginning in 1898, American businessmen engaged in a frenzy of merger activity. By 1904, three hundred giant firms controlled nearly two-fifths of American manufacturing capital. As corporations grew, effective control was concentrated in fewer hands.

The financier J. P. Morgan organized the biggest new combination in 1901: U.S. Steel, created from 150 corporations, including Carnegie's, and capitalized at over $1 billion. Competition in the steel industry virtually disappeared. U.S. Steel was large enough to dictate prices, and like Carnegie's earlier company, the giant corporation was vertically integrated, making it invulnerable both to suppliers' price increases and to labor problems.

Some attempts at combination failed. Although General Electric and Goodyear became household names, U.S. Leather and United Button did not survive. In industries that did not require large investments in expensive machinery, new competitors could still challenge trusts. By 1910, manufacturing had been divided into two distinct sectors. Very large corporations dominated industries that required heavy capital investments, while small firms competed feverishly in industries that did not. Thus, the leather, printing, clothing, and construction industries remained highly competitive, with thousands of firms battling for a slice of the market. Many small manufacturing firms that made clothing, jewelry, and furniture still did "batch work," producing many styles, colors, and sizes rather than mass-producing identical items. And small business still dominated retailing. Although Sears and Montgomery Ward had both grown huge through their catalog sales, and chain stores had emerged in the groceries, drugs, and general merchandise, most retail stores were small and run by individual proprietors.

Eat, Drink, and Be Merry. The managers of the nation's competing steel companies gathered together in 1901 to celebrate their merger into the giant U.S. Steel Corporation. **Source:** The Carnegie Library of Pittsburgh.

But big business dominated business-government relationships and business ideology. Only big businesses had the resources to lobby Congress or to create combinations large and powerful enough to ensure dependable supplies, markets, transportation, and banking connections. The problem of how to deal with these huge concentrations of wealth and power became one of the driving issues of the day. Though agitation against big combinations like Standard Oil had begun in the 1880s, the Sherman Antitrust Act, passed in 1890, was vaguely worded and did not define either *trust* or *monopoly*. As a result, the courts threw out cases against the sugar and whiskey trusts. Ironically, although the biggest businesses did not suffer from the Sherman Antitrust Act, the labor movement did.

"An Alphabet of Joyous Trusts." A segment of cartoonist Frederick Opper's "Nursery Rhymes for Infant Industries," published in the *New York American* in 1902. Opper closed his primer with these words:

> With these alphabet pictures the artist took pains,
> But he's got to stop now, and with grief nearly busts—
> 'Cause our language but twenty-six letters contains,
> Though our country contains twenty-six hundred Trusts.

Source: Frederick Opper, *New York American,* September 1902—Prints and Photographs Division, Library of Congress.

Organized Labor in a Time of Recovery

As the economy expanded following the depression, AFL-affiliated craft unions enjoyed a brief resurgence. Industrial growth created a labor shortage, especially among skilled workers. Knowing they were in demand, workers became less fearful of the consequences of collective action, and they renewed their struggle to build unions and preserve their control over the work process. Between 1897 and 1904, the number of unionized working people more than quadrupled, to over 2 million.

The resurgence of craft unionism was concentrated in the Northeast and Midwest, in basic industries like railroads, metal working, construction, and coal mining. Skilled workers—primarily men of northern and western European stock—fought, often with great militancy, to retain and extend shop-floor rights won in earlier scuffles with management. Established craft unions, most of them members of the American Federation of Labor led these battles.

Less-skilled workers, generally immigrants and African Americans, were excluded from AFL unions, as were women. Women were barred from most skilled occupations, but unions were hostile even to the women who customarily worked alongside men, as in the cigar industry. Focusing narrowly on "bread and butter" wage goals, craft unions fought for the "family wage," to enable men to support their families "in a manner consistent with their responsibilities as husbands, fathers, men, and citizens." Though the demand for a family wage dignified male workers'

"The Labor Question and Its Solution." A two-panel cartoon in a 1902 issue of the satirical weekly *Judge* endorsed the National Civic Federation. The first panel shows British labor relations, "capital and labor fighting to the death, at the same time destroying English commercial life," while the second panel depicts American "labor and capital on friendly terms, aiding each other, and together making the United States the greatest commercial nation in the world."

Source: Victor Gilliam, *Judge,* January 25, 1902—American Social History Project.

struggles at the expense of women's, the two were not entirely separable; most working women would have benefited from higher wages paid to their fathers and husbands.

Even on occasions when the rank and file showed solidarity with workers of other races and nationalities, AFL leaders typically resisted the integration of nonwhite workers. In Oxnard, California, 1,200 Mexican and Japanese farm laborers won a hard-fought strike against sugar beet growers in 1903. But the AFL, which had attacked Asian labor in a widely read pamphlet co-authored by Samuel Gompers and subtitled "Meat vs. Rice," refused to charter the group unless they excluded the Japanese workers. Indignant, the beet workers refused to accept a charter under those conditions. "In the past we have counseled, fought and lived on very short rations with our Japanese brothers, and toiled with them in the fields," their Mexican leader wrote to Gompers. "We would be false to them and to ourselves and to the cause of unionism if we now accepted privileges for ourselves which are not accorded to them."

Samuel Gompers thought of unions in more pedestrian terms, as "business organizations of wage-earners." AFL unions were stable, centralized organizations, directed by well-paid professional leaders who held their posts for years. In the building trades, full-time union officials known as "business agents" negotiated with contractors and assigned jobs to union members. These officials, although they helped craft unions to grow more stable and effective, also tended to frame union goals concretely, solely in terms of wages and working conditions.

The upsurge of craft unionism prompted some industrialists to seek peaceful solutions to industrial conflict. In that spirit, corporate leaders, bankrolled by financiers August Belmont and J. P. Morgan, founded the National Civic Federation (NCF) in 1900. Seeking employer acceptance of "responsible" unions, NCF leaders denounced both radicals and anti-union employers. They encouraged mediation as a method for settling disputes and fostered "welfare capitalism"—the pension plans, insurance, and recreational activities some employers hoped would frustrate union organizers. The NCF urged employers to negotiate industrywide labor agreements through trade associations; such agreements were signed in the metalworking, newspaper, mining, ironmolding, and pottery industries. For a brief moment, the war between owners and skilled workers appeared to be over.

That moment soon passed, however. In one industry after another, rank-and-file skilled workers refused to accept the weakening of their workplace control. Displays of worker militancy, such as a nationwide machinists' strike called in 1900 at the insistence of insurgent locals, convinced most corporate leaders that peace with labor was too costly. They rejected union demands and crushed ensuing strikes. By 1903 many employers had broken with the NCF and reverted to their old union-busting tactics: blacklists to prevent union activists from getting jobs, spies to gather information on organizing efforts, and strikebreakers to keep factories running when strikes did occur.

The National Association of Manufacturers (NAM) led employers in these efforts. Founded in 1895, the NAM united primarily small and medium-size manufacturers. In 1903 it took command of the employers' battle for "the open shop"—a contractual guarantee of the right to work without union membership—and of the employers' right to bar unions from factories.

Together with fluctuations in the economy, the open-shop drive slowed and then halted the spread of craft unionism. After nearly seven years of growth, membership in the AFL dropped by nearly 200,000 in 1905. New technology and the reorganization of factories made it easier for capitalists to replace skilled workers with the less skilled, and thereby resist the demands of craft unions. At the same time, organizations such as the NAM had enhanced businessmen's ability to shape public opinion. Permanent organizations were more difficult to sustain among workers, where social divisions between the skilled and the less-skilled, between immigrant and native-born, black and white, male and female undercut the union movement. More important, the AFL itself helped undermine the movement through its reluctance to bridge those gaps.

End of a Century; End of an Era

Class conflict defined the final two decades of the nineteenth century as working people confronted, with extraordinary creativity, the profound changes wrought by industrial capitalism. The first truly national working-class movement emerged in these years out of the militant protests and oppositional ideas of workers and farmers across the country. In creating a culture of resistance, the late–nineteenth-century labor movement rejected not only capitalists' growing control over the nation's economic and political life but also the twin ideologies of acquisitive individualism and Social Darwinism that served to justify that control. While the movement's programs were eclectic, its philosophies diverse, and its outright victories few, it nonetheless succeeded in galvanizing millions of people with an alternative vision of industrial America.

But the bitter defeats suffered by the Knights of Labor in 1886, the Homestead workers in 1892, the industrial armies in 1893 and 1894, the Pullman workers in 1894, and the Populists in 1896 eroded the power of this alternative vision and marked the end of an era. As a result, many working people in cities and the countryside retreated into insular cultures that included strong elements of racism and nativism. The nineteenth century closed with the labor and agrarian movements fragmented and their broad, organizing efforts defeated. The return of economic prosperity, the expansion of American corporations abroad, and the wave of mergers that swept through the economy further consolidated the power of giant corporations.

The bitter defeats of the 1880s and 1890s left permanent scars. The United States would never again witness such a broad or fundamental challenge by working people to the claims of capital. Racial, ethnic, gender, skill, and ideological divisions would define the labor movement after 1900, displacing the working-class unity of the preceding decades. Thus, as the new century dawned, neither popular movements nor the government imposed serious constraints on the actions of the nation's capitalists. Working people, African Americans, immigrants, and women would need to find new ways to mitigate their subordinate position in American society.

The Years in Review

1881

- Booker T. Washington founds Tuskegee Institute in Alabama to train African Americans to work with their hands.

1882

- Congress passes the Chinese Exclusion Act.

1887

- American Protective Association is formed to drive Catholics out of American politics.

1890

- Mississippi enacts legislation to prevent African Americans from voting, setting a precedent that all southern states will follow over the next two decades.
- Congress passes the Sherman Antitrust Act, the first federal antitrust law, in an effort to regulate big business.
- Farmers' Alliance moves into politics and captures 4 governorships and more than 40 congressional seats.

1892

- Congress renews the Chinese Exclusion Act.
- People's (Populist) party holds its first convention and adopts the Omaha Platform, attacking economic and social conditions and calling for action; Populists win more than one million votes and elect governors in Kansas and Colorado in fall election.
- Grover Cleveland is elected president for a second term.

1893

- Chicago's World Fair celebrates the four-hundredth anniversary of Columbus's arrival in the Americas.
- Five-year economic collapse begins as the stock market crashes on May 3.
- U.S. sugar planters led by Sanford B. Dole overthrow Hawaii's Queen Liliuokalani with the support of U.S. Marines. Hawaii is proclaimed an American protectorate.

1894

- Jacob S. Coxey's army of unemployed workers marches on Washington, D.C.
- Pullman strike ends in defeat for workers.

1895

- First U.S. pizzeria opens in New York City.
- Booker T. Washington's "Atlanta Compromise" speech accepts racial separatism.

1896

- Republican William McKinley is elected president over Democratic and Populist candidate, William Jennings Bryan.
- U.S. Supreme Court decision in *Plessy v. Ferguson* sanctions racial segregation.

- Gold is discovered along the Klondike River in Yukon Territory, which leads to the Alaska Gold Rush.
- Richard Outcault's "The Yellow Kid"—the first comic strip—appears in *New York World.*

1897

- Jell-O is introduced.

1898

- United States enters the Spanish-American-Cuban war after the U.S.S. *Maine* explodes in Havana Harbor, killing 266 sailors on February 15.
- Treaty of Paris ends the war with Spain; Spain relinquishes its claim to Cuba, sells the Philippines to the United States for $20 million, and transfers Puerto Rico to U.S. control.
- United States annexes Hawaii.
- Emilio Aguinaldo declares Philippine's independence, but the United States refuses to recognize the republic and fights a guerilla war against the Filipino nationalists.

1899

- Coca-Cola is bottled for the first time.
- Secretary of State John Hay issues "Open Door" notes to European powers, arguing that all industrialized nations should be given equal access to Chinese trade.

1900

- Corporate leaders found the National Civic Federation to seek peaceful solutions to industrial conflict and to condemn anti-union employers. By 1903 many employers had broken with the NCF and reverted to union busting.
- George Eastman's Kodak Co. introduces the $1 Brownie Box camera; photography spreads as a hobby.
- "Boxer Rebellion" attacks foreigners and foreign influences in China.

1901

- Platt Amendment grants the United States the right to intervene and build naval bases in Cuba.
- J. P. Morgan underwrites creation of U.S. Steel, earning $7 million in creation of first billion-dollar corporation.

1902

- Colombian government rejects U.S. proposal to build a canal across Panama.
- U.S. Army replaces blue uniforms with less-visible olive-drab ones.

1903

- 1,200 Mexican and Japanese farm laborers win a hard-fought strike against sugar beet growers.

- New leaders declare Panama an independent nation and grant the United States rights to build the Panama Canal.

1904

- Roosevelt Corollary to the Monroe Doctrine asserts U.S. right to intervene in Latin America.
- Ice-cream cones and iced tea are introduced at the St. Louis exposition.

1905

- Niagara Movement demands an end to segregation and racial discrimination in every area of U.S. life; it leads to founding of National Association for the Advancement of Colored People four years later.

1907

- President Theodore Roosevelt concludes a "gentleman's agreement" with Japan to exclude Japanese workers from the United States.

1909

- U.S. troops are dispatched to Nicaragua.

1914

- The Panama Canal opens.

Suggested Readings

Ayers, Edward L., *The Promise of the New South: Life After Reconstruction* (1992).
Brecher, Jeremy, *Strike!* (1972).
Cell, John W., *The Highest Stage of White Supremacy: The Origins of Segregation in South Africa and the American South* (1982).
Foner, Philip S., *The Spanish-Cuban-American War and the Birth of American Imperialism* (2 vols., 1972).
Gilmore, Glenda, *Gender and Jim Crow: Women and the Politics of White Supremacy in North Carolina, 1896–1920* (1996).
Goodwyn, Lawrence, *Democratic Promise: The Populist Moment in America* (1976).
Harlan, Louis R., *Booker T. Washington: The Making of a Black Leader* (1972).
Higham, John, *Strangers in the Land: Patterns of American Nativism, 1860–1925* (1973).
Kaufman, Stuart B., *Samuel Gompers and the Origin of the American Federation of Labor, 1848–1896* (1973).
Keyssar, Alexander, *Out of Work: The First Century of Unemployment in Massachusetts* (1986).
Kinzer, Donald L., *An Episode in Anti-Catholicism: The American Protective Association* (1964).
Kleppner, Paul, *The Third Electoral System, 1853–1892* (1979).
Kousser, J. Morgan, *The Shaping of Southern Politics: Suffrage Restriction and the Establishment of the One-Party South* (1974).

LaFeber, Walter, *The Cambridge History of Foreign Relations: The Search for Opportunity, 1865–1913* (1993).
Lamoreaux, Naomi, *The Great Merger Movement in American Business, 1895–1904* (1985).
Lindsey, Altmont, *The Pullman Strike: The Story of a Unique Experiment and of a Great Labor Upheaval* (1942).
McMath, Robert C., *American Populism: A Social History, 1877–1898* (1993).
McMurray, Donald L., *Coxey's Army: A Study of the Industrial Army Movement of 1894* (1929).
Miller, Stuart Creighton, *"Benevolent Assimilation": The American Conquest of the Philippines, 1899–1903* (1979).
Oestreicher, Richard Jules, *Solidarity and Fragmentation: Working People and Class Consciousness in Detroit, 1875–1900* (1986).
Palmer, Bruce, *"Man over Money": The Southern Populist Critique of American Capitalism* (1980).
Rosenberg, Emily, *Spreading the American Dream: American Economic and Cultural Expansion, 1890–1945* (1982).
Salvatore, Nick, *Eugene V. Debs: Citizen and Socialist* (1982).
Saxton, Alexander, *The Indisputable Enemy: Labor and the Anti-Chinese Movement in California* (1971).
Schwantes, Carlos A., *Coxey's Army: An American Odyssey* (1985).
Serrin, William, *Homestead: The Glory and Tragedy of an American Steel Town* (1992).
Trask, David, *The War with Spain in 1898* (1981).
Williams, R. Hal, *Years of Decision: American Politics in the 1890s* (1978).
Williams, William Appleman, *The Tragedy of American Diplomacy* (rev. ed., 1972).
Williamson, Joel, *The Crucible of Race: Black-White Relations in the American South since Emancipation* (1984).
Wolff, Leon, *Lockout, the Story of the Homestead Strike of 1892* (1965).
Woodward, C. Vann, *The Strange Career of Jim Crow* (3rd ed., 1974).
Woodward, C. Vann, *Tom Watson: Agrarian Rebel* (1963).
Wright, James Edward, *The Politics of Populism: Dissent in Colorado* (1974).

And on the World Wide Web

Jim Zwick, *Anti-Imperialism in the United States, 1898–1935* (http://www.boondocksnet.com/ail98-35.html)

Library of Congress, *The Spanish-American War in Motion Pictures* (http://memory.loc.gov/ammem/sawhtml/sawhome.html)

chapter 4

Change and Continuity in Daily Life

1900–1914

In January 1912, the Procter and Gamble Company (P&G) announced to the readers of the *Ladies' Home Journal* "An Absolutely New Product, A Scientific Discovery Which Will Affect Every Kitchen in America." The "new and heretofore unknown food" was Crisco, a solid vegetable shortening made from cottonseed oil. P&G hoped the new shortening would replace the pork lard and beef tallow that had long dominated American cooking. If successful, Crisco would not only expand P&G's consumer products offerings but would also ensure that the company would have greater control over the market for cottonseed oil, a key raw material in the manufacture of its most famous brand-name product, Ivory Soap. After patenting Crisco in 1910, P&G launched it with the most elaborate and expensive marketing campaign ever seen. The company tested a variety of promotion plans, analyzed the shortening market, sent full-size free samples to every grocer in the United States, and advertised the new product in newspapers and magazines.

Crisco exemplified many of the dramatic changes in America's economy and everyday life at the turn of the century. "Science" and "progressive reform" would dominate the rhetoric of consumer culture. Giant (often global) corporations like P&G would reorganize factories around new principles of "continuous-process" or "flow" production. Everything from cars and cigarettes to soap and shortening would be produced in massive operations in which abundant and reasonably priced raw materials were a precondition of success. And to move these vast quantities of products into the hands and households of millions of Americans, the manufacturers would pioneer new methods of distribution—brand names, advertising, national sales forces, chain stores—to convince people that they "needed" these goods.

Fashion Sense. This illustration from a 1910 *McClure's Magazine* showed young women employees leaving a New York department store at the end of the workday.

Source: Wladyslav T. Benda, *McClure's Magazine,* October 1910—General Research Division, New York Public Library, Astor, Lenox and Tilden Foundations.

This remarkable new system of production and distribution reflected and contributed to the even more remarkable economic growth and prosperity that emerged in the United States after the end of the depression of the 1890s. Between 1896 and 1914, the per capita gross national product (GNP) increased by almost 50 percent (in constant dollars). By 1910, the United States was the world's greatest industrial power. The productivity of the nation's industrial economy brought with it a wealth of mass-produced goods—packaged foods and cleaning products, ready-made clothing, and factory-made furniture—that reshaped everyday life. Some of the new factory-produced goods (like canned tomato soup and dining room tables) supplanted items formerly produced at home and in small crafts shops. Others (like safety razors and cornflakes) were entirely new products that could be made only in factories. New products and technologies made old ones obsolete: electric lights replaced kerosene lamps, for example, and Crisco displaced lard. New national, commercial forms of leisure—movies, vaudeville, and spectator sports—similarly undermined home-made and local entertainments.

But for all the enormous changes that the new century brought, there were clear signs of continuity as well. The factories that pioneered mass production may have been bigger and more efficiently powered by electricity, but the conditions of work remained harsh and demanding. Even if some employers sugar-coated the new regime with lunchrooms and picnics, the scientific management techniques and assembly-line discipline they imposed on their workers made twentieth-century factory work even more dehumanizing than it had been in earlier times. The remarkable prosperity of the new century also remained strikingly unequal in its distribution. Mass production and mass leisure made new products and attractions available to a much wider market, but they remained beyond the reach of many people. Rural African Americans, for example, could not afford even cheap consumer products like Crisco. Few urban working people had telephones or electric lights. And, although a few women like Helen Landsdowne, who wrote the Crisco ads, played leading roles in the consumer economy, the most common job for women remained domestic service.

Moving-picture films with their nickel admission fees and silent pictures attracted immigrant workers whose knowledge of English was limited. But many Americans were denied access even to the cheap amusements they could afford—amusement parks did not welcome African Americans, and farm folk lived too far from the bright lights of the city to benefit from urban forms of recreation. Meanwhile, middle-class arbiters of morality tried to direct working-class audiences into "uplifting" forms of recreation.

This era of mass production, mass consumption, mass leisure, and mass markets catered to a "mass" that still retained many interior distinctions. P&G, for example, realized that to sell Crisco it needed to accommodate ethnic cooking preferences. To Jews, it pointed out that Crisco was kosher and provided a substitute for non-kosher lard in cooking all-American apple pie. P&G even persuaded a New York rabbi to endorse the product with the declaration that "the Hebrew Race had been waiting 4,000 years for Crisco." But in making their appeals to cooks accustomed to using chicken fat or olive oil in their recipes, even P&G's clever marketers failed to anticipate some opportunities—as when the

Yup'ik and Inupiaq women of Alaska adopted Crisco for use in a berry confection called *akutaq,* which was traditionally made from caribou fat or seal oil.

Gradually and unevenly the outline of the "modern" order was emerging in what would become known as the "Progressive Era." But the outline was not yet filled in: these years were marked by the coexistence of extraordinary prosperity and desperate poverty, the mass market and the rule of Jim Crow, female advertising executives and women domestic servants, Crisco and chicken fat.

Mass Production

Long before 1913—the year Henry Ford created the first assembly line to manufacture automobiles—other industrialists were isolating the elements and applying the principles of mass production. Manufacturers developed interchangeable parts in making firearms, millers moved grain on conveyor belts, and slaughterhouses set up "disassembly lines" that reduced whole animals to packaged meat. All shared one fundamental idea: mass production would set up systems that would enable materials to flow through the workplace in a continuous process, from the arrival of raw materials at the entrance of the building to the dispatch of finished goods at the exit.

A Disassembly Line. As shown here, workers at the Swift and Company meatpacking plant in Chicago performed specialized, repetitive tasks based on many of the same principles Henry Ford used in the automobile assembly line.

Source: Brown Brothers.

Small flour mills had run a continuous process since the eighteenth century, and soon after the metal-working industries applied some of its principles. During the 1880s, inventors developed new machinery to pack meat, brew beer, and can vegetables. Using conveyer systems, rollers, and gravity slides, these machines automatically sent materials through the production process in a continuous stream. The first automatic canning line opened in 1883, soldering cans at the rate of fifty a minute. Heinz pickles, Campbell's Soup, and Borden's Milk were among the first products canned in this way. Other companies soon used similar machines to manufacture a variety of products, including soap, cigarettes, matches, and breakfast cereals.

For workers, high-speed machinery brought unremitting and repetitious work. In some industries, the continuous process—and the introduction of electric lights—meant that factories could operate around the clock. In 1908, the Homestead works of United States Steel ran two shifts: a day shift of ten and a half hours and a night shift of thirteen and a half. "The men are too tired to take an active part in family life; they are usually ready after smoking a pipe to go to bed," wrote one observer.

The new factories employed huge workforces. The McCormick plant in Chicago had 15,000 workers in 1916; Ford's Highland Park plant employed 16,000. These immense plants had their own railroad terminals, water supplies, energy sources, telephone networks, fire departments, and security forces. As a result, they were often completely independent of the municipalities and companies that supplied goods and services to households and small businesses.

Of course, some consumer goods were created without mass production. Ready-made clothing was manufactured in thousands of small factories and tenement sweatshops at the turn of the century. Jewelry, furniture, and other items were produced by small firms that did "batch work." But even small factories produced unprecedented quantities of consumer products by relying increasingly on the division of labor.

Scientific Management

Despite differences in production methods, nearly all workers experienced new kinds of discipline and control. Time clocks, first patented in 1889, carried an unambiguous message: workers must submit to the machine's—and the boss's—account of their arrival and departure times. Employers continued to perfect the techniques of "scientific management," also called "Taylorism," after Frederick Winslow Taylor, who pioneered the movement. Taylor insisted there was "one best way" to perform every job, and that way could be scientifically determined, planned by managers, and taught to workers. In his quest for maximum efficiency, Taylor analyzed how workers performed their jobs, broke the jobs down into steps, and timed workers with a stopwatch. He then set standards for each task, paying a high piece rate for high output and a lower one for substandard results. In 1911, Taylor published *The Principles of Scientific Management,* and Taylorism became all the rage—except among workers.

Baking a Better Apple Pie

As the principles of scientific management came to play a more significant role in the workplace, some reformers sought to apply standardization and routine to aspects of daily life. Nowhere was this more apparent than in the kitchen. The domestic science movement (or "home economics," as it was later called) attempted to standardize routines and recipes, thereby relieving housewives of the anxieties of inexact cooking and bringing the supposed benefits of efficiency into the home. Fannie Merritt Farmer was a leader in the movement for scientific cooking, helping to entrench the notion of exact measures and procedures designed to produce a uniform product. The following two recipes for apple pie demonstrate the difference between Farmer's precisely measured approach and an earlier "inexact" set of instructions.

Starting from Scratch: Catherine Beecher's Apple Pie

Pare your apples, and cut them from the core. Line your dishes with paste, and put in the apple; cover and bake until the fruit is tender. Then take them from the oven, remove the upper crust, and put in sugar and nutmeg, cinnamon or rose water to your taste; a bit of sweet butter improves them. Also, to put in a little orange peel before they are baked, makes a pleasant variety. Common apple pies are very good to stew, sweeten, and flavor the apple before they are put into the oven. Many prefer the seasoning baked in. All apple pies are much nicer if the apple is grated and then seasoned.

Source: Catherine Beecher, *Domestic Receipt Book* (1846).

Apple Pie by the Book: Fannie Farmer's Recipe

4 or 5 sour apples
1/8 teaspoon salt
1/3 cup sugar
1 teaspoon butter
1/4 teaspoon grated nutmeg
1 teaspoon lemon juice
Few gratings lemon rind

Line pie plate with paste. Pare, core, and cut the apples into eighths, put row around plate one-half inch from edge, and work towards the centre until plate is covered; then pile on remainder. Mix sugar, nutmeg, salt, lemon juice, and grated rind, and sprinkle over apples. Dot over with butter. Wet edges of under crust, cover with upper crust, and press edges together. Bake forty to forty-five minutes in moderate oven. A very good pie may be made without butter, lemon juice, and grated rind. Cinnamon may be substituted for nutmeg. Evaporated apples may be used in place of fresh fruit. If used, they should be soaked overnight in cold water.

Source: Fannie Merritt Farmer, *Boston Cooking-School Cook Book* (1905).

Taylorism and mass production went hand in hand. Although efficiency theories were applied to work in many fields—even education and housework—Taylor's program was best suited to large-scale, mechanized production processes. The new system separated manual from mental labor, unskilled from skilled tasks. Skilled work was broken into smaller steps that could be done by low-paid semiskilled or unskilled workers. The work of a shoemaker, for instance, was subdivided into forty

The Science of Repetition. The small lights attached to the arms and hands of this worker enabled efficiency experts to track his movements. The resulting "cyclegraph," a photograph taken by an open-shutter still camera and invented by time-and-motion specialist Frank Gilbreth, was then studied in an attempt to eliminate useless movement and turn mass-production work into a rigid arrangement of "efficient" motions.

Source: National Museum of American History, Smithsonian Institution.

tasks. Unlike the shoemaker, the semiskilled workers learned to operate a single machine, but they were not trained to set it up, repair it, or operate similar equipment. Lacking any generalized knowledge of production, these workers had less bargaining power than the skilled shoemakers they replaced. This strategy not only increased employers' control over the labor force but also improved their production and profits. After 1900, factory owners increasingly hired unskilled and semiskilled workers (including women and new immigrants) rather than the skilled craftsmen who had once dominated the industrial workforce.

Workers understood this managerial strategy, and they equated Taylorism with diminished autonomy, close supervision, regimentation, and pressure to produce. Some less-skilled workers, new to industrial work, took the new jobs eagerly. But between 1909 and 1913, unskilled immigrant workers in industrial towns throughout the East and Midwest—including Lawrence, Massachusetts, and Paterson, New Jersey—went on strike against wage cuts, unsafe conditions, and the dehumanizing work patterns required by scientific management and the new mass production methods. For skilled workers, scientific management meant the loss of craft control and the routinization of labor. In 1912 the American Federation of Labor (AFL) came out against Taylor's time-study methods. "We don't want to work as fast as we are able to," one machinist declared in 1914. "We want to work as fast as we think it's comfortable for us to work."

Welfare Capitalism

The close supervision and careful timing of Taylorism was the most important new managerial strategy of the early twentieth century, but it was not the only approach employers used to regulate workers. Haunted by

Amenities. The male employees' bathroom at the National Cash Register (NCR) Company in Dayton, Ohio, in 1900. The facility was part of NCR's extensive welfare program, which also included clubs, sports teams, and landscaping of the company grounds.
Source: Courtesy NCR.

the specter of bitter labor strife, some innovating employers responded by offering incentives to secure greater productivity, higher profits, and workers' loyalty. A few large capitalists, such as the Pittsburgh food processor H. J. Heinz, provided lunchrooms, showers, and company-owned housing in an effort to "humanize the business system" and "end the spirit of enmity between capital and labor." Various companies offered a panoply of other programs aimed at promoting workers' "welfare"—savings clubs, English classes, company picnics, in-house magazines, and on-site nurses. Many businesses limited these benefits to skilled workers, however.

Some companies provided more direct monetary benefits, profit-sharing plans, pensions, and the opportunity to buy a home. These plans—intended to persuade workers to remain loyal to the company and give them a stake in their community—often were introduced when strikes were brewing and were available only to workers who took the boss's side.

Companies frequently promoted themselves as families, modeled on small-town entrepreneurs who prided themselves on their ability to call every employee by name. The "family" of employees sometimes consisted of real families. In New Hampshire's huge Amoskeag Mills, as in California and Colorado agriculture, people often got jobs through family ties, and relatives substituted for one another on the job. When workers knew of an opening they would bring in their relatives, even after companies established formal employment offices. Working alongside a brother in a factory or picking crops in the same field with a father or daughter sometimes made harsh working conditions easier to bear. But there was also a down side: whole families working in the same place were more vulnerable to wage cuts, layoffs, and shutdowns.

Many companies included "Americanization" in their welfare programs—classes intended to teach immigrant workers English and acculturate them to American ways. These company programs were part of a broader Americanization movement supported by social workers, civic groups, and government agencies. Some emphasized English and civics and encouraged immigrants to apply for citizenship. Others had a harder edge, emphasizing obedience, discouraging radicalism, and stressing the need to break with Old World customs.

"Amoskeag Did All This to Keep Harmony . . ."

The Amoskeag Corporation in Manchester, New Hampshire, operated the world's largest textile mill, employing some 14,000 workers. The company ran a whole series of welfare programs for workers and their families. Joseph Debski, who began working at Amoskeag in 1910 when he was fourteen years old, described one company benefit.

The Amoskeag had a textile club; anybody over eighteen who worked there could belong to it. It had a reading room, canteen, billiard and pool tables, and card tables; and they used to have dances, probably once a month in the wintertime. They had a golf course with a clubhouse; and in 1927 they took over the Intervale Country Club. . . . Then they had the Amoskeag Textile Field, which was a baseball field.

There was a general fund to operate things like a Christmas party for employees' children. They'd take all the equipment out of the garage—it was all bare floor—and prepare it for fifteen to twenty-five hundred children from five to fifteen, free of charge. They would try to take the hard cases, people who probably couldn't afford a good Christmas party of their own.

The textile club had an annual meeting at the Jolliet Hall . . . and there'd be fifteen hundred to two thousand people there. They'd have a big dinner and entertainment. We had committees on bowling, athletics, photography. . . . They had about twenty different committees. . . .

Amoskeag did all this to keep harmony amongst its employees. The board of directors established the textile club. . . . During the strike of 1922, the textile club functioned the most because people didn't have anywhere else to go. They would go play cards, play pool. They didn't draw any lines and say people couldn't come in because of the strike. . . . The club kept going . . . until the mid-thirties. . . . It was when the mill was shut down [in 1936] that everything was demolished.

Source: Tamara K. Hareven and Randolph Lagenbach, *Amoskeag: Life and Work in an American Factory-City* (1978).

Employers' special interest in Americanization stemmed from two beliefs: that the instruction would help them retain experienced workers in a time of severe labor shortages, and that it would instill positive attitudes and values in their workforce. After inaugurating English language classes in 1911 with help from the YMCA, International Harvester took over the program one year later and revised it to stress safety, shop discipline, and welfare work. Lesson One began: "I hear the whistle. I must hurry." As one company spokesman explained, every immigrant employee should simultaneously "learn to speak English correctly and also have impressed upon him the rules he should follow while in and around the works."

Of course, many immigrants welcomed the opportunity to learn English, become a citizen, and share more fully in American life. Ethnic community leaders often encouraged newcomers to participate in such programs. Many workers also appreciated the fact that company-provided benefits improved their work and home environment. Others, however, viewed the welfare programs as an invasion of their privacy and a poor substitute for higher wages.

New Standards of Living

Mass production, urbanization, and new technologies brought new products and services to both rich and poor in the decades after the depression of the 1890s. By the turn of the century, food products, cleaning supplies, and other grocery store items were mass produced, sold for a few cents, and promoted to workers on billboards and streetcar placards and to the middle classes in magazine advertisements. Quaker and Pillsbury now sold prepackaged oats and flour to people once accustomed to scooping them from grocers' barrels. Heinz and Campbell's supplied prepared sauces and soups, while Procter and Gamble offered a variety of brands and grades of factory-made soap—products that were once made at home. Some packaged goods were luxuries; Franco-American, for example, advertised its canned vichyssoise in yachting magazines. But as the firms that put food in cans exploited the economies of mass production, prices began to drop and these luxuries became affordable to more people.

Still, there was a huge gap between the lifestyles of the rich and the poor. Electricity, natural gas, telephones, central heating, and indoor plumbing were common among the urban upper classes by the turn of the century. At the other end of the scale, tenement-dwellers fueled their kitchen stoves with scavenged scraps of coal and wood, lit kerosene lamps, and drew water from hydrants located in courtyards near overflowing privies. A new tenement building might

A Well-Appointed Bathroom. A customized shower stall was one of the many features in a 1910 bathroom in a New Rochelle, New York, residence. **Source:** Byron Collection—Museum of the City of New York.

include a bathroom, and possibly even hot water, but most housing built for workers had neither heating nor lighting systems.

Within the working class, the level of comfort between skilled and unskilled workers also differed widely. An unskilled worker cobbled together a life for his family on an average of $10 a week. That was barely enough to rent a dilapidated two-room apartment with no running water; buy food, crude furniture, and some ready-made clothing; and purchase the most minimal private insurance—a necessity for workers who were unprotected by any form of government insurance. A survey done in 1910 concluded that if an unskilled steelworker worked the standard shift—twelve hours a day, 365 days a year—he still could not earn enough to support a family of five.

Privies. Toilet facilities, such as this backyard outhouse, remained minimal in some immigrant urban neighborhoods.

Source: Prints and Photographs Division, Library of Congress.

Skilled workers' families, in contrast, lived in relative comfort on an average of $20 a week. The additional income enabled them to rent or buy one- or two-family houses far away from the smoke and stench of the mill and the bright lights of the central city. They shared neighborhoods with families headed by small businessmen and low-level white-collar

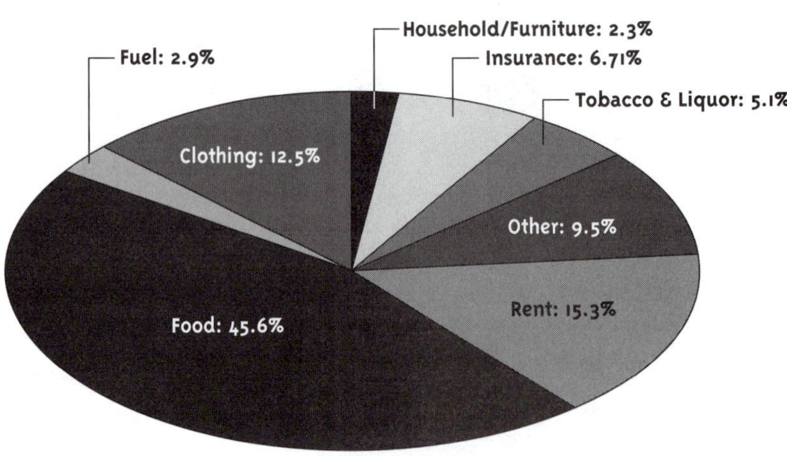

The Bottom Line: Family Budgets in Homestead Standards of living were rising in the early twentieth century. But unskilled workers, many of them immigrants, still spent about half of their meager incomes on food and had very little left over for recreation or the other pleasures of life. This chart is based on family budgets collected in 1908 from twenty-nine Slavic families in the steelmaking community of Homestead, Pennsylvania.

workers, an occupational group that grew as corporations expanded their managerial ranks. They could eat a varied, healthy diet and take comfort and pride in decent housing and furniture. If they were careful with their money, they could afford pianos and hand-operated washing machines and even accumulate some savings.

Indoor plumbing—like household appliances—was a real indicator of status. Wealthy homes had been equipped with indoor plumbing for much of the nineteenth century, but middle-class plumbing systems remained rudimentary until the mass production of pipe and fitting. In Muncie, Indiana, in 1890, no more than two dozen houses had complete bathrooms, and only one family in six or eight had even a hydrant in the yard or a faucet in the kitchen. Even eighteen years later, a study of working families in New York found that although many used indoor toilets, few had full bathrooms.

Plumbing was a godsend to women in all working-class families. Those without this convenience had to carry chamber pots and heavy buckets to and from tenement courtyards, streams, wells, and privies and had to heat washwater on wood- and coal-burning stoves. Leonard Covello's mother cried at the party welcoming her to the United States in 1896, but she smiled through her tears when her husband's landlady, Carmela Accurso, showed her how to bring water into the kitchen with the turn of a handle. "Courage! You'll get used to it here," insisted Accurso. "See. Isn't it wonderful how the water comes out."

Plumbing, gas, and electricity—whether at home or at the commercial laundries that working people patronized when they had no sinks—also enabled higher standards of personal cleanliness. As electricity, gas, and plumbing eliminated the work of making fires, cleaning lamps, and hauling wood, coal, and water, people began to keep their bodies, clothes, and houses considerably cleaner. New levels of cleanliness were also noticeable on city streets, where automobiles and electric streetcars were reducing horse droppings. And the new theory that disease was caused by germs—popularized in newspapers and magazines and by home economists in colleges, high schools, and settlement houses—raised public awareness of the dangers of thoughtless disposal of sewage and garbage.

Wiring a Nation

Electricity created a new landscape of light in the turn-of-the-century decades. Thomas A. Edison had produced his first electric lamp in 1879; even more important, he created a delivery system for generating and transmitting the new form of energy. By 1890, Edison's company was manufacturing more than one million light bulbs a year. They were used in shop windows, streetlights, and theater marquees, all of which were electrified during the 1880s. By 1900, advertising signs flashed changing words in blinking lights; New York's Madison Square displayed a forty-five-foot electric pickle promoting Heinz products.

Factories and businesses installed electric lighting in the workplace between 1880 and 1900. Electric light did not flicker or heat up rooms as did gas lighting. It also reduced the danger of fire and made possible round-the-clock shifts. In 1893 the Columbia Mills Company of Columbia, South Carolina, became the first textile mill to run on electricity, which was generated by water power. By 1919, electricity supplied about half of the power used by U.S. factories.

Many workers relied on electricity to get them to their jobs. Electric streetcars—first used in Richmond, Virginia, in 1887—caught on quickly because they were faster, cheaper, and cleaner than horse-drawn cars. Within three years, 15 percent of urban transit was electric-powered, and that figure rose to 94 percent by 1902. Between 1890 and 1902, the amount of track operated by electric railways almost tripled, and the number of passengers they carried more than doubled. Electric streetcars offered inexpensive rides all over American cities, giving workers new mobility and creating "streetcar suburbs," residential districts that were separated from industrial centers.

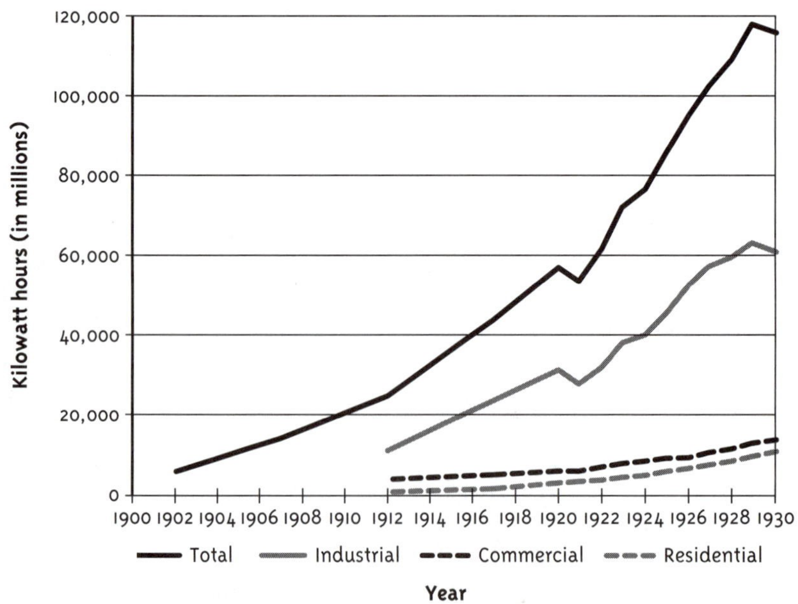

Uses of Electric Energy, 1902–1930 Use of electricity grew at an incredible clip—almost twentyfold—between 1900 and 1930. Although industries were by far the heaviest consumers, residential use grew at the fastest rate after 1912.

Telephone Operators. The work of telephone operators, such as these women at the New England Telephone Company switchboard in 1915, resembled industrial labor. Closely watched by supervisors who monitored their speed and enforced rigid work rules, switchboard operators handled up to six hundred calls an hour.

Source: Print Department, Boston Public Library.

Consumers could not just decide to buy electricity; it had to be made available by private companies and public utilities, which generally served industry and business first. Until 1910, only the wealthy were potential customers. But power companies soon realized that domestic demand, which was high at night, could balance the industrial load, which peaked during the day. After 1918, nationwide home electrification—which had been 10 percent in 1910—proceeded rapidly, reaching 70 percent by 1930. Initially, however, most homes used only a few electric lights, and few had electric toasters, irons, fans, or other appliances.

Working people were also late users of the telephone wires crisscrossing the urban sky. The telephone—first shown at the Centennial Exposition in 1876 by Alexander Graham Bell—had become a common tool of business during the 1880s and 1890s. In 1891 the New York and New Jersey Telephone Company had more than five times as many commercial customers as residential ones. But phones would remain too expensive for most urban workers for several decades. Families who needed to call a doctor or a druggist might ask to use the phone of a friendly grocer.

Marketing to the Masses

As Americans became consumers, linked to the complex distribution network of a national market, their longstanding relationships with local craftspeople and storekeepers were weakened. Customers now got information about products not from the people who made or sold them, but from persuasive advertisements. They purchased the mass-produced goods from stores conceived on principles similar to those of mass production. These new patterns were by no means universal or complete by the time the United States entered World War I, but they had taken a firm hold on the American way of life.

Advertised brand names gave manufacturers power over wholesalers and storekeepers. Before the 1880s, for example, wholesalers who distributed soap bought it from the manufacturer who offered the best price. But after 1881—when Procter and Gamble accidentally produced a floating soap and started pitching it to the nation—people began to ask for Ivory. Because the product could be obtained only from Procter and Gamble, wholesalers had to buy from that company. Manufacturers who created successful brands and convinced people to trust their advertising rather than the grocer's opinion had other advantages, too. They could charge more for their products, and they were protected from competition and price fluctuations.

"Picturesque America." Harry Grant Dart's illustration in a 1909 issue of *Life* magazine portrayed the increasingly aggressive and intrusive character of advertising in turn-of-the-century America.
Source: Harry Grant Dart, *Life*, 1909—Prints and Photographs Division, Library of Congress.

The most advanced advertising agencies and the biggest companies conducted sophisticated marketing campaigns that coordinated advertising with market research and other kinds of promotion, such as free samples. By 1911, the large Heinz sales force could coordinate 25,000 store displays with the firm's monthly magazine advertisements. New marketing campaigns took advantage of and contributed to major developments in the advertising media. Newspapers and magazines had published commercial messages for centuries, usually in separate sections full of small, closely packed ads. But the newest periodicals, designed to highlight full-page ads, functioned literally as advertising media and depended on advertising, not subscriptions, for their revenues. Similarly, billboards had been used for many years, but advances in lithographic techniques now enabled the reproduction of huge color images. After 1890, national and regional firms could post thousands of signs at the same time, offering advertisers systematic control over billboards and streetcar placards across the country. And Heinz's pickle in New York and other electric signs kept ads in view around the clock.

Even the foreign-language press came to depend on national advertising. *Il Progresso Italo-Americano* promoted few American brands in 1905, but in less than a decade brand advertisements were eclipsing ads by Italian undertakers and dentists and by local merchants selling pasta, olive oil, cheese, and wine. In the Yiddish press, the National Biscuit Company advertised Uneeda Biscuits next to ads for Coca-Cola, Vaseline, Heinz, and Colgate.

Manufacturers were now segmenting their markets by income, producing different versions of a product for different segments. Arbuckle Brothers packaged Yuban coffee for wealthy urbanites and Ariosa for rural and poor city people. The Edison Company offered a range of phonographs in 1910, from the $200 Amberola, with sapphire needle and oak or mahogany cabinet, to a bare-bones model for $12.50.

The face-to-face personal relationships that went along with retail credit and delivery were challenged during the first decades of the twentieth century by new kinds of retailing. Small merchants felt the competition of new kinds of stores—big city department stores, mail-order houses, and chain stores such as Woolworth's and the Great Atlantic and Pacific Tea Company (A&P)—which differed from traditional retailing not only in size but in distribution principles and techniques. Mass merchandising was based on the idea of *turnover:* moving goods into and out of the store as quickly as possible. The principle of turnover was honed to a fine edge by Sears, Roebuck and Montgomery Ward. These big Chicago mail-order houses offered a wider range of products than any other stores, and for farmers in remote areas, they were a boon. Montgomery Ward was selling about 24,000 different items in the early 1890s, when Richard Sears and Alvah C. Roebuck began to expand their watch business. By 1900 Sears had surpassed Ward, and in 1906—still doing only mail-order business—the company moved to a forty-acre tract where merchandise was carried, as in mass production, by gravity chutes and conveyer belts. Two thousand Sears employees opened and processed more than nine hundred sacks of mail every day. Sears owned or held a major interest in sixteen manufacturing plants, and it used those facilities to produce its own line of goods.

Chain stores had entered the grocery trade well before 1890, but they remained small until around 1912. In that year the A&P introduced "economy stores," small operations that did not offer credit and delivery and could be run by two people. By 1915, A&P had 2,200 stores. Consumers were shopping in tobacco, newsstand, variety, and drug chain stores by 1914. A few chains also ran clothing stores, piano stores, bookstores, and lumber yards. Some, like Sears, owned manufacturing plants; others offered low prices on nationally advertised brand merchandise. Local merchants viewed the chains, like the mail-order houses, as a serious threat to their business. And for consumers with cash to spend, the appeal was real—the new retailers offered lower prices and often a better selection. Industrial workers who lived from paycheck to paycheck remained with the local merchants. Prices were higher, but the local stores still offered credit.

Leisure Time and Public Recreation

Central to the consumer culture of the early twentieth century was a new concept: leisure. Free time—an idea that would have mystified most farmers and artisans of a hundred years before—emerged as more people became wage earners, owing employers a certain number of hours a day or week, and no more. Eight- and nine-hour days became widespread, the result of decades of dedicated union activity, new technologies, rationalized production, and protective legislation.

Like so much else in American life, leisure activities became commercialized. Home-made and local entertainment gave way to dance halls, vaudeville acts that toured the nation, and eventually to moving-picture films. Boxing, baseball, and other sports became big business. Designed for profit and engineered by experts in the developing entertainment industry, these diversions turned individuals into audience members. But for all the excitement, there was also a loss, as amateurs who had sung, danced, and played music in their homes and neighborhoods were replaced by highly talented paid performers.

Young people seeking to escape big-city tenements, which offered no place to hold parties and precious little privacy, were drawn to public meeting places. By the 1910s, greater New York had more than five hundred dance halls. "The town is dance mad," wailed a reformer. Dancing had long been popular in working-class neighborhoods. Workers in cities all over the country had danced not only at weddings and other family celebrations but also at parties sponsored by unions and fraternal lodges, held in rented halls usually located next door to saloons. As time passed, hall owners opened their ballrooms to the public.

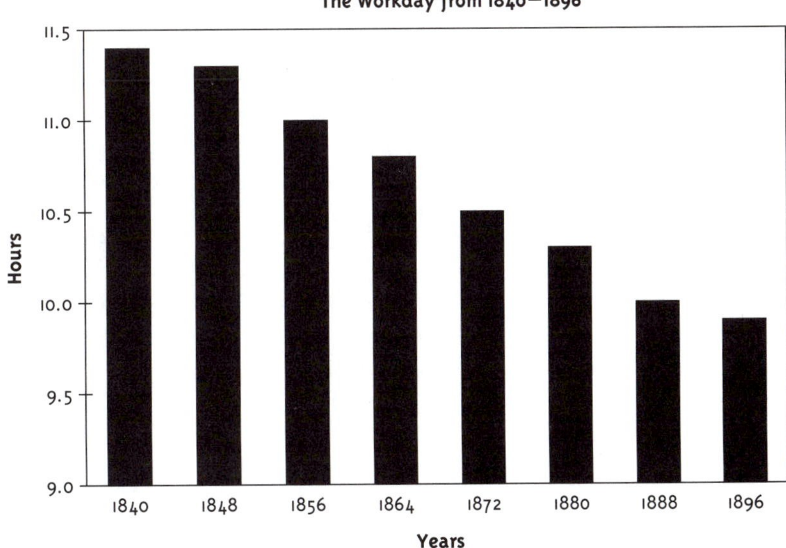

Note: Full-time workers, 6-day week, average of 21 selected industries.

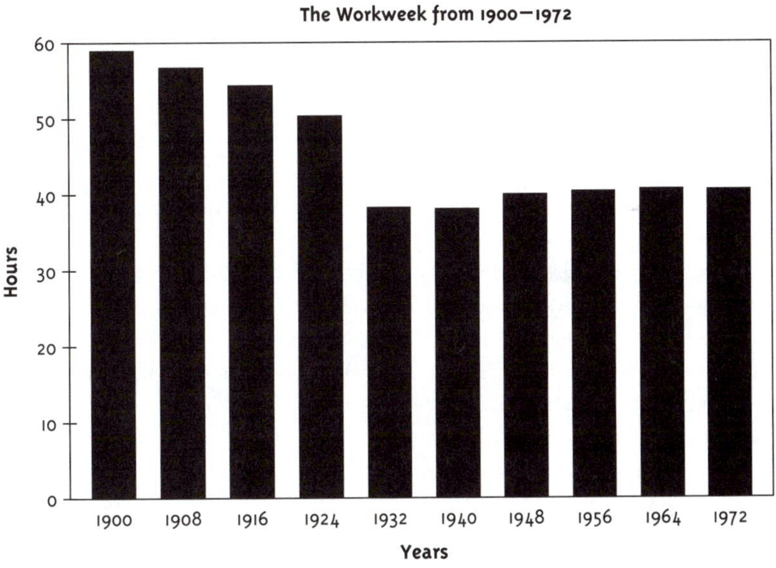

Note: Full-time workers, median of all manufacturing industries.

Counting the Hours: The Workday and the Workweek, 1840–1972 As these two graphs indicate, the shorter-hour workweek emerged gradually and unevenly over the nineteenth and early twentieth centuries. Until 1940, the trend continued steadily downward.

Dance halls ranged from the respectable to the tawdry. The ones that featured and welcomed female prostitutes and homosexual men were often located in poor areas where residents had little power to object to what went on in neighboring establishments. Gay men and their culture were highly visible in the urban sexual underworld and were more publicly and fully integrated into working-class culture than into that of the middle class. But the mainstays of the dance halls were young working women, who were expected to contribute most of the little they earned to their families. They stretched their pennies by "dating" young men, who paid for an evening's food, drink, and entertainment in return for female companionship and the possibility of sexual experimentation. These young working women were the pioneers of a new mixed-sex realm of leisure; previously, women's entertainment had been restricted largely to family outings or activities meant for women only. Dance halls and amusement parks offered young people a place to meet and enjoy each other's company unsupervised. Seeking excitement and independence, young immigrant women and men established the norms of modern romantic companionship.

Watch Your Steps. Aware of dancing's popularity, many urban reform organizations arranged alternatives to commercial dance halls. The People's Institute organized this dance on New York's Lower East Side, in a setting in which young men and women's behavior could be supervised.

Source: People's Institute Papers—General Research Division, New York Public Library, Astor, Lenox and Tilden Foundations.

Dancing could also be found at commercial amusement parks, which developed during the late 1890s. By 1919, at least 1,500 parks took their place alongside vaudeville shows, movies, and professional sports events, offering diversion to people who were not wealthy. Amusement parks used technology to manufacture pleasure, and they encouraged people to spend money on transitory enjoyment. By 1910, every major city had at least one park that could be reached by trolley. They featured picnic groves, dance halls, skating rinks, pony and boat rides, a penny arcade, a carousel, a Ferris wheel, a roller coaster, and perhaps other rides in addition to nightly entertainment like fireworks, band concerts, or musical shows. Elaborately decorated and highly mechanized, amusement parks like the Chutes in San Francisco, Pittsburgh's Kennywood Park, Boston's Revere Beach, and Denver's Manhattan Beach offered release from the dullness of the workaday world. "It is just like what I see when I dream of heaven," one young woman exclaimed on her first visit to Brooklyn's Coney Island. The Tun-

Summer in the City. Bathers enjoyed the Coney Island surf in 1903.

Source: Prints and Photographs Division, Library of Congress.

nel of Love had distinctly sexual overtones: "Will she throw her arms around your neck and yell?" advertisements asked.

Coney Island hotels, beaches, and boardwalks catered to a range of pocketbooks; one 1899 guidebook claimed the area was "divided equally amongst the rich and the poor." Luna Park, a fantasy land of minarets, turrets, and 250,000 electric lights, had a relatively high admission price and was aimed at the respectable middle class. Steeplechase Park, with its fun houses, circus-like sideshows, and rougher rides, attracted working-class youths.

Many individuals crossed class lines in seeking their pleasure. Some frequented bars where prostitutes or gay men spent time and money. On the whole, however, most entertainment was tame enough for the average American, wealthy or not. The Coney Island guidebook urged guests of the luxury hotels to spend some time at "the great resort for the crowds." People who could not afford Luna Park on a regular basis went as an occasional treat. Immigrants were welcome if they could afford it; the diverse crowds were for many part of the draw. But one form of diversity was excluded. Amusement parks generally did not admit African Americans.

Entertainment for the Masses

An outing to an amusement park was an occasional treat, but plenty of everyday entertainment was also available, and at popular prices. The theater was alive in immigrant neighborhoods, from participatory, hiss-the-villain melodrama to Shakespeare. By the 1890s, vaudeville was competing with other forms of live entertainment by offering "something for everybody": shapely women for the men, romantic singers for the women, slapstick comedians for the boys, animal acts for young children. Vaudeville ran almost nonstop—six days a week, from around noon to near midnight—at popular prices, based on the same principle of turnover used by department stores. "If I were to sell an orchestra chair for twenty-five cents, four times a day, it would be just as lucrative to me as if sold once for a dollar," declared Benjamin Franklin Keith, the most famous vaudeville impresario.

Over the next decades, nationwide vaudeville circuits emerged, controlled by booking syndicates that promoted big stars. To attract the largest possible audience, vaudeville promoters sought respectability: they sold no liquor, they excluded prostitutes, and controlled smoking and drinking. Women were admitted free on "Ladies Night" and were sometimes courted with gifts of coal, hams, dress patterns, and bonnets. To attract men, the master of ceremonies announced sports scores, and the boxers John L. Sullivan and Jack Johnson performed song-and-dance routines, told jokes, and sparred onstage. By 1910, more than half the vaudeville audience was middle class, and about one-third of all tickets were sold to women.

At the big vaudeville houses, performances were given in English, which limited the immigrant audience. But much of the entertainment was ethnically oriented. Singers, acrobats, and comedians were listed on the program as "Irish," "German," "colored," "Hebrew," or "blackface" acts, each with its typical routine, jokes, and costumes. Many African Americans performed in vaudeville, but in both northern and southern cities, black audience members were segregated in a balcony accessible only from a separate entrance in the alley. Middle-class black Americans refused to patronize these places, but they were still seg-

"Blaybt er Lign Toyt im Hol" (He Lies Dead in the Hall)

The "new" immigrants of the Progressive Era added to the diversity of American culture by bringing with them the cultural forms and practices of their homelands. Drawing on the Yiddish language and musical traditions of eastern Europe, Jewish immigrants created expressive musical shows in Lower East Side bars and theaters. This Yiddish song "Di Nyu Yorker Trern" (New York Tears), written earlier but first published in 1910, comments on the difficulties and tragedies of immigrant life in urban America.

New York bubbles like a pot
There's constant tumult and hubbub
You see a lot of people rushing around and
Often you see people's tears.
Misfortunes happen here at every step
And yet this hell is called Freeland
They put a family out on the street
Because they can't pay the rent on time
It rains, it pours, the tears flow
And the poor things sit depressed and forlorn

That's the New York tears
Which can never stop
A sob, a scream, a sigh and a woe
That's what you hear all the time
That's nothing new; wherever you go
You see the New York tears

Who hasn't heard of the murder
That took place not long ago on Montgomery Street
They found three people stabbed
A man, a wife, and a mother-in-law in a pool of blood
And there you hear a boy shot his friend
Two children were playing with a pistol
A boy of fourteen, what has he seen of life
The second boy, still younger, aimed at him
When he felt the shot
He screams "mama" loudly
And, running from the third floor
He lies dead in the hall

Source: Mark Slobin, *Tenement Songs: The Popular Music of the Jewish Immigrants* (1982).

"The Line at the Ticket Office." This illustration from the reform magazine *Outlook* depicted a scene outside of a "moving-picture show" in a New York immigrant neighborhood.

Source: Wladyslav T. Benda, *Outlook* (June 24, 1911)—General Research Division, New York Public Library, Astor, Lenox and Tilden Foundations.

regated—illegally, in cities like New York, Chicago, and Los Angeles—in the first-class playhouses they attended.

Vaudeville houses had shown "magic lantern" slide shows before the invention of the movies, and after that invention they were quick to include one-reel films between live acts. Moving pictures had evolved quickly from the 1893 peep shows that one person viewed by looking into a hand-wound Kinetoscope. Within three years, large-screen projection cinema had been perfected, and vaudeville audiences could watch "the movies" as part of the show. By 1905 entrepreneurs were setting up small storefront theaters featuring continuous shows composed entirely of one-reel films. These "nickelodeons," so named because the price of admission was a nickel, were an instant success. By 1907 there were more than two thousand of them in the United States. Three years later, about twenty-six million Americans were attending weekly shows at ten thousand nickelodeons.

At first, as the comedian Milton Berle later remembered, "the movies were something for the lower classes and immigrants. Nice people didn't go to the 'flickers.' " Low admission prices that even children could afford soon made the movies the rage in workers' districts. Silent movies crossed many barriers of language and culture. "It doesn't matter whether a man is from Kamchutka or Stamboul," wrote one movie theater manager, "he can understand pictures." Immigrant life was the topic of many early films, and immigrant producers built the early filmmaking industry. For much of the audience, silent films offered the first sustained contact with mainstream American culture.

Just before World War I, entrepreneurs began to build larger theaters. Equipped with carpets, ushers, and other marks of refinement, these movie halls showed new, longer feature films to the middle classes. Like vaudeville promoters, the most successful theater owners organized nationwide syndicates and circuits. Marcus Loew, who offered combina-

"Moving Day in Hogan's Alley." Richard F. Outcault's color comic, first appearing in the *New York World* in 1896, lovingly portrayed the immigrant, working-class urban neighborhood as energetic and comically chaotic. "Hogan's Alley" (also known as "The Yellow Kid," named after the strange, hairless child in a yellow dress who appeared in each installment) instituted the serialized color comic strip as one of the many features in the new mass-circulation newspapers. Like the movies, newspapers now gained a broad audience by offering a range of features designed to please every taste.

Source: Richard F. Outcault, *New York World,* May 3, 1896—Prints and Photographs Division, Library of Congress.

tion film and vaudeville shows, owned more than a hundred theaters throughout the United States and Canada.

Entrepreneurial energy also went into sports promotion. Although baseball had been played for decades, it took off as a spectator sport after the turn of the century, as clubs built stadiums along trolley, subway, and railroad lines. But the game was played everywhere, in all kinds of neighborhoods. Sandlot baseball diamonds were sometimes the only open spaces in the smoky, dirty, crowded inner cities. Hard-hitting, slick-fielding sons of immigrants worked their way up from neighborhood pickup games to local semipro teams and even the major leagues. As working people jammed the bleachers to see these men, immigrants began to feel they were part of mainstream American society. African Americans, however, were again excluded. They played on separate teams for separate leagues.

Uplifting the Masses

The new commercial culture of spectator sports, dance halls, vaudeville theaters, movies, and amusement parks challenged the middle-class ideals and values of thrift and sobriety, moderation and order. Unlike saloons, these recreations mixed the sexes, providing new arenas for courting; they promised excitement, romance, and adventure and supplanted older, community-organized amusements. An easy escape from the daily stresses of industrial life, these entertainments were especially attractive to young people, who made them the foundation for a new kind of working-class youth culture.

Commercial entertainment was exuberant, sensual, and irreverent. Genteel reformers considered it exploitative and dangerous. "Looping the loop amid shrieks of stimulated terror or dancing in disorderly saloon halls are perhaps natural reactions to a day spent in noisy factories," one critic admitted, "but the city which permits them to be the acme of pleasure and recreation to its young people commits a grievous mistake." Another reformer called Coney Island "a disgrace," a place where "humanity sheds its civilization and becomes half child, half savage."

Though the genteel wealthy had never successfully controlled the cultural lives of working Americans, they had long held sway over middle-class and mainstream culture. Beginning in the Gilded Age, their spokesmen—ministers, college presidents, political leaders—had sponsored high culture for the masses, seeking to instill in working people the values of thrift, sobriety, moderation, diligence, self-control, and moral uplift. In Pittsburgh, Andrew Carnegie funded a museum, library, and music hall that opened in 1895. Free Sunday organ recitals—excluding "all music of low or vulgar character"—were given to "develop the musical instincts of the people." Working people patronized such "uplift" institutions but turned them to their own ends. In 1891 eighty thousand people—more than half of them residents of the Lower East Side—signed a petition to open the Metropolitan Museum of Art on Sundays.

"How the Workingman Enjoys the Museum on His Only Day of Liberty." Some advocates of gentility endeavored to create cultural preserves sequestered from the taint of "cheap amusements." Prominent among such patrons of high art were the directors of New York's Metropolitan Museum of Art, who until 1891 resisted demands for opening on Sundays—when working people could attend.

Source: Samuel D. Ehrhart, *Puck,* January 2, 1889—New-York Historical Society.

Carnegie's best-known philanthropy was a new urban institution, the free public library, directed at the reform of working-class reading habits. New paper, printing technologies, and distribution networks were bringing reading material to more people than ever before, and literacy was increasing. by 1900, about 95

"The Most Important and Fruitful Discovery . . ."

Literacy was not just for English-speaking workers. For Oscar Ameringer, who spoke and read only German when he first immigrated to the United States, the opportunity to read books in his native language opened up a whole new world. In this selection from his autobiography, Ameringer describes his discovery of American history books, translated into German, at the local public library.

The most important and fruitful discovery I made in the winter of 1887–88 was the public library of Cincinnati, Ohio. I stumbled on the place by sheer accident. . . . The place looked good. It was warm and comfortable. In one of the large rooms of the ground floor people were reading newspapers and other periodicals, some of them in German, and all this was free. So I made myself at home. . . .

I discovered that the Cincinnati Public Library harbored the very place I hankered for. It was the history room up on the third floor, and there I settled down. The few others who patronized it occasionally were bespectacled young men who tended strictly to their own business, never spoke, and usually walked on tiptoe. There was the regular librarian, an elderly maiden lady who was always too busy crocheting to disturb the tranquility of the room. My particular method of reading history was to extract a large volume from the bookshelves, lay it on the table, spread my elbow-cradled face between hands and if there were illustrations, look at the illustrations. If there were no illustrations, I would snooze over the English text. . . .

One day when I passed too close to the elderly maiden lady, she looked up from her crocheting and asked me . . . "If you are so fond of history, would you mind if I selected a course of reading for you? I have noticed your reading is rather indiscriminate. You rarely selected the same book a second time."

I was caught. From now on, it was either read history or keep out.

The first book she handed me was a life of Tom Jefferson. It was written by a [18]48 revolutionist. . . . I should add that this life of Tom Jefferson was printed in German, thereby closing my last avenue of escape from reading it. I didn't snooze over that book. On the contrary, it kept me so wide awake that when "lights out" sounded that night I was still reading, and next morning was first on deck in the history room. This Tom Jefferson was a man after my own heart! His whole crowd belonged to my league. These fellows had no more respect for high priests, princes, kings, and hand-me-down authority than I had. They were rebels from the word go. They . . . had dissolved the unholy partnership between church and state. Declared that one man was as good as the next one and maybe a darned sight better. Had reveled in force and violence, going as far as I had in throwing bricks at scabs, or loyalists as they called them, when not riding the Tory strikebreakers tarred and feathered out of town on a fencerail.

The life of Jefferson swallowed in two bolts, the good teacher handed me the *Life of George Washington* by Washington Irving—still in German.

Source: Oscar Ameringer, *If You Don't Weaken: The Autobiography of Oscar Ameringer* (1983).

percent of white native-born Americans, almost 90 percent of white immigrants, and more than half of all African Americans could read and write. And they did read—a flourishing labor and ethnic press for news and political analyses, and "dime novels" for romance and adventure. Middle-class critics called the ethnic press subversive and the dime novels cheap and immoral, but their effort to direct working-class reading were

"Sunday Afternoon in Union Square." At the turn of the century, a group of painters, later termed the Ashcan School, were inspired by the city's diverse population and popular institutions. In particular, John Sloan recorded and celebrated the ways that New Yorkers dealt with living in a new, heterogeneous environment populated by strangers. In this 1912 painting, for example, he showed how public spaces like city parks offered people opportunities to watch and assess one another.

Source: John Sloan, 1912, oil on canvas, 16 1/4 × 32 inches. Bowdoin College Museum of Art, Brunswick, Maine. Bequest of George Otis Hamlin.

only partly successful. Most library buildings were forbidding in structure and located outside working-class neighborhoods. Borrowers had to display a respectable demeanor and slog through a considerable amount of red tape to get a library card. As a result, many workers preferred using union reading rooms. In the South, African Americans were prohibited from using public libraries.

Philanthropists and reformers also tried to lure the "lower orders" to enjoy nature in the parks, away from the debauchery of back alleys, brothels, gaming dens, and saloons. Frederick Law Olmsted, the most influential landscape architect of the nineteenth century, declared that his major work, Central Park in Manhattan, "exercises a distinctly harmonizing and refining influence upon the most unfortunate and lawless classes of the city." Many working people seized the opportunity to get outside. Those newly arrived from the countryside or desperate to escape crowded tenements used public parks extensively and with great respect. Unions and fraternal organizations sponsored gatherings in parks. Families spent whole Sundays there, bringing a meal or two along as picnics. Before Adriana Valenti and her family would go to Central Park, she remembered, her mother "would make us all sit on the chair and we all had high shoes at the time—and she would see that they were all buttoned, and if we looked presentable."

But philanthropists and middle-class Americans sometimes differed over the use of parks by working people. In Worcester, Massachusetts, middle-class spokespeople constantly complained about the "unsavory and idle appearance" of the working people who relaxed on the city common. Similar complaints inspired Manhattan's park commissioner to license rental chair businesses in city parks in 1901. After a major public protest and much newspaper publicity, however, park seats were again made free, and 20,000 people rallied to celebrate victory.

Middle-class people were more likely to entertain themselves at home, considering it the appropriate thing to do. There they conducted their private lives in quiet, orderly neighborhoods far from the noise and overcrowding of rough-and-tumble working-class districts. They had room to socialize and money to patronize restaurants or private clubs instead of public saloons. In African-American communities, too, the people who cared about respectability stayed away from working-class dance halls like "Funky Butt Hall" in New Orleans; they did their socializing at church-sponsored suppers, fairs, concerts, and excursions, where drinking and often dancing were forbidden.

White Collars and Middle-Class Values

For many, being middle class was as much a state of mind as a matter of money: "respectable" people observed rules about good taste and conduct. Many aspects of the growth of urban-industrial life seemed menacing to these people, including the huge factories and unbridled greed of capitalists and the extreme poverty and "alien" culture of the urban immigrants. But middle-class Americans also realized that the growth of corporations—the new bureaucratic institutions of the industrial economy—fostered their lifestyle by creating new sectors of the economy and expanded job opportunities.

This explosion of white-collar work—clean work—expanded the white middle class, which had been quite small for most of the nineteenth century. More than factory work, the new jobs required good English-language skills and a willingness to behave according

"The Hurry Habit." This 1914 cartoon, which appeared in *Life* magazine, commented on the increasingly frenetic nature of middle-class life in the early twentieth century.

Source: M. Fenderson, *Life,* November 1911—General Research Division, New York Public Library, Astor, Lenox and Tilden Foundations.

to company rules. Some children of immigrants took such jobs, which their parents could never get, while others followed their folks to the factories. Immigrants' daughters often entered the white-collar world before their brothers could. The new jobs therefore fostered more complex experiences of social class and changing ideas about its meaning.

Above all, corporations expanded opportunities for people who could sell products and maintain records. At the lowest levels, new entrants to the middle class functioned as clerks. At the highest levels, white-collar workers directed and controlled the expansion of the businesses they worked for. Before the turn of the century, many middle-class

"She Didn't Fire Me—I Fired Myself": Beulah Nelson Protests

Black women were twice as likely as white women to pursue paid employment, but they were more constrained in their choice of occupations. Nonetheless, the shortage of servants gave them some leverage in their jobs. The prospect of migration lent new resolve to black domestic workers as they confronted difficult employers, as revealed in Beulah Nelson's account, told to historian Elizabeth Clark-Lewis.

Before I left, a lady, who was named Miss Addie, and a member of my mother's church—my people all were sanctified—stayed home to have a baby. . . . And I worked [there] . . . three days. Why? Mama sent me, and they was paying a quarter a week! Now, you had to cook the breakfast, you wait on all of them, all the children, and get them ready for school. . . . Fix their lunch and everything. Then you wash up all the dishes. Then you had to go make up all the beds and pick up all the things behind all the children, and then after that you had to go out behind the house, honey, and pick the garden. And pick what kind of vegetables you got to have. You got to wash them and cook them. And they had three meals a day. They would eat they breakfast, and then twelve o'clock they had to have a big dinner. And then they had supper later in the evening.

But they didn't want no nigger to put they hand on their bread. Understand me good now. I set the table up and put the food on the table. But the bread be the last thing. Never bring the bread in until after they say the grace, so the bread would be seeping hot. I wait just as good until they said the grace, and I wouldn't move because I would have had to pick up the bread out of the pan, and I still would have to take knife or fork to lift it to put in the plate to take to the table, and I know she didn't want me to touch it. Right? Well, if she didn't want me to touch it, if I couldn't touch it, I wasn't going to try not to touch it to carry it to the table to give it to them. She said to me, "How long are you going to wait before you bring that bread in here?" I said, "I'm not even going to bring it in there." I said, "You put it in there. You cook it, you don't want me to touch it. If you don't want me to touch it, you don't need me to bring it in there." . . . And that's when she got mad, arguing with me so. She jumped up from table and she said to me, "Beulah, you fired." But she didn't fire me—I fired myself, 'cause I intended to do what I did. . . . I said, "No, if that's the way it's to be—not me!" I said, "For what? Six days a week for twenty-five cents? Not me!" You see, I didn't have to do it—I was leaving.

Source: Elizabeth Clark-Lewis, *Living In, Living Out: African American Domestics in Washington, D.C., 1910–1940* (1994, pp. 65–66).

men had aspired to entrepreneurial independence and had viewed their status as employees as a temporary one. Those views changed as large firms grew and gained control over vital sectors of the economy. Men in salaried jobs ranging from mail boy to chief executive officer now began to think in terms of lifelong employment with corporations.

Women dominated the lowest clerical positions, staffing typing and stenography pools, large bookkeeping staffs, and telephone switchboards. These women generally earned more than other women who worked for wages, but they were subjected to rigid discrimination and segregation. Jobs were defined by gender: the mail room was a male preserve, while the telephone switchboard was staffed by women. Gender segregation went well beyond job categories: men and women entered the Metropolitan Life building through different doors and used separate stairways, hallways, and elevators.

Virtually all the new white-collar jobs were denied to black Americans. As a result, middle-class African Americans of the segregated South debated whether to stay or move north. In the South, they could hold a few professional positions as teachers, doctors, and ministers to their own community, but they faced Jim Crow and the threat of lynching on a daily basis. In the North, most could get jobs only as waiters or house maids.

Some clerical and sales jobs offered workers a lifetime of low-paying, regimented—and rarely unionized—labor. But a few paid well, and many held the promise of advancement—the key to an escape from drudgery at work and scarcity at home. Sales work offered great possibilities for financial advancement to men who were willing (or eager) to forgo the comforts of a home life and able to adjust to life on the road. Salesmen were central to the developing mass-distribution system. Between 1880 and 1920, the number of commercial travelers increased at least sixfold. With good English and an attractive personality, a small-town boy or an immigrant's son might dream of expense accounts, good clothes, automobiles, and relative independence from the boss.

Women Making Money

A few women worked as commercial travelers for smaller firms, but many companies simply would not hire women to travel. More women searched for mobility in department store work, "the Cinderella of occupations," in the words of one business researcher. Bessie Harrison, who began as a duster in the china department of a San Francisco department store, doubled her $4 weekly wage in a sales job five months later. Within ten years she had a buyer's position at $80 a week.

But the glamour of the occasional Cinderella story obscured the real-

Gibson Girls. In the 1890s, Charles Dana Gibson's magazine illustrations of fashionable young women gained wide popularity. The physical type he portrayed became the standard of beauty, a romantic ideal that suggested a new independence while also celebrating the privileges and glamor of elite society.

Source: Charles Dana Gibson, *Ladies' Home Journal,* April 1895—American Social History Project.

ity of low wages and tedious jobs held by many retail saleswomen. Compared with laundries and factories, stores offered full-time employees steady work without seasonal layoffs. But this security was supported by the insecurity of many part-time workers, who worked only during special sales and heavy seasons, and at a lower pay scale. These women earned very little, but store owners argued that their wages were appropriate because women who worked part time needed only to supplement their families' income. In fact, most part-time saleswomen eked out a meager living for years, hoping to be hired as part of the regular staff. Even saleswomen on regular staff were paid roughly half the wages their male counterparts received in departments such as sporting goods and appliances.

Despite discrimination in the workplace, more and more women worked for wages, feeding growing corporate demands for clerical workers to cope with mountains of paperwork and retailers' demands for saleswomen and stock people to serve crowds of new customers. The shift from home production to factory, and the abolition of child labor, also drew increasing numbers of women into manufacturing. As the idea of women working for pay became more acceptable, the prevailing attitude that married women belonged at home faded, and an increasing proportion of wives joined the workforce. In 1890, just under 5 percent of married women worked for wages; thirty years later, twice as many did so. Altogether, the female labor force more than quadrupled

Women's Labor Force Participation Rates. Women's participation in the paid workforce grew steadily before World War II, but the most dramatic increases were among married women.

The Expansion of the Female Labor Force, 1900–1940

Year	Percentage of All Women Working	Percentage of Married Women Working
1900	20.6%	5.6%
1920	23.7	9.0
1930	24.8	11.7
1940	25.8	15.6

between 1880 and 1930. Industrial homework—the piecework manufacture of clothing, artificial flowers, or costume jewelry—enabled young mothers to earn money at home. In 1902, about 25,000 to 30,000 women did piecework at home in New York City.

Women's participation in the workforce varied by ethnic and racial group. Unmarried Polish women in Buffalo, New York, often took jobs in factories or as domestic servants, while their counterparts from southern Italy preferred to take in piecework or do seasonal farm labor. Many married African-American women worked for wages; few married immigrant women did so. But all kinds of women workers found themselves in new situations. Virtually every type of work women did—in offices, stores, factories, domestic service, and at home—was in the process of profound change.

"The Return from Toil." John Sloan's cover illustration for the radical magazine *The Masses* presented working women in a new way. *The Masses* often portrayed women as the victims of oppressive working and labor conditions. Here, however, the magazine's artists broke away from the standard sentimental or wretched stereotypes, instead showing working women as strong, independent, and exuberant individuals.

Source: John Sloan, *The Masses,* July 1913—Tamiment Institute Library, New York University.

Domestic service remained the foremost occupation for single white women in the North and for married black women in the South. In 1910 more than 2.5 million women—more than a third of the female workforce—were servants. African-American women who worked as domestics in the South generally lived in their own homes, while northern maids lived in their employers' attics and basements. Domestic service was both physically and psychologically taxing, involving intimate surveillance by an ever-present employer. Women with other choices abandoned this work in droves: one former servant reported how happy she was to leave behind the "degrading sense of servility." Factory work at least offered group camaraderie and genuine free time.

Even the most desirable of women's jobs had serious drawbacks, reflecting women's second-class position in the labor market. At the top of the female job hierarchy was nursing, which remained a preserve of native-stock Americans. During their apprenticeship in hospital schools, student nurses were used as cheap labor. After graduation, most of these women went into private nursing, caring for patients at home or in hospitals and charging a fee for their service. The isolation of private duty weighed heavily on them. Nurses took pride in their skills, knowledge, and independence, but they were subordinate to patients' families. Some of their work was disconcertingly similar to that of domestic servants.

Whatever their field—nursing, teaching, domestic service, garment and textile manufacturing, retail sales, or clerical work—women held jobs that usually paid less and carried less prestige than equivalent male positions. With no women in positions of power in either companies or unions, sexual harassment was widespread. Antonia Bergeron remembered that the bosses at the Amoskeag Company "were very fresh. The boss would chase the girls and slap their behinds, give them kicks in the rear end."

Fordism

Many of the new trends in workers' lifestyles and labor conditions came to be symbolized by the ideas and labor policies of Henry Ford and the Ford Motor Company. The term *Fordism* has been used to describe the modern industrial regime, which combined rationalized and mechanized production with mass consumption of standardized products. Henry Ford understood that increased production required increased consumption, which in turn required that factory workers be paid well enough to buy what they produced. High wages and a high standard of living were the reward for monotonous, repetitive, and alienating labor on the assembly line.

Automobiles had been built in America since the 1890s, but these early models were luxury items. Henry Ford, a machinist and engineer born on a Michigan farm during the Civil War, was manufacturing medium-price automobiles in 1908 when he introduced his Model T. A simple, low-cost car that could travel even over unpaved roads intended for horses and wagons, the Model T was an instant success. Ford's company grew rapidly, thanks to his constant innovation of the manufacturing processes. By 1914 the Ford Motor Company was producing 250,000 Model T's a year. When production was finally halted in 1927, 15 million Model T's had been made.

Unlike previous cars, the Model T was a standardized product designed for a mass market. "I will build a motor car for the great multitude," Henry Ford declared. The creation of a complicated product for a mass market was Ford's personal mission. "The way to make automobiles," he declared, "is to make one automobile just like another . . . to make them come through the factory alike—just like one pin is like another pin." For twelve years, the only cars Ford sold were black Model T's. Having just one model lowered costs and allowed Ford's engineers to scrutinize every phase of the production process.

As in many other industries, mechanization was the key to mass production, and technological innovation was central to success. To produce the Model T, Ford built a state-of-the-art plant for 16,000 workers in Highland Park, Michigan, on the edge of Detroit. The capstone of the Ford production method was the assembly line. Early on, Ford had posi-

Making Model T's. The Ford assembly line in Highland Park, Michigan, was a prime example of continuous-process production. In this photo, taken in 1913, automobile bodies are secured to chassis.

Source: Henry Ford Museum and Greenfield Village.

tioned machines according to their sequence in the production process, so that identical parts were hand carried from one machine workstation to the next. In 1913, Ford's engineers began experimenting with the gravity slides, endless chains, and conveyor belts used in the continuous-process production of flour, beer, and other products. Rather than assigning workers numerous tasks on stationary objects, they trained each worker to perform a few simple operations on parts that passed before him. The crowning achievement of their new system was the final assembly of the car by means of a continuous moving chain, to which the car frames were attached. The new continuous-process design reduced assembly time for a Model T from twelve and a half man-hours to less than two.

Although Ford did not acknowledge the influence of scientific management, or Taylorism, his new organization followed its general principles. Separating mental from manual labor and using time studies to plan work were becoming standard practice in many industrial enterprises. Ford's achievement was to apply those principles and the technology of continuous materials-handling to a highly complex product. Company after company soon adopted "Fordist" methods. The assembly line transformed the very nature of manufacturing, by addressing in a new fashion the old problem of increasing the work pace. Instead of quotas, piecework wages, or foremen who set the pace of production, the machinery itself determined how fast the work would be done.

Fordism meant enormous savings for companies, but exhausting, nerve-racking, and alienating labor for workers. Though it alleviated some heavy lifting, assembly-line work was draining. "The weight of a tack," one worker noted, "is insignificant, but if you have to drive eight tacks in every Ford cushion that goes by your station within a certain time, and know that if you fail to do it you are going to tie up the entire platform, and you continue to do this for four years, you are going to break under the strain." Monotony and boredom were severe; as another employee put it, "a man checks his brain and his freedom at the door when he goes to work at Ford's."

Worker discontent increased dramatically, and Ford, like most other employers, was threatened by extraordinarily high worker turnover. With little chance for advancement and few ties to their employers, semiskilled and unskilled workers were prone to quit if they disliked the boss, wanted a vacation, or saw a better opportunity elsewhere. Their mobility was costly to employers, who constantly had to hire and train new workers. At Ford, the problem was extreme. In 1913, the year the assembly line was developed, Ford had to hire 52,000 workers to maintain a workforce of 13,600. His worries mounted as a number of unions, including the radical Industrial Workers of the World, began organizing in the plants.

To keep out unions and reduce turnover, Ford announced a dramatic scheme, the Five-Dollar Day in 1914. He reduced the workday from nine hours to eight and offered a profit-sharing plan that brought wages up to a full five dollars a day—double the prevailing pay of laborers and semi-skilled workers in Detroit. Job seekers rioted at the doors to the Highland Park plant. But the wage policy had some catches. Ford fired workers who did not produce. Those who did produce could get the full profit-sharing payment only if they met certain standards both at work and at home. He set up a "sociological department" to investigate workers' home lives and administer the plan.

Out of the Melting Pot and into . . . These 1916 graduates of the Ford English School are shown at the finale of commencement exercises. The graduation included a ritual of citizenship where the graduates, dressed in traditional national costumes, disembarked from an immigrant ship and disappeared into a gigantic melting pot (center of photo). Their teachers then vociferously stirred the pot with ladles and the graduates finally emerged dressed in "American" clothes and waving flags.

Source: Henry Ford Museum and Greenfield Village.

After 1914, Henry Ford tied the profit-sharing payments to his Americanization program. He believed that immigrants had to "be taught American ways, the English language, and the right way to live." The program encouraged immigrant workers to move out of ethnic neighborhoods and discouraged them from taking in boarders. As at International Harvester, lessons at the Ford English School concerned safety, shop discipline, personal hygiene, and the company's welfare programs, as well as Henry Ford's personal benevolence. The company even taught racism to immigrants: according to one Ford text, black Americans "came from Africa where they lived like other animals in the jungle. White men brought them to America and made them civilized." Ford's policies were contradictory, however; despite its statements, the company hired more black workers than other auto manufacturers.

Ford argued that high wages and a forty-hour week would increase consumer demand and bind workers more securely to their jobs, creating both disciplined workers and mass consumers. These were necessary goals, he believed, because mass production would lead nowhere if the masses—the workers—could not afford to buy what they produced. And indeed, Ford made it possible. The price of a Model T—$950 in 1909—dropped to $290 by 1924.

Change and Continuity

The changes that swept the United States at the turn of the century were evident in the landscape in New York, Chicago, Pittsburgh, and other cities in the Northeast and Midwest. Public architecture celebrated the dynamic power of urban America. Travelers entered major cities through magnificent new railroad stations built of granite and steel, with vast train sheds and high-ceilinged waiting rooms. Nearby tall office buildings, made possible by new construction techniques, housed the headquarters of large corporations, proclaiming their dominant position in the U.S. economy. Downtown department stores competed to present the most opulent displays and the greatest assortment of goods, while expensive restaurants, music halls, and nightclubs offered the middle and upper classes exciting and varied entertainment.

But in individual lives, new ways coexisted with old ones: people bought some new things but not others, and they put their new purchases next to their treasured keepsakes. Farmers ordered from the Sears catalog but continued to barter eggs and butter for other goods sold by country storekeepers. Urban workers bought some goods from pushcarts and others from department stores. Yet the future was clear:

young people insisted on new levels of convenience, leisure, and material comfort. The children of immigrants understood the "land of the dollar" better than their parents ever would. But before immigrants, workers, women, and African Americans could fully share in the bounty, they would have to overcome economic, social, and political barriers that limited their participation. Those inequities and barriers—low wages, dirty streets, unsafe working conditions, racial and gender discrimination—fueled the conflicts of the Progressive Era and the decades that followed it.

The Years in Review

1876

- Alexander Graham Bell introduces the telephone at the Centennial Exposition in Philadelphia.

1879

- Thomas A. Edison produces the first electric lamp; by 1890, Edison manufactures more than one million light bulbs a year.

1881

- Procter and Gamble introduce Ivory soap, which becomes the model for nationally distributed brand-name merchandise.

1883

- The first automatic-line canning factory opens, soldering cans at the rate of fifty per minute.

1887

- The first urban electric streetcar system is installed in Richmond, Virginia, by Frank J. Sprague; by 1902, electricity will power 94 percent of all urban transit.

1889

- First patent is granted for a time clock; many factories will adopt time clocks within the next five years.

1890

- Enameled steel pots and pans are introduced into the average American kitchen.

1891

- Eighty thousand people, many of them working class, sign petition to open the Metropolitan Museum of Art on Sundays.

1893

- Columbia Mills Company of Columbia, South Carolina, becomes the first textile mill to run on electricity.
- Alexander Graham Bell's key telephone patents expire, opening the field to competition and reducing prices.
- First moving pictures are introduced. By 1910, twenty-six million Americans attend weekly shows at ten thousand nickelodeons.

1899

- New York cabbie Jacob German becomes first person arrested for speeding; he was driving at the "breakneck speed" of twelve miles an hour.

1900

- George Eastman's Kodak Co. introduces the one-dollar Brownie box camera; photography spreads as a hobby.

1901

- Japanese-American chemist Satori Kato invents the first soluble "instant" coffee.

1903

- Luna Park, one of the first "modern" amusement parks, opens at Coney Island, New York, with spectacular rides and attractions.
- Milwaukee draftsman William Harley and mechanics Arthur and Walter Davidson introduce the Harley-Davidson motorcycle.
- Wilbur and Orville Wright make the first sustained (852 feet; 59 seconds) manned flight in a gas-powered airplane at Kitty Hawk, North Carolina.

1904

- Post Cereal Company renames its cereal Post Toasties after the original name, Elijah's Manna, arouses the wrath of clergymen.

1905

- Neon signs become part of American culture.
- First theater dedicated to moving pictures opens in Pittsburgh, Pennsylvania and charges customers five cents to watch "The Great Train Robbery."

1906

- Americans hear the nation's first radio broadcast of a voice and music program.
- San Francisco sets up segregated schools for Japanese immigrants.

1907

- YMCA offers English language and temperance lessons to immigrant workers.

- First Mother's Day is observed in Philadelphia through the efforts of Anna M. Jarvis.
- New York follows Paris's example and introduces metered taxis.

1909

- Strawberries are frozen for market for the first time.

1910

- Electric washing machines become available.
- White mobs attack African Americans in Boston, New York City, Cincinnati, Houston, and Norfolk following black boxer Jack Johnson's defeat of the "Great White Hope," James Jeffries.
- Father's Day is observed for the first time in Spokane, Washington.
- The United States becomes the world's greatest industrial power.

1911

- Frederick Winslow Taylor publishes *The Principles of Scientific Management.*
- Charles Kettering invents the first electric self-starter for car and truck engines.
- Calbraith P. Rogers accomplishes the first transcontinental air flight in 82 hours, 4 minutes.

1912

- The Great Atlantic and Pacific Tea Company—better known as the A&P—introduces "economy stores," small operations that can be run by two people; by 1915, the number of A&P stores reaches 2,200.
- New Mexico and Arizona become the 47th and 48th states to join the Union; Alaska is given territorial status.
- S.S. *Titanic* sinks in the North Atlantic with 1,513 aboard, including traction heir Harry Elkins Widener and copper heir Benjamin Guggenheim.
- Procter and Gamble markets Crisco shortening in innovative advertising and marketing campaign.
- Morton's Salt, Hellmann's Mayonnaise, Prince Macaroni, Oreo Biscuits, Lorna Doones are introduced.
- L.L. Bean opens in Freeport, Maine.

1913

- Henry Ford creates the first assembly line to manufacture the Model T; by 1914, 250,000 low-cost Model T's are produced each year.
- U.S. Postal Service introduces domestic parcel-post service.
- U.S. share of world industrial production reaches 40 percent.

1914

- Lord & Taylor's Department Store opens in New York, with a lounge, dining room, gymnasium, infirmary, and library for its employees.
- Henry Ford introduces the Five-Dollar Day in an effort to reduce worker turnover and prevent unionization.

Suggested Readings

Adams, Judith A., *The American Amusement Park Industry: A History of Technology and Thrills* (1991).

Benson, Susan Porter, *Counter Cultures: Saleswomen, Managers, and Customers in American Department Stores, 1890–1940* (1986).

Boorstin, Daniel, *The Americans: The Democratic Experience* (1973).

Boris, Eileen, *Home to Work: Motherhood and the Politics of Industrial Homework in the United States* (1994).

Butsch, Richard, ed., *For Fun and Profit: The Transformation of Leisure into Consumption* (1990).

Byington, Margaret, *Homestead: The Households of a Mill Town* (1910).

Chandler, Alfred D., *The Visible Hand: The Managerial Revolution in American Business* (1977).

Chauncey, George, *Gay New York: Gender, Urban Culture, and the Making of the Gay Male World, 1890–1940* (1994).

Cohen, Lizabeth, *Making a New Deal: Industrial Workers in Chicago, 1919–1939* (1990).

Ewen, Elizabeth, *Immigrant Women in the Land of Dollars: Life and Culture on the Lower East Side, 1890–1925* (1985).

Fischer, Claude S., *America Calling: A Social History of the Telephone to 1940* (1992).

Gamber, Wendy, *The Female Economy: The Millinery and Dressmaking Trades, 1860–1930* (1997).

Glickman, Lawrence B., *A Living Wage: American Workers and the Making of Consumer Society* (1997).

Hall, Jacquelyn Dowd, et al., *Like a Family: The Making of a Southern Cotton Mill World* (1987).

Hareven, Tamara K., *Amoskeag: Life and Work in an American Factory-City* (1978).

Harris, Neil, *Cultural Excursions: Marketing Appetites and Cultural Tastes in Modern America* (1990).

Heinze, Andrew R., *Adapting to Abundance: Jewish Immigrants, Mass Consumption, and the Search for American Identity* (1990).

Hounshell, David, *From the American System to Mass Production, 1800–1932: The Development of Manufacturing Technology in the United States* (1984).

Hoy, Suellen, *Chasing Dirt: The American Pursuit of Cleanliness* (1995).

Jacoby, Sanford, *Employing Bureaucracy: Managers, Unions, and the Transformation of Work in American Industry, 1900–1945* (1985).

Marchand, Roland, *Advertising the American Dream: Making Way for Modernity, 1920–1940* (1985).

May, Lary, *Screening Out the Past: The Birth of Mass Culture and the Motion Picture Industry* (1980).

Meyer Stephen III, *The Five Dollar Day: Labor Management and Social Control in the Ford Motor Company, 1908–1921* (1981).

Meyerowitz, Joanne J., *Women Adrift: Independent Wage Earners in Chicago, 1880–1930* (1988).

Nasaw, David, *Going Out: The Rise and Fall of Public Amusements* (1993).

Norwood, Stephen H., *Labor's Flaming Youth: Telephone Operators and Worker Militancy, 1878–1923* (1990).

Nye, David E., *Electrifying America: Social Meanings of a New Technology* (1991).

O'Malley, Michael, *Keeping Watch: A History of American Time* (1990).

Peiss, Kathy, *Cheap Amusements: Working Women and Leisure in Turn-of-the-Century New York* (1986).

Rosenzweig, Roy, *Eight Hours for What We Will: Workers and Leisure in an Industrial City, 1870–1920* (1983).

Rosenzweig, Roy and Elizabeth Blackmar, *The Park and the People: A History of Central Park* (1992).

Ruiz, Vicki L., and Ellen Carol DuBois, eds., *Unequal Sisters: A Multi-Cultural Reader in U.S. History* (1994).

Scranton, Philip, *Endless Novelty: Specialty Production and American Industrialization, 1865–1925* (1997).

Spears, Timothy B., *100 Years on the Road: The Traveling Salesman in American Culture* (1995).

Strasser, Susan, *Never Done: A History of American Housework* (1982).

Strasser, Susan, *Satisfaction Guaranteed: The Making of the American Mass Market* (1989).

White, Shane and Graham White, *Stylin': African American Expressive Culture from the Beginnings to the Zoot Suit* (1998).

Zunz, Olivier, *Making America Corporate, 1870–1920* (1990).

And on the World Wide Web

- Library of Congress. *An American Ballroom Companion: Dance Instruction Manuals, ca. 1490–1920* at http://memory.loc.gov/ammem/dihtml/dihome.html
- Library of Congress. *Inventing Entertainment: The Early Motion Pictures and Sound Recordings of the Edison Companies* at http://memory.loc.gov/ammem/edhtml/edhome.html

chapter 5

Radicals and Reformers in the Progressive Era

1900–1914

On the warm spring afternoon of March 25, 1911, a small fire broke out in a bin of rags at the Triangle Shirtwaist Company, a crowded garment factory on New York City's Lower East Side. The factory's fire escapes were faulty and the exits were locked or blocked by foremen fearful that workers would sneak out to rest or leave with stolen needles and thread. As the fire spread, the workers were trapped. In less than an hour, 146 people—most of them young Italian and Jewish women recently arrived in America—perished from smoke inhalation or from injuries sustained in a desperate ten-story leap to escape the flames. Many more workers were injured.

The Triangle fire horrified Americans of all classes and focused public attention on the human costs of industrialization. In the aftermath of the tragedy, middle-class reformers, socialists, and working people, including survivors of the fire, united to pressure lawmakers for factory regulation. In response, New York's state legislators established a factory commission to investigate the disaster and recommend ways to prevent future incidents. Even New York City's machine politicians embraced the issue.

This outpouring of concern by the general public and by legislators was emblematic of the times. By the turn of the century, many Americans—wageworkers, the middle class, elite humanitarians—sensed that corporate power was out of control and that the industrial order needed fundamental reform. The same giant corporations that had brought an incredible new array of products from Crisco to the Model T had also brought incredible exploitation, indignities, and even death. The bitter defeats of the Homestead and Pullman strikes had confirmed the dominance of corporate enterprise and large-scale production and distribution. The United States was now the greatest industrial power in the world, and the Populist vision of a nation of yeoman farmers had faded. Even the republican and producer ideals of the Knights of Labor, which were rooted in the world of the artisan, were clearly no longer viable. But millions of ordinary Americans had grown indignant over the inhuman living and working conditions endured by many laborers and with the corruption that had been rife in U.S. political and economic spheres since the Gilded Age. In the first decades of the new century, this indignation was expressed as a growing chorus of public criticism of corporate giants such as Standard Oil and U.S. Steel, and as increasing friction between labor and

Solidarity and Skates. These children were distributing socialist leaflets during a New York streetcar drivers' strike in September 1916.

Source: Prints and Photographs Division, Library of Congress.

capital. Running for president in 1912, Woodrow Wilson would declare that in this era of corporate capitalism, "the individual has been submerged" and "people are coming to feel they have no control over their affairs." In that election, three out of four voters agreed that something needed to be done to rein in great wealth and restore individual autonomy, even if they disagreed on who should do the job. Most backed Wilson, who ran as a Democrat. Others placed their faith in the Progressive party candidate, Theodore Roosevelt. And 6 percent of the popular vote went to the Socialist Eugene V. Debs. Even the most conservative candidate, Republican President William Howard Taft—who received less than one-quarter of the vote—had taken steps in his previous term to curb the power of giant corporations.

This statement at the polls was a reflection of a wide-ranging set of movements or coalitions that had sprung up to address the cultural, economic, social, and political dislocations and inequities caused by the growth of industrial capitalism. Historians use the term *progressivism* to describe these movements. The term is confusing because it does not refer to a single movement or party but rather applies to a network of overlapping and sometimes conflicting organizations and coalitions that campaigned to reform American society between 1890 and the outbreak of World War I in 1914. The breadth of this network enabled Wilson, Roosevelt, and Taft to run against each other for the presidency and still claim the mantle of progressivism. And radicals like Debs both drew upon and influenced progressivism.

Millions of Americans from all walks of life marched under the progressive banner. Some were working people battling for better pay and control over their lives. Others were urban reformers striving to improve living and working conditions in the slums. Some "reformers" were actually what we might consider conservative in their goals—they wanted to "Americanize" millions of new immigrants, to close working-class saloons, or to make city government more businesslike. Progressive politicians set goals of "trust busting," regulating corporate activity, and conserving the natural environment. And some parts of the movement addressed issues specific to a certain gender, race, or social group, such as women campaigning for the right to vote and African Americans protesting disfranchisement and lynching.

In retrospect, progressivism accomplished less than it promised. Big business managed to avoid or subvert some of the most significant restrictions on its power, and African Americans actually experienced reversals during this period. Still, the ferment of the Progressive Era did bring important improvements in the lives of many ordinary Americans—the Triangle Fire, for example, led to tougher municipal building codes and stricter factory inspection codes. And it is significant that working

"Come, Brothers, You Have Grown So Big You Cannot Afford to Quarrel." William A. Rogers's 1901 cover of *Harper's Weekly* depicted capital and labor as evenly matched—with commerce a beleaguered referee. Variations on this theme appeared frequently in the Progressive Era's mainstream press. Commerce alternated with other allegorical figures like "The Nation" or "The Public," suggesting that organized labor now represented a powerful interest, equal to capital and equally oblivious to how its actions affected the well-being of ordinary Americans.

Source: William A. Rogers, *Harper's Weekly,* June 1, 1901—American Social History Project.

people and women provided the impetus for many of the important changes during this era.

But if less than promised, progressivism was also more than is reported in standard accounts, where the story is often told as a series of events in the lives of a few famous men—particularly the most notable political figures: Roosevelt, who served as president from 1901 to 1909, and Wilson, who was president from 1913 to 1921. Progressivism was much more than that: it was an insurgency from below. Women of all classes were important in spearheading major reforms. Another critical influence came ironically from radicals skeptical of progressivism's potential for effectiveness. Socialists, Wobblies, and other groups who wanted a more thoroughgoing transformation of the system than that offered by progressive reformers mobilized pressure that would lead to more moderate reforms. As these popular insurgencies moved party politics to the left, national political leaders—for one of the few times in U.S. history—competed to be known as "reformers" and "progressives." Even if feminists, radicals, African Americans, and industrial workers failed to win all of their demands, they succeeded in setting the political agenda to which the more famous progressives like Roosevelt and Wilson would respond.

Andru Karnegi and Mr. Rucevelt: Simplified Spelling and the Contours of Progressivism

One of the strangest of the many early twentieth-century reform movements was the effort to simplify the spelling of words. This seemingly peripheral movement was actually a microcosm encompassing the themes and forces found in progressivism in that era—its focus on rationality and technical expertise; its strong support among the middle classes; its disdain for traditional political parties; its optimistic faith in the power of the state; its diverse constituency; its shifting coalitions, depending on the specific social, economic, cultural, and political issue; its international character; and its limited success.

Spelling reform was promoted by the Spelling Reform Association. Supporters of the reform complained bitterly that the English language lent itself to innumerable variations in spelling (one obsessive reformer counted 1,690 different spellings of *diarrhea* in Civil War pension applications) and that officially approved spellings were illogical and irrational. *Could,* they argued, should really be spelled *kud* or *cud,* and there were at least twenty ways of spelling the sound of *sh*—as in *ship, sure, ocean, partial,* and *mansion*. *Foolish,* they noted (in what was not the best choice of an example), could be just as logically spelled 613,975 different ways.

Like many other early twentieth-century reformers, the advocates of simplified spelling were engaged in what one historian calls a "search for order." They viewed the lack of standardization in American spelling as chaotic, inefficient, and irrational—hence, badly in need of reform. They complained about the "appalling and incalculable waste of nervous energy" on the teaching of English spelling and calculated that the *Encyclopedia Britannica* could (or *kud*) be twenty volumes instead of twenty-four.

This quest in spelling was part of a wider search for order and efficiency that relied increasingly on professionals and experts. Progressives differed on many points, but they generally shared an optimistic belief in progress and trust in the ability of professionals to find rational, scientific solutions to social problems. Such ideas appealed particularly to members of the new professional class—physicians, businessmen, engineers, managers, and scholars—who believed they could build a better society by analyzing social ills and taking intelligent, informed action. As shock troops of the progressive causes, these middle-class professionals and experts were often joined by other young members of the middle class—especially women—who brought a moral and sometimes religious fervor to reform. Crusading writers and photographers (dubbed "muckrakers" by Theodore Roosevelt), for example, played a vital role in spreading progressive ideas, linking reform elements, and informing the public about corruption and monopoly. Investigative reporters such as Lincoln Steffens and Ida Tarbell (who wrote for magazines like *McClure's*) and political novelists such as Upton Sinclair revealed political and corporate wrongdoing, targeting such major institutions as Rockefeller's Standard Oil Company, the stock market, and the meatpacking industry.

These young middle-class progressives tended to distrust political parties. Although the Progressive party was founded in 1912, most reformers worked outside the political party system; this was particularly true for women, who were denied the right to vote at the time. While disdaining traditional political parties, however, progressives favored governmental action. Thus, the spelling reformers counted as their greatest success President Theodore Roosevelt's 1906 executive order directing that government publications would henceforth follow such simplified spellings as *kisst* for *kissed,* and *thru* for *through.* This use of governmental power reflected the broader progressive conviction that the government should intervene in market relationships on behalf of the poor and of the public.

"The Crusaders—Marching Embattled 'Gainst the Saracens of Graft." This February 1906 *Puck* cartoon celebrated "muckraking" journalists and publications.

Source: Hassman, *Puck,* February 21, 1906—New-York Historical Society.

Despite the prominence of the middle-class experts in simplified spelling and other reforms, the progressive movement appealed to a much broader social spectrum. Radical activists worked side by side with more conservative colleagues, endorsing moderate reforms and spreading their more militant ideas at the same time. Black and white women campaigned together for municipal trash collection, bridging the chasm of race. At times (as in the aftermath of the Triangle fire), working-class Americans with their own agendas worked with progressives. And on some issues—spelling reform was one of them—the reform agenda attracted leading industrialists like Andrew Carnegie or politicians from old-line wealthy families like Theodore Roosevelt. (Satirists lampooned them as Andru Karnegi and Mr. Rucevelt.) In this sense, the progressive movement is better viewed as a series of shifting coalitions than as an internally coherent social movement with an easily definable program.

The ideas and values that became part of progressivism in the United States flowed across national boundaries. Factory reformers and public health activists studied the work of their colleagues abroad and met with them despite the expense and time involved in transatlantic travel. Sometimes—as with spelling reform, which the English protested vociferously—the proper nature of reform was debated internationally.

The diversity of participants reflected, in turn, the diverse range of issues that progressives addressed, from seemingly trivial matters like spelling reform to profound questions about the control of corporate enterprise. Broadly speaking, progressives worked in three areas that all

Steelworkers at a Russian Boarding House. Some progressive reformers turned to social science to understand the impact of industrial capitalism on turn-of-the-century America, and photography was one of the new documentary tools available to them. From 1907 to 1908 Lewis Hine was hired to photograph immigrant steelworkers in Homestead, Pennsylvania, for the Pittsburgh Survey, the first extensive study of a major industrial city. In addition to their value as documentary evidence, Hine's photos conveyed a new reform message about the immigrant to the American public. In contrast to the detachment and distaste apparent in Jacob Riis's pictures, Hine constructed a positive view of worthy newcomers, deserving of a role in American society and all the benefits that would bring.
Source: 4 1/2 × 6 1/2 inches—Photograph Library, The Metropolitan Museum of Art. Gift of Mr. And Mrs. Wolfgang Pulverman, 1969. Copyright The Metropolitan Museum of Art.

responded in some way to the vast social and economic transformations accompanying industrial capitalism in the United States. *Social and economic reformers* most directly confronted the inequities of the new order. They crusaded for better housing, cleaner streets, improved sanitation, safer factories, and more humane working conditions, and they challenged the untrammeled power of giant corporations and "trusts." Not surprisingly, such reforms most often had working-class support. Working people were much less likely to share the agenda of *cultural reformers,* who campaigned against what they saw as the immorality and vice embodied in prostitution, gambling, and—most especially—drinking. The third group, the *political reformers,* tried to rein in urban political machines and political corruption. Sometimes they worked for expanded political franchise (as in the movement for women's suffrage), but at other times they actually restricted voting rights (by backing literacy tests).

Spelling reform ultimately did not transform the written form of American English. Public protests led Roosevelt to rescind his order, although he vowed to continue it in his private correspondence. But some limited changes stuck—*labour* became *labor,* and *humour* and *rumour* also dropped their second *u* in the United States, although England retains the original forms. Progressivism had a similarly mixed fate. Despite the enormous energy and lofty ideas of progressives, their achievements were limited. But their legacy of an optimistic belief in the positive potential of government marked the beginning of a new relationship between working people and the government.

Social Settlements and Municipal Housekeeping

Among the earliest and most dynamic vehicles of progressivism were the settlement houses established in working-class neighborhoods, largely by young women from middle- and upper-class homes who sought to ease the transition of immigrants into American life. Beginning in the late 1880s, hundreds of young people moved into immigrant working-class neighborhoods across the United States to live in nonreligious communities devoted to reform. Jane Addams's Hull House in Chicago was the best known, but settlements were to be found in every urban center. In New York, Atlanta, and some smaller southern cities, middle-class African-American women ran settlements in poor black neighborhoods. Seeking to provide social services otherwise unavailable to their neighbors, black and white settlement workers all over the country organized

"Then We'd Have Some Cake and Coffee"

Immigrant men and women had a wide range of experiences with settlement house reformers. For some immigrants, the settlement houses were places of refuge and caring; others encountered reformers who were arrogant and patronizing. This document, which describes a positive encounter, is drawn from the oral memoirs of Rosa, an Italian immigrant who lived and worked at a Chicago settlement house, Chicago Commons.

In the first beginning we always came in to the club and made two circles in the room. One circle was for those ladies who could talk English and the other was for the ladies who talked German. Mrs. Reuter talked German to the German ladies and Miss Gray talked English to the other ladies. But I guess they both did the same preaching. They used to tell us that it's not nice to drink the beer, and we must not let the baby do this and this. Me, I was the only Italian woman—where were they going to put me? I couldn't talk German, I went in the English Circle. So after we had about an hour or an hour and a half of preaching, they would pull up the circle and we'd play the games together. All together we'd play the games—the Norwegian, the German, the English and me. Then we'd have some cake and coffee and the goodnight song. . . .

Pretty soon they started the classes to teach us poor people to talk and write in English. The talk of the people in the settlement house was different entirely than what I used to hear. I used to love the American people, and I was listening and listening how they talked. That's how I learned to talk such good English. Oh, I was glad when I learned enough English to go by the priest in the Irish church and confess myself and make the priest understand what was the sin! But I never learned to do the writing in English. I all the time used to come to that class so tired and so sleepy after scrubbing and washing the whole day—I went to sleep when they starting the writing. . . .

I have to tell about another good thing the settlement house did for me. That winter my [baby] Leo died we were still living in that little wooden house in the alley. All my walls were thick with frosting from the cold, and I got bronchitis on the lungs, with blood coming up. So one of those good ladies from the Commons, she arranged and sent me to a kind of home in the country where people go to get well. They had the nice nurses in that place and they cured me up good. I had a good time there, too.

Source: Marie Hall Ets, *Rosa: The Life of an Italian Immigrant* (1970).

kindergartens, adult education classes, health programs, and unemployment bureaus. By 1910, hundreds of thousands of working people were using more than four hundred settlement houses nationwide.

For a new generation of college-educated women searching for suitable work, settlement houses offered homes and occupations. Living and working in immigrant neighborhoods, settlement workers had a close-up view of the intense emotional bonds and self-sacrifice that sustained the immigrant urban working class. But most middle-class progressives viewed immigrant customs with incomprehension or disdain, and even the most sensitive settlement workers saw their mission as "uplifting" working-class culture. Lillian Wald, founder of New York's Henry Street Settlement, defended her neighbors fiercely against charges that they were "degraded," encouraged them to form trade unions, and mediated disputes between immigrant women and their Americanized daughters. But she also staged "coming-out" parties for them, modeled on the debutante balls of the elite. In spite of their good intentions, settlement workers and other middle-class progressives often found themselves taking stands against workers' preferences on certain issues. One was the movement to impose a total ban on alcohol. Middle-class progressives tended to view saloons and drinking with horror, whereas most male immigrant workers saw the saloon as a central social and cultural institution.

Settlement Worker and Immigrants. This photograph documenting the activities of a settlement-house worker captures the complicated relationship between reformers and the people they "served." The reformers' altruism was offset by their belief in the superiority of middle-class mores, which they imposed on immigrants to get them to relinquish "un-American" customs.

Source: People's Institute Papers—General Research Division, New York Public Library, Astor, Lenox and Tilden Foundations.

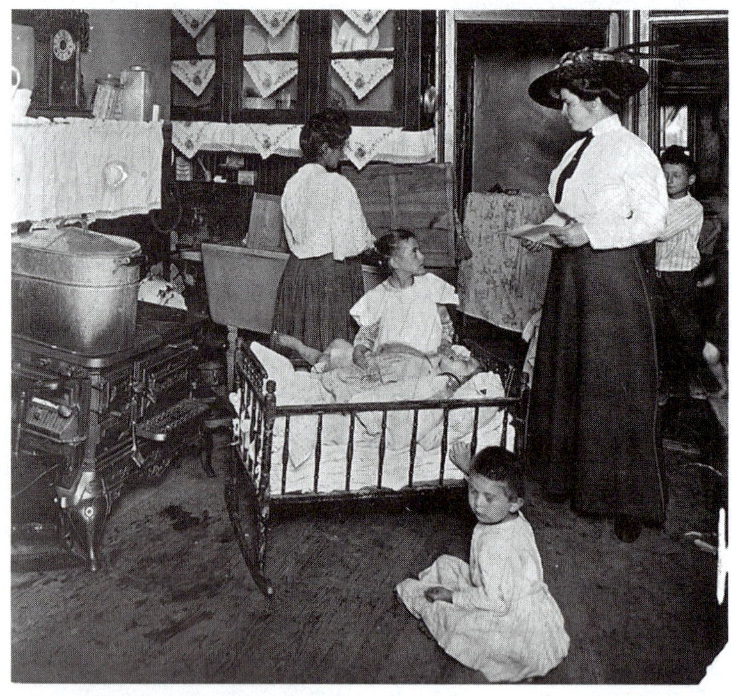

Settlement houses trained not only immigrants but an entire generation of reformers. Many were unmarried, college-educated women unwilling to restrict their lives to maintaining a Victorian home. Typically, they spent a few years helping immigrants in the urban slums before moving into better neighborhoods and wider political arenas and campaigning for social justice, improved public health and urban sanitation, and labor reform. Influenced by their experiences in the settlement houses and movements for women's rights, these women became "spearheads of reform" in a

"For Why Must I Tell You All My Business?"

Some immigrants found reformers to be interfering and insensitive. This excerpt from "The Free Vacation House," a short story written by Jewish immigrant Anna Yezierska, illustrates this unpleasant aspect of the encounter between immigrants and reformers.

How came it that I went to the free vacation house was like this:

One day the visiting teacher from the school nursery comes to find out why don't I get the children ready for school in time; for why are they so often late.

I let out on her my whole bitter heart. I told her my head was on wheels from worrying. . . .

"My dear woman," she says, "you are about to have a nervous breakdown. You need to get away to the country for a rest and vacation. . . . "

Later, in a few days, I just finished up with Masha and Mendel and Frieda and Sonya to send them to school, and I was getting Aby ready for kindergarten, when I hear a knock on the door, and a lady comes in. She had a white starched dress like a nurse and carried a black satchel in her hand.

"I am from the Social Betterment Society," she tells me. "You want to go to the country?"

Before I could say something, she goes over to the baby and pulls out the rubber nipple from her mouth, and to me she says, "You must not get the child used to sucking this; it is very unsanitary."

"Gott im Himmel!" I beg the lady. "Please don't begin with that child, or she'll holler my head off. She must have the nipple. I'm too nervous to hear her scream like that."

When I put the nipple back again in the baby's mouth, the lady takes herself a seat, and then takes out a big black book from her satchel. Then she begins to question me. What is my first name? How old I am? From where come I? How long I'm already in this country? Do I keep any boarders? What is my husband's first name? How old is he? How long he is in this country? By what trade he works? How much wages he gets for a week? How much money do I spend out for rent? How old are the children, and everything about them.

"My goodness!" I cry out. "For why is it necessary all this to know? For why must I tell you all my business? What difference does it make already if I keep boarders, or I don't keep boarders? If Masha had the whooping-cough or Sonya had the measles? Or whether I spent out for my rent ten dollars or twenty? Or whether I come from Schnipshnock or Kovner Gubernie?"

"We must make a record of all the applicants, and investigate each case," she tells me. "There are so many who apply to the charities, we can help only those who are most worthy."

"Charities!" I scream out. "Ain't the charities those who help the beggars out? I ain't no beggar. I'm not asking for no charity. My husband, he works. . . . "

"If your application is approved, you will be notified," she says to me, and out she goes.

Source: Anzia Yezeirska, "The Free Vacation House," *Hungry Hearts* (1920).

variety of movements, many of them steering middle-class women's clubs toward social and political issues. Although their work was initially humanitarian and nonpolitical, settlement-house workers and their allies ultimately helped transform U.S. politics and government.

Women working in settlement houses joined forces, for example, with public health reformers to campaign for better sanitation. The Hull House

Woman's Club documented more than a thousand violations of Chicago's sanitary ordinances, and Jane Addams became the garbage inspector for her ward. She and her colleagues were among the many women activists who flew the banner of "municipal housekeeping." Describing clean cities as extensions of clean houses, they lobbied municipal officials and volunteered to inspect the work of city contractors charged with picking up the garbage. A common interest in these issues united black and white women's groups, at least temporarily.

"End of an Era." Around 1900, a photographer captured the unwholesome combination of children's play, open street sewers, and a dead horse. Such scenes prompted reformers to campaign for better sanitation in U.S. cities.

Source: Library of Congress.

Sanitary reformers in government worked closely with activists concerned about public health, personal cleanliness, and civic beauty. As cities increased in population and density, the street-cleaning problem alone became cause for alarm. Over three million horses lived in U.S. cities at the turn of the century. Milwaukee's horses produced 133 tons of manure every day. City streets everywhere were littered with dead animals. Garbage and sewage disposal was an equally staggering problem. Reformers viewed piles of trash as both a menace to health and an eyesore. But landowners and merchants viewed efforts at reform as an infringement of their property rights and a threat of higher property taxes for sanitary improvements. To bridge this impasse, sanitary reform in many cities became part of a more general attack on the inadequacies of municipal government and the unchallenged power of the wealthy.

Women's Political Culture

Women's activism was central to the development of progressivism. Decades before the formation of the Progressive party in 1912, progressive causes and organizations were identified with women leaders. Throughout the nineteenth century, women reformers had challenged the idea of separate spheres for men and women. Shut out of party and electoral politics, women had created organizations and movements that transferred their authority from the home to the rest of the world. They sought legislative action on a number of fronts—education, child care, health, public morality, and social welfare—and they did so through private charities, churches, and volunteer groups.

"Heavy, Heavy, Hangs o'er Thy Head." A 1911 antisuffrage cartoon published in a satirical weekly (and, unusually, drawn by a woman) presented woman suffrage—and its female proponents—as a threat to conventional family roles.

Source: Laura Foster, *Life,* September 28, 1911—General Research Division, New York Public Library, Astor, Lenox and Tilden Foundations.

What was new at the end of the nineteenth century was the scale of women's activism and the ability of women's organizations to forge alliances among women of different classes and with powerful men interested in reform. Asserting a role that did not depend on the right to vote, women activists represented themselves as the embodiment of civic virtue. New types of women leaders—some with college and graduate school training in the analysis of social problems, some with experience in settlement work, some with backgrounds as activists in labor, suffrage, and temperance struggles—concluded that only the power of government could solve deep-rooted social problems. Undertaking new strategies and alliances based on this understanding, they formed highly organized groups with constitutions, officers, and bylaws, and they called upon well-organized local activists in the temperance and woman suffrage movements. Both movements blossomed during the Progressive Era, eventually producing the Eighteenth Amendment (Prohibition, 1919) and the Nineteenth Amendment (woman's suffrage, 1920).

A black women's political culture paralleled, and occasionally intersected with, many white women's movements, particularly the Woman's Christian Temperance Union (WCTU), the largest women's organization of the era. As Jim Crow restricted the political activity of black men, the women of the small but growing black middle class in the South had come to see themselves as leaders of their race and sex. Some supported themselves, primarily as teachers; others could afford to do volunteer work. Many of these women activists came from well-off families, but others, like Julia Sadgwar, a North Carolina teacher and activist, had struggled to rise from poverty.

Black women usually moved into community improvement from church organizations. Blending their religious values with activism legitimized their public role: they were working for what they called the "uplift" of their race. Like so many white women, they claimed a distinctly female moral authority. They organized in their communities and went downtown to interact with white officials and bureaucrats. They formed mothers' clubs, built playgrounds, and lobbied for better sanitation. And they campaigned for temperance. In these activities they adopted white women's political styles, but unlike their white counterparts, black women had to build private institutions—schools, community centers, homes for the aged—to provide services their communities were denied because of race.

Black women activists sometimes prodded white women to recognize their common class and gender across racial lines. Journalist and activist Ida B. Wells-Barnett brought her antilynching campaign to many white groups, including the WCTU, and worked with Jane Addams to block the segregation of Chicago public schools. But relationships between black and white women's organizations were sometimes strained or nonexistent. They were weakened especially by white women whose idea of their own political role was limited to influencing men. They believed that, since black men could not vote, black women were politically weak because they would be unable to influence the votes of their fathers, brothers, husbands, and sons. The national WCTU condemned lynching at its 1893 convention but assigned African-American delegates to a separate banquet table. The segregated delegates left the hall in protest before "their sisters had enough good sense and Christianity," reported a black woman teacher in a religious journal, "to call them back and treat them like sisters." But at least some of the time women created coalitions that transcended race, class, and ethnicity. And, although not always radical, women's political culture was inherently dedicated to changing the prevailing order.

Some women activists lived their private lives as well as their public ones in communities of women. In women's colleges, settlement houses, and reform organizations, a growing number of women began to live together as lifelong partners, passionately committed and devoted to each other. Mary Dreier of the Women's Trade Union League shared a home with Progressive

In Black and White: Eighty Years of Lynching This graph illustrates the nearly five thousand deaths by lynching (broken down by race) that were officially recorded in the United States between 1882 and 1965. Lynchings of African Americans were at their worst in the 1890s, but the annual numbers remained high in the early twentieth century.

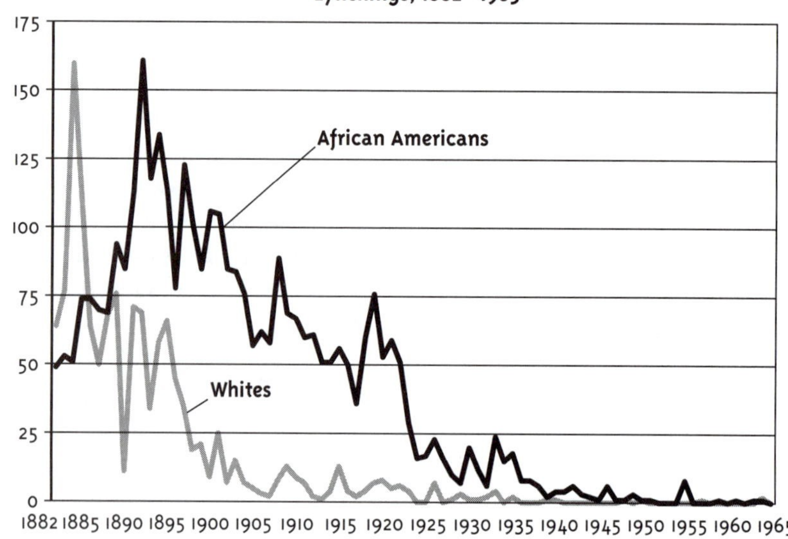

party activist Frances Kellor. Countless others forged ties with other women out of the public eye. Accepted as couples within reform circles, and moving among networks of women with similar commitments, they lived and worked independent of men. Outside those circles, however, such relationships were considered deviant and "unnatural"; career women and political activists who did not marry were even branded an "intermediate sex."

Woman Suffrage

Women had been campaigning for the right to vote since the middle of the nineteenth century. In 1869, women activists had split into two rival groups, based on differing opinions on the priority that should be given to black male suffrage. The National Woman Suffrage Association, led by Elizabeth Cady Stanton and Susan B. Anthony, opposed the male-only Fifteenth Amendment; the American Woman Suffrage Association, led by Lucy Stone, regarded black male suffrage as a step in the right direction. The development of the broader women's political culture motivated the two factions to unite in 1890, forming a revitalized National American Woman Suffrage Association (NAWSA).

The ultimate strength of the suffrage movement was not in NAWSA, however, but at the local level. Three-quarters of the states had to ratify a constitutional amendment, which meant that suffragists had to win the vote state by state. Victories came first in the West. By 1914 women could vote in state, local, and school board elections in ten states west of the Mississippi (including Utah and Wyoming), in the territory of Alaska, and in Illinois. The woman suffrage movement in the West had skilled and articulate leaders, including the editors of women's rights papers in Colorado and Oregon, and Jeannette Rankin in Montana, who would become the first woman elected to Congress. Coalitions between middle-class suffragists and laboring people could be sustained more easily in the West than in the East, where opponents of woman suffrage exploited the divisions between Catholic immigrants and native-born Protestants over issues like drinking and temperance. The coalition that won woman suffrage in Colorado in 1893 mobilized women's clubs, labor union women, and the WCTU to work with male Populists and organized labor. Oregon's Abigail Scott Duniway addressed her women's rights paper to women farmers and working-class women; she called for divorce reform, women's education, and equal responsibility for housework and child care.

Working-class women saw the vote as only one element in the larger working-class struggle. As one woman wrote to a labor newspaper, "If

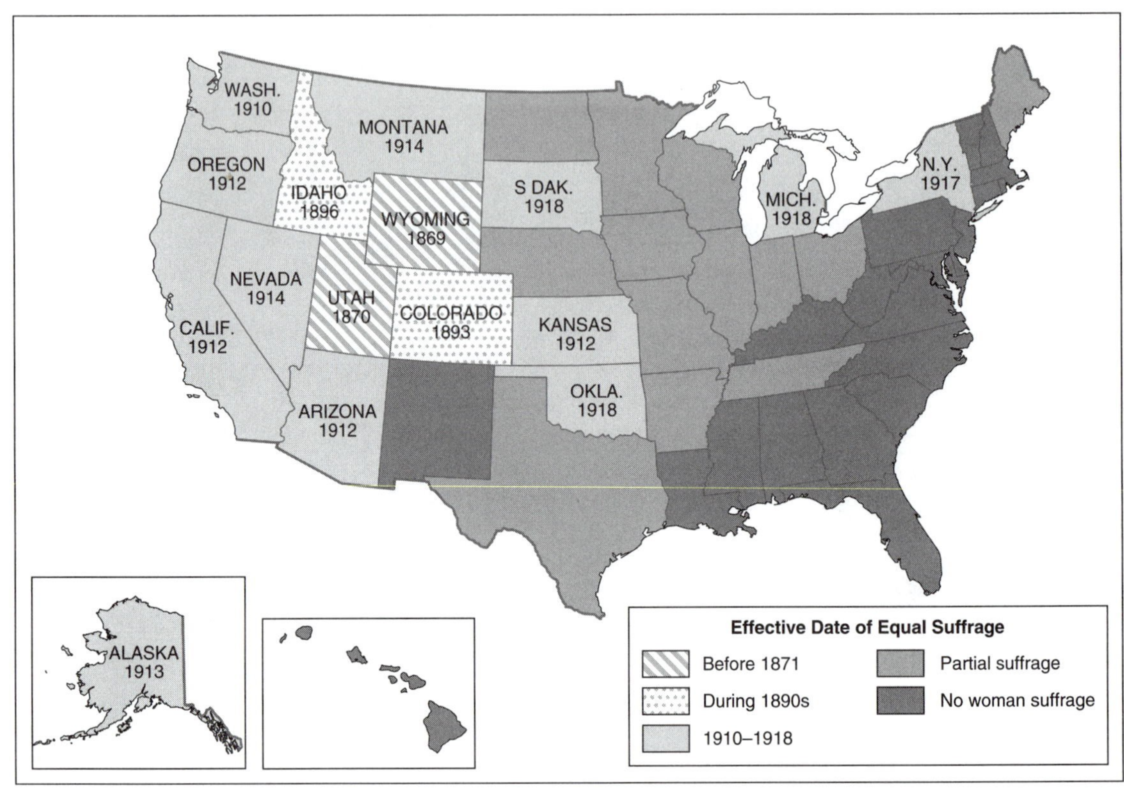

Where Women Could Vote, 1869–1918 This map shows the extent of American women's voting rights (especially in the West) in the years prior to the passage of the constitutional amendment granting woman suffrage in 1920.

women have the right of suffrage it will double the number of voices in the hands of the working people." After women reformers rallied to support striking female shirtwaist makers in 1909, young women from the sweatshops began marching in suffrage parades. Settlement-house workers and members of the Women's Trade Union League infused the suffrage movement with their commitment to social justice and the labor movement with their feminism. They forged alliances with working women and broadened the base of the suffrage movement.

But not all suffragists took a broad view. Some, in fact, mobilized conservative arguments that enfranchising women would improve the "quality" of the electorate by increasing the percentage of voters who were white and native born. They abandoned earlier demands for suffrage based on "justice" or "equal rights" and instead argued that women voters would bring special "female" qualities to the political process and would defend traditional family life in a time of stress and change.

Opposed to the Vote. A 1915 cartoon wryly commented on standard antisuffrage positions; the housewife is explaining to the door-to-door canvasser that her husband "ain't for wimmin votin'. He says he can take care of me good enough—besides the polls is too rough for ladies."

Source: Anna Goldthwaite, *Woman Voter*, May 1915—Sophia Smith Collection, Smith College.

Nevertheless, by the 1910s, woman suffrage became a mass movement, embracing wealthy socialites and garment workers, local black and white women's clubs, left-wing and conservative women, and increasing numbers of men. As the movement grew, it shifted tactics. Local suffrage organizations with large working-class memberships held open-air meetings and massive parades—organizing techniques that had long been used by socialists and labor groups in both Europe and the United States.

But as support for the movement grew, so did resistance—from liquor interests, machine politicians, the Catholic Church, and some business groups who were concerned that women voters would support other progressive reforms. The battle over a constitutional amendment enfranchising women grew heated during the early 1910s but then stalled, as referenda on woman suffrage were defeated in Pennsylvania, Massachusetts, and New York.

Factory Reform and the Conditions of Labor

The women of the settlement houses spearheaded the successful drive to improve wages and working conditions in factories and to outlaw child labor. Hull House resident Florence Kelley led a coalition that in 1893 achieved passage of an Illinois law providing for state investigation of factory conditions. As the state's first chief factory inspector, Kelley campaigned tirelessly for better working hours and conditions and against child labor, in Illinois and elsewhere. Women reformers worked closely with labor activists as they battled for protective legislation that would regulate the hours and conditions of labor for women and children. Many argued that such laws would establish precedents for regulating working conditions for men as well. Progressive politicians, such as Wisconsin's governor Robert La Follette, broadened their concerns to include women's and labor issues, realizing that they would need working people's support to prevail against political machines.

In 1908, the U.S. Supreme Court broke with previous legal doctrine and set a precedent for certain kinds of protective legislation. The Court's decision in *Muller v. Oregon* upheld an Oregon law limiting women's work in certain kinds of businesses (including the Portland laundry involved in the case) to ten hours a day. *Muller* overturned a 1905 decision, *Lochner v. New York,* in which the Court had refused to uphold a state law limiting the workday of bakers to ten hours. At the time of the *Lochner* decision, some progressives had concluded that if they could not win limitations on hours for all workers, they might be able to make a case in defense of limits for women. Progressive lawyer Louis Brandeis argued the *Muller* case, basing his brief on research by Kelley and her National Consumers' League (NCL) colleague Josephine Goldmark. Brandeis's case for limitations was based on the arguments that the "two sexes differ . . . in the amount of physical strength [and] in the capacity for long continued labor" and that long hours were detrimental to the health, safety, and morals of employed women. In upholding the Oregon law, the Court observed that women would always depend on men for "protection." This double-edged decision benefited working women but reinforced male domination in its underlying logic. Nevertheless, unlike previous legal doctrine, the decision set limits on employers' control over the terms of workers' employment. *Muller* was also the first time the Court had sanctioned "sociological jurisprudence": an argument based as much on sociological evidence—such as the reports of factory inspectors—as on abstract legal reasoning.

The state's victory in *Muller* greatly increased the legislative pace, at least in the North and the West. In 1912 alone, thirty-eight states passed child-labor laws and twenty-eight set maximum hours for women workers. By 1915, workers' compensation laws were on the books in thirty-five states. Twenty-five states had passed legislation limiting the working hours of some categories of male workers. Legislators in southern states resisted such reforms. Child labor legislation was especially difficult to pass in parts of the South where textile mills were coming to dominate the economic landscape. More than one-quarter of the employees of southern cotton mills were children, half of them below age twelve. These children earned less than older workers, but their wages helped support the family in homes where parents took home too little to pay the bills.

In 1900, more than a quarter of a million children under age fifteen were working in mines, mills, and factories. Others worked the streets: boys (and a few girls) as young as ten sold newspapers, polished shoes, and scavenged for rags and scraps of metal. The Knights of Labor had advocated the abolition of child labor, but the progressives broadened the coalition of reformers agitating on behalf of children's welfare. Led by professional social workers and educators, activists promoted the building of playgrounds and compulsory school attendance. Settlement house

Breaker Boys in Coal Chute, South Pittston, Pennsylvania, January 1911. Lewis Hine took hundreds of pictures as staff photographer for the National Child Labor Committee from 1908 to 1918. Hine traveled across the country, photographing children in textile mills, canneries, glass and shoe factories, mines, and fields to reveal the extent of child labor and the need for enforcement of reform laws. "No anonymous or signed denials can contradict proof given with photographic fidelity," Hine wrote. "These pictures speak for themselves, and prove that the law is being violated."

Source: Lewis Hine, January 1911—International Museum of Photography at George Eastman House, Rochester, New York.

founder Lillian D. Wald had proposed the creation of a federal Children's Bureau to safeguard children's welfare. In 1912 Julia Lathrop, an Illinois reformer who had lived at Hull House, became the head of the new agency. Under Lathrop's direction, the bureau investigated such topics as infant mortality, juvenile delinquency, and mothers' pensions—an important forerunner of social welfare provisions that emerged fully only during the New Deal years in the 1930s.

Despite the creation of the federal Children's Bureau, the child-labor movement's work was far from finished. At the forefront of the movement was the National Child Labor Committee, one of a number of organizations that pioneered nonprofit advocacy by publicizing its cause through pamphlets, mass mailings, and lobbying. The committee sponsored investigations by experts, and it sent its staff photographer Lewis Hine around the country to photograph children working in cotton mills, mines, and canneries, and on the streets as newsboys and scavengers. Congress passed federal laws regulating child labor in 1916 and 1918, but a conservative Supreme Court declared them unconstitutional. The movement had greater success at the state level. By 1920, most states forbade the employment of children under fourteen, set an eight-hour day for workers under sixteen, and mandated compulsory education.

But simply having laws on the books did not solve fundamental problems. Pauline Newman, a labor activist who had worked as a child in a New York City garment factory, remembered the monotony of cutting threads from 7:30 in the morning until 9:00 at night. "Well, of course, there were [child labor] laws on the books," she recalled, "but no one bothered to enforce them. The employers were always tipped off if there was going to be an inspection. 'Quick,' they'd say, 'into the boxes!' And we children would climb into the big boxes the finished shirts were stored in. Then some shirts were piled on top of us, and when the inspector came—no children. The factory always got an okay from the inspector, and I suppose someone at City Hall got a little something, too."

The Garment Industry and Working Women's Activism

The Triangle Shirtwaist fire that galvanized activists in 1911 occurred in an industry known for its labor militancy. Concentrated in New York City, the ready-made clothing industry was relatively new. For most of the nineteenth century, women had made their own clothing and their children's clothing at home, with or without the help of hired seamstresses, and men with money had used tailors. Consequently, workingmen's clothing dominated the small nineteenth-century ready-made industry. Much of that had changed by the end of the century, as new sewing and cutting machines increased workers' productivity and an organizational innovation—the sweatshop system—developed. Sweatshops employed a handful of workers, almost all of whom were immigrant Jewish or Italian women. They were supervised by contractors of their own nationality, mostly men, who got materials on credit from manufacturers, bought sewing machines on the installment plan, and rented lofts or tenement apartments for factories.

Thousands of small, marginal firms competed with a few large manufacturers. Shops were hot in summer, cold in winter; workers were charged for needles, thread, and electricity. Workers were paid by the piece rather than by the hour, and at low piecework rates, they pushed themselves hard and worked long days to make a living. Many workers participated in short, spontaneous strikes, but lasting labor organizations were rare.

In the fall of 1909 the industry exploded. Wage cuts and other grievances sparked a wave of small walkouts by workers who produced shirtwaists, the blouses urban working- and middle-class women wore. The workers were mostly young women whose earnings not only helped to support their families but also gave them a small measure of independence. In November, they turned out for a huge meeting at New York City's Cooper Union auditorium. The most dramatic and inspiring speaker that night was Clara Lemlich, a fifteen-year-old Ukrainian-born activist who called for a general strike

On the Picket Line. This photograph captures the spirit of the young immigrant women shirtwaist workers who resisted strikebreaker violence and police intimidation during the 1909 Uprising of the Twenty Thousand.

Source: Library of Congress.

"A Pint of Trouble for the Bosses . . ."

The 1909 shirtwaist workers' strike saw young immigrant women step to the forefront of the labor struggle. Fifteen-year-old shirtwaist worker Clara Lemlich, a Jewish immigrant from Russia, emerged as a key organizer and speaker. A reporter from the *New York Sun* witnessed this attack by anti-union thugs on Lemlich and other strikers.

The girls, headed by teen-age Clara Lemlich, described by union organizers as "a pint of trouble for the bosses," began singing Italian and Russian working-class songs as they paced in twos before the factory door. Of a sudden, around the corner came a dozen tough-looking customers, for whom the union label gorilla seemed well-chosen.

"Stand fast, girls," called Clara, and then the thugs rushed the line, knocking Clara to her knees, striking at the pickets, opening the way for a group of frightened scabs to slip through the broken line. Fancy ladies from the Allen Street red-light district climbed out of cabs to cheer on the gorillas. There was a confused melee of scratching, screaming girls and fist-swinging men and then a patrol wagon arrived. The thugs ran off as the cops pushed Clara and two other badly beaten girls into the wagon.

I followed the rest of the retreating pickets to the union hall, a few blocks away. There a relief station had been set up where one bottle of milk and a loaf of bread were given to strikers with small children in their families. There for the first time in my comfortably sheltered, Upper West Side life, I saw real hunger on the faces of my fellow Americans in the richest city in the world.

Source: McAlister Coleman, "All of Which I Saw," *The Progressive* (May 1950).

against all the companies in the industry. Within two days, between twenty thousand and thirty thousand workers had walked off their jobs. A month later, the strike—which became known as The Uprising of the Twenty Thousand—spread to Philadelphia.

The strikers appealed to the Women's Trade Union League (WTUL) for help in countering police harassment. Founded in 1903, the WTUL was a coalition of women—some from the working class, some professionals like Lillian Wald and Jane Addams, and some extremely wealthy women—devoted to bringing women into trade unions as a means of empowerment. League members believed that working women were more oppressed as workers than as women, but that women of all classes shared important "bonds of womanhood." The elite WTUL members allied with their working colleagues. They provided funds for strikers, spoke to the press, and arranged for volunteer lawyers, but they also did their share of picket duty and even went to jail. Not everyone trusted them or their financial support. "I've almost come to the conclusion," wrote socialist Theresa Malkiel in a fictionalized account of the strike, "that the gulf between us girls and these rich ladies is too deep to be smoothed over by a few paltry dollars." Still, despite disputes between women of different classes, the women shared a commitment to making the WTUL a genuine arena for working-class feminism.

Off to Jail. A garment worker was arrested by the Chicago police during a 1910 strike in which workers protested a cut in their piece rate. Some forty-thousand workers throughout the clothing industry eventually walked off the job.

Source: Chicago Historical Society [DN-56132].

The industrywide strikes of garment workers during 1909 and 1910 brought tens of thousands of women into the International Ladies' Garment Workers Union (ILGWU), which had been established a decade earlier. Most of these new members were Jewish, but some were from other ethnic groups. Both in Philadelphia and New York, African-American women joined the union and the strike. The conflict dragged on until February 1910, when the ILGWU reached an arbitrated settlement with manufacturers. Employers refused to recognize the union, but they reduced hours, improved working conditions, and agreed to arbitrate future disputes through a board of community and religious leaders.

Within months of the February victory, two other groups of garment workers walked out. At Hart, Schaffner, and Marx, a huge Chicago manufacturer of men's clothing, fourteen young women struck over a cut in their piece rate. They picketed alone for three weeks before coworkers took them seriously, but eventually forty thousand workers throughout the city's clothing industry joined them. That number was exceeded in New York when sixty thousand cloakmakers, mostly male, began a general strike that ended with an agreement devised by Louis Brandeis, acting on behalf of Boston department store owner A. Lincoln Filene. Like some other large garment manufacturers and buyers, Filene realized that stabilizing wages and working conditions might reduce cutthroat competition and ensure more predictable prices and supplies. By the eve of World War I, unions had made deep inroads into the clothing, fur, and millinery industries. Nearly four hundred thousand clothing workers became union members between 1909 and 1913.

But as the Triangle fire demonstrated, these partial settlements with garment industry employers did not provide for adequate fire escapes and open doors. By naming American Federation of Labor (AFL) president Samuel Gompers and New York Consumers' League representative Frances Perkins to the Factory Commission established after the disaster, politicians acknowledged well-established national reform forces. Crucial to the commission's success were two politicians allied with the Democratic political machine known as Tammany Hall, Robert Wagner and Alfred E. Smith, who served as its chairman and vice chairman. Over the course of four years, hundreds of workers testified to the commission about unsafe working conditions. To improve wages and protect the health and safety of New York workers, the commission sponsored fifty-six laws, many of which were passed by Democrats eager not only to wrap themselves in the banner of reform but also to undercut the growing influence of socialists among working-class constituents.

Democrats felt no pressure to enact reforms to maintain working-class allegiance in the South, however, where a weak trade union movement and virulent racism divided and undermined reform efforts. Two weeks after the Triangle fire, a violent explosion ripped through the Banner coal mine outside Birmingham, Alabama, killing 128 convict miners, mostly African Americans jailed for minor offenses. Although evidence supplied by the federal Bureau of Mines indicated high levels of dangerous methane gas, a state investigating commission declared that the miners' ineptitude had caused the explosion. Middle-class reformers and Alabama's trade union movement called for abolition of the policy of leasing out convicts as laborers, but they were a poor match for the strong coalition of Democratic state legislators and big businessmen who opposed them. Both groups continued to receive substantial profits from convict labor until 1928, when Alabama finally abolished the system.

Socialists, Marxists, and Anarchists

Many garment union activists belonged to or sympathized with the Socialist party, whose best-known spokesperson was the labor leader Eugene V. Debs. "I am for Socialism," he wrote, "because I am for humanity. We have been cursed with the reign of gold long enough. Money constitutes no proper basis of civilization." American socialism developed from a variety of movements, some home-grown and others imported from abroad. For much of the nineteenth century, religious and secular utopian communities exemplified the possibilities of egalitarian living. Germans who immigrated after the failed European revolutions of 1848 brought with them the radical ideas of Karl Marx, whose writings about the historical inevitability of class struggle had stimulated socialist organizing in industrialized countries everywhere. Although marxism did not dominate

American socialist thought, immigrants who had been influenced by Marx and the international socialist movement had had a major impact on the national railroad strike of 1877 and the eight-hour movement.

The first American socialist political party, the Socialist Labor party, was formed in 1877, with Daniel De Leon at its head. It and a number of other socialist groups suffered from poor organization and infighting, but the ideal of socialism spread nevertheless. Edward Bellamy's utopian novel *Looking Backward* (1888), for example, sparked considerable interest in the idea of a classless society brought about without bloodshed. Thousands of Americans joined clubs promoting Bellamy's ideas; others devoted their lives to socialist ideals.

Debs joined the Socialist Labor party in 1897 and was active in the merger of several groups that combined to create the Socialist party in 1901. Within seven years, the party had 41,000 dues-paying members in more than three thousand local branches. Running for president on the Socialist ticket in 1908, Debs received more than 400,000 votes. Urban workers formed the core of the party's strength. At first it was popular mostly with skilled workers, including many German immigrants, but by 1909 it was winning more and more support from newer immigrants from eastern and southern Europe. The party also enjoyed substantial rural backing, especially in the Southwest, where many farmers were losing ownership of their land. Middle-class women reformers and Christian socialists added to the mixture of groups and traditions that made the Socialist party a volatile and exciting organization. Its influence went well beyond its membership because its electoral and legislative successes helped to radicalize the debates about progressive reform. At the time of the presidential election of 1912, for example, party membership would peak at 118,000, but Debs, the Socialist candidate, would receive 900,000 votes.

Socialists had considerable influence in many unions, including those of the machinists, mineworkers, and garment workers. Many attacked the AFL for neglecting unskilled workers, arguing that organizing unions only of skilled workers along narrow craft lines instead of more broadly by industry, had turned the federation into the "American Separation of Labor." Critical of AFL policies, they denounced Samuel Gompers for cooperating with businessmen.

Within the labor movement and in radical organizations, socialists associated with—and sometimes opposed—representatives of another radical force, the anarchists. Anarchists believed that the ideal society must be achieved without increasing the power of governments, which were inevitably oppressive. Resistance to political organizations sometimes inspired solitary acts of violence directed against government, big business, and their leaders. The best known anarchist in the United States was Emma Goldman. After emigrating from Russia in 1885 at age sixteen to avoid an arranged marriage, she worked in the garment industry in

Happy Hooligan. Beginning in 1900, Frederick Opper's comic strip featuring the hapless tramp was a major attraction of William Randolph Hearst's *New York Journal.* Unlike Riebe's Mr. Block (see page 230), Happy Hooligan was the undeserving victim of the abuses and insanities of American society—including, in this strip, popular hysteria about anarchists and police penchant for summary justice. **Source:** Fred Opper—Hyperion Press, Inc., Westport, Connecticut.

Rochester, New York. A charismatic speaker, Goldman lectured on topics ranging from anarchism and the modern theater to birth control and free love, asserting that women had the right to decide not to bear children and to enter into spiritual and sexual unions outside of marriage.

Militant Communities

Although most working people were neither anarchists nor socialists, radical ideas about the need for fundamental changes had substantial influence in working-class communities in the early twentieth century. The clearest indication of this sentiment was the creation of a new labor organization, the Industrial Workers of the World—the IWW, or Wobblies, as they were popularly known. "An injury to one is an injury to all," the IWW declared; "the working class and the employing class have nothing in common."

The IWW sought to abolish the wage system and to create a society in which workers would own and control the factories, mines, and railroads where they labored. IWW leaders believed that the vehicle for revolutionary change should be a union not a political party. Organizing all workers into one militant union, they asserted, would lead to a massive general strike. Capitalism would be overthrown, and the people would run industry in a decentralized, democratic fashion.

Dissident socialists, including Eugene V. Debs, together with other radicals and industrial unionists organized the IWW in 1905. Leadership came, in part, from the Western Federation of Miners (WFM), which represented thirty thousand hard-rock miners in the Rocky Mountains.

Mr. Block. Ernest Riebe's comic strip about a willfully ignorant and gullible worker appeared in the IWW's *Industrial Worker.* The strip conveyed the organization's attitude toward workers who lacked class-consciousness or subscribed to the AFL's conservative craft unionism, inspiring IWW songwriter Joe Hill's lyrics: *Oh, Mr. Block, you were born by mistake. / You take the cake. / You make me ache. / Tie a rock to your block and jump in the lake. / Kindly do that for Liberty's sake.* The adventures of the beleaguered Mr. Block, as indicated here, also took swipes at the reform wing of the Socialist party.

Source: Ernest Riebe—Charles H. Kerr Publishing Co., Chicago, Illinois.

During a decade of bitter strikes against some of the largest corporations in America, the WFM's leaders had come to reject capitalism and to embrace unions that spanned an entire industry (steelworkers or railroad workers) rather than a specific craft (carpenters or machinists). The federation's efforts to build alliances with workers in the East culminated in the founding convention of the IWW in Chicago. "Fellow workers," western miner Big Bill Haywood proclaimed, "this is the Continental Congress of the working class." The new movement, he declared, "shall have for its purpose the emancipation of the working class from the slave bondage of capitalism."

Spirited, colorful, and proud in the face of jail sentences and vigilante attacks, the IWW was the most egalitarian labor organization in American history. It was committed to organizing all workers—skilled and unskilled, men and women, black and white, Mexican, Chinese and Japanese. The Wobblies drew upon longstanding traditions: the Knights' belief in organizing across ethnic and racial lines; the shop-floor control enjoyed by skilled craftsmen; and the industrial unionism of coal miners and the American Railway Union.

At first, factionalism, government harassment, and an economic downturn frustrated the IWW. But in 1909 it won nationwide attention by leading a successful strike among unskilled immigrant steelworkers in McKees Rocks, Pennsylvania. In 1909 and 1910 the IWW also led a series of "free speech" fights in western cities, which served as hiring centers for jobs in forests, mines, and fields. But the union's reputation soared in 1912, when it led a massive textile strike in Lawrence, Massachusetts. A new Massachusetts state law requiring employers to cut workers' hours had backfired when employers retaliated by speeding up the looms to compensate for the lost time. The last straw for Lawrence's thirty thousand textile workers came when mill owners announced a pay cut. Half of the mills' labor force were young women between the ages of fourteen and eighteen, many of whom suffered from malnutrition and overwork. Two days after the pay cut announcement, more than twenty thousand workers of forty nationalities went on strike. "We want bread

"We Want Bread and Roses, Too." Shouting that slogan, strikers confronted national guardsmen during the Lawrence, Massachusetts, textile strike of 1912.

Source: Archives of Labor and Urban Affairs, Wayne State University, Detroit.

and roses, too" was the strikers' memorable slogan.

The IWW organized separate strike and relief committees for workers of different nationalities and translated speeches and literature into every language. Strikers threw up massive picket lines around the mills and paraded through the streets. Mill owners and government officials responded with a massive show of force, including a declaration of martial law and a ban on public meetings. With an entire town deprived of the workers' meager wages, hunger was widespread. Eventually, New York socialists, concerned about the effects of hunger on the strikers' children, organized to care for them. Margaret Sanger, a nurse who later became famous for promoting birth control, arrived in Lawrence to transport children out of the strife-torn town. "Out of the 119 children, only four had underwear on . . . their outerwear was almost in rags . . . their coats were simply torn to shreds," she later testified.

The departure of the children generated so much sympathy for the strikers that Lawrence authorities decreed that children would no longer be allowed to leave the city. Two days later, a group of Philadelphia socialists arrived to transport two hundred children. As a member of the Philadelphia Women's committee testified, "The police closed in on us with their clubs, beating right and left with no thought of the children who were in the most desperate danger of being trampled to death. The mothers and children were thus hurled in a mass and bodily dragged to a military truck, and even then clubbed, irrespective of the cries of the panic-stricken women and children." This was the turning point. Across the country, public opinion turned against the employers. In March, the mill owners agreed to a settlement providing raises and overtime pay to workers.

The Lawrence textile strike demonstrated that immigrant workers could unite to win a strike, but the victory did not open the way for widespread industrial organization. A year later, in 1913, the IWW met serious defeat in a silk workers' strike in Paterson, New Jersey, where thousands of immigrant women, men, and children had walked out of the mills. Over the course of seven months, IWW leaders again organized picket lines and called enthusiastic rallies, and again the authorities responded with repression, even arresting socialist Frederick Sumner Boyd for reading the free-speech clause of the New Jersey state constitution at a strike meeting. But Paterson employers, unlike their Lawrence counterparts, exploited divisions within the silk workers' ranks. The skilled, English-speaking workers and their craft unions, put off by the radicalism and anarchism of many of the Italian and Jewish workers, were slow to join the strike. The strike collapsed when the English-speaking mill workers agreed to return to work on a shop-by-shop basis, leaving the unskilled immigrants without support.

In mining communities in the Appalachian and Rocky mountains, the United Mine Workers of America (UMWA) overcame the cultural difficulties that defeated the strikers in Paterson. Although highly skilled, coal miners had no tradition of apprenticeship and therefore little control over who entered their trade. Thus recent immigrants or African Americans could find work as miners more easily than in other trades. Drawing on the legacy of interracial unionism inherited from the Knights of Labor and black UMWA activists, the UMWA extended itself to organize all who worked in and around the mines. By 1910, nearly one-third of all coal miners were unionized, compared with one-tenth of the broader U.S. labor force.

But the mine owners fought back fiercely. In late 1913, John D. Rockefeller's Colorado Fuel and Iron Company led other companies in an open-shop drive—an attempt to guarantee the right to work without union membership—that prompted more than ten thousand miners to strike. The battle was long and bitter. Despite the determination of the miners and their wives, who were active in the struggle, the owners refused to recognize the union. They evicted strikers from their company-owned homes and brought in deputies and the state militia to quell the protest. On Easter night in 1914, the troops attacked a strikers' tent camp in Ludlow. Firing machine guns and setting fire to the tents, they killed sixteen people, including twelve children.

In the wake of the Ludlow massacre, the UMWA issued a "call to arms." For ten days war raged between miners and the state

Class War in Colorado. John Sloan's April 1914 cover for *The Masses* was unusual: portraying the devastation and death wrought by the national guard and Rockefeller-hired private police on the miners' tent colony, Sloan nevertheless emphasized the strikers' continued resistance.

Source: John Sloan, *The Masses,* June 1914—Prints and Photographs Division, Library of Congress.

"It Was a Murder and Nothing Less"

The brutal massacre of strikers and their families at Ludlow, Colorado, stunned the nation and led to numerous investigations and reports. Below are two documents about the massacre. The first is an excerpt from a newspaper reporter's account that appeared in the *New York World.* The second is a portion of John D. Rockefeller's testimony before the Commission on Industrial Relations, set up by the U.S. government in 1914 to investigate labor conditions. Rockefeller was questioned by Commission chairman Frank Walsh, a noted reformer.

New York World

Then came the killing of Louis Tikas, the Greek leader of the strikers. We saw the militiamen parley outside the tent city, and a few minutes later, Tikas came out to meet them. We watched them talking. Suddenly an officer raised his rifle, gripping the barrel, and felled Tikas with the butt.

Tikas fell face downward. As he lay there we saw the militiamen fall back. Then they aimed their rifles and deliberately fired them into the unconscious man's body. It was the first murder I had ever seen, for it was a murder and nothing less. Then the miners ran about in the tent colony and women and children scuttled for safety in the [underground] pits which afterwards trapped them.

We watched from our rock shelter while the militia dragged up their machine guns and poured murderous fire into the arroyo from a height by Water Tank Hill above the Ludlow depot. Then came the firing of the tents. . . . The militiamen were thick about the northwest corner of the colony where the fire started and we could see distinctly from our lofty observation place what looked like a blazing torch waved in the midst of militia a few seconds before the general conflagration swept through the place.

Testimony of John D. Rockefeller

Chairman: And you are willing to go on and let these killings take place . . . rather than go out there and see if you might do something to settle those conditions?

Rockefeller: There is just one thing . . . which can be done, as things are at present, to settle this strike, and that is to unionize the camps; and our interest in labor is so profound . . . that interest demands that the camps shall be open [nonunion].

Chairman: And you will do that if it costs all your property and kills all your employees?

Rockefeller: It is a great principle.

Chairman: And you would do that rather than recognize the right of men to collective bargaining? Is that what I understand?

Rockefeller: No, sir. Rather than allow outside people to come in and interfere with employees who are thoroughly satisfied with their labor conditions—it was upon a similar principle that the War of the Revolution was carried on. It is a great national issue of the most vital kind.

Source: New York *World,* May 5, 1913; *Final Report and Testimony Submitted to Congress on Industrial Relations,* 64th Congress, 1st Session (1916).

militia, until federal troops finally disarmed the miners. IWW leader Bill Haywood concluded that the country was gripped by "an irreconcilable class struggle" between workers and capitalists. Most progressives would have avoided those terms, but many of them agreed that in Lawrence, Paterson, and Ludlow, the industrial system had generated a terrifying conflict that threatened the very stability and promise of American society.

Like the electoral challenge by the Socialist party, the militant agitation of the Wobblies and mine workers moved the terms of progressive debate to the left. Moderate reformers took up more radical ideas for two reasons. First, they were worried about the threat posed by socialists and Wobblies. They sought to counter the appeal of the radicals—and prevent the more fundamental changes those groups favored—by offering changes that responded, in part, to the radical critique. When the radicals publicized the inequities and degradations brought by industrial capitalism, progressives proposed ways that reform and regulation could make capitalism more humane while also preserving it.

The second reason moderate reformers incorporated some radical ideas is that they found them attractive. They agreed with the radicals about the threats posed by unregulated big business and great concentrations of wealth. They also adopted the radicals' view that only a strong national state could tame the giant national corporations—an idea that socialist activists had long argued, but that broke with deep-seated U.S. traditions of limiting the power of the federal government. Although the role of the state espoused by Democratic and Republican progressives was not as vast as that endorsed by the socialists, the moderate reformers did come to accept and endorse a new regulatory function for the federal government.

Local and State Reform Politics

Reformers on the local and state levels borrowed some ideas from radicals and socialists. Many reformers viewed the corporations providing municipal services—streetcars, water, gas, and electricity—as rapacious monopolies. The socialist idea of public ownership seemed an attractive alternative, and many urban reformers—even though they rejected the concept of public ownership of *all* corporate enterprises—endorsed public ownership of public utilities. The appeal of municipal socialist programs was reinforced by the Socialist party's success in providing clean and efficient government to cities like Milwaukee. In elections in 1910 and 1911, Socialist party candidates were elected to more than four hundred public offices, including twenty-eight mayors, in such communities as Butte, Montana; Schenectady, New York; and Reading, Pennsylvania. In most cases, however, these administrations lasted only one or two terms.

Although urban reformers were attracted to some socialist views and

The Boss. The standard reform perspective of the urban political machine was illustrated in *Collier's* in 1906. Graphically, the conception of the Boss had changed very little since Thomas Nast's Tweed Ring caricatures of the 1870s.

Source: Walter Appleton Clark, *Collier's,* November 10, 1906—Prints and Photographs Division, Library of Congress.

coalitions, the goals of the two groups differed substantially. Where socialists campaigned for social justice, most urban reformers worked for efficient and responsive government. Above all, they wanted to stamp out corruption and curb the power of machines and bosses, some of whom had working-class ties. On the East Coast and in the South, businessmen and other elites seeking more efficient and less costly government dominated local reform efforts. These municipal reformers aimed to destroy corrupt political machines, but they often saw working-class voters—especially immigrants and African Americans—not as allies but as antagonists. Consequently, they sought to strip them of their votes. In the urban East, reformers pushed social programs to "improve" immigrant behavior, and immigration reform to reduce the influx of "undesirable" newcomers.

The influence of businessmen and professionals was also evident in new governmental systems established in hundreds of small and middle-size cities, especially in the South. These city commission or city manager systems shifted power from popularly elected councilmen to professional administrators. Designed, as president John Patterson of the National Cash Register Company put it, to place municipal government "on a strict business basis," such systems took power away from working-class communities. One new form, the commissioner system, originated in Galveston, Texas, in the wake of a 1900 flood that killed six thousand people. When the local government proved incapable of handling the emergency, a group of businessmen proposed a new charter that gave authority to five commissioners who would serve as both the city council and the city administration. By 1917, more than five hundred cities had adopted the plan. Another system, first tried in Staunton, Virginia, in 1908, combined an elected city council with an appointed city manager, a professional executive. The council set broad policies, and the city manager administered them.

A more democratic type of reform had grown up in midwestern cities such as Milwaukee and St. Louis and in western ones such as San Francisco. In these areas, reformers' attacks on corrupt state and local governments had a strong antibusiness character, and reforms opened up the political system to the influence of working people. One of the

"Give the Property Owner a Fair Show"

Some reformers sought to eliminate from urban government the power and influence of what they thought of as the ignorant working masses. The first document comes from the elite Voters' League of Pittsburgh, which campaigned in 1911 for removing workingmen from local school boards, suggesting that "a man's occupation ought to give a strong indication of his qualifications for membership." In the second document, Rear Admiral F. E. Chadwick, a leader in the municipal reform movement in Newport, Rhode Island, argued for changing local government to ensure a larger voice for "property owners."

Voters' League of Pittsburgh

Employment as ordinary laborer and in the lowest class of mill work would naturally lead to the conclusion that such men did not have sufficient education or business training to act as school directors. . . . Objection might also be made to small shopkeepers, clerks, workmen at many trades, who by lack of educational advantages and business training, could not, no matter how honest, be expected to administer properly the affairs of an education system . . . where millions of dollars are spent each year.

Rear Admiral F. E. Chadwick

Our present system has excluded in large degree the representation of those who have the city's well-being most at heart. It has brought in municipalities . . . a government established by the least educated, the least interested class of citizens.

It stands to reason that a man paying $5,000 in taxes in a town is more interested in the well-being and development of his town than the man who pays no taxes. . . . It equally stands to reason that the man of the $5,000 tax should be assured a representation in the committee which lays the tax and spends the money which he contributes. . . . Shall we be truly democratic and give the property owner a fair show or shall we develop a tyranny of ignorance which shall crush him?

Source: Samuel P. Hays, "The Politics of Reform," in Blaine A. Bronell and Warren E. Stickle, eds., *Bosses and Reformers: Urban Politics in America, 1880–1920* (1973).

leaders of the more democratic reform movement was four-term Detroit mayor Hazen Pingree. First elected in 1889, Pingree increased corporate taxes and provided public services such as electricity and sewers. This program and his support of striking railroad workers won Pingree the backing of immigrants and trade unions. In 1896 he began to draw national attention when he organized a municipal streetcar company. Within a few years, campaigns for public ownership of urban utilities were triumphing throughout the nation.

In St. Louis in 1900, a reform movement blossomed during a strike against the local street railway monopoly, which charged high prices for inadequate services. This working-class action spurred reformers to undertake legal and political battles with the railway and its allies, bankers, corporate leaders, and machine politicians. St. Louis district attorney Joseph Folk then took the crusade against corruption to a new level in his campaign for governor in 1904. After working people helped sweep him to victory, Governor Folk successfully prosecuted monopolies like Standard Oil for overcharging Missouri consumers.

Folk, Pingree, Wisconsin progressive governor Robert La Follette, and others moved to strengthen their reform coalition by opening up the political process to their working-class allies. With the support of unions and some middle-class groups, they pushed for direct primaries, which shifted the power to choose candidates from party bosses to voters. They also established the initiative and the referendum, which put popular issues directly on the ballot, and they fought for the Seventeenth Amendment (1913), which provided for the direct popular election of U.S. senators (instead of by state legislators).

Progressivism and Participation

While some reformers worked to open up the political system to working people, others were instituting changes that would restrain the power and influence of marginal groups. Some of the most far-reaching measures were ballot reforms, which created barriers to voting and to third-party political movements. For example, after decades of promotion, reformers had succeeded in having the publicly printed "Australian ballot," which listed all the candidates, replace ballots issued by political parties for voters to carry to the polls. Although the new system discouraged corruption, it made voting more difficult for immigrants who could not read English. It also gave public officials the power to eliminate minor party candidates from the ballot.

"Antifusion" laws further diminished the effectiveness of electoral protests in the South. Throughout the late nineteenth century, disgruntled workers and farmers had organized their own parties and had later thrown their support to major party candidates who backed their demands. The "fusion" of the Populists and Democrats in 1896 was the most powerful example of this tactic. But by the turn of the century, numerous states had passed laws prohibiting two parties from supporting the same candidate, thus making it more difficult for third parties to wield power. In some instances, reformers changed electoral procedures specifically to check the growth of the Socialist party, which was achieving considerable success on the local level.

Literacy requirements offered a more direct method of limiting workers' political power. They were often applied unfairly to disfranchise African Americans and, in some places, poor whites. By 1920 all southern

Reductions in Southern Voter Turnout After Suffrage Restriction

State	Elections	Percentage Reduction: Overall Turnout	Percentage Reduction: Estimated White Turnout	Percentage Reduction: Estimated Negro Turnout
Alabama	1892–1896 Gov.[a]	19	15	24
Alabama	1900–1904 Pres.	38	19	96
Arkansas	1890–1894 Gov.	39	26	69
Florida	1888–1892 Gov.	61	31	83
Louisiana	1896–1900 Gov.	66	46	93
Mississippi	1888–1892 Pres.	57	34	69
So. Carolina	1892–1896 Pres.	13	17	51
Tennessee	1888–1892 Gov.	19	4	68
Texas	1902–1904 Gov.	32	29	36

[a]The notation means that the elections compared are the 1892 and 1896 governor's races.

Source: J. Morgan Kousser, *The Shaping of Southern Politics: Suffrage Restriction and the Establishment of the One-Party South* (1974).

Stamping Out the Vote: The Impact of Suffrage Restriction in the South Various forms of suffrage restriction imposed in the South at the turn of the century led to massive declines in voter turnouts among both white and black southerners. Between 1896 and 1900 in Louisiana, turnouts dropped by 46 percent for white voters and 93 percent for black voters.

states and nine states outside the South had adopted such laws. Literacy requirements were one factor in a dramatic decline in voter participation across the country. In an average 1870s election, 80 percent of those legally eligible had voted; by 1920, the figure had fallen to 60 percent in the northern states and less than 30 percent in the South. The decline in voting also reflected a broader erosion of popular politics—the intense partisanship and heated election campaigns—that had flourished in the nineteenth century. Once-vibrant party loyalties declined, and a new, less participatory style of party politics emerged.

The decline in formal voter participation was in part countered—and possibly generated—by the spread of nonelectoral forms of citizen participation. Large numbers of Americans employed other means to confront the problems of the industrial age. Some favored municipal and national commissions, which gave wide publicity to issues and problems. Others joined voluntary associations, such as the National Association for the Advancement of Colored People (NAACP), founded in 1909–1910 by white and black reformers to fight the rise of segregation and the lynching of African Americans. Women reformers, who had never had the option of voting, had pioneered the practice of participating in nonparty organizations in order to influence politicians. Their methods would con-

Working Against Discrimination. An undated photograph shows editor W. E. B. DuBois and his young staff preparing an edition of the NAACP's publication, *The Crisis.*

Source: The DuSable Museum of African American History, Chicago.

tinue to define the struggle for political and social change well beyond the Progressive Era.

Reform Comes to National Politics

The broad-based impulse for reform that infected so many arenas of American life was not shared by all political leaders. But at the end of the nineteenth century, few would have predicted that such a broad spectrum of national politicians—including all three presidents in the first two decades of the twentieth century—would have backed at least a moderate version of progressive reform. The United States seemed a more conservative place in 1896, when the pro-business Republican William McKinley triumphed decisively over the populist Democrat William Jennings Bryan. The Republicans dominated Congress, led by such Old Guard conservatives as the wealthy Senator Nelson Aldrich of Rhode Island and the autocratic House Speaker Joseph G. Cannon of Illinois.

But then the party regulars made a mistake. Theodore Roosevelt, who had turned himself into a national hero through his role in the Spanish American War, was posing a threat to the conservative Republican leadership of the major state of New York, where he was a reform-minded governor. Why not "bury" him in the then-insignificant job of vice president, the regulars cleverly proposed? Their proposal became history, and McKinley and Roosevelt won an easy victory in the 1900 rematch with William Jennings Bryan. Mark Hanna, part of the conservative Republican leadership, was uneasy at the ploy: "Don't you realize that there's only one life between that madman and the White House?" he warned. In September 1901, that one life fell to the bullet of Leon Czolgosz. "Now look," declared an exasperated Hanna, "that damned cowboy is president of the United States."

Roosevelt's path to reform was both implausible and inconsistent. The offspring of an old and established family, he had thrown himself into the rough and tumble of New York politics, becoming a state assemblyman in 1881 at age twenty-three. His energetic opposition to machine politics and his push for civil service reform won him the nickname of "Cyclone Assemblyman." With the same energy and intensity, he threw himself into a series of other careers—cattle rancher in the Dakotas, member of the U.S. Civil Service Commission, president of the New York City Police Board, and assistant secretary of the Navy. Despite his reputation for reform, Roosevelt always insisted that he was a conservative who supported progressive reform as the best alternative to the radicalism represented by the socialists and Wobblies. "The friends of property, of order, of law," he argued, "must realize that the surest way to provoke an explosion of wrong and injustice is to be shortsighted, narrow-minded, greedy, and arrogant."

As president, Roosevelt followed policies in line with this view of conservative reform. He was initially sympathetic to mine owners when the United Mine Workers of America (UMWA) called a major strike in Pennsylvania's anthracite coalfields in 1902, a year after he took office. Then public opinion began to turn against the mine owners after they refused to bargain with the UMWA. Worried that a strike would cripple the economy and leave the nation without fuel for the winter, Roosevelt pressed the operators to settle. By threatening to seize the mines and by calling on the influence of the financier J. P. Morgan, he finally got them to negotiate. The ensuing settlement boosted the cause of the UMWA and of the union movement nationwide.

The coal strike taught Roosevelt that bashing big business could be good politics. That same year, he took the popular step of ordering the Justice Department to prosecute the Northern Securities Company, a monopolistic combine of northwestern railroads organized by J. P. Morgan. This was the first use of 1890 Sherman Antitrust Act against such a powerful corporation, but not the last. The Justice Department filed forty-five cases under the act during Roosevelt's presidency, earning him the nickname "Trustbuster." The most celebrated case was in 1907 against Standard Oil, whose monopoly control of the nation's oil business had been exposed in Ida Tarbell's muckraking articles in *McClure's* and her *History of the Standard Oil Company* (1904). In 1911, the Supreme Court upheld the forced breakup of the company. Roosevelt, a passionate outdoorsman, also restricted business in the interest of conservation. He brought 125 million acres of public land into the national forest system, doubled the number of national parks, and established numerous national monuments and wildlife refuges.

But Roosevelt was not a radical and did not oppose all trusts. Many government actions against corporations were dropped after industry leaders visited the White House seeking presidential assistance. The president believed, in fact, that "bigness" had become inevitable; what was important, in his mind, was that the federal government have the power

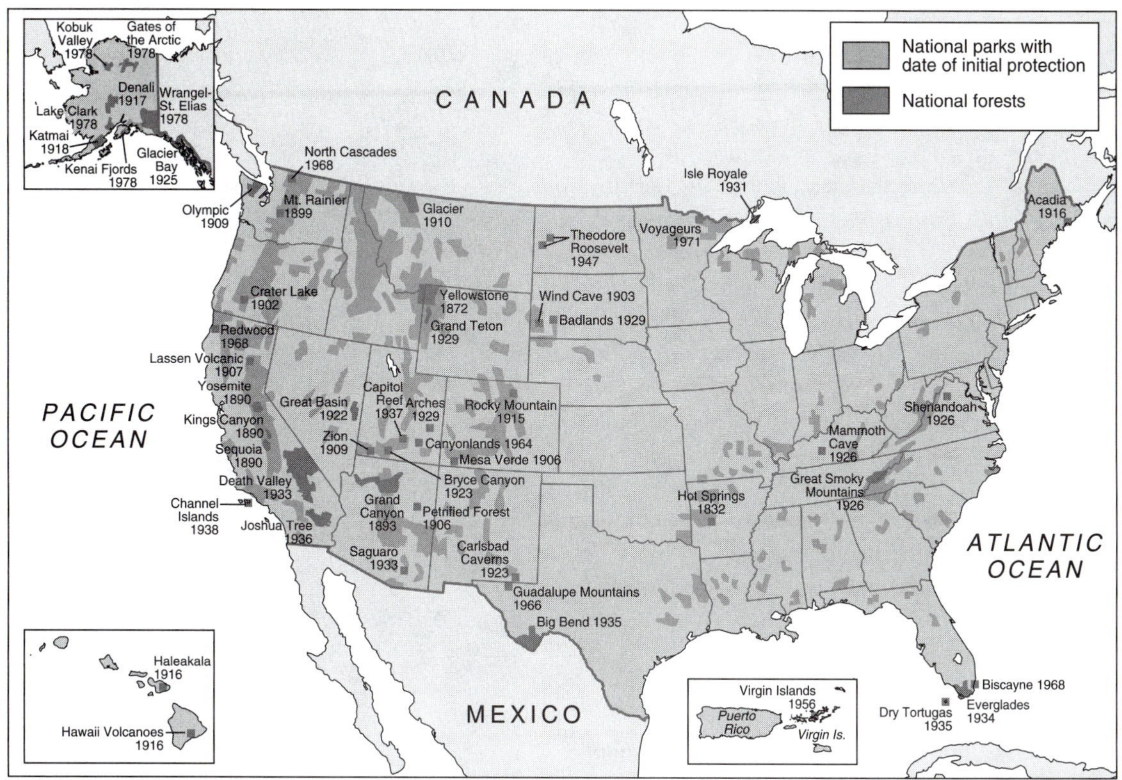

Expanding the Public Domain: National Parks and Forests "To waste, to destroy, our natural resources," Theodore Roosevelt warned, "will result in undermining in the days of our children the very prosperity which we ought by right to hand down to them amplified and developed." As president, Roosevelt practiced what he preached, adding 125 million acres to national forests and creating six new national parks—Crater Lake, Lassen Volcano, Mesa Verde, Petrified Forest, Wind Cave, and Zion.

to regulate corporate behavior so that no corporation would be above the law.

This view of an activist federal government seemed an extension of Roosevelt's activist personality and his craving for the limelight. It was once said of him that he wanted to be "the bride at every wedding, the corpse at every funeral." The flamboyant Roosevelt easily won reelection in 1904 over the colorless Democrat Alton B. Parker, a New York judge. Elected on the promise of a "square deal" for all Americans, Roosevelt used his second term to move in more decisively reformist directions and toward expanded government regulation of the economy. In 1906, for example, he won passage of the Hepburn Act, which enabled the previously weak Interstate Commerce Commission (ICC) to regulate railroad rates. The same year, after Upton Sinclair's sensational novel *The Jungle* exposed unhealthy practices in the meatpacking industry and *McClure's* and *The Ladies' Home Journal* exposed fraud in patent medicines, a popular uproar spurred passage of the Meat Inspection Act and the Pure Food and Drug Act.

Some big corporations actually supported some of these reforms or turned them to their advantage. The biggest meatpacking companies, for example, supported federal inspections because they would place a burden on smaller competitors. But at the time, most Americans had trouble finding an appropriate label for this president. Many conservatives viewed him as a dangerous radical, but radicals did not recognize him as one of their own. The more aggressive reformer Robert La Follette complained that Roosevelt "filled the air with noise and smoke" but accomplished little. Whatever the label, Roosevelt did take some increasingly progressive stances, supporting an eight-hour day for federal workers, a workmen's compensation law, and federal income and inheritance taxes. He also angered conservative defenders of the sanctity of private property by putting his conservation principles ahead of the interests of western cattlemen, lumbermen, and mine owners.

"One of the Little Victims." An April 1907 article in *The Ladies' Home Journal* featured a young victim of patent medicine, Baltimore toddler John D. Goddard. The article's title succinctly stated the danger posed by patent medicines: "Their Well-Meaning Parents Just 'Gave Them a Little Something' to Soothe Them or Make Them Sleep,—and They Slept!"

Source: *The Ladies' Home Journal,* April 1907—General Research Division, New York Public Library, Astor, Lenox and Tilden Foundations.

As Roosevelt became bolder in his advocacy of reform, Republican conservatives, who still dominated Congress, became increasingly uncooperative. Some blamed his attacks on big business for the financial panic that hit the nation in 1907. When Roosevelt announced that he would honor his earlier pledge to leave office after one full term, they breathed a sigh of relief. In response to the news that Roosevelt would go on an African safari, conservatives in Congress reportedly raised their glasses in the toast: "Health to the lions!"

Although William Howard Taft, who defeated William Jennings Bryan in the 1908 election, was Roosevelt's handpicked successor, they were a study in contrasts. Where Roosevelt was flamboyant and gregarious, the Cincinnati judge was shy. Where Roosevelt was energetic and physically fit, Taft was slow moving and struggled with a serious weight problem. (In college, he was known as "Big Lub;" as president his weight reached 332 pounds and he once got stuck in the White House bathtub.) Taft, did, however, share some of Roosevelt's reform inclinations—backing the eight-hour workday, mine safety legislation, the graduated income tax (which was ratified as the Sixteenth Amendment in 1913), and a federal Children's Bureau, as well as helping to strengthen the ICC and filing ninety more antitrust suits.

Teddy the Trustbuster. A critical view of Theodore Roosevelt's reputation as a regulator of corporate abuses appeared in the *Columbus* (Ohio) *Dispatch* during the 1912 presidential campaign. **Source:** William A. Ireland, *Columbus* (Ohio) *Dispatch,* reprinted in *Cartoons Magazine,* November 1912—Prints and Photographs Division, Library of Congress.

But Taft's conservative judicial temperament made him reluctant to use the office of the presidency as aggressively as Roosevelt had done. He also annoyed reformers by going along with the Payne-Aldrich Tariff, which did not cut tariffs as progressives had hoped. And he failed to back progressive efforts to limit the powers of conservative House Speaker Cannon. Particularly irritating to Roosevelt and other conservationists was Taft's support for Secretary of the Interior Richard Ballinger over Chief Forester Gifford Pinchot, a Roosevelt friend and appointee. Pinchot charged Ballinger with abetting a coal-mining syndicate in a plan to plunder government coal reserves in Alaska. When Taft backed Ballinger and fired Pinchot, progressives saw it as capitulation to corporate greed. "For the first time in the history of the country," editorialized the *Louisville Courier-Journal,* "a president of the United States has openly proclaimed himself the friend of thieves and the enemy of honest men."

The Highpoint—and the Limits—of Progressivism

Taft's support of Ballinger, his embarrassment of Roosevelt in a controversy over U.S. Steel, and the Republican's loss of control of the House of Representatives in 1910 led the former president to challenge his successor for the 1912 Republican nomination. Although Roosevelt won most of the primaries, the Republican bosses handed the nomination to Taft. As a result, Roosevelt left the party to run as the nominee of the insurgent

Progressive party. His proposed program, dubbed "the New Nationalism," called for greater government involvement in regulating industrial capitalism, including labor legislation to prevent, in the words of progressive reformer and Roosevelt-supporter Jane Addams, "industrial accidents, occupational diseases, overwork, involuntary unemployment, and other injurious effects incident to modern industry." Although Taft had some progressive credentials, he ran—"walked" might be a better description of his lethargic campaign—as the candidate of conservative Republicans.

If the Democrats had also nominated a conservative, Roosevelt might have been able to win a third-party victory. But the Democratic nominee turned out to be Woodrow Wilson, who had established a reform reputation as governor of New Jersey. A stern Presbyterian, Wilson differed sharply from the effervescent Roosevelt in both style and rhetoric. Whereas Roosevelt's "New Nationalism" called for an expanded national state to regulate capitalism, Wilson trumpeted a "New Freedom," in which antimonopoly policies would restore competition and small-scale business. But the two men shared a fundamental critique of the excesses of industrial capitalism. An even more thoroughgoing critique came from the Socialist candidate, Eugene V. Debs. He dismissed Roosevelt's Progressive party as "a party of progressive capitalism" and called for "the abolition of this monstrous [capitalist] system" rather than for its reform.

The split in the Republican party and support from the South, the West, and AFL unions gave Wilson a clear victory (though not a majority of voters). Debs won a surprising 6 percent of the vote (more than any Socialist presidential candidate). Perhaps most startling is that three-quarters of the electorate backed one of the three candidates who had championed the interests of the people over monopoly capitalism, in one of the most resounding endorsements of reform in U.S. history.

As president, Wilson responded to some but not all of the items on the reform agenda. He dragged his feet on the call for woman suffrage and showed almost no sympathy for the problems of immigrants. Wilson—the first southerner elected president since before the Civil War—probably received more black votes than any previous Democratic presidential candidate. African Americans had abandoned Taft, in part because he had appointed or retained only thirty-one black officeholders. But Wilson's record on African-American rights was even more dismal; he ended up making only nine black appointments, eight of them Republican carryovers. Worse still, he extended and defended segregation in the federal civil service. Black workers were forced to use inferior and segregated washrooms and to work behind screens that separated them from white workers in government offices. And like his predecessors, Wilson repeatedly ignored both the lynching of hundreds of African Americans by

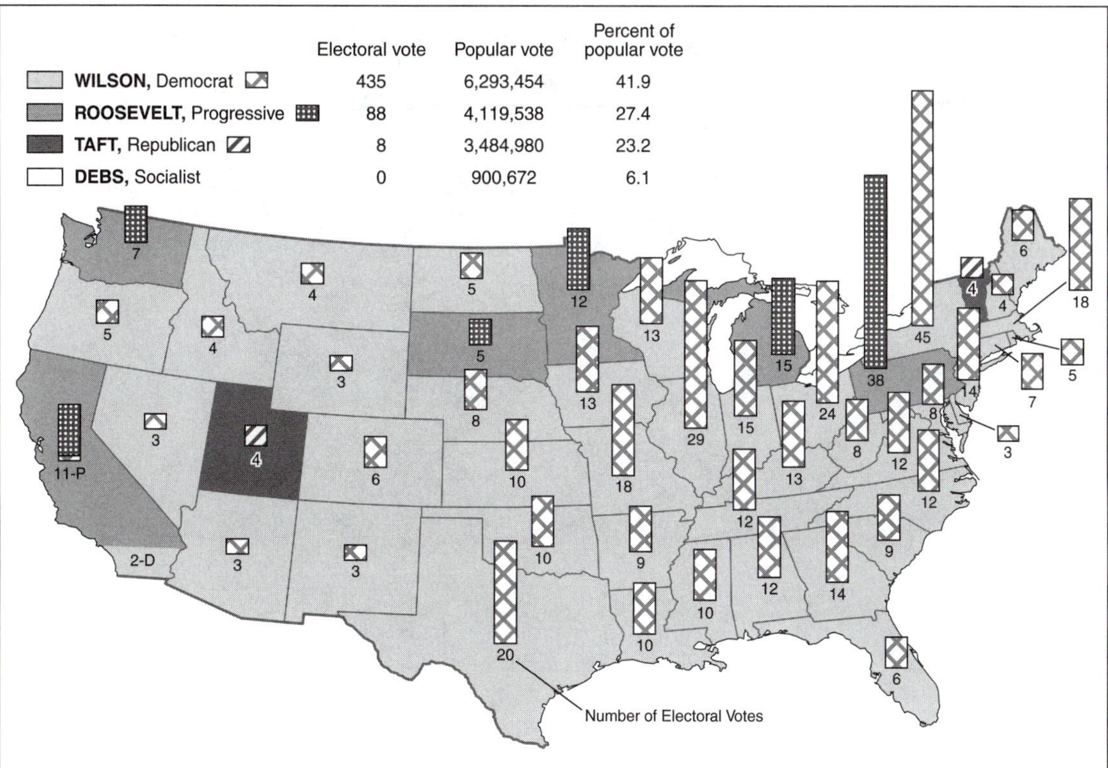

The Election of 1912 No other election in American history produced such a strong endorsement of reform as that of 1912. Three-quarters of the popular vote went to candidates (Woodrow Wilson, Theodore Roosevelt, and Eugene V. Debs) who championed the "people" against monopoly capitalism. William Howard Taft, the one conservative candidate, only won the electoral votes of Utah and Vermont.

white southerners and the disfranchisement and Jim Crow laws that reversed the modest political and economic gains black Americans had made during Reconstruction.

Organized labor, which had also backed Wilson, did much better. Wilson rewarded the labor movement by backing the Clayton Antitrust Act. It replaced the Sherman Act (1890), which had not offered a strong definition of monopolies and trusts and had been used more effectively against labor (especially in the Pullman strike) than against big business. Samuel Gompers called the Clayton Act labor's Magna Carta because not only did it precisely define such prohibited practices as "interlocking directorates" and "discriminatory pricing," but it also specifically stipulated that labor unions and farmers' organizations should not be considered conspiracies in restraint of trade. Wilson also championed a model federal workers' compensation statute, an eight-hour law for railroad workers, and a federal child labor law. The result of years of pressure from working people and reformers, these bills established, for the first time, the federal government's interest in regulating the conditions of labor.

Eight Hours for What We Will! Maurice Becker in the radical monthly *The Masses* celebrated the passage of the Adamson Act in 1916, which specified an eight-hour workday (with additional pay for overtime labor) for employees of railroads engaged in interstate commerce.

Source: Maurice Becker, *The Masses,* November 1916—Prints and Photographs Division, Library of Congress.

One of Wilson's first acts in 1913 had been to appoint the Commission on Industrial Relations, authorized by Congress in response to labor radicalism and violence. The commission's chairman, Frank P. Walsh, a Kansas City reformer sympathetic to labor, had used a series of public hearings to expose what he called "industrial feudalism." The commission's 1915 report asserted that poor working conditions, autocratic business management, and the concentration of wealth underlay labor violence. It called for an inheritance tax to finance education, social services, and public works; a child-labor law; equal pay for women and men; and protection of the right to join a union and bargain collectively.

Although the Wilson administration ignored most of these recommendations, it did offer some important concessions to labor. The Seamen's Act of 1915 eliminated the oppressive financial arrangements and semi-military discipline inflicted on merchant sailors. In 1916 came the first federal child-labor law and the Adamson Act, which granted railroad workers the eight-hour day—the first time private workers' hours came under federal regulations. The courts eventually undercut some of labor's legislative victories: the labor provisions of the Clayton Act were severely weakened by judicial interpretation, and the child-labor law was declared unconstitutional. Still, Wilson's accommodation of labor was a dramatic step and responded to both the growing power of the AFL and the mass insurgencies represented by the Socialist party, the IWW, and other radical unionists.

Wilson also expanded the government's economic role. He set up the Federal Reserve System (1913), which reestablished a central banking system, and the Federal Trade Commission (1914), which was charged with the task of preventing corporate attempts to inhibit competition. These efforts continued a trend begun a decade earlier under Roosevelt, of concentrating federal power in the executive branch and creating a large administrative bureaucracy to mediate conflicting social

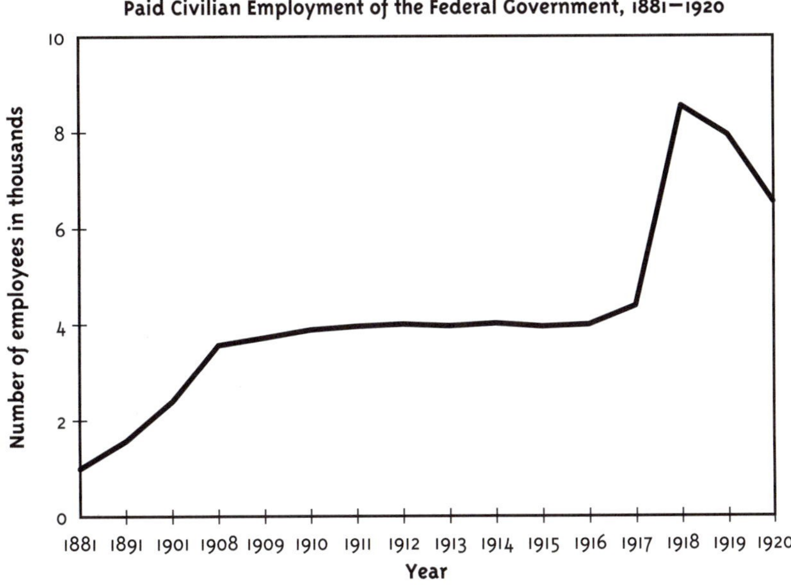

Creating a National Bureaucracy: Growth in Federal Employment, 1881–1920 As this graph shows, the federal government grew during the Progressive Era, but the most rapid growth came during World War I.

and economic pressures. In that sense, Wilson's New Freedom turned out to look a lot like Roosevelt's New Nationalism. As before, however, businessmen were often able to capture control of the regulatory process. Under the Federal Reserve Act of 1913, bankers dominated the regulation of the nation's currency and credit systems, controlling the boards of the regional Federal Reserve banks and shaping the policies of the Federal Reserve Board.

Toward the Modern State

Progressivism responded to the economic, social, and political dislocations that accompanied industrial capitalism's dramatic growth during the Gilded Age: rapid technological change; intense and episodic conflict between capital and labor; the influx of enormous numbers of immigrants from southern and eastern Europe, Asia, and Latin America; and the growing national and international reach of American capitalism. Each of these problems posed a special challenge to older American ideals of individual independence and equality.

Progressivism looked to an active government to blunt the worst of capitalism's economic and social problems. Working people, in coalition with socialists, radicals, and feminists, were key participants in progressive reform struggles, helping to win passage of pro-labor legislation, especially the federal Clayton Act. These reforms helped lay the foundation for our modern notion of government and were among progressivism's most lasting contributions to American political life.

But by the time war broke out in Europe in 1914, the central role many progressives desired for government had been only partially realized: federal, state, and local laws minimally regulated the economy and industrial relations while extending limited protections to consumers and women and children. Assembling the cross-class coalition that made progressive reforms possible had involved significant compromises. Only a relatively small number of working people—those organized into skilled-craft unions and those working in industries covered by limited factory reforms—fully benefited from the passage of progressive legislation. Many others—unskilled and manual laborers, domestic servants, agricultural wageworkers, and sharecroppers—remained outside progressivism's protective sphere.

"The 'Open Road.'" This 1916 cartoon celebrating the insurgent Progressive party drew its title from a quote by Woodrow Wilson, stating that Americans discontented with traditional party politics proposed to "find an open road for themselves."

Source: Robert Carter, *American Review of Reviews* (1912)—Prints and Photographs Division, Library of Congress.

African Americans experienced the Progressive Era quite literally as a tightening noose: the federal government repeatedly ignored the wanton lynching of hundreds of African Americans in the South. At the same time, the modest political and economic gains these Americans had made during Reconstruction were rolled back in a flood of Progressive Era disfranchisement laws and the purging of African Americans from federal jobs by the Wilson administration. Women had been central to the movements that made up progressivism and had succeeded in expanding their public role in American life. Yet their most important demand—for the right to vote—remained stalled as the United States entered World War I.

Despite these very real limitations, progressivism represented a watershed that marked the beginning of a new relationship between working people and the government. The era's limited reforms inaugurated a period of governmental involvement in economic and social affairs that would intensify in coming decades. As a result, working people would look increasingly to government to ameliorate the worst excesses of industrial capitalism. Progressivism set the terms of this new relationship, as working people's experiences in their struggle for a better life were now linked inextricably to national political, economic, and social developments.

The Years in Review

1874

- Woman's Christian Temperance Union founded; becomes largest women's organization.

1889

- Jane Addams establishes Hull House.

1890

- Two major factions join to form the National American Woman Suffrage Association.

1900

- Reform movement begins in St. Louis when local unions strike against the street railway monopoly; four years later it will elect District Attorney Joseph Folk as reform governor.
- Hamburger pioneered by Louis Lassen at Louie's (three-seat) Lunch.

1901

- Socialist party founded by the merger of several socialist groups; party membership would peak in 1912 at 118,000 members.
- Leon Czolgosz assassinates William McKinley; Theodore Roosevelt becomes president.

1902

- 140,000 anthracite coal miners strike for an eight-hour day; Roosevelt convinces mine owners to accept arbitration.
- U.S. Army drops its traditional blue uniforms and adopts less-visible olive drab.

1903

- Women's Trade Union League founded by a coalition of working-class and elite women.
- Teddy bears, modeled on Roosevelt's hunting exploits, become a popular toy.

1904

- Republican candidate Theodore Roosevelt wins the presidential election, defeating Democrat Alton B. Parker and Socialist Eugene V. Debs.

1905

- Industrial Workers of the World is founded to abolish the wage system.
- Albert Einstein publishes paper on general theory of relativity: $E = MC^2$.

1906

- Hepburn Act enables the previously weak Interstate Commerce Commission to regulate railroad rates.
- Congress passes Pure Food and Drug Act and Meat Inspection Act following the publication of Upton Sinclair's *The Jungle*.
- Roosevelt issues executive order calling for "simplified spelling"—a typical "scientific" reform of the Progressive Era.

1907

- Financial panic, which results from irresponsible speculation and industrial overproduction, brings minor depression after general prosperity of the early 1900s.

1908

- *Muller v. Oregon:* U.S. Supreme Court upholds an Oregon law limiting women's work to ten hours a day in certain kinds of businesses.
- Republican candidate William Howard Taft defeats Democrat William Jennings Bryan and Socialist Eugene V. Debs in the presidential election.

1909

- Uprising of the Twenty Thousand: garment strikes lead to reduced hours, improved conditions, and system for future arbitration.
- President Taft signs Payne-Aldrich protective tariff.
- Eighteen-man expedition—including four Inuits and an African American, Matthew Henson—reaches the North Pole; expedition leader Robert E. Peary is credited as the "first man" to get there.
- Taft's support for Secretary of the Interior Richard Ballinger over Chief Forester Gifford Pinchot angers Roosevelt and other conservationists.

1910

- Thousands of garment workers strike in New York and Chicago, leading to major union victories in the clothing industry.
- Boy Scouts of America and the Campfire Girls are founded.
- National Association for the Advancement of Colored People (NAACP) is formally established.

1911

- Triangle Shirtwaist Company fire leaves 146 workers dead because of faulty fire escapes and intentionally blocked exit routes; public outcry leads to factory safety and health reforms.
- Coal mine explosion outside of Birmingham, Alabama, kills 128 convict miners.

1912

- Democrat Woodrow Wilson wins presidential election over Theodore Roosevelt (candidate of new Progressive party), Republican William Howard Taft, and Socialist Eugene V. Debs.

- IWW organizes successful Lawrence, Massachusetts ("Bread and Roses"), textile strike.
- IWW meets with defeat in silk workers' strike in Paterson, New Jersey.

1913

- Sixteenth Amendment (income tax) is adopted.
- Seventeenth Amendment (direct election of U.S. senators) is adopted.

1914

- Women in eleven states—most in the West—and the territory of Alaska have the right to vote in state, local, and school board elections.
- Federal Reserve Act passed—first comprehensive reorganization of banking system since Civil War.
- World War I breaks out in Europe.
- Clayton Antitrust Act, labor's "Magna Carta," is passed; it exempts unions from antitrust laws and limits the use of injunctions against labor.
- Troops attack a strikers' tent camp in Colorado, killing sixteen people, including twelve children, in what will be known as the Ludlow Massacre.
- George Washington Carver reveals results of his peanut experiments.
- Mary Phelps Jacob, New York debutante, patents the elastic brassiere.

1915

- Commission on Industrial Relations report asserts that poor working conditions, autocratic business management, and the concentration of wealth led to labor violence.

1919

- Eighteenth Amendment (Prohibition) is adopted.

1920

- Nineteenth Amendment (woman's suffrage) is adopted.

Suggested Readings

Bordin, Ruth, *Women and Temperance: The Quest for Power and Liberty, 1873–1900* (1981).

Boyer, Paul, *Urban Masses and Moral Order in America, 1820–1920* (1978).

Brody, David, *Workers in Industrial America: Essays on the Twentieth-Century Struggle* (1980).

Buenker, John, *Urban Liberalism and Progressive Reform* (1973).

Chambers, John Whiteclay II, *The Tyranny of Change: America in the Progressive Era, 1900–1917* (2nd ed., 1992).

Cooper, John Milton, Jr., *The Warrior and the Priest: Woodrow Wilson and Theodore Roosevelt* (1983).

Davis, Allen, *Spearheads of Reform: The Settlements and the Progressive Movement, 1890–1914* (1967).

Dawley, Alan, *Struggles for Justice: Social Responsibility and the Liberal State* (1991).

Diner, Steven J., *A Very Different Age: Americans of the Progressive Era* (1998).

Dubofsky, Melvyn, *We Shall Be All: A History of the Industrial Workers of the World* (1969).

Dubofsky, Melvyn, *When Workers Organize: New York in the Progressive Era* (1968).

Dye, Nancy Schrom, *As Equals and as Sisters: Feminism, Unionism, and the Women's Trade Union League of New York* (1980).

Filler, Louis, *The Muckrakers: Crusaders for American Liberalism* (1968).

Flexner, Eleanor, *Century of Struggle: The Woman's Rights Movement in the United States* (1975).

Gilmore, Glenda Elizabeth, *Gender and Jim Crow: Women and the Politics of White Supremacy in North Carolina, 1896–1920* (1996).

Green, James R., *Grassroots Socialism: Radical Movements in the Southwest, 1895–1943* (1978).

Hays, Samuel P., *The Response to Industrialism, 1885–1914* (1957).

Hofstadter, Richard, *The Age of Reform* (1955).

Holli, Melvin, *Reform in Detroit: Hazen Pingree and Urban Politics* (1969).

Kloppenberg, James, *Uncertain Victory: Social Democracy and Progressivism in European and American Thought, 1870–1920* (1986).

Kolko, Gabriel, *The Triumph of Conservatism: A Reinterpretation of American History, 1900–1916* (1967).

Kraditor, Aileen S., *The Ideas of the Woman Suffrage Movement, 1890–1920* (1965).

Link, Arthur S., and Richard L. McCormick, *Progressivism* (1983).

McGerr, Michael, *The Decline of Popular Politics: The American North, 1865–1928* (1986).

Muncy, Robyn, *Creating a Female Dominion in American Reform, 1890–1935* (1991).

Rodgers, Daniel T., *Atlantic Crossings: Social Politics in a Progressive Age* (1998).

Salvatore, Nick, *Eugene V. Debs: Citizen and Socialist* (1982).

Sklar, Kathryn Kish, *Florence Kelley and the Nation's Work: The Rise of Women's Political Culture, 1830–1900* (1995).

Sklar, Martin J., *The Corporate Reconstruction of American Capitalism, 1890–1916: The Market, the Law, and Politics* (1988).

Skocpol, Thead, *Protecting Soldiers and Mothers: The Political Origins of Social Policy in the United States* (1992).

Skowronek, Stephen, *Building a New American State: The Expansion of National Administrative Capacities, 1877–1920* (1982).

Tax, Meredith, *The Rising of the Women: Feminist Solidarity and Class Conflict, 1880 – 1917* (1980).

Thelen, David, *The New Citizenship: The Origins of Progressivism in Wisconsin, 1885 – 1900* (1972).

Weinstein, James, *The Corporate Ideal in the Liberal State, 1900 – 1918* (1968).

Wiebe, Robert H., *The Search for Order, 1877 – 1920* (1967).

And on the World Wide Web

Thomas Dublin and Kathryn Kish Sklar, *Women and Social Movements in the United States, 1830 – 1930* (http://womhist.binghamton.edu).

Library of Congress, *The Evolution of the Conservation Movement, 1850 – 1920* (http://memory.loc.gov/ammem/amrvhtml/conshome.html).

War, Depression, and Industrial Unionism

1914-1945

When the first U.S. Army troops landed in war-ravaged Tokyo early in September 1945, they were commanded by scores of young officers, many born just before World War I. These confident commanders, ex-civilians still in their 30s, had been part of a vast wartime expansion of American power to almost every corner of the globe. But their memories stretched back to the grim Depression years, to high school in the 1920s, and to childhood memories of World War I itself.

Their generation had already seen a transformation in American life as dramatic and fundamental as any since the founding of the Republic. When they attended elementary school, the nation's social and political rhythms were still attuned to those of a nineteenth-century agrarian world; by the time they learned that B-29 bombers had dropped atomic bombs on Hiroshima and Nagasaki, U.S. diplomacy, politics, and society had far more in common with the end of the twentieth century than with its start.

In just a third of a century, from 1914 to 1945, Americans fought two world wars, survived the Great Depression, and saw the emergence of the most powerful trade union movement in the nation's history. As war and revolution convulsed nation after nation, U.S. politics became saturated with debate over the great "isms" of the twentieth century: imperialism, capitalism, socialism, fascism, and communism. The federal government became far more powerful but also more intimately involved with the lives of ordinary Americans. Women got the vote, African Americans demanded it, and immigrant Americans began to exercise the franchise in huge numbers. New modes of communication, consumption, and transport—movies, radio, chain stores, buses and cars—recast the texture of everyday life.

Four great developments transformed the United States and its place in the world during this third of a century. First, the nation became the world's greatest power, in terms both of its economic infrastructure and its capacity to project military power across the oceans. In 1914 the United States was already the productive equal of Great Britain and Germany; but whereas both world wars sapped the economic vitality of the European combatants—and bled white an entire generation of young men—the American republic emerged from each conflict with ever greater economic and military strength. U.S. industry perfected mass production, put an automobile in the hands of most families, and developed the kind of technologies—like aviation, radar, telecommunications, and nuclear fission—that paid off in time of war. Early in 1941 *Life* magazine publisher Henry Luce proclaimed his era "The American Century." Indeed, by the end of Word War II the relative power of the United States was so great that to measure it one had to recall the strength of Great Britain at the high noon of its Victorian empire, or Rome in the reign of the Caesars.

Second, the federal government became enormously more powerful during these three short decades. In 1914 the post office was about the only agency of the national government that touched the lives of ordinary Americans. But war and depression soon changed all that. U.S. participation in World War I proved a dress rehearsal, not just for the next world conflict, but for the transformative, intrusive impact of the New Deal fifteen years later. During the First World War, the Wilson administration mobilized the American people as never before. It regulated business, took over the railroads, tested and trained millions of military recruits, censored the mail, and sold war bonds in a huge propaganda effort. In the 1920s Republican presidents tempered the growth of federal power, but even in that more conservative decade President Herbert Hoover, who had been a highly effective World War I administrator, argued for the kind of nation-state activism that would have surprised his nineteenth-century predecessors.

Many veterans of World War I, including Assistant Secretary of the Navy Franklin D. Roosevelt, would deploy this same kind of organizational energy and ambition when the nation faced its next great crisis, the Great Depression. The New Deal built dams and reads, subsidized millions of farmers, regulated corporations, banks, and the stock market, and established Social Security, which would eventually become the single largest, most expensive, and, for many years, the most popular of all government programs. And then came World War II, when the federal government achieved stupendous size and power: It raised an army and a navy that enlisted 16 million; it mobilized the nation's leading universities for military research; and it launched the industrialization of southern California, large sections of the south, Long Island, and other new war production centers. By 1944 the military was spending more than 40 percent of the nation's entire gross domestic product.

Third, these were the years during which the labor movement moved to the center ring of American politics and culture. This took place in two stages, during both of which rank and file activism and government policy combined to generate an explosive growth in union size and influence. During World War I the Wilson administration repressed antiwar radicals, but to advance U.S. war aims the government also linked victory over German autocracy to the spread of an industrial democracy at home. American workers were therefore emboldened to denounce "Prussian" managers and "Kaiserism" in industry; and they joined unions in a vast wave that crested during the nationwide strikes of 1919, the largest working-class upheaval in the history of the republic.

Fifteen years later, industrial unionism finally won the kind of political support and legislative backing that had been absent during the First World War and the tragic years immediately thereafter. The 1935 Wagner Act encouraged trade unionism as a spur to economic recovery and a bulwark of American democracy. But no matter how favorable the law was to labor, the mass unionism of the 1930s required the courageous activism of thousands of women and men. Organizing the most basic industries of their time—automobiles, steel, rubber, and electrical products—they built the new Congress of Industrial Organizations (CIO) and put its power and values close to the heart of a New Deal impulse that stretched well into the post–World War II years.

Fourth, this era of war and depression also generated a remarkable transformation in the character of the American people. Shipping shortages and dangers during the First World War—and the immigration restriction laws that followed—stanched the great transatlantic migrations, but the impact of that European diaspora would have a long afterlife. In the 1930s and 1940s the sons and daughters of the prewar immigrant wave—the ambitious, assimilationist "second-generation"—helped refound the Democratic party, gave new energy to the labor movement, and provided much of the creativity that characterized science, film, and music during those years. Immigrant daughters figured prominently in the labor upsurge of the 1930s, but a large number of women took advantage of new opportunities in industry and office. They poured into jobs vacated by men during the two world wars and they began to stay in the workforce longer. In 1914 the typical woman worker was an unmarried teenager; after 1945 she was married and a decade or more older.

Southerners, both black and white, filled the workplace vacuum left by the absence of European immigrants. Fleeing a generation-long agricultural depression, white southern immigrants poured into the North all during the 1920s and 1930s. But the wartime "Great Migration" of African Americans proved even more dramatic. Starting in the First World War, and renewing itself in the Second, a huge exodus out of the rural South swelled the African American population of Chicago, New York, Baltimore, Washington, D.C., Detroit, and Oakland, California, moving the aspirations of this community toward the center of U.S. politics. In 1914 African Americans were voteless, voiceless, and hidden behind a veil of nearly unchallenged white supremacy. Thirty years later a vigorous civil rights movement, powerfully reinforced by hundreds of thousands of black factory workers, had begun to challenge the old racial order on almost every front.

chapter 6

Wars for Democracy
1914–1919

In mid-1918, as the clouds of war rolled over the United States, socialist leader Eugene Debs rose from his sickbed to protest the massive government repression that had led to the arrest of thousands of radicals and opponents of U.S. participation in the war. "They tell us that we live in a great free republic," he told a cheering crowd in Canton, Ohio, "that our institutions are democratic, that we are a free and self-governing people. This is too much, even for a joke." Debs knew his own remarks placed him at risk of arrest, but he insisted he "would rather a thousand times . . . be a free soul in jail than . . . be a sycophant and coward in the streets." Rejecting the claim that the United States was fighting "to make democracy safe in the world," Debs believed that wars were waged for conquest and plunder. "The master class," he insisted, "has always declared the wars; the subject class has always fought the battles. The master class has had all to gain and nothing to lose, while the subject class has had nothing to gain and all to lose—especially their lives."

Debs was prophetic. As he perhaps expected, he wound up as a "free soul in jail"—this very exercise of free speech led to a ten-year sentence for violating the 1917 Espionage Act. And while munitions makers and a small number of other corporations grew rich from what would later be known as World War I, millions, most of them from the "subject class," died. Ten million (including 112,000 U.S. soldiers) perished; twice that number died from hunger and disease attributable to the war. Rather than make the world safe for democracy, as President Woodrow Wilson had asserted, the bungled peace enacted at the end of the so-called War to End All Wars would only pave the way for a second, even deadlier world war.

But, like most political speakers, Debs painted on a broad canvas. In hindsight, we can see that the war years brought some gains as well as some grievous losses for ordinary Americans. Although the United States did not enter the conflict until 1917, nearly three years after it began, World War I affected virtually every aspect of American life. More than four million men found themselves in the armed forces as the federal government greatly expanded its role in everyday life. Workers benefited from the labor shortage that developed as war production increased. Rural black southerners moved north to fill industrial positions. The flow of immigration from Mexico swelled. Women were recruited for traditionally male jobs. With jobs easy to get, workers pressed for better

No Man's Land. A soldier's corpse, caught on one of the barbed-wire barricades that criss-crossed European battlefields during the First World War, hung unburied between the trenches of the opposing armies.

Source: Imperial War Museum.

wages and conditions and for recognition of their unions. To win working-class cooperation in war production, the government paid attention to their concerns. Working people made unprecedented organizational and political gains in the war years. From below, workers, immigrants, women, and African Americans pressed the meaning of a war for democracy beyond the boundaries that President Wilson had intended.

The victory of the United States and its allies in the war, as well as the Russian Revolution of 1917, seemed to open up further promises not only of a new and fairer social order, but also of greater economic and social democracy. Unions staged massive strikes to redeem the idea of economic democracy; African Americans proclaimed their rights to long-delayed civic equality. But the postwar strikes met defeat at the hands of repressive employers, and a government-sponsored "red scare" soon crushed most signs of radicalism. Newly assertive African Americans were beaten and killed in a series of brutal race riots. Not all the gains and promises of the war years melted away; women finally won the vote that had been denied them for so long. Nevertheless, by 1920 many Americans would have agreed with the imprisoned Debs that World War I had neither enshrined democracy around the world nor advanced it more than modestly at home.

From Assassination in the Balkans to War in Europe

On June 28, 1914, Gavrilo Prinčip, a Serbian nationalist, assassinated Archduke Franz Ferdinand, the heir to the Austro-Hungarian throne. The Archduke was visiting Sarajevo, the capital of Bosnia, part of the Austro-Hungarian Empire that Serbia sought to annex. Less than three weeks after the assassination, Austria-Hungary declared war on Serbia, and European nations joined in, declaring their loyalty to one side or the other. Russia quickly came to Serbia's aid, and Germany rushed to Austria-Hungary's defense by attacking France, Russia's ally. The next day Britain joined the conflict, on behalf of both France and neutral Belgium, which had come under attack by German troops. Within five weeks virtually all of Europe was at war. Today the circumstances surrounding the outbreak of World War I seem absurd. Indeed, Prinčip himself could not believe he had started what Europeans called the "Great War."

How *did* a single shot from an unknown student terrorist set in motion a conflagration that would leave millions of people dead? Part of the answer lies in the intense ethnic and nationalist rivalries in the Balkans in southeastern Europe—conflicts that remain explosive at the beginning of the twenty-first century. The nineteenth century had seen the decay of the longstanding Turkish Ottoman Empire, and the rise of nationalist senti-

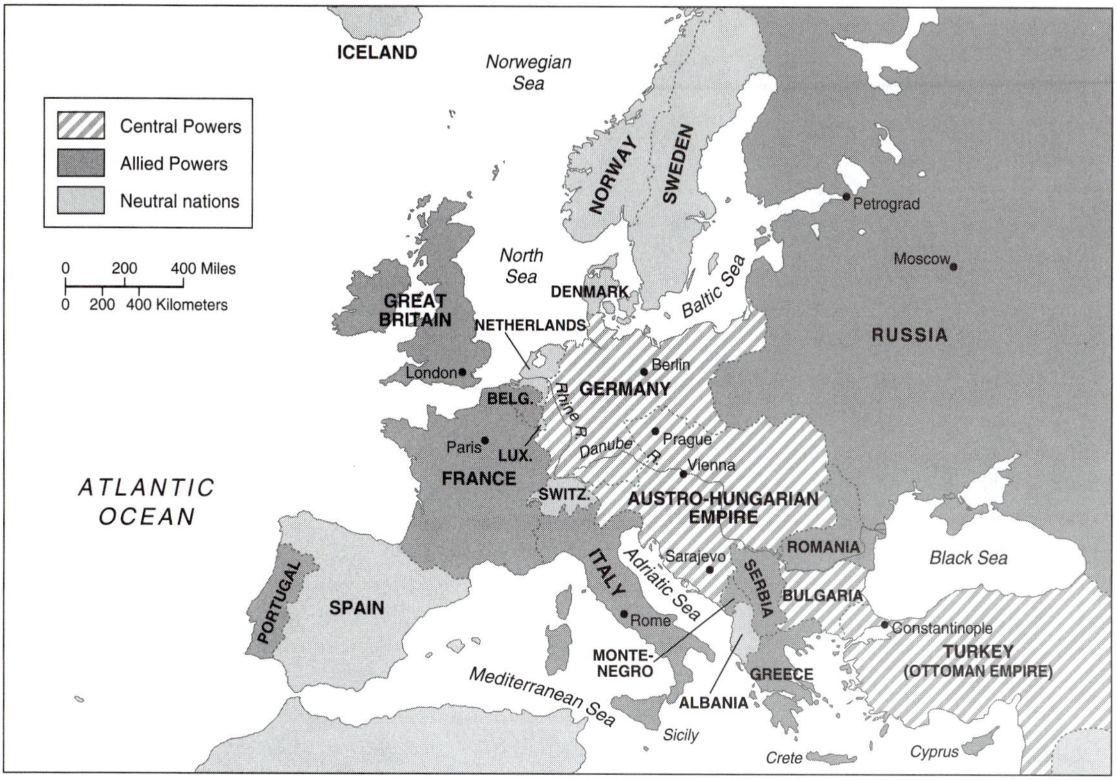

Before and After: Europe at the Beginning and End of World War I. World War I dramatically reshaped Europe. Out of the defeated Central Powers—Germany and the Austro-Hungarian Empire—came a host of new nations. Russia, weakened by revolution, also lost territory.

ment among the different ethnic groups living in the Balkans—Serbs, Croatians, Bosnians, Montenegrins, and others. In 1912 and 1913, these small nations had engaged in two wars without resolving their differences. These conflicts would not have led to global war had they not played into larger European tensions. Rising nationalism posed a fundamental threat to Austria-Hungary's already crumbling multicultural empire; Serbian expansionism would further stir up those nationalist aspirations. Even more important, Russia—a fierce defender of the Serbs—and Austria-Hungary sat on opposing sides of two sets of alliances that had emerged in Europe in the previous half-century. In 1882, Germany, Austria-Hungary, and Italy had formed the Triple Alliance. Russia and France had become allies in 1894; ten years later, France signed an *Entente Cordiale* (friendly understanding) with Britain. When Britain and Russia came to a similar understanding in 1907, the Triple Entente of France, Great Britain, and Russia was born. These two alliances soon encompassed smaller European nations as well, binding each member to come to the aid of the others in the event of an attack.

Though they had been formally at peace since 1871, European powers competed intensely for markets, colonies, and raw materials—in short, for the fruits of empire. The most intense rivalry existed between the two greatest powers, Britain and Germany. The Entente Cordiale was, in fact, an imperialist pact allowing Britain a free hand in Egypt in return for British support of French—over German—claims in Morocco. (Although the United States had also joined in this imperial competition, its strategy, with some notable exceptions, was to maintain an "open door" for investment and trade rather than to colonize distant territories.) Britain and Germany each sought to dominate the world, politically and economically. A prize of such magnitude, they believed, justified reckless and deadly actions.

These competing ambitions fostered an arms race in which each major power feared falling behind its rivals. From 1887 to the eve of the First World War, British military expenditures more than doubled. Expenses for both the German and British navies quadrupled during that period. At the same time, Europe became increasingly militarized. Except in Britain, which did not institute compulsory military service, the draft turned local-minded villagers into citizens of the nation-state. Military bands played at public events, and armies mobilized at times of social crisis. The ideology of nationalism also proved useful in quieting domestic turmoil caused by restive workers, feminists, and ethnic minorities.

This lethal mix—ethnic tensions, nationalism, global imperial ambitions, escalating militarism, and a convoluted system of alliances and treaties, many of them secret—proved explosive. When Germany decided to back Austria-Hungary against Serbia and Russia, the die was cast. Neither the Allies (Britain, France, and Russia) nor the German-led Central Powers could or would back down. The chain reaction that followed would turn a seemingly obscure incident into a war more terrifying and destructive than anything Europe had ever seen.

Total War in Europe

Even though the Allies and the Central Powers each confidently predicted a quick victory, the war turned into a gruesome stalemate. By fall of 1914, the French and British had stopped the German advance toward Paris in northeastern France in a narrow strip of land known as the Western Front, where millions of troops fought from a vast network of parallel trenches. The Eastern Front, running across Poland, was more fluid, with cavalry battles and sweeping troop movements.

On the Western Front, infantry troops endured rain and cold and trenches filled with mud and rats. Soldiers ordered "over the top," out of the trenches, were mowed down by machine guns in a "no man's land" strung with barbed wire to separate the opposing front lines. During 1915 and 1916, both sides tried to break through enemy lines. The German attack on Verdun, France, in February 1916 involved unprecedented firepower. Ten months and almost seven hundred thousand deaths later, the position of the front had barely changed. The new strategy became one of wearing down the enemy in an intentional war of attrition—holding ground no matter how many men died. In July the British launched an offensive on the Somme River; 19,000 died on just the first day. Before the attack ended (and the Allies gained a pathetic 125 miles of

"Won't They Be Edified!" A 1914 cartoon published in the *Chicago Daily News* used racial chauvinism to condemn the European war for undermining the moral supremacy of "Western Civilization." **Source:** *Chicago Daily News*, 1914—American Social History Project.

mud), casualties on both sides would exceed one million. By contrast, only 150,000 soldiers had died in the entire Franco-Prussian War (1870–1871), the preceding major European conflict.

For the European participants, World War I was "total war," a phrase coined by French premier Georges Clemenceau. The expression suggests the war's exceptional intensity and magnitude: huge armies and millions of casualties, a global character, and the utter destruction and collapse it caused. War on this scale demanded complete mobilization and the extension of warfare beyond the battlefield. Entire economies and societies focused on providing the labor and moral support needed to fuel the machine of war.

The armed forces on each side required huge mountains of supplies and equipment, which were supplied by the new technologies and large-scale production of the industrial age. Well-developed railways and telegraph lines made it possible to move and manage these mass armies; long-range artillery and rapid-fire infantry weapons multiplied their firepower. Machine guns, flame throwers, and tanks changed warfare forever. The sound of artillery on the Western Front was so loud that it could be heard miles away in London and Paris. Airplanes and zeppelins dropped bombs from the sky. Poison gas—forbidden by international law—caused horrendous suffering among the troops. At sea, submarines altered traditional naval strategy with their stealth, surprise, and capacity for sudden destruction.

Crucial to these operations were the working men and women who labored on the "home front" to produce the materials that would be used in this prolonged conflict. They and other civilians became, for the first time, "legitimate" military targets. Cities were bombed from the air; ports and seaside resorts were blockaded or shelled from the sea. The blockades cut off food supplies, causing widespread malnutrition and vulnerability to disease among civilians, especially the young and the old. Though civilian populations at first responded with extraordinary enthusiasm, within two years many had become not just weary of war but hostile to the slaughter.

American Neutrality and American Business

The machine of world war required more food and weapons than Europe could produce. The increased demand proved profitable for the United States, stimulating the economy and pulling it out of the recession that had plagued it since 1913. By 1917 the nation's gross national product—the sum of all the goods and services the United States produced—was 20 percent higher than it had been three years earlier.

In 1914 Wilson's administration urged strict U.S. neutrality. The war seemed to have little to do with the United States, whose international activity had been confined to the Caribbean, South and Central America, and the Pacific. But U.S. citizens *were* involved—carrying goods from the United States to Europe, traveling on American and European ships, and doing business with the warring governments and their citizens. Both sides turned to the United States to finance the war: the British sold Americans more than $3.5 billion worth of investments they had in the United States, and the Allies borrowed over $2 billion from American banks and the federal government. By the end of the war, the United States had reversed its historic position as a debtor nation and become a net lender. New York was well on its way toward replacing London as the world's financial capital, and the United States was on the verge of becoming the world's strongest economy.

Much of the money the United States loaned European nations came back immediately in payment for food, raw materials, and manufactured goods. J. P. Morgan & Co., the exclusive purchasing agent for England and France, placed over $3 billion worth of wartime orders. By the end of 1915, U.S. goods were flowing to Europe in massive quantities. The Allied Powers' purchases of wheat alone increased sevenfold.

As the conflict dragged on, U.S. businesses developed stronger ties to England and France, and a greater economic stake in their victory. Because of both the British blockade and longstanding patterns of international commerce, U.S. firms traded more extensively with the Allies than with the Central Powers. Between August 1914 and March 1917 the United States sold the Allies about $2.2 billion in armaments—an amount nearly equal to the value of all American exports in 1913. It also shipped iron, steel, copper, and oil to the Allies, paid for by loans from U.S. bankers. Moreover, with the warring countries concentrating on military production, U.S. businesses could increase their sales in Latin America and other regions—enlarging their share of markets long dominated by Europeans—and could develop new ties to producers of raw materials.

But profitable as this trade was, it also posed a problem. Under international law, the belligerents could intercept and detain neutral ships, inspect them, confiscate goods they considered contraband, and remove enemy personnel. While U.S. foreign policy was based on freedom of the seas, neutrality was difficult to maintain in this total war. Countless supplies were needed to sustain massive armies and civilians, and each side tried to prevent neutral countries from supplying its enemies. In February 1915, the British navy, the most powerful in the world, began turning back ships carrying war-related goods, including food, to Germany. The Germans retaliated with their new *Unterseeboot,* or U-boat, launching surprise submarine attacks on Allied ships. They also declared the waters around the British Isles a war zone and warned that misuse of neutral flags would put neutral ships at risk. Incidents involving Americans became inevitable, and the clash occurred in May 1915, when 128 Americans died as a German U-boat torpedoed the British passenger ship *Lusitania,* rumored to be carrying contraband, off the Irish coast. Responding to a huge public outcry, the United States protested immediately. The Germans, unwilling to push the United States into the war on the Allied side, expressed regret and agreed to respect international agreements on naval warfare.

Secretary of State William Jennings Bryan urged Wilson to avoid any appearance of taking sides in the European conflict and even recommended breaking commercial ties with the combatants. The president refused, arguing that the United States had to maintain free trade and freedom of the seas, and that submarine warfare was immoral, a clear reason to oppose Germany. Bryan—one of the only members of the administration who was genuinely committed to neutrality—resigned over Wilson's reaction to the *Lusitania* affair. The British blockade, Bryan insisted, was equally immoral, because it was starving Germany's civilian population, and he warned that Wilson's actions would lead to war. Bryan's successor, the pro-British Robert Lansing, believed as early as 1915 that the United States "would ultimately become an ally of Great Britain." Lansing's appointment further tilted U.S. policy toward the Allies.

The Debate over American Involvement

Increasingly, the war was presenting Americans with a profound dilemma. Wilson agreed with most business and political leaders that continued U.S. prosperity and tranquility depended on international investment and trade. The main obstacle, in his view, was European-style imperialism—the competitive rush for colonies and exclusive spheres of influence that had secured European domination of world markets and, indeed, the world's people. Wilson believed that high tariffs denied American producers their share of world markets. In 1913 he had promoted the Underwood Tariff, which reduced U.S. import duties. He had done so not only because of its domestic effects—increased competition, a lower cost of living, and a curb on the trusts—but also as a first step toward an international free-trade system. U.S. producers, Wilson explained in 1912, "have expanded to such a point that they will burst their jackets if they cannot find a free outlet to the markets of the world." Similarly, the Federal Reserve Act of 1912 not only had curbed the excesses of the biggest banks by applying public supervision to the banking system but had also permitted U.S. banks to establish overseas branches. Wilson meant his policies not simply to aid industry and raise the standard of living in the United States; a devout Presbyterian, he also saw the spread of free trade and democratic capitalism as a concrete expression of Christian values.

The war raging in Europe epitomized the very sort of imperialism Wilson detested, and violations of neutral rights now threatened U.S.

peace. The United States faced no immediate military threat. But the president was emotionally and ideologically sympathetic to Great Britain, and he feared that if the Allies were defeated, Germany would emerge as a dangerous economic and military rival and an opponent of the U. S. Open Door policy. Furthermore, he worried that a neutral America would be powerless to help shape the postwar world and would ensure that world markets would be open to what he called "righteous conquest" by American business.

The public was deeply divided by the war. One in nine Americans had been born in a Central Powers country or had a parent who was born there. German Americans generally favored the Central Powers; those with British backgrounds tended to back the Allies. Most Irish Americans, though no special friends of Germany, opposed aid to Britain. Their opposition intensified—as did the struggle for independence in Ireland—after the British crushed the abortive Easter Rebellion of 1916. Nonetheless, when war broke out, the strongest impulse in America was for peace. Peace forces mobilized activists who had previously focused on domestic issues.

Across the country, people rallied to oppose U.S. intervention in the conflict. Many radicals and reformers argued that war would suspend

"Let the Capitalists Do Their Own Fighting"

Radical and socialist opposition to the war was near-absolute, growing out of a sense that the war resulted from inevitable capitalist rivalry for international markets and raw materials. Eugene Debs, industrial union leader and Socialist party presidential candidate, expressed this intense antiwar attitude immediately after the outbreak in Europe in the following editorial, published in August 1914 in the working-class newspaper *National Rip-Saw*.

The capitalists tell us it is patriotic to fight for your country and shed your blood for the flag. Very well! Let them set the example.

It is their country; they own it and therefore according to their logic it is their patriotic duty to fight and die for it and be brought home riddled with bullets and covered with flowers as shining examples of patriotric duty to the youth of the nation. . . .

You never had a country to fight for and never will have as much as an inch of one as long as you are fool enough to make a target of your bodies for the profit and glory of your masters.

Let the capitalists do their own fighting and furnish their own corpses and there will never be another war on the face of the earth.

Source: Frederick C. Griffin, *Six Who Protested: Radical Opposition to the First World War* (1977).

"Babes on Bayonets." Many American newspapers and magazines featured prowar cartoons depicting German atrocities in Belgium. This cartoon appeared in a 1915 edition of the weekly magazine *Life*. Although the German slaughter in Belgium did not actually occur, tens of thousands of Africans had died in the Belgian Congo by 1915, victims of Belgium's ruthless exploitation of its colony's resources.

Source: A. B. Walker, *Life*, 1915—American Social History Project.

domestic reform, endanger civil liberties, and profit big business. Some activists joined an internationalist movement that promoted world order based on international law. Those opposing the war included many progressive journalists, the old Populist Tom Watson, the midwestern progressives George Norris and Robert La Follette, and a large bloc of Democratic congressional representatives from the South and the Midwest. William Jennings Bryan, commenting on what he saw as the pro-British, pro-war bias of the East Coast, complained to his daughter that "the president does not seem to realize that a great part of America lies on the other side of the Allegheny Mountains."

Most feminists and suffragists opposed the war. Jane Addams and Carrie Chapman Catt, president of the National American Woman Suffrage Association, together founded the Women's Peace Party, which attracted 40,000 members. In 1915 Addams became the central U.S. spokesperson at an international conference of women held at The Hague. There, delegates from both sides of the war united in support of woman suffrage and the peaceful resolution of international conflicts. The resolutions they passed eventually became the basis for most of President Wilson's famous Fourteen Points peace plan.

Almost all political and labor radicals opposed U.S. intervention. The Industrial Workers of the World (IWW or Wobblies), the Socialist party, and most anarchists denounced the war as an imperialist conflict—rich men sending poor ones to fight for the cause of empire. "We as members of the industrial army," announced the IWW, "will refuse to fight for any purpose except the realization of industrial freedom." Although relatively few Americans belonged to radical organizations, a growing number were sympathetic to their perspective. In 1914 a Socialist from New York City's Lower East Side was elected to Congress; two years later another was elected mayor of Milwaukee. Tens of thousands of recent immigrants joined Socialist-sponsored ethnic federations. Soon artists, writers, college students, and reformers were caught up in a wave of socialist enthusiasm.

At the other extreme were Americans urging preparedness—a military buildup that would outfit the United States for war. Many advocates of preparedness had ties to banking and commercial interests and were therefore strongly pro-British and pro-French; they anticipated that war profits might be higher than those from neutral trade. Conservative businessmen used preparedness as a patriotic cover for anti-union, antiradical, and nativist campaigns. Theodore Roosevelt and other militarists argued that military discipline would restore men's masculinity, in the same way as the "strenuous life" of competitive sports and outdoor activity he had long promoted. When "I Didn't Raise My Boy to Be a Soldier" became a popular song in 1915, Roosevelt found it so antithetical to his notion of manhood that he suggested it was akin to singing, "I Didn't Raise My Girl to Be a Mother."

Toward Intervention

As the debate over the war raged, President Wilson vacillated. After first supporting neutrality, in the fall of 1915 he recommended a military buildup. A few months later he again switched positions, this time with an eye on the 1916 presidential election. In 1912 Wilson had won the presidency in a three-way contest, with only a minority vote; to be reelected, he would have to woo a sizable bloc of new supporters.

He therefore launched a liberal campaign aimed at attracting progressive, labor, and anti-interventionist voters. In 1916 he appointed the progressive leader Louis Brandeis to the U.S. Supreme Court. Next, he supported important bills to benefit labor and farmers. Once the presidential campaign got under way in the summer of 1916, Wilson began to champion the cause of peace. Although his foreign policy positions were not much different from those of the Republican candidate, Supreme Court Justice Charles Evans Hughes, Wilson campaigned on the slogan "He kept us out of war."

This election-year stance won Wilson strong progressive support. Wilson seemed to back everything progressives believed in: an active federal role in upgrading working and living conditions; the settlement of domestic and international conflicts through conciliation rather than war;

and more broadly, the notion of a new world built on principles of rationality and social harmony. Still, Wilson won the popular vote only narrowly, by fewer than 600,000 votes.

Many progressives believed that Wilson's reelection would usher in an era of peace, progress, and social cooperation. Beginning in 1915, Wilson had attempted to play the role of peacemaker, sending his confidant Colonel Edward House on two peace missions to Europe and urging the establishment of an international organization to enforce peace treaties. Operating on the assumption that world peace was linked to domestic stability and the global expansion of American capitalism, Wilson promoted foreign trade. "Go out and sell goods that will make the world comfortable and more happy, and convert them to the principles of America," he told a group of businessmen visiting the White House. Thus the United States would provide the leadership in establishing a stable international order that Europeans had not.

Wilson renewed his peacemaking efforts after the 1916 election, but neutrality became increasingly difficult to sustain. The $10 million a day the Allies were spending in the United States tied Americans ever closer to the British-French alliance. For Wilson, the "moral obligation . . . to keep us out of this war" conflicted with the "moral obligation . . . to keep free the courses of our commerce and finance."

Meanwhile, sensing imminent victory over the Russians on the Eastern Front, the Germans gambled that blocking vital American supplies would bring quick victory on the Western Front. On February 1, 1917, Germany announced the resumption of unrestricted submarine warfare. Two days later Wilson broke diplomatic relations with Germany. Later that month, British intelligence officers intercepted a telegram from the German foreign secretary, Arthur Zimmermann, to Mexican leaders, proposing that if the United States were to enter the war, Mexico should ally itself with Germany to recover its "lost provinces" in the southwestern United States. Although such an alliance was never a real possibility, the Zimmermann telegram further inflamed U.S. public opinion against Germany.

A Recruiter's Dream. "At last," an army medical examiner exults, "a perfect soldier." Robert Minor's cartoon in the July 1916 *The Masses* was published before the United States entered the war. A year later the magazine's antiwar position would lead to its suppression under the 1917 Espionage Act.

Source: Robert Minor, *The Masses,* July 1916—Tamiment Institute Library, New York University.

At the same time that Americans began to look more harshly on the Central Powers, they also began to view the Allies more favorably. In March 1917, when Russians replaced their autocratic tsar with a liberal democratic government, Wilson could argue that the Allied cause was the cause of democracy. But what finally moved the president to action was his belief that he had to defend U.S. commerce and that he could have a hand in the peace only by joining in war.

Still, when the president went before Congress on April 2, 1917, to seek a declaration of war, he spoke in soaring tones of the need to make the world "safe for democracy." "We shall fight," he told an applauding Congress, "for democracy, for the right of those who submit to authority to have a voice in their own Governments, for the rights and liberties of small nations, . . . and [to] make the world itself at last free." Even though commerce and practical politics underlay the decision for war, this democratic rhetoric would inspire many Americans and Europeans during the closing year and a half of the war.

Nevertheless, some remained skeptical. When Congress voted for war four days later, six senators and fifty members of the House of Representatives dissented, including Jeannette Rankin of Montana, the first woman elected to Congress. Some progressives who had sup-ported Wilson joined the antiwar camp, bitterly disillusioned with the president. Ideological opponents of the war included isolationists, internationalists, pacifists, socialists, Wobblies, and agrarian radicals. In local elections held during the summer and fall of 1917, the Socialist party vote was unusually high—an expression, observers felt, of antiwar sentiment. In the Southwest, clandestine tenant farmer groups urged armed resistance to military conscription. "Now is the time to rebel against this war with German boys," read a poster for an abortive antiwar insurrection in eastern Oklahoma, dubbed the Green Corn Rebellion. "Get together, boys, and don't go. Rich man's war. Poor man's fight."

Mobilizing the Home Front

Fearing that dissent would hinder the nation's ability to win the war, the Wilson administration launched a prowar propaganda campaign. A week after war was declared Wilson set up the Committee on Public Information (CPI). Led by George Creel, a prominent progressive journalist, the committee used sophisticated mass marketing techniques to sell the war. It distributed 75 million pamphlets explaining government policy, placed slick ads in magazines, produced prowar films, and sent out 75,000 speakers to give short talks before any audience they could find, often in movie theaters. As the war went on, the CPI abandoned the pretense that

The Power of Pictures. In the mobilization for war, the U.S. government quickly recognized the power of effective, if often fantastic, imagery to shape public opinion. Most illustrators, and especially editorial cartoonists, eagerly produced prowar work. The government even instituted a Bureau of Cartoons, which issued the weekly *Bulletin for Cartoonists* with suggestions about appropriately patriotic themes and, in some cases, instructions for specific pictures.

Source: Joseph Peunell, chromolithograph, c. 1918—Prints and Photographs Division, Library of Congress.

it was a neutral source of information and began to spread exaggerated stories alleging German atrocities. More propaganda issued from the Treasury Department, which sold Liberty Bonds through patriotic campaigns employing Boy Scouts, movie stars, and local community leaders.

Employers, civic groups, local governments, and the U.S. Congress eagerly joined the crusade. Steel companies sponsored parades, flag-raising ceremonies, and bond drives. School districts instituted loyalty oaths and offered federally prepared "war study courses." Colleges taught similar courses and enlisted students in the new Reserve Officers' Training Corps. More ominously, Congress passed the Espionage Act (1917) restricting freedom of speech during wartime through harsh penalties for antiwar activity and banning treason-ous material from the mails. The law was strengthened the next year by the Sedition Act, which made it illegal to "utter, print, write or publish any disloyal, profane, scurrilous, or abusive language" about the government or the military. Thousands of pacifists and radicals who opposed the war (Eugene Debs among them) were arrested under these laws, which weakened the Left by censoring its press and prosecuting its leadership.

The government also moved to mobilize the nation economically. Through agencies like the War Industries Board, it took greater charge of the nation's economy than it had at any time since the Civil War. Businessmen literally went to work for the government, attempting to rationalize the economy through cooperative agreements. They worked in federal agencies that determined production priorities, fixed prices, and facilitated orderly operations. It was in effect a system of government-sponsored industrial self-regulation, which partially fulfilled the progressive vision of the promotion of social wellbeing through public-private cooperation. The financier Bernard Baruch, who headed the War Industries Board, later recalled that "many businessmen . . . experienced, during the war, for the first time in their careers, the tremendous advantages, both to themselves and to the general public, of combination, of cooperation and common action." The government also took direct control of a few strategic industries: the Railroad Administration ran the nation's entire railroad system as a single unit, while the Shipping Board managed existing merchant ships and launched a massive shipbuilding program.

The Food Administration, a key wartime agency, was typical of the new economic bureaucracy. Its head was Herbert Hoover, a mining engineer who had led a European relief organization. In 1916 and 1917, European demand, bad weather, and small harvests had driven U.S. food prices sky-high. Hoover resisted pressure to institute food rationing or retail price fixing. Instead he used persuasion, threats, patriotic appeals, and the profit motive to increase production, streamline distribution, and encourage conservation. He guaranteed high prices to American wheat farmers so they would plant larger crops. He fixed the profit margin for food processors and coordinated food storage and transportation facilities. And he sent out tens of thousands of volunteers to ask housewives to conserve food through "meatless" and "wheatless" days.

Other wartime agencies increased production by standardizing parts, products, and procedures. Before the war, for example, typewriter ribbons had been produced in 150 different colors; by its end, in only five. Manufacturers expanded their facilities and introduced new production methods, taking advantage of steady wartime demand and "cost-plus" government contracts, which guaranteed a fixed profit plus costs. Thus the government's military budget subsidized private innovation, laying a foundation for postwar profits.

But the wartime measures with arguably the most lasting significance were the Revenue Acts of 1916 and 1917, setting up a progressive tax on incomes. The Sixteenth Amendment to the Constitution (1913) had sanctioned a federal income tax but had affected few Americans and brought in little money. Now, faced with the necessity of raising $33 billion to under-write the cost of the war—an enormous sum for a federal government that was then relatively small—Wilson and progressive Democrats turned to taxes on incomes and corporate profits as sources of federal revenue. Their approach was progressive because it placed the largest tax burden on the wealthiest individuals and corporations (as opposed to a national sales tax, which would have taxed rich and poor alike). By the end of the war, a corporate excess profits tax was generating $2.5 billion per year—more than half the federal government's tax revenues.

Wartime Labor Gains

Expanded industrial production—and after May 1917 the draft—created labor shortages, which benefited the organized labor movement. Individually, workers switched jobs and even moved across the country seeking better wages and working conditions. Collectively, they formed new unions and joined established ones. By 1919 the International Association of Machinists had more than 330,000 members—six times its membership a decade earlier. The Amalgamated Clothing Workers' Union doubled in size during the war, in part because its president, Sidney Hillman, skillfully cultivated ties to federal officials in charge of uniform purchases and labor policy. The railroad brotherhoods mushroomed. Virtually all white railroad workers became union members (most nonwhites were barred), making transportation the country's most heavily unionized industry. Total union membership increased by nearly 70 percent between 1914 and 1920, to over 5 million. Close to one of every five nonagricultural workers belonged to a union.

But even as the number of jobs expanded, and companies with steady, highly profitable orders accepted higher labor costs, labor unrest intensified. Consumer prices rose sharply in 1915 as a result of the war; by 1920 they had doubled. Despite steady employment and higher wages, workers found themselves falling behind as inflation cut their purchasing power. Once the United States entered the war, they had more complaints: state

"Schwab's Bonus Men." A May 1916 cover of *Collier's* weekly magazine presented a romantic portrait of the industrial worker, reflecting the steel companies' sudden turn to extolling the virtues of their workers in the face of a labor shortage.

Source: Herbert Paus, *Collier's*, May 13, 1916—General Research Division, New York Public Library, Astor, Lenox, and Tilden Foundations.

governments suspended safety, hour, and child labor regulations that had been hard won by progressives and unions, and wartime regulations capped workers' wages but not employers' profits.

As the war went on, strikes and threats of strikes became common. Each year from 1916 through 1920, more than one million workers went on strike—a higher proportion of the workforce than during any similar period before or since. And all kinds of workers struck: union and nonunion, skilled and unskilled, male and female, immigrant and native, day laborer and steady worker.

Many war-era walkouts were huge, involving workers from different companies and different industries striking in support of one another. In the summer of 1915, for instance, a wave of strikes hit the booming northeastern munitions industry. In Bridgeport, Connecticut, machinists from eighteen different shops—including a giant Remington Arms plant—demanded an eight-hour day and union recognition. When employers quickly agreed to a shorter workweek, thousands of unskilled workers left their jobs in Bridgeport's corset and textile factories, garment shops, and laundries, demanding similar concessions. "A ten-hour center like Bridgeport," the *New York World* observed, "was converted overnight into an eight-hour community, a result that ten years of agitation under normal conditions might not have accomplished."

During the six months following the U.S. declaration of war in April 1917, union workers in shipbuilding, coal mining, and the metal trades led a massive wave of strikes, collectively withholding more than six million workdays. They struck for many reasons. Most hoped to offset higher prices with increased wages; many sought shorter hours or union recognition. Often strikers made radical demands for control of their work processes, challenging the scientific management and incentive plans employers had implemented in response to government pressure to increase production. Because the thriving economy required full employment, workers' power was enhanced and many of these strikes were successful.

Wartime labor militancy forced the federal government to establish labor relations agencies, which built on the progress labor had made during the first Wilson administration. Labor representatives sat on a number of commissions, along with business and government representatives, a system pioneered by the National Civic Federation. Never before had unions been given so extensive a role in determining and administering federal labor policy. Progressives who were sympathetic to unionism, like Frank Walsh, were appointed to key agency positions. Walsh became cochair of the War Labor Board, an advisory body that advanced the principles of collective bargaining, the eight-hour day, and equal pay for women as part of a government effort to achieve no-strike guarantees.

The wartime labor bureaucracy generally accepted the then-novel idea that strikes resulted from real grievances and the denial of collective bargaining rights. Hoping to forestall strikes and reduce job turnover, government officials pressured employers to raise pay, shorten working hours, and improve working conditions. Many believed that a strong union movement would channel workers' discontent into orderly contract negotiations and conflict resolution. As President Wilson declared, "Our laws and the long-established policy of our government recognize the right of workingmen to organize unions if they so desire."

Although some government officials who opposed unionism failed to enforce the new policy, organized labor generally benefited from the federal government's directives. In the meat-packing industry, a combination of pressure from Washington, federal arbitration, and an aggressive union-organizing campaign won the long-sought eight-hour day. "It is a new day," proclaimed union leader William Z. Foster to a meat-packers' rally. The stockyard unions grew rapidly; by the end of the war, the national membership of the Amalgamated Meatcutters' Union exceeded 62,000.

Wilson's support for labor convinced most labor leaders to rally behind the war effort. Many saw it as an opportunity; by supporting the administration they hoped to win more influence over federal labor policy and to boost public support for organized labor. Not only the labor movement, but also working people themselves benefited. Steady work and higher pay raised their living standard. Families that had once struggled to survive could now hope for a decent life.

The Great Migration

Even before the United States entered the war, expanding industrial production had dramatically altered patterns of work and residence. Just when more workers than ever were needed in mines, factories, and fields, the flow of immigrants across the Atlantic dropped sharply because of the war. In 1914 more than 1 million Europeans had come to America; in 1915 the number fell to under 200,000, and in 1918, to only 31,000. That year the unemployment rate fell to just 2.4 percent, down from over 15 percent just three years earlier.

Previously disdained groups—immigrants, African Americans, Appalachian whites, and women—suddenly became desirable employees. Immigrant men who had known only unskilled or semiskilled employment found better jobs; more foreign-born women found paid work. Steel companies that once had counted on rapid turnover to defuse worker discontent now built housing for immigrant workers, raised their wages, granted them promotions, and offered citizenship classes. The general manager of the Youngstown Sheet and Tube Company urged his foremen in

March 1917 to show a "spirit of helpfulness and consideration" toward foreign-born workers. "These men are needed by our company," he explained.

The war also accelerated the movement of Americans from the countryside to the city. The rapidly expanding auto industry, in particular, attracted workers from rural areas in the Midwest, Canada, and the South. Between 1910 and 1920 more than half a million white southerners moved out of their region. The mountainous areas of the upper South were particularly ripe for an exodus. Farming had always been difficult in the Appalachian Mountains; by the time war broke out, much of the area's timber had been cut, and many coal mines were worked out. When the war opened up high-paying jobs in nearby northern cities, an estimated 50,000 West Virginians moved to Akron, Ohio, center of the booming rubber industry.

The "Great Migration" of black southerners offered the most visible example of the shift from country to city. Although African Americans had been moving north in small numbers since the end of Reconstruction, the geographic distribution of the country's black population was much the same in 1910 as it had been half a century earlier. Nine of every ten African Americans lived in the South, chiefly in rural areas. During the next ten years about 500,000 blacks left the South, most of them after

Tracking the Great Migration: Railroad Routes Followed by Black Migrants. As this map shows, African-American migrants to the North chose their destinations primarily based on their state of origin: those from Georgia and the Carolinas headed to cities along the eastern seaboard like New York and Philadelphia; migrants from Alabama and Mississippi headed for the midwestern cities like Chicago; and those from Texas, Louisiana, and Tennessee often headed west to California.

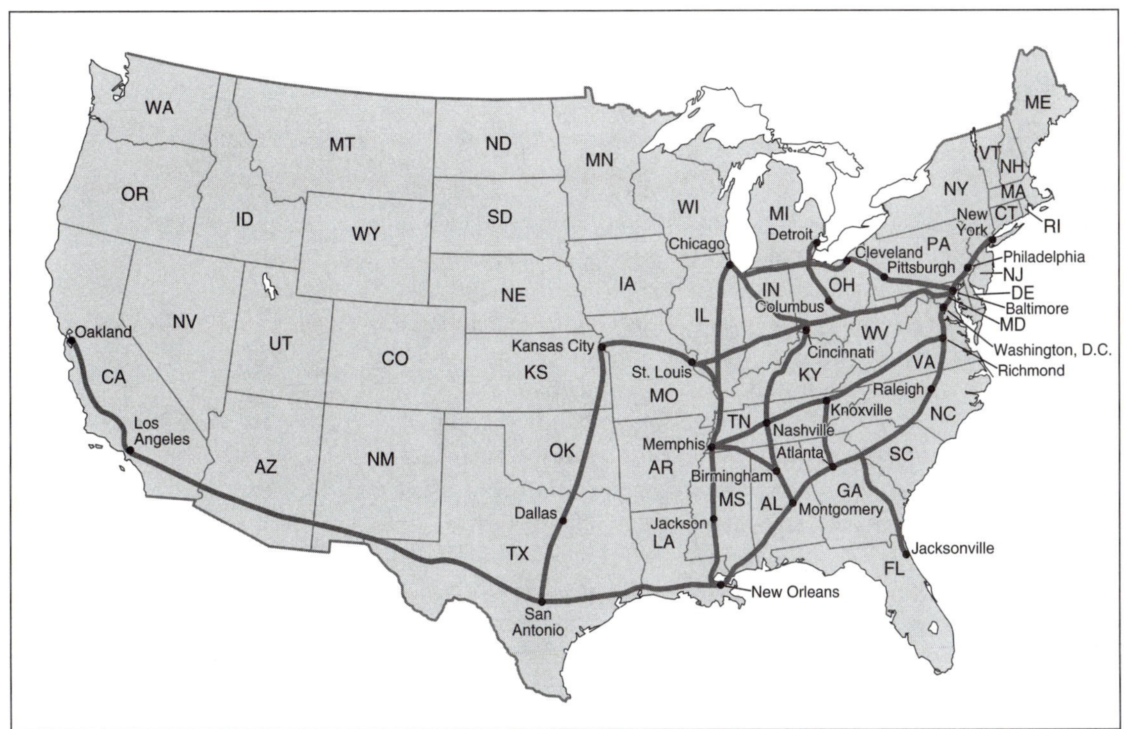

1916. The African-American population of Chicago nearly doubled, to more than 100,000. New York, with 150,000 black residents, became the largest African-American center in the country.

Black Americans had plenty of reasons to leave the rural South: disfranchisement, segregation, poverty, racial violence, lack of educational opportunities, the drudgery of farm life, and just the daily indignities of living under Jim Crow laws. For Joseph Brown, the turning point came when he was ill and asked an Atlanta druggist for a glass of water. Despite a shelf of glasses and a soda fountain, the druggist directed Brown to a bucket of dirty, soapy water out back. "When I left that store and walking back up the hill home, I said, 'God, if you give me strength and give me my health,' I says, 'this will never happen to me again.'" Another migrant, Alphonse Oliver, from rural Tennessee, recalled that he had to walk five miles to get to the nearest black school, even though there was a white schoolhouse across the road from his house.

Hard times accelerated the migration of rural black farmers like Oliver. In 1916, a particularly bad year in the South, the boll weevil attacked the cotton crop and floods caused extensive damage. "The two calamities," wrote one black Georgian, "left the average farm laborer with nothing to start out with to make a crop for next year . . . [H]e wants to migrate to where he can see a chance to get work." Of course, neither the push of southern poverty and racism nor the pull of northern jobs caused most southern blacks to migrate. As late as 1940, three-quarters of all African Americans remained in the South. Even in the worst years, black southerners managed to endure.

Before the war stepped up the need for workers, racial discrimination had severely limited job possibilities in the North. Only with the war did employers begin hiring African Americans for jobs they once had been shut out of. Some companies even sent agents to the South to recruit black workers. More often southern African Americans learned about jobs and conditions from northern black newspapers, such as the *Chicago Defender*.

Leaving was not always easy. In addition to the usual concerns about relocating, African Americans had to cope with white southerners who tried to prevent an exodus of workers crucial to southern agriculture. Plantation overseers used violence and threats; state and local governments passed laws designed to put labor recruiters out of business. But the Great Migration quickly developed its own momentum. Migrants wrote home urging others to join them, enclosing money when they could. Kinship and social networks soon linked particular places. Migrants from Virginia, the Carolinas, and Georgia tended to move to the Northeast. African Americans from Mississippi, Alabama, Louisiana, Arkansas, and Texas usually headed to the Midwest—especially Chicago—or West, particularly to Oakland, California, the western terminus of the Southern Pacific Railroad.

"People We Can Get Along Without." A series of cartoons by Leslie Rogers, published during the 1920s in the *Chicago Defender,* conveyed everyday tensions between recently arrived southern migrants and longtime residents in the city's African-American community. Rogers's *Defender* comic strip, "Bungleton Green," which started in 1920, featured the misadventures of a naive migrant from the South.

Source: Leslie Rogers, *Chicago Defender,* July 9, 1921—*Chicago Defender.*

Leaving the South did not mean escaping racism. Kept out of white neighborhoods by law or custom, African Americans crowded into inner-city neighborhoods that became ghettos. In heavy industry—steel, meat packing, autos, shipbuilding, and mining—black men were restricted to unskilled jobs, which were often the dirtiest and most physically taxing. Black workers were generally paid less than white workers, although more than they could earn in the South. Black women usually worked as domestic servants; in 1920 fewer than 7 percent of them worked in industry. Hard as their work might be, the continuing shortage of domestic servants gave black women the opportunity not only to move north, but to shift from job to job in search of better working conditions. In a five-year period starting in 1911, Beatrice Bingham worked as a domestic and a hairdresser, moving from Connecticut to California to New York, then back to California, to Chicago, and back to New York.

Some black northerners, embarrassed by the migrants' unsophisticated ways and anxious about their own tenuous positions, resented the southern newcomers. And as the white and black population competed for jobs, housing, and political power, racial tensions worsened. White workers, motivated by a deep-seated racism and fearful that black workers would take their jobs or force down wage levels, staged wildcat strikes against employers who hired black workers. White progressives in the meat-packing and coal-mining unions tried to sign up the newcomers, but most unions either barred black workers entirely or segregated them in all-black locals with restricted voting and job rights.

Some African Americans responded to racism by forming their own unions. In Newport News, Virginia, a former IWW organizer established the National Brotherhood Workers of America, which enrolled hundreds of black shipyard workers. But more often African Americans rejected unionism entirely. Black ministers, politicians, and editors often argued, as had Booker T. Washington, that black workers were more likely to find allies among white employers than among white workers. Though the AFL used black organizers in its wartime campaign to organize Chicago stockyard workers, only 15 percent of African Americans joined, compared with nearly 90 percent of Poles and Slovaks. One southern black migrant expressed a common view: "Unions ain't no good for a colored man. I've seen too much of what they don't do for him."

The vicious cycle of job competition and racism exploded in July 1917 in East St. Louis, Illinois. When black workers helped to break a strike at an aluminum factory, white union workers launched a campaign

Silent Parade. Thousands of Harlem residents marched down Fifth Avenue on July 28, 1917, in a demonstration organized by the NAACP to protest race riots in East St. Louis, Illinois.

Source: Schomburg Center for Research in Black Culture, New York Public Library, Astor, Lenox, and Tilden Foundations.

to drive recently arrived African Americans out of town. A shooting incident touched off a full-scale riot. White mobs invaded black neighborhoods; bystanders were assaulted, shot, and lynched. At the end of two days of fighting, forty black people (including a two-year-old child who was shot and thrown into a burning building) and nine white people had been killed.

In spite of all the problems African Americans encountered, many kept coming North. One former southerner wrote back home: "I should have been here twenty years ago. I just begin to feel like a man. . . .

"We Lost Everything But What We Had On"

In the following letter to a friend, a victim of the 1917 East St. Louis riot recounted the terror of being caught in the middle of the violence.

3946 W. Belle
St. Louis, Mo.

Dearest Louise:

Was very glad to hear from you. Your letter was forwarded from what used to be my house.

Louise, it was awful. I hardly know where to begin telling you about it. First I will say we lost everything but what we had on and that was very little. . . .

It started early in the afternoon. We kept receiving calls over the phone to pack our trunks and leave, because it was going to be awful. We did not heed the calls, but sent grandma & the baby on to St. Louis & said we would "stick" no matter what happened. At first, when the fire started, we stood on Broadway & watched it. As they neared our house we went in & went to the basement. It was too late to run then. They shot & yelled some thing awful, finally they reached our house. At first, they did not bother us (we watched from the basement window), they remarked that "white people live in that house, this is not a nigger house." Later, someone must have tipped them that it was a "nigger" house, because, after leaving us for about 20 min[utes] they returned & yelling like mad "kill the 'niggers,' burn that house."

It seemed the whole house was falling in on us. Then some one said, they must not be there, if they are they are certainly dead. Then some one shouted "they are in the basement. Surround them and burn it down." Then they ran down our steps. Only prayer saved us, we were under tubs & any thing we could find praying & keeping as quiet as possible, because if they had seen one face, we would have been shot or burned to death. When they were about to surround the house and burn it, we heard an awful noise & thought they were dynamiting the house. (The Broadway Theater fell in, we learned later.) Sister tipped the door to see if the house was on fire. She saw the reflection of a soldier on the front door—pulled it open quickly & called for help. All of us ran out then & was taken to the city hall for the night—(just as we were). The next morning we . . . were sent on to St. Louis. Had to walk across the bridge with a line of soldiers on each side . . . in the hot sun, no hats, & and scarcely no clothing . . .

On Tuesday evening . . . our house was burned with two soldiers on guard. . . . We were told that [the crowd] looted the house before burning it. . . .

Source: Robert Asher, "Document of the Race Riot at East St. Louis," *Journal of the Illinois State Historical Society* (1972).

My children are going to the same school with the whites and I don't have to humble to no one. . . . Will vote in the next election and there isn't any 'yes, sir, and no, sir.' "

Tension on the Southern Border

While African Americans headed north, U.S. relations with countries in Central and South America grew tense. Though Wilson supported nonintervention in Europe, he took a different stance toward the Western Hemisphere, using troops to defend U.S. property in Cuba, Haiti, Nicaragua, and the Dominican Republic. "I am going to teach the South American republics to elect good men!" the president declared. American Marines and naval forces intervened in Haiti in 1915, and the next year began an eight-year military occupation of the Dominican Republic. In these places, Americans appointed financial advisers, supervised elections, and maintained law and order by putting down popular insurrections. The United States also became deeply involved in the Mexican Revolution.

The Mexican Revolution had begun in 1910 with an armed revolt against the thirty-five-year dictatorship of Porfirio Diaz. At first a fight over the presidential succession, the conflict broadened into widespread strife that lasted a decade and cost a million lives. Wilson backed first one Mexican faction and then another, hoping to protect U.S.-owned property, especially oil interests. The United States intervened twice. In 1914, U.S. troops occupied the city of Vera Cruz. Two years later, General Pershing led a U.S. expedition into northern Mexico, after Mexican troops loyal to the agrarian radical Francisco "Pancho" Villa raided a town in

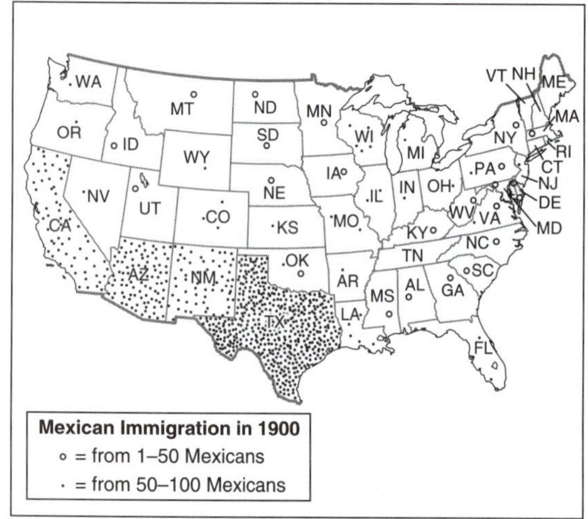

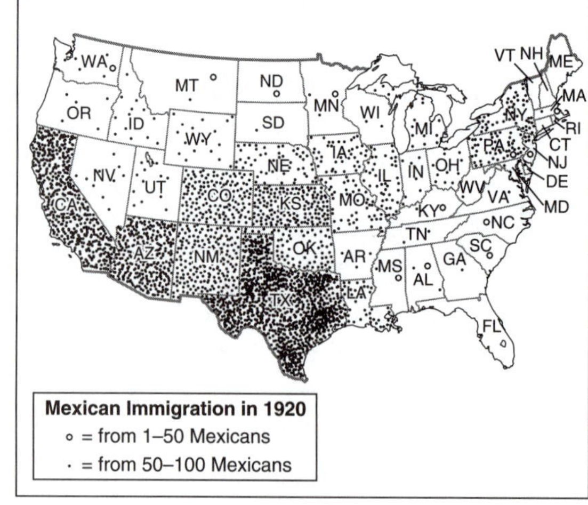

From Mexico to the United States, 1900–1920. These maps, covering the years 1900–1920, illustrate the growth of Mexican immigration and the spread of immigrants into the Midwest.

New Mexico. There was talk of war, but both countries stepped back. Still, U.S. leaders were uncomfortable with Mexican self-rule, in part because Mexico's new constitution nationalized that country's mineral resources and restricted foreign ownership of its oil.

To avoid the inflation, violence, and social chaos that accompanied the revolution, many Mexicans fled to the United States. In the years before the war, new railroads had opened up the northern part of Mexico, drawing many individuals from the crowded central provinces to the region near the U.S. border. Soon they were pulled across the border by economic opportunities in the rapidly growing American Southwest. There was no quota on Mexican immigration, and according to official statistics, more than 185,000 Mexicans entered the United States between 1910 and 1919. Many more crossed the border unofficially. Some estimates indicate that the total number of people of Mexican heritage living in the United States doubled during the decade, to about 750,000.

Crossing the border was easy. Officials and border patrols understood that the economy of the American Southwest, not legal restrictions, determined Mexican immigration. They were concerned primarily about Chinese immigrants who might try to enter the country through Mexico. As Charles Armijo, who crossed the border between Juárez and El Paso during the Mexican Revolution, explained, "Well, we just came over. . . . Everybody was allowed to go back and forth whenever they wanted. . . . We came over on the streetcar."

Invading Forces. A 1914 Mexican postcard shows a company of U.S. soldiers marching along the Avenida Independencia in Vera Cruz. **Source**: Photography Collection, Harry Ransom Humanities Research Center, University of Texas at Austin.

Some Mexicans came temporarily, hoping to save money and return home quickly. Others, intending to stay, settled in established Mexican-American communities. However long they planned to stay, most worked in agriculture, especially in Texas, California, Arizona, and Colorado. Railroads and mines also hired large numbers of workers; by 1911 about 60 percent of Arizona's smelter workers were Mexicans. Wages were seven to twenty times those paid in Mexico, but still very low by U.S. standards. As the southwestern labor supply swelled, some Mexican Americans, including many with roots in the region that went back to the 1840s, left for better-paying industrial jobs in the Midwest.

World War I created some new opportunities at military bases around San Antonio, especially in construction, transportation, and maintenance work. After the United States entered World War I, many Mexicans working in the United States feared they would be drafted. But Mexican labor had become vital to the southwestern economy, and employers pushed the federal government to assure Mexican workers they would be exempt from the draft. To protect agricultural, mine, and railroad workers, the

"Iron Road"

Many songs composed by Mexican immigrants expressed homesickness, disappointment, and concern over the adoption of "American" values. In the song below, the completion of a railroad line stretching over six hundred miles from Victoria, Texas, to central Mexico is portrayed as an occasion for alarm rather than celebration.

El Ferrocarril

La máquina pasajera
No puede hacer cosa buena
Porque "oscurece" en su casa
Y amanece en tierra ajena.

¡Ay! ¡qué dolor!
Tendrían los mexicanos
Al ver el ferrocarril
Que traen los americanos.

La máquina chiquitita
Ws la que ha quedado aquí
Y la quieren llegar
Hasta San Luis Potosí.

Oigan y oigan
El ferrocarril bramar
Él que lleva a los hombres
Y nunca los vuelve a traer.

Iron Road

She's like a bird of passage
Who never can do the right thing.
She leaves her home every evening
Just to see what the morning might bring.

Oh, what a pain
Will visit those Mexicans
When they hear her steaming down the track,
The train of the Americans.

Just a little bitty steam engine
Is all they left for me
And they really think it'll go from here
To San Luis Potosí.

Listen, listen,
Hear her roar down the track
She's coming for a load of men
That she won't be bringing back.

Source: Manuel Gamio, *Mexican Immigration to the United States* (1930).

government also suspended a 1917 immigration law that banned contract labor and imposed a literacy test and a head tax on immigrants. Nevertheless, Mexican Americans encountered discrimination all over the Southwest, in segregated schools, theaters, restaurants, and neighborhoods. Often Mexican workers were paid less than the Anglos who worked beside them. Most unions ignored or excluded them or relegated them to separate locals.

Here as elsewhere in the United States, discrimination sometimes produced violent reactions. In the lower Rio Grande Valley, Mexicans and Mexican Americans fought the Texas Rangers in hundreds of incidents between 1915 and 1917. Most of the disorder occurred in areas where commercialized farming of vegetables and cotton had displaced the old Mexican rancho society. The farmers often used violence and intimidation to wrest Mexicans' land from them. Displaced ranchers fought back by raiding farms and sabotaging trains and irrigation systems. The Mexicans saw themselves as part of the *Plan de San Diego,* a group of as many as three thousand men, most of whom had been driven off the land—sometimes at gunpoint by Texas Rangers—and had pledged to fight "Yankee tyranny." Twenty-one Anglo Americans were killed in these clashes; in reprisal, three hundred Mexican Americans were executed without trial. The sheriff of Cameron County, Texas, attributed the conflict to the "unwillingness of American newcomers to the valley to accept the Mexican," and claimed the Rangers often shouted, "We have to make this a white man's country!!" In the end, the ranchers were reduced to wage laborers.

There was a strong radical strain in the Mexican-American community. Before the revolution many critics of the Mexican government had gone into exile in the United States, where they organized political parties, put out newspapers, and developed ties with U.S. radicals. The revolution strengthened Mexican-American radicalism. Soon the Socialist party and the IWW had large Mexican-American memberships. In New Mexico and Arizona in 1917, the Western Federation of Miners and the United Mine Workers of America brought Anglo and Mexican miners together to cooperate in a series of mine strikes. But their struggle to eliminate unequal wages and win union recognition ended when thousands of Mexican-born strikers were arrested, and many of them deported.

Other Mexican immigrants avoided political activity, concentrating instead on saving money to buy land or businesses back home. But like many Slavs and Italians before them, many Mexican immigrants gave up plans to return home and settled permanently in the United States. Over time, the long-established Spanish-speaking communities of the West and Southwest became increasingly important in this, the fastest-growing region of the country. Unlike European immigrants, however, Mexican Americans lived not across an ocean from their homeland, but across a nearby border. Many went back and forth, to work or to stay with family. In individual lives and in the character of the border towns, two cultures coexisted.

Women Workers and Woman Suffrage

Like Mexicans, women workers found new opportunities in the wartime economy. For the first time they were hired for traditionally male jobs—for example, as railroad workers and streetcar conductors. Others found metalworking and munitions jobs, often as part of a management decision to hire less-skilled workers. Most of these women moved up from lower-paying jobs they had held before the war in female-dominated occupations, although some had never worked for pay. Male unionists, fearing for their own jobs and pay rates, generally resisted the practice of hiring women. Their worries were unfounded, for the gains women made in traditional blue-collar work proved temporary; once the war ended, most women left or were forced out of their jobs.

But the war did hasten the expansion of one area of work—clerical jobs—that had been open to women since the 1890s. Women worked in government bureaucracies, which expanded with the U.S. entry into the war. Even more worked for the growing corporations, which found that achieving and then maintaining horizontal and vertical integration of production and resources demanded considerable paperwork. By 1920 there were nearly eight times as many women clerical workers as there had been in 1900. Despite the loss of blue-collar jobs at the end of the war, there were still 700,000 more women in the labor force in 1920 than in 1910.

Arms and the Woman. Recently hired women operating equipment in a Bloomfield, New Jersey, munitions plant, 1917.

Source: Sophia Smith Collection, Smith College.

The war also opened up some new opportunities for black women, the least advantaged group in the workforce. Even in Southern cities like Atlanta, some factories hired black women; between 1910 and 1920, the percentage of black women in domestic service dropped from 84 to 75 percent. Worried employers used legal and illegal coercion to reverse this trend. "Work or Fight" laws, ostensibly intended to force unemployed men into military service, were used in the South to prosecute black women who declined jobs as household workers. A vigilante group in Vicksburg, Mississippi, harassed "idle" black workers, a group that included women who didn't want to work as domestics. They tarred and feathered Ethel Barrett while her husband was away fighting in France.

On other fronts, some women war workers were better situated to demand social and political rights and advance the movement for woman suffrage. In New York City, working-class suffragists saw a close link between the vote and the conditions on the job. "Why are you paid less than a man?" asked a leaflet put out by the Wage-Earners' Suffrage League there. "Why do you work in a firetrap? Why are your hours so long?" The answer: "Because you are a woman and have no vote. Votes make the law. Votes enforce the law. The law controls conditions."

The war years saw new divisions within the suffrage movement, particularly over tactical questions. A new militant suffrage group, the National Woman's Party (NWP), formed in 1916. Led by Alice Paul, a social worker who had studied in England, the NWP was founded on the tactics of British suffragists, who held the party in power responsible for the denial of the vote to women. To publicize their grievance, the NWP began picketing the White House. Arrested, the imprisoned pickets went on a hunger strike and were brutally force-fed. The more conservative women's groups, led by the largest suffrage group, the North American Woman Suffrage Association (NAWSA), took the opposite tack, energetically supporting the war by knitting socks, selling war bonds, and preparing Red Cross supplies. They cemented an alliance with Wilson and united local and state suffrage groups in a centrally directed effort.

In different ways, both groups tried to use Wilson's democratic rhetoric to their own advantage. As one historian points out, "Wilson's 'safe for democracy' speech was analogous to Lincoln's Emancipation Proclamation, which did not free any slaves but probably made freeing them inevitable." By asking Americans to fight for "democracy versus autocracy," Wilson put compelling logic behind the drive for universal suffrage.

The combination of the NWP's militant agitation and NAWSA's pragmatic political alliances worked. In 1914, women had acquired the right to vote in the territory of Alaska and in eleven states—all of them except Illinois west of the Mississippi. NAWSA spent the next three years conducting vigorous campaigns throughout the East, while the NWP kept up the pressure in Washington. By 1917, women had won at least partial voting rights in eight additional states, including New York, long a major battleground, and Arkansas, the first southern state to grant suffrage.

Hands Across the Water. Demonstrators in front of the White House in July 1917 appealed to representatives of the new Russian government to support American woman suffrage as a condition for Russia's remaining in the Allied camp. The banner roused the ire of patriotic passersby, and soon after this photograph was taken an angry crowd attacked the suffragists. **Source:** Harris and Ewing, 1917—National Archives.

In January 1918 the House of Representatives passed a constitutional amendment giving women the right to vote. Despite Wilson's endorsement of the measure as "vital to the winning of the war," anti-suffrage Republicans and southern Democratic Senators blocked the amendment. In response, the NWP and NAWSA mobilized a massive outpouring of marches, parades, and meetings to overcome lingering opposition in the Senate and state legislatures, three-quarters of which had to ratify the amendment. On August 18, 1920, Tennessee became the crucial thirty-sixth state to ratify the Nineteenth Amendment, after a twenty-four-year-old legislator changed his vote at the insistence of his elderly mother. The Nineteenth Amendment went into effect in time for that year's presidential election. Among the first voters was ninety-one-year-old Charlotte Woodward, who as a teenager had witnessed the start of the women's rights movement at Seneca Falls seventy-two years earlier.

Working-Class Protest and Political Radicalism

The same radical spirit that infected the most militant suffragists infused some working-class struggles as well. In some cases the new radicalism had foreign sources. Many Europeans who came to America in the decade prior to World War I had been proponents of socialism, anarchism, and trade unionism in their native lands. As their influence spread through immigrant communities, workers grew increasingly receptive to collective action and political radicalism. The sense of radical possibility—that society could be fundamentally transformed—grew in November 1917, when V. I. Lenin and his Bolshevik party led a successful Communist revolution in Russia. Other leaders, like Eugene Debs, drew their radicalism from American sources, and insisted that the United States live up to the democratic promises Wilson and others trumpeted.

The new militancy often came from people who had previously seemed indifferent to radicalism and collective action. Among them were many unskilled immigrant workers who had planned to return to their native lands but now were stranded by the wartime disruption of transatlantic travel. Miserable job conditions once seen as temporary became

"We Don't Want Other Women Ever to Have to Do This Over Again"

Polish-born suffragist Rose Winslow (her given name was Ruza Wenclawska) started working in a Pennsylvania textile mill at age eleven, quitting eight years later when she developed tuberculosis. In 1917 she was one of five protesters sentenced to seven months in prison for obstructing traffic in front of the White House. After she and National Woman's Party founder Alice Paul began a hunger strike, they were transferred to a prison hospital. Winslow smuggled out an account she kept of her stay.

If this thing is necessary we will naturally go through with it. Force is so stupid a weapon. I feel so happy doing my bit for decency—for *our* war, which is after all, real and fundamental.

The women are all so magnificent, so beautiful. Alice Paul is as thin as ever, pale and large-eyed. We have been in solitary for five weeks. There is nothing to tell but that the days go by somehow. I have felt quite feeble the last few days—faint, so that I could hardly get my hair brushed, my arms ached so. But to-day I am well again. Alice Paul and I talk back and forth though we are at opposite ends of the building and a hall door also shuts us apart. But occasionally—thrills—we escape from behind our iron-barred doors and visit. Great laughter and rejoicing!

My fainting probably means nothing except that I am not strong after these weeks. I know you won't be alarmed.

I told about a syphilitic colored woman with one leg. The other one was cut off, having rotted so that it was alive with maggots when she came in. The remaining one is now getting as bad. They are so short of nurses that a little colored girl of twelve, who is here waiting to have her tonsils removed, waits on her. This child and two others share a ward with a syphilitic child of three or four years, whose mother refuses to have it at home. It makes you absolutely ill to see it. . . .

Alice Paul is in the psychopathetic ward. She dreaded forcible feeding frightfully, and I hate to think how she must be feeling. I had a nervous time of it, gasping a long time afterward, and my stomach rejecting during the process. I spent a bad, restless night, but otherwise I am all right. The poor soul who fed me got liberally besprinkled during the process. I heard myself making the most hideous sounds. . . . One feels so forsaken when one lies prone and people shove a pipe down one's stomach.

This morning but for an astounding tiredness, I am all right. I am waiting to see what happens when the President realizes that brutal bullying isn't quite a statesmanlike method for settling a demand for justice at home. At least, if men are supine enough to endure, women—to their eternal glory— are not. . . .

. . . Don't let them tell you we take this well. Miss Paul vomits much. I do, too. . . . We think of the coming feeding all day. It is horrible. The doctor thinks I take it well. I hate the thought of Alice Paul and the others if I take it well. . . .

All the officers here know we are making this hunger strike that women fighting for liberty may be considered political prisoners; we have told them. God knows we don't want other women ever to have to do this over again.

Source: Doris Stevens, *Jailed for Freedom* (1920).

Just Before the Firing Started. Moments after these striking workers were photographed confronting guards outside the Bayonne, New Jersey, Standard Oil Works, the private police opened fire, killing five strikers.

Source: Prints and Photographs Division, Library of Congress.

intolerable when viewed as permanent. In Bayonne, New Jersey, Polish refinery workers had long accepted low pay, long hours, and dangerous working conditions. But when they walked off the job in 1915, virtually the entire Polish community supported them. Only police violence and hired thugs broke the strike: five strikers were killed by gunfire. Visiting Bayonne, wrote journalist Mary Heaton Vorse, "you realize that you are in a terrorized city, and that fear is in the very air that you breathe." Still, refinery workers struck again the next year.

Housewives as well as workers took to the streets, protesting high food prices. Wartime inflation had pushed food prices to astonishing levels—potatoes more than doubled in price during one month in 1916—and wages, though increasing, could not keep up. In early 1917, a desperate Brooklyn woman overturned a peddler's pushcart. Running after her, the vendor was attacked by hundreds of other women; eventually a thousand rioters battled police. One officer, who refused to arrest rioting women in another Brooklyn neighborhood the next day, explained, "I just didn't have the heart to do it. They were just crazy with hunger, and I don't see how I could blame them."

Women in Philadelphia and Boston took similar action. In Manhattan, women marched on City Hall, shouting "We want food for our children." The socialist, Meyer London, who represented the East Side of New York, defended them on the floor of the House of Representatives: "When women and children cry for bread you cannot designate it a riot. It is an outcry to heaven for relief."

In this atmosphere of militancy, the Industrial Workers of the World found new life. The organization had been in decline when the war started, but during the war years shifted its focus from eastern factory towns like Lawrence, Massachusetts, and Paterson, New Jersey, to the West and the Midwest. There the Wobblies recruited migratory workers—semiskilled and unskilled farm workers, lumberjacks, railroad men, and miners who moved from job to job, often weathering long bouts of unemployment. Most were single; many were immigrants. They were attracted to the IWW because they were alienated—literally

Food Riot, 1917. Wartime inflation severely taxed the limited budgets of working-class families. After confronting pushcart peddlers who were charging exorbitant rates for necessities, thousands of women marched to New York's City Hall on February 20, 1917, to demand relief. The "food riot" precipitated a boycott campaign that eventually forced pushcart prices down. **Source**: National Archives.

rootless and terribly exploited, on the job and in the miserable barracks employers provided to house them. The IWW organizers understood their needs and offered social networks as well as union leadership.

In 1916 the Wobblies led a strike of ten thousand miners in the Mesabi iron range of northern Minnesota, and they then began an intensive campaign to organize northwestern lumber workers. Around the same time, a new unit of the IWW, the Agricultural Workers' Organization (AWO), signed up thousands of midwestern harvest workers. Most of them were single men who lived in Chicago, Kansas City, Minneapolis, and other midwestern cities during the winter and spent their summers riding the rails, following the harvest. The AWO won better pay and working conditions from wheat farmers more eager to take advantage of high grain prices than of cheap labor.

In response to these successes, government at all levels attacked the radical Wobblies, trying to stigmatize them as illegitimate. IWW organizers were repeatedly arrested, and strikers were beaten or shot by police and hired thugs. In Everett, Washington, sheriff's deputies removed forty Wobbly prisoners from jail in October 1916, took them to a wooded park, stripped them, and made them run a gauntlet of vigilantes, who beat the naked prisoners with guns and whips. A later confrontation left seven people dead. In September 1917 federal agents raided every IWW office in the country, arresting some three hundred leaders on charges of espionage and sedition. Within six months, two

The Bisbee Deportation, July 12, 1917. All over the country Wobblies faced coordinated government-employer attacks. In Bisbee, Arizona, a local sheriff, with the aid of the Phelps-Dodge mining company, deputized townspeople to break up an IWW-led strike. Vigilantes arrested twelve hundred alleged Wobblies, aliens, and subversives and, as shown in this photograph, loaded them into cattle cars. The cars were towed to the middle of the New Mexico desert and abandoned.

Source: Archives of Labor and Urban Affairs, Wayne State University.

thousand Wobblies were in jail awaiting trial, including the entire executive board. Most were eventually convicted of violating wartime statutes and sentenced to long jail terms. The IWW would never recover from these setbacks.

Repression and Nativism

The attack on the IWW was only one part of a government effort to end protest and silence dissent. Press censorship was extensive. In the summer of 1917, the Post Office Department refused second-class mailing privileges to newspapers and magazines that were critical of the war, the draft, or even the way the war was being conducted. Socialist periodicals, with a combined prewar circulation exceeding half a million, were banned from the mails. The foreign-language press was closely watched: a federal law required that articles discussing the war or the government be submitted in translation for prior approval—a process so costly that many papers folded, and others adopted a pro-government stance in hopes of winning exemption from the rule. Professors who protested the use of educational institutions to promote the war were fired. Their dismissal prompted the formation of the American Association of University Professors (AAUP) and the demand for job tenure to protect faculty members' freedom of speech.

"The I.W.W. and the Other Features That Go With It." By using the acronym "I.W.W." in place of the features of Kaiser Wilhelm, this 1917 *New York Globe* cartoon accused the Wobblies of treason.

Source: Harold Tucker Webster, *Cartoon Magazine,* September 1917—Prints and Photographs Division, Library of Congress.

Critics of the war were also silenced through arrest. Fifteen hundred people were put on trial for opposing the war or counseling draft resistance. Over six thousand German and Austrian nationals were detained as potential threats to national security. The Wilson administration was especially concerned about antiwar sentiment among workers. To counteract the widespread belief that the United States was fighting a businessmen's war, the Department of Labor and the Committee on Public Information deluged factories with posters, slogans, and speakers. The government also launched an unprecedented campaign to manipulate the political direction of the union movement, aiding unions that supported the war and harassing or destroying those that opposed it.

Government repression bred a vigilante spirit. Radical opponents of the war, and even those who simply refused to buy Liberty Bonds, were harassed and beaten. Members of "loyalty" organizations spied on neighbors and coworkers; in the name of patriotism, reactionaries and businessmen used their reports to harass radicals and unionists. The Department of Justice granted funding and quasi-official status to the largest loyalty organization, the American Protective League, which claimed a quarter of a million members.

Immigrants had a particularly hard time. Even before the United States had joined the conflict, the loyalties of "hyphenated" Americans (German Americans, Polish Americans, and so forth) had been questioned. Immigrants were seen as potentially more loyal to their countries of birth than to their adopted land. In fact, the opposite was often true: the experience of war led many immigrants to identify closely with the United States. Tens of thousands of them entered the armed forces, fought in the war, and embraced the rhetoric of democracy and self-determination that Wilson trumpeted.

Even so, fears of divided loyalties lingered. Wilson spoke of the need for "100 percent Americanism," while Theodore Roosevelt called for "America for Americans." Suspicion and hostility focused particularly on German Americans. Mobs attacked German-American stores and drove German-American performers off the stage. German Americans were harassed, beaten, tarred and feathered, forced to kiss the flag, and, in at least one instance, lynched. Not surprisingly, many Americans with German names changed them.

"This Is for Traitors." The pillory, a device used in colonial New England to punish through public ridicule, was resurrected in Cincinnati in 1918. Placed in a public square, this pillory was "a warning to citizens of Cincinnati as to what they may expect in case of disloyalty." Unable to find a convenient dissenter immediately, the photographer of this picture had to make do with an acquiescent volunteer. **Source**: J. R. Schmidt, 1918—National Archives.

Amid this hysteria, Congress passed several nativist measures. In 1917 a law enacted over Wilson's veto imposed a literacy test and other restrictions on immigration. The same year, Congress passed the Eighteenth Amendment to the Constitution, which banned the manufacture or sale of alcoholic beverages; it was ratified in 1919. Though temperance supporters had long advocated Prohibition on moral grounds or as a means of increasing productivity, nativism was involved, too. Alcohol was commonly associated with immigrants, specifically German Americans, who dominated the brewing industry.

Like many other aspects of the wartime loyalty campaign, Prohibition had little to do with the direct requirements of fighting a war. Rather, the international crisis seemed to validate nativist fears, legitimizing the use of government power to enforce social, political, and cultural orthodoxy. Although many wartime measures were only temporary, the campaign for enforced consensus also had permanent effects: radical groups were severely weakened, and in the next decade immigration was nearly cut off. The atmosphere of fear and intolerance would persist in the postwar era.

American Troops and the Battles They Fought

When the United States declared war in 1917, the Allies had hoped U.S. troops would quickly be integrated into the French and British combat units already fighting in Europe. Instead, Wilson accepted his military staff's recommendation that separate American units be organized under U.S. command. To this end, Congress authorized the draft in May 1917. A quarter of the registrants were found to be illiterate and a third of them physically unfit, but an army was raised, equipped, and trained in a year. The U.S. Army—about 122,000 strong when war was declared—would grow to 3,623,000 by the time the war ended. Even this huge number was a smaller commitment of manpower, in a population of 105 million, than that of the European nations.

Proponents of conscription had argued that a draft would strengthen American democracy by bringing young men from different ethnic and class backgrounds into close, cooperative relationships. The reality was quite different. Immigrants who had not filed naturalization papers were exempt from the draft. Some foreign-born men who did get drafted were put into ethnically segregated "development battalions," where they were taught English and civics. The army at first declined to take black draftees but eventually established separate units for them. The marines remained exclusively white, and the navy employed African Americans only as cooks and kitchen help.

In the fall of 1917, African Americans began to be drafted in large numbers; eventually nearly 370,000 were inducted. Assigned to segregated units and subjected to racist harassment (including demeaning insults from white officers), they were continually reminded of their second-class citizenship. Under pressure from African-American groups and the National Association for the Advancement of Colored People, the army put more than half the black soldiers into combat units rather than support groups. But these men remained segregated from white soldiers.

Standardized testing, administered as part of the induction procedure, lent a pseudoscientific gloss to prejudices that lay behind the segregation of troops. Nearly two million soldiers had been given a newly developed "IQ" test, which purported to measure innate intelligence. The psychologists in charge maintained that the tests "proved" northern and western Europeans were more intelligent than southern and eastern Europeans, who in turn were more intelligent than African Americans. In reality, the IQ tests were flawed in both design and administration, and the results were virtually meaningless. The tests actually measured literacy in English and familiarity with mainstream American culture, not intelligence. A typical question read: "Christy Mathewson is famous as a: writer, artist, baseball player, comedian." (The correct answer was baseball player.)

Nonetheless, the army's program legitimized IQ testing, which was administered widely after the war. The IQ test would be used to justify quotas established in the 1920s to limit immigration from southern and eastern Europe.

Segregated or not, the American troops and the supplies that accompanied them proved crucial to the Allied victory, in part because it undercut German resolve to continue the war. The American Expeditionary Forces were commanded by General John Joseph Pershing, a veteran of the Wounded Knee massacre of the Lakota Sioux, the 1898 charge of San Juan Hill in Cuba, extended warfare in the Philippines, and the American intervention in Mexico. Between May and September 1918 a million American troops arrived in France; another million came in the next two months. They reinforced French positions in June 1918 and were engaged in large numbers by mid-September.

At the end of September Pershing launched a drive through France's Argonne forest, pushing the Germans back. German troops, exhausted by an offensive the previous spring and undercut by revolution in Berlin, began to mutiny. One by one Germany's allies surrendered—Bulgaria in September, Turkey in October, and Austria-Hungary on November 3. Eight days later, the Germans signed an armistice. Argonne was America's major contribution to the war. Though many American soldiers saw battle, few experienced the prolonged trench warfare that ended the lives of 1.8 million Germans, 1.7 million Russians, 1.4 million French, 1.2 million Austro-Hungarians, and over 900,000 British. In contrast, only 112,000 American soldiers and sailors died, over half of them from disease. To put these figures into

P.O. 7th U.S. Corps

To the colored soldiers of the U. S. Army.

Hallo boys, what are you doing over here? Fighting the Germans? Why? Have they ever done you any harm? Of course, some white folks and the lying English-American papers told you that the Germans ought to be wiped out for the sake of humanity and democracy. What is Democracy? Personal Freedom, all citizens enjoying the same rights socially and before the law! Do you enjoy the same rights as the white people do in America, the land of Freedom and Democracy? Or aren't you rather treated over there as second class citizens? Can you go into a rest urant where white people dine, can you get a seat in a theater where white people sit, can you get a Pullman seat or berth in a railroadcar or can you even ride, in the South, in the same street car with white people? And how about the law? Is lynching and the most horrible cruelties connected therewith a lawful proceeding in a democratic country?

Now, all this is entirely different in Germany, where they do like colored people, where they treat them as Gentlemen and not as second class citizens. They enjoy exactly the same social privileges as every white man, and quite a number of colored people have migthy fine positions in business in Berlin and other big German cities.

Why then fight the Germans only for the benefit of the Wallstreet robbers to protect the millions they have lent to the English, French and Italians? You have been made the tool of the egotistic and rapacious rich in England and in America, and there is nothing in the whole game for you but broken bones, horrible wounds, spoiled health or — death. No satisfaction whatever will you get out of this unjust war. You have never seen Germany, so you are fools if you allow [illegible] to teach you to hate it. Come over to see for yourself. [illegible] do the fighting who make profit out of this war; do[illegible] them to use you as cannon food. To carry the gun in th[illegible]ce is not an honor but a shame. Throw it away and come over to the German lines. You will find friends who help you along.

"To the Colored Soldiers of the U.S. Army." This propaganda leaflet was dropped by German airplanes behind American lines. By stressing racist conditions in the United States, the leaflets attempted to destroy morale and encourage desertion among African-American troops. **Source:** National Archives.

"You Boys Give 'Em Hell for Me"

Even a brief experience with front-line combat could be harrowing. The following entries from the diary of Elmer Sherwood, a corporal from Linton, Indiana, described fighting on the Western Front near the end of the war.

Oct. 8. . . . Two of our fellows had already been wounded by an explosion near our kitchen this morning, but I was determined to go back for some mess because I was so confounded hungry. . . . I had just got a panful of slum and started eating, when I saw part of the temporary trench I had left, screened by an exploding shell. I thought it had come over the trench, but no—just then Smithy and Netterfield jumped out calling for stretchers.

I dropped my mess and ran to the trench and looked in. Poor Art was dead, one arm completely severed from his body. Danny had a hole in his stomach and we placed him on a stretcher and sent him back to the first aid station. . . . Dan looked at me with a smile on his face as we loaded him into an ambulance. I gave him a word of cheer and he said, "I don't know, Doc, old boy. I've got a pretty bad wound in my stomach. You boys give 'em hell for me." [He died the same day.]

I have seen many die, but none have been so close to me as these fellows. I have worked with them and fought beside them every day since I joined the outfit, and they have been my best pals.

But we must carry on, whatever happens. I ran back to the trench and rescued the battered switch board. . . . We are experiencing a fierce cannonading as I jot down these lines.

Oct. 30. Last night Fritz [the Germans] put on a whale of a bombardment, and I don't see how any of us escaped to tell the story. In the thick of it our communications were knocked out and I was detailed to repair the telephone line. How kind they are to me! Well, I thought of all the mean things I had done in my life, breathed a little prayer, climbed out of my fox hole, and darted out into the inferno.

Flashes of exploding artillery at intervals lighted up the blackness of the night. Explosions of enemy shells on every hand and the scream of big ones going over head to back areas added to the thunderous roar so that I could not have heard my own voice had I dared to speak. Boy! I was glad when I came to that break in the line. I was splicing the wire when—Shriek! Bang! a ton of steel came over me. Just as I finished the job—hell's bells—another hit knocked the line out of place.

For once I lost my cocky self-assurance, for I wasn't so certain that I would ever see home and Mother again. But finally, after stumbling over the body of a dead German, I came upon the next break and spliced it in a hurry. Then I raced back to my hole after reporting communications in order.

Source: William Matthews and Dixon Wecter, *Our Soldiers Speak, 1775–1918* (1943).

perspective, consider that nearly 24,000 Americans were killed on the job during 1917 and 1918, and nearly 3 million suffered industrial injuries.

At the end of the war Europe was devastated. Governments had collapsed; widespread famine had decimated whole populations. Weakened by starvation, millions of people died from a worldwide influenza epidemic. A century of optimism and "progress" had been reversed by four years of war.

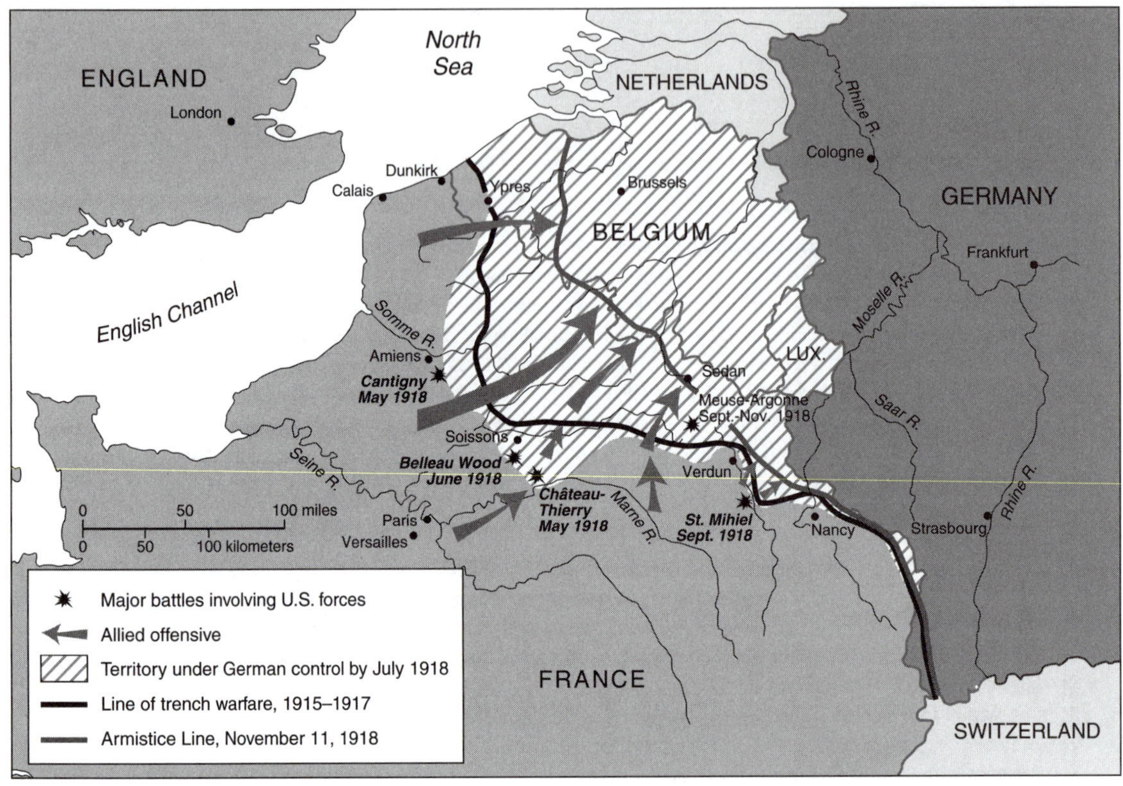

Not So Quiet on the Western Front: America in World War I. U.S. troops—commanded by General John J. Pershing—finally arrived on the Western front of battle in the summer of 1918. They played a crucial role in pushing back the exhausted German troops in battles at Saint-Mihiel, Belleau Wood, Château-Thierry, and especially Meuse-Argonne. Large numbers of American troops saw battle, but the United States suffered many fewer casualties than the other combatants.

Wilson and the Shape of the Peace

As noted earlier in this chapter, Wilson promoted World War I as a crusade that would make the world "safe for democracy." He argued that all the Allies—including Russia, which had overthrown its czar in the 1917 revolution—were democracies, battling an autocratic German Kaiser and an Austro-Hungarian emperor. Casting the conflict in this light helped Wilson to win popular support for the war.

But the second phase of the Russian Revolution, which began in November, created a profound crisis for Wilson and the Allies. When Lenin's Bolshevik party seized control of Russia, it quickly initiated peace talks with Germany and urged European workers and soldiers to stop the war. Lenin also published secret treaties, in which Allied governments agreed to carve up the territory and colonies of the Central Powers at the war's end. This revelation undercut Wilson's claims of a war for democracy. Finally, the Bolsheviks promised a far-reaching social transformation that appealed to downtrodden peoples around the world. For some, the revo-

New Faces. This display of plaster casts showed soldiers' mutilated faces (top row) and their reconstructions with the aid of new prosthetic devices (bottom row). In spite of its original purpose, the display now serves as a reminder of the damage inflicted on those who fought in World War I, and the imperfect attempts to contend with those gruesome effects.

Source: Prints and Photographs Division, Library of Congress.

lutionary Lenin, not the reformist Wilson, seemed the towering figure of the age.

In March 1918 Lenin's new government signed a separate treaty with Germany and withdrew from the war. Within months the United States, England, and France sent troops to Russia, which would soon be reorganized as the Union of Soviet Socialist Republics, in an ill-fated effort to weaken Bolshevik forces and maintain military pressure on Germany's Eastern Front. Even before the war ended, Wilson seemed to repudiate his principle of national self-determination.

Nonetheless, that principle—that each nation had the right to choose its own government—became central to Wilson's famous Fourteen Points, which he first proposed in a speech to Congress in 1918. The Fourteen Points called for free trade, freedom of the seas, arms reduction, arbitration of international disputes, and the adjustment of European borders along ethnic lines—all to be achieved through open negotiation of public treaties. To maintain peace, Wilson proposed that an international association of nations be formed to guarantee its members' "political independence and territorial integrity." Although the Allies never formally endorsed the Fourteen Points, they were the main platform on which the war was sold, both in the United States and Europe, during the last year of the war.

Wilson was a popular hero, and when he arrived in Europe late in 1918 to begin peace negotiations, he was greeted by cheering crowds grateful for American intervention in the war's final months. Some diplomats, however, did not share in the popular adulation. French President Georges Clemenceau complained that "Wilson thinks he is another Jesus Christ come upon earth to reform men." And at the peace conference in Paris, Wilson found little support for a treaty based on his Fourteen Points. Italy, France, and Britain had suffered great losses, and their delegates to the conference were determined to impose severe penalties on Germany, and to promote their own interests at their enemy's expense. Both Germany and Russia were excluded from the peace conference.

"Society Note from Moscow." This cartoon, one of a series by Alfred Frueh in the radical weekly *Good Morning* celebrated the Bolshevik Revolution's impact on Russia's aristocracy: "Count Parasitsky will not occupy his palatial residence in the mountains this summer," reads the caption. "He expects to remain in the city and do uplift work."

Source: Alfred Frueh, *Good Morning,* May 15, 1919—Prints and Photographs Division, Library of Congress.

A number of factors weakened Wilson's bargaining position. First, the United States had contributed least to the war, declaring war last, spending less of its national resources, and losing relatively few men. Second, Wilson was unwilling to ally with European socialists, who offered the strongest opposition to the punitive peace treaty the Allied leaders envisioned. Third, Wilson compromised his commitment to self-determination when he agreed to the takeover of German colonies by the Allies. Continued U.S. intervention in the Caribbean, including the occupation of Haiti and the stationing of troops in Cuba in 1917, did not help matters. Irish Americans decried Wilson's acquiescence to the British, who refused to consider granting independence to Ireland. Finally, the president had just suffered political defeat at home: in the 1918 elections, the Republicans had captured control of both houses of Congress.

The treaty that was finally signed at Versailles forced Germany to acknowledge guilt for the war, to cede territory to other countries, and to make huge reparation payments to the Allies for damage to their land and economies. To fulfill the national aspirations of various ethnic groups (as well as to surround the Soviet Union with hostile states), the treaty carved new countries—sometimes illogically—from the old Austro-Hungarian and Russian empires and from parts of Germany. The new nations of Austria, Hungary, Poland, Yugoslavia, Czechoslovakia, Estonia, Latvia, Finland, and Lithuania took their places on the redrawn map of postwar Europe.

Wilson's major achievement at the conference was persuading the other Allies to include his plan for a League of Nations in the peace treaty. But when the president returned to Washington after months of bargaining, it became clear that Congress disapproved of the plan. Even before he presented the Versailles treaty to the U.S. Senate for ratification, isolationist Republicans voiced strong opposition. As proposed, the League—meant to resolve disputes and guarantee member nations' territorial integrity—was empowered to consider collective action in response to aggression. Opponents suggested that the League would put restraints on U.S. foreign policy and that the treaty restricted congressional authority to declare war. Frustrated by lengthy hearings by the Senate Foreign Relations Committee, Wilson embarked on a speaking tour in September 1919 to arouse popular support for the pact. Late that month, exhausted by the trip, he collapsed from a severe stroke. For the remaining seventeen months of his presidency, Wilson was an invalid, often unable to conduct business. The U.S. Senate twice refused to ratify the Versailles treaty and instead concluded separate peace treaties with the Central Powers. The League of Nations was established without U.S. participation, but it never became an effective force for peace.

Postwar Strikes and Race Riots

While Congress debated the Versailles treaty, strikes and riots erupted across the country. African Americans and workers—men and women, black and white—sought to consolidate and expand gains they had won during the war, to make good on the war's democratic promise. Their opponents sought to roll back wartime advances. A series of titanic clashes rocked the nation as the two sides met. Four million workers—one-fifth of the nation's workforce—went on strike in 1919. Organized labor and political radicals put forth the most startling and fundamental challenge to the established order seen in the twentieth century; business and government responded with a wave of repression.

Early in 1919, the Seattle General Strike set the tone for the year. Seattle was a strong union town. Its 35,000 shipyard workers had won higher wages than workers who lived elsewhere, but a wartime government panel had limited further increases. In January 1919 the shipyard workers responded by striking. Two weeks later, 65,000 workers left their jobs in a general strike that paralyzed the city; tens of thousands more were idled by the shutdown. Streetcars and other commercial traffic

The Seattle General Strike. These strikers were photographed with groceries that the General Strike Committee had issued to union families.

Source: Museum of History and Industry, Puget Sound Maritime Historical Society, Seattle, Washington.

ground to a stop. For five days the city was run largely by a General Strike Committee, which set up milk delivery for children and laundry service for hospitals and organized some five hundred uniformed war veterans to patrol the streets. Because so many Seattle workers were single men who ate at unionized restaurants, the cooks' union served more than 20,000 meals a day out of community kitchens. Working people, the General Strike Committee exuberantly declared, were "learning to manage" the local economy.

Although the strike had been peaceful, the mayor and local businessmen, calling up the specter of Bolshevism, charged the labor movement with attempted revolution. Fearful of a backlash, national labor leaders successfully pressured the Seattle committee to call off the strike before workers won their demands. The strike was nevertheless a remarkable demonstration of working-class unity and organization.

In city after city and industry after industry, workers went on strike in 1919. In New York, 50,000 men's clothing workers struck for thirteen weeks, winning a forty-four-hour workweek. Theater workers struck, too, under the banner of Actors' Equity. In New England and New Jersey, 120,000 textile workers stayed away from their jobs. Striking women telephone operators in New England forced the Post Office Department, which was still running the nation's telephone system under wartime authority, to grant higher wages. Late in the year 400,000 coal miners walked out, defying a plea from Wilson and a federal court injunction that barred them from striking. Despite determined federal efforts to put down the uprising, the miners stayed off the job until they were granted an immediate wage hike of 14 percent and arbitration of their grievances.

In Boston even the police struck, walking out when the police commissioner suspended nineteen officers who were leading a movement to affiliate with the AFL. During the walkout the city was hit by a wave of rowdyism, theft, and violence. Massachusetts governor Calvin Coolidge, outraged, established a national reputation by announcing that none of the strikers would be rehired. Coolidge mobilized state troops while he recruited unemployed veterans for an entirely new police force.

Although the demands of these strikes centered on wages, hours, and other traditional issues, the radical spirit that was evident during the war continued to pervade the labor movement. The war had given railroad workers and miners experience with coordinated bargaining and government administration of industry. In 1919, the railroad unions endorsed a plan for government ownership of all rail lines, and the United Mine Workers debated nationalization of the coal industry. The Bolshevik victory in Russia and the growing strength of Britain's Labour party encouraged their fervor. "Messiah is arriving," the Amalgamated Clothing Workers' Sidney Hillman had written to his daughter the year before. "He may be with us any minute. . . . Labor will rule and the world will be free."

The most important strike of 1919 began in September, in the steel industry. Dominated by U.S. Steel, the largest corporation in the world, the industry had since the turn of the century used its financial strength and political connections to crush organizing efforts, exploiting tensions among workers and between competing unions. But wartime labor shortages and democratic rhetoric had revived steelworkers' interest in unionism. Once again, working people took Wilson's democratic rhetoric further than he intended. As a Hungarian-born steelworker named Frank Smith told a Senate Committee, "this is the United States and we ought to have the right to belong to the union."

When the steel companies rejected workers' demands, the unions struck. On September 22 more than 350,000 steelworkers left their jobs, shutting down virtually the entire industry in ten states. Gompers and other conservative AFL leaders, fearful of the potential of industrial unionism, gave the strikers little support, although they formally led the strike. The steel companies responded by unleashing a reign of terror, with the cooperation of local governments. Strikers and their supporters

BlackSmith

BALLOT

IRON & STEEL WORKERS

The Union Committees are now seeking to get higher wages, shorter hours and better working conditions from the steel companies. Are you willing to back them up to the extent of stopping work should the companies refuse to concede these demands?

TAJNO GLASANJE

Odbor junije sada traži da se dobije bolja plaća, kraći radni satovi i bolji uvjeti za rad od kompanija čelika. Dali ste voljni isti do skrajnosti podupreti da se prestane sa radom ako bi kompanija odbila da udovolji zahtevima?

SZAVAZZON!

Az Union Bizottsága, az Acél Társaságoktól való—magasabb fizetés, rövidebb munka idő és jobb munka feltételek—elnyeréseután törekszik. Akar ezek után törekedni? s a végsőkig kitarta—ni? és ha a társaságok ezen kivánalmaknak nem tesznek eleget a munkát beszüntetni?

VOTAZIONE.

I comitati dell'Unione stanno cercando di ottenere paghe piu' alte, ore di lavoro piu' brevi, e migliori condizioni di lavoro. Desiderate voi assecondarli, anche quando dovesse essere necessario di fermare il lavoro se le Compagnie rifiutassero di accettare le domande?

HLÁSOVACI LÍSTOK

Výbor uniový chce dosiahnuť podvyšenie mzdy, menej hodín robiť a lepšie robotnícke položenie od oceliarskych spoločností. Ste vy ochotní ich podporovať do krajnosti, až do zástavenia práce, v páde by spoločnosť odoprela žiadosťučiniť tým požiadavkám.

BALOT

Komitet Unii stara się obecnie o uzyskanie od Stalowych Kompanij większej płacy, krótszych godzin i lepszych warunków pracy. Czy jesteś gotów poprzeć nas aż do możliwości wstrzymania pracy na wypadek, gdyby Kompanie odmówiły naszym żądaniom?

VOTE YES OR NO. **Mark X in square indicating how you vote**

IPEU **Yes** [X] **No** [ ]

National Committee for Organizing Iron and Steel Workers

WM. Z. FOSTER, Secy-Treas. 303 Magee Bldg., Pittsburgh, Pa.

9

STRIKE BALLOT

How Do You Spell Strike? The strike ballot distributed by the National Committee for Organizing Iron and Steel Workers—printed in English, Croation, Hungarian, Italian, Slovak, and Polish—indicates the range of nationalities that contributed to the industry's workforce in 1919.

Source: William Z. Foster, *The Great Steel Strike and Its Lessons* (1920)—General Research Division, New York Public Library, Astor, Lenox, and Tilden Foundations.

were beaten, arrested, shot, and driven out of steel towns. In Pittsburgh the sheriff deputized five thousand loyal U.S. Steel employees and prohibited outdoor meetings. In Clairton and Glassport, Pennsylvania, state troopers clubbed strikers who were attending peaceful gatherings. Federal troops occupied the city of Gary, Indiana.

The steel companies' refusal to meet with the unions, even at the president's request, won them widespread scorn. To gain popular sympathy, they portrayed the conflict as an attempted revolution by foreign-born radicals. They split the strikers along ethnic and racial lines by bringing in African-American and Mexican-American strikebreakers. And they launched campaigns to encourage skilled and native-born workers to go back to work. Many native-born skilled workers had joined the strike, but some—reflecting longstanding tensions between unskilled immigrants and skilled "American" workers—stood on the sidelines. Over time, growing numbers of skilled workers fell away from the strike. One Youngstown, Ohio, steelworker, John J. Martin, professed satisfaction at wages and working conditions, maintaining that "the foreigners brought the strike on." Slowly the strike weakened; in January 1920 it was officially called off.

It was a terrible defeat. The immigrant steelworkers had demonstrated a capacity for sustained militancy and discipline, but the steel industry had shown itself capable of crushing even the most massive of walkouts. It would be fifteen years before the next major effort to organize basic industries like steel, autos, and electrical equipment manufacturing.

African Americans, too, found 1919 to be a cruel year. A resurgent Ku Klux Klan and other racist organizations urged terrorist attacks on black communities. Meanwhile, African Americans, many of them returning veterans, sought to defend the gains they had won during the war and redeem the war's democratic promise. The resulting tensions—over jobs, housing, and the basic position of black Americans in postwar society—erupted in twenty-five race riots during the second half of 1919. In July, whites attacked blacks in Washington, D.C., in a riot that killed six people and injured a hundred. Later that year four deaths were recorded in a racial incident in Omaha, Nebraska. Perhaps as many as twenty-five African Americans and several white people died in rural Arkansas, where black sharecroppers had begun to organize and arm themselves.

Chicago was the site of the worst riot. Like many racial clashes, it began on a hot summer day at a public facility—a beach—shared uneasily by white and black bathers. When a young black swimmer drifted toward a white section of the beach, someone threw a rock and killed him. Fighting broke out and quickly spread to the city proper, fed by pent-up resentment over housing, job competition, and segregation. In the past, when white rioters had invaded black neighborhoods, the inhabitants had hidden or fled. But in 1919 black Chicagoans fought back, refusing to accept second-class citizenship. Full-scale battles erupted along the borders between black and white neighborhoods, and sometimes between black and white workers from the same factories. By the time the violence ended five days later, thirty-eight people had died and more than five hundred were injured.

The Red Scare

The mobilization of municipal police forces, state militias, and federal courts against strikers and rioters was part of a larger postwar offensive against radicals and labor militants, which focused on the foreign-born. "Loyalty" organizations intensified their antiradical crusade, even though the worldwide advance of radicalism—often associated with the Bolshevik Revolution—had been largely checked by fall 1919, after an attempted revolution was violently suppressed in Germany and a Soviet government toppled in Hungary.

"Under the Stars and Stripes." Daily representations of subversion and menace, like this Bolshevik serpent in the *Philadelphia Inquirer,* also carried a strong anti-immigrant message, fueling the 1919 red scare.

Source: Morgan, *Philadelphia Inquirer,* March 13, 1919—General Research Division, New York Public Library, Astor, Lenox, and Tilden Foundations.

In the United States the radical movement had been seriously weakened. The IWW was feeble, its energies drained by defending members who were facing trial on wartime charges. The socialist movement had splintered, weakened by repression, Debs's imprisonment, and internal disagreements. In the summer of 1919 the party split. One faction kept the name Socialist party and continued to field candidates, believing they could win enough votes to legislate democratic control of the economy. Debs received nearly a million votes for president in 1920, running from his cell in the Atlanta Federal Penitentiary. A small group modeled on the Bolsheviks went underground to organize a revolutionary movement, and eventually established the U.S. Communist party.

American radicals posed little threat to the status quo, but their opponents were unrelenting in their ruthless search for revolutionaries and repression of working-class immigrants. Foremost among the "red-hunters" was Attorney General A. Mitchell Palmer, who led arrests and deportations of thousands of immigrants and radicals. Most had never been charged with a crime. Some, like the well-known anarchist Emma Goldman, had lived in the United States for decades.

The largest of the "Palmer raids" took place in January 1920: in one night, federal agents arrested six thousand alleged radicals in thirty-three cities. Many were held without warrants, were never formally charged,

After the Execution—Boston, August 1927. Thousands of mourners follow behind the funeral carriages of Sacco and Vanzetti.
Source: *Labor Defender,* August 1928—General Research Division, New York Public Library, Astor, Lenox, and Tilden Foundations.

and were not allowed to contact lawyers or relatives. Some had no connection to radical activities; others signed coerced confessions. Six hundred of them were eventually forced to leave the country.

The excesses of the January raids eroded support for the anti-red campaign. The Labor Department, which had legal jurisdiction over alien deportations, stopped cooperating with the Justice Department. Protesters targeted the New York State Assembly after it expelled five Socialist legislators in April. Palmer finally overplayed his hand when he warned that revolutionaries were planning a wave of violence on May Day, the traditional labor holiday. Police mobilized to protect buildings and political leaders, but the day passed quietly. Discredited, the anti-red drive went into decline.

Nevertheless, the Department of Justice continued its antilabor, antiradical activities until 1924, working closely with state governments, businesses, and private detective agencies. Military intelligence agents issued an infamous Spider-Web Chart showing connections between activists in national women's organizations, including the American Home Economics Association and the Parent-Teachers Association, as well as political and pacifist groups. The implication was that they were all part of an international socialist conspiracy. Private citizens' groups also continued to harass left-wing activists.

One case in particular would keep the issue of political repression alive for much of the 1920s. Two Italian-born anarchists, shoemaker

Nicola Sacco and fish peddler Bartolomeo Vanzetti, were arrested on May 5, 1920, and charged with killing two men during an armed robbery in South Braintree, Massachusetts. Both men professed their innocence, insisting they were being persecuted for their political beliefs. Following a trial marred by questionable evidence and judicial procedures, Sacco and Vanzetti were convicted of first-degree murder and sentenced to death.

For many people in the United States and abroad, Sacco and Vanzetti's case came to symbolize governmental injustice. Protests flared, first among Italian Americans, then among non-Italian radicals, and finally among a broad spectrum of intellectuals and civil libertarians. Under pressure, the governor of Massachusetts appointed a committee of prominent citizens to review the case, but it found no reason to reverse the sentence. On August 23, 1927, as crowds gathered throughout the world to protest, Sacco and Vanzetti were executed. A few months before he died, Vanzetti offered an eloquent summary of his case. His words, as rendered by a New York reporter, were: "If it had not been for these thing, I might have live out of my life, talking at street corners to scorning men. I might have die, unmarked, unknown, a failure. Now we are not a failure. This is our career and our triumph. Never in our full life can we hope to do such work for tolerance, for justice, for man's understanding of man, as now we do by an accident."

Toward a Postwar Society

World War I began as the culmination of longstanding European rivalries, but it ended in a political and economic crisis that seemed to threaten the very existence of capitalism. The war undercut the moral, political, and economic bases of all the old European regimes. In Russia the collapse was complete: a revolutionary socialist government replaced the czarist regime. In half a dozen other countries revolutions were either attempted or threatened. Never before had the foundations of capitalism seemed so shaky.

America's domestic battles in 1919 were part of this larger struggle over the shape of the postwar world. For a brief moment during and just after the war, progressives thought their hopes for domestic reform and international order might be realized, and radicals thought socialism might spread beyond the Soviet Union. But neither came to pass. Indeed, U.S. isolationism and the failure of the peace helped to set the stage for another global confrontation twenty years later.

The United States was nevertheless forever changed by the war. The government continued to play a larger role in the economy, in labor relations, and in shaping public opinions. Workers continued to move from the South to the North and West and from Mexico to the southwestern United States. Women gained the vote. Although alien radicals were silenced or deported, and wartime suspicion of "foreigners" contributed to the end of open immigration a few years later, most immigrants continued to think of themselves as full-fledged Americans.

When the war ended, so did many of the conditions that favored working-class activism and the development of strong, radical unions. As production levels returned to normal and four million military men reentered the civilian workforce, the labor shortage abated. Intolerance, fear of foreigners, and a dread of radicalism played into employers' hands. Factional bickering and government repression weakened labor and its radical allies, while wartime profits bolstered corporations, enabling them to withstand long interruptions in production. By the early 1920s, businessmen no longer had to deal with a confident, politicized working-class movement. It would be well over a decade before the labor movement would again be able to exert its power nationally.

The Years in Review

1913

- Underwood Tariff reduces U.S. import duties.

1914

- Serbian nationalist assassinates heir to the Austro-Hungarian throne and precipitates World War I; United States declares neutrality.
- First red and green traffic lights are installed in Cleveland.
- President Woodrow Wilson proclaims the first national Mother's Day—a boon to restaurants and florists.

1915

- Wilson endorses military "preparedness."
- (February) Germany begins submarine warfare; 128 Americans die when the *Lusitania* is torpedoed in May; a huge public outcry follows.
- U.S. Marines begin a 19-year occupation of Haiti.
- First taxis take to streets.

1916

- Brigadier-General John J. Pershing leads 6,000 men into Mexico in an unsuccessful pursuit of General Francisco "Pancho" Villa.

- 600,000 soldiers die in the German offensive at Verdun.
- Wilson, running under the slogan "He kept us out of war," defeats Charles E. Hughes in the presidential election.
- The Industrial Workers of the World (IWW; Wobblies) finds new life by organizing western migratory workers but also faces sharp government attacks.
- Southern farmers suffer as boll weevils attack cotton crops and floods cause extensive damage.
- Increasing numbers of African Americans leave the South in the Great Migration, which sends 500,000 north in the 1910s.
- Revenue Acts of 1916 and 1917 impose the first substantial income taxes.
- Clarence Saunders opens Piggly-Wiggly in Memphis, Tennessee, the nation's first supermarket chain.

1917

- United States enters World War I in April; draft begins in May; first U.S. troops reach France in June.
- Women in New York, Philadelphia, and Boston take to the streets to protest wartime inflationary price hikes for food and other necessities.
- White rioters attack black neighborhoods of East St. Louis for two days in July; forty African Americans and nine white people are killed.
- Federal government sets up Committee on Public Information (CPI) to disseminate war news and government propaganda.
- Russian czar is overthrown in March revolution; in October, Bolshevik (Communist) party, headed by V. I. Lenin, seizes power.
- National Woman's party pickets the White House, demanding that "democracy should begin at home."
- Espionage Act gives federal authorities wide powers to suppress dissent.
- National Hockey League is organized in Montreal; the league will have no U.S. teams until the Boston Bruins became members in 1924.

1918

- Charles Strite patents the automatic pop-up toaster.
- Wilson issues his statement of war aims, the Fourteen Points.
- U.S. troops push back German troops in France's Argonne forest, in America's major contribution to the fighting.
- The German army, exhausted by an offensive the previous spring, collapses, and an armistice is signed in November; more than 13 million people died in the conflict.
- "Spanish" influenza spreads through Europe, Asia, and America, killing 22 million people in the worst epidemic since the Black Death in the Middle Ages.

1919

- Cincinnati Reds defeat the Chicago White Sox in a World Series later shown to have been fixed; eight "Black Sox" are banned from baseball.

- The Eighteenth Amendment to the Constitution, banning manufacture and sale of alcoholic beverages, is ratified.
- The Treaty of Versailles, including Wilson's proposed League of Nations, is signed in Paris; the U.S. Senate refuses to ratify it.
- Four million workers—fully one-fifth of the nation's workforce—strike; more than 300,000 steelworkers stage the biggest strike and suffer the worst defeat.
- Race riots sweep through the nation, killing six people in Washington, D.C., and thirty-eight in Chicago.
- George B. Hansburg patents his pogo stick.

1920

- The Nineteenth Amendment is ratified on August 26, granting women suffrage.
- Italian-born anarchists Sacco and Vanzetti are arrested for murder and convicted in a trial marred by questionable evidence and procedures.
- In the largest "Palmer raid," federal agents arrest six thousand radicals in thirty-three cities, culminating in wholesale violations of civil liberties.
- Ohio man invents the Good Humor bar—an ice-cream bar covered with chocolate and held on a stick.

1927

- Sacco and Vanzetti are executed despite worldwide protest.

Suggested Readings

Brody, David, *Labor in Crisis: The Steel Strike of 1919* (1965).

Chambers, John W., *To Raise an Army: The Draft Comes to Modern America* (1987).

Chickering, Roger, and Stig Foerster, *Great War, Total War: Combat and Mobilization on the Western Front, 1914–1918* (1991).

Coffman, Edward M., *The War to End All Wars: American Military Experience in World War I* (1968).

Conner, Valerie Jean, *The National War Labor Board: Stability, Social Justice, and the Voluntary State in World War I* (1983).

Dawley, Alan, *Struggles for Justice: Social Responsibility and the Liberal State* (1991).

Dubofsky, Melvyn, *We Shall Be All: A History of the Industrial Workers of the World* (1969).

Eisenhower, John S. D., *Intervention! The United States and the Mexican Revolution, 1913–1923* (1993).

Eksteins, Modris, *Rites of Spring: The Great War and the Birth of the Modern Age* (1989).

Ferrell, Robert H., *Woodrow Wilson and World War I, 1917–1921* (1985).

Flexner, Eleanor, *Century of Struggle: The Woman's Rights Movement in the United States* (rev. ed., 1975).

Frank, Dana, *Purchasing Power: Consumer Organizing, Gender, and the Seattle Labor Movement, 1919–1929* (1994).

Gardner, Lloyd C., *Safe for Democracy: The Anglo-American Response to Revolution, 1913–1923* (1984).

Green, James R., *Grassroots Socialism: Radical Movements in the Southwest, 1895–1943* (1978).

Greenwald, Maurice W., *Women, War, and Work: The Impact of World War I on Women Workers in the U.S.* (1980).

Grossman, James R., *Land of Hope: Chicago, Black Southerners, and the Great Migration* (1989).

Grubb, Frank L., *Samuel Gompers and the Great War* (1982).

Hawley, Ellis W., *The Great War and the Search for Modern Order: A History of the American People and Their Institutions, 1917–1933* (1979).

Hobsbawm, Eric, *The Age of Empire, 1875–1914* (1987).

Hobsbawm, Eric, *The Age of Extremes: A History of the World, 1914–1991* (1994).

Hunter, Tera W., *To Joy My Freedom: Southern Black Women's Lives and Labors After the Civil War* (1997).

Iriye, Akira, *The Cambridge History of American Foreign Relations, Vol. III: The Globalizing of America, 1913–1945* (1993).

Kennedy, David M., *Over Here: The First World War and American Society* (1980).

Knock, Thomas, *To End All Wars: Woodrow Wilson and the Quest for a New World Order* (1992).

LaFebre, Walter, *The American Age: United States Foreign Policy at Home and Abroad* (1994).

Link, Arthur S., *Woodrow Wilson: Revolution, War, and Peace* (1979).

Mayer, Arno, *The Politics and Diplomacy of Peacemaking: Containment and Counter-revolution at Versailles, 1918–1919* (1967).

Montgomery, David, *The Fall of the House of Labor: The Workplace, the State, and American Labor Activism, 1865–1925* (1987).

Murray, Robert K., *Red Scare: A Study in National Hysteria, 1919–1920* (rev. ed., 1980).

Preston, William, Jr., *Aliens and Dissenters: Federal Suppression of Radicals, 1903–1933* (1963).

Thelen, David, *Robert M. La Follette and the Insurgent Spirit* (1976).

Tuttle, William M., Jr., *Race Riot: Chicago in the Summer of 1919* (1970).

And on the World Wide Web

- Mike Iavarone, *World War I: Trenches on the Web,* at http://www.worldwar1.com/
- Jane Plotke, Richard Hacken, Alan Albright, and Micheal Shackelford, *The World War I Document Archive* at http://www.lib.byu.edu/~rdh/wwi/
- Library of Congress, *Votes for Women: Selections from the National American Woman Suffrage Association Collection, 1848–1921* at http://memory.loc.gov/ammem/naw/nawshome.html

chapter 7

A New Era
1920–1929

On January 1, 1929, the editors of the *Washington Post* prepared a special business supplement to welcome the New Year. "Good Times Are Predicted for 1929," read the banner headline. The *Post* hardly seemed to be going out on a limb with this forecast. After all, two other headlines trumpeted "Record Year Just Ended" and "Gains in Stock Exchange." Further fueling the business community's optimism was the feeling that the federal government took their views to heart. "Hoover's Policies Looked Forward to as Great Aid to Business," another headline declared.

The *Post*'s optimistic prediction could, in fact, have been made almost anytime during the 1920s. And at least for the wealthiest Americans, these were indeed good times. "The whole upper tenth of a nation," novelist F. Scott Fitzgerald wrote, was "living with the insouciance of a grand duc and the casualness of chorus girls." Fitzgerald, the emblematic and most celebrated writer of the decade, gave the new era a label that stuck, "The Jazz Age"—an invocation of a carefree time of high living, bootleg liquor, and illegal drinking in speakeasies. Fitzgerald himself spent much of the decade in Paris, drinking and dancing till dawn with his wife Zelda.

More than just the "upper tenth" enjoyed some of the good times. For the first time, substantial numbers of workers lived above bare subsistence levels, thanks in part to expanded consumer credit. Even automobiles and houses became attainable for many. As working hours decreased and incomes rose, leisure time and ways to enjoy it mushroomed, feeding the entertainment industry. Movies and radio promoted consumerism, undermining the traditional ideals and values of the family, community, and ethnic and regional subcultures.

Even so, few Americans lived like grand dukes or like chorus girls. Prosperity was uneven. While the rich got much richer, the average worker saw only a slow rise in income. Workers in some industries suffered falling wages and massive unemployment. On the whole, skilled and white-collar workers did much better than the unskilled. Farmers suffered for most of the decade. And as usual, African Americans fared worse than whites. A resurgent Ku Klux Klan spewed venom at them as well as at Catholics and Jews. Hostility toward immigrants impelled the nation to shut its doors to foreigners more firmly than at any time in the past.

But perhaps the most basic problem of the 1920s was the one no one seemed to notice. The unequal distribution of the nation's wealth made its

Raids and Refreshment. As wine poured into the streets of a Brooklyn neighborhood after federal agents raided an illegal distillery, local children rushed to catch as much of the illegal drink as they could.

Source: *New York Daily News.* Used by permission of the *Daily News.*

economy fundamentally unsound. Before the year was out, the *Post* would be running very different headlines announcing the crash of the stock market and the early signs of hard times. When a discouraged Fitzgerald, now battling alcoholism, returned to America in 1931, he found a country racked by depression.

Conservatism and Corruption in Political Life

The 1920 presidential election set the political tone for the decade. Both major parties nominated middle-of-the-road politicians from Ohio: Republican Senator Warren G. Harding and Democratic Governor James Cox. Since the last election, many Americans had tired of Wilson and his moral righteousness, and they wanted relief from the rampant inflation and social turmoil that had come with the end of World I—the strikes, race riots, and Red scares of 1919. Harding, capitalizing on this weariness, declared that the country needed "not heroism but healing, not nostrums but normalcy, not revolution but restoration." The election results—a landslide for the Republicans—showed that he had captured the public mood.

Although Harding's vision of "normalcy" embraced generous acts, like pardoning the imprisoned socialist Eugene Debs, it translated more fundamentally into extraordinary corporate influence on national policy. During the 1920s, the political power of big business climbed to new heights. Secretary of the Treasury Andrew Mellon, one of the wealthiest men in the nation, and Secretary of Commerce Herbert Hoover dominated Harding's cabinet.

After Harding's sudden death in 1923, his modest reputation was destroyed by the discovery of considerable corruption. Subsequent polls of historians have consistently ranked him one of the worst presidents in U.S. history. "Harding was not a bad man," Alice Roosevelt Longworth (Theodore Roosevelt's daughter) later observed. "He was just a slob." Although her own husband, Nick, an Ohio Republican congressman, was an associate member of what was known as Harding's "poker cabinet," she recalled with distaste Harding's drinking and carousing with political buddies in the "Ohio Gang." When she visited the White House study, she found the "air heavy with tobacco smoke . . . every imaginable brand of whisky . . . cards and poker chips ready at hand." Fortunately, she did not open the closet doors, or she might have discovered the president making love to his mistress, Nan Britton. While still a senator, Harding had fathered a child with Britton; as president, he sent Secret Service agents to deliver support payments for his child.

"The National Gesture." A 1926 cartoon by Clive Weed in the satirical weekly *Judge* commented on the escalation of governmental corruption during Prohibition.

Source: Clive Weed, *Judge,* June 12, 1926—American Social History Project.

Whatever his personal failings, Harding himself was never accused of public wrong-doing, but he generally looked the other way when his friends put their hands in the government till. The head of the Veterans Bureau, aided by its general counsel, Charles F. Cramer, sold government medical supplies at ludicrously low prices to private contractors and extracted kickbacks in return. When the scam seemed about to unravel, Cramer committed suicide. So did Jess W. Smith, private secretary to Harding's closest ally, an Ohio politician named Harry Daugherty, whom Harding had made attorney general. Smith had been lining his pockets by selling paroles and liquor licenses. Daugherty himself was later indicted for fraud, but a "lucky" fire that destroyed some key records prevented his conviction. The most notorious scandal of Harding's administration involved the secret leasing, at discount prices, of government-owned oil reserves in California and Wyoming—one of which was called "Teapot Dome." The grateful oil companies rewarded Secretary of the Interior Albert Fall, who arranged the deal, with more than $400,000 in bribes.

These gradually unwinding scandals probably contributed to Harding's depression and high blood pressure, and finally his death, probably from a stroke. His successor, Vice President Calvin Coolidge, was a very different sort of man—upright, cautious, and introverted. (Coolidge's legendary taciturnity led to many jokes. One woman allegedly told him she had made a bet that she could get him to say more than two words. "You lose," he retorted.) Under Coolidge, Alice Longworth commented, the White House was "as different as a New England front parlor is from a backroom in a speakeasy." But if Coolidge's style was different, his conservative policies were very much the same. "Normalcy" remained the watchword of the day.

The Business of America Is Business

More than most of their predecessors, Harding, Coolidge, and the men who served in their administrations identified the fortunes of America with those of business. Coolidge described business as "one of the greatest contributing forces to the moral and spiritual advancement of the race." "The chief business of the American people is business," he concluded.

Pro-business conservatives like Secretary of the Treasury Mellon believed that the government could best aid business by cutting taxes and minimizing federal intervention in the economy. In 1926 Mellon succeeded in persuading Congress to halve the income tax rate for the top bracket of taxpayers and drastically lower the taxes on inherited wealth. Mellon also wanted to return quickly to private hands those businesses the government had operated during the war. Although the American Federation of Labor and the railroad brotherhoods, which had prospered with government control of the trains, wanted the nation to buy the railroads, Congress instead restored them to corporate control in 1920. Nationalization of basic industries was reduced to a goal only of radicals and some diehard Progressives.

Some cabinet officials, however, believed that the government should actively promote and coordinate private economic initiatives. To keep farm prices up, Secretary of Agriculture Henry C. Wallace created cooperative marketing arrangements and voluntary crop reduction programs. Secretary of Commerce Herbert Hoover, the engineer and business executive who had served as head of the Food Administration during the war, sponsored studies of industrial waste and inefficiency, pushed for further standardization in industry, and worked with the State Department to increase exports. Hoover also encouraged state and local governments to use public works to stimulate the economy. Still, Hoover was a Republican, and he shared his party's probusiness ideology.

The business–government alliance became an issue in the 1924 presidential election, when discontented farmers and unionists joined together to back a third-party presidential bid by Wisconsin Senator Robert La Follette. The senator's platform harked back to prewar Populism and Progressivism. "The great issue," it asserted, was "the control of government and industry by private monopoly." Nationalization of railroads and water power, a ban on antilabor injunctions, increased aid for farmers, and a tax system restructured to benefit working people were some of the planks in the platform.

The Democrats might have been expected to join La Follette in attacking the business-dominated Republican administration, or at least Harding-era corruption. But deep cultural issues divided the Democrats and deadlocked their 1924 convention. Southern Democrats supported

The Business of America Is Accommodation. In a 1927 ceremony set in front of the Capitol and supervised by President Calvin Coolidge, battle flags captured by northern troops during the Civil War were returned to aged Confederate veterans. Such rites of reconciliation obscured the repressive state of race relations in the South during the 1920s.

Source: Prints and Photographs Division, Library of Congress.

Prohibition and refused to denounce explicitly the racist and anti-Catholic Ku Klux Klan. But the immigrant-led urban political machines opposed Prohibition and wanted to nominate a Catholic, Governor Alfred E. Smith of New York, for president. After a record 103 ballots, the two factions compromised on an obscure and relatively conservative Wall Street lawyer, John W. Davis, who could neither unite his divided party nor offer voters a clear alternative to Coolidge. Although both Davis and Coolidge sharply attacked La Follette as a dangerous radical, he received one-sixth of the popular vote—an extraordinary showing for a third-party candidate. Coolidge, however, won the election easily, and the business-government alliance remained intact.

The United States and the World

The business-government alliance guided domestic policy and also helped form U.S. foreign policy in the 1920s. To open the "door" for American business, Charles Evans Hughes, secretary of state under Harding and Coolidge, used federal power to assist American businesses wishing to expand overseas. Critics charged that Wall Street was dictating American foreign policy, but a State Department official retorted that "in these days of competition . . . capital . . . and statecraft go hand in hand." Working with Herbert Hoover, who as secretary of commerce exercised great influence over American foreign policy, Hughes sought to create a new world order that would bring stability and allow for the expansion of American capitalism—a "Pax Americana," as Hughes put it.

American businesses would have to exercise this global power while the United States stood aloof from the organization that Woodrow Wilson had designed precisely to promote world stability—the League of Nations. Without American involvement, the League remained permanently weak. Nevertheless, the U.S. government, American businesses, and American citizens became increasingly active in world affairs during the

1920s. At the Washington Conference of 1921, Hughes, a brilliant diplomat, engineered a halt to the naval arms race, which threatened peace and the ability of American businesses to expand abroad. Astonishingly, the major powers agreed to scrap millions of tons of warships and to adhere to limits of 500,000 tons for the British and American navies, 300,000 for the Japanese navy, and 175,000 for the French and Italian navies. But although the Japanese, whose growing power Hughes wanted to restrain, had seemingly agreed to second-class status, they had in fact won dominance in the Pacific. Hughes, however, thought he had gained more important concessions: access for American businesses to most of the vast China market, and Japanese dependence on New York banks.

American bankers were central to another key diplomatic agreement of the 1920s. By 1924, the Germans were no longer able to pay the $33 billion in reparations imposed on them at the end of World War I. Hughes sponsored a Washington conference in which American bankers worked out a deal—called the Dawes Plan, after Chicago banker Charles Dawes—that sharply reduced German reparations payments and provided massive private loans to restart the German economy. But what looked like a brilliant success ultimately proved a dismal failure. Increasingly, the loans went into speculative ventures or simply propped up the crippled German economy rather than rebuilding it.

Bankers and businessmen were not the only Americans to look overseas in the 1920s. Private voluntary organizations like the YMCA and Rotary International founded branches in other countries. Like the Coolidge administration, these organizations favored the spread of American business and opposed radical alternatives like the Socialist and Communist movements that had large numbers of adherents in Europe. Another group of Americans formed a loosely defined "peace movement." Committed pacifists who had opposed World War I joined with a new breed of Wilsonian internationalists to promote the free flow of ideas and capital and to oppose the use of military force to resolve conflicts. The peace movement's greatest victory was the Kellogg-Briand Pact of 1928; signed by most of the world's nations, the treaty outlawed war but failed to set up an effective enforcement mechanism.

Business, however, was the real engine of American internationalism. American companies scrambled to build factories in other countries to take advantage of cheap labor, low tariffs, and easy access to raw materials and markets. By 1929, eight American automakers were running assembly plants abroad. Other companies invested in foreign enterprises: General Electric, for example, held shares in every major electric company in the world. Soon, mass retailers like Montgomery Ward, Woolworth's, and A&P began to expand into foreign countries. The high-tech firms of the day—General Electric, International Telephone and Telegraph, and West-

Distribution of World's Industrial Production, 1870–1938 (in percentages)

Years	United States	Great Britain	Germany	France	Russia	Japan	Rest of world
1870	23	32	13	10	4	—	17
1881–1885	29	27	14	9	3	—	19
1896–1900	30	20	17	7	5	1	20
1906–1910	35	15	16	6	5	1	21
1913	36	14	16	6	6	1	21
1926–1929	42	9	12	7	4	3	22
1936–1938	32	9	11	5	19	4	21

Source: W. W. Rostow, *The World Economy: History and Prospect*, 1978.

American Industry in the Global Economy. Three nations—the United States, Great Britain, and Germany—overwhelmingly dominated the world's industrial production in the late nineteenth and early twentieth centuries. By 1881, the United States had overtaken Britain as the leading industrial power, and it increased its lead further in the subsequent years. The Great Depression, however, devastated the capitalist economies and led to the emergence of the Soviet Union (Russia) as a major industrial power.

ern Electric—laid the cables and created the communications systems that made it possible for these companies to do business abroad. Finally, U.S. companies took an increasingly active hand in exploiting the raw materials of Latin American countries: Venezuelan oil, Chilean copper, Cuban sugar, Argentine beef, and Central American fruit. Direct U.S. investment abroad doubled in the 1920s; by 1930, the United States also led the world in exports.

In selling and investing, American companies received generous assistance from the federal government. Worried about a potential oil shortage, U.S. diplomats helped to identify foreign oil sources that companies might use to satisfy the growing needs of American motorists. Cars also needed rubber tires, so Secretary of Commerce Hoover encouraged Firestone and other tire companies to expand their rubber plantations in West Africa and Southeast Asia in order to break British dominance of the world rubber market.

The growth of U.S. investment abroad was also facilitated by the government's willingness to "send in the marines." Wilsonian principles of self-determination, Secretary of State Hughes argued, did not apply to poor countries. Over and over, the U.S. military intervened when rebels demanding self-rule threatened American industry. The United States occupied Nicaragua almost continuously from 1912 to 1933 and Haiti from 1915 to 1934. U.S. Marine Corps General Smedley Butler later gave this blunt summary of U.S. military interventions in Central America, many of which he had commanded: "I helped in the raping of half a dozen Central American republics for the benefit of Wall Street. I spent most of my time being a high-class muscle man for Big Business, for Wall Street and the bankers. In short, I was a racketeer for capitalism."

While the United States stood firmly for the free flow of goods and capital around the globe, it backed away from its earlier commitments to the free flow of people. During World War I, anti-immigrant sentiment had led to a literacy test for immigrants, and wartime conditions had sharply curtailed the influx of foreigners. With the end of the war, immigration returned to previous levels—800,000 people arrived in 1921—and anti-immigration sentiment rose with it. First, Congress passed the Quota Act of 1921, then, in 1924, the even more restrictive Immigration (Johnson-Reed) Act, which shaped U.S. immigration policy for the next four decades. Initially, the 1924 law limited immigration from all countries to a total of 165,000 a year, less than 20 percent of the pre–World War I average. A 1927 law set even lower limits. Both the 1924 and 1927 laws set quotas by countries, based on the percentage of a particular nationality in the United States as recorded in the 1890 census. This maneuver was a blatant effort to limit immigration from southern and eastern Europe, which occurred primarily after 1890. In the first decade of the twentieth century, an average of 200,000 Italians had entered the United States each year; in 1924, the annual quota for Italians was set at less than 4,000.

Goodwill. The 1928 Havana Pan-American Conference found President Calvin Coolidge defending U.S. intervention in Nicaragua from attacks by Latin American delegates. U.S. press coverage largely ignored the controversy, preferring to herald transatlantic aviator Charles Lindbergh's arrival in Havana with a message of "goodwill." "How sweet it sounds in the ears of the Pan-American delegates," commented the *New Masses* in the caption to this cartoon, "but how different it looks to Sandino and the Nicaraguan patriots."

Source: Hugo Gellert, *New Masses,* February 1928—Prints and Photographs Division, Library of Congress.

Asians fared even worse under the new law, which barred all immigrants who were ineligible for citizenship. That included Asian Indians, Japanese, and Chinese, all of whom were judged ineligible based on past judicial rulings. In 1922, the Supreme Court had ruled the Japanese ineligible for citizenship; the following year another court ruling barred Asian Indians, who had begun emigrating to work in the northwestern lumber mills and on California farms in the early twentieth century. A resurgent nativism and racism was evident in these new immigration restrictions. During the Senate debate on the 1924 Johnson-Reed Act, Ellison DuRant Smith of South Carolina urged lawmakers to "shut the door" to preserve "the pure, unadulterated Anglo-Saxon stock" that had made America "the foremost nation in her progress."

The one exception to these new restrictions was immigration from within the Western Hemisphere. In part because the United States wanted to maintain good relations with its neighbors and in part because farmers (and especially agribusiness) in the Southwest insisted on a ready supply of cheap labor, Mexicans and Canadians could immigrate freely. Almost half a million Mexicans entered the United States in the 1920s—double the number in the previous decade. Some settled in industrial cities like Detroit and Chicago, but most remained in the Southwest and continued to work in agriculture. In the Northeast, French Canadians bound for

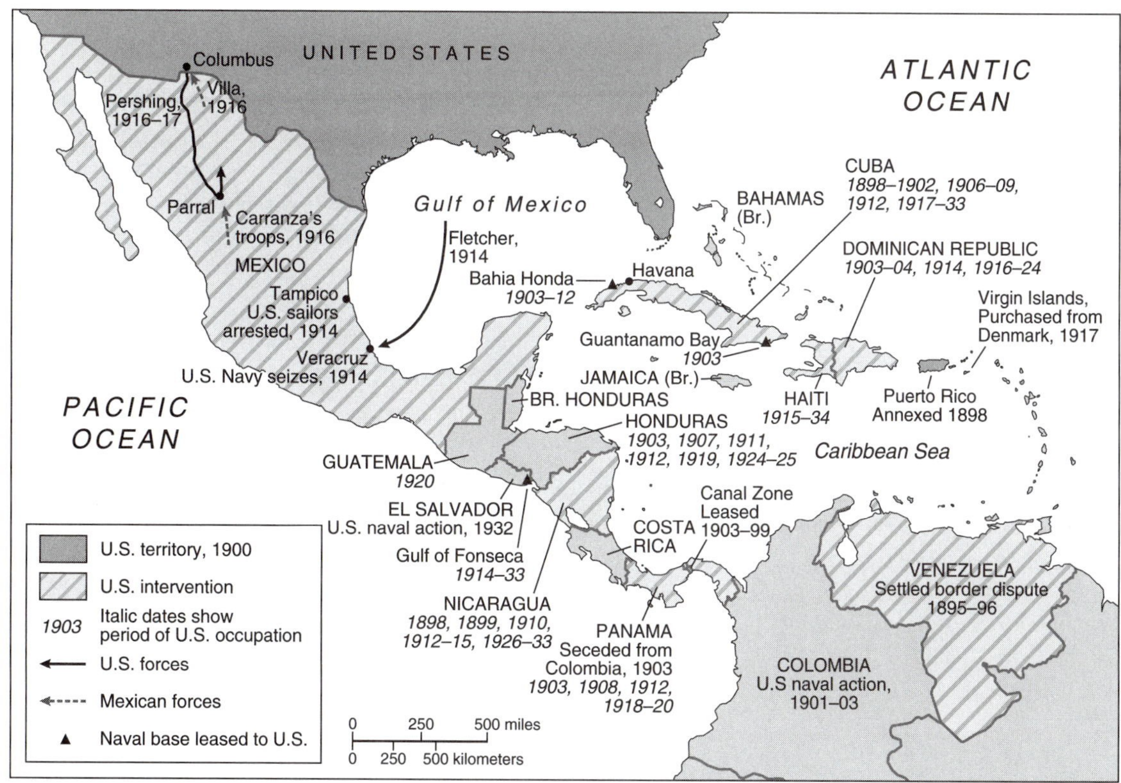

Big Stick Diplomacy: U.S. Military Invasions of Central America, 1898–1930. In the first third of the century, the United States was not reluctant to "send in the Marines" to defend what it saw as American interests in Central America. This map shows the locations of U.S. military invasions from 1898 to 1917 and the continuing presence of American troops in the 1920s and 1930s.

New England factories joined established French Canadian communities. But without a similar influx of youths from the old country, most other immigrant communities began to struggle to maintain their traditions and cohesion.

Shifts in Manufacturing

The U.S. economy experienced a fundamental shift during the 1920s. Many industries like coal and textiles were labeled "sick," and scores of railroads were in bankruptcy. The old economy, based on typical nineteenth-century industries—steel, coal, textiles, railroads, lumber, meatpacking and shipping—was being replaced by one more directly responsive to consumer demand for automobiles, entertainment, processed food, ready-made clothing, petroleum chemicals, home appliances, and other mass-merchandized goods. Demographic changes were part of the engine driving this change. Americans were having fewer children, and they were moving to cities. In 1900, three-fifths of the American population had lived in rural areas. By the time the 1920 census was taken, the urban population had surpassed the rural, and it would continue to grow throughout the decade. Households were growing more numerous but smaller. In 1890, about a third of American households had fewer than four people; by 1930, over half did. The increase in the number of households fed the demand for household goods. So did the growth of cities, which meant less time and space for home production.

Consumer goods accounted for more economic activity than ever before, and for most of the increase in manufacturing. Yet while manufacturing output nearly doubled between 1921 and 1929, the manufacturing workforce barely grew; almost the same number of workers now produced twice as many goods. During and after the war, manufacturers invested heavily in new machines, which reduced the number of workers needed, especially skilled workers. For example, a machine that painted decorative strips on cars eliminated ten jobs. Many factories also converted from steam to electric power, a more efficient source of energy. Productivity gains (and cuts in employment) also came from speed-ups, the practice of forcing employees to work harder and faster. This was especially prevalent in the southern textile industry. One southern mill hand recalled her nightmares: "I just sweated it out in my dreams just like I did when I was there on the job; wanting to quit but I couldn't afford to."

Service industries, finance, construction, and public utilities all grew more than manufacturing during the 1920s. Most new jobs were in construction—both residential and road building boomed—or in commerce, services, and finance. Clerical employment alone increased by nearly a million jobs during the 1920s, while the proportion of workers engaged in manufacturing, mining, agriculture, and railroading declined. With the exception of construction, most expanding sectors of the economy employed large numbers of women. By 1930, more than half the country's clerical workers were female.

Economic Growth and Instability

Throughout the 1920s, industrialists and bankers hailed what they called "the new capitalism." Banker Charles E. Mitchell claimed that this new era was bringing "all classes of the population to a more equal participation in the fruits of industry." Even the boom-bust business cycle had been conquered, according to another banker, Nelson A. Taylor. "We need not fear a recurrence of conditions that will plunge the nation into the depths of the more violent financial panics such as have occurred in the past."

"Times Look Pretty Dark to Some." A cartoon in the *Chicago Tribune* prescribed "good old fashioned hard work" as the cure for the depression of 1920 and 1921.

Source: Carey Orr, *Chicago Tribune,* 1921—American Social History Project.

But the truth was more complicated than these rosy statements suggested. Rather than shrinking the gap between the rich and the poor, economic growth increased it. While corporate profits nearly doubled in the 1920s, factory workers' wages rose only modestly—less than 15 percent, by one estimate. Workers in some industries did considerably better than those in others. Between 1923 and 1929, workers in the automobile, electrical, and printing industries received wage increases of 10 to 28 percent, but those in the shoe, coal, and textile industries watched their wages drop. In general, skilled workers (in construction, for example) and white-collar workers (such as postal clerks) did much better than the unskilled (domestic servants and others). Between 1923 and 1929, when skilled railroad brakemen won wage increases totaling 14 percent, their unskilled counterparts—one-third of the railroad work force—found themselves earning 2.5 percent less.

Moreover, unemployment often undercut workers' wage gains. According to one estimate, unemployment in manufacturing, transportation, mining, and building averaged 13 percent between 1921 and 1926. Unsteady work meant insecurity for working-class Americans. "You couldn't save very much," recalled the wife of a steelworker, "because my husband was more out of work than working." Even skilled workers' employment was often seasonal; the "fully employed" got laid off frequently.

The ups and downs of the business cycle, which continued despite assertions to the contrary, exacerbated joblessness and insecurity. The initial postwar boom gave way to hard times in late 1920. Prices fell sharply and a hundred thousand firms went bankrupt. The economy recovered in 1923, but two more recessions soon followed. In spite of these fluctuations, *the nation as a whole* experienced rising standards of living in the 1920s. In the aggregate, the real earnings of all employed wage earners (not just working-class or blue-collar workers) rose about 25 percent. Americans were also becoming better educated: 27 percent of all seventeen-year-olds graduated from high school in 1929, up from 16 percent in

1920. People were living longer: Life expectancy went from age forty-seven in 1900 to fifty-nine in 1930. And they were eating better, as fruits and vegetables became a more important component of the urban diet.

Despite the overall prosperity, signs of deeper economic trouble were surfacing. Part of the problem lay in the painful and disruptive shift from the old industries that were ailing to the new industries that were not yet mature. But those troubles were compounded by financiers who speculated in new enterprises and engaged in a variety of unsound financial practices, including buying stock on borrowed money and creating dummy corporations that existed only to hold the stocks and bonds of other companies. Stock prices rose steadily throughout the decade, accelerating to speculative heights in 1928 and 1929.

A third sign of trouble came from what analysts of the Great Depression would eventually label "overproduction." By 1928, commercial real estate and consumer-oriented industries like housing, automobiles, and electrical products were slowing down. Sales lagged, inventories rose, factories cut their output, and unemployment rose. Even before the stock market crash of 1929, many executives thought their markets were saturated—that is, everybody who was going to buy their products was already doing so. For example, in 1923, new cars had outsold used cars three to one; by 1927, that ratio had been reversed and Chevrolet was paying dealers a bounty of $25 for each old car they destroyed.

But what was overproduction to the businessman was underconsumption to the many workers who could not afford to buy the new consumer items the nation's factories were churning out. Workers and farmers were buying all those used cars in the late 1920s because they couldn't afford new ones. In one Indiana city, almost three-quarters of all families earned less than the Bureau of Labor's minimum cost of living standard. By one estimate, two-fifths of all Americans lived in poverty in the 1920s.

Meanwhile, the rich were getting richer. In 1929, the 36,000 wealthiest families received as much income as the 12 million poorest. Wealth—in stocks, bonds, and real estate—was concentrated among these fortunate few to an unprecedented degree. This growing social inequality was paralleled by the concentration of productive capacity among a handful of enormous corporations, such as General Motors, General Electric, and AT&T. By 1929, the two hundred largest U.S. corporations controlled half of all corporate assets. These institutions were no longer merely private enterprises; their ability to establish prices and to direct investment held enormous consequences for millions of working Americans. In 1927, a single industrialist, Henry Ford, touched off a brief nationwide recession when he shut down his plants and laid off 100,000 workers in order to retool his assembly lines.

Daily Life in the New Consumer Culture

The underlying problems of the economy were not immediately obvious, however. Across the country, builders scrambled to ease a serious housing shortage. Six million new homes went up between 1922 and 1929, twice as many as in any previous seven-year period. Well over half were single-family dwellings. Although fewer than half of all American families owned their homes, and brand-new houses were beyond the means of most working-class families, the growth of mortgage financing allowed more of them than ever before to become homeowners. Banks were not the only lenders; some employers provided low-cost mortgages to skilled workers, hoping to win their loyalty. A few unions also underwrote mortgages; the Amalgamated Clothing Workers, for example, sponsored cooperatively owned apartment buildings.

Residential patterns remained economically and racially segregated. As cities grew, better-off workers moved outward, while poorer families took over the neighborhoods they abandoned. Suburban areas grew twice as rapidly as the center cities. To keep out African Americans, Asians, Mexicans, and Jews, some suburban towns adopted zoning regulations or "restrictive covenants," special clauses written into deeds to regulate the sale of land and houses.

But wherever Americans lived, dramatic changes were taking place inside their homes. Oil furnaces, radios, toasters, irons, and wringer washing machines appeared even in working-class homes during the 1920s. Sociologists Robert and Helen Lynd, who studied daily life in Muncie, Indiana, in 1924, commented on the vacuum cleaner: "The homely broom, unchanged since the time of the early Egyptians, is giving way to an expensive piece of electrical equipment." Prepared

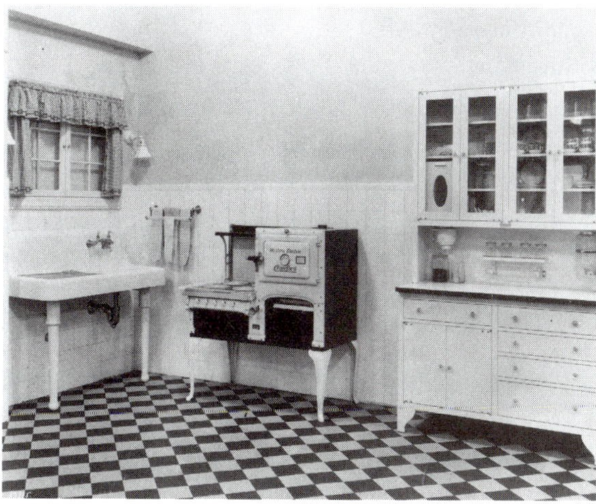

Model Kitchens. A quarter of a century separated these two "model kitchens" that demonstrate how technology and new consumer products—including gas stoves, washing machines, and vacuum cleaners—changed housework. The wood stove in the 1899 kitchen, for example, stands in sharp contrast to the 1924 showcase electric stove. Nevertheless, some innovations were far beyond the means of many American families; over one-third of all U.S. households still had wood or coal stoves in 1940.

Source: Anna Leach, "Science in the Modern Kitchen," *Cosmopolitan*, May 1899—American Social History Project; Prints and Photographs Division, Library of Congress.

and packaged foods could be found on many working people's tables; cleaning products were now purchased rather than made at home, as in the past.

Throughout the decade, as appliances multiplied, the use of electricity increased. Over two-thirds of U.S. households were wired by 1930—double the proportion of a decade before. Some electric companies offered wiring services on the installment plan. As new power plants came on line, the price of power dropped by one-third between 1912 and 1930. At first, most homes used only a few electric lights, but as electricity got cheaper, people installed more lights, bought more appliances, and used more current. By 1926, more than half the houses in Zanesville, Ohio, had electric irons and vacuum cleaners, and one-fifth had toasters. Still, the average residential customer in 1930 used only 547-kilowatt hours annually; customers in the 1990s would use sixteen times that much.

Farm homes lagged far behind city ones in household technologies and utilities. Nearly three of every four urban families had bathrooms, but only one in three rural families did. Similarly, only about 10 percent of farms had electricity in 1930, compared with 85 percent of urban and small-town dwellings. Many prosperous farmers bought appliances that ran on gas, but almost three-quarters of the farm homes in the Midwest had no modern household equipment at all, although many had automobiles and tractors.

Farm women, like urban women, bought more clothing ready-made than ever before. Those who lived far from stores shopped from catalogs. "Tell us this," Sears asked on its 1927 order blank, alongside spaces for body measurements, "do you like to wear your garments loose-fitting or close fitting?" Answers and orders could be given in any language. Sewing—once a task that occupied most women's every spare moment—became a choice. The Lynds found that two-thirds of the working-class women in Muncie spent less than six

A Consumer Revolution? The Production of Consumer Goods, 1900–1930. New consumer goods and appliances spread unevenly across the nation in the 1920s. The most rapid growth came in the production of cars and radios. Labor-saving devices for the home appeared much more slowly. As late as 1930, fewer than a quarter of American families owned washing machines and fewer than a third had vacuum cleaners.

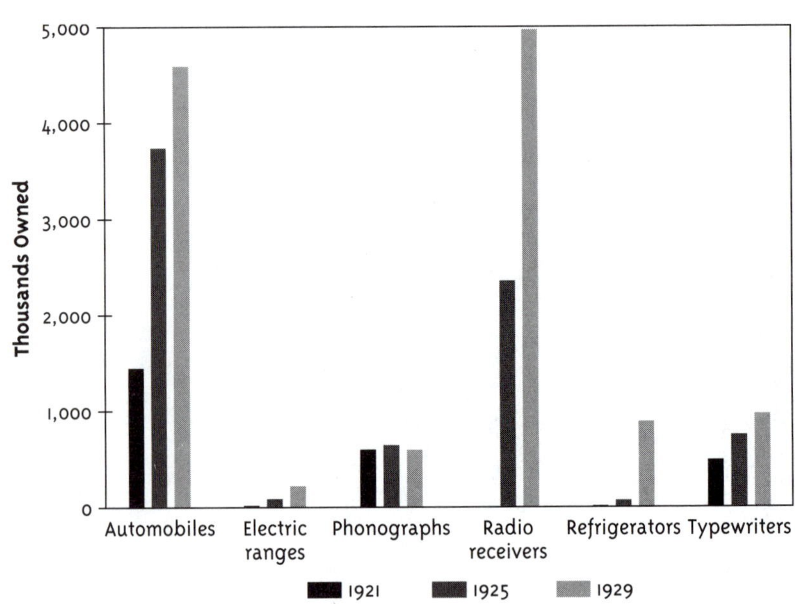

hours a week sewing and mending. The head of the fabric department of Muncie's largest department store reported that demand for yard goods was "only a fraction of that in 1890."

Still, tens of millions of Americans lived outside the boundaries of the consumer economy, unable to afford new clothes, automobiles, or the many other products that were part of Americans' rising expectations during the 1920s. A third of all families lived in houses categorized by one expert as below "any decent standard." Times of unemployment, seasonal layoffs, or sickness threw blue-collar workers into hard times. "When my husband's working steady," a roofer's wife explained, "I can just manage, but when he's out [of work], things go back." First she stopped sending her wash to the commercial laundry and did it by hand in the kitchen sink. Then she cut back on food. Then, she explained, "the rent goes behind."

Autos for the Masses

The single most important product in the new culture of consumption was the automobile, and the number of cars manufactured more than tripled during the 1920s. By 1929, almost half the families in the United States owned a car—a level not reached in England until 1970. "Why on earth do you need to study what's changing this country?" a Muncie resident asked Robert and Helen Lynd. "I can tell you what's happening in just four letters: A-U-T-O!"

The automobile transformed not only the way Americans spent their leisure time, but also the economic and physical landscape. The automobile industry in 1929 accounted for nearly 13 percent of the value of all manufactured goods; it employed 375,000 workers directly and millions more indirectly. Fifteen percent of the nation's steel went into auto bodies

America Goes Driving: Automobile Sales and Registrations, 1900–1946. This chart documents the rapid increase in car ownership in the first half of the twentieth century. War-time restrictions on driving and automobile production led to the fall off in car sales and registrations in the early 1940s.

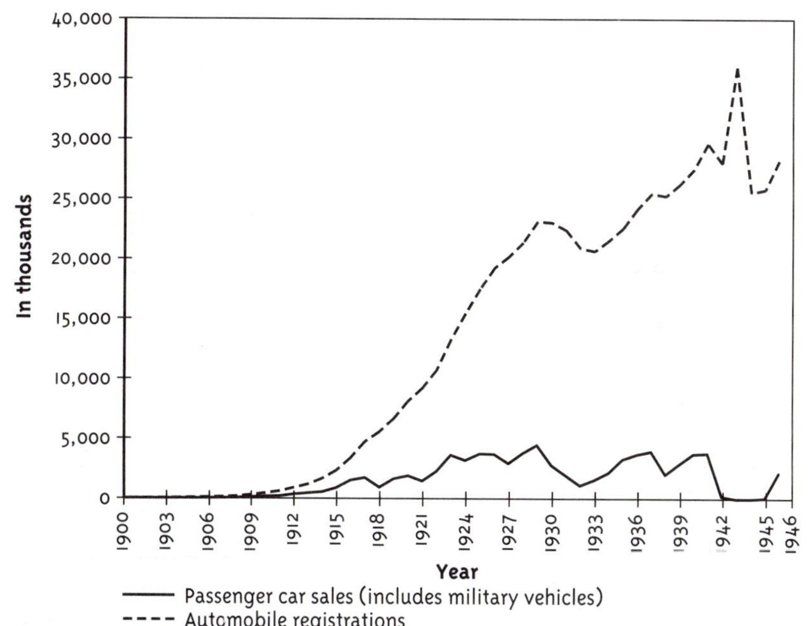

and parts, and 80 percent of its rubber into tires. What's more, the auto industry generated and supported secondary industries and businesses, supplying Americans with tires, new highways, and parking lots. New demands for insurance and consumer credit stimulated financial markets. Whole cities grew up around automobile production. Detroit grew from a population of 285,000 in 1900 to 1.5 million in 1930. Flint, Michigan, where General Motors had numerous plants, increased twelvefold in the same period.

At the beginning of the decade, Henry Ford and the Ford Motor Company dominated the automobile market. Ford was selling transportation, not style, and he emphasized production: the most efficient factories, the lowest price for cars, the largest market. To those ends, during World War I, Ford had developed the huge River Rouge complex in Dearborn, Michigan. This vertically integrated manufacturing operation had its own port, steel mill, power plant, and railroad, and it operated the world's largest foundry. At its height, the River Rouge complex was the largest factory in the United States, employing more than 75,000 workers. "Fordist" methods—reducing labor costs and increasing output through the use of machinery, keeping prices low and wages high—paid off. In 1921, the Ford Motor Company controlled 55 percent of the U.S. automobile market. The price of a Model T—$950 in 1909—dropped to $290 by 1924.

Ford's main rival, General Motors (GM), took a different approach. GM president Alfred P. Sloan, Jr., believed that Americans with rising incomes would choose cars not only for their price but also for their comfort and style. Accordingly, GM began to offer a wide range of styles and prices, changing them every year. Sloan called this approach "the 'laws' of Paris dressmakers": "keep the consumer dissatisfied" and eager to buy a new and fancier model. Thus the company maintained five separate car divisions, ranging from Cadillac, which made the fewest, most expensive automobiles, to Chevrolet, which mass-produced low-priced vehicles.

Assembly Line, 1928. Automobile workers at the end of an assembly line at the Ford River Rouge plant are shown here putting the finishing touches on the stylish new Model A, which replaced the basic black Model T in 1927.

Source: Henry Ford Museum and Greenfield Village.

Increasingly, working people found it easier to afford cars, although perhaps not the models they longed for. For many decades, the installment plan had enabled seamstresses and farmers to buy sewing machines and harvesters. Now three major companies—including the General Motors Acceptance Corporation, established in 1919 as part of Sloan's marketing plan—financed the postwar auto boom by offering loans to buyers. Many bought used cars, creating a market for secondhand autos that kept the new-car market afloat and broadened automobile ownership. In 1927, used-car sales surpassed new-car sales for the first time.

Farmers and people in small towns were the first to purchase cars in massive numbers. About three of every ten farm families in the Midwest bought their first cars during the 1920s; by 1930, almost nine of every ten farm families in Iowa, Kansas, Minnesota, Nebraska, and the Dakotas owned cars. For these people, living far from stores and neighbors, automobiles filled a real need and transformed rural social life. One farm woman thought it obvious why her family had bought a Model T before equipping their home with indoor plumbing. "Why, you can't go to town in a bathtub," she told an inquiring government official.

Automobiles to Match Milady's Mood. This 1927 advertisement for Paige-Jewett cars suggests how manufacturers and advertising firms used colors and new styles to differentiate their products from those of competitors. Buying became confused with self-expression as consumers were urged to purchase products as a way to display individual taste and distinction.

Source: *Ladies' Home Journal*, February 1929—American Social History Project.

Even some poor farmers scrimped and saved to buy secondhand vehicles. In Georgia, about half of white sharecroppers and somewhat fewer black ones owned cars by the mid-1930s. Some lived in their cars, others traveled to Florida in them to pick crops. Autos weakened the tyrannical grip of southern plantation owners and local merchants, because farmers could now patronize more distant stores, banks, and cotton gins. But black drivers in the rural South could not outrun Jim Crow: They were still expected to yield to white drivers and pedestrians. Ned Cobb, a black sharecropper from Alabama, bought his car as a kind of work incentive for his growing sons: "My boys, anyway, they done got big enough to go and correspond girls," he later recalled, so he decided to "buy me a new Ford to please them."

The automobile changed life in the city, too. Cars enabled people to live

"We Rode the Public a Little Ourselves"

To sell its Model T, the Ford Motor Company established a national network of sales agencies. These were independent businesses, but as one rural dealer recalled, they were forced by Ford to meet sales quotas. To do so, they sometimes used unethical practices.

When I first took the agency I was my own boss like any other business man, selling as many cars as I could and buying more when I needed them. . . . Then one day a representative of the [Ford] Company came to see me . . . and said ten cars a month was not enough for a dealer like me to sell. It seems the Company had made a survey of my territory and decided that the sales possibilities were much greater. Benson [the Ford representative] said my quota had been fixed at twenty cars a month, and from then on that number would be shipped to me.

Naturally, I got a little hot under the collar at this kind of proposition, and I told Benson where he could get off at. . . . Benson was pretty hard boiled. . . . Either I could buy twenty cars a month or the Company would find another agent. . . .

Well, I finally decided to take a chance on twenty cars a month rather than lose the agency. . . . But I sure got it in the neck when the slump of 1920 came on. If anyone wants to know what hard times are he ought to try to do business in a Western farming community during a panic. . . . From September to January of that year I sold exactly four cars. . . .

I am willing to confess that we rode the public a little ourselves while we were getting rid of our big surplus of cars. There are always people that you can sell anything to if you hammer them hard enough. We had a salesman named Nichols who was a humdinger at running down prospects, and one day he told me he had a fellow on the string with a couple of hundred dollars who would buy a car if we would give him a little extra time on the balance. This prospect was a young fellow that had come out West on account of his health and was trying to make a living for his family as an expert accountant. Just at that time the referee in the bankruptcy was doing most of the accounting business around town, and I knew the young fellow wasn't getting on at all. He had about as much use for a car as a jack rabbit. . . .

Well we went ahead and made the sale, but we never got any more payments. The young fellow took to his bed just after that, and the church people had to look out for him and his family until he died. In the final showdown it turned out that the two-hundred dollar equity in the car was everything they had on earth, and by the time we [repossessed] it and sold it as a trade-in there wasn't anything at all. I gave twenty dollars toward his funeral expenses.

Source: "Confessions of a Ford Dealer, as told to Jesse Rainsford Sprague," *Harper's Monthly Magazine,* June 1927.

farther from work. No longer dependent on public transportation, Americans moved away from older working-class neighborhoods and into the suburbs. The new mobility was accompanied by a sense of freedom and control. For young people, the automobile offered the means to socialize away from their parents. For workers in increasingly routinized jobs, it fueled a growing tendency to make recreation a part of everyday life, not just an occasional event. Like other consumer industries, the automobile makers began manufacturing not only products, but desires. Ultimately, GM's emphasis on marketing proved more effective than Ford's stress on manufacturing. Ford was forced to abandon the Model T, to introduce and advertise new models and colors, and to move toward more flexible manufacturing methods. Henry Ford's vision of extreme standardization and continuous price reduction was on its way out. Replacing it was a more sophisticated form of mass production, based on creating and then fulfilling ever-changing consumer demands.

"Smoked Continuously from Trepassey to Wales." In this 1928 advertisement, aviator Amelia Earhart, the first woman to complete a solo flight across the Atlantic, testifies to the pacifying virtues of Lucky Strikes.

Source: American Social History Project.

The Creation of Customers

If manufacturers like Ford were the captains of industry, advertising men could be seen as the captains of consumerism, charged with manufacturing dreams and creating new wants. Some advertisements associated products with a desirable lifestyle: "Men at the top are apt to be pipe-smokers," read an ad for Edgeworth Pipe Tobacco. Others tried to undermine people's reliance on traditional sources of advice and authority—parents, friends, and neighbors—so they would trust manufacturers' claims instead. Some pointed out the dire consequences of not purchasing a product: "A single contact with inferior toilet paper," warned a Scott Paper ad, "may start the way for serious infection—and a long, painful illness." Celebrities from the world of entertainment, sports, and occasionally politics also endorsed products.

Despite advertisers' suggestion that everybody had to have the latest of everything, most families set their own priorities and purchased the things they wanted most. "It is not uncommon," the Lynds wrote about Muncie, "to observe 1890 and 1924 habits jostling along side by side." A family might have "primitive back-yard water or sewage habits" but own an automobile, an electric iron, or a vacuum cleaner.

Consumption varied from town to town and from region to region, but was particularly conspicuous in places like Flint, Michigan, which were experiencing an economic boom. Flint's auto industry drew large numbers of young workers to the city. Unrestricted by community traditions and family obligations, they eagerly adopted the ethic of consumption, buying cars and clothing on the installment plan. Young single women, too, went into debt to buy stylish clothes. Dressed for a night out, workers flocked to Flint's movie theaters, dance halls, and bowling alleys.

Some businessmen argued that the Flint situation was ideal, that the high wages common in the auto industry would not only maintain labor peace, but also enlarge the pool of purchasers for consumer products. Boston reformer and department store owner Edward A. Filene believed that the very idea of mass production was "based upon a clear understanding that increased production demands increased buying, and that the greatest total profits can be obtained only if the masses can and do enjoy a higher and ever higher standard of living. . . . Mass production is . . . *production for the masses.*"

Mass Culture: Radio, Music, and the Movies

The new consumer culture was accompanied by the rise of a truly national popular culture. Popular entertainments like radio, recorded music, and motion pictures pulled previously isolated social groups into the mainstream. At the same time, however, they divided families by appealing differently to members of different generations. As they reached their wide audiences, these entertainment forms created new desires and aspirations, reinforcing the development of a consumer culture.

When broadcasting started in 1920, radio was a primarily male hobby. Men and boys wearing headsets assembled and listened to broadcasts made by local amateurs. Stations were supported by wealthy individuals, colleges, churches, newspapers, municipalities, and manufacturers of radio equipment. By 1926, more than four million radios made their way into American homes. Soon, loudspeakers replaced headphones, allowing entire families to listen together. Families and neighbors gathered in homes and shops to listen to drama, comedy, and crop and weather reports. For the first time, millions of Americans could hear the voice of the president, the roaring crowds at the World Series, and the very best professional musicians. Radio created a mass audience for sports and music far from the ballpark and the concert hall.

Businesspeople quickly realized that radio offered a wonderful new medium for peddling their wares. Within a few years, companies were sponsoring programs that incorporated commercials featuring "branded performers" like the Ipana (toothpaste) Troubadours, the A&P Gypsies, and "Paul Oliver" and "Olive Palmer," who performed for the Palmolive Company. By 1928, national networks had been established on an explicitly commercial basis to sell expensive radio time. Filling that time were new forms of sponsored programming, like Pepsodent toothpaste's "Amos 'n' Andy," an enormously popular comedy show about African Americans (played by white actors), which premiered in 1928.

Radios were common even in rural areas, where they were powered by batteries or windmills. The news of commodity prices and weather reports that the radio brought was vital information. Soon the Department of Agriculture was providing radio stations with scripts for lessons on dairy production, livestock feeding, and cooking. The "National Farm and Home Hour," which debuted on NBC stations in 1928, provided forty-five minutes of music, weather and crop forecasts, and information on soil improvement and home economics. Just as important, the radio kept farm women company as they churned butter and made beds. As one Missouri farmer wrote to a radio station in 1923: "We hill-billies out in the sticks look upon radio as a blessing direct from God. We farmers are going broke anyway, but we would like to have our radios to sort of ease the pain."

Music and Milking Time. Pausing to tune in to his favorite program, this farmer was an extreme example of radio's broad popularity during the 1920s.

Source: Prints and Photographs Division, Library of Congress.

Local and ethnic radio broadcasts flourished alongside the emerging national shows. In every city, scores of low-powered stations carried foreign-language programs. In neighborhoods like Boston's Italian-American North End, many more people listened to such broadcasts than to English-language programming. Stars of foreign-language radio shows became important figures in the ethnic enclaves, making frequent personal appearances at neighborhood restaurants, dance halls, and cultural centers.

Ethnic audiences could also buy phonograph records made in foreign languages. By the mid-1920s, phonographs were affordable luxuries for working people. Like radios, they were sold at widely ranging prices, depending on the quality of their cabinets as well as their working parts. "Race records," marketed to black audiences, brought black music to far-flung corners of the United States. In just six months, leading blues singer Bessie Smith's first recording, "Downhearted Blues," made in 1923, sold 750,000 copies.

The movies, too, were adapted to the needs of ethnic communities. Eastern European Jews created a Yiddish film industry in the 1920s, with its own directors, movie stars, and theaters. The conflicting aspirations of European-born parents and their "American" children were a major theme of this emerging cinema. Another small, independent movie industry served blacks.

For most of the decade, movies were only part of a show that included live entertainment. In the packinghouse district of Chicago, a Polish play accompanied the film; in Little Sicily, Italian music could be heard at the movie house. In "The Stroll," Chicago's African-American entertainment district, blues artists played on the same bill as the movie. Nor was the film showing entirely silent: Live music—a piano in a small theater, an organ in a larger one, an orchestra in the big downtown movie palaces for the middle class—accompanied the screen images.

Before World War I, moviegoers had been mainly urban, working-class immigrants, but during and after the war, movie theaters sprang up even in remote towns. By the mid-1920s, there were more than twenty thousand movie theaters in the United States. In Carrboro, North Carolina, a small mill town without electricity, the only entertainments had once been baseball, hunting and fishing, music, and conversation. Now, with a movie house equipped with a gasoline-powered generator, mill families could see the latest newsreels and Hollywood movies. Carrboro was becoming less isolated.

At the same time movies were arriving in small towns, film distributors began building large, ornate movie palaces in the cities. One Baltimore theater featured a 110-person orchestra, a mammoth organ, and fourteen pianos. Workers took the streetcar, and middle-class people drove downtown, to see new kinds of films at these theaters—at first, silent features running an hour or more; eventually, in the late 1920s, "talking pictures." By 1930, a total of 100 million movie tickets were being sold every week.

Businessmen embraced the new popular culture because it stimulated consumption. People wanted to own the cars and clothes they saw in

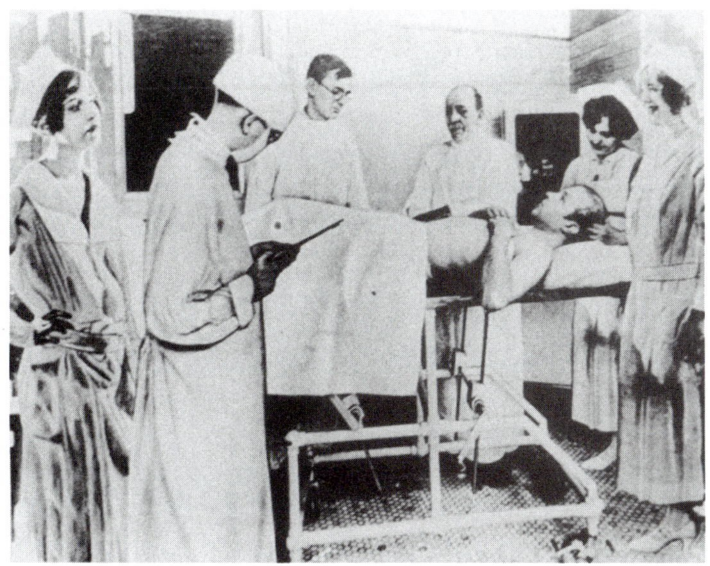

Composograph. When it began publication in 1924 Bernarr Macfadden's *New York Graphic* claimed to inaugurate a new brand of journalism. Its brazen exploitation of the sensational; focus on crime, gossip, sex, and scandals; and utter disregard for the truth set a model followed by tabloid journalism to this day. Its inventiveness extended to publication of "composographs," retouched photographic collages that claimed to show events that were never actually caught on film—such as movie idol Rudolph Valentino's 1926 operation, from which he never recovered. The *Graphic* itself was short-lived, going out of business in 1932.

Source: *New York Graphic*, 1926—Prints and Photographs Division, Library of Congress.

movies and magazines. Young people, and adults, too, began modeling their clothing, speech, and behavior after stars of movies, vaudeville, radio, and professional sports.

Many of the new celebrities came from working-class, immigrant backgrounds. Rudolph Valentino, Hollywood's top male romantic lead, had been born in Castellaneta, Italy, and had worked as a gardener and busboy when he first came to the United States. The great magician Harry Houdini was the son of a Jewish tailor. And baseball slugger Babe Ruth's parents, the children of German immigrants, lived in a poor neighborhood on the Baltimore waterfront. These celebrities were popular in part because they spurned the Protestant middle-class values of self-restraint, hard work, and "character." Valentino's erotic portrayal of exotic and passionate characters in movies like *The Sheik* challenged the Victorian ideal of restrained and decorous masculinity. Ruth was celebrated not only for his extraordinary athletic accomplishments (his career home-run record lasted thirty-five years) but for his oversized appetites for food, clothes, alcohol, and sex.

These icons of mass culture competed with the traditional values of families and local communities in providing the primary channels for children's access to the outside world. Generational conflict often resulted, especially in immigrant homes. Grace Gello, who grew up in an Italian family on New York's Lower East Side, remembered that she and her fiancé would occasionally take the afternoon off from work to go to the movies. "We didn't do this too much because we were afraid of my father. He would say, 'If I catch you, I'll break your neck.'"

For immigrants and their children, and for farmers, miners, millworkers, and laborers, movies provided a window on the middle- and upper-class world, with which they had no direct contact. Kate Simon, a writer who grew up among immigrants in the Bronx, New York, recalled that from movies "we learned how tennis was played and golf, what a swimming pool was and what to wear if you ever got to drive a car . . . and of course we learned about Love, a very foreign country like maybe China or Connecticut."

In a sense, all of America was Americanizing. Mass culture was not only Americanizing immigrants, it was redefining the nation's values. Such changes proved threatening, particularly to traditional arbiters of public values—ministers, political leaders, police officials, social workers, and academics—who generally opposed change. Although the movie moguls profited from their role as the nation's new cultural brokers, they also worried that if they went too far, they would provoke censorship and attack, a serious concern, since so many of them were themselves immigrants. After a young actress was found dead in the aftermath of a drunken party hosted by "Fatty" Arbuckle, one of the nation's favorite film comedians, the producers realized they needed a frontman. For $150,000 a year, they hired Will Hays, President Harding's postmaster general and an elder of the Presbyterian Church, to set up a system of industry self-policing. A few years earlier, baseball owners had followed a similar strategy after gamblers fixed the 1919 World Series. They appointed as baseball commissioner the federal judge and former semipro ballplayer Kenesaw Mountain Landis, who ruled the sport with the same autocratic style that had made him a feared opponent of radicals in the Industrial Workers of the World (IWW) sedition trials.

Women as Workers and Consumers

"In an age where the emphasis is on consumption," social scientist Lorine Pruette commented in 1929, "women need wages . . . to keep themselves afloat on the tide. . . . The manufacturers need the women as consumers, need the two-wage family and its demands to keep the factories going." Indeed, to help their families survive or simply to live more comfortably, increasing numbers of married women took jobs outside the home during the 1920s. Their numbers were still modest: In 1930, fewer than 12 percent of all married women worked for wages, for women who could afford to stay home generally did so. But those who did take jobs were part of a long-term trend; since 1900, the percentage of married working women had doubled. In essence, women were replacing children as second wage earners in families that could not live on one paycheck. Because poverty remained the most important determinant of whether a woman worked, married black women were five times as likely as married white women to be in the paid labor force. They were also more likely to occupy the lowest paid positions: as farm laborers or domestic servants, and in the least desirable factory jobs.

Household appliances and other manufactured products eased the burden of housework, allowing more married women to take jobs. Urban women with electricity and indoor plumbing no longer had to clean and fill kerosene lamps or haul water. Most women now bought soap and clothing instead of making them. But working women spent whatever they earned on the new products, and most had to juggle their families' finances carefully. One Philadelphia worker bragged that his wife was "a good manager"; she could "squeeze every cent out of a nickel."

Women were also freed for the labor force by a drop in the birth rate throughout the decade. As child labor became less common, children had become an expenditure for poor families rather than an economic asset. Popular psychological literature encouraged parents to have fewer children and to pay closer attention to childrearing.

"They Raised the People's Children"

In the South as well as the North, domestic service was one of the few occupations in which African-American women could find work. In an interview with the author Susan Tucker, Cecelia Gaudet described what it was like. Gaudet, born in Mobile, Alabama, in 1897, had moved to Chicago in the early 1920s. But the man she married there—another Mobile native—preferred the South.

My husband was a boner . . . for Swift's [a Chicago meatpacker]. But he heard from his sister that they were losing some of their property [in Mobile]. So we came back in 1924. I got a job working at housekeeping for a gentleman. He had lost his wife, and he had a sister there. She was an old maid, but they were rich, and she never didn't know nothing about housekeeping.

She and his two children and him, they fell in love with me. He said I was a perfect housekeeper and cook. I was like their mother. I stayed there until I bought me a place in town. They lived too far out, and my husband said it was too hard on me to go out there.

Then, for a good while, I just did work here and there. This family I'd worked for some before, her son got typhoid pneumonia. I nursed him. Then, her daughter she got grown and married, and whenever she wanted something special done, then she'd come around me—for serving parties. And when these babies in white families were born premature, well, I nursed them.

I took a little girl—she wasn't but six years old—and I raised her because I didn't have no children of my own that lived. So I took care of her and sewed at home and sold vegetables, flowers, chickens, eggs. And sometimes I'd go out and serve parties or weddings. . . .

The majority of [black] people here in Mobile worked. And the majority of them made their living working for white people or washing and ironing for them. Everybody couldn't be teachers, and that was the only thing for them to do. They had to work for white people as cooks, housekeepers, maids.

And it's some people that just done it for a lifetime . . . from young people till they got old for the same family. They raised the people's children, and they raised the children's children.

Source: Susan Tucker, *Telling Memories Among Southern Women: Domestic Workers and the Fmployers in the Segregated South* (1988).

Although more women entered the workforce in the 1920s, they did not do so on an equal basis with men. In 1929, the average working woman earned only fifty-seven cents to a man's dollar. A key reason for the disparity was that jobs were generally designated as "male" or "female." Women were considered suitable for service jobs and precise but routine tasks; jobs requiring independent action and policymaking were reserved for men. The classification of jobs by sex varied from industry to industry. Automakers employed only a few women, nearly a third of whom operated sewing machines. But electrical equipment manufacturers hired women to do many kinds of assembly work, giving them a third of all jobs in the industry.

More women were employed in offices than in manufacturing. New methods of accounting and record keeping required an ever-growing number of clerks, bookkeepers, and accountants. Both men and women, most of them white, could be found in all types of clerical jobs, but employers preferred women for routine tasks, men for sales and general clerical posts. Women were rarely promoted to managerial positions.

To lower costs, companies introduced a variety of calculating machines and Dictaphones (recording machines that eliminated the need for shorthand skills). Following scientific management practices, companies divided the work process into narrow, highly routinized jobs, and the pace of clerical production increased. In large "typing pools," women typed documents for bosses they never saw. These pools more resembled light manufacturing plants than the small company offices of an earlier era.

More satisfying career opportunities opened up in professions that were filled primarily by college-educated women: social work, nursing, teaching, and librarianship. A small but growing number of women found jobs as lawyers, bankers, religious leaders, and editors. Although a handful of these women became well known, most were marginalized, excluded from power even in professions they dominated. Some professions were largely closed to women. Most medical schools had quotas of just 5 percent for women students; only a handful of hospitals would hire women interns. The law schools of Columbia and Harvard would not consider admitting women. All told, only 14 percent of wage-earning women occupied professional positions in 1930, while 19 percent held clerical positions and 30 percent worked in domestic service or as waitresses and beauticians.

One traditional women's profession, midwifery, was outlawed in states across the country. The process of suppressing midwives in favor of male physicians had begun in the eighteenth century among the upper classes. By the 1920s, midwives served mostly blacks, immigrants, and the rural poor. Despite midwives' successful professional records, both male doctors and female reformers accused them of being dirty, ignorant, and dangerous. Between 1910 and 1930, birthing moved increasingly from home to hospital.

As women began to gain some economic independence, their legal and social status began to change. Ratification of the women's suffrage amendment to the Constitution led to the extension of other legal rights; by the early 1920s, women could serve on juries in twenty states. But women did not use the vote to win greater social and economic equality, as suffragists had long hoped. Property, marriage, and divorce laws remained unfavorable to women. Fewer women than men voted throughout the decade, and the choices of women voters were much like men's: shaped less by gender than by class, region, age, race, and religion. As a result, the major political parties were indifferent to women voters and women's issues. An Equal Rights Amendment (ERA) to the Constitution repeatedly failed to pass Congress, although it was the focus for many middle- and upper-class women activists. Supporters of hard-won legislation to protect women workers opposed the ERA, fearing that it would invalidate those protections. The only important legislative triumph for the women's movement in the 1920s was the Sheppard-Towner Maternity and Infancy Protection Act of 1921, which for the first time provided federal funds for health care.

Cultural habits may have changed more than politics. The popular 1920s stereotype of the "flapper"—a "new woman" who wore short, loose dresses and used cosmetics, smoked and drank in public, and embraced the sexual revolution—both mirrored and exaggerated the popular rejection of the genteel, corseted Victorian feminine ideal of the

The Equal Rights Amendment

Suffragist Alice Paul wrote the Equal Rights Amendment in 1921. It has been introduced in every session of Congress since 1923. It passed the House and Senate in 1972 and was ratified by thirty-five states, but it failed to attain the necessary thirty-eight states by the July 1982 deadline.

Section 1. **Equality of Rights under the law shall not be denied or abridged by the United States or any state on account of sex.**

Section 2. **The Congress shall have the power to enforce, by appropriate legislation, the provisions of this article.**

Section 3. **This amendment shall take effect two years after the date of ratification.**

late nineteenth century. These changes did not come about overnight, or affect all women equally; working-class women had pioneered some of the new attitudes before World War I. And while the 1920s brought much franker and more open discussions of sexuality, sexual behavior had probably begun to change earlier than that. Whatever the date of the change, Americans in the 1920s were waking up to the realization of a sexual revolution. One study found that women born after 1900 were twice as likely as those born earlier to have premarital sex. Birth control, more widely available and more reliable in the 1920s, was one force behind the change in behavior. "Rubber has revolutionized morals," declared family court judge Ben Lindsey in 1929.

Agriculture in Crisis

While the consumer economy boomed, agriculture was plagued by overproduction, falling prices, and declining income. Farmers had been relatively prosperous until 1920: agricultural prices had risen faster than industrial prices before World War I, and the extraordinarily high wartime demand for farm products further improved farmers' purchasing power. But the economic downturn of 1920 hit agriculture particularly hard. In 1910, a suit of clothes cost the equivalent of 21 bushels of wheat; a decade later, that suit was worth 31 bushels. A bushel of corn that had sold for $1.22 in 1919 brought just forty-one cents a year later. "'Leven-cent cotton, forty-cent meat, How in the world can a poor man eat?" asked a popular song of the late 1920s.

Overexpansion and debt were at the heart of the farm crisis. During wartime, large European orders for American farm products had prompted farmers to expand, often on borrowed money. When conditions in Europe returned to normal, demand dropped, but output was still increasing thanks to farmers' investments in new fertilizers, seed strains, and machinery. At the same time, farms in Canada, Australia, Argentina, and Brazil joined in flooding the world mar-

"Teaching Old Dogs New Tricks." The slinky style of the flapper was celebrated in the popular press, most notably in the cartoons of John Held, Jr. Cartoons of high-stepping, boot-legging high society, however, quickly lost their appeal after the stock market crashed in 1929.

Source: *Life,* February 18, 1926—Prints and Photographs Division, Library of Congress.

ket with excess produce. There was no market for all that farmers could grow. Nearly half a million Americans lost their farms, unable to meet their mortgage payments and equipment loans. Many independent farmers, rather than mortgaging their farms or becoming tenants, simply gave up. Some moved to cities and worked for wages. For the first time in the nation's history, the total number of farms dropped. Thirteen million acres of cultivated land were abandoned between 1920 and 1930.

The crisis in agriculture brought a revival of rural protest and political activism. The Non-Partisan League, founded in North Dakota in 1915 and concentrated in the upper Midwest, called for government assistance. The League campaigned for state ownership of grain elevators, packinghouses, and flour mills; state hail insurance; easy rural credit; and tax exemptions for farm improvements. In Minnesota, the League allied itself with organized labor and eventually formed the Farmer-Labor Party. In North Dakota, the League had elected a state governor and other officials and had instituted much of its program by 1920. But in 1921, League opponents forced a recall election that ousted the governor and attorney general and weakened the League's influence.

The American Farm Bureau Federation also promoted farmers' interests, but through more conservative channels, stressing cooperative marketing to increase farmers' bargaining power. It lobbied political leaders to support and protect these cooperatives. In the early 1920s, the federal government exempted cooperatives from antitrust action, raised import duties for certain agricultural products, and made more farm credit available. County agricultural extension agents (appointed in every rural county under the federal Agricultural Educational Extension Act of 1914) encouraged farmers to join the Federation rather than more radical farm organizations.

"The 'Snake Doctor' Invades New Fields." This *New York Evening Mail* cartoon ridiculed the efforts of the Non-Partisan League to spur radical reforms in U.S. agricultural policies. **Source:** Albert Reid, *New York Evening Mail,* 1921—American Social History Project.

The McNary-Haugen bill, a more comprehensive solution to the problem of falling farm prices, was introduced in Congress in the 1920s. This complex legislation was designed to restore the prewar relationship between farm prices and industrial prices—a balance that came to be known as parity. The bill would have set up a government corporation to purchase the agricultural surplus and sell it abroad; tariffs were to protect domestic prices. Congress passed the bill in 1927 and 1928, but President Coolidge vetoed it. The plan was adopted during the New Deal, however, and has been a cornerstone of U.S. farm policy ever since.

Farmers rallied around La Follette's presidential campaign in 1924 and continued to press for government aid after the election, but with little success. A gradual rise in agricultural prices diminished their political fervor. Organizing efforts were also hampered by growing differences in income, lifestyle, and political perspective among farm families. A new pattern was emerging in American agriculture. Large, well-financed farms now produced more and more of the country's agricultural output. By 1930, half the nation's farms yielded nearly 90 percent of the cash crop. Large midwestern grain growers prospered by using mechanized equipment. Identifying themselves as businessmen, many were hostile to unions. Immense truck farms and fruit orchards thrived in California and Florida by shipping fresh produce to colder regions during the winter. But California's fruit and vegetable industry was dependent on migrant labor and huge government-financed irrigation projects. Planting and harvesting an acre of lettuce took ten times as much labor as an acre of wheat.

As many as 200,000 farm laborers worked in California during the 1920s, 75 percent of them Mexican. Because demand for agricultural labor peaked at harvest time, these workers moved from region to region as the crops ripened. Children and parents worked side by side in the fields, with little opportunity for social life or schooling. Living conditions were atrocious. A minister described a migrant camp in California's Imperial Valley thus: "Shelters were made of almost every conceivable thing—burlap, canvas, palm branches." Cows and horses deposited manure near the shelters, and water for cooking, drinking, and washing was dipped from irrigation ditches.

Huge farms exploited both impoverished workers and new technologies, and settled farmers without much land or capital could not compete with them. For the quarter of all Americans who still lived on the land, economic hard times were a fact of life well before the rest of the country experienced them in 1929. Southern cotton growers particularly faced hard times in years when bumper crops drove prices down. Even worse off were the millions of sharecroppers and tenants. As Alabama sharecropper Ned Cobb put it, "Every time cotton dropped, it hurt the farmer. Had to pay as much rent, had to pay as much for guano [fertilizer], but didn't get as much for his crop." Millions of farmers never recovered from the drastic fall in tobacco, cotton, and wheat prices that followed the giddy expansion of World War I.

Organized Labor in Decline

Like farmers, unions suffered in the 1920s. The once militant labor movement that had led the 1919 strikes virtually disappeared, for the Red scare had crushed the IWW and other radical groups. Conservative labor leaders provided a small elite of craft workers with union representation, but most other workers had to fend for themselves.

Employers used the economic downturn of 1920 and 1921 as an opportunity to reverse labor's wartime gains; they slashed wages and increased hours, often in violation of union contracts. Building on wartime patriotism and the Red scare, they portrayed union shop contracts, which required all employees to join unions, as an infringement on American liberties. They launched a drive for the open shop, a workplace in which union membership was either not required or was forbidden; this was called the "American Plan." Some unions fought back with major strikes. In Seattle, union leaders organized a six-month boycott of the Bon Marché, the city's largest department store, forcing managers to abandon their open-shop drive.

But nationwide, the antiunion drive took its toll. By late 1923, union membership had fallen to 3.6 million, from a high of over 5 million in 1920. For the rest of the decade, membership continued to decline. Weakened by membership losses, disheartened by defeat, and confronted by hostile employers and unsympathetic government officials, unions made virtually no progress in organizing the rapidly growing automobile, electrical equipment, and petrochemical industries.

In industries dominated by a few large companies, employers promoted stable labor relations with relatively high wages, benefits, or employee welfare programs. Ford's five-dollar day was only the most generous of a wide range of paternalistic plans adopted by large employers. Some offered stock-purchase

Welfare Capitalism and Its Conceits. A 1929 installment of J. R. Williams's popular comic strip *Out Our Way* poked fun at the illusions held by some workers who bought stocks in the companies that employed them.

Source: J. R. Williams, *Labor Age,* March 1929—American Social History Project.

plans, pensions, subsidized housing and mortgages, insurance, and sports programs. In southern textile towns, companies even built churches and paid ministers' salaries. Some of these programs were aimed specifically at reducing labor turnover, particularly among skilled workers. Many welfare programs were run through "company unions," created to keep out worker-controlled unions, build employee loyalty, and settle grievances. Workers were pressured or required to join these employer-sponsored groups.

Workers in industries with many small, competing producers were generally paid less and treated worse than those in industries controlled by a few large firms. In the bituminous, or soft-coal, industry, high wartime prices had prompted the opening of many new mines, particularly in Kentucky and West Virginia. But when demand fell after the war, with competition from oil, natural gas, and hydroelectric power, there were too many mines and miners. As a result, most miners, union and nonunion, were cut back to part-time work. Families lived in poverty and struggled to make ends meet, borrowing from the grocer rather than the auto dealer. Discouraged, many young men left the mining towns for growing industrial cities like Akron, Ohio, and Flint, Michigan.

In 1922, 600,000 members of the United Mine Workers of America (UMWA), the country's largest and most powerful union, struck for over four months in response to pay cuts. In unionized mines in the North, most operators gave in, but the union failed to win new contracts in nonunion mines. By 1926, more than 65 percent of the nation's soft coal came from nonunion pits. Hard-pressed owners, determined to compete with new low-priced international competition, broke the unions and slashed workers' pay. Safety standards deteriorated, working hours increased, and wages fell. By 1928, union membership among soft-coal miners had fallen to 80,000 from about half a million in 1920.

Faced with stiff business opposition, a conservative political climate, and declining membership, American Federation of Labor (AFL) leaders grew increasingly cautious, especially after 1924, the year of Samuel Gompers's death and the La Follette campaign. Unions confronted new legal barriers after a series of U.S. Supreme Court decisions that upheld "yellow-dog" contracts, in which workers promised when they were hired that they would never join a union. No charismatic new leader rose to the occasion. Gompers's replacement, UMWA secretary-treasurer William Green, was, a contemporary remarked, "as plain, as plodding, and as undramatic as his name." (The head of the miners' union, John L. Lewis, unkindly reflected: "Explore the mind of Bill Green. . . . I have done a lot of exploring of Bill's mind and I give you my word there is nothing there.") Green reinforced the conservative and conventional direction in which the labor movement was already heading when he took charge. Radicals

A. F. of L. Delegates. A cartoon by William Gropper published in the Communist Yiddish newspaper *Freiheit* (and reprinted in English in the *New Masses*) caricatured delegates to a 1926 American Federation of Labor convention in Atlantic City. "Well, boys," the caption read, "We had a swell convention. Now for the gravy."

Source: William Gropper, *New Masses,* November 1926—Prints and Photographs Division, Library of Congress.

viewed AFL leaders like Green as overpaid functionaries who were more interested in feathering their own nests than in organizing the unorganized.

Some unions tried to attract or hold members by offering new services; they set up their own banks and began offering insurance and other benefits. Others tried publicity, using "union labels" and "shop cards" to identify and advertise union-made goods and places of business. But such nonconfrontational tactics failed to stop organized labor's decline.

Unions did emerge in a few new places. In 1925, the most important black union in U.S. history, the Brotherhood of Sleeping Car Porters (BSCP), was founded. About fifteen thousand sleeping-car porters worked for the Pullman Company, the manufacturer and administrator of railroad sleeping cars and the country's largest black employer. A porter might work four hundred hours and travel eleven thousand miles every month, but the pay was good compared with most other jobs that were open to African Americans. Even politically sophisticated, well-educated community leaders took jobs as Pullman porters.

The small group that organized the BSCP recruited the socialist A. Philip Randolph to lead the union. Thousands of porters soon joined. But the Pullman Company refused to recognize the union, fired several of its leaders, and began hiring Filipino porters to warn African Americans that they could be replaced. Then the AFL, reflecting in part the labor movement's racism in the 1920s, refused to charter the union. By the end of the decade, the BSCP was down to a few hundred members, mirroring the general decline of organized labor in the conservative climate of the 1920s. But it kept alive the dream of a national labor union for blacks.

African-American Life in the 1920s

Most black Americans remained poor in the 1920s; they neither shared in the new profits nor enjoyed the new consumer goods. But the Great Migration continued to bring profound changes, as 824,000 African Americans moved north between 1920 and 1930. The black populations of New York, Chicago, and Cleveland more than doubled; that of Detroit tripled. Some growth came from West Indian immigration; by 1930, there were fifty thousand foreign-born blacks in New York alone. Blacks who remained in the South moved to cities; by the end of the decade, one in five African Americans lived in a southern city, and more African-American men held blue-collar jobs than farmed. These growing black communities provided the basis for a relatively prosperous black urban culture, extraordinary for its intellectual and artistic accomplishments and significant for its new political militancy.

The movement into urban and blue-collar jobs did not end discrimination. African Americans were usually given the least attractive jobs. Auto companies hired few blacks; indeed, most auto plants were all white. Ford was an exception; 5 to 10 percent of its Detroit-area workers were black, and by 1926 the company had roughly ten thousand African-American employees. Henry Ford believed that white people were a "superior" race, obligated to help black people establish decent lives. But his hiring practices were not entirely altruistic. The African-American workers his company recruited, generally through local ministers, were unusually loyal—an important consideration, given Ford's fear of unions.

As the northern black working class expanded, opportunities developed for black professionals and businesspeople, and the African-American class structure became more complex. Most northern cities had a small black elite that included college-educated lawyers, doctors, and ministers who served black clienteles, along with successful musicians, saloonkeepers, and dressmakers, many of whom catered to whites. A new black middle class emerged to provide services—newspapers, hotels, drugstores, insurance, funerals—to their community. Black women's clubs, which drew on

"The Shame of America." During November 1922, the NAACP ran this full-page advertisement in the *New York Times* and other newspapers, pressing for passage of the Dyer antilynching bill. Although the bill passed in the House of Representatives by a two-to-one majority, southern opponents subsequently filibustered and defeated it in the U.S. Senate.

Source: *New York Times,* November 23, 1922—American Social History Project.

THE SHAME OF AMERICA

Do you know that the United States is the Only Land on Earth where human beings are BURNED AT THE STAKE?

In Four Years, 1918-1921, Twenty-Eight People Were Publicly BURNED BY AMERICAN MOBS

3436 People Lynched 1889 to 1922

For What Crimes Have Mobs Nullified Government and Inflicted the Death Penalty?

Is Rape the "Cause" of Lynching?

83 WOMEN HAVE BEEN LYNCHED IN THE UNITED STATES

AND THE LYNCHERS GO UNPUNISHED

THE REMEDY

The Dyer Anti-Lynching Bill Is Now Before the United States Senate

THE DYER ANTI-LYNCHING BILL IS NOW BEFORE THE SENATE
TELEGRAPH YOUR SENATORS TODAY YOU WANT IT ENACTED

NATIONAL ASSOCIATION FOR THE ADVANCEMENT OF COLORED PEOPLE
70 FIFTH AVENUE, NEW YORK CITY

THIS ADVERTISEMENT IS PAID FOR IN PART BY THE ANTI-LYNCHING CRUSADERS.

this new middle class, campaigned for community issues and held social events.

These developments fostered a new political militancy and heightened racial pride throughout black America. African Americans who had fought in or supported World War I demanded greater democracy at home. The National Association for the Advancement of Colored People (NAACP) benefited from this new spirit; by 1919, it had 91,000 members. The organization worked, largely through lobbying and the courts, for civil rights and an end to lynching. It won some notable victories, such as a 1927 Supreme Court decision that outlawed Texas's practice of excluding blacks from voting in Democratic party primaries. But southern senators blocked the NAACP's antilynching efforts. Moreover, the organization failed to win the allegiance of poor African Americans, who viewed it as a club for liberal whites and well-to-do blacks. In contrast, Marcus Garvey's Universal Negro Improvement Association (UNIA) garnered massive support. Garvey, a printer by trade, founded the UNIA in his native Jamaica in 1914 and brought it to the United States two years later. The UNIA sought black nationhood and the redemption of Africa from colonialism, and it promoted self-help and self-respect. Garvey preached pan-Africanism, the idea that black men and women throughout the world were one people and that the struggle for black rights outside of Africa was fundamentally linked to the fight to free Africa from colonial rule. To help liberate Africa, he encouraged skilled African Americans to return to their "African homeland."

Garvey's appeal rested on black pride. He publicized black achievements, opposed interracial marriage, and, in a reversal of convention, looked down on light-skinned African Americans. Arguing that blacks should

The Black Star Line. This advertisement ran in Marcus Garvey's newspaper, *The Negro World,* urging African Americans to help establish and support a black-owned shipping company.

Source: *The Negro World*—Schomburg Center for Research in Black Culture, New York Public Library, Astor, Lenox and Tilden Foundations.

THE NEGRO WORLD

LET US GUIDE OUR OWN DESTINY

BY FINANCING OUR OWN COMMERCIAL VENTURES.
HELP US TO HELP YOU HELP YOURSELF AND THE NEGRO RACE IN GENERAL
YOU CAN DO THIS BY PLAYING A MAN OR WOMAN'S PART IN THE WORLD OF COMMERCE;
DO YOUR FULL SHARE IN HELPING TO PROVIDE
A DIRECT LINE OF STEAMSHIPS OWNED, CONTROLLED AND MANNED BY NEGROES TO
REACH THE NEGRO PEOPLES OF THE WORLD
AMERICA, CANADA, SOUTH AND CENTRAL AMERICA, AFRICA AND THE WEST INDIES

There should be no trouble about making up your mind to help your race to rise to a position in the maritime world that will challenge the attention and command the admiration of the world. "Men like nations fail in nothing they boldly attempt when sustained by virtuous purpose and firm resolution."
Money awaiting an advantageous investment should go to purchasing shares in the Black Star Line and reap the reward that is bound to follow.

DO A MAN'S PART RIGHT NOW

Send In and Buy Your Shares Today

"THE BLACK STAR LINE," Inc.

Capitalized at $10,000,000 Under the Laws of the State of Delaware

2,000,000 shares of common stock now on sale at par value of $5.00 each for a limited time only at the office of the corporation, 56 West 135th Street, New York City. Phone Harlem 2877.

The Black Star Line, Inc., is the result of a Herculean effort on the part of Hon. Marcus Garvey, world-famed Negro orator, who in July, 1914, founded a society known as the Universal Negro Improvement Association and African Communities League, of which he is now President-General.

The Association now has a membership of over three million persons, with branches all over the United States, Canada, South and Central America, the West Indies and Africa.

THE BLACK STAR LINE, Inc.

is backed today in its operations by the full strength of its organization—to say the least, of millions of other Negro men and women in all parts of the world.

BUY SHARES TODAY AND NOT TOMORROW

CUT THIS OUT AND MAIL IT

SUBSCRIPTION BLANK

"THE BLACK STAR LINE, Inc."
56 West 135th Street, New York City

Date........................

Gentlemen:
I hereby subscribe for........shares of stock at $5.00 per share and forward herewith as full payment $........on same.

Name ....
Street ....
City ....
State ....

develop their own separate institutions and commercial enterprises, he criticized the NAACP's goal of racial integration. Under Garvey's charismatic leadership, the UNIA attracted followers from virtually every segment of black America, especially West Indians, recent migrants from the South, and members of the new black middle class. Within a few years it had a million members in the United States, as well as branches in Africa and the Caribbean.

But the UNIA's success made it a target, and mishandled finances and political infighting devastated the organization. A wide range of black leaders—NAACP officials, socialists, and followers of Booker T. Washington—denounced Garvey for financial mismanagement of a UNIA-owned shipping company, the Black Star Line. The U.S. and British governments also harassed the UNIA. In 1922, Garvey was indicted for mail fraud. The next year he lost the support of the African Blood Brotherhood, a group composed largely of West Indian immigrants, which espoused both socialism and nationalism. Garvey went to prison in 1925 and was deported to Jamaica two years later. His removal shattered the UNIA, although his ideas remained influential.

Other political groups, including the major political parties, competed for black support. As the northern African-American population grew, black votes became significant to the urban machines. Most black voters were Republican, the party of Lincoln; one black New Jerseyite said that "being a black Democrat was like announcing one had typhoid." But Democrats courted blacks anyway, and by maneuvering between the two parties, black political leaders won influence and patronage. In New York City, police, fire, and other municipal departments began to hire blacks. Soon black candidates were running for office. Oscar De Priest, the Alabama-born son of ex-slaves who was Chicago's first African-American alderman, became, in 1928, the first northern black representative elected to Congress.

Postwar African-American political activism was paralleled by a flowering of black culture known as the Harlem Renaissance. Reflecting the racial self-confidence nourished by the growing northern black communities, the writers and artists of the Harlem Renaissance expressed a new pride in black racial identity and heritage. "Negro life," wrote Alain Locke, the movement's leading philosopher and publicist, "is seizing its first chances for group expression and self determination." In music, poetry, novels, plays, dance, painting, sculpture, and photography, black artists and intellectuals celebrated African-American spiritual and cultural traditions, rejecting white values and stereotypes.

In an era when pan-Africanism was emerging as an intellectual and political movement, some black artists looked to Africa for inspiration.

"I Could Not Eat the Poems I Wrote"

Langston Hughes, one of the country's leading twentieth-century poets, recalls the spirit of the Harlem Renaissance, and its underside.

When I came back to New York in 1925 the Negro Renaissance was in full swing. Countee Cullen was publishing his early poems, Zora Neale Hurston, Rudolph Fisher, Jean Toomer, and Wallace Thurman were writing, Louis Armstrong was playing, Cora Le Redd was dancing, and the Savoy Ballroom was open with a specially built floor that rocked as the dancers swayed. Alain Locke was putting together *The New Negro* [an anthology of black writing]. Art took heart from Harlem creativity. Jazz filled the night air—but not everywhere—and people came from all around after dark to look upon our city within a city, Black Harlem. Had I not had to earn a living, I might have thought it even more wonderful. But I could not eat the poems I wrote. Unlike the whites who came to spend their money in Harlem, only a few Harlemites seemed to live in even a modest degree of luxury. Most rode the subway downtown every morning to work or look for work.

Downtown! I soon learned that it was seemingly impossible for black Harlem to live without white downtown. . . . It was not even an area that ran itself. The famous night clubs were owned by whites, as were the theaters. Almost all the stores were owned by whites, and many at that time did not even (in the very middle of Harlem) employ Negro clerks. . . . And almost all the policemen in Harlem were white. Negroes couldn't even get graft from themselves for themselves by themselves. Black Harlem really was in white face, economically speaking. So I wrote this poem:

Because my mouth
Is wide with laughter
And my throat
Is deep with song,
You do not think
I suffer after
I have held my pain
So long?

Because my mouth
Is wide with laughter,
You do not hear
My inner cry?
Because my feet
Are gay with dancing,
You do not know
I die?

Source: Langston Hughes, *Freedomways* (1963).

Alain Locke's writings and speeches about black culture echoed Woodrow Wilson's references during World War I to a people's need for self-determination. That theme recurred in black efforts to win liberation for colonized Africans and to identify with them. In "The Negro Speaks of Rivers," Langston Hughes, perhaps the greatest poet of the Harlem Renaissance, tied together the Euphrates, the Nile, and the Mississippi as "ancient, dusky rivers [that] I've known." Other writers, however, like Zora Neale Hurston and Jean Toomer, concentrated instead on the folk culture of the South. In the innovative and experimental novel *Cane,* Toomer combined fiction, poetry, and dramatic dialogue to evoke the world of black rural southerners. Still other writers explored urban black middle-class life, as did Nella Larsen in her novel *Passing,* the story of two friends, one of whom could pass for white.

More popular African-American cultural forms flourished too. Singers such as Florence Mills and Ethel Waters, and dancers such as Bill Robinson traveled a growing circuit of black nightclubs, theaters, and vaudeville houses. Noble Sissle and Eubie Blake broke new ground in musical theater with their all-black Broadway play *Shuffle Along.* In the South, string bands, blues singers, and jug bands reached new heights of popularity, entertaining at house parties, in "juke joints," and in traveling tent shows.

Jazz, an immensely popular and sophisticated musical form, thrived in the developing black communities of the North. The culmination of centuries of African-American musical development, jazz emerged particularly in New Orleans, Kansas City, Chicago, and New York. By the early 1920s, Louis Armstrong and other important New Orleans jazzmen had moved to Chicago. Edward "Duke" Ellington moved from Washington, D.C., in 1927 to New York City and began playing at Harlem's Cotton Club.

Some middle-class whites were drawn to black culture to escape the sterility and materialism of their own. In a variant of older stereotypes, they saw African Americans as symbols of freedom, passion, and sensuality. "Slumming"—the practice of venturing

The Crisis. Heralding the style and substance of the Harlem Renaissance, the NAACP's magazine, edited by W. E. B. Du Bois, reached between sixty and one hundred thousand readers monthly.

Source: *The Crisis,* May 1929—Schomburg Center for Research in Black Culture, New York Public Library, Astor, Lenox and Tilden Foundations.

into black neighborhoods to go to cabarets, dance halls, jazz clubs, and literary salons—became fashionable. Some of the largest Harlem clubs, in fact, admitted only whites. But most whites encountered African-American culture only secondhand, through white entertainers who copied black styles. Racist depictions of blacks still prevailed in white mass culture, most notably in the movies. The nation's first talking picture (and one of the most influential movies of all time), *The Jazz Singer* (1927), featured a white performer, Al Jolson, singing "My Mammy" in blackface; this perpetuated a crude racial stereotype inherited from nineteenth-century minstrel shows.

Cultural Conflicts

American cultural diversity emerged as a crazy quilt of conflicts in the 1920s and met with resistance of many kinds. Ethnic enclaves in large cities continued to preserve old traditions and respect for family obligations. Tens of millions of Americans were raised in homes where English was not spoken except by the children, who went to religious schools that fostered Old World traditions. As late as 1940, New York had 237 foreign-language periodicals. But although their parents bought radios to listen to the foreign-language programs, the children changed the stations and sneaked off to the movies.

High-brow culture, too, was centered in the large cities. Many of the best-known writers of the 1920s, including Sinclair Lewis, Sherwood Anderson, and H. L. Mencken, portrayed people who lived in small towns as narrow, hypocritical, and spiritually impoverished. *Babbitt,* the title of Lewis's satirical novel about a small-town businessman, entered the language as a synonym for a narrow and self-satisfied conformist.

Cities permitted behaviors and institutions unacceptable in small towns. Major cities like New York became the center of an increasingly visible homosexual subculture that could be found in certain bars, tearooms, rooming houses, bathhouses, restaurants, and cafeterias, as well as in particular neighborhoods like Greenwich Village and Harlem. Prohibition pushed gay and lesbian life further out in the open. By criminalizing drinking behavior that even many middle-class people sanctioned, Prohibition undercut conventional moral authority and fostered a set of institutions ("speakeasies") and an amusement district (Times Square) where gay men and lesbians could flaunt social convention. By the late 1920s, New York was in the throes of a "pansy craze," with drag balls that attracted thousands of spectators and Broadway plays that featured gay themes. Gladys Bentley, an openly lesbian performer, began her own Harlem nightclub and married her white girlfriend in a very public ceremony.

"We Didn't Join American Organizations"

Joe Rudiak, a Polish-American steelworker, described growing up in the ethnic enclave of Lyndora, Pennsylvania, home to coal miners and steelworkers.

And of the things my mother insisted on, education . . . was one of them. Mother insisted, with a few other families, at least to educate us [in] our own native tongue and [in] writing [at the] language schools. They formed language schools through the churches. And that was a must with most families. . . . I don't know why they did it. I guess it was on account of their background, [out of] loneliness and everything for their own countries. And my mother insisted that we all become musicians. . . . Seven of us became musicians. Every day—about two hours every day—there was catechism. And during . . . school vacation we had to attend the language schools. The Polish church was a good distance away. There was the problem of shoes, clothing, and weather conditions and all that. And sure we were down a good distance away also from the public school. Mother insisted that we go to the Greek [Orthodox] church; they had the language school. When they had a problem of not having any money, we joined the Ukrainian Orthodox. So I've learned how to speak Ukrainian, but it wasn't my mother's tongue. It meant another language, which came in very handy.

We celebrated various holidays together. We did it as musicians, you see, in our family. And different churches went out caroling, and they gathered money for support of the band and their cultural activities. And this was done during Christmas. We each had costumes of our own native lands. You know, the Slovaks had [boys dressed as] sheep herders going from house to house singing. The women would have embroideries of different colors. It was beautiful, beautiful, made out of linen. It was all hand made. . . .

Since we went to the Ukrainian school, [we kids spoke Ukrainian. And] my mother spoke very good Ukrainian and my father spoke good Ukrainian because he spoke it in Europe. So there was no problem as far as learning the language [was concerned], because you got to repeat [it] at home after you came from elementary school. But when the Polish friends would come in, then it was Polish language. It just happened that most of them lived around their own churches, tried to get as close as possible to their social activities. And the church was part of their social activity.

We didn't join American organizations though. There was no drive on among the nationality people, no drive on by the politicians. You've got to understand that they didn't want these people to vote in the first place. The companies controlled the towns. They controlled the courthouse. They controlled the police. They controlled the state police, the coal mine police. There was no encouragement for people to vote up until the Depression.

Source: John Bodnar, ed., *Workers' World* (1982).

Not surprisingly, such transgressions against sexual and gender conventions brought a backlash. In 1927, New York police raided plays like *The Captive* and *Sex* and arrested their casts, including the flamboyant Mae West. The New York state legislature quickly followed with a ban on plays "depicting or dealing with the subject of sex degeneracy, or sex perversion." Four years earlier the legislature had lashed out against gay bars and "cruising" by defining homosexual solicitation as a form of disorderly conduct—a statute often interpreted to mean that all gay and lesbian gathering places were "disorderly." By the 1930s, continued legal harassment and police raids had erased gay life from public view.

Culturally conservative Americans saw the growing visibility of urban gay culture as one of many signs that cities were the source of sin, depravity, and irreligion. Many of these Americans were part of a Protestant fundamentalist movement that had been gaining strength since the late nineteenth century. The movement was a reaction against modern urban life, modern science, and liberal Protestants who tolerated both challenges to traditional religion. The term *fundamentalist* came into use in 1909, after publication of a series of pamphlets called *The Fundamentals,* which denounced as corrupt modern scientific theories such as evolution and modern life pastimes such as dancing. Intellectuals and urban Americans in the 1920s (as now) saw fundamentalism as a sign of rural backwardness and opposition to change. H. L. Mencken relentlessly mocked "the forlorn pastors who belabor half-wits in the galvanized iron tabernacles behind the railroad yards." Yet fundamentalist and evangelical Christians had a strong presence in the cities, and readily adopted modern means of communication in their proselytizing. The evangelist Aimee Semple McPherson, for example, may have started out preaching at revival meetings in tents, but by the mid-1920s she was presiding over the spectacular Angelus Temple in Los Angeles, where tens of thousands heard her sermons, which were also broadcast over the radio. McPherson's success flowed not just from her message and effective use of the new technology (and her legendary beauty), but from the incredible growth of the city of Los Angeles, which added 1.3 million new residents in the 1920s.

But if adherents of fundamentalism could be found in cities all over the country, the decade's most famous confrontation over the truth of the Bible erupted in the small southern town of Dayton, Tennessee, in 1925. There, fundamentalists, hostile to any idea that ran counter to a literal reading of the Bible, rallied against the teaching of Charles Darwin's theory that human beings shared an evolutionary link with other primates. They had persuaded the Tennessee legislature to pass a law prohibiting teaching that "man has descended from a lower order of animals." When the American Civil Liberties

Billy Sunday. George Bellows's 1923 lithograph of William Ashley Sunday, the professional baseball player turned evangelical minister, captures the atmosphere of revival meetings during the 1920s. Preaching a return to "old time religion," traveling evangelists like Sunday relied on techniques inspired by forms of mass entertainment.

Source: George Bellows, 1923, lithograph, 9 × 16 1/2 inches—Courtesy of the Boston Public Library, Print Department. Gift of Albert H. Wiggin.

Union (ACLU) chose Dayton high school teacher John T. Scopes to defy the law intentionally as a test of its constitutionality, fundamentalists were outraged. They enlisted former secretary of state and Democratic presidential candidate William Jennings Bryan to aid the prosecution. Clarence Darrow, a prominent liberal lawyer who had defended many political and criminal celebrities, headed Scopes's defense team. The trial was a carnival of journalists and onlookers; on the street outside, vendors sold Bibles and toy monkeys. It was the first jury trial to be broadcast live on the radio.

The most famous moment in the Scopes trial came when the defense—prohibited by the judge from calling scientists to defend evolution—put Bryan on the stand as an expert on the Bible. Darrow ridiculed him before the court and the nation, forcing Bryan to admit that some biblical passages could not be interpreted literally. But Bryan's testimony had no real bearing on the case, and it exaggerated the differences between Darrow and Bryan, both of whom actually shared a commitment to social justice. In fact, Bryan's fundamentalism was linked to his populism. He had long opposed social Darwinism, or the application of Darwin's principle of "survival of the fittest" to human society—to struggling farmers, laborers, and small businessmen.

Both fundamentalists and scientists emerged from the trial as losers. In the face of the scorn heaped on them by intellectuals, fundamentalists retreated from political life, and did not fully reenter politics until the 1980s. Scopes was convicted (although his sentence was later thrown out on a technicality), and Tennessee's antievolution law remained on the books until the 1960s. A few other states passed antievolution laws, and publishers meekly complied by removing discussions of evolution from biology textbooks sold across the nation.

Like fundamentalists, the Ku Klux Klan is also often associated with southern rural life. Yet in the 1920s, the Klan, too, had a major following in the cities. In its heyday, in the early 1920s, roughly half of the Klan's three million members lived in metropolitan areas. And although it had considerable support in the South, the Klan was strongest in the Midwest and the Southwest. Founded in 1915 and inspired by the Reconstruction-era organization of the same name, the Klan shared with its nineteenth-century namesake a deep racism, a fascination with mystical regalia, and a willingness to use violence to silence its foes. Unlike its predecessor, it professed anti-Catholicism and anti-Semitism as strongly as it affirmed racism.

The intolerance and vigilantism that was prevalent during World War I had paved the way for the Klan's rise. Farmers going through hard times, underpaid workers facing competition from immigrants and African Americans, small businessmen who were losing out to national manufacturers and chain stores all lashed out through the Klan against

White Sheets in Washington, D.C. Forty thousand members of the Ku Klux Klan marched down Pennsylvania Avenue on August 8, 1925. Organized to counter reports of faltering enrollment, the "konklave" succeeded in attracting national attention, but it marked the peak of Klan power in the 1920s.

Source: Prints and Photographs Division, Library of Congress.

those they believed were threatening their economic well-being. Country dwellers resented the diminishing importance of rural virtues; city dwellers associated foreigners with gangs and crime. Old-stock urban Protestants felt displaced by Catholics and Jews, and those who remembered the Red scare were left with the suspicion that immigrants were inherently subversive.

Riding on fears of immigrants, communists, labor unions, African Americans moving north, and Jews and Catholics rising in the economic and social order, the Klan staged parades and cross-burning rallies across the country. Klan leaders gained strong influence over state governments in Texas, Oklahoma, Oregon, Louisiana, Kansas, and especially Indiana. Within a few years, however, a series of sexual, financial, and political scandals had tainted the Klan, and political leaders in several states moved against it.

Although the Klan retreated, the cultural antagonisms that supported it remained strong and surfaced in conflicts over Prohibition. In 1919 the Eighteenth Amendment to the Constitution was ratified, making it illegal to manufacture, sell, transport, import, or export drinking alcohol. Ratification, however, did not reflect a national consensus on drinking. Although the law was not openly flaunted at first, liquor flowed into the country across U.S. borders. Bootlegging and the production of alcohol for medical and religious purposes added to the supply. Alcohol consumption did decline, perhaps by as much as half, but tens of millions of normally law-abiding Americans either broke the law or abetted those who did. Even President Harding had a favorite bootlegger. It became apparent that enforcing Prohibition would require huge police forces.

Opponents of Prohibition argued that because the law could not be enforced, it bred crime, corruption, and a disregard for the rule of law in general. Indeed, the vast profits to be made from illegal liquor fed gangsters who were involved in prostitution and high-interest loans. With profits rolling in, these types of organized crime provided poor Italians, Jews, Poles, and Irish with a means of upward mobility. Gangster

"There Was Another Unusual Feature of the Flower Shop Basement"

The criminal lawyer George Bieber's first job was in a Chicago bootlegging establishment. The job paid well enough, according to Bieber, to enable him to pay his college tuition.

I was fifteen when the Volstead Act [enforcing prohibition] went into effect, working in the Division Flower Shop. . . . The owners weren't interested in selling flowers. They kept a dozen bunches in the windows, but if some stranger came in and placed a big order, they'd fill it through a genuine florist nearby and send it out under the Division label. That was my job, standing around in the front of the shop and handling people who actually wanted to buy flowers.

The boss was Vincent "Schemer" Drucci. They nicknamed him that because of the wild schemes he was always thinking up to defeat the law. The real business of the Division Flower Shop was converting denatured alcohol into drinkable liquor. Drucci and his partners had first set up a hair tonic plant. This entitled them to buy No. 39B alcohol. . . .

Up to a point, the Cosmo Hair Tonic Company was legitimate. They advertised widely. . . . And they sold quite a few bottles. Not nearly as many as their books showed. To deceive the government inspectors, they would sell a few hundred cases to a friendly wholesale distributor and throw in a few hundred more as a bribe. The books would then show sales of thousands, and on the basis of such a big volume the government would allot the company corresponding amounts of 39B alcohol.

The conversion to drinkable liquor took place in the basement of the flower shop under the direction of the chemist we all called Karl the Dutchman, who was formerly employed by a toothpaste manufacturer. . . . To fake scotch, bourbon, rye, or whatever, Karl would let the rectified alcohol stand for a few weeks in charred barrels in which authentic whiskey had been aged. I would pick up those barrels from a cooperage on Lake Street. They brought enormous prices—as high as $50 or $60 a barrel. The owner's son would help me load them onto a truck, and I remember he wore a diamond ring the shape of a barrel. . . .

Some of Drucci's customers came from out of town, and if he figured a man was a *shnook,* he would sell him the liquor in a trick 5-gallon can. This can had a tube soldered inside to the top and bottom. Only the tube contained whiskey. The rest of the can was filled with water to give it weight, as the *shnook* would discover when he got it home.

There was another unusual feature of the flower shop basement—a life-size picture of a cop. The boys used it for target practice. . . .

Source: John Kobler, *Ardent Spirits: The Rise and Fall of Prohibition* (1973).

organizations grew in size, sophistication, and power, fighting to establish regional fiefdoms using the latest technology, from fast automobiles to submachine guns. Politicians and police were bought off wholesale. In some cities, gangs became an integral part of local politics. Al Capone and other flamboyant gangsters became celebrities: Their latest exploits—and their elaborate funerals—received detailed newspaper coverage. Capone, who turned crime into a big business, was said to have grossed more than $100 million from bootlegging, gambling, prostitution, and other rackets.

Two Celebrities. Catcher Gabby Hartnett was photographed as he exchanged pleasantries with "Scarface" Al Capone (who was known to wield a bat himself on occasion). The Chicago Cubs player was autographing a baseball for the gangster's twelve-year-old son at a charity game in Comiskey Park.

Source: UPI/Corbis-Bettmann.

"The very fact that the law is difficult to enforce," an official of the Anti-Saloon League commented in 1926, "is the clearest proof of the need of its existence." But by then the failure of Prohibition was obvious, especially in urban areas. Organized opposition, once confined to the unions and the liquor interests, began to mount. Of nine state referenda held in an attempt to modify the law, the "wets" (opponents of Prohibition) won seven. Public opinion polls showed that especially in the large industrial states, wets predominated. In the new urban culture, influenced by the automobile, the radio, and the movies, the protection of the Victorian home and family was no longer a central issue; individualism, personal freedom, and consumerism were the dominant values.

American Indians defended another front in the cultural wars of the 1920s. Backed by Christian missionaries, Hubert Work, Secretary of the Interior in the mid-1920s, attacked Indian culture and religion, especially the peyote cult, in which worshippers ingested a hallucinogen during a holy rite. Work charged that "gross immorality . . . accompanies native dances." Others lashed out at "Indian paganism" and what they described as "horrible, sadistic, and obscene" heathen practices. Defenders of Indian culture, including both Indians and white supporters, argued for reform of federal Indian policy, based on the Wilsonian principle of self-determination. Conservative critics of Indian culture labeled these defenders "Red Progressives," "anti-American, and subversive . . . agents of Moscow." Over the course of the 1920s, however, Indians won some modest concessions from government officials and a Congress that was often hostile to Indian interests. In 1924, for example, Congress finally passed a law conferring citizenship on all Indians born in the United States. But many states continued to prevent Indians from voting. More far-reaching reform of the nation's Indian policy would not come until the next decade.

Hoover and the Crash

The urban-rural tug of war made its way into the voting booths in the 1928 presidential election. By 1928, the balance of power within the Democratic party had shifted decisively toward the cities. New York Governor Al Smith easily won the party's presidential nomination. The contrast—at least in image—between Smith and Republican Herbert Hoover could not have been greater. Smith was a "wet," a Catholic, a product of urban ethnic working-class life. Radio coverage of the campaign broadcast his heavy New York accent throughout the nation. Hoover stressed his boyhood in rural Iowa, professing his love for fishing and the simple, small-town life. In fact, he was a sophisticated businessman, the first president to rise to power from the ranks of the managerial elite rather than through party politics.

Prohibition was a powerful issue in the election. Smith was attacked as the candidate of foreigners and drinkers. Because many immigrants had no taboos about alcohol, the "drys" had long identified their crusade with

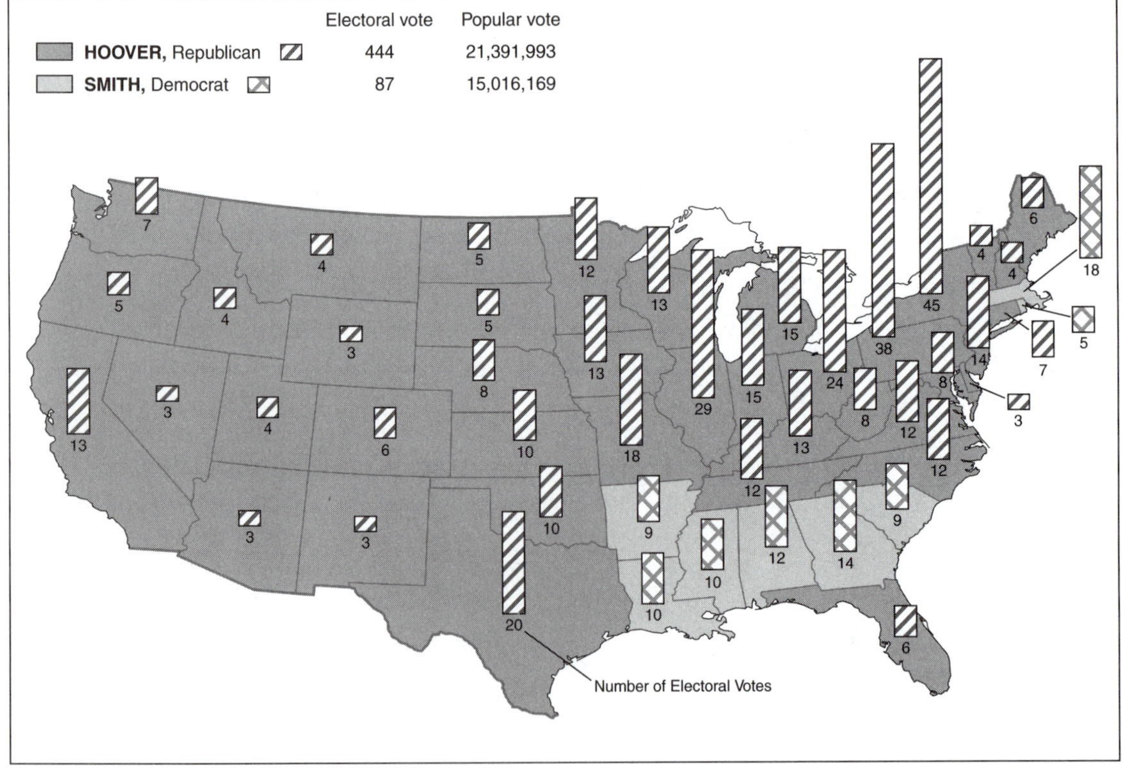

Engineering a Victory: The Election of 1928. Republican presidential candidate Herbert Hoover—aided by a strong economy and religious prejudice against his Catholic opponent Al Smith—won a landslide victory in 1928 with 21 million votes to Smith's 15 million. The silver lining in the defeat for the Democrats was their victory in the nation's largest cities, an indication that they were becoming the party of urban America.

the "100 percent Americanism" ideas of the war era and with the preservation of the American way of life. But it was probably religion, more than anything else, that shaped voting patterns in 1928. Smith faced a vicious campaign of anti-Catholic attacks, including rumors that he planned to extend the recently built Holland Tunnel across the Atlantic, so that it would connect the White House with the Vatican, and that he would annul all Protestant marriages and declare all the children of these marriages to be bastards. Hoover was not only a Protestant with a rural image, he also had another basic advantage: The Republicans got credit for the nation's prosperity. With both a strong economy and religious prejudice behind him, Hoover won by a landslide, receiving 444 electoral votes to Smith's 87. Thanks to increased participation by immigrant voters, however, Smith won in the nation's twelve largest cities, marking the Democrats as the party of urban America.

Hoover's victory capped his long successful career in industry, relief work, and government. But he had little time to enjoy it. Within a year, the country was plunged into a devastating depression. Hoover could not remedy the economy's fatal weakness, the tendency of industrial production to far outstrip the American people's ability to consume. The stock market crashed in October 1929. The "motor city" of Detroit—the exemplar of 1920s prosperity—soon had the highest jobless rate in the nation. By August 1931, Ford Motor Company, which employed 128,000 workers in 1929, had only 37,000 workers. By the early 1930s, Hoover's political reputation had been destroyed. The man who, along with Henry Ford, perhaps best symbolized America in the 1920s became one of the most hated men in the country. In a popular joke of the day, Hoover asked Secretary of the Treasury Mellon for a nickel—the price of a pay-phone call—to "call a friend." Mellon replied: "Take a dime; call all your friends."

The shattering of the idols of the vaunted new era—F. Scott Fitzgerald, Henry Ford, Herbert Hoover—suggested to many Americans that they would need to look in very different directions to cope with the hard times ahead.

The Years in Review

1920

- Republican Warren Harding defeats James Cox for the presidency.
- Commercial radio broadcasting begins.

1921

- Congress enacts the Emergency Quota Act to control the flow of immigrants.
- Opponents of the populist Non-Partisan League oust its state officials in North Dakota.
- Washington Conference begins negotiations on agreements to reduce naval armaments among leading powers.
- Sheppard-Towner Maternity and Infancy Protection Act provides first federal funds for health care.
- Economic recession hits the nation.
- Johnson & Johnson introduce Band-Aid bandages.
- Wise Potato Chips and Peter Paul Mounds bars make their debut.

1922

- Some 600,000 coal miners strike and win some gains, but the union is in sharp decline.

1923

- The Ku Klux Klan, which was refounded in Atlanta in 1915, reaches peak membership.
- The U.S. Supreme Court declares Asian Indians ineligible for U.S. citizenship.
- President Warren Harding dies; Teapot Dome and other scandals are revealed in his administration.
- *Time* magazine publishes its first issue.
- Colonel Jacob Schick patents an electric razor.
- John D. Hertz inaugurates the Hertz Drive-Ur-Self System, with twelve used cars.

1924

- Banker Charles Dawes brokers a plan to reduce German reparations and save the German economy; the plan fails.
- Congress enacts a law that limits new immigration to 2 percent of each nationality present in the United States in 1890; the law totally excludes the Japanese.
- Calvin Coolidge, who had succeeded Harding in 1923, is reelected president. Discontented farmers and unionists back a third-party bid by Wisconsin Senator Robert La Follette.
- Macy's stages its first Thanksgiving Day parade.

- Trinity College changes its name to Duke University; in return, American Tobacco Co. president James Duke gives the school $40 million.
- Kimberly-Clark Corporation markets Kleenex Kerchiefs as the "Sanitary Cold Cream Remover," but they soon become popular as disposable handkerchiefs.

1925

- Alain Locke's *The New Negro* is published.
- Congress passes the McNary-Haugen bill, designed to restore the prewar relationship between farm prices and industrial prices; Coolidge vetoes it.
- A. Philip Randolph organizes the Brotherhood of Sleeping Car Porters.
- John T. Scopes is arrested in Tennessee and convicted for teaching that "man has descended from a lower order of animals."
- Children compete in the first National Spelling Bee.

1926

- American Marines suppress the Nicaraguan nationalist rebellion led by Augusto Sandino and impose a dictatorship under General Anastasio Somoza.
- Secretary of Treasury Andrew Mellon, one of the nation's richest men, pushes through a tax cut for the wealthy.
- Slide fasteners (invented in 1913) are renamed zippers; they come into wide use only after the patent expires in 1931.
- Gertrude Ederle of New York becomes the first woman to swim the English Channel.
- Notre Dame wins its first football championship under Knute Rockne.

1927

- U.S. deports Marcus Garvey to Jamaica; his departure shatters the Universal Negro Improvement Association, which had won mass support after World War I.
- After making 15 million Model T's, Ford ceases their production and switches to the more stylish Model A.
- Charles Lindbergh completes the first nonstop solo transatlantic flight.
- The "talkies" arrive with *The Jazz Singer.*
- Al Capone's income of $105 million (mostly from bootleg liquor) is the highest in the nation.
- John Willard Marriott opens his first Hot Shoppe in Washington, D.C., leading to a hotel and food service empire.
- Nan Britton's *The President's Daughter* describes her affair with Warren Harding.

1928

- Oscar DePriest becomes the first black representative ever elected to Congress from the North.
- More than sixty nations sign the Kellogg-Briand Pact, renouncing war, but it lacks any enforcement mechanisms.

- Herbert Hoover defeats Al Smith for the presidency; Smith's Catholicism is a major factor in his defeat.
- Children start chewing Fleer's Dubble Bubble, the first bubble gum.
- Mickey Mouse debuts in *Plane Crazy* and *Steamboat Willie*.
- NBC premieres "Amos 'n' Andy," a fifteen-minute comedy show that becomes the most popular program on radio.

1929

- The stock market reaches speculative heights and then crashes on "Black Thursday," October 24.

Suggested Readings

Benson, Susan Porter, *Counter Cultures: Saleswomen, Managers, and Customers in American Department Stores, 1890–1940* (1986).

Bernstein, Irving, *The Lean Years: A History of the American Worker, 1920–1933* (1960).

Black, George, *The Good Neighbor: How the United States Wrote the History of Central America and the Caribbean* (1988).

Chafe, William H., *The American Woman: Her Changing Social, Economic, and Political Role, 1920–1970* (1972).

Chandler, Alfred D., Jr., *Scale and Scope: The Dynamics of Industrial Capitalism* (1990).

Cohen, Lizabeth, *Making a New Deal: Industrial Workers in Chicago, 1919–1939* (1990).

Cott, Nancy F., *The Grounding of Modern Feminism* (1987).

Dumenil, Lynn, *The Modern Temper: American Culture and Society in the 1920s* (1995).

Edsforth, Ronald William, *Class Conflict and Cultural Consensus: The Making of a Mass Consumer Society in Flint, Michigan* (1987).

Ewen, Elizabeth, *Immigrant Women in the Land of Dollars: Life and Culture on the Lower East Side, 1890–1925* (1985).

Ewen, Stuart, *Captains of Consciousness: Advertising and the Social Roots of Consumer Culture* (1976).

Frank, Dana, *Purchasing Power: Consumer Organizing, Gender, and the Seattle Labor Movement 1919–1929* (1994).

Hall, Jacquelyn Dowd, et al., *Like a Family: The Making of a Southern Cotton Mill World* (1987).

Harris, William H., *The Harder We Run: Black Workers Since the Civil War* (1982).

Hawley, Ellis W., *The Great War and the Search for a Modern Order* (1979).

Hicks, John D., *The Republican Ascendancy, 1921–1933* (1960).

Higham, John, *Strangers in the Land: Patterns of American Nativism, 1865–1925* (1955).

Huggins, Nathan, *Harlem Renaissance* (1971).

Katzman, David M., *Seven Days a Week: Women and Domestic Service in Industrializing America* (1981).

Kessler-Harris, Alice, *Out to Work: A History of Wage-Earning Women in the United States* (1982).

Lears, T. J. Jackson, *Fables of Abundance: A Cultural History of Advertising in America* (1994).

Levine, Lawrence, *Defender of the Faith: William Jennings Bryan: The Last Decade, 1915–1925* (1965).

Lichtman, Allan J., *Prejudice and the Old Politics: The Presidential Election of 1928* (1979).

Lynd, Robert, and Helen Lynd, *Middletown: A Study in Modern American Culture* (1929).

Marchand, Roland, *Advertising the American Dream: Making Way for Modernity, 1920–1940* (1985).

Marsden, George S., *Fundamentalism in American Culture* (1980).

McMillan, Neil, *Dark Journey: Black Mississippians in the Age of Jim Crow* (1989).

Nasaw, David, *Going Out: The Rise and Fall of Public Amusements* (1993).

Rosengarten, Theodore, *All God's Dangers: The Life of Nate Shaw* (1975).

Schatz, Ronald W., *The Electrical Workers: A History of Labor at General Electric and Westinghouse, 1923–1960* (1983).

Sklar, Robert, *Movie-Made America: A Cultural History of American Movies* (1976).

Smulyan, Susan, *Selling Radio: The Commercialization of American Broadcasting, 1920–1934* (1994).

Stein, Judith, *The World of Marcus Garvey: Race and Class in Modern Society* (1985).

And on the World Wide Web

The James S. Coleman African Studies Center, University of California, Los Angeles, *The Marcus Garvey and Universal Negro Improvement Association Papers Project* (http://www.isop.ucla.edu/mgpp/).

chapter 8

The Great Depression and the First New Deal

1929–1935

"We in America today are nearer to the final triumph over poverty than ever before in the history of any land. We shall soon . . . be in sight of the day when poverty will be banished from this nation." So spoke Herbert Hoover as he accepted the Republican nomination for president in 1928. And apparently the people agreed, for Hoover was elected by a wide margin that November.

But within a year the new president would preside over an economic crisis that proved to be the most severe test of the American people and their institutions since the Civil War had divided the nation seventy years before. The Great Depression struck the United States like some biblical plague, shuttering factories, closing banks, foreclosing farms, and putting as many as one out of three workers on the street. Mass unemployment and economic insecurity lasted for a full decade, searing the memory and transforming the politics of an entire generation. By 1931 the Depression had spread to Europe and East Asia, where it rocked the political institutions under which hundreds of millions of people lived and worked. There the economic and social tensions that grew out of this modern catastrophe fueled the growth of mass movements hostile to liberal capitalism: on the Left, communism and socialism; on the Right, an even more powerful surge toward militarism, fascism, and ethnocentric nationalism. In the United States the Depression did not overturn the government or threaten the nation's constitutional democracy, but it did strike a blow at the prestige and power of those who had long considered themselves the nation's elite. The big banks, the big corporations, and the old Protestant upper class had failed to sustain the very prosperity of which they had boasted. As they declined in public esteem, new ideas and new forces moved to the forefront.

The Great Depression still lives in our imaginations, even among those whose grandparents and great-grandparents were children when the Wall Street stock market crashed, signaling the onset of mass unemployment. In the decades since then, the stock market has had some terrible days, but few compare to the string of disastrous trading sessions that began on "Black Thursday"—October 24, 1929. In the next seven days, panicked American investors would lose more money than the U.S. government had spent fighting World War I. At the time, many traders and economists considered the market plunge a healthy response to frothy

Detroit, July 1930. During the Depression, unemployment struck the nation's large industrial cities with particular ferocity. In Detroit automobile production dropped by half. Nearly a third of all families there had no breadwinner. This unemployed worker took to the streets in search of work.

Source: Milton (Pete) Brooks, July 1930, *Detroit News—Detroit News.*

speculation, which had continued despite a decline in industrial production that began several months earlier. But none of these experts thought that the 1929 Wall Street crash would signal the onset of a worldwide, decade-long Great Depression. Their surprise has cast a long shadow forward, lengthened by the failure of historians and economists to reach a firm conclusion as to precisely why the Great Depression lasted almost an entire generation. Thus today, when trillions of dollars ride on the constantly changing expectations of hundreds of millions of investors, the stability of world capitalism can never be taken for granted. It remains under some of the same clouds that darkened American skies nearly three generations ago.

The Onset of the Great Depression

Although the vast majority of Americans owned no stock, few escaped the social impact of the market crash. The number of unemployed workers jumped from fewer than five hundred thousand to more than four million between October and December 1929. Yet many politicians and experts still believed the economy was sound and the downturn temporary. "Let the slump liquidate itself," asserted Andrew Mellon, Hoover's ultraconservative secretary of the treasury. Mellon predicted that the economy would right itself if government didn't worry too much about the human cost: "Values will be adjusted, and enterprising people will pick up the wrecks from less competent people." But in mid-1931 the economy took another sickening plunge, and by the spring of 1933, fifteen million people were out of work—nearly one of every four wage-earners. Millions more were working only part time. Average real wages had fallen 16 percent in just two years.

Between 1929 and 1933 the gross national product, the

Going Bust: Business Failures, 1929–45. Bankruptcies, already high in the late 1920s, peaked in 1932—the nadir of the Depression. Although unemployment stayed high, New Deal measures stabilized the business economy. Business failures almost vanished during the prosperous years of World War II.

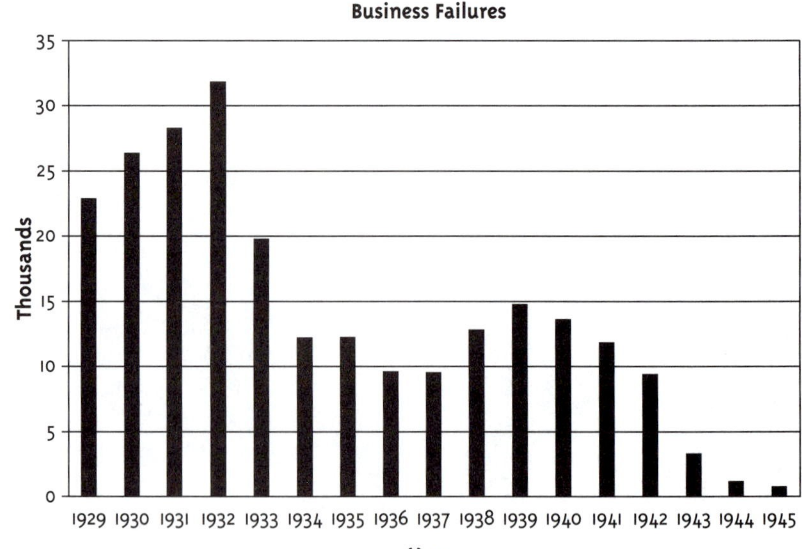

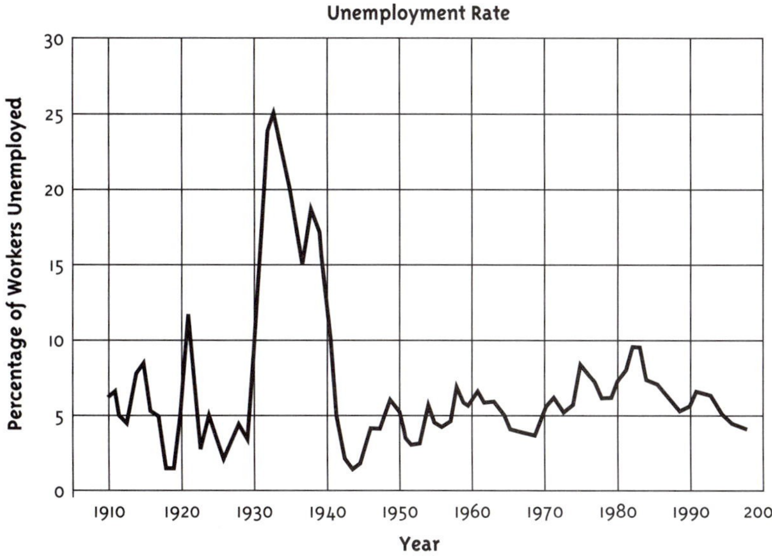

U.S. Unemployment during the Great Depression. A much higher proportion of all workers were without jobs during the Great Depression than at any other time in the twentieth century. Joblessness declined sharply after 1933, but prospects for an end to the Depression evaporated in 1937 and 1938 when the "Roosevelt Recession" demonstrated that without massive government intervention, the instability of capitalism was chronic.

sum of all the goods and services produced in the country, fell 29 percent. Construction was down 78 percent, manufacturing 54 percent, and investment a staggering 98 percent. By the summer of 1932, the steel industry was operating at only 12 percent of its capacity. Fewer miles of railroad track were laid that year than in any year since the Civil War. Many cities went broke: Detroit and Chicago paid their employees in paper scrip—government IOUs. A single share of Montgomery Ward stock, which had sold for $138 in September 1929, was worth just $4 three years later.

The government itself, through the Federal Reserve Board, had fueled Wall Street's frenzied speculation during the late 1920s by keeping interest rates low. Cheap money enabled many investors to buy huge amounts of stock "on margin." In effect, they had borrowed against the shares' value and had used that borrowed money to purchase additional shares. While the market continued to boom, investors made a real killing; but when it declined, brokerage firms called in their loans—which often amounted to 90 percent of the stock's value at its highest price—and investors lost their entire stake.

After the market crashed in October 1929, low interest rates would have been genuinely helpful to an economy fast losing steam. But the Federal Reserve Board blundered again, this time by raising interest rates. The rate hike put enormous pressure on the banking system, especially on unstable rural banks and ethnic savings and loans, whose fortunes were linked to the farmers, merchants, and tradesmen who always needed plenty of easy credit. Uninsured by either state or federal authorities, more than five thousand of these smaller financial institutions failed during the first three years of the Great Depression. Nine million people lost their savings accounts, often during panicked bank runs touched off by rumors of an institution's impending collapse.

Even with all these difficulties, the Great Depression might well have ended in the early 1930s had it not been for the simultaneous collapse of the international economic system. Because New York was now the center of world capitalism, the Wall Street crash sent tremors throughout the shaky system that had emerged after World War I. In an atmosphere of spreading panic, nations enacted measures to protect their own economies. The United States, for example, passed the Smoot-Hawley Tariff in 1930, which raised import duties to the highest levels in our history. The goal was to protect U.S. farmers from international competition; the result was disaster, as other countries retaliated by increasing their own tariffs. World trade plunged.

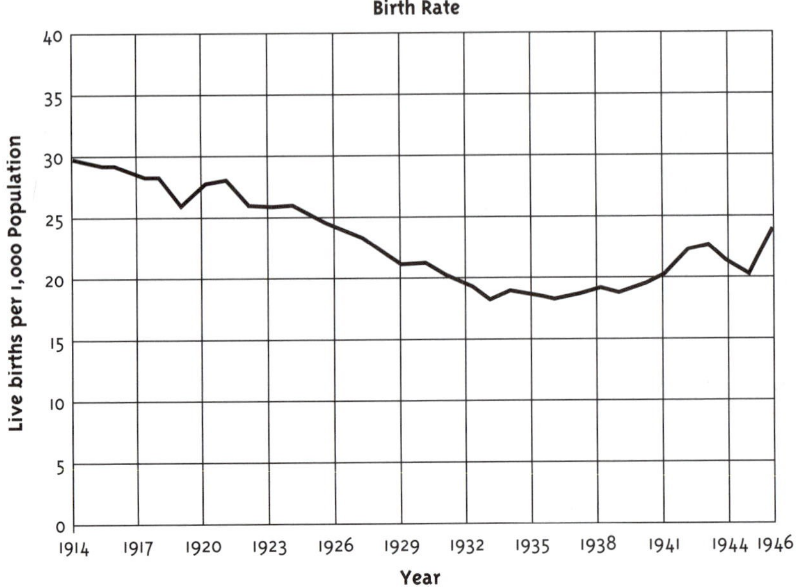

Depressing the Birth Rate. Birth rates had been declining throughout the early twentieth century—in part, a continuation of a long-term demographic shift away from the high birth rates characteristic of a more rural society. But they fell even further with the onset of the Great Depression, especially in the dark years of the early 1930s. After 1933, families began to have more children as the economy slowly recovered. In 1946 there was a sharp increase—the first sign of the postwar baby boom.

The new economic system was particularly vulnerable because Germany, France, and Great Britain had not yet recovered from the devastation of World War I. Europeans still owed massive war debts to one another and to the United States, and they were able to make payments on those debts only because U.S. banks lent billions of dollars to Germany. That country in turn passed them on to Britain, France, and Belgium in the form of reparations, and those countries returned the money to the United States, as payments on their war debts. The money flowed back and forth across the Atlantic in an endless cycle.

The stock market crash halted the American loans. Germany defaulted on its reparation payments to France and Britain, whose governments then stopped paying their American debts. Central European banks, dependent on the American loans, went bankrupt. When Austria's largest bank collapsed in May 1931, an atmosphere of economic crisis spread across Europe and the United States. Hard-pressed European investors sold their American stocks to raise cash, further depressing the stock market. Some European nations also abandoned the gold standard and devalued (lowered the value of) their currency in relation to the U.S. dollar. The United States clung to the gold standard, which made American goods more expensive abroad and further undercut the American economy. The international economic crisis also had ominous political consequences: As

German banks collapsed and unemployment rolls soared, the National Socialist party (Nazis) grew in power.

Hard Times

While the international monetary crisis played itself out, bread lines, soup kitchens, and desperate apple vendors became familiar features of the large cities in the United States. In Colorado, more than half of all schoolchildren were undernourished. With inadequate diets came a rise in dysentery, tuberculosis, pellagra, and typhoid. In the fall of 1930, one New Jerseyite wrote to President Hoover, "Can not you find a quicker way of executing us than to starve us to death?"

Joblessness struck hardest in large cities, in single-industry towns, in the Northeast and the Midwest, and among male blue-collar workers, both black and white. In Detroit and Pittsburgh, mass unemployment followed the collapse in production of autos and steel. California escaped the high levels of joblessness until 1932, but in that year the ripples of distress that had begun in the East finally made their way into California's diversified light industry, shipping, and agriculture. Unemployment was not quite as bad in the South as it was in the North, in part because many southern manufacturers were so marginal and debt-ridden that they could not afford to reduce production and risk a reduction in income. In the nation as a whole, white-collar workers in retail and wholesale trade, communications, banking, and insurance fared somewhat better than blue-collar workers. Government employees were less likely to lose their jobs than were private-sector workers.

The country's largest manufacturing firms tried to retain their experienced workers. Rather than fire valuable employees, they reduced the number of hours or days each worked, so that more people could be kept on the payroll. At General Electric Company (GE), one worker remembered, "They'd just say, 'You come in Monday. Take the rest of the week off.'" Some companies fired unskilled workers and gave skilled workers their jobs, at lower pay rates. By reducing hours and reassigning jobs, Westinghouse Electric Corporation managed to retain almost all employees with more than ten years' seniority at its huge East Pittsburgh plant.

But most construction companies and smaller manufacturers could not afford to retain excess workers, even part time. Between 1929 and 1933, employment in the construction trades dropped by more than 80 percent. People without money bought neither new houses nor new clothes. At one point, only 10 percent of the members of the Amalgamated Clothing Workers' Union in New York City were working.

Joblessness was the worst problem workers faced, but not the only one. The income of those who retained their jobs was greatly reduced because of the shorter hours and lower pay. Many people, employed and unemployed, fell behind on their rent or mortgage payments and eventually lost their homes. In Philadelphia, thirteen hundred homes and apartment buildings were sold at sheriff's sales—each month. Evictions became so common that young children included the event in their play. "We ain't go no money for the rent, so's we moved into a new house," a youngster who was "playing house" told his teacher. "Then we got the constable on us, so we's moving again."

Some Americans kept moving, leaving town altogether. By 1932 a quarter of a million youths under age twenty-one (as well as many older counterparts) had left home in search of work or shelter, hitching rides or hopping freight trains in what one government agency called a "migration of despair." Woody Guthrie, the hoboes' balladeer, provided this description of the traveling life: "I could see men of all colors bouncing along in the boxcar. . . . We used each other for pillows. I could smell the sour and bitter sweat soaking through my own khaki shirt and britches, and the work clothes, overalls and soggy, dirty suits of the other guys." But not all vagabonds were "guys." Kay, an undernourished fifteen-year-old, told an investigator: "Dad hasn't worked steady for four years. Sis, for two. Mother got a job scrubbing—$7 a week, and that's all we had to live on except for some clothes we got from a lodge. . . . There wasn't much else for me to do but go."

Hooverville, 1933. This squatter settlement was built by homeless Americans in Seattle, Washington, in 1933.

Source: J. Lee, March 30, 1933—no. 20102, Special Collections Division, University of Washington Libraries.

As female unemployment rose, so did discrimination against working women, especially if they were married. Many people agreed with the man who signed himself "A Good Citizen" in a letter to the president: "I know that something can be done about the married women. . . . They have no right taking the jobs and positions of single girls, single men, and married men." People assumed that married women worked only to make "pin money." That was rarely the case, but when layoffs occurred, even progressives thought married women should be the first to go. Thus, both New England Telephone and Telegraph and the Northern Pacific Railroad fired all married women in 1931. In most cities, married women were banned from teaching. Even the American Federation of Labor, which had hundreds of thousands of female members, was so distressed by widespread unemployment that in 1931 it adopted a program to counter this "unfortunate trend in family life," the employment of married women. Federation leaders proposed that "preference of employment" be given to "those upon whom family or dependency rests," by which they meant men.

When they had jobs, women were routinely paid less than men, even for the same work. Because their employment was irregular—for example, women worked an average of only twenty-six to thirty-five weeks a year in the garment, glove, and textile industries—their average annual income was roughly half that of men. Millions of women, many the sole support of their children, lived on the edge of destitution. As their household income shrank, women's unpaid work at home greatly expanded. Whereas once they might have bought new clothes, now they darned socks, shortened pants, let out waistlines, and hemmed dresses. Finally, the Depression imposed one more cost on working women: it diminished their opportunity to improve their job status. White women had rapidly entered white-collar office and sales work between 1910 and 1930, but in the 1930s their upward mobility came to a halt. Hundreds of thousands of women had to lower their expectations and face a working life of diminished pay and satisfaction.

Growing joblessness also fed a rise in racial and ethnic discrimination. Many employers and white workers insisted that native-born white workers receive preference in employment. Mexican Americans were among the foremost victims of this revived racism. In California, joblessness and the immigration of white Americans—"Anglos"—from other parts of the country mushroomed at the same time that agricultural production declined, swelling the pool of desperate agricultural workers. By 1933, two people were competing for every available job on California farms. In such cases, Anglos routinely got the job, even though many of the Mexicans had been recruited by the growers themselves.

Nearly five hundred thousand Mexican nationals and their U.S.–born children returned to Mexico during the Depression, most of them before 1933. Emigration from rural areas was heavier than the flight from the cities, so that by 1940, most Mexican Americans lived in urban areas. Many of those who emigrated left voluntarily, but others left under pressure. Several states encouraged emigration by barring noncitizens from employment on public works projects. Many local governments and private relief agencies offered free rail fare to the Mexican border for those

"Where Women Go"

Meridel LeSueur, poet and journalist, described the plight of unemployed women, of which she was one, in the worst years of the Depression. *Jungle* was a common term for a homeless encampment.

It's one of the great mysteries of the city where women go when they are out of work and hungry. There are not many women in the bread line. There are no flop houses for women as there are for men, where a bed can be had for a quarter or less. You don't see women lying on the floor at the mission in the free flops. They obviously don't sleep in the jungle or under newspapers in the park. There is no law I suppose against their being in these places but the fact is they rarely are.

Yet there must be as many women out of jobs in cities and suffering extreme poverty as there are men. What happens to them? Where do they go? Try to get into the Y.W.[C.A.] without any money or looking down at the heel. Charities take care of very few and only those that are called "deserving." The lone girl is under suspicion by the virgin women who dispense charity.

I've lived in cities for many months broke, without help, too timid to get in bread lines. I've known many women to live like this until they simply faint on the street from privation, without saying a word to anyone. A woman will shut herself up in a room until it is taken away from her, and eat a cracker a day and be as quiet as a mouse so there are no social statistics concerning her.

Source: Meridel LeSueur, *Women on the Breadlines* (1984).

who were willing to leave, and they sometimes gave emergency relief only to those willing to leave the United States. In Michigan, the Immigration Service transported "welfare cases" as well as deportees to the Mexican border. Three out of four of Detroit's Mexican inhabitants returned to Mexico in 1932. In Chicago, relief authorities organized a massive repatriation campaign that resulted in the departure of several thousand Chicano steelworkers. In some places, groups such as the Chamber of Commerce began campaigns to scare Mexicans into leaving the country. The federal government cooperated in these efforts. Although relatively few Mexicans were formally deported—a process that required lengthy, complex hearings—the deportations that did occur were heavily publicized.

Economic competition also provoked a new wave of anti-Asian racism. Hard-working Chinese Americans had long dominated the laundry business in New York and other large cities, where such small enterprises were among their few opportunities for employment. This dominance was threatened during the 1920s, when other Americans began opening large-scale steam laundries, complete with mechanized washing machines and steam presses. Competition between these large operations and the small hand laundries (usually owned and operated by a single individual or family) increased dramatically during the Depression. When Chinese-American launderers in New York refused to abide by a minimum price scheme set by a citywide laundry organization in 1932, the trade association organized a massive boycott of Chinese-owned establishments. A racist pro-boycott poster, showing a bucktoothed Chinese laundryman spitting into a pile of wet clothing, appeared in store windows throughout the city.

Like Chinese Americans, African Americans were poor to begin with, but the Great Depression made their plight worse. African-American workers were concentrated in occupations that were particularly affected by the economic downturn: unskilled manufacturing, construction, mining, and the lumber industry. White workers displaced black ones in many of these difficult, low-status jobs, reversing much of the progress African Americans had made in moving into industrial jobs. Sometimes drastic measures were used to oust black workers. In Atlanta, African-American bellhops were arrested on trumped-up charges so that their jobs could be given to white men. In Louisiana, vigilantes launched a reign of terror against black railroad firemen, killing ten, to force them off the rails. In Milwaukee, white workers at the Wehr Steel Foundry struck, demanding that their African-American coworkers be fired. Depression-era joblessness drove hundreds of thousands of African Americans to the brink of starvation—and beyond. After surveying conditions in Cleveland, where half the workers in the largest African-American ghetto were without work, one observer worried that "the race is standing on a precipice of economic disaster."

In the South, where three-quarters of the African-American population still lived, a bitter drought in the summer of 1930 compounded the misery engendered by rock-bottom cotton and tobacco prices. Red Cross investigators sent to the parched areas reported that both black and white families were suffering from hunger, but racist fears prevented a quick response. Community leaders—fearful that African-American day laborers would refuse to pick the cotton if there was any other way to put food on the table—refused to start relief programs before the fall harvest. Racial tensions rose and planter violence increased. For the first time in a decade, lynchings of African Americans increased; twenty-four were killed in 1932 alone.

The Scottsboro case focused national attention on the growing terror in the South. In 1931, nine young black males, one only twelve years old,

Daily Worker

CENTRAL ORGAN COMMUNIST PARTY U.S.A. (SECTION OF COMMUNIST INTERNATIONAL)

NATIONAL EDITION

Vol. XI, No. 251 — NEW YORK, SATURDAY, OCTOBER 20, 1934 — (Eight Pages) — Price 3 Cents

Press Run Yesterday—48,700

ALL OUT FOR SCOTTSBORO MARCH!

CALL CONFERENCE ON SOCIAL INSURANCE

JOBLESS WILL BE IN CAPITAL IN JANUARY

Local Groups in All Cities Will Elect Delegate Bodies

APPEAL TO UNIONS

Will Ask Insurance Equal to Average Normal Wage

C.P. Districts–Attention!

The following telegram was sent yesterday to all large districts of the Communist Party by the Management Committee of the Daily Worker.

DAILY WORKER MUST HAVE HELP FROM YOUR DISTRICT STOP WIRE ALL FUNDS AT HAND AT ONCE STOP FOLLOW UP WITH EMERGENCY APPEAL THROUGHOUT DISTRICT FOR IMMEDIATE ADDITIONAL COLLECTIONS BY PERSONAL VISITS TO MASS ORGANIZATIONS, TRADE UNIONS, ETC. STOP DRIVE RECEIPTS MUST BE DOUBLED AT ONCE TO INSURE NEW DAILY WORKER!

'Industrial Adjustment' Agencies Uncovered As Network of Stoolpigeons

DYERS VOTE TO STRIKE NEXT WEEK

Will Mobilize Today in Paterson to Make Final Preparations

MASS MARCH CALLED

Lovestone's Henchman Attempts to Disrupt Rank and File Meet

DEMOCRATIC FAKERS BARED BY I. AMTER

Communist Candidate for Governor of N.Y. Analyzes Platform

MASS MISERY RISES

C.P. Leads Struggle of Masses Against the Bosses' Program

By I. AMTER

MASS PARADE BEGINS 11 A.M. TODAY; MANY GROUPS TO SEND DELEGATES TO EMERGENCY PARLEY TOMORROW

Conference Will Map Plans to Spread Mass Defense

LEADERS TO ATTEND

Davis to Tell Facts of Leibowitz Maneuvers Against I. L. D.

New Terror Drive Launched in Atlanta With Inquiry Plan

Hathaway, Haywood and Other Leaders To Be Among Speakers

BEN DAVIS TO SPEAK

Marchers Will Converge at Lenox Avenue and 126th Street

Scottsboro Defense. The *Daily Worker* announced one of the many demonstrations sponsored by the Communist Party in support of the Scottsboro defendants.

Source: *Daily Worker,* October 20, 1934—Scott Molloy Labor Archives.

were falsely accused of raping two white women on a freight train near Scottsboro, Alabama. In a trial based on questionable evidence and riddled with prejudice and procedural error, eight of the defendants were convicted and sentenced to death. The case of the "Scottsboro boys," championed first by the Communist party and then by the National Association for the Advancement of Colored People (NAACP), became an international cause célèbre, much like the Sacco and Vanzetti case during the 1920s. Eventually the death sentences were overturned, but not before five of the defendants had served long prison terms for a crime that never occurred.

Depression and Drought in the Farm Belt

While African Americans fought against racism, American farmers battled against falling prices and lack of rain. Between 1929 and 1932, net farm income plummeted. Wheat prices sank 50 percent, and the price of raw cotton fell by more than two-thirds. Many farmers did not even bother to harvest the crops they had planted. Although farm families could provide some of their own food, their cash income was too low to meet mortgage payments, repay loans, or pay taxes. Hundreds of thousands of families lost their farms. During just two years in Iowa County, Iowa, a once-prosperous corn-growing area, one of every eight farms was sold at auction. A discouraged Indiana woman wrote to the secretary of agriculture in 1930 protesting that her family was about to lose its 250-acre farm: "[We are] worked to death with no income, no leisure, no pleasure, and no hope of anything better. . . . We are a sick and sorry people. . . . My nearest neighbor has turned bootlegger, I can smell the mash brewing in his still."

Dust Bowl. Many people saw the dust storms as a natural disaster, but the more fundamental problem was rooted in destructive farming practices on the Great Plains. When drought hit the region in the early 1930s, dust storms darkened the skies of parts of Kansas, Oklahoma, Colorado, New Mexico, and the Texas Panhandle.

Had farmers faced only economic problems, their situation would have been bad enough, but during the very depths of the Depression another disaster arrived: drought. At first the lack of rain was most severe in the East, but then the dry spell moved to the Great Plains, where temperatures reached 118 degrees in 1934. Normal rainfall did not return until 1941.

With the drought came a series of dust storms that hit the Plains states from 1932 through the end of the decade. The storms, which could last from an hour to several days, were terrifying. Clouds of dirt as high as eight thousand feet would roll in, sometimes accompanied by thunder, lightning, and powerful winds. One storm, in March 1935, carried off twice as much dirt as had been dug during the building of the Panama

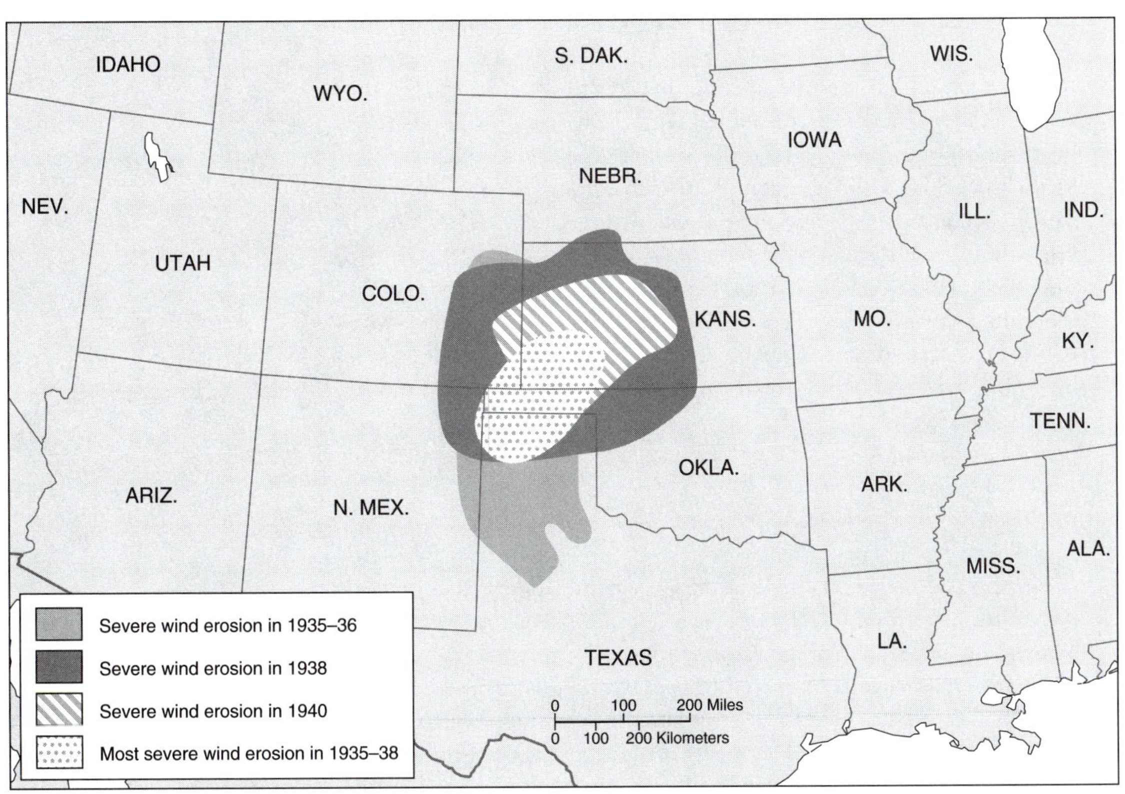

Canal, destroying half the wheat crop in Kansas and the entire wheat crop in Nebraska. Occasionally, children caught outside in the dust storms died of suffocation in drifts of dirt. Dust made its way into homes, beds, food, and clothes. Some places turned into virtual deserts as crops, livestock, and a whole way of life were destroyed. The worst-hit area, dubbed the Dust Bowl, encompassed parts of Kansas, Oklahoma, Colorado, New Mexico, and the Texas Panhandle.

Dust Storm. A wall of dirt and sand descended on Spearman, Texas, on August 14, 1935. **Source:** Franklin D. Roosevelt Library.

Dry weather was the immediate cause of the Dust Bowl, but its effects were compounded by the destructive way farmers had been cultivating the land. When farmers began settling in the southern plains in the 1890s, they had plowed up the grasses that kept the topsoil in place. The region had experienced droughts before, but the dry spell that hit in the 1930s, combined with the new cultivation patterns, produced one of the worst man-made ecological catastrophes ever.

This ecological disaster coincided with a massive exodus of residents of the southern plains, which became known as the "Okie" or "Dust Bowl" migration to California. John Steinbeck's 1939 novel *The Grapes of Wrath* (and the popular film made from it) reinforced the mistaken view that the migrants were all fleeing the dust. The sixteen thousand farmers who fled the farming areas devastated by dust storms were only a small part of a much larger migration of about four hundred thousand people. They came from a wider area of the Southwest and migrated for a variety of reasons, including drought, the drop in agricultural prices, and the mechanization of agriculture.

Material deprivation was only part of the human cost of the Depression. The psychological strains were severe, too. Almost everyone felt insecure. Those who had jobs feared losing them; those without work worried about what would become of their families. In the early years of the Depression, people generally blamed themselves for their troubles. Sherwood Anderson wrote of a ruined wheat farmer he met on the road: "It's my own fault," the farmer said. "I was not smart enough." Many men who had lost their jobs felt that their status in their families and communities had been diminished. With these deeply depressed men moping around at

"And Then We Were in California"

Propelled by hard times, families streamed into California. Cesar Chavez's father owned a small plot of land in Arizona until a bank foreclosed on his loan. He and his family were forced to become migrant farm workers in the mid-1930s at a time when labor was plentiful, wages extremely low, and discrimination against Mexican Americans growing. Many years later, Chavez help found the United Farm Workers' Union.

We all of us climbed into an old Chevy that my dad had. And then we were in California, and migratory workers. There were five kids—a small family by those standards. . . . I was about eight. Well, it was a strange life. We had been poor, but we knew every night there was a bed *there,* and that *this* was our room. There was a kitchen. It was sort of a settled life, and we had chickens and hogs, eggs, and all those things. But that all of a sudden changed. When you're small you can't figure these things out. . . .

"Following the crops," we missed much school. Trying to get enough money to stay alive the following winter, the whole family picking apricots, walnuts, prunes. We were pretty new, we had never been migratory workers. We were taken advantage of quite a bit by the labor contractor and the crew pusher. . . .

Coming into San Jose, not finding—being lied to, that there was work. We had no money at all, and had to live on the outskirts of town under a bridge and dry creek. . . .

We got hooked on a real scheme once. We were going by Fresno on our way to Delano. We stopped at some service station and this labor contractor saw the car. He offered a lot of money. We went. We worked the first week: the grapes were pretty bad and we couldn't make much. We all stayed off from school in order to make some money. Saturday we were to be paid and we didn't get paid. He came and said the winery hadn't paid him. We'd have money next week. He gave us $10. My dad took the $10 and went to the store and bought $10 worth of groceries. So we worked another week and in the middle of the second week, my father was asking him for his last week's pay, and he had the same excuse. This went on and we'd get $5 or $10 or $7 a week for about four weeks. For the whole family.

So one morning my father made the resolution no more work. If he doesn't pay us, we won't work. We got in a car and went over to see him. The house was empty. He had left. The winery said they had paid him and they showed us where they had paid him. This man had taken it.

Source: Studs Terkel, *Hard Times* (1970).

home, women also found it hard to keep going. Larry Van Dusen, whose father was a carpenter, remembered: "My father led a rough life: he drank. During the Depression, he drank more. There was more conflict in the home." Young people, uncertain of their futures, held off starting families; marriage and birth rates dropped in the early 1930s.

On the Road. Their worldly possessions piled on two run-down vehicles, this migrant family paused en route to California in February 1936.

Source: Dorothea Lange, 1936—Prints and Photographs Division, Library of Congress.

Middle-income Americans were financially better prepared for the Depression than were most workers, but they were psychologically vulnerable. Committed to an ethic of individual accomplishment, many of them felt deep shame about even modest economic setbacks. Often isolated in cities, they lacked an extended family to whom they could turn for emotional and material support. In the face of adversity, they stopped going to churches and clubs, shunned their former friends, and turned down social invitations. As the journalist Marquis Childs observed of the middle class early in 1933, "What is surprising is the passive resignation with which the blow has been accepted: this awful pretense that seeks to conceal the mortal wound, to carry on as though it were still the best of all possible worlds." When a once-prosperous North Carolina cotton merchant went bankrupt, his daughter, who had been raised in one of the town's oldest and most attractive houses, was unprepared for what followed. The phone was cut off, and then, "Our own house was sold . . . . Imagine my shock when it was sold for $5,000 in back taxes."

Hoover's Response to the Crisis

When the Depression struck, few Americans expected the federal government to take dramatic action, for its reach was weak and tenuous. Washington, D.C., was still a segregated, sleepy southern town where offices shut early during the steamy summer months. The government had barely 750,000 civilian and military employees (compared with more than 5 million today). The Post Office was the only federal agency that touched the lives of most Americans. There was no military draft, no federal aid for cities, schools, farmers, or the unemployed. The annual national budget was only $4 billion—less than 5 percent of the entire

No Laughing Matter. "Mama," runs the caption of this illustration published in the December 12, 1930, issue of *Life* magazine, "it's so nice to have Daddy home all the time now." By winter 1930, the situation was too grim a subject to lampoon, even for a magazine that favored arch commentary and collegiate humor. *Life,* a humor magazine, soon became another victim of the Depression; its name was quickly adopted in 1936 by Henry Luce for his new photojournalism magazine.

Source: Victor Anderson, *Life,* December 12, 1930—American Social History Project.

gross domestic product. Only the very rich paid income taxes.

Yet President Herbert Hoover seemed to exemplify all that was modern, efficient, and humane in American politics and social thought. Hoover embodied the Horatio Alger myth. Born in 1875 and orphaned at age nine, he had become an internationally known self-made millionaire by age forty. Hoover had won national acclaim during World War I, when he organized relief efforts in Belgium and later headed up a successful drive to boost U.S. food production. During the 1920s, he had served as a dynamic and influential secretary of commerce, after which the Republican party had handed him the 1928 presidential nomination. In the general election that year he easily defeated Alfred E. Smith, a New Yorker whose Catholicism, big-city roots, and rejection of Prohibition had lost him votes in the once solidly Democratic South.

Faced with America's economic collapse, President Hoover thought that the primary role of the federal government should be to coordinate private, state, and local relief and recovery efforts rather than to launch major initiatives. The key to recovery, he believed, was restoring business confidence, which meant avoiding unsettling actions and keeping the budget in balance. Although Hoover sometimes had his doubts, he assured Americans that the nation's dilemma was largely a product of the economic crisis in Europe and the breakdown of international trade and monetary relations. The U.S. economy itself was "on a sound and prosperous basis" and would soon recover. The president did succeed in winning a one-year moratorium on intergovernmental debt reparations payments, but he failed to achieve the broader agreements he felt were necessary to restore world trade. In May 1931 he told an Indianapolis audience that the idea that the nation could get out of the Depression through congressional action was no different from the belief one could "exorcise a Caribbean hurricane by statutory law."

Neither passive nor reactionary, Hoover set about encouraging the kind of voluntary cooperation among businessmen and local governments that he had championed during World War I and later as commerce secretary. At his request, many major corporations agreed not to cut wages in order to maintain consumers' spending power. A host of presidentially endorsed business committees sprang up to promote relief and recovery through voluntary private action. Charitable giving reached record levels, but it was not enough. Many companies that had agreed to maintain hourly wages negated any beneficial impact of the agreement by cutting workers' hours and laying them off. Then, in 1931, U.S. Steel announced a 10 percent wage cut that was widely copied in other industries.

"Fundamentally the Ship Was Sound." *New Yorker* cartoonist Richard Decker commented on the obstinate outlook of conservative business leaders in the face of the nation's mounting economic and social crisis.

Source: Richard Decker, *New Yorker,* March 5, 1932—Copyright 1932, The New Yorker Magazine, Inc.

Hoover was an activist compared with the pre–World War I presidents, who had stood by passively during financial panics and long-term slumps. He responded to the crisis of the agricultural economy, which preceded the stock market crash, by winning passage of the Agricultural Marketing Act of 1929. In line with Hoover's preference for government-sponsored voluntary cooperation, this legislation made available $500 million for loans to marketing cooperatives, which, in theory, would foster efficiency, limit surpluses, and raise prices. But the unprecedented government effort to bring order to the agricultural sector foundered on Hoover's insistence on voluntarism: The marketing act lacked authority to limit production, and farm prices continued to fall.

Hoover also supported other unprecedented, but equally inadequate, measures in answer to the growing economic crisis. He sharply increased spending on public works to $700 million, an unheard-of sum at the time. He set up the Reconstruction Finance Corporation (RFC) to provide billions of dollars in loans to failing banks and businesses. And when drought swept the agricultural South, Hoover authorized direct federal aid.

But Hoover's activism coexisted uneasily with a persistent conservatism that limited his effectiveness. The RFC gave most of its loans to larger and healthier banks and corporations and favored public works projects that were likely to pay for themselves, such as toll bridges. And when RFC spending raised the deficit, the president won passage of the Revenue

Interviewed On Unemployment

J. Egbert Haggle, prominent Chicago packer, is encouraging a movement for the rich to devote two minutes of silent meditation before beginning their Christmas dinners. "This should cheer up the unemployed by letting them know they are being thought about," Mr. Haggle said.

Salomon De Pischer, leading department store owner of New York thinks the trouble with the unemployed is that they are hoarding their money. When asked for his cure for unemployment, the great merchant, without a moment's hesitation, said: "Spend More."

Graves S. Close-Fist, eminent Brooklyn banker, thinks high-living has caused poverty and unemployment. Addressing the exclusive "Four Hours For Lunch Club," Mr. Close-Fist summed up his advice to the unemployed in two words: "Save More."

Act of 1932, increasing taxes (and hence reducing purchasing power).

Hoover was also a stubborn moralist when it came to the relief of hunger and unemployment. Refusing to commit federal funds to supply basic needs, Hoover argued that relief was a local responsibility. Federal involvement, he believed, would strike at "the roots of self-government" and destroy the "character" of its recipients. Such thinking led to his endorsement of a $45 million appropriation to feed the livestock of Arkansas farmers during a 1930 drought but his rejection of a congressional grant of $25 million to provide food for the farmers' families. Hogs and bankers, it seemed, were in one category, farmers and the unemployed in another.

Hoover's program was clearly inadequate. At a time when countries such as Germany, Britain, Sweden, and Australia had national pension and unemployment insurance systems, no such program existed on the federal level in the United States. Only eight American states had any form of unemployment compensation, and few workers received retirement pensions from their employers. Worse, many relief agencies treated the poor as if their plight was the product of personal failings, requiring applicants to submit to humiliating interviews before extending aid to them. When provided, relief often took the form of "food orders" that could be used only to purchase groceries, with little or no money for rent, clothes, or medical care. Most recipients found this system demeaning. As one Pittsburgh relief recipient put

"Interviewed on Unemployment." The December 1930 edition of the League for Industrial Democracy's *The Unemployed* presented three business perspectives on the unemployment "problem."

Source: Art Young, *The Unemployed,* December 1930—General Research Division, New York Public Library, Astor, Lenox and Tilden Foundations.

Stiff Upper Lip. Rather than call for the creation of federal relief programs, this 1931 advertisement placed by the President's Organization on Unemployment Relief opted for local voluntary charity as a response to the Depression. Hoover firmly believed that relief was a local responsibility. **Source:** *Literary Digest,* November 21, 1931—General Research Division, New York Public Library, Astor, Lenox and Tilden Foundations.

it, "Does a man's status change when he becomes unemployed, so that, while he was perfectly able to handle money while he had a job, he can't be trusted with it when he is out of work?"

In New York, the average family grant was $2.39 a week, and only half of all qualified families received that tiny sum. New York's plight was repeated in many other locations, and by 1931—even with such small forms of relief—most local governments and many private agencies were running out of money. Sometimes they responded by simply removing needy people from the relief rolls. In Hamtramck, Michigan, welfare officials cut off relief to all families with fewer than three children. Some cities pared down relief rolls by discriminating against nonwhites. In Dallas and Houston, government officials denied assistance to African Americans and Mexican Americans.

By 1932 only about one-quarter of the jobless were receiving aid, and cities began taking desperate measures. In Detroit, Mayor Frank Murphy, who had been elected in 1930 with strong labor backing, set up municipal feeding stations that served fourteen thousand people daily. Murphy also opened emergency lodging in empty factories and promoted "thrift gardens" for the jobless on vacant city land. But within two years of his election, deteriorating city finances forced him to give in to fierce pressure from the banks (from whom the city needed loans) to cut spending on relief sharply.

Self-Help and Its Limits

As the Depression deepened, workers and farmers looked first to the institutions and individuals that had sustained them in earlier crises. They expected a measure of care, sustenance, and protection from their employers, merchants, churches, landlords, and local banks. In what one historian has characterized as "moral capitalism," American workers believed that the chaos and pressures of the market would be tempered by the resources and good will of traditional elites. Thus in many parts of the South, sharecroppers, both black and white, expected landlords and merchants to extend credit, food, and supplies to tide them over the drought and the collapse in cotton prices. And in the mills and factories of the North, workers expected the welfare programs and work-sharing schemes begun in the 1920s to make the economic slump tolerable. In some cases, owners and executives seemed to share this perspective. One steel company executive asserted, "Let it be said of the steel industry that none of its men was forced to call upon the public for help." In most big cities, working-class families looked to their ethnic associations, religious institutions, and neighborhood savings and loans to help them through the crisis. "Let's have pride enough *not* to sponge upon public support when Catholic charity is still able to care for its own interests," one Chicago priest urged his flock.

As the Depression ground its way through working-class lives, however, American capitalism proved less than moral. In a widely read book, *Moral Man and Immoral Society* (1932), the theologian Reinhold Neibuhr, who had spent nearly a decade as pastor of a Detroit congregation, declared that capitalism was dying and that the only remaining question was when it would finally expire. This would have come as no surprise to working-class Americans, who did not need a learned churchman to tell them that something was fundamentally wrong with the system.

What made the Depression so catastrophic for working-class families was not simply the loss of a job, a home, an insurance policy, or a bank account. Rather, these losses called into question the sustaining institutions of the 1920s, threatening the patterns of loyalty that working people had taken for granted in their families, their communities, and their workplaces. So severe was the Depression that most corporations abandoned their highly touted welfare schemes, slashing wages, hours, and employment. General Electric, for example, stopped paying bonuses to workers with good attendance records, eliminated paid vacations for blue-collar workers, and stopped subsidizing home mortgages. Meanwhile, ethnic benefit societies, churches, and religious charities failed to provide the material support expected of them. In Chicago, more than 80 percent of all neighborhood banks—institutions such as the Italo-American Building and Loan Association and the Lithuanian Dollar Savings—closed their doors. By 1933 both the corporate elite and the immigrant bourgeoisie had failed working-class America.

"A Wise Economist Asks a Question." In a 1931 *Chicago Tribune* cartoon, John McCutcheon suggested the extent to which commonplace American beliefs about thrift were undermined by the onset of the Great Depression.

Source: John Tinney McCutcheon, *Chicago Tribune* (1931)—

In this crisis, Americans turned first to neighbors and relatives to keep food on the table and a roof over their heads. The great urban migrations of the 1920s, which had swelled the population of cities such as Detroit, Los Angeles, Chicago, and Atlanta, suddenly came to a halt as nearly two million urban residents returned to their birthplaces and the impoverishment and hidden unemployment of rural life. Between 1930 and 1935, people who had fled the cities farmed more than a million acres of previously uncultivated land. Even some intellectuals, such as the well-known radicals Scott and Helen Nearing, turned to rural self-sufficiency. From Vermont, the Nearings extolled organic farming and the simple life.

But only a minority of the unemployed could return to the land. For the rest, help had to be improvised on the spot, and Americans strained their creativity and pooled their resources to survive. After a Connecticut rubber company laid off several thousand workers, investigators found that "whole families combine in a sort of super family, so that one rent will do instead of two. Relatives of all degrees gather round an income like flies round a honey pot." Likewise, in New York's Harlem and on Chicago's South Side, unemployed African Americans devised the end-of-the-month "rent party," a last-ditch attempt to raise money to keep the landlord at bay. "A hundred people would crowd into one seven-room flat until the walls bulged," recalled the young jazz musician Willie "The Lion" Smith, who provided entertainment. "Food! Hog maws and chitlins with vinegar—you never ate nothing until you ate 'em. Beer and gin." Meanwhile, in the anthracite fields of western Pennsylvania, more than 6,500 miners made their living by gleaning coal from abandoned mines.

Even in such desperation, most working-class people did not initially turn to the state for help. Following the lead of the American Federation of Labor officials, who distrusted the government, many working men and women opposed unemployment insurance, old-age pensions, and government-mandated minimum wages. The unions expected members to look to them for such support. Some leaders of the unemployed shared this preference for self-help over government programs; they developed mechanisms to enable the jobless to produce their own food and other necessities. For example, in Seattle during the summer of 1931, jobless workers founded the Unemployed Citizens' League. This "republic of the penniless" arranged for idle fishing boats to be made available to unemployed workers. It convinced farmers to allow the jobless to dig potatoes and pick apples and pears, and it gained permission from landowners for trees to be cut down for firewood. As league members mended clothing, rebuilt furniture, gave haircuts, and repaired shoes, the city's economy reverted to barter. The league's success inspired imitation; by the end of 1932, more than three hundred similar organizations were active in thirty-seven states, with a total membership exceeding three hundred thousand.

Poor People's Movements

Political radicals played a key role in turning the American people's attention to the federal government as a solution to their problems. In 1930 and 1931, under banners reading "Work or Wages" and "Fight, Don't

Starve!" communists and socialists organized scores of demonstrations of the unemployed. The communists declared March 6, 1930, to be "International Unemployment Day" and held a series of rallies to demand government jobs, relief, and an end to evictions. In city after city, the turnout far exceeded expectations. In Boston and Chicago, fifty thousand protesters showed up; in Milwaukee, forty thousand; and in Detroit, as many as one hundred thousand. In New York, where demonstrators tried to march on City Hall, police attacked the huge throng; the *New York Times* reported that "hundreds of policemen and detectives, swinging nightsticks, blackjacks, and bare fists, rushed into the crowd, hitting out at all with whom they came into contact." Leaders of the demonstration were arrested and sentenced to six months in jail.

Anti-eviction battles organized by communist "Unemployed Councils" may have had an even bigger impact. When landlords or banks evicted families, local radicals rounded up as many people as possible and moved the families and their furniture back into their homes. Delegations also went to housing courts to pressure judges not to issue eviction orders. Police and sheriff's deputies clashed with tenants during many of these battles, but the pressure made landlords think twice before putting a family on the street. In some black neighborhoods in Chicago, the Unemployed Councils became so well known

Seattle Unemployed Worker

Capturing the Times. The desperation of hard times was mirrored in the modest appearance of the official publication of the Seattle Unemployed Council.

Source: *Seattle Unemployed Worker,* April 17, 1932—Scott Molloy Archives.

that, according to two contemporary observers, when eviction notices went out, "it was not unusual for a mother to shout to the children, 'Run quick and find the Reds!' "

Family farmers took radical direct action as well. By 1932 more than a third of the farmland in states such as Mississippi and Iowa was scheduled for sale at auction because the farm owners had fallen behind on taxes or mortgage payments. Neighbors often aborted these sales by intimidating potential bidders, buying the farm themselves at a token price, and returning it to its original owner. Emil Loriks of Arlington, South Dakota, remembered that in his county, "farmers would crowd into the courtroom, five or six hundred, and make it impossible for the officers to carry out the sales." Such near-violent conflicts soon compelled even conservative state legislators to press for laws blocking the sale of farms for taxes or debt.

Conflicts with police and sheriffs were common in the industrial North and the agricultural Midwest, but nowhere were they more deadly than in the rural South, where a pervasive climate of repression and racial violence forced communists and socialists to organize what they called "the black peasantry" in an underground fashion. In May 1932, for instance, when a young African-American communist, Angelo Herndon, tried to organize a demonstration of the unemployed in Atlanta, he was charged with insurrection under an 1866 law and sentenced to twenty years in prison. (The U.S. Supreme Court eventually overturned his conviction.)

The Communist party was particularly active in Alabama, where its membership was predominantly black. In Birmingham, the party attracted steelworkers; in the countryside, black sharecroppers. As cotton prices plummeted, planters' paternalism vanished. Some cut off food advances to their tenants, reduced the wages for day labor, or forced sharecroppers to work off real estate taxes—the landowner's responsibility—by doing roadwork. When the communists organized the Sharecroppers' Union (SCU) in Tallapoosa County, Alabama, in 1931, many African Americans joined despite enormous risk.

Within months, local landowners and authorities struck back. In July 1931, a sheriff's party raided a Sharecroppers' Union meeting near the town of Camp Hill, touching off a series of gun battles that resulted in the wounding of two officials and the death of a sharecropper. As the Communist party's role in organizing the SCU and in defending the "Scottsboro boys" became known, more black Alabamans joined the party. In 1932, a second shoot-out between authorities and SCU members ended in the death of at least three sharecroppers and the imprisonment of five others.

These conflicts with police and sheriffs, as well as the demonstrations by the unemployed, were failures that nevertheless had lasting

"Weren't No Use Under God's Sun to Treat Colored Folks Like We Been Treated"

Ned Cobb, a sharecropper and staunch supporter of the Alabama Sharecroppers' Union, describes how he resisted an attempt by his landlord, Mr. Taylor, to foreclose on another sharecropper, Clint Webster, in 1932. Cobb ended up spending twelve years in prison for defying the authorities in this incident.

I happened to be at Clint Webster's house one mornin' when Mr. Taylor sent the deputy sheriff [Mr. Woods] over to attach everything the man had and bring it away from there. . . . Well, I knowed I had to take a stand right there because . . . I was going to be next. . . . I stretched out my arms and said, "Mr. Woods, please, sir, don't take what he's got. He's got a wife and children and if you take all his stock and everything else, you'll leave his folks hungry." He told me . . . "I got orders to take it, and I'll be damned if I don't." . . . So I just politely told him that he weren't goin' to do it. . . .

Then the deputy raised sand with me about it. He jumped up and told me, "I'm going to Dadeville to get [Sheriff] Carl Platt and bring him down here. He'll come down here and kill the last damn one of you, shoot you in a bunch."

Now, a organization is a organization, and if I don't mean nothin' by what I say and do, I ought to keep my ass out of it; but if I'm sworn to stand up for myself and stand up for all the poor class of farmers, I have to do it. Weren't no use under God's sun to treat colored folks like we been treated here in the state of Alabama, weren't no sense in it. Work hard and look what's done to me. . . .

Mr. Woods come back that same day . . . with four sheriffs. . . . There were several men in Clint Webster's house when that bunch of sheriffs arrived, five or six of them. But when the sheriffs walked up in the yard, I was standin' outside. . . . I said, "Fellas, here they come, here come the officers." God Almighty, they jumped up and run out of that house goin' out the back way into the field and the forest, clean out of there. . . . Then [Deputy Sheriff] Grant, be standin' in front of me holdin' a shotgun straight on me; wouldn't budge, just standin' there lookin' at me, wouldn't say nothin' . . . just lookin' at me and holdin' that gun, the muzzle part of it. . . .

And bless your soul, I got tired standin' there. . . . So I walked off. I just decided I'd go on in the house. And when I started up the doorstep, [Deputy Sheriff] Meade . . . grabbed me by my right arm and just pressured it, but I absolutely flung him off like you would fling off a leech. . . . I just commenced a steppin' right on in the house. And Mr. Grant shot me three times, in the back. . . . But I didn't stop walkin' when he shot me. Shot me twice more, right quick before I could get in the house. Boom! Boom! Same place, every time he shot me. I just still kept walkin', never did weaken.

Now the door to the north room of that house was open comin' off a hallway. I just walked in that door to the north room and looked back. Mr. Grant still had that gun on me, and I started workin' out with him. He jumped behind a big oak tree and I just kept working' out with my .32 Smith and Wesson. I had that gun on me when I come there that mornin', and they didn't know it. I didn't go there actin' a fool, less'n a person will call me a fool for what I said. My finger was on that trigger all the time and the gun was in my hand. I had on a pair of big overalls, brand new, and the pockets was deep and my hand in the pockets. And I had on a white cowboy hat—that's the way I was dressed and my jumper and a pair of Red Wing boots, about knee-high. . . . And when Mr. Grant shot me—shot me three times, in the same place—my blood came near to fillin' them boots. . . . I was just sloshin' in my blood every step I took.

Well, I shot six times, and when I got done shootin', all of them deputies done cleared out from that house, every one of 'em run away from there.

Source: Dale Rosen and Theodore Rosengarten, "Shoot-Out at Reeltown," *Radical America,* November—December 1972.

consequences. The stark confrontations of the early 1930s helped to radicalize thousands of impoverished men and women who later built potent industrial unions and social movements. And—despite much radical rhetoric denouncing the government—these early Depression protests helped workers and farmers to turn their attention beyond their neighborhoods and employers and to look to the state for help with their problems. This in turn pushed the nation toward the creation of work relief programs and unemployment insurance.

In 1932, two great protests demonstrated the potential of the Depression to mobilize people for more far-reaching changes. Of all the unemployment demonstrations that year, the most dramatic was the Ford Hunger March. By 1932 Henry Ford, America's most famous industrialist, had dumped sixty thousand workers onto Detroit's relief rolls. On March 7, 1932, more than three thousand protesters organized by the small, Communist-led Auto Workers' Union marched on Ford's giant River Rouge complex in Dearborn, Michigan. The protesters demanded jobs for laid-off Ford workers, a slowdown of the company's assembly line, and a halt to evictions of former Ford workers. As the marchers neared the factory gate, Dearborn police and Ford guards first threw tear gas, then leveled their guns at the retreating crowd and fired. Hundreds of shots rang out, killing four marchers and wounding more than sixty others. Within days, hundreds of suspected "Reds" had been arrested throughout the region in a police dragnet.

But Ford's reaction to the march only hardened the participants' determination to effect change. For Dave Moore, who began his political activity fighting evictions in Detroit, the Hunger March was "the turning point in my life. . . . When I saw the blood flowing there on Miller Road, that was the point I became a radical." The following Sunday, an interracial crowd of more than twenty thousand people followed the caskets of the slain men to a cemetery, where they were lowered into the ground to the strains of the "Internationale," the Communist anthem. Henry Ford, a hero of the 1920s, became a much-hated man in the city of Detroit.

Four months later, in the summer of 1932, a veterans' march on Washington, D.C., had an even greater impact on the nation. After World War I, Congress had passed a bill promising each veteran a cash bonus to be paid in 1945. As the Depression deepened, veterans demanded that the bonuses be distributed immediately. In May 1932, a group of veterans from Portland, Oregon, set out for Washington to press their case. Their Bonus March, which was reminiscent of Coxey's Army forty years earlier, quickly gathered followers. Twenty thousand ex-servicemen soon were encamped in the capital. The House responded by passing a new bonus bill but the Senate defeated it. When Congress adjourned, some veterans left town, but others stayed and set up camps in unoccupied government buildings. Some demonstrators invited their families to join them. In late July, the Hoover administration evicted the protesters. In the skirmishes that followed, two veterans were killed. Prodded by Army Chief-of-Staff General Douglas MacArthur, who considered the Bonus Army a "mob" driven by the "essence of revolution," Hoover called out the regular army.

Anacostia Flats and Flames. The Bonus Marchers' shantytown burned down within sight of the Capitol on the afternoon of July 28, 1932. Federal troops had set fire to the camp after dispersing the unemployed and homeless World War I veterans who were asking for an early release of their war bonuses.

Source: National Archives.

Although the president urged restraint, MacArthur was determined to force the demonstrators out of their camps. Launching an attack that was spearheaded by tanks, cavalry, and foot soldiers firing tear gas, the U.S. Army quickly routed the veterans and their families, setting fire to their tents in the process. Hoover defended the attack, agreeing with MacArthur that many of the protesters were communists or "persons with criminal records." But few Americans accepted the president's rationale. Millions of citizens were horrified by the image, reproduced in newspapers and on newsreels, of a battle-equipped army driving off a ragtag collection of men who had faithfully served their country and were now desperately seeking help. "So all the misery and suffering had finally come to this," reported journalist Thomas Stokes, who witnessed the assault, "soldiers marching with their guns against American citizens." Hoover's reputation, like Henry Ford's, collapsed.

Roosevelt's Promise of a New Deal

Herbert Hoover's monumental unpopularity in the third year of the nation's economic crisis virtually guaranteed that a Democrat would win the presidential election in 1932. The man the Democrats selected at their Chicago convention was the governor of New York, Franklin Delano Roosevelt, a distant cousin of Theodore Roosevelt. Roosevelt ran a cautious campaign, pledging a balanced budget and a cut in the federal payroll. Even so, he sailed to an easy victory, winning more than 57 percent of the poplar vote and taking every state outside New England except Pennsylvania. With his victory came a Democratic Congress that was itching to do something about the Depression.

Franklin Roosevelt stands with Abraham Lincoln as a refounder of the American nation. He was elected four times and served more than twelve years, longer than any president before or since. During those years, the United States put in place the social legislation, economic regulations, and governmental apparatus that serves as the foundation for the powerful, politically intrusive state that has been a prominent feature of American life during the second half of the twentieth century. Under Roosevelt, liberalism came into its own as an ideology of governance, an electoral coalition, and a social and cultural force. Roosevelt was such a towering figure that every president who has succeeded him has measured his own statecraft by the standard Roosevelt set in the 1930s.

Roosevelt was born in 1882 into a patrician family of New York estate owners whose wealth, although substantial, was no match for the spectacular fortunes then being amassed by the Rockefellers and Carnegies. Schooled at Groton, Harvard, and Columbia Law School, Roosevelt used his charm, money, and social prominence to climb the political ladder. After moving from the New York Assembly to the Democratic party's vice-presidential nomination in 1920, Roosevelt was eyeing the governorship of New York when he was stricken with polio and lost the use of both legs in 1921. He would never walk again without heavy braces and much assistance, but Roosevelt's misfortune probably made him more expansive, mature, and socially concerned. Soon he was battling his way back into public life with the help of his wife, Eleanor, who displayed a talent for political organization and public speaking that surprised those who had known her as a shy, awkward woman. Although the Roosevelts' marriage was one of growing estrangement, Eleanor proved a loyal, liberal political ally, a woman Franklin often called his "eyes and ears."

Roosevelt, who was known simply as FDR, served as governor of New York during the same dark era when Hoover held the White House. He proved a more imaginative administrator than Hoover was in those crisis years, but still he had to position himself carefully to win his party's presidential nomination in 1932. His approach was laissez-faire on the issues of religion and drink (he pledged to repeal Prohibition) but interventionist on the economy and social welfare. In accepting the Democratic nomination, Roosevelt promised "a new deal for the American people."

Between Roosevelt's election in November 1932 and his inauguration in March 1933, the economy dipped to the lowest point of the entire Depression. Particularly worrisome was a new wave of bank failures. In mid-February 1933, Michigan's governor ordered all state banks closed, to prevent the collapse of the big Detroit institutions. Panic spread in state after state—forty altogether—forcing authorities to declare bank "holidays." Even the New York Stock Exchange shut down.

"A Real Mother to the Nation"

Millions of Americans felt a close personal bond with Franklin and Eleanor Roosevelt. In letters sent to the White House, they recounted their personal troubles and expressed their gratitude to the president and First Lady. Below are excerpts from letters addressed to Eleanor Roosevelt. The first correspondent begged for a loan to buy baby clothes; the others praised the Roosevelts in strikingly religious terms.

Jan. 2, 1935
Troy, New York

Dear Mrs. Roosevelt,

About a month ago I wrote you asking if you would buy some baby clothes for me with the understanding that I was to repay you as soon as my husband got enough work. Several weeks later I received a reply to apply to a Welfare Association so I might receive the aid I needed. Do you remember?

Please Mrs. Roosevelt, I do not want charity, only a chance from someone who will trust me until we can get enough money to repay the amount spent for the things I need. As a proof that I really am sincere, I am sending you two of my dearest possessions to keep as security, a ring my husband gave me before we were married, and a ring my mother used to wear. Perhaps the actual value of them is not high, but they are worth a lot to me. If you will consider buying the baby clothes, please keep them until I send you the money you spend. It is very hard to face bearing a baby we cannot afford to have, and the fact that it is due to arrive soon, and still there is no money for the hospital or clothing, does not make it any easier. . . .

Ridley Park, Pennsylvania
9/1/34

Dear Mrs. Roosevelt,

I was delighted but I dont believe I was very much surprised when I received your letter. Just to look at your picture and that of our President seems to me like looking at the picture of a saint. So when you answered my letter and promised to have some one help me it only proved you are our own Mrs. Roosevelt. I have told everyone what you done for me. I want them to know you are not too busy to answer our letters and give us what help and advice you can. You hold the highest place any woman can hold still you are not to[o] proud to befriend the poorest class. . . . Thank you and God bless you both.

Nov. 25, 1934
Arkansas City, Kansas

Dear Madam:

I beg to inform you that I have been reading your writings in the *Wichita Beacon* and I must say that the whole nation should be enthused over them. I was especially carried away with the one on Old Age Pensions. It brought my mind back to the day of the Chicago Convention, when Mr. Roosevelt was nominated for the presidency.

In our little home in Arkansas City, my family and I were sitting around the radio . . . and when he spoke it seems as though some Moses had come to alleviate us of our sufferings. Strange to say when he was speaking to see the moisten eyes and the deep feeling of emotions that gave vent to every word and when you spoke then we knew that the white house would be filled with a real mother to the nation.

Source: Robert S. McElvaine, *Down and Out in the Great Depression: Letters from the "Forgotten Man"* (1983).

Not since the days of Lincoln had a president taken office in such dramatic and difficult circumstances. For Roosevelt, it was a golden opportunity. A master of the radio, he used his inaugural address to assure the nation that "the only thing we have to fear is fear itself." Hoover had made similar appeals on numerous occasions, but Roosevelt's enormous self-confidence, combined with paternal warmth and a plain, friendly manner, gave hope to millions. He later broadcast a series of "fireside chats" in which he explained his programs to the public, using easily digestible anecdotes. Within weeks of his election, Roosevelt had come to embody the state as friend and protector. "My mother looks upon the president as someone so immediately concerned with her problems and difficulties that she would not be greatly surprised were he to come to her house some evening and stay to dinner," remarked an insurance salesman. The volume of White House mail exploded: While Hoover had required just one clerk to answer correspondence, Roosevelt needed a staff of fifty to handle the letters that poured in to the president and first lady.

Harold Ickes, FDR's secretary of the interior, described the first hundred days of Roosevelt's administration as "a new world. . . . It's like quitting a morgue for the open woods." Unlike Hoover, Roosevelt was an opportunist and an experimentalist who surrounded himself with politically savvy academics and bold administrators. Many key New Deal officials and advisers, such as Ickes, Felix Frankfurter (whom FDR later appointed to the Supreme Court) and Secretary of Agriculture Henry Wallace, were veterans of the Progressive movement or the World War I bureaucracy. Young men and women just out of Harvard or Columbia filled other vital positions, assuming extraordinary responsibilities. Many of these young people were Jewish or Catholic law school graduates unwelcome in the Protestant world of the big corporate law firms. And women long active in social reform movements, including Secretary of Labor Frances Perkins, the first female cabinet officer, filled several posts dealing with relief or labor relations.

Have Faith. Instead of blaring its usual movie advertisement, this theater sound truck toured the streets of Boston in December 1931 chiding citizens who, fearing impending financial failure, had withdrawn their deposits from local banks.
Source: Courtesy of the Boston Public Library, Print Department.

The quintessential New Dealer may well have been Harry Hopkins. A social worker by training, Hopkins broke all the conventions of that heavily Protestant, moralistic profession. He was divorced, belonged to no church, and liked to bet on the horses. Roosevelt put him in charge of the administration's emergency relief program the minute Congress authorized it. Within two hours Hopkins had set up a desk in a hallway and spent $5 million.

In his inaugural address, Franklin Roosevelt had asserted, "The nation calls for action and action now." But the president was not a radical, nor were the overwhelming majority of his key appointees. In fact, much of the legislation put forward during the first, famous hundred days of the New Deal was drawn from the program of the most conservative wing of the Democratic party or from proposals Herbert Hoover had failed to pass. Even as the government took on new responsibilities, Roosevelt sought to preserve as much of the economic and social status quo as possible. Mistrustful of labor radicals, and worried that "the dole," as he referred to cash relief, undermined self-respect, Roosevelt courted business support and strove to balance the budget as soon as possible. And neither Roosevelt nor his principal advisers were willing to challenge the power of the southern white oligarchy or to question neo-Victorian gender roles in framing emergency relief and social welfare legislation.

Financial Rescue and Emergency

Roosevelt's first task was to restore confidence in the financial system. Two days after taking office he declared a national bank holiday, closing all banks; he then called Congress into special session. Although popular anger at the banking system was at such a pitch that Congress might well have nationalized the banks outright, the Roosevelt administration pushed through an Emergency Banking Act that merely empowered the government to lend money to troubled banks, to reorganize failed ones, and to stop the hoarding of gold. Banks judged to be solvent were allowed to reopen within a week. In general, Roosevelt acted decisively but avoided the most radical solutions proposed. Farmers and others with large debts, for example, urged inflationary policies of the sort favored by the Populists in the late nineteenth century. Roosevelt resisted, but he still shocked conservatives by taking the nation off the gold standard in April 1933. One Roosevelt adviser pronounced that this act would bring "the end of Western Civilization."

Civilization survived and so did the financial system. In fact, Roosevelt's efforts over the next two years served largely to restore public confidence shattered by the crash. The Glass-Steagall Banking Act of 1933 increased Federal Reserve supervision over banks and created the Federal Deposit Insurance Corporation, which guaranteed the security of most family savings. And the Securities Acts of 1933 and 1934 initiated long-overdue regulation of the nation's stock exchanges by requiring what Roosevelt called "truth telling" in the marketing of securities and establishing a Securities and Exchange Commission to oversee the stock market.

Meanwhile, Roosevelt and Congress fulfilled two Democratic campaign promises. First, they passed a constitutional amendment ending Prohibition. Second, they slashed veterans' benefits and lowered federal salaries.

Roosevelt's efforts to save the banks and cut spending were hardly different from those of Herbert Hoover, but his decision to launch a national relief program was a major policy innovation. To provide funds for the unemployed, Congress at the president's request set up the Federal Emergency Relief Administration (FERA), which over the next three years spent about $1 billion a year—roughly 2 percent of the national income. Congress also approved one of Roosevelt's pet projects, the Civilian Conservation Corps (CCC). Like his cousin, Theodore Roosevelt, FDR believed that outdoor life was morally and physically curative. The CCC provided temporary work to three million young men, who lived in semi-military camps, constructed recreation facilities, and carried out conservation projects under the direction of army officers. Later in 1933, Roosevelt launched the Civil Works Administration (CWA). Under Harry Hopkins, the CWA hired four million of the unemployed and put them to work on four hundred thousand small-scale projects, mainly road building and repair work.

"We Can Take It!" A photograph of a young Civilian Conservation Corps (CCC) worker epitomized the agency's slogan. "Building strong bodies is a major CCC objective," the accompanying caption stated. "More than half of the enrollees who entered CCC during the last year were seventeen years of age. Work, calisthenics, marching drills, good food, and medical care feature the CCC health program."

Source: Wilfred J. Mead—National Archives.

These emergency work relief programs employed more than ten million Americans. By putting real money in the pockets of the poor, they offered tangible evidence that the New Deal could touch the lives of ordinary Americans. Hopkins insisted that only public agencies receive federal funds, a policy that undercut the role of private charity, and he tried to hold state and local officials accountable to government-established federal guidelines. Overnight, the public's expectations of federal officials underwent a dramatic change. "Clients are assuming that the government has a responsibility to provide," reported Hopkins, with some misgiving. "The stigma of relief has almost disappeared except among white-collar groups."

Despite the efforts of Hopkins and other liberals, the distribution of government aid largely replicated the racial, regional, and gender divisions that plagued the nation. Congress appropriated money, but entrenched local elites usually administered the funds. Thus benefits varied greatly from state to state. Monthly FERA payments were ten times higher in New York than in Mississippi because the planter class in the Delta wanted a ready supply of harvest labor. In the West, fruit growers often forced relief agencies to cease making relief payments when pickers were needed. And in the CCC, which was administered by the army, black and white workers received equal wages but lived in segregated camps that reflected military recruitment practice.

Women were largely excluded from these work relief programs. The major concern of most New Deal policymakers, working-class radicals, and social service administrators was the restoration of male dignity and livelihood. The CCC accepted no women; and of the millions of FERA and CWA beneficiaries, fewer than 10 percent were female, despite the fact that women made up a quarter of the unemployed. New Deal workers built roads and dams; teaching, child care, and public health were lower priorities.

Agricultural Supports and Industrial Codes

To restore stability to the agricultural and industrial sectors, the Roosevelt administration developed two major programs, the Agricultural Adjustment Act (AAA) and the National Industrial Recovery Act (NIRA). Both sought to tame the economy but not to abolish the free market.

For more than a decade, agriculture had been in crisis because of low prices and chronic overproduction. In 1931, several southern states had actually passed laws prohibiting farmers from sowing that year's crop. But the movement for a moratorium on cotton planting collapsed when Texas refused to participate. Midwestern farmers turned to more violent action. The next year, in an effort to raise prices an Iowa-based Farmer's Holiday Association blocked rural highways to prevent milk, corn, and other farm products from going to market.

In a nation in which rice, wheat, cotton, and tobacco were raised in thousands of counties, such regional efforts were doomed to failure. The New Deal solution was the Agricultural Adjustment Act, passed by Congress early in the spring of 1933. The AAA was meant to raise the purchasing power of farmers by restoring "parity," the relationship between farm prices and industrial prices during World War I. To achieve parity, the government made payments to farmers, who agreed to reduce the size of their crops in return. New Deal officials argued that, just as

The Spirit of '32. Three striking farmers mimicked Archibald Willard's "The Spirit of '76," the popular 1876 painting celebrating the American Revolution. When asked by a reporter how he justified Farm Holiday protest actions that broke the law, one elderly man replied, "Seems to me there was a Tea Party in Boston that was illegal, too." **Source:** August 31, 1932—Scott Molloy Labor Archives.

major industrial companies manipulated their sales and prices, so a government-mandated reduction in the amount of land under cultivation could force up commodity prices. To finance the payments to farmers, the government taxed food processors, who generally passed the tax on to consumers in the form of higher costs. The Agricultural Adjustment Administration ran the program. Separate agencies promoted soil conservation and made loans at favorable rates to farmers who reduced their cultivated acreage.

Since the planting season had already begun by the time Roosevelt's farm bill became law, farmers who wanted benefit payments had to destroy their crops and livestock. So farmers slaughtered six million baby pigs and plowed under ten million acres of cotton. The destruction of food and fiber in the midst of want was entirely logical, given that the AAA's purpose was to cut the supply of agricultural commodities. But it created a furor nonetheless, in part because it highlighted the larger irrationalities embedded within the government's market-taming program.

The AAA did boost agricultural income. By 1936, crop prices were higher and gross farm income had risen by 50 percent. Large commercial farmers benefited most, since they could make the greatest reductions in their crops and thereby receive the largest payments. Many of those farmers used the money to retire debts, expand their farms, and purchase new equipment. Smaller farmers did not benefit nearly as much, and some tenant farmers and sharecroppers found themselves worse off. Legally, landowners were obligated to share their crop-reduction payments with tenants and sharecroppers, but with the help of local officials, they commonly evaded the responsibility. Furthermore, as the amount of land being cultivated was reduced and cash became available through the crop-reduction program, many landowners stopped renting fields to tenants, forcing them to become sharecroppers or day laborers. Some evicted tenants entirely.

The impact of the AAA on these small farmers provoked a new wave of protest. In 1934, Arkansas sharecroppers and laborers—both black and white—organized the Southern Tenant Farmers' Union (STFU). The

STFU sought to pressure landowners and federal officials to stop the widespread eviction of tenants and sharecroppers and give them their fair share of government parity payments. The union soon grew to ten thousand members, and through its ties to the Socialist party it made the plight of the Arkansas rural poor known to a sympathetic public in the North. Planters and local authorities responded with a wave of beatings, arrests, and shootings. Although this reign of terror forced the STFU underground, the union still managed to organize cotton pickers' strikes in five states in 1936. Black tenant farmers became some of the union's most effective organizers.

At the Department of Agriculture, many of the young New Dealers were deeply sympathetic to the plight of tenant farmers. But Roosevelt, Secretary of Agriculture Wallace, and other top aides were more interested in conciliating the powerful, conservative cohort of southern Democrats they considered so vital to New Deal legislative majorities. Wallace therefore fired the Agriculture Department radicals in 1935, making clear that the New Deal would do little to threaten the power of planters and agribusiness interests. To provide some help for poor farmers and farmworkers, the administration set up a new agency, the Resettlement Administration. But its low budget and even smaller group of political supporters meant that it could aid only a fraction of the displaced rural poor. Meanwhile, the STFU collapsed; its defeat was a harbinger of the massive, decades-long reorganization of American agriculture, a period when millions of small farmers were pushed off the land. The New Deal agricultural revolution demonstrated that an intrusive set of government controls and incentives could make American agribusiness the most prosperous and efficient in the world, but the human costs of that transformation were never properly calculated.

Organizing in Arkansas. Black and white farmworkers listened to a speaker at a Southern Tenant Farmers' Union meeting.

Source: Louise Boyle—Southern Tenant Farmers' Union Papers no. 3472, Southern Historical Collection, Library of the University of North Carolina at Chapel Hill.

Industrial recovery posed even more complex problems than those facing farmers. How could the downward cycle of falling wages, prices, profits, and employment be stopped? One remarkably popular solution was to legislate a thirty-hour workweek. Such a law, which would have created millions of new jobs, actually passed the Senate early in 1933. But big business opposed it, and so did the president, who thought it merely spread the misery around. In its stead Roosevelt pushed through the National Industrial Recovery Act, which mandated a government-sanctioned system of business self-regulation, coordinated by a National Recovery Administration (NRA). Like the AAA, the NRA would use government power to regulate the market, raise prices, and increase wages. The NRA was more than a Washington bureaucracy. FDR's flamboyant NRA chief, Hugh Johnson, used many of the propaganda techniques he had learned during his Great War service to turn the recovery effort into a national crusade. Companies that agreed to cooperate with the NRA were allowed to display a blue eagle. Parades, speeches, and posters urged the public to spend money only where the symbol was displayed.

In an effort to restrain competition and thereby end the downward cycle of wage cuts and price reductions, a detailed NRA code spelled out permissible production and marketing practices for each industry. The textile industry, for example, agreed to limit mills to two forty-hour weekly shifts, to end child labor, and to set minimum wages at $12 to $13 per week. Johnson argued that the act would "eliminate eye-gouging and knee-groining and ear-chewing in business." In theory, consumers, labor, and the government would help to write the codes. Such was the case in the coal and garment industries, where the unions were making a spectacular comeback. But in most other industries, the codes were written at the behest of the largest and most politically influential producers. "The lumber code is not an edict handed us by Congress or the president," bragged a West Coast lumberman to industry associates. "We went to Washington and asked for it."

"We Do Our Part." Three unlikely spots for the display of the otherwise ubiquitous NRA eagle.

Source: Pare Lorentz, *The Roosevelt Year: A Photographic Record* (1934)—American Social History Project.

The NRA generated more than five hundred industry codes, some of great complexity. Trade unionists, New Dealers, and a few businessmen recognized that a strong labor movement was essential to industry self-regulation because unions possessed an intimate, internal knowledge of business conditions. If unions had sufficient power, they could ensure that employers complied with the minimum wage standards and maximum hour regulations set out in the codes. But labor power would come only with successful union organizing. Thus Section 7a of the NRA proved an important and controversial part of each industry code. Section 7a gave employees "the right to organize and bargain collectively through representatives of their own choosing . . . free from the interference, restraint, or coercion of employers." Employers were forbidden to require their workers to join company-sponsored unions or to make them sign yellow-dog contracts promising not to unionize. Labor leaders hailed the provision, but a closer look revealed that it offered few enforcement measures.

The New Deal in the South and West

Many New Dealers believed that national economic growth was stifled by the monopolization of capital and manufacturing in the Northeast. Compared with that region, the South and West were virtually undeveloped countries. Because private investment in those regions had evaporated entirely, reform alone would not end poverty. Massive public investment was necessary not only to provide construction jobs but also to build highways, bridges, and other elements of infrastructure essential to future prosperity.

The Tennessee Valley Authority (TVA) was the New Deal's most ambitious and celebrated experiment in regional economic planning. Launched in 1933, this giant project had its roots in the Progressive era, when development of the nation's water resources as a source of inexpensive electric power was a priority. The TVA, a government-owned corporation set up by the first New Deal Congress, planned the comprehensive redevelopment of an entire river watershed spanning seven southern states. With twenty new dams, the authority soon tamed the flood-prone rivers of the Tennessee Valley and, in the process, became the largest producer of electric power in the United States. Private utility executives thought the TVA socialistic, but the otherwise conservative farmers and manufacturers of the Appalachian South thankfully reaped the benefits of improved navigation on the Tennessee River, flood control, recreational facilities, industrial development, and cheap electricity. Beginning in 1935, the Rural Electrification Administration brought running water and electric lights to remote farmhouses nationwide by making cheap, government-backed credit available to hundreds of electric power cooperatives.

More government-financed dams, airports, courthouses, and bridges were the product of the $3.3 billion Public Works Administration (PWA), enacted as part of the NIRA in 1933. Managed with an incorruptible hand by Interior Secretary Harold Ickes, the PWA put in place much of the infrastructure on the Pacific Coast. In California alone, the PWA helped to finance the world's largest dam at Shasta; the longest and

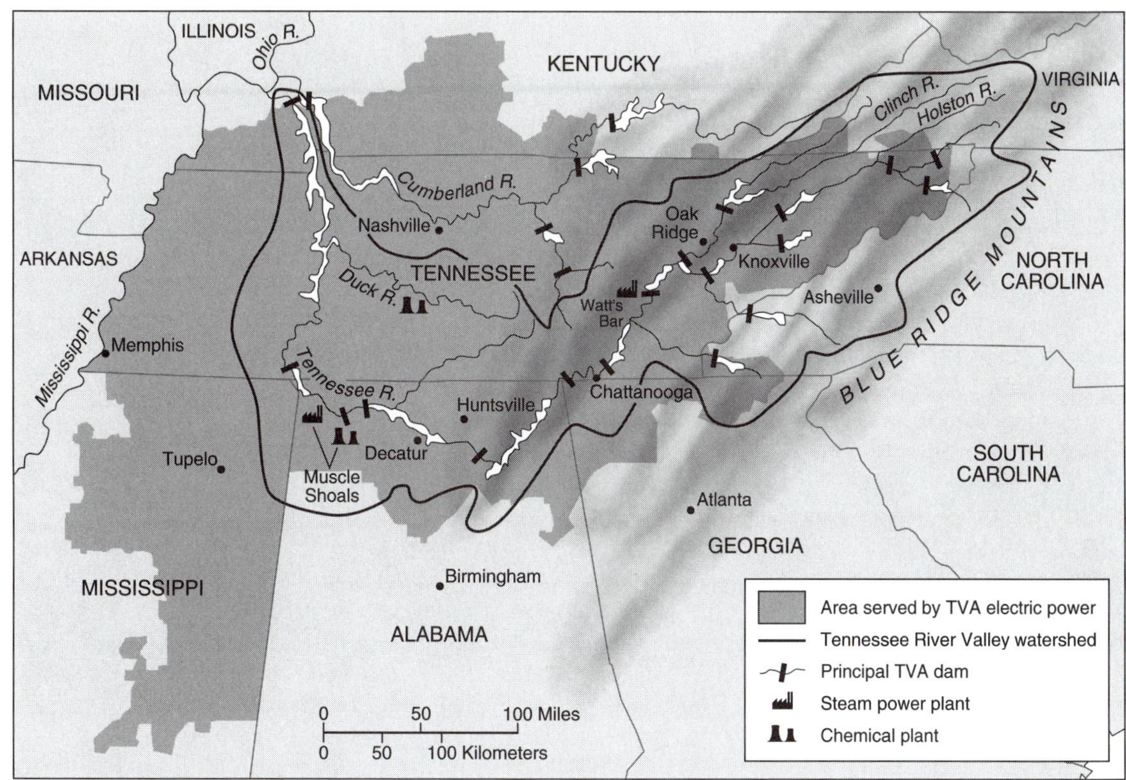

Tennessee Valley Authority. Between 1933 and 1952, the Tennessee Valley Authority improved five dams and built twenty others, taming the flood-prone rivers of the Tennessee Valley and bringing affordable electricity to remote rural areas. TVA, therefore, represented social and ecological engineering on a grand scale.

most expensive suspension bridge, between San Francisco and Oakland; and the nation's first freeway, from downtown Los Angeles to Pasadena. Following the Long Beach earthquake of 1933, it rebuilt the entire school system of Los Angeles County, including Hollywood High and Pasadena City College, which were designed in the distinctive "Streamline Moderne" style of southern California architecture.

At the same time that the New Deal modernized the American West, it was more respectful of the traditions of one group that was heavily represented there—American Indians. Ever since the adoption of the Dawes Act in 1887, the federal government had tried to force Indians to assimilate into white society by ending communally owned reservations and insisting that they take up "allotments"—individually owned plots of land. This policy proved disastrous for the nation's more than three hundred thousand Native Americans. Between 1887 and the early 1930s, tribal lands decreased from 135 million acres to 52 million acres (much of it in poor condition), and tribal funds dropped from $500 million to $12 million. More than one hundred thousand Indians survived only through begging.

In 1933 John Collier, FDR's reform-minded commissioner of Indian affairs, set out to transform the relationship between the federal government and American Indians. His Indian Reorganization Act of 1934 dramatically changed federal policy. It ended the allotment of tribal lands to individuals and made possible the reconsolidation of allotted land into tribal hands. It restored surplus lands to tribes. It allowed tribes to adopt constitutions giving them self-government. And it opened the way for Indians to seek jobs in the white-dominated Bureau of Indian Affairs. Collier also pushed for the restoration of traditional Native American cultural expressions, including ancient dances and religious practices that had been discouraged or banned under the Dawes Act.

Collier's reforms, known as the New Deal for Indians, encountered opposition from Protestant missionaries and other conservatives who preferred the assimilationist policy. In addition, a number of Indian groups who had previously embraced assimilation were suspicious of the new government endorsement of traditional ways. More than a quarter of the nation's tribes (including the Navajo, the largest tribe) rejected the Indian Reorganization Act. Still, those that accepted the new policy gained a measure of autonomy. Most American Indians remained poor, but the New Deal had at least brought them a more sympathetic hearing in Washington.

Section 7a and the Revival of Organized Labor

Before the Depression, unions were clustered in a few industries: coal mining, construction, railroads, garment manufacturing, and public utilities. Organizing efforts in other fields had been effectively blocked by management hostility, restrictive court decisions, postwar prosperity, and company-sponsored unions.

The collapse of the economy compounded labor's problems. As unemployment rose, union membership dropped sharply. By early 1933, it had fallen below 3 million—less than 10 percent of the national workforce, about what it had been in the early years of the century. Even well-established unions were devastated. In 1933, for instance, there were only 583,000 unionized construction workers, down from 919,000 four years earlier. The number of walkouts also fell during the early Depression years, to the lowest level of the century. With unemployment so high, few workers were willing to risk their jobs by going on strike. Union leaders, too, became extremely cautious.

In 1933, however, workers suddenly and dramatically embraced collective action. The number of strikes jumped sharply, and unions launched organizing drives in industry after industry. Anger had been building among workers since the beginning of the Depression; pay cuts, hour reductions, speedups, and layoffs had caused widespread discontent. Many workers particularly resented the tremendous power foremen and supervisors held over their lives. Workers who had connections in management or who gave presents or kickbacks to supervisors often kept their jobs while more senior employees were laid off. Corporations further undercut workers' loyalty by eliminating the health, recreational, and profit-sharing benefits they had provided during the more prosperous years of the 1920s.

The NIRA's Section 7a, which gave workers in some industries the right to organize and bargain collectively, proved the catalyst that turned discontent into action. Although Section 7a was only a vague statement of policy, it had enormous psychological and political impact. The NIRA enabled union organizers to suggest that joining a union was a patriotic contribution to the national recovery effort. This was a big change from the 1920s, when open-shop employers had sought to brand unions as un-American—an outlook that had frequently been sustained by the use of army and National Guard troops against strikers in the tumultuous years after World War I. Meanwhile, anti-union executives were losing their nerve. Confused and demoralized by the Depression, by Roosevelt's election, and by the desperate, experimental tenor of the new Congress, businessmen were no longer sure they could count on backing from the police, state and local officials, or even the federal courts. Thus Section 7a gave workers confidence that they could organize, perhaps with the government's blessing.

The working-class upsurge of 1933 and 1934 had uneven consequences. In those industries and regions that had once had a tradition of collective bargaining, trade unionism reemerged nearly uncontested. But on the frontiers of organizing—in agriculture, autos, textiles, steel, longshoring, and trucking—corporate resistance and police violence produced bitter confrontations that pitted strikers against an entrenched and hostile coalition of old-line managers and political elites, whose supporters were often organized into club-wielding paramilitary groups.

Steel Strike, October 1933. Armed with shotguns and machine guns, steel company private police fired on pickets outside the Spang-Chalfant Tube factory in Ambridge, Pennsylvania. One striker was killed and fifteen were wounded.

Source: United Steel Workers of America Archive, Historical Collections and Labor Archives, Pettee Library, Pennsylvania State University. Print by Associated Photographers.

The amazingly rapid rebirth of the United Mine

Workers of America (UMW) demonstrated how quickly the New Deal could transform working-class consciousness. The UMW had been decimated by the coal industry's chronic slump and by the Depression. In February 1933, a UMW member reported that "as far as West Kentucky is concerned there is no sign of organization . . . you could not organize a baseball team." But once it became clear that the NIRA would be passed, the miners' union gambled its remaining resources on a lightning-quick organizing campaign, throwing a hundred organizers into the field. Organizers leaned heavily on workers' patriotism and President Roosevelt's popularity. A circular they distributed in Kentucky claimed that the NIRA "recommends that coal miners . . . organize in a union of their own choosing." Some leaflets stretched the truth even further, stating, "The president wants you to join the union."

The response was tremendous. By June 17, the day after Roosevelt signed the NIRA, 80 percent of Ohio miners had signed union cards. The miners "organized themselves for all practical purposes," UMW veteran John Brophy observed. UMW chief John L. Lewis, backed by the swelling membership and the close ties he had carefully developed with the Roosevelt administration, pressed mine operators to accept the union's proposed codes for the bituminous coal industry. A series of unauthorized wildcat strikes added to the pressure. In September 1933 the mine operators gave in, accepting a code that raised wages, reduced regional variations in pay, outlawed child labor, established an eight-hour day and a five-day week, banned the use of scrip for wage payments, and gave miners the right to select representatives who would ensure that they were properly paid for the weight of the coal they produced. Almost overnight, the UMW had reversed the balance of power in the coal industry.

This same process of rapid reunionization took place in the garment industry, where the Amalgamated Clothing Workers (ACW) and the International Ladies' Garment Workers' Union (ILGWU) rebuilt their memberships and won important concessions from employers immediately following passage of the NIRA. In the summer of 1933 the two unions launched a series of strikes designed to increase their influence in the code-writing process, to win back former members, and to sign up new ones. "The NRA protects your right to have a union and will punish the boss if he tries to stop you," read an ACW leaflet. "The president is behind you." Within months, the needle-trades unions had signed up more than two hundred thousand new members and had begun a drive to organize the industry's nonunion shops.

In other industries workers wanted to make their voices heard as well, but the NRA proved far less useful to them. Some frustrated workers began to call the NRA the "National Run Around." Section 7a had no enforcement mechanism, and the idea that "employees had the right to representatives of their own choosing" was subject to multiple interpretations. In August 1933 the Roosevelt administration set up a tripartite National Labor Board (NLB) to resolve labor conflicts. The board established an important precedent when it ruled that employers were obligated to hold secret-ballot elections to determine who would represent workers in negotiations. But many employers, especially in the steel and electrical products industries, set up company-dominated unions run by managers and foremen. Still others fired union advocates and used pro-employer codes to set wages and hours unilaterally. Employers frequently ignored the NRA and the Labor Board, especially when they confronted unions led by radicals, African Americans, or Mexican Americans.

The New Union Leaders

Under such difficult circumstances, it took courage and political commitment to offer union leadership. Pioneer unionists tended to be highly skilled, relatively well-paid workers, a sizable minority of whom had emigrated from the British Isles or Germany, where union traditions were strong. Women activists typically were less skilled and younger. Many came from union households, and they were often the children of Eastern or Southern European immigrants. Rose Pesotta, for example, had joined the International Ladies' Garment Workers' Union soon after emigrating from Russia in 1913. By the early 1930s she had become a leading organizer for that union, and in 1933 she helped organize women garment workers in Los Angeles. Among those joining the union during that campaign was a young Mexican immigrant, Anita Andrade Castro, who herself went on to become a lifelong union activist.

In an anti-union environment, skilled and experienced organizers were the most likely to succeed. The leading unionist at Cleveland's White Motor Company was Wyndham Mortimer, a lathe operator who had begun working in the Pennsylvania coal mines at age twelve. A lifelong communist, Mortimer knew that patience and thorough organization were essential to any lasting movement. With a group of fellow workers he unionized White Motor in 1934—and even won a wage increase. But Mortimer believed that without a national union of all autoworkers, his Cleveland local could not survive. He therefore spent an increasing proportion of his time in Michigan, where hundreds of thousands of autoworkers were still unorganized.

Clarence Irwin, the president of a new union at the Brier Hill works of the Youngstown Sheet and Tube Company, was typical of the new breed of union organizers. In 1934, Irwin was forty-two, but he had worked in the steel industry for twenty-eight years, had belonged to the American

Federation of Labor (AFL) for twenty-four years, and had been active in the 1919 steel strike, and was a skilled roller. He was married, had three children, and was a long-time Democrat. Most other leaders of the new steel locals, he noted, were also "middle-aged family men, well paid, and of Anglo-Saxon origin."

Joining these older skilled workers at the forefront of the new unions were many young workers who had been humbled by the Depression. Douglas Lincoln MacMahon, the son of a Brooklyn real estate broker, had lost his Wall Street job when the stock market crashed. After taking an unskilled maintenance job in the New York City subways, he had begun reading socialist literature in an attempt to understand what had happened to the nation's economy. Within a few years he had joined the Communist party and become a top officer of the Transit Workers Union. Similarly, James Carey, the first president of the United Electrical Workers, had attended college at night, hoping to become an electrical engineer. But during the Depression he was transferred from his laboratory job at Philco Radio in Philadelphia to factory work. Soon he was leading a union that successfully struck for recognition by the company.

Building the new industrial unions required more than a core of able and enthusiastic activists. The masses of workers, historically divided along ethnic, racial, gender, craft, and political lines, had to be won over. Several changes in American life since World War I facilitated this task. First, the working class had become more homogeneous. By the early 1930s, immigration had been slowed for nearly two decades; the proportion of foreign-born men and women in the workforce had declined, while the children of immigrants had become an increasingly significant presence. These second-generation workers generally spoke English. Second, the tensions that had long existed between skilled craftsmen and less skilled workers had been reduced by the rise of the assembly line and the emergence of giant mass-production factories. A new category of worker, the semiskilled machine operator, played a particularly important role in the rise of the new unions. And finally, the Depression (and the difficulty of finding employment) made workers more reluctant than in the past to simply quit their jobs when they were dissatisfied with conditions. Increasingly, they saw the solution not in looking for a better job but in improving the one they had.

A Wave of Strikes

By the middle of 1934, the industrial union movement was spreading rapidly. New unions were popping up across the country, and strikes were becoming more frequent. Whole communities were mobilized in support of these strikes, even in the face of violent resistance from local political elites and well-armed vigilante groups. While officials of the AFL usually stood on the sidelines, political radicals proved willing and able to assume the leadership of these labor conflicts. Three almost simultaneous strikes—in Toledo, Minneapolis, and San Francisco—signaled how far things had come and how far they might go as a wave of labor militancy swept the country.

Street Warfare. A Minneapolis truckers' strike turned violent in May 1934 when an alliance of businessmen, backed by the police and city officials, sought to break union picket lines and run scab trucks. But, led by a militant, democratically elected set of officers, the Minneapolis Teamsters local sparked a general strike and organized hundreds of workers into para-military groups that fought police. By the end of the 1930s, the Teamsters were one of the fastest growing unions in the United States.

Source: UPI/Bettmann.

In Toledo, a major center for automobile parts manufacturing, workers joined in the first rush of enthusiasm for unionism in 1933. That summer they organized an independent local union with a direct charter from the AFL. The next February, four thousand Toledo autoworkers struck and won a modest wage hike and an agreement to negotiate other issues. But when one large company, Electric Auto-Lite, spurned negotiations, the walkout resumed. This time the employers hired scabs (strikebreakers) and kept their plants open.

As the strike faltered, a local group of unemployed workers, affiliated with the socialist American Workers party, joined the struggle, throwing up mass picket lines in defiance of a court injunction. On May 23, 1934, the local sheriff and his special deputies arrested several picket leaders, and the "Battle of Toledo" erupted. For seven hours a crowd of ten thousand blockaded the Auto-Lite factory, preventing the scabs inside from leaving. Deputies used tear gas, water hoses, and occasional gunfire to clear the crowd, which responded by stoning the plant and burning cars in its parking lot. The next day the National Guard arrived. They killed two protesters but failed to break the strike. Strikers won recognition of their union, a higher minimum wage, and a 5 percent pay hike.

An even more dramatic confrontation unfolded in Minneapolis. Local 574 of the International Brotherhood of Teamsters—several of whose leaders were followers of the dissident, exiled Russian communist leader Leon Trotsky—had successfully organized the city's truck drivers and warehousemen during the spring of 1934. On May 15, after their employers had all but ignored the local's demands, five thousand truck drivers and warehousemen walked off their jobs, with the support of thousands of the city's unemployed.

The union set up a huge strike headquarters (staffed largely by the daughters, wives, and sisters of the strikers) equipped with sleeping, meeting, and eating facilities, a makeshift hospital, and a center for dispatching "cruising picket squads." On May 19 the Citizens' Alliance (a secretive businessmen's group) and the Minneapolis police lured a group of pickets into an alley and beat them with nightsticks and leather saps. Over several days, strikers armed with clubs, pipes, and bats engaged police and deputies recruited by the Alliance in street fighting, and even in a full-scale battle at the city's central market in which two Alliance supporters, including a prominent Minneapolis businessman, were killed.

A compromise settlement lasted only two months. When the strike flared up again in July, the workers took the heaviest casualties: Police gunfire killed two and wounded dozens of others. The National Guard was called out and, as federal pressure for a settlement increased, the

"Labor Was in Control"

The following description of the San Francisco general strike was written by rank-and-file journalist Mike Quin.

The paralysis was effective beyond all expectations. To all intents and purposes industry was at a complete standstill. The great factories were empty and deserted. No streetcars were running. Virtually all stores were closed. The giant apparatus of commerce was a lifeless, helpless hulk.

Labor had withdrawn its hand. The workers had drained out of the shops and plants like life-blood, leaving only a silent framework embodying millions of dollars worth of invested capital. In the absence of labor, the great machinery loomed as so much idle junk. . . .

Everything was there, all intact as the workers had left it—instruments, equipment, tools, machinery, raw materials and the buildings themselves. When the men walked out, they took only what belonged to them—their labor. And when they took that they might as well have taken everything, because all the elaborate apparatus they left behind was worthless and meaningless without their hand. The machinery was a mere extension of labor, created by and dependent upon labor.

Labor held the life-blood and energy. The owners remained in possession of the corpse.

Highways leading into the city bristled with picket lines. Nothing moved except by permission of the strike committee. Labor was in control.

Source: Mike Quin, *The Big Strike* (1949).

employers finally surrendered and signed a contract favorable to the union.

In Toledo and Minneapolis, unionists had talked about escalating their struggles into general strikes. In San Francisco such a mass walkout actually occurred as an outgrowth of a fierce clash on the city's waterfront. In the early 1930s a new West Coast local of the International Longshoremen's Association (ILA), led by Harry Bridges, an Australian-born longshoreman who worked closely with the Communist party, rapidly signed many new members. From the start, Bridges and his colleagues had to do battle not only with employers but also with the corrupt, conservative national leaders of the East Coast–based ILA, who had negotiated secret deals with the big waterfront companies.

Defying the national ILA leadership, the San Francisco longshoremen went on strike on May 9, 1934, for a shorter workweek, higher pay, union recognition, and union-run hiring halls. They were soon joined by dockworkers in West Coast ports from Seattle to San Diego. Sailors and waterfront truckers also stopped work. Forty thousand maritime workers walked out in the largest maritime strike ever. For nearly two months, the strike lingered. Then local employers and politicians decided to retake the waterfront by force. On "Bloody Thursday," July 5, police killed a striker and a strike supporter and injured scores more.

Outraged workers called for a general strike. Local union officials reluctantly went along. By July 16, San Francisco was at a virtual standstill, as 130,000 workers—including trolley drivers, construction workers, teamsters, bartenders, and even entertainers—walked off their jobs. Strikers also shut down Oakland, Berkeley, and other nearby California cities. For several days nothing—not even food—moved into or out of San Francisco and other Bay Area cities without the approval of the strike committee.

The general strike was short-lived. Local businessmen, newspapers, and government officials maneuvered furiously to split the ranks of labor, denouncing

Popeye Versus the Goon. During 1933 and 1934, readers of E. C. Segar's comic strip were introduced to the Goons, powerful, mindless servants of the sailor's nemesis, the horrible Sea Hag. The name was soon applied to violent strikebreakers who patrolled the San Francisco waterfront.

Source: Elzie Crisler Segar, "Thimble Theatre," 1934—Reprinted with special permission of King Features Syndicate.

the longshoremen as dangerous radicals while egging on vigilante groups that destroyed the offices of the Communist party and several allied organizations. The strike committee finally called off the general strike on July 19, 1934. With their backing gone, the striking waterfront unions accepted arbitration. In October an arbitration decision granted the longshoremen union recognition, hiring halls controlled by the union, a thirty-hour workweek, and a pay increase.

The Toledo, Minneapolis, and San Francisco strikes had certain common features. In each case, radicals defied conservative AFL leaders and mobilized thousands of working people in concerted, militant action. Workers developed innovative tactics and countered force with force. And when employers and police launched attacks, thousands of other workers came to the strikers' aid. The strikes ended in compromise, but each laid the groundwork for future gains. Toledo unionists played a major role in the creation of the United Automobile Workers' Union. The leaders of the Minneapolis strikes went on to organize long-distance truckers throughout the Midwest, contributing to the phenomenal growth of the International Brotherhood of the Teamsters. And the San Francisco strike led to the formation of the International Longshoremen and Warehousemen's Union and to the growth of maritime unionism up and down the Pacific Coast.

In spite of these dramatic union victories, 1934 also witnessed failures, including unsuccessful efforts to organize unions in the fruit and vegetable fields of California and in the textile mills throughout the Piedmont region of the Carolinas. In California, commercial agriculture depended on a multiethnic workforce. Three of every four of the state's two hundred thousand farm laborers were Mexican Americans, but workers of Filipino, Armenian, Chinese, and Japanese descent, as well as "Okie" migrants from middle America, also sweated in the cotton fields and fruit orchards. The Mexican-American workers had been influenced by the radical political ideas that took hold in their homeland following the 1911 revolution. But these workers, many of whom had been born in the United States, were also inspired by the promise of the New Deal and by the presence of Communist party organizers in their midst.

Nearly fifty thousand workers, the vast majority of them Mexican Americans, undertook more than forty strikes between April and December 1933, against growers of almost all the major crops in the state. In June, fifteen hundred berry pickers employed by Japanese ranchers in El Monte, a suburb of Los Angeles, struck for higher wages. The berry strikers were soon joined by five thousand celery-field workers (including a sizable number of Japanese Americans and Filipino Americans) in Santa

Monica and Culver City, small towns near Los Angeles. In October twelve thousand workers left the cotton fields of the San Joaquin Valley, north of Los Angeles. During these strikes whole communities organized for a long and bitter struggle. In the town of Corcoran in Kings County, the strikers erected a tent city for three thousand people. In 1934 these agricultural strikes, often led by young communists from the Cannery and Agricultural Workers Industrial Union, spread across the state, from the Imperial Valley on the Mexican border to the Santa Clara Valley near San Francisco.

Almost all these work stoppages ended in violence and defeat. NRA and state officials urged growers to raise wages but gave the workers no help in establishing a permanent union or fending off anti-union lawmen. (Section 7a had excluded agricultural workers from federal labor protection.) A San Francisco rabbi who observed the activities of armed Anglo vigilante groups during a 1933 strike wrote to the governor, "Gangsterism has been substituted for law and order in the cotton area." The next year, police tear-gassed union meetings in the Imperial Valley, forcibly evicted more than two thousand families, and burned workers' homes. Many strike leaders were arrested, tried, and jailed under California's draconian criminal syndicalism act, which made it a crime to belong to a group that sought a change in industrial ownership by force. An entire generation would pass before another drive succeeded in improving the lot of California agricultural workers.

The East Coast also had its share of strikes, including the biggest strike of 1934. In September of that year, 376,000 textile workers along the East Coast walked off their jobs. The Depression had devastated the textile industry, shortening workweeks and lowering wages to the point that malnutrition and disease were common in textile workers' families. Many children under age fourteen worked in the mills, and thousands of families had to live in decaying company housing. But the loudest complaint of the mill workers was of "stretch-outs," the

Cotton Strike, October 1933. Strikers demanded that local police take action after cotton growers in Pixley and Arvin, California, opened fire on unarmed Mexican pickers, killing three people. Instead, authorities issued additional gun permits to growers and appointed many as deputies. Eventually, several growers in the Pixley incident were prosecuted for murder (and later acquitted by a friendly jury), while a strike leader was charged with criminal syndicalism.

Source: The Bancroft Library, University of California, Berkeley.

assignment of more and more looms to each worker until the pace of work became unbearable.

Textile executives wrote and administered the NRA textile code. Consequently the shorter hours and higher wages put into effect during the summer of 1933 came at a high price — vicious stretch-outs that most workers found intolerable. "Please do something," wrote thirteen mill workers to a federal official. "There is many here that will give you a glad welcome and tell you of the Dirty Deal this eight hour law has given us." As it had for other workers, Section 7a proved a hollow promise for textile workers. Soon after its passage, they flocked to the United Textile Workers' Union (UTW), which grew dramatically from fifty thousand members in 1933 to three hundred thousand in mid-1934. Then mill owners fired some four thousand union members while NRA officials looked the other way.

The 1934 textile strike was a massive protest by the mill hands against the brutality of the mill owners and the betrayal by New Deal officials. Stretching from Maine to Alabama, the work stoppage crippled production in every major textile center. Southern mill workers organized "flying squadrons" of automobiles that spread the strike up and down the Piedmont. But mill owners, who saw the walkout as an opportunity to crush unionism once and for all, hired spies and thugs and convinced local authorities to evict strikers from company housing and throw them off relief rolls. In state after state, governors called out the National Guard to intimidate workers and defend the mills. Violent incidents were common, and the number of strikers killed escalated rapidly.

To help settle the strike, President Roosevelt appointed a board of inquiry. The UTW, whose leadership was based in the North, used the federal initiative as an excuse to end the strike in its third week, much to the surprise and anger of tens of thousands of southern mill workers. Some fifteen thousand strikers were not rehired, and many staunch unionists were permanently blacklisted. Those who did return were required to "humble down," acting apologetic and meek to supervisors before they could resume work. In the South, textile unionism collapsed, and with it the prospect that New Deal liberalism might secure a firm foothold in the region. Textile workers continued to live in misery, and southern labor remained without a voice even in the years after 1937, when industrial unionism swept across the North and West.

Organized labor's major victories and defeats during 1934 contributed to a heightened awareness among FDR and his advisers that changes in the New Deal's labor policies were necessary if militancy and employer intransigence were to be contained and controlled.

The Collapse of the First New Deal

By 1934, there was a growing sense among working-class and middle-class Americans that the New Deal had failed to confront the economic crisis successfully. In 1933 and 1934, national income had risen by one-quarter, unemployment had dropped by two million, and total factory wages had leapt upward. But the nation's annual output was still only slightly more than half of what it had been in 1929. Ten million workers were without jobs, and almost twice that many people were at least partially dependent on relief. The recovery had stalled, and Secretary of the Treasury Henry Morgenthau, Jr., frankly admitted that "we are not making any headway." With the economy stagnating, criticism of the Roosevelt administration grew. Many businessmen feared growing government intervention in the economy. Labor leaders were disappointed by the administration's half-hearted support. And a series of mass movements demanded radical action to end the Depression and redistribute the nation's wealth.

The NRA came under particularly fierce attack; the process of writing and enforcing industry codes had brought to the surface sharp conflicts among competing interests. Many farmers, small businessmen, and consumer groups argued that NRA price and production controls had been written primarily by and for large corporations; their effect was to prop up prices, stifle competition, and retard economic expansion. Even corporate leaders had begun to doubt the value of the NRA. Section 7a, weak as it was, had added to their labor problems. They also feared that the growing debate over corporate influence on the recovery agency might lead to revised regulations that would limit their freedom to act.

Business criticism of the NRA spilled over into general criticism of the New Deal. Most businessmen opposed the government's deficit spending, fearing it would undermine the economy and lead to higher taxes. They also worried about the effects of government relief efforts. "Five Negroes on my place in South Carolina refused to work this spring," complained retired DuPont vice president R. R. M. Carpenter to his friend John J. Raskob, a DuPont executive and adviser to Al Smith. "A cook on my houseboat at Fort Myers," he continued, "quit because the government was paying him a dollar an hour as a painter."

As time went on, more and more business leaders blamed the economy's ills on government functionaries, labor leaders, and individual "chiselers." Government power and budgets, they insisted, should be reduced drastically, while business should be given a greater voice in setting national policy. To promote this view, Raskob, Pierre DuPont, and General Motors chairman Alfred P. Sloan resigned from Roosevelt's Business Advisory Council in 1934 to found the American Liberty League, which soon came to represent the most reactionary wing of the business com-

"The Square Deal." Most nationally syndicated comic strips avoided politics, but a conservative political agenda consistently shaped the characters and stories in the popular "Little Orphan Annie." Debuting in 1924, the comic strip reached the height of its popularity in the 1930s even though the adventures of its spunky orphan hero conveyed a faith in self-reliance that was at odds with the cooperative spirit of the New Deal. But it was Annie's benefactor, the industrialist Oliver "Daddy" Warbucks, who epitomized cartoonist Harold Gray's beliefs: a self-made, inventive, and generous millionaire who invariably arrived in the nick of time to save the day.

Source: Harold Gray, *New York Daily News,* July 11, 1935—

munity. Well financed and influential, the League campaigned in the courts, the newspapers, and the political arena against the New Deal and its labor-liberal supporters. In California, meanwhile, opponents of Roosevelt and the labor movement organized under the leadership of the Associated Farmers, a powerful statewide organization that provided money, manpower, and influence to all those opposed to unions, social reform, and civil liberties in the Golden State.

Class divisions were also polarizing American politics. Just as businessmen were beginning to criticize the government for doing too much, the tremendous popularity of the New Deal became evident in the 1934 congressional elections. In the Senate, the Democrats won nine new seats, a gain that gave them well over a two-thirds majority. In the House, the Republicans were left with less than a quarter of the votes, the lowest portion since the party had been founded. Most of the newly elected Democratic senators and representatives were strong backers of the New Deal; if anything, they sought more radical measures. Indeed, a variety of mass movements were gathering strength by attacking the government for doing too little.

Populist Critics of the New Deal

The New Deal was soon under attack from all sides. Its most prominent southern critic was the Louisiana senator Huey Long, who rose to power by attacking corporate interests and portraying himself as a champion of the common man. Elected governor in 1928, he completely dominated Louisiana's government. Under Long, Louisiana built hundreds of schools, hospitals, and bridges; paved thousands of miles of roads; distributed free textbooks; and increased taxes on oil and gas interests.

Inauguration. This illustration of Huey Long taking the presidential oath of office appeared in his *My First Days in the White House.* In his fantasy presidency, Long instituted a range of social and fiscal reforms, aided by a National Share Our Wealth Committee, composed of cooperative bankers and industrialists. Long also fantasized about assembling a distinguished cabinet—including Franklin Delano Roosevelt as Secretary of the Navy. The book was published in 1935, shortly after Long's assassination.

Source: Cleanthe, Huey P. Long, *My First Days in the White House* (1935)—American Social History Project.

Long supported Roosevelt in 1932, when he himself won election to the Senate, but he soon broke with the president. He criticized the New Deal both for creating huge bureaucracies that interfered in local affairs and for failing to curb the power of the rich. In 1934 Long proposed the "Share Our Wealth Plan," a system of confiscatory taxes on large fortunes and incomes that would enable the government to provide every family with "enough for a home, an automobile, a radio, and the ordinary conveniences," plus a guaranteed annual income. By setting up thousands of Share Our Wealth Clubs, Long developed a large national following.

Other critics of the New Deal took their cues from Charles E. Coughlin, a Catholic priest from the suburbs of Detroit whose weekly radio broadcasts reached an audience of thirty to forty-five million listeners. Like Long, Coughlin at first supported Roosevelt but quickly grew disillusioned. A vehement anticommunist, Coughlin nevertheless blamed the Depression on "Wall Street" and "international bankers." Inflationary monetary policy, he believed, would spark a recovery. More broadly, Coughlin promoted "social Catholicism"—a call for class harmony, "living wages," and social legislation to combat the evils of industrialism. Increasingly influenced by European fascism and anti-Semitism, Coughlin was soon calling for government control over production, profits, working conditions, and unions.

On the West Coast, Francis Townsend, an elderly doctor from Long Beach, California, proposed that every citizen over sixty who was not working should receive $200 a month from the government "on the condition that they spend the money as they get it." These pensions, to be financed by a national sales tax, would pump money back into the economy and, by encouraging retirements, would open up jobs for the young. At least ten million people signed petitions in support of Townsend's plan, and two million Americans, most of them elderly, joined seven thousand Townsend clubs.

Townsend, Coughlin, and Long capitalized on popular discontent with the Depression and the unequal distribution of wealth and power. But in spite of their attacks on the rich, they all firmly rejected collective ownership of the means of production, the basic tenet of socialism. Instead, they combined nostalgia for an older, community-based way of life with simple plans they claimed would solve all social ills. The possibility that the Long, Coughlin, and Townsend movements might join forces and enter national politics in 1936 deeply worried Roosevelt and his advisers.

Administration leaders were also concerned about the impressive electoral achievements of left-liberal alliances in several states. In California, the novelist Upton Sinclair resigned from the Socialist party in 1933 to form the End-Poverty-in-California (EPIC) movement within the Democratic party. Sinclair called for "Production for Use and Not for Profit," proposing that the state turn idle farmland and factories into self-sustaining cooperatives of the unemployed and impose higher taxes on corporations and the rich than on others. Sinclair shocked the Democratic establishment by winning the party's nomination for governor of California in the 1934 primary. Many New Deal Democrats, including FDR, refused to back him in the general election. Attacked as a communist and a crackpot, Sinclair lost the governorship but received well over a third of the votes, helping twenty-three EPIC-backed candidates to win election to the state legislature.

In the state of Washington, EPIC sympathizers helped to elect a U.S. senator and to form the Washington Commonwealth Federation, which became a powerful force in that state's politics. In Minnesota, the labor-backed, left-wing Farmer-Labor party took control of the state's governorship for most of the 1930s. Behind the scenes, the Communist party—which in 1935 adopted a "popular front" strategy of building broad alliances with liberals and moderates—gained considerable influence in both organizations. Meanwhile, in Wisconsin, Senator Robert M. La Follette, Jr., and his brother Phil, a former governor, left the Republican party to revive the old Progressive party. The possibility that a national, left-leaning third party might form in time for the 1936 presidential election seemed plausible.

By the spring of 1935, then, the New Deal was in a state of disarray and its main industrial recovery agency, the NRA, was falling apart. The final blow came on May 27, when in *Schecter v. United States* the Supreme Court declared the NIRA unconstitutional. The case involved NRA code violations by a New York slaughterhouse that had been convicted of selling diseased chickens. The Court ruled that Congress, in allowing the NRA to write legally enforceable codes, had unlawfully delegated its own authority, and by applying the codes to local concerns, like the Schecter brothers' slaughterhouse, had unconstitutionally extended the federal power to regulate interstate commerce. This decision was correctly seen as an indication that the Court would strike down much of the legislation of the first New Deal. Roosevelt, whose first year in office had raised so many hopes, now faced an uncertain future. The structures of government, politics, and labor relations had proved inadequate, as they had during the Gilded Age, for dealing with profound economic and social crisis. By the middle of the decade, most Americans agreed that basic economic and political changes were necessary. But the questions remained: What sort of changes, and in whose interest?

The Years in Review

1929

- Herbert Hoover is sworn in as president in March, after having decisively defeated Democrat Al Smith in the fall election.
- A U.S. entrepreneur acquires the rights to an ancient Filipino weapon and introduces it to Americans as the yo-yo.
- The stock market crashes on Black Thursday, October 24.

1930

- Communists rally thousands on International Unemployment Day (March 6) to demand government action in the face of mounting joblessness.
- The protectionist Smoot-Hawley Tariff Act sharply raises tariffs on imported goods to the highest levels in U.S. history.
- An international Naval Conference takes place in London in an attempt to take steps toward disarmament.

- Dick and Maurice (Mac) McDonald flee economically depressed New Hampshire and move to California; ten years later they found a drive-in hamburger stand, serving the first of what will be billions of hamburgers.
- The Wonder Bread Company introduces sliced bread.
- Mickey Mouse, who had first become a film star in 1928 in *Steamboat Willie,* makes his first appearance as a comic strip character.

1931

- Nine African-American youths are falsely accused of rape in the Scottsboro case, which will attract international attention.
- Japanese troops occupy the Chinese province of Manchuria.
- Austria's largest bank collapses as economic crisis spreads across Europe.
- Seattle's unemployed create the Unemployed Citizens' League, one of many self-help organizations of the jobless.
- The "Star Spangled Banner" becomes the U.S. official national anthem, despite protests that it is "unsingable."

1932

- Twenty thousand World War I veterans stage a Bonus March to the capitol, demanding that their war bonuses be distributed immediately; U.S. troops led by General Douglas MacArthur use force to disperse the protesters.
- More than three thousand protesters march on the main Ford plant in Dearborn, Michigan, demanding jobs for the unemployed; four marchers are killed and many more are wounded.
- Hoover establishes the Reconstruction Finance Corporation, which proves an inadequate response to the Depression.
- Franklin Delano Roosevelt is elected president, promising a "New Deal."

1933

- Nazi leader Adolf Hitler is appointed chancellor of Germany.
- Unemployment peaks at 15 million; the U.S. gross national product has fallen 29 percent since 1929.
- The Twenty-First Amendment nullifies Prohibition.
- In his first one-hundred days, President Roosevelt declares a bank holiday and establishes the Federal Emergency Relief Administration (FERA), Civilian Conservation Corps (CCC), Agricultural Adjustment Administration (AAA), and National Recovery Administration (NRA).
- The Roosevelt administration announces a Good Neighbor policy toward Latin America.
- Section 7a of the National Industrial Recovery Act (NIRA), which (on paper) gives workers right to organize, sparks nationwide upsurge of labor activism.
- The first National Professional Football League Championship game takes place, and Chicago defeats New York 23 to 21.

- Civil Works Administration puts four million people to work.
- The United States recognizes the Union of Soviet Socialist Republics.

1934

- Democrats sweep the fall elections and gain overwhelming dominance in Congress—a sign of the popularity of the New Deal.
- A "New Deal for Indians," centered around the Indian Reorganization Act, alters the relationship between the federal government and Native Americans.
- Black and white Arkansas sharecroppers organize the Southern Tenant Farmers' Union (STFU) to stop evictions of tenants and croppers.
- Huey Long proposes the "Share Our Wealth Plan," a system that taxes large fortunes and incomes and redistributes the money to poor Americans.
- A wave of militant strikes sweeps the nation, with particularly dramatic confrontations in Toledo, Minneapolis, and San Francisco; strikes in East Coast textile mills and California farm fields have little success.
- Drought hits the Great Plains; terrifying dust storms create the Dust Bowl in Kansas, Oklahoma, Colorado, New Mexico, and Texas.
- U.S. Marines leave Haiti, where they have been stationed since 1915.
- Father Charles Coughlin grows in popularity as a radio preacher and critic of the New Deal.
- Novelist Upton Sinclair wins one-third of the votes in his run for governor of California as the leader of the radical EPIC—End Poverty in California—movement.

1935

- The U.S. Supreme Court declares the NIRA unconstitutional, setting off warnings that much of the New Deal legislation will be declared unconstitutional.

Suggested Readings

Badger, Anthony, *The New Deal: The Depression Years, 1933–1940* (1989).

Balderrama, Francisco E., and Raymond Rodriguez, *Decade of Betrayal: Mexican Repatriation in the 1930s* (1995).

Bellush, Bernard, *The Failure of NRA* (1975).

Bernstein, Irving, *The Lean Years* (1960).

Bernstein, Michael, *The Great Depression: Delayed Recovery and Economic Change in America, 1929–1939* (1987).

Brinkley, Alan, *Voices of Protest: Huey Long, Father Coughlin, and the Great Depression* (1982).

Burns, James MacGregor, *Roosevelt: The Lion and the Fox* (1956).

Cohen, Elizabeth, *Making a New Deal: Industrial Workers in Chicago, 1919–1939* (1990).

Cohen, Robert, *When the Old Left Was Young, 1929–1941* (1993).

Crease, Walter, *TVA's Public Planning: The Vision, the Reality* (1990).

Dubofsky, Melvyn, *The State and Labor in Modern America* (1994).

Fraser, Steve, *Labor Will Rule: Sidney Hillman and the Rise of American Labor* (1991).

Galbraith, John Kenneth, *The Great Crash, 1929* (1954).

Gerstle, Gary, *Working-Class Americanism: The Politics of Labor in a Textile City, 1914–1960* (1989).

Goodman, James, *Stories of Scottsboro* (1994).

Gordon, Colin, *New Deals: Business, Labor, and Politics in America, 1920–1935* (1994).

Gordon, Linda, *Pitied But Not Entitled: Single Mothers and the History of Welfare* (1994).

Gregory, James, *American Exodus: The Dust Bowl Migration and Okie Culture in California* (1989).

Grubbs, Donald, *Cry from the Cotton: The Southern Tenant Farmers' Union and the New Deal* (1971).

Hall, Jacquelyn Dowd, et al., *Like a Family: The Making of a Southern Cotton Mill World* (1987).

Hawley, Ellis W., *The New Deal and the Problem of Monopoly* (1966).

Howe, Irving, and Louis Coser, *The American Communist Party: A Critical History* (1957).

Iriye, Akira, *The Globalizing of America, 1914–1945* (1993).

Kazin, Michael, *The Populist Persuasion: An American History* (1995).

Kindleberger, Charles, *The World in Depression* (rev. ed., 1986).

McElvaine, Robert S., *The Great Depression* (1984).

Mitchell, Greg, *The Campaign of the Century: Upton Sinclair's EPIC Race for Governor of California and the Birth of Media Politics* (1992).

Ribuffo, Leo, *The Old Christian Right* (1983).

Scharf, Lois, *Eleanor Roosevelt: First Lady of American Liberalism* (1987).

Schlesinger, Arthur, *The Age of Roosevelt: Crisis of the Old Order* (1957).

Schwartz, Jordan A., *The New Dealers* (1993).

Simon, Bryant, *A Fabric of Defeat: The Politics of South Carolina Millhands, 1910–1948* (1998).

Sitkoff, Harvard, *A New Deal for Blacks* (1978).

Terkel, Studs, *Hard Times: An Oral History of the Great Depression* (1970).

Watkins, T. H., *The Great Depression: America in the 1930s* (1993).

Wilson, Joan Hoff, *Herbert Hoover: Forgotten Progressive* (1985).

Worster, Donald, *Dust Bowl: The Southern Plains in the 1930s* (1979).

And on the World Wide Web

- Library of Congress, *California Gold: Northern California Folk Music from the Thirties* (http://memory.loc.gov/ammem/afccchtml/cowhome.html)
- Franklin and Eleanor Roosevelt Institute, *The New Deal Network* (http://newdeal.feri.org/)

chapter 9

Labor Democratizes America
1935–1939

In the second half of the 1930s, America's working people—organized into new industrial unions and allied with President Franklin D. Roosevelt's New Deal coalition—moved the nation toward a more democratic political and economic order. The political roots of that transformation could be seen in the 1934 fall elections. Many of the members of Congress elected in that Democratic sweep stood well to the left of Roosevelt, in favor of an "industrial democracy" that would curb business power, enhance labor's voice, and increase government social spending. "Boys—this is our hour," exulted Harry Hopkins, FDR's top relief official. "We've got to get everything we want . . . now or never." Much of the new legislation Hopkins and his liberal allies sought was passed by Congress between January and August 1935, the period known as the Second New Deal.

But the greater challenge to the status quo came not from the Capitol's well-polished corridors, but from America's working people, who had launched a surge of popular protest with the 1934 strike wave. Two years later, they gave Roosevelt's Second New Deal a powerful vote of ratification. In November 1936 the president won reelection by a massive landslide, and working-class support became the foundation for a generation-long dominance of a New Deal political coalition in American life. Just a few months later, a great wave of strikes rolled through the heartland, establishing the centrality of labor in that new order.

By the end of the 1930s, however, a resurgent conservatism stymied further progress. Moreover, the progress that had been made fell short of the aspirations of the more radical participants in the New Deal and industrial union coalitions. Still, the adoption of progressive legislation and the transformation of workplace relations made the United States a very different—and more democratic—place.

Just Before the Tear Gas. On September 16, 1936, at the height of the Salinas Valley, California, lettuce strike, members of the Fruit and Vegetable Workers' Union blocked a downtown Salinas street. Their intent was to stop a convoy of trucks carrying produce harvested by strikebreakers. California State Police attacked the strikers shortly after this photo was taken.

Source: Harold Ellwood, *San Francisco Examiner,* September 17, 1936—California Section, California State Library.

An Expanded Jobs Program

Although production had risen by almost 30 percent since early 1933, unemployment remained high in 1935. New Dealers blamed "underconsumption"—a chronic weakness in consumer demand caused by low wages, an inequitable distribution of income, and a capitalist system that was no longer growing. Big business and the rich, they insisted, would have to give up some of their wealth and power. They pushed for measures that would break up the giant utility holding companies, raise taxes, and limit the power of banks. Business and commercial interests battled furiously against these measures—they called Roosevelt's tax plan a "soak the rich" scheme—and in the end New Dealers had to settle for laws that were less sweeping than most wanted. But the conflict made it clear that the nation's politics had tilted to the Left.

New Dealers tackled the unemployment issue directly, with a series of programs more permanent and substantive than the ones the Civil Works Administration had thrown together so hurriedly two years before. In the spring of 1935, Congress passed a $5 billion Emergency Relief Appropriations Act that funded new agencies designed to provide useful and creative employment to millions. One—the National Youth Administration—initiated work projects for more than 4.5 million students and young workers; another—the Resettlement Administration—aided the rural homeless, agricultural tenants, and owners of small farms. But Harry Hopkins's Works Progress (later Projects) Administration (WPA) was the most important of these new programs. Unlike the Civil Works Administration, the WPA provided productive jobs: WPA workers built or improved more than 2,500 hospitals, 5,900 schools, 1,000 airport landing fields, and nearly 13,000 playgrounds. Because they were exchanging labor for wages and earning nearly double the weekly sums received by clients of earlier emergency relief programs, WPA employees saw themselves as workers and citizens, not as welfare cases. They organized unions, demanded higher pay, and lobbied for the continuation of the program when Congress began to cut it back at the end of the 1930s. Roosevelt had insisted that WPA wages be pegged at a level below those in the private sector; even so, the huge jobs program fulfilled a demand that spokesmen for the unemployed had been making for nearly a century. By the time of its demise in 1943, the agency had provided employment for eight million Americans. The WPA had its greatest impact in the hard-hit industrial centers of the Northeast and Midwest, but it also

Federal Spending in Depression and War. Although the New Deal doubled federal spending, budget deficits remained modest throughout the 1930s. A vast expansion in military spending during World War II pushed federal expenditures upward tenfold and generated massive budget deficits. During the war years, the federal debt jumped fivefold to $260 billion.

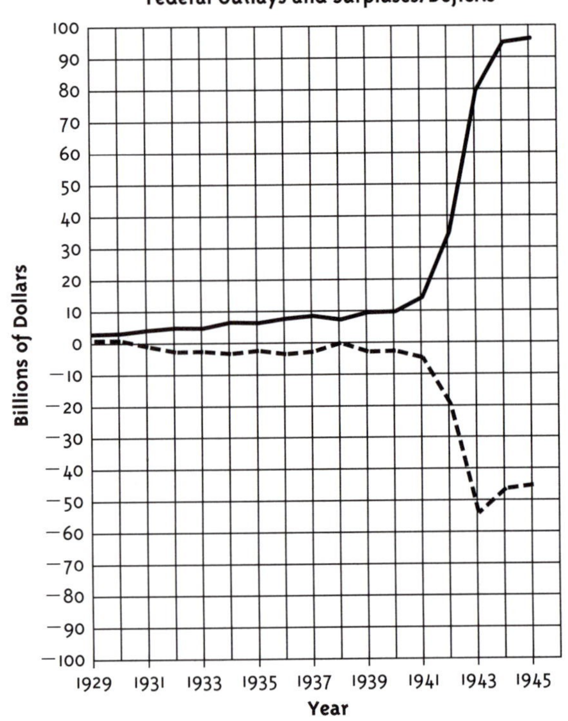

provided jobs in rural areas of the South and West. In just three years, WPA workers in Wyoming (a state with only two towns having more than ten thousand residents) built or improved 375 bridges and 341 public buildings and also constructed thousands of miles of roads and dozens of parks and playing fields.

A program that began as part of the WPA but that quickly became an independent agency had an enormous impact on American families. The Rural Electrification Administration quadrupled the number of farms with electricity between 1930 and 1945, largely as a result of its support for rural cooperatives. This "power revolution" transformed the lives of rural Americans by bringing them into the social and cultural mainstream.

The Social Security Act

During the first half of the twentieth century many industrialized Western nations, most notably Great Britain, Germany, and the Scandinavian democracies, built "welfare states" that offered their working populations protection against the hazards of a market economy: unemployment, sickness, old-age insecurity, and the loss of the family breadwinner. American reformers had failed to establish a similar system of universal social insurance during the Progressive era. Veterans of that period, such as Secretary of Labor Frances Perkins, viewed the Second New Deal as an opportunity to compensate for that failure. A women's network of New Dealers and social reformers (including First Lady Eleanor Roosevelt) joined forces to enact laws that would protect women as well as male workers from destitution.

The president himself called for legislation that would provide cradle-to-grave security "against the hazards and vicissitudes of life." In the late twentieth century, Social Security became synonymous with old-age insurance, but the Social Security Act passed by Congress in 1935 embodied a far larger conception of the government's role. In providing social protection to all citizens (including not just help for the elderly, but also unemployment insurance and aid for poor families), the law represented a fundamental break with traditional elitist notions that the poor and the unemployed were to blame for their condition.

The law contained two types of support for the elderly. Those who were destitute in 1935 could receive relatively small amounts of immediate aid from the federal government: $15 a month in the mid-1930s. But in a longer timeframe, many working Americans—especially those employed by large corporations—anticipating retirement within a few years could look forward to a federal pension financed by a payroll tax split evenly between themselves and their employers. Under the new system, an individual's pension check would vary according to marital status and past earnings, but not according to state of residence or type of employment. This old-age insurance system accommodated two groups of Americans. On the one side were the clamorous demands of Dr. Francis Townsend's popular old-age movement, which advocated a monthly $200 pension for everyone over age sixty. On the other side were those representing the interests of employers, who sought to limit costly pension expenditures and to standardize benefits across states, regions, and industries.

The Social Security Act also established a cooperative federal-state program of unemployment insurance, which also had its roots in the reform initiatives of the Progressive era. The program was meant to counteract the financial insecurity workers experienced during the temporary layoffs that plagued the auto, textile, clothing, and construction industries. It, too, was financed by a special tax, but unlike the pension program, the unemployment insurance program was administered by the states. Consequently eligibility requirements varied widely from state to state, as did benefits: payments were high in the North and low in the South.

Still, the old-age insurance and unemployment programs won nearly universal support. Most Americans saw these entitlements not as relief for the poor but as insurance purchased with taxes deducted from their paychecks. Both programs were redistributive—they transferred income from the rich to the poor—but their advocates, including Roosevelt, who abhorred "the dole," downplayed this fact. The president saw the Social Security tax largely as a political rather than a fiscal issue. He told his advisers, "We put those payroll contributions there so as to give the contributors a legal, moral, and political right to collect their pensions and their unemployment benefits. With those taxes in there, no damn politician can ever scrap my social security program."

But if the New Deal effort to legitimize social insurance proved enormously successful for workers and recent retirees, the moral and social biases attached to welfare would become increasingly debilitating for those who were unable to work. Thus the Social Security Act's provisions for the elderly poor and for dependent children in single-parent families were far less generous and equitable, and far more demeaning, than were the provisions for those who had "earned" their benefits. For example, the Social Security Act provided matching funds to the states to finance an Aid to Dependent Children program, but these benefits were not treated as an automatic entitlement as were monthly unemployment benefits. A woman with dependent children received financial support only if it was granted by a social worker or other state official based on the family's degree of need, her adherence to a code of acceptable sexual conduct, and the stability of the home life she provided. In the 1930s, when most eligible women were white and widowed, welfare aid of this sort generated little controversy. But when an increasingly large number of deserving children began to come from families in which the mother was neither white nor widowed, mainstream Americans developed a negative opinion about what came to be disparagingly called "welfare."

The Social Security Act was also racially coded—in part because of the power of southern Democrats in the New Deal coalition. Southern politicians, reported one architect of the new law, were determined to block any "entering wedge for federal interference with the handling of the Negro question." Southern employers worried that federal benefits would discourage black workers from taking low-paying jobs in their fields, factories, and kitchens. Thus neither agricultural laborers nor domestic servants—a pool of workers that included at least 60 percent of the nation's black population—were covered by old-age insurance. Further, sharecroppers—black or white—and farm laborers (many of whom were of Mexican descent in the West) were also ineligible for unemployment insurance. Meanwhile, state administration of the program for dependent children resulted in huge inequities; in the 1930s, monthly payments for a typical family in Arkansas were less than one-eighth those in Massachusetts.

The same racial and regional disparities shaped the last major piece of welfare legislation passed during the Second New Deal: the Fair Labor Standards Act (FLSA), passed in 1938. Once again, New Dealers completed an agenda first put forward in the Progressive era. The FLSA banned child labor in manufacturing industries, established the first nationwide minimum wage, and made the forty-hour workweek a national norm by mandating that employers pay time and a half for work over and above that standard. Though those in the labor movement who had sought a thirty-hour workweek in order to generate new jobs were disappointed, the act did end the traditional half day of Saturday work, granting a two-day "weekend" to both white- and blue-collar workers.

In a concession to the increasingly conservative congressional representatives from the white South, the FLSA pegged the minimum wage to the low pay in the southern textile and lumber industries. Once again, workers in agriculture, domestic service, and the restaurant trade were left uncovered by even those minimal wage standards. One liberal congressman facetiously proposed an amendment to the act: "Within 90 days after the appointment of the Administrator, she shall report to Congress whether anyone is subject to this bill." But if few workers actually received wage increases under the act in the 1930s, employers and social conservatives had nevertheless conceded the ideological high ground to New Deal liberals. The United States was acknowledged as a single economic unit in which the federal government held much of the responsibility for workers' well-being.

"The Wagner Bill Is Behind You!" This leaflet distributed by the United Automobile Workers (UAW) captured the impact of the Wagner Act on union organizing.

Source: Scott Molloy Archives.

Ford Workers

UNIONISM NOT FORDISM

Now is the time to Organize!
The Wagner Bill is behind you!
Now get behind yourselves!

General Motors Workers, Chrysler Workers, Briggs Workers have won higher wages and better working conditions. 300,000 automobile workers are marching forward under the banner of the United Automobile Workers Union.

JOIN NOW IN THE MARCH AND WIN:

Higher Wages and Better Working Conditions
Stop Speed-up by Union Supervision
6 Hour Day, 8 Dollars Minimum Pay
Job Security thru Seniority Rights
End the Ford Service System
Union Recognition

Organize and be Recognized - JOIN NOW!

Union Headquarters for Ford Workers: Michigan Avenue at Addison; Vernor Highway West, and Lawndale

Sign up at Union Headquarters for Ford Workers or at any office of the United Automobile Workers

1324 Clay at Russell
2441 Milwaukee at Chene
11725 Oakland at Tuxedo
4044 Leuschner at Dwyer
11640 East Jefferson
10904 Mack at Lemay
77 Victor at John R.
8944 Jos. Campau at Playfair
11440 Charlevoix at Gladwin
1343 East Ferry at Russell
3814—35th Street at Michigan
2730 Maybury Grand at Michigan
4715 Hastings Street
Room 509 Hofmann Bldg.

Distributed by

United Automobile Workers of America

License No. 4

Printed by Goodwill Printing Co. 33

The Wagner Act

Undoubtedly the most radical and far-reaching piece of legislation passed during Roosevelt's second "hundred days" of 1935 was the National Labor Relations Act, known as the Wagner Act, for New York's Senator Robert Wagner, who introduced it. The president was not initially an advocate of Wagner's bill, but he reluctantly put it on his agenda because it would encourage the growth of trade unions, which seemed to offer a solution to two central problems confronting the nation. The first problem was the industrial unrest and social turmoil that had been so notable during the New Deal's first two years, especially during the 1934 labor upsurge. "Men versed in the tenets of freedom become restive when not allowed to be free," Senator Wagner had argued. "Until the promises made by [Section 7a of the National Industrial Recovery Act (NIRA)] are given definite meaning . . . increasing unrest is inevitable." (Section 7a gave workers the rights to organize but lacked enforcement powers.) Roosevelt shared Wagner's viewpoint, so when the U.S. Supreme Court struck down the NIRA in May 1935, the president finally agreed to endorse Wagner's bill, which the House of Representatives had just passed.

The second problem Roosevelt hoped the Wagner bill would help solve was that neither the Social Security Act nor the WPA could cure wage stagnation and underconsumption, on which most liberals blamed the Depression's persistence. The missing ingredient was an increase in the purchasing power of the working class—and unions were the only institutions then capable of implementing an industrywide wage standard.

But if the trade unions had only raised wages, their appeal would have been limited. To the mass of American workers, a huge proportion of whom were immigrants or African Americans, unions represented a doorway into the mainstream of American life. Thus by encouraging the growth of trade unions, the Wagner Act helped not only to raise incomes but also to democratize the world of work through a set of protections and procedures that enabled wage earners to exert their collective power. Unions gave workers a voice, and sometimes a club, with which to settle their grievances and organize themselves to bargain and take political action.

The Wagner Act guaranteed workers the right to select their own unions by majority vote, and to strike, boycott, and picket their employers. It banned "unfair labor practices" by employers, including the maintenance of company-dominated unions, the blacklisting of union activists, the intimidation or firing of workers who sought to join an independent union, and the employment of industrial spies. To determine the will of the workers, the new law established a National Labor Relations Board, which would hear employee complaints, determine union jurisdictions, and conduct on-site elections. It stated that whenever a majority of a company's workers voted to be represented by a union, management had a legal obligation to negotiate exclusively with that union over wages, hours, and working conditions. Collective bargaining, wrote a leading economist, was a method of "introducing civil rights into industry, that is, of requiring that management be conducted by rule rather than by arbitrary decision." It was the essence of the industrial democracy that many New Dealers and labor activists sought to build.

The Committee for Industrial Organization

A law is not a social movement, however. Seemingly progressive labor laws stand unenforced on the statute books of many nations. To give the Wagner Act real social and political meaning, the nation needed a working-class alliance of explosive power and institutional strength. In June 1935, when Franklin Roosevelt signed the new labor act into law, the obstacles to the creation of such a movement were considerable. The Supreme Court, having invalidated the NIRA, seemed likely to declare the even more sweeping provisions of the Wagner Act unconstitutional as well. Large corporate employers were so certain that the Wagner Act was unenforceable that they fought the unions and ignored the new statute. Indeed, companies such as General Motors, Goodyear, and Republic Steel did more than simply challenge the Wagner Act; they hired scores of labor spies, fired union activists, stocked up on guns and tear gas, and waged a public relations campaign against the act and the unions.

Meanwhile, the leadership of the American Federation of Labor (AFL) seemed both unwilling and unable to wage the necessary fight on behalf of industrial unionism. The AFL, whose leaders were steeped in the craft tradition, had no comprehensive strategy for organizing the semiskilled workers who comprised the majority of employees in the great mass-production industries. These sometimes volatile workers wanted an inclusive form of unionism that incorporated employees of many different skills and trades in a single industrial union. But the AFL adhered to a longstanding philosophy of "exclusive jurisdiction," meaning that the various craft unions—carpenters, machinists, electricians, and so forth—would seek to organize only a narrow slice of the skilled workforce in each factory and mill. More important, the AFL leadership mistrusted workers who were not of northern European or U.S. ancestry. Teamsters president Daniel Tobin betrayed his prejudice when he derided "the rubbish that have lately come into other organizations." And William Collins, another AFL official, once joked, "My wife can always tell from the smell of my clothes what breed of foreigners I have been hanging out with."

Such attitudes infuriated unionists such as the United Mine Workers' (UMW) John L. Lewis and the Amalgamated Clothing Workers' Sidney Hillman, both advocates of industrial unionism. In their view, passage of the Wagner Act, the insurgent mood of the working class, and the increasingly antibusiness tenor of the White House meant that there would never be a better time to unionize industrial workers. If unions could seize this opportunity, organized labor would multiply its membership, economic power, and political clout.

By the fall of 1935 Lewis, Hillman, and a few like-minded colleagues had concluded that any mass organizing effort would have to take place outside the AFL framework, under the banner of a new Committee for Industrial Organization (CIO). Although this split in labor's ranks did not become permanent until 1937, when the new union federation renamed itself the Congress of Industrial Organizations (also CIO), it was neatly symbolized in October 1935 at the AFL's convention in Atlantic City. When William Hutcheson, the stand-pat president of the Carpenters' Brotherhood, tried to silence an advocate of industrial unionism by raising a point of order, Lewis shouted, "This thing of raising points of order all the time . . . is rather small potatoes." Hutcheson rose to the bait, calling Lewis a "bastard," whereupon Lewis jumped to his feet. "Quick as a cat," an observer recalled, "he leaped over a row of chairs toward Hutcheson, jabbed out his right fist, and sent the carpenters' president sprawling." Hutcheson left the floor with blood on his face, while "Lewis casually adjusted his tie and collar, relit his cigar, and sauntered slowly through the crowded aisles."

Lewis was no radical. The burly, sonorous-voiced UMW leader voted Republican in most elections and had a well-deserved reputation as an autocrat. But he was determined to organize the labor movement by industry, not by craft. "Great combinations of capital," he argued, "have assembled to themselves tremendous power and influence, and they are almost 100 percent effective in opposing . . . the American Federation of Labor. . . . If you go in there with your craft union they will mow you down like the Italian machine guns will mow down Ethiopians in the war now going on in that country."

The success of the CIO's organizing campaign in 1936 and 1937 rested on its ability to tap the energy of thousands of grass-roots activists and to provide the national coordination and leadership that would enable the new unions to confront large corporations such as U.S. Steel and General Motors. Lewis hired scores of communists and socialists, because of their exceptional ability as mass organizers, and he backed their efforts with money from the UMW treasury. When reporters probed his decision to hire so many communists, Lewis replied, "Who gets the bird, the hunter or the dog?" As it turned out, the "dog" got quite a few birds: the

"We Done It!"

The CIO victory in the Akron, Ohio, rubber factories was made possible by the workers' use of a new tactic: the sit-down strike. Instead of walking out of the factory and picketing outside, the workers simply occupied the plant. Ruth McKenney, a novelist, graphically described the occupation of the Firestone tire plant in January 1936.

It was 1:57 A.M. January 29, 1936.

The tire builders worked in smooth frenzy, sweat around their necks, under their arms. The belt clattered, the insufferable racket and din and rhythm. The clock on the south wall, a big plain clock, hesitated, its minute hand jumped to two. A tire builder at the end of the line looked up, saw the hand jump. The foreman was sitting quietly staring at the lines of men working under the vast pools of light. . . .

The tire builder at the end of the line gulped. His hands stopped their quick weaving motions. Every man on the line stiffened. All over the vast room, hands hesitated. The foreman saw the falter, felt it instantly. He jumped up . . . his eyes darting quickly from one line to another.

This was it, then. But what was happening? Where was it starting? He stood perfectly still, his heart beating furiously, his throat feeling dry, watching the hesitating hands, watching the broken rhythm.

Then the tire builder at the end of the line walked three steps to the master safety switch and, drawing a deep breath, he pulled up the heavy wooden handle. With this signal in perfect synchronization, with the rhythm they had learned in a great mass-production industry, the tire builders stepped back from their machines.

Instantly, noise stopped. The whole room lay in perfect silence. The tire builders stood in long lines, touching each other, perfectly motionless, deafened by the silence. . . .

Out of the terrifying quiet came the wondering voice of a big tire builder near the window: "Jesus Christ, it's like the end of the world."

He broke the spell, the magic moment of stillness. For now his awed words said the same thing to every man, "We done it! We stopped the belt! By God, we done it!" And men began to cheer hysterically, to shout and howl in the fresh silence. Men wrapped their long sinewy arms around their neighbors' shoulders, screaming, "We done it! We done it! . . . "

Source: Ruth McKenney, *Industrial Valley* (1939).

leftists with whom Lewis cooperated were energetic, young, and confident. Union radicals, many of whom were communists or socialists—such as the auto worker Walter Reuther, the longshoremen's leader Harry Bridges, and the Transport Workers' Mike Quill—would soon emerge as the new generation of labor leaders.

The Roosevelt Landslide

The CIO organizing drive was closely linked with Roosevelt's 1936 re-election campaign. Lewis wanted "a president who would hold the light for us while we went out and organized," so the nascent industrial union movement broke new ground by making an unprecedented half-million-dollar contribution to the national Democratic party. As a result, in sharp contrast to virtually every other labor upsurge during the preceding half-century, the CIO enjoyed at least the friendly neutrality of the federal government during the most crucial phase of its organizing work.

To challenge Roosevelt for the presidency, the Republicans nominated Governor Alfred M. Landon of Kansas. Landon's campaign emphasized themes cherished by the conservative Liberty League, the U.S. Chamber of Commerce, and the National Association of Manufacturers. He blasted Roosevelt for swelling the federal deficit. He heaped blame on him for undermining the Constitution, the dollar, and the free market. But Landon was not a reactionary: in a tribute to the powerful New Deal coalition, he endorsed much of Roosevelt's program, while promising to administer it more efficiently.

Like the Man Says . . . A CIO recruiting poster quoted President Franklin Delano Roosevelt's statement supporting unions and collective bargaining.

Source: The George Meany Memorial Archives, AFL-CIO.

Leaders of the Coughlin, Long, and Townsend movements formed the short-lived Union party, an uneasy coalition that nominated Congressman William Lemke of North Dakota for the presidency. (Huey Long, who would have been the obvious choice of the new party, had been assassinated in September 1935.) On the Left, both the Socialist and Communist parties ran half-hearted campaigns, implicitly backing Roosevelt. Earl Browder, the Communist presidential candidate in 1936, later recalled conducting an "ambiguous campaign in favor of 'my rival,' Roosevelt." Earlier in the decade, the Communists had sharply attacked the New Deal. But now, to fight against big business and the Republicans at home and the rise of fascism abroad, they promoted a "Popular Front" of labor, liberals, New Dealers, and other radicals, while proclaiming that "communism is twentieth-century Americanism."

Evicted. These black sharecroppers were forced off farms by landlords eager to receive federal crop subsidies. They gathered along Highway 60 in New Madrid County, Missouri, in January 1939.

Source: Arthur Rothstein—Prints and Photographs Division, Library of Congress.

Roosevelt ignored the small parties, directing his fire against the Republicans and the "economic royalists" who, he said, took "other people's money" to "impose a new industrial dictatorship." The forces of "organized money," he charged, "are unanimous in their hate for me—and I welcome their hatred." He concluded, "I should like to have it said of my first Administration that in it the forces of selfishness and of lust for power met their match." Such rhetoric paid off. As one mill worker in the South noted, Roosevelt "is the first man in the White House to understand that my boss is a son of a bitch." Thus, when the Roosevelt motorcade passed through Michigan's industrial belt, virtually every assembly line ground to a halt as workers, union and nonunion alike, crowded to the windows.

Roosevelt also benefited from a shift in the loyalties of African-American voters. Since the end of the Civil War, African Americans had been steadfast Republicans, but during the 1930s they moved in massive numbers to the Democratic column. On the surface, this turnaround seemed puzzling: Roosevelt had never added black equality to his legislative agenda, and many of his programs discriminated against African Americans. The Agricultural Adjustment Act, in fact, had enabled landlords to dispossess so many African-American tenants and sharecroppers that the bill was often referred to as the "Negro Removal Act." Relief programs regularly shortchanged African Americans, and work programs often assigned them to segregated units. And the Tennessee Valley Authority (TVA) ran its construction, administration, and settlement programs on an openly discriminatory basis. "You can raise all the rumpus you like," confided one TVA official. "We just aren't going to mix Negroes and white folks in any village in TVA."

Nor had FDR thrown his support behind the antilynching law proposed in November 1933 by the National Association for the Advancement of Colored People (NAACP). In 1934, a dozen governors—including the governor of Florida—had voiced support for the bill. Roosevelt had publicly denounced lynching, but he had acceded to the power of the southern racists ensconced in the Democratic party and

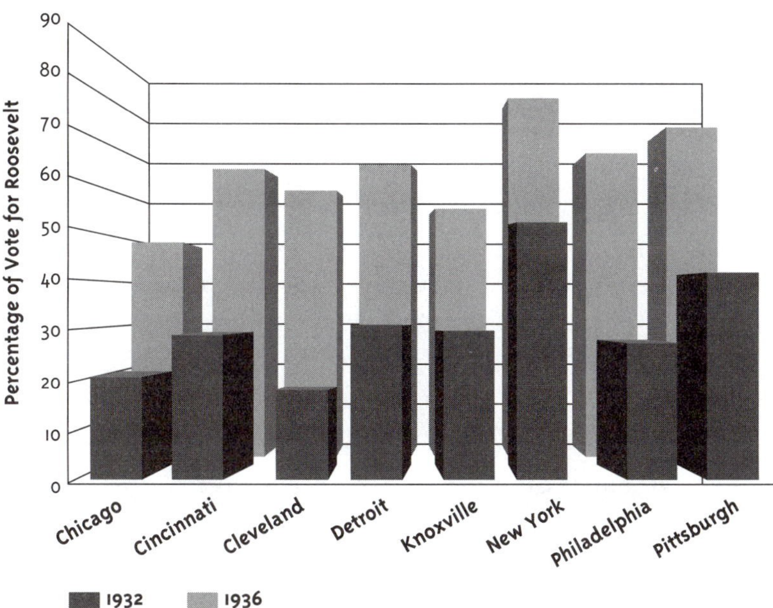

African Americans Vote Democratic. Although the Roosevelt administration never supported civil rights legislation, as it would be defined after World War II, African Americans began to abandon the Republican party in the 1930s because the New Deal offered them jobs, relief, and a modicum of political power—especially in the urban North. This graph, which was developed by historian Nancy Weiss, shows the dramatic change in black voting patterns between 1932 and 1936. Weiss compiled data on voting in precincts that were predominantly black, which she defined as having a black population of 90 percent or greater in 1940.

refused to endorse the bill. "The southerners . . . are chairmen or occupy strategic places on most of the Senate and House committees," FDR explained. "If I come out for the antilynching bill now, they will block every bill I ask Congress to pass to keep America from collapsing."

Nevertheless, African-American support for Roosevelt mushroomed midway through his first term. Part of the reason for the shift was that the Roosevelt administration had begun to respond to the needs of rural African Americans when the disastrous impact of the Agricultural Assistance Act on tenant farmers became apparent. New Deal agencies granted loans to struggling black farmers, helped some tenants buy land, and created agricultural settlements where displaced farmers could begin anew. Hundreds of thousands of poor rural families, black as well as white, benefited from the initiatives.

But the primary reason African Americans abandoned the party of Abraham Lincoln to support Roosevelt was that New Deal relief measures and employment projects had a huge impact on black Americans, rescuing many from the brink of starvation. In Cleveland, for example, the federal government had become the largest employer of African Americans, whose jobless rate fell from 50 to 30 percent. New Deal agencies also built more than three thousand housing units for the city's minority residents—fully half the public housing built in Cleveland. On Chicago's South Side, one resident recalled how "the WPA came along and Roosevelt came to be a god. . . . You worked, you got a paycheck, and you had some dignity." In Columbia, South Carolina, a registrar of voters reported that black Americans "say Roosevelt saved them from starvation, gave them aid when they were in distress, and now they were going to vote for him."

Although some New Deal agencies—such as the Civilian Conservation Corps, which was administered by a conservative southerner—actively discriminated against African Americans, others had much better records. The Public Works Administration (PWA), the Farm Security Administration (FSA), and the WPA were most notable on this score. The PWA did spend proportionately more for projects for southern whites than for their African-American neighbors, but it also expended four

"President Roosevelt Is a Friend to the Laborin' Men"

African Americans wrote and sang many songs during the Depression to acknowledge the debt they felt to President Roosevelt or to tell the story of how joining unions changed their lives. Many of these songs used the rhythms and style of old spirituals or prison work songs. The lyrics of one such song, "Union Dues," were written in a more modern musical idiom, the blues, which became popular in southern African-American communities in the 1920s. "Union Dues" was recorded by the folklorist George Korson during the 1940s.

President Roosevelt is a friend to the laborin' men,
Gives us the right to organize an' be real union men,
Union, union is all over the wide worl',
Back on the farm an' tobacco barns.
I'm glad I'm a union man; long may it live on,
The union will be livin' when I'm dead an' gone.

I got the union blues, don't care where I go,
I got the union blues, don't care where I be,
It's good for you an' good enough for me;
I'm goin' down the road feelin' mighty glad,
I'm goin' down the road feelin' mighty glad,
The union is the best friend that labor ever had.
I'm goin' to write a letter, goin' to mail it in the month o' May.
I'm goin' to write a letter, goin' to mail it this very day.
I'm goin' to thank the President for that seven-hour day.
I'm goin' to close my song, but won't close my mind,
I'm goin' to close my song, but won't close my mind—
That laborin' man was not left behind.

Source: George Korson, *Coal Dust on the Fiddle* (1943).

times more for black schools and hospitals than all government agencies combined had done in the previous three decades. The WPA was particularly successful in stopping discrimination against African Americans on projects in northern cities—and it was the North, not the South, where blacks could more readily vote. By 1939 upwards of a million black families were supported by WPA jobs. "Let Jesus lead you and Roosevelt feed you," proclaimed the president's black supporters.

By stressing the social welfare and union rights legislation of the Second New Deal and identifying himself with the aspirations of small property owners and wage earners, Roosevelt garnered 60 percent of the popular vote in 1936 and carried every state but Vermont and Maine. His victory was one of party as well as personality: the Republicans lost twelve more seats in the House of Representatives, giving the Democrats three-quarters of the total. In the Senate, seven new Democrats took office, giving the president's party nearly eight of every ten seats in that body. Democratic gubernatorial candidates won in Michigan, Ohio, Pennsylvania, and New York, four states where the battles for union organization were sure to be fought.

The Roosevelt landslide included traditionally Democratic strongholds in the western mountain states and the deep South, but urban working people made up the core of the new Democratic electorate. Overwhelming support came from the newly enfranchised children of turn-of-the-century Southern and Eastern European immigrants and from the native-born millions, black and white, who had left the farms for the cities during the 1920s. For them a vote for Roosevelt and the New Deal was practically a requirement of citizenship. On the local level, the Roosevelt landslide seemed a dramatic repudiation of the old industrial order.

Times had changed. In the 1920 election, the Republicans had captured the twelve largest cities with a plurality of more than 1.5 million votes. In 1936, Roosevelt and the Democrats swamped their opponents in those cities by a margin of more than 3.5 million. The black vote for Roosevelt was 56 percent in Knoxville, Tennessee; 75 percent in Pittsburgh; and 81 percent in New York City. In some midwestern industrial cities, the Polish and Italian Democratic vote was over 90 percent. These urban ethnic and African-American working-class voters would remain the backbone of the Democratic party for the next third of a century.

The Flint Sit-Down Strike

Buoyed by Roosevelt's smashing reelection, CIO efforts to organize basic industries—steel, rubber, meatpacking, autos, and electrical products—climaxed during a dramatic six-week sit-down strike at General Motors

Corporation (GM) in the winter of 1937. General Motors was the largest and most profitable corporation in the United States, and one of the most sophisticated. *Fortune* magazine called GM "the world's most influential industrial unit in forming the life patterns of the machine age," and said that, with 110 manufacturing and assembly plants across the nation, a quarter-million employees, and half a million stockholders, GM was "the perfect exemplar of how and why American business is Big." Not surprisingly, GM managers were increasingly hostile to both the New Deal and the new industrial unions. The CIO's political objectives, reported GM's president Alfred Sloan to stockholders, were an "important step toward an economic and political dictatorship." In the mid-1930s GM spent more money on labor spies than did any other company in the nation.

Someone Didn't Like the Message. The day after arsonists tried to burn it down, union members repaired this Detroit billboard set up by the Ford Organizing Committee of the United Automobile Workers. **Source:** Archives of Labor and Urban Affairs, Wayne State University.

Autoworkers sought to counter GM's enormous power with a companywide industrial trade union that could defend their health and dignity on the shop floor, their job security during layoffs, and their standard of living. The grievances of these relatively well-paid workers did not involve wages so much as arbitrary supervision, economic insecurity, and the dehumanizing speedup characteristic of assembly-line production. The foremen "treated us like a bunch of coolies," a Chevrolet employee later remembered. " 'Get it out. If you cannot get it out, there are people outside who will get it out.' That was their whole theme." Because of the industry's seasonal production cycle, employees worked long, hard hours during the winter and spring, only to be laid off for up to three months when the company retooled the factories during the off season. "The fear of being laid off," one journalist noted, "hangs over the head of every worker. He does not know when the sword will fall."

What was more, foremen and other managers had the right to discipline, fire, lay off, and rehire workers at their own discretion. The corporation had successfully resisted union and NRA efforts to make seniority (the length of time a worker had been employed) the basis for promotion and recall. Managers argued that they needed the flexibility to hire, fire, and promote in order to keep operations efficient. But the experience of thousands of workers was quite different: they saw such managerial prerogatives as a weapon with which to penalize unionists and reward favorite employees. Such was especially the case during the annual layoff, explained another Chevrolet worker: "If he [the foreman] happened to like you or if you sucked around him and did him favors . . . you might be picked to work a few weeks longer than the next guy."

Throughout November and December 1936, as leaders of the fledgling United Auto Workers (UAW) formulated their plans, autoworkers became impatient and began strikes in South Bend, Kansas City, Detroit, and Atlanta. Following the example of Akron, Ohio, rubberworkers, who had occupied the Firestone plant in January 1936, autoworkers staged "sit-down" strikes: they seized control of the plants where they worked, remaining inside rather than picketing outside, until management capitulated. This innovative tactic, which demonstrated the workers' willingness to violate owners' private-property rights to win concessions, prevented companies from replacing strikers with scabs. It also discouraged the use of violence against strikers, because the deployment of police, troops, or other armed groups to oust the men could result in damage to expensive company-owned buildings, machinery, and materials.

Catching Up on the News. During the sit-down strike, strikers who occupied General Motors' Fisher Body Plant No. 1 avidly followed newspaper coverage of their action.

Source: Archives of Labor and Urban Affairs, Wayne State University.

The UAW leadership, aware of the spreading wildcat (without formal union approval) strikes, decided to attack GM head-on by striking the company's key Fisher Body plants in Cleveland and Flint. The strike was scheduled for right after New Year's Day, following the inauguration of New Dealer Frank Murphy as governor of Michigan.

But events raced ahead of the union leaders' plans. When workers in one department in the Cleveland Fisher Body plant sat down to protest wage cuts on December 28, the rest of the factory's seven thousand employees joined them. In Flint, an attempt by managers in Fisher Body Plant No. 2 to discipline three union members on December 30 prompted fifty workers to occupy that building. The next day, angry workers from Fisher No. 1 gathered at Flint's UAW hall, shouting at their leaders, "Shut her down! Shut the goddamn plant!" Streaming back into Plant No. 1, between five hundred and one thousand workers took control of the factory in minutes, shutting down the assembly line. The month-long sit-down strike that followed proved to be the pivotal labor struggle of the decade. If Flint autoworkers could beat General Motors—the largest producer of automobiles, parts, and accessories in the world—their victory would galvanize workers not only in the auto industry but also in other basic industries.

The Flint strike was emblematic of countless other labor battles between 1936 and 1942 because it revealed rank-and-file workers' extraordinary creativity and bravery in the struggle for industrial unionism. Located sixty miles northwest of Detroit, Flint was the corporation's key production center and a near-classic company town. General Motors employed four of every five workers in the city. For the UAW, the burden of conducting the actual confrontation with General Motors rested on a relatively narrow base: a few hundred sit-downers in each plant; an energetic group of radicals (many of whom were Socialist and Communist party members) who ran the strike from day to day; and a few older unionists of national reputation posted to Flint during the conflict. But the UAW also drew on the courage and determination of thousands of autoworkers and their families, in Flint and elsewhere, in maintaining a sit-down strike that effectively stopped most of GM's production. The tactic was not new, but the UAW deployed it on an aggressive scale to maximize the leverage of a militant minority and avoid clashes with police and strikebreakers. During the course of the occupation, sit-downers held frequent meetings, conducted classes

Meanwhile, Outside . . . The UAW's Women's Emergency Brigade, along with members of the union local's Women's Auxiliary, marched in front of an occupied Chrysler plant in March 1937. **Source:** Archives of Labor and Urban Affairs, Wayne State University.

in labor history, put on plays, and scrupulously avoided damaging the factories or their products. They felt as though they had ownership rights in the jobs and factories they were defending.

The union's allies in the Democratic party kept Michigan's powerful state militia at bay, even though the sit-down strike was of questionable legality and Flint police had sought to oust the strikers on more than one occasion. The transformation of the 1936 presidential election into a referendum on the industrial status quo had convinced key politicians, including Governor Murphy and President Roosevelt himself, to refrain from using the National Guard or army to evict the strikers.

As in several other industrial conflicts of the late 1930s, the unionists often organized themselves into paramilitary formations called flying squadrons to prevent companies and police from bringing in strikebreakers or dislodging sit-downers. In Flint, the Women's Emergency Brigade, led by the twenty-three-year-old socialist firebrand Genora Johnson (Dollinger), was one of the most effective and celebrated. The red-bereted brigade served as the female shock troops of the solidarity movement; its members carried two-by-fours when they joined in violent confrontations, placing themselves between strikers and police and militia.

Everybody's Doing It. These employees of Detroit's Goody Nut Shops staged a sit-down strike in March 1937.

Source: *Detroit News.*

In fact, company-sponsored violence often worked to the strikers' advantage. On January 11, sheriff's deputies and police, using tear gas, billy clubs, and guns, tried to retake Chevrolet Plant No. 2. After strikers twice repelled them by turning on the plant's fire hoses and raining two-pound car hinges down on the police, the police opened fire, wounding several strikers. A third charge, at midnight, also failed. Defeated, the police (known in the jargon of the day as "bulls") abandoned the field. The "Battle of the Running Bulls" galvanized GM workers dispirited by years of company intimidation. The next morning, Flint workers lined up two abreast at UAW headquarters to sign membership cards and pay dues.

A month later, with car production at a near standstill, GM finally caved in. The signed contract was merely four pages long, but it proved an enormous victory, not only for the employees of America's largest corporation but for millions of other workers as well. GM recognized the union as the sole voice of its employees and agreed to negotiate with UAW leaders on a multiplant basis. For the first time, union activists had the right to speak up, recruit other workers, and complain to management without fear of retribution. "Even if we got not one damn thing out of it other than that," declared a GM employee in St. Louis, "we at least had a right to open our mouths without fear." Indeed, an enormous sense of self-confidence, democratic participation, even liberation swept through working-class ranks. Huge crowds thronged the streets of Flint in a celebration that Roy Reuther, an auto union militant, likened to "some description of a country experiencing independence."

Industrial Unionism at High Tide

Across industrial America, the GM settlement transformed the expectations of workers and managers alike. In Flint and elsewhere, few workers had actively supported the first strikes, picket lines, and demonstrations. Although only a committed minority had led the way, their coworkers were neither pro-company nor even neutral in the conflict; most were fearful bystanders whose loyalty would crystallize only after the CIO had stripped management of its capacity to penalize workers. In the wake of the GM victory, workers in almost every industrial district poured into the new unions, where for a time many were organized into citywide units that cut across corporate, ethnic, and political boundaries.

A fever of organization gripped working-class communities in a huge arc that spread from New England through New York, Pennsylvania, and the Midwest. In 1937 nearly 5 million workers took part in some kind of industrial action, and almost 3 million became union members. In Detroit alone, a rolling wave of sit-down strikes hit dozens of factories. "Somebody would call the office," recalled a UAW organizer, "and say, 'Look, we are sitting down. Send us over some food.' " Workers in Detroit occupied every Chrysler Corporation facility, twenty-five auto-parts plants, four downtown hotels, nine lumberyards, ten meat-packing plants, a dozen industrial laundries, three department stores, and scores of restaurants, shoe stores, and clothing outlets. When the police evicted female strikers from a cigar company and a few stores along lower Woodward Avenue, the labor movement shut down the entire city and put 150,000 protesters in front of City Hall.

Such raw power made the kind of headlines that influenced even the most conservative elite. There were no sit-down strikes at U.S. Steel, but its president, Myron Taylor, read GM's capitulation in Flint as a sign that

Celebration. A May 1937 union demonstration of Aliquippa, Pennsylvania, steelworkers and their supporters was portrayed on the cover of *Photo-History* (a short-lived, pro-CIO magazine).

Source: *Photo-History* (July 1937)—Prints and Photographs Division, Library of Congress.

"complete industrial organization was inevitable." To avoid a violent conflict with steelworkers, Taylor, who presided over the second-largest manufacturing company in the world—the corporation that had smashed the nationwide steel strike in 1919—agreed to raise wages and to recognize the CIO's Steelworkers Organizing Committee (SWOC) as the sole bargaining agent for employees. That was in early March; scores of other major corporations followed suit. In April the Supreme Court, whose conservative members also recognized the popular impetus behind the Roosevelt landslide and the labor upsurge, surprised almost everyone by declaring the Wagner Act constitutional.

Thus CIO unionism had a profound impact on the daily lives of millions of ordinary workers. Although the new unions negotiated for higher wages and lobbied for much-needed social legislation, they had their greatest impact inside the factory itself, where dramatic changes were taking place on the shop floor in the relationship between boss and workers. There shop stewards elected by their workmates gave voice and power to the heretofore inarticulate. "Everybody wants to talk. Leaders are popping up everywhere," reported an organizer from Flint. Shop stewards used their newfound power to argue with the foreman, backed sometimes by employees in their departments, who dropped their tools and gathered around until the grievance was settled.

"Before organization came into the plant, foremen were little tin gods in their own departments," declared a 1941 union handbook. "With the coming of the union, the foreman finds his whole world turned upside down. His small time dictatorship has been overthrown, and he must be adjusted to a democratic system of shop government." The grievance procedures and seniority systems instituted by the new unions established a rough system of industrial jurisprudence, which for the first time brought something of the orderliness and predictability of democratic society to the shop floor of privately managed factories.

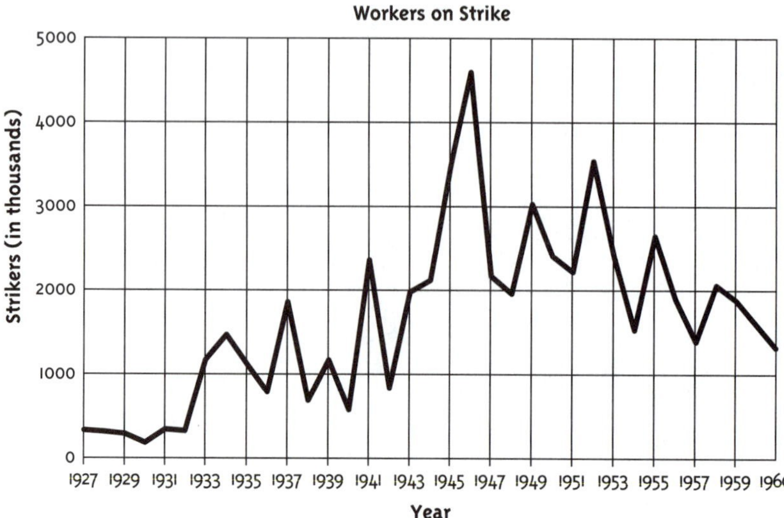

On Strike! The number of American workers participating in strikes increased rapidly in the 1930s, reaching a Depression-era peak during the sit-down strikes of 1937. But the immediate postwar era found even more workers on strike. For decades thereafter, the existence of a powerful trade union movement ensured that strike levels remained high.

The AFL, which had sharply rejected the call for industrial unionism two years earlier, reaped many benefits from this upsurge of worker militancy and industrial unionization. When AFL leaders such as Teamsters president Dan Tobin and Carpenters president William Hutcheson saw that the CIO was winning victories, they began to organize the same workers they had once scorned. Machinists and boilermakers transformed many of their affiliated locals into industrial unions so as to compete directly with the CIO. In meatpacking, food processing, and the retail and service trades, the AFL's network of central labor bodies provided effective political, legal, and financial support to union organizers. Many anti-union employers, frightened by the CIO's successes, were suddenly happy to negotiate with AFL unions so they could avoid "Lewis's Reds." The AFL gained one million new members during 1937; within a few years it was once again the nation's largest labor federation. Total union membership rose from three million in 1934 to eight million at the end of the 1930s.

One of the most important AFL success stories was the Teamsters. Before the Depression the union had limited its ranks to truck drivers who hauled goods in the nation's urban areas. But after radicals in Minneapolis demonstrated in 1934 that organizing warehousemen and other goods handlers could strengthen the union, Teamster locals throughout the nation began to organize workers they had previously ignored. They also began signing up long-distance intercity drivers. Within five years the union had grown to 440,000 members and had secured a powerful grip on the motor transport industry. Its success was the product not of mobster muscle, although such parasitic and corrupt influence would grow rapidly a decade later, but of dedicated organizers and militant truck drivers.

Working-class empowerment had its impact not only at the work site but also in the community. Union-sponsored baseball teams and bowling leagues, singing groups, tenant organizations, food cooperatives, and health clinics—all were part of a new participatory culture that gave life and spirit to the industrial unionism of the era. In many company-dominated towns throughout the East and Midwest, old-line Republican officials—white, Protestant, and of northern European heritage—were either defeated or forced to share power with ethnic Democrats allied

"Made in the U.S.A."

Thomas Bell's 1941 novel *Out of This Furnace* spans three generations in the life of a family of Slovak immigrants who toiled in Pittsburgh's steel mills. The story spans the years from the grandfather's arrival in 1881 to the grandson's participation in the CIO organizing drives of the late 1930s. In the closing pages of the novel, Dobie, the grandson, reflects on the sense of empowerment he and his fellow steelworkers now enjoy, concluding that, despite his ancestry, his participation in the formation of the Steelworkers' Union had made him feel as American as if his family had arrived with the Puritans.

And he realized now what it was that had once puzzled him about the CIO men. Whatever their ancestry, they had felt the same way about certain things; and because Dobie had been born and raised in a steel town, where the word meant people who were white, Protestant, middle-class Anglo-Saxons, it hadn't occurred to him that the CIO men were thinking and talking like Americans.

"Maybe not the kind of American that came over on the *Mayflower,*" he reflected, "or the kind that's always shooting off their mouths about Americanism and patriotism, including some of the God damndest heels you'd ever want to see, but the kind that's got 'Made in U.S.A.' stamped all over them, from the kind of grub they like to the things they wouldn't do for all the money in the world."

He stared down at the sleeping town without really seeing it.

"Made in the U.S.A.," he thought, "made in the First Ward. Mikie was right; it's too bad a person can't pick their own place to be born in, considering what it does to you. I'm almost as much a product of that mill down there as any rail or ingot they ever turned out. And maybe that's been part of the trouble. If I'm anything at all I'm an American, only I'm not the kind you read about in history books or that they make speeches about on the Fourth of July; anyway, not yet. And a lot of people don't know what to make of it and don't like it. Which is tough on me but is liable to be still tougher on them, because I at least don't have to be told that Braddock [Pennsylvania] ain't Plymouth Rock and this ain't the year 1620."

. . . Made in the U.S.A., he thought, made in the First Ward. But it wasn't where you were born or how you spelled your name or where your father come from. It was the way you thought and felt about certain things. About freedom of speech and the equality of men and the importance of having one law—the same law—for rich and poor, for the people you liked and the people you didn't like. . . . About the uses to which wealth and power could honorably be put. . . . About human dignity, which helped a man live proudly and distinguished his death from an animal's; and, finally, about the value to be put on a human life, one's enemy's no less than one's own.

Source: Thomas Bell, *Out of This Furnace* (1941).

with the union movement. CIO industrial unions laid a solid foundation for citizenship. They gave first- and second-generation immigrant workers a collective political voice, transformed relations at the work site, and began to equalize wage scales that all too often mirrored invidious ethnic and racial hierarchies. In western Pennsylvania steel towns and New England textile centers, the new citizenship and the new unionism were virtually synonymous, linking union membership, New Deal politics, and income stability. "Unionism is the spirit of Americanism," asserted a typical union paper.

This working-class Americanism represented a new departure. In the past, conservative defenders of the status quo had frequently manipulated patriotic and nationalist sentiment in their own interest, for example, denouncing radical and union movements as "un-American." In earlier conflicts, police and vigilantes had forced organizers to kneel and kiss the American flag as a sign of their loyalty to the nation and its institutions.

But during the 1930s liberals, labor, and the Left successfully captured the flag. A telling moment came in 1934 when Secretary of Labor Frances Perkins visited unorganized steelworkers in Homestead, Pennsylvania, to hear their grievances and explain New Deal labor policy. When union militants sought to make their voices heard, the mayor of the town, which was tightly controlled by the United States Steel Corporation, abruptly cut short her speech and ushered her out of the city hall. Out on the street, amid a crowd of angry steelworkers, Perkins spotted an American flag flying over the local post office. In the lobby of that federal building, under the symbol of national unity, she resumed her speech, detailing, for the largely Catholic, immigrant audience, their rights under federal law.

Soon the Depression-era labor movement would deploy huge American flags in all its struggles, symbolizing the ethnically diverse Americanism of the new unionism and the New Deal. But working people's appreciation of such patriotic symbols was not simply the product of manipulation by union organizers. When victorious sit-down strikers emerged from GM's plants in Flint in February 1937, proudly waving the flag, they were announcing that they, too, belonged to a venerable patriotic tradition and were entitled to all the rights of American citizens.

Women's Place in the New Unions and the New Deal

In these union struggles, women workers won their own kind of industrial citizenship—albeit one limited by the sexist assumptions of the period. The unions recruited almost a million women in the 1930s, especially in the garment trades, electrical products, clerical and sales work, canning, and tobacco processing. Women sit-down strikers occupied hotels, drugstores, restaurants, and auto-parts factories. In Detroit, the women who took over a Woolworth store ridiculed the heiress who owned the chain, Barbara Hutton, in a take-off on an army ditty from the Great War:

> Barbara Hutton has the dough, parlez-vous
> Where she gets it, sure we know, parlez-vous
> We slave at Woolworth's five-and-dime
> The pay we get is sure a crime
> Hinkey-dinkey parlez-vous.

"Hello, Mama. We're Makin' History." Denys Wortman's cartoon in the March 25, 1937, *New York World-Telegram* captured the excitement and sense of power felt by many working men and working women when they participated in militant labor action.
Source: Denys Wortman, *New York World-Telegram* March 25, 1937—General Research Division, New York Public Library, Astor, Lenox and Tilden Foundations.

Women often played an essential role in linking a union's shop activism to the larger community. Most unions organized women's auxiliaries, whose very existence testified to a sense of family solidarity. During the 1934 Firestone strike in Akron, for example, the local newspaper reported, "Shoulder to shoulder with their men, the wives, daughters, and sisters of strikers marched through the business district to strike headquarters in a great victory parade." But such dramatic linkages were far less important than the more subtle ways in which women made the unions present in their neighborhoods and communities. Labor-based tenant organizations, soup kitchens, food cooperatives, recreation halls, singing societies, and education programs drew both women workers and the wives and daughters of male unionists into a dense, supportive social network that strengthened the ties of solidarity inside the factory and out.

But women's activism did not win them equality. Organized labor's posters and billboards invariably portrayed the working-class movement as a powerful white male with muscles, even when the workers represented by the unions were dark-skinned women. There were no feminists among the men who led the AFL and the CIO. Stella Nowicki, a Communist party member and Chicago Packinghouse Union activist, noted that union officials, most of whom were leftists, "didn't take up the problems women had," nor did they "encourage women to come to meetings."

Though official CIO pronouncements demanded "equal pay for equal work," the sign carried by one male picketer proved more eloquent and revealing: "Restore Our Manhood," it implored; "We Receive Girls' Wages." Even in industries in which most workers were women, male union activists did not welcome female leadership. Thus those women who played leading roles in the labor movement were remarkably atypical: divorcees, widows, political radicals, or members of intensely union-conscious households.

Florence Luscomb, for example, received an architecture degree from MIT in 1909 but soon abandoned architecture (at that time a very unusual occupation for a woman), first to campaign for women's suffrage and later to work for prison reform. When the CIO started the United Office and Professional Workers' Union, she became president of the Boston local. Although she helped win higher pay, she had trouble building a large union. One problem was that female clerical workers often felt socially superior to factory workers and above trade unionism; another was that stenographers and typists worked in isolated settings and small groups. And, as Luscomb later recalled, "the CIO didn't give much assistance in having secretaries organized; they'd be too busy trying to organize the textile workers, and the railroad workers, and large 'important' bodies of the working class."

The sexism of male unionists and the structural isolation of many women workers were not the only problems. As the populist, communal unions of the mid-1930s became part of an industrywide labor organization, and as many in that organization came to see the contractual relationship at the work site as the essence of successful modern unionism, the opportunities for women's participation in the movement dwindled. Meetings were held less frequently and at night, the women's auxiliaries were replaced by women's departments inside the union bureaucracy, and many food cooperatives and drama workshops were discontinued.

Like the new unions, the New Deal had a decidedly mixed record on issues of concern to women. Women political activists, led by Eleanor Roosevelt, had a greater role than in any other previous presidential administration. President Roosevelt appointed the first woman cabinet member, Secretary of Labor Frances Perkins, the first woman director of the U.S. Mint, and the first woman judge on the federal Circuit Court of Appeals. But the success of these few individuals translated into only modest gains for women as a group: few women found jobs in the Civil Works Administration or the Public Works Administration; none in the Civilian Conservation Corps. The Works Progress Administration did

"It Was a New Idea for Office Workers to Organize— . . . A Very Unusual Idea"

In this selection from an oral interview, Florence Luscomb recalls the CIO drive to organize women office workers, an increasingly important occupational category, into industrial unions. Luscomb had a long and distinguished career as a Progressive reformer, suffragist, trade unionist, and peace activist. Educated as an architect at MIT, Luscomb was an officer in the NAACP, an organizer for the International Ladies Garment Workers' Union, and, as she recalls, president of the Boston local of the CIO's United Professional and Office Workers of America.

I joined the American Federation of Labor, what they called, the Stenographers, Typewriters, Bookkeepers, and Accountants Union. Not typists, but typewriters. I joined it in the early thirties, because I believed in labor unions, and so I wanted to be a member. And it was really just a fake union. There was just this one public stenographers' office in Boston, and that was a union office. . . . When I became president in 1936, I wanted to put on big campaign to unionize more office workers. And they [the AFL union] wouldn't do it. . . . When the Congress of Industrial Organizations came along and started to establish a United Office and Professional Workers Union . . . we set up local No. 3 of the UOPWA in the CIO. I was the president for several years, and we did a lot of very active work without getting a very large union.

For example, there was one big firm which had quite a large office staff, and they paid very low wages. We used to go around and find one girl in the office who would think that they ought to be organized, and she'd give us the names and addresses of all the office workers. We'd go and visit them in their homes, and talk union with them. And we got a large group of girls in this office who were very much interested in having the union there. The firm got wind of it, that they were probably going to have a strike on their hands. So they raised their girls' pay, whereupon the girls lost all interest in joining the union! And that happened various times. We got more stenographers with pay raises than we got members of the union, but we did gradually build up the union. It was a new idea for office workers to organize—it was a very unusual idea. They felt themselves socially superior to the person working in a factory, although they might get much less pay than the girls who were working in the factory.

Source: Ellen Cantarow with Susan Gushee O'Malley and Sharon Hartman Strom, *Moving the Mountain: Women Working for Social Change* (1980).

employ hundreds of thousands of women, but it was still a smaller percentage than the female share of the workforce. Social Security coverage failed to include some of the most important categories of female employment, such as waitresses and maids. Women New Dealers, moreover, were generally committed to an older Progressive agenda of providing "special protection" for female workers rather than demanding equal rights for them. Feminism never made it onto the agenda of either the New Deal or the CIO in the 1930s. Liberals, trade unionists, and even many radicals thought of women as the loyal and supportive comrades of the male worker rather than as equal citizens in the new political and economic order.

The New Deal and Popular Culture

Just as mass production typified American industry in the 1930s, mass culture characterized entertainment, journalism, and the arts during that era. Fifty million Americans went to the movies each week. Radio entered almost every home, and news magazines such as *Time* and *Newsweek* brought East Coast reportage to remote rural areas. And for the first time, the federal government employed writers, photographers, actors, and artists on a massive scale.

What was the relationship of this new mass culture to the politics of the era? Almost all newspapers were hostile to labor and the New Deal, and most of the new Hollywood moguls were staunch Republicans. Nevertheless, creative artists who were sympathetic to labor and the Left had an unprecedented impact on mass culture in the 1930s. This was the era of the Popular Front, in which radicals in or close to the Communist party played a major role in organizations devoted to everything from modern dance to student politics, public housing, and minority rights. The cultural movement had a broad reach, combining a modernist, experimental sensibility in arts and letters with an appreciation of the

The Rise of Radio. By the end of the 1930s, almost every electrified home contained a radio. In 1922, 30 stations broadcast to just 60,000 radio sets. But seventeen years later, more than 700 stations beamed music, news, drama, and comedy to more than 27 million households.

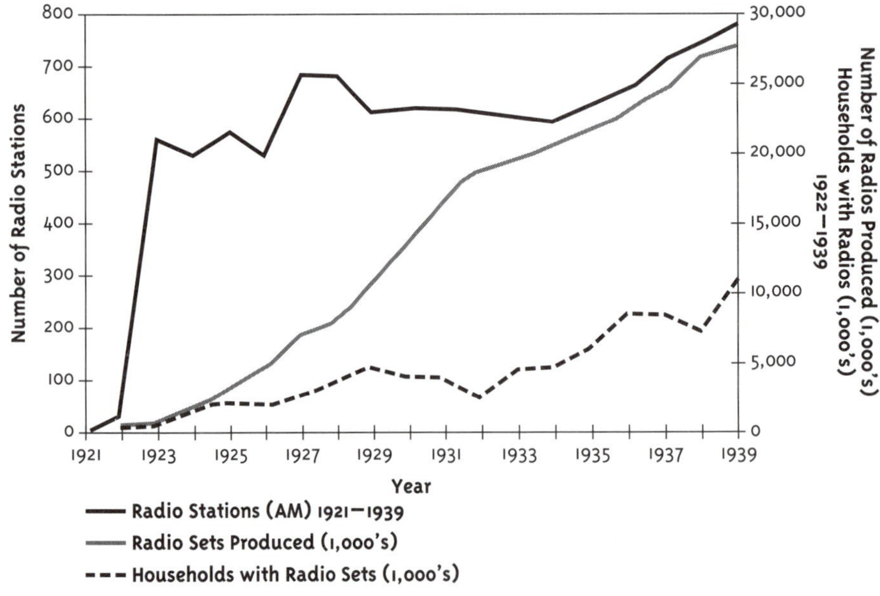

"Pocahontas Rescuing Captain John Smith." At times, local tastes clashed with individual artists' expressions. In the case of Paul Cadmus's mural for Richmond's Parcel Post Building, it was male nudity that roused concern. Although Pocahontas's breast and the foreground Indian brave's buttocks remained bare, Cadmus had to retouch a suggestive foxhead he had mischievously placed over another brave's groin.

Source: Paul Cadmus, *Pocahontas Rescuing Captain John Smith,* 1939, mural—National Archives.

critical role of workers and farmers in American society. Simultaneously nationalistic and regionally rooted, it celebrated as inherently democratic and creative the folk cultures of the Southwest, the Appalachian South, and small-town New England.

The Roosevelt administration fostered support for New Deal programs by helping artists to create and disseminate works of democratic mass culture. In the early 1930s the drama, color, and political subjects of the great left-wing Mexican muralists Diego Rivera, José Clemente Orozco, and David Alfaro Siqueiros inspired those who sought to develop socially relevant public art in the United States. Such was the appeal of their work that even the Rockefeller family commissioned them to produce murals for Dartmouth College and Rockefeller Center in New York, while Henry Ford's son Edsel sponsored a Rivera mural on industrial labor at the Detroit Institute of the Arts (But Nelson Rockefeller ordered the removal of the Rockefeller Center mural because Rivera included a portrait of Lenin.). Late in 1933, New Deal relief and public works agencies began to fund similar works, employing thousands of artists to produce more than fifteen thousand murals, oils, watercolors, and prints. As part of the Works Progress Administration, employees of the Federal Art Project created murals for the walls of federal and state buildings and established community art centers in remote communities. The project

"The Corn Parade." Few of the post-office murals commissioned by the Treasury Department Section of Fine Art displayed the humor of Orr C. Fisher's paean to corn. But the Iowa-born Fisher's work suggests the kind of regional boosterism and pride of place that characterized many murals painted by local artists.

Source: Orr C. Fisher, *The Corn Parade,* 1941, oil on canvas—National Archives.

employed as many as six thousand painters, sculptors, and muralists, 90 percent of whom were on relief.

New Deal public art embodied the hope of John Dewey, the nation's foremost philosopher, that "our public buildings may become the outward and visible sign of the inward grace which is the democratic spirit." Reflecting the leftist politics of many of the artists, the representational subject matter was often that of ordinary Americans, at work or in struggle, rendered in a heroic, larger-than-life style. Like other elements of New Deal culture, the murals and paintings were overtly masculinist. Women were portrayed as sturdy partners in the American pageant but were not presented as heroines in their own right.

Another WPA undertaking, the Federal Writers Project, gave important and creative work to thousands of unemployed white-collar workers—not just writers and poets, but insurance salesmen, librarians, and middle managers as well. Writers project employees published guidebooks, collected folk songs, and recorded interviews with ex-slaves, cowboys, and immigrants. These works and documents fostered a more democratic vision of the American past and present that celebrated the "common hero" and the "forgotten American."

Other New Deal arts projects, such as the Federal Music Project, brought art and culture to ordinary people. Before the launch of that project, the United States had only eleven recognized symphony orchestras. The music project created thirty-four more, not just in the biggest cities of the East and West Coasts, but in cities in Oklahoma and Utah. WPA-sponsored music teachers gave lessons to seventy thousand people

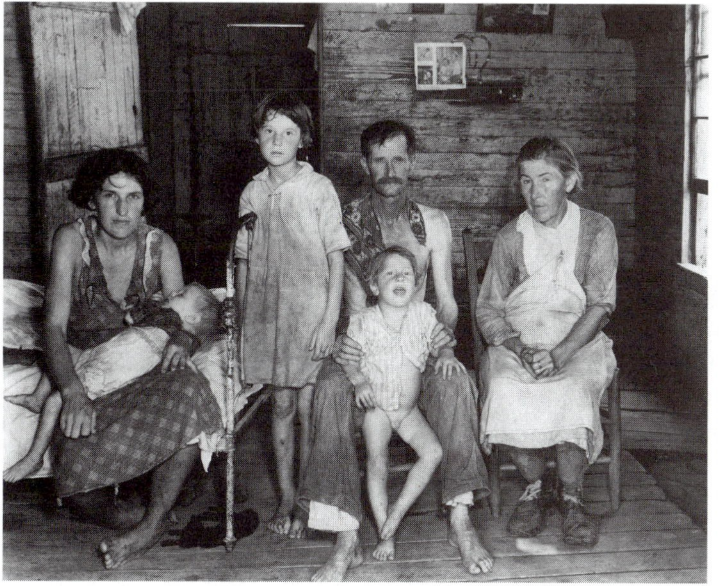

The Fields Family, Hale County, Alabama, Summer 1936. From 1935 to 1943, photographers working for several government agencies, principally the Farm Security Administration (FSA), produced the most enduring images of the Great Depression. This Walker Evans picture of rural poor, like Dorothea Lange's photographs in Chapter 8, was part of that massive documentation effort. Wishing to convey both suffering and dignity, FSA photographers searingly presented conditions to the American public, selecting effective compositions and poses influenced by advertising and mass-market magazine formats.

Source: Walker Evans, 1936—Prints and Photographs Division, Library of Congress.

in Mississippi and sparked a boom in the sale of secondhand pianos. The Federal Music Project also cooperated with other agencies to gather and preserve the nation's folk music. In New Mexico, for example, it collected folk tunes with roots going back to Spain, Cuba, and Mexico. In Oklahoma, it recorded the songs and dances of five Native American tribes, as well as the fiddle tunes popular throughout the state.

But perhaps the most outstanding contributions to the nation's cultural archives came from photojournalists. To build broad public support for its programs, the Roosevelt administration encouraged the directors of New Deal agencies to document the human suffering caused by the Depression. For this purpose, the WPA, the Department of Agriculture, and the Farm Security Administration (formerly the Resettlement Administration) hired amateur and professional photographers to travel the Depression-ravaged country. Some of the hundreds of thousands of "social-realist" photos they shot—particularly Dorothea Lange's haunting portraits of poor farm women, Arthur Rothstein's shots of dust storms, and Walker Evans's despairing images of sharecroppers—became icons of the Depression. They were widely circulated in the popular press, including *Time, Look,* and *Life* magazines, and they appeared in major museum exhibits and best-selling books.

Folk singer Woody Guthrie and the novelist John Steinbeck combined the social realism of the Depression-era photojournalists with the populist cultural sensibilities of the left-wing Popular Front. Guthrie, who had taught himself to sing country music and folk ballads in Texas and Oklahoma, wrote songs that celebrated hobos, cowboys, fruit pickers, and New Deal monuments such as the Bonneville Dam. His best lyrics captured the spirit of America in a style so poetic and direct that one of his songs, "This Land Is Your Land," became a kind of national anthem. John Steinbeck's 1939 novel *The Grapes of Wrath,* a mythic tale of suffering, migration, and redemption, immortalized the Okies who fled the Southwestern Dust Bowl for California. Guthrie's and Steinbeck's work proved powerful and lasting in part because the protagonists were white, rural,

"One-Third of a Nation." Taking its title from FDR's Second Inaugural Address, the 1938 Federal Theatre Project production played to packed houses in New York and ten other cities. Arthur Arent's "living newspaper play" combined documentation and drama—and an imposing four-story tenement set—to convey the causes of and solutions to America's housing crisis.

Source: Library of Congress, Federal Theatre Project Collection.

and Protestant; their strength and dignity made them icons of the mainstream national culture.

Theater enjoyed a renaissance during the New Deal years as well. In New York, Lee Strasberg and Harold Clurman organized the radical, labor-oriented Group Theatre, which discovered playwrights Clifford Odets, William Saroyan, and Irwin Shaw. Odets's play *Waiting for Lefty,* the story of a taxi strike, was the most widely performed—and most widely banned—American play of 1935. In the labor movement, skits, plays, and radio dramas became an integral part of union propaganda. In 1935 the International Ladies' Garment Workers Union established the Labor Stage. One of its productions, *Pins and Needles,* became a Broadway hit. Employing actors drawn from the garment shops, the show satirized contemporary politics and the lives of ordinary workers.

The government supported dramatic arts through the WPA's Federal Theatre Project, which hired actors, writers, and directors from the relief rolls. It produced classics by Shakespeare, Molière, and Marlowe, as well as socially avant-garde works such as the *Living Newspaper* and Sinclair Lewis's *It Can't Happen Here,* a drama about fascism coming to America. Many plays were produced in multiple versions, with African-American, Spanish, and Yiddish casts. Led by Hallie Flanagan, the exuberant, politically engaged director of Vassar College's Experimental Theatre, the Federal Theatre Project became a lightning rod for conservative criticism of the New Deal, both because it employed so many radicals and bohemians and because many Americans thought theatrical work was hardly work at all.

Following the addition of sound to motion pictures in 1927 and the establishment of the major movie studios, Hollywood and its stars had moved to center stage in American mass culture. Though most Depression-era films had little social or political content—Busby Berkeley's extravagant production numbers, such as *Gold Diggers of 1933,* were escapist fantasies—there were some exceptions. The dark crime films of the early Depression, including *Little Caesar* (1930) and *Public Enemy* (1931), explored the gangster underworld, while *I Am a Fugitive from a Chain Gang* (1932) exposed the South's brutal penal institutions. Frank Capra's films, especially those starring Jimmy Stewart, contrasted a Popular Front version of small-town America with the corrupt and self-interested world of powerful politicians and businessmen. And comedians such as the Marx Brothers, Charlie Chaplin, W. C. Fields, and Mae West lampooned the social pretensions of the wealthy.

Many of the film stars of the 1930s, including Eddie Cantor, Joan Crawford, James Cagney, and Robert Montgomery, were partisans of the New Deal. They helped build the powerful Screen Actors Guild, which not only advanced the economic interests of its membership but also demonstrated that trade unionism was not just for factory workers.

"I Am a Fugitive from a Chain Gang." Mervyn LeRoy's 1932 film, starring Paul Muni as a wrongly imprisoned World War I veteran, exposed the abuses of the penal system in the South.

Source: Museum of Modern Art/Film Stills Archive.

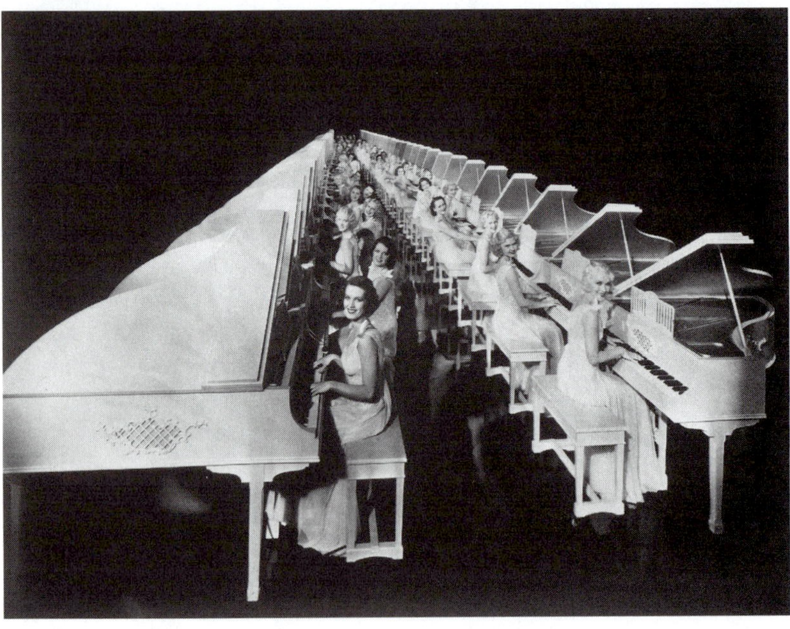

"Gold Diggers of 1933." Dance director Busby Berkeley excelled at creating extravagant musical numbers, such as this one in Mervyn LeRoy's sunnier treatment of "making it" in the Depression-era theater world.

Source: Museum of Modern Art/Film Stills Archive.

"The Ideal Picket." In 1941, trade union activism reached the workplace where some of the nation's favorite fantasies were produced. After Walt Disney fired union organizers on his art staff, his studio cartoonists went on strike. This cartoon from a newspaper report indicated how Disney strikers brought new skills to labor organizing. "There are mighty few labor disputes," the caption stated, "in which just about every striker can make his own picket signs. Consequently, the signs are bright and lively . . . attracting the passerby and winning friends for the Screen Cartoon Guild." **Source:** *PM,* June 6, 1941—General Research Division, New York Public Library, Astor, Lenox and Tilden Foundations.

Unionism in Hollywood entered Walt Disney's studios in 1941, when cartoonists successfully struck for higher pay and greater artistic freedom. Such activities were enormously controversial because they seemed to subvert the hierarchical celebrity culture promoted by the major studios.

The African-American Struggle for Equal Rights

In the 1930s African Americans took a half-step toward winning the civil rights and equality long denied them. They did not directly attack racial segregation of schools, jobs, and government programs, but their social and political agenda did demand racial equality—in citizenship, economic justice, and treatment under the law.

The legal strategy of the National Association for the Advancement of Colored People (NAACP) exemplified this approach. Lawyers Charles Houston and Thurgood Marshall attacked educational segregation by insisting that southern states abide by the potentially expensive requirements inherent in the Supreme Court's "separate but equal" doctrine (*Plessy v. Ferguson,* 1896). By demanding actual equality of educational opportunity, the NAACP opened border-state professional schools to African Americans. It also campaigned to equalize the salaries of black and white teachers throughout the South.

This strategy had its counterpart in the New Deal, for the administration's accommodation of southern segregationists was balanced in part by the racial liberalism of top government officials. Secretary of the Interior Harold Ickes and First Lady Eleanor Roosevelt helped recruit Roosevelt's "black cabinet," a group of subcabinet-level officials and outside advisers who fought hard against discrimination in New Deal programs. Members of this group—for example, Mary McLeod Bethune, an African-American educator and close friend of the First Lady, and William Hastie, the dean of the law school at Howard University—wanted to abolish segregation. But they often had to settle for equal access to government programs, and even that was not always forthcoming. Activists scored a great symbolic victory for racial equality in 1939, after the Daughters of the American Revolution (DAR) refused to permit the world-famous contralto and African American Marian Anderson to sing in the DAR's Washington concert hall. With the backing of Eleanor Roosevelt, a coalition of black civic leaders and NAACP officials won the Roosevelt administration's approval for Anderson to perform on Easter Sunday at the Lincoln Memorial. The performance established a powerful association between civil rights and a key symbol of American nationalism. "Genius, like justice, is blind," said Ickes, as he introduced Anderson to an audience of 75,000 people.

"Don't Buy Where You Can't Work." The women walking this picket line were asking customers to boycott one of the many white-owned stores that refused to hire black employees in West Baltimore, Maryland. Similar demonstrations appeared in New York, Chicago, and other large cities in the early 1930s.

Source: Afro-American Newspapers Archives and Research Center.

African-American workers demanded economic justice as well as the rights of equal citizenship. In Baltimore, New York, Chicago, and other large cities they launched "Don't Buy Where You Can't Work" campaigns, insisting that white owners of stores in their communities employ black clerks and salespeople. In the early 1930s these campaigns had a black nationalist and sometimes anti-Semitic flavor. But they took on an increasingly interracial, pro-union character, especially under the leadership of Adam Clayton Powell, Jr., a charismatic young minister from

Harlem, whose talent for oratory would later earn him a career in Congress. In New York, the Uptown Chamber of Commerce agreed to fill a third of all retail jobs with African Americans and to give preference to black applicants until that goal was reached. Thousands of Americans of African descent also obtained employment with public utilities, municipal services, and city transit lines.

During the Depression years the trade union movement became an increasingly important vehicle for the advancement of workers of color, but they overcame the legacy of white working-class racism and official union exclusion only with great effort. Officials of AFL craft unions, who sought to monopolize the labor market for their members, simply excluded African Americans from their trades. In Richmond, Virginia, for example, no black worker, union member or not, was permitted in the AFL Labor Temple. And when diesel locomotives reduced the number of firemen needed by the railroads, the white railroad brotherhoods waged a virtual war against black workers who remained in the occupation. Thus many black organizations, including the Urban League and the NAACP, remained skeptical of the union movement, and many African Americans remained loyal to paternalistic employers.

Attitudes shifted rapidly in the late 1930s, however. First, an inspiring, progressive trade union of African Americans gave a voice to all black workers. In the mid-1930s, under the superb leadership of A. Philip Randolph, the Brotherhood of Sleeping Car Porters took advantage of the nation's pro-labor mood to win union recognition, higher wages, and job security from the Pullman Company. For the 35,000 black and Filipino porters and maids who comprised the union's rank and file, the victory also meant a shorter workweek. More important, the protection offered by a signed contract gave these newly empowered people the freedom to press for civil rights in the railroad towns where they lived. And Randolph successfully used the union as a platform from which to denounce the AFL's continued racist practices.

Randolph also played a leading role in the organization of the National Negro Congress (NNC), an interracial group that flourished in the Popular Front culture of the late 1930s. Though Randolph was a socialist, for a time the NNC cooperated closely with both the communists and the CIO to support union organizing drives, agitate for public housing, and picket discriminatory employers. The Chicago branch, for example, fought for more relief jobs, organized a rent strike, forced the addition of black motormen to the all-white streetcar workforce, and mobilized ten thousand citizens in defense of a public housing project opposed by real estate interests. NNC activists in Richmond, Virginia, led black tobacco workers to victory in their strikes against employers wedded to conservative social and racial views.

In the tobacco, cannery, longshore, and foundry industries, African Americans often built all-black local unions. But the future of black labor lay with the interracial unions in the industries organized by the CIO. African Americans comprised about 25 percent of all packinghouse workers in Chicago, 15 percent of employees in the steel industry, 4 percent of autoworkers (10 percent at Ford), and a large portion of the workers in southern lumber and mining camps. Leaders of the CIO, such as Philip Murray, who presided over the organizing drive in steel, forthrightly promised that "there shall be no discrimination under any circumstances, regardless of creed, color, or nationalities."

Such sentiments flowed not just from the liberalism of the new labor leaders but also from a realization that the allegiance of African-American workers was essential to the success of the new movement. Not only were black workers numerous, but they also occupied jobs vital to the production process, from the hot and dirty foundries where engine blocks were poured to the stinking and bloody packinghouse kill floor, where African Americans controlled the flow of carcasses to every department.

The CIO's campaign to unionize the steel industry put its egalitarian claims to the test. Black-white conflict had helped to undermine the great steel strike of 1919. Now, the recruitment of black organizers to the Steel Workers Organizing Committee helped reassure skeptical African-American steelworkers that the union would take their interests seriously. Indeed, during the 1930s the committee's proportion of black officers exceeded that of its black members. The union's success brought an end to some of the most glaringly discriminatory practices in the steel industry. As the lowest-paid workers won large raises, the enormous wage inequities between workers began to shrink. Meanwhile, the CIO's culture of solidarity earned black workers some real social dividends. "Well, you know, I'll tell you what the CIO has done," reported a black worker in Chicago. "Before, everyone used to make remarks about, 'that dirty Jew,' 'that stinkin' black bastard,' 'that low-life Bohunk,' but you know I never hear that kind of stuff anymore. I don't like to brag, but I'm one of the best-liked men in my department. If there is ever any trouble, the men usually come to me."

Others were not so sanguine. Interracial unionism did little to end the social and residential segregation that pervaded working-class America. Although union meetings were integrated—often they were the first integrated event workers of either race had ever attended—activities that even hinted at social equality remained a flashpoint. "If you ask them to your dances, they'll come and they won't just dance with each other," complained the white president of a women's auxiliary of the Steel Workers Organizing Committee. African Americans were cautious as well. Asked whether "the white union men are sincere, this time," in urging Negroes to join the union, a black steelworker offered a shrewd analysis. "They're sincere enough, because it's the only way out, or else they'd have the same thing as in 1919. They realize this, so whether they like it or not, they have to include Negroes. We know it, and they know it. They're sincere, if you can call that sincereness."

Conflict between black and white workers emerged on the shop floor, too, where trade unions tended to reinforce the segregated, hierarchical job structures established in the pre-union era. At issue was the seniority system. Unions demanded rigid, plantwide rules regarding promotions and recalls from layoffs. Managers and white workers usually insisted on narrowly defined departmental seniority, which protected the rights of relatively well-paid whites who held the better jobs against the claims of black workers with longer overall seniority in the plant.

Though such issues proved increasingly divisive, African-American workers did not flinch in their growing loyalty to the new unions. Despite structural discrimination, the new unionism, with signed contracts, grievance procedures, and elected shop stewards, generated a kind of industrial citizenship that liberated African Americans from the paternalism, deferential subordination, and overt racism of the old social order. And it gave them new organizational weapons with which to fight. The Packinghouse Union would have failed "if it hadn't been for the Negro joining with you," a Kansas City black worker reminded his white brothers and sisters. "We are not asking for favors. We will take what is coming to us."

Backlash Against Labor and the New Deal

Although the labor movement and the New Deal seemed to sweep all before them in 1936 and 1937, their very success generated resistance and countermobilization from those who had long opposed their progressive goals. By 1937 the U.S. economy was producing as many goods and services as it had in 1929. Businessmen who had been desperate for federal help five years earlier suddenly resented new government initiatives. "The life preserver which is so necessary when the ship is sinking," observed an official of the Chamber of Commerce, "becomes a heavy burden when a man is back on dry land."

In California, right-wing mobilization began in 1934. It was a response set off by many triggers—the agricultural strikes in the Central Valley, Upton Sinclair's radical campaign for the governorship, and the general strike in San Francisco, among them. Vigilante groups terrorized the state's agricultural districts, kidnapping and beating labor organizers and their supporters. But the most powerful new opponent of labor and the New Deal was the Associated Farmers, a statewide interlocking network of packers, shippers, utilities, and employers of migrant labor. This association possessed strong ties to local sheriffs and police departments, and it maintained well-organized files on thousands of radicals and union organizers at its San Francisco headquarters. In 1936, urged on by the Associated Farmers, the California Highway Patrol sealed off the state to Okie migrants and crushed a strike by lettuce harvesters in Salinas. In 1937 California business interests broke a sit-down strike at Douglas Aircraft; they managed to keep most of Los Angeles an open-shop town until the early 1940s. Although California voters elected a liberal, Culbert Olson, to the governorship in 1938, the state's economic and political elite never made peace with the New Deal or with organized labor.

Resistance to New Deal liberalism and unions came not only from corporate executives but also from other branches of government. The 1937 sit-down strikes occurred just as Roosevelt placed before the U.S. Senate an ambitious plan to "pack" the Supreme Court with judges favorable to New Deal programs. Roosevelt saw his reelection in 1936 as a sweeping mandate, but he feared that the courts, which had invalidated much of the work of the New Deal's first Hundred Days, would soon strike down the fruits of the Second Hundred Days, including the Wagner Act and the Social Security Act. To preclude this possibility, the president wanted the authority to name up to fifty additional federal judges, including six Supreme Court justices, whenever an incumbent with ten years seniority reached the age of seventy. His plan would have increased the executive power over the judiciary and given him a solid majority of opinion on the Supreme Court.

To many Americans, not just the Republican old guard, both the CIO's sit-down strikes and Roosevelt's court-packing plan were an assault on the social order and on established property rights. Their fears and resentments exploded on the Senate floor on April 1, 1937, when both Democrats and Republicans denounced the CIO, its sit-down tactic, and what they considered to be Roosevelt's hunger for dictatorial power. Outrage at what many considered to be "changing the rules" in midgame by packing the Supreme Court turned not only many New Deal congressmen but also public opinion against the president. The court-packing plan went down to an embarrassing defeat—although the president soon got his chance to name several distinguished judges to the High Court, including Hugo Black, Felix Frankfurter, and William O. Douglas. But even before that happened, the Court, mindful of the wide public support enjoyed by New Deal programs, broadened its constitutional interpretation

"The Memorial Day Massacre." This photograph was one of many taken of the May 30, 1937, incident outside the gates of the Republic Steel Company's South Chicago factory. During the subsequent investigation by the U.S. Senate's La Follette Committee, these images—including motion-picture newsreel footage—proved that the brutal attack was unprovoked by the unarmed strikers. Only two words were audible on the newsreel sound track: "God Almighty!" The newsreel was never exhibited in Chicago.
Source: Chicago Historical Society.

and validated most of the legislative initiatives of the Second New Deal, including the Wagner Act and the Social Security Act.

The labor movement itself was not so fortunate. Buoyed by the upsurge of anti–New Deal sentiment touched off by Roosevelt's court-packing fiasco, the nation's "Little Steel" companies (large corporations that were small only in comparison to U.S. Steel)—Bethlehem, Republic, Inland, and Youngstown Sheet and Tube—resolved to resist the CIO's unionizing efforts. Employing nearly two hundred thousand workers altogether, the Little Steel companies usually dominated political and civic life in the middle-size industrial towns that depended on steel for jobs. The Steel Workers Organizing Committee (SWOC) rejected the sit-down tactic and deployed mass picket lines instead. Although the strikers shut many mills, the Little Steel companies were determined not to dismantle their company unions or to sign contracts with the steelworkers.

The standoff came to a bloody end on May 30, 1937. That afternoon, a crowd of more than a thousand steelworkers, family members, and supporters marched to the main gate of Republic Steel, on Chicago's South Side. Carrying large American flags, the demonstrators represented a cross-section of the ethnically diverse workforce in Chicago's steel industry, from Southern Europeans, who probably constituted a majority, to smaller groups of African Americans and Mexican Americans. The mood of the crowd was peaceful; Mayor Edward Kelly had promised to respect the union's right to picket at the plant.

Two blocks north of the plant gate, the demonstrators encountered a force of two hundred Chicago police, wielding clubs, ax handles, and guns. For a few minutes, marchers talked with the police. When the police refused to give strikers permission to set up a picket line, a few people in the crowd began throwing rocks. The police immediately opened fire. As men, women, and children ran for their lives, police shot at their backs, killing 10 demonstrators and wounding 30 others, including 3 children. Nine people were permanently disabled, and another 28 were hospitalized with injuries inflicted by police clubs and ax handles.

The next day, headlines in one of Chicago's newspapers proclaimed, "Reds Riot at Steel Mill." A coroner's jury pronounced the killings "justifiable homicide." A graphic Paramount Pictures newsreel, which showed fleeing strikers being shot in the back, was never exhibited in the city for fear of "inciting riots." Only the workers recognized the event for the massacre it was. On June 2, the SWOC gave the 10 slain marchers a mass funeral in downtown Chicago.

The Hilo Massacre. Demonstrators trying to escape police gunfire were driven into Hawaii's Hilo Harbor on the morning of August 1, 1938. In support of striking Honolulu workers, more than two hundred Hilo trade unionists had peacefully gathered to protest the unloading of the SS *Waialeale*.

Source: Grand Jury Exhibit 33, Hawaii State Archives.

The Memorial Day Massacre set the tone for aggressive police action elsewhere. Across the Midwest, 8 strikers were killed in June, another 160 seriously wounded, and many more subjected to tear gas and arrests. In Monroe, Michigan, an anti-union crowd brutally beat the black SWOC organizer Leonidies McDonald. Afterward, Republic Steel's private police tear gassed union pickets and set fire to the SWOC's Monroe headquarters. In Youngstown, Ohio, deputies shot 2 strikers outside Republic Steel's gates; another 42 men and women were injured. The National Guard, sent in by Governor Martin Davey and welcomed at first by SWOC leaders, jailed all the union's organizers and hundreds of its members.

That Davey would betray the CIO forces who had helped him win election testified to the strength of the backlash against labor and the New Deal. Elected on President Roosevelt's coattails, with strong support from the CIO, Davey sensed that the mobilization of anti-union elements in his state, combined with journalists' fierce attacks on "violent" and "radical" union activists, had turned many of his constituents against labor. Declaring that the "right to work is no less sacred than the right to strike," Davey forbade picketing and union meetings and ordered the National Guard to protect and escort strikebreakers into the steel plants. Ohio National Guardsmen killed and wounded dozens of strikers and jailed hundreds more in the confrontations that followed.

Staggered by such unexpected opposition from Democratic officeholders, the CIO's Philip Murray called on President Roosevelt to offer at least a verbal endorsement of union steelworkers who had supported him so loyally during his 1936 electoral sweep. But Roosevelt, weakened by his Supreme Court defeat, considered the Little Steel strike "a real headache" and spurned Murray's plea for help. "The majority of the people are saying just one thing," FDR declared during a June press conference: " 'A plague on both your houses.' " On Labor Day in 1937, labor leader John L. Lewis offered a rejoinder: "It ill behooves one who has supped at labor's table and who has been sheltered in labor's house to curse with equal fervor and fine impartiality both labor and its adversaries when they become locked in deadly embrace."

Defeat of the New Deal in the South

Although Roosevelt left the CIO in the lurch during the spring of 1937, he actually stepped up his efforts to make the Democratic party a more consistently liberal organization. Many New Dealers wanted to industrialize the South, equalize wages there with those in the North, and democratize the political system. In a speech in Georgia in 1938, Roosevelt brought the campaign for an expanded New Deal to the heart of Dixie. He attacked those southerners who were content to maintain a "feudal economic system." "There is little difference between the feudal system and the fascist system," he declared, referring to the rise of reactionary governments in Italy and Germany. "If you believe in one, you lean to the other." Voicing the views of a small but energetic group of southerners allied with the New Deal, Roosevelt declared the South "the nation's number one economic problem."

But southern political leaders rejected Roosevelt's gambit. During the court-packing fight and in the debates over relief and the minimum wage, Democratic congressmen and officeholders from the South had proven increasingly hostile to New Deal reformism. The white southern oligarchy was more secure in 1938 than it had been in the depths of the Depression. Massive New Deal financial subsidies had revived cotton and tobacco cultivation and begun a program of farm mechanization that tilted the balance of power still further toward the landed gentry. Especially as the CIO turned its attention to the mills, factories, and refineries of the industrial South, the benefits of federal relief began to pale beside the threat of federal intervention in labor and race relations. As one southern white crudely summed up his fears, "You ask any nigger in the street who's the greatest man in the world. Nine out of ten will tell you Franklin Roosevelt. That's why I think he's so dangerous."

This conservative turn did not reflect the views of the majority of southerners, black and white, who overwhelmingly favored federal regulation of industry and economic aid. But the states of the old Confederacy were not then governed by institutions that would today be considered democratic. Black southerners were systematically denied suffrage, and in most states the poll tax and other obstacles also prevented poor whites from voting. In Virginia and Mississippi, less than 10 percent of the adult population voted, even in presidential elections. In the long run, New Deal agricultural policies would force millions of rural black Americans off the land and set the stage for the transformation of the South and the Democratic party. But in the 1930s, such displacement merely generated surplus labor, depopulating the countryside and intensifying racial competition at the bottom of the labor market. As a result, a CIO effort to organize southern textiles—still the nation's largest industry—collapsed late in 1937.

Roosevelt's effort in 1938 to "realign" the Democratic party and purge opponents of the New Deal from southern congressional delegations was doomed to failure. In a series of Democratic primaries, the president supported Democrats who backed the Second New Deal against conservatives who opposed his program. He attempted to "purge" outspoken conservatives such as Senator Walter George of Georgia, who saw the president's program as "a second march [by Union General Sherman] through Georgia," and Senator Ellison ("Cotton Ed") Smith of South Carolina, who sharply attacked the fair labor standards bill. But the fall 1938 elections handed the administration another political setback. Not only did the conservative southern Democrats retain their seats, but Republicans also gained eighty-one seats in the House and eight in the Senate.

Roosevelt also failed to bring about a realignment in the West, where conservative Democrats and Republicans won many state and federal races in 1938. The reverses were ironic, for no region had benefited more from federal generosity in the 1930s. In Montana, for example, federal agencies spent five times per capita what they laid out in North Carolina. Federal assistance totaling more than $500 million went to help out western cattlemen hurt by overgrazing and falling prices, but many resented the help. "For this salvation," one historian observed, "many cattlemen never forgave the government."

New Deal support remained healthy in the Southwest, California, and Washington state; New Mexico, once solidly Republican, had become a one-party Democratic stronghold by 1938. But the losses in the South and elsewhere in the West had more lasting consequences. The failure to realign the Democratic party resulted in a generation-long alliance between conservative "Dixiecrats" and Republican opponents of the New Deal, one that effectively frustrated liberal efforts to expand the welfare state, advance African-American civil rights, and encourage the growth of the labor movement. As a reform movement, the New Deal was over. For the next quarter century and beyond, the nation would be governed by a schizophrenic Democratic party. At the presidential level, the Democrats would make an effective play for the votes of the northern, urban, working-class majority; once in power, however, Democratic presidents would be unable fully to deliver real reforms. With the institutional power their long years of congressional seniority assured them, southern Democratic legislators and their Republican allies would block most initiatives that threatened the industrial or racial status quo.

"I Am Hanging On to the Principles of the New Deal"

In his classic 1941 study of rubberworkers in Akron, Ohio, the sociologist Alfred Winslow Jones painted a complex picture of workers' political consciousness at the close of the New Deal era. Jones's study revealed that despite participating in various industrial actions (including the 1936 sit-down strike) and their anger at the abuses of banks, bosses, and corrupt policemen, a large majority of Akron's unionized rubberworkers continued to accept the basic right of capitalists to use their property as they saw fit. This belief was tempered, however, by a strong sense of social justice growing out of the workers' own experiences in fighting to organize a union. The following interview with James Hunt, a tirebuilder whose family had been coalminers in Ohio for four generations and who had moved to Akron to work in the rubber plants twenty years earlier, typified the attitudes of many Akron workers and unionists. Hunt's comments suggest that while American workers might be angry about the way employers and political leaders denied them the right to a decent job and fair wages, they still believed that they would win those rights within the framework of the existing political and economic order.

All my spare time I devote to the union—to meetings and activities. That's my social enjoyment. I want to see the union eventually a sound and steady organization. I am not at all satisfied with it the way it works at present. . . . Don't get me wrong. I'm a hundred per cent for unions and I think we are twice as well off since the union was organized. . . . Since the union was organized we have had more freedom, security, dependability, and stability in wages. The union has sprung up as a sort of social change in the face of the present fast speed-up system. In the beginning the union grew so fast that . . . anybody and everybody just jumped in and went along. Socialism has crept in and I'm no socialist so I greatly disapprove of that. I want to see majority rule in a union as well as in our government, but that is not true in either at present. . . . We must build a constructive organization instead of a destructive one.

. . . The big trouble with the New Deal is that a few people run the country instead of the majority like they should. Although I have been non-partisan all my life, I am hanging on to the principles of the New Deal, but I really know that it won't solve our problems.

. . . Every worker should make more than just living expenses, but the average one certainly does not. There ought to be a limit on how much the rich can earn and on the profits of any factory or corporation. There ought also to be a minimum for everybody. There is no sense in one man making a dollar an hour and another working twice as hard and making fifty cents. But I don't contend that everyone should make equal wages for that would be wrong too.

Source: Alfred Winslow Jones, *Life, Liberty, and Property* (1941).

"Un-American!" A cartoon published in the *Washington Post* ridiculed the hearings held by Texas congressman Martin Dies's House Committee on Un-American Activities during August 1938.

Source: Elderman, *Washington Post,* August 24, 1938—Copyright 1938, *Washington Post.* Reprinted with permission.

Labor Divided and Besieged

The attack on labor and the New Deal came not merely from the conservative elite but also from working people who feared the effects of reform on their own lives. The enormous changes at work in industry and politics opened up deep social and cultural fissures within America's working population. On one side stood the lower middle class and the old labor aristocracy, largely of Northern European descent. These men and women had a substantial stake in the old order, be it the comfortable politics of a small midwestern town or the chance to climb a few steps higher on the job ladder. Through organizations such as the Masons, the Knights of Columbus, and the evangelical churches, as well as through kinship and friendship, they had forged social and cultural links with those above them socially and economically. Those links seemed threatened by workers on the other side, including the CIO, with its leaven of radical Jews and anticlerical Catholics and its rationalizing, modernizing, and cosmopolitan outlook. These fissures became a deep chasm in the late 1930s, with a revival of right-wing agitation and Red-baiting by white workers. The terroristic Black Legion flourished in Ohio and Michigan factory towns; the Ku Klux Klan, in Indiana, Missouri, and Texas. Company-sponsored vigilante groups held sway in California and upstate New York. Such divisions penetrated the CIO as well, fueling the political factionalism that fractured unions in the electrical, farm equipment, automobile, and transit industries.

The AFL took full advantage of these divisions to wage an unrelenting war on its upstart CIO rivals and on those government agencies that had supported the new unions. For more than a decade, an episodic civil war in union ranks weakened labor's voice, both in politics, where liberals often split ranks, and in industries such as construction, shipbuilding, aircraft, and public utilities, where the AFL and CIO competed for members.

In Washington, AFL hostility to the CIO aligned the AFL with some of the bitterest opponents of the New Deal. In 1938 Congress authorized the formation of a new investigative House Committee on Un-American Activities (popularly known as "HUAC"). Under the leadership of Congressman Martin Dies of Texas, the committee attacked Popular Front political organizations and exposed left-wing influence in the Federal Theatre Project, which was ultimately closed down. The AFL used HUAC's hearings to denounce sit-down strikes and to publicize the role played by Communists and other radicals in the formation of the CIO.

A year later, the National Labor Relations Board came under sharp attack by the House Rules Committee, led by the conservative Virginian Howard Smith. Working closely with Smith and other anti-union southerners, the AFL charged that the National Labor Relations Board (NLRB) favored the CIO. Reeling from his recent defeats, President Roosevelt quickly appointed a new set of NLRB members who accommodated the AFL's point of view. The new board stressed the importance of stability and the validity of craft union claims. Hence the NLRB soon proved far less amenable to the industrywide union structures favored by the CIO and by those who saw the labor movement as a regulator of working-class income and purchasing power.

"The Charge Has Been Made That This Article of Yours Is Entirely Communistic"

The election of a large number of new conservative congressional representatives and senators in 1938 and the subsequent attack on and rollback of federal programs had ominous implications for the New Deal coalition. In 1938, congressional conservatives established the House Committee on Un-American Activities (HUAC) to investigate communist influence both in and out of government. Among those called to testify in December was Hallie Flanagan, director of the Federal Theatre Project, who was questioned by Democratic representative Joseph Starnes of Alabama about an article on workers' theater she had written seven years earlier. Despite its ridiculous qualities, the exchange between Starnes and Flanagan reveals the lengths to which conservative Democratic and Republican politicians would go to to discredit progressive institutions and individuals and smear them with the taint of communism.

Mr. Starnes: I want to quote finally from your article "A Theater is Born" . . . "The power of these theaters springing up everywhere throughout the country lies in the fact that they know what they want. Their purpose—restricted, some will call it, though it is open to question whether any theater which attempts to create a class culture can be called restricted—is clear. This is important because there are only two theaters in the country today that are clear as to aim: one is the commercial theater which wants to make money; the other is the workers' theater which wants to make a new social order. The workers' theaters are neither infirm nor divided in purpose. Unlike any art form existing in America today, the workers' theaters intend to shape the life of this country, socially, politically, and industrially. They intend to remake a social structure without the help of money—and this ambition alone invests their undertaking with a certain Marlowesque madness." You are quoting from this Marlowe. Is he a Communist?

Mrs. Flanagan: I am very sorry. I was quoting from Christopher Marlowe.

Mr. Starnes: Tell us who Marlowe is, so we can get the proper reference, because that is all that we want to do.

Mrs. Flanagan: Put in the record that he was the greatest dramatist in the period immediately preceding Shakespeare.

Mr. Starnes: Put that in the record because the charge has been made that this article of yours is entirely Communistic, and we want to help you. . . . Of course, we had what some people call Communists back in the days of the [ancient] Greek theater.

Mrs. Flanagan: Quite true.

Mr. Starnes: And I believe Mr. Euripides was guilty of teaching class consciousness also, wasn't he?

Mrs. Flanagan: I believe that was alleged against all of the Greek dramatists.

Mr. Starnes: So we cannot say when it began.

Source: Eric Bentley, *Thirty Years of Treason: Excerpts from Hearings Before the House Committee on Un-American Activities, 1938–1968* (1971).

The "Roosevelt Recession"

As if all these problems were not enough, toward the end of 1937 the economy took a nosedive and unemployment soared. In a single year industrial production declined by a third, manufacturing employment fell by a quarter, and in the big cities, WPA rolls rose fivefold. The nation seemed close to returning to the conditions of 1933: employed factory workers were cut back to a one- or two-day workweek, and some of the unemployed went hungry once again.

The so-called "Roosevelt Recession" was a product both of the president's political blunders and of far-reaching economic problems. By 1937 a remarkable economic recovery had convinced administration policymakers that the Depression was nearly over; indeed, rising prices now seemed the real threat. So despite continued high unemployment, FDR cut WPA expenditures, laying off 1.5 million relief workers. This premature effort to balance the federal budget sucked purchasing power out of the economy, as did the $2 billion tax increase required by the new Social Security program (the pension checks would not begin flowing until 1941). But the sharp recession of 1937 and 1938 also had more ominous causes. American capitalism was still an unstable system; none of the New Deal reforms had transformed its fundamental character. Instead, Roosevelt's smashing victory in 1936, the rise of labor, and the growth of federal regulation may well have inhibited investment by businessmen worried about the effects of these trends on their enterprises.

The Depression Continues. These migrants camped along U.S. Route 99 in Kern County, California, in November 1938. **Source:** Dorothea Lange, 1938—Prints and Photographs Division, Library of Congress.

The administration's response to the recession helped to define the contours of liberal thought and politics for the next generation. After much internal debate, Roosevelt announced two partially complementary initiatives in April 1938. The first was a massive spending bill inspired by the theories of British economist John Maynard Keynes, who argued that in time of economic stagnation, government should "prime the pump" by raising public expenditures. Admitting that a large budget deficit was unavoidable, Roosevelt asked Congress to appropriate $5 billion for public works and relief programs. The government added two million new workers to the payroll, and soon another recovery was tentatively under way.

Public Housing. Legislators and real estate lobbyists tried to keep expenditures for public housing low, contributing to the drab uniformity of many government-sponsored projects. But some public housing offered inexpensive homes with the style and amenities of a locality's private residences. With their tall windows and cast-iron balconies, these St. Thomas Houses, for example, fit comfortably into New Orleans's traditional architectural design.

Source: *Public Housing: The Work of the Federal Public Housing Authority* (1946)—General Research Division, New York Public Library, Astor, Lenox and Tilden Foundations.

But Roosevelt and his more radical advisers did not see this strategy as an adequate response to what many considered a stagnant economy. These left-leaning New Dealers believed that the concentration of economic power kept prices high and wages low. To generate significant spending, the nation needed more than budget deficits and public relief; it needed a shift in power from the corporations to workers and consumers. To explore this thesis, Roosevelt appointed Thurmond Arnold as head of the Justice Department's Antitrust Division, where he launched a vigorous attack on business monopolies. Working with Congress, Roosevelt also set up a Temporary National Economic Committee to study corporate power and obstacles to competition. Unlike some progressives, these New Dealers fought business monopolies not out of moral opposition to bigness but because they thought that the concentration of power undermined democracy and thwarted the expansion of consumer purchasing power. Ultimately, however, this broad vision lost out to a strategy that focused on manipulation of consumer demand through either tax cuts or spending programs. New Deal liberalism would, as a result, become defined by efforts to regulate and stabilize the economy through tax measures and spending policies rather than by intervening directly in the private sector and redistributing wealth or limiting the power of giant corporations.

Some New Deal initiatives got through Congress in the late 1930s, but they rarely matched the bold measures of the middle part of the decade. In 1937, New York Senator Robert Wagner finally won passage of the Wagner-Steagall Housing Act to stimulate construction of public housing. But Congress sharply limited appropriations for loans and restricted the size of grants to New York and other big cities, where the need for housing was most urgent. Even so, southern antagonism toward urban housing and Republicans' animosity to what they called "the cutting edge of communism" killed housing appropriations after 1939. In its short lifetime, the act financed 117,000 new housing units, which working-class residents found vastly superior to the dilapidated housing available to them in the private real estate market.

The power of rural interests in Congress ensured the continuation of farm programs and subsidies. In January 1936, the Supreme Court had declared the Agricultural Adjustment Act unconstitutional on the grounds that agricultural problems were local and not national issues. In response, Congress passed the Social Conservation and Domestic Allotment Act, justifying government limits on production on environmental grounds. When that program's voluntary limits proved inadequate, farm lobbyists won passage of a new Agricultural Adjustment Act in 1938, which brought both tighter controls and larger government subsidies. Overall, the New Deal agricultural programs did enable many farmers to survive the Depression—farm income more than doubled between 1932 and 1939, in part because of direct government payments totaling more than $4.5 billion. As usual, sharecroppers and tenant farmers were the last to benefit from the federal government's largesse.

Part of the reason for the gradual narrowing of New Deal liberalism was a sharp and increasingly effective corporate assault on programs that attacked their power and prerogatives. Businessmen routinely condemned Washington bureaucrats, left-wing New Dealers, and the new labor bosses. Such rhetoric had its appeal, especially among the affluent, but the major corporations were more successful when they projected a bright future in which they would bring the bounty of new technology and consumer goods to the whole population. Like the New Dealers, executives at companies like DuPont, General Motors, and Standard Oil of New Jersey looked beyond the Depression to a new era of high-wage consumption. But they celebrated the remarkable technical and organizational innovations industry had made during the Depression. For example, managers at DuPont transformed a company known for the profitability of its munitions business and the paternalism of its labor relations into a modern enterprise that boasted "Better Things for Better Living . . . Through Chemistry." The corporate counteroffensive reached full flower at the 1939 New York World's Fair, where scores of corporations advertised their vision of an abundant future under the guidance of giant conglomerates. GM's Futurama exhibit, which featured an elaborately crafted world of express highways, green suburbs, and well-planned cities, proved the highlight of the fair and offered a corporate alternative to the social democratic vision of New Deal partisans and labor activists.

Legacies of the New Deal and the CIO

By the end of the 1930s the resurgence of congressional conservatism and corporate power had checked further progress in democratizing American society. Even before then, some much-needed changes—full equality for women and African Americans—had failed to win much support even within the New Deal coalition and the labor movement. Still, the working-class upsurge and the New Deal had accomplished a great deal.

The biggest achievements, however, were not in solving the problems of the Depression. The New Deal was, in fact, an economic failure. None of Roosevelt's recovery programs ended mass unemployment or restored long-term economic growth. At the end of the 1930s, the effort to construct a new mass market for American industry was still incomplete. The labor movement was but half-built, commercial investment remained tepid, and trading blocs and war tremors shaking Europe and the Far East threatened the prospect of any revival of overseas trade. Working-class standards of living were still restricted, and working people still feared sudden layoffs. Half a decade of military mobilization and ultra-Keynesian government spending would be required to eradicate mass unemployment and restore economic growth and investment.

But if the New Deal failed to make capitalism work, its supporters nevertheless transformed the nation's politics. Roosevelt had assembled a governing coalition that would dominate presidential politics until the 1960s. White supremacists from the South belonged to it, but so did progressive farmers from the upper Midwest, urban politicians whose machines had been reinvigorated by the federal relief funds they administered, middle-class liberals anxious for social reform, African Americans who saw the new power of the federal government as a weapon they could turn to their economic and political benefit, and industrial unions that gave weight and influence to the Democratic party's left wing. Roosevelt often functioned as a power broker juggling those interests—and even those of his opponents. It was not always a pretty sight, but compared with the far more monolithic power wielded by the pre-Depression Protestant elite, the Roosevelt coalition had more legitimacy.

Culturally, the New Deal and the new industrial unionism represented a triumph because they transformed Americans' vision of themselves and of their nation. No longer a distant authority, the state became an active—even a protective—presence in citizens' lives. The welfare state and the labor laws enacted during the Second New Deal had many flaws, but they held the promise of new social and political enfranchisement. For at least half of the industrial working class—not only African Americans but also immigrants from Southern and

Eastern Europe—citizenship had been merely a formality, underused or unrealized. Despite the power of the coalition of Dixiecrats and Republicans, the new unionism and the New Deal played a decisive role in mobilizing these new Americans into an organized body of citizens whose political power and distinctive outlook gave birth to a new kind of patriotism. In the 1930s, after a thirty-year decline, the rate of voter participation began to rise. In the approaching world conflict, the nation would be more unified than ever, because its patriotism arose from a pluralism far more genuine than that of earlier—or later—times. In the 1930s, America's working people had transformed themselves from subjects into citizens.

The Years in Review

1935

- The Second New Deal, which includes the Works Progress Administration, Social Security Act, and Wagner Act, greatly expands the role of the federal government.
- American Federation of Labor (AFL) dissidents establish the Committee for Industrial Organization (later the Congress of Industrial Organizations, or CIO) under John L. Lewis to back aggressive organizing of industrial unions.
- Populist senator Huey Long is assassinated.
- The Communist party of the United States proclaims support for a "Popular Front" of labor, liberals, and New Dealers to fight business and the rise of fascism.
- The first canned beer appears on America's store shelves.
- Parker Brothers markets Monopoly, a board game based on the Landlord's Game, which was developed to popularize the ideas of reformer Henry George.
- Chain letters make their first appearance; the real winners are postal workers who receive overtime pay to sort the letters.

1936

- The Supreme Court invalidates the Agricultural Adjustment Act.
- The National Negro Congress (NNC) is founded to support union organizing drives, agitate for more public housing, and picket discriminatory employers.
- California's Associated Farmers crush the lettuce harvesters' strike in Salinas.
- African-American Jesse Owens wins four gold medals representing the United States at the Olympic Games in Berlin; Hitler, distressed when his "Aryan" athletes lose to Owens, walks out of the stadium.
- Roosevelt is reelected in a massive landslide over Republican Alfred Landon

and third-party candidates William Lemke, Norman Thomas, and Earl Browder.

- Scientific polling gains credibility when Gallup predicts a landslide for Roosevelt.
- GM employees initiate a massive sit-down strike in Flint, Michigan, which will lead to GM's recognition of the United Autoworkers Union in early 1937.
- Bandleader Fred Waring invents the blender as a tool for bartenders to whip up mixed drinks.

1937

- Strikes sweep the nation—nearly five million workers take part in some kind of industrial action and almost three million become union members.
- Roosevelt announces his court-packing plan.
- U.S. Steel recognizes the Steel Workers' Organizing Committee, but smaller steel companies resist; workers at Republic Steel in South Chicago stage a strike that turns into a Memorial Day massacre by police.
- Joe Louis knocks out James Braddock and becomes the World Heavyweight Boxing Champion and a hero to African Americans.
- Roosevelt signs the Marijuana Traffic Act, which outlaws possession and sale of the drug.
- The U.S. Housing Authority is created and assigned the task of building public housing.
- A sharp decline in the economy, "the Roosevelt Recession," saps the president's popularity.
- The Brotherhood of Sleeping Car Porters wins union recognition, higher wages, and shorter hours.
- An Oklahoma City supermarket introduces shopping carts to enable its customers to buy more than their usual wicker baskets can hold.
- The Hormel Company markets Spam, which soon becomes the nation's best-selling brand of canned meat.

1938

- The House Committee on Un-American Activities holds hearings suggesting that many of America's problems are caused by communist agitators.
- The Fair Labor Standards Act prohibits child labor, sets a minimum wage, and writes the forty-hour workweek into federal law.
- Democrats lose eighty-one seats in the House and eight seats in the Senate, as Roosevelt's effort to "realign" the Democratic party fails.
- Disney releases *Snow White,* the first full-length animated cartoon feature.
- Chester Carlson makes the first Xerox copy.
- Two young cartoonists from Cleveland sell the rights to their creation, "Superman," to Detective Comics, Inc.
- DuPont receives the first patent for nylon and begins manufacturing toothbrushes with bristles made from the "miracle" fabric.

1939

- New York World's Fair in Flushing Meadows presents vision of an abundant future under the guidance of giant corporations.
- African-American contralto Marian Anderson gives a concert on the steps of the Lincoln Memorial after the Daughters of the American Revolution bar her from performing in Constitution Hall.
- Germany invades Poland, beginning World War II.
- The Baseball Hall of Fame is created at Cooperstown, New York, and celebrates the myth that baseball was invented there one hundred years earlier.

Suggested Readings

Bernstein, Irving, *A Caring Society: The New Deal, the Worker, and the Great Depression* (1985).

Bernstein, Irving, *The Turbulent Years: A History of the American Worker, 1933–1941* (1970).

Brinkley, Alan, *The End of Reform: New Deal Liberalism in Recession and War* (1995).

Caro, Robert, *The Years of Lyndon Johnson: The Path to Power* (1982).

Chateauvert, Melinda, *Marching Together: Women of the Brotherhood of Sleeping Car Porters* (1997).

Cobble, Dorothy Sue, *Dishing It Out: Waitresses and Their Unions in the Twentieth Century* (1991).

Dallek, Robert, *Franklin D. Roosevelt and American Foreign Policy, 1932–1945,* 2nd ed. (1995).

De Hart, Jane S., *The Federal Theater, 1935–1939: Plays, Relief, and Politics* (1967).

Denning, Michael, *The Cultural Front: The Laboring of American Culture in the Twentieth Century* (1996).

Dubofsky, Melvyn, and Warren Van Tine, *John L. Lewis: A Biography* (1977).

Faue, Elizabeth, *Community of Suffering and Struggle: Women, Men, and the Labor Movement in Minneapolis, 1915–1945* (1991).

Fine, Sidney, *Sit-Down: The General Motors Strike of 1936–37* (1969).

Fraser, Steve, and Gary Gerstle, eds., *The Rise and Fall of the New Deal Order, 1930–1980,* (1989).

Freeman, Joshua, *In Transit: The Transport Workers Union in New York City, 1933–1966* (1989).

Hauptman, Laurence, *The Iroquois and the New Deal* (1981).

Jacoby, Sanford M., *Modern Manors: Welfare Capitalism Since the New Deal* (1997).

Kelley, Robin D. G., *Hammer and Hoe: Alabama Communists During the Great Depression* (1990).

Klein, Joe, *Woody Guthrie: A Life* (1980).

Leff, Mark, *The Limits of Symbolic Reform: The New Deal and Taxation, 1933–1939* (1984).

Lichtenstein, Nelson, *Walter Reuther: The Most Dangerous Man in Detroit* (1997).

Melosh, Barbara, *Engendering Culture: Manhood and Womanhood in New Deal Public Art and Theater* (1991).

Patterson, James T., *Congressional Conservatism and the New Deal* (1967).

Pells, Richard, *Radical Visions and American Dreams: Culture and Social Thought in the Depression Years* (1973).

Pike, Frederick, *FDR's Good Neighbor Policy* (1995).

Ruiz, Viki, *Cannery Women / Cannery Lives: Mexican Women, Unionization, and the California Food Processing Industry, 1930–1950* (1987).

Sanchez, George, *Becoming Mexican American: Ethnicity, Culture and Identity in Chicano Los Angeles, 1900–1945* (1993).

Starr, Kevin, *Endangered Dreams: The Great Depression in California* (1996).

Sullivan, Patricia, *Days of Hope: Race and Democracy in the New Deal Era* (1996).

Susman, Warren, *Culture as History: The Transformation of American Society in the Twentieth Century* (1984).

Tomlins, Christopher, *The State and the Unions: Labor Relations, Law and the Organized Labor Movement in America, 1880–1960* (1985).

Wald, Alan, *The Rise and Decline of the Anti-Stalinist Left from the 1930s to the 1980s: The New York Intellectuals* (1987).

Ware, Susan, *Beyond Suffrage: Women in the New Deal* (1981).

Watkins, T. H., *Righteous Pilgrim: The Life and Times of Harold L. Ickes, 1874–1952* (1990).

Weiss, Nancy J., *Farewell to the Party of Lincoln: Black Politics in the Age of FDR* (1983).

Williams, William A., *The Tragedy of American Diplomacy* (1959).

Ziegler, Robert, *The CIO, 1935–1955* (1995).

And on the World Wide Web

- Library of Congress, *America from the Great Depression to World War II: Photographs from the FSA-OWI, 1935–1945* (http://memory.loc.gov/ammem/fsowhome.html)
- Library of Congress, *American Life Histories: Manuscripts from the Federal Writers' Project, 1936–1940* (http://memory.loc.gov/ammem/wpaintro/wpahome.html)

chapter 10

UNITED
we are strong

UNITED we will win

A Nation Transformed: The United States in World War II

1939–1946

Fascism, militarism, communism, capitalism—these were the world-shaking "isms" that captured the nation's attention at the end of the Depression. When Ford Motor Company employees beat up labor organizers in 1937, the unions charged "fascism;" when President Roosevelt increased the budget for the army and navy in 1938, critics cried "militarism." When a recession began in late 1937, critics on the Left said it exemplified the recurring stagnation of "capitalism" and when the CIO attempted to organize the aircraft industry, manufacturers branded the effort a plot to advance "communism."

Even before the end of the 1930s, then, domestic events were linked to battlefronts and propaganda wars in Europe and Asia. The outbreak of World War II in Europe in 1939 and the U.S. entry into the war two years later further narrowed the gap between life in the United States and events taking place around the world. By the time the war came to an end in August 1945, those events would transform both American life and the global society to which the nation had become inextricably tied.

Militarism and Fascism Abroad

Just as the Depression of the 1930s had intensified antagonisms within the United States, so too had it bred international conflict. Industrialized nations responded to the widespread decline in consumer buying power by shutting foreign competitors out of their markets and scrambling for additional customers abroad. "Foreign markets must be regained if America's producers are to rebuild a full and enduring domestic prosperity for our people," President Roosevelt had warned in the mid-1930s. Such concerns were even stronger in Germany, Japan, and Italy, whose domestic markets and resources were relatively limited. The militaristic leaders of those countries believed that the existing world order served solely to maintain the supremacy of Great Britain, France, and the United States.

In East Asia, the Depression had sharply reduced exports and generated mass unemployment. Japan's authoritarian government moved to eliminate European colonies in Asia and create instead an empire—the "Greater East Asia Co-prosperity Sphere"—intended to ensure Japan's access to vital raw materials. In 1931 the Japanese Imperial Army took

War Production and Victory. Belching defense industry smokestacks resemble cannonfire in this Office of War Information poster, which urged higher industrial production.

Source: West Point Museum Collections, United States Military Academy.

over Manchuria and then gradually extended control over all of northern China. Although the League of Nations condemned the invasion, it imposed no sanctions. In 1937 full-scale war broke out between Japan and China. That year the Japanese captured the Chinese capital of Nanking, slaughtering close to 300,000 civilians. A civil war between Chinese Communists, led by Mao Zedong, and Chiang Kai-shek's nationalists crippled the Chinese resistance movement.

As the Far Eastern conflict spread, racial animosity and racist imagery were never far from the surface. The Japanese saw the Chinese as an inferior people upon whom the Imperial Army could impose their will, and they viewed the United States and Great Britain as decadent and materialistic colonial powers, whose strength would crumble when confronted by the pure spirit of Japan. American officials were equally blinded by racial stereotypes. They often sentimentalized the Chinese as an inherently peaceful peasant people who needed U.S. beneficence to achieve their destiny. In contrast, they characterized the Japanese as a "yellow peril," a devious, rodentlike race threatening to bring economic ruin to the West with exports of "cheap Jap goods."

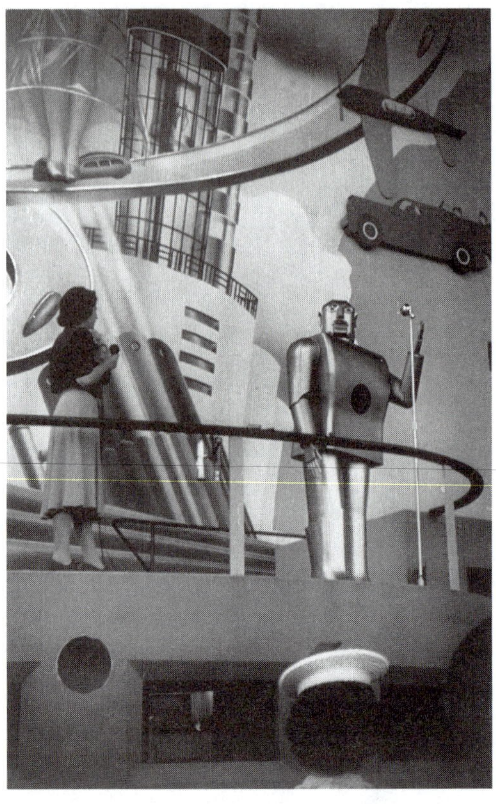

"The World of Tomorrow." The 1939 New York World's Fair opened in the shadow of approaching war, yet its theme and exhibits optimistically predicted a prosperous, pollution-free future based on the technological expertise provided by American corporations. Among its many attractions was Elektro, a seven-foot "moto-man" in Westinghouse Corporation's "Singing Tower of Light." Elektro—who "talks, sees, smells, sings, and counts with his fingers"—represented the benefits of electrical power. **Source:** Queens Museum of Art.

The success of Japan's aggressive actions encouraged European dictators, especially in Italy and Germany, where fascist leaders were dreaming of new empires. In Italy, Benito Mussolini's followers had seized power in 1922, ruthlessly suppressing labor unions, parliamentary government, and civil liberties. Mussolini's brand of fascism resembled other authoritarian, right-wing, nationalist movements, all of which were defined as much by what they opposed (liberalism, socialism, and communism) as by what they favored. But its leadership style differed, in that it involved mobilizing the masses of ordinary people in support of a particular leader: Mussolini came to be venerated as *Il Duce* (the leader). He appealed to Italian nationalism, trumpeting complaints about Italy's unfair treatment under the 1919 Treaty of Versailles and reminding Italians of their humiliating defeat by Abyssinia (today's Ethiopia) in 1896—the first time Africans had turned back European imperialists. An aroused Italy invaded Ethiopia in 1935, arraying airplanes, machine guns, and poison gas against the poorly organized riflemen of one of the few independent states left in Africa. When Ethiopia's Emperor Haile Selassie appealed to the League of

Nations, the League condemned Mussolini's act of aggression, but its members could not agree to impose a sanction on Italy's oil imports. In the end, Italy's subjugation of Ethiopia went unchallenged.

The rise of the German version of fascism—National Socialism, or Nazism—worried Americans more than any other overseas development. Americans had strong cultural ties to Germany, whose scientific, literary, and musical traditions were influential throughout the Western world. And although the Weimar Republic had become politically unstable by the 1930s, it still seemed to embody much that was cosmopolitan, modern, and democratic in twentieth-century art and culture. Given the advanced character of German science and technology and Germany's enormous economic power, Americans viewed the rise of Nazism with great alarm.

Like the Italian fascists, the Nazis repudiated both the terms of the Treaty of Versailles and also democracy, in all its forms. Nazi leader Adolf Hitler, elected chancellor in 1933, quickly seized dictatorial powers, taking the title of *Der Führer* (the leader), proclaiming a thousand-year *Reich* (empire), and outlawing all other political parties. Americans were appalled at Hitler's brutal destruction of Germany's democratic institutions, and they also recognized that his systematic and aggressive anti-Semitism marked the Nazi regime as something genuinely new and dangerous. When the Nazis burned nearly two hundred synagogues and looted thousands of Jewish shops on *Kristallnacht* (November 9–10, 1938), a shocked President Roosevelt confided that he "could scarcely believe that such things could occur in a twentieth-century civilization."

Although many in the West sympathized at first with Hitler's efforts to revise the punitive Versailles Treaty, sympathy soon turned to alarm as it became clear that the Nazis sought to unite all the Germans in Europe in a single German fatherland. In 1933 Hitler withdrew from the League of Nations and began secretly rearming Germany in violation of the Versailles Treaty. Then, using "salami tactics," he annexed slices of territory, none of which was large or vital enough to provoke outright hostilities with his opponents. In August 1936, he dispatched part of Germany's new air force to aid Spain's General Francisco Franco and his fascist forces in their attack on that country's democratically elected government. A series of pacts in late 1936 and 1937 united Japan, Italy, and Germany in an alliance that would become known as the "Axis," ostensibly to protect themselves against the Soviet Union.

The leaders of Britain and France, hoping to avoid another bloody war, sought to appease the German dictator. In the spring of 1936, when Hitler violated the Versailles Treaty by sending the German army into the Rhineland, a demilitarized zone in western Germany, neither Britain nor France attempted to force him to withdraw. Within two years, Germany had annexed Austria and then demanded that Czechoslovakia surrender the German-speaking border area known as the Sudetenland. Again, British and French leaders capitulated, agreeing at a conference held in Munich in September 1938 to Hitler's occupation of the Sudetenland. For decades afterward, British Prime Minister Neville Chamberlain's proclamation that the Munich agreement guaranteed "peace with honor . . . peace for our time" would be seen as a cowardly and shortsighted appeasement that fed the dictator's appetite for aggression. Only six months after the Munich agreement, Germany had gobbled up all of Czechoslovakia.

Within a year, the Nazis and the Soviets signed a "nonaggression" pact, opening the door to a violent partition of Poland by Germany and the Soviet Union. Many were stunned by the opportunistic agreement between bitter ideological foes—each of whom saw short-term advantages in a peace treaty. Nine days after the pact was signed, the German army invaded Poland on September 1, 1939. Unable to ignore the attack on their Polish ally, Great Britain and France finally declared war on Germany. World War II had begun.

Germany proved stronger, and the "Allies" (the term for the nations that fought Germany, Italy, and Japan in World War II) weaker, than most observers expected. Poland surrendered within a month, and the next spring German troops swept through Denmark, Norway, Belgium, and the Netherlands. In mid-June 1940, the French army collapsed and the Germans marched into Paris. Hitler continued his offensive, launching a bombing attack on London. In 1940 and 1941 Hungary, Romania, and Bulgaria joined the Axis alliance, and German troops moved into Yugoslavia and Greece. Finally, on June 22, 1941, Hitler broke his nonaggression pact with Josef Stalin and invaded the Soviet Union. The huge German army pushed to the gates of Moscow and Leningrad. Within three months, the Nazis had killed or captured more than three million people inside the Soviet borders.

From Isolationism to Internationalism

President Roosevelt condemned foreign aggression while the United States remained steadfastly isolationist through much of the 1930s. Fueling this self-contradictory stance was a highly publicized Senate investigation that uncovered evidence that Wall Street bankers, corporate munitions makers, and other "merchants of death" had led America into the Great War and then reaped huge profits from the conflict. Fear of engagements abroad proved so potent that in 1935 the Senate rejected U.S. membership in the League of Nations' World Court. Congress then passed the Neutrality Acts, mandating an arms embargo against both the victim and aggressor in any military conflict, renouncing President Wilson's aggressive definition of "neutrality rights," and establishing a "cash-and-carry" trading policy that deprived belligerents of access to American credit, ships, and military goods.

Late in the 1930s, however, the powerful isolationist current gradually ebbed as Americans came to appreciate the threat posed by the rise of fascism abroad. Chinese Americans spearheaded a boycott of Japanese goods; Jews and civil libertarians urged a similar ban on German products. Liberals and leftists sympathetic to the Spanish Republic attacked

Just Before the Battle. Members of the Abraham Lincoln Battalion marched in the streets of Barcelona in January 1937 shortly after their arrival in Spain. Within a month they would face their first action against Franco's rebels in the ten-day Battle of Jarama. The 450-member Lincoln Battalion, along with other International and Spanish Republican forces, succeeded in preventing the rebels from severing the strategic Madrid-Valencia road. But the cost was high: two of every three Americans who fought in the battle were either killed or wounded.

Source: Marx Memorial Library, London.

U.S. neutrality laws, which prevented the Spanish Loyalists from securing the military supplies necessary to fend off the fascists in that nation's Civil War. Some American radicals supported the Spanish Republican cause directly by enlisting in the Abraham Lincoln Brigade, which fought alongside 35,000 anti-fascists from fifty-two countries in what some later saw as a dress rehearsal for World War II.

This shift in the public's mood, especially among supporters of the New Deal, enabled Roosevelt to align the nation's diplomacy more closely with that of Britain, France, and China. When Japan renewed its assault on China in 1937, Roosevelt told an audience in Chicago that the United States must help the international community to "quarantine" aggressors and prevent the contagion of war from spreading. After war broke out in Europe in 1939, Roosevelt began mobilizing public opinion against the Neutrality Acts and even urged "measures short of war" to bolster England, France, and other "Allied" powers engaged in the conflict.

The Nazi conquest of Western Europe in the spring of 1940 pushed the United States toward active engagement in the war. Americans were shocked by the speed—just seventy days—with which Hitler's troops rolled into Paris. Congress reacted by tripling the War Department's budget, enacting the nation's first peacetime draft, and agreeing in March 1941 to lend or lease war material to enemies of the Axis nations (chiefly Great Britain, and later the Soviet Union). Through the Lend-Lease program, Roosevelt declared, the United States would become "a great arsenal of democracy." White House officials recognized that a Nazi-dominated Europe, combined with Japanese supremacy in East Asia, would endanger the capitalist world order that policymakers saw as synonymous with U.S. interests. John J. McCloy, a key figure in the War Department, warned that the Germans might "shut off our trade with Europe, with South America, and with the Far East."

In August 1941, President Roosevelt and British Prime Minister Winston Churchill issued the Atlantic Charter, a joint declaration of war aims. British and U.S. military officers and war production officials began to coordinate their strategy and planning. In return for this virtual cobelligerency on the part of the United States, Churchill agreed to an increase in U.S. trade and investment in the British empire. The U.S. Navy was soon patrolling the North Atlantic, an action that was just short of outright naval warfare against Germany.

U.S. and British leaders cooperated in the Pacific as well. Japan's invasion of the French colonies in Indochina provoked Congress to freeze all Japanese assets in the United States. Great Britain and Holland followed suit, preventing Japan from purchasing oil, steel, and other essential materials. Between August and November 1941, U.S. and Japanese diplomats exchanged a series of fruitless peace proposals. When their talks collapsed, Secretary of State Cordell Hull declared, "I have washed my hands of the Japanese situation, and it is now in the hands of . . . the Army and Navy." The only problem remaining, Secretary of War Henry Stimson confided to his diary in 1941, "was how we should maneuver [Japan] into . . . firing the first shot."

The nation's gradual move from isolationism to rearmament was accompanied by a bitter political and ideological debate. Even after the fall of France, not all Americans shared Roosevelt's predisposition toward intervention in the war. For example, Irish Americans, who hated British imperialism, were leery of an alliance with Britain, and many German Americans were reluctant to go to war against their homeland. A revitalized isolationist movement developed around the America First Committee, led by Sears Roebuck Chairman Robert Wood, aviation hero Charles A. Lindbergh, and numerous political and business leaders, most from the Middle West. Although well represented in the Republican party, the isolationists could find no presidential candidate in 1940. Instead, the GOP nominated Wendell Willkie, a Wall Street utilities executive aligned with the internationalist wing of the Republican party. Willkie's positions differed little from those Roosevelt held in 1940: he would keep the country out of war but would extend generous assistance to the Allies. A magnetic figure, Willkie tried to convince voters that giving the president an unprecedented third term would threaten the nation's democratic traditions. But he was no match for Roosevelt, who won reelection with 55 percent of the popular vote.

The isolationists' political defeat was matched by a moral one: many isolationists seemed oblivious to the danger of fascism and thought German domination of Europe was inevitable. Isolationist sentiment was also tinged with anti-Semitism, even in the face of Hitler's increasingly murderous policies. Charles Lindbergh undercut the isolationists' credibility when he asserted that Jews were among the most active of American groups pressing for the United States to enter the war. Conservative isolationists called the New Deal the "Jew Deal."

Leftist alternatives to internationalism collapsed just as quickly. In the months following Germany's invasion of France, most American trade unionists came to support Roosevelt's program of active U.S. involvement in the conflict. When labor leader John L. Lewis denounced Roosevelt and endorsed Willkie during the 1940 campaign, few workers followed his lead, prompting Lewis to resign as president of the CIO. Unionists such as Philip Murray, the new CIO chief, and Sidney Hillman of the Amalgamated Clothing Workers' Union saw U.S. participation in the war as politically advantageous to labor. Roosevelt, recognizing Hillman as an ally and a sympathetic spokesman in the labor movement, appointed him to important defense mobilization posts. In his new role, the CIO's co-founder worked to make unions full partners in the development of government economic and social policy. American communists also lined up behind U.S. intervention. They did so, however, only after alienating many former allies by a rapid about-face, first arguing that the war was merely one of imperialist rivalry and then, after Germany's invasion of the Soviet Union in June 1941, declaring the conflict a great crusade against fascism.

Pacifist antiwar sentiment also evaporated by 1941. Reinhold Neibuhr, America's leading theologian, renounced the socialism he had espoused early in the Great Depression and endorsed instead a neo-orthodox "Christian realism" that justified the nation's growing military mobilization. Such views were popularized with the release of the Warner Brothers' film *Sergeant York,* the drama of a young soldier's passage from Christian pacifism to military heroism during World War I.

The End of the New Deal

With the approach of war, the era of New Deal social reform, already weakened by the late 1930s, came to an end. Roosevelt's attention was focused increasingly on the international situation, and he directed his special adviser and campaign organizer Thomas Corcoran to "cut out this New Deal stuff. It's tough to win a war." The president, Corcoran later explained, had "heard complaints from the people who could produce the tanks and other war stuff. As a payoff, they required an end to what they called New Deal nonsense."

In July 1940 Roosevelt filled several influential government posts with conservative advocates of intervention, including Henry Stimson, who had served in President Hoover's cabinet, and Frank Knox, Alfred Landon's running mate in 1936. These men recognized the impossibility of repealing the New Deal and rolling back labor's victories. Their aim was to block a new round of social reforms and to prevent big business's power and prestige from further decline.

Nevertheless, labor leaders managed to take advantage of the defense employment boom to rebuild and expand the industrial union movement, so gravely damaged by the Roosevelt recession of 1937 and 1938. Between June 1940 and December 1941 the unions launched a wave of strikes that boosted wages and enrolled 1.5 million new members. Almost 2.5 million men and women engaged in some kind of work stoppage, more than two-thirds of them under CIO leadership. Because the Supreme Court had declared sit-downs to be a violation of employers' private property rights, many strikers resorted to another militant tactic, mass picketing: they kept out scabs—and police—by surrounding plants with a huge picket line, densely packed and constantly moving. These strikes demonstrated the unions' renewed power, and they won wage increases for workers from the southern Appalachian coal fields to the factories of General Motors, U.S. Steel, and General Electric.

Many of these work stoppages were strikes to gain union recognition from the nation's most reactionary employers. The most dramatic occurred at the Ford Motor Company, the only large automaker that had successfully resisted the United Auto Workers' (UAW) organizing drive in 1937. On April 1, 1941, tens of thousands of Ford workers walked out of the gigantic River Rouge complex in support of the union. Using their own automobiles as a barricade, the strikers formed a mobile picket line that stretched for miles around the Dearborn, Michigan, plant. Within a few weeks, more than 100,000 new workers had joined the UAW, under a union-shop contract that turned the pioneer auto firm into a bastion of militant unionism almost overnight.

Despite the UAW's victory, the organizing drive of 1940 and 1941 foundered on the shoals of national politics. In January 1941, Roosevelt declared that "whatever stands in the way of speed and efficiency in defense preparations must give way to the national need." Building on that premise, defense contractors, congressional conservatives, the military, and the White House demanded an end to industrial disputes, which the War Department called "an unpredictable drain on defense production." At Sidney Hillman's urging, a number of CIO unions called off their strikes, and the AFL agreed to curtail work stoppages on defense-related construction sites.

But neither Hillman nor the president could guarantee compliance at the local level. When union-busting tactics at a Milwaukee defense plant triggered a violent strike early in 1941, the Roosevelt administration set up the National Defense Mediation Board. The new board, which included representatives of organized labor, management, and the government, established a system of government-supervised wage agreements and voluntary arbitration of industrial disputes. The CIO agreed to cooperate, and its president, Philip Murray, became one of the board's members. He did so, however, while recognizing that a war-oriented labor-relations system would automatically "find its attention directed against labor in order to maintain the status quo as much as possible."

A California aircraft strike in June 1941 demonstrated the extent to which the federal government would use the defense emergency to throw its weight against union militancy and political radicalism. Wages were low and profits enormous at the North American Aviation plant in Inglewood, California, which supplied vitally needed training planes to the Army Air Corps. But when a strike erupted in early June, Sidney Hillman and the National Defense Mediation Board joined with the army's top brass to persuade UAW officials in Detroit to declare the strike a "wildcat," or unauthorized, work stoppage, motivated by communist opposition to the war. When strike leaders, a few of whom were indeed identified with the Communist party, resisted orders from UAW officials to return to work, President Roosevelt dispatched 2,500 active-duty troops to disperse the pickets and ban all gatherings within a one-mile radius of the factory. Within a few days, the strike had been broken.

At Inglewood and elsewhere, government authorities did not seek to smash trade unionism outright, only to tame and contain it. In California, the army pressured the National Defense Mediation Board to give workers at North American Aviation a big wage increase, thus helping national UAW leaders to reclaim the loyalty of the workforce. When wages at the plant were finally boosted in July 1941, a UAW paper greeted news of the award with the triumphant headline "Responsible Unionism Wins at Inglewood."

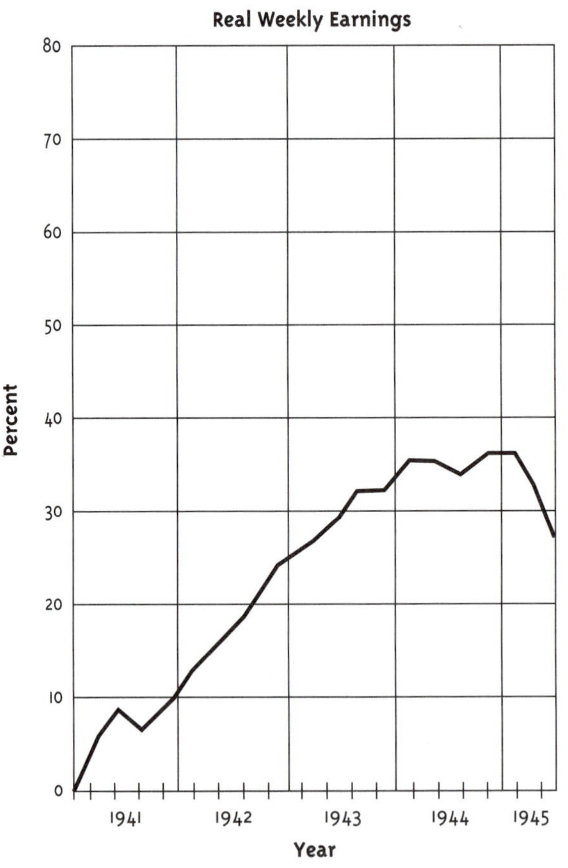

We're in the Money: War Time Pay. Despite wage controls and inflation, real weekly income increased by more than 30 percent during World War II. This was because millions of workers migrated to higher paying jobs and put in long hours of overtime. Weekly pay dropped sharply when the opportunity to earn overtime shrank at the end of the war.

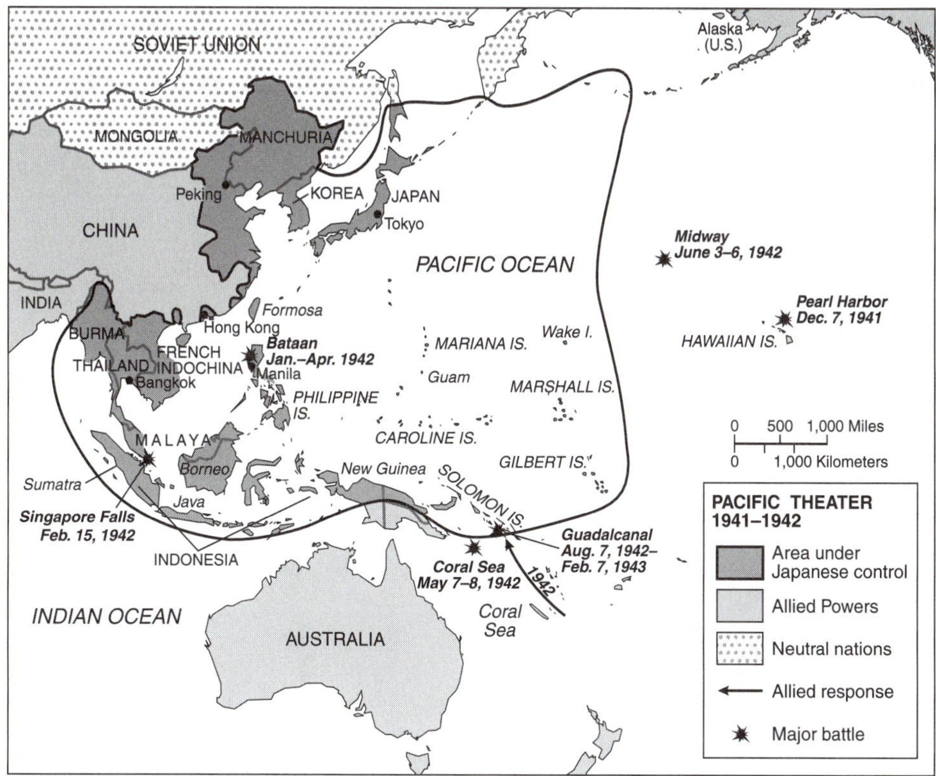

The Japanese Advance. Only five months after the Japanese bombing of Pearl Harbor, Japan controlled the oil of Sumatra, the railroads of Manchuria, the Philippines, parts of New Guinea, and dozens of strategic islands. Many feared that Australia would fall next.

War in the Pacific and in Europe

The United States was well on its way toward full wartime mobilization by December 7, 1941. The decision to enter the war was made final when the Japanese launched a surprise attack on the U.S. forces in Hawaii and the Philippines. At Hawaii's Pearl Harbor, Japanese planes sank or disabled several of the heaviest ships in the U.S. Pacific Fleet, killing 2,400 soldiers and sailors. The next day, Great Britain and the United States declared war on Japan, and Germany declared war on the United States. The Japanese attack—"A day that will live in infamy," Roosevelt called it—swept away nearly all popular resistance to U.S. involvement in the war.

Over the next six months, the Allies took a terrible beating in the Pacific. By May 1942 Japan had seized Indonesia from the Dutch, Indochina from the French, the Philippines from the Americans, and Hong Kong, Malaya, and Burma from the British. Japan also occupied most of eastern China. Americans were horrified when they learned three years later of a brutal "death march," in which thousands of American and Filipino soldiers perished on a long trek out of the Bataan Peninsula in the Philippines. "If you fell out to the side," recalled Anton Bilek, then a 22-year-old soldier from Illinois, "you were either shot by the guards or you were bayoneted and left there." Most Americans came to hate the Japanese, with a passion not equally directed at their German or Italian enemies. U.S. propaganda portrayed the Japanese as subhuman apes, insects, rats, and reptiles; Japanese propaganda, in turn, depicted Western leaders as devils, demons, and ogres.

In the Pacific, U.S. strategists sought first to contain the Japanese naval advance. Early in May 1942, relying on a handful of aircraft carriers left undamaged at Pearl Harbor, Americans turned back the Japanese fleet in the Battle of the Coral Sea. In June, during a four-day carrier battle near Midway Island, the United States regained control of the central Pacific. Japanese ships and planes outnumbered those of the United States, but

The Enemy 1. The cover of a December 1942 issue of *Collier's* magazine commemorated the first anniversary of the Japanese attack on Pearl Harbor. The vampire-bat portrayal of Prime Minister Hideki Tojo indicates one way the Japanese were presented in American popular media and war propaganda. Unlike images of the European enemy, the Japanese were depicted as vicious animals, most often taking the form of apes or parasitic insects.

Source: Arthur Szyk, *Collier's,* December 12, 1942—American Social History Project.

The Enemy 2. A 1942 poster depicting the Nazi enemy used a stereotype of a monocled Prussian officer that dated back to the war-propaganda images of World War I. Germans were portrayed as sinister but not as the nonhuman predators featured in the anti-Japanese posters.

Source: Victor Ancona and Karl Koehler, *This Is the Enemy*, 1942, offset lithograph, 34 1/4× 23 3/4 inches—Poster Fund, The Museum of Modern Art.

Americans enjoyed superior radar technology, better pilots, and success in breaking the enemy's wireless codes. By mid-1943, the Americans, aided by Australians and New Zealanders, had halted the Japanese advance and regained the initiative in the Pacific war.

The U.S. push across the Pacific proceeded slowly on two broad fronts. Under General Douglas MacArthur, the army leapfrogged from the Solomon Islands to New Guinea and on to the Philippines, where they landed in late 1944. Meanwhile, a huge naval force under the command of Admiral Chester Nimitz used amphibious assault tactics to fight its way through the central Pacific, from Tarawa to the Marianas. From there, U.S. B-29 bombers began raiding Japan. Such advances were bathed in blood. In August 1942, the United States launched its first offensive of the war, invading Guadalcanal, one of the Solomon Islands. By the time the Japanese finally gave up the island six months later, 25,000 Japanese and 1,500 Americans lay dead.

Determined as Americans were to "Remember Pearl Harbor," the Pacific Theater took second place to Europe, both as a battleground and as a strategic priority. The Soviet Union bore the brunt of the fighting in Europe. Facing almost two hundred German divisions along a huge front, Soviet soldiers and civilians halted, drove back, and then encircled 330,000 troops of the German Sixth Army in the four-month-long Battle of Stalingrad. When the Germans finally surrendered to the Red Army in January 1943, cold, hunger, and constant fighting had cut their numbers in half. The Germans lost 140,000 troops at Stalingrad, with another 91,000 taken prisoner. Tens of thousands of Soviet soldiers and civilians also died. The Battle of Stalingrad was the turning point in the titanic conflict that engulfed Eastern and Western Europe, where military and civilian deaths rose to nearly 40 million, including 6 million Jews murdered by the Nazis. The Soviet Union alone lost 20 million people during the war—the most casualties suffered by any nation.

For British and American planners, debate over a "second front" proved the major strategic issue of the first half of the war. Stalin was desperate for an Anglo-American invasion of France, to divert some of Hitler's forces away from the Eastern ("first") Front. Soviet Foreign

Minister Vyacheslav Molotov raised the issue repeatedly, and with increasing irritation; he was said to know only four English words, *yes, no,* and *second front.* But Winston Churchill and others in the British high command feared enormous battlefield losses in an early invasion of Western Europe. In 1942 and 1943, therefore, the Western allies concentrated their forces on Hitler's Mediterranean periphery, where they confronted a total of just twenty German divisions. Between October 1942 and September 1943, British and U.S. forces regained control of North Africa, conquered Sicily, and slowly fought their way up the Italian peninsula toward Rome.

"An American Soldier of the Antitank Co., 34th Regiment, Who Was Killed by Mortar Fire." Until September 1943, government censors blocked the publication of all photographs showing dead American soldiers. After that, censors continued to withhold many pictures—such as this photograph taken on Leyte Island in the Philippines on October 31, 1944—that did not, even in death, conform to the heroic image of the American fighting man.

Source: National Archives.

In lieu of a second front, the British and the Americans launched an aerial bombardment of German industry. Flying out of air bases in England, thousands of B-17s, Lancasters, and other four-engine bombers pounded aircraft factories, munitions plants, railroad centers, and oil refineries in Central Europe. Air combat gripped the imagination of both military planners and the public, for it promised to substitute advanced technology and industrial capacity for the blood and mud of ground fighting. But the campaign was a failure. Clouds, wind, darkness, and enemy fighters made a mockery of "precision bombing." Meanwhile, the Germans successfully decentralized much of their production capacity, pushing their aircraft and tank output to new heights in 1943 and 1944. In response, the Allies resorted to area bombing of German cities, including tightly packed working-class neighborhoods, an approach some Americans condemned as a terror tactic.

Life in the Armed Forces

Until the final year of the war, only a small fraction of the 16 million Americans who served in the armed forces actually saw combat. For most soldiers and sailors, training and supplying a vast and complex organization were the primary duties. GIs (so-called because their clothing and supplies were "General Issue" or "Government Issue") learned to march,

"The Home of One of Our Distinguished Personnel." A March 1944 sketch by twenty-year old Corporal Ben Hurwitz of the U.S. Army 351st Regiment, 88th Infantry Division, First Battalion, shows a GI in front of his makeshift "home away from home" in Tufo, Italy.

Source: Used with permission of Eleanor A. Brown.

shoot, drive a truck, repair a radio, type, and keep accurate records. As in the Civil War and World War I, life in uniform broadened the horizons of almost all soldiers. Wartime service introduced provincial Americans to Europeans, North Africans, and Asians. The draft was egalitarian, touching men from all classes and regions. "The first time I ever heard a New England accent," a Midwesterner recalled, "was at Fort Benning." For white youths in particular, military service helped to reduce the ethnic and regional differences that had long divided the working class.

Those GIs who were sent to the front entered a nightmarish world of violence and death. The combatants in World War II possessed far greater firepower than ever before. Consequently, the incidence of death and mutilation in units actually fighting the enemy was extremely high, sometimes one in three. World War II was the first war in which combat deaths actually outnumbered fatalities from disease or accident. Most of the 405,000 deaths suffered by U.S. forces came in the war's final year, when American armies spearheaded the assault against German and Japanese forces. War correspondent Ernie Pyle, who lived in the foxholes with the GIs, reported, "We see from the worm's-eye view, and our segment of the picture consists only of tired and dirty soldiers who are alive and

"'Fresh, Spirited American Troops, Flushed with Victory, Are Bringing in Thousands of Hungry, Ragged, Battle-Weary Prisoners' (News Item)." Sergeant Bill Mauldin's cartoons in *Stars and Stripes,* the Army newspaper distributed to troops, contradicted the American press's upbeat and sanitized coverage of the war. Mauldin's unromantic and biting cartoons, often celebrating the insubordinate spirit of American soldiers, were reviled by officers such as General George S. Patton (who personally reprimanded the cartoonist for "undermining the morale of the army"). But Mauldin's work, featuring the weary and cynical archetypal GIs Willie and Joe, was eagerly read by the troops.

Source: Bill Mauldin, *Up Front* (1945)—Copyright 1944 Bill Mauldin. Reprinted with permission of Bill Mauldin.

don't want to die . . . of shocked men wandering back down the hill from battle . . . of smelly bed rolls and C rations . . . and of graves and graves and graves."

American sailors also experienced the war's brutality first hand. In early November 1943 the *U.S.S. Montpelier* and other U.S. battle ships engaged the Japanese in a fierce battle off the island of Bougainville, ultimately defeating the Japanese naval force. James Fahey, a gunner on the *Montpelier,* described one typical incident in the diary he kept: "The [Japanese] ship was a mass of flames and red hot steel as the [U.S. Navy's] big guns covered it with exploding shells. . . . It must have been a

"We Were Fighting and Sleeping in One Vast Cesspool"

The historian William Manchester served as a marine in the Pacific Theater. He described the horror of hand-to-hand combat in the Battle of Okinawa, as U.S. troops neared Japan in the war's final months.

All greenery had vanished; as far as one could see, heavy shellfire had denuded the scene of shrubbery. What was left resembled a cratered moonscape. But the craters were vanishing, because the rain had transformed the earth into a thin porridge—too thin even to dig foxholes. At night you lay on a poncho as a precaution against drowning during the barrages. All night, every night, shells erupted close enough to shake the mud beneath you at the rate of five or six a minute. You could hear the cries of the dying but could do nothing. Japanese infiltration was always imminent, so the order was to stay put. Any man who stood up was cut in half by machine guns manned by fellow Marines.

By day, the mud was hip-deep; no vehicles could reach us. As you moved up the slope of the hill, artillery and mortar shells were bursting all around you, and if you were fortunate enough to reach the top, you encountered the Japanese defenders, almost face to face, a few feet away. To me, they looked like badly wrapped brown paper parcels someone had soaked in a tub. Their eyes seemed glazed. So, I suppose did ours.

Japanese bayonets were fixed; ours weren't. We used the knives, or, in my case, a .45 revolver and MI carbine. The mud beneath our feet was deeply veined with blood. It was slippery. Blood is very slippery. So you skidded around, in deep shock, fighting as best you could until one side outnumbered the other. The outnumbered side would withdraw for reinforcements and then counterattack.

During those 10 days I ate half a candy bar. I couldn't keep anything down. Everyone had dysentery, and this brings up an aspect of war even Robert Graves, Siegfried Sassoon, Edmund Blunden and Ernest Hemingway avoided. If you put more than a quarter million men in a line for three weeks, with no facilities for disposal of human waste, you are going to confront a disgusting problem. We were fighting and sleeping in one vast cesspool. Mingled with that stench was another—the corrupt and corrupting odor of rotting human flesh. . . .

After my evacuation from Okinawa, I had the enormous pleasure of seeing [John] Wayne humiliated in person at Aiea Heights Naval Hospital in Hawaii. Only the most gravely wounded, the litter cases, were sent there. . . . Each evening Navy corpsmen would carry litters down to the hospital theater so the men could watch a movie. One night they had a surprise for us. Before the film the curtains parted and out stepped John Wayne, wearing a cowboy outfit—and 10-gallon hat, bandanna, checkered shirt, two pistols, chaps, boots and spurs. He grinned his aw-shucks grin, passed a hand over his face and said, "Hi ya, guys!" He was greeted by a stony silence. Then somebody booed. Suddenly everyone was booing.

This man was a symbol of the fake machismo we had come to hate, and we weren't going to listen to him. He tried and tried to make himself heard, but we drowned him out, and eventually he quit and left. If you liked [John Wayne's film] *Sands of Iwo Jima,* I suggest you be careful. Don't tell it to the Marines.

Source: William Manchester, "The Bloodiest Battle of All," *New York Times,* Sunday Magazine, 14 June 1987. Reprinted by permission of Don Congdon Associates, Inc.

nightmare in hell for the Japs as they were roasted and blown to bits. I don't see how anyone could escape. It was a horrible way to die, it was a slaughter. . . . There is no safe place to hide and if you land in the water the huge sharks that are longer than a good-sized room are always close by."

In contrast to Americans who fought in the Civil War and World War I, when many men enlisted with and fought side by side with their neighbors, most GIs were strangers initially. Nonetheless, they quickly formed bonds that enabled them to fight and survive. "The reason you storm the beaches is not patriotism or bravery," one ex-GI explained. "It's that sense of not wanting to fail your buddies. That's sort of a special sense of kinship." Living close together and depending on one another for survival under the shadow of death, soldiers often formed intense emotional attachments. Their camaraderie became the basis for lifelong friendships,

"True Towel Tales . . . As Told to Us by A Solider." One of a series of towel advertisements published during 1943 and 1944 that framed its sales-pitch in homoerotic imagery inspired by purported testimony from GIs overseas. The ads, which are sexually ambiguous, suggest how the same-sex environment in the military afforded young men, both gay and straight, with opportunities for sexual self-discovery.

Source: *McCall's,* June 1944—Prints and Photographs Division, Library of Congress.

and for the veterans' organizations and unit reunions that proved so popular after the war.

Life in the armed services also had a long-lasting impact on America's homosexual population. Far from home, many gay men and lesbian women felt less social pressure to conform to heterosexual social norms. Bob Ruffing, a naval officer, remembered that when he entered the navy, "there'd be eye contact, and pretty soon you'd get to know one or two people and kept branching out. All of a sudden you have a vast network of friends." Many who first expressed their sexual orientation during the war later became pioneers in the gay and lesbian rights movement.

As in other wars, the military's need for soldiers tended to make it more tolerant, albeit silently, of the homosexual men and women in its ranks. Nevertheless, the U.S. military for the first time began to act not just against homosexual acts but also against gays as a group during World War II. Those whose sexuality was discovered received stigmatizing "blue discharges," which denied them GI benefits, adversely affected their employment prospects, and jeopardized their reputation in their hometowns. The military also launched investigations into lesbianism, although WAC officers were told to root out service women for homosexuality only in "extreme cases." At the end of the war, the army instituted anti-lesbian purges that coincided—not accidentally—with the military's decreasing need for female labor.

Patterns of discrimination also confronted black soldiers, despite the battlefield valor of African-American troops in previous wars. In 1940, African Americans were excluded from the U.S. Marine Corps, the Coast Guard, and the Army Air Corps. In the U.S. Navy, African-American sailors at first served only in the ship's mess, although by the spring of 1942 they were allowed to perform general labor.

The army accepted African Americans—more than 700,000 of them by 1944, including 4,000 women in the WACS—only on a segregated basis. These enlistees and draftees trained in segregated camps like Camp Shenango in Pennsylvania, where Dempsy Travis was sent:

> The troop train was Jim Crow. They had a car for black soldiers and a car for whites. They went to their part and sent us to the ghetto. It seems the army always arranged to have black soldiers back up against the woods someplace. Isolated. . . . If you went through camp as a visitor, you'd never know black soldiers were there, unless they happened to be working on some menial detail.

Early in the war, African-American GIs found themselves not only segregated but also restricted to duty in transportation, construction, and other support units. As one ex-sergeant in the Quartermaster Corps recalled bitterly, "We serviced the service. We handled food, clothing,

"You Can't Fight All of Them"

The African-American novelist, photographer, and filmmaker Gordon Parks served as a reporter-writer assigned to an all-black air force unit during the war. He recalls a small but telling racial incident that occurred in Virginia.

Our plane took off in a blinding rainstorm—and it landed in another one at Norfolk, Virginia. A taxi took me to the ferry landing where I would cross over into Newport News. I sat there in the waiting room for an hour on top of my battle gear among a boisterous group of white enlisted men. Four Negro soldiers were huddled in a nearby corner. Two of them were propped against each other, sleeping. . . .

We filed out when the ferry whistled. It was still raining and we stood near the edge of the dock watching the boat fasten into the slip. Through the wetness I noticed a sign reading COLORED PASSENGERS and another one reading WHITES ONLY. The four black soldiers moved automatically to the colored side, and so did I. How ironic, I thought; such nonsense would not stop until we were in enemy territory.

After all the outgoing passengers were off and the trucks and cars had rumbled past, we started forward. Then I saw a Negro girl step from the ferry. She . . . was in the direct line of the white enlisted men, who stampeded to the boat screaming at the tops of their voices. I saw the girl fall beneath them into the mud and water. The four Negro soldiers also saw her go down. The five of us rushed to her rescue. She was knocked down several times before we could get to her and pull her out of the scrambling mob.

"You lousy white bastards!" one of the Negro soldiers yelled. "If I only had a gun!" Tears were in his eyes, hysteria in his voice. A long knife was glistening in his hand.

"Soldier!" I shouted above the noise, letting him get a look at my officer's cap. "Put that knife away!"

He glared at me fiercely for a second. "But you saw what they did!"

"Yes, I saw, but we're outnumbered ten to one! You can't fight all of them. Get on the boat!" He looked at me sullenly for another moment, then moved off. We cleaned the mud from the girl's coat and she walked away without a word. Only proud anger glistened on her black face. Then the four of us joined the soldier I had ordered away. He was standing still tense beneath the sign reading COLORED PASSENGERS."

"Sorry soldier," I said. "We wouldn't have had a chance against a mob like that. You realize that, don't you?"

"If I gotta die, I'd just as soon do it where I got real cause to." His tone was resolute. I had to answer. I was tempted to hand him the bit about the future and all that, but the future was too uncertain. The yelling was even louder now on the other side of the boat. "Sons-of-bitches," he muttered under his breath.

Source: Gordon Parks, *A Choice of Weapons* (1966).

equipage. We loaded ammunition, too. We were really stevedores and servants."

The military's rising need for manpower eventually lowered some racial barriers. White air force officers dismissed "the Negro type" as lacking "the proper reflexes to make a first-class fighter pilot," but President Roosevelt nevertheless established the all-black 99th Fighter Squadron known as the Tuskegee Airmen and led by Colonel Benjamin Davis. The squadron won accolades in the Allied offensive in Italy for shooting down twelve German fighters on two successive days in January 1944. Another racial barrier fell January 1945, after the Germans smashed through the Allied lines, killing or capturing thousands of Americans at the Battle of the Bulge. The 2,500 African Americans who volunteered to replace those troops fought side by side with white troops to repel the final Nazi counteroffensive.

The military experience of Mexican Americans contrasted sharply with that of African Americans, in large part because Latino soldiers were never officially segregated. Nearly three million Hispanic people lived in the United States at the outbreak of the war. Most were residents of California, Texas, and the Southwest. About 350,000 went into the armed forces, nearly all of them as draftees. Most Mexican Americans were welcomed into combat units, and the army encouraged publicity about their outstanding records under fire. By the war's end, seventeen Mexican Americans had earned the Congressional Medal of Honor. Mexican-American soldiers were invariably placed in the infantry, where they suffered casualties disproportionate to their numbers in the general population.

American Indians could not vote in three states, but they could be—and were—drafted. About 25,000 Indians served in the military, many of whom had enlisted enthusiastically, as they had in World War I. By war's end, about half of all able-bodied Indians either had joined the military or had served in war industries. Among them were 300 Navajo marine "code talkers" who baffled Japanese electronic eavesdroppers by transmitting radio messages in their little-known language. They baffled some Americans as well: a few Navajos were temporarily taken prisoner by fellow marines who thought they were Japanese spies.

Mobilizing the Home Front

World War II ended the Depression with a massive dose of government-stimulated demand, doubling the gross national product within four years. At the peak of the war, the military commanded about 47 percent of all production and services. But because of chronic shortages in machinery, raw materials, and labor, the government could not let the cost and pace of either military or civilian production be determined by the free market. That much became clear in 1941, when Detroit's auto makers, enjoying their best year since 1929, delayed converting their factories to military production of tanks and aircraft. Government officials concluded that the whole economy would have to be centrally planned, with controls placed on the distribution and cost of virtually everything, from steel and machine tools to chickens, chocolate, and clothing.

Government propaganda encouraged Americans to support the war effort. Civilian volunteers collected scrap metal and old newspapers, donated blood, and served on local defense and ration committees. Twenty million families planted victory gardens, which produced more than a third of the nation's vegetables. Millions more bought Liberty Bonds to support the war during a series of morale-building campaigns publicized by Hollywood movie stars.

Roosevelt assigned the primary responsibility for mobilizing industry to the military and to corporate executives. The armed services set overall production requirements, and executives took the key posts in the mobilization agencies in Washington, D.C., serving as "dollar-a-year-men" while remaining on their company payrolls. They established what Sears vice president Donald Nelson, who became chairman of the War Production Board, called "a set of rules under which the game could be played the way industry said it had to be played." The government suspended antitrust laws, paid most of the cost of constructing new defense plants, and lent much of the rest at low interest rates. Cost-plus contracts guaranteed a profit on the production of military goods.

To fight inflation, other government agencies regulated wages, prices, and the kinds of jobs people could take. Following Pearl Harbor, the president set up the War Labor Board to arbitrate labor-management disputes and set wage rates for all workers. The Office of Price Administration began the complicated and controversial task of setting price ceilings for almost all consumer goods and of distributing ration books for items in short supply. Finally, the Selective Service and the War Manpower Commission determined who would serve in the military, whose work was vital to the war production effort, and when a worker could transfer from one job to another. These federal agencies were highly political institutions. By the end of the war labor, capital, consumers, and government policymakers were in constant conflict over the administration and enforcement of programs and policies.

Government planning of this sort fostered further concentration of the U.S. economy. In 1940, the top one hundred companies turned out 30 percent of the nation's total manufactured goods. By the end of the war, the same one hundred companies held

To Buy Is Patriotic. From smoking to skin care, advertisers rushed to identify their products with the war effort after the United States entered the conflict.

Source: *McCall's,* August 1942—American Social History Project.

70 percent of all civilian and military manufacturing contracts. Executives used their connections to key military procurement officers to obtain prime contracts, as well as the material and labor needed to meet production requirements. Coca-Cola accompanied the troops overseas, where bottling plants followed the battle lines; a piece of Wrigley gum went into each soldier's K-rations. Small businesses were pushed aside; if they went under, one War Production Board official explained, they could blame "the process of natural selection in the business world."

Not unexpectedly, military officials and dollar-a-year men came to share similar political and economic visions. Lieutenant General Brehon Somervell, the chief of supply for the U.S. Army, established an elite school at Fort Leavenworth, Kansas, where business leaders attended seminars and classes on the military's new role in U.S. economic life. General Electric's president, Charles E. Wilson, the powerful second in command of the War Production Board, proposed that business executives receive reserve commissions, so that close cooperation between defense contractors and the military might continue after the war ended. This relationship came to be known as the military-industrial complex.

The Wartime Industrial Boom

World War II was a metal-turning, engine-building, multiyear conflict that required an enormous amount of manual labor. Unemployment, which had been 14 percent in 1940, virtually disappeared by early 1943. World War II–era factories were gigantic, not only because production requirements were huge, but also because the technology of the assembly line brought together vast numbers of men, women, and machines. In the aircraft industry, for example, 100,000 Americans worked at the Douglas Aviation plants in El Segundo and Long Beach, California; 50,000 at a Curtiss-Wright plant in New Jersey; and 40,000 at Ford's bomber plant in Ypsilanti, Michigan. Forty-three percent of all nonagricultural workers were now blue-collar workers, the highest proportion in U.S. history.

The war proved especially beneficial to the American West, whose Pacific ports, favorable climate, and huge federal landholdings, suitable for testing new airplanes and weapons, attracted military procurement contracts. The big winner was California, which received one-eighth of all war orders. Aircraft worker Don McFadden remembered that Los Angeles "was just like a beehive. . . . The defense plants were moving full-time. . . . Downtown movies were staying open twenty-four hours a day." The University of California, California Institute of Technology, and Stanford University became key links in the military's weapons-development program. "It was as if someone had tilted the country," noted one observer. "People, money, and soldiers all spilled west."

Full employment had a radical impact on the lives of ordinary Americans. Fifteen million workers—a third of the prewar workforce—used their new labor power to change and upgrade their jobs. Some shifted from one factory department or office to another; at least 4 million—triple the prewar total—crossed state lines to find better jobs. The rural South experienced the largest exodus, California and Michigan the greatest influx. As factory work, especially in defense facilities, grew in prestige and earning power, office and service employment declined in status and pay.

To reduce absenteeism during the labor shortage, the federal government funded workplace amenities, such as in-plant training and cafeterias. "For the majority of workers the war was an experience of opportunity rather than limitation," observed Katherine Archibald of her fellow shipyard workers in Oakland, California. "It was like a social," Peggy Terry of Paducah, Kentucky, said, remembering her first months in a defense plant. "Now we'd have money to buy shoes and a dress and pay rent and get some food on the table. We were just happy to have work."

Most servicemen and urban workers enjoyed an unprecedented rise in their standard of living. Between 1939 and 1945, real (controlled for inflation) wages grew 27 percent. Indeed, the wages of those at the bottom of the social scale grew more rapidly than the highly taxed incomes

Guns Make Butter. July 1941 listings of available industrial jobs cluttered a Detroit labor-exchange blackboard, showing the dramatic effect that the war in Europe had on the U.S. economy.

Source: Scott Molloy Labor Archives.

of those at the top, generating the most progressive redistribution of American wealth in the twentieth century. George Peabody, who worked as a machinist at Lockheed, remembered the fat paychecks of those years:

> My income increased very rapidly because of the number of hours I worked. By 1944 . . . it was eight hours a day on Saturdays and Sundays and ten to twelve hours a day all during the week. . . . Even though the wages per hour didn't increase a great deal, the take-home pay was tremendous by comparison.

The military provided medical and educational benefits for a substantial portion of the male population, while a larger proportion of the working class could afford to take advantage of schools, hospitals, and clinics. Life expectancy, after remaining stagnant for a decade, increased by three years for the white population and five years for African Americans. Infant mortality declined by more than a third between 1939 and 1945.

For white workers from immigrant backgrounds, there was an added benefit. Unlike the anti-immigrant Americanization campaigns of World War I, propaganda used in this war attempted to unify the American people around a vision of cultural pluralism. The *Detroit News* praised the nearly spotless attendance records of six workers at GM's Ternstedt Division in Detroit, whose names were Kowalski, Netowski, Bugai, Lugari, Bauer, and Pavolik. "Look at the names . . . the sort of names one finds on an All-American football team . . . and at Ternstedt's, management and workers alike are hailing them as the plant's All-American production team." In many factories and mills, new opportunities for promotion, combined with vigilance by the industrial unions, enabled "ethnics" to break into the skilled trades or the ranks of first-line supervisors. These wartime developments accelerated the decline of immigrant working-class institutions—foreign-language radio programs and newspapers and immigrant fraternal organizations, for example—that had begun in the previous decade.

Women in the Workforce

The wartime mobilization also transformed the roles of women in the workplace. Shortly after the nation entered the war, the War Manpower Commission mounted a special campaign to recruit women, especially married housewives, into the defense industries. Government propaganda sounded a patriotic—if hardly feminist—trumpet: women workers were backing their men at the front, not pioneering a pathway out of the kitchen. As *Glamour Girls of '43,* a government-produced newsreel, announced, "Instead of cutting the lines of a dress, this woman cuts the pattern of aircraft parts. Instead of baking a cake, this woman is 'cooking' gears to reduce the tension in the gears after use."

But of course, work in a factory *was* an enormous transition from the kitchen, one that enhanced the self-confidence and expanded the horizons of millions of American women. War worker Delle Hahne remembered a Sunday dinner at a friend's house where "his mother and grandmother talk[ed] about which drill would bite into a piece of metal at the factory. . . . My God, this was Sunday dinner in Middle America, and to hear, instead of a discussion of the church service, a conversation

Industrial Chic. She now operates a drill press, but her lipstick is still unsmeared. The September 1942 cover of *McCall's* magazine imbued the new female industrial worker with the same kind of clean, unruffled glamour that the magazine had conferred on women's household work before the war.

Source: *McCall's,* September 1942—McCall's is a trademark licensed for use by Gruner & Jahr USA Publishing. Used by permission.

After Work. Men and women workers begin to unwind as they finish their shift in a Richmond, California, shipyard.

Source: Dorothea Lange—Prints and Photographs Division, Library of Congress.

about how to sharpen tools—it was a marvelous thing." Soon a popular song was being heard frequently on the radio, celebrating a young defense worker named "Rosie the Riveter," who could "do more than a male can do."

In munitions factories and pink-collar offices, World War II created new opportunities for women to have independent lives and to work and socialize exclusively with other women. With so many men overseas, women socializing together attracted little attention. And for lesbians, who were already leading women-centered lives, the war provided a protective cover, giving them new latitude to dress (pants were just becoming acceptable for women) and behave as they saw fit.

The expanding war industries allowed larger numbers of women than ever before to enter the previously male domain of heavy industry, and women responded eagerly to the new opportunities. The number of employed women rose from 11 million to nearly 20 million during the war, although only about 5 million had never before worked for wages. Hundreds of thousands of women moved from low-paying jobs to higher-paying industrial work. In 1940, one of every twenty production workers in the auto industry was a woman; by 1944, the number of women had grown to one in five. In a dramatic—and in some cases bitterly resisted—move, African-American women, who had been confined largely to agricultural labor and domestic work before the war, entered higher-paying and more dignified factory, clerical, and sales jobs.

The growth of female employment during the war did not generate a radical transformation in the way most Americans defined the rights and proper role of women. Many male workers were profoundly prejudiced against working women, greeting them with a barrage of hisses and whistles as they made their way through formerly all-male workplaces. And most employers, unions, and government officials were united in insisting that "Rosie" would be "the Riveter" only for the duration of the war and would gratefully turn over her job to a returning veteran at war's end. Jobs were segregated by sex in virtually all factories, and women workers were often denied specialized training. Although the War Labor Board insisted on "equal pay for equal work," employers frequently assigned women to inspection or small assembly jobs, or simply reclassified jobs to escape equal pay provisions. Women remained heavily segregated in a low-wage ghetto.

"We Were Determined to Stay"

Celia Saparsteen Yanish, who worked as a machinist in New York City, recalls the trials and tribulations of breaking into "men's work" during the war.

Before the war I worked in metal shops, assembling locks and doing other assembly work, until 1941 when the government set up a defense training school where they taught you to operate a bench lathe and drill press. . . . I was one of three girls in the school.

When the class was over we were sent to the machine shop. I was very happy. For the first time in my life I was going to be able to do skilled work. . . . I didn't know what it was, but I knew that until then only men had done this work.

[The men] were afraid we women were taking away jobs and they resented us. They complained they wouldn't be able to undress in the shop and work half nude like they did before. They said the women would interfere with their work, would distract them. . . .

I was about 24 at the time and I knew how to handle myself. I didn't laugh at the men's dirty jokes. But another girl who was only 17 did laugh and so the men got more and more brazen. They would be looking up her skirt until she would start to cry.

We worked on a competitive system. You had to keep up with the man standing next to you because he made more money if he could increase his production. If you slowed down, they would say, "we knew these women would be no damn good." We were exhausted all the time. The men would go home and sit down to a prepared meal, but when the women came home they had to get the meal ready for their family. . . .

It was very rough for a while, but we were determined to stay, and eventually the majority of the men learned to accept us and respect us as co-workers and union sisters.

Source: Miriam Frank, Marilyn Ziebarth, and Connie Field, *The Life and Times of Rosie the Riveter* (1982).

A large proportion of the female workforce were married women with children. Working wives and mothers bore the double burden of homework and wage work. Housing was cramped, and rationed foods were more difficult to prepare in the overcrowded housing in which many women lived. The government did build hundreds of child-care facilities during the war—far more than ever before—and more than 50,000 children attended such centers by 1943. But federal day-care programs were inadequate, and many women refused to use them because of the centers' inaccessibility, high cost, low quality, and restricted hours. By 1944, working mothers were being blamed for a new social phenomenon, the "juvenile delinquency" of unsupervised children.

By war's end, women's membership in unions had doubled, from 10 to 20 percent, but the unions' response to the needs of their new female members was mixed. Trade unions staunchly supported equal pay for equal work, if only to protect male members who might otherwise lose their jobs or their high pay to the tide of women workers. But most unions were apathetic or even hostile to the idea of maternity leave with continuous seniority or improved child care. A 1944 UAW conference of women workers endorsed such demands, but as Millie Jeffrey, the first head of the auto union's Women's Bureau, recalled, "The policies of the UAW were always very good. Getting them implemented was another story." When the auto companies began to fire women workers at the end of the war, unions such as the UAW raised few objections—perhaps not surprisingly, given the union's overwhelmingly male leadership.

The Limits of Pluralism

World War II created new opportunities for immigrants and women, but American pluralism and tolerance had limits. While the United States was fighting anti-Semitic Nazi Germany on the battlefield, perceptible anti-Semitism existed at home. As millions of Jews perished in concentration camps in Europe, the U.S. State Department and other government officials opened America's doors to only a handful of refugees. In 1939, the ship *St. Louis,* filled with more than nine hundred Jews fleeing Nazi Germany, sailed from one closed U.S. port to another, searching for a place where passengers could disembark. But there was no room in the nation, and the ship was forced to return to Europe. Most of the passengers ultimately were sent into Nazi death camps.

Conscientious objectors to the draft—especially Jehovah's Witnesses—had an extremely difficult time in World War II. At least six thousand objectors went to prison, sentenced to an average of five years;

beatings by guards and other prisoners were common. Many Jehovah's Witnesses, who refused to salute the flag because of their religious beliefs, were kept in solitary confinement for months, often on rations of bread and water.

But U.S. treatment of Japanese Americans proved to be the government's most egregious wartime abridgment of civil liberties. Unlike German Americans or Italian Americans, Americans of Japanese descent were presumed to be disloyal simply by virtue of their national origin. General John L. DeWitt, chief of the West Coast Defense Command, charged that "the Japanese race is an enemy race. It makes no difference whether he is an American citizen or not."

In March 1942, the government began rounding up all Japanese Americans on the West Coast, citizens and noncitizens alike, and transporting them to specially constructed detention camps. In California, nativists and racists who had long resented successful Japanese-American merchants, fishermen, and fruit and vegetable farmers supported the relocation and detention campaign. Japanese-American citizens on the West

Geography of Shame. More than 100,000 Japanese Americans would ultimately be forced to leave their homes and businesses on the West Coast. They then traveled to one of fifteen assembly centers where they were first processed and then transported by train to one of ten permanent relocation centers, or camps, hundreds and even thousands of miles from their homes. A much smaller number of Japanese Americans (about 17,000, most of whom were considered "enemy aliens") were placed in internment camps.

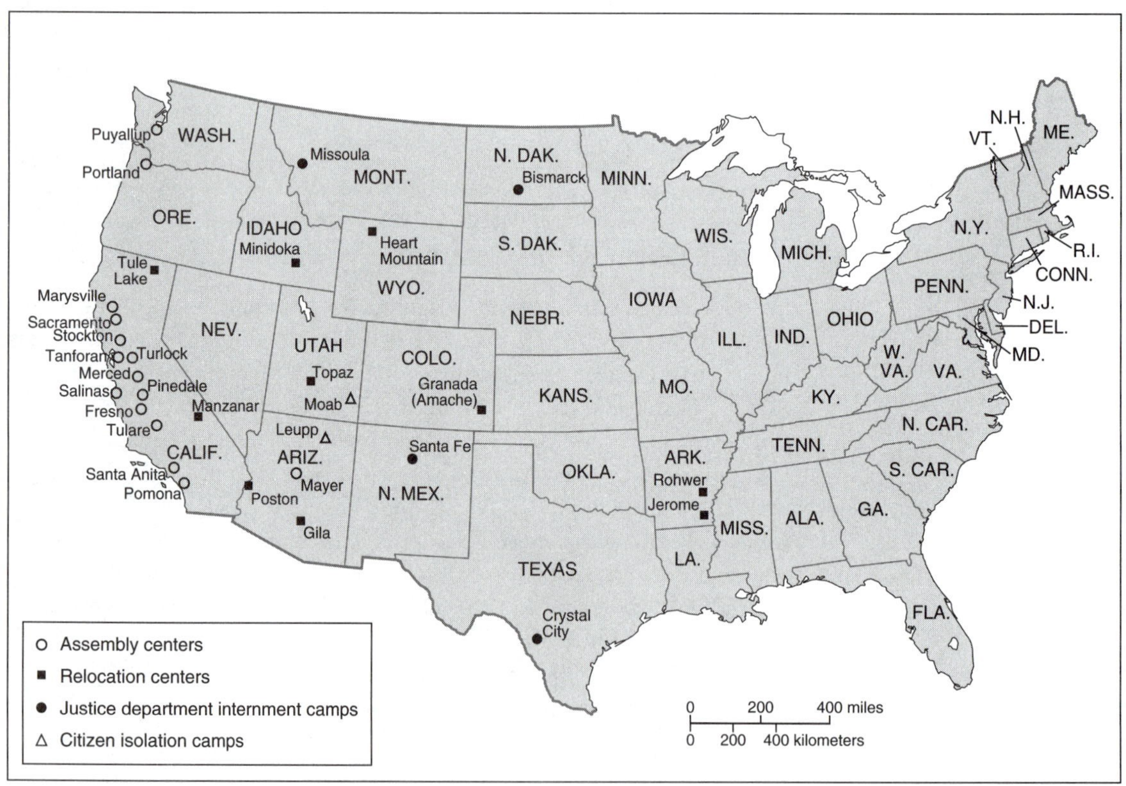

Coast were required to go to assembly centers for processing prior to assignment to a relocation or detention center further inland. One of the largest was the Santa Anita Assembly Center, a converted race track in southern California that ultimately held 22,000 detainees. Amy Uno Ishii, a Los Angeles teenager who arrived there in April 1942 with her mother and nine siblings, described the center as "a terribly dusty, dirty, smelly area," where people were forced to live in horse stables.

By the fall of 1942, more than 100,000 Japanese had been forced to abandon their jobs, businesses, and homes for a life in one of ten camps scattered throughout the West. Conditions in the remote and desolate detention camps were spare at best, deplorable at worst. Families crowded into long, wooden barracks with a minimal amount of privacy

"I'm as Loyal as Anyone in This Country"

In July 1943, government investigator Morris Opler interviewed a Japanese man, identified only as "an Older Nisei" (the first generation of Japanese Americans born in the United States), who was interned at Camp Manzanar. The man was indignant at having to sign a formal declaration of loyalty to the United States.

If this country doesn't want me they can throw me out. What do they know about loyalty? I'm as loyal as anyone in this country. Maybe I'm as loyal as President Roosevelt. What business did they have asking me a question like that?

I was born in Hawaii. I worked most of my life on the west coast. I have never been to Japan. We would have done anything to show our loyalty. All we wanted to do was to be left alone on the coast. . . . My wife and I lost $10,000 in that evacuation. She had a beauty parlor and had to give that up. I had a good position worked up as a gardener, and was taken away from that. We had a little home and that's gone now. . . .

What kind of Americanism do you call that? That's not democracy. That's not the American way, taking everything away from people. . . . Where are the Germans? Where are the Italians? Do they ask them questions about loyalty? . . .

Nobody had to ask us about our loyalty when we lived on the coast. You didn't find us on relief. . . . We were first when there was any civic drive. We were first with the money for the Red Cross and the Community Chest or whatever it was. Why didn't that kind of loyalty count? Now they're trying to push us to the east. It's always "further inland, further inland." I say, "To hell with it!" Either they let me go to the coast and prove my loyalty there or they can do what they want with me. If they don't want me in this country, they can throw me out. . . .

Evacuation was a mistake, there was no need for it. The government knows this. Why don't they have enough courage to come out and say so, so that these people won't be pushed around? . . .

I've tried to cooperate. Last year I went out on furlough and worked on the beet fields in Idaho. There was a contract which said that we would be brought back here at the end of the work. Instead we just sat there. . . . We had to spend our own money. The farmers won't do anything for you. They treat you all right while you're working hard for them but as soon as your time is up, you can starve. . . . When I got back to Manzanar, nearly all my money that I had earned was gone. . . .

Source: Michi Weglyn, *Years of Infamy: The Untold Story of America's Concentration Camps* (1976).

and furnished only with cots, blankets, and bare lightbulbs. Internees had to fend for themselves, making their own furniture and tending their own meager vegetable gardens.

At first, Japanese Americans, like other first- and second-generation Americans, were overwhelmingly loyal to the United States. But among a sizable minority, detention bred precisely the hostility and resistance that government officials feared. In 1943, more than one out of every four Japanese-American males born in the United States refused to pledge "unqualified allegiance" to the nation.

Still, when young Japanese-American internees were drafted, starting in 1944, only a minority resisted. Some 3,600 of these young Americans proved their loyalty, serving in the segregated 442nd Regimental Combat Team, the most decorated unit in the U.S. Army. Ironically, while their own families remained in an American prison camp, the fighting 442nd helped liberate the Nazis' infamous Dachau concentration camp.

The Supreme Court affirmed the legality of Japanese American internment in 1943 (*Hirabayashi* v. *U.S.*) and again in 1944 (*Korematsu* v. *U.S.*). By the time of the second decision, a few justices had doubts about

Manzanar Relocation Center, April 1942. These Japanese Americans in the newly opened California internment camp had gathered to watch the arrival of fellow internees. **Source:** War Relocation Authority Photo 210-GID-B3, from Edward H. Spicer, Asael T. Hansen, Katherine Luomala, and Marvin R. Opler, *Impounded People* (1969)—Used by permission of Rosamond B. Spicer.

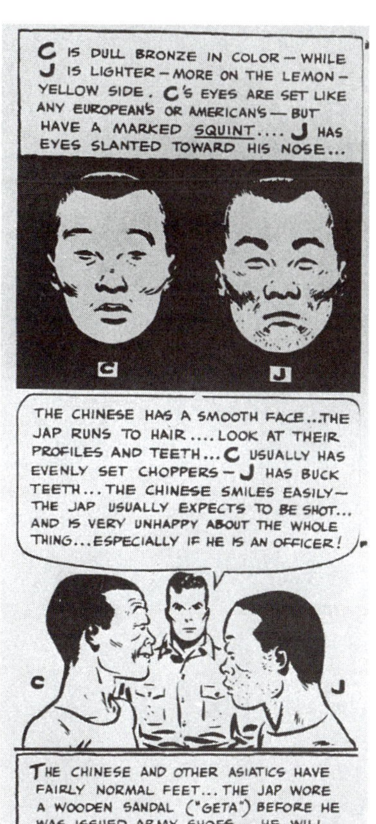

How to Tell a Chinese from a 'Jap.' These three panels appeared in the *Pocket Guide to China,* a U.S. Army pamphlet illustrated by cartoonist Milton Caniff (best known for the comic strips *Terry and the Pirates* and, after the war, *Steve Canyon*). This pamphlet and other official wartime publications distributed to American soldiers used outrageous racial stereotypes to distinguish between Asian friends and foes.

Source: American Social History Project.

the detention policy. The internment order, Justice Frank Murphy wrote in a dissenting opinion, went "over the brink of constitutional power" and into "the ugly abyss of racism." But only in 1988, after decades of legal action and public protest, did the U.S. government finally offer the surviving detainees modest financial restitution and a formal apology.

Chinese Americans, who had often been lumped together with other Asians and even called "Japs," worried that anti-Japanese hatred would be directed at them. They put up signs in their stores explaining that "This is a Chinese shop" and even wore buttons proclaiming "I am Chinese." Many Chinese Americans also proved their patriotism by joining the military. Charlie Leong, a resident of San Francisco's large Chinatown, later recalled that "to men of my generation, World War II was the most important historic event of our times. For the first time we felt we could make it in American society." Almost one-quarter of all Chinese adult males were drafted or enlisted.

Many other Chinese men and women broke out of their employment ghetto in laundries and restaurants as labor shortages opened up new opportunities. In the San Francisco Bay Area, Chinese Americans filled 15 percent of the shipyard jobs. A further breakthrough came in 1943, when Congress finally repealed the hated Chinese Exclusion Act. Although the new law set a token immigration quota of only 105 people per year, it allowed Chinese permanent residents to apply for citizenship. Asian Indians, who had also been excluded, sought similar naturalization rights around the same time and finally won them in 1947.

Origins of the Modern Civil Rights Movement

Although African Americans continued to endure victimization and discrimination during the war years, the early 1940s saw the first flowering of the modern civil rights movement. A dramatic shift in the social structure of black America gave rise to a surge of activism: for the first time, African Americans possessed the collective resources to inaugurate a nationwide liberation movement. Almost 10 percent of the southern black population moved to northern cities during the war, while an approximately equal number migrated from farm to city within the South. The number of African Americans who held industrial jobs almost doubled, and earnings—although still below par—soared from 40 percent of the average white wage in 1939 to nearly 60 percent after the war. This movement of black southerners from rural marginality to urban empowerment, one of the most important social and political transformations in American history, accelerated dramatically during World War II and continued for decades afterward.

Life was far from easy in overcrowded war production centers such as Detroit and Los Angeles, but African Americans joined together in an unprecedented fashion to make their aspirations known. NAACP membership increased nearly tenfold during World War II. The civil rights organization's national office also began assembling a talented legal team led by Charles Houston, dean of Howard University Law School, and future Supreme Court justice Thurgood Marshall to challenge Jim Crow practices in the South. In 1944, this team won a crucial Supreme Court decision that outlawed "whites-only" primaries. (Since victory in the Democratic primary was equivalent to winning elections in the one-party South, these primaries effectively disenfranchised African Americans.) The NAACP also joined with other groups such as the CIO to work against the poll tax, which was common in the South and which discouraged poor people of all races from voting. Some small victories against the poll tax and an end to the white primaries led to big gains in black voting—between 1940 and 1947, the proportion of black southerners registered to vote jumped from 3 percent to 12 percent.

As African Americans gained access to better jobs and higher incomes, they began using official war propaganda, which emphasized democracy and equality, to legitimize their demands. In 1943, the War Labor Board ordered an end to wage differentials based on race, explaining that "whether as vigorous fighting men or for production of food and munitions, *America needs the Negro.*" Removal of racial barriers at home, the board added, "is a test of our sincerity in the cause for which we are fighting." The African-American–owned *Pittsburgh Courier* popularized the "double-V" symbol, which stood for victory over fascism abroad and over discrimination at home. And Swedish scholar and social democrat Gunnar Myrdal sounded the same theme in his influential book *An American Dilemma* (1944), in which he argued that racial discrimination violated the deeply held precepts for which the nation was then shedding its blood.

The CIO's wartime organizing efforts also transformed African Americans' consciousness. Despite continuing racism among white workers and corporate managers, the CIO's campaign to organize a multiracial workforce into plantwide industrial unions gave black workers enormous leverage to press their grievances. Calling the CIO a "lamp of democracy,"

"Tests Have Shown . . . That Our Three Average Men Are Equal." A frame from *Brotherhood of Man,* an animated short produced by United Productions of America, a studio created by former Walt Disney animators, for the United Automobile Workers' 1946 interracial organizing drive.

Source: *Ammunition,* February 1947—United Automobile Workers of America.

an NAACP journalist wrote, "The South has not known such a force since the historic Union Leagues in the great days of the Reconstruction era."

But if wartime conditions made African-American advancement possible, forceful and well-organized protests of black workers were necessary to persuade unions and the federal government to root out discrimination in jobs, housing, and politics. The first, and in many ways the most dramatic, protest movement began in 1940, when A. Philip Randolph and other leaders of the Brotherhood of Sleeping Car Porters decided that only a show of strength would win African Americans access to good jobs in the new defense plants. Randolph announced plans for a July 1, 1941, March on Washington, in which thousands of African Americans would descend on the still-segregated capital city unless the federal government took vigorous steps to end racial discrimination in war industries and the military. Throughout the nation, the chance to act stirred thousands of black Americans never before touched by a civil rights movement. One week before the march was scheduled to take place, President Roosevelt, fearing the political consequences of such a demonstration, issued Executive Order 8802, creating a Fair Employment Practices Committee (FEPC) and directing government agencies, job-training programs, and contractors to avoid racial and religious discrimination. In return, Randolph canceled the march.

The FEPC, which had the same sort of far-reaching implications as the Wagner Act and the Fair Labor Standards Act, asserted that all Americans had a right to fairness on the job and at the hiring gate. As the Urban League's Lester Granger put it, "Employment is a civil right." But the FEPC was pitifully weak as a legal and administrative entity. FEPC officials could do nothing to modify segregation in the armed forces; and in the South, federal policy was little more than a legal fiction. In Baltimore, the Maryland State Employment Service systematically discriminated against African Americans who were seeking work. "Even if you had a graduate degree in electronics," remembered Alexander Allen, who worked for the Baltimore Urban League, "you would still be sent to the black entrance (for common labor and unskilled work). And there were police to enforce it."

In the North, however, the federal government often acted more forcefully, especially if war-related production or services were at stake. In Philadelphia, which was second only to Detroit as a center of defense production, the FEPC and the War Manpower Commission ordered the city's transit system to promote eight African Americans to positions as streetcar drivers. When the system's white employees responded with a protest strike in 1944, closing down Philadelphia's entire transit system and paralyzing the city's wartime industries, the federal government sent in eight thousand armed soldiers to enforce FEPC orders and end the stoppage. Afterward, Philadelphia employers opened more good jobs to the city's African Americans.

Even more important, the FEPC's well-publicized hearings legitimized racial progressivism and engendered a new sense of citizenship, which soon turned into a wave of direct, forceful action by black workers and their allies. "I am for this thing called Rights," a disgruntled woman wrote to the FEPC. And another asked President Roosevelt to help her find a job because "we are citizens and we pay taxes."

Detroit was a center of rights-conscious activism. African-American employees at Chrysler's Dodge Division walked out three times during 1941 to protest racial discrimination, both by management and the union. The next year, with NAACP backing, two busloads of black women who were seeking jobs occupied the personnel office at Ford's new Willow Run factory. And in 1943, three thousand black foundrymen quit work for three days over issues of job discrimination at Ford's River Rouge complex. Shortly thereafter, an integrated crowd of ten thousand, carrying banners proclaiming "Jim Crow Must Go" and "Bullets and Bombs Are Colorblind," marched to Detroit's Cadillac Square. There, union and NAACP leaders joined together to declare that "full and equal participation of all citizens is fair, just, and necessary for victory and an enduring peace."

Such assertiveness on the part of African Americans generated white resistance. Southern segregationists like Mississippi's Democratic senator James Eastland denounced the FEPC as a "Communist program for racial amalgamation." And white resistance often exploded in those urban factories and neighborhoods where the two races competed for jobs, housing, and political power. As black workers broke out of their job ghettos and moved into formerly all-white departments, a spectacular wave of racist strikes shut down scores of factories and shipyards.

These hate strikes were in part a product of one of the New Deal's most significant effects: the transformation of an ethnically heterogeneous, episodically employed working class into the self-confident, race-conscious, working class of the postwar era. This new Americanism subordinated older ethnic identities within a transcendent sense of "whiteness," drawing confidence and strength from full employment, the new union movement, and the still-segregated military. In many factories and mills, white workers came to see the union's representatives and seniority system as protectors of their job rights, which they defended with almost as much steadfastness as they did their racially segregated neighborhoods. With the continuing influx of southern migrants, many northern cities became fertile soil for the racist propaganda of the Ku Klux Klan and other demagogues.

Black workers were not intimidated, however. Supported by many union-conscious white workers, they insisted that the unions and the government take steps to contain the inflammatory work stoppages. When three thousand workers shut down a factory in North Canton, Ohio, to protest the first African-American hires there, the United Electrical Workers sent organizer Henry Fielding to town in 1943. North Canton was a "lily-white community," he remembered:

> There was a mass meeting during working hours and I took them on . . . a screaming, hysterical audience of three thousand people calling me everything under the sun and threatening me. . . . It took a couple of hours, and although I did not convince the workers that it was right, I did persuade them to go back to work, that there was no alternative.

Racial conflicts over housing were equally intense. When African Americans attempted to move into Detroit's federally financed Sojourner Truth housing project early in 1942, a crowd of rock-throwing working-class whites jeered and blocked the way. Bowing to white pressure, city and federal officials moved to bar occupancy by African Americans. But a coalition of black civic groups and CIO activists forced them to back down and open the apartments to black and white occupants.

Racial violence peaked in 1943, with 250 incidents in forty-seven cities. The worst riot erupted in Detroit,

The Detroit Riot, June 21, 1943. While police stood by, white crowds terrorized African Americans on Detroit's Woodward Avenue. As shown here, African-American motorists were pursued and beaten, their cars destroyed. Shortly after this photo was taken, the victim's car (halted in front of the bus) was overturned and set on fire. **Source:** *Detroit News.*

Zoot-Suit Riot. In the weeks preceding the riots, a nationally syndicated comic strip satirically skewered the zoot suiters. Li'l Abner Yokum, cartoonist Al Capp's good-natured and dullwitted hero, became the pawn of zoot-suit manufacturers. As "Zoot-Suit Yokum," he performed heroic deeds that prompted a nationwide fashion fad—much to the horror, as this panel shows, of more levelheaded citizens. Capp's treatment reflected general hostility toward the defiant style favored by many young Mexican Americans. After the riots, the Los Angeles City Council passed a law that made wearing a zoot suit a misdemeanor.

Source: *Mercury Herald and News,* April 25, 1943—

where a fight at the Belle Isle amusement park ignited thirty hours of violence and left nine whites and twenty-five blacks dead and almost seven hundred people seriously injured.

Race riots flared in wartime Los Angeles, too, but with a difference: this time the violence also targeted Mexican-American males. Resentment against Mexican Americans—especially those who defied mainstream society by wearing the distinctive, loose-fitting "zoot suits" favored by young Chicanos—mushroomed as discriminatory barriers to employment fell. In June 1943, local newspapers played up a story about Mexican youths arrested for assaulting a group of Anglo sailors. In response, thousands of marines, sailors, soldiers, and civilians visited a reign of terror on Mexican-American neighborhoods in Los Angeles, beating up young zoot suiters, stripping off their clothes, and cutting their long hair. More than a hundred people were injured in the riots, which inspired anti-Mexican activity in seven other cities as well. Only when the Mexican ambassador interceded—and fear grew that the Axis countries would make effective propaganda of the riots—did the U.S. government declare downtown Los Angeles off-limits to naval personnel.

Labor's War at Home

The war brought about permanent changes not only in race relations but also in the relationship between labor and capital, both in the factory and in the corridors of power in Washington. At the outset of the conflict, most labor leaders had quickly agreed to a no-strike pledge. The resulting decline in shop-floor strife pleased the Roosevelt administration and business leaders alike. But patriotic unionism created other problems. In arbitrating the wages of millions of workers, the War Labor Board gave priority to increasing production and resisting inflation, not to settling workers' grievances. The keystone of the board's policy was a July 1942 decision in the Little Steel case, which raised wages for workers at the nation's smaller steel companies only 15 percent above the level of January 1, 1941. Since most union workers had already won a negotiated wage increase of that size in the spring of 1941, the board's ruling meant that few workers could expect a further wage boost for the duration of the war.

Board officials and even some employers recognized the dilemma for trade union leaders. If unions could not strike or bargain for higher wages, then why should workers join them? The War Labor Board therefore put in place a "maintenance of membership" policy, which virtually mandated that any employee at a unionized workplace must join and pay dues to the union. Thus the expansion of war production led automatically to an expansion of union membership, which jumped from fewer than ten million to nearly fifteen million. An organizer in the electrical industry recalled: "We'd circulate membership cards in front of the management. . . . I remember a two-year period, 1942–43, where we went through some sixty-six or sixty-eight plants, organized them, and held elections. We lost one!"

But the growth of unions hardly eliminated workers' grievances. Wage-rate inequalities were one vexing and persistent cause of discontent on the shop floor. Workers also clashed with managers and government officials over control of work on the shop floor. Foremen and managers often took advantage of labor's no-strike pledge to regain some of the power unions had wrested from them in the turbulent prewar years. And the wartime demand for more and more production also generated conflicts over speed-ups and safety. Edward Osberg, who made airplane engines for Chrysler during the war, remembered that "whenever engineers and general superintendents devised a new process to make something faster or better, they went ahead and did it. They didn't care if it killed someone or if the fumes and dust were dangerous." Workers challenged management over the right to set production standards and piece rates, assign work, and discipline employees. Unauthorized strikes over such issues mounted steadily from 1942 until the end of the war. Government officials denounced these stoppages as "unpatriotic," but rank-and-file pressures kept many unions in turmoil.

The largest wartime labor confrontation took place in the coal industry. John L. Lewis, head of the United Mine Workers, had never thought the War Labor Board's Little Steel wage formula was equitable, and during 1942 he came under increasing pressure from dissatisfied miners to obtain pay increases for them. To break the "Little Steel formula," Lewis called 500,000 miners out on strike four times in 1943 alone. These strikes generated a storm of protest. All the major newspapers denounced Lewis, and public-opinion polls condemned the strikes. In June

"Zero Hour." A cartoon in the March 29, 1943, issue of *Time* magazine interpreted John L. Lewis's challenge to the War Labor Board's Little Steel wage formula in military terms. Lewis, arguing that "bayonets cannot mine coal," extracted a wage increase for miners in spite of the wartime wage ceiling.

Source: James Cutter, *Time,* March 29, 1943—American Social History Project.

1943, Congress passed (over Roosevelt's veto) the Smith-Connally War Labor Disputes Act, which gave the president the power to seize strikebound mines and factories. The legislation made it a crime to advocate work stoppages and it prohibited unions from contributing to electoral campaigns. This was the first anti-union measure passed by Congress since the early 1930s, and it foreshadowed the more conservative legislative climate of the postwar years.

But that did not stop Lewis. On November 1, 1943, the miners struck again. Roosevelt seized the coal mines and threatened to end the miners' draft deferments. At the same time, however, the president understood that the nation and the war effort ran on coal and that, as Lewis had always maintained, "bayonets cannot mine coal." Roosevelt ordered Secretary of the Interior Harold Ickes to negotiate a contract acceptable to the miners, even though it punched a big hole through the wartime wage ceiling.

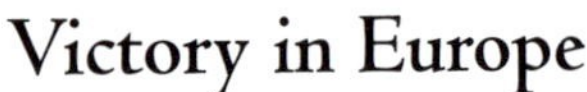

Victory in Europe

Despite the tensions in the nation's defense plants, U.S. arms production far outstripped that of any other nation. By 1944 the United States was producing nearly half of all the world's goods. With a continuous supply of American-made planes, tanks, ships, and guns, the Allied war effort soon ground down the German, Italian, and Japanese forces.

On June 6, 1944 (D-Day), the long-awaited British-American invasion of Western Europe began. In the largest amphibious landing in military history, 150,000 troops jumped from their boats onto the beaches of Normandy, France. Reinforcements soon swelled the Allied forces to two million, under the command of American General Dwight Eisenhower. By September the Allies had retaken most of France and Belgium; in November they reached the Rhine River, on Germany's western border.

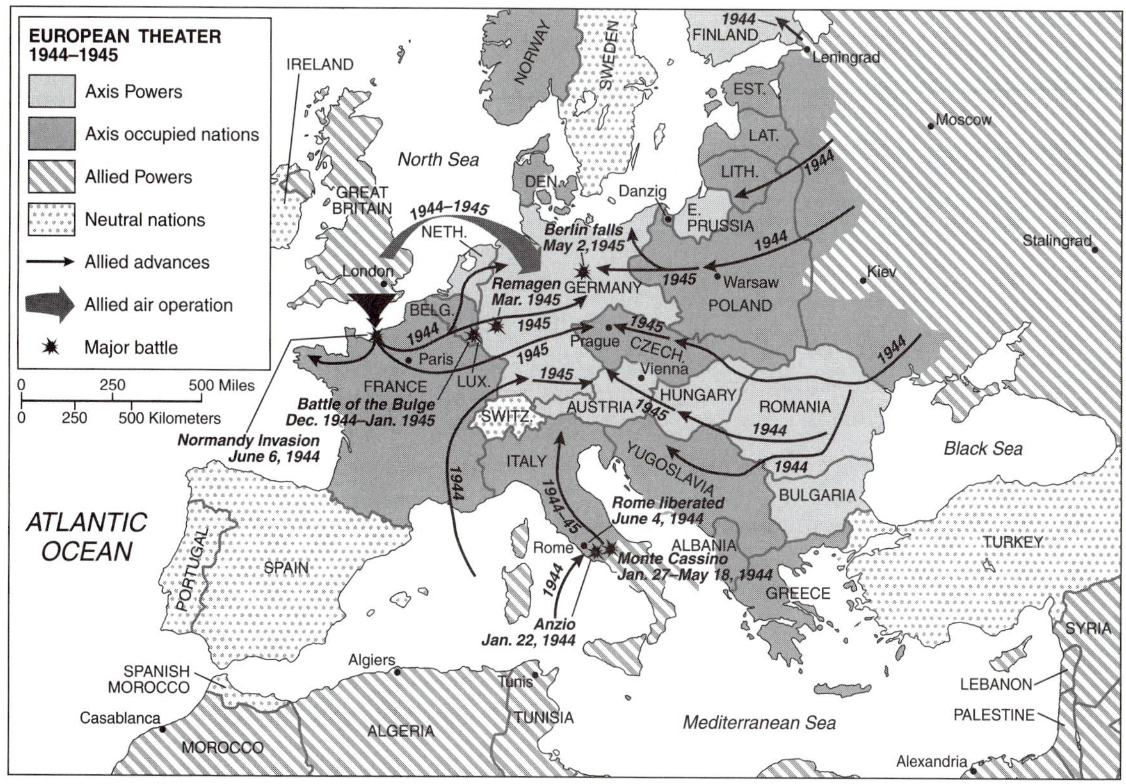

Europe At War, 1944–1945. Until June 1944, most fighting in World War II in the European Theater took place between the German and Russian armies on a vast Eastern Front. With the British and American invasion at Normandy on June 6, 1944, a Western Front forced the Nazis to divide their forces. Eleven months later on May 8, 1945, the Germans surrendered.

But in December the German Army staged a desperate counterattack—the Battle of the Bulge—pushing across the Rhine into France. The fierceness of the attack surprised Americans. "Where in hell has this son-of-a-bitch gotten all his strength?" asked General Omar Bradley. The answer, in part, was from conscripting teenagers; many of the 30,000 Germans killed in the assault were only 15 or 16 years old. That the Americans prevailed was due in large part to the tenacity and skill of ordinary soldiers. American military planners had failed to anticipate the German attack, and U.S. troops were outgunned and outmanned. But in the largest battle ever fought by the U.S. Army, they halted the German offensive and made the Allied victory all but inevitable.

Eisenhower's army crossed the Rhine in March 1945, entering southern Germany in the early spring. American soldiers soon encountered horrifying evidence that the Nazis had been exterminating millions of Jews as well as Gypsies, homosexuals, political prisoners, and others in a string of concentration camps that stretched from Buchenwald in Germany to Auschwitz in Poland. "I was totally unprepared for what I saw," recalled Leon Bass, a nineteen-year-old black sergeant of his encounter with Buchenwald. "I saw what I can refer to now as the walking dead." Much later, the world would discover that the leaders of the Roosevelt administration had known about the genocide, but they had failed to appreciate the extent of the atrocities and did nothing to stop the slaughter.

Roosevelt, whose physical condition deteriorated rapidly following his reelection to a fourth term in November 1944, died on April 12, 1945. Vice President Harry Truman, a former senator from Missouri, later said he felt as if "the moon and all the planets" had fallen on his ill-prepared shoulders. Truman had spent his youth as a dirt farmer and unsuccessful investor and businessman. In the 1920s and 1930s he had been the protégé of Tom Pendergast, Kansas City's powerful political boss. Truman had won national stature early in the war when he presided over a Senate investigation into corruption and inefficiency in the mobilization effort. In 1944, when Roosevelt allowed Democratic conservatives to cut the liberal Henry Wallace from the ticket, Truman had proved to be the perfect compromise candidate for vice president.

Truman had none of Roosevelt's great self-confidence, nor did he inspire the same public loyalty or hatred as the man who had been elected four times to the White House. But in foreign affairs Truman did not deviate from Roosevelt's strategy: the war would be concluded with an unconditional surrender, in both Europe and the Far East. In the days after Truman took office, the mighty Soviet, American, and British armies blasted their way into the heart of Germany. On April 30, with Soviet

Death Camp. When British soldiers liberated the concentration camp in Bergen-Belsen, Germany, in April 1945, they found thousands of unburied dead. Of the 60,000 camp survivors, almost half would die in the next few weeks, most succumbing to typhus. In an attempt to quell the epidemic, the British liberators buried the dead in mass graves and eventually burned the camp to the ground. The systematic extermination of almost 6 million European Jews during World War II was part of an overall death toll that claimed at least 55 million lives.

Source: Imperial War Museum.

troops encircling Berlin, Hitler committed suicide. In the next few days, American troops swept through Munich and on into Czechoslovakia, the Soviets captured Berlin, the British took Hamburg, and German troops finally gave up fighting in Italy. On May 7, 1945, Germany surrendered unconditionally. The war in Europe was over.

Japan's Surrender

In Asia, the Allies generally avoided direct confrontation with the main body of the Japanese Army on the mainland. Instead, U.S. forces closed in on Japan by island-hopping across the Pacific. Savage hand-to-hand combat on the islands of Tarawa, Saipan, and Guam put long-range B-29 bombers within striking distance of the Japanese home islands by 1944. In October of that year, American troops began the reconquest of the Philippines with a devastating defeat of the Japanese Navy at the Battle of Leyte Gulf. The next spring, after ferocious fighting, the United States took the islands of Iwo Jima and Okinawa, near the Japanese homeland. In early May 1945, British, Indian, and Nationalist Chinese troops retook Burma in South Asia.

By the middle of 1945, Japan had lost most of its navy and much of its air force, along with its holdings in the Pacific. The Japanese army remained in control of Korea, Manchuria, and much of China and Southeast Asia. But massive and continuous bombing raids on Japanese civilian and military targets had terrorized and demoralized Japan's population, smashed its industry, and further isolated its forces on the Asian mainland from those on the home islands. During June and July of 1945, high Japanese officials in a pro-peace faction of the government made repeated efforts to open negotiations with both the Soviets and the Americans. Allied leaders agreed that when Japan

The Battle of Peleliu Island, September 1944. Oppressed by 115-degree heat and trapped by withering Japanese fire, U.S. Marines took cover in the sandy terrain of the small Central Pacific island.
Source: National Archives.

surrendered, they would allow the emperor to keep his throne and that the nation eventually would regain self-rule. The end of the war was in sight.

After Germany surrendered in May, British and American intelligence agencies expected that Japan would also stop fighting—especially if the Soviet Union entered the war in the Far East. Therefore, Great Britain and the United States pushed for the earliest possible Soviet attack on Japanese-held Manchuria. Stalin agreed to open hostilities against Japan on or about August 8, three months after Germany's surrender. "Fini Japs when that comes about," President Truman wrote in his diary.

But Truman did not wait for a Soviet declaration of war. On August 6 and 8, U.S. planes dropped atomic bombs on the Japanese cities of Hiroshima and Nagasaki. The Hiroshima blast leveled nearly five square miles and instantly burned to death nearly 80,000 people. Tens of thousands more died soon afterward from injuries, burns, and radiation. In Nagasaki, where poor visibility reduced the accuracy of the bombing, about one and a half square miles were destroyed; 35,000 people were killed immediately, and another 60,000 injured. In less than a week, Japan agreed to surrender. The war in Asia formally ended on September 2, 1945 (V-J Day).

Miyuki Bridge, Hiroshima, August 6, 1945. Three hours after the United States detonated an atomic bomb over Hiroshima, shocked and wounded survivors wandered near a bridge a little over a mile from ground zero.
Source: Yoshito Matsushige—Hiroshima Peace Culture Foundation.

Americans soon learned that the atomic bombs dropped on Japan were the products of an enormous wartime mobilization of scientific talent and engineering skill called the Manhattan Project. The project inaugurated not just a new age of weaponry, but an era of bureaucratically organized and government-funded big science. After news of the enormous effort required to build the bomb had been reported, the prestige of atomic physicists, radar engineers, military planners, and other technical experts reached extraordinary heights. Vannevar Bush, an architect of the Manhattan Project, declared science "the endless frontier," the quest that would sustain American power, purpose, and democracy now that the era of pioneer migrations west was over.

President Truman persuaded most Americans that the bombings of Hiroshima and Nagasaki had been necessary to compel Japan's surrender without the enormous loss of life that would have resulted if Allied forces had invaded Japan. After the devastating bombing raids by both sides on civilian targets, two more bombs, even though they were atomic bombs, did not seem particularly excessive to Americans. "We're sitting on the pier in Seattle," one GI remembered, "sharpening our bayonets, when Harry [Truman] dropped that beautiful bomb. The greatest thing that ever happened."

But others raised pointed questions about Truman's decision. Hadn't the Japanese signaled their readiness to surrender months earlier? Why was Truman in such a rush? The Americans had had no major military operations planned for the next three months—not until November 1—and in any case, the projected full-scale invasion of Japan was not to occur before spring 1946. Why couldn't Truman have waited for the Soviet Union to enter the war? Questions like these led General Eisenhower to conclude that "it wasn't necessary to hit them with that awful thing." Admiral William Leahy, head of the U.S. joint chiefs of staff, concurred: "The use of this barbarous weapon at Hiroshima and Nagasaki was of no material assistance in our war against Japan. The Japanese were already defeated and ready to surrender."

Why, then, were the atomic bombs dropped? Less for military than for political reasons, it seems. With victory in sight by 1945, tension was quickly rising between British and American leaders and their Soviet ally over the shape of the postwar world. When Churchill, Stalin, and Roosevelt, the leaders of the "Grand Alliance," met together for the last time in February 1945 at the Russian resort city of Yalta, those tensions started coming to a head. The leaders did reach agreements on contentious issues like the future of Germany and plans for a new international organization (the United Nations), but many of the compromises were vague and subject to multiple interpretations. For example, on the question of Poland, Roosevelt won a fence-straddling compromise between Stalin and Churchill that gave the Soviets part of eastern Poland, installed a coalition government (including the pro-Communist Polish government in Lublin and the anti-Communist government-in-exile in London), and promised free elections in the future. Stalin interpreted the agreement as tacit acceptance that Poland would fall within the Soviet sphere of influence. The ambiguities were less a failure of diplomacy than a triumph of the cooperative wartime spirit of the Grand Alliance, which viewed winning the war as paramount. But by July, when Truman met at Potsdam, Germany, with Churchill and Stalin to complete the work begun in Yalta, the end of the war was in sight, and jockeying for postwar position replaced wartime cooperation. Truman later described the conference as a "brawl." Just as World War II was winding down, a new conflict loomed on the horizon—a Cold War that would pit the United States and Western Europe against the Soviet Union.

In that context, the atomic bomb offered a means not only to win the war against Japan but also to give American diplomacy the upper hand over the Soviets. Just before the first atomic test, Truman noted that "if it explodes, as I think it will, I'll certainly have a hammer on those boys"—and he meant the Soviets, not the Japanese. More immediately, by quickly ending the war, the bomb would limit Soviet participation in the war against Japan. If the Soviet Army were to move into northern China, the Soviet Union would be in a position to aid the Chinese Communists against the Nationalists. Soviet participation might also entitle Stalin to participate in the occupation and administration of postwar Japan.

The White House wanted to ensure America's supremacy in postwar Asia. American officials expected the bomb's immense destructive power to intimidate the Soviet Union and to make the United States the dominant power in the postwar world. Secretary of State James F. Byrnes later recalled the hope, widely shared in Washington at the time, that the bomb's use would enable the United States "to dictate our own terms at the end of the war."

Conversion to a Peacetime Economy

On the home front, Americans celebrated the end of the war but also searched for signs that the United States could avoid a postwar depression and sustain the wartime prosperity that had pulled so many people out of poverty and fear. In 1944 President Roosevelt had outlined a "second bill of rights" that included the right to a job, medical care, education, housing, food, clothing, and recreation, and Congress had passed the G.I. Bill of Rights to provide returning veterans with access to education and job training. But the transition to a peacetime economy would take place in an atmosphere charged with the fearful memories of an earlier peace: the economic collapse after World War I, the bitter labor wars of 1919 through 1923, and the bread lines and Hoovervilles of the Great Depression. The World War II economy had generated millions of new jobs, but what would happen when the defense plants shut down and 12 million GIs came home? Could a free market economy successfully reemploy these workers, keep inflation under control, and raise the real incomes of a vastly expanded labor force? Or would the nation need to retain and expand wartime controls over wages, prices, and investment?

Most business leaders wanted to dismantle wartime controls as soon as possible and undercut the public support that had sustained New Deal liberalism. Unlike their counterparts in continental Europe or Great Britain, who had been tarred with the brush of appeasement or even of collaboration with the Nazis, American business leaders had emerged from the war in a stronger economic and political position. While their companies had profited handsomely from their alliance with the government, they had little interest in the state-sponsored economic planning

"Add Post-War Adjustments." Reflecting male fears rather than postwar reality, this cartoon suggested that returning veterans would confront a job market in which prewar gender roles were now reversed. In fact, few women workers kept their jobs at war's end.

Source: Jay N. ("Ding") Darling—Courtesy of the J. N. "Ding" Darling Foundation.

and labor-management collaboration they saw in postwar Western Europe. They remained intensely suspicious of the kind of New Deal social engineering favored by organized labor, and they wanted to be free of government or union interference in determining wages and prices. As GM's Alfred P. Sloan put it, "It took fourteen years to rid this country of prohibition. It is going to take a good while to rid the country of the New Deal, but sooner or later the ax falls and we get a change."

Unions, together with their liberal and consumer allies, put forth their own ambitious postwar planning agenda. Few union leaders, especially in the CIO, believed that the welfare of the working class would be advanced only, or even primarily, by postwar collective bargaining. Instead, they were hopeful that labor would continue to exert an influence on economic and business decisions, both public and private. Thus, in the early years of the war, the CIO's Philip Murray had urged the creation of a series of industry councils that would fuse economic and political bargaining—"a program for democratic economic planning and for participation by the people in the key decision of the big corporations."

For a while, a democratic reconversion of the wartime economy seemed possible. Organized labor had increased its membership by half during the war, to almost 15 million—about a third of the nonfarm workforce. In 1944 the industrial unions had established a pioneering political action committee that played a key role in reelecting Roosevelt to a fourth term. Nine months later, liberals and progressives in the United States took heart from the smashing victory of the Labour Party in Great Britain's first postwar election. As one observer put it, "Union leaders no longer regard themselves as a force merely reacting to managerial decision . . . but as a force which itself can influence the whole range of industrial economic activity."

The UAW's Walter Reuther embodied this ambition. A trade unionist who was equally at ease among the shop-floor militants of Detroit and the policymaking bureaucrats of Washington, Reuther called on the government to convert taxpayer-financed war plants to the mass production of badly needed housing and railroad equipment. Most strikingly, he demanded a 30 percent increase in autoworkers' wages, which would just about make up for the income those workers had lost when the postwar workweek shrank to forty hours. But Reuther did not limit his argument to a narrow consideration of wages. A believer in Keynesian economics, he wanted to boost working-class "purchasing power." He challenged management to keep car prices at prewar levels, in order to stave off an inflationary surge, raise working-class living standards, and win labor support from middle-class consumers. Reuther demanded that General Motors "open the books" to show that its profits and productivity made an inflation-proof wage increase possible.

In their efforts to extend their positions into postwar America, business leaders and unions differed in their views of the Office of Price Administration (OPA). The fate of the OPA was central to the success of an orderly and progressive conversion of the war economy to a peacetime footing. In 1945 this popular and effective government agency helped sustain working-class living standards by enforcing price and quality standards for hundreds of different hard-to-find products. Bolstered by the voluntary efforts of almost 300,000 OPA "price checkers," the agency's leverage over business pricing policies gave millions of consumers a stake in the outcome of the labor-liberal effort to sustain a postwar New Deal. OPA chief Chester Bowles, a spirited liberal, called the agency's housewife volunteers "as American as baseball," even as some merchants denounced them as a "kitchen Gestapo," an allusion to the Nazi secret police.

The leaders of America's major corporations asserted that the OPA had to go, and with it all constraints on corporate power and profits. They were willing to increase wages about 10 percent, but they were determined to keep pricing decisions under management control. As General Motors pronounced late in 1945, "America is at the crossroads! It must preserve the freedom of each unit of American business to determine its own destiny."

These tensions erupted in a massive postwar strike wave. Beginning late in the fall of 1945, a five-month wave of strikes, the largest such action since 1919, put three million workers on the street. These stoppages had a twofold purpose: to win substantial wage increases that would set the pattern for all American workers in the postwar years and to preserve government-mandated price ceilings, so that inflation would not erode working-class living standards. Strikes shut down the steel, electrical, oil, coal, and meatpacking industries. In contrast to the strikes of 1919 and 1937, union efforts to stop production went largely uncontested, so most of the strikes were peaceful and effective. When the police did intervene against the unions, labor responded with mass picket lines or with a general strike. Citywide stoppages to protest anti-union policing brought commerce to a halt in Stamford and Hartford, Connecticut; Lancaster, Pennsylvania; Houston, Texas; Rochester, New York; Camden, New Jersey; and Oakland, California. Autoworker Stan Weir later recalled the exuberance of the Oakland strike: "That first 24-hour period of the 54-hour strike had a carnival spirit. A mass of couples danced in the streets" to jukeboxes playing 'Pistol Packin' Mama,'" the number one hit.

The wave of strikes in 1945 and 1946 may well have marked the height of union strength and social solidarity during the twentieth century. It was the final episode in the great cycle of industrial confrontations that began with the railroad strikes of the 1870s and erupted again every

Welcome Back. During the war, housing construction came to a virtual standstill. The return of millions of servicemen to civilian life in 1945 set off a national housing crisis.

Source: American Social History Project.

decade, reminding the nation of the seemingly insolvable conflict between labor and capital. Certainly, this was one of the last times union workers could claim, with the public's general agreement, that their struggle embodied the hopes and aspirations of all Americans. The claim extended even to military veterans and active service personnel. After V-J Day, U.S. troops in Asia organized a "bring the troops home" movement, demanding rapid demobilization of U.S. troops from North China, the Philippines, and Indonesia. Savvy unionists and radicals in uniform led this effort, which often resembled a labor protest. In December 1945, when four thousand troops marched on an army headquarters depot in Manila, the commander ordered them back to their barracks with the quip, "You men forget you're not working for General Motors. You're still in the Army."

By February 1946, presidential fact-finding boards in both the auto and steel industries had recommended substantial wage hikes, with no corresponding rise in OPA price guidelines. But steel industry leaders responded flatly that "until [the Office of Price Administration] authorizes fair prices, nothing can be settled through collective bargaining." Thus the strikes of the winter of 1946 took on a fundamentally political character. They were a struggle over the fate of the Truman administration's program to sustain price controls and give noncorporate voices a full hearing in planning the nation's economic reconversion. But with unemployment on the rise and industry spokesmen adamant, President Truman caved in, announcing that in return for a wage increase of about eighteen cents per hour, he would allow the steel corporations to raise the price of steel five dollars a ton.

Most labor leaders concluded that the political winds had shifted against them, and they would have to settle for Truman's offer. Moreover, AFL unions such as the Carpenters and the Teamsters had never subscribed to the CIO's brand of social unionism. The CIO's president, Philip Murray, who also led the steelworkers, made it clear that his organization had little stomach for a long and bitter strike that might well turn into a political confrontation with the Truman administration. Even UAW lead-

"People Were Literally Dancing in the Streets"

Autoworker Stan Weir, an enthusiastic participant in the 1946 general strike in Oakland, California, described the workers' jubilant mood in the early hours of the strike and the way they took control of the city for more than two days.

The Oakland general strike was called by no leader. It was unique, I think, in general strikes in this country. There was a strike of women who were the clerks at Kahn's and Hastings' department stores and it had been going on for months. The Teamsters had begun to refuse to make deliveries to those department stores and the department stores needed commodities badly.

Not many people had cars right after the war and you took public transportation to work in the morning. You had to go downtown to the center of Oakland and then out in the direction of your workplace. So thousands and thousands of people traveled through the heart of town every morning on the way to work, on public transportation. Very early one morning, here were the policemen of Oakland herding in a string of trucks, operated by a scab trucking firm in Los Angeles, with supplies for these department stores. Some truck driver or some bus driver or street car conductor asked some policeman about the trucks. . . . Well, that truck driver, that bus driver, or that street car conductor didn't get back on his vehicle . . . and that increased till those trucks and those buses and those street cars just piled up and thousands of people were stranded in town.

In a small way it was a holiday. The normal criteria for what was acceptable conduct disappeared. No one knew what to do and there were no leaders. No one called it. Pretty soon the strikers began forming into committees on the street corners. Certain shopkeepers were told to shut down and drug stores to stay open. Bars could stay open if they didn't serve hard liquor, and they had to put their juke boxes out on the sidewalk. People were literally dancing in the streets in anticipation of some kind of new day. Soon the strikers began to direct traffic and only let union people into town and keep out those who it was feared might be against the strike. It lasted fifty-four hours.

Source: Stan Weir, "The Informal Work Group," in Alice Lynd and Staughton Lynd, eds., *Rank and File: Personal Histories by Working Class Organizers* (1973).

ers at Ford and Chrysler abandoned their support of the GM strike. By March 1946 Reuther, too, had settled with GM.

The great strikes of 1946 proved a costly victory for organized labor. True, every major corporation had agreed to negotiate with the union that represented its employees—thus demonstrating the permanence of the industrial unions that had been built during the 1930s and expanded during the war. But businessmen also insisted that postwar contracts include a "management security" clause giving them more power to set production standards and to limit the authority of shop stewards and union officials. More important, the wage increases won during the walkouts evaporated quickly under the galloping inflation let loose when government price controls were lifted in the summer and fall of 1946.

Unions that sought to break the wage patterns negotiated in the winter of 1946 found that the government now considered their goals incompatible with the national welfare. Late in the spring of that year the mine workers and the railroad brotherhoods challenged the Truman administration; both unions shut down their industries in a vain effort to win concessions beyond those the president thought reasonable. With labor strife becoming increasingly unpopular, Truman decided the unions were an easy target. Adopting a tough, uncompromising attitude, he briefly placed both the railroads and the coal mines under government control. In private, the president railed against the stoppages, at one point threatening, "We'll draft 'em first and think about the law later."

With inflation running at more than 12 percent, most of the big unions had to return to the bargaining table for another round of wage hikes in 1946. Although the settlements were reached without strikes, most manufacturers again raised their prices, blaming "Big Labor" for the inflationary spiral that gripped the economy. Middle-class consumers and industrial workers alike turned against the unions, and the entire country soon grew hostile toward the labor movement. The incapacity of either the Truman administration or the unions to stop the inflationary surge discredited the Rooseveltian state and demoralized millions of working-class voters. Responding to the Republican campaign slogan, "Had Enough?" voters in 1946 deprived the Democrats of control of Congress for the first time since 1930. Apathy and discontent robbed the Democrats of more than ten million voters who had cast their ballots for Roosevelt just two years before: voter turnout was one of the lowest in the twentieth century. Democrats sustained their greatest losses in the industrial regions stretching from Connecticut to Illinois—precisely the area with a heavy urban-labor constituency.

The New Deal was over, and reaching an end with it was the cycle of union growth and working-class recomposition that had transformed the structure of American society. Labor, both as an organization and as a social construct, was now an established part of the American political order. And the federal government continued to exercise far greater power than it had a generation earlier. But perhaps the most profound transformation of all was the evolution of the United States from an isolationist nation into a global power, with immense influence over the economic and political affairs of a world divided along economic and ideological lines. Within that context, America would have to confront a host of issues that had been raised, but not always resolved, by the Depression, the New Deal, and World War II. For the next half-century, the nation would puzzle over the proper degree of government involvement in the economy and social welfare legislation, the fate of the burgeoning labor movement, the nascent civil rights insurgency, and the still small movement for women's equality.

The Years in Review

1922

- Benito Mussolini's fascists seize power in Italy.

1931

- The Japanese Army captures Manchuria and then gradually extends control over all of northern China.

1933

- Nazi leader Adolf Hitler seizes dictatorial powers.
- President Franklin D. Roosevelt proclaims the Good Neighbor Policy toward Latin America.

1935

- Italy conquers Abyssinia (Ethiopia).
- Congress passes the Neutrality Act; two more such acts pass in the next two years and limit U.S. action in world crises.

1936

- Hitler takes and rearms the Rhineland.
- Japan, Italy, and Germany sign pacts with one another, giving birth to the Axis military alliance.
- The Spanish Civil War begins; Congress prohibits the United States from sending arms to either side, but individual Americans join the International Brigade of volunteers defending the Republic, which is defeated by Francisco Franco in 1939.

1937

- Japan launches a new invasion of China.

1938

- Nazis smash Jewish shops and loot homes and synagogues in Germany, in a wave of destruction known as *Kristallnacht*.
- France and Britain sign the Munich Pact, hoping to appease Germany and limit expansion; British Prime Minister Neville Chamberlain heralds it as "peace in our time."

1939

- The Soviet Union signs a nonaggression pact with Germany.
- Germany invades Poland; Britain and France declare war; World War II begins.

1940

- Germans sweep through Western Europe in *blitzkrieg* attacks, launching simultaneous air and land campaigns.
- President Roosevelt defeats Wendell Willkie for an unprecedented third term.
- A Vermont widow becomes the first recipient of Social Security benefits, which she continues to receive until her death forty-five years later.

1941

- Germany invades the Soviet Union.
- Japan launches a surprise attack on U.S. forces at Pearl Harbor, Hawaii, bringing the United States into the war.
- A. Philip Randolph threatens a march on Washington, D.C., to protest racial discrimination; Roosevelt heads it off by creating the Fair Employment Practices Commission.
- Cheerios cereal finds its way to American breakfast tables.

1942

- The United States forces 100,000 Japanese Americans to abandon their homes and jobs and live in concentration camps throughout the western states.
- Japanese troops capture the Philippines; more than 5,000 captured U.S. servicemen die during the Bataan Death March.
- Allied troops invade North Africa.
- The United States wins crucial battles at Guadalcanal and Midway.
- U.S. government imposes gasoline rationing and bans pleasure driving to help reduce rubber consumption.
- U.S. soldiers popularize M&M candies, which are issued as part of their rations because, as later slogan puts it, "The milk chocolate melts in your mouth—not in your hand."

1943

- Congress repeals the Chinese Exclusion Act, but sets a new quota of only 105 Chinese immigrants per year.
- White Americans attack Mexican Americans in the "zoot-suit riots."
- Edward Noble, who made his fortune in Life Savers, buys the National Broadcasting Company's Blue Network and creates the American Broadcasting Company (ABC).
- Racial violence peaks in 1943, with 250 incidents in forty-seven cities; the worst riot is in Detroit, where 34 people die.

1944

- On D-Day (June 6) 176,000 Allied troops land on the beaches of Normandy, France.
- President Roosevelt defeats Republican challenger Thomas Dewey for a fourth term in the White House.

- United Fruit brands its bananas with the "Chiquita" name.

1945

- The last meeting of the Big Three—Churchill, Roosevelt, and Stalin—takes place at the Yalta Conference.
- Franklin D. Roosevelt dies on April 12; Harry Truman becomes president.
- Germany surrenders unconditionally on May 4, ending the war in Europe.
- On August 6 and 8, U.S. planes drop atomic bombs on the Japanese cities of Hiroshima and Nagasaki; Japan surrenders, ending World War II.
- Truman meets with Churchill and Stalin at the Potsdam Conference to decide the shape of the postwar world.
- At war's end, an outbreak of strikes occurs; 5 million workers go on strike, losing 120 million days of work over the next twelve months.
- Chemist Earl W. Tupper founds the Tupperware Corporation to sell plastic bowls with a leak-proof seal.
- Frozen orange juice, a spin-off from the wartime production of powdered orange juice, appears.

1946

- A French designer creates the first "bikini," which draws its name from the Bikini Atoll, where the United States tested atomic bombs.
- Dr. Benjamin Spock's manual on childrearing appears just as the "baby boom" begins; the book will become an all-time bestseller, second only to the Bible and Shakespeare's works.

Suggested Readings

Alperovitz, Gar, *Atomic Diplomacy: Hiroshima and Potsdam* (rev. ed., 1995).

Ambrose, Stephen E., *Citizen Soldiers: The U.S. Army from the Normandy Beaches to the Bulge to the Surrender of Germany, June 7, 1944 to May 7, 1945* (1998).

Bailey, Beth, and David Farber, *First Strange Place: The Alchemy of Race and Sex in World War II Hawaii* (1994).

Baughman, James, *Henry R. Luce and the Rise of the American News Media* (1987).

Bernstein, Alison R., *American Indians and World War II: Toward a New Era in Indian Affairs* (1991).

Berube, Allan, *Coming Out Under Fire: The History of Gay Men and Women in World War Two* (1990).

Blum, John Morton, *V Was for Victory: Politics and American Culture During World War II* (1977).

Dower, John, *War Without Mercy: Race and Power in the Pacific War* (1986).

Fussell, Paul, *Wartime: Understanding and Behavior in the Second World War* (1989).

Garfinkel, Herbert, *When Negroes March* (1959).

Gropman, Alan, *Mobilizing U.S. Industry in World War II* (1996).

Harris, Howell John, *The Right to Manage: Industrial Relations Policies of American Business in the 1940s* (1982).

Hirsch, Susan E., and Lewis A. Erenberg, eds. *The War in American Culture: Society and Consciousness During War World II* (1996).

Honey, Maureen, *Creating Rosie the Riveter: Class, Gender, and Propaganda During World War II* (1985).

Honey, Michael K., *Southern Labor and Black Civil Rights: Organizing Memphis Workers* (1993).

Horowitz Roger, *Negro and White, Unite and Fight: A Social History of Industrial Unionism in Meatpacking, 1930–90* (1997).

Iriye, Akira, *Origins of the Second World War in Asia and the Pacific (Origins of the Modern War)* (1987).

Irons, Peter H., *Justice at War* (1993).

Isserman, Maurice, *Which Side Were You On? The American Communist Party During the Second World War* (1993).

Kimball, Warren F., *The Juggler: Franklin Roosevelt as Wartime Statesman* (1994).

Koppes, Clayton R., and Gregory D. Black, *Hollywood Goes to War* (1987).

Lichtenstein, Nelson, *Labor's War at Home: The CIO in World War II* (1984).

Lipsitz, George, *Rainbow at Midnight: Labor and Culture in the 1940s* (1994).

Meulen, Jacob Vander, *Building the B-29* (1995).

Meyer, Leisa D., *Creating GI Jane: Sexuality and Power in the Women's Army Corps During World War II* (1996).

Milkman, Paul, PM, *A New Deal in Journalism, 1940–1948* (1997).

Milkman, Ruth, *Gender at Work: The Dynamics of Job Segregation by Sex During World War II* (1987).

Perrett, Geoffrey, *Days of Sadness, Years of Triumph: The American People, 1939–1945* (1985).

Polenberg, Richard, *War and Society: The United States, 1941–1945* (1972).

Rhodes, Richard, *The Making of the Atomic Bomb* (1995).

Sherry, Michael S., *The Rise of American Air Power: The Creation of Armageddon* (1989).

Sherwin, Martin J., *A World Destroyed: The Atomic Bomb and the Grand Alliance* (1975).

Spector, Ronald H., *Eagle Against the Sun: The American War with Japan* (1985).

Terkel, Studs, ed., *"The Good War": An Oral History of World War II* (1997).

Weir, Margaret, Ann Shola Orloff, and Theda Skolpol (eds.), *The Politics of Social Policy in the United States* (1988).

Winkler, Allan, *The Politics of Propaganda: The Office of War Information, 1942–1945* (1978).

Wyman, David, *The Abandonment of the Jews: America and the Holocaust, 1941–1945* (1998).

And on the World Wide Web

National Archives and Records Administration, *A People at War [World War II]* (http://www.nara.gov/exhall/people.html).

San Francisco Exploratorium, *Remembering Nagasaki* (http://www.exploratorium.edu/nagasaki/).

U.S. Holocaust Memorial Museum (http://www.ushmm.org)

Cold War America—and After

part three

On January 7, 1946, twenty thousand American servicemen held a mass meeting in Manila, where they listened to sergeants, corporals, and other veteran GIs demand that the Army ship them home. They were homesick, but many also protested U.S. plans to station troops in North China, Indonesia, and the rest of the Philippines, where Communist insurgencies and nationalist revolts challenged old oppressors. This "Bring the Boys Home" movement quickly spread throughout the Far East and won widespread support back in the States. Bowing to the popular pressure, the War Department soon accelerated troop demobilization schedules to fill every available ship with veterans eager for the return voyage home.

The revolt of the overseas servicemen dissipated within weeks, but it encapsulated much of the tension that would govern U.S. diplomacy and politics during the post World War II years. The United States was then the world's preeminent military and economic power, with millions of troops spread all over the globe. Much of Europe and Asia lay in ruins, while the U.S. industrial machine remained untouched by the ravages of war. But the deployment of American strength—and for what purposes—generated unexpected controversy both at home and abroad.

For all their prosperity, Americans did not feel secure in 1946. The planet was dividing into two armed and hostile camps, embodying different social and ideological systems: one composed of nations allied to or occupied by the Soviet Union; the other, a slightly looser network of states led by the United States. This military and ideological rivalry—dubbed the "Cold War" by American financier and presidential adviser

Bernard Baruch—generated an expensive and dangerous arms race and bloody conflicts in China, Greece, Korea, Vietnam, and Central America.

America's protracted struggle with the Soviets gave rise to a dual set of containments: abroad the U.S. helped erect a worldwide set of anti-Communist alliances; at home the Cold War generated a sharp turn to the right, containing within well-policed boundaries the ideas and activities now considered politically acceptable. The unions recruited new members and conducted frequent strikes early in the postwar era, but radical anti-capitalist ideas no longer had a place in the house of labor. "McCarthyism"—which first took its name from the inquisitorial investigations conducted by Wisconsin senator Joseph McCarthy—provided a convenient label for the repressive atmosphere generated by a political obsession with the miniscule influence still exercised by American Communists.

Since the 1950s American politics and society has been transformed in two fundamental ways. First, an amazingly creative mass movement of black and white citizens swept aside the structures of legal segregation and discrimination that for almost one hundred years had mocked the Union victory in the Civil War. The civil rights revolution gave enormous energy to the reforming impulse that culminated in the 1960s in President Lyndon Johnson's "Great Society." Medical care for the poor and elderly, greater access to education, a more liberal and less racist immigration law, and a highly-touted "War on Poverty" seemed but a continuation of the New Deal social agenda. The movement for African-American liberation made all Americans more "rights" conscious, raising the expectations and aspirations of young people, women, gays, the disabled, American Indians and all those who once felt marginal to the mainstream of American life. The women's movement that began late in the 1960s offered a particularly potent political and cultural challenge to the gender inequalities that were so thoroughly embedded within the very structure of marriage, work, and public life.

The "rights" revolution of the 1960s also transformed working-class America. The typical worker of the 1950s—a male breadwinner in a blue-collar union job supporting a family—had virtually ceased to exist. The massive entry of women into the paid labor force has radically altered the character American family life. Moreover, since 1965 a wave of immigrants from Asia, Latin America and Eastern Europe has made the working class of most cities even more cosmopolitan than in the years of transAtlantic immigration before World War I.

But these great social and ideological changes shifted American politics to the right, not the left. Indeed, the second signpost to the history of the last half century has been the unexpected rise of a powerful conservative current in American politics. Liberalism had but a brief flowering in the 1960s because the polarization generated by the War in Vietnam, the revival of feminism, and the upheaval in race relations fractured the coalition that had long sustained the majority status of the Democratic Party. Then, just a decade later, the unexpected stagnation in U.S. living standards brought into question the even older New Deal linkage between economic prosperity and activist government. In the 1970s and early 1980s a sharp decline in the productivity and profitability of American business ended the great postwar boom that had doubled Americans' living standards in just a generation. As high-paying industrial jobs vanished and the unions shrank in size, white working-class loyalty to the Democrats declined as well.

Jim Crow. A southern liquor store entrance in 1951.

Source: Schomburg Center for Research in Black Culture, New York Public Library, Astor, Lenox, and Tilden Foundations.

The collapse of liberalism in the 1970s helped pave the way for the presidency of a conservative Republican, Ronald Reagan, whose successful efforts to roll back taxes, cut social spending, curb union power, and expand the military represented a decisive postwar break with the political legacy of the New Deal. The influence of Reaganite Republicanism proved as great as that of any twentieth-century president. The Democratic Party itself became much more conservative. And even with the end of the Cold War, the election of Democrat Bill Clinton to the presidency, and the return of economic good times, efforts to expand the welfare state and legitimize a socially activist government proved largely unsuccessful. At the end of the twentieth century, jobs were once again plentiful and real wages rising, but racial harmony, social equality, and workplace justice remained unfulfilled ideals on the American agenda.

April 1968. Demonstrators protesting the Vietnam War prepare to march to a rally in New York's Central Park.

Source: *The Militant.*

chapter 11

BURN ALL REDS
ROSENBERG TRAITORS MUST DIE FOR THEIR CRIME
NO MERCY FOR SPIES

The Cold War Boom

1946–1960

"America at this moment stands at the summit of the world," announced Winston Churchill in August 1945. That same month, Walter Lippmann wrote, "What Rome was to the ancient world, what Great Britain has been to the modern world, America is to be to the world of tomorrow." The former British prime minister and America's most respected newspaper columnist stood in awe for good reason. During World War II, the United States had mobilized an army of 12 million, and had bankrolled or equipped an equal number of Allied troops. It had assembled the world's largest navy and air force, and built the atomic bombs that wiped out two Japanese cities. But most impressive to observers such as Lippmann and Churchill was the extraordinary strength of the U.S. economy. In the four wartime years U.S. income, wealth, and industrial production had all doubled or more than doubled. By 1947 the United States produced roughly half the world's manufactures: 57 percent of the steel, 43 percent of the electricity, and 62 percent of the oil. And America dominated in precisely those industries—aviation, chemical engineering, and electronics—that spelled victory in modern war. This enormous military and industrial power enabled the United States to become the guardian of a postwar *Pax Americana,* to restructure international politics and finance in a way that made them more responsive to American interests.

After World War I, U.S. citizens had voted for a "return to normalcy," turning their attention away from European and Asian affairs. But such isolation was impossible after World War II, which had so dramatically confirmed the United States as the leading world power. U.S. interests were now indissolubly linked to a global order that depended on American economic strength and political will. In the postwar years, more than ever before, the everyday lives of American women and men were shaped by international developments.

Smile when you say that. Despite the calm demeanor of this anti-Rosenberg picketer at a 1953 Washington, D.C., demonstration, the message on his sign suggests the intensity of anti-Communist hysteria in the period. **Source:** Elliott Erwitt/Magnum.

Origins of the Cold War

Economic growth and political stability in the United States stood in stark contrast to the radical transformations sweeping the rest of the globe in the years immediately following World War II. In 1947 Churchill described Europe as "a rubble-heap, a charnel house, a breeding ground of pestilence and hate." There, depression and war had so discredited the old elites that many doubted capitalism could long survive. In France, the Communists and Socialists, who had led the anti-Nazi resistance, were far more popular than business leaders, and even many conservatives there supported the postwar nationalization of the country's most important banks and manufacturing firms. In Britain the Labour party swept Churchill and the Conservatives out of power, raising the possibility that America's closest ally might embrace socialism. In Greece, Italy, and Yugoslavia, Communist parties seemed on the verge of assuming power. Meanwhile, powerful independence movements emerged in Asia and Africa, shaking the colonial empires built by France, Britain, and the Netherlands.

In this moment of uncertainty, only two nations — the United States and the Soviet Union — had the ideological confidence and military strength to construct a new world order. The two countries began a protracted conflict in which the clash of ideas and values was as important as military and diplomatic rivalry. Though the Soviet dictator Joseph Stalin had betrayed the ideals of the Russian Revolution to establish a brutal and despotic regime, millions of people throughout the world still looked to the Soviet Union as an alternative to capitalism, which they identified with the chaos of the Great Depression and World War II. The Soviets sought to dominate a buffer zone of friendly states along Russia's historic borders, while at the same time probing for political and social weaknesses in western Europe.

In wartime conferences, American policy makers had seemed to accept the idea of a Soviet sphere of influence in eastern Europe, if only as compensation for Russia's wartime sacrifices. After meeting with Stalin in Teheran, Iran, late in 1943, Roosevelt reported, "I got along fine with Marshall Stalin . . . and I believe that we are going to get along very well with him and the Russian people." At a meeting in the Ukrainian resort city of Yalta in February 1945, Roosevelt and Churchill thought it fruitless to oppose Soviet dominance in Poland once the Red Army had fought its way across that nation. Churchill had already conceded all of eastern Europe to the Soviets in return for assurances that Britain would have a free hand in Greece. Roosevelt won a Soviet pledge of "free elections" in Poland, but U.S. policy makers knew that with the Red Army occupying most of eastern Europe, the region clearly lay within the Soviet orbit. After mid-1945, however, President Harry Truman grew uncomfortable with these arrangements. Although Stalin showed no interest in an invasion of western Europe, the Soviet Union's suppression of nationalist aspirations in eastern Europe, combined with its encouragement of anticapitalist and anticolonial movements worldwide, led Western leaders to believe the USSR was an inherently expansionist power.

Nothing is inevitable in history or politics, but the Cold War antagonism that soon divided "East" and "West" would have been exceedingly hard to avoid. Given the enormous ideological, military, and geopolitical divisions between the Soviets and the Americans, tension and conflict were almost inevitable. "Russia," *Life* magazine editorialized in July 1945, well before the Cold War erupted, "is the number one problem for Americans because it is the only country in the world with the dynamic power to challenge our own concepts of truth, justice, and the good life."

Still, the intensity of the Cold War—the costly and dangerous militarization of the rivalry; the all-encompassing, global character of the antagonism; and its protracted, half-century length—might have been mitigated or ameliorated through careful statesmanship. But America's military and diplomatic elite were bursting with self-confidence. The financial strength of the United States was so great that at the Bretton Woods Conference, held in New Hampshire in 1944, the American dollar became the reserve currency upon which all others depended. Despite the objections of the British and French as well as the Soviets, the United States insisted that its currency be used to determine the value of all international monetary transactions. In this and other matters, U.S. leaders felt they had the right and the duty to shape the new global order. Henry Luce, an influential spokesman for American internationalism and the publisher of *Time* and *Life,* urged readers of those magazines to "go over the earth, as investors and managers and engineers, as makers of mutual prosperity, as missionaries of capitalism and democracy."

In the year following the defeat of Germany, tensions rose quickly between the USSR and the United States. Although the Soviets were in desperate need of assistance in rebuilding their country, President Truman canceled lend-lease aid to the USSR almost immediately after Germany's surrender. In Poland, where Americans wanted free elections, the Soviets began to suppress opposition parties in order to keep that buffer state's puppet government firmly in their own hands. And much haggling took place over the international control of atomic energy. Although some U.S. leaders were willing to give the newly formed United Nations a role in this area, President Truman

Number 1, 1948. The postwar movement of Abstract Expressionism, exemplified in Jackson Pollock's work, marked a sharp break from earlier representative painting. Unlike the previous generation of artists, the Abstract Expressionists rejected political themes, developing techniques that reflected the irrationality of Cold War hostilities and potential nuclear annihilation. But the obscurity of these paintings made them malleable propaganda tools in U.S. government-sponsored cultural festivals and exhibits. Ironically, Abstract Expressionism became a symbol of America's postwar power. **Source:** Jackson Pollock, 1948, oil on canvas, 68 inches × 8 feet 8 inches—The Museum of Modern Art.

and leaders of the U.S. military insisted on a system of mandatory international inspections that would preserve the relative U.S. advantage in the development of atomic weapons. The Soviets, rejecting this U.S. plan, forged ahead with a secret program to build their own A-bomb, which they would test in 1949. By the end of 1945, President Truman had become convinced that the United States had to "stop babying the Soviets." "Unless Russia is faced with an iron fist and strong language," he mused privately, "another war is in the making."

The Division of Europe

Two influential individuals helped to codify and globalize the meaning of these growing tensions. Early in 1946, the highest-ranking U.S. diplomat in Moscow, George F. Kennan, cabled an explosive 8,000-word assessment of Soviet intensions to State Department officials in Washington. Kennan's "long telegram" quickly circulated throughout the federal government, and an even more ideological, anti-Communist version was published in the influential journal *Foreign Affairs,* under the pseudonym "Mr. X." It proved a landmark statement of U.S. Cold War strategy. Soviet leaders, wrote Kennan, were motivated both by traditional Russian insecurities and by Marxist–Leninist dogma. Their totalitarian rule in the USSR was based on an irrational fear of capitalist encirclement and of foreign hostility. And they wanted to expand everywhere, "like a persistent toy automobile wound up and headed in a given direction, stopping only when it meets unanswerable force." To counter the Soviets, Kennan wrote, the United States should pursue a policy of "firm containment, designed to confront the Russians with unalterable counterforce at every point." Kennan's strategy of "containment" would come to characterize the Cold War posture the West adopted toward the Soviets for more than a generation. Although Kennan had construed containment largely in economic and diplomatic terms, the strategy soon took on a decidedly military cast as Cold War antagonisms deepened.

The idea of containment was given a powerful rhetorical flourish in March 1946, when Winston Churchill accepted President Truman's invitation to address the faculty and students of Westminster College in Fulton, Missouri. Although Churchill had at first acceded to Soviet domination of eastern Europe, he had become deeply pessimistic about the USSR's "expansive tendencies." In one of the most famous speeches of the twentieth century, Churchill warned that an "Iron Curtain" of Soviet domination had descended across central Europe, and he called for a new Anglo-American military alliance to oppose it. Many Americans, including some within the policy-making elite, thought Churchill's harsh speech unnecessarily provocative: in early 1946 the Soviets tolerated some pluralism and multiparty competition in Finland, Austria, Hungary, and Czechoslovakia. But Churchill's "Iron Curtain" speech helped convince U.S. policy makers that compromise or negotiation with the Soviet Union would prove fruitless. Churchill's eloquent warning, together with Kennan's blunt analysis, relieved officials of the need to agonize over the problem of accommodating legitimate Soviet interests.

Thus, the ideological confrontation with the Soviets soon turned into a military and economic projection of U.S. power, first in the eastern Mediterranean and then throughout all of western Europe. In Greece, President Truman faced a crisis early in 1947. There, as in so many other eastern European societies, the royal family and the landowning elite had been discredited by their collaboration with the fascists during World War II. Local Communists, emerging from the anti-Nazi resistance, took up arms; soon civil war engulfed the nation. The British government had backed the Greek monarchists with troops and financial aid, but in February 1947 officials of the new Labour government informed Truman that Britain could no longer afford to assist anti-Communist forces.

Although Stalin refrained from aiding the Communist guerrillas in Greece, as he had promised, President Truman and his advisers were determined to fill the political and military breech left by the British. However, they faced a skeptical American public and a fiscally conservative Republican Congress. Truman resolved this difficulty by announcing what came to be known as the "Truman Doctrine." Requesting $400 million in economic and military aid for Greece and Turkey, the president framed his goals in sweeping terms: "At the present moment in world history, nearly every nation must choose between alternative ways of life." To win popular support for the new financial and military commitment, Truman took the advice of Republican senator Arthur Vandenberg "to scare the hell out of the country." Whatever the merits of the conflict, Truman argued, the Greek civil war had a far larger meaning: "I believe that it must be the policy of the United States to support free peoples who are resisting attempted subjugation by armed minorities or by outside pressures." Truman had defined political upheaval as inherently undemocratic. With money and arms,

UFOs. For some Americans, fears about the escalating Cold War abroad were mitigated by a new problem emerging from above. Beginning in 1947, many people (including United Airlines pilot E. J. Smith) saw—or thought they saw—mysterious "flying discs" in the skies over the United States.

Source: *Life* Magazine, July 21, 1947, AP/Wide World Photos.

America would guarantee the political status quo in Greece and defend friendly regimes elsewhere in the world.

The Truman Doctrine was followed within a few months by an even more ambitious program, the $16-billion Marshall Plan for the reconstruction of Europe. About a $140-billion undertaking in current U.S. dollars, the plan was proposed by Secretary of State George Marshall in a June 1947 speech. It offered aid even to the Communist regimes of eastern Europe, but only under conditions that would have linked their economies to the West — and thus threatened their role as buffer states for the Soviet Union. When the USSR forced those nations to reject Marshall Plan assistance, the economic partition of Europe was confirmed. And when Czech Communists seized control of Prague's coalition government in what became known as the "coup" of February 1948, Congress overwhelmingly approved funding for the Marshall Plan.

A tangible symbol of American wealth and generosity, the Marshall Plan scored a twofold victory in much of Europe. It strengthened the hand of conservatives in countries such as France, Italy, Greece, and Belgium, where Communist movements were strong. And it sparked a powerful economic recovery in countries with an educated work force, a well-built infrastructure, and a social democratic tradition, such as Germany, Norway, the Netherlands, Great Britain, and France. Those countries were able to take advantage of Marshall Plan aid and to share its fruits relatively equitably. But in other parts of Europe — such as Italy, Portugal, Greece, and Spain — the Marshall Plan was less successful. There foreign aid merely reinforced existing inequalities and inefficiencies, lending support to corrupt or authoritarian governments for more than two decades.

The economic and political division of Europe led inexorably to a military divide as well. The central issue was the revival of German power, feared both by the Soviets and by many in the West, especially the French. In June 1948, U.S.-led efforts to link the currency in Berlin's western sector to that of West Germany alarmed the Soviets: Berlin lay deep within the Soviet zone of occupation. They responded with a blockade of all highway, rail, and river traffic into the former German capital. American military leaders considered driving an armed convoy through Soviet lines, but President Truman instead ordered a spectacular airlift, which successfully supplied the city's residents with coal, food, and clothing for nearly a year. By May 1949, when Stalin lifted the blockade, Berlin had become an international symbol of resistance to Soviet intimidation.

Against the backdrop of the Berlin airlift, the United States pushed for the creation of a western European military alliance, called the North Atlantic Treaty Organization (NATO), and the eventual rearmament of West

Cold War Europe. By the mid-1950s, most of Europe was sharply divided into two opposing camps. In 1949, the North Atlantic Treaty Organization (NATO), which was led by the United States, brought together twelve Western nations in an anti-Communist alliance. Responding to the addition of West Germany to NATO in 1955, the Soviet Union created an opposing alliance, known as the Warsaw Pact. The map above shows the political situation in Europe in 1955.

Germany. Policy makers and analysts saw NATO as part of a strategy of "double containment," in which the revival of Germany, contained by a military alliance sensitive to French fear of German economic and military power, would in turn help to contain the USSR. The Soviets replied with another alliance, the Warsaw Pact, the cornerstone of which was the rearmament of East Germany. Europe was polarized into two mutually hostile camps. In eastern Europe, Communist governments suppressed all opposition political parties and institutions; in western Europe, NATO froze the Communists out of the governments of France and Italy, halting the political and economic experimentation under way there.

The Cold War in Asia

While the Cold War solidified European political allegiances, upheaval continued in much of the rest of the world. From Africa to Iran, from India to Southeast Asia and China, World War II had undermined Western colonial powers, unleashing a great wave of nationalism. Burma, Indonesia, India, and the Philippines soon achieved independence, followed a decade later by most of the Western colonies in Africa. Anticolonial nationalists were often linked to revolutionary social movements. In Vietnam and China, Communists under the leadership of Ho Chi Minh and Mao Zedong created powerful military insurgencies that championed the peasants' need for land as well as the nationalism of most urban workers and intellectuals. In India, the British imprisoned Mohandas Gandhi, Jawaharlal Nehru, and other nationalists during World War II, but jail merely enhanced their political and moral stature. By 1947, both Muslim Pakistan and predominantly Hindu India had achieved nationhood.

During the war, the United States had looked with some favor on anticolonial movements in Asia, especially those that fought against the Japanese occupying forces. American foreign service officers who met with Chinese Communists during the war praised them as patriots and "land reformers," even as U.S. military advisers grew increasingly frustrated with the corrupt rule of the pro-Western Chinese dictator Chiang Kai-shek, who preferred to deploy his army against the Communists rather than the Japanese. In September 1945, U.S. intelligence agents were honored guests when the Vietnamese Communist Ho Chi Minh, borrowing language from Thomas Jefferson's Declaration of Independence, declared Vietnam's freedom from France.

But Cold War tensions transformed U.S. attitudes toward these left-wing, anticolonial movements. Although the United States had provided Chiang with billions in military aid, Mao's Communist army took power in October 1949, forcing the Nationalists to flee to Taiwan. Many Americans soon asked, "Who lost China?" Truman's new secretary of state, Dean Acheson, argued that the civil war there "was the product of internal Chinese forces, forces which this government tried to influence but could not." But Republicans and other conservatives, many with prewar missionary experience on the Asian mainland, accused the State Department of being "soft" on the Red Chinese. For more than a decade thereafter, this powerful "China lobby" influenced the nation's Far Eastern policy. The United States tried to isolate Red China, kept it out of the United Nations, and, unlike most of its European allies, recognized Chiang's Taiwanese regime as the only legitimate Chinese government. American policy makers became more hostile to nationalist and reform movements in the colonial world. In 1950, the United States began to send military aid to the French, who were fighting Ho Chi Minh's forces in Indochina.

The Soviet explosion of an atomic bomb in August 1949, followed by the "loss" of China, accelerated both the arms race and the militarization of U.S. diplomacy. Thus, in January 1950, President Truman gave the go-ahead for the development of a controversial new "super" bomb, a thermonuclear weapon hundreds of times more powerful than the 10,000-kiloton device that had destroyed Hiroshima. First tested late in 1952, the new H-bomb threw off a fireball—five miles high and four miles wide—that vaporized Eniwetok Atoll in the Marshall Islands. Within a year, the Soviets began their own H-bomb tests, eventually exploding a leviathan with the power of 50 million tons of TNT.

The United States accompanied this new stage in the nuclear arms race with a plan for tripling the nation's arms budget. A secret report by

Better Safe Than Sorry. An advertisement in a 1951 edition of the professional periodical *School Executive* sells "dog-tag" necklaces for children to help identify their presumably mutilated remains after nuclear war. New York City's public school system issued tags during that year.

Source: *School Executive,* August 1951—Special Collections, Milbank Memorial Library, Teachers College, Columbia University.

SE-23

CITIES FROM COAST TO COAST

adopt identification necklaces of Bead Chain for students

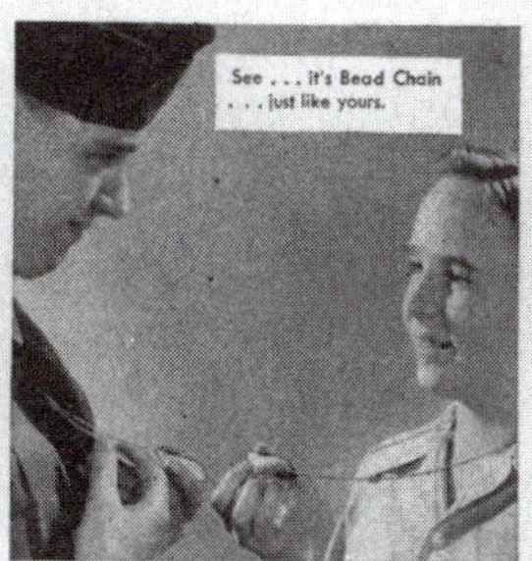

From New York City to Redwood, California, many cities across the country are ordering Identification Necklaces as a safeguard for their school children. Each student is being issued a necklace carrying a tag on which is stamped the student's identity and other information necessary for civilian defense.

For this purpose, Bead Chain has long been accepted as standard by our Armed Forces, for whom we have made identification necklaces for many years.

So flexible that it can't kink . . . economical, attractive, comfortable and very strong . . . Bead Chain is also preferred for religious chains and many other products made for personal wear. Write for catalog and complete information.

the National Security Council, NSC-68, had proposed such an increase, rejecting the possibility that any diplomatic or political initiative could moderate the Cold War. Instead, Paul Nitze, Robert Lovett, and other high-placed authors of NSC-68 assumed that the Soviets were preparing a military assault on one or more of the "Free World's" outposts. "We must realize that we are now in a mortal conflict; that we are now in a war worse than any we have experienced," argued Lovett in an apocalyptic memo. "It is not a cold war; it is a hot war. The only difference between this and previous wars is that death comes more slowly."

The "hot war" fears of NSC-68, as well as its budgetary hope, seemed fulfilled on June 25, 1950, when a Communist North Korean army crossed the 38th parallel into South Korea, where American troops had once been stationed. Though Stalin approved of the invasion, the driving force behind it was the North Korean revolutionary Kim Il Sung, who sought to forcibly reunify his homeland and oust the American-backed conservatives who ruled the South. American policy makers instantly imposed a global, strategic template on what was essentially a regional struggle. Korea, Truman told one of his associates, "is the Greece of the Far East. If we are tough enough now, if we stand up to them like we did in Greece three years ago, they won't take any next steps."

Cold War Illusions. The September 26, 1950, issue of *The Reporter,* an influential liberal weekly, featured an article by a Russian colonel who had defected to the United States in 1949. Kyril Kalinov's "How Russia Built the North Korean Army" was presented as proof of Soviet treachery. Kalinov, however, did not exist; the article was written by a Central Intelligence Agency operative.

Source: *The Reporter,* September 26, 1950—General Research Division, New York Public Library, Astor, Lenox, and Tilden Foundations.

Truman quickly won United Nations backing for the dispatch of U.S. Army troops to South Korea. (The Soviets, who might have vetoed this U.N. action, had absented themselves from meetings of the U.N. Security Council in protest over U.N. failure to admit Red China.) Under the command of General Douglas MacArthur, U.S. troops took the offensive in September 1950, pushing the North Koreans well north of the 38th parallel dividing the country. But when Chinese troops confronted U.S. forces later that fall, the Korean War settled into a bloody, three-year stalemate. Korean casualities mounted to more than a million killed and wounded, while the United States lost 34,000 men before signing a July 1953 truce that left the Communists still in control of North Korea.

The outbreak of the Korean War made it politically possible for the Truman administration to triple defense spending to nearly $50 billion a year, in accordance with the NSC-68 proposal. Thereafter, the defense budget remained high in order to support the capacity of the U.S. military to project its power onto every continent. By 1955, the United States had hundreds of military bases in thirty-six countries. New alliance systems, such as the Southeast Asia Treaty Organization and the Rio Pact, kept Asian and Latin American states friendly through a combination of diplomacy, foreign aid, and covert manipulation of their newspapers, politicians, and trade unions. In Korea, Spain, and the Philippines, the mere presence of large U.S. military bases bolstered authoritarian governments. But clandestine operations, often orchestrated by the newly formed Central Intelligence Agency, sometimes supported pro-U.S. military coups d'états. In Iran (1953) and Guatemala (1954), and later in Brazil (1964) and Chile (1973), the CIA cooperated closely with right-wing military officers in removing popularly elected liberal or leftist leaders. U.S. troops also intervened directly in conflicts in Vietnam, the Congo, and the Dominican Republic. Filled with what Senator J. William Fulbright, chairman of the Senate Foreign Relations Committee, later called "the arrogance of power," American policy makers had little patience with, or respect for, nations that refused to enlist in the fight against Soviet power and Communist ideology.

Labor Loses Ground

As the Cold War transformed America's role abroad, politics became more conservative at home. Although the Great Depression had discredited business leaders, the successful wartime production effort seemed to prove that American capitalism worked and that, in government and outside it, corporate managers should once again be trusted public figures. As H. W. Prentis, a prominent spokesman for the National Association of Manufacturers, had asserted during the war, "it is not government that has wrought the miracle that is being accomplished today in the production of war materials but the initiative, ingenuity and organizing genius of private enterprise." As for corporate executives, their experience as wartime administrators, and their service in government after the war, had enhanced their sense of entitlement and self-confidence. Business leaders knew they might have to pay higher wages to organized workers, but they rejected the idea of democratic power-sharing in shops and offices. "In industry as in government or anywhere else, there are two classes of people," argued one businessman. "There are those who decide and those who carry out." Industrial unions, executives complained, deprived them of the power to assign work as they saw fit, to fire unsuitable employees, and to speed up production. "We recognize that in some of our shops the union committeeman exercises greater authority than the foreman," asserted the industrial relations director of a large rubber firm. An angry auto executive was even more blunt: "If any manager in this industry tells you he has control of his plant he is a damn liar."

Executives had reluctantly accepted such constraints during the war, but now they seemed intolerable, especially since the political winds had shifted so strongly with the 1946 elections. Both in Washington and in their own companies, employers sought to win "the right to manage." Still, this was not the early 1920s, when another generation of managers and officials had battled for the outright destruction of the unions following World War I. Instead, executives wanted to contain the labor movement's power—to channel workers' demands toward issues that could be safely and routinely negotiated, and as much as possible to transform the unions into disciplinarians of the workforce. "During the New Deal, labor unions were coddled, nursed, and pampered," argued Republican congressman Fred Hartley of New Jersey, calling for an end to what he saw as the excessive power of labor.

Employers made the state an ally in their campaign against the labor movement. In the eighteen months after the Japanese surrender, more than seventy antilabor bills were introduced in the House of Representatives alone. Managers in core industrial sectors, such as auto manufacture and shipbuilding, wanted to halt the spread of unionism within the lower ranks of supervision. Smaller companies in construction, transport, and retail sales wanted to outlaw the secondary boycott, which the Teamsters and Longshoremen used to pressure anti-union employers and appeal to less well organized workers. Employers in the South and West simply wanted to stop the spread of unionism in their regions. Republicans, and not a few Democrats, especially feared the CIO, whose Political Action Committee had helped insure Roosevelt's reelection in 1944. Finally, conservatives wanted to force the Communists out of the union movement. The Republican-dominated Congress that took power early in 1947 lent a sympathetic ear to such anti-union interests: by June a coalition of Republicans and southern Democrats had overridden Truman's veto of the Taft-Hartley Act, a landmark revision of the New Deal labor law, named for its two principal sponsors, Hartley of New Jersey and the GOP stalwart, Senator Robert Taft of Ohio.

The Taft-Hartley Act signaled a major shift in the tenor of class relations in the United States. The new law deprived foremen of the protection afforded workers under the Wagner Act; made sympathy strikes and boycotts more difficult to carry out; and allowed states (in practice, those in the South and mountain West with weak union movements) to ban the union shop. The act also legalized employer "free

Don't Go Daft with Taft. Ohio Republican Senator Robert Taft, co-sponsor of the Taft-Hartley Act, is confronted by trade union demonstraters in Seattle, Washington, in August 1947.

Source: Corbis / Bettmann-UPI.

speech" during union organizing campaigns, which gave managers a greater opportunity to intimidate workers before a National Labor Relations Board (NLRB) election. And it gave the federal government considerable veto power over union politics and strikes. Labor leaders had to declare themselves to be non-Communist if they wanted their unions to participate in NLRB elections. And if they headed large unions, they had to bargain knowing that the president could postpone for eighty days any strike deemed a "national emergency"—a power Truman used thirty-seven times in the remainder of his term. None of these restrictions made the Taft-Hartley Act the "slave labor law" unionists called it, but together they helped to deradicalize the union movement, curb interunion solidarity, and keep the movement from organizing new regions and new workers. To survive, unions would have to function less as a social movement mobilizing grass-roots discontent and more as a set of interest groups protecting their own well-established turf.

Though the tides of public sentiment, congressional votes, and administration policy were all shifting against unions, the labor movement and its liberal allies were not without resources to mount a counterattack. The unions' postwar political strategy was two-pronged: (1) a concerted campaign to organize the South, called Operation Dixie, and (2) a political comeback in 1948, based on the reform and realignment of the Democratic party.

In Operation Dixie, the CIO sought to break the political power of reactionary landlords and employers in the South by striking at the racial discrimination and low-wage labor that sustained the conservative elite. During World War II, labor shortages and government wage guidelines had pushed wages upward more rapidly in the South than in any other region, and the unions had organized more than 800,000 southern workers, one-third of them black. In Winston-Salem, North Carolina, wartime unionization of the Reynolds Tobacco Company had enabled 3,000 African Americans to register to vote and had opened local politics to black participation for the first time since the Populist era. Along the Gulf Coast, the CIO had mobilized wartime workers into a progressive force that ended the political careers of two archconservative congressmen. In the deep South, black veterans, many in uniform, had marched boldly into rural courthouses to demand the right to register and vote. This patriotic, labor-based civil rights movement helped double African-American voting registration during the 1940s.

Beginning in 1946, the labor movement sought to extend these wartime breakthroughs. Northern unions, especially those in the CIO, hired hundreds of organizers, opened scores of offices, and began vigorous organizing campaigns in textiles, lumber, tobacco processing, and other southern industries. "When Georgia is organized," predicted a leader of the union drive, "you will find our old friend Gene Talmadge [the conservative governor of Georgia] trying to break into the doors of the CIO conventions and tell our people that he has always been misunderstood."

But Operation Dixie was a complete failure. Resistance from the political and industrial leadership of the white South proved overwhelming: during the next few years, the proportion of unionized southern workers actually declined. One problem was that many textile and lumber mills were located in tightly controlled company towns, where city officials, churches, and police were bitterly hostile to "outside" organizers. And though black workers proved exceptionally union-conscious, many southern whites rejected interracial solidarity. Union organizers found that "mixed" meetings could only be held outdoors, that interracial handshakes were taboo, and that African-American participation had to be downplayed. But most important, Operation Dixie's organizers faced physical intimidation. A Louisiana organizer recalled the dangers of organizing African Americans in a company town: "We went over and had a meeting down the railroad tracks with the blacks that worked in the plant. . . .

And someone rode around the street there and shot the meeting up. They just shot the little wooden church full of holes."

In short, organizing the South in the late 1940s would have required a massive, socially disruptive interracial campaign by a militant CIO leadership. But the national labor movement had lost much of its vitality, and its ranks were increasingly divided over the role of Communists and other radicals. This ambivalence toward radicalism proved particularly damaging in the South, where some of the most dynamic unionists, including the tobacco workers of North Carolina and the boatmen of Memphis, were African Americans who were hospitable to radical ideas. The crisis came to a head in Alabama, where conflict broke out between the United Steel Workers (USW) and a local of the Mine, Mill, and Smelter Workers' Union, which represented African-American iron miners in the area around Birmingham. Blending a flag-waving anti-communism with overt racism, the USW actually raided the Mine, Mill, and Smelter local, destroying one of the black community's most progressive institutions.

The 1948 Election

The failure of Operation Dixie meant that unions would not transform southern politics. But labor leaders still hoped to "realign" the American political system, either by building the power of labor, small farmers, and African Americans within the Democratic party (and thereby pushing most of the conservatives into the GOP), or by creating an entirely new third party based on a liberal–labor coalition. Until the spring of 1948, most union leaders therefore opposed Harry Truman as the Democratic presidential candidate. Many, including more than half of all CIO officials, expressed interest in forming a third party.

In 1948, the Communists, supported by a slice of the old New Deal coalition, formed a new Progressive party, nominating former vice president Henry Wallace for president. Wallace's vision of an expanded New Deal, of racial egalitarianism, and of peaceful coexistence with the Soviet Union differed sharply from the outlook of policy makers in the Truman administration: late in 1946, he had been dismissed as secretary of commerce after making a speech critical of the administration's tough line toward the Soviets. But rather than realigning American politics, the Wallace effort put an end to political experimentation and wed labor even more closely to the Democrats. The Progressives were bitterly attacked by anti-Communist liberals, including Eleanor Roosevelt, Walter Reuther, and the young mayor of Minneapolis, Hubert Humphrey. Joining together to form the Americans for Democratic Action (ADA), a pro-labor, pro-civil rights organization, they denounced Wallace as politically naive, called for the elimination of Communist influence in all liberal and labor organizations, and supported Truman's tough stance toward the Soviet Union. In February 1948, after Wallace failed to denounce the Communist coup in Czechoslovakia, still more liberals turned away from his candidacy. The CIO and the AFL rejected the Progressive party and endorsed Harry Truman's candidacy.

The support of organized labor proved crucial to the Democrats in the 1948 election. Most observers assumed that voters would put Republican Thomas Dewey, the financially well-connected governor of New York, into the White House. But Truman surprised everyone. He and his advisers understood that in order to win, they would have to remobilize the old New Deal coalition. A border-state politician with traditional racial attitudes, Truman knew that his reelection would hinge, in the words of his adviser Clark Clifford, on winning the support of "labor and the urban minorities." His administration therefore shifted leftward. Fearful that Wallace's Progressive party would steal votes from him, Truman made civil rights a major presidential priority for the first time in seventy-five years. Early in 1948, he called on Congress to pass a new Fair Employment Practices Act that would end job discrimination. In July, he capitulated to a protest campaign led by the African-American union leader A. Philip Randolph, signing an executive order that desegregated

'Jim Crow Must Go'

HENRY WALLACE

WALLACE SHOWS IT CAN BE DONE

Wins Battle Against Segregation

See story on page 3

Picture and caption courtesy Pittsburgh Courier

KKK "SCARE" FAILED!—Crowds gathered to hear former Vice President Henry Wallace speak to non-segregated audiences in the deep South. This definitely mixed audience reflects the keen feeling and interest aroused by Mr. Wallace's words. In Atlanta, despite KKK threats, never in the city's history did so many white photographers and writers seek entry to an affair at a Negro institution. The rally was held in the Wheat Street Baptist Church. Above, the New Orleans' audience was typical of the mixed crowds which came from far and near to hear Wallace.

The Wallace Campaign. A Progressive party flyer promotes integration in the deep South.

Source: Tamiment Institute Library, New York University.

the armed forces. And he appointed a civil rights commission that recommended sweeping reforms aimed at dismantling Jim Crow in the South.

Although Truman often sought to moderate liberal social initiatives in order to retain the loyalty of white Southerners, the Democratic party could not reconcile opposing factions. At the 1948 nominating convention in Philadelphia, a coalition of delegates from unions, the Americans for Democratic Action, and northern urban political machines pushed through a civil rights plank calling for the federal government to guarantee voting and equal employment rights. "To those who say the civil rights program is an infringement of states' rights," Hubert Humphrey told the convention, "I say this, that the time has come for the Democratic party to get out of the shadow of states' rights and to walk forthrightly into the bright sunshine of human rights."

Such sentiments proved anathema to the white South. Waving the battle flag of the Confederacy, delegates from Mississippi and Alabama marched out of the convention in protest. Three days later, a convention of southern Democrats chose South Carolina's governor, Strom Thurmond, as the candidate of a new States Rights party. Though the so-called Dixiecrats took only four states in the deep South in the November election, their revolt was highly significant: southern whites no longer saw the Democratic party as a reliable bulwark of white supremacy. Over the next third of a century, they would abandon their old party and shift to either the Republicans or an even more conservative third party.

In the final stretch of the campaign, Truman called for a system of national health insurance and a massive program of public housing. He promised to work with a new Democratic Congress to repeal the Taft-Hartley Act. Denouncing "Wall Street Republicans" on a frenetic whistle-stop campaign across the country, he thwarted Wallace and Dewey by galvanizing midwestern farmers and urban workers who had been part of the old Roosevelt coalition. That November, to a greater degree than ever before in the twentieth century, voters in large industrial states cast their ballots along class lines. As Truman excitedly told the press, "Labor did it!"

Truman's victory in 1948 put the Democrats back in control of Congress. But the split with the Dixiecrats had damaged party unity. When Truman sought to pass a "Fair Deal" program, including national health insurance, public housing, repeal of the Taft-Hartley Act, and agricultural subsidies for small farmers, a coalition of southern Democrats and Republicans blocked his initiatives at every turn. Moreover, without a sense of general crisis to mobilize the electorate, powerful interests such as the National Association of Real-Estate Boards (representing the private housing market), the Farm Bureau Federation (representing large farmers), and the American Medical Association also helped to defeat the initiatives.

Congress did pass a National Housing Act in 1949, but it led primarily to the building of low-cost urban housing projects, which soon turned into slums.

The drive toward civil rights stalled as well. Once the Progressive party was smashed, most Democratic leaders sought to regain the loyalty of the white South. Truman's commitment to black equality flagged during his second term, and in 1952 the Democratic presidential nominee, Adlai Stevenson, downplayed civil rights even further, choosing for his running mate an Alabama senator who stood for the maintenance of the status quo. Republicans also stood aloof: many hoped to build support in the South among the growing number of conservative white suburbanites there.

Southern politicians and business leaders soon mobilized against the extension of federal power, the spread of unions, and the push for civil rights. In the Senate, they used Rule 22 to filibuster—block by nonstop speechmaking—any legislation that threatened white supremacy in the South. The growth in the number of black voters came to a halt in the early 1950s. Thereafter, southern election campaigns were increasingly characterized by a xenophobic anti-Communism and outright appeals to racism. "Northern political labor leaders have recently ordered that all doors be opened to Negroes on union property," declared one election flyer. "This will lead to whites and Negroes working and living together. . . . Do you want that?"

The Weapon of Anti-Communism

America's encounter with the specter of domestic Communism proved a crucial contribution to the political stalemate and cultural conservatism of the early postwar years. Scores of Americans, perhaps as many as 300, did indeed provide information to Soviet agents, largely during the era of the Popular Front and World War II, when the politics of a fervent antifascism generated an apparent common bond among liberals, Communists, and the Soviet Union. Some of the people who provided information held high office, including Harry Dexter White, an assistant secretary of the Treasury, and Alger Hiss, a State Department official who participated in the Yalta conference with Roosevelt. But post–World War II anti-Communism was motivated far less by the actions of a treasonable few than by a pervasive antiradicalism that was now merged with a postwar hostility to the New Deal and its partisans.

Anti-Communism was both a partisan strategy exploited by top politicians and a popular grass-roots movement. The most prominent anti-Communist campaigns were led by national politicians, who turned

The Enemy Within. Hollywood producers, cowed by the House Committee on Un-American Activities' witch-hunts, strove to prove their loyalty. *The Red Menace* (1949) was but one of a flurry of films that melodramatically "exposed" a gangster-like network of Communists subverting America. Audiences, however, seemed to prefer science-fiction fantasies that portrayed malevolent intergalactic creatures infiltrating American society.

Source: Michael Barson Collection.

the issue into an obsessive quest for "internal security." In 1947, fearing he might be outflanked on the issue by the Republicans, Truman had boosted funding for the FBI, set up a loyalty program for federal employees, and asked the attorney general to draw up a list of subversive organizations. And between 1945 and 1952, congressional committees conducted eighty-four hearings on Communist subversion, the most infamous of which were held by the House Committee on Un-American Activities (HUAC), which investigated Hollywood, higher education, unions, and the federal government.

In the well-publicized HUAC hearings, investigators demanded that witnesses not only affirm their loyalty to the government but also prove it by naming former Communist associates. "Don't present me with the choice of either being in contempt of this committee and going to jail," pleaded the Hollywood actor Larry Parks, "or forcing me to really crawl through the mud to be an informer." Though Parks did name his former left-wing friends and associates, his career, like those of many others, was ruined when film studios and other large employers backlisted suspect employees. Some Americans lost more than their careers. When the biochemist William Sherwood received a HUAC summons in 1957, he poisoned himself. "The Committee's trail," he wrote in a suicide note, "is strewn with blasted lives, the wreckage of useful careers. . . . The scientific mind cannot flourish in an atmosphere of fear, timidity and imposed conformity."

The most relentless interrogator, Republican senator Joseph McCarthy of Wisconsin cast himself as the ultimate patriot, directing his inquisitorial skills against "respectable" targets in the State Department, Ivy League universities, and the U.S. Army. McCarthy achieved national stature early in 1950 by exploiting public frustration over the "loss" of China and the consolidation of Soviet power in eastern Europe. To McCarthy and his followers, these events were not just diplomatic setbacks. "The reason why we find ourselves in a position of impotency," the senator told a Republican audience, "is not because our only powerful potential enemy has sent men to invade our shores, but rather, because of the traitorous actions of those who have been treated so well by this nation." At one point, McCarthy claimed to have a list of 205 Communists employed in the State Department. In his eyes, Secretary of State Dean Acheson was the "Red Dean . . . Russian as to heart, British as to manner"; the years of Roosevelt and Truman he called "twenty years of treason." Using his chairmanship of a minor Senate subcommittee to launch wide-ranging and often crudely partisan investigations, McCarthy charged that Communist sympathizers in the highest reaches of government were shielding Soviet spies. Though such charges were nonsense in the 1950s, McCarthy's manipulation of the press and the new medium of television (which broadcast many of the hearings) proved so masterful that he became one of the most feared political figures of the early 1950s.

Well-known officeholders, actors, and scientists were not the only ones who came under the scrutiny of the FBI or congressional probes. HUAC furnished data on 60,000 people to inquiring employers. As a result of investigations by government loyalty boards, at least 15,000 federal employees were fired or forced to resign. Hundreds of high school teachers, community college instructors, and municipal librarians were forced out of their posts, either because they failed to pass a security review or because they refused to sign the loyalty oaths most cities and states instituted. In San Francisco, as many as a fifth of all seamen and longshoremen were denied clearance to work on vessels owned or chartered by the government. By one estimate, 13.5 million Americans fell within the scope of various federal, state, and private loyalty programs. Roughly one of every five working people had to take an oath or receive a security clearance as a condition of employment.

Liberals, non-Communist radicals, labor activists, and others who questioned the direction of postwar society were often the real target of

The Informer as Hero. *I Led Three Lives,* a syndicated series about the infiltration of the Communist party by an FBI informer, ran on television from 1953 to 1956. Starring Richard Carlson (left), best known for roles in low-budget science-fiction movies, as informer Herbert Philbrick (right), the series depicted Philbrick as an intrepid hero. In the series, while leading an ordinary life (Philbrick was an advertising manager for a Boston movie theater), he consistently foiled the party's attempts at espionage and murder.

Source: The Everett Collection.

anti-Communist probes. As the head of one government loyalty board noted, "The fact that a person believes in racial equality doesn't prove he's a Communist, but it certainly makes you look twice, doesn't it?" "We may get information on a man through anonymous letters, phone calls, or personal visits," reported Republic Aviation's security director. "Several years ago we encouraged employees up and down the line to report suspicious activities of fellow workers. . . . We're alert to which men are becoming prominent in plant organizations, ranging from hobby and sport to religious and political groups." By 1954, the company had fired at least 250 workers considered to be security risks.

Indeed, many businessmen found Communist subversion to be a convenient explanation for labor conflict. "Whoever stirs up needless strife in American trade unions advances the cause of Communism," asserted the *Nation's Business* late in 1946. Employers worked closely with congressional investigators and state officials, who were happy to "red-bait" union officials when a strike or certification election was imminent. In 1947, for example, members of the House Education and Labor Committee berated the left-wing leaders of a Milwaukee UAW local, then in the midst of a bitter and unpopular strike against Allis-Chalmers, Wisconsin's leading industrial firm. Two ambitious congressmen, Richard Nixon of California and John F. Kennedy of Massachusetts, were among the most hostile and persistent interrogators. Nongovernmental groups such as the American Legion, with 17,000 posts, also played a powerful role in the anti-Communist movement. Feature articles in the Legion's magazine asked such questions as "Does Your Movie Money Go to Commies?" and "Do Colleges Have to Hire Red Professors?"

Not surprisingly, anti-Communism polarized the labor movement. In the 1930s and 1940s, Communists and other radicals had played an indispensable role in building the new unions; now they were accused of "infiltrating" these organizations. In 1949, anti-Communist leaders of the CIO denounced the half-million-member United Electrical Workers, labeling it "the Communist Party masquerading as a trade union." Such invective reflected not only the Cold War but also the way in which working people defined themselves. In the late 1940s, millions of workers were still first- or second-generation immigrants, whose sense of "Americanism" had only recently been affirmed by the patriotism that surged through their communities during the New Deal and the wartime years. Although many immigrants, especially Germans, Finns, and Russian Jews, had once sought to combine socialist politics with patriotic Americanism, the Cold War forced them to choose. To be a radical, let alone a Communist, seemed now to be un-American.

Are You Now or Have You Ever Been a Member of the Communist Party? Autoworker Basil Gordon kneels on the sidewalk outside a Los Angeles Chrysler Corporation plant in July 1950 after receiving a beating from fellow workers. Gordon and two other workers were attacked when they refused to say whether they belonged to the Communist party.

Source: AP/Wide World Photos.

Ironically, the Communists had been among the most zealous patriots of World War II. Their lockstep support of the war effort had helped to disarm their critics and to twist antifascism into a celebration of anything labeled "American." But after the war, this resurgent nationalism turned against the Communists. In the million-member UAW, Walter Reuther denounced his Communist-backed opponents for their wartime antistrike activities, appealing to workers' reawakened sense of patriotism. "UAW Americanism for Us" read the slogan propped on the desks of many local union officers. Not all left-wingers were ejected from the unions; those who were effective trade unionists sometimes retained the support of the rank and file. But a virulent anti-Communism became the official policy. In 1949 the CIO expelled nine unions representing 900,000 workers for refusing to purge themselves of Communist leaders and to support government policies such as the Marshall Plan.

Religious, ethnic, and racial loyalties often determined the ways in which working Americans responded to the anti-Communist impulse. Catholics, especially those of Irish or eastern European extraction, who had themselves been the subject of nativist prejudice in the 1920s, were among the most anti-Communist of all working-class Americans. The Red Army's occupation of eastern Europe had had an electrifying impact on millions of Slavs and Hungarians, who constituted perhaps half of the CIO's membership. When the Soviets arrested Church leaders in Poland, the Catholic Church mobilized tens of thousands of adherents to protest the "Satan-inspired Communist crimes." Priests from working-class parishes played an aggressive part in the effort to oust Communists from the leadership of unions such as the United Electrical Workers, which enrolled many second-generation Slavs, and New York's heavily Irish Transport Workers' Union. In working-class Catholic neighborhoods, even rosary clubs, often led by women, joined the anti-Communist crusade. Catholics backed Joseph McCarthy by a margin considerably greater than that among either Jews or Protestants.

In contrast, relatively few African Americans joined in the anti-Communist crusade. Their lack of enthusiasm reflected the Communist party's long commitment to civil rights and its active recruitment of black workers as members. But more important, the discrimination African Americans endured made them skeptical of white efforts to define "Americanism." Coleman Young, who had once been a Ford worker and would later become the first African-American mayor of Detroit, denounced a congressional investigating committee that questioned his loyalty:

> I am a part of the Negro people. I fought in the last war and . . . I am now in process of fighting against what I consider to be attacks and discrimination against my people. I am fighting against un-American activities such as lynchings and denial of the vote. I am dedicated to that fight, and I don't have to apologize or explain it to anybody.

Of all the nation's ethnic groups, Jews were most divided and devastated by McCarthyism. By the late 1940s, anti-Semitism had seemed to be on the wane and the prospects for assimilation had seemed good: second- and third-generation Jewish Americans were entering the middle class more rapidly than any other ethnic group. Yet Jews, who had been solid Roosevelt partisans and had provided a large share of Henry Wallace's support in cities such as New York and Los Angeles, were often victims of the anti-Communist witch-hunt. In New York City, 90 percent of all teachers fired by the Board of Education were Jewish; in Detroit and Flint, Michigan, Communists who were "run out" of the auto plants were often taunted with anti-Semitic epithets.

A notorious espionage case accentuated Jewish fear of renewed anti-Semitism. In 1950, Julius and Ethel Rosenberg, both active Communists and the children of Jewish immigrants, were tried for and convicted of delivering atomic secrets to the Soviet Union; in June 1953, they were executed. Julius was clearly guilty of giving the Soviets information provided to him by his brother-in-law, a machinist at the Los Alamos weapons laboratory. But the death penalty meted out to the couple—Ethel was but marginally involved—nevertheless generated a worldwide uproar. They were the first American citizens ever to be executed for treason in time of peace, and their deaths frightened Jewish progressives, causing many to abandon their longtime participation in radical causes.

I Like Ike

McCarthyism's hold on American politics lost some of its power once the Republicans regained control of the White House and both houses of Congress in the 1952 elections. For Republicans like the new president, Dwight D. Eisenhower, Joseph McCarthy's strident brand of anti-Communism paid few political dividends; meanwhile, the death of Joseph Stalin in March 1953, followed three months later by armistice in the Korean War, eased Cold War tensions and national anxieties. McCarthy still made headlines, but he came under increasing attack: from the newspapers, from a growing band of Senate Republicans, and from television. In November 1954, the Senate voted to censure him. Thereafter he quickly lost influence, though the political and ideological constraints imposed by the anti-Communist impluse did not fully ebb until well into the 1960s.

Eisenhower called himself a "modern Republican:" he ran for president in 1952 as an internationalist determined to keep the right wing of his party in check. Born in Abilene, Kansas, in 1890, Eisenhower had made the Army his career. He was not a dashing front-line commander, like George S. Patton or Douglas MacArthur; rather, he rose through the ranks as the consummate planner and military diplomat. As Supreme Commander in Europe during World War II, he used these skills to organize the Normandy landings on D-Day and to coordinate the Anglo-American push into Germany. After the war, he served briefly as president of Columbia University and as NATO commander.

Known to the public as Ike, Eisenhower and his vice-presidential candidate, Richard Nixon, won 55 percent of the popular vote, swamping the Democratic ticket of Illinois governor Adlai Stevenson and Senator John Sparkman of Alabama. Because of his eloquence and wit, Stevenson won the fervent support of many liberals, but his politics were actually to the right of both FDR and Truman: he was cool to labor, opposed a system of national health insurance, and thought racial issues should be left to the states. Eisenhower was clearly more conservative, but his fatherly demeanor and war-hero self-confidence appealed to those Americans who sought political and social stability after more than twenty years of turmoil. When Eisenhower and Stevenson squared off again in 1956, Ike proved even more personally popular, though his political coattails were too short to carry either house of Congress for the Republicans.

An admirer of businessmen, Eisenhower put eight millionaires in his first cabinet. He pushed for private development of off-shore oil and hydroelectric power, which the old New Dealers wanted to keep in federal hands. And he favored balanced budgets, even when the two recessions that took place during his administration cut federal income and generated high levels of unemployment. The corporate spirit of his

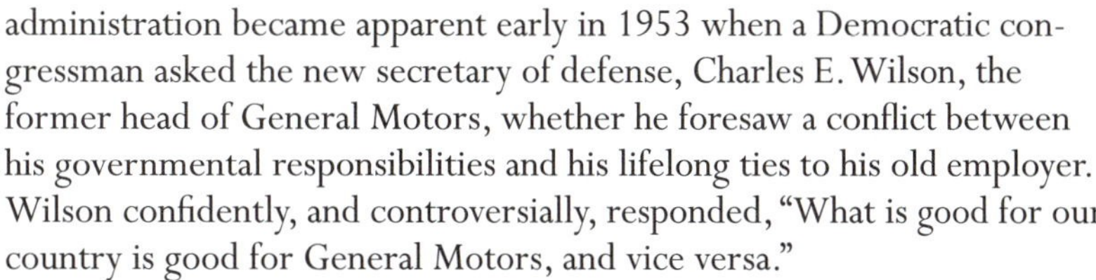

administration became apparent early in 1953 when a Democratic congressman asked the new secretary of defense, Charles E. Wilson, the former head of General Motors, whether he foresaw a conflict between his governmental responsibilities and his lifelong ties to his old employer. Wilson confidently, and controversially, responded, "What is good for our country is good for General Motors, and vice versa."

But Eisenhower was hardly a reactionary. Although most of the leading figures in his administration had fought New Deal labor and social welfare reforms, once in power they did nothing to undermine them. Indeed, the Eisenhower administration locked the New Deal in place. The president created a new cabinet office (Health, Education, and Welfare), raised the minimum wage, and broadened Social Security coverage. After the Soviet Union launched the first earth-orbiting satellite, *Sputnik,* in 1957, Eisenhower endorsed the liberal view that federal funds were needed to improve American education in science, technology, and languages. Eisenhower had no enthusiasm for school integration, but neither did he pander to white racism in the South. Indeed, African Americans gave him more of their votes in 1956 than any Republican presidential candidate had received in twenty years.

Eisenhower and his secretary of state, John Foster Dulles, were orthodox Cold Warriors who believed the Communist bloc to be an implacable foe of Western civilization. But as fiscal conservatives who feared high taxes and an intrusive "garrison" state, they also sought to wage the Cold War without a huge army and an ever-spiraling military budget. Eisenhower and Dulles therefore relied on relatively less expensive nuclear weapons and a worldwide aerospace delivery system. Dulles, a master of provocative speech and imagery, condemned the Truman era's containment doctrine as "appeasement" and instead declared that the United States would employ "massive retaliation" to protect Free World interests.

Critics called Dulles's policy nuclear "brinksmanship" because it involved repeatedly taking the nation to the verge of war in order to force its opponents to back down. It was necessary "to remove the taboo" from the use of atomic weapons, Dulles informed the press, thus making the nuclear threat a routine part of American diplomacy. This atomic specter certainly had an impact at home. Civil defense exercises were soon being conducted in factories, offices, and

Robots. During the 1950s, science-fiction stories and films became increasingly popular, although their vision of the future was often pessimistic. Besides alien invasions and atomic disasters (including devastating destruction wrought by gigantic monsters created or awakened by nuclear experiments), another favorite theme was the mixed blessing of automation: the robot as a labor-saving device that all too easily could turn against humankind.

Source: Virgil Finlay, *Amazing Stories,* October–November 1953.

schools, where "duck and cover" drills became a routine part of public education. Hollywood produced a series of end-of-the-world movies, from the fantastic *Them* (1954), in which giant, mutating ants destroyed Los Angeles, to the realistic *On the Beach* (1957), which portrayed the extinction of humankind as the aftermath of nuclear war.

But nuclear brinkmanship proved virtually useless in the real world. When French troops were on the verge of defeat in Vietnam, in May 1954, Eisenhower refused to order a nuclear air strike to save them. When Hungarians revolted against Communist rule two years later, the United States refused to intervene, fearing that any direct support it might offer the Budapest fighters would generate a military confrontation with the Soviets. In 1958 and 1959, during a protracted crisis over the status of Berlin, nuclear brinkmanship was abandoned outright for painstaking diplomacy that downplayed the nuclear threat and forestalled a clash of arms. By the time he left office in 1961, Eisenhower himself was a critic of what he called the "military-industrial complex" and an advocate of vigorous U.S. diplomacy as a means of reducing Cold War tensions.

The Postwar Economic Boom

From the end of World War II until the early 1970s, a period of more than a quarter-century, the United States enjoyed an unprecedented era of sustained economic growth. Even with five short recessions, the production of goods and services doubled, while unemployment and inflation stayed below 5 percent most of the time. This newfound material affluence deeply affected Americans on the job and at home, reshaping the way they thought about themselves and their society.

Nothing symbolized the boom so well as the automobile. Production of civilian vehicles had been halted during World War II; for nearly a decade afterward, car-starved Americans bought whatever Detroit turned out. In the late 1940s and early 1950s, hundreds of thousands of consumers flocked every year to New York, where the major automakers unveiled their new models. A near-riot took place there in 1949, when Ford displayed its first all-new model since the war in the grand ballroom of the Waldorf-Astoria Hotel. That year 5 million cars were sold, surpassing sales in the banner year of 1929. Afterward, auto production rarely flagged; by the early 1970s, there were two cars on U.S. roads for every three adult citizens.

The auto industry stood at the center of American society. Auto manufacturing represented the epitome of postwar production technology, the source of secure, high-wage jobs for more than a million members of the UAW, the nation's most prominent union. The car culture spurred the

"If You Had a Fast Car . . . You Were a Big Man"

In the 1950s tens of thousands of Americans, most of them white working-class men, transformed the standardized consumer automobiles coming out of Detroit into personalized masterpieces. Among them were Ed Schafer and Boyd Pennington of St. Louis. Interviewed in the late 1970s, they recalled their teenage passion for "hot rods."

Ed Schafer: I had my first car when I was 14 in 1953. I was the only guy in the 8th grade that drove to school. I lived in the country and drove to school on the back roads. I had a 1940 Chevrolet that you had to tie the doors shut, but I could tear the engine down and put it back together. I bought it for $25, a piece of junk, but it ran and I could keep it running. . . . You had to have fender skirts and you had to have the rear end of the car dropped almost to the axle. . . . I think what we tried to do was make it as different as possible to what Detroit put out and it was neat to watch Detroit follow us; decking, cleaning the chrome and the ornaments off, lowering the silhouette, lowering the entire car.

Boyd Pennington: If two guys had exactly the same color car within two days somebody had something different. There was quite a lot of rivalry between cars even though they were old cars, of course some of it was show; terrycloth seat covers and mud flaps.

Ed Schafer: Our interest was stimulated by California, by the news we got from there and by the movies and songs that were prevalent then.

Boyd Pennington: The West Coast always led. You could travel out to California and it would take a year for that trend to move to the Midwest. In the early 1950s there was *Honk, Hot Rod, Rod and Custom, Car and Custom,* just a whole stack of West Coast magazines.

Boyd Pennington: There are some things I'm not too proud of. We did steal from other people; we did make regular trips into South St. Louis because it was so easy to steal fender skirts, hubcaps, tail-lights or whatever was big at the time. . . . People knew what we were doing, I mean it's hard to conceal from your parents that you have, probably four, five thousand dollars of equipment in your garage. . . .

Ed Schafer: We had a fairly large group of people, 15, 16 guys, and the camaraderie was unbelievable. There was no way one guy would rat on another. . . . Your importance in the club increased by your performance on the dragstrip. It didn't matter if you were a nerd; if you had a fast car and could make it down a quarter mile faster than anyone else, you were a big man.

Source: George Lipsitz, "They Knew Who We Were: Drag Racing and Customizing," *Cultural Correspondence* (Summer–Fall 1977).

growth of suburbs, the proliferation of interstate highways, and the emergence of drive-in movies, restaurants, and shopping centers. Each year station wagons, hot rods, sports cars, and sedans became bigger, flashier, and more powerful, with tail fins, bold colors, and automatic transmissions. To American consumers, they embodied excitement, mobility, and material gratification.

The automobile industry's success was possible only because the nation's economic boom put real money into the average citizen's pocket.

Television Dreams. Enacting the American fantasy of achieving instantaneous fame and fortune, television quiz shows were wildly popular in the 1950s. Columbia University English instructor Charles Van Doren (left) was the most renowned quiz-show celebrity, going on from his triumph on NBC's *Twenty-One* to become one of the stars of the network's *Today* show. However, a 1959 congressional investigation revealed that many of the big-money game shows were rigged. Van Doren was implicated in the scandal, which led to fraud indictments and his disappearance from television.

Source: Photofest.

Between 1941 and 1969, family income almost doubled. This economic growth fed a baby boom of unprecedented proportions. Because Americans felt more secure economically, they went ahead with marriages and pregnancies they had postponed during the Depression and World War II. The birth rate, which had fallen to nineteen per thousand in the mid-1930s, leaped by 25 percent after 1945 and remained high throughout the 1950s. "It seems to me," wrote a British visitor in 1958, "that every other young housewife I see is pregnant."

Moreover, the increase in the standard of living improved the general health of the population. Americans ate better, lived in more spacious homes, and could afford to see the doctor more often. Besides boosting the number of successful pregnancies, these improvements meant that people lived longer. During the 1940s, white Americans' life expectancy increased from sixty-three to sixty-seven years, while African-Americans' rose from fifty-three to sixty-one.

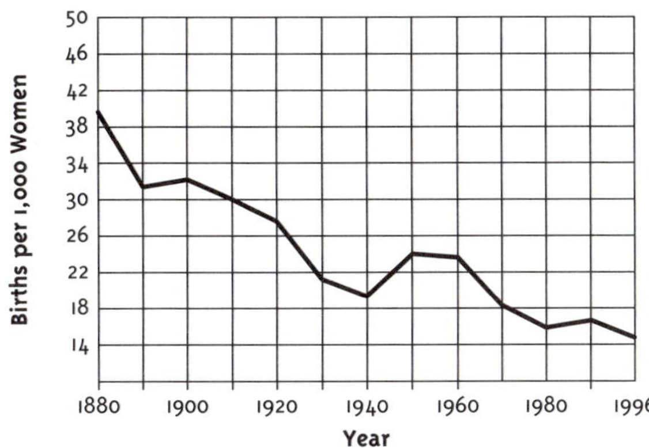

Baby Booms and Busts: The U.S. Birth Rate, 1880–1996. The birth rate has been declining in the United States for more than a century. The one exception was the post–World War II "baby boom." In the 1950s, families grew larger, and the American rate of population growth approached that of India.

Postwar affluence was no accident; it arose out of New Deal politics, the experience of World War II, and America's new role in the world. To many Americans, the great lesson of World War II was that federal money and political will power could vanquish unemployment. As *The Nation,* a liberal magazine, editorialized in 1943, mobilization for war had discredited "the defeatist thinking that held us in economic thralldom through the thirties, when it was assumed that we could not afford full employment or full production in this country. The war has shown the absurdity of this contention." Congress passed the Employment Act of 1946, which committed the federal government to promote "maximum employment, production, and purchasing power" and set up a Council of Economic Advisers charged with developing "national economic policies."

During the next quarter-century, government fiscal policy was based largely on theories developed by the British economist John Maynard Keynes. Keynes argued that in modern capitalist societies, governments could combat business slumps by using its power to tax and spend in order to regulate consumer demand for goods and services. Liberals wanted to sustain consumer purchasing power through government spending on public works, schools, housing, Social Security, and unemployment insurance. Conservatives, who feared such programs would erode market incentives and open the door to government planning, favored tax reductions for business instead. Throughout the 1950s, liberals and conservatives fought to a standoff on these issues. Though business taxes remained at the high levels established during World War II, government spending on social programs grew slowly.

Two new forces dominated the nation's economy in this era: a strong union movement and an enormous peacetime military establishment. Though the Taft-Hartley Act (1947) and the failure of Operation Dixie had signaled the end of labor's challenge to the hegemony of capitalism, large unions still negotiated for higher wages and pushed for increased government spending. The labor movement enrolled more workers than at any other time in U.S. history, reaching a high point of nearly 35 percent of the labor force in 1953. In cities such as Pittsburgh and Detroit, 60 percent of all households included a union member. For the first time, American unions had the kind of economic influence enjoyed by organized labor in western Europe. Key unions such as the Steelworkers and the United Auto Workers negotiated wage increases that set the standard

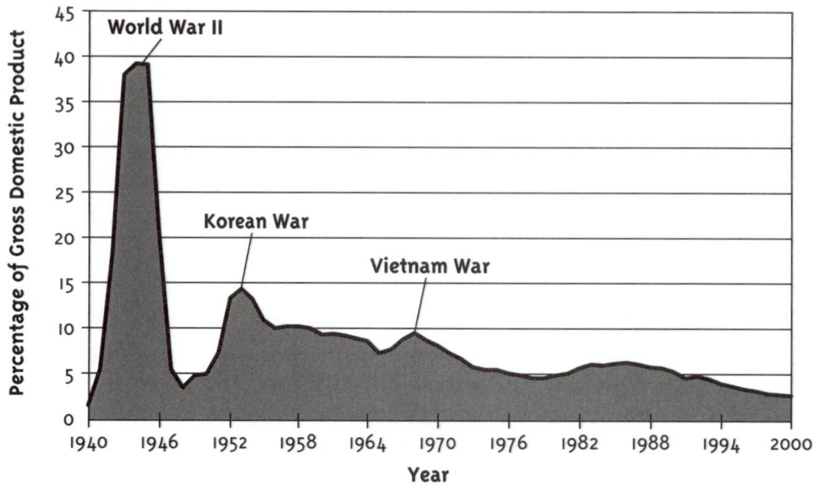

The Military Industrial Complex: Defense Spending as a Percentage of U.S. Output, 1940–2000. Military spending has been central to the American economy in the post–World War II era. After the end of the war, defense spending (as a percentage of the entire economy defined as gross domestic product) dropped sharply. But the Cold War (and the hot wars of Korea and Vietnam) pushed it much higher. It gradually dropped as the United States became less actively engaged in Vietnam; a further decline came with the end of the Cold War.

for millions of other workers, union and nonunion alike. Because wages increased independently of market pressures, workers' purchasing power remained intact during the periodic recessions of the postwar era, and the economy rebounded quickly.

The second pillar of the postwar boom was military spending. By 1950, about half of the federal budget, or more than 10 percent of all goods and services consumed in the United States, went to the armed services. Because of the Cold War, massive government outlays in the form of military spending were acceptable to most citizens, including conservatives who were otherwise hostile to high taxes and large federal expenditures. "Government planners figure they have found the magic formula for almost endless good times," reported the conservative columnist David Lawrence in 1950. "Cold war is the catalyst. Cold war is an automatic pump primer. Turn a spigot, and the public clamors for more arms spending. Turn another and the clamor ceases."

Arms production helped to fuel the growth of key sectors of the economy, such as aircraft manufacturing and electronics. It fostered economic growth and urbanization in the South, where many new military bases were built, and in southern California, Seattle, and Long Island, where the growing aviation industry contributed to a vibrant postwar sprawl. Military spending acquired a permanent economic constituency in these regions, represented by powerful political spokesmen such as Senator Henry Jackson of Washington, dubbed the "senator from Boeing," and Congressman L. Mendel Rivers, who put so many military facilities around Charleston, South Carolina that people joked it would sink into the sea. The political consensus on military spending allowed the federal government to fund social programs that otherwise would have been controversial. Educational, medical, housing, and pension benefits for veterans all expanded in the late 1940s. In 1956, Congress used the military's ostensible need for an improved transportation system to vote funds for the multibillion-dollar Interstate and Defense Highway Program, the largest public works project in the nation's history.

Together, the unions and the military helped to sustain high wages, high employment, and endless consumption. The whole system seemed a never-ending spiral of growth and abundance, prompting contemporary observers to conclude that American capitalism had found the solution to all economic problems. "The world revolution of our times is 'Made in the USA,'" wrote the business consultant Peter Drucker in 1949. "The true revolutionary principle is the idea of mass production."

A Classless Society?

The boom had a profound impact on the way Americans thought about economic and social problems. In the 1930s, many New Deal theorists had assumed the U.S. economy was permanently crippled. Its strength, they believed, could be restored only by breaking up big corporations and redistributing wealth and income. But the postwar boom made that political agenda irrelevant; it reduced class and ideological tension over the distribution of power and resources in American society. Though the distribution of income did not change in the postwar years—the top tenth of the population consistently took home almost 40 percent of the national income—the economic pie was getting bigger, so there seemed no need to redivide it. Had the "labor problem" been solved? Many influential Americans thought so. "The union," wrote the editors of *Fortune,* "has made the worker, to an amazing degree, a middle class member of a middle class society." "Of all the great industrial nations," *Life* magazine pointed out, "the one that clings most tenaciously to private capitalism has come closest to the socialist goal of providing abundance for all in a classless society."

Of course, these were not new ideas; from the Revolution onward, many Americans—especially those who enjoyed a measure of economic security—had wanted to believe that the United States was a nation in which social class was unimportant, wealth widely shared, and social conflict muted. In the postwar era, however, this vision was remarkably pervasive, not only among conservatives but also on college campuses and in union halls, newsrooms, and television studios. As even Philip Murray, the president of the CIO, asserted to a union audience: "We have no classes in this country."

In retrospect, economic growth clearly did not solve all the problems of American society. Nor did all Americans become members of a unified middle class. The lines dividing American society did not disappear in the 1950s; rather, they were redrawn. Affluence united white male adults of the working and middle classes, who became more homogeneous. At the same time, new rifts divided high-wage unionized workers from low-wage nonunion workers, young from old, and city dweller from suburbanite. Historical divisions remained between men and women and between those with white skins and those whose skin color was black, brown, or yellow. These were the fault lines on which political debate and social conflict would increasingly center in the postwar years.

The Labor – Management Accord

In the late 1940s, the union movement began to grope its way toward a less confrontational relationship with management. Though labor organizations had more members than at any other time in American history, their failure to realign the party system or forestall the rise of McCarthyism had drastically narrowed the range of strategic options. The result was a labor – management accord that would last for more than a quarter century. It guaranteed high wages to union members and insulated well-established unions from a direct corporate assault. At the same time, the accord protected management's decision-making power on the shop floor and in the boardroom. Though the accord was reached by large unions and major employers such as General Motors and U.S. Steel, it spread to many other firms, both union and nonunion.

There were two main elements to the postwar settlement. First, corporations in the same industry agreed not to compete over labor costs. Once a leading firm such as Goodyear or Boeing reached an agreement with a union, other major companies in the industry would copy the settlement, meeting the resulting rise in labor costs through a general price increase. Thus the system removed wages as a factor in business competition. Only the overall health of the U.S. economy and the small number of companies within major industries made such an arrangement possible.

Second, workers were protected against inflation by a cost-of-living adjustment (COLA), first suggested by General Motors in negotiations with the United Automobile Workers in 1948. Two years before, during a long, costly strike, GM had staved off the UAW's efforts to link the prices it charged customers for cars to the wages it paid its workers. But the corporation's head, Charles Wilson, realized that disruptive strikes and contentious wage negotiations — especially if they were part of a broad offensive against corporate power — would embitter relations on the

"UAW Americanism for Us"

As industrial unions' relationship to corporations changed, so did life within the union. The journalist Samuel Lubell visited a UAW local in 1948, and he found it "hard to believe it was the same place" he had visited in 1940.

When I first visited Chrysler Local Seven of the United Automobile Workers a few days after Franklin Roosevelt's third term victory [in 1940], the scene was one of belligerent activity. Bulletin boards bristled with photographs of police clubbing strikers and of tear gas riotings. When the union's educational director heard that I was analyzing the election . . . he [had] stiffened suspiciously and seemed about to have me thrown out. Then, he began boasting freely of how class conscious the auto workers were and how ready they were to vote Roosevelt a fourth or a fifth term. He wore a lumber jacket. With his feet on his desk and a buzzer by his hand, he looked the very picture of newly arrived power.

Returning eight years later, after Truman's victory, the whole atmosphere of the local had changed. The strike photographs had come down from the bulletin boards and had been replaced by idyllic snapshots of the union's annual outings and sporting events. An honor roll listed fifty-nine union members who had been killed in the war. Nearby stood a cabinet filled with loving cups and other trophies won in city-wide UAW tournaments. The "class-conscious" educational director was gone—ousted in the UAW-wide fight against Communists which Walter Reuther led. On their desks, the new officers had propped the slogan, "UAW Americanism for Us."

In 1940 the flavor of the local was one of street barricades and sit-down strikes; eight years later it was almost like a lodge hall.

Source: Samuel Lubell, *The Future of American Politics* (1951).

shop floor and hamper the company's long-range planning. In 1948, GM offered the UAW a contract that included two pillars of the postwar accord: an automatic COLA keyed to the consumer price index and an unconditional 2-percent "annual improvement factor," designed to give workers a share of GM's productivity gains.

The 1948 GM–UAW agreement was a dramatic departure from past union–management practice. It was premised on the emergence of a new era of prosperity and social peace—a development that a few years earlier had seemed unimaginable. When a 1949 recession turned out to be milder than expected and economic growth quickly resumed, the door was opened to broad accommodation between large unions and major corporations. In 1950 the UAW pioneered a new agreement, a five-year

"Treaty of Detroit" that provided pensions and a COLA in addition to a wage increase. *Fortune* hailed the new contract as "the first that unmistakably accepts the existing distribution of income between wages and profits as 'normal' if not as 'fair' . . . thus throwing overboard all theories of wages as determined by political power and of profits as 'surplus value.'" By the end of the 1950s, the COLA principle had been incorporated into more than 50 percent of all major union contracts. Nonunion firms such as IBM and DuPont, anxious to keep unions out, copied the pattern, paying top wages, matching union benefits, and establishing employee grievance systems.

This economic settlement had a steep price, however: the decline of democracy and activism in the unions and the workplace. "This kind of collective bargaining," wrote economist Frederick Harberson, "calls for intelligent trading rather than table pounding . . . for internal union discipline rather than grass roots rank-and-file activity." In return for their acceptance of unions and of high-wage contracts, corporate managers insisted that "wildcat" strikes (actions not authorized by the union) stop, that contracts be negotiated for the long term, and that all disputes be handled through official channels (in most cases, a multistep grievance procedure). Shop stewards were often replaced by full-time committeemen, who functioned less as shop floor leaders than as contract police.

Although contemporary journalists and later scholars have often argued that working-class affluence subverted union militancy in the 1950s, those years saw much shop floor militancy, often at a level scarcely less vigorous than in the tumultuous Depression decade. Workers were delighted to receive higher pay, but they did not find a trade-off between money and dignity on the job acceptable; they wanted both. One-third of all strikes in the 1950s were wildcat stoppages that arose when workers balked at speedups or contested efforts to erode their workplace rights. In 1959, rank-and-file steelworkers pressured USW officials into calling a 119-day strike that forestalled the elimination of work rules and safety standards labor had won in the 1930s and 1940s.

Such massive stoppages did not have the political impact of those that made headlines in 1937 or 1946, however. After 1950, most company-wide strikes were aimed at adjusting the wage and benefit package, not at changing the distribution of power in the workplace. And wildcat strikes had little long-range effect, even when they were temporarily successful. "We're moving rapidly away from the crusading spirit of the thirties," admitted a shop steward in an aircraft union at the end of the decade. "In 1953 we had one of the most militant unions in the labor movement. We had wildcat strikes, direct job action. . . . Today there is much less of this. People no longer file grievances because they think it is no use."

The merger of the AFL and the CIO in 1955 ratified these changes in the union movement. With the CIO's expulsion of Communist-

Mobbed Up. Inspired by the notoriously corrupt leadership of the International Longshoremen's Association, the 1954 film *On the Waterfront* portrayed trade union officials as gangsters.

Source: Photofest.

dominated unions, few substantial differences remained between the two federations. The AFL, dominated by the construction trades and other "business" unionists, was almost twice the size of the CIO. It was therefore fitting that the chief of the new AFL-CIO would not be the CIO's visionary president, Walter Reuther, but George Meany, a Bronx plumber who had risen to leadership in the AFL during the 1930s and 1940s. Meany, who would later boast that he had never led a strike, had won high wages for union members by adapting the labor movement to the contours of American capitalism. "We do not seek to recast American society in any particular doctrinaire or ideological image," Meany asserted. "We seek an ever rising standard of living."

The merger proved, in the words of the economist Richard Lester, a "sleepy monopoly." In the years after 1955 the amount of energy and money unions devoted to organizing new workers declined, as did their relative independence from the Democratic party. Moreover, because both labor law and management practice encouraged an insular, depoliticized form of collective bargaining, some trade union leaders became little better than corrupt businessmen, who undercut the price of labor they "sold" for kickbacks and payoffs from employers.

Union corruption, exposed in a series of congressional hearings presided over by Senator John McClellan in 1957 and 1958, proved especially prevalent in decentralized, highly competitive industries, such as trucking, the restaurant business, and dock work, in which autocratic union leaders could cut "sweetheart" deals with employers and ignore rank-and-file sentiment. Gangsters actually ran some locals; nepotistic families presided in many others. Teamster president Jimmy Hoffa clashed repeatedly with Senator John F. Kennedy and his brother Robert, then chief counsel to the McClellan committee, during the nationally televised hearings. The union image was deeply morally damaged—one reason that contributed to the decline in the proportion of American workers

"Sweetheart Deal"

Trade union corruption became big news in the 1950s, after Senate investigating committees found Mafia influence at the highest levels of the Teamsters, the International Longshoremen's Association, and the Hotel and Restaurant Workers. Allen Friedman, a Teamster strongarm man in Cleveland in the 1950s, later described how he had worked with a local attorney to "organize" the workers at local Italian restaurants while "shaking down" the restaurant owners.

The attorney's idea was for me to go to each of the restaurants he represented, signing up the members so that he would have to be called in to negotiate the contracts. In exchange for his giving me the list of names of the restaurants involved, I would negotiate a "sweetheart deal" which wouldn't cost the restaurant owners very much more than they were already paying. It was a good arrangement for everyone. . . .

The idea that unions organize workers isn't always true. With big places we had to work hard to sign people to pledge cards, then present enough pledge cards to the boss to show that the workers were behind us. . . . With smaller places we didn't always bother to organize. We'd just tell the boss we had the members pledged to join, flashing phony cards, not all of which were even filled out by the employees. Sometimes we'd have two or three signatures. Sometimes we'd have none. It didn't matter. If we could bluff our way through, we would.

I worked with a partner from Local 10, which was created from the combined unions serving restaurant and hotel workers. We walked into the restaurant . . . and demanded that the union be recognized. The owner would yell at us and throw us out of the restaurant. Then we could go to the car, pull out the picket signs, and start walking back and forth in front of the business.

John Felice, an acquaintance of mine, headed the local that controlled the beer truck drivers. When the beer arrived, I'd tell the driver that he wasn't supposed to deliver the beer that day because John Felice sanctioned the strike. The driver would go on to his next stop. . . . It was easy to organize those places. Stop the supplying of essential services and they're out of business.

Generally the meetings would be similar. The restaurant owner would start yelling, the attorney talking with him in his native language, quieting him. He then would explain that the owner should slip me a few hundred dollars and I would give him a sweetheart contract. The owner understood the bribe, paid it, and got a good deal. The employees didn't care because they kept their jobs and got a little better deal than they had had.

Source: Allen Friedman and Ted Schwarz, *Power and Greed: Inside the Teamsters Empire of Corruption* (1989).

who were AFL-CIO members, from about 33 percent of the workforce in 1955 to little more than 20 percent two decades later.

Flight from the Farms

In the quarter-century after the war, the U.S. economy generated two sorts of jobs. At its productive core, big firms and big government bureaucracies expanded steadily. Corporations were making money, governments were hiring more teachers and policemen, and the unions were upgrading many jobs that had once been casual or low paid, such as telephone repair, warehousing, and seafaring. Jobs in this core sector, both white- and blue-collar, provided relatively well paid, virtually lifetime employment.

But millions of other jobs—perhaps as many as 40 percent—shared none of these characteristics. Farm laborers, cabdrivers, cannery workers, and dime-store clerks were poorly paid and lacked job security. Such jobs are often thought of as belonging to a distinct, "secondary" labor market—segregated from the more secure work in the core economy, but still essential to the functioning of the system. Though casual employment has long been part of the working-class experience in America, in the postwar era the secondary labor market, once comprised mostly of manual labor, evolved to include clerical and service employment. Workers in those fields tended to come from "marginal" groups: racial minorities, teenagers, and women.

The growth of this secondary labor market was spurred by three major changes in the composition of the American workforce: a dramatic rise in service, sales, and clerical work; the increasing employment of women; and, most of all, a flight from farming. Mining and agriculture had together supported one in four American families before the war, but consolidation and mechanization eliminated 15 million of these jobs in one generation. The nation's agricultural population fell from one in five to one in twenty. In midwestern states such as Iowa and Ohio, rural migrants, mainly whites with some education, were readily absorbed into the factories and offices of the region's cities. But in the rural South, Puerto Rico, and the Mexican borderlands, the process of depopulation was far more traumatic.

In the South, the plowing, weeding, and picking of cotton were mechanized, thus displacing more than 4 million farmers and farm laborers. African Americans were the hardest hit; by 1960, fewer than 10 percent of them worked on the land. The great black migration out of the South, which had begun early in the twentieth century, generated a demographic revolution. Between 1940 and 1970, more than 5 million African Americans moved from the South to the North, most of them to the largest cities. At one point in the 1950s, the black population of Chicago was swelled by more than 2,200 new arrivals each week.

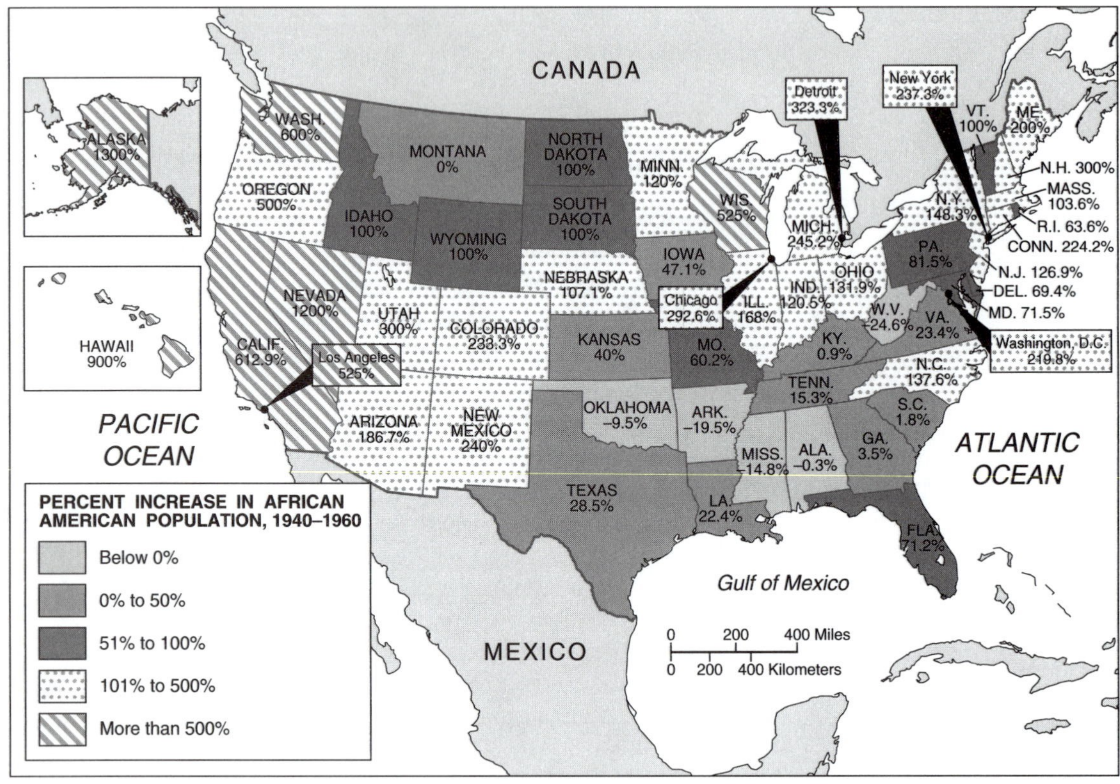

Great Migrations: African Americans Move North and West, 1940–1960. African Americans were pushed and pulled out of the South during and after World War II. The mechanization of cotton farming decreased the need for a large rural black population at the same time that urban areas in the North and West beckoned with industrial and service jobs.

The South Side of Chicago now rivaled Harlem as the cultural capital of black America. New arrivals swelled a ghetto that offered thousands of good jobs in nearby packing plants, steel mills, and warehouses. The community was home to the renowned boxing champion Joe Louis, the longtime member of Congress William Dawson, the gospel singer Mahalia Jackson, and the nation's largest black congregation, the Mount Olivet Baptist Church. The South Side boasted substantial homes and apartment complexes, access to Lake Michigan's beaches, and famous nightclubs where the world's finest jazz and blues artists played. It also had crowded slums, decaying tenements, and the familiar urban problems of prostitution, crime, and alcoholism.

The same economic transformation that drove African Americans north also drove Puerto Ricans from their island farms and into the mainland cities. During the 1940s, a U.S. government program, "Operation Bootstrap," had encouraged the mechanization of the island's sugarcane plantations and the growth of low-wage, tax-free industries in cities such as San Juan. Rural employment plunged, and the island's urban popula-

". . . We Consider This Part of the City to Be Ours"

When Puerto Ricans began arriving in New York City in massive numbers in the late 1940s, they found already established Latino communities. In this excerpt from Guillermo Cotto-Thorner's autobiographical novel, *Trópico en Manhattan (Tropic in Manhattan),* Juan Marcos, a new arrival, travels with his friend Antonio, a seasoned New Yorker, from the airport to El Barrio, the Puerto Rican community in uptown Manhattan.

. . . The plane prepared for a graceful landing in the mysterious city of hope. Off in the distance, Juan Marcos saw the vertical zig-zag of the Manhattan skyline. The streets seemed so wide to him; he hadn't yet adapted to the dimensions of the metropolis. . . .

In a few minutes he found himself "walking underground" for the first time in his life. The subway captivated him. He began to feel that sensation of mystery and splendor that the city instills. . . . Their car of the subway filled up at the first stop, and the newly arrived greenhorn saw a beautiful blonde balanced before him clinging to one of the stiff, enameled handles that hung from the ceiling. Juan Marcos thought he was in Puerto Rico where courtesy hasn't suffered the sad fate that it has in New York. He stood up and in broken English said to the woman: "Lady, dis is a sit for yu." The girl looked him up and down and said in a rude, contemptuous tone, "Don't be a sucker."

Juan Marcos felt as though he'd been slapped across the face. . . . Juan Marcos thought: "What a shameless girl. Are all the women here like that?" He was extremely agitated. He felt like giving the girl a piece of his mind, but how, if his English wasn't even good enough to sell a bag of tomatoes? . . .

Juan Marcos had read and heard so much about El Barrio, the Puerto Rican colony in Manhattan scattered all over lower Harlem. Leaving the subway station, he stopped instinctively to look it over, while Antonio carried his suitcase as a gesture of courtesy. . . . On both sides of the wide street, the newly arrived friend could only distinguish two large buildings which stretched from corner to corner. Parallel windows, identical stairs reaching down to the sidewalk from six floors above the street. No, they weren't two buildings: they were many apartment buildings stuck together. . . . Hundreds, thousands of fellow Puerto Ricans lived there who, like him, had left the island to try their luck in New York. . . .

Two men were playing checkers on a little table they had brought out onto the sidewalk, while two others watched. They were in front of "The Cave," a Puerto Rican "greasy spoon," which exuded the delicious aromas of fried pork rinds, *pasteles,* and fried codfish. Next to the table where the two men were playing, there was a wooden box full of coconuts and pieces of ice. The players spoke not a word, their concentration was total in spite of the hustle and bustle around them. . . .

"This," [said] Antonio, "is our neighborhood, El Barrio. It's said that we Latins run things here. And that's how we see ourselves. While the Americans take most of the money that circulates around here, we consider this part of the city to be ours. Notice the store signs—'La Fe' (The Faith), 'La Mallorquina' (The Mallorcan), 'El Nuevo Gardel' (The New Gardel), 'El Atómico' (The Atomic), 'Las Tres Marías' (The Three Marys) and that's not all. The stores, barbershops, restaurants, butcher shops, churches, funeral parlors, greasy spoons, pool halls, everything is all Latino. Every now and then you see a business run by a Jew or an Irishman or an Italian, but you'll also see that even these people know a little Spanish."

Source: Juan Flores, ed., *Divided Arrival: Narratives of the Puerto Rican Migration, 1920–1950* (1987).

tion tripled. Yet Puerto Rico's unemployment rate remained among the highest in the Caribbean.

These conditions prompted a large migration to the mainland. Since the 1920s, a small but steady stream of Puerto Ricans had been moving to New York and other eastern cities. In the postwar years, cheap airfares, family connections, and the hope of steady employment lured 40 percent of all islanders to make the move. By the end of the 1960s, New York City had a larger Puerto Rican population than San Juan. The center of Puerto Rican life there was El Barrio in East Harlem, the home of salsa music, scores of social clubs, and hundreds of small Puerto Rican grocery stores, or bodegas, which served as the center of social and economic life for many immigrants. Like Italian immigrants of the early twentieth century, many Puerto Ricans hoped to earn enough money to return home and buy a piece of land.

Mexican immigrants fleeing the poverty of their homeland also poured into American cities. Though many crossed the border illegally, hundreds of thousands of Mexicans came to the Southwest in the 1950s through a government-sponsored *bracero* work program. Some of the new immigrants found employment on the vast factory farms that dominated California and Arizona agriculture, but many went to the growing cities of California and the Southwest. From 1950 to 1960, the Chicano (Mexican-American) population in Los Angeles County more than doubled, growing from 300,000 to more than 600,000. By 1968 the Chicano community in East Los Angeles was approaching 1 million. In that year, 85 percent of the nation's Chicano population lived in urban areas.

Thus, the postwar era marked a watershed in the history of American cities. The arrival of millions of Mexican Americans, blacks, and Puerto Ricans reshaped the character of the nation's urban centers. In some ways, the lives of these postwar migrants and immigrants resembled those of earlier immigrants, such as the Irish in the 1850s or the Jews, Italians, and eastern Europeans of the early twentieth century. They, too, had to make the change from rural to urban life, figure out the city's ways, and in some cases learn a new language. Much like earlier immigrants, Chicanos, Puerto Ricans, and African Americans drew on their traditional cultures while adapting to the new world of the city.

In other ways, however, the postwar arrivals confronted new challenges, perhaps the biggest of which was economic. Although the U.S. economy grew rapidly after the war, it no longer generated an ever-increasing number of unskilled and semiskilled construction and manufacturing jobs, which had been the mainstay of earlier immigrant groups. By the late 1950s, in fact, many industries had moved out of the inner cities. In Chicago, economic changes eliminated more than 90,000 jobs, many in high-wage, unionized industries such as meatpacking and steel manufacture. As urban unemployment rose, many of the new migrants and

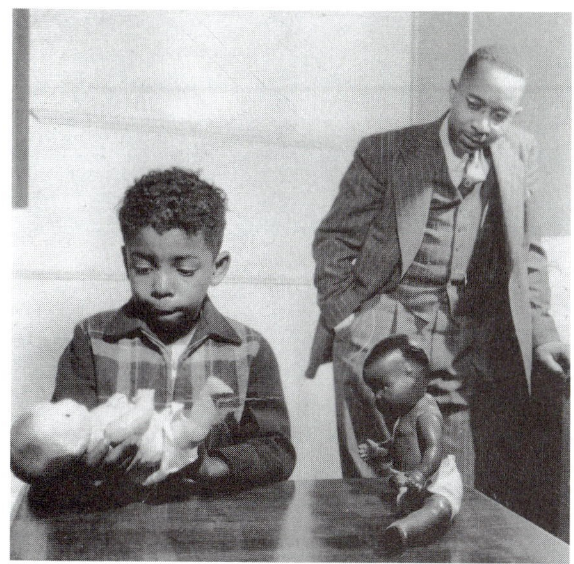

Dolls and Discrimination. Studies conducted by sociologists Kenneth Clark (right) and Mamie Phipps Clark at their Northside Center for Child Development in Harlem demonstrated the detrimental impact of segregation on African-American children. For example, when asked to choose between a white and black doll, African-American children from segregated environments preferred and identified with the white one. These studies were instrumental in convincing the Supreme Court in its 1954 *Brown versus Board of Education* decision that racial segregation in public schools was unconstitutional.

Source: Gordon Parks—Prints and Photographs Division, Library of Congress. Courtesy of Gordon Parks.

immigrants were forced into insecure, low-wage positions at the bottom of the job ladder.

Racial discrimination added to the problem. In many cities, the job market remained rigidly divided along racial lines. In Chicago, African Americans could get jobs in large mail-order houses and post offices, but not in insurance companies and construction. Puerto Ricans, including many women, found work in New York's garment industry, but generally in the lowest-paid positions; others found work as janitors, doormen, or hospital service workers. Both Puerto Ricans and Chicanos had to overcome language barriers. Many Chicanos faced the added problem of being illegal immigrants, which meant that they had few legal rights and had to be constantly alert to avoid deportation.

To be sure, earlier immigrant groups had faced prejudice and discrimination. But African Americans, Puerto Ricans, and Chicanos confronted what W. E. B. Du Bois had called "the color line." Though the three groups possessed distinct cultures and histories, and often did not get along well with each other, most white Americans saw them as a single dark-skinned mass. Puerto Ricans, Chicanos, and African Americans faced discrimination not only in hiring but also in housing, schooling, and social services. Many were forced to live in the poorest housing and attend the worst city schools. When they tried to move into traditionally white neighborhoods, they faced discrimination by realtors and landlords and, in some instances, violence at the hands of angry white homeowners.

Urban police forces, virtually all-white in the 1950s, clashed repeatedly with the new urban migrants. The trouble was a product not only of white racism but also of the aggressive professionalism with which urban police departments now did their job. To police driving radio-equipped cruisers, the ghettos and barrios were no longer alien territory, off limits to the foot patrolman. And though police in Oakland and Los Angeles were then among the most innovative in the nation, they were also among the most brutal. On Christmas night in 1951, Los Angeles police dragged six Chicano youths from a bar. When other youths protested, the police arrested all of them for assaulting an officer and took them to the central jail, where gangs of officers took turns beating the youths so severely that they later had to be hospitalized. Despite a community outcry, none of the offending officers were disciplined.

Political remedies for such problems were not easily available to the new arrivals. Since many Chicanos were not U.S. citizens, and thus could not vote, they had few political representatives. And though Puerto Ricans had been granted full U.S. citizenship in 1917, most Puerto Ricans found mainland literacy tests an obstacle to voter registration. Not until 1965, when the federal Voting Rights Act ended the use of literacy tests to qualify voters, did Puerto Ricans begin to vote in large numbers. Urbanized African Americans could and did vote in the 1950s, which gave them some political leverage. But urban political machines, such as the one headed by Richard Daley in Chicago, managed to contain African-American demands.

Integration, Peanuts, and Crackerjacks. Jackie Robinson steals home plate during the fifth inning of a Braves-Dodgers game at Ebbets Field, August 22, 1948. Robinson broke baseball's race barrier, but major league teams continued to resist integration. By 1953, only six teams had African-American players. **Source:** UPI/Corbis-Bettmann.

Throughout the 1950s, then, most African Americans, Puerto Ricans, and Chicanos lived in relatively segregated and culturally isolated communities, even in the most cosmopolitan of cities. Symbolic changes, such as the integration of major league baseball after Jackie Robinson joined the Brooklyn Dodgers in 1947, did not change the realities of everyday life. Though each group mounted limited protests against job discrimination and police brutality, such campaigns did not generate mass involvement or media attention until the rise of an African-American civil rights movement late in the 1950s. For the most part, these communities remained inwardly focused, sustained by their own institutions and cultural traditions.

The Growth of the Service Sector

The flight from agricultural work took place during the same post–World War II years in which millions of new workers sat behind a desk, stood behind a counter, or presided over a classroom. In the two decades after 1950, 9 million jobs opened up for secondary school teachers, hospital support staff, and government office workers. The growing demand for consumer goods spurred the creation of new department stores and supermarkets, staffed by 3 million additional employees. And in almost every large corporation, new white-collar jobs were created. Hundreds of thousands of supervisors and personnel managers were hired to control workers and keep unions out of the workplace. Millions more were assigned to planning, advertising, sales, and public relations. Finance, real estate, and insurance companies added 4 million new workers in the twenty years after 1950.

In 1956, for the first time in U.S. history, white-collar workers outnumbered those whose collars were blue. Professional, managerial, clerical, and sales workers, who had composed less than a third of the work force in 1940, swelled to almost half of all those employed by 1970. Meanwhile, blue-collar employment was declining steadily as a proportion of the work force, to 35 percent by 1970. The sociologist C. Wright Mills captured the new world of work in his influential study *White Collar* (1951): "What must be grasped is the picture of society as a great salesroom, an enormous file, an incorporated brain, a new universe of management and manipulation." Declared one journalist, "Increasingly, the representative wage earner became a pencil pusher working for a large, impersonal entity."

Holocaust or No Holocaust, A Woman's Place Is in . . . An illustration in the widely circulated 1950 book *How to Survive an Atomic Bomb* designates "appropriate" civil-defense jobs for men and women.

Source: Richard Gestell, *How to Survive an Atomic Bomb* (1950)—General Research Division, New York Public Library, Astor, Lenox, and Tilden Foundations.

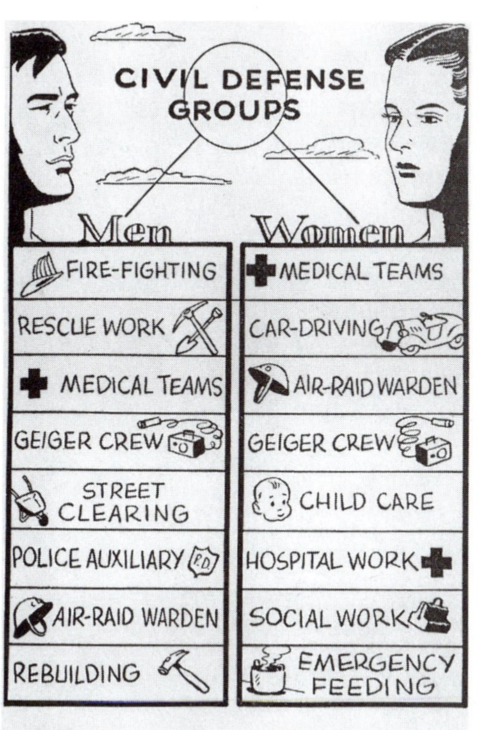

The growth of the service industry reinforced the popular, but misleading, notion that the United States had become a classless, "postindustrial" society. Despite the deployment of much highly touted automated machinery, factory work still required an army of manual workers. Although they were a declining proportion of the workforce, manufacturing workers actually increased in number from 22 million to 26 million between 1950 and 1970. Moreover, half of all service jobs involved manual labor—trash collection, maintenance, and food preparation, for example. The greatest growth in so-called white-collar employment came in sales and clerical work: jobs that might be considered white-collar, in the sense that a typist did not spot-weld body joints, but that involved little creativity or autonomy. "My job doesn't have prestige," bank teller Nancy Rogers noted. "It's a service job. Whether you're a waitress, salesperson, anything like that . . . you are there to serve them. They are not there to serve you."

Most of the half-million women who worked for the telephone company, for instance, were classified as service or clerical staff, though their work was as routinized as any factory job. AT&T employees were rigidly divided between an all-male craft unit, whose unionized staff repaired and installed equipment, and the largely female departments that handled long-

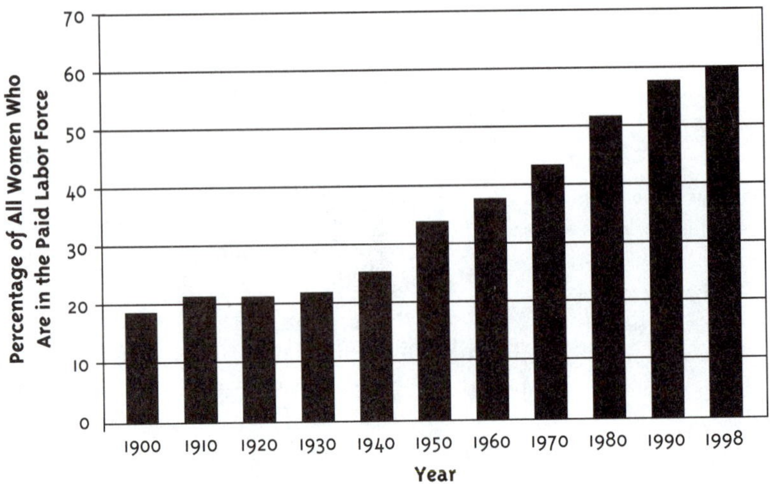

Women in the Workforce (1900–1998). Since 1940, the percentage of working women has more than doubled. In 1998, there were 63.7 million women in the labor force, compared to 12.8 million in 1940.

distance calls and took sales and installation orders. Operators were confined to their consoles, monitored closely, and held to a daily work quota. "You've got a clock next to you that times every second," reported a Chicago operator. "They do keep track. How many calls you take, how well you mark your tickets, how many errors you make. You're constantly being pushed. It's hectic." Like many workers in the casual labor market, the operators' turnover was high and their pay low. In the big cities, such jobs were increasingly held by African Americans or Latinos.

The postwar shift to service and clerical work would have been impossible without the influx of 20 million women into the workforce. In 1950, a total of 31 percent of all women were employed outside the home; twenty years later, the figure was 42 percent. Unlike women workers during the war, women in the postwar work force were confined to a female job ghetto. Ninety-five percent of them worked in just four job categories: light manufacturing (home appliances and clothing), the retail trade, clerical work, and health and education. Within those categories, high-status work was usually assigned to men; low-status work, to women. In 1960, for example, 90 percent of high school principals were male, while 85 percent of elementary school teachers were female.

Such job segregation helped to keep women's work low-paid and dead-end. During World War II, women's wages in manufacturing had risen to about two-thirds of those earned by men. But within a few years of the war's end, women's median earnings in that sector had dropped to only 53 percent of men's. In Baltimore, women who were clerical employees were allowed to stay on the job after the war, but women who worked in high-wage aircraft assembly were forced to take lower-paying jobs as waitresses or service workers. Women's average weekly wages in that city fell from $50 to $37. The same process of exclusion took place in other types of work. Because professional schools discouraged women from enrolling, and because World War II veterans took so many seats at the nation's colleges and universities, there were actually fewer women doctors and lawyers in the 1950s than there had been two decades before.

Young Mother. New Rochelle, New York, 1955.

Source: Elliott Erwitt / Magnum.

The relegation of women to the secondary labor market was sustained by the sexual ideology of the early postwar years. All too quickly the wartime self-confidence of "Rosie the Riveter" gave way to a rigid definition of gender roles reminiscent of mid-nineteenth-century social spheres. Experts celebrated women's submissiveness and domesticity, branding sexual freedom as potentially subversive, even pro-Communist. In the popular media, women were portrayed largely as incompetent and vulnerable, fulfilled only in the context of a stable and secure marriage. By the late 1940s, women's magazines such as the *Ladies' Home Journal* and *Redbook* were full of articles with such titles as "What's Wrong with American Women?" "Isn't a Woman's Place in the Home?" and "Really a Man's World, Politics." The author Betty Friedan labeled all this the "feminine mystique" in her best-selling book of the same name (1963).

American men, too, were subjected to a new sexual orthodoxy, one that equated masculinity with rationality and control over one's emotions. They, too, were expected to marry. To be a "family man," even in late adolescence, was considered a sign of maturity and reliability. Men who were still single in their thirties were considered suspect by many employers. Homosexuality was a criminal offense that was thought to sap the moral fiber of both the individual and the nation. Indeed, the anti-Communist movement engendered a wave of homophobia, intensifying the persecution of male and female "perverts." When the FBI mounted an all-out effort to discover the sexual habits of those suspected of subversive political behavior, gay-baiting rivaled Red-baiting in its ferocity, destroying careers, encouraging harassment, and forcing those who "confessed their guilt" to name their lovers and friends.

Despite the heavy emphasis on marriage and the family, or perhaps because of it, Americans indulged an appetite for vicarious sex. The postwar era gave birth to the cosmopolitan, sexually permissive *Playboy* magazine, which was a huge success when it was first published in 1953. The magazine, which was filled with advertisements for liquor, stereo equipment, and cars, demonstrated that lust itself was a consumer commodity eminently suitable to the upwardly mobile. Though *Playboy* had a predominantly male audience, the new interest in sexuality was for women, too. *Peyton Place,* the steamy story of a town in rural New England, became the best-selling novel of the century. Published in 1956, it sold 10 million copies, largely to women.

These rigid gender roles made the lives of midcentury working women particularly difficult. Most American men saw cooking, cleaning, and changing the baby's diapers as "women's work." Consequently, women who did work outside the home were usually burdened with housework and childrearing as well. And though American homes were filling up with dishwashers, vacuum cleaners, and other labor-saving appliances, housework still demanded as much time as it had thirty years earlier for the average woman. According to one survey taken during the 1950s, half of all working women said they had no leisure time at all.

The gender orthodoxy of the period was also used to justify the low pay and discriminatory employment practices women faced. Many working women came to see themselves as temporary employees working toward a specific goal: school clothes for the kids, a new refrigerator, a larger house. A supervisor's handbook of this era noted that such sex discrimination made sense, because "the role of achievers still belongs to men. . . . Women as a rule don't seek job promotion—their emotions are secure in a limited job."

Women workers made the best of a bad situation. In workplaces large and small, postwar women, like their mothers before them, created a rich work culture that both accommodated and resisted the sexist system. With ample opportunity for talk, clerical workers and saleswomen created a social world of birthdays, bridal showers, and shopping trips that gave them some compensation for unrewarding paper-shuffling and order-taking. Though large firms sometimes took advantage of such social networks to generate group competition and esprit de corps, more often women and men found in their friendships and office rituals a source of work-life satisfaction and self-organization, in some cases counterpoised to managerial authority.

The Decline of Ethnicity

In the 1950s and 1960s, ethnic and religious divisions were growing less important to white Americans. Almost two generations had passed since the end of mass European immigration. Because there were only half as many foreign-born residents in the United States as there were during the Depression, ethnic differences were becoming increasingly irrelevant to institutions such as the church, the military, and the public schools. Enrollment in Catholic schools, especially those organized along ethnic lines, began a long-term decline. And though churches and synagogues benefited from increased attendance in the 1950s, many worshipers had come to see their faith as part of a homogenized "civic religion" that validated the "American way of life." Perhaps President Eisenhower put it best when he affirmed, "Our government makes no sense unless it is founded in a deeply religious faith—and I don't care what it is."

The growth of the comprehensive high school had the same homogenizing effect. After the war, secondary school enrollment rose to 80 percent of its potential constituency. Virtually all white Americans spent three or four formative years in an institution whose official ideology was one of classless homogeneity. Elaborate sports contests and the emergence of a distinct teen culture in the 1950s soon eclipsed the ethnic antagonisms that had bitterly divided white youths since the late nineteenth century. For millions of working-class youths, for whom "the service" was a rite of passage from adolescence to adulthood, the postwar military draft, which lasted from 1948 until 1971, further diluted ethnic, religious, and regional parochialism.

The explosive growth of college and university enrollments also contributed to the process. The enactment of the G.I. Bill (officially known as the Servicemen's Readjustment Act) in 1944 had democratized higher education by making it broadly available to those who had served in the armed forces. World War II veterans took advantage of generous government payments to jam college classrooms and hastily expanded living facilities at state universities and private colleges. "Everybody went to college," remembered a Sicilian-born architect who had spent his childhood in the Bronx, where his father kept a wine press in the basement. "Suddenly we looked up, we owned property. Italians could buy. The G.I. Bill, the American dream. Guys my age had really become Americanized."

Still, upward mobility was clearly structured along class and racial lines. The "tracking" of high school students into academic or vocational courses usually replicated social-class divisions in the local community; and many of the white working-class youths who found higher education suddenly within reach enrolled in community colleges and technical schools rather than in the prestigious liberal arts colleges. Until the late 1960s, African Americans found that managerial and professional jobs were largely closed to them.

Suburban America

The explosion of suburban housing tracts in the postwar era was almost as much a product of the New Deal as were the new unions and the new sense of citizenship held by ethnic Americans. New Deal planners had believed in cheap credit, which they extended to farmers, hospitals, homeowners, and veterans. After the war, with interest rates running at 2 and 3 percent, the government had continued to guarantee loans through the Veterans Administration and other government agencies. For the first time in their lives, huge numbers of working people could afford better housing. And their demand was desperate. The Depression and war had virtually halted residential construction; now millions of veterans and cash-rich workers needed homes for their growing families. The demand was so great that, in 1945, the city of Chicago had put 250 old streetcars up for sale as potential homes. An ad in an Omaha newspaper read, "Big Ice Box, 7 × 17 feet, could be fixed up to live in."

The construction of new suburbs was only one of a range of possible solutions to the housing crisis. Before World War II, the suburbs had been reserved largely for the well-to-do. Working-class Americans lived near their work, often in apartments or cramped row houses in ethnic neighborhoods. Except in the Midwest, most workers rented, because purchasing a house required putting as much as 50 percent down on a ten- or fifteen-year mortgage.

Reformers had experimented with a variety of housing programs in the 1930s and 1940s. During the New Deal, the government had helped to plan and construct several "greenbelt" towns in which garden apartments were clustered close to work places and recreational facilities. And during the war, to meet the desperate need to house defense employees, the government had financed the construction of thousands of new rental units. Many were convenient to public transportation, and some were designed with the needs of single workers or working mothers in mind. Vanport City, Oregon, which housed 40,000 shipyard workers during the war, included child-care centers, restaurants, and recreational facilities in its original city plan.

In the postwar era, however, such experiments quickly gave way to single-family suburban tract homes, best symbolized by the three huge Levittowns that sprouted in potato fields outside New York and Philadelphia. William Levitt's wartime experience in constructing family quarters on a navy base had convinced him that if financing were available, a contractor could make millions housing veterans and their families. He and other builders prodded officials of the Veterans Administration and the Federal Housing Administration (FHA) to guarantee low-interest loans that would make suburban homes cheaper than rental apartments. Assured of a mass market, Levitt used assembly-line methods to erect thousands of identical Cape Cod–style homes. Sold at a modest $6,990, each small house was a self-contained world with a white picket fence, green lawn, and well-equipped kitchen. Buyers snapped up 1,400 houses in the first three hours after sales began in March 1949.

Suburban Development, 1957. An aerial view of Levittown, Pennsylvania, under construction.

Source: Margaret Bourke-White, *Life* Magazine, Copyright Time, Inc.

By 1960, homeownership had become the norm for the first time in U.S. history: three out of every five families owned their own dwelling. Some thought the new suburbs would transform feisty urban white ethnics into conservative homeowners concerned chiefly with keeping the crab grass at bay. "No man who owns his own house and lot can be a Communist," Levitt asserted. "He has too much to do." Indeed, during the 1950s sociologists, intellectuals, and other social commentators denounced the new developments as breeders of conformity and conservatism. As the folk singer Malvina Reynolds wrote in a 1962 ballad satirizing postwar conformity, the new suburbanites lived in "little boxes made of ticky-tacky," and "they all look just the same." The sociologist David Riesman compared life in suburbia to "a fraternity house at a small college in which like-mindedness reverberates upon itself."

But the residents of the Levittowns, South San Francisco, Rockville (Maryland), and Troy (Michigan), were more creative and independent than their critics thought. Even when their incomes were pinched, working-class families quickly transformed both their communities and their living space. Thus, when the Smithsonian Institution sought an unmodified Levittown house for display in the early 1980s, not one could be found among the tens of thousands that had been built. Indeed, the entire suburban phenomenon lasted but a third of a century. By the mid 1970s, the homogeneous, exclusively residential "bedroom" community no longer existed in most parts of the nation, for the suburbs were no longer subordinate to the central city. Jobs, shopping, education, entertainment—all had migrated to the new "edge cities" that had sprung up just over the horizon.

The suburbs did little to ameliorate social-class divisions, for blue-collar workers remained part of a working-class world. Although workers might own homes nearly identical to those of their middle-class neighbors, they were unlikely to vote Republican or repudiate their unions. Autoworkers who followed a relocated Ford plant from Richmond, California, to a new tract near Milpitas liked the spaciousness of their new suburban homes, but most did not believe they had left the working class. More than mobility, blue-collar families valued security. In a suburban community, one sociologist reported, "the people of working-class culture stay close to home and make the house a haven against a hostile, outside world."

Married women had mixed feelings about the new suburban world. They loved the spaciousness and convenience of their new homes, the safety of the neighborhood, and the access to good public schools. But at a time when millions of married women were entering the labor market, most suburban housing developments were designed for families in which Mom stayed home, Dad worked in the city, and relatives remained at a distance. Thus, the early housing tracts contained few of the social institutions—the corner grocery store, the nearby grandparent, the convenient streetcar—women had long relied on to ease their burden of shopping, housework, and childrearing. By making work outside the home more difficult for women, and cutting them off from traditional support networks, the insular suburban neighborhood enforced conformity to postwar gender roles.

As the suburbs grew, government housing policies actually deepened racial and class divisions across metropolitan America. The FHA, which financed about 30 percent of all new homes in the 1950s, advised developers to concentrate on a particular housing market based on age, income, and race. To ensure neighborhood homogeneity and preserve property values, the agency endorsed "restrictive covenants" that barred Jews and blacks from buying homes. (William Levitt permitted neither blacks nor single women to sign a mortgage.) And because federal housing agencies followed private lenders in "red-lining"—refusing to write mortgage loans—in the cities, where millions of working Americans still lived, housing stock in the central cities deteriorated in the 1950s. Such neglect slowly turned the inner cities into slums. Millions of African-American and Puerto Rican migrants found that their race and low income barred them from decent housing stock. As minority ghettos pressed against the boundaries of traditionally white neighborhoods, racial tensions flared. In cities such as Chicago, Philadelphia, and Buffalo,

Public Housing. In the years following World War II, as many middle-class families moved to the suburbs, inner-city public housing increasingly became identified with poor Americans. Living in public housing was viewed by many as a stigma, and new high-rise projects took on a harsh and regimented appearance.

Source: Prints and Photographs Division, Library of Congress.

white families typically fled to the suburbs a few years after the appearance of the first African Americans on the block. Soon northern housing became more rigidly segregated than it had been at any time since the Civil War.

The nation's public housing failure exacerbated urban apartheid. Because of resistance from realtors, mortgage bankers, and home builders, only 320,000 units of public housing were funded in the decade after Congress passed President Truman's housing act (1949). Still, the country might have been better off had no new units been built, since acres of old housing stock were bulldozed and reconstructed in the most brutal, utilitarian style. In the new public housing projects, closets were left without doors (to ensure tenants' neatness) and cinder blocks were left exposed in hallways. To minimize land costs, most projects were built in massive blocks. Apartments were cramped, and many mothers found the barren play areas, wedged between high rises, too unpleasant or dangerous for their children. "You feel like you can't breathe," reported a St. Louis public housing resident in the mid-1960s. "People are everywhere. Children are in the bathroom when you are using the toilet, somebody is sitting in every chair in the house, you've got to eat in shifts."

Unlike the tax subsidies for single-family suburban homes, public housing was thought of as welfare, so local governments usually imposed income restrictions on project residents. Families with rising incomes had to leave, ensuring the economic segregation of those who remained. In the end, no one liked American-style public housing—not the taxpayers, not the housing industry, not the politicians, not even the people who lived there. Adding insult to injury were the massive expressways that slashed through urban neighborhoods in the late 1950s. The new superhighways, which replaced more accessible trolleys and interurban trams, often disrupted stable working-class communities. When residents protested, they were told "You can't stop progress." Like low mortgage rates for single-family homes, the government-sponsored freeway boom represented a massive subsidy for suburban commuters and a tax, both fiscal and social, on city dwellers.

The Splintering of the Working Class

Like housing and education, the union movement fostered the homogenization of one group of workers while separating it from the rest of the working class. Unions greatly reduced wage differences between skilled and unskilled workers, so that by 1958, tool and die makers in an auto plant made only 20 percent more than unskilled assembly-line workers. Through grievance and seniority systems, organized labor also reduced the influence of personal or ethnic favoritism in the workplace. In many steel mills, Catholic workers of eastern European extraction, who had labored for three generations at heavy, sweaty jobs, finally got a chance to do skilled work. And because a definite set of rules now governed the foreman's authority to assign work, the old saying "It's not what you know, but who you know" was laid to rest, even at Ford.

But the stagnation of the union movement fostered increasingly sharp divisions within the working class. Race and gender prejudice had always separated American workers, but the inability of the unions to organize white women, African Americans, and others in the growing secondary labor force hardened these divisions in the working class. Meanwhile, union policy on two key issues of the period, automation and employee fringe benefits, further divided workers. In the 1930s, unions had sought to spread the burden of unemployment by reducing the length of the workweek, even if that meant smaller paychecks for everyone. Though unemployment was far less of a problem in the 1950s, workers faced rapid technological change—then called automation—that threatened to eliminate many of the best blue-collar jobs. In the hosiery industry, new high-speed knitting machines destroyed the skilled jobs of highly paid unionized workers; in telephone offices, the introduction of direct local dialing eliminated the work of many operators. And on the West Coast docks, the shift to shipping freight in uniform, sealed containers generated a two-tier work force: a small group of well-paid, steadily employed machine operators and a large group of casual workers who did the dangerous work of lifting and hauling.

A subtle but more pervasive division of the working class took place when unions focused their energy on bargaining over health and pension plans, which came to constitute a sort of private welfare state for union members. In the late 1940s, the labor–liberal effort to expand Social Security and inaugurate national health insurance had stalled, so unionists turned to the bargaining table to secure pensions and medical care for their members. John L. Lewis won a health and pension fund for the United Mine Workers in 1947, after which most other big unions also bargained for an increasingly wide assortment of "fringe benefits." Many large nonunion firms, as well as government at the state and federal level, quickly followed suit. By the end of the 1960s, almost all unionized workers had some sort of employer-paid health insurance, two-thirds were covered by pensions, and about half had won an automatic cost of living adjustment (COLA), which protected their real income from inflationary erosion.

Union success in these efforts had unforeseen consequences, however. In the inflationary postwar economy, COLAs and hefty benefit packages gave unionized industrial workers a tremendous financial advantage over unorganized, poorly paid service and clerical workers. The relatively egalitarian wage pattern of the mid-1940s eroded steadily during the next two decades. Soon high-wage workers came to resent the taxes they paid to fund those on state-supported welfare, especially after 1970, when the tax structure became more regressive. Thus, the weakness of the postwar welfare state, and the resulting creation of a privatized substitute, helped split the American working class into two segments, one relatively secure and the other—predominantly young, minority, and female—left out in the cold.

The World of *Father Knows Best*

Television reinforced the family-oriented privatization of American society in the postwar era. By 1960 TV was a fixture in 90 percent of all homes, and TV programming mirrored the nation's social and cultural landscape, if often in an exaggerated form. In the early days of television, just after the end of World War II, radio-inspired situation comedies had offered TV viewers a sympathetic glimpse of urban working-class families enmeshed in a world of tenements, street-corner stickball, and manual labor. The most successful of the comedies was *The Goldbergs,* which made the transition from radio to television in 1948. As each episode in the life of this Jewish working-class family began, Molly Goldberg leaned out the window of her Bronx tenement to "schmooze" with her neighbors. Molly, played by Gertrude Berg (who later became the victim of anti-Communist blacklisting), was a strong, sharp-witted woman with opinions on everything. Like the show's other adult characters, she spoke English with an accent, interspersed with Yiddish phrases. Molly's teenage kids were Americanized; many episodes explored the comic possibilities of the family's hybrid culture. The Goldberg family approached life in America with a warm humanism that dignified and made universal their struggle with urban, workaday life.

During the 1950s, shows such as *The Goldbergs, The Life of Riley* (about the travails of an aircraft worker and his family), and *The Honeymooners* (starring Jackie Gleason as a New York bus driver) were replaced by situation comedies and westerns that bleached ethnicity, class, and social commentary out of their story lines. *Father Knows Best,* introduced in 1953, exemplified the new world of suburban respectability: the Andersons lived in a large house on Maple Street in "Springfield," U.S.A. Jim Anderson, the father (played by Robert Young), would never have dreamed of going to work carrying a lunchpail with two bologna sandwiches, as William Bendix did on *The Life of Riley.* Anderson's work as an insurance executive remained offscreen; he had no politics, held few strong opinions, and never had a bad day at the office. All the action in *Father Knows Best* took place at home, where the middle-class father exercised a benevolent despotism over three not particularly rebellious children. Jane Wyatt, who played the mother, maintained perfect order in her house and, in contrast to Molly Goldberg, kept her opinions to herself. Though TV viewers sensed that *Father Knows Best* was hardly a realistic portrayal of the average American family, the insular, classless world it portrayed seemed an appropriate model of contemporary life, and they tuned in faithfully every week.

Though small-town domesticity was clearly the dominant cultural ideal, there were some unexpected challenges to the placid world of *Father Knows Best.* In the mid-1950s, a small group of rebels mocked the values of the American mainstream in poetry and literature. Led by Allen Ginsberg and Jack Kerouac, the "beat" poets idolized African Americans, especially jazz musicians, and denounced what they saw as the materialism, sexual repression, and spiritual emptiness of middle-class American life. "These have been years of conformity and depression," wrote Norman Mailer in 1957, voicing a critique common among intellectuals sympathetic to the beats. "A stench of fear has come out of every pore of American life, and we suffer from a collective failure of nerve."

Though the beats attracted only a small following, they stirred widespread controversy and comment. Newspaper and magazine reporters sneered at the "beatnik" style of dress and speech, hinting darkly about "racial mixing" and sexual immorality at beat parties. *Life* magazine derided the beats as a group of "sick little bums" and "hostile little chicks." And writing in *Esquire,* the critic Norman Podhoretz charged

Beats—By Way of Hollywood. A publicity still from the 1959 film *The Rebel Set* displays some of the stereotyped characteristics ascribed to "beatniks." Dressed in black, wearing sandals, and sporting distinctive hairstyles (goatees for men; severe yet flamboyant ponytails for women), the two beats crouch on a bare mattress and "groove" on poetry. The paintings in the background display drug-induced nightmare themes. **Source:** Photofest.

The Pulp Threat. A 1954 montage that appeared in newspapers presents what many Americans saw as a new danger threatening the nation's youth. In Senate committee hearings and other forums, parents, social scientists, and public officials called for censorship laws, claiming that crime and horror comic books, along with other sensational publications, contributed to the growing problem of juvenile delinquency.

Source: Prints and Photographs Division, Library of Congress.

that the beats were conspiring to replace Western civilization with "the world of the adolescent street gangs."

The comparison of the beats to juvenile delinquents was no coincidence. At the same time the beats were writing their poems and books, a nationwide debate over juvenile delinquency erupted in Congress, among educators, and in the news media. The near-hysterical attention focused on "JDs" by the FBI, the mass media, and Hollywood did not arise from any significant growth in youthful criminality or adolescent rebellion. Instead, it reflected fears about the stability of the family and alarm at the growing assimilation by some middle-class teenagers of the cultural values found in the black ghetto and among urban working-class youth. Disrespect for teachers and the police, underage drinking, "hot-rodding," rock-and-roll music, "going steady," black slang, and blue jeans gave many otherwise middle-class high schoolers of the 1950s a distinct, alienated identity. The growth of this teenage subculture was shaped not only by the vitality of African-American music in the postwar years but also by the cross-class fertilization taking place in big-city high schools—and by the business world's discovery and exploitation of a multibillion-dollar teenage market.

Rock-and-roll, one of the most prominent features of the new teenage lifestyle, originated in the music that dominated black working-class communities during and after World War II. Many of the leading artists were newly urbanized migrants from the rural South; among the most important was the blues singer Muddy Waters, who moved from rural Mississippi to Chicago in 1941. Waters and his band brought the pulse and energy of the electric guitar to the traditional country blues form. By the mid 1950s, he and other black singers such as Big Joe Turner in Kansas City, Chuck Berry in St. Louis, and Ray Charles, who performed throughout the South, had created and refined a new musical genre, rhythm-and-blues. It was Charles's gospel-inspired piano-playing in "I Got a Woman" that launched the rock-and-roll revolution in 1954. Joe Turner's hit "Shake, Rattle, and Roll" (1954) became the first of many rhythm-and-blues tunes to be "covered" (copied) by a major white artist. And Chuck Berry's distinctive guitar playing and upbeat performance in songs such as "Johnny B. Goode" inspired rock-and-roll's youthful sound and style.

Elvis Presley, a white Memphis teen, made rock-and-roll a national craze when he combined the drive of African-American rhythm-and-blues with the lyrics and sentiments of southern white "country music." Flaunting his sexuality and his working-class demeanor, Presley scandalized an older generation of viewers when he appeared on the normally staid *Ed Sullivan Show* in 1956. But he immediately became a teenage idol and his songs, rock-and-roll anthems. African-American artists were equally creative and equally subversive of established social norms. Little Richard composed

Fear of Teenagers. Teenagers exhibit behavior many adults thought bordered on the criminal. From dancing to grooming to just "hanging out," teenage popular culture seemed to undermine society's notions of innocence and propriety.

Source: *Rock, Baby, Rock* (1957)—Frank Driggs.

one of his first songs after a long day spent washing dishes in a Georgia bus station. "I couldn't talk back to my boss man. He would bring all those pots back for me to wash, and one day I said, 'I've got to do something to stop that man . . .' and I said, 'Awop bopa-lop bop-a-wop bam boom, take'em out!' and that's how I came to write 'Tutti Frutti.' "

While some parents and conservative social critics denounced rock-and-roll as an evil influence on the young, Hollywood quickly discovered that money could be made from the rebellious youth culture. Films such as *The Wild One, Rebel Without a Cause,* and *The Blackboard Jungle,* which featured Bill Haley's classic recording of "Rock Around the Clock," offered sympathetic portraits of teenage "delinquents" trapped in a crass adult society that neither cared nor understood them. Brilliant acting performances by the young actors Marlon Brando and James Dean communicated the personal alienation of a generation. Partly as a result of the popularization of such attitudes, millions of Americans would, within a decade, come to see the rejection of middle-class values not as semicriminal but as a "counterculture"—an alternative way of looking at, and perhaps changing, an unhappy world.

The Years in Review

1944

- Bretton Woods Conference makes dollar the basis for international financial transactions.
- Democrat Franklin Roosevelt wins a fourth presidential term with Harry S Truman as vice-president.

1945

- A-Bomb dropped on Hiroshima. World War II ends.
- United Nations formed.

1946

- George F. Kennan lays out "containment" doctrine.
- Operation Dixie: Effort by unions to organize southern workers, which fails ultimately.
- Dr. Benjamin Spock's *Baby and Child Care,* a radically different approach to childrearing focused on the needs of the child, first published.
- Massive postwar strike wave raises wages, but also sparks rapid inflation.

1947

- Taft-Hartley Act, which undercuts unions, passes over President Truman's veto.

- Truman boosts funding for the FBI, sets up a loyalty program for federal employees, and asks the attorney general to draw up a list of subversive organizations.
- Jackie Robinson integrates major league baseball.
- United Mine Workers win first health and pension fund package in labor history from mine owners.
- Truman Doctrine commits the United States to assisting countries in fighting Soviet expansion or internal Communist threats.
- Secretary of State George Marshall announces $16-billion plan for the reconstruction and integration of Europe; the Marshall Plan.

1948

- Soviets blockade Berlin; the United States responds with airlift.
- Truman elected in four-way presidential race, defeating Republican Thomas Dewey, Progressive party candidate Henry Wallace, and Dixiecrat Strom Thurmond.
- United Nations approves partition of Palestine to create the new state of Israel.
- Edwin H. Land's Polaroid Land Camera, which processed prints in one minute, goes on sale.

1949

- CIO expels nine unions for refusing to purge themselves of Communist leaders and support government policies.
- Congress passes Truman's public housing bill. Only 320,000 units built in the first decade because of resistance from realtors, mortgage bankers, and homebuilders.
- Pro-Western Chinese dictator Chiang Kai-shek overthrown by Mao Zedong's Communist army.
- North Atlantic Treaty Organization (NATO) formed. In response, Soviets later created Warsaw Pact alliance of eastern European nations.
- Soviets explode their first nuclear bomb.

1950

- Communist North Korea invades South Korea and UN-backed American troops enter conflict. Truce leaving the Communists in control of North Korea reached in 1953 after a three-year stalemate that resulted in 34,000 American deaths.
- Communists Julius and Ethel Rosenberg charged with delivering atomic secrets to the Soviet Union. Convicted in 1951, they are executed in June 1953 despite worldwide protests.
- Truman administration announces new foreign policy plan NSC-68, which commits the United States to an expensive military buildup in the fight against Communism.

1951

- First color television program broadcast but no color sets are available for purchase yet.
- First transcontinental direct-dial telephone call.

1952

- Republican Dwight D. Eisenhower defeats Democrat Adlai Stevenson for the presidency.

1953

- CIA supports military coup in Iran, restoring the Shah to power.
- *Playboy* magazine first published.
- Soviet premier Joseph Stalin dies, temporarily encouraging hope for a new U.S.–Soviet relationship.

1954

- Senate votes to censure Joseph McCarthy, who had led anti-Communist crusade.
- Black singers Ray Charles and Chuck Berry launch rhythm-and-blues, which leads to rock-and-roll.

1955

- AFL and CIO merge.
- Dr. Jonas E. Salk's polio vaccine administered to millions of children.
- Disney TV show launches Davey Crockett craze; millions of coonskin hats sold.

1956

- Congress funds multibillion-dollar Interstate and Defense Highway Program, the largest public works project in U.S. history.
- Rock-and-roll star Elvis Presley creates a national scandal when he dances suggestively during an appearance on *The Ed Sullivan Show.*
- Capturing 57 percent of the popular vote, President Eisenhower easily defeats Adlai Stevenson in presidential election.

1957

- Soviet Union launches *Sputnik* satellite into orbit.
- Brooklyn Dodgers and New York Giants move to California.
- Surgeon general reports that scientific evidence shows link between cigarettes and lung cancer.

1958

- The United States launches its first space satellite.
- Major recession temporarily ends postwar boom.

1959

- Around 700,000 steelworkers strike for 119 days to successfully defend work rules and safety standards.
- U.S. Army launches two monkeys into space for a 300-mile-high flight.

1960

- Planned U.S.–Soviet summit canceled when American U-2 spy plane shot down over Russia.

Suggested Readings

Ambrose, Stephen E., *Eisenhower* (1987).
Biskind, Peter, *Seeing Is Believing: How Hollywood Taught Us to Stop Worrying and Love the Fifties* (1983).
Chinoy, Ely, *Automobile Workers and the American Dream* (1992).
Coontz, Stephanie, *The Way We Never Were: American Families and the Nostalgia Trap* (1992).
Ehrenreich, Barbara, *The Hearts of Men: American Dreams and the Flight from Commitment* (1983).
Engelhardt, Tom, *The End of Victory Culture: Cold War America and the Disillusioning of a Generation* (1998).
Findlay, John M., *Magic Lands: Western Cityscapes and American Culture After 1940* (1992).
Fones-Wolf, Elizabeth A., *Selling Free Enterprise: The Business Assault on Labor and Liberalism, 1945–1960* (1994).
Gaddis, John Lewis, *We Now Know: Rethinking Cold War History* (1997).
Gans, Herbert J., *The Levittowners: Ways of Life and Politics in a New Suburban Community* (1982).
Gilbert, James B., *A Cycle of Outrage: America's Reaction to the Juvenile Delinquent in the 1950s* (1988).
Griffith, Barbara S., *The Crisis of American Labor: Operation Dixie and the Defeat of the CIO* (1988).
Guralnick, Peter, *Last Train to Memphis: The Rise of Elvis Presley* (1994).
Halberstam, David, *The Fifties* (1993).
Halle, David, *America's Working Man: Work, Home, and Politics Among Blue-Collar Property Owners* (1987).
Halliday, Jon and Bruce Cumings, *Korea: The Unknown War* (1988).
Hamby, Alonzo L., *Man of the People: A Life of Harry S Truman* (1998).
Hogan, Michael J., *A Cross of Iron: Harry S Truman and the Origins of the National Security State, 1945–1954* (1998).
Horowitz, Daniel, *Betty Friedan and the Making of the Feminine Mystique: The American Left, the Cold War, and Modern Feminism* (1998).
Iriye, Akira, *Cultural Internationalism and World Order* (1997).
Jackson, Kenneth T., *Crabgrass Frontier: The Suburbanization of the United States* (1985).
Kaledin, Eugenia, *Mothers and More: American Women in the 1950s* (1984).
Lacey, Michael J., ed., *The Truman Presidency* (1989).
Leffler, Melvyn P., *A Preponderance of Power: National Security, the Truman Administration, and the Cold War* (1992).
Lichtenstein, Nelson, *Walter Reuther: The Most Dangerous Man in Detroit* (1997).
May, Elaine Tyler, *Homeward Bound: American Families in the Cold War Era* (1999).

Metzgar, Jack, *Striking Steel: Solidarity Remembered* (2000).
Meyerowitz, Joanne, ed., *Not June Clever: Women and Gender in Postwar America, 1945–1960* (1994).
Pells, Richard H., *The Liberal Mind in a Conservative Age: American Intellectuals in the 1940s and 1950s* (1994).
Plummer, Brenda Gayle, *Rising Wind: Black Americans and U.S. Foreign Affairs, 1935–1960* (1996).
Radosh, Ronald and Joyce Milton, *The Rosenberg File: A Search for the Truth* (1997).
Schrecker, Ellen, *Many Are the Crimes: McCarthyism in America* (1998).
Solinger, Rickie, *Wake Up Little Susie: Single Pregnancy and Race Before Roe v. Wade* (1992).
Stebenne, David, *Arthur J. Goldberg: New Deal Liberal* (1996).
Sugrue, Thomas J., *The Origins of the Urban Crisis: Race and Inequality in Postwar Detroit* (1998).
Ward, Ed., Geoffrey Stokes, and Ken Tucker, *Rock of Ages: The Rolling Stone History of Rock & Roll* (1986).
Weinstein, Allen, *Perjury: The Hiss–Chambers Case* (1977).

And on the World Wide Web

Al Filreis, University of Pennsylvania, *The Literature and Culture of the American 1950s*
(http://dept.english.upenn.edu/~afilreis/50s/home.html)

chapter 12

The Rights Conscious 1960s

At the inauguration of President John F. Kennedy in January 1961, poet Robert Frost articulated the hopes of most Americans when he forecast a new age of "poetry and power," matching the nation's influence abroad with a new surge of self-confidence and harmony at home. The "Sixties" did renew the nation's great postwar boom, but the decade also saw a higher degree of ideological and social polarization than any time since the Civil War. The civil rights movement shook the country, sparking a broad wave of popular activism that called for the full realization of America's democratic promise. And just as the African-American freedom struggle reached its peak, the Vietnam War brought the political contradictions of the Cold War to the surface of national life. Meanwhile, on the political Right, growing hostility to the movement for African-American liberation, to antiwar activism, and to the invigoration of federal power gave American conservatism a more pointed ideological profile.

Millions of ordinary Americans came to feel that they could make their collective weight felt on issues once handled behind the closed doors of the county courthouse or the corporate board room. A growing sense of "rights consciousness" encompassed not just the advancement of formal citizenship rights, such as voting and equal access to the courts, but an entirely new set of social and economic expectations. This expanded sense of citizenship brought to public attention the hitherto unfocused grievances of group after group in American society: those defined by ethnicity, such as African Americans, Latinos, and American Indians, as well as those defined by age, gender, income, and sexual orientation.

Social activism in the 1960s had its ideological roots in a sense that all things were finally possible in affluent, postwar America and that hypocrisy, of either a personal or a social sort, would no longer be tolerated. This earthly "perfectionism," like that which had motivated abolitionists William Lloyd Garrison and John Brown before the Civil War and socialist Eugene V. Debs and reformer Jane Addams early in the twentieth century, gave enormous spirit and energy to the social movements around which so much of the politics of the 1960s revolved. Like the antebellum reformers who linked temperance and abolition, social reform and salvation, many activists of the 1960s affirmed that there was a political dimension to private life—or to use a phrase coined by feminists in the late 1960s, "The personal is political." The politicized

Birmingham, Alabama, 1963.

Source: Charles Moore, copyright 1963 Black Star.

spiritualism of the African-American church, the counterculture of the New Left, and the consciousness-raising groups of the women's movement nourished a strong "movement" culture, which filled a void in the lives of many. "In most basic terms," a student activist of the mid 1960s remembered, "what the Movement provided for me was a sense of purpose and a feeling of community which had been missing from my life before then." Such sentiments resonated across the political and religious spectrum.

By the early 1970s, the spread of new social values had begun to transform the workplace as well, creating demands for equity in hiring and promotion, for a healthy and safe environment, and for personal recognition and dignity where none had existed before. The leadership of American unions played a relatively limited role in the progressive political changes of the period, but the social movements of the 1960s revived for a time the grass-roots militancy that had once been part of the culture of an insurgent, rights-conscious working class.

Birth of the Civil Rights Movement

In May 1954, civil rights attorneys led by Thurgood Marshall won a unanimous Supreme Court decision, *Brown* v. *Board of Education,* which decreed that, in education, the old "separate but equal" standard was inherently discriminatory against African-American children. Basing the Court's opinion on the Fourteenth Amendment, adopted at the height of the Reconstruction era, and new evidence on the psychological impact of segregation, Chief Justice Earl Warren declared segregated public schools unconstitutional. This was the most significant Supreme Court decision of the twentieth century because it would eventually put the full weight of the federal government behind a radical transformation of the nation's entire system of public education.

Back of the Bus, 1951. Segregated seating on a southern streetcar.

Source: Schomburg Center for Research in Black Culture, New York Public Library, Astor, Lenox, and Tilden Foundations.

But it took fifteen years for *Brown* to bear fruit because neither the courts nor the government took decisive action to implement school desegregation. In 1955, for example, the Supreme Court itself accommodated those opposed to integration by ruling that desegregation need only take place with "all deliberate speed." This proved a confusing and cautious approach, ratified by President Dwight D. Eisenhower himself, who once asserted, "It's all very well to talk about school integration — if you remember that we may also be talking about social disintegration." Federal ambivalence encouraged white segregationists. In their 1956 "Southern Manifesto," 101 congressmen and senators vowed opposition to the Court's order, while a quarter-million of their constituents joined local White Citizens' Councils to defend segregation. African Americans pushing for the implementation of *Brown* were met with harassment and intimidation. Southern politicians, led by Senator Harry F. Byrd of Virginia, called for "massive resistance" to school integration, African-American voting rights, and social reform.

The 1957 battle to integrate Central High School in Little Rock, Arkansas, dramatized the political conflict. Although local school officials were prepared to desegregate, Governor Orville Faubus generated a violent crisis by sending National Guardsmen to block the entry of black students, ostensibly to preserve "order" at Central High. When a shrieking crowd chased six black teenagers from the school, President Eisenhower reluctantly federalized the Arkansas Guard and sent a thousand U.S. Army paratroopers to Little Rock. In response, Faubus shut Little Rock public high schools for the entire year, a strategy also adopted in several Virginia counties. Across the South, the number of school districts engaging in even token desegregation fell from 712 in the first three years after the *Brown* decision to just 49 between 1957 and 1960.

This stalemate was broken by a reborn civil rights movement that once again captured the imagination of millions of Americans, both white and black. This movement was not based in the unions, as it had been just after World War II, but rather found much of its leadership in the African-American church and the National Association for the Advancement of Colored People (NAACP), whose attorneys' long march through the courts had begun to dismantle the legal foundations of America's Jim Crow order.

The new movement was born in the heart of Dixie—Montgomery, Alabama, where the Confederate flag still flew over the state capitol building. Montgomery had felt the stirrings of postwar social change: the African-American population had doubled; nearby Maxwell Air Force Base was largely integrated; and the city had even begun to build a new sports stadium without separate entrances for white and "colored." But the city's theaters, schools, parks, and restaurants remained rigidly segregated. And nothing rankled Montgomery's black community more than the segregated bus system. It was a twice-daily humiliation. Blacks had to pay their fare in the front, then get off the bus and reenter in the back. If the bus began to fill with whites, white drivers would often shout "Niggers get back!"

On a cold December afternoon in 1955, Rosa Parks, a longtime NAACP activist, refused to cooperate with this humiliating ritual. Tired

"We Were Prepared . . ."

Groups in Montgomery's African-American community had organized against segregationist laws for many years before Rosa Parks refused to give up her seat on the bus. The Women's Political Council, an organization of black working-class and middle-class women formed in 1946, had vigorously protested the segregated bus system. Jo Ann Robinson, president of the WPC and an English teacher at the all-black Alabama State College, describes what her organization did to help organize the bus boycott.

Fred Gray told me Rosa Parks was arrested. Her case would be on Monday. He said to me, "Jo Ann, if you have ever planned to do anything with the council, now is your time." I called all the officers of the three chapters, I called as many of the men who had supported us as I could reach, and I told them that Rosa Parks had been arrested and she would be tried. They said, "You have the plans, put them into operation." We had worked for at least three years getting that thing organized.

The Women's Political Council had begun in 1946, after just dozens of black people had been arrested on the buses for segregation purposes. By 1955, we had members in every elementary, junior high, and senior high school, and in federal, state, and local jobs. Wherever there were more than ten blacks employed, we had a member there. We were prepared to the point that we knew that in a matter of hours, we could corral the whole city.

I didn't go to bed that night. I cut stencils and took them to the college. . . . We ran off thirty-five thousand copies. After I had talked with every WPC member in the elementary, junior high, and senior high schools to have somebody on the campus during the day so I could deliver them, I took them to school with me in my car. I taught my classes from eight o'clock to ten o'clock. When my ten o'clock class was over, I took two senior students with me and I had the flyers in my car, bundled and ready to be given out. I would drive to the place of dissemination, and a kid would be there to grab them. I was on the campus and off before anybody knew that I was there.

Most of the people got the message, but there were outlying areas that didn't. And one lone black woman, who was so faithful to her white lady, as she called it, went back to work and took one of the circulars to this woman so she would know what the blacks had planned. When the woman got it, she immediately called the media. After that, the television, the radio, and the evening newspapers told those persons whom we had not reached that there would be a boycott. So the die was cast.

Monday morning, December the fifth, 1955, I shall never forget because many of us had not gone to bed that night. It was the day of the boycott. We had been up waiting for the first buses to pass to see if any riders were on them. It was a cold morning, cloudy, there was a threat of rain, and we were afraid that if it rained the people would get on the bus. But as the buses began to roll, and there were one or two on some of them, none on some of them, then we began to realize that the people were cooperating and that they were going to stay off the bus that first day. What helped us to keep them off, too, was that the police department had decided that they would put a police on a motorcycle with a white cap who would accompany the buses and any of the blacks who wanted to get on. They would help them to get on without what they called "the goon squads" keeping them from riding. And that helped out the cause because those few blacks who were going to ride were afraid that the police who were following the buses would hurt them. So they didn't ride. As a result, a very negligible number of riders rode that first day.

Source: Henry Hampton and Steve Fayer, with Sarah Flynn, *Voices of Freedom: An Oral History of the Civil Rights Movement* (1990).

from a long day at the department store where she worked as a seamstress, she kept her seat as whites crowded into the bus. "I felt it was just something I had to do," she later recalled. She was taken to jail and charged with violating a city segregation ordinance. A spirited group of female teachers spread word of her arrest through the black community; within hours, African-American leaders decided to boycott the city bus system in protest. E. D. Nixon, president of the Alabama NAACP and head of the local Brotherhood of Sleeping Car Porters, knew that the black community would rally around Rosa Parks, for she was no ordinary seamstress. For twelve years she had worked as NAACP secretary. "She was decent, and she was committed," Nixon remembered, "so when she stood up to talk, people'd shut up and listen. And when she did something people just figured it was the right thing to do."

While Nixon and a host of churchwomen organized black-owned taxis and church vans to replace the buses, Montgomery's African-American ministers chose as their spokesperson the Reverend Dr. Martin Luther King, Jr., an Atlanta-born, twenty-six-year-old minister in his first pulpit. King, who quickly proved himself one of the great tribunes of American democracy, skillfully linked Old Testament prophecy and the legacy of African-American suffering to inspire a new generation of civil rights activists. As he told more than five thousand on the first night of the boycott, "If you will protest courageously and yet with dignity and Christian love, in the history books that are written in future generations, historians will have to pause and say 'there lived a great people—a black people—who injected new meaning and dignity into the veins of civilization.' "

Montgomery, Alabama, 1956. Evidence of the effectiveness of the year-long bus boycott. **Source:** Dan Weiner. Courtesy of Sandra Weiner.

The thirteen-month-long boycott demonstrated how a social movement creates its own momentum. African-American demands were initially modest: greater courtesy toward black passengers; employment of African-American drivers in black neighborhoods; and an easing—but not an end to—segregated seating on the buses. But, as week after week passed, Montgomery's black citizens grew more confident of their ability to stick together and resist white intimidation. By the time the

U.S. Supreme Court ruled that Montgomery buses must integrate, in December 1956, a new civil rights movement had been born.

Freedom Now!

Black college students took the lead during the movement's next stage, which began in February 1960 as a wave of "sit-ins" swept through the South. The protests started when four neatly dressed African-American students from North Carolina A&T College violated a Greensboro segregation ordinance by taking seats at a Woolworth lunch counter to demand the service traditionally denied them. While Franklin McCain, Ezell Blair, Joe McNeil, and David Richmond had only decided to "sit in" a few days before, the whole of their lives had prepared them for this struggle. Barely teenagers when the U.S. Supreme Court declared public school segregation unconstitutional, they had ruefully attended segregated schools, followed news of the Montgomery bus boycott, and joined the activist NAACP Youth Council.

"All of us were afraid," recalled David Richmond, "but we went and did it." When a nervous waitress refused them service, the four pulled out their books and prepared for a long stay. The sit-in galvanized other A&T students. Several dozen came to Woolworth's the next day, followed by hundreds more each afternoon, until the city closed the store a week later. By then, a network of church and student activists had begun leading sit-ins throughout the upper South. "I felt at the time it was like a crusade," Nashville sit-in leader John Lewis remembered. Although gangs of white youths often taunted and abused the African-American students, at least 70,000 persons participated in sit-ins in more than a hundred cities during the winter and spring of 1960.

Woolworth Sit-In, May 28, 1963. White youths shower abuse and food on a Tougaloo College professor and students staging a sit-in at a segregated lunch counter in Jackson, Mississippi. After soda, ketchup, mustard, and sugar failed to deter them, the civil rights demonstraters were doused with spray paint and beaten.

Source: State Historical Society of Wisconsin.

The sit-ins demonstrated that mass civil disobedience and nonviolent confrontation were effective tactics. Activists soon organized the Student Nonviolent Coordinating Committee, or SNCC, which served as a vanguard within the civil rights movement during the new decade. SNCC was never a large organization, but its members, predominantly young African Americans, were creative and dedicated: "commando raiders," one observer called them, "on the more dangerous and exposed fronts of the racial struggle." Television broadcasts and magazines put their message before millions of people. "Here were four students from Greensboro who were suddenly all over *Life* magazine," a white student at Oberlin College later remembered. "There was a feeling that they were us and we were them."

Like any grand social movement, civil rights activism made its political and moral weight felt on many levels. In their numerous confrontations with white city politicians, businessowners, and police, civil rights activists proved to be successful only episodically. Many lunch counters were desegregated, but others were not. Seeking to register black voters in Mississippi, Alabama, and Georgia, SNCC workers and those they sought to organize were frequently beaten and jailed; and despite numerous demonstrations and jailings, white officials in Albany, Georgia, and St. Augustine, Florida, refused to open jobs or beaches to the black community.

But stalemate at the local level focused the eyes of the nation on southern racial injustice, thus prompting federal intervention. In May 1961, the Congress of Racial Equality (CORE), a civil rights group based primarily in the North, organized a series of "Freedom Rides" to test recent court orders mandating the integration of southern bus terminals. "Our intention," CORE leader James Farmer later explained, "was to provoke the southern authorities into arresting us and thereby prod the Justice Department into enforcing the law." When the integrated group of Freedom Riders reached Alabama, white mobs burned one of their buses and, with the tacit approval of local police, savagely attacked the riders. But SNCC bolstered the Freedom Riders with new volunteers, who quickly filled Mississippi's jails. Federal marshals then moved in to stop the mob violence and ensure compliance with the desegregation orders.

Movement activists also aimed to create grass-roots organizations to serve as vehicles of empowerment within African-American communities. Most participants in the early sit-ins and Freedom Rides were students, but local organizers helped enlist all segments of the black community. African-American maids, tenant farmers, and laborers who worked for white employers had traditionally been more cautious than ministers and businessmen who derived their income from the black community. But the sit-ins and Freedom Rides opened the way for a new sense of citizenship and participation. This change became clear during a year-long series of demonstrations in Albany, Georgia, in 1961 and 1962.

"They Shot The Tires Out . . ."

Volunteers from all over the country arrived in the South to integrate the segregated southern buses on a series of "Freedom Rides" organized by the Congress of Racial Equality. One Freedom Rider, Hank Thomas, recalls the destruction of an integrated bus by a white mob in Anniston, Alabama, on May 14, 1961.

The Freedom Ride didn't really get rough until we got down in the Deep South. Needless to say, Anniston, Alabama, I'm never gonna forget that. When I was on the bus they [whites] threw some kind of incendiary device on. I got real scared then. You know, I was thinking—I'm looking out the window there, and people are out there yelling and screaming. They [whites] just about broke every window out of the bus. . . . I really thought that that was going to be the end of me. They shot the tires out, and the bus driver was forced to stop. . . . And we were trapped on the bus.

It wasn't until the thing [smoke bomb] was shot on the bus and the bus caught afire that everything got out of control. . . . First they [whites] closed the doors and wouldn't let us off. But then I'm pretty sure . . . that somebody said, "Hey, the bus is gonna explode . . ." and so they started scattering, and I guess that's the way we got off the bus. Otherwise, we probably all would have been succumbed by the smoke. . . . I got whacked over the head with a rock or I think a stick as I was coming off the bus.

The bus started exploding, and a lot of people were cut by flying glass. . . . Took us to the hospital, and it was incredible. The people at the hospital would not do anything for us. They would not. And I was saying "You're doctors, you're medical personnel." They wouldn't. . . . But strangely enough, even those bad things don't stick in my mind that much. Not that I'm full of love and goodwill for everybody in my heart, but I chalk it off to part of the things that I'm going to be able to sit on my front porch in my rocking chair and tell my young'uns about, my grandchildren about.

Source: Milton Meltzer, ed., *The American Promise* (1990).

There SNCC activists mobilized the entire community for a precedent-setting civil disobedience campaign. Demanding integration of stores, restaurants, bus stations, and schools, African-American students, farmers, laborers, and churchwomen filled Albany's jails week after week. Children as young as eleven and twelve were prominent in these demonstrations. Going to jail, ordinarily a shameful as well as a dangerous experience, now became a badge of courage. One in twenty Albany blacks spent time behind bars.

African-American women formed the backbone of the Albany protests and other community organizations built by the civil rights movement. "There is always a 'mama,' " commented SNCC's Georgia

The Reenfranchisement of African Americans: Black Voter Registration, in the South, 1940–1968. Black voter registration leapt forward in two stages. During World War II and the immediate years afterwards, the first wave of the modern civil rights movement generated widespread interest in voting, which multiplied by seven times the proportion of blacks voting in the South. White resistance in the 1950s slowed further increases until the Civil Rights Act of 1965 generated another dramatic increase in black voter registration.

project director, Charles Sherrod. "She is usually a militant woman in the community, outspoken, understanding, and willing to catch Hell, having already caught her share." These women were often the largest and most dynamic element within the black church, sometimes forcing ministers to open their churches to civil rights workers.

In Ruleville, Mississippi, Fanny Lou Hamer emerged as the determined leader of a voter registration drive launched by SNCC in early 1962. A tenant farmer, Hamer was forced off her land after she refused her landlord's demand that she take her name off the voter registration list. Repeatedly arrested and beaten, Hamer was not intimidated. "The only thing they could

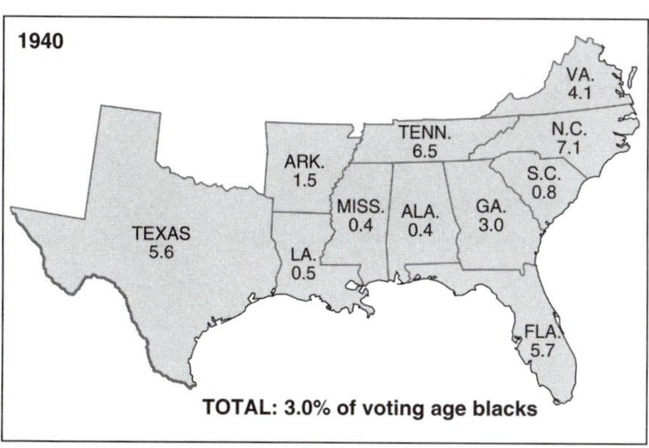

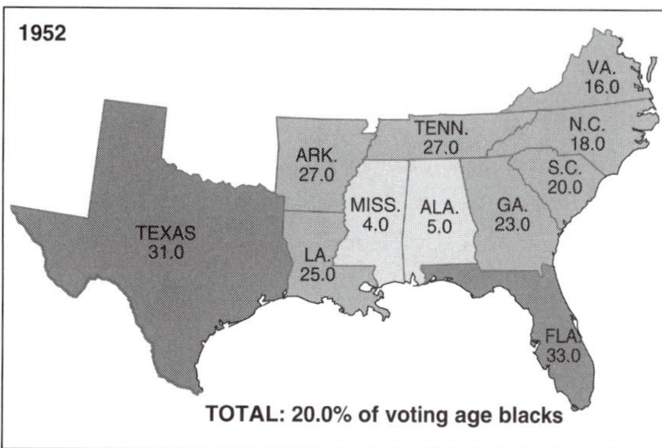

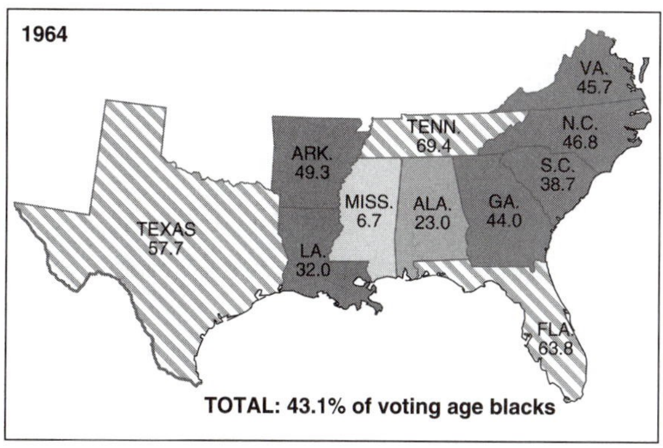

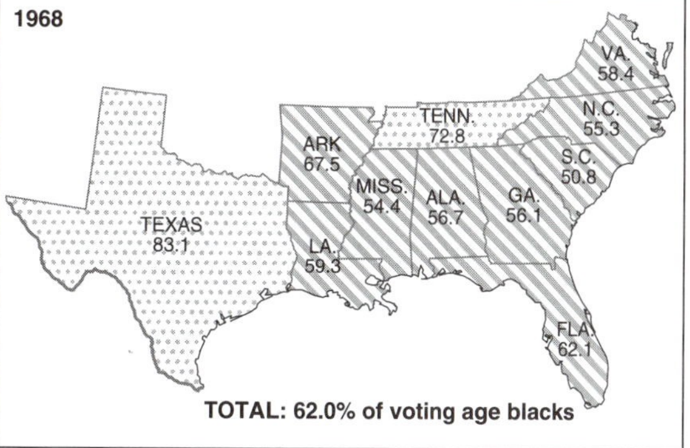

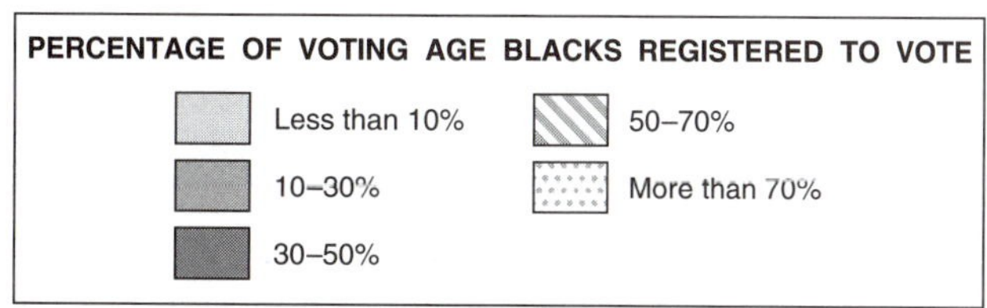

do to me was kill me, and it seemed like they'd been trying to do that a little bit at a time ever since I could remember." Hamer's courageous spirit soon made her a leader of the statewide movement.

The battle to desegregate Birmingham, Alabama, begun in April 1963, transformed the nation's political and moral dynamic. Birmingham African Americans, working closely with Martin Luther King's Southern Christian Leadership Conference (SCLC), forged a tightly knit community of struggle. They held mass meetings for sixty-five consecutive nights, often followed by marches to the downtown business district that ended in arrest or police attack. City police, under command of a reactionary segregationist, Eugene "Bull" Connor, used fire hoses and police dogs to disperse marchers. Thousands of high school students singing "freedom songs" joined the protests, as did hundreds of African-American workers from the city's steel mills and coke ovens. "I have stood in a meeting with hundreds of youngsters and joined in while they sang 'Ain't Gonna Let Nobody Turn Me 'Round,' " King told a northern audience. "It is not just a song, it is a resolve. . . . These songs bind us together, give us courage together, help us to march together."

The Birmingham protests sent a political shock wave throughout the nation. City officials and white merchants agreed to open downtown businesses to African-American patronage and employment; even more importantly, however, these protests fully nationalized the impact of the civil rights movement. Televised images of Birmingham police dogs attacking defenseless marchers helped swing northern public opinion massively against segregation. During the summer of 1963, there were 758 demonstrations and marches, more above the Mason–Dixon line than below it. In San Francisco, Detroit, and New York City, hundreds of thousands of blacks and whites marched side by side. Scores more demonstrations followed: construction-site protests demanding more jobs for minority youth; school boycotts designed to end segregation and increase funding at inner-city schools; picket lines protesting police brutality. More than half of all African Americans polled by a national newsmagazine reported a sense of "personal obligation" to get involved.

A. Philip Randolph, the African-American trade unionist whose threat of a 1941 march on Washington had helped integrate World War II war plants, now unveiled plans for a new mass demonstration in the capital to demand jobs, housing, and higher wages for blacks. Backed by the United Auto Workers and other liberal trade unions, the August 1963 "March on Washington for Jobs and Freedom" brought to the capital a crowd of almost a quarter-million, at that time the largest political gathering in U.S. history. Refuting predictions of a drunken riot, the racially integrated march was peaceful and dignified. On the steps of the Lincoln

Memorial, Dr. King delivered a speech that articulated a broad moral vision of the civil rights movement, a singular synthesis of Christian idealism and appeals to America's highest principles of freedom and equality. "I have a dream," he declared, "that one day this nation will rise up and live out the true meaning of its creed . . . when the sons of former slaves and the sons of former slave owners will be able to sit together at the table of brotherhood."

The Kennedy Administration

Civil rights activity put Washington officials on the spot. In 1960 Massachusetts Senator John F. Kennedy had defeated Vice President Richard Nixon in the closest presidential race of the twentieth century. Kennedy's paper-thin victory was a product of a lingering recession, which hurt the Republicans, as well as substantial support from the white South, which still maintained a traditional loyalty to the Democrats. Kennedy, the first Catholic president, was not a passionate liberal. His father had made a fortune on Wall Street, and he had entered Congress in 1947 as a budding Cold Warrior. In Kennedy's view, a bitter military and economic competition with the Soviets was the central issue confronting the nation: he wanted to boost economic growth and contain Communism abroad. "Foreign affairs," he once remarked to Nixon, "is the only important issue for a President. . . . I mean, who gives a shit if the minimum wage is $1.15 or $1.25, compared to something like Cuba."

Kennedy found civil rights issues divisive and embarrassing. By exposing America's racism, the movement seemed to give the Soviets a propaganda tool and made it more difficult for Kennedy to woo the newly independent nations of Africa and Asia. And in Congress, he needed the support of southern Democrats, who held a near-veto over all legislation. Although the president supported integration, he also sought political stability and compromise, working closely with his brother Robert, the new attorney general, to achieve these. During the Freedom Rides, the Kennedys called on southern governors to suppress white violence, but they also urged CORE and SNCC to end the rides and focus their energies on activities the White House saw as less disruptive: voter education and registration. In 1962, Kennedy mobilized federal troops to guarantee the admission of James Meredith to the all-white University of Mississippi, but until 1963 he did not put the reform of American race relations at the top of his agenda. Indeed, the Kennedys worried that an increasingly radical movement might move beyond the influence of politicians like themselves; thus, in 1962, Robert Kennedy approved FBI wiretaps on the telephones of movement leaders, including King.

President Kennedy finally put his administration behind a sweeping desegregation bill after the Birmingham demonstrations forced civil rights issues to the top of the nation's agenda. In a nationally televised speech on June 11, 1963, the president declared the denial of civil rights not only a constitutional problem but also a powerful "moral issue" that required tough new laws outlawing segregation in public accommodations, integrating public schools, and prohibiting discrimination in programs receiving federal funds. That very night the necessity for such federal law was again made clear when a Mississippi sniper assassinated Medgar Evers, the NAACP field secretary whose leadership of the civil rights struggle in his home state had been steadfast and courageous.

The Liberal Hour

The civil rights movement reopened the door to reform in American politics, a door that had been shut tight since the waning years of the Great Depression. For more than a generation, the conservative alliance between the white South and northern business had successfully resisted extension of the liberal social legislation pioneered during the presidency of Franklin Roosevelt. For more than two decades, they had blocked new laws that would have provided more health insurance, funded public education, and offered opportunity and income to the poor. The civil rights movement broke this stalemate by isolating southern conservatives and breathing new life into the liberal–labor coalition that had backed New Deal reforms a generation earlier.

Lyndon Baines Johnson, a Texas-born president, presided over the nation's liberal hour. Johnson had been an ardent New Dealer during the 1930s when he was first elected to Congress, but as a senator and then as Majority Leader of the Democrats during the 1950s, he had proven far more cautious. Because he had presidential ambitions, Johnson did not sign the segregationist Southern Manifesto, but neither did he challenge President Eisenhower's conservative domestic policies. Indeed, Kennedy had chosen him as his vice-presidential running mate in 1960 in order to keep Texas in the Democratic column and reassure southern conservatives.

Lyndon Johnson took the presidential oath of office inside Air Force One, at Love Field in Dallas, on the afternoon of November 22, 1963, just hours after the murder of John F. Kennedy as his motorcade wound through Dallas. The assassin, Lee Harvey Oswald, struck the forty-three-year-old president with two shots from a high-powered rifle. Oswald was an unstable twenty-four-year-old ex-Marine who had lived in the Soviet Union for nearly two years. His precise motivation remains unknown because just two days later Oswald, then in police custody, was himself killed by Jack Ruby, a Dallas strip-joint owner well-known to the local police.

Kennedy's assassination had two great consequences for American politics. In the long run, it put a dark question mark over the legitimacy of the nation's institutions and the motivations of its highest officials. Although a high-profile commission chaired by Chief Justice Earl Warren concluded that Oswald was not part of an assassination conspiracy, an increasingly large proportion of the American people came to think otherwise. Many came to see the Kennedy years as a mythic "Camelot," a luminous, hopeful moment in U.S. history transformed on November 22, 1963, into a turbulent era of social upheaval, domestic violence, and unpredictable politics.

In the short run, however, Kennedy's assassination advanced the liberal agenda. President Johnson championed the nation's reform impulse, as a way to both legitimate his unexpected assumption of presidential power and to accommodate the remarkable pressure that arose from the African-American community. Johnson was determined to demonstrate to Kennedy loyalists and skeptical liberals that he had outgrown his conservative Texas roots. In January 1964, the new president declared an "unconditional war on poverty" in his State of the Union address; then, in the spring and summer, he added his considerably legislative and lobbying clout to the movement that won long-delayed passage of Kennedy's Civil Rights Act in June of that year.

Missing. The notice issued by the FBI in June 1964 for missing civil rights workers Andrew Goodman, James Chaney, and Michael Schwerner.

Source: Federal Bureau of Investigation.

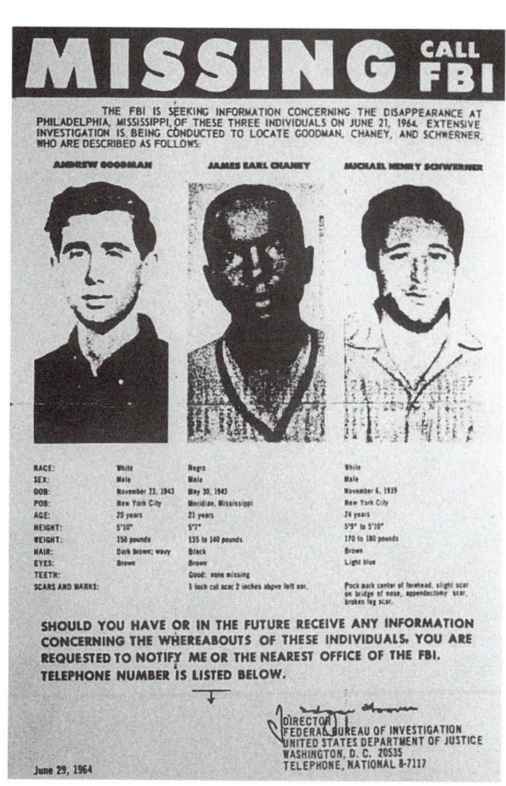

American liberalism was expansive, but President Johnson marked out clear political limits during the months leading up to the Democratic National Convention in August 1964. That summer all eyes were on Mississippi, where SNCC and CORE had brought hundreds of northern white students to teach in "Freedom Schools" and conduct voter registration drives in the black community. Civil rights leaders expected the presence of white students to focus the nation's attention on the racism of the deep South. The strategy worked, all too tragically. In mid-June, three civil rights workers were reported missing: James Chaney, an African-American civil rights worker from Meridian, Mississippi; Michael Schwerner, a white CORE activist from New York City; and Andrew Goodman, a summer volunteer from Queens College in New York City. Federal agents eventually uncovered their mangled bodies: Klansmen and Mississippi police had kidnapped the activists and beaten them to death with clubs and chains.

Mississippi civil rights forces now challenged the credentials of the segregationist white Democrats who composed the state's convention delegation. Their Mississippi Freedom Democratic Party (MFDP) hoped the convention, meeting in Atlantic City, would throw out the segregationists and seat the MFDP instead. At a credentials committee meeting, African-American civil rights leader Fannie Lou Hamer described her efforts to vote in Mississippi. "I was beaten until I was exhausted," she told a huge television audience. "All of this on account we wanted to register, to become first-class citizens. [If] the Freedom Democratic Party is not seated now, I question America."

This was Lyndon Johnson's convention, however, and he would brook no challenges to his authority. Johnson wanted to sweep the fall elections, and to do so he felt he needed votes from the white South, votes that would be lost if the MFDP challenge were sustained. The president ordered Minnesota senator Hubert Humphrey, his prospective running mate and one of the party's foremost liberals, to turn back the MFDP challenge. Humphrey recruited other key liberals, including the UAW's Walter Reuther. Humphrey and his allies forged a "compromise" plan that seated the white Mississippians, gave the MFDP two delegate slots, and mandated racially integrated state delegations in future years.

The MFDP angrily rejected this plan. "We want much more than 'token' positions," explained SNCC's Charles Sherrod. "We want power for our people." The MFDP experience convinced many activists that "white liberals" such as Humphrey and Reuther could not be trusted and that a radical break with mainstream politics was necessary. "We are a country of racists, with a racist heritage, [and] a racist economy," thundered the normally soft-spoken Sherrod, "and we need a naked confrontation with ourselves." The MFDP challenge was like a stroke of heat lightning in a summer sky. It foretold the coming storm that would divide liberals from radicals in the years to come.

But in the presidential election that fall, Lyndon Johnson won the sweeping mandate he had craved. In a highly polarized contest, Johnson and Humphrey won 61 percent of the popular vote, defeating Republican Barry Goldwater, the ideologically conservative senator from Arizona whose Senate vote against the Civil Rights Act won him heavy support in the deep South. There he picked up four states, but defections among moderate Republicans in the North gave the Democratic presidential ticket the electoral votes of every other state except Arizona. Riding on Johnson's coattails, the Democrats won staggering majorities in both the House (295 to 140) and Senate (68 to 32). This landslide ushered in a brief but heady era of liberal politics during which almost every piece of Lyndon Johnson's "Great Society" legislation was written into law.

At the heart of the Great Society was the legal revolution in civil rights. For the first time since Reconstruction, the federal government used the full reach of its power to dismantle the racial hierarchies long presided over by local white elites in education, business, and government. They were now expected to conform to a national standard mandating legal equality for minorities and women. The 1964 Civil Rights Act ended segregation in all public accommodations, including theaters, restaurants, and swimming pools. Under Title VII, an Equal Employment Opportunity Commission championed demands for equitable hiring and promotion practices in private employment. The long-prevailing practice of listing jobs for "white" and "colored," as well as for "men" and "women," in newspaper help-wanted ads was soon abolished.

In a similar fashion, the Voting Rights Act of 1965, passed after the nation watched Alabama authorities use police and National Guardsmen to suppress a massive voter registration drive in Selma, gave the U.S. attorney general the right to intervene in those counties where less than half of all eligible voters were registered. The new law sent hundreds of federal voter registrars into the "Black Belt" counties of the South: within a decade, 2 million additional African Americans were on the voting rolls. And an equally large number of whites registered for the first time. As a result, the South underwent its greatest political transformation since the end of Reconstruction. By the 1970s a biracial, two-party system had emerged. There were thousands of black elected officials in the South, from mayors and sheriffs to state legislators and congressional representatives.

Liberal majorities in the House and Senate also allowed President Johnson to secure enactment of his broader program of social reform, which he called "The Great Society." Since the 1930s, the benefits of New Deal–era social programs and legislative reforms had been largely limited to white, urban wage-earners, for whom Social Security, state unemployment benefits, hospital subsidies, and the federal labor law had all been tailored. But now the sense of social citizenship inherent in these reforms expanded to include millions of additional Americans, those who were black, brown, poor, aged, or employed in agriculture and service industries.

The most important and far-reaching of the Great Society programs extended government-financed medical care to the aged and the poor. Medicare, which provided health insurance as part of the Social Security program, was enacted in 1965, temporarily ending a bitter, twenty-year debate between those who believed in the concept of national health insurance and those who denounced it as "socialized medicine." The next year, Congress again broadened the social safety net by passing Medicaid, which offered federal medical assistance to welfare recipients of all ages. Both programs proved popular, especially Medicare, whose beneficiaries were almost all solidly middle-class retirees; meanwhile, once-resistant doctors and hospitals found the stream of government dollars an unexpected bonanza. But this was the problem: without effective cost controls, these social programs stoked the fire of inflation in the health care system, whose spiraling costs were often borne by employers and individuals still excluded from these government benefits. Although one-quarter of all Americans now held some kind of government-financed medical insurance, fiscal and administrative problems blocked the extension of this system to the remainder of the population.

Congress also overcame the racial and religious impasse that had long stymied a federal program of aid to schools. In the South, conservatives no longer feared that federal dollars would be used to advance racial integration, because desegregation of the schools was rapidly becoming an accomplished fact. And in the North, Catholic advocates of federal aid to parochial schools were accommodated when President Johnson crafted a school aid bill that distributed aid based not on the needs of the schools themselves but on the poverty of their student populations. Total federal expenditures for education and technical training tripled in the decade after 1964.

Finally, a dramatic liberalization of America's immigration policy proved one of the Great Society's lasting legacies. The Immigration Act of 1965 eliminated the quota system that had favored northern European immigrants since the 1920s. In its place, the new bill opened the door to many more immigrants from Asia, Africa, and Latin America, whose ranks would swell in the 1970s and 1980s when political instability and economic crisis swept those regions.

Prime-Time Poverty. By the early 1960s, television news programs regularly reported on poverty in the nation's cities. But most prime-time dramatic programs ignored life in the inner city. One exception was the 1963 CBS series *Eastside/Westside,* featuring George C. Scott (right) and Cicely Tyson as idealistic New York City social workers. While the series' characters won small victories against discrimination and inequality—as in the episode pictured here, with Ruby Dee and Earle Hyman portraying a black couple living in a previously all-white neighborhood—*Eastside/Westside*'s view of urban poverty as an insurmountable problem was unusually pessimistic. The program lasted only one season. **Source:** The Everett Collection.

The War on Poverty

Great Society programs doubled the proportion of the nation's total income going to pay for the social welfare of its people. Because the bulk of this spending went for so-called entitlement programs available to the middle class as well as to the poor, they were largely free of controversy. But the War on Poverty, launched by Johnson in early 1964, proved far more controversial. In the early 1960s, socialist Michael Harrington's *The Other America* had

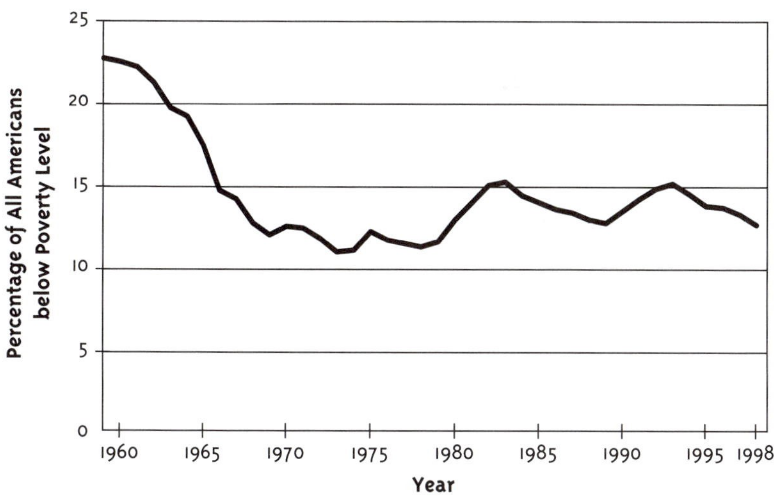

Poverty's Decline and Persistence: Poverty Rates, 1959–1998. Full employment, a rise in real wages, and government anti-poverty programs sharply decreased the proportion of Americans, both black and white, living in poverty during the 1960s and early 1970s. Thereafter, economic stagnation as well as a loss of government interest in the problem of poverty halted the dramatic gains won in the 1960s.

called national attention to the existence of pervasive poverty amid growing affluence. President Kennedy responded by asking advisers to draft plans for a "War on Poverty," and after JFK's death, Johnson made the project his own.

Economic policy makers in the presidential administrations of both Kennedy and Johnson believed that persistent poverty was a function of tepid economic growth combined with inadequate levels of education, training, and motivation among many poor and minority Americans. In 1964, an $11-billion tax cut, much of it directed toward business investment, provided the stimulus that Walter Heller, the influential chairman of the Council of Economic Advisers, predicted would spur annual growth rates and lower unemployment to 4 percent. By the late 1960s it did so, aided by an increase in military spending that supercharged the economy.

The successful turnaround reinforced the belief that the overall economy worked rather well; therefore, persistent poverty was seen to be a product of the failure of the poor to take advantage of the opportunities generated by a booming American capitalism. The War on Poverty did increase some direct income support to poor people in the form of food stamps, rent supplements, and Aid to Families with Dependent Children. But most new funding went to programs designed to help the poor get an education and secure a job. Head Start, the most popular of these programs, provided nutritious food and intellectual stimulation to preschoolers. Upward Bound sought to aid disadvantaged teenagers. The Job Corps retrained unskilled adults and those who had dropped out of school, while VISTA (Volunteers in Service to America) offered a vehicle for college-trained young people to help residents in Appalachia and other pockets of rural poverty. Such educational programs were far cheaper than the relief and public works projects of the New Deal. Indeed, expenditures in what LBJ declared "a total commitment to pursue victory over the most ancient of mankind's enemies" amounted to less than 1 percent of the federal budget during the 1960s. As a New Jersey antipoverty official later remarked, "The antipoverty program was premised on the assumption that poverty existed primarily in the heads of the poor."

Despite its relatively small budget and its emphasis on motivation, the War on Poverty proved highly controversial because it was linked to a rights-conscious mobilization of the poor. To encourage a new self-help attitude among the poor, the administration's antipoverty agency, the Office of Economic Opportunity (OEO), established the Community Action Program to encourage "maximum feasible participation" by residents of impoverished areas in programs that affected their communities. Within two years, more than a thousand Community Action agencies had sprung up across the nation, many infused with the spirit of the civil rights movement. Taking the Johnson administration at its word, the new agencies challenged the way local officials used federal antipoverty funds. This often involved mobilizing the poor to picket City Hall or filing lawsuits against city and state officials. OEO liberals hoped that Community Action would do for the poor what the Wagner Act had done for labor—give them leverage, recognition, and a voice.

Welfare recipients, largely female, adopted much of the outlook generated by the civil rights movement. Since the 1930s, Aid to Families with Dependent Children (AFDC) had often been doled out in a discriminatory, condescending manner, especially against women of color. Yet these welfare grants provided merely one-third of the amount necessary to maintain a family above the poverty line defined by the federal government. In the 1960s, this was $3,000 a year for a Family of four. Led by groups like the National Welfare Rights Organization (NWRO), poor people challenged the system's longstanding paternalism and proclaimed welfare to be a right of citizenship. Poverty, argued many welfare rights activists, was a result not of individual weakness but of structural imbalances in the labor market and the larger economy.

NWRO chapters sprouted in forty-five cities; welfare recipients led demonstrations for better treatment and fought for special grants for housing, food, and children's school clothing. "The mood of applicants in welfare waiting rooms had changed," reported two observers. "They were no longer as humble, as self-effacing, as pleading. They were indignant, angrier, more demanding." Increased numbers of poor people eligible for welfare began requesting assistance. By the early 1970s, more than 3 million families had applied for AFDC grants, more than quadruple the number a dozen years before.

Governors and mayors who had long controlled federal largess were naturally outraged by such activism. "We are experiencing a class struggle in the traditional Karl Marx style," asserted one city official in Syracuse,

New York. This assessment was an exaggeration, but it did point to very real conflict. When these officials demanded an end to this federally sponsored challenge to their power, the White House and the OEO flinched. After 1966, funding for experimental antipoverty programs declined, and state officials assumed the right to take over any community-based agency they did not like. Funds specifically targeted for federal War on Poverty programs remained static during the late 1960s, although expenditures for Social Security, Medicare, Medicaid, and secondary education increased substantially.

Was the War on Poverty a failure or a success? Poverty rates did fall in the 1960s, even if the expanding economy and low overall unemployment probably deserve the lion's share of the credit. As measured by the Department of Labor, the number of poor people decreased from 23 percent in 1962 to 11 percent in 1973. There was a 30-percent reduction in infant mortality, a three-year increase in life expectancy, and a leap in school attendance for African Americans, Hispanics, and low-income whites. But when measured against Lyndon Johnson's extravagant rhetoric, the War on Poverty seems to have been a failure. African-American unemployment remained at double the level for whites, and among inner-city youths, who were the presumed beneficiaries of so much attention, crime, poverty, and unemployment increased to three times the rate among their white suburban counterparts. All such comparative social indexes would worsen in the 1970s when economic growth dropped sharply.

The problem was that Johnson administration officials ignored the most important cause of postwar poverty: structural changes in the economy that made it increasingly difficult for poor people to earn a decent living. The decline of the Appalachian coal industry had thrown more than half a million miners out of work. The mechanization of southern cotton production had pushed millions of African Americans off the land. Economic changes in both Puerto Rico and Mexico had crippled labor-intensive agriculture, forcing millions of Latinos with few economic resources into northern cities. These massive population movements took place at precisely the time that industry was fleeing to the suburbs, stripping central cities of more than a million blue-collar jobs. Minority workers would become trash collectors, janitors, dishwashers, hospital orderlies, and office clerks, but these insecure service-sector jobs were just a step above outright poverty. Thus, whatever the usefulness inherent in War on Poverty education and job-training programs, these structural changes doomed millions of Americans, especially minorities and women, to a secondary labor market characterized by high turnover and low pay.

The Riots and Black Power

Just as Great Society liberalism failed to shift the structures of power in American society, so, too, did it prove inadequate to the new mood that swept black America. In 1963, the year of the March on Washington, the civil rights movement had seemed the culminating affirmation of a liberal faith in the harmonious perfectibility of American institutions. But in the years that followed, the battle against racial injustice took on an increasingly bitter tone. Beginning in the summer of 1965, Los Angeles, Cleveland, Newark, and other cities were swept by fierce street battles and massive fires as African Americans fought police and focused the national spotlight on racial tensions in the North. Hundreds were killed, thousands injured, and millions of dollars' worth of property destroyed as upheavals scarred more than two hundred American cities.

Urban racial violence was hardly new in American history: in 1919 and 1943, race riots had churned through Chicago and Detroit with murderous result. But until the end of World War II, such disturbances had largely consisted of white vigilante attacks on African-American city dwellers. The riots of the 1960s were different: in response to incidents of police hostility and discrimination, blacks took angry action against white-owned ghetto property. Fires and looting erupted. Police and National Guardsmen escalated the violence with mass arrests, brutal beatings, and murderous, indiscriminate gunfire. In Detroit and Washington, D.C., armored troop carriers rumbled through city streets. America's cities were transformed into deadly combat zones.

Bayonets on Linwood and Hazelwood. African-American residents gaze at a National Guard patrol on the second day of the 1967 Detroit riot. **Source:** Copyright 1967 *The Detroit News.*

Newspaper headlines blamed the violence and bloodshed on small groups of radical agitators and heavily armed black snipers. Later investigations revealed that the vast majority of casualties were African Americans shot by government forces. In Detroit, where newspapers' claims of sniping were shrill, reporters later admitted that such gunmen had caused at most three of the city's forty-three riot-related deaths and that two of those cases were doubtful. A presidential commission found that the riots were not the work of a small group; large numbers of African Americans had taken part, including many who held steady jobs and helped support their families. Property destruction was targeted, not indiscriminate. Much like the patriot crowds who had stormed the houses of Tory officials during the American Revolution, rioters demonstrated a rough sense of social justice. Looting and arson was generally directed against stores that charged excessive prices or sold inferior goods. Homes, churches, and schools usually were spared.

Investigators also spotlighted the social problems that lay behind the upheavals. Detroit, for example, had long been a Mecca for black migrants; but in the 1950s and early 1960s, the auto companies built new manufacturing plants in all-white suburbs such as Livonia and Wyandotte, leaving the central city with outmoded factories and a decaying downtown shopping district. Although manufacturing boomed in Michigan during most of the 1960s, Detroit's unemployment rate rarely dropped below 10 percent. As a result, the median income of African Americans remained at about 55 percent that of whites. As the city's tax base dwindled, schools were understaffed and poorly maintained, and social services began to unravel. The civil rights movement brought hope that something could be done to end these problems, but the persistence of rats, rapacious landlords, and racial prejudice fed bitterness and anger.

In the Watts ghetto of Los Angeles the situation was even worse: unemployment remained stuck at 20 percent; three of every five Watts residents depended on some sort of welfare benefit. On the street, teenagers bitterly resented the treatment meted out by the nearly all-white Los Angeles Police Department (LAPD), which many saw as an alien, occupying army. The LAPD seemed to make arrests less to enforce the law than to intimidate young African Americans. One study showed that 90 percent of juveniles arrested never had charges filed against them. Meanwhile, Watts residents confronted other reminders that they lived in a racist society. In 1964, a huge majority of white Californians voted to repeal a state law banning racial discrimination in the sale and rental of housing. "Everyone was angry that it had even come up," said a black teacher active in the election. "Everybody in Watts was aware that they were being rejected by somebody, by somebody white."

Blacks' frustrations were heightened by the sense that other Americans were enjoying growing affluence. In 1965, when the Watts riot erupted, involving as many as 80,000 people, one Los Angeles resident explained that it was as if the community were saying, "We're hungry. Our schools stink. We're getting the shit beat out of us. We've tried the integration route. It's obvious the integration route ain't going to work. Now we've got to go another way."

Many civil rights activists saw the riots as compelling evidence that the movement had to turn its attention to the North. But the causes of poverty and discrimination there were harder to identify than the formalized segregation found in the South. Northern whites, once eager to condemn southern racism, were less willing to address problems in their own local governments, corporations, or unions. Moreover, activists learned that urban ghettos were fragmented and difficult to organize, in part because the black church was less of a community center in the urban North than in the rural South.

Even the movement's most prominent leaders found this new terrain difficult. When in 1966 Martin Luther King tried to bring the movement's moral fervor to bear on the housing discrimination and employment problems faced by African-Americans in Chicago, the city's powerful mayor, Richard Daley, skillfully deflected most of the demands King and his lieutenants put forward. Meanwhile King's campaign met fierce, sometimes violent, resistance from angry white homeowners when blacks marched through Chicago's working-class suburbs. The Southern Christian Leadership Council ended its Chicago campaign with little to show for his efforts.

As King and his allies seemed to stumble, a new set of African-American leaders emerged. For many young urban blacks, the most inspiring figure was a charismatic Black Muslim named Malcolm X. A dope peddler and pimp in his teenage years, Malcolm Little converted to Elijah Muhammad's separatist, puritanical Nation of Islam early in the 1950s while in a Massachusetts prison. With other Black Muslims, Malcolm adopted a new last name and saw integration with the "white devil" as an illusory solution to black problems; instead, he advocated self-reliance, black pride, and unity. "The worst crime of the white man has been to teach us to hate ourselves," Malcolm declared to the ghetto youths who were his most devoted following. "We hated our head, we hated the shape of our nose. . . . Yeah, we hated the color of our skin."

By the early 1960s Malcolm X was the nation's leading black nationalist and the best-known leader of the Nation of Islam. Jealous of his protégé, Elijah Muhammad expelled him from the organization in 1964, after which Malcolm sought to accommodate his nationalist ideology to the cosmopolitan spirit of the mainstream civil rights movement. However, early in 1965, before such a creative symbiosis could be brought to fruition, Malcolm X was assassinated, probably by followers of Elijah Muhammad and his heir apparent, Louis Farrakhan. After his death, Malcolm's ideas became even more widely popular among African Americans, especially after the publication of Alex Haley's best-selling *Autobiography of Malcolm X* in 1966.

This new brand of racial assertiveness won another articulate spokesman when the young SNCC leader Stokely Carmichael popularized the slogan "Black Power" during civil rights marches in the summer of

". . . Fight Them and You'll Get Your Freedom"

In December 1964, less than two months before his assassination, Malcolm X spoke with a group of African-American teenagers from McComb, Mississippi. The group, composed of youthful activists, had come to New York City under the auspices of SNCC. When they visited Malcolm, he applauded their efforts and urged them toward an even bolder stance.

One of the first things I think young people, especially nowadays, should learn, is how to see for yourself and listen for yourself and think for yourself. Then you can come to an intelligent decision for yourself. This generation, especially of our people, has a burden, more so than any other time in history. The most important thing that we can learn to do today is think for ourselves. . . .

My experience has been that in many instances where you find Negroes talking about nonviolence, they are not nonviolent with each other, and they're not loving with each other, or forgiving with each other. Usually when they say they're nonviolent, they mean they're nonviolent with somebody else. I think you understand what I mean. They are nonviolent with the enemy. A person can come to your home, and if he's white and wants to heap some kind of brutality on you, you're nonviolent; or he can come to take your father and put a rope around his neck, and you're nonviolent. But if another Negro just stomps his foot, you'll rumble with him in a minute. Which shows you that there's an inconsistency there.

I myself would go for nonviolence if it was consistent, if everybody was going to be nonviolent all the time. I'd say, okay, let's get with it, we'll all be nonviolent. But I don't go along with any kind of nonviolent unless everybody's going to be nonviolent. If they make the Ku Klux Klan nonviolent, I'll be nonviolent. If they make the White Citizens' Council nonviolent, I'll be nonviolent. But as long as you've got somebody else not being nonviolent, I don't want anybody coming to me talking any nonviolent talk. . . .

I think in 1965, whether you like it, or I like it, or they like it or not, you will see that there is a generation of black people becoming mature to the point where they feel that they have no more business being asked to take a peaceful approach than anybody else takes, unless everybody's going to take a peaceful approach.

So we here in the Organization of Afro-American Unity are with the struggle in Mississippi one thousand per cent. We're with the efforts to register our people in Mississippi to vote one thousand per cent. But we do not go along with anybody telling us to help nonviolently. We think that if the government says that Negroes have a right to vote, and then some Negroes come out to vote and some kind of Ku Klux Klan is going to put them in the river, and the government doesn't do anything about it, it's time for us to organize and band together and equip ourself and qualify ourselves to protect ourselves. And when you can protect yourself, you don't have to worry about being hurt. . . .

I hope you don't think I'm trying to incite you. Just look here: look at yourselves. Some of you are teenagers and students. How do you think I feel—and I belong to a generation ahead of you—how do you think I feel to have to tell you, "We, my generation, sat around like a knot on a wall while the whole world was fighting for its human rights—and you've got to be born into a society where you still have that fight." What did we do, who preceded you? I'll tell you what we did: nothing. And don't you make the same mistake we did. . . .

You get freedom by letting your enemy know that you'll do anything to get your freedom; then you'll get it. It's the only way you'll get it. When you get that kind of attitude, they'll label you as a "crazy Negro," or they'll call you a "crazy nigger"—they don't say Negro. Or they'll call you an extremist or a subversive, or seditious, or a red or a radical. But when you stay radical long enough, and get enough people to be like you, you'll get your freedom. . . .

So don't you run around here trying to make friends with somebody who's depriving you of your rights. They're not your friends, no, they're your enemies. Treat them like that and fight them, and you'll get your freedom; and after you get your freedom, your enemy will respect you. And we'll respect you. And I say that with no hate. I don't have any hate in me. I have no hate at all. I don't have any hate. I've got some sense. I'm not going to let somebody who hates me tell me to love him. I'm not that way-out. And you, young as you are, and because you start thinking, are not going to do it either. . . .

Source: George Breitman, ed., *Malcolm X Speaks* (1966).

1966. Insisting that African Americans must control their own institutions, both within the movement and in the larger society, Carmichael stirred African-American crowds with the impatient declaration "It's time we stand up and take over; move on over, or we'll move on over you." The California-based Black Panther party soon adopted equally aggressive language. These urban militants argued that African Americans were the vanguard of the socialist revolution they forecast for the United States. The Panthers got their start in Oakland, when they mounted armed street patrols designed to ward off police harassment against the black community. By 1969 their inflammatory rhetoric—"Off the pig" was a favorite insult hurled at the police—drew heavy media attention, and it provoked several shootouts with the police and the FBI, who now targeted the Panthers as dangerous revolutionaries.

XIXth Olympiad Protest. As the "Star-Spangled Banner" is played during the 1968 Mexico City Olympics, the American gold and bronze medalists in the 200-meter dash raise their fists in the Black Power salute. Outraged by this silent tribute to black dignity and protest against racial discrimination in sports, the International Olympics Committee ejected Tommie Smith (center) and Juan Carlos (right) from the Olympic Village.
Source: UPI/Corbis-Bettmann.

Although Black Power was denounced by moderate African-American leaders and used by many whites as an excuse to turn against civil rights reforms, the phrase captured the consciousness that was stirring within the black community. Black Power encouraged African Americans to take increased pride and interest in their African roots and in their history of struggle and cultural innovation in America. For some it meant building black institutions and communities that depended as little as possible on whites. Many blacks began to celebrate African-American food, fashion, poetry, prose, theater, dance, and music. And within little more than a decade, black voters united to elect a score of black mayors in cities such as Newark, Detroit, and Oakland. Though the movement could not dismantle the structural inequality in the larger society, African-American political activists gained a certain degree of control over their immediate environment.

Rights Consciousness in the Workplace

An assertive rights consciousness also took hold in the workplace, where African Americans, Puerto Ricans and Mexican Americans had long held the worst jobs. Title VII of the 1964 Civil Rights Act forbade employment discrimination on the basis of race, creed, sex, or national origin, and it established an Equal Employment Opportunity Commission to investigate and litigate such bias. As with the Wagner Act thirty years earlier, the government put its moral and administrative weight behind a new set of employee rights, which soon had a profound impact on the U.S. workplace.

African-American workers rejected second-class treatment. In factories, restaurants, and government offices, black employees filling "white" job slots soon proved to be some of the most militant workers. They stiffened the backbone of union drives in janitorial services, blue-collar government employment, and the textile industry. "Back in the late 1960s," remembered one union organizer, "whenever you went into one plant the first thing you looked to was how many blacks are there working. . . . And if there were forty blacks you could count on forty votes."

Some unions linked themselves directly to the civil rights struggle. Seeking to organize New York City's hospital service workers, such as orderlies and cafeteria workers, the leaders of Local 1199, the Drug and Hospital Employees' Union, proclaimed that their campaign ran on "union power plus soul power." To black hospital workers such as Doris Turner, their own activism was but an extension of the civil rights movement in the South: "Really and truthfully, they were one [struggle], just being waged in different places." By the end of the 1960s, Local 1199 had begun to transform the very character of hospital work in many big cities. No longer "involuntary charity," it soon provided a living wage for a workforce that was predominantly African American, Puerto Rican, and female.

Union Rights and Civil Rights. Malcolm X and trade union leader A. Philip Randolph share a platform during a 1962 rally celebrating a successful hospital workers' strike organized by Local 1199 of the Drug and Hospital Employees' Union.

Source: *1199 News*, Local 1199, Health Care Employees Union, New York City.

Two thousand miles away, in California's Central Valley, a farm labor workforce composed largely of Mexican and Filipino immigrants also adopted the tactics and ideas pioneered by the civil rights movement. Unionization efforts among workers on California's giant commercial farms had a long, bitter history. In the post-war years, Mexican-American workers made up the vast majority of the state's agricultural workforce, and like southern blacks, they suffered poverty and powerlessness within a hierarchical and discriminatory social structure

"The Women Have to Be Involved"

Jessie Lopez De La Cruz came from a family of migrant farmworkers living in California's San Joaquin Valley. Her experiences as a farmworker and a mother of six children helped her effectively organize for the UFW. Her ability to relate to the workers in the field and to involve the women in the unionization struggle were important contributions to the battle for farmworkers' rights. Here she tells of her experiences as an organizer.

Growing up, I could see all the injustices and I would think, "If only I could do something about it! If only there was somebody who could do something about it!" That was always in the back of my mind. And after I was married, I cared about what was going on, but felt I couldn't do anything. So I went to work, and I came home to clean the house, and I fixed the food for the next day, took care of the children and the next day went back to work. The whole thing over and over again. Politics to me was something foreign, something I didn't know about. I didn't even listen to the news. I didn't read newspapers hardly at all. *True Romance* was my thing!

But then late one night in 1962, there was a knock at the door and there were three men. One of them was Cesar Chavez. And the next thing I knew, they were sitting around our table talking about a union. I made coffee. Arnold had already told me about a union for the farmworkers. He was attending their meetings in Fresno, but I didn't. I'd either stay home or stay outside in the car. But then Cesar said, "The women have to be involved. They're the ones working out in the fields with their husbands. If you can take the women out to the fields, you can certainly take them to meetings." So I sat up straight and said to myself, "*That's* what I want!"

When I became involved with the union, I felt I had to get other women involved. Women have been behind men all the time, always. Just waiting to see what the men decide to do, and tell us what to do. . . . I'd hear [women] scolding their kids and fighting their husbands and I'd say, "Gosh! Why don't you go after the people that have you living like this? Why don't you go after the growers that have you tired from working out in the fields at low wages and keep us poor all the time? Let's go after them! *They're* the cause of our misery!" Then I would say we had to take a part in the things going on around us. Women can no longer be taken for granted—that we're just going to stay home and do the cooking and cleaning. It's way past the time when our husbands could say, "You stay home! You have to take care of the children! You have to do as I say!"

I think I was made an organizer because in the first place I could relate to the farmworkers, being a lifelong farmworker. I was well-known in the small towns around Fresno. Wherever I went to speak to them, they listened. I told them about how we were excluded from the NLRB in 1935, how we had no benefits, no minimum wage, nothing out in the fields—no restrooms, nothing. I would talk about how we were paid what the grower wanted to pay us, and how we couldn't set a price on our work. I explained that we could do something about these things by joining a union, by working together.

It was very hard being a woman organizer. Many of our people my age and older were raised with the old customs in Mexico: where the husband rules, he is king of his house. The wife obeys, and the children, too. So when we first started it was very, very hard. Men gave us the most trouble. . . . They were for the union, but they were not taking orders from women, they said. When [the union] formed the ranch committee [to represent workers' grievances to management] at Christian Brothers [a large wine company], the ranch committee was all men. . . .

That year, we'd have a union meeting every week. Men, women, and children would come. Women would ask questions and the men would just stand back. I guess they'd say to themselves, "I'll wait for someone to say something before I do." The women were more aggressive than the men. And I'd get up and say, "Let's go on, let's do it."

When the first contract was up, we talked about there being no women on the ranch committee. I suggested they be on it, and the men went along with this. And so women were elected.

Source: Ellen Cantarow, et al., *Moving the Mountain: Women Working for Social Change* (1980).

dominated by a powerful and entrenched elite. They worked long hours in the blazing sun for piecework wages so low that the labor of an entire family was required to make ends meet.

Led by Cesar Chavez, a charismatic organizer who had spent his childhood as a migrant laborer, California farmworkers struck the Delano vineyards early in 1965. Had these desperately poor workers relied only on their own resources, their union would have been smashed like other agricultural labor unions before them. Farmworkers were not covered by federal labor laws, and the growers easily imported thousands of strike-breakers from Mexico. But the United Farm Workers (UFW) held on for five years by presenting their strike not as a simple union–management conflict, but rather as *La Causa,* an awakening of the Mexican-American community to both its ethnic heritage and its full citizenship rights. UFW rallies, marches, and picket lines featured huge, blood-red banners imprinted with the black Aztec eagle that symbolized Mexican pride and power. When UFW strikers marched 300 miles to the state capital at Sacramento to call attention to their working conditions, they sang "We Shall Overcome" in Spanish and English.

Chavez won the large following that was essential to the success of his union's national boycott against California grape growers. With the help of thousands of students and hundreds of priests and nuns, the UFW challenged the growers in supermarkets and freightyards across America. "We got to the point where we could track a grape shipment from California to Appleton, Wisconsin, and have pickets waiting for them at the loading docks at two o'clock in the morning," remembered one organizer. The UFW won formal recognition from many growers and made the union an important political force in the Southwest. By the 1970s, the UFW could mobilize more campaign workers than all the other unions in California combined, and in Arizona the union registered 100,000 new Mexican-American voters. By adopting the tactics of the civil rights movement, Mexican Americans in the Southwest gained new respect and increased political clout.

The Road to Vietnam

If the burgeoning social movements of the 1960s revealed the domestic problems of post–World War II society, the Vietnam War brought to the surface the tensions inherent in the U.S. effort to manage the global political economy. The road to Vietnam was paved with the arrogance of American Cold War statecraft. Like Presidents Truman and Eisenhower before him, John F. Kennedy wanted the United States to appear strong, command respect from foe and friend, and thereby keep world markets open, maintain the international balance of power, and carefully orchestrate the pace of social and economic change. Anything less, they thought, would invite instability, especially in the agricultural, underdeveloped nations of the Third World. President Kennedy and his principal advisers favored democracy and development, but when it came to a choice between a leftist insurgency and an authoritarian but pro-Western regime, American policy makers invariably supported the kind of strongman of whom JFK once said, "[He's] a bastard, but at least he's our bastard."

During his first months in office, Kennedy faced three reversals that seemed to demonstrate a systemic weakness in the Western camp. In April 1961, a CIA-organized invasion of Cuba, at the Bay of Pigs on the island's southern coast, failed to overthrow Fidel Castro's young revolutionary regime. Five months later, East German Communists erected an ugly concrete wall across Berlin in order to halt the flow of refugees to the increasingly prosperous West. Then a pro-Western government in the Southeast Asian kingdom of Laos collapsed. None of these setbacks was of overriding importance, but they suggested to the Kennedy administration that the United States would have to demonstrate its will to stand up to the Communists somewhere.

Toughness seemed to pay off in the fall of 1962, when the Soviets installed intermediate-range ballistic missiles in Cuba. Kennedy responded with a U.S. naval blockade of the island. For a moment, the world seemed poised on the brink of nuclear war. The crisis ended when the Soviet Union agreed to remove the missiles. Kennedy's victory won him much support at home and gave him the political strength to negotiate a treaty with the USSR banning the above-ground testing of nuclear weapons. But the long-term consequences of the Cuban missile crisis were ambiguous. Determined never to be outgunned again by the United States, the Soviets built up their naval and long-range missile forces and ended a five-year period of internal reforms. Meanwhile, Kennedy, Johnson, and their key aides concluded that they could control the escalation and character of military force as an effective tool of statecraft.

This reasoning helped lead the United States into a tragic war in Vietnam. There an independence movement led by the Communist and nationalist Ho Chi Minh had won substantial support among Vietnamese peasants, students, intellectuals, and urban workers. By 1954, Ho's forces had defeated the French colonial forces and won independence for the northern half of Vietnam. The United States quickly stepped in to replace France as the dominant power in South Vietnam. The United States backed the authoritarian regime of Ngo Dinh Diem, a Catholic aristocrat, in a vain effort to build up a viable political alternative to Communism, but Diem's support never spread much beyond the army and a narrow circle of landlords and urban Catholics.

Tet Offensive of 1968: Turning Point in the Vietnam War. On January 31, 1968, North Vietnamese troops and supporters of the National Liberation Front attacked scores of sites throughout South Vietnam. Although routed by U.S. and South Vietnamese forces, the surprise attack demonstrated that U.S. victory in the war was not in sight and turned U.S. public opinion against the war. Soon after, President Johnson announced that he would not run for re-election and the U.S. inaugurated a partial bombing halt of the North.

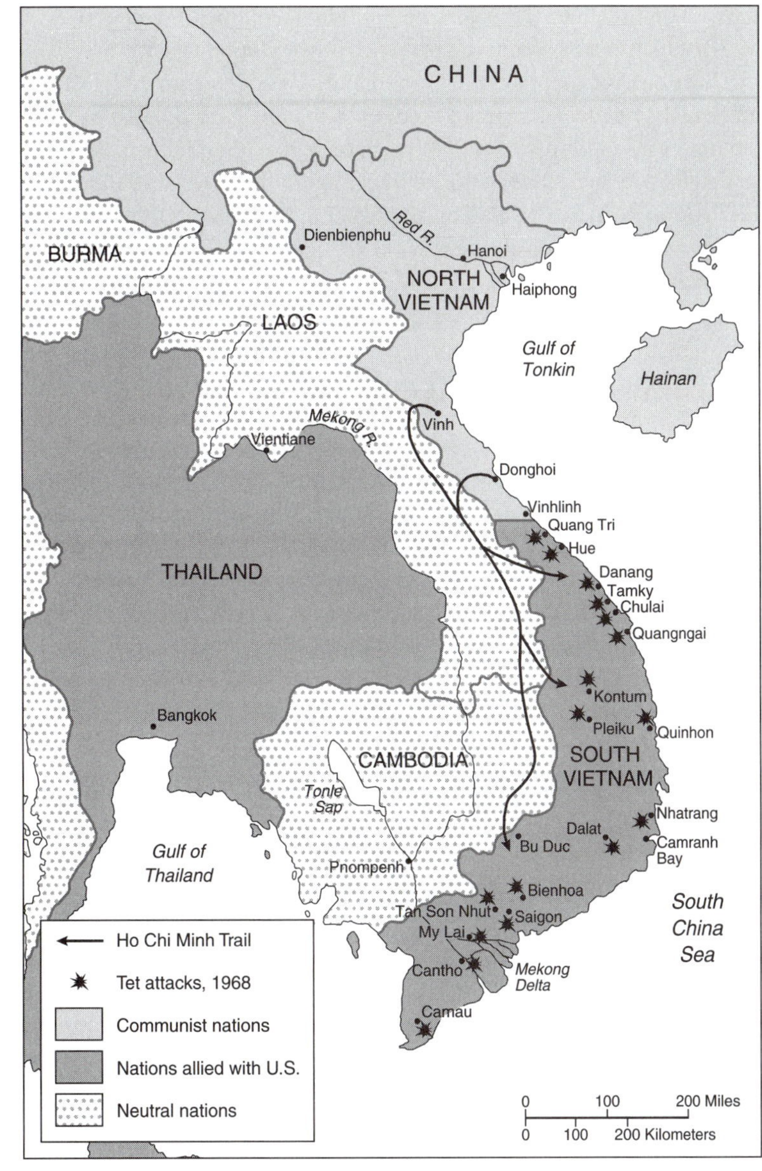

Kennedy and his advisers were aware of Diem's weaknesses but were determined to demonstrate U.S. power and steadfastness. Vietnam would be the place to do it, not so much because of its strategic or economic value but because the president wanted to prove, in the words of one Pentagon analyst, that the United States was "willing to keep promises to its allies, to be tough, to take risks, get bloodied, and hurt the enemy badly." If Vietnam was a "domino" in the worldwide conflict with the Soviet Union and China, then the United States was determined that it would not fall. But such an understanding of the civil war thereby put the United States in opposition not only to Vietnamese Communism but also to the nationalist, anticolonial passions championed by Ho Chi Minh. Steadily, Kennedy increased the number of U.S. military advisers in Vietnam; at the time of his death in November 1963, they numbered more than 16,000.

Escalation of the Vietnam War

Like John Kennedy, Lyndon Johnson saw Vietnam as a proving ground for U.S. global power. But the new president stepped up U.S. involvement even further than Kennedy had. Early in August 1964, Johnson won from Congress a virtual blank check for expansion of the war. By that time, South Vietnam patrol boats had already conducted raids against North Vietnamese shore defenses while U.S. destroyers hovered nearby. On August 2, 1964, North Vietnamese torpedo boats skirmished with the American destroyer *Maddox* in the Gulf of Tonkin; two days later radar operators on the *Maddox* and another destroyer, the *C. Turner Joy,* reported another attack (though the Navy soon concluded that, as a result of stormy seas, the nervous sailors had probably generated a false report). But whatever its actual character, this naval incident was too useful to ignore. Johnson labeled it "open aggression on the high seas against the United States," and he secured congressional passage of the Gulf of Tonkin Resolution mandating the president "to take all necessary steps, including the use of armed force" to aid South Vietnam.

The Gulf of Tonkin Resolution was the closest the United States ever came to an open declaration of war. LBJ thought that "like Grandma's nightgown, it covered everything." In February 1965, the U.S. Air Force began a sustained bombing campaign known as Rolling Thunder against North Vietnam, after which the United States sent an ever-increasing number of ground combat troops to Southeast Asia. There were 125,000 there by the end of 1965, 300,000 in 1966, and more than half a million by the middle of 1968.

As troop levels in Vietnam rose, hundreds of thousands of teenagers were swept into the military. In the first years of the war, most soldiers were actually enlistees rather than conscripts, but for high school males there was not much of a distinction between the two. Most working-class young men thought of their years in "the service" as something akin to high school, a rite of passage from adolescence to manhood. At first, few

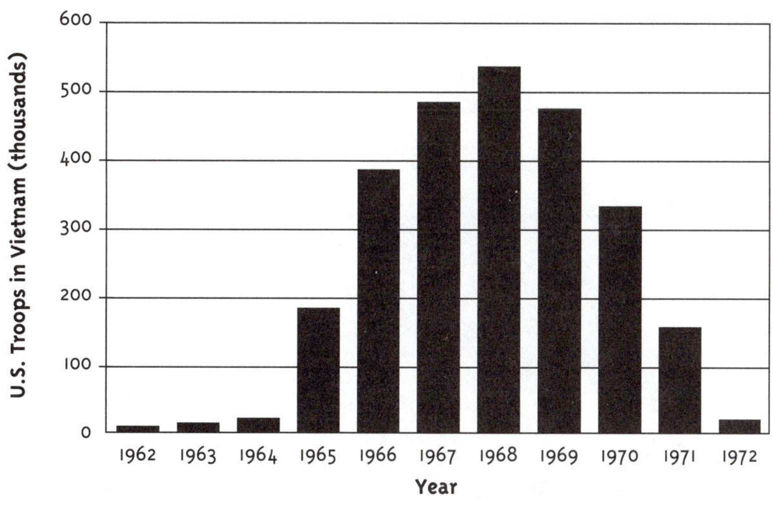

Escalation and Deescalation: U.S. Troops in Vietnam, 1962–1972. Although President Kennedy sent more than 16,000 military "advisers" to Vietnam in the early 1960s, the dramatic expansion of American troops did not begin until the spring of 1965. Anti-war protests and disillusionment with the war effort grew along with the escalating commitment of troops. In 1969, President Nixon began a "Vietnamization effort" designed to reduce the number of American soldiers in Vietnam and quiet the furor at home.

young men gave much thought to the politics of the war. "I didn't have any feelings one way or the other," one draftee remembered. "I figured it was more or less right, because why would I be going if it wasn't right?"

The military draft, or Selective Service System, was indeed selective. Because college students initially enjoyed deferments, most escaped the first years of the draft. If they did end up in the Army, they usually served as officers or in noncombat posts. Of all the graduates of Harvard, Princeton, and Yale during the 1960s, precisely two had been drafted and killed in Vietnam as of June 1970. In contrast, poor Americans, white as well as black and Latino, were far more likely to be drafted and assigned to combat. Draftees, only about a quarter of the army, represented 88 percent of infantry riflemen in 1970 and two-thirds of all battle deaths. A Veterans Administration survey concluded that "while minority Americans may have suffered a disproportionate share of the exposure to combat and combat fatalities, their suffering was the product not of racial discrimination, but of discrimination against the poor, the uneducated, and the young." This represented a major change from World War II, when college deferments were far harder to come by. Then the draft had reached deep into the middle class and to those already established in jobs and careers. World War II GIs had averaged twenty-six years of age, almost seven years older than those who served in Vietnam.

Politics and new technology helped shape U.S. military strategy in Vietnam. Since World War II, the navy and air force had dominated the American military: big ships, fast planes, and lots of bombs could hold the peace or win a war, or so it was thought. Vietnam-era strategy assumed that expensive technology and sophisticated organization would substitute for the blood and sweat of ground combat. In practice this meant that day after day U.S. bombers piloted by young, college-educated officers took off from Southeast Asian air bases and U.S. Navy aircraft carriers to bomb Vietnam, Laos, and, after 1970, Cambodia as well. More than 700 U.S. planes were eventually shot down in Southeast Asia, but the air war had a bureaucratic routine about it that belied both its destructiveness and its futility. A B-52 run from the U.S. territory of Guam had the feel of an interstate haul in a big truck, except that the cargo consisted of more than 200 bombs unloaded by computer decision from an elevation of 30,000 feet. Eventually the United States dropped more than four times as many bombs on Southeast Asia as were dropped in all of World War II.

Operation Barrel Roll, 1982. The Plain of Jars in northern Laos, pockmarked with bomb craters, nine years after the United States ended its aerial campaign.

Source: Hiroji Kubota / Magnum.

But the air war proved ineffective against a rifle-carrying, foot-soldier enemy that usually fought in small combat units. Even massive U.S. bombing could not stop the infiltration of personnel and supplies from North Vietnam or destroy the southern bases of the insurgent National Liberation Front (NLF), or Viet Cong. The Vietnam War would have to be fought by individual soldiers operating in small units in unfamiliar and dangerous jungle terrain. At first the United States used Marines to guard the air bases it had constructed in South Vietnam, but after July 1965 U.S. troops sought out the enemy in a series of "search-and-destroy" operations. The enemy proved elusive; neither the NLF nor regular units of the North Vietnamese Army wanted to fight pitched battles with U.S. forces. Frustrated, U.S. military leaders came to define victory not by the seizure of land or even the defeat of enemy battalions but by the physical annihilation of individual enemy soldiers.

This war of attrition led to a bureaucratic fixation with the daily "body count." U.S. soldiers were soon reporting as an enemy fatality any Vietnamese killed by U.S. firepower. To American soldiers, the distinction between civilians and combatants became hopelessly confused, not only because they were ignorant of the Vietnamese language and customs but also because the nature of the war made such distinctions meaningless. As a guerrilla army, the NLF relied on its ability to blend in with the rest of the population. U.S. soldiers came to fear that the street urchins who asked for candy doubled as NLF couriers and that the "friendlies" who washed your clothes in the morning might take part in a deadly ambush that night. A T-shirt worn by some U.S. soldiers expressed their frustration: "KILL THEM ALL! LET GOD SORT THEM OUT!"

The ultimate consequence of such attitudes came in the village of My Lai, where an American platoon landed one morning in 1968. "When the

"But We Are Not Alone . . ."

This poem, written by Corporal William Ehrhart in the early 1970s and entitled "A Relative Thing," expresses the sense of futility experienced by many American foot soldiers during the Vietnam War. VC and ARVN are abbreviations, respectively, for "Vietcong" and the "Army of the Republic of Vietnam," the South Vietnamese military.

We are the ones you sent to fight a war
You didn't know a thing about.

It didn't take us long to realize
The only thing that we controlled
Was covered by the bottom of our boots.

When the newsmen said that naval ships
Had shelled a VC staging point,
We saw a breastless woman
And her stillborn child.

We watched ourselves becoming insensitive.
We laughed at old men stumbling in the dust
In frenzied terror to avoid our three-ton trucks.

We fought outnumbered in Hue City
While the ARVN soldiers looted bodies
In the safety of the rear.
The cookies from the wives of Local 104
Did not soften our awareness. . . .

We are the ones who have to live
With the memory that we were the instruments
Of your pigeon-breasted fantasies.
We are inextricable accomplices
In this travesty of dreams;
But we are not alone. . . .

Just because we will not fit
Into the uniforms of photographs
Of you at twenty-one
Does not mean you can disown us.

We are your sons, America,
And you cannot change that.
When you awake,
We will still be here.

Source: Jan Berry and W. D. Ehrhart, eds., *Demilitarized Zones: Veterans After Vietnam* (1976).

attack started," one sergeant recalled, "it couldn't have been stopped by anyone. We were mad and had been told that the enemy was there and we were going in there to give them a fight for what they had done to our dead buddies." The U.S. platoon took no enemy fire, but within a matter of minutes the village exploded with American grenades and machine-gun bursts. "People began coming out of their hooches [huts] and the guys shot them and burned the hooches—or burned the hooches and then shot the people when they came out," another soldier recalled. That day more than 350 Vietnamese villagers were murdered. There was one American casualty: a GI who shot himself in the foot out of disgust at what he was witnessing.

The My Lai Massacre. Quang Ngai province, March 16, 1968.
Source: Ron Haeberle, *Life* Magazine.

The Antiwar Movement and the New Left

The Vietnam War was fought on two fronts: at home and abroad. U.S. policymakers conducted the war with one eye always focused on national opinion. At first Presidents Kennedy and Johnson worried that militant Cold Warriors would criticize them as being "soft on Communism" if South Vietnam fell. But at the same time, neither president was confident that the American public would support a large military conflict in Asia. The escalation of the war therefore took place step by step: Johnson never formally declared that U.S. ground troops would fight in Vietnam; and although U.S. troop strength climbed to 550,000 by 1968, the military reserves were never called up, nor was a general war tax imposed.

Until the very end of the 1960s, most Americans supported the Vietnam War. But its length, cost, and character generated a growing opposition, or, rather, two kinds of antiwar sentiment. A highly ideological, and at first a largely youthful, antiwar movement emerged out of a broader New Left set of political ideas that were themselves inspired by the civil rights movement. But this radical opposition to the war was accompanied by a late-blooming, far more conservative rejection of the war whose slogan might well have been "Win Now or Get Out." Conservative opponents of the war considered themselves traditional patriots and had nothing but contempt for the students of the New Left, but they were unwilling to bear the costs of what seemed an endless struggle. By 1968, Washington policy makers faced domestic opposition to the war in the streets, in congressional hearing rooms, and at the ballot box. Antiwar sentiment on both the Left and Right had become so great that continued escalation of the war was no longer a tenable military policy.

The New Left came to life on college and university campuses in the early 1960s, when many contemporary observers were still bemoaning a "silent generation" of college conformists. Students in the 1960s were children of the baby boom, products of America's postwar economic growth and affluence, young people who could look forward to comfortable, middle-class futures. Yet it was at places such as Stanford, Oberlin, and the Universities of Chicago, Michigan, California, which drew the smartest and often the most affluent young Americans, that students rediscovered a radical critique of American society, and it was from these campuses that the antiwar movement drew its initial strength.

Despite the emphasis on being "new," the New Left was linked in many ways to previous radical movements, including the Communist-dominated Left of the 1930s. The early New Left differed from previous radicalisms primarily in its rejection of Marxist ideology and the need for well-structured political organizations. Activists identified with the civil rights movement, which promised to restore moral vision to American life, and with the university, which seemed a place where ideas could have immediate and beneficial consequences. Unlike most working-class students, whose social outlook was often shaped by an urgent desire to find a secure job, middle-class students in the prosperous 1960s were "free" for a few crucial years to reflect skeptically on the gap between the liberal promise of American life and social reality.

The 1962 Port Huron Statement, a founding manifesto of the leading New Left organization, Students for a Democratic Society (SDS), called on America to live up to its highest democratic ideals. SDS urged activists to respond not only to issues of poverty but also to the problems of modern life, from alienation and bureaucratic impersonality to the threat of nuclear war. "A new left," SDS proclaimed, "must give form to the feelings of helplessness and indifference, so that people may see the political, social, and economic source of their personal troubles and organize to change society."

Early SDSers such as University of Michigan student Tom Hayden hoped that organized labor might regain its "missing idealism" and thought a revitalized labor movement essential to the new America they envisioned. Such sentiments won SDS the warm regard of many labor liberals in the early 1960s. UAW leaders, for example, thought SDS might help the labor movement get its message across on college campuses and among unorganized white-collar workers, and it provided the college group with funds for some of its early organizing activities.

But early New Leftists did not see labor as the sole engine of progressive social change. Instead, they saw the civil rights movement as proof that other groups, including students, intellectuals, and African Americans, could pick up the mantle of leadership. "SDS seemed hip and bold," recalled Jeremy Brecher, an Oregon student in the early 1960s. "It had an enthusiasm for direct action, an attitude of defiance towards the establishment, and a constant looking for points where change could be stimulated and supported." From 1963 to 1966, SDS sent groups of students to Chicago, Newark, and elsewhere to organize "interracial movements of the poor."

In the fall of 1964 student activists first made the New Left a force on campus when they mounted huge demonstrations at the University of California at Berkeley. Influenced by the radical politics of the northern California labor movement and the cultural dissidence that radiated from San Francisco's "beat" community, Berkeley became a flashpoint for civil rights activity in the early 1960s. Scores of Berkeley students went South as civil rights workers, and thousands joined demonstrations in the Bay Area. When in 1964 local politicians and businessmen demanded that university officials crack down on such activism, the university prohibited the collection of funds for civil rights work or the distribution of political literature on campus. In response, activists organized a "Free-Speech Movement" (FSM) that waged a nonviolent, disruptive, and, in the end, largely successful struggle against paternalistic university officials.

The student movement swept into its ranks thousands who had never thought of themselves as political, especially after 800 students were arrested during a December 1964 civil rights–style sit-in at Sproul Hall, the administration building. Many student radicals came to see the university as bureaucratic, impersonal, and linked to corporate interests. FSM leader Mario Savio, a Freedom Summer veteran, denounced higher education's "sophisticated powers of manipulation" and compared the student movement in California to the civil rights struggle in Mississippi. "The same rights are at stake in both places," he told Berkeley students, "the right to participate as citizens in democratic society and the right to due process of law."

Conflicts over university governance spread to hundreds of schools, but campus reform issues were soon overshadowed by a fierce debate over the politics and morality of the war in Vietnam. After President Johnson ordered massive air strikes and troop deployments in 1965, a generation of radical students moved into the forefront of the antiwar movement. Their opposition had many sources. A few were pacifists

From Protest to Resistance. Confronted by a phalanx of soldiers, federal marshals, and police, antiwar demonstrators block the Pentagon on October 21, 1967.

Source: Marc Riboud / Magnum.

who opposed the use of organized violence for any purpose. Others came to sympathize with and even glorify the NLF as heroic nationalists. Most agreed that the war—and America's role as global policeman—violated the ideals of democracy and freedom. "We'd been brought up to believe in our hearts that America stood for fighting on the side of justice," remembered one student of the mid 1960s. "World War II was ingrained in us—my father had volunteered. So there was this feeling of personal betrayal."

The antiwar movement expanded rapidly. Antiwar marches, which had drawn but a few thousand in 1965, grew in size; by 1967 there were a million marchers in the streets of New York, San Francisco, and Washington, D.C. SDS membership mushroomed. In addition to national protest marches, activists organized local demonstrations, targeting universities that conducted war-related research, the Central Intelligence Agency, and Dow Chemical Company, the manufacturer of napalm (jellied petroleum), an incendiary weapon used in Vietnam. Students held vigils, tried to block troop trains, petitioned government officials, and supported "peace candidates" who ran for public office.

For young Americans, the draft stood as a prime symbol of the war. Millions of young men tried to evade it: some fled to Canada; many feigned physical or psychological problems in hopes of winning deferments; others used family connections to gain safe berths in the National Guard. A few thousand took public stands as draft resisters, burning their draft cards and challenging the government to imprison them. Catholic priests Philip and Daniel Berrigan inspired a wave of clandestine attacks against local draft boards, burning files or drenching them with blood. By the late 1960s, draft resistance—organized and unorganized, overt and covert—was so widespread that the nation's legal system could no longer effectively handle the flood of cases.

Although the antiwar movement was initially based in the middle class, it won thousands of working-class recruits after 1968. By then, nonelite universities such as Wayne State in Detroit, Kent State in Ohio, and all-black Southern University in Baton Rouge, Louisiana, had become centers of movement activity. Long hair, marijuana, and rock music, which had first symbolized campus political and social alienation, soon spread to factory night shifts, construction sites, and mail rooms staffed by young workers.

The radicalization of working-class youth had a direct effect on the military, where internal conflict undermined the morale of many Vietnam combat units. After 1967, drug use soared, desertions quadrupled, and hostility toward officers took on a political coloration. Peace symbols and Black Power fists appeared on GIs' helmets. "Almost to a man, the members of my platoon oppose the war," explained one sergeant in 1971. "There is a great deal of pressure on leaders at the small-unit level to conduct what are popularly referred to as 'search and avoid' missions, and to do so as safely and cautiously as possible." Officers who failed to accommodate their men might find a grenade rolled under their bunk — more than a thousand such "fragging" incidents were recorded after 1969. As thousands of bitter Vietnam veterans joined peace marches, antiwar and anti-authority sentiment spread across the United States, to European bases, and to naval vessels, undermining U.S. military strength around the globe.

Operation Dewey Canyon III. Facing a barricade erected to keep them off the steps of the Capitol, hundreds of veterans — many in wheelchairs or on crutches — return medals they received during tours of duty in Vietnam. Perhaps the most moving of all antiwar demonstrations, this ceremony was the culmination of a week-long campaign during April 1971 organized by the Vietnam Veterans Against the War to dramatically publicize atrocities committed by the United States. The VVAW named the protest after secret American invasions of Laos in 1969 and early 1971.

Source: Leonard Freed / Magnum.

Political and social radicalism in the United States also helped spark an international student movement that challenged leaders on both sides of the Cold War. As in the United States, the first generation to come of age in postwar Europe felt stifled by the rigid social structures of the Cold War era. Young people in France, Germany, and Italy campaigned against the Vietnam War and helped revitalize socialist traditions, and even in Poland and Czechoslovakia many glimpsed the possibility that Soviet control might be loosened and Communism given a human face. In Mexico a mass student movement reached a tragic climax in October 1968, on the eve of the Olympic Games in Mexico City, when government troops killed hundreds protesting one-party rule.

The international New Left reached a peak in the spring of 1968, when student demonstrations and university occupations at the Sorbonne in Paris, at Columbia University in New York, and at the Free University of Berlin seemed to shake the structures of world politics. In the "Prague Spring," students were in the vanguard of the effort to humanize east European Communism. In France, university protests initially directed against the rigidities of the centralized educational system struck a nerve in the whole society, touching off factory occupations and strikes involving almost 10 million workers.

In the United States, however, many New Leftists felt that unions had no role to play in transforming American society. The AFL-CIO leadership supported the Vietnam War; and in the eyes of many activists, the "affluent" white working class had bargained away its radical potential. "The next time some $3.90-an-hour AFL–type workers go on strike for a 50-cent raise," exploded Berkeley activist Marvin Garson in 1967, "I'll remember the day they chanted 'Burn Hanoi, not our flag,' and so help me, I'll cross their picket line."

Instead, many activists looked to the Black Power movement or to the Cuban and Vietnamese revolutions for models. Frustrated by the failure of peaceful protests to halt the war and increasingly disillusioned with American institutions, some New Leftists sought to emulate the urban rioters in the United States or the guerrilla warriors in Latin America and Asia. Repressive police activity encouraged this shift toward confrontation. While state and local police attacked marchers and harassed demonstrators, an FBI counterintelligence program spearheaded a nationwide effort to "expose, disrupt, and otherwise neutralize" civil rights and antiwar activity. Intelligence agents sometimes posed as radicals, so-called agents provocateurs who sought to discredit antiwar groups and individuals. A 1976 U.S. Senate report condemned this government effort as "unworthy of a democracy and occasionally reminiscent of the tactics of totalitarian regimes."

The Students for a Democratic Society self-destructed in the summer of 1969. One SDS splinter group known as the Weathermen identified themselves as urban guerrillas waging underground warfare as part of the global struggle against the "Amerikkkan" empire. Between September 1969 and May 1970, there were at least 250 bombings linked to radical groups in the United States. Campus Reserve Office Training Corps buildings and draft board headquarters were a favorite target. The spate of bombings slowed in 1970 after three Weathermen accidentally killed themselves when a homemade bomb exploded in their Greenwich Village townhouse. Although hundreds of thousands, adults as well as students, still turned out for protests, the New Left fragmented at the very moment when broad layers of the American people might have been most receptive to its political and moral arguments.

Rise of the Counterculture

The impact of the New Left was cultural as well as political. Like antebellum reformers in the 1830s and the Populists in the 1890s, New Left radicals generated a multifaceted "counterculture" that expressed itself in the values and rituals of daily life. Millions of Americans sought new

Comix! In the spirit of the counterculture, underground cartoonists rejected the style and substance of commercial comics and enthusiastically embraced every taboo. The starched suburban antics of "Archie" were replaced by the slovenly inner-city iconoclasm of Gilbert Shelton's "Fabulous Furry Freak Brothers" (represented here by brother Fat Freddy). The standard paternal and patriotic superheroes were rearranged into Shelton's sadistic and super-patriotic "Wonder Wart Hog," Spain Rodriguez's vengeful guerrilla-fighter "Trashman," and others. Meanwhile, Robert Crumb and S. Clay Wilson delved into the darker recesses of consciousness, producing a range of characters who revelled in the violent excesses of "sex, drugs, and rock-'n-roll."

Source: Gilbert Shelton, *Gothic Blimp Works,* 1969—Copyright Rip Off Press, Inc.

forms of community, questioning traditional forms of monogamy and family, suburban life, the headlong pursuit of material possessions, and the value placed on scientific rationality and emotional repression. The rise of rock music, the end of many sexual taboos, and the growing use of marijuana and psychedelic drugs represented only the most obvious indications that American culture was in the midst of a great change.

Music was central to the 1960s counterculture. Early in the decade, folk musicians such as Bob Dylan set the tone for the era's political idealism by reviving such songs as Woody Guthrie's "This Land Is Your Land," which celebrated a democratic, populist America. By 1963, however, the year of the Birmingham demonstrations and President Kennedy's assassination, Dylan's "Blowin' in the Wind" reflected impatience with a liberalism turning sour. About the same time, soul singers such as Otis Redding and Aretha Franklin, Motown stars such as Marvin Gaye, and British rock-and-roll groups such as the Beatles and the Rolling Stones were renewing rock-and-roll's connection to its African-American roots. After 1965, San Francisco bands such as The Grateful Dead, which performed routinely at protest rallies, enlivened the robust Bay Area radical culture. Popular music now seemed to spread the messages of social criticism and possibility. "The music and the world it created," recalled one former activist, "helped give us a sense that we were defining the culture, and the whole society was following."

The counterculture pioneered a new form of journalism as well. Hundreds of "underground" community newspapers sprang up in the late 1960s. Their very names—*Los Angeles Free Press, Berkeley Barb, Austin Rag*—

Wearing Your Politics. Political buttons adorn the sleeve of an antiwar demonstrator in the fall of 1968. During the 1960s, political buttons were produced in the millions, providing people with an inexpensive and stylish way to publicly express their beliefs and commitments.

Source: Copyright Charles Harbutt/Actuality, Inc.

announced their viewpoint. These newspapers celebrated rock music and the drug scene, publicized movement protests, and experimented with a journalistic style that was intensely personal and committed to radical perspectives. Many of these papers collapsed along with the New Left, but they had a lasting influence on the news media, helping to open the doors to a new generation of investigative journalists.

American culture seems to have an endless capacity to absorb and transform what is new and different. Advertising agencies understood that the cultural winds were shifting even in the early 1960s when they identified a new, youthful "Pepsi Generation," proclaimed a "Dodge Rebellion," and celebrated the homely Volkswagen Beetle. Such was the fate of the counterculture, especially after it became divorced from the radical movement that gave it direction. Record companies, clothing manufacturers, and other purveyors of consumer goods quickly found a new market. Soon rock albums accounted for two-thirds of the sales of large record companies. Expensive stereo systems sold briskly, and *Rolling Stone* made an easy journalistic transition from New Leftism to rock music capitalism.

While the counterculture was not intrinsically radical, its impact spread to almost every segment of the population. American Catholicism, for instance, underwent a surprising transformation, in response to both the reformist Second Vatican Council of 1962 and the new social movements. Among the laity, obedience to church authority declined, and as popular mores changed, millions of Catholics came to ignore church teachings on sexual matters. By the mid 1970s, three-quarters of all Catholics polled said that, if necessary, they would have an abortion or advise their wives to do so, and in Chicago two-thirds of those Catholics under thirty who considered themselves pious approved of premarital sex. A small but growing group of Catholics plunged into the civil rights movement, farm-worker support activities, and opposition to the

If You Can't Beat 'em, Absorb 'em. Columbia Records denounces the "Establishment" in an advertisement placed in underground newspapers in December 1968. Abbie Hoffman, a leader of the anti-establishment Yippies, later commented that such corporations "were taking the energy from the streets and using it for a commercial value, saying, 'If you are in the revolution, what you got to do is buy our records,' while we were saying, 'You got to burn your draft card, you can't go to Vietnam, you have to come to the demonstrations and the protests.' It was a conflict and we called their process cooptation: . . . They were able to turn a historic civil clash in our society into a fad, then the fad could be sold."

Source: *Rolling Stone,* December 7, 1968—General Research Division, New York Public Library, Astor, Lenox, and Tilden Foundations.

Vietnam War. A growing corps of outspoken nuns and priests helped push the American Catholic Church toward an increasingly liberal stand on issues of war, peace, and nuclear weapons.

1968: A Watershed Year

Some years in American history are milestones that every schoolchild knows: 1492, 1776, 1861, 1919, 1941. The year 1968 joins this short list, not only because it was full of dramatic and unexpected events but also because the nation's Cold War consensus seemed to break apart. By the end of the year, Americans were no longer willing to pay the price of "winning" the war in Vietnam. Though the conflict dragged on for seven more years, Johnson's presidency suddenly disintegrated, and modern American liberalism went into sharp decline.

Late in January, during Tet, the Vietnamese New Year, the National Liberation Front launched a massive offensive that put its combatants inside almost every Vietnamese town and city. Hue, the ancient capital of all Vietnam, was occupied by the NLF, and the nightly news brought graphic pictures of a gun battle between Marines and NLF troops inside the American embassy compound in Saigon. The bitter fighting, which raged through February and March, killed thousands of enemy soldiers. American generals claimed victory, but the Tet Offensive actually dealt President Lyndon Johnson's Vietnam policy a political deathblow. The war might continue indefinitely. There was no longer a "light at the end of the tunnel."

The Tet Offensive transformed the way Americans saw the Vietnam War. Until then, most newspapers and the television networks had covered the war in a fashion largely favorable to the U.S. government. The news media were themselves big businesses that framed the news in ways that legitimized social order at home and U.S. interests abroad. Moreover, the most respected correspondents, such as CBS anchorman Walter Cronkite, had learned about combat journalism in World War II, when newsmen proudly saw their job as telling the army's story to the folks back home.

The Tet Offensive shattered the optimistic story line. "To say that we are mired in a stalemate seems the only realistic, if unsatisfactory, conclusion," reported Cronkite from Vietnam. Thereafter, the news media greeted official government pronouncements with skepticism and gave antiwar activity increased coverage and respect. The mass-circulation magazine *Life* demonstrated how far this shift had gone in June 1969, when it underlined the human cost of the war by publishing on its front cover the youthful pictures of the 247 American servicemen killed in the fighting during one week.

The NLF offensive shook the Democratic party as well. Until Tet, party liberals hesitated to criticize President Johnson; in late 1967, when antiwar senator Eugene McCarthy of Minnesota announced he would challenge the incumbent president for the 1968 Democratic nomination, his prospects seemed marginal. After Tet, however, the news media spotlighted McCarthy's effort, student volunteers poured into his campaign, and he startled Johnson with a near-upset in the New Hampshire primary. New York senator Robert Kennedy, the former U.S. attorney general, sensed Johnson's vulnerability and declared his own presidential candidacy, calling for a halt to the bombing and a revival of the War on Poverty.

In the next three months, McCarthy and Kennedy demonstrated that, if given the choice, Democratic party voters would choose a candidate committed to deescalation of the war. McCarthy was an inept campaigner, but his willingness to challenge Johnson won him the fierce loyalty of many antiwar activists. In contrast, Kennedy was a more traditional liberal and a latecomer to the antiwar cause. Nevertheless, Kennedy had become a passionate advocate of social justice, and he won the hearts of many Latinos and African Americans as well as a substantial portion of the white working class. His ties to established urban politicians also helped propel him to the front of the race.

Meanwhile, Tet precipitated a reevaluation of the war by the elite lawyers, bankers, and State Department officials who had presided over U.S. foreign policy since World War II. The war had generated disquiet on Wall Street and complaints from America's allies in Europe. By 1968 the costs of the war had spiraled well beyond those forecast just two years before, superheating the economy, generating inflationary pressures at home, and weakening the value of the dollar abroad. To men such as Dean Acheson, a corporate lawyer and former secretary of state, and Clark Clifford, a powerful lawyer whom Johnson had just appointed secretary of defense, the war was an open wound that sapped America's global strength. Acheson told Lyndon Johnson: "We need to stand back and get our priorities right. Enemy number one is Russia. Enemy number two is China. The vital strategic areas in their proper order are Western Europe particularly Germany, Japan, the Middle East, Latin America—and only then Southeast Asia. The most crucial priority of all, of course, is the home front."

President Johnson caved in. On March 31 he announced that he would stop bombing North Vietnam, cancel a planned troop increase, and end his reelection campaign. The antiwar movement had split the Democratic party and forced a powerful president to repudiate his own foreign policy and renounce another term in office. These dramatic developments might well have opened the way for America to make a decisive turn to the left, toward a new foreign policy and a more radical program of social reform at home. Yet 1968 proved a turning point that did not turn. Within two months, the two most visible opposition figures in American politics, Robert Kennedy and Martin Luther King, Jr., lay dead, struck down by assassins' bullets.

King was the first to fall. Convinced that the black movement had to take up the demand for economic as well as political justice, King had gone to Tennessee to help organize support for striking Memphis sanitation workers. Led by the American Federation of State, County, and Municipal Employees, the strike had lasted for two months. Marches, demonstrations, and arrests gave the strike much of the flavor of the early civil rights movement; the slogan boldly printed on their picket signs, "I AM A MAN," spoke as clearly to the real meaning of the conflict as did the union's demand for higher wages and a contract. On April 4, hours before King was to lead another mass march on City Hall, a white ex-convict named James Earl Ray shot him from ambush. After King's death, ghettos across the United States exploded in riots, signaling a bitter end to the once-hopeful civil rights era.

After helping to lead the mourning for King, Robert Kennedy returned to the primary campaign. In June, he won the California Democratic primary, thus positioning himself to make a strong bid for his party's presidential nomination. But after Kennedy made a triumphant speech to California campaign workers in Los Angeles, a Palestinian nationalist, Sirhan Sirhan, shot him as he returned to his hotel room. "I won't vote," one black New Yorker later told a pollster. "Every good man we get they kill."

The murders of King and Kennedy eroded the sense of legitimacy and democratic fairness that were the prerequisite for the nation's political institutions to work. They were brought into question yet again at the Democratic National Convention in Chicago, where liberals within the Democratic party felt deprived of an antiwar standard-bearer and resentful of party rules that unfairly limited the representation of dissident views. Meanwhile, in the streets and parks of Chicago, antiwar radicals were harassed and beaten by a police force whose brutality was encouraged by Chicago mayor Richard J. Daley. With solid backing from Lyndon Johnson, conservative Democrats, and organized labor, Vice President Hubert H. Humphrey easily captured the Democratic presidential nomination, but the prize seemed tarnished and his party still bitterly divided.

Humphrey's Republican opponent was Richard Nixon, the former vice president. Nixon was not an ideologue like Barry Goldwater. He was a Republican centrist, an opportunist remarkably adept at manipulating the political passions of his era. In a carefully scripted campaign, Nixon

"There Were Police Chasing Them with Billy Clubs"

In August 1968 a few thousand antiwar activists and "Yippies" — a flamboyant group led by Abbie Hoffman and Jerry Rubin — gathered in Chicago to protest the Democratic National Convention. The activists' presence — and, in some cases, their acts of provocation — spurred a stunning display of police violence. The Chicago police broke up protests with tear gas and billy clubs, beating hundreds of activists, bystanders, and reporters. Vivid reports of the battle fed a widespread sense that American society was being torn apart. Barry Edmonds, a prize-winning photographer for the Booth Newspaper chain, covered the demonstrations. Here, he describes what he saw one night as he drove down Wells Street in Chicago.

After about two blocks, a running mob of people — about fifty — burst out of an alley in front of our station wagon. I stopped to avoid running over them. There were police chasing them with billy clubs.

A young man in a tan summer suit — he was well-dressed and carried one camera — ran in front of our vehicle. A cop yelled, "Get out of here with that camera." The man ran to the sidewalk, but one cop circled a parked car to cut him off, and another cop was just five feet behind him with a raised club.

The young man raised his hands when he saw the cop in front, like he was surrendering, but both cops grabbed him, one on each side. A third cop came up behind him with a billy club and made a running swing at the man's head. It didn't knock him out. He began screaming in a high pitched voice, like a girl, it sounded. He dropped to the sidewalk, and the two cops turned away, but the cop who had clubbed him from behind — he was a short, stocky man — was still clubbing the man, who lay on the pavement, still screaming. Then the cop left, and "Yippie medics" came up, wearing white smocks. . . .

I drove on, slowly. . . . Some more "Yippies" in their white smocks with crude red crosses sewn on the sleeves were kneeling by another man down on the sidewalk. The man's face was bloody. . . . I heard somebody ask, "Can you take this man to the hospital? . . ." They laid the man across the back seat of our station wagon. He had a bandage around the crown of his head. . . .

There were police all over, and we told the man to stay down. He kept saying, "I'm sorry. I'm sorry. Gee, my wife is really going to be worried." He didn't look like a Yippie or a hippie or a newsman — he was just a person.

Source: *Ann Arbor News,* August 28, 1991.

denounced the campus upheavals, the ghetto riots, and many Great Society reforms, aiming his message at what he called the "silent majority" of "forgotten Americans, the non-shouters, the non-demonstrators." But Nixon also went after the peace vote, declaring he had formulated a plan — never spelled out during the campaign — to bring "peace with honor" in Vietnam.

Humphrey's difficulties were compounded by third-party candidate George Wallace, who stepped into the void created by liberalism's disarray. Wallace, a former governor of Alabama, was a Vietnam hawk and a racist who had learned to substitute new code words, such as "law and or-

CHICAGO'S AMERICAN, THURSDAY, AUGUST 22, 1968 ** 3

Here's Cast of Characters in Drama of Streets

"Identify Them by Their Garb." As Democratic National Convention delegates and protestors arrived in Chicago in late August 1968, the *Chicago American* published a guide to the "cast of characters" converging on the city. Illustrating student supporters of Eugene McCarthy, activists identified with the National Mobilization Against the War ("the Mobe"), liberal Democrats opposed to the Johnson administration, hippies, Yippies (whose presidential candidate was a pig), apolitical greasers, and outlaw bikers, the guide identified political attitudes through stereotypes of dress and hair style. The *American* failed to notice any African Americans among the dissenting delegates and demonstrators.

Source: Bruce Darrow, *Chicago American,* August 22, 1968—Chicago Historical Society.

der," for the old segregationist cant. At the end of September, polls gave Wallace 21 percent of the national vote, with his greatest strength among Democratic voters in the white South, in the lower middle class, and among blue-collar workers in the industrial Midwest.

Northern white workers' support for Wallace did not necessarily mean that they were more racist or prowar than the rest of the population. Surveys taken in the late 1960s showed that racial hostility was as prevalent in upper-middle-class suburbs as in white ethnic neighborhoods and that opposition to the war was greatest in workers' communities. Rather, Wallace attracted many supporters by tapping a deep vein of alienation and social resentment among working-class Americans. He appealed, in his own words, to the "average man," the "steelworker, paper worker, small businessman, the cabdriver" who was "sick and tired of theoreticians in both national parties and in some of our colleges and some of our courts telling us how to go to bed at night and get up in the morning."

Wallace attracted support from two kinds of northern workers: older skilled workers, often of Polish or Italian extraction, who feared African-American encroachment in their neighborhoods; and rebellious young production workers alienated from their unions and the established order. As one young autoworker noted, if "[UAW President Walter] Reuther was for Wallace, we'd be for Humphrey." Frightened by the Wallace phenomenon, the AFL-CIO and the UAW deluged their members with leaflets and pamphlets pointing out Wallace's anti-union, pro-employer record. This appeal worked, and Humphrey won the votes of many northern workers who had once favored Wallace. In the end the Alabaman took only 8.4 percent of the national vote, mostly in the South. Humphrey also won back the support of some on the antiwar left when he belatedly broke with Johnson's war policy and pledged to halt the bombing of North Vietnam. But Nixon and his vice-presidential running mate Spiro Agnew, the governor of Maryland, squeaked through in November 1968, capturing the White House with but 43 percent of the popular vote. (The Republican ticket took 56 percent of the electoral college vote.)

The Nixon Administration

Richard Nixon's tepid mandate set the stage for drama on the foreign policy stage. Nixon's program was to diffuse Vietnam as a domestic political issue in order to give his administration more political space in which to maneuver, both at home and abroad. Like Johnson, Nixon believed that rapid, unilateral withdrawal of American support from South Vietnam would lead to the domino-like fall of all Southeast Asia to the Communists. His "peace plan" therefore turned out to mean a "Vietnamization" of the war: a slow reduction in the combat role played by U.S. troops, accompanied by the more active engagement of the South Vietnamese military, an intensification of the U.S. air war, and dramatic incursions into neighboring Cambodia and Laos.

The political contradictions inherent in this policy were demonstrated in May 1970, when U.S. troops invaded Cambodia. In response to this unexpected escalation, hundreds of American college campuses erupted in the most massive, disruptive set of antiwar demonstrations of the entire Vietnam era. At Kent State University in Ohio four undergraduates were killed when the National Guard fired rifles into a crowd at an antiwar rally, and at Jackson State University in Mississippi police killed two more students. As hundreds of thousands of antiwar demonstrators converged on Washington, the Nixon administration was forced to announce that U.S. ground troops would be withdrawn from Cambodia within a few weeks. Shortly thereafter, an angry Democratic-controlled Senate repealed the Gulf of Tonkin Resolution and forbade the further use of American troops in Laos or Cambodia.

U.S. troop levels and battle deaths thereafter declined. From a peak of 540,000 in 1969, the number of U.S. soldiers stationed in Vietnam dwindled to about 60,000 three years later. A new lottery system made the draft more equitable, even as the emergence of a smaller, all-volunteer military virtually eliminated the Selective Service System itself. Meanwhile, there were plenty of high-profile political figures, inside and outside the Democratic party, who now championed the demand for immediate U.S. withdrawal, a sentiment once associated only with the most radical New Leftists. After 1971, there were no major antiwar demonstrations in the United States.

Nixon's search for a politically acceptable end to the Vietnam War also led his administration to seek the cooperation of China and the Soviet

Union in brokering a peace settlement and in reducing tensions among the great powers. Advised by the brilliant but devious Henry Kissinger, who headed Nixon's National Security Council, the president sought a balance-of-power "detente" with these erstwhile enemies. When he visited "Red" China in February 1972, Nixon seemed to repudiate twenty-five years of American hostility, demonstrating that the nation's Cold War posture was just that, a politically motivated manipulation of popular sentiment and elite self-interest. The U.S. rapprochement with China soon led to a new set of arms and trade agreements with the Soviet Union, which feared a Chinese–American alliance. The Strategic Arms Limitation Treaty, signed by Nixon and Soviet premier Leonid Brezhnev in a May 1972 Moscow ceremony, did little to slow the qualitative escalation of the arms race, but the agreement itself, which limited the total number of missiles and bombers, ratified elite accommodation, on both sides of the Iron Curtain, to the geopolitical status quo.

Despite the cordiality in Beijing and Moscow, Nixon could not find "peace with honor" in Vietnam, even after years of negotiations with the North Vietnamese in Paris. When Henry Kissinger announced that "peace is at hand" in a 1972 election-eve press conference, America's Vietnamese allies in Saigon objected to any agreement that left Communist troops in the South. Nixon and Kissinger sought to break this stalemate in December with a massive B-52 bombing campaign that for the first time targeted Hanoi itself; but little changed, and when the Paris peace accords were finally signed early in 1973, the North Vietnamese military advantage remained intact. The United States did win release of several hundred airmen who had spent years in North Vietnamese prison camps; and the Hanoi government waited two years before launching its war-winning military offensive in the South. By that time the South Vietnamese no longer had the will to fight, and Congress refused to authorize further bombing or funding for the Vietnamese war effort. As Communist tanks rumbled into Saigon late in April 1975, U.S. officials and their Vietnamese civilian supporters left in humiliating disarray, many in helicopters from the rooftop of the American embassy.

Like John F. Kennedy, Nixon thought domestic policy making full of second-rate issues, which helps explain the contradictory character of many of his domestic initiatives. Nixon did have one overriding goal, however: to build a Republican majority by winning to a new conservative coalition the white South, heretofore Democratic, and the national constituency energized by George Wallace. Toward this end, Nixon pursued a "southern strategy" that downplayed desegregation of schools and jobs, sought a more conservative tilt to the Supreme Court, cut back Great Society social programs, and demonized both the New Left and Democratic party liberals. Nixon appealed to what he called "the silent majority," seeking a curb on government activism and a return of spending power to the business and political elites that were so influential at the state and local level.

Nixon's strategy would eventually prove a political success, but during most of his first term it was a policy failure. The Senate refused to confirm Nixon's first two nominees to the Supreme Court: both Clement Haynsworth and G. Harold Carswell were southern conservatives tainted by a segregationist past. And Nixon could not stop the rapid, court-ordered desegregation of southern schools. The president did succeed in abolishing the Johnson-era Office of Economic Opportunity, and for a time he "impounded" other funds Congress had already appropriated, but the Democrats saved most of the Great Society social programs. The Nixon administration escalated the government's clandestine war against New Left activists, but government prosecution of prominent radicals such as Benjamin Spock, Jerry Rubin, and Tom Hayden ended in acquittal or mistrial.

Nixon appointed four mainstream conservatives to the Supreme Court, including Warren Burger, who replaced Earl Warren in 1969. But the Burger Court continued much of Warren's activist tradition, especially on racial matters. In *Alexander* v. *Holmes* (1969) the Supreme Court unanimously decreed that it was the "the obligation of every school district to terminate dual school systems at once." It strengthened this ruling in *Swann* v. *Charlotte-Mecklenburg Board of Education* (1971) by ruling in favor of the use of busing to achieve racial balance in the schools. For a majority of African-American schoolchildren in the South, integration was finally becoming a reality.

The Burger Court also struck a blow against discrimination in hiring and promotions when it decreed in *Griggs* v. *Duke Power* (1971) that employment tests and standards that had a "disparate impact" on blacks and other minorities were inherently racist. Henceforth, employers could protect themselves against charges of discrimination only by showing a statistical parity between the racial composition of their workforce and that of the local population. Finally, in *Roe* v. *Wade* (1973) the Burger Court helped push forward a social revolution by declaring that a woman's right to privacy invalidated most state laws forbidding abortions.

Because social and economic liberalism remained powerful during the early 1970s, Nixon often accommodated himself to this ideological current if he thought it politically advantageous. He approved congressional efforts to boost spending for Medicaid, food stamps, and Aid to Families with Dependent Children; he also signed the costly legislation that indexed Social Security to inflation and brought the indigent aged, blind, and disabled into the system. Nixon even supported a Family Assis-

"Zap FAP!" As part of the campaign against the Nixon administration's Family Assistance Plan, a National Welfare Rights Organization poster shows the limited daily diet supported by the welfare reform proposal. The complicated and controversial reform plan would have provided federal assistance to states and cities to relieve the burden of rising welfare expenses. Many critics argued, however, that FAP's real aim was to cut welfare rolls.
Source: Madeleine Adamson.

tance Plan (FAP), drafted by the liberal social theorist Daniel Patrick Moynihan, that would have replaced AFDC with a guaranteed annual income for all poor families. A political crossfire soon doomed the plan: liberals thought the benefit levels were too low and objected to the requirement that some recipients work, while conservatives denounced the Family Assistance Plan as another government giveaway.

More successfully, Nixon linked the interests of the Republican party to elements of the urban civil rights community to make himself the father of the nation's much-debated affirmative action initiative. Late in 1969 the federal government endorsed the "Philadelphia Plan," which required construction unions in Philadelphia employed on government contracts to set up "goals and timetables" for the hiring of black apprentices. Within a year, this mechanism was incorporated into regulations governing all federal hiring and contracting, thereby covering more than a third of the entire national labor force. Affirmative action programs were politically advantageous to Nixon. They appealed to middle-class African Americans, cost practically nothing, and exacerbated tensions between unions and blacks, both of which were core constituencies of the Democratic party.

The Environmental Movement

Whatever the merits of Nixon's clever statecraft, American politics, culture, and social expectations still bore the democratic imprint of "the Sixties." The giant Woodstock rock festival of August 1969 and massive antiwar protests in November 1969 and May 1970 demonstrated that a self-conscious youth culture and a new capacity for political mobilization had spread far beyond the campuses that had first spawned radical thought and action.

The environmental movement, which overnight became a major political force in the 1970s, was an offspring of this new participatory political culture. Ecological awareness had its roots in the early-twentieth-century conservation impulse that had helped establish the national park system. However, this movement had dwindled during the midcentury decades when depression, war, and the rush to suburbia absorbed so much energy and imagination. By the 1960s, however, the growth of America's high-consumption, "throwaway" economy had begun to generate a new environmental awareness, especially among many affluent suburban whites. During the 1950s and 1960s the California-based Sierra Club transformed itself from a hiking group into an influential national organization that blocked the construction of new dams on several western rivers; and in 1962 Rachel Carson's *Silent Spring* aroused widespread public concern about the effect of insecticides, such as DDT, on the everyday environment. Then, in early 1969, a major oil spill off the coast of Santa Barbara hit the evening news, with dramatic film of thousands of dead seabirds and blackened coastal beaches.

President Nixon signed legislation setting up the Environmental Protection Agency early in 1970. But environmental consciousness truly became a national preoccupation three months later, on April 22, 1970, when hundreds of thousands of Americans participated in a set of "Earth Day" demonstrations. In the words of the naturalist René Dubos, Americans now shared the widespread conviction that "Gross National Product and technological efficiency are less important than the quality of the organic world and the suitability of the environment for a truly human life."

The environmental movement borrowed direct-action tactics from the New Left and resonated with the back-to-nature ethic of the counterculture. Ecology groups held sit-ins and demonstrations; Chicago activists dumped sludge and garbage in the executive suite of a polluting company. But most environmental activists shunned such confrontations in favor of either local politics or effective lobbying in Washington. In the 1970s environmental activism played a large role in blocking new freeway construction, development of a noisy supersonic transport plane, and the spread of nuclear power. For many, this new movement rechanneled some of the passions that had once been aroused by opposition to the Vietnam War. "We are beginning to realize," wrote one group of activists, "that our life-styles, our industries, and our population growth are leading to the extinction of more and more species, to the poisoning of our air, water, and food, and to the exhaustion of resources on earth. This growing destruction threatens the continued existence of the human species."

Although environmentalists and unionists often clashed over industrial regulation issues and infrastructure construction in the 1970s, millions of workers also became increasingly conscious of their right to a safe and healthy workplace environment. The industrial boom of the 1960s and early 1970s pushed industrial accident rates and health problems up nearly 50 percent, as managers urged workers and machines to

. . . And the Breathing *Isn't* Easy. A cloud of dust containing harmful crystalline silica envelopes a plumber sawing a concrete floor.

Source: Mine Safety and Health Administration.

the limits of their capacities. By 1970 the Labor Department estimated that 2.2 million workers were disabled each year from job-related health problems, proportionately far more than in western Europe or Japan.

Before the early 1970s, neither workers nor their unions had made health and safety top issues. "In the past," noted one labor official, "the union practice . . . was to trade and barter its safety and health demands for a couple of cents an hour in wages." For many workers, a combination of fatalism and masculine stoicism had forestalled earlier action on safety and health issues. "When it came to safety, the older guys would say 'If you die, you die,' " recalled one construction worker. For other workers, including utility linemen and hard-rock miners, the dangers of the work sustained their pride in the skill needed to do the job. But these sentiments changed in the 1960s, especially when it came to dangers generated by chemicals and air pollution. Male workers could find little "manliness" in being exposed to lead and mercury poisoning, asbestos, cotton and coal dust, pesticides, and radiation.

In the late 1960s, unions in steel, coal, and oil pressured Congress for health and safety laws. In response, Congress passed the 1970 Occupational Safety and Health Act (OSHA), which created a new set of workplace rights and, like the U.S. Supreme Court's 1954 *Brown* v. *Board of Education* decision, helping legitimize a grass-roots struggle. Although OSHA had many limitations, including a cumbersome regulatory mandate, it did offer union activists a new tool with which to assert employee rights to a healthy workplace. At the Olin Corporation's Film Division works in North Carolina, unionist James Reese used his chairmanship of the plant safety committee to confront management over the safe use of many chemicals. Proudly, he memorized the OSHA standards for each. "For once," he explained, "I had something that they had to listen to. I finally had a law to back me up."

More than a thousand miles away, Karen Silkwood felt the same. The new consciousness about safety issues motivated her to become a union activist for the Oil, Chemical, and Atomic Workers' Union (OCAW) at Kerr-McGee's plutonium-processing plant in Oklahoma. Silkwood had never taken much interest in activism until she discovered that Kerr-McGee policies often exposed her and her fellow workers to radioactive hazards. Her death in a mysterious auto accident followed months of harassment at the hands of company personnel. Silkwood became a martyr for the growing safety and health movement; her story dramatized a new social issue.

Industrialists were caught unaware when OSHA became law, but once they saw how it empowered workers, they lobbied Congress for cuts in inspection funds, exemptions for small firms, and delays in implementation of health standards. Governmental action to assure safe working conditions proved to be dependent on the extent to which workers in each industry forcefully pressed their claims. In the coal fields, where the respiratory disease known as black lung disabled thousands of miners each year, a dynamic movement led by miners, antipoverty activists, and liberal doctors forced Congress to establish the Mine Safety and Health Administration, better funded and more sympathetic to workers than OSHA; accident rates in the coal fields declined sharply. In contrast, workers in the largely nonunion textile industry gained little from OSHA. Their employers, contemptuous of the claim that brown lung, a respiratory disease similar to black lung, was a serious malady, were able to dominate the debate over health and safety in the mills. OSHA failed in its efforts to force the industry to reduce factory cotton dust, and brown lung went largely uncompensated by insurance companies and local workers' compensation boards.

Pluralism in American Life

Since the New Deal era, cultural pluralism in the United States had been an important element of the country's unofficial creed, but in the early 1970s a multicultural sense of the nation's ethnic and racial diversity took on a far more tangible reality. These were the years in which black studies programs spread in many institutions of higher learning, helping to pave the way for new attention to Hispanic and Indian culture and heritage, as well as providing a template for renewed interest in women's studies as well.

In the 1960s and 1970s, Hispanic Americans were the fastest-growing minority group in the United States, about 5 percent of the population. Miami housed more Cubans than any other city except Havana, and more Mexicans lived in Los Angeles than in any other urban place except the Mexican capital. The Miami Cubans—middle-class, entrepreneurial, and intensely anti-Communist—were among the most politically and culturally conservative of all Americans, but many Puerto Ricans and Mexican Americans, especially the youth, had been inspired by the American civil rights movement and the farmworkers' struggle.

In the spring of 1968, Chicano students in Los Angeles and other cities held a series of school boycotts, or "blowouts." Poor-quality education was a key issue for the whole community, according to participant Carlos Vasquez. "Chicano students became radicalized," he recalled, "when they asked, 'Why are our schools the way they are?' " The student protests spurred a broader movement seeking increased power for the Mexican-American community and an end to social, economic, and political discrimination.

Meanwhile, across the continent, in Chicago and New York City, a similar movement emerged in the Puerto Rican community. There the catalyst was the Young Lords, an organization that drew members from urban street gangs as well as from college campuses. According to Pablo Guzman, a New York Young Lords leader, "We tapped an intense nationalistic fervor among Puerto Rican people. In this way we were able to cut across all ages and types and reach a broad segment of the population."

The pluralistic effervescence of this era also encouraged a movement among American Indians. By the 1960s Indian life had reached a crisis: life expectancy was twenty years below that of the national average, unemployment was ten times higher, and suicide among Indian youth had reached epidemic proportions. But the rights-conscious spirit of the 1960s brought signs that Indians would no longer suffer in silence. They sought not only good jobs and federal antipoverty aid but also recognition that they constituted a separate people with a distinctive cultural and legal claim to their heritage and land.

In 1964, the Puyallup in the state of Washington held "fish-ins" to protest state court decisions that denied them their treaty-guaranteed fishing rights. Then in the spring of 1969, the Navajo and Hopi attacked Peabody Coal Company mining operations in the Southwest, complaining, as one Navajo tribal elder put it, that "Peabody's monsters are digging up the heart of the earth, our sacred mountain, and we also feel the pain." Indian protests of this sort made their first high-profile impact late in 1969 when a group of seventy-eight Indians, calling themselves "Indians of All Tribes," occupied Alcatraz island in San Francisco Bay, turning the site of a notorious federal prison into "liberated" territory for some eighteen months.

Wounded Knee, South Dakota, 1973. An American Indian Movement activist rejoices after hearing that the federal government has agreed to a cease-fire and negotiations at the Pine Ridge Reservation in South Dakota. The three-month confrontation between AIM and federal marshals began in February 1973 when AIM seized hostages at a reservation trading post to dramatize their protest against Bureau of Indian Affairs policy and conservative tribal leadership.

Source: UPI/Corbis-Bettmann.

An even more dramatic confrontation came in 1973, when three hundred Oglala Sioux seized the town of Wounded Knee in South Dakota, where the U.S. cavalry had massacred hundreds of Indians in 1890. These militant, youthful American Indian Movement (AIM) activists demanded a democratization of reservation governance and U.S. adherence to long-forgotten treaty obligations. Scores of heavily armed FBI agents lay siege, but Indian activists held out for seventy-one days before agreeing to a cease-fire and a court trial of the principal leaders. The occupations at Alcatraz and Wounded Knee provided an ideologically charged backdrop to a wave of Indian lawsuits that reestablished land claims and tribal institutions from Maine to Alaska. By the 1980s, Indian poverty was still widespread, but no one doubted their claim to cultural and political recognition in a multicultural America.

The Women's Movement

The women's movement was by far the largest and most influential of all the social movements of the early 1970s, for it touched almost every fiber of American life. The stunning rebirth of American feminism emerged in part from the New Left's probing of the political dimension of personal life. As an ideology and a social movement, feminism had flourished in the years before World War I and faded in the 1920s and 1930s; it was reborn in the late 1960s as a result of the merger between the self-emancipatory impulse of the New Left and the political agenda long put forward by an older generation of women reformers.

Beginning in the late 1950s, a small group of well-placed American women sought to achieve equality between the sexes in much the same way that the NAACP used the courts and Congress to fight racial discrimination. Prodded by such veteran liberals as Eleanor Roosevelt, President Kennedy appointed a Commission on the Status of Women in 1961, but women's issues won popular notice only with the 1963 publication of Betty Friedan's best-selling book *The Feminine Mystique*.

Friedan's commitment to women's rights had been shaped during her decade of left-wing union activism in the 1940s, but now she offered an even broader critique of women's status at home and at work. According to Friedan, a "feminine mystique" stifled millions of women whose suburban imprisonment unnaturally deprived them of creativity, careers, and their very humanity. In the early 1960s few liberals felt passionate about ending gender inequality. Most partisans of the 1964 Civil Rights Act thought the ban on sex discrimination was inserted into the proposed law merely as a conservative ploy to divide civil rights advocates. In 1966, Friedan and twenty-seven other professional women established the National Organization for Women (NOW) "to take action to bring American women into full participation in the mainstream of American society now." Inspired by the African-American civil rights movement, NOW prodded the federal government to actually enforce the ban on sex discrimination in employment and public accommodations included in the 1964 Civil Rights Act.

The feminist impulse might have remained confined to these relatively elite women had their ideas not been given a dynamic moral vision and intense personal meaning by the explosion of feminist consciousness within the New Left. Young women had joined the political movements of the 1960s with fervor and dedication. But many were dismayed to discover that their male comrades did not think of them as equals. At SDS meetings, remembered one participant, "Women made peanut butter sandwiches, waited on tables, cleaned up, got laid. That was their role." This gap between radical vision and discriminatory practice drove tens of thousands of young women out of the antiwar and student movements. Bringing with them skills, networks, tactics, and a language for describing their oppression, these young women built an explosive and ultimately massive movement for women's liberation. As one woman remembered, "In the black movement I had been fighting someone else's oppression. Now there was a way I could fight for my own freedom, and I was going to be much stronger than I ever was."

Flowering in the early 1970s and continuing to grow throughout the decade, the women's movement then sent shock waves into every recess of American society. NOW membership multiplied rapidly; and *Ms.* magazine, which first appeared in 1971, sold out its first 300,000 copies in little more than a week. Hundreds of thousands of women took part in consciousness-raising (CR) groups, where they discussed every aspect of their lives, ranging from discrimination on the job, to the destructive results of competition over men, to failed sexual relationships with boyfriends and husbands.

CR. A consciousness-raising group at the New York Women's Center in December 1970.

Source: Bettye Lane, 1970.

These groups served as springboards for action. Feminists argued that not only should men share in the responsibilities of childrearing but that government should fund a universal system of child-care centers. Likewise, women demanded wage parity. In 1968, women's pay averaged less than 60 percent that of men. And because of systematic discrimination, fewer than 10 percent of the nation's doctors, lawyers, college

". . . Personal Problems are Political Problems"

Consciousness-raising (CR) groups, a common feature of the women's liberation movement, helped women discover the social roots of their individual problems. These quotations suggest the diverse ways that different CR groups grappled with the link between the personal and the political. The first quotation is from a woman talking in 1970 about her ongoing group. The other statements were made by women in the 1980s, recalling their experiences in the late 1960s and early 1970s.

Carol H: So the reason I participate in these meetings is not to solve any personal problem. One of the first things we discover in these groups is that personal problems are political problems. There are no personal solutions at this time. There is only collective action for a collective solution. I went, and I continue to go to these meetings because I have gotten a political understanding which all my reading, all my "political discussions," all my "political action," all my four-odd years in the movement never gave me. . . . I believe at this point, and maybe for a long time to come, that these analytical sessions are a form of political action. . . .

Arlene S.: Our group was very different, nonpolitical. Other groups seemed to have a harshness to them. The message was you had to move forward, you had to deal with issues. There was a sense of confrontation and judgment. Our group, I feel, accomplished so much more, but in a different way. We just talked about ourselves, and it was very warm.

Frances H.: It was a time of tremendous turmoil. And I think the turmoil may have preceded our understanding of what was really going on. It was like being a little boat on a rocky sea, and you think it's your fault that you are rocking the boat. But in fact you are on this tremendously disturbed social ocean. So that's how I think of CR now. We were this little boat battering around, having our conversations, but, now, as I look back, in fact, I see a much larger panorama.

Abby T.: When I first joined consciousness-raising, I was aware of its being part of large political ferment. There were the civil rights movement, the assassinations, the antiwar stuff, the SDS organizations on campus. The Women's Movement just seemed to flow out of all of this, and so right from the beginning I thought of it as political.

Phyllis F.: We perpetuate sexism until we become conscious of the part that we play. That's what women's groups were meant to do because they were really well thought out. They were actually political groups. They really got me. You know, if you said politics to me back then, I would have left the room. I came from the dead 1950s, and I didn't know from radical politics. But in the group, they just said, well, the personal is political. Just work on yourself, that's politics. Okay, I could deal with that. And you know, it works. Not immediately that minute, maybe, but over time. There are battered women's shelters and rape crisis services across the state of New York that did not exist in the early 1970s. These came out of CR groups.

Source: Anita Shreve, *Women Together, Women Alone: The Legacy of the Consciousness-Raising Movement* (1989).

professors, business executives, and architects were women in 1970. Feminists used petitions, picketing, and legal action to push employers to increase wages and open upper-level jobs to women. The Women's Equity Action League brought class-action suits against nearly 300 colleges and universities, forcing them to agree to change their employment and admission policies. One woman physician confronted a male colleague who had publicly disparaged the capacity of women to perform difficult surgery. "I said, 'Doctor, I want to watch you work. I want to see what part of your anatomy you use in performing surgery that I am not equipped with.' "

The new feminists also acted to change the ways in which women were perceived and represented in American culture. In August 1968, a group of women startled the nation by disrupting the Miss America pageant, charging that beauty contests encouraged the notion that women were merely objects for men's sexual pleasure. Believing that language was crucial to the formation of attitudes, feminists attacked the use of such demeaning labels as "chicks" and urged women who married to keep their own surnames as symbols of their individuality. Feminists challenged television producers to begin portraying women in a more diverse and realistic fashion, and they pushed newspapers and magazines to address women's social and economic concerns. Arguing that traditional scholarship ignored women, feminist authors wrote women back into American history and demanded an end to gender stereotyping in educational materials.

Health care was another major area of concern to feminists. They charged that medical schools excluded women and taught male doctors to treat women patients condescendingly. As a result, feminists felt, women were often pushed into unnecessary hysterectomies, radical breast surgery, and cesarean childbirth. Activists sought the reform of medical education as well as the creation of independent health care clinics run by and for women.

Feminists frequently linked their health care reform efforts to the campaign for the legalization of abortion. Before 1970, this procedure was illegal in virtually every state in the country. Women seeking to end unwanted pregnancies were forced to seek out illegal abortions or to self-induce miscarriages; thousands of women died each year as the result of botched operations. Arguing that a woman had a right to "control her own body," feminists mounted abortion rights rallies and joined population-control advocates in lobbying state legislatures for more liberal legislation. They made slow, state-by-state progress until 1973, when the U.S. Supreme Court's landmark *Roe* v. *Wade* decision guaranteed women access to abortions in the early stages of pregnancy.

The women's movement was highly controversial, and many Americans resisted both the concrete reforms its activists demanded and the feminist ideology that stood behind them. But most polls in the early 1970s recorded a steady shift in public opinion toward feminist positions on such issues as pay equity, child care, and abortion. By 1976, the conservative *Reader's Digest* conceded: "Women's Liberation has changed the lives of many Americans and the ways they look at family, job and sexual equality." Even those who rejected feminism embraced the transformations it had wrought. As one secretary put it, "I'm no women's libber, but I believe women should get equal pay." Millions of women office workers helped transform the work culture: they refused to serve coffee, wore slacks to work, insisted on being addressed as an adult, and demanded the right to promotions and better pay.

The feminist challenge to traditional sex roles also encouraged the growth of the gay and lesbian rights movement. Throughout the postwar years most gay men and women had kept their sexual orientation secret, fearful of job loss or public humiliation if they openly acknowledged it. But a dramatic change took place following a riot between New York City Police and gay patrons of the Stonewall Inn in June 1969. Immediately, homosexual men raised the demand for "Gay Power," consciously linking their struggle for dignity and sexual freedom with that of African Americans and other "oppressed minorities." Much the same dynamic took hold among lesbians. Some feminists endorsed sexual relationships with women, hoping they would be less oppressive and more fulfilling than relationships with men. Many lesbians who had long hidden or denied their sexual orientation found that the women's movement provided them with a broader community in which they could openly profess their sexuality. Gay men and women denied that homosexuality was a crime or a sickness and moved aggressively into the open, holding marches, pushing for legislation to end decades of bias and discrimination, and calling for "gay liberation." The effort paid off: in 1973 the American Psychiatric Association ended its classification of homosexuality as a mental disorder, and by

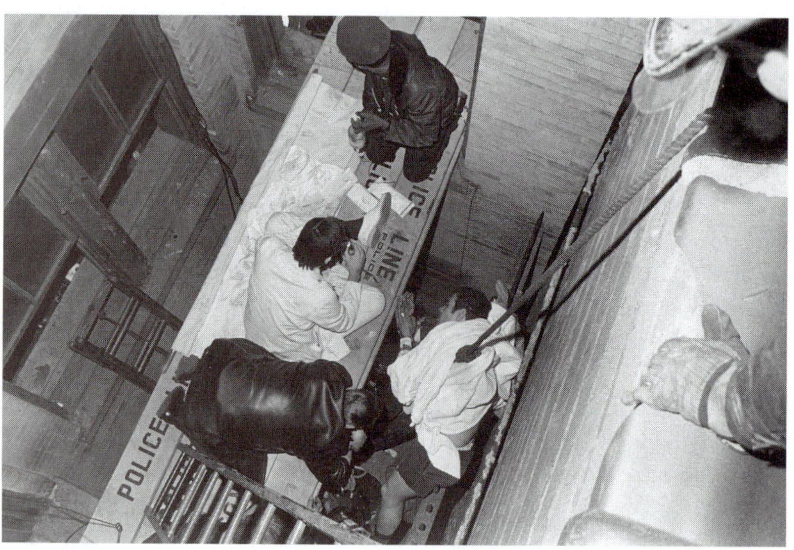

After Stonewall I. In the months following the June 1969 Stonewall Rebellion, New York police continued to raid bars where lesbians and gay men gathered. In the early morning hours of March 9, 1970, police raided the Snake Pit, a Greenwich Village bar, arresting all 167 employees and patrons. After the "suspects" were taken to a local stationhouse, Alfredo Vinales, an illegal alien afraid of being deported if his homosexuality was discovered, tried to escape. After leaping from a second-floor window, he was impaled on an iron picket fence.

Source: Frank Giorandino, New York *Daily News,* March 9, 1970.

After Stonewall II. Vinales's act of desperation graphically articulated the oppression of gays. "No matter how you look at it," as one gay activist slogan went, "Vinales was pushed." The horror of the Snake Pit incident helped mobilize hundreds of gays to join the new movement. In June 1970, the first march commemorating the anniversary of the Stonewall Rebellion was organized—an event now observed every June by hundreds of thousands of gays and lesbians around the world.

Source: Bettye Lane, August 20, 1977.

the mid 1970s a slight majority of Americans opposed job discrimination based on sexual orientation.

Militancy and Dissention in the Labor Movement

American unions had many things going for them in the 1960s. The AFL-CIO had a cordial relationship with Presidents Kennedy and Johnson, and its leaders supported the Great Society programs of the mid 1960s and the occupational health and safety legislation of the early 1970s. The unions enjoyed the longest era of sustained high employment since World War II. Protected by cost-of-living adjustments written into their contracts, many blue-collar workers won real wage increases even in the inflationary years after 1966. Most big unions won employer-funded health insurance, higher pensions, and increased vacation pay.

At the same time, a democratic sensibility surged through the nation's factories. Workers sought respect, equality, and a sense of workplace citizenship from their employers. "The worker wants the same rights he has on the street after he walks in the plant door," asserted Jim Babbs, a twenty-four-year-old white worker at a Ford plant outside Detroit. "This is a general feeling of this generation, whether it's a guy in a plant or a student on campus, not wanting to be an IBM number."

Union leaders faced a rebellious rank and file. Contract rejections, a rarity before 1962, soared after 1965; unauthorized wildcat strikes reached a postwar high. In the steelworkers', miners', teachers', and postal employees' unions, top union leaders who seemed too complacent failed to be reelected. Between 1961 and 1973, every national auto contract signed by the UAW generated at least a score of local strikes by workers determined to humanize conditions.

This new working-class mood had its greatest impact among public employees, especially those who worked for the 80,000 units of state and local government. Before World War II, public employment meant secure, high-status jobs, often reserved for those with close ties to the city machine or the local ethnic political club. But by the 1960s, civil service employees' wages had fallen well behind those of organized labor, while overcrowded classrooms, deteriorating public transit systems, and teeming welfare offices reduced the quality of public employees' work life. Public employees therefore unionized rapidly and sometimes struck. Their work stoppages grew nearly tenfold in the decade after 1965. Because many of these strikes were illegal, public-sector unionism had the feel of an underground movement, a consciousness-changing social crusade. In Hamtramck, Michigan, in 1965, junior high school teachers defied state law and staged a twenty-four-hour-a-day "prolonged teachers' meeting" to force the local school board to recognize their union. Leaders of the American Federation of Teachers frequently courted arrest and jail during their still-illegal strikes in the 1960s.

The most startling expression of the new militancy erupted in the postal system in March 1970, when 200,000 workers struck urban post offices across the North and West. Postal employees had once been mostly older white males, but by the late 1960s the number of blacks and white females had risen, and many mail carriers were young "hippies" with shaggy hair. As the Post Office Department mechanized, many of the half-million postal workers bridled under the factory-like discipline. When postal workers walked out, their strike amounted to a revolt—not only against their employer, the federal government, but also against their own union leaders, who had long functioned largely as Capitol Hill lobbyists. President Nixon countered by sending troops to sort the mail, but the strike succeeded in forcing Congress to raise wages and reorganize the postal system.

Despite growing worker militancy, the labor movement did not hold its own in the 1960s. Though unions recruited 2 million additional members in the decade, largely in public-sector employment, the proportion of all workers who belonged to unions declined from 29 percent in 1960 to 23 percent fifteen years later. The unions failed to grow because they were unable to link their fortunes to the dynamic social movements that had emerged in those years. On the two great issues of the 1960s—race and Vietnam—unions stood divided and hesitant. While some organizations, such as Hospital Workers Local 1199 and the United Farm Workers, took advantage of the idealism and energy of the New Left and the civil rights movement, no major trade union leader was prepared to give 1960s-era radicals the kind of backing Communists and Socialists had enjoyed in the 1930s when John L. Lewis put some of them in high-profile CIO jobs.

Indeed, when it came to civil rights, unions were as much a part of the problem as they were part of the solution. Since the 1940s, the trade union movement had been the most integrated major institution in American life, and in the early 1960s, black and minority workers made up about a quarter of total union membership. The AFL-CIO forbade discrimination in its new constitution and worked hard to pass civil rights laws, but the federation lacked the will to combat racial discrimination within its own affiliates, many of which excluded minority workers. AFL-CIO head George Meany disliked socially disruptive civil rights demonstrations, including the 1963 March on Washington. And he resented efforts by A. Philip Randolph of the Sleeping Car Porters to organize a black caucus within the AFL-CIO. "Who the hell appointed you the guardian of all the Negroes in America?" Meany once shouted at the venerable civil rights leader.

Throughout the civil rights era, craft unions in the construction trades, which limited membership tightly, remained almost all-white. "We don't take any new members, regardless of color," asserted one building trades leader. When apprenticeships did open up, many construction workers felt union cards should go to their sons and relatives as a sort of patrimony, much like a family-run business. Such exclusionary practices were naturally offensive to urban African Americans, who often saw white workers from the suburbs earning good pay on construction projects just a few blocks from the ghetto. Though the Nixon administration's Philadelphia Plan targeted discriminatory recruitment patterns among these craft unions, it proved relatively ineffective because a recession in the early 1970s cut employment and intensified job competition between whites and blacks.

School's Open, But . . . A Brooklyn public school classroom during the 1968 New York City teachers strike.
Source: AP/Wide World Photos.

Racial tensions were not confined just to the traditionally conservative wing of the union movement. An even more ominous conflict emerged in 1968 as the New York City local of the American Federation of Teachers (AFT) fought a decentralization plan that offered parents a limited form of community control of the schools. The AFT claimed that some local school boards were dominated by black nationalists hostile to Jewish teachers and that the new plan would give these activists the power to ignore seniority rights and grievance procedures. Community-control advocates, on the other hand, argued that the AFT was unwilling to share power with African-American and Puerto Rican parents and their increasingly assertive leaders. This bitter conflict, which began in the Ocean Hill–Brownsville school district in Brooklyn, generated four strikes in the fall of 1968 and drove a wedge between groups that had long been allies in the fight against discrimination.

Even the UAW, whose progressive leaders put money and muscle behind the civil rights movement, found itself at odds with black activists. By the early 1960s, 200,000 African-American workers made up more than a fifth of total UAW membership. They were confined largely to the most grueling work in the most dangerous and dirty departments. Encouraged by A. Philip Randolph and the burgeoning civil rights struggle, black activists, many veteran union organizers from the 1930s and 1940s, fought Walter Reuther and other white UAW leaders for more blacks in high union office, a more vigorous union fight against workplace racism, and political power in Detroit. But UAW pioneers of both races were surprised by the explosion of black nationalism and workplace militancy that swept Detroit factories in the aftermath of the city's 1967 riot. When young African-American workers, organized into groups such as the Dodge Revolutionary Union Movement (DRUM), briefly shut down several inner-city plants, UAW secretary-treasurer Emil Mazey, once a fiery union militant, branded the dissidents "black fascists." Tension declined only after the auto corporations rushed hundreds of African Americans into the supervisory ranks, the UAW hired more black staff, and the recessionary layoffs of the early 1970s purged Motown factories of some of their most militant workers.

Vietnam proved just as problematic an issue for the labor movement as race. Under the leadership of George Meany, the AFL-CIO steadfastly defended U.S. conduct of the war, even after business leaders had begun to waver. Calling opponents of the war a "coalition of retreat," Meany used secret files supplied by the FBI to discredit antiwar activists in the union movement. The AFL-CIO also received millions of dollars from the U.S. government, some from the Central Intelligence Agency (CIA), to undermine Asian, African, and Latin American trade unions that appeared to be anti-American or Communist-led. In Guyana, Brazil, and Chile, the AFL-CIO cooperated with the CIA to topple populist political leaders the U.S. government considered hostile to its interests. In Vietnam, it worked with the U.S. military to make sure supplies flowed smoothly over the Saigon docks.

Not all union leaders supported the Vietnam War. In traditionally liberal unions such as the UAW, the Packinghouse Workers' Union, Local 1199, and the American Federation of State, County and Municipal Employees, union officials criticized the war and Meany's hawkish politics. In New York, San Francisco, and Los Angeles, local unions participated in mass antiwar marches; and in 1968 Walter Reuther, who had grown frustrated with Meany's knee-jerk anti-Communism, pulled the UAW out of the AFL-CIO. With the Teamsters, the UAW formed the Alliance for Labor Action (ALA), which Reuther hoped would "revitalize" the labor movement. But the ALA disintegrated in the early 1970s, after the Teamsters raided the Ceasar Chavez's United Farm Workers in California and endorsed President Nixon for reelection in 1972.

Political Polarization

Conflict between the social movements of the 1960s and organized labor was not confined to top-level disputes over foreign policy or civil rights legislation. In his 1968 campaign, George Wallace demonstrated the extent to which white working-class discontent with high taxes, declining neighborhoods, black militancy, and student radicalism could be turned toward a populism of the Right. In the years that followed, most workers remained liberals when it came to such welfare-state programs as Social Security, unemployment compensation, AFDC, and job training, and they grew increasingly hostile to the war, as polls and referendums demonstrated. But on other social issues of the era—affirmative action, school busing to achieve racial balance, a woman's right to an abortion, and the rejection of the traditional symbols of American patriotism—white working-class men grew increasingly willing to attack the New Left and its allies.

This became clear in New York City on May 8, 1970. Antiwar demonstrators had gathered at a federal building near Wall Street to protest the U.S. invasion of Cambodia. Suddenly a shining wave of yellow and orange surged through the crowd. A contingent of 200 construction workers wearing bright plastic hard hats and armed with pliers and hammers pounced on the "longhairs." To the chant of "All the way with the USA," the hard hats roughly elbowed the young protesters aside and returned the flag, lowered to half mast in homage to the four antiwar students just slain at Kent State University, back to full height.

Although the hard-hat demonstration had been carefully orchestrated by the White House and the conservative leaders of the New York building trades, it created a new social stereotype: the tough, pro-war, blue-collar worker; a hardworking taxpayer hostile to blacks on welfare; a family man who spurned marijuana and the liberation of women. The hard hats seemed to stand for working-class anger and resentment against all the social changes and political innovations of the 1960s. When officials of the construction trades presented Nixon with an honorary hard hat, the latter described the gift "as a symbol, along with our great flag, for freedom and patriotism to our beloved country."

The popular TV comedy series *All in the Family* captured this mood. Centered on the character of Archie Bunker, a gruff and opinionated white warehouse foreman from Queens, the show broadcast the language of racial and political insult. Caught in a world he had not made, Archie lashed out against the forces of change, revealing an undisguised hatred for imagined enemies. "If your spics [Hispanics] and spades [African Americans] want their rightful share of the American dream," Archie told his liberal son-in-law, "let 'em go and hustle for it just like I done." *All in the Family* had been created by the liberal producer Norman Lear to poke fun at what he saw as blue-collar parochialism, but its popularity partially reflected the genuine anger that existed within sections of the white working class.

Yet Archie Bunker was more myth than reality. In the early 1970s, white workers were not the reactionaries portrayed on television. On the issue of the Vietnam War, for example, opinion polls indicated that rank-and-file workers were substantially less hawkish than the college-educated. "The whole goddamn country of South Vietnam is not worth the life of one American boy," declared a construction worker, "no matter what the hell our politicians tell us."

But precisely because a disproportionate number of working-class men were drafted and sent to Vietnam, blue-collar Americans resented the college students who led antiwar protests. At issue was not a difference over foreign policy, but class antagonism. Working-class opponents of the Vietnam War hated antiwar demonstrators even more than they disliked the war. One worker whose son was serving in Vietnam lamented the inability of poorer boys to "get the same breaks as the college kids. We can't understand how all of those rich kids—the kids with beards from the fancy suburbs—how they get off when my son has to go over there and maybe get his head shot off."

The women's liberation movement sparked similar patterns of reaction and resentment. Many Americans, male and female, felt threatened by the renewal of the women's movement and its challenge to cherished traditional values. Though increasing numbers of women were entering the paid labor force, most held routine jobs that offered few psychic or emotional rewards. To many such women, the role of mother in the traditional family seemed more likely to provide a sense of security and dignity. Seeing "women's libbers" as privileged professionals, many working-class women interpreted feminist criticism of traditional women's roles as a threat to their own sense of self-worth. President Nixon appealed to this antifeminist reaction in 1971 when he vetoed federal support for day-care centers, arguing that they would undermine the nation's "family centered traditions" and "commit the vast moral authority of the national government to . . . communal approaches to childrearing."

This new attack on social liberalism and New Left radicalism bolstered support for a conservative movement that had been growing for several years. While the 1960s are generally remembered as a decade in which left-wing activism characterized the political commitments of a whole generation, ultraconservative groups such as Young Americans for Freedom and the John Birch Society had begun to recruit many ardent followers well before the rise of the New Left. Their hostility was directed toward the entire legacy of the New Deal, and they thought even John F. Kennedy and Richard Nixon insufficiently anti-Communist. As early as 1961, for example, the Young Americans for Freedom drew more than 3,000 to a New York rally that celebrated anti-union employers, conservative intellectuals, and congressmen whose efforts to eliminate Communist influence in government and the professions had never flagged. Despite his loss in the 1964 presidential election, Barry Goldwater remained a conservative icon, but many conservative activists transferred their loyalty to actor Ronald Reagan, who was elected governor of California in 1966. His denunciations of New Left students and environmental activists won him an enthusiastic following.

President Nixon drew on the energy of all streams of conservatism in his 1972 reelection campaign. His acerbic vice president, Spiro Agnew, targeted radicals, hippies, black activists, and welfare mothers as the causes of America's problems. Nixon himself conducted a "Rose Garden" campaign, emphasizing his personal commitment to world peace and stability. Nixon's opponent was Senator George McGovern of South Dakota, a staunch liberal who urged the nation to "come home" from Vietnam. But the Democratic campaign proved inept and disorganized. The AFL-CIO refused to endorse McGovern because of his dovishness on the war in Indochina; and McGovern wounded his own credibility when he cut his running mate, Senator Thomas Eagleton of Missouri, from the ticket when it became known that Eagleton had undergone electrical shock treatments for an emotional disturbance. Meanwhile, Nixon won the allegiance of many former supporters of George Wallace, whose candidacy ended when a would-be assassin paralyzed and nearly killed him in May 1972. Nixon easily won reelection with more than 60 percent of the popular vote, including many southerners and blue-collar workers who normally voted Democratic.

The Watergate Crisis

Nixon's reelection seemed to mark the consolidation of conservative power. But his second term unraveled quickly as the constitutional crisis known as "Watergate" ignited public passion and consumed administration energy. The stunning, precipitous fall of Richard Nixon was a product of both grand politics and personal failure. The origins of the crisis, which forced a sitting president from office for the first time in American history, were threefold: the rapid growth of unfettered presidential power during the Cold War era; the polarization of the political process that arose out of the debate over the Vietnam war; and the secretive, resentful character of Richard Nixon himself.

Like so many presidents before him—Truman, Eisenhower, Kennedy, and Johnson—Richard Nixon claimed that in the interest of national security, the White House had the right to take extraordinary action against its opponents. Thus, during his first term Nixon had not only escalated covert police activity against black and antiwar activists but had also begun using government spies against an "enemies list" of elite journalists, Democrats, and even some dovish Republicans. This mentality soon saturated Nixon's own Committee to Reelect the President, which took in millions of dollars in illegal contributions and funded a variety of "dirty tricks" designed to sabotage the election effort of their Democratic opponents.

The June 1972 break-in at the Watergate offices of the Democratic National Committee was one of many such actions; this time, however, a security guard caught the intruders, two of whom had been White House security consultants. Nixon's press secretary dismissed the break-in as a "third-rate burglary attempt," but the subsequent effort by the White House to cover up these illegal activities proved Nixon's undoing. "Play it tough," Nixon ordered top aide H. R. Haldeman right after news of the Watergate break-in became public. "That's the way they play it, and that's the way we are going to play it." Nixon arranged to pay the burglars almost $500,000 in hush money from secret reelection committee funds. And the president tried to get the CIA to stop an FBI investigation of the affair. This was clearly illegal, a deliberate obstruction of justice.

The Nixon White House successfully managed the Watergate scandal all through the 1972 campaign, but the cover-up unwound rapidly in 1973. John Sirica, a tough federal judge, was unwilling to let justice stop

"I Am Not a Crook." In 1973, as the Watergate scandal grew, political cartoonist Edward Sorel likened the Nixon administration to a band of trapped gangsters.

Source: *Ramparts,* August-September 1973—Edward Sorel.

with jail terms for a handful of low-level operatives. Meanwhile, a press corps—led by Bob Woodward and Carl Bernstein, two young *Washington Post* reporters—grown suspicious of presidential power during the Vietnam years doggedly pursued the Watergate money trail back to Nixon's reelection committee and his top White House aides.

In the spring and summer of 1973, televised hearings by a select Senate investigating committee revealed the White House role in an ever-expanding network of deceit and unconstitutional governance. Nixon fired Haldeman and other top Oval Office aides in a vain effort to purge the White House of officials tainted by the Watergate cover-up, but Nixon's own criminality soon became the central focus of the Senate probe, especially after the stunning news, in July 1973, that the president himself had ordered the secret taping of all conversations that took place in the Oval Office. By the autumn of 1973, all concerned—Sirica, the Senate investigating committee, and Archibald Cox, a Harvard Law School professor Nixon had been forced to appoint as an independent special prosecutor—were battling Nixon and his lawyers for release of these incriminating presidential conversations.

In October 1973, the White House lost virtually all moral credibility. Vice President Agnew unexpectedly resigned when evidence surfaced that he had accepted bribes and kickbacks while serving as governor of Maryland and as vice president. He was replaced by Michigan congressman Gerald Ford. Meanwhile, an investigation of Nixon's own financial affairs revealed a set of criminal irregularities in his tax returns. Then on the night of October 20, Nixon fired Cox, but only after the president's own two top Justice Department appointees had resigned in protest. A firestorm of protest at this "Saturday Night Massacre" forced Nixon to appoint a new independent prosecutor, Leon Jaworski, who proved just as tough as Cox.

Congressional sentiment, public opinion, and the federal courts now turned steadily against Nixon. When the president himself released a heavily edited version of the White House tapes late in April 1974, they proved embarrassing because in many passages his lawyers had inserted the phrase "expletives deleted." In July a unanimous Supreme Court forced the release of all the tapes, including a devastating conversation of June 23, 1972, in which Nixon ordered his aides to obstruct an FBI investigation of the break-in. Faced with certain congressional impeachment for "high crimes and misdemeanors," Nixon resigned the presidency on August 7, 1974. Although the new president, Gerald Ford, soon pardoned Nixon, twenty-five other members of his administration, including several top advisers and the attorney general, served time in prison.

Nixon's downfall marks an end to the long "Sixties." The nation's drift toward what historian Arthur Schlesinger called an "imperial presidency" did moderate because the memory of Watergate put in place a set of sturdy warning signals against greater centralization of executive power. Likewise, even after the fragmentation of the civil rights movement and the New Left, the experience of the 1960s left in place a far greater sense of rights consciousness than had existed at any time during the previous century. In law and in practice, at work and at play, for women and men, and among white, brown, and black, the U.S. could never go back to the unexamined assumptions that had governed social intercourse and workplace hierarchy in the 1950s and the years before. A new freedom had been enshrined not only in the civil rights laws of the 1960s but in the pervasive transformation of American political culture itself. But rights consciousness is not an abstraction: it must have a very concrete social and economic foundation. In the coming decades, the greatest threat to American liberties would come not from an overweening executive or racial bigots but from an economic earthquake that was reshaping the world of work, both at home and around the globe.

The Years in Review

1954

- *Brown* v. *Board of Education:* U.S. Supreme Court declares segregated public schools unconstitutional.

1955

- Refusing to give up her seat to a white rider, Rosa Parks sparks a thirteen-month-long bus boycott in Montgomery, Alabama.

1956

- Elvis Presley appears on Ed Sullivan Show.
- Martin Luther King founds Southern Christian Leadership Council.

1957

- U.S. Army paratroopers sent to Little Rock, Arkansas, to enforce desegregation of Central High School.

1958

- Liberal Democrats win big in Congressional Elections.

1959

- Fidel Castro takes control of Cuba from corrupt U.S.-supported dictator Fulgencio Batista.

1960

- Four black college students demand service at a Woolworth lunch counter in Greensboro, North Carolina, and initiate a wave of sit-ins throughout the South.
- Democrat John F. Kennedy defeats Vice President Richard Nixon in presidential election.

1961

- Congress of Racial Equality (CORE) organizes a series of "Freedom Rides" to test the desegregation of southern bus terminals.
- CIA organizes an invasion of Cuba in an attempt to overthrow Fidel Castro.
- East German Communists erect a concrete wall across Berlin in effort to stop the flow of refugees to the West.

1962

- Cuban missile crisis: After U.S. blockade of Cuba and threatened air attack, Soviet premier Nikita Khrushchev agrees to remove Soviet missiles.
- New Left organization Students for a Democratic Society (SDS) founded.
- Publication of Rachel Carson's *Silent Spring* arouses widespread concern about the use of insecticides.

1963

- Betty Friedan's *The Feminine Mystique* becomes a best-seller and brings women's issues to public notice.
- "March on Washington for Jobs and Freedom" mobilizes nearly a quarter-million people; there Martin Luther King, Jr., delivers "I have a dream" speech.
- John F. Kennedy assassinated in Dallas, Texas. Lyndon Johnson becomes new president.

1964

- Freedom Summer campaign mobilizes hundreds of northern student volunteers to help register black voters in Mississippi.
- Lyndon Johnson defeats conservative Republican Barry Goldwater by a record margin in presidential election. Democrats sweep congressional elections.
- Civil Rights Act passes, ending segregation in all public accommodations.
- Congress passes Tonkin Gulf Resolution, giving President Johnson a blank check to expand the war in Vietnam.
- Free-Speech Movement (FSM) organized at the University of California campus in Berkeley.
- English rock-and-roll sensation, the Beatles, tour United States.
- President Lyndon Johnson declares War on Poverty.

1965

- Voting Rights Act passes Congress, ending most barriers to African-American voting in the Southern states.
- Congress enacts Medicare and the following year establishes Medicaid.
- New Immigration Act eliminates the racist quota system that had favored northern European immigrants since the 1920s.
- Malcolm X assassinated.
- United Farm Workers, led by Ceasar Chavez, organize a five-year protest and boycott against California grape growers.

1966

- Betty Friedan and other feminists found the National Organization for Women (NOW).

1968

- U.S. troops murder more than 350 Vietnamese villagers in My Lai massacre.
- NLF's Tet Offensive convinces Americans that the Vietnam War is at a stalemate.
- President Johnson announces that he will stop bombing North Vietnam, cancel a planned troop increase, and end his reelection campaign.
- James Earl Ray assassinates Martin Luther King, Jr.
- Sirhan Sirhan asassinates Robert Kennedy.
- Republican Richard Nixon defeats Vice President Hubert Humphrey and third-party candidate George Wallace to become president.

- Young Indians found American Indian Movement.

1969

- Woodstock rock festival.
- Stonewall Riot launches gay liberation movement.

1970

- U.S. troops invade Cambodia, sparking massive antiwar demonstrations, which result in deaths at Kent State and Jackson State universities.
- First "Earth Day."

1971

- President Nixon imposes wage and price controls to staunch accelerating inflation.

1972

- President Nixon visits Communist China.
- Security guard apprehends intruders at the Democratic National Committee offices in the Watergate complex. President Nixon and other White House officials attempt to cover up the burglary and other illegal activities.

1973

- Paris peace accords signed, ending much direct U.S. involvement in Vietnam War. American POWs return home.
- *Roe* v. *Wade:* U.S. Supreme Court rules that women have right to abortion.
- Three hundred Oglala Sioux seize the town of Wounded Knee, South Dakota, and resist an FBI siege for seventy-one days.

1974

- President Nixon resigns the presidency.

1975

- North Vietnamese regular troops capture Saigon. U.S. officials and Vietnamese civilian supporters flee in helicopters from roof of U.S. embassy. Led by Pol Pot, Khmer Rouge seize all of Cambodia.

Suggested Readings

Andrew, John A., *The Other Side of the Sixties: Young Americans for Freedom and the Rise of Conservative Politics* (1997).

Appy, Christian G., *Working-Class War: American Combat Soldiers in Vietnam* (1993).

Baritz, Loren, *Backfire: A History of How American Culture Led Us into Vietnam and Made Us Fight the Way We Did* (1998).

Branch, Taylor, *Parting the Waters: America in the King Years, 1954–1963* (1989).

Blight, James G., and David A. Welch, *On the Brink: Americans and Soviets Reexamine the Cuban Missile Crisis* (1990).
Brenes, Wini, *Community and Organization in the New Left, 1962–1968: The Great Refusal* (1989).
Carson, Clayborne, *In Struggle: SNCC and the Black Awakening of the 1960s* (1995).
Carter, Dan T., *The Politics of Rage: George Wallace, the Origins of the New Conservatism, and the Transformation of American Politics* (1996).
Chester, Lewis, Godfrey Hodgson, and Bruce Page, *An American Melodrama: The Presidential Campaign of 1968* (1969).
D'Emilio, John, *Sexual Politics, Sexual Communities: The Making of a Homosexual Minority in the United States, 1940–1970* (1998).
Dickstein, Morris, *Gates of Eden: American Culture in the Sixties* (1997).
Dittmer, John, *Local People: The Struggle for Civil Rights in Mississippi* (1994).
Echols, Alice, *Daring to Be Bad: Radical Feminism in America 1967–1975* (1990).
Evans, Sarah, *Personal Politics: The Roots of Women's Liberation in the Civil Rights Movement and the New Left* (1980).
Fink, Leon, and Brian Greenberg, *Upheaval in the Quiet Zone: A History of Hospital Workers' Union, Local 1199* (1989).
Garrow, David, *Bearing the Cross: Martin Luther King, Jr., and the Southern Christian Leadership Conference* (1999).
Garrow, David J., *Liberty and Sexuality: The Right to Privacy and the Making of* Roe *v.* Wade (1998).
Gitlin, Todd, *The Sixties: Years of Hope, Days of Rage* (1993).
Goldman, Peter Louis, *The Death and Life of Malcolm X* (1979).
Graham, Hugh Davis, *The Civil Rights Era: Origins and Development of National Policy, 1960–1972* (1990).
Harrison, Cynthia, *On Account of Sex: The Politics of Women's Issues, 1945–1968* (1989).
Hays, Samuel P., *Beauty, Health, and Permanence: Environmental Politics in the United States, 1955–1985* (1989).
Hoff, Joan, *Nixon Reconsidered* (1995).
Isserman, Maurice and Michael Kazin, *America Divided: The Civil War of the 1960s* (1999).
Kutler, Stanely I., *Wars of Watergate: The Last Crisis of Richard Nixon* (1992).
Lemann, Nicholas, *The Promised Land: The Great Black Migration and How It Changed America* (1992).
Levy, Peter B., *The New Left and Labor in the 1960s* (1994).
Lichtenstein, Nelson, *Walter Reuther: The Most Dangerous Man in Detroit* (1997).
Matusow, Allen J., *The Unraveling of America: A History of Liberalism in the 1960s* (1984).
McAdam, Doug, *Freedom Summer* (1990).
McDougall, Walter A., *The Heavens and the Earth: A Political History of the Space Age* (1997).
Miller, James, *"Democracy Is in the Streets": From Port Huron to the Siege of Chicago* (1994).
Patterson, James T., *America's Struggle Against Poverty 1900–1994* (1995).

Posner, Gerald, *Case Closed: Lee Harvey Oswald and the Assassination of JFK* (1994).
Powers, Thomas, *Vietnam: The War at Home, Vietnam and the American People 1964–1968* (1973).
Reeves, Richard, *President Kennedy: Profile of Power* (1994).
Rieder, Jonathan, *Canarsie: The Jews and Italians of Brooklyn Against Liberalism* (1987).
Schandler, Herbert, *The Unmaking of a President: Lyndon Johnson and Vietnam* (1977).
Schlesinger, Arthur Meier, Jr., *Robert Kennedy and His Times* (1996).
Scott, Daryl Michael, *Contempt and Pity: Social Policy and the Image of the Damaged Black Psyche, 1880–1996* (1997).
Shawcross, William, *Sideshow: Kissinger, Nixon, and the Destruction of Cambodia* (1987).
Sheehan, Neil, *A Bright Shining Lie: John Paul Vann and America in Vietnam* (1989).
Stein, Judith, *Running Steel, Running America: Race, Economic Policy, and the Decline of Liberalism* (1998).
Terry, Wallace, ed., *Bloods: An Oral History of the Vietnam War by Black Veterans* (1992).
Wilkinson, J. Harvie, *From "Brown" to "Bakke": The Supreme Court and School Integration, 1954–1978* (1979).
Young, Marilyn B., *The Vietnam Wars, 1945–1990* (1991).

And on the World Wide Web

The Digital Scriptorium, Rare Book, Manuscript, and Special Collections Library, Duke University, *Documents from the Women's Liberation Movement* (http://scriptorium.lib.duke.edu/wlm/).
National Archives, *When Nixon Met Elvis* (http://www.nara.gov/exhall/nixonelvis/).

chapter 13

Economic Adversity Transforms the Nation

1973–1989

Like his father before him, Steve Szumilyas worked at Wisconsin Steel on Chicago's Southeast Side. At 4 p.m. on Friday, March 28, 1980, he was checking steel slabs before they went into the reheating furnace when his foreman came by with news that would shatter his world. The gates were being locked at the end of the shift; the mill was going down; 3,400 steel-workers were out of a job. Szumilyas was on the street. Had it not been for his wife's new job, his family would have lost their suburban home. Steve Szumilyas would work again, but at only half the wages he earned in basic steel.

Szumilyas's layoff would prove symptomatic of an era. "Nobody," wrote *Time* magazine "is apt to look back on the 1970s as the good old days." This was a decade in which American society was being transformed by forces most people could neither control nor understand. It was an era of growing insecurity in which the world economy turned sour and unpredictable. After a quarter-century of rapid growth, wages, productivity, and output dropped sharply in all of the great industrial nations. Recessions became more severe and more frequent, while unemployment rose to double the average level of the immediate postwar years. This economic turmoil seemed to discredit government activism and traditional liberalism, thus paving the way for conservative Ronald Reagan's election to the presidency in 1980.

Pornography Hearings. Attorney General Edwin Meese's Commission on Pornography was appointed during Ronald Reagan's second presidential term to appease conservative and fundamentalist supporters who felt the "Reagan Revolution" had not sufficiently altered the nation's social agenda. During 1985 and 1986, public hearings were held in six U.S. cities, featuring testimony of anonymous witnesses who claimed to be "victims" of pornography as well as displays of sexually explicit pictures and films. The hearings focused on visual images to support otherwise unsubstantiated arguments about the harmful effects of pornography—and sexual behavior in general.

Source: U.S. Department of Justice.

End of the Postwar Boom

In the United States, the growth in the efficiency of the economy—what economists call productivity—dropped like a stone. Over the next quarter-century, economic growth would continue, but at an annual rate of about 2 percent—far lower than during the twenty-five years after World War II. Meanwhile, West Germany and Japan, once vanquished on the military battlefield, would forge ahead, competing successfully for the American market in steel, autos, machine tools, and electrical products. In the United States, the value of imported manufactured goods nearly tripled, from less than 14 percent of domestic production in 1970 to nearly 40 percent in 1979.

Die American. Many Americans believed the end of the postwar boom in U.S. industry was caused by Asian competition and blamed the Japanese in particular for "stealing" American jobs. Anti-Asian sentiments were expressed in U.S. trade union publicity campaigns urging consumers to "buy American," and some frustrated workers resorted to violence against Asian Americans. One of the most prominent cases occurred in 1982 in Highland Park, Michigan, when Vincent Chin, a Chinese American, was beaten to death with a baseball bat. Chin's autoworker assailants were sentenced to probation and mild fines.

Source: *Detroit News.*

With inflation levels soaring—reaching a high of more than 18 percent in one year—and the unemployment rate rarely below 7 percent, the decade after 1973 brought the postwar boom in the United States to an unsettling end. Indeed, for two full decades, from the early 1970s to the early 1990s, real wages stagnated for most Americans, and for young males they actually dropped by 25 percent. At the end of these two decades a freshly minted male college graduate could look forward to earning only slightly more each year than a typical high school graduate of the previous generation. Family income increased during these decades of slow growth, but this was largely because Americans were working longer hours and because women and teenagers were more likely to hold a paying job. Meanwhile, income inequalities widened dramatically. Top corporate executives had earned about 20 times as much as ordinary workers in the 1960s; thirty years later, the multiplier was an astounding 115 times.

What accounted for this new era of economic hard times and social inequality? To begin with, the Vietnam War's spiraling costs had set off the first of several great waves of inflation, which soon made U.S. products more expensive than those of its other countries. In 1971, monies paid to foreign producers for imported goods exceeded those paid for U.S. exports: the first time in the twentieth century that the nation had registered a balance-of-payments deficit. Consequently, the United States could no longer maintain the dollar as the world's currency standard, so in August 1971 President Nixon had allowed the value of a dollar to "float"—to go up or down in relationship to the price of gold and to other currencies according to the world's shifting economic and political currents. In effect, Nixon had devalued the dollar, which made U.S. exports cheaper but imports more expensive. Oil was one import that soon became much more costly. In October 1973, in the midst of a war between Israel and its Arab neighbors, Arab oil producers declared an embargo on oil shipments to the United States and Western Europe. The Organization of Petroleum Exporting Countries (OPEC) manipulated the resulting shortage to raise prices from $3 to $12 a barrel. Just five years later, after a revolution in Iran toppled the pro-Western monarch, oil prices peaked at $34 a barrel.

Although many economists and pundits thought the oil shortage signaled the onset of a worldwide drop in the production of fossil fuels, the energy crisis of the 1970s was actually a political phenomenon, reflecting in the marketplace the U.S. defeat in Vietnam and the subsequent shift in power from Western consumer countries to the Latin American and Mid-

The Post-War Boom Slows: Median Family Income, 1947–1997 Family income increased dramatically in the first quarter century after World War II. Thereafter, family income grew much more slowly and would have actually declined had not more wives and teenagers entered the workforce.

Source: Lawrence Mishel, Jared Benstein, and John Schmitt, *The State of Working America, 1998–99* (1999).

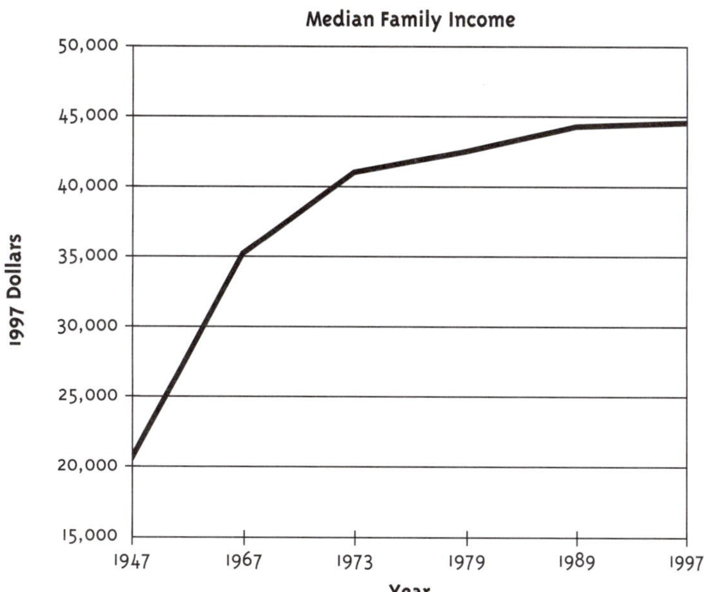

dle Eastern states that controlled OPEC and other producer cartels. In 1974, the disruption of energy supplies and the dramatic rise in the price of oil led to federally mandated gasoline rationing. To conserve fuel, Congress also decreed a nationwide speed limit of 55 miles per hour. Panicky motorists lined up at gas stations to buy a commodity most had taken for granted only weeks before. Conservation measures, new oil-field discoveries, and a reassertion of Western economic power would end the worldwide energy crisis about a decade later, but while the oil shortage lasted Americans began to feel increasingly insecure, hostage to economic forces well beyond their control.

As the oil "shock" reverberated through the U.S. economy, the rising price of gas and oil forced many energy-reliant industries to close. American consumers, fearing the worst, drastically reduced their purchases of gas-guzzling, U.S.-made automobiles, as well as other American manufactured goods. In 1974 alone, factory output fell 10 percent and unemployment nearly doubled. Inflation rose into the double digits, eroding the value of pensions and paychecks. Economists coined a new term—"stagflation"—to describe this unusual mix of economic problems: low levels of economic growth, high unemployment, *and* persistent inflation. Overnight, Americans became far more pessimistic. "You always used to think in this country that there would be bad times followed by good times," commented a Chicago housewife. "Now, maybe it's bad times followed by hard times followed by harder times." Federal Reserve Chairman Arthur F. Burns did not disagree. "Inflation at anything like the

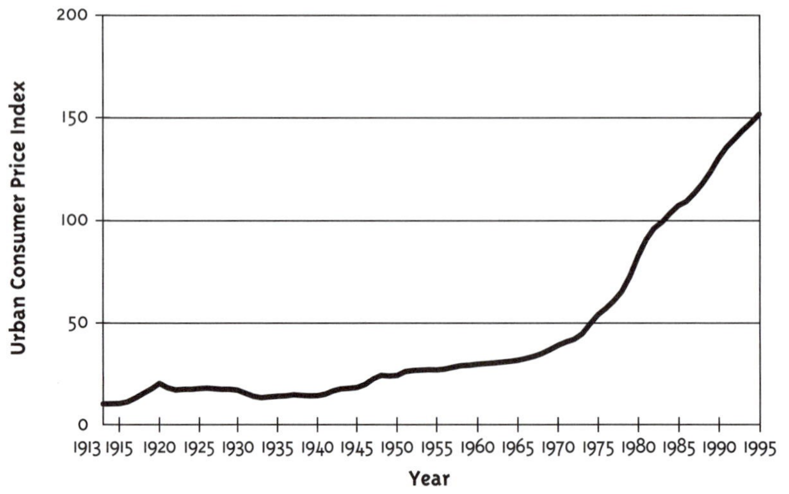

The Higher Cost of Living: Twentieth Century Inflation In the twentieth century, prices leaped upward during and after major wars—World War I, World II, and Vietnam. Post-Vietnam inflation was made worse by a world-wide increase in the price of oil, wheat, and other major commodities.

present rate would threaten the very foundations of our society," the head of the nation's central bank warned in May 1974.

Higher oil prices and growing competition from foreign producers would have been less of a problem had not thirty years of Cold War militarization distorted key sectors of the U.S. economy. Encouraged by huge government procurement contracts, American businesses—especially electronics and aviation—had focused their capital resources and technological know-how on producing armaments. Nearly one of every two federal dollars expended in the 1950s went to the military. Such massive spending provided employment for large numbers of defense workers in the postwar years. But ultimately the nation's huge military budget—on a proportionate basis twice as great as Germany's and seven times that of Japan—sapped America's productive strength, diverting resources from the development of commercially competitive products.

Worse, the expertise that developed sophisticated, high-tech military products was not readily transferable to the increasingly competitive consumer market. One writer noted that while American electronics manufacturers were engrossed in building " 'smart bombs,' people sniffers, and other warlike wizardry," they lost their ability to produce televisions, stereos, and videocassette recorders. For example, during the 1960s managers at the venerable Singer Sewing Machine Company, whose product had stood for Yankee ingenuity in every hamlet from Spain to Surinam, focused corporate research efforts on missile and warplane guidance systems. Singer's share of the world sewing machine market spiraled downward when the company failed to retool its U.S. factories and lost its reputation for high-quality production. Sewing machines from Sweden and Korea took over the American market, forcing Singer to close its flagship New Jersey factory in 1979. By the 1980s, Singer sewing machines were made only in Hong Kong.

Finally, a legacy of the 1960s, the growing sense of "rights consciousness" in the workplace, created legal and regulatory difficulties for many U.S. companies. Workplace safety and health as well as the equitable treatment of white women and African Americans, became inflammatory issues during the 1970s. A new feminist consciousness in the workplace helped generate laws and court decisions covering areas of interpersonal relations and employer–employee contact once considered exclusively private. The Equal Employment Opportunity Commission received more than 100,000 complaints per year. After much debate and protest throughout the 1970s and 1980s, Congress finally enacted the Americans with Disabilities Act in 1990 and the Family and Medical Leave Act in 1993, both of which prohibited employers from discriminating against their employees because of physical incapacity or absence from work because of childbirth or family emergency. Thus, the hiring, pay, promotion, and layoff of employees became subject to governmental review and private litigation to an extent unmatched even during the heyday of the union movement three decades earlier.

No Nukes. Many activists opposed to the proliferation of nuclear weapons and nuclear power facilities used direct-action tactics to forestall the building of reactors. On May Day 1977, thousands of demonstrators affiliated with the Clamshell Alliance blocked construction of a nuclear plant in Seabrook, New Hampshire. Almost 1,500 were arrested and jailed in armories around the state. After two weeks, the armories were still filled because many demonstrators refused to leave until all "clams" were unconditionally released. Governor Meldrin Thompson, who had hoped to stem protest with mass arrests, relented, releasing them all.

Source: Ellen Shub/ Impact Visuals

The ecological consciousness that had emerged after 1970 also demonstrated the extent to which a sense of democratic empowerment had transformed the corporate economy. Until the early 1970s, nuclear power had seemed the embodiment of technological progress, national security, and economic efficiency. Powerful, authoritative supporters in Congress, industry, and science argued that "the mighty atom" would end U.S. dependence on foreign oil and dirty coal. But commercial nuclear power was neither as safe nor as cheap as its advocates claimed, and some "experts", radicalized by the Vietnam War, defected from the pro-nuclear consensus. Thus, when thousands of anti-nuclear protestors took to the streets in the late 1970s, numerous engineers and scientists bolstered the credibility of this new social movement. Hollywood amplified this nuclear skepticism in *The China Syndrome* and *Silkwood,* which warned of the potential for a catastrophic accident involving radioactive material. Dramatic confirmation of such fears came in 1979 when a near-meltdown at Pennsylvania's Three Mile Island utility near Harrisburg forced the evacuation of 100,000 people. Radioactive contamination outside the facility seemed slight, but the actual cleanup of the reactor proved a time-consuming, billion-dollar project. Soon after the incident at Three Mile Island, thirty energy companies canceled plans to build nuclear reactors. The demise of the U.S. nuclear power industry was sealed in 1986 when a genuine meltdown at the Soviet Union's Chernobyl nuclear reactor killed scores of workers and spread radioactive fallout over a wide swath of the Ukraine.

The New Shape of American Business

With economic hard times in the offing, many conservatives in the business community and politics argued that the nation would have to shift resources from labor to capital and cut back the environmental programs and regulatory laws that investors and industrialists thought burdensome. Thus *Business Week* editorialized in 1974, right after the first oil shock: "it will be a hard pill for many Americans to swallow—the idea of doing with less so that big business can have more." American corporations did face a profit squeeze in the 1970s. Earnings were down one-third from those of the previous two decades; in manufacturing, they were only about one-half what they had been. Although an excess of managers, the growth in foreign competition, and the rise in energy prices accounted for the lion's share of the difficulties, the new rights-conscious activism proved highly visible and vexing. In the decade that ended in 1975, Congress had passed more than twenty-five major pieces of regulatory legislation that required 40,000 new federal workers to administer. In response, corporations stepped up their efforts to influence government decisions, increasing fivefold their lobbying operations in the nation's capital. Naturally, all this activity required more lawyers, whose presence in Washington doubled during the 1970s.

Corporations sought to resolve their problems largely by driving down their costs: by cutting wages, acting to reduce their taxes, and attempting to end the governmental regulations they found most burdensome. For generations, American firms had periodically moved their factories from one state to another to take advantage of low wages and cheap land. In the 1920s, for example, New England textile manufacturers had transferred their mills to the South. In the 1970s, this trend accelerated as firms moved out of the Northeast and into the Sunbelt, a broad crescent stretching south from Virginia to Florida and west through Texas and southern California. Federally funded superhighways and more efficient telecommunications linked this vast region to the population centers of the North and enabled firms to build a new archipelago of small, highly efficient factories and warehouses. Generous tax incentives encouraged the move, and the introduction of air-conditioning made the region more suitable to office work. Finally, the massive influx of Latin American and Southeast Asian workers into Florida, Texas, and California offered corporations an even larger pool of cheap, Sunbelt labor.

The South, including Texas, gained more than a million manufacturing jobs during the 1970s, while the Northeast and Midwest lost nearly 2 million. By the 1980s, formerly rural North Carolina had the highest percentage of manufacturing workers of any state. It also had the lowest blue-collar wages and the lowest unionization rate in the country. But the North lost more than manufacturing jobs. The computerization of clerical work made it possible for large financial service firms such as Merrill Lynch, American Express, and Citibank to shift many operations to the South and the West. According to the *Wall Street Journal,* these companies targeted "low-cost Sun Belt areas for future growth, such as industrial companies did decades ago when they moved from the Northeast to the South. They seek places where labor, land, electricity and taxes are cheap."

If jobs could be moved to Texas, they could also be shifted to Mexico, Taiwan, and Indonesia. Until the 1960s, U.S. investment in Latin America and the Pacific basin had focused largely on the extraction and processing of raw materials mined or grown in those regions. But beginning in the 1970s, a number of American firms began producing some of their most sophisticated components in low-wage foreign factories. Between 1971 and 1976, manufacturers of color TVs shifted more than 90 percent of their subassembly production to Asia. Similarly, the Ford Motor Company chose to build its most advanced automobile manufacturing complex in Hermosillo, Mexico. Such foreign "outsourcing" of high-value goods and parts sustained the profitability of many "American" product lines. But in the long run, such policies eroded the U.S. manufacturing base and the technical expertise of its workers, managers, and engineers.

The conservative economist Joseph Schumpeter once described capitalism as a system of "creative destruction" in which a powerful set of technological and organizational winds continually reshape the business landscape. The fates of two great companies exemplify this phenomenon. General Motors remained the largest manufacturing company in the world through the last third of the twentieth century. But from the 1970s onward, the corporation's failure to build fuel-efficient or stylish cars cost it more than 15 percent of the entire U.S. automobile market. And because of its cumbersome, hierarchical bureaucracy, GM, which had once been the most cost-efficient of all automobile firms, now lagged behind both foreign rivals and U.S. competitors. In response, GM managers closed more than twenty factories and outsourced billions of dollars in parts production to low-wage firms in the American South and Mexico. As a result, the corporation's blue-collar payroll fell by half, devastating once bustling centers of GM production such as Flint and Pontiac in Michigan.

The rise of the retailing giant Wal-Mart exemplified the job shift from manufacturing to services and from high-wage northern cities to the low-wage Sunbelt countryside. At the end of the 1980s, Wal-Mart was the nation's leading retailer, a firm whose payroll was second in size only to the U.S. Post Office. When Sam Walton founded it early in the 1960s, this pint-sized, Arkansas-based retailer had been dwarfed by Sears, Woolworth, and other long-established chains that dominated the big cities and their nearby suburbs. But with the completion of the interstate highway system and the growth of exurban communities in the Sunbelt, the big shopping centers lost much of their convenience and appeal. Walton therefore located his stores in the once-neglected small-town hinterlands, especially in the South and Midwest, where land was cheap, labor nonunion, and competition limited. Although Walton gave his firm a "just folks," small-town image, Wal-Mart was among the most sophisticated of global corporations, importing huge quantities of clothing and household goods from fifty countries. Managers used the latest computer technology to track sales, minimize inventory expenses, and squeeze suppliers. Wal-Mart's success made the Walton family multibillionaires, but the company's rapid growth bankrupted thousands of independent merchants whose viability had sustained Main Street life throughout small-town America.

Stagflation Politics: From Nixon to Carter

As corporate concerns moved to the center of American politics, the liberal statecraft that had once animated the New Deal and the Great Society became unworkable. With global trade now such an important determinant of the nation's economic well-being, efforts to apply the fiscal remedies of the economist John Maynard Keynes—increasing taxes and government spending to dampen inflation, boost employment, and encourage business investment—proved increasingly ineffective. During the inflationary 1970s, taxes, government spending, and the federal budget deficit—the gap between income and spending—rose higher each year, but the problem-solving capacity of the federal government seemed to falter. For example, the policy of spending to end an economic slump, which liberal economists of the 1960s had seen as a remedy for high unemployment, proved politically unattractive a decade later when such federal budget deficits also stoked the inflationary fires.

Of the three presidents who sought to revive the fortunes of American capitalism during the 1970s, Republican Richard Nixon was actually the most "liberal." During his administration Congress passed, and the president signed, laws indexing Social Security benefits to inflation, extending unemployment benefits, and regulating oil and gas prices during the first energy crunch. Declaring himself a "Keynesian," Nixon also used government power to directly attack both inflation and the growing trade imbalance. In August 1971, for example, when the Nixon administration devalued the dollar, it also froze wages and prices and raised the tariff on foreign cars. This "New Economic Policy" (NEP) was designed to keep a lid on pay increases and rein in organized labor, but it also sought to avoid the kind of massive unemployment and high interest rates that a later generation of more conservative policy makers would routinely adopt as the orthodox anti-inflation remedy.

President Nixon's economic activism gave him enough inflation-free breathing space to win the 1972 election, but his NEP proved unequal to the profound shifts transforming the world economy. When U.S. price controls were eliminated in 1973, the cost of living rocketed upward, fueled by sharp increases in the prices of grain, oil, lumber, and other internationally traded commodities. Nixon's successors never again sought to regulate the market or avoid unemployment in such a forthright manner. Vice President Gerald Ford had the misfortune to move into the Oval Office in August 1974, just weeks before the nation plunged into the deepest recession since the Great Depression itself. As production declined by more than 10 percent in 1974 and 1975, nearly a tenth of the workforce became unemployed. Ford's unimaginative, passive response reminded many of the kind of economic conservatism that had last prevailed in the White House during the 1920s. Ford vetoed most congressional efforts to increase countercyclical spending on education, jobs, and infrastructure construction. His rhetorical "Whip Inflation Now" campaign, which involved distributing tens of thousands of WIN buttons, proved a flop.

Ford's conservatism became apparent in 1975 when he confronted a budget crisis in New York City. The metropolis was in trouble for the same reason as the nation: the city's traditional industrial base—garment manufacturing, printing, and electrical products—had shrunk, but New York remained a mecca for low-wage, unskilled immigrants and migrants from the U.S. South, the Caribbean, Latin America, and Asia. At the same time, New York's vigorous union movement, especially strong in the public sector, managed to sustain a relatively generous level of wages and benefits. This financial squeeze forced the city to borrow heavily against future revenues and later seek outside loan guarantees. When Mayor Abraham Beame appealed to the White House for help, New York's *Daily*

News captured the president's response in an earthy headline: "FORD TO CITY: DROP DEAD." To avoid bankruptcy, New York fired thousands of police officers and teachers, put the city's financial affairs in the hands of a banker-dominated control board, and slashed numerous social programs, including the egalitarian "open admissions" and free-tuition policies at the City University of New York.

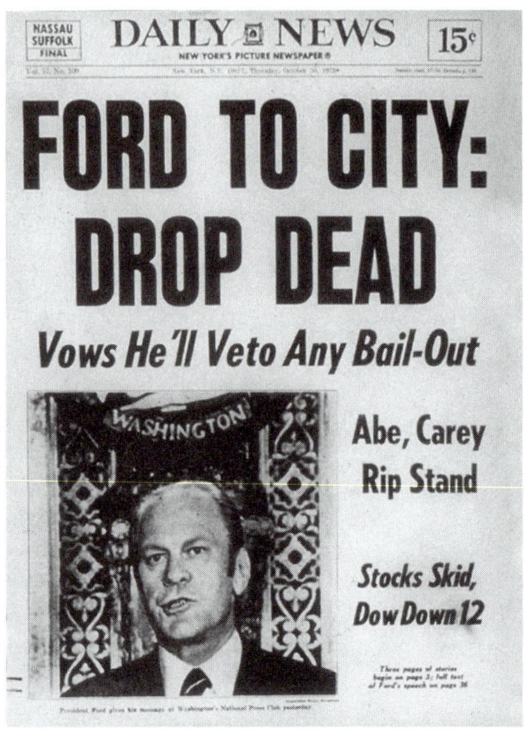
DAILY NEWS

NASSAU SUFFOLK FINAL

15¢

NEW YORK'S PICTURE NEWSPAPER

FORD TO CITY: DROP DEAD

Vows He'll Veto Any Bail-Out

Abe, Carey Rip Stand

Stocks Skid, Dow Down 12

Fiscal Crisis, Federal Neglect. The front page of New York's *Daily News* on October 30, 1975, the morning after President Gerald Ford announced his opposition to federal aid for the nearly bankrupt city. **Source:** New York *Daily News*, October 30, 1975.

Gerald Ford's ineffectual domestic leadership gave James Earl Carter, a little-known former governor of Georgia, the opportunity to win the Democratic presidential nomination in 1976 and then edge his way into the White House. Carter was something of a technocrat who had learned nuclear engineering in the U.S. Navy, but he was also a Christian moralist who argued that his lack of experience in Washington gave him a fresh, honest perspective. "I will never lie to you," he told campaign audiences in a not-so-subtle reference to the Watergate scandal. Carter was far more conservative than the other Democrats who campaigned for the presidency that year, but he had broken with the tradition of southern racism. Georgia-based civil rights leader Andrew Young was a confidante, and Carter appointed numerous veterans of that 1960s movement to posts in his administration.

Jimmy Carter's single-term presidency was a failure because he never managed to tame the double-digit inflation that frightened so many Americans. With few ties to organized labor or to traditional liberals, Carter had won the White House by appealing to the anti-incumbent mood that dominated political life in the years following Watergate and President Ford's unpopular 1974 pardon of ex-president Richard Nixon. Carter advocated energy conservation, but he avoided even Nixon-style price controls as ineffective and counterproductive. Carter also rejected most efforts to restart Great Society–style social welfare initiatives, including Democratic proposals for national health insurance and federal programs to promote full employment and fund abortion services for poor women. And he gave but tepid support to the labor movement's 1978 effort to reform the National Labor Relations Board. An increasingly well-organized and outspoken business community successfully lobbied against the bill, which would have reduced employers' ability to resist union-organizing drives.

"Carter and the Killer Rabbit." A sketch by political cartoonist Pat Oliphant commented on a peculiar incident that occurred when President Carter was on vacation in Georgia during the summer of 1979. Carter was fishing when a swimming rabbit "attacked" his rowboat. The president managed to fend off the animal with one of his oars. The story, which was widely disseminated by the press, epitomized for many Americans the weakness of the Carter administration.

Source: Pat Oliphant, 1982, pencil on paper (sketchbook), 4 × 6 inches. Reproduction courtesy of Susan Conway Gallery, Washington, D.C.

Instead, the president sought to curb wages and prices by presiding over the radical deregulation of the airline, trucking, railroad, and telephone industries. New Deal–era liberals had thought that enterprises in these industries required close government supervision, either because of the vital services they rendered or because of their inherent instability. But Carter Democrats now came to see such price and market regulation as economically inefficient and hostile to consumer interests. Administration officials believed that prices would fall and service improve if they took a laissez-faire approach. For example, the abolition of the Civil Aeronautics Board in 1978 eliminated most guidelines that governed fares, schedules, and mergers. A fiercely competitive environment flourished briefly in which new nonunion airlines—like People Express—won a slice of the market by offering rock-bottom fares and no-frills service.

The Carter administration's conservative tilt became apparent in its rescue of the Chrysler Corporation, which in 1979 stood at the brink of bankruptcy. Chrysler's aging factories were inefficient compared to those of Japan, and its products were equally outmoded. The financially troubled corporation needed billions of dollars to retool, but the big banks would not extend credit. Chrysler executives argued that only a government loan guarantee—a federal bailout—could save the company and thousands of well-paid jobs. Such loan guarantees were not new: in 1971 the Lockheed Corporation, one of the nation's major defense contractors, had secured this type of federal help. But the conditions under which Washington guaranteed the Chrysler loan opened the door to a further decline in the standard of living of millions of American workers. Together with the big banks, federal officials demanded that Chrysler's workers make hundreds of millions of dollars in wage concessions as part of the bailout package. As Chrysler's president, Lee Iacocca, explained in the midst of the crisis, "It's freeze time, boys. I've got plenty of jobs at seventeen dollars an hour; I don't have any at twenty." The leadership of the UAW convinced autoworkers that such concessions were the only way to save their jobs. Chrysler went on to earn record profits in the mid

1980s, but the Chrysler bailout proved the first in a long wave of concession contracts and wage rollbacks that swept through almost every unionized industry.

Carter's break with traditional economic liberalism was also evident when in 1979 he appointed Paul Volcker, a conservative Wall Street banker, to replace Arthur Burns as the chairman of the powerful Federal Reserve Board. Volcker's appointment signaled the death of Keynesianism as a government policy tool. Although unemployment was rising, so, too, were inflationary expectations. This meant that the financial markets where borrowers and lenders interact might well have recoiled had Carter sought a Keynesian fiscal stimulus to boost demand and fight unemployment. The president therefore abdicated economic stewardship of the economy in favor of Volcker, who instituted a set of "monetarist" policies that severely restricted the growth of the money supply and thereby pushed interest rates toward 20 percent—their highest level since the Civil War. By the early 1980s, his program had cut the annual inflation rate from 12 percent to 4 percent.

Volcker's monetarism had a huge impact, especially on the goods-producing sectors of the economy. Big-ticket consumer items became far more expensive. "Those interest rates have killed me and my business," complained Bruno Pasquinelli, whose Illinois homebuilding firm faced near-bankruptcy. "When I come to negotiate with a banker, I don't negotiate. It is a card game, but I don't have any cards." High interest rates also pushed up the value of the dollar against foreign currencies, making American cars, steel, and electronic products even less competitive overseas. Smokestack America was devastated as wave after wave of plant closings swept through the Midwest and Middle Atlantic states. In 1982 alone, 2,700 mass layoffs eliminated more than 1.25 million industrial jobs. Cities such as Youngstown, Buffalo, Cleveland, Gary, Milwaukee, and Detroit, once the industrial crown jewels of the nation, now exemplified a declining "Rustbelt." In 1982, almost 11 percent of the total U.S. workforce was unemployed, the highest proportion since 1940. In industrial states such as Michigan, Illinois, and Pennsylvania, unemployment reached levels not seen since the Great Depression.

This blue-collar depression had a devastating impact on older male breadwinners, who had often thought of the factories where they worked as the social center of their world. When plants closed, they experienced a deep sense of loss. "I feel like I've been robbed—robbed of 25, 26 years of my life really," complained fifty-year-old Victor Gonzales when he lost his job as a carpenter. Many felt that their inability to "bring home the bacon" reflected on their masculinity. "I've had to change my life-style completely," reported Pete Jefferson, an African American who lost his job when his steel mill closed its doors. "I come from a Southern family.

They always looked up to me because I'd done so well financially. I used to be head of the family; now I'm just a member." Many workers sank into depression and alcoholism in the months and years that followed a factory shutdown. Some fought with their wives; others abandoned their families altogether. Few blue-collar men over age forty were able to retrain; most would find new work, but rarely at the same high levels of pay or with the same pension and health care benefits.

The Collapse of Détente

In what seemed an increasingly unstable geopolitical environment, American foreign policy also moved to the right. During the last two years of Jimmy Carter's presidency, U.S. foreign policy shifted from détente with the Soviets to a renewal of Cold War tensions. Guided by Henry Kissinger, secretary of state from 1973 to 1977, the United States had sought a relaxation of the political and military competition that had characterized U.S.–Soviet relations for more than twenty years. Neither Kissinger nor the Republican presidents under whom he served had grown "soft" on Communism, but they thought it was in the U.S. interest to stabilize relations with both Communist China and the Soviet Union. Kissinger and other U.S. diplomats believed that such a policy would enable the nation to extract itself from Southeast Asia, moderate the arms race, and demilitarize Cold War tensions in Africa, Latin America, and eastern Europe. In 1975 a Strategic Arms Limitation Treaty (SALT) put a ceiling on the number of nuclear missiles that each side could deploy, and under the Helsinki accords reached that same year, the United States officially recognized the boundaries of Europe that the Soviets had helped establish at the end of World War II. Four years later, the United States recognized the Communist regime in Bejing as the sole legitimate government of all China, posting labor leader Leonard Woodcock there as the nation's first ambassador.

Jimmy Carter started his presidency determined to deepen détente. During his presidential campaign, he had denounced the nation's "inordinate fear of Communism," urged negotiation of a second SALT treaty, and advocated modest reductions in the U.S. military budget. More important, Carter emphasized a U.S. commitment to human rights—not only behind the Iron Curtain but also among the nation's "Free World" allies, including Argentina, Uruguay, Nicaragua, South Korea, and South Africa. Although the president's attempt to modify the behavior of these authoritarian regimes had mixed results, his human rights rhetoric did help to restore U.S. moral influence abroad in the years following the Vietnam disaster.

In the Middle East, the era of détente gave the United States a stronger hand. Like Kissinger before him, Carter urged Israel to return its occupied territories in exchange for Arab pledges to respect its pre-1967 borders. But unlike previous administrations, Carter supported the formation of a Palestinian "homeland." In 1978, after inviting Israeli prime minister Menachem Begin and Egyptian president Anwar Sadat to the presidential retreat at Camp David, Maryland, Carter brokered a set of 1978 accords that returned the Sinai to Egypt, in return for which Cairo extended formal diplomatic recognition to Israel. The next year Sadat and Begin won the Nobel Peace Prize, but the Camp David accords satisfied neither the Palestinians nor the other Arab states. The bitterness generated by the agreement came to an explosive climax in 1981 when dissident elements within the Egyptian military assassinated Anwar Sadat.

The revolutionary upheavals that engulfed Africa, Central America, Iran, and Afghanistan made détente increasingly untenable in the late 1970s. Although geopolitical stability was the goal of most diplomats on both sides of the East–West divide, the U.S. defeat in Vietnam generated a wave of instability in those regions where colonial or neocolonial regimes still clung to power. The bipolar model of a world neatly divided between an Atlantic-centered "West" and a Soviet-dominated "East" had clearly broken down. Revolutions in Angola and Rhodesia (soon renamed Zimbabwe) overturned white minority rule in those African nations. In Central America, leftist coalitions of peasants, intellectuals, and urban workers fought brutal dictators who had exercised power with the support of the U.S. government. In 1979 a Nicaraguan guerrilla movement, taking its inspiration from the 1930s insurgency led by Augusto Sandino, toppled a longstanding dictatorship run by the wealthy, pro-American Somoza family. Reaching out to both the United States and Cuba for aid and assistance, the Sandinistas redistributed much rural land, nationalized leading industries, and aided leftist guerrillas in nearby El Salvador.

Yellow Ribbon. Inspired by the 1973 pop song "Tie a Yellow Ribbon Round the Ole Oak Tree," many U.S. communities displayed yellow ribbons during the Iran hostage crisis. **Source:** UPI/Corbis-Bettman.

Revolutionaries of a very different sort deposed an even more important U.S. client, Iran's monarch

Reza Shah Pahlavi, late in 1978. For decades the shah had been a bulwark of U.S. influence in the Persian Gulf. But the billions of dollars in oil revenue that washed over his nation of 35 million had set off explosive tensions among both secular radicals, who fought for a constitutional democracy, and Islamic fundamentalists, who sought to impose an anti-Western theocracy. As the Shah's army disintegrated, Islamic religious leaders (the ayatollahs) led by the exiled Ayatollah Ruhollah Khomeini, consolidated their power. The 1979 Iranian revolution precipitated a second oil shock, which tripled world prices and further strained the already weak American economy. Islamic militants added to U.S. woes when they seized the U.S. embassy in November 1979, after the Shah, who was ailing from cancer, had entered a New York hospital. The youthful radicals held fifty-two embassy personnel hostage for 444 days. A long-running TV news show entitled *America Held Hostage* reflected a widespread sense of U.S. impotence and frustration, which was exacerbated in April 1980 by a failed rescue mission, during which eight U.S. commandos died.

Amid this turmoil, détente collapsed. Though the Soviets had not instigated the revolutionary movements in Central America, Africa, or Iran, they were quite prepared to take advantage of them to extend Soviet hegemony. In Afghanistan, where a pro-Soviet faction had gained power, Communist rule was tenuous at best, especially after Islamic radicals seized power in neighboring Iran. To forestall the collapse of their Afghan clients, the Soviets airlifted thousands of troops into the capital, Kabul, in December 1979. President Carter called the invasion the "gravest threat to peace since 1945." He suspended grain sales to the Soviets, orchestrated a Western boycott of the 1980 Summer Olympics in Moscow, and withdrew from Senate consideration a second SALT treaty. Then, shifting gears, Carter called for an increase in the military budget, reinstated draft registration for eighteen-year-old men, and accelerated the development of a new generation of medium-range Pershing missiles to be deployed in Europe. In Afghanistan itself, the Central Intelligence Agency shipped sophisticated arms to Muslim guerrillas, who soon stalemated more than 100,000 Soviet troops.

Fantasies of Invasion. Hollywood exploited the new Cold War in John Milius's *Red Dawn,* a 1984 film about a Soviet takeover of the United States. Such fantasies, however, failed to anticipate the direction that invasion would actually take: six years later, McDonald's opened its first fast-food franchise in Moscow. **Source:** Photofest

Carter's about-face was a product of domestic pressure as well as overseas upheaval.

Many conservatives, and some liberals, thought détente a poor bargain for the United States. Within the Democratic party, a faction led by Senator Henry Jackson of Washington opposed both trade liberalization with the Soviets and a new arms agreement until the Kremlin respected the human rights of Jews and other minorities within the USSR. Among Republicans, a powerful nationalist current, in part a compensatory response to the defeat in Indochina, opened a breach within party ranks. Thus when President Carter sent to the Senate a treaty relinquishing U.S. sovereignty over the Panama Canal, ratification proved unexpectedly contentious, even though the agreement had been negotiated largely by diplomats of the Nixon–Ford State Department. Indeed, by the last year of his presidency, Carter's foreign policy lay in ruins. In Europe détente had collapsed; in Central America the United States once again threw its weight to the side of conservative elites, and in Iran President Carter faced the kind of humiliation that bolstered the growth of chauvinistic sentiment at home.

Rise of the New Right

American politics turned right late in the 1970s, as the multiple traumas of that decade—Vietnam, Watergate, the oil shocks, and the Iranian hostage crisis—generated a pervasive sense of cynicism and alienation. In the quarter-century after 1973, the percentage of Americans who agreed with the statement, "The best government is the government that governs the least," nearly doubled, to 56 percent. Not unexpectedly, electoral participation dropped sharply: many who had traditionally supported an activist, governmental solution to the nation's problems now stayed home on election day. After 1968, barely half of all potential voters cast ballots in presidential elections—about one-third less than in the New Deal era or the early 1960s.

This withdrawal from the electoral process was concentrated among working people and the poor. Between 1968 and 1988, turnout rates among those who never finished high school declined by one-third, while among college graduates, almost always more affluent, voting participation held steady. In 1976, the two congressional districts with the lowest voter turnout in the nation—Bedford-Stuyvesant and the South Bronx, both in New York City—were overwhelmingly poor, African American, and Latino. Only about one-fifth of eligible voters there cast ballots, in sharp contrast to the 70 percent who voted in districts with the highest turnout—wealthy suburbs outside Chicago and Minneapolis. The disappearance of poor and working-class voters had an enormous consequence: it pushed all American politics to the right. Had voter turnout in 1976 equaled that of a decade earlier, Jimmy Carter would have defeated Gerald Ford in a landslide, rather than by a narrow margin (50 percent to 48 percent of the popular vote), and Congress would have been overwhelmingly Democratic.

The decline in voter turnout had many sources, but two stand out. First, institutions that traditionally linked individual voters to national politics, such as trade unions and urban political machines, had become far less influential. They were replaced by the professionally crafted thirty-second television clip and computer-generated direct-mail fund-raising letters. These political tools were simply not effective in mobilizing those at the bottom of the social ladder. Second, political participation declined among poor and working-class voters because the Democratic party failed to offer alternative policies around which these voters, once its most loyal supporters, might be mobilized. Although African Americans continued to vote Democratic by a ratio of more than nine to one, their turnout declined sharply in the 1970s. The Democratic party had moved so forcefully toward conservative positions on economic issues that it no longer appealed to inner-city ghetto dwellers or blue-collar workers. Thus in California, Jerry Brown, an otherwise liberal Democratic governor, declared that the Golden State had entered a new "era of limits," while President Jimmy Carter, in his famous "malaise" speech of 1979, made known his doubts that any governmental action could resolve the nation's pressing social and economic problems.

Many Americans began to see electoral politics, especially at the national level, as a spectator sport that bore no relation to their needs and aspirations. "Why don't people vote?" one welfare worker asked rhetorically. "Because it doesn't make a difference." Between the end of the 1960s and the end of the 1970s, the number of Americans who agreed with the polling statement that government will "do what is right most of the time" fell from 56 to 29 percent. At the same time, the proportion who affirmed that the "people running the country don't really care what happens to you" shot up from 26 to 60 percent.

Political demobilization among once-stalwart supporters of the Democratic party was soon matched by the rise of a "New Right," which made a powerful bid for the allegiance of many of these same voters. For most of the twentieth century, political conservatism in the United States had been closely linked to the views of affluent white Anglo-Saxon Protestants, who looked with some disdain upon blacks, Catholics, Jews, labor unions, and immigrants. This brand of "Old Right" conservatism mistrusted activist government, denounced international Communism, and defended laissez-faire economics. Though traditional conservatism did not disappear in the 1970s, its elite spokesmen lost much of their influence to a New Right, dedicated to mobilizing the body politic against secular culture, feminist ideas, and the government social programs first launched during Lyndon Johnson's presidency.

The New Right grew in response both to the decline in popular confidence in the nation's institutions and to the transformations taking place in American culture. Social and ideological changes during the 1960s had challenged what many saw as their traditional values and proper place in the social hierarchy: the father-centered family, the Christian character of American public life, and an unproblematic patriotism. Thus the New Right appealed to millions of Americans who had once been reliable supporters of the New Deal: white southerners, urban Catholics, and disaffected unionists.

But the New Right was not simply a backlash against "the Sixties," for a militant brand of conservatism had begun to flourish long before the end of that decade. Barry Goldwater's 1964 presidential campaign was a crystallizing event, transforming the nascent New Right from a circle of collegiate intellectuals into something of a broad political movement. Key conservative leaders of the 1970s and 1980s, including the columnist George Will, Chief Justice William Rehnquist, Equal Rights Amendment opponent Phyllis Schlafly, TV pundit Pat Buchanan, and direct-mail entrepreneur Richard Viguerie had all been passionate Goldwater partisans. Viguerie, who raised millions of dollars for New Right initiatives in the 1970s, proved an imaginative organizer and a master of direct-mail fundraising. He discovered the power of these targeted postal solicitations when he worked in the Washington office of the Young Americans for Freedom early in the 1960s. Viguerie hand-copied the Goldwater campaign donor list and later combined it with one from George Wallace's 1972 presidential campaign, for which Viguerie had also worked. Soon, he was a power in the Republican party. "Direct mail," asserted Viguerie, "is like having a water moccasin for a watchdog. Silent but deadly."

Revolt Against Taxes and Busing

Throughout much of the 1970s, racial conflict and anxiety proved the most compelling issue pushing white voters to the right. The civil rights revolution had a huge impact upon the urban white working class—the Irish of Boston, the Slavs of South Chicago, the Italians of Brooklyn—as well as once-poor southern whites. Many of these Americans now lived in cities presided over by black mayors such as Cleveland's Carl Stokes, elected in 1967, and Detroit's Coleman Young, who began a twenty-year tenure in 1973. The schools, jobs, and neighborhoods of these white workers were the first to be integrated. As long as cities were prosperous and schools well funded, it seemed possible that a multiracial set of urban institutions might emerge with relatively little social tension. But economic hard times in the 1970s, combined with the decline of the cities and their school systems, made it virtually certain that racial conflict would erupt and white working-class voters would shift rightward in response.

Tensions exploded over court-ordered busing to achieve racial balance in the schools. By the early 1970s, racial integration of public schools in the rural South had largely ended the state-supported dual system there, but in most large urban areas segregated schools continued to mirror the racial divide that persisted in residential neighborhoods. To remedy such de facto segregation, courts often ordered local school boards to institute cross-neighborhood busing. Despite the loss of familiar neighborhood schools, African-American parents supported these plans, hoping that their children's attendance at resource-rich, formerly all-white schools would enhance their educational opportunity and performance. But many white parents denounced court-ordered busing. In Pontiac (Michigan), Louisville (Kentucky), and Kansas City (Missouri), busing programs quickly generated organized opposition and even some violence. But the most spectacular clash over school busing came in Boston, the city that had spawned nineteenth-century movements for free public education and the abolition of slavery.

For years the Boston school board—controlled by Irish-American politicians who saw the school system as part of their patronage machine—had kept the city's schools racially segregated. In 1975, after a long, NAACP-initiated legal battle, a federal district court issued a sweeping integration order that mandated, among other remedies, the busing of pupils from all-black Roxbury to South Boston, an economically declining, Irish section of the city. Thus the burden of the busing plan fell almost entirely on the children of the urban working class, both black and white. Federal courts in Massachusetts, as elsewhere, excluded from integration plans the white, middle-class suburbs that surrounded Boston and most other American cities.

The stage was set for an ugly confrontation when the first black students were bused into "Southie," Charlestown, and other predominantly white neighborhoods in September 1975. For the next three years, Boston police struggled to protect black children from angry residents screaming "Nigger go home!" More than 20,000 white students left the Boston public schools to escape desegregation. The city's inflamed racial climate finally subsided in the 1980s when a new generation of politicians, both black and white, launched a set of biracial electoral campaigns to defuse the tension and revive the city. By then the busing controversy had faded from the news, in part because a new cohort of conservative judges backed away from the tactic, and in part because the racial integration of most big-city school systems had become unworkable. White flight and the growth in immigrant and minority populations gave most urban school systems a substantial African-American and Latino majority enrollment.

South Boston Backlash. The Boston busing controversy turned violent in the spring of 1976. On April 5, a group of white high school students from South Boston and Charlestown opposed to busing visited City Hall to meet with a councilwoman who supported their boycott of classes. Outside the building, the teenagers encountered and then assaulted labor lawyer Theodore Landsmark. The attack sparked a series of violent racial incidents that extended into the summer.

Source: Stanley Forman.

Because of the enfranchisement of millions of African-American voters, direct appeals to racial intolerance largely vanished from public political discourse during the 1970s and 1980s. High public officials who used words such as "nigger," "Jap," or "kike" invariably apologized for the gaff. But American political discourse remained saturated with an array of code words, phrases, and substitute issues that spoke indirectly to white racial prejudice. Urban crime, escalating drug use, and the growing number of people receiving Aid to Families with Dependent Children were real issues, but much conservative rhetoric denouncing welfare "queens," "drug lords," and "forced busing" gave the public debate a thinly disguised racial edge.

Such rhetoric helped discredit many government functions and fuel a series of an antigovernment tax revolts that swept the nation in the late 1970s. In states such as California, an inflationary surge had pushed housing prices skyward, putting the purchase of a first house—a central part of the American Dream—beyond the reach of many young couples. Those middle-class and working-class citizens who already owned their homes were shocked by huge property tax bills. Substantial increases in the Social Security payroll tax added to their burden. The tax system was regressive and unfair, and in the 1970s it was becoming more so as double-digit inflation raised the nominal income of working men and women, pushing them into tax brackets originally designed for the rich and affluent.

In 1978, passage of California's Proposition 13, a ballot initiative limiting property taxes and slashing local government revenues, signaled the ability of New Right conservatives to turn the tax issue against liberal governance itself. As one state legislator put it, Proposition 13 was "a bullet from a loaded gun that went off in California on its way to its ultimate target—the high level of Federal spending." Soon conservative activists mounted antitax campaigns in Michigan, Idaho, Nevada, Massachusetts,

Oregon, and Arizona. They argued that at issue was not only the fairness of the tax system but also wasteful government expenditures for education, welfare, and other social programs. Surveys taken at the time showed that most of those who voted for such tax-limitation laws did not actually reject these government programs. Indeed, most of the tax savings went to business, not to ordinary taxpayers. But the antitax agitation of these years had a profound impact on civic life. Combined with the stale taste left by Watergate, it helped to mobilize public sentiment against government responsibility for social problems. Many Americans were beginning to think of themselves not as citizens but as self-interested taxpayers.

Gender Politics

School busing and taxes were not the only issues that mobilized conservatives in the 1970s; explosive moral and cultural questions about the role of women and the status of homosexuals proved just as powerful. Before the 1970s, most evangelical Protestants had avoided politics, which they saw as hopelessly corrupt. But court rulings that legalized abortion, curbed school prayer, and deprived segregated Christian academies of their tax-exempt status unleashed a wave of activism. In the South, Carter administration efforts to eliminate tax breaks for hundreds of new religious academies mobilized thousands of Protestant conservatives to participate in Republican party politics, the Moral Majority, and other Christian political groups.

For Protestant fundamentalists, gender issues took on the air of a religious war. In these conflicts, denominational lines had less meaning than the split between theological liberals and conservatives. The former had little quarrel with the nation's pluralist, secular culture; the latter, regardless of denomination, saw the United States as an increasingly amoral nation in which the difficulties faced at home and abroad were but the outward sign of an inner debasement. Perhaps for this reason, evangelical Christianity enjoyed an extraordinary renaissance in the 1970s among both black and white Americans. Between 1965 and 1985, membership in liberal Protestant churches declined, but the conservative Southern Baptists, America's largest Protestant denomination, gained 3 million members. By the start of the 1980s, more than 45 million Americans considered themselves fundamentalists. Scores of congregations moved to the suburbs and built huge new churches, often with money donated by the Sunbelt's energy, real estate, and banking entrepreneurs. Evangelical ministers, such as Virginians Jerry Falwell, founder of the politically influential Moral Majority, and Pat Robertson, used the latest in television technology and programming to spread their conservative message well beyond the traditional southern Bible Belt.

Three gender issues served as New Right cultural and religious lightning rods: the Supreme Court's 1973 decision in *Roe* v. *Wade,* which legalized abortions; the feminist-backed effort to pass the Equal Rights Amendment (ERA) to the U.S. Constitution; and the increasing rights consciousness and public visibility of gay Americans.

Before 1973, abortion was an option exercised primarily by young unmarried women, most of whom either attended school or had just entered the workforce. Feminists and civil libertarians argued, and the Supreme Court came to agree, that governmental prohibitions against a medical abortion were not only unenforceable but also a violation of a woman's right to privacy, especially during the first trimester of pregnancy. Most women who sought abortions were not vocal feminists, but conservatives linked the exercise of the new abortion rights to what they perceived as the sexual licentiousness of the 1960s. They denounced legalized abortion as murder of the unborn, a spur to sexual promiscuity, and, as one activist put it, an attack on "the right of a husband to protect the life of the child he has fathered in his wife's womb."

Antiabortion forces across the country rallied quickly after the *Roe* v. *Wade* decision. In the North, Catholic Church leaders organized the first antiabortion demonstrations. Among many Catholics, as among most evangelical Protestants, the depth of one's religious commitment was judged by the degree of opposition to abortion and the defense of what many saw as the sanctity of "God-given" gender roles within the family. In state and local jurisdictions "pro-life" groups waged a vigorous legal and legislative campaign to restrict abortion rights when they could not eliminate them outright. Activists often picketed abortion clinics and courted arrest in order to stigmatize this medical procedure and the doctors who performed it. But across the picket lines they faced an equally fervent "pro-choice" movement, whose members argued that the right of a woman to choose an abortion was fundamental to her dignity and citizenship.

Pro-life Props. Antiabortion demonstrators brandish fetal images as they protest outside a New Jersey abortion clinic in February 1990. Pictures played a significant role in promotion of the "pro-life" cause, reducing a complex debate over women's rights and the development of life into a single figure, "the unborn child." Ignoring developmental stages in the womb, they presented images that either depicted full-term, baby-like "fetuses" (such as the rubber doll shown here) or focused on the most developed parts of the fetal anatomy (such as the head, hands, and feet) while avoiding those that are less identifiably human.

Source: Donna Binder/ Impact Visuals.

The ERA, which both houses of Congress approved in 1972, also proved a controversial issue in the 1970s and early 1980s. The proposed amendment stated simply that "equality of rights under the law shall not be denied or abridged by the United States or by any State on account of sex." It thus ratified, in symbolic and legal terms, the new roles that women were exploring and the new gender egalitarianism that was reshaping so many aspects of American life. In education, for example, coeducation came to scores of all-male colleges and universities, including Yale, Dartmouth, Princeton, the University of Virginia, and the military academies. And when Congress amended the Civil Rights law in 1972 to require an equal expenditure of federal funds on both male and female students, the visibility and popularity of women in competitive sports leaped forward, both on the college circuit and off. Women's

"Liberate Us from the Liberators"

Teddi Holt, a full-time homemaker from Georgia with three sons, helped found "Mothers on the March (MOM)" in the late 1970s, a New Right organization dedicated to "preserv[ing] and strengthen[ing] the home."

I am pleased that God blessed me with the privilege of being a woman. I have never been envious of the role of men but have had respect for both sexes. There's no doubt that there has been discrimination against women, but that is past history, just as discrimination against blacks is past history in the US. . . .

NOW's [The National Organization for Women's] primary goal was to pass the Equal Rights Amendment (ERA) without amendment. Second, it included as a secondary goal—"right to abortion on demand." And third, it supported "a woman's right to . . . express her own sexuality and to choose her lifestyle. . . . " Such goals were foreign to me. I could not imagine any woman with my background having such goals, because they did not hold to traditional values and/or Judeo-Christian ethics on which the Constitution and our laws are based. . . .

It was obvious to me that ERA was certainly not a protection of women's rights. In fact, it would remove many protections and exemptions that were specifically placed in our laws, recognizing the fact that our Creator had most certainly created us male and female: two separate, very different, equally important human beings. . . .

Just what were we women to be liberated from? These women [feminists] were calling for liberation from the things women like me love most—our husbands, our children, our homes. My cry became: "God, liberate us from the Liberators!" . . .

We believe that the mothers of this and other nations must stand up for the protection of our homes and our children. In no way are we extremists, unless we be guilty of extreme devotion to our husbands, our children, and our homes. It is our sincere belief that if we do not unite against the threats to the home, if we retire to the convenience and security of our houses and do not speak out, then it will not be long until we, the "keepers at home" (Titus 2:5) will not have a home to keep!

Source: Robyn Rowland, ed., *Women Who Do and Women Who Don't Join the Women's Movement* (1984).

basketball, tennis, track, and swimming soon filled athletic venues with thousands of cheering spectators.

Although many Republicans had once been staunch supporters of the ERA, a new generation of social conservatives attacked it as little more than a proxy for the entire feminist agenda. As debate on the proposed constitutional amendment rolled through key state legislatures in Illinois, North Carolina, and Pennsylvania, New Right leaders such as Phyllis Schlafly and Jerry Falwell organized thousands of activists against it. Falwell told his large television audience, "The Equal Rights Amendment is a delusion. In families and in nations where the Bible is believed, Christian women are honored above men. . . . The Equal Rights Amendment strikes at the foundation of our entire social structure." Twenty-eight state legislatures had approved the ERA by the end of 1973, but Schlafly, Falwell, and their allies successfully turned public opinion against the amendment during the remainder of the decade. It never became part of the U.S. Constitution because supporters could not win passage in the two-thirds of all state legislatures (thirty-eight) necessary for final ratification.

The key to the New Right's victory in this battle lay in the very different meaning the idea of women's equality held for men and women divided by age, class, and economic expectations. Many working-class men feared that passage of the ERA would undercut whatever control they still possessed over their work and family lives. For their part, working-class women did not identify with many of the feminist leaders who had injected the ERA into national politics. To them, the spread of feminist ideas seemed to undermine the implicit bargain upon which traditional marriage and family life were based. One otherwise liberal trade unionist explained her distrust for *Ms.* magazine publisher Gloria Steinem in this way: "Maybe I have my own stereotype of her, but I think maybe she looks above us. I feel she's fighting for women like herself, professional women. . . . So I don't consider myself part of her movement."

The new visibility and rights consciousness projected by gay Americans also polarized American politics and culture. In the surge of "gay pride" that followed the 1969 Stonewall Inn riot in New York City, many homosexuals expressed their sexual orientation with an openness denied previous generations. They built a new kind of urban counterculture, which included gay and lesbian bars, newspapers, and magazines, as well as numerous social and political groups. The once-buried history of gay Americans came alive in an outpouring of books and movies. For the first time, local politicians acknowledged a definable gay vote. In the 1970s, the victorious mayoral campaigns of George Moscone in San Francisco and Edward Koch in New York City benefited from the support of a mobilized gay electorate. Following in the footsteps of feminist women and African-American civil rights advocates, homosexual Americans struggled for passage of state and local laws forbidding discrimination against them.

Horrified, fundamentalist Christians attacked the public display of homosexuality as blasphemous. In 1977, Anita Bryant, a popular singer and celebrity, won national attention when she campaigned against the specter of "militant" homosexuals corrupting young students in Florida's public schools. Bryant spearheaded the successful movement to repeal a Dade County ordinance that protected homosexuals from employment discrimination. Her success reflected a new climate of hostility toward homosexuals, especially when they openly declared their sexual orientation. Physical attacks on gay people increased, reaching an ugly crescendo in 1978 after Dan White, a conservative former San Francisco politician, assassinated Mayor Moscone and Harvey Milk, the city's first openly gay member of its board of aldermen. When White was found not guilty of the crime by reason of insanity, San Francisco's gay community erupted in a night of street violence.

The New Right's hostility toward homosexuals intensified in the early 1980s when AIDS, the deadly acquired immune deficiency syndrome, began to ravage the male homosexual communities of San Francisco, New York, Los Angeles, and other big cities. Within a decade, more than 100,000 people had died, while another 2 million (both gay and straight) were infected by HIV (human immunodeficiency virus), the virus that causes AIDS. To many heterosexual Americans, not only those in the New Right, AIDS seemed less a disease than a moral judgment on the gay lifestyle. A wave of homophobia, including a sharp increase in physical assaults, swept the nation's cities in the mid 1980s. But the AIDS epidemic soon spread well beyond the gay community, first to intravenous drug users and then to heterosexuals, the latter reminding moralists that gay people had no monopoly on promiscuity. Indeed, a burst of gay community health care activism late in the 1980s won homosexual Americans grudging respect within much of the cultural mainstream. By the

News-breaking. An ACT-UP protestor, shouting "Fight AIDS, not Arabs," interrupted anchor Dan Rather during the January 22, 1991, broadcast of the *CBS Evening News*.

Source: Mario Suriani, AP/World Wide Photos.

mid 1990s, a combination of new medicines and a decline in gay sexual promiscuity had limited, within the United States, the devastating impact of the AIDS epidemic.

Ronald Reagan: Enter Stage Right

The demise of détente, the rise of the New Right, and the persistence of stagflation doomed the presidency of Jimmy Carter and opened the door to Republican Ronald Reagan's sweeping victory in the 1980 presidential contest. Born in Tampico, Illinois, Reagan had won modest fame as a Hollywood actor in the 1930s and 1940s. He was then a pro-labor, New Deal liberal who was active in the Screen Actors Guild. But after the war, Reagan sided with conservative anti-Communists during a violent set of film industry strikes. In the 1950s, as a corporate spokesperson for General Electric, then one of the nation's most aggressively anti-union firms, he became an active Republican and an opponent of what he called "big government." His political star rose quickly during the 1964 presidential campaign when he proved an exceptionally effective advocate for Barry Goldwater. Elected governor of California in 1966, Reagan served two terms, during which he fought to slow the growth in state spending for health, education, and welfare. He won national attention as a bitter opponent of the student movement on California campuses and a strong supporter of the Vietnam War. By the time he left the governor's mansion in 1975, he was defacto leader of the resurgent Republican Right. In 1976, he nearly edged Gerald Ford aside for the GOP presidential nomination.

Reagan was by far the most conservative figure in the 1980 presidential race. He easily defeated the mainstream Republican candidate, ex-CIA director George Bush, for the Republican nomination, and in the general election he marginalized support for the GOP moderate John Anderson, who ran as an independent. Reagan attacked détente, emphasizing the need to increase the military budget and project American power abroad. He took skillful advantage of the nation's economic difficulties to denounce government efforts to manage the economy and regulate business. Reagan was an outright opponent of corporate taxation and an advocate of sharply lower personal tax rates for the rich. In rhetoric, if not always in practice, he supported the New Right's conservative social agenda. "Government is not the solution to our problem," he would assert in his first inaugural address, "government is the problem."

Reagan had overwhelming financial support from virtually the entire U.S. business community. But unlike so many other GOP opponents of the New Deal legacy, such as Robert Taft and Barry Goldwater, Reagan

Photo Op. Press photographers are shown here taking pictures of Ronald Reagan during a "photo opportunity." Formal photography sessions, scheduled by the White House staff, dated back to the 1930s, when FDR's press secretary instructed photographers to avoid showing the polio-afflicted President in a wheelchair. During the Reagan administration, however, photographic access to the president was controlled and orchestrated to virtually guarantee that no unflattering or negative picture would be recorded. Believing that the "look" was more important than the meaning of an event, White House staff dictated the time, place, and even the angle of vision of "photo ops." The resulting pictures helped shape a positive, upbeat image of Reagan for the public. **Source:** National Archives.

projected a sunny disposition and Rooseveltian self-confidence that helped put his radical initiatives in the most favorable light. In contrast, Jimmy Carter, who had fought off a primary challenge from the Massachusetts liberal, Senator Edward Kennedy, often seemed pessimistic about the ability of Americans to resolve their economic and social problems.

Although Reagan took only 51 percent of the total popular vote (compared to 41 percent for Carter and 7 percent for Anderson), his electoral count was an impressive 489 to 49. The Republicans won the election by retaking the white South from the Democrats and increasing their victory margin among middle-class, suburban voters. Most striking, Reagan captured the votes of half of all blue-collar workers and more than 40 percent of union households. These "Reagan Democrats," who had once been core supporters of the New Deal and the welfare state, now helped tilt American politics against new taxes and social spending initiatives. Only African Americans voted solidly Democratic. On Reagan's coattails, the Republicans gained twelve Senate seats, giving them a majority in that body for the first time since the early 1950s. The House kept a slim but dispirited Democratic majority.

Reagan and the Republicans promised to transform American politics in a fashion just as sweeping as that inaugurated by Roosevelt's New Deal nearly fifty years earlier. The new administration soon won a 40-percent increase in arms spending, including expensive new weapons systems such as the B-1 bomber and the "Star Wars" antimissile shield. Reagan labeled the Vietnam War a "noble effort," while declaring the Soviet Union an "evil empire." Reaganite intellectuals, such as U.N. ambassador Jeane Kirkpatrick and State Department official Elliot Abrams, defined most insurgencies in developing countries as Soviet-inspired, Soviet-supported terrorism. The Reagan administration therefore adopted a "rollback" strategy that targeted revolutionary movements in Africa and Latin America. The administration also sought to overcome what some pundits called the "Vietnam syndrome," defined as a lingering reluctance to commit U.S. military forces abroad. To this end, the administration increased military aid to the Afghan rebels; organized and armed a group of counterrevolutionary Nicaraguans; sent the Marines into the Lebanese civil war; and in 1983 launched a military invasion of the tiny Caribbean island of Grenada, where pro-Cuban radicals had taken power.

The Reagan administration sought to restore economic growth and pay for its military buildup by cutting taxes, government regulations, and social spending. By "getting the government off our backs," Reagan hoped to unleash a tide of entrepreneurial energy. In 1981, with the cooperation of many conservative Democrats in Congress, the new president cut business and income taxes by 25 percent and pared $25 billion from domestic social programs. Meanwhile, Reagan's new secretary of the interior, James Watt, worked to open federally controlled land, coastal waters, and wetlands to mining, lumber, oil, and gas companies. Under the new Republican administration, both the Environmental Protection Agency and the Occupational Safety and Health Administration became much more solicitous of the business point of view. Commentators called Reagan's program of tax cuts and regulatory reforms "supply-side economics," or just "Reaganomics." Its partisans argued that business profits, sales, investment, and employment would soar in an economic environment so much more favorable to capital investment. And Reagan administration officials claimed that despite lower tax rates, overall tax revenue would actually rise because of the resulting economic boom.

Such was the theory. Reaganomics did cut taxes sharply for corporations and the wealthy, reducing the top individual tax rate from 70 percent in the 1970s to 28 percent in 1986. A family with an income between $100,000 and $200,000 gained an average of $8,400 in extra income from the Reagan tax cuts. However, families whose total income was less than $10,000 actually found that their total tax bill had risen. They did pay just $58 less in federal taxes, but because state and local taxes increased to make up for reductions in federal aid, and because Social Security deductions rose almost every year, the tax rate on most working-class Americans did not fall. Many actually paid a higher proportion of their income in taxes than the rich in the Reagan era.

The Reagan tax policy had an additional consequence, which its architects understood from the outset but did not admit. Between 1981 and 1986, federal income tax receipts plummeted by $750 billion. This loss of income, combined with huge increases in military spending, generated staggering federal budget deficits of some $150 billion to $200 billion a year. Thus Reaganomics assured that regardless of which party controlled Congress or the White House—and however great the social need—the federal government would find it virtually impossible to initiate new programs. Moreover, because the government had to borrow so much to cover the tax shortfall, interest rates remained at double-digit levels. The value of the dollar therefore soared against the yen and the mark. The strong dollar drove down the cost of imported Japanese cars and German machine tools, but it also ensured that domestic manufacturing would continue to struggle and blue-collar unemployment would remain at near-depression levels.

Reaganomics also forced deep cuts in welfare spending. The social programs inaugurated or expanded in the late 1960s had helped reduce poverty in the United States, but in the 1970s inflation and recession began to undermine this progress. During the 1980s, conservative ideologues such as Charles Murray and George Gilder argued that poverty was the product of liberal social policy itself, which had generated a self-perpetuating "underclass" dependent on government handouts. Declaring such social programs a failure, Reagan administration policy makers set out to destroy them. Large cuts in food-stamp, child-nutrition, and job-training programs followed; Aid to Families with Dependent Children, public service employment programs, and low-income housing projects also suffered. Half a million working families, all headed by women, lost their child-assistance benefits. Seventy percent of the savings in the food-stamp program came from families already living below the poverty line.

Not all welfare programs were cut so drastically. Those social programs and tax policies that benefited those with a solid attachment to paid work—Social Security, Medicare, and the tax deduction for interest on home mortgages—were largely spared the cutbacks targeted at the poor. There was no stigma attached to these middle-income entitlement programs; most Americans considered them a right rather than a handout. Thus, in the 1980s, even conservative Republicans considered Social Security, which was by far the nation's most expensive income-transfer program, the "third rail" of American politics: touch it and you die.

The Reagan Boom

The same economic policies that devastated the country's industrial heartland generated regional booms that gave the nation an aura of prosperity. In California and New England, defense spending, foreign investment, and the maturation of the baby-boom generation sent real estate values soaring. In financial centers such as New York, Dallas, Los Angeles, and Miami, Reagan policies that deregulated the banking industry and the stock market set off a wave of speculation. New York City recovered from its fiscal crisis to become an international financial and real estate mecca for the superrich. In Chicago, the nation's commodity trading center, mammoth new skyscrapers dotted the Loop, just fifteen miles from empty, decaying steel mills and packinghouses.

The dramatic surges in real estate, finance, the retail trade, and high-tech manufacturing also became visible in the suburban and exurban centers, whose overnight growth threatened the very existence of downtown office and shopping districts. Tysons Corner, Virginia; the Route 1 corridor to Princeton, New Jersey; Clayton, Missouri; Newport Beach, California; Rockville Pike, Maryland; and the Route 580 corridor just east of the Oakland hills in northern California—these were not the bedroom suburbs of the 1950s, but entirely new towns complete with gleaming officeparks, huge shopping malls, and high-priced homes and condominiums. In them lived a workforce segregated by race, class, and personal expectations from those still struggling in the nation's older, urban manufacturing and service sectors. In the 1980s and afterward, these "edge cities" represented a physical manifestation of the great social divisions generated by Reaganite capitalism.

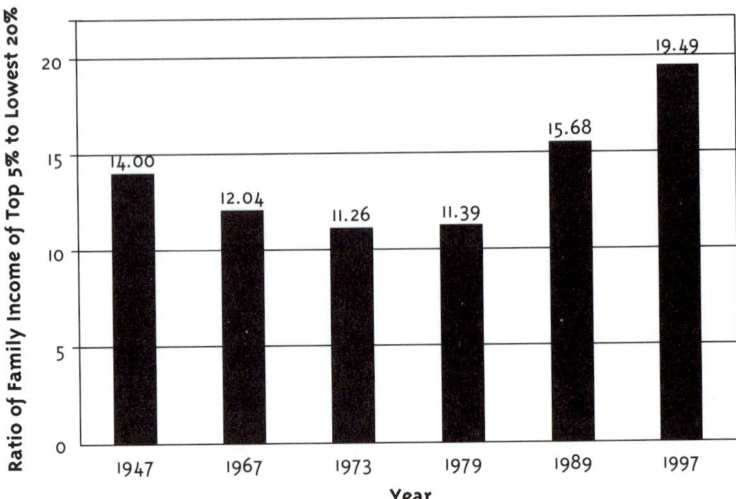

The Rich Get Richer: Ratio of Average Family Income of Top 5% to Lowest 20% After World War II, the average income of the wealthiest Americans (the families in the top 5 percent) declined relative to the average income of the poorest fifth of the population. But in the 1970s and 1980s, higher unemployment and more favorable tax treatment of the rich reversed this trend and increased income inequality dramatically. Both rich and poor doubled their income in the first twenty-five years after World War II. But in the next quarter century, incomes for the poor stagnated while those of the rich continued to grow substantially.

Source: Lawrence Mishel, Jared Benstein, and John Schmitt, *The State of Working America, 1998–99* (1999).

Thus did Reaganomics help to widen the gap between rich and poor. Income distribution in the United States, though far less egalitarian than in most other industrial democracies, had remained fairly stable for a quarter-century after the end of World War II. But in the early 1980s, the United States, in the words of economists Barry Bluestone and Bennett Harrison, took a "Great U-Turn" that widened the distance between the well and poorly paid to an extent greater "than at any point in the lifetimes of all but our most senior citizens, the veterans of the Great Depression." Between 1977 and 1990, the income of the richest fifth of the population rose by one-third; that of the top 1 percent almost doubled. In these years, when the net worth of the richest 400 Americans nearly tripled, the total income of the bottom 60 percent actually fell, with the income of those who lived below the poverty line dropping most sharply.

There were critics aplenty, of course, but, in general, American popular culture celebrated the new rich. Greed and extravagance became the stuff of television dramas such as *Dallas* and *Dynasty,* whose ruthless but stylish characters owned the hot stocks, luxury homes, and designer clothes coveted by most viewers. Their real-life counterparts paraded

Haves. The ostentatious display of self and wealth became a hallmark of 1980s America. In this case, a young, upwardly mobile professional couple posed in their high-rise apartment for a magazine photograph—unselfconsciously displaying the nanny as one of their possessions.

Source: Patricia Morrisroe, "The Yupper West Side: The New Class," *New York*, May 13, 1985—Diego Goldberg/SYGMA.

across the fashion and society pages of glossy magazines, daily newspapers, and the aptly named television series, *Lifestyles of the Rich and Famous.*

Financial speculation alone generated hundreds of thousands of extremely well-paid jobs. During the 1970s, inflationary fears kept the stock market flat, but in the half-decade after 1982, the Dow Jones Average almost tripled. Young lawyers, bankers, stockbrokers, and businessmen—the young urban professionals sometimes mocked as "yuppies"—flocked to the thriving financial districts in New York, Los Angeles, and Chicago. There they sought to win their share of the vast fortunes created by corporate consolidations and leveraged buyouts in what *Business Week* dubbed the "casino economy." Their heroes were investment wizard Peter Lynch, whose giant Magellan Fund churned out year after year of capital gains; Donald Trump, who parlayed his father's substantial real estate business into an empire of prestige hotels and gambling casinos; and "junk bond" king Michael Milken, whose trading prowess earned him $550 million in one extraordinary year. The film *Working Girl* captured the lure of this new era of deal-making wealth, while Tom Wolfe's novel *Bonfire of the Vanities* revealed its darker, amoral side.

Millions of white-collar professionals, managers, and small businessmen stood well below these high rollers on the American income pyramid. Constituting perhaps 25 percent of the working population, this slice of the middle class also seemed to bask in the glow of the Reagan revolution: their salary increases kept pace with inflation, their income taxes were lower, and they voted Republican in overwhelming numbers. By living, working, and shopping in the new edge-city world of office parks and shopping malls, many managed to remove themselves from the urban blight and racial conflict that typified even such Sunbelt cities as Miami, Houston, New Orleans, and Atlanta.

But this seemingly prosperous middle stratum was not immune to the economic and social difficulties of the 1980s. Since the end of World War II, white-collar workers had enjoyed job stability in return for their loyalty to corporate employers. While large firms routinely matched the hiring and layoff of blue-collar workers with the ebb and flow of their sales, white-collar workers had come to expect uninterrupted employment. Indeed, corporations in the United States employed three or four times as many managers and supervisors as those in Japan and Europe. They were a costly burden—too costly in an era of corporate mergers and rising international competition. Thus, when top executives began reorganizing their enterprises to make them "lean and mean," many long-service middle managers found themselves unemployed for the first time in their lives. "I was hurt," remembered a middle manager nudged into retirement by a large pharmaceutical company. "After thirty-four years with the company, I was surprised that it came down to an economic relationship. . . . I thought I was in—a family kind of thing."

During a typical eighteen-month period in 1985 and 1986, DuPont dismissed or pushed into retirement 11 percent of its white-collar workforce; Exxon, 17 percent; General Electric, 8 percent; and AT&T, 10 percent. Downsizing, a polite term for mass dismissals, intensified during the recession that began in 1989, when a new wave of reorganizations and layoffs swept through the banking, stock brokerage, and real estate sectors. These sweeping white-collar layoffs became a routine management practice and continued well into the boom of the 1990s. Of course, total professional and managerial employment increased during the 1980s and 1990s, even in some newly restructured companies, but this churning of the white-collar labor force generated widespread middle-class insecurity, even among those who kept their jobs. Among all workers, the proportion with the same employer for nine years fell dramatically—from 67 percent during the 1970s to 52 percent in the 1980s.

Despite the erosion in the pay and job security of many male breadwinners, family incomes rose modestly in this era, because more members of the family went to work. The most important additions to the workforce were women, primarily wives, whose labor-force participation increased from about 40 to 60 percent in the quarter-century following 1970. By the 1990s, paid work was virtually universal among middle-class and working-class women under age forty. Indeed, their labor represented the difference between comfort and hardship for the broad middle stratum of the U.S. population. Virtually all of the income gain among white two-parent families in the years after 1967 can be accounted for by the wages of wives and daughters.

As a result of these new employment patterns, white middle-class family life changed dramatically. "Traditional" families—husband and father as sole breadwinner, wife as mother and homemaker—now represented only one of every ten American households. Nearly 60 percent of all women with children under age six worked outside the home. Likewise, teenage employment, even among middle-class families, increased dramatically in the 1970s and 1980s. Teenagers helped to pay for the spiraling cost of a college education, their own cars, and a well-stocked wardrobe. They also proved essential to the nation's giant service economy: Wal-Mart, McDonald's, and Foot Locker could hardly have remained open without a vast teenage labor force.

The relative affluence of the American middle class was sustained by what can only be called family speed-up. To the surprise of optimistic social forecasters, the growth of office automation and the deployment of a wide array of technological gadgets—from personal computers to faxes and car phones—did not reduce the working hours of professionals and office workers. One aggressive CEO told his top managers: "People who work for me should have phones in their bathrooms." For Motorola executive Sheila Griffin, a cell phone and voice mail started the workday during her early-morning commute. "I get to the office and check the faxes. I get Europe out of the way and then work on things in our own time zone." By 6:30 p.m.—thirteen hours after she left home in the predawn darkness—Griffin is back with her family. "Then at about 9:30 p.m. the phone rings, and it's Japan."

In the two decades after 1969, the average employed American worked an extra month a year: about two and a half weeks more for men, seven and a half weeks more for women. Vacation time declined, overtime rose, and moonlighting soared. Women, whose workday did not end when they arrived back at home, bore the brunt of this family speed-up. Columnist Ann Landers pronounced herself "awestruck at the number of women who work at their jobs and go home to another full time job." One study found that employed mothers average more than 80 hours a week of housework, child care, and employment. "These women talked about sleep the way a hungry person talks about food," reported a California sociologist.

The New Immigration

In the 1970s and 1980s, huge numbers of Asian and Latino immigrants flocked to U.S. shores to fill millions of new service, retail, clerical, and light manufacturing jobs. This new wave of immigrants rivaled in sheer numbers the great trans atlantic flows a century earlier. In the 1960s, annual immigration had totaled only a quarter-million; by the 1990s, the United States was admitting more than 800,000 legal immigrants a year, and perhaps half again as many illegal immigrants, mainly from Mexico. More than 40 percent of the newcomers were from Asia, especially the Philippines, China, South Korea, and Vietnam; about 35 percent came from Latin America and the Caribbean.

One of every three new immigrants entered the United States through California, making the nation's most populous state its unofficial Ellis Island as well. By the 1990s, one-third of the population of Los

"Round Up." U.S. Border Patrol agents arrest a group of Mexicans who illegally crossed into the United States near San Diego, California. In 1990, more than 1 million migrants were arrested while crossing the border between Mexico and the United States; 400,000 were caught and deported in the San Diego area alone. **Source:** U.S. Border Patrol.

Angeles, the nation's second-largest city, was foreign-born, making the City of Angels the second-largest Spanish-speaking city on the North American continent. As hundreds of thousands of Mexicans and Central Americans streamed into poor neighborhoods and communities in East Los Angeles and the San Gabriel Valley, tens of thousands of Koreans settled in an old working-class neighborhood just west of downtown Los Angeles. At the same time, equally large numbers of immigrants from Taiwan, Hong Kong, 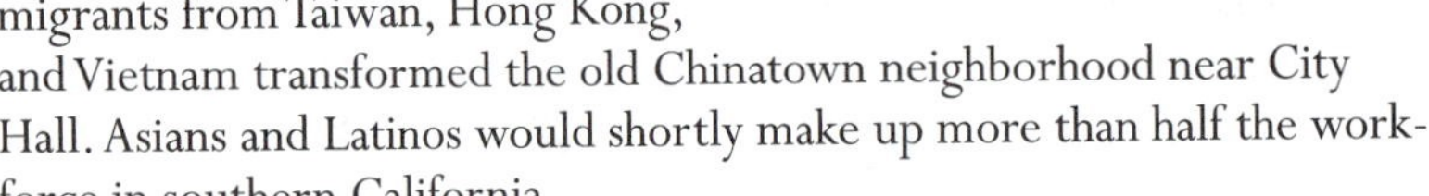and Vietnam transformed the old Chinatown neighborhood near City Hall. Asians and Latinos would shortly make up more than half the workforce in southern California.

New York's foreign-born population, like that of Los Angeles, also approached 35 percent of its total populace in the 1990s — a level the city had last reached in 1910, at the height of southern and eastern European immigration. Long-established immigrant communities, including those composed of Puerto Ricans, Irish, and Poles, grew rapidly during the 1970s and 1980s, even as hundreds of thousands of Haitian, Dominican, Colombian, East Indian, Chinese, and Russian immigrants settled into the city's poorer neighborhoods. Nearly 200,000 Mexican immigrants arrived after the peso was devalued in 1986. Mostly undocumented, they had traveled thousands of miles by truck and car from some of the poorest rural regions in search of work. "We came because we are poor farmers and our parents did not have enough to send us to school," explained a young food deliverer.

Miami, too, was transformed by the newcomers; by the 1980s it had the highest percentage of foreign-born residents of any U.S. city. First came an influx of nearly 600,000 Cubans, many of them well-to-do exiles from the Cuban Revolution of 1959. Then, in the late 1970s and early 1980s, tens of thousands of political and economic refugees arrived from Haiti, Guatemala, El Salvador, and Nicaragua. The huge number of Latino immigrants changed the face of the city: as Spanish became the language of foreign trade, Miami became the commercial "capital of Latin America," a politically stable, financially well-regulated marketplace hospitable to businesspersons from a dozen countries. Latin business flourished in the North as well. In old industrial cities such as Passaic, Paterson, and Union City, New Jersey, Latinos from Cuba, Chile, Colombia, Ecuador,

"There is Blood in Every Dollar I Make . . ."

Mr. Ji (not his real name) was a quality control officer in a pharmaceutical factory in Canton, China; his wife worked in a factory day-care center. The Jis decided to come to the United States in the early 1980s in order to get better medical care for their twelve-year-old daughter. The Ji family bags and tags garments in a New York City sweatshop, working long hours at below minimum wage. Mr. Ji, age sixty-two, recounts the difficulties he and his family have had to endure in coming to America.

It was very crowded with over ten people living in [his brother-in-law's] apartment. There's no room for our luggage and we were sleeping in the living room. This is a complete surprise for us. We thought in the U.S. there are all high rises and big apartments. We started searching for the apartment right away. We found a one bedroom apartment on 56th St., Brooklyn, from the classified ads in the Chinese newspapers. It's two blocks from my father-in-law. The rent was $480 and the landlord is very nasty. . . .

I was disappointed with my relatives. . . . The first thing people ask you here is "How much money do you make?" They measure you by how much you can make. My circle of friends are too busy. It's not like China. Here they don't have time to see you at all. They just ask you to call. My in-laws put me down. They said, "You are a college graduate. See how much you are making. What good is going to school?" They said I'm lazy, that I don't work hard enough. . . .

I don't understand America's policy. They let you come. But once you are here, they don't care at all. They don't care if you can get a job or what you do. You are all on your own. It's one thing to let immigrants in. But once they are here, you have to digest them. We get below minimum wages. This is the tenth factory we worked in. It's all the same. Finally we decided to stop hopping around. There is no labor law here. The government is acting like an idiot who doesn't know what's going on. The minimum wages are not for real. . . . In China, I just do desk work, giving people ideas. Now I'm doing this totally meaningless work. America is a world where the strong devours the meek.

I am at a point of no return. If I go back, I'll be looked down on by everybody. They'll think I'm such a failure. . . . I can't go back empty-handed. It'll be so embarrassing. . . . I want to learn English, I felt handicapped. I feel I'm without my limbs. I don't want to be dependent on other people. But I don't have any time at all. . . . Now I'm so tired when I get home, sometimes I don't even cook, just make some instant noodles. . . .

We have to work so hard for so little money. Last Saturday we worked from 9 until 10:30 p.m. Between us we made eighty dollars. It's the best day since I came to the U.S. . . . I am tied down to my job. I feel like a slave. I can't go anywhere. Even if there is gold out there, I won't have time to pick them up. . . . There is blood in every dollar I make. . . . We all thought U.S. is such an advanced country. I don't see too much personal freedom here. You are free if you have money.

Source: Interview conducted by Ying Chan, New York City, 1990.

and Guatemala soon outnumbered both Anglos and African Americans. Latino-owned businesses, including restaurants, nightclubs, cigar shops, fruit stands, and clothing stores, transformed the look, sound, and smell of the main shopping areas in these municipalities. As one Union City resident noted, a few years earlier many shops "used to [have] signs saying, 'We speak Spanish.' Now the signs say, 'We speak English.' "

The new immigration touched even small-town America. Late in the 1970s, church and civic leaders in Wausau, Wisconsin, a homogeneous city of 37,500, welcomed hundreds of Southeast Asian refugees. Many were from the nomadic Hmong Mountain tribes of Laos, who had been recruited by the CIA to fight against North Vietnam during the war in Indochina. Soon a pattern of "chain migration" made Wausau the destination for other family members and friends, increasing the town's Asian population to nearly 5,000. By the mid 1990s, social tensions between the new immigrants and older residents had created in Wausau the same kind of conflict — at school, on the job, and in city government — last seen there a century before when an influx of working-class Germans had challenged the city's old Yankee establishment.

In the United States, immigrants with skills, family connections, and an entrepreneurial outlook could do very well. In Los Angeles, New York, and other cities, many Korean families owned and managed fruit and vegetable markets. Vietnamese, Chinese, Thais, Mexicans, and Iranians opened tens of thousands of new restaurants, making the American dining experience far more cosmopolitan. Indian, Pakistani, and Chinese immigrants with English-language, engineering, and computer electronics skills won a solid beachhead in Silicon Valley and other cyberworld enclaves. And a small number of wealthy individuals from Hong Kong, Saudi Arabia, and Japan took advantage of the undervalued dollar to make substantial investments in commercial real estate, residential property, and stateside industry.

Most of the new immigrants were solidly working class, however. They came because even minimum wage work in the United States paid five or ten times more than they could earn in the cities, barrios, and villages of their homelands. Like the Italians and Irish who arrived in the nineteenth century, many hoped to return to their native countries to buy a farm or open a business. But like their predecessors, most did not succeed. In New York and Los Angeles, Latino and Asian immigrants labored in hundreds of sweatshops of the sort once condemned by progressive reformers. Likewise, in Nebraska, Colorado, and South Dakota, a new generation of immigrants labored in slaughterhouses, under conditions similar to those portrayed in Upton Sinclair's 1904 novel, *The Jungle*. "We came with illusions of earning a little money, investing it, and doing something in Mexico," noted one undocumented immigrant

Sweatshop. Asian workers were photographed in 1991 laboring in a garment shop in lower Manhattan. The setting was reminiscent of sweatshop conditions in the clothing industry earlier in the twentieth century.

Source: Andrea Ades Vásquez—American Social History Project.

"It's the Freon . . ."

Silicon Valley production workers not only labor in tedious and low-paying jobs (often at or just above the minimum wage); they are also frequently exposed to an array of toxic chemicals. At Q.E.S., where the journalist Diana Hembree worked in the early 1980s, production workers were exposed to freon 113, which caused skin rashes, drowsiness, nausea, giddiness, and nervous-system depression.

From the outside, the plant looked more like a real estate office than a factory. Along with hundreds of other "board shops" in the area, it makes printed circuit boards—the brains and memory banks of computers—for other high-tech firms. . . .

At first I was so pleased to have persuaded Q.E.S. to hire me that I clipped the tiny wires with unfeigned enthusiasm. But as the morning wore on, my neck and shoulders ached from craning over the boards, my eyes smarted, and I felt drowsy. After what seemed like interminable hours clipping boards, I stole a glance at the clock: only 9:45. I could smell a peculiar odor, but had no idea what it was.

"Sleepy?" asked the older woman beside me when I tried to stifle a yawn. "It's the freon," she said confidentially, nodding at a machine a few feet away. "Go to the bathroom and splash cold water on your face and arms; that helps a little. Or, if you can't keep your eyes open a second longer, drop something on the floor and take your time picking it up. That's what I do. . . ."

Since [Angel, a co-worker had] been working with the freon, he had broken out in a rash and he had painful, recurring stomach aches. . . . Richard, a friendly, awkward twenty-year-old who was clipping beside Angel, said he didn't know if freon could actually hurt him, but washing circuit boards made him feel dizzy and disoriented. "The last time I did it," Richard said, "I felt like I was in a white cloud. . . ."

Gloria Luna, Angel's twenty-four-year-old sister, worked in the assembly room next door. Having learned English as a teenager, she served as unofficial translator for the other Mexican women. She was two-and-a-half months pregnant with her second child. . . .

[The] new floor supervisor, Ray Burks, told me . . . : "Worrying about chemicals is fine if you have money and options, but compared to being evicted tomorrow if you can't pay the rent, chemical fumes and skin rashes seem pretty minor. . . ."

At the back of the assembly room stands a large machine in which circuit boards are coated with molten tin-and-lead solder. For the past three weeks, the machine has blanketed the room with noxious fumes, causing dizziness among the work force and sending several women to the bathroom to vomit. . . .

"I've never been sick so much in my life," Laura, a single mother in her twenties, told me today. "Since I've been here, I've been sick at least once a week. . . ."

Supervisors traced the problem to a new kind of oil used in the machine, but some employees were not satisfied with the explanation. Worried, I called OSHA [Occupation Safety and Health Administration] and asked that an inspector do air sampling for lead.

At least three other employees have called OSHA to ask for an investigation of the foul-smelling fumes; they talk about it daily in excited whispers. But so far, no inspectors have shown up.

Source: Diana Hembree, "Dead End in Silicon Valley," *The Progressive,* October 1985.

in New York City. "But those who get $180 for working seven days, what can they do? They return defeated to Mexico."

Even where the work was technology-based and legal, job hierarchies resembled those of the pre–New Deal era. Many of California's most successful new computer firms maintained a pyramidal job structure: a few optimistic professionals with an innovative concept at the top; English-speaking clerical, sales, and research and development workers in the front office; and in the back shop, scores of Asian and Latino women building chips, stuffing circuit boards, or moving inventory. Their work was as routine and insecure as that of a sweatshop garment worker a hundred years before. Seventy percent of all the electronics manufacturing jobs in northern California's Silicon Valley were held by women, half of whom were Latino and Asian immigrants.

The Ranks of the Poor

At the very bottom of the American social hierarchy stood the one in eight Americans whose incomes fell below the U.S. government's poverty line during the 1980s. The proportion of all Americans considered poor reached its postwar low in 1973, but stagflation drove this number upward until it peaked at 15 percent in the early 1980s. Increasingly low levels of unemployment, especially in the 1990s, decreased the number of people living in poverty, but even during the most prosperous times, about one-tenth of all whites were poor, as were one-third of the nation's African Americans and one-quarter of all Latinos.

Low pay, structural changes in the economy, and institutional racism were the chief causes of poverty in late-twentieth century America. During the 1980s and into the early 1990s, American business generated some 30 million new jobs, but most of them were in the service sector, which paid on average about 20 percent less than did manufacturing or transportation. Although a substantial number of white-collar "knowledge worker" jobs were created in the health professions, finance, entertainment, and high technology, the majority of these new service-sector jobs did not pay enough to keep even a two-paycheck family in middle-class comfort. The most rapidly growing occupations—home health care attendant, salesclerk, food server, janitor, and office clerk—were unglamorous. Most of these jobs were low-paid and part time, offering few pension or health care benefits and affording little opportunity for promotion. McDonald's, the largest employer of black youth in the nation, hired almost all its workers on a part-time, minimum wage basis, which assured a turnover rate of more than 100 percent per year. "You make minimum wage," complained one Baltimore resident, "and there are so many people applying that the jobs are snapped right up."

"You Don't Have to Know How to Cook . . ."

Over the years more than ten million Americans have found work at McDonald's; most are paid the minimum wage. In the name of efficiency and profitability, McDonald's has reduced formerly semiskilled jobs such as short-order cook to unskilled and mindless grill-tending. A teenager describes cooking hamburgers on a computerized grill in the allotted ninety seconds.

They called us the Green Machine 'cause the crew had green uniforms then. And that's what it is, a machine. You don't have to know how to cook, you don't have to know how to think. There's a procedure for everything and you just follow the procedures. . . .

You're on the ten-in-one grill, ten patties in a pound. Your basic burger. The guy on the bin calls, "Six hamburgers." So you lay your six pieces of meat on the grill and set the timer. Beep-beep, beep-beep, beep-beep. That's the beeper to sear 'em. It goes off in twenty seconds. [Then press the patties down with a spatula.] Sup, sup, sup, sup, sup, sup. Now you turn off the sear beeper, put the buns in the oven, set the oven timer and then the next beeper is to turn the meat. This one goes beep-beep-beep, beep-beep-beep. So you turn your patties, and then you drop your re-cons [handfuls of reconstituted onions] on the meat, t-con, t-con, t-con. Now the bun oven buzzes. This one turns itself off when you open the oven door so you just take out your crowns [tops of buns], line 'em up and give 'em each a squirt of mustard and a squirt of ketchup.

Now, you get to put on the pickles. Two if they're regular, three if they're small. That's the creative part. Then the lettuce, then you ask for a cheese count ("cheese on four please"). Finally the last beep goes off and you lay your burger on the crowns. . . .

Then scoop up the heels [the bun bottoms] which are on top of the bun warmer, take the heels with one hand and push the tray out from underneath and they land (plip) one on each burger, right on top of the re-cons, neat and perfect. It's like I told you. The procedures makes the burgers. You don't have to know a thing. . . .

You follow the beepers, you follow the buzzers and you turn your meat as fast as you can. . . . To work at McDonald's you don't need a face, you don't need a brain. You need to have two hands and two legs and move 'em as fast as you can. That's the whole system. I wouldn't go back there again for anything.

Source: Barbara Garson, *The Electronic Sweatshop: How Computers Are Transforming the Office of the Future into the Factory of the Past* (1988).

Government welfare programs and wage standards, designed to compensate for the economy's inability to generate enough high-paying jobs, were cut back or abandoned during the Reagan era. By 1989, state and local welfare payments had dropped by an average of 40 percent from their 1973 level. Job-training programs were also sharply curtailed, and the minimum wage, which the Reagan administration froze at 1981 levels, lost some 44 percent of its value through inflation. The U.S. Labor Department admitted that a full-time minimum wage worker could not keep a family of four out of poverty.

Many Americans fell out of the world of work. The decline in the value of unemployment compensation and welfare, coupled with sharp hikes in urban rents and the elimination of federally supported housing programs, generated a new, or at least a vastly more visible, phenomenon: homeless Americans, between 1 million and 3 million of them during the 1980s. When homeless people first appeared in large numbers in the late 1970s, many Americans labeled them as "bag ladies, winos, and junkies," or people just released from mental hospitals. But within a few years it became clear that for millions of working Americans, homelessness was only a layoff or a family crisis away. In fact, one of every five homeless people held a full-time or part-time job. On cold winter nights, whole families, not just single men, searched for food and warmth at the crowded, squalid shelters that opened in almost every American city. By the end of the 1980s, families with children constituted one-third of the urban homeless population.

Unlike those in poverty during the Great Depression, who lived everywhere, the new poor, especially African Americans, often lived in isolated ghetto communities. The civil rights revolution of the 1960s had helped to expand the small black middle class to perhaps one in four African Americans by the end of the 1980s. But the fair employment and housing laws passed during the civil rights era also facilitated the exodus of solid income earners from many black inner-city neighborhoods. As a result, African-American poverty, as the sociologist William Julius Wilson pointed out, became geographically isolated, thus depriving ghetto residents of the kind of community leadership and socially positive role models found in neighborhoods and schools where jobs were more plentiful.

Have-nots. Homeless people found shelter during a cold January 1990 night in New York City's Pennsylvania Station.

Source: George Cohen/ Impact Visuals.

Endemic poverty and social isolation contributed to a fearful wave of criminality and drug addiction that washed over inner-city neighborhoods during the 1980s. A wave of hard drugs, especially inexpensive "crack" cocaine, generated a

". . . I Fear for My Children"

Deborah M., a homeless single mother in New York City, speaks about trying to raise her children while shifting from one dormitory-style public shelter to another. Early in 1991, a city agency finally placed her and her children in their own apartment.

This could happen to anyone. As for me, I finished high school, I've done a year and a half of college, I'm a certified nurse's aide and a bank teller, and I'm homeless. . . . I have four children: fourteen, thirteen, nine, and the baby was two. . . . I had teenage girls so we had to sleep in [our] clothes. . . . You don't have locks on your doors. . . . The worst part of being there is that I fear for my children. . . . Whatever place we moved, I took them to [school in] Queens. We had to get up at five. It took us in traveling time an hour and a half to an hour and forty-five minutes. . . .

From the little timid children that they were, they're not that anymore. . . . My oldest daughter had to stop her cheerleading, swim meets, her gymnastics because we didn't know where we would be living day by day. I have a lot of problems with her now. . . . There is a lot of bad kids in the shelter. I don't blame the mothers or nothing. A year from now I see her not in school, pregnant. . . . She thinks that she's so much older and wiser now . . . like nobody can tell her anything.

My son said that he is tired of moving around, he's sleepy: "Do we have to move tomorrow again?" We moved to six different shelters, most of them was overnight. My children changed drastically, they got hostile, disrespectful, angry, they just got the attitude that they just didn't care anymore. . . . Like they lost their self-identity. . . . My children lost all sense of security.

When they just saw the place [temporary apartment-style shelter] they ran through the whole apartment. "This is going to be my room. Oh, we have a bathroom!" The first thing my daughter said is, "I'm just going to love it here, I'm so glad that we're not in the shelters anymore." My children have improved greatly since we moved here. They have found me an apartment back in Queens, it's a whole house, and hopefully in the next two or three weeks, we'll be out of here.

Source: *Homeless with Children,* WNYC-TV, June 1991.

violent world of well-armed drug lords and street-corner salesmen. By the 1980s, homicide was the leading cause of death among urban black males aged fifteen to twenty-four, a rate six times greater than that of other Americans. In many large metropolitan areas such as New York City, one of every four African-American men in their twenties and one of every eight Latino men of the same age were in prison, on probation, or on parole.

Prisons, in fact, were one of the great growth industries of the 1980s and 1990s. For most of the twentieth century, the U.S. incarceration rate was comparable to that in other industrialized nations — about one in every thousand. But as the idea of rehabilitation faded during the 1970s, government at all levels began to jail criminals simply to keep them off the street. Fueled by a set of stiff drug laws that hit African Americans the hardest, the prison population tripled to nearly 2 million between 1980 and 1998. This gave the United States both the most prisoners and the highest incarceration rate of any nation in the world. Arrests of African Americans for drug possession soared sevenfold in the decade following 1985. The United States was also one of the few Western nations to retain the death penalty. After the Supreme Court affirmed its legality in 1975, southern and western states carried out executions with increasing frequency. And like the drug laws, the death penalty was applied to a disproportionate degree to African Americans, who made up half of all inmates on death row.

The Labor Movement Under Fire

Reaganomics proved disastrous for American trade unions. In the 1970s, the unions had represented almost one in four working Americans, but during the 1980s this proportion dropped to one in six. In the private sector, organized labor represented but 11 percent of all workers — a huge decline from the early postwar years, when trade unions were pervasive in manufacturing, utilities, transport, mining, and the telephone industry. Moreover, unions became weak and their leaders fearful: in the 1980s strikes practically ceased, even when management cut wages, pensions, and health care benefits.

What accounted for this debacle? The plant closings and layoffs that swept through many heavily unionized industries provided one answer. U.S. Steel, which had once employed a unionized workforce of 200,000, transformed itself into USX Corporation, shut down a dozen steel mills, and acquired Marathon Oil, from which it soon derived the bulk of its sales and profits. The United Steelworkers of America lost almost half its members in the process, as imports and automation slashed jobs in Pittsburgh (Pennsylvania) and Gary (Indiana), and as small southern, nonunion mills cut themselves a slice of the market. When the union finally undertook a strike against USX in 1986, only 20,000 union steelworkers remained at the company.

The United Auto Workers lost half a million members after 1978, when Japanese auto sales captured a quarter of the U.S. market. Dozens of Big Three factories were shut down, and auto-parts makers fled the

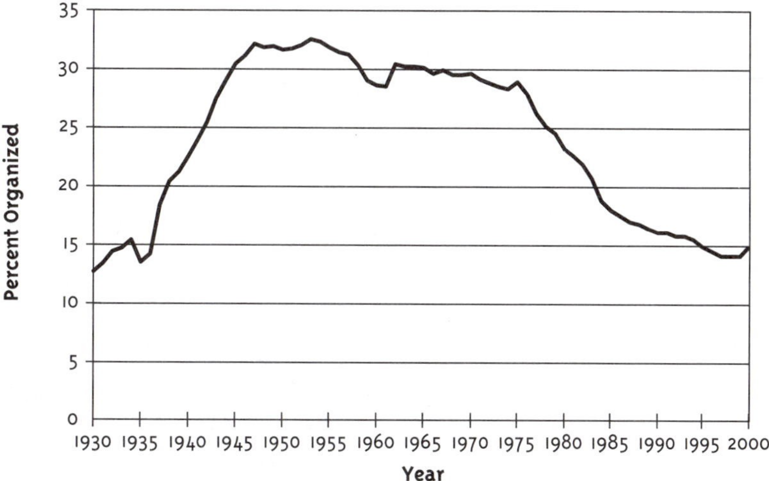

The Decline of American Unionism: Union Membership, 1930 to 1999 Unions grew rapidly in the 1930s and 1940s and maintained their strength for most of the next three decades. But because they were unable to organize white-collar and service workers who were employed by firms like Wal-Mart, McDonald's, and Microsoft, unionism remained confined to public employment and the declining manufacturing sector. Therefore, the proportion of all Americans who were members of a trade union declined sharply in the 1980s and 1990s.

unionized North for low-wage Tennessee, Alabama, and Mexico. Union strongholds such as Chicago, Detroit, Baltimore, and Philadelphia lost population, while anti-union Sunbelt cities such as San Diego, Phoenix, and Dallas mushroomed in size. These latter three cities were now the sixth, seventh, and eighth largest, respectively, in the nation.

Beginning in the 1970s, many employers became much more aggressive in their efforts to avoid or break trade unions, even in the once labor-friendly North. Their tactics skillfully combined both a paternalistic carrot and an anti-union stick. Corporations in such growing fields as finance, information technology, and health care offered workers an attractive menu of new benefits, often including on-site health clubs and child care. But most of these same companies remained bitterly anti-union. Management consultants advised executives of a group of New Jersey hospitals to figure out "who is going to be most vulnerable if the union knocks," then "weed 'em out. Get rid of anyone who's not going to be a team player." Such tactics violated both the spirit and the letter of existing labor law, but they were punished only mildly by the National Labor Relations Board. Managers who engaged in such "unfair labor practices" considered the penalties merely part of the cost of doing business in a union-free environment. By 1984, pro-union workers were fired at a rate four times higher than in 1960.

Hardball anti-union tactics went hand in hand with another old-fashioned management strategy—cutting wages. In the 1980s, employers slashed wages in industries facing foreign competition—auto, steel, and garment manufacturing—as well as in profitable industries whose only competition was domestic. U.S. meatpackers, for example, began shifting their operations away from unionized packinghouses in Chicago and

Omaha to save money. Soon a string of low-wage, nonunion meatpacking plants flourished in Iowa, Illinois, and Nebraska. By the early 1980s, wages in this once thoroughly organized industry varied by as much as $3 an hour from one plant to another. As a business spokesperson summed up the situation, "An abundant supply of labor makes it more possible than ever before to operate during a strike. This possibility constrains union demands." During the first half of the 1980s, American workers lost about $500 billion in wage givebacks and other concessions.

Plant Closing. A northern California lumber company auctioned off its works and equipment in the fall of 1988. **Source:** Evan Johnson/ Impact Visuals.

In the midst of this wave of "concession bargaining," President Reagan's destruction of a trade union of government employees, the Professional Air Traffic Controllers Organization (PATCO), immeasurably strengthened business's hand against organized labor. Ironically, PATCO, a politically conservative craft union, had been one of the few unions to support the Republican presidential candidate in 1980. But these well-educated, well-paid workers, many of them U.S. Air Force veterans, complained of the intense mental stress and physical strain inherent in air traffic control work. The union wanted Reagan to restaff and reform the Federal Aviation Administration (FAA), which employed most PATCO members. When the air traffic controllers struck the FAA in August 1981, Reagan waited only three days to fire more than 10,000 of the striking workers and fill their jobs with supervisors and other replacements. Not since Massachusetts governor Calvin Coolidge broke the Boston police strike in 1919 had the government so thoroughly smashed a union of its own employees.

Reagan's destruction of PATCO transformed every strike in the nation into a union-busting opportunity. In both private companies and public agencies, managers had little trouble finding unemployed or underpaid workers willing to replace union strikers. Most "scabs," or strikebreakers, were motivated by sheer economic necessity, given the wage stagnation and high unemployment of the early 1980s. But worker solidarity could hardly be expected to flourish in an era that celebrated

A Warning. This illustration is from a leaflet distributed during the summer and fall of 1981 by the Los Angeles local of the Professional Air Traffic Controllers Organization (PATCO). The leaflet urged other airline and airport workers to support PATCO and warned that the Reagan administration's suppression of the union would permit the airline companies to force layoffs and contract concessions from all workers in the industry.

Source: Los Angeles Professional Air Traffic Controllers Organization, 1981.

entrepreneurial freedom, wage inequality, and the virtue of corporate downsizing. In almost every long strike during the 1980s, management found it relatively easy to recruit replacement workers eager to keep their enterprise afloat. This shift in sentiment and public perception was graphically revealed during a strike of professional football players in 1984. Thousands of fans flocked to the stadiums, jeering picket lines manned by players they considered too well paid, to cheer on football teams composed entirely of third-string replacement players.

Corporate attacks on unions were especially vicious in industries that were deregulated during the late 1970s. Nonunion upstart companies grabbed market share from industry stalwarts, but in the new, competitive environment some firms went bankrupt, while others cut wages, broke their unions, and even skimped on safety precautions. In 1983, after selling hundreds of millions of dollars' worth of high-interest "junk bonds," Frank Lorenzo bought Continental Airlines, declared it bankrupt, and then slashed the pay of thousands of pilots, machinists, and flight attendants. When the workers struck, Lorenzo broke their unions by hiring replacement workers from the tens of thousands of unemployed pilots and machinists laid off during the recession of the early 1980s. He then moved on to Eastern Airlines, which he added to his empire in 1986. Using similar tactics, Lorenzo again demanded massive wage concessions certain to precipitate a strike. But this time, well-paid airline pilots joined machinists and flight attendants in a highly effective work stoppage that won sympathy from passengers, solidarity from the labor movement, and even grudging admiration from Wall Street. Their lengthy strike threw the airline into bankruptcy, forced Lorenzo out of the airline business, and put the brakes on deregulation of the airline industry.

The organized working class was on the ideological and economic defensive throughout the 1980s. In almost every strike and negotiation, unions sought to defend the status quo: to save jobs and maintain their existing wage levels and health benefits in the face of the concessions, or givebacks, demanded by employers. The battleground for these struggles was often a single factory, company, or community where embattled unionists tried to mobilize families, neighbors, and community activists in defense of an entire way of life. In the coal fields of Appalachia, in the Arizona copper mines, on California factory farms, and in midwestern manufacturing towns, unionists demonstrated that they could still organize for long, bitter social struggles reminiscent of those waged during the last quarter of the nineteenth century.

Austin, Minnesota. Local P-9 strikers and supporters confronted the Minnesota National Guard outside the Hormel plant on a cold January morning in 1986.

Source: Hardy Green.

In Austin, Minnesota, for example, Local P-9 organized retirees, high school students, family members, and sympathetic unionists in a battle against wage concessions at the venerable Hormel Meatpacking Company. Throughout the bone-chilling winter of 1985, the Austin working-class community, "P-9 Proud," mobilized tens of thousands of supporters throughout the upper Midwest. But unlike the great railroad strike of 1877 or the Homestead steel conflict of 1892, labor protests of the 1980s had few defenders beyond the ranks of working-class militants. The Democratic party was becoming more conservative, and many liberals thought of the unions as white male institutions that were hostile to feminism, civil rights, and environmental concerns. In Austin, Local P-9 had to fight not only the company, but a Democratic governor, who sent in National Guard troops, and the leadership of United Food and Commercial Workers, who thought the workers should accept another round of wage concessions. The Austin strike ended late in 1986 with the community divided, P-9 defeated, and Hormel victorious.

Reaganism in Triumph and at an Impasse

As fiscal austerity and the liberal–labor retreat shifted American politics to the right, the long recession of the early 1980s began to lift. Thus Ronald Reagan and his party entered the 1984 campaign season at the height of their popularity. The Democrats were deeply divided. Jesse

Jackson, an African-American minister whose Rainbow Coalition aspired to represent a multiracial alliance of the poor and working class, proved a dynamic spokesman for the party's social democratic wing. In contrast, Senator Gary Hart represented a growing neoliberal current, progressive on social issues such as abortion and gun control but increasingly cool toward the labor movement and the welfare state. Both candidates were bested by the party's titular leader, former vice president Walter Mondale, who sought to inject some excitement into his campaign by selecting New York congresswoman Geraldine Ferraro as his running mate.

Ronald Reagan won the election in a landslide, taking 59 percent of the popular vote and every state except Minnesota, Mondale's home state. Reagan's campaign, epitomized by a widely broadcast TV spot, "It's Morning in America," projected a new era of national pride, moral certitude, and economic well-being. Although African Americans and Jews voted solidly Democratic once again, Republicans kept the allegiance of blue-collar "Reagan Democrats," swept the white South and the suburbs, and won a majority of votes even among white women and union members. As usual, white Protestant men were the most solidly Republican group in the nation.

But Reaganism reached an impasse after the start of the new term, both as an economic doctrine and as a foreign policy prescription. Though unemployment began to fall and the stock market to boom, supply-side economics had little to do with it. Rather, the surge in military spending, combined with lower interest rates and a large federal budget deficit, pulled the U.S. economy out of the recession. Indeed, Congress repudiated much of Reagan's supply-side tax program early in his second term. In 1985, a coalition of Republicans and Democrats passed the Gramm–Rudman–Hollings Act, which established a maximum federal debt level and required across-the-board cuts if the budget exceeded that target. Both the White House and Congress would later circumvent this law, but the idea that tax cuts in and of themselves would generate revenue sufficient to balance the budget was henceforth taken seriously only by the extreme right wing. Thus in 1986, another bipartisan congressional coalition revised the tax law: by closing numerous tax loopholes and subjecting capital gains to the same tax rate as ordinary income, it raised more revenue from corporations and the rich.

Reagan's aggressively anti-Communist foreign policy also ran into trouble. Outraged by the administration's policy of "constructive engagement" with white South Africa, U.S. students spearheaded a broad national movement demanding that universities and companies divest themselves of their investments in the apartheid regime. Early in 1985, thousands of protesters were arrested at South African embassies and consulates. Their activism spurred Congress to pass, over President Reagan's veto, a law banning new investments in South Africa or loans to the South African regime. Another broad movement opposed U.S. intervention in the civil wars in Nicaragua and El Salvador, in part because many saw in the American military involvement there the specter of another Vietnam. Although Reagan hailed the Nicaraguan counterrevolutionaries ("Contras"), as "freedom fighters," Congress remained skeptical; in 1984, it passed the Boland Amendment banning U.S. military aid to the Contras. Finally, Reagan's support for a new round of Cold War military spending encountered stiff resistance, especially after reformer Mikhail Gorbachev assumed power in the Soviet Union.

Crisis engulfed the presidency in 1986 when the public learned that officials from the Central Intelligence Agency (CIA), the National Security Council (NSC), and the State Department had conspired to organize a covert and illegal government operation to aid the Contras in violation of the Boland Amendment. At the instigation of CIA director William Casey and national security adviser Robert McFarlane, the United States secretly sold millions of dollars worth of military equipment to Iran, a regime the United States publicly denounced for supporting terrorism. The profits from this illegal arms trade, along with other money raised secretly from foreign governments, were then used to fund the Contras in their war against Nicaragua's radical Sandinista government. Although several NSC officials went to jail and much evidence suggested that Reagan had condoned the illegal acts, Democratic lawmakers shied away from an effort to impeach the still-popular president. But the televised hearings into the Iran–Contra affair, which brought to national prominence the telegenic NSC staffer Lieutenant Colonel Oliver North, nonetheless deprived Reagan of his ability to set the national political agenda for the remainder of his term. In the 1986 congressional elections, the Democrats recaptured control of the U.S. Senate, an outcome that was heavily influenced by Jesse Jackson's campaign to mobilize liberals and African Americans in normally conservative states such as Alabama and Louisiana.

Symbols Speak Louder than Words. Oliver North appeared before the House Foreign Affairs Committee on December 9, 1986, to testify about his role in the Iran–Contra scandal. Dressed in his Marine uniform, North presented himself as a symbol of American patriotism in an effort to counterbalance his refusal (citing his Fifth Amendment rights) to discuss his illegal activities in the basement of the White House. **Source:** Corbis/Bettmann-UPI.

The Reaganite impasse became more evident in 1987, when a liberal coalition that included feminists, civil libertarians, trade unionists, and civil rights activists successfully blocked Senate approval of Robert Bork, Reagan's nominee to the U.S. Supreme Court. Reagan had already made three conservative appointments to the Supreme Court. In 1981 he had named Sandra Day O'Connor, an Arizona judge and the first woman to serve on the high court. Then in 1985 he promoted Justice William Rehnquist to the position of chief justice and nominated the conservative legal scholar Antonin Scalia to the Court. O'Connor, Rehnquist, and Scalia were all "strict constructionists" who did not accept an expansive interpretation of the Supreme Court's constitutional mandate. But Bork was a right-wing ideologue. A believer in adherence to what he considered the original intent of the Constitution, Bork had opposed both the 1964 Civil Rights Act and *Roe* v. *Wade,* the 1973 Supreme Court decision legalizing abortion. After a bitter and partisan hearing, the Senate rejected Bork's appointment 58 to 42. In his place, the Senate easily approved Anthony M. Kennedy, who, with O'Connor, would become the core of a centrist bloc that sustained in the 1990s most of the liberal judicial decisions handed down during the 1960s and 1970s.

The defeat of the Bork nomination was followed by another setback. In October 1987 the stock market crashed, forcing the Dow Jones Index down 22 percent in one day, proportionally more than that of "Black Tuesday," which marked the beginning of the Great Depression. Although no economic collapse followed this stock market tumble, the speculative boom of the 1980s was over. Real estate and junk bond prices plummeted. A recession followed, beginning on both coasts and then spreading to the Midwest and South. Meanwhile, several of the most celebrated financial wizards of the era, including Michael Milken, were found guilty of illegal stock market manipulation and sent to jail.

An even more widespread and costly pattern of financial chicanery plunged the nation's savings and loan (S&L) industry into near-bankruptcy in the late 1980s. The deregulation of S&Ls had begun during the Carter administration, but it was greatly advanced by Reagan-era legislation, which gave S&Ls virtually unlimited freedom to invest their depositors' funds in risk-laden ventures. Unsophisticated S&L executives now transformed thousands of cautiously managed home-mortgage institutions into speculative enterprises that gambled federally insured deposits on questionable real estate loans and junk bonds. The personal profligacy of some S&L executives soon became a national scandal. One group of Beverly Hills S&L officials paid themselves well enough to enjoy the use of two $17-million jets, on which they flew family and friends to vacation condominiums bought with depositors' money. Others contributed heavily, and illegally, to friendly politicians in both parties. But when the boom in southwestern oil, suburban officeparks, and Sunbelt defense production ended after 1987, hundreds of S&Ls plunged into bankruptcy. Because most S&L deposits were guaranteed by an agency of the U.S. government, taxpayers were left holding a multibillion-dollar bill. In the early 1990s, a federally chartered Resolution Trust Company sold off the depreciated S&L properties and cleaned up their books, at a total cost to American taxpayers of $150 billion.

Culture Wars

Reaganism was far more of a political than an economic success. If at the end of the 1980s the Reagan administration itself stood at a policy impasse, its eight years of governance had nevertheless shifted the nation's politics well to the right. The Republican party no longer had room for a liberal, pro-welfare-state wing. The Democrats still controlled Congress, though they had neither the votes nor the will to propose social or economic legislation of the sort once championed by Lyndon Johnson and Hubert Humphrey. Reagan Republicans set the nation's political agenda, even if they could not always carry the day on any particular issue. If the culture of the university and the old-line philanthropies remained largely liberal, conservative intellectuals were a growing presence on the television talk shows, on newspaper opinion pages, and in such influential, well-funded think tanks as the Heritage Foundation and the Cato, Hudson, and American Enterprise Institutes.

But Reaganite political power was not matched by a conservative capacity to transform the nation's social mores or restrain the increasingly adventuresome character of U.S. culture, entertainment, and social thought. This was an enormous frustration to many intellectuals and politicians of the Right, who saw Reaganism not merely as a political or economic doctrine but also as a movement to reverse some of the dramatic cultural changes that had transformed American society since the 1960s. William Bennett, Reagan's secretary of education, denounced "relativism" and "mulitculturalism" in university curricula, arguing instead for a return to the study and celebration of what he called the "Judeo-Christian tradition." Likewise, Allan Bloom, a neoconservative political theorist, briefly soared to prominence with publication of *The Closing of the American Mind,* a 1986 best-seller that assaulted student activism, cultural relativism, academic Marxism, and rock-and-roll. Columnist George Will warned that "everything connected with culture, from literature through science, depends upon a network of received authority."

But American culture never conformed to this Reaganite orthodoxy. Evangelical Protestantism continued to

Heritage USA. A scene in the Baptism Pool in Jim and Tammy Bakker's 2,300-acre revivalist theme park and campground, located on the border between North and South Carolina. By 1986, Heritage USA was one of the nation's top tourist attractions, drawing more than 6 million visitors a year to its rides, water park, petting zoo, hotel, and shopping mall. But in 1989, Jim Bakker was convicted of defrauding investors of hundreds of millions of dollars and subsequently served five years in federal prison.

Source: Jerry Valente/Sipa Press.

grow in numbers, and in 1986 allies of the conservative televangelist Pat Robertson won control of the Southern Baptist Convention, the nation's largest religious denomination. But the influence of the religious Right did not extend far beyond its own ranks. Several states did impose some restrictions on the right of women to secure an abortion, especially if they were teenagers or in the last trimester of pregnancy, but this medical practice remained legal and widely available in the United States. Women continued to increase their numbers within the workforce, and at the end of the 1980s affirmative action programs still benefited those racial minorities who sought employment, job promotions, or admission to college. Meanwhile, several well-known fundamentalist ministers, including Jimmy Swaggart and Jim Bakker, became embroiled in embarrassing sex and financial scandals. Enthusiasm for their TV programs waned after 1987, prompting Jerry Falwell to disband his Moral Majority. In 1988, when Pat Robertson ran for the GOP presidential nomination, his campaign was a flop.

On network television, the celebration of wealth and ruthless entrepreneurship that had helped define the Reagan era, such as *Dallas* and *Falcon Crest,* were canceled in the late 1980s. They were replaced by successful situation comedies such as *Roseanne, Married . . . with Children,* and *The Simpsons,* which revolved around the many frustrations and occasional joys of hard-pressed working families. On the music scene, "country" still held the greatest radio audience, but rock-and-roll, which dominated record sales, continued to showcase the nation's cultural avant garde. The two biggest pop stars of the 1980s, Michael Jackson and Madonna, were not only fabulously successful entertainers but also racial and gender experimentalists. Jackson, whose 1982 album *Thriller* sold more copies than any other record in history, transformed himself into a racially and sexually ambiguous icon. Likewise, Madonna, an indefatigable exhibitionist, redefined a modern sexuality that deployed an earthy feminist sensibility, exemplified in her "Material Girl" and other best-selling songs.

Scratching. DJs work out "scratch" rhythms on records at a Bronx playground party in 1984. "Hip-hop" culture emerged out of black inner-city neighborhoods in the 1980s, appropriating fragments of previous musical forms to construct a new genre of popular music. By the end of the decade, hip-hop style and rap music had spread to the suburban mall. Yet while young Americans embraced hip-hop and businesses packaged youth-oriented products in hip-hop style, the African-American reality continued to be dominated by unemployment, the crack epidemic, and "black-on-black" violence. By 1990, homicide was the leading cause of death for black men between the ages of fifteen to twenty-four, a rate six times greater than for other Americans.

Source: Henry Chalfant/City Lore.

Popular music defined a technological and aesthetic frontier. Cassettes replaced vinyl records as the Sony Walkman and the portable boom-box made listening both more all-pervasive and more private. Music Television (MTV), a genuinely new art form, burst onto the scene in 1981. Rap, or hip-hop, emerged from the African-American ghetto early in the 1980s. Combining rhythmic verse with a driving beat derived from scratching the surface of a record and sampling the music of other rhythm-and-blues and rock-and-roll performers, rap spoke to the daily experiences of black inner-city youth facing gang violence, the crack epidemic, police brutality, and economic strain. By the end of the decade, many Chicanos, who introduced bilingual lyrics, and white suburban teenagers had enthusiastically embraced the music, the accompanying hip-hop style in fashion, and rap's outlaw image. Rap stimulated the resurgence of a black nationalist sensibility. Groups such as Public Enemy, whose *Fight the Power* was an openly Afrocentric anthem, and KRS-One, who preached a more inclusive "edutainment" message, moved the music onto political terrain, as did the controversial recordings of 2 Live Crew and N.W.A. ("Niggahs With Attitude"). So did Spike Lee's hip-hop-inspired 1989 film *Do the Right Thing,* which depicted the escalating, sometimes violent racial tensions that still divided America's multi-ethnic cities.

The Reagan Legacy

In the 1970s and 1980s, the United States entered an era of post–New Deal politics and political economy. The globalization of trade, finance, and manufacturing put enormous pressures for profit and productivity on American firms and made far less efficient and effective the kind of liberal interventionist economic policies that had worked so well when the North American continent coincided with U.S. labor and product markets. But politics still trumped market forces. Thus the price of oil, which seemed to rise inexorably during the 1970s, plunged after 1984, largely because of political disarray among the oil-producing nations in the Middle East, government-mandated conservation measures, and slower economic growth.

Likewise, the stagnation in the American standard of living was not a product of what some politicians of the 1970s liked to call "an era of limits"; it reflected instead the increasingly successful effort waged by corporations and the government to make American workers pay for the return of U.S. business to a more profitable and competitive status. The key events here were threefold. Carter's appointment of Paul Volcker to the Federal Reserve in 1979 signaled that the government would tolerate a recession and high unemployment in order to lower the rate of inflation. Then Reagan's massive tax cut in 1981 slashed social spending and offered the wealthy billions in tax relief. And his destruction of the air traffic controllers' union later that same year inaugurated a generation-long assault on the organized working class as debilitating as the defeat of the Homestead strikers in 1892 and the immigrant steelworkers in 1919.

But Reaganism did not realign American politics and culture. Reagan's electoral victories in 1980 and 1984 were decisive, but they were not of the same consequence as those of 1860, 1896, and 1932. The new conservatism did win new recruits in the white South and among northern blue-collar Democrats, but Reaganism never had the same thoroughgoing impact on American life as had Lincoln's triumphant abolitionism, McKinley's anti-Populist Republicanism, or the New Deal of Franklin Roosevelt. Anti-Communism constituted much of the glue that held together the Reaganite majority, but at the end of the 1980s even that ideology would become increasingly anachronistic.

The Years in Review

1970

- Congress creates Environmental Protection Agency, one of many signs of growing environmental consciousness in the 1970s.

1972

- Congress approves the Equal Rights Amendment (ERA), but it fails to win ratification by states after the New Right mobilizes against it.
- Sally J. Preisand ordained as the first female rabbi in the United States; five years later, first woman Episcopal priest, Jacqueline Means, is ordained.

1973

- The Organization of Petroleum Exporting Countries (OPEC) raises oil prices from $3 to $12 a barrel. The resultant energy crisis leads to federally mandated gasoline rationing in 1974 and a nationwide speed limit of 55 miles per hour.

1974

- In September, President Ford pardons Richard Nixon, who had resigned a month earlier to avoid impeachment.
- Little League baseball opens team membership to girls.

1975

- New York City narrowly averts bankruptcy; President Ford refuses to provide federal assistance.
- Boston plunges into crisis when working-class whites oppose school busing.

- Strategic Arms Limitation Treaty (SALT) puts ceiling on nuclear missile development.

1976

- Georgia Democrat Jimmy Carter defeats Gerald Ford for president.

1977

- New climate of homophobia evident when singer Anita Bryant spearheads successful movement to repeal a Florida antidiscrimination ordinance.

1978

- California voters pass Proposition 13, capping property taxes.
- Camp David accords return the Sinai Peninsula to Egypt in return for Egypt's formal diplomatic recognition of Israel.
- Iran's Shah Reza Pahlavi deposed; the next year Islamic militants take over U.S. embassy and hold fifty-two persons hostage for 444 days.
- Resorts International opens the first legal casino outside of Nevada in Atlantic City, New Jersey.

1979

- Near-meltdown at Pennsylvania's Three Mile Island nuclear utility.
- President Carter appoints conservative Paul Volcker chairman of the Federal Reserve Board; interest rates climb to 20 percent, and the U.S. economy plunges into a recession.
- U.S. government officially recognizes Communist China.
- Sandinistas topple Somoza family dictatorship in Nicaragua.

1980

- Former Beatle John Lennon is murdered by Mark Chapman.
- United States boycotts Moscow Olympics in response to Soviet invasion of Afghanistan, signaling breakdown of détente.
- Easily defeating Jimmy Carter, Republican Ronald Reagan is elected President; Republicans gain control of the Senate for the first time in almost thirty years.

1981

- Reagan administration and Congress cut taxes and domestic social programs, and raise military spending.
- President Reagan fires more than 10,000 air traffic controllers for striking against the Federal Aviation Administration (FAA).
- Reagan appoints the first woman, Sandra Day O'Connor, to the U.S. Supreme Court.
- MTV first appears on cable television.

1982

- First case of AIDS reported in the United States.
- National Collegiate Athletic Association (NCAA) holds first major college basketball championship for women.

1983

- Cabbage Patch Dolls are toy craze.

1984

- Ronald Reagan captures 59 percent of the popular vote, defeating Democrat Walter Mondale and the first female vice presidential candidate, Geraldine Ferraro.
- Congress bans U.S. military aid to Nicaraguan Contras, but Reagan administration secretly sells arms to Iran and uses the profits to support the Contras.
- First birth of a baby to a surrogate mother.

1985

- Local packinghouse union in Austin, Minnesota, wages an unsuccessful strike against Hormel.
- Congress passes the Gramm–Rudman–Hollings Act requiring a balanced budget in response to ballooning federal debt.
- Congress bans new investment in South Africa or loans to its apartheid regime.
- President Reagan pushes the U.S. Supreme Court to the right with the appointment of Antonin Scalia and promotion of William Rehnquist to Chief Justice.
- Coca-Cola introduces new formula; public hostility leads to reintroduction of "Coca-Cola Classic."

1986

- Meltdown at the Chernobyl nuclear plant in the Ukraine.

1987

- Enthusiasm for televangelism wanes after Jimmy Swaggart and Jim Bakker are involved in sex and money scandals.
- Half-million people assemble for Gay Pride march in Washington, D.C.

1989

- Indictment of junk bond king Michael Milken, who earned $550 million in 1987, for racketeering and securities fraud provides symbolic end to 1980s "casino capitalism."

1990

- Congress passes Americans with Disabilities Act.

Suggested Readings

Barlett, Donald L., and James B. Steele, *America: Who Stole the Dream?* (1996).

Bensman, David, and Roberta Lynch, *Rusted Dreams: Hard Times in a Steel Community* (1988).

Berman, William C., *America's Right Turn: From Nixon to Clinton* (The American Movement) (1998).

Blumberg, Paul, *Inequality in an Age of Decline* (1980).

Blumenthal, Sidney, and Thomas Byrne Edsall, eds., *The Reagan Legacy* (1988).

Cannon, James M., *Time and Chance: Gerald Ford's Appointment with History* (1998).

Carroll, Peter N., *It Seemed Like Nothing Happened: America in the 1970s* (1990).

Cowie, Jefferson R., *Capital Moves: RCA's Seventy-Year Quest for Cheap Labor* (1999).

Dionne, E.J., Jr., *Why Americans Hate Politics* (1992).

Edsall, Thomas Byrne, *The New Politics of Inequality* (1985).

Ferguson, Thomas, and Joel Rogers, *Right Turn: The Decline of the Democrats and the Future of American Politics* (1987).

Geoghegan, Thomas, *Which Side Are You On? Trying to Be for Labor When It's Flat on Its Back* (1992).

Greider, William, *One World, Ready or Not: The Manic Logic of Global Capitalism* (1997).

Greider, William, *Secrets of the Temple: How the Federal Reserve Runs the Country* (1989).

Halliday, Fred, *From Kabul to Managua: Soviet–American Relations in the 1980s* (1989).

Harrison, Bennett, and Barry Bluestone, *The Great U-Turn; Corporate Restructuring and the Polarizing of America* (1998).

Hochschild, Arlie, *The Second Shift: Working Parents and the Revolution at Home* (1989).

Hodgson, Godfrey, *The World Turned Right Side Up: A History of the Conservative Ascendancy in America* (1996).

Holland, Max, *When the Machine Stopped: A Cautionary Tale from Industrial America* (1990).

Judis, John B., *William F. Buckley, Jr.: Patron Saint of the Conservatives* (1990).

Kaufman, Burton I., *The Presidency of James Earl Carter, Jr.* (1993).

Kingsolver, Barbara, *Holding the Line: Women in the Great Arizona Mine Strike of 1983* (1997).

Klatch, Rebecca E., *Women of the New Right* (1988).

Krieger, Joel, *Reagan, Thatcher, and the Politics of Decline* (1986).

Kuttner, Robert, *Revolt of the Haves: Taxpayer Revolts and the Politics of Austerity* (1980).

Lukas, J. Anthony, *Common Ground: A Turbulent Decade in the Lives of Three American Families* (1986).

Mansbridge, Jane J., *Why We Lost the ERA* (1986).

Martin, William, *With God on Our Side: The Rise of the Religious Right in America* (1996).

Moody, Kim, *An Injury to All: The Decline of American Unionism* (1997).

Morris, Edmund, *Dutch: A Memoir of Ronald Reagan* (1999).

Morris, Kenneth E., *Jimmy Carter: American Moralist* (1996).

Newman, Katherine S., *Falling from Grace: Downward Mobility in the Age of Affluence* (1999).

Petchesky, Rosalind Pollack, *Abortion and Woman's Choice: The State, Sexuality, and Reproductive Freedom* (1990).

Reich, Robert B., *The Work of Nations: Preparing Ourselves for 21st Century Capitalism* (1992).

Reich, Robert B., and John D. Donahue, *New Deals: The Chrysler Revival and the American System* (1986).

Samuelson, Robert J., *The Good Life and Its Discontents: The American Dream in the Age of Entitlement, 1945–1995* (1997).

Schor, Juliet B., *The Overworked American: The Unexpected Decline of Leisure* (1993).

Sidel, Ruth, *Women and Children Last: The Plight of Poor Women in Affluent America* (1992).

Stacey, Judith, *Brave New Families: Stories of Domestic Upheaval in Late Twentieth-Century America* (1998).

Stein, Judith, *Running Steel, Running America: Race, Economic Policy and the Decline of Liberalism* (1998).

Thelen, David, *Becoming Citizens in the Age of Television: How Americans Challenged the Media and Seized Political Initiative During the Iran–Contra Debate* (1996).

Tolchin, Susan J., and Martin Tolchin, *Dismantling America: The Rush to Deregulate* (1985).

Wilson, William Julius, *The Truly Disadvantaged: The Inner City, the Underclass, and Public Policy* (1990).

And on the World Wide Web

- Paul Halsall, *People with a History: An Online Guide to Lesbian, Gay, Bisexual, and Trans* History* (http://www.fordham.edu/halsall/pwh/)

chapter 14

The American People in an Age of Global Capitalism

1989–2000

For twenty-eight years, the Berlin Wall had symbolized the Cold War division of Europe and the power of political ideology to shape the economic and social lives of millions of people in the alliance systems that enfolded most of the globe. Then, early on the evening of November 9, 1989, a young East German couple—we don't know their names—walked to the Invalidenstrasse gate to see if the political upheavals in their homeland had opened the barrier to ordinary Berliners. To their amazement, the once fearsome Volkspolice, who were now the demoralized agents of a rapidly crumbling system, let them pass to the bright lights of the West. Within hours, men and women from both sides of the Wall attacked the edifice with hammers, picks, and any other instruments they could find. Communism was in collapse, and the Cold War would soon be history.

The startlingly abrupt end of European Communism revolutionized international politics. For the first time in nearly half a century, the United States faced no superpower rival. Indeed, for the first time since the end of World War I, capitalism was once again truly a world system, unchallenged on any continent, including Asia, where the Communist rulers of China and Vietnam welcomed foreign investment and encouraged a new class of entrepreneurs.

An increasingly unfettered system of global trade and finance undermined national sovereignty and economic autonomy, not only in Europe and North America, where barrier-free markets were being put in place, but also throughout East Asia and Latin America, where the International Monetary Fund and other supranational bodies came to play a highly prominent role. McDonald's, Nike, Toshiba, and the other transnational corporations actively sought to shed their old national attachments. But the power and pervasiveness of capitalist consumer culture hardly eliminated the search for ethnic, racial, and linguistic identity in the years leading up to the turn of the millennium. In the United States, the debate over cultural values and racial identity has been chronic, though never as tragic and bloody as the warfare that erupted over similar issues in the Caucasus region of the former USSR, the Balkan region of Southeastern Europe, and Central Africa.

Uniformity. The 1990s saw the reemergence of dress codes in many urban school systems. Primarily directed at elementary school-aged students, these measures were an attempt to address the crisis in inner-city schools by promoting discipline. However, no clear correlation has been found between wearing uniforms and increased academic achievement.

Source: Hazel Hankin/Impact Visuals.

End of the Cold War

The Cold War cost more than $11 trillion. But the collapse of the Soviet Union and its satellites was not a result of such enormous military expenditures. No NATO tank fired a shot. No bomb fell on the Kremlin. Instead, a massive, home-grown insurgency, led by workers, dissident intellectuals, and advocates of national self-determination, cracked the Communist bloc regimes. The downfall began in 1980 when striking Polish workers organized Solidarity, an independent trade union of nearly 10 million members. Solidarity, which had strong support from the powerful Polish Catholic Church, demonstrated how a working-class movement could offer an entire nation moral and political leadership. The Polish military drove Solidarity underground late in 1981, but when it reemerged later in the decade, Solidarity won a smashing electoral victory, which soon installed Lech Walesa, a shipyard unionist, as the first freely elected president of the Polish nation in more than sixty years.

Solidarity's example had an impact throughout eastern Europe. Under a relatively youthful party secretary, Mikhail Gorbachev, the Soviet Union in the late 1980s undertook a series of reforms: *perestroika,* designed to restructure the production system, and *glasnost,* meant to open the society to political and artistic debate. Gorbachev knew that in a world of increasing technical complexity and communications, Soviet-style authoritarianism had become economically dysfunctional. No regime could keep track of all the computers, copiers, and communication devices necessary to modern production in the information age. Gorbachev therefore wanted to liberalize Communist rule, but strikes and demonstrations soon erupted throughout the Soviet Union. Coal miners, railroad workers, Baltic nationalists, and urban intellectuals all formed independent organizations that called on Gorbachev to quicken the pace of political and economic reform. In Hungary and Poland, like-minded officials lifted most of the old restrictions on travel and emigration beyond the Iron Curtain.

Then came the revolution. Beginning in September 1989, a wave of huge demonstrations shook Communist regimes across eastern Europe. A massive tide of East German emigrants surged through Czechoslovakia and Hungary to the West, undermining the authority of the Communist hard-liners who still clung to power in the German Democratic Republic (GDR). Finally, on the night of November 9, 1989, ordinary Germans poured through the Berlin Wall. The GDR quickly disintegrated, and by the end of 1990, all of East Germany had been incorporated into the wealthy, powerful Federal Republic of Germany. The Communist government in Czechoslovakia also tumbled, and reformers strengthened their hand in Hungary and Bulgaria. In Romania, the Communist dictatorship

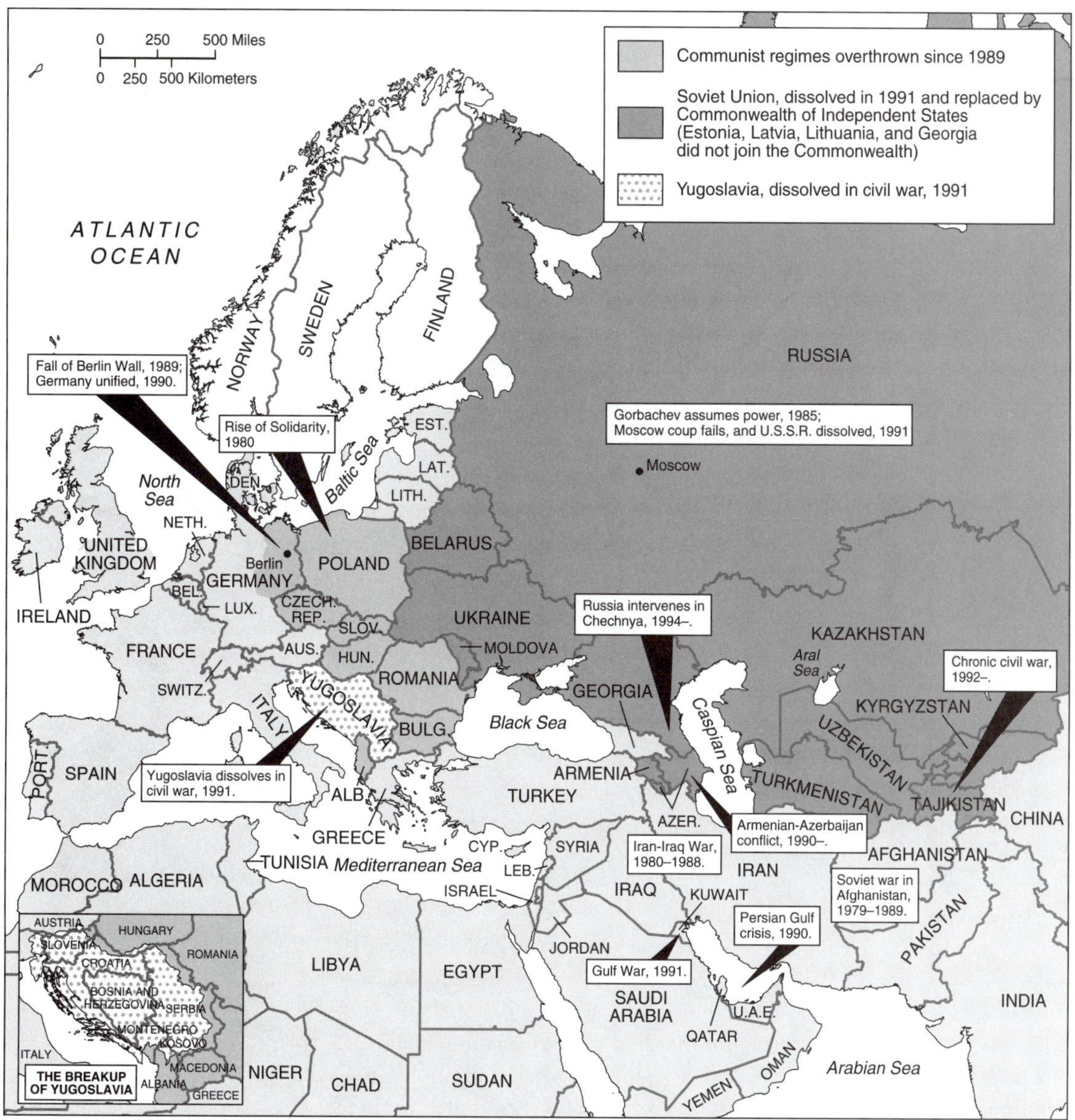

New States and New Conflicts: The Post-Cold War Map of Europe and Asia The decline of Soviet power and the breakup of the Soviet Union enabled Eastern European nationalism to flourish once again. A series of stable states emerged in central and northern Europe. But in the former Yugoslavia and the Caucasus (between Russia and Turkey), upheaval and civil war proved endemic.

fell only after a week of bloody street battles between ordinary citizens and police, who defended the old order to the bitter end.

Radical change finally reached the Soviet heartland in August 1991, when thousands of Russian citizens poured into the streets to defeat a reactionary coup d'état. The Communist party quickly collapsed, and the Soviet Union began the painful and uncertain process of reorganizing itself as a loose confederation of independent republics. Boris Yeltsin, who headed the Russian Republic, replaced Gorbachev as president of a much-diminished state.

Collectibles. News photographs and footage depicting the dismantling of the Berlin Wall in November 1989 powerfully symbolized the end of the Cold War. Less noted was the subsequent commercialization of that symbol, including the sale of pieces of the notorious wall to souvenir-hunting Germans and foreign tourists.

Source: Corbis/Wolfgang Kaehler.

The Cold War was over, brought to a close not by the missiles and tanks of the principal protagonists, but by the collective courage and willpower of ordinary men and women. Most insurgents had sought civil rights and political democracy, not a capitalist revolution, but they got one nonetheless. New governments in the Soviet Union and eastern Europe began opening their economies to Japan and the West, selling off state-owned enterprises and even establishing stock markets. In Poland, Hungary, Estonia, Latvia, and the Czech Republic, the process generated relatively successful economic systems oriented toward the West, but in Ukraine, Russia, Romania, Slovakia, and Bulgaria, the standard of living plunged amid political instability and plummeting production. Cuba, China, Vietnam, and North Korea remained authoritarian regimes, but almost all the Asian Communist countries abandoned state planning and encouraged capitalist trade and enterprise.

In the United States, partisans of Ronald Reagan claimed much of the credit for ending the Cold War, greeting the demise of European Communism in a triumphant mood. Reagan's forthright denunciation of the Soviet Union as an "evil empire," along with his administration's military buildup, were said to have heartened eastern bloc dissidents at the same time the arms race exhausted the productive capacity of the Soviet Union and other inefficient Communist regimes.

Confrontation. In the immediate aftermath of the June 1989 Tiananmen Square massacre, one image that symbolized the spirit of the student demonstrators was printed and broadcast around the world. A lone Chinese citizen blocked a convoy of tanks on Beijing's Avenue of Eternal Peace. After a tense standoff, in contrast to the government's earlier bloody suppression, the tanks did not harm the protester but instead drove around him.
Source: Corbis/Reuters.

But the Cold War doves had the stronger case. The West's militarized posture had long helped the Communists to rationalize their authoritarian rule. As the historian and diplomat George Kennan put it, the more U.S. policies had followed a hard line, "the greater was the tendency in Moscow to tighten the controls . . . and the greater the braking effect on all liberalizing tendencies in the regime." Indeed, U.S. policy makers encouraged such liberalization only with great caution. After the Chinese regime crushed a huge student demonstration in Beijing's Tiananmen Square in 1989, President George Bush suspended sales of military equipment to China, but at the same time sent his national security adviser, Brent Scowcroft, to Beijing to secretly reassure the Communists that large-scale trade would continue. Moreover, conservatives in both the Reagan and Bush administrations mistrusted the initial Soviet reforms, claiming that Mikhail Gorbachev sought merely to strengthen the USSR's capacity to wage a new Cold War.

George Bush's "New World Order"

George Herbert Walker Bush presided over the United States during this revolution in international statecraft. Although Bush had been Ronald Reagan's loyal vice president for eight years, he was hardly touched by

New Right fervor. Bush was a traditional upper-class conservative whose father, Prescott Bush, had been a New York investment banker and Connecticut senator. Unlike Reagan, Bush easily weathered the Great Depression but faced real danger as a naval flier in World War II. After he graduated from Yale University, his father staked him to a business career in Texas, where Bush adapted himself both to the entrepreneurial unpredictability of panhandle oil operations and to the hard-edged politics of southwestern Republicanism. After serving two terms in the House of Representatives, Bush held a series of high-profile appointments under Presidents Nixon and Ford, including U.S. ambassador to the United Nations and director of the Central Intelligence Agency. His gold-plated resume proved of but modest value when he entered the 1980 Republican presidential primaries, although it did earn him the second spot on the GOP ticket headed by Ronald Reagan.

Bush stood for Reaganite continuity during the 1988 presidential campaign, even as he implicitly criticized the Reagan presidency by calling, in his acceptance speech at the Republican National Convention, for a "kinder, gentler" society. But such moderation would have to wait until after the campaign. Because Bush enjoyed little of Reagan's popularity among conservative Republicans, he campaigned and later governed with one eye always cocked over his right shoulder. Thus Bush chose a brashly conservative Indiana senator, J. Danforth Quayle, for his running mate, and during the fall his campaign slandered his opponent, Massachusetts governor Michael J. Dukakis, calling him unpatriotic and soft on crime. In an infamous commercial, the GOP touched a racist nerve when it charged Governor Dukakis with responsibility for rapes committed by a black convict named Willie Horton during a work furlough from a Massachusetts prison.

Dukakis and his running mate, Senator Lloyd Bentsen of Texas, ran a far more successful campaign than had Democrat Walter Mondale four years before. They took 500 counties Reagan had carried in 1984 and almost captured California, whose population nearly equaled that of Texas and New York combined. But Bush and Quayle won more than 53 percent of the popular vote. Dukakis, a northeasterner of Greek ancestry, ran especially poorly in the South, where his brand of technocratic liberalism stirred little response. There the Democrats captured about 90 percent of the black vote but only 32 percent of white ballots.

President Bush felt sufficiently emboldened by the collapse of Communism to announce an American-dominated "new world order." During his administration, several of the most troublesome proxy wars that had been energized by the larger East–West conflict rapidly wound down. The Soviets withdrew from Afghanistan in the late 1980s, after which the CIA stopped supplying the Afghan rebels with advanced weapons. The brutal war there, waged among rival religious factions, did not stop, but it no longer played a role in superpower politics. Likewise, in Central America, the Bush administration ended U.S. support for the antigovernment Contra forces in Nicaragua, in return for a pledge that the Soviets and Cubans would stop supplying arms and aid to the ruling Sandinista party. The deal paid off handsomely for Bush when free elections held in 1990 gave the presidency to a pro-U.S. candidate. And in neighboring El Salvador, a peace treaty signed in 1992 ended the civil war there, allowing left-wing rebels to participate in electoral politics.

Finally, the end of the Cold War created a far more advantageous atmosphere for the liberation of South Africa. There the apartheid regime headed by F. W. de Klerk finally released from prison the African National Congress leader Nelson Mandela, who had spent twenty-seven years in confinement. The ANC had long maintained an alliance with the Communists, and Mandela had publicly defended such anti-U.S. leaders as Cuba's Fidel Castro and Libya's Muammar el-Qaddafi. U.S. governments had therefore kept the ANC at arm's length, especially during the Reagan presidency, when administration policy favored a "constructive engagement" with the white South African government. But as Mandela and the ANC swept to power in the early 1990s, even conservative U.S. diplomats applauded. The disintegration of South Africa's all-white regime quickly reduced the level of violence throughout southern Africa. Namibia, a vast South African protectorate on the Atlantic coast, achieved independence in 1990, after which the intensity of the civil war in nearby Angola diminished dramatically.

The end of the Cold War left the United States as the world's only superpower. Thus, even as international tensions declined, the United States had a relatively free hand to deploy its military might abroad, unhampered by a countervailing Soviet response. This new state of affairs became clear in December 1989, when President Bush dispatched thousands of troops to Panama to oust a corrupt dictator, Manuel Noriega, in an overt display of U.S. military power that echoed early-twentieth-century interventions in Latin America. A short, bloody war ended with Noriega's capture and extradition to the United States, where he was convicted in a Miami courtroom of drug-related offenses. But little actually changed in Panama, which remained one of the major transshipment points for illegal drugs in the Western Hemisphere.

Little more than a year later, in an even more massive deployment of its military might, the United States confronted the troops of the Iraqi dictator Saddam Hussein, whose invasion and annexation of the oil-rich emirate of Kuwait threatened to destabilize U.S. allies in the Persian Gulf. The Bush administration assembled an international coalition, including the Soviets, Germany, Japan, and most Arab states, to endorse the dispatch of nearly 500,000 U.S. troops to the region by the end of 1990. Britain, France, and Saudi Arabia committed an additional 200,000 troops. Although many Americans, including most congressional Democrats, believed that economic sanctions imposed by the United Nations might force Iraq to withdraw from Kuwait, Bush administration officials argued that economic pressure alone would prove ineffective.

On January 15, 1991, U.S. forces launched a massive air assault against Iraq. The high-tech bombing campaign, which deployed a new generation of post-Vietnam "smart" bombs, lasted over a month, killing and wounding tens of thousands of Iraqi citizens and soldiers and destroying much of Iraq's infrastructure and military hardware. A ground assault launched in February took but 100 hours to reclaim Kuwait and enter southern Iraq. Antiwar demonstrations briefly filled the streets of Washington and San Francisco, but light casualties and a swift victory soon generated a wave of patriotic fervor. As U.S. troops returned home to a series of huge victory parades down Broadway in New York City and Pennsylvania Avenue in Washington, D.C. — the first such parades since World War II — the president's approval ratings soared past 90 percent.

But the Gulf War left a mixed legacy. President Bush had hoped that the successful, massive use of military power against Iraq would shatter the nation's "Vietnam syndrome" by confirming a renewed U.S. willingness to intervene abroad as the world's unchallenged superpower. But U.S. public opinion remained skittish when it came to the deployment of U.S. troops, especially when diplomatic interventions or humanitarian missions turned violent, as they would in Somalia and the former Yugoslavia. In the Persian Gulf itself, Kuwait was once again an independent nation, but the Bush administration had chosen to end the war with Saddam Hussein still in power, largely because the United States saw his regime as a regional counterweight to Iran. However, this meant that the Iraqi dictator would retain the power to suppress domestic opposition and rebuild his military. The United Nations therefore con-

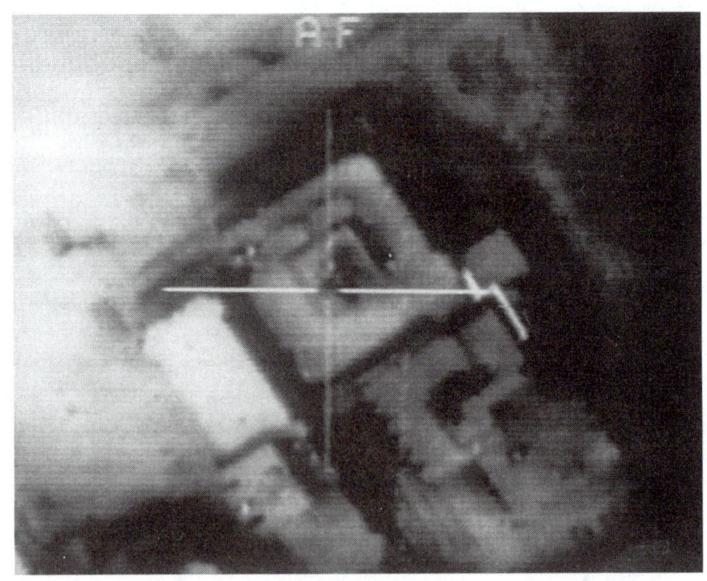

High-Tech War. Americans glimpsed the Persian Gulf War largely through television, often seeing images that were in fact composed of other video images. In this case, a video display aboard a Stealth F-117 bomber locks a Glide "smart" bomb's infrared guidance camera onto a target in Baghdad. The accuracy and glamour of such high-tech weapons were highlighted in news coverage that was heavily censored by the military. Only after the war did the military reveal that "smart" weapons comprised only 7 percent of the 81,980 tons of bombs dropped on Iraq and Kuwait — and of that total figure, 70 percent, or 62,137 tons, missed their targets.

Source: Reuters/Corbis-Bettmann.

tinued an economically debilitating trade boycott, while the United States maintained an active military presence in the region, periodically bombing Iraqi targets.

A New Economy

The U.S. military victory in the Persian Gulf was not matched by a sense of economic well-being at home. By the fall of 1990, the economy was once again in recession. The Iraqi invasion of Kuwait had generated a huge spike in the price of oil, which shook consumer confidence and depressed corporate profits and investment. Though oil prices soon moderated, the recession did not lift until a full two years later, after which the recovery proved initially quite tepid. Unemployment declined slowly, and real wages remained stagnant until the second half of the 1990s.

Unlike the early 1980s, when blue-collar workers opened most of the pink slips, this time professional, managerial, and other white-collar workers were just as likely as factory workers to become victims of corporate "downsizing." Nearly 2 million people lost their jobs in the three years that followed the Persian Gulf War; 63 percent of American corporations cut their staffs during that time. The California economy, which had sailed through the 1980s, was particularly hard hit by post–Cold War layoffs in the high-paying defense industries. Indeed, even in the mid 1990s, with the recovery well under way, large, successful corporations continued to announce stunning layoffs: IBM would shed 63,000 employees; Sears, 50,000; AT&T, 40,000; Boeing, 28,000. Though the economy produced millions of new jobs as well, the perpetual churning of the workforce generated a pervasive insecurity. As AT&T's vice president of human resources explained: "People need to recognize that we are all contingent workers in one form or another." No wonder some called the downturn of the early 1990s the "silent depression."

But U.S. corporations staged a remarkable turnaround once the recession began to lift. In contrast to the 1970s and 1980s, American businesses again competed successfully at home and abroad. Productivity growth finally rebounded to levels not seen since the late 1960s, profits leaped upward, and the stock market soared more than fourfold between 1991 and 1999 in one of the great Wall Street booms of all time. Key industries—steel, automobiles, telecommunications, microchip manufacturing, computer software, entertainment, aircraft, and finance—were once again creative, innovative, and profitable. By the late 1990s, unemployment, inflation, mortgage rates, and oil prices had fallen to levels not seen in three decades. Most experts once again counted the United States the most competitive industrial nation in the world. *Time*

"You Work Your Hardest, Then the Next Thing You Know, You're on the Streets Looking. . . ."

In 1994, *Mother Jones,* a socially progressive journal named for labor organizer Mary Harris Jones, who was active during the progressive era, interviewed working Americans in different parts of the country on their views about their jobs and about President Clinton's economic performance. Their opinions were as diverse as their occupations.

Charlie Seda, 26
Construction worker
$10/hour
High school graduate
Married, 2 kids

I've worked a lot of temporary jobs. They aren't reliable. The agencies tell you, "OK, we got you a job. It's up to you to keep it." You work your hardest, then the next thing you know, you're on the streets looking.

I didn't want to work at minimum wage anymore. I had a hard time getting union work, but with a union, the pay's more reliable. I've had the job I'm on now two months. It's only the second job I've had that I feel confident when I wake up in the morning that I still have a job.

If you don't have training and a certificate, no one wants to train you on the job. Clinton wanting to train the workforce is great, but what if you don't get a job after the training? What then? With construction, I'm afraid we'll build so much, there won't be anything left to build. Then what will be left? It'll just be maintenance and doctors.

Ana Nolasco, 26
Garment worker
$5.50/hour
High school graduate
Single, 1 kid

I came to the United States to find honest work. I had done hand embroidery for my family in El Salvador—hearts and birds mostly. One day I read in the paper they were hiring people to run embroidery machines.

I've had to learn how to handle a computer and load disks with designs on them. Our machines are able to do a lot more now, and it's not as hard as it was when we did it by hand. I don't think it's cut work down, but it makes it much faster.

Even with jobs moving to Latin America, the living in America is still better than in El Salvador. The wages they earn in a week, I earn in a day here.

Most factories are closing down or moving away. I worry about it. I take English lessons on Saturdays because I want to do something besides factory work. That way, if the factory closes down, I could do something else. I'd like a job in an office—something that was more intellectual, less physical.

This country was founded by immigrants, but we're made to feel we're not wanted. People come here to better themselves. The government should help, give them opportunities to learn English and get training.

Karen Tarlow, 47
Asst. vice president
Wall Street bank
$65,000/year
MBA in finance
Divorced

I always thought, "If I get more credentials, I'll get what's due me." So I went for my MBA at night. I still have not gotten the raises and promotions I should have. It's not that I didn't work hard; it's not that I didn't give things up. I gave up an awful lot. But I didn't get rewarded properly. I hit the glass ceiling hard.

I don't want to go to another job where I'm told the sky is pink and I have to swallow it along with lunch. But the finances are compelling. Every night I think about my dream job. Owning a bookstore would be great, but I'm not sure I want to spend all my savings on a bookstore. I might have to use my savings to eat someday.

I'm 47, I've had all this education, and I find myself asking, "Where do I go now?" There is no job security anymore. The dream is gone; it's not going to get better. As we export jobs, other places will get better, but look at all the people here who aren't buying goods and services. We're becoming a Third World country.

It's very insidious how the rich get richer. They do it beyond the government, no matter what the government tries to do. Insider trading is the norm.

Brenda Bettencourt, 43
Correctional officer
$20,000/year
3 years college
Married, 1 kid

My brother's a retired policeman, and I have two uncles in law enforcement. My aunt was a matron at a prison in Arizona. I can't see myself working anywhere but at an institution. I'm not the type to go looking for trouble, but I won't walk away from it either.

I used to be an executive secretary. I got a job with the state for job security and better benefits. As a security officer, I get better benefits than other state employees. I don't know that people who work for institutions should make more money, but we work very hard for the money we do make. My job is as secure as a job can be these days. We never run out of inmates.

Marie Dupuy, 43
Day care center owner
$25,000–$30,000/year
Bachelor's degree
2 kids

In Haiti I was from a privileged family. When I came to the United States, I stayed as a legal alien for 10 years. It's a big decision for a black, foreign-born person to become a citizen. Now I make sure I fulfill my civic duties.

I taught French in public schools for four years. I don't think teachers are paid what they're worth. They get frustrated, they hate the kids, hate their jobs. But teachers need to be more conscientious about their responsibilities. All children deserve better. I looked for a better way to help. I opened a day care center, and now I'm satisfied in my work.

My children are going to be successful Americans. Their names will be known all over. I'm not talking about how much money they make; I hope they will make a difference.

Source: Ashley Craddock, "American Workers Talk About Their Jobs and the Future," *Mother Jones,* March/April 1994. (http://www.motherjones.com/mother_jones/MA94/craddock.html).

magazine captured the ambiguity of this accomplishment in a 1994 cover story headlined, "We're Number 1. And It Hurts."

What accounted for this simultaneous sense of productive accomplishment and economic insecurity? The two phenomena were closely linked, because corporations benefited enormously from the wage stagnation, deunionization, low taxes, and deregulatory business climate that characterized the Reagan era. The virtual abandonment of antitrust action during the 1980s and 1990s had led to a massive wave of corporate mergers and reorganizations, which opened the door both to cost-cutting layoffs and speculative stock market recapitalizations. "There is no job security anymore," reported Karen Tarlow, a Wall Street bank officer in her late forties. "It's very insidious how the rich get richer."

In oil, telecommunications, health care, and finance a new set of powerfully competitive firms emerged almost overnight. Exxon bought Mobil, Bell Atlantic acquired GTE, WorldCom bought MCI, and Daimler-Benz merged with Chrysler. Between 1992 and 1998, the value of all corporate mergers advanced nearly tenfold to more than a trillion dollars. In real dollar terms, this was the biggest merger wave in nearly a century.

The U.S. government had also spurred the competitiveness of corporations headquartered in North America by devaluing the dollar against the currencies of other industrial nations. Beginning in the late 1980s, the Treasury and the Federal Reserve had abandoned the Cold War effort to sustain the dollar as the world's reserve currency. When the dollar dropped in value by more than 50 percent against the Japanese yen and the German deutsche mark, U.S. corporations that traded abroad, such as Boeing, or faced import competition, such as General Electric and the au-

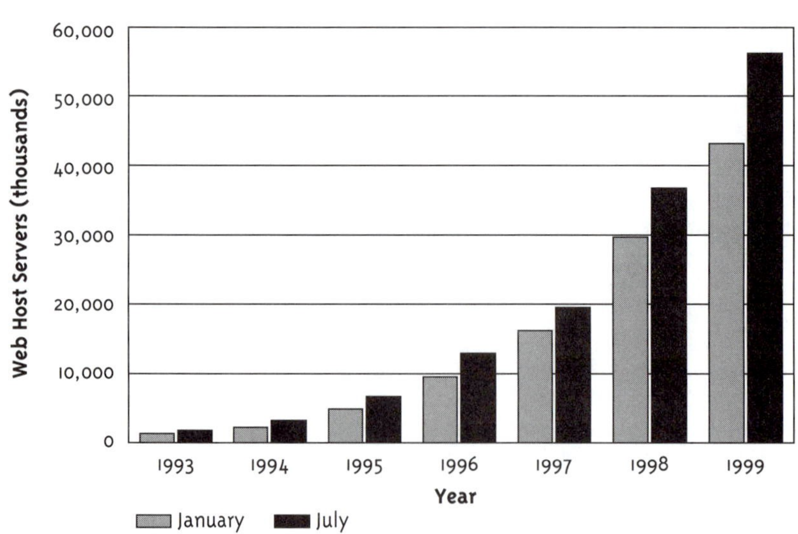

Web Mania: Internet Hosts, 1993–2000 The appearance in 1993 of Mosaic (the predecessor to Netscape), the first graphical browser for the World Wide Web, led to the explosive growth of the Internet. Between 1993 and 1999, the number of Web "hosts" (basically computers housing Web sites) grew more than fifty times.

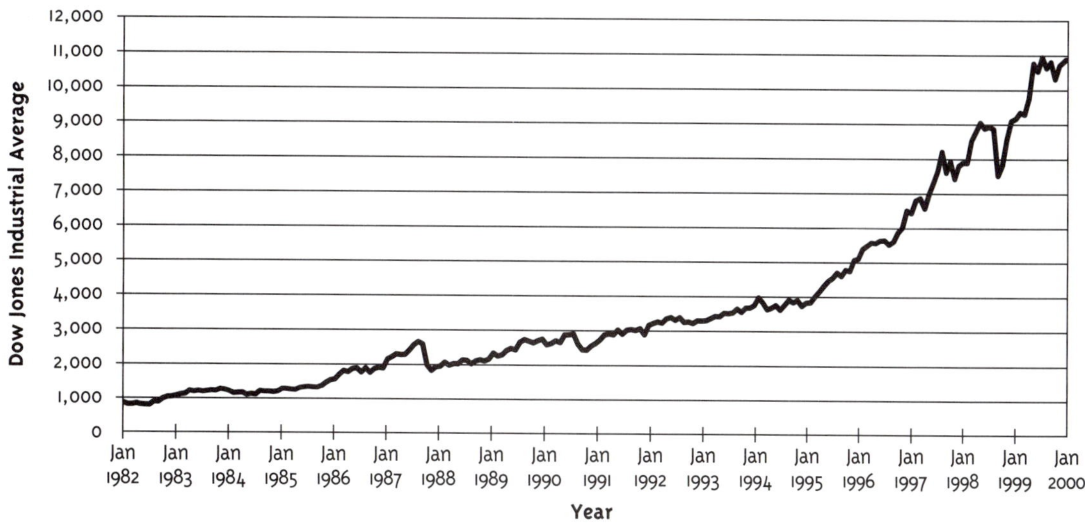

Stock Mania: The Stock Market, 1982–2000 The more than ten-fold rise in stock averages in the eighteen-year period after 1982 had two sources. The Reagan-era redistribution of income from labor to capital powered the stock market boom of the 1980s and early 1990s. After that, a combination of pure speculation and anticipated profits from a new computer-based economy sent the market even higher.

tomotive giants, found themselves on more favorable competitive terrain. Suddenly, their products sold more cheaply than those of many foreign competitors. Further easing the competitive pressure on U.S. firms, wages had risen far more rapidly in Europe and Asia than in the United States during the 1980s. Additionally, foreign nations faced some unique challenges in this period. The German government had to raise taxes to pay the huge costs of reunification, while Japan struggled with a decade-long recession brought on by the near-collapse of its overheated banking and real estate sectors. Thus, after decades of decline, the U.S. share of world manufacturing exports began to rise in the years after 1986.

U.S. firms also benefited in the 1990s from adopting the most advanced organizational and technological techniques. In the steel industry, the introduction of German-style mini-mills slashed by more than half the number of hours required to produce a ton of steel. In autos, Japanese inventory and production scheduling methods and new levels of automation enhanced quality, cut labor costs, and shortened new-model engineering time, enabling Chrysler and Ford to earn record profits. And the telecommunications revolution, which made fax machines, e-mail, cellular telephones, and overnight package delivery pervasive, enhanced productivity in factories, offices, and hospitals.

Perhaps most important, the computer revolution finally began to pay off. Despite the fanfare that accompanied dramatic advances in technology, computerization had been slow to boost white-collar service-sector productivity, whose growth lagged far behind that of even run-of-the-mill factories during the 1970s and 1980s. But by the early 1990s, a generation of employees had been trained on the new machines, which sat on the desks of more than six out of ten workers (compared to less than two out of ten in Japan). As *Business Week* put it, "Networking [the linking together of large numbers of small computers] finally united all the systems, and voila! Productivity began to take off."

Indeed, the deployment of millions of easy-to-use computers began to replicate the productivity breakthrough brought on by the birth of the mass-production assembly line early in the twentieth century. Then skilled tool and die craftsmen built the precision metal-cutting machinery that would be operated by so many untutored farm hands and immigrants. In the 1990s, skilled programmers churned out thousands of different computer programs ("software") that allowed clerical workers and managers to perform tasks once restricted to well-trained professionals. "Up until the early 1980s, the only people able to use personal computers were a very tiny elite," reported a Princeton economist. "Now, a lot of software is for numskulls."

Soon the Internet and the World Wide Web linked together millions of terminals all across the globe. The Internet had its origins in Pentagon efforts, begun in the 1960s, to build a communications network capable of surviving a nuclear war and to share expensive computer resources. But imaginative scientists and clever hackers soon spread this network well beyond the military laboratories and university research facilities of its inception. By the late 1980s, e-mail was becoming commonplace, and in the mid-1990s the development of colorful, interactive Web pages generated an explosive new stage in the growth of this medium. The Web doubled in size every eighteen months, transforming the locus of commerce, entertainment, and information retrieval.

The imaginative hold of this vast network approached that of the great world-transforming technologies: steam power and the railroad in the early nineteenth century, electricity fifty years later, and the internal combustion engine during the first third of the twentieth century. Like these technologies, computerization promised a revolutionary transformation in the structure of production, the organization of society, and the meaning of work. And for those in the right place at the right time, it generated enormous wealth.

Like Rockefeller and Ford before him, Microsoft president Bill Gates combined the technical expertise and business savvy to make himself the richest man of his era. Born to a wealthy Seattle family in 1955, Gates dropped out of Harvard to join the

"The Truth about Y2K." Discussion about the Year 2000 computer problem, better known by the acronym Y2K, was ubiquitous at the close of the 1990s. The problem originated in the mid-twentieth century when computer programmers opted for two rather than four digits to represent a year. With the change from 1999 to 2000, this shorthand method was potentially disastrous because "oo" might be read by computers as progressing to the first year of the twenty-first century *or* the first year of the twentieth. The realization that many date-sensitive computers running crucial service, transportation, fiscal, and other activities might malfunction at the turn of the century prompted some panic and widespread, expensive reprogramming. But the passage to the new year brought no disruptions.

Source: © 1999 Randy Glasbergen.

wave of youthful West Coast computer "hackers" who refounded the computer industry in the late 1970s. Like Steve Jobs and Steve Wozniak, creators of Apple Computer Corporation and pioneers in personal computing, Gates put his entrepreneurial faith in the proliferation of millions of inexpensive desktop machines. But he was not interested in building the hardware; instead, his firm purchased, rewrote, and *owned* DOS, the essential operating system for the machines. Microsoft got its big break in 1981 when mighty IBM licensed the personal computer system software from Gates. Within a decade, Microsoft programming became the de facto standard for more than 80 percent of all the personal computers sold in the world.

Not only did Gates become fabulously wealthy, but Microsoft and other software firms transformed the entire structure of the computer industry. In just a few years, market power and creativity came to lie not with the vertically integrated hardware giants, such as IBM, Hewlett-Packard, and Digital Equipment Corporation, but with a plethora of small firms that employed hundreds of thousands of technically proficient software programmers. The growth requirements of this key industry meshed seamlessly with many of the characteristics peculiar to late-twentieth-century U.S. capitalism: entrepreneurial flexibility, a close partnership with a large number of commercially oriented universities, a cosmopolitan and multi-ethnic workforce, and "ownership" of the cyberworld's lingua franca—American English.

Exploitation of Web commerce built a new generation of Internet companies and Silicon Valley billionaires. As in the mid-nineteenth-century railroad boom and the Texas oil rush of the early twentieth century, much of this new wealth was a product of Wall Street speculation and entrepreneurial hype. Many Internet companies saw their stock valuation soar into the billions, even as they continued to lose money. In December 1999, *Time* magazine made Jeff Bezos, the 35-year-old founder of Amazon.com, its "Man of the Year." Even though Bezos's Web-based shopping service continued to lose millions, the stock market valued his company at $33 billion and his own holdings made him one of the richest men in the United States. Stock options and IPOs (initial public offerings) generated remarkable wealth for tens of thousands of computer-technology employees, whose ninety-hour workweeks and eccentric work habits made them unlikely millionaires.

Speculative mania aside, creativity, camaraderie, and cutting-edge technology had built a vast new industry. The craftworkers of this cyberworld revolution were the driven, youthful programmers, whose workaday role actually had much in common with that of the skilled machinists, technicians, and draftsmen who had been crucial to the industrial transformation of the nation nearly a century before. Like the proud

Dilbert. The popular newspaper comic strip portrays the trials and tribulations of employees in an unnamed high-tech company in northern California. Cartoonist Scott Adams started the strip in 1989, inspired by his experience working for Pacific Bell.
Source: Dilbert © 1999 United Feature Syndicate, Inc.

craftsmen of Bridgeport, Philadelphia, and Cincinnati, college-educated programmers stood at the very nexus of production. "It is their skill in coding, in turning strings of numbers into life-altering software, that is Microsoft's lifeblood," observed a computer-savvy journalist. But for most programmers and other skilled workers, thirty-five percent of whom were immigrants, loyalty lay with the craft, not with any single company. Job-hopping proved endemic throughout cyberworld industries. Indeed, a growing proportion of these skilled technical workers were "temps," temporary employees who received few benefits other than a paycheck from the companies in whose offices they spent their months and years. "Programmers are like artists," reflected an executive, recently risen from the ranks. "When you're writing code you're not thinking in English. It's like a play—there's motion, things work, it's not static. You know where you're going. Things just flow."

But a rising economic tide—including the powerful surge flowing out of Silicon Valley—could not lift all boats or solve all problems. The reconfiguration of the American economy brought real social and psychological costs, which were borne not only by the unemployed and the Rustbelt factory workers but also by millions of suburban families and college-educated "knowledge workers" who might otherwise seem the beneficiaries of the new economy. Real family income continued to drop throughout the first half of the 1990s, even as record numbers of women and teenagers entered the workforce. Health care expenses rose inexorably, twice as fast as the overall consumer price index. In response, insurance companies and corporations restricted coverage and demanded co-payments. By 1992, more than 37 million Americans were uninsured.

The 1992 Election

The Bush administration had neither the will nor the wherewithal to ameliorate such problems. President Bush did sign legislation that raised the minimum wage, stiffened clean-air regulations, and protected disabled

Americans against discrimination. But he was basically a caretaker executive who saw his domestic policy goals in largely negative terms—avoiding, as he once put it, "stupid mistakes" in order to "see that the government doesn't get in the way." He once told his chief-of-staff, John Sununu, "We don't need to remake society." In the recession that followed the Gulf War, the Bush administration's passivity cost the president virtually all the goodwill the U.S. military victory had generated. Throughout his term, the one piece of legislation Bush championed with the greatest consistency was a reduction in the capital gains tax, whose benefits would flow largely to the wealthy.

Democratic prospects therefore looked bright in 1992 when William Jefferson Clinton, the forty-six-year-old governor of Arkansas, emerged from the crowded primary field to become the party's presidential nominee. Clinton called himself a "New Democrat," and he was anything but a conventional liberal. He supported the death penalty, favored a work requirement for parents receiving welfare support for their children, and proved indifferent to organized labor. As a five-term governor of a conservative southern state, he had accommodated himself to the interests of the region's economic elite. Within the Democratic party, he allied himself with pro-defense, free-trade conservatives. His wife, Hillary, was a partner in the state's most powerful law firm and a member of Wal-Mart's board of directors.

Though his political career had tilted toward the center, Clinton was in many ways a product of the 1960s. The son of a widowed nurse growing up in a small Arkansas town, he became a consummately ambitious student-politician. He had identified with the civil rights movement in high school, and as a Rhodes Scholar at Oxford University he took part in anti–Vietnam War demonstrations. Though Clinton was not as radical as some activists in his generation, he did avoid the draft, smoke marijuana, and campaign for left–liberal Democrats, including George McGovern, the Democratic presidential nominee in 1972. After graduating from Yale Law School he returned to Arkansas, where his large circle of friends helped him to win the governorship in 1978. He was just thirty-two, the youngest U.S. governor in four decades.

The 1992 campaign was the most ideologically engaging since 1972, the first election contest since 1964 in which domestic political issues held center stage. George Bush stood for the status quo, but he faced a determined challenge from the party's right wing. In 1988 when he accepted the Republican nomination for president, Bush had pledged to the convention delegates, "Read my lips: no new taxes." But two years later Bush broke that pledge to reach a budget deal with the Democrats that sought a much-needed reduction in the federal budget deficit, which had climbed to more than 3 percent of the entire gross domestic product. His pact with the Democrats infuriated conservative Republicans and sparked a primary challenge from Pat Buchanan, a former high-level aide to Presidents Nixon and Reagan. A prominent New Right warrior, Buchanan was hostile to abortion and gay rights. He also exemplified a new strain of post–Cold War conservatism that rejected Wilsonian internationalism and trade liberalization. Buchanan therefore campaigned against the highly controversial North American Free Trade Agreement (NAFTA), supported by most multinational corporations and the leadership of both major political parties.

The billionaire computer services entrepreneur Ross Perot proved an even more significant political outsider. Although Perot had once been a conservative Republican and a right-wing backer of the Vietnam War, he spent $60 million of his own money to run an independent campaign for president as a common-sense "populist." His United We Stand political organization opened branches in almost every state. Unlike Buchanan, Perot was something of a libertarian on social issues, but he proved even more militantly opposed to NAFTA and other free-trade agreements, which he charged would "suck" American manufacturing jobs to Mexico and the Far East. An engaging TV personality, Perot put the chronic $200-billion federal budget deficit at the top of the campaign agenda. Unlike Bush and other mainstream Republicans, who proposed to cut government expenditures largely by slashing social welfare programs, Perot argued for more education and training and a kind of hands-on economic governance at odds with laissez-faire doctrine. "It's time to take out the trash and clean up the barn," he told TV audiences in his folksy, down-home manner. Perot struck a nerve among both liberals and conservatives, because budget gridlock in Washington seemed symptomatic of the political stalemate and economic difficulties that dogged the nation in the early 1990s.

Presidential Chops. Bill Clinton played a saxophone at a gala celebration following his inauguration on January 20, 1993. His predilection for (if not his talent on) the saxophone on the campaign trail had become a symbol of Clinton's political platform, suggesting to some Americans his allegiance to the "alternative" values of the 1960s.
Source: Corbis/Reuters.

Bill Clinton and his running mate, Al Gore, an environmentally conscious senator from Tennessee, promised to break that gridlock and raise living standards by rebuilding the nation's infrastructure, restoring higher taxes on the rich, launching a federally funded jobs program for welfare recipients, and, perhaps most important, reorganizing the nation's entire health care system. Clinton saw himself in the tradition of Franklin Roosevelt and the New Deal. As the candidate promised to focus, "like a laser," on the work-related anxieties of ordinary Americans, campaign strategist James Carville tacked a soon-to-be famous note above his desk: "It's the economy, stupid!"

Clinton and Perot crushed Bush in the election. The Republican took only 37 percent of the popular vote, while the mercurial Texas businessman garnered a remarkable 19 percent—the best third-ticket showing since Theodore Roosevelt's Progressive party campaign of 1912. Clinton and Gore won 43 percent, which translated into 370 electoral college votes, 100 more than they needed to win. As usual, African Americans voted for the Democratic ticket by almost nine to one. And the proportion of women who voted for Clinton and Gore was some eight points higher than that of men. Clinton's popularity with women was not due primarily to the fact that Clinton favored abortion rights and Bush did not. Nor was it a tribute to Hillary Clinton, an influential and articulate role model some found reminiscent of Eleanor Roosevelt. Rather, poll after poll demonstrated that women were particularly likely to favor and benefit from the kind of social programs advocated by Clinton and most Democrats. Women were less likely than men to enjoy employer-funded health insurance, and they were the prime beneficiaries of food stamps and Medicare. Because of their child-care needs and employment status, many women endorsed what conservatives derisively called "the Nanny State." Liberals and feminists therefore labeled 1992 "The Year of the Woman." Female representation in the House of Representatives nearly doubled—from twenty-eight to forty-seven—and the number of women in the Senate tripled, from two to six. African Americans increased their number in the House to forty-one, an all-time record.

The Clinton Administration

The political trajectory of the Clinton administration falls into two phases. Between late 1992 and the fall of 1994, Clinton and his advisers sought to implement an ambitious program of social reform that harkened back to issues last debated during the liberal heyday of the mid-1960s. But Clinton's failures, both personal and political, led to a sweeping Republican victory in the 1994 congressional elections, after which his administration sought little more than survival in office, even at the cost of a programmatic accommodation to congressional conservatives.

Clinton's initial cabinet appointments were unusually diverse. He put African Americans in charge of the Departments of Agriculture, Commerce, and Energy, heretofore the reserve of conservative white businessmen, and he made Janet Reno, a Florida law enforcement official, the first female attorney general. Hispanic politicians from Colorado and Texas took over stewardship of the Departments of Transportation and of

Housing and Urban Development. Clinton named the liberal economist Laura Tyson as head of the Council of Economic Advisers and Robert Reich, a well-known critic of the nation's growing inequality of wealth, education, and wages, as Secretary of Labor. Not long after his inauguration, Clinton had the chance to appoint to the Supreme Court Ruth Bader Ginsberg, a pioneer in the legal fight against gender discrimination. And in 1994 he nominated Stephen Breyer, an economic conservative whose social views tended toward liberalism, to the High Court.

Early in 1993, Clinton signed social legislation that Bush would have vetoed: the Family and Medical Leave Act, which guaranteed workers their jobs when they returned from childbirth or a family medical emergency; the Brady bill, which regulated handguns; and the "Motor-Voter" bill, which made voter registration available through many state agencies, including those that issued driver's licenses. He ended the Reagan-era ban on abortion counseling in family-planning clinics and won new funding for more police and prisons, as well as a youth-oriented job corps.

But on the big economic issues, the Clinton administration came to demonstrate much continuity with the policies of his Republican predecessors. In his presidential campaign Clinton had downplayed deficit reduction and emphasized the need for new social investment: in infrastructure, education, environmental technology, and health care. He wanted a new tax on business to encourage energy conservation and job training. Once in office, however, he dropped the fight for large-scale infrastructure spending—and the jobs it would have created—when his more conservative advisers, including Secretary of the Treasury Lloyd Bentsen and Robert Rubin of the National Economic Council, warned that the federal government needed to sacrifice social spending and instead emphasize deficit reduction. Clinton did push through Congress a substantial tax increase on wealthy individuals, which restored some of the tax progressivity lost during the Reagan era. Otherwise his administration remained fiscally conservative, not unlike the "Eisenhower Republicans," complained Clinton in one Oval Office meeting. Such restraint mollified Wall Street bond traders and generated the lower interest rates Clinton's more orthodox advisers thought necessary for business investment and economic recovery.

Despite this accommodation to the fiscal conservatives within his own administration, Clinton proved a polarizing figure, whose person and presidency evoked social and cultural controversies smoldering since the Vietnam era. To many Americans, Clinton never seemed to be an entirely legitimate president, especially with regard to military issues. Although they maintained a facade of apolitical neutrality, many military officers were contemptuous of their commander-in-chief, who had "dodged" the draft during the Vietnam War. Thus Clinton's effort to support gay rights

Don't Ask, Don't Tell—Just Boycott! In 1992 gay activists and their supporters protested in Atlanta, Georgia, after the Cracker Barrel Restaurant chain in that city fired at least four gay employees. The restaurant chain quickly rescinded its antigay hiring practices, but in 1999 the NAACP filed a lawsuit charging that Cracker Barrel discriminated against its employees based on skin color.

Source: Bill Clark/Impact Visuals.

within the armed services generated a storm of criticism, forcing his administration to promulgate a confusing "Don't Ask, Don't Tell" doctrine regarding the homosexual orientation of enlisted personnel. Fearing similar attacks on his judgment and patriotism, Clinton did little to reduce the post–Cold War military budget.

When it came to the use of American military forces abroad, the Clinton administration was hesitant and inconsistent. This was a product not only of the president's primary focus on domestic policy but also of the divided character of American opinion in a post–Cold War world. The anti-Communist ideology and geopolitical rivalry with the Soviet Union that had long provided the raison d'être for an internationalist foreign policy had all but evaporated. For the first time in more than half a century, a powerful, isolationist current emerged within the ranks of both political parties. Clinton and his key advisers continued to support United Nations peacekeeping missions and NATO military interventions in unstable regions, but they sought to avoid, at almost all costs, the death of American troops in foreign combat.

This first became clear in Somalia, where a U.N. humanitarian effort to end political anarchy and provide food and relief supplies had turned into a military conflict with regional warlords. When a firefight cost the lives of seventeen U.S. servicemen in October 1993, Clinton responded to disquiet at home by withdrawing all American troops within a few months. A year later Clinton deployed 15,000 U.S. troops in Haiti, ousting the military strongmen there and restoring to office Jean Bertrand Aristide, the democratically elected president. But this relatively peaceful transfer of power took place only after lengthy negotiations that left in place many armed partisans of the old regime.

In the former Yugoslavia, where Serbian and Croatian nationalists battled each other and the Serbs instigated a series of bloody "ethnic cleansing" campaigns against Bosnian Muslims, the Clinton administration was unwilling to use sufficient military force to actually stop the massive bloodshed. In Bosnia, therefore, the United States and other Western powers stood aside while Serbian nationalists shelled Muslim Sarajevo for more than two years. Finally, in late 1995, after NATO bombed Serbian gun emplacements and tank units, the United States brokered a settlement—reached at an air force base outside Dayton, Ohio—that sent American and other U.N. troops to Bosnia as peacekeepers for a set of new, ethnically based mini-states. Three years later, the same dynamic played itself out in Kosovo, a Serbian province inhabited largely by ethnic Albanians. By early 1999, Kosovo was in near-rebellion and the Serbs on the verge of yet another bloody ethnic cleansing. When the Serbian strongman Slobodan Milosevic balked at a NATO military occupation of Kosovo, U.S. and other NATO warplanes inaugurated a bombing campaign against all Serbia. After seventy-eight days Milosevic capitulated, but not before Serbian forces had murdered thousands of Albanian civilians and precipitated a refugee exodus of almost a million people.

Clinton considered his economic diplomacy of even greater importance than these skittish military interventions. His administration backed U.S. membership in the North American Free Trade Association over the adamant opposition of organized labor and most Democratic liberals. NAFTA made it far easier for Canadian and U.S. corporations to buy low-cost goods from Mexico, sometimes produced by the American subsidiaries that fled south to take advantage of the low wages there. Although the movement of jobs to Latin America did not amount to the "giant sucking sound" Ross Perot had predicted, NAFTA did prove a powerful weapon in the hands of employers, who used the specter of a factory shutdown to forestall employee drives for higher pay and unionization. Some economists estimated that nearly a quarter of all the recent growth in wage inequality derived from this downward pressure on U.S. wages. Thus when Congress enacted NAFTA legislation in the fall of 1993, the lion's share of the votes came from Republicans.

Robert Rubin, who became Treasury secretary in 1994, played a key role in sustaining the Clinton administration's commitment to free trade and unregulated financial markets, even when such policies required austerity in developing nations. Rubin orchestrated a controversial, multibillion-dollar bailout of the Mexican economy—and of the U.S. banks that had lent money there—after the peso collapsed in 1994. But in 1997 and 1998 the International Monetary Fund (heavily influenced by the U.S. Treasury) exacerbated an Asian financial crisis when, in return for new loans to Thailand, South Korea, and Indonesia, it demanded high interest rates and government-spending cutbacks certain to generate business bankruptcies, massive layoffs, and a lower living standard. The crisis precipitated a near-revolution in Indonesia, repression in Malaysia, and factory occupations in South Korea.

IMF. A protester at a December 1997 demonstration in Seoul, South Korea, displayed a poster that adroitly explained the impact of the International Monetary Fund's harsh loan policies on many Asian workers.

Source: Sung So Cho/Sygma.

Health Care Reform

Clinton's effort to establish a system of universal health care was the most important legislative battle fought by his administration. The issue was red-hot in the early 1990s for two reasons. First, the American health care delivery system was a failure, compared to those of other Western nations. More than 20 percent of all people under the age of sixty-five had no insured access to a doctor. Moreover, health care costs were rising at twice the level of inflation, and the United States was spending more of its total income, 14 percent, on medical care than any other nation. America's fragmented, employment-based commercial system was a paperwork nightmare. A Toronto hospital administrator familiar with Canada's "single-payer" system of universal coverage (the government paid doctors and hospitals from tax revenues) found U.S. health care costs bloated by "overwhelming duplication of bureaucracies working in dozens of insurance companies, no two of which have the same forms or even the same coverage."

Second, the health insurance system had become a political and social issue of great contention. During the 1980s, management efforts to trim health insurance costs had precipitated more than 80 percent of all strikes that took place in the United States. The United Mine Workers (UMW) of America fought the most spectacular of these struggles in 1989 – an eleven-month siege of the Pittston Coal Company — in defense of miners' health care benefits and pension rights. Some 3,000 miners and

Stop Joe Camel. In the late 1990s, new evidence about cigarette smoking's contribution to rising rates of lung cancer prompted a public outcry against American tobacco companies, in particular their manipulation of nicotine levels to keep smokers addicted and their targeting of advertising toward young adults. In 1998, in the face of class-action suits lodged by 46 state attorneys-general to cover increased smoking-related health care costs, tobacco companies agreed to restrict marketing, reveal previously secret trade documents, and pay state governments $206 billion to cover medical costs and finance education campaigns to deter tobacco use.

Source: Dan Habib/ Impact Visuals.

UMW supporters were arrested during a campaign that resurrected the sit-down tactics and mass demonstrations characteristic of the union movement in its formative years. Such industrial conflicts soon had their political echo. The death knell of the Bush presidency may well have been sounded during a 1991 Senate contest in Pennsylvania, when Harris Wofford, a former aide to President John Kennedy, came from forty points behind to defeat Bush's former attorney general, Richard Thornburgh. The key issue was universal health coverage. As Wofford put it, "Americans should have the same right to a doctor as they do to a lawyer."

President Clinton and his wife Hillary, who was in charge of the health care project, rejected a Canadian-style single-payer system. Although recognizing its economic efficiency and political popularity, they argued that health care reform had to be built on the existing system of employer-paid benefits and private insurance. The Clinton plan, which was reminiscent of the Roosevelt reform of capitalism under the 1933 National Recovery Act, would have regulated the largest insurance companies through a system of "managed competition" contained within a "global budget" set by the federal government. With this lid on insurance costs, the government could mandate employers to provide health insurance for all their employees. The plan did provide for a universal system of health care, but it was highly complex—the proposed law required more than 1,350 pages of text—because the Clintons sought to regulate and expand an inherently heterogeneous system of privately funded health insurance.

Mass murder. Students fled Columbine High School in Littleton, Colorado, after two teenagers armed with automatic weapons and explosives murdered twelve of their classmates and a teacher before committing suicide. The April 1999 incident highlighted the fearful toll of the estimated 200 million guns in circulation in the United States, and particularly their impact as a major "health problem" for young Americans. According to the Centers for Disease Control and Prevention, 4,643 children and teenagers were killed with guns in 1996 (including 1,309 suicides and 468 unintentional shootings). The *Journal of the American Medical Association* estimated that the cost of medical care for gun-related injuries amounted to $4 billion in 1995 alone. Since 1960, a half-million people have died from gunshots. **Source:** Corbis/AFP.

Despite these problems, the Clinton health program was the most ambitious and progressive effort to expand the American welfare state in three decades. By guaranteeing health insurance to every worker, the plan would have taken a large step toward reversing the growth in social inequality; and it would have provided employers with a powerful incentive to transform part-time jobs into forty-hour-a-week positions. The Clintons counted on support from those high-wage business sectors that already provided health insurance: employer mandates cost them nothing, but instead spread insurance costs equally among all employers. American auto companies paid more for health insurance than for steel, but Wal-Mart, Marriott, and hundreds of thousands of other low-wage service-sector firms shifted the health care costs of their employees to the state, to charity, or to other firms' payrolls. Thus Pizza Hut, a PepsiCo subsidiary that employed 93,000 workers, offered health insurance to only 3,000, most of them managers.

But the Clintons miscalculated. American capitalism had transformed itself dramatically since the last era of health care reform in the 1960s, and low-wage, low-benefit companies in the swollen service sector, especially restaurants and retail outlets, bitterly resisted employer mandates. In addition, almost all the smaller insurance companies, who sought the youngest and least risky clients, assailed the plan. These companies bankrolled a widely viewed set of television commercials that pointed to the complexity and regulatory burden inherent in the Clinton plan. Among the strongest backers of the Clinton plan were American trade unions, but after more than two decades of waning strength, organized

Newt Gingrich's "Contract with America"

In the 1994 elections Conservative Republican Congressman Newt Gingrich, who would subsequently become Speaker of the House, had sought to unify the Republicans around an election manifesto, "The Contract with America," that aimed to dismantle the New Deal and the Great Society. His efforts produced government grid-lock but not the sweeping right-wing change that he had forecast. In this selection, Gingrich provides the ideological franework for the Republican program.

We have to replace the welfare state with an opportunity society. It is impossible to take the Great Society structure of bureaucracy, the redistributionist model of how wealth is acquired, and the counterculture value system that now permeates the way we deal with the poor, and have any hope of fixing them. They are a disaster. They ruin the poor, they create a culture of poverty and a culture of violence which is destructive of this civilization, and they have to be replaced thoroughly from the ground up.

This should be done in cooperation with the poor. The people who have the most to gain from eliminating the culture of poverty and replacing it with a culture of productivity are the people currently trapped in a nightmare, living in public housing projects with no one going to work, living in neighborhoods with no physical safety, their children forced to walk into buildings where there will be no learning, and living in a community where taxes and red tape and regulation destroy their hope of creating new entrepreneurial small businesses and doing what every other generation of poor Americans have done, which is to leave poverty behind by acquiring productivity.

We simply need to reach out and erase the slate and start over, and we need to start with the premise that every American is endowed by their Creator with certain inalienable rights, among which are life, liberty, and the pursuit of happiness, and that extends to the poorest child in Washington, D.C., and the poorest child in West Virginia, and the poorest child in American Indian reservations. And we have been failing all of them because we have lacked the courage to be mentally tough enough to get the job done. I think it can be done, but I think it's very deep and represents a very bold change.

We have to recognize that American exceptionalism . . . is real; that this has been the most successful civilization in the history of the human race at liberating people to pursue happiness. There is no other society in history where as many people from as many cultures speaking as many languages could come together and become a nation, and where they could then be liberated to go off and be who they wanted to be. This is a country where Colin Powell and John Shalikashvili can both be chairman of the Joint Chiefs and nobody even thinks about the remarkable difference in ethnicity because they're Americans, and that's the way it should be.

That means we have to say to the counterculture: Nice try, you failed, you're wrong. And we have to simply, calmly, methodically reassert American civilization and reestablish the conditions, which I believe starts with the work ethic. You cannot study 300 years of American civilization without coming to the conclusion that working and being expected to work and being involved—and work may be for money or it may be at home, it may be a hobby that you pursue, but the sense of energy, the pursuit of happiness, which is not—it's an active verb—not happiness stamps, not a department of happiness, not therapy for happiness. Pursuit. This is also a muscular society and we've been kidding ourselves about it. The New Hampshire slogan is "Live free or die." It is not "Live free or whine."

labor commanded far less congressional influence than when Congress had enacted Medicare three decades before.

Indeed, the fate of the Clintons' plan turned into a referendum on the capacity of the state to resolve social problems. Their reforms would have instituted a new layer of social citizenship, symbolized by a health security card the government would issue to every American. But conservatives feared such an entitlement, both because of the expense and because of the legitimacy it conferred on governmental activism. The crisis of confidence in all levels of government greatly strengthened the right-wing critique. In the 1960s more than 60 percent of all Americans had trusted the federal government. Thirty years later, after Vietnam, Watergate, and three severe recessions, less than half as many thought as well of their government.

Thus by August 1994, when the Clinton health plan expired in Congress, even many Democrats had abandoned the ambitious effort to restructure one-seventh of the economy. Health care inflation did moderate in the mid 1990s, both because of the regulatory scare and because of the rapid rise of health maintenance organizations (HMOs), which had eclipsed hospitals and individual physicians as the primary provider of medical services. But health insurance was still linked primarily to employment, which meant that at the end of the 1990s more than 44 million Americans were without medical insurance.

Challenge from the Right

The collapse of the Clinton health care initiative generated a large vacuum in American politics, which a reinvigorated Republican party promptly filled. With conservatives out of the Presidency for the first time in twelve years, the leading spokesmen for the cause were both more strident and more ideological. Talk-show hosts such as Rush Limbaugh piled denunciations of Clinton's ineffectiveness onto their daily attack on "feminazis," "Washington insiders," and "political correctness." Georgia congressman Newt Gingrich codified much of this right-wing militancy in a 1994 election manifesto, the "Contract with America," which sought to ideologically unify scores of Republican congressional campaigns. Gingrich and other GOP conservatives avoided divisive cultural issues such as abortion rights and school prayer, calling instead for large reductions in federal social spending, congressional term limits, partial privatization of Medicare and public education, the elimination of five cabinet departments, and a new set of tax cuts.

Like Clinton, Gingrich was a baby boomer who had avoided the draft during the Vietnam War. But this articulate, historically minded ideologue moved steadily rightward in the 1970s and 1980s. He led the GOP revolt that nearly sank the Bush administration's budget in 1990. Then he pushed aside Robert Michel, a more conventional conservative, to become House Minority Leader. Although many voters were apparently unaware of Gingrich's Contract with America during the 1994 elections, liberals were dispirited during the campaign. Labor did not mobilize its troops, and among women, turnout was the lowest in twenty years. The Republicans captured control of both the House and Senate for the first time in forty years, won several governorships, and gained ground in most state legislatures. In the House of Representatives, the elections sent to Washington a large, unified class of GOP freshmen whose politics were ideologically right-wing. As the newly chosen Speaker, Gingrich embodied a dramatic transformation within the Republican party, whose legislative leadership now shifted from the old Midwest to the deep South.

Clinton's moment for neo-Rooseveltian reform was finished. He staged a successful rearguard defense of his presidency after 1994, but only by shifting his politics to accommodate Gingrich conservatives. The president quickly distanced himself from the remaining liberals in Congress, later announcing, in his 1996 State of the Union address, "The era of big government is over." Clinton did win much public support in his effort to preserve existing programs when House Republicans closed many government agencies during a late 1995 showdown over their proposed budget cuts. Just nine months later, he signed into law a drastic revision of U.S. welfare law that ended the federal government's sixty-year commitment to families with dependent children. Henceforth, caregivers—most of whom were young mothers—would be eligible during their entire lifetime for only five years of federal benefits. Many states soon enacted even more restrictive guidelines. Although the government provided no new monies for child care or job training, most welfare recipients were expected to get a job in the private sector, a task that was eased in the late 1990s by the boom in fast-food and other service-sector employment. Conservatives claimed this reform would break the welfare "cycle of dependency."

Gingrich Republicanism had its echo in California, where voters enacted a state ballot initiative in 1994 curbing the social citizenship rights of illegal immigrants. Proposition 187 denied unlawful residents of the United States access to prenatal and childbirth services, child welfare, public education, and nonemergency health care. Its passage, which reflected the severity of the recession in California, was a belated effect of a 1978 ballot proposition that had frozen most property taxes, costing local government more than $200 billion in badly needed revenue. (California schools, once among the best funded in the country, had deteriorated sharply, to quality levels historically characteristic of the far poorer South.) In a pattern reaching back to the anti-Chinese riots of the late nineteenth century, conservatives lay the blame for economic insecurity on non-white immigrants. An infamous TV spot broadcast during the 1994 campaign replayed video footage of Mexican illegals rushing through a San Diego border checkpoint, with the ominous voiceover: "They keep coming."

Two years later, voters in the nation's largest state enacted the California Civil Rights Initiative, which banned affirmative action at the University of California and in state agencies. Affirmative action guidelines were strongly backed by most university administrators, as well as by corporate executives, who saw diversity as essential to the legitimacy and effectiveness of their businesses in a multiracial society. Indeed, an exhaustive 1998 study authored by two former Ivy League college presidents demonstrated that African-American students admitted under affirmative action guidelines graduated as readily as any other group of students. They then went on to careers in the professions, government, and business in proportions even greater than that of their white peers. But affirmative action remained highly controversial in the United States in the mid 1990s. Most conservatives argued that it contravened the idea of a color-blind society, of a social order based on merit, and that the civil rights laws of the 1960s had successfully ended most racism, eliminating the necessity for such policies. Indeed, the conflict over affirmative action had turned into an argument over the degree to which racism remained a force within American politics and society. President Clinton possibly spoke for many when he proposed to "mend it, don't end it."

Gingrich's brand of conservatism soon generated its own backlash. As House Speaker, Gingrich was perceived by the public as a brash radical: public opinion polls gave him some of the lowest approval ratings of any national political leader since Richard Nixon was forced from the White House. Although Gingrich retained the fervent loyalty of many right-wingers, other Republicans began to distance themselves from his leadership. In the 1996 Republican primaries, pro-Gingrich conservatives such as *Forbes* magazine owner Steve Forbes and Texas senator Phil Gramm spent considerable money but won few primary votes. Pat Buchanan once again ran as an anti-abortion cultural conservative, but he generated the most excitement by denouncing NAFTA and big corporations. The more moderate Senate Majority Leader Robert Dole, who won his party's nomination for president, ran a spiritless campaign that advanced few Contract with America themes.

Although Clinton and Gore also ran a relatively muted, apolitical campaign, they had little trouble winning reelection, albeit with only 49 percent of the popular vote. (Ross Perot took only 8 percent this time.) Turnout in the election fell to levels not seen since 1924. But for one group of voters, the election was a political coming of age. The Latino electorate, which had increased substantially, swung sharply to the Democrats. Although this rapidly growing population had given Ronald Reagan more than 40 percent of their vote, many Latinos were furious with the GOP's anti-immigrant politics. In both 1996 and 1998, their wholesale shift into the Democratic column locked up California for Clinton and his party.

New Leadership and New Ideas for the Labor Movement

By the early 1990s, American trade unions were in decline. Unionized labor represented only 16 percent of all American workers; each year the proportion dropped. Trade unions no longer set the wage standard in any major industry—not even in autos or steel, where nonunion factories and mills represented an increasingly large production sector. Perhaps most threatening, the union idea seemed stale and antiquated. " 'Organized Labor.' Say those words, and your heart sinks," wrote Thomas Geoghegan, an embattled pro-union attorney. "Dumb, stupid organized labor." Liberals such as Robert Reich, Clinton's secretary of labor, seemed equally skeptical about the future of unionism. Reich thought traditional unionism of doubtful usefulness to workers in the knowledge industries of the new economy. Under the leadership of Lane Kirkland, whose politics had been molded by the conservative labor chieftain George Meany, the AFL-CIO devoted few resources to organizing, and it had little presence on television or in other media.

But the Republican sweep of Congress during the 1994 elections generated a leadership revolt at the top of the AFL-CIO. Under Kirkland, the unions had counted on the Democrats to pass laws that would aid collective bargaining and make organizing easier. But now, for the first time since the 1950s, Republicans controlled both houses of the federal legislature. In this crisis, an insurgent group of top union officials, mostly representing workers in public employment, the service trades, and manufacturing, overthrew Kirkland's leadership. It was the first successful challenge to a sitting AFL or AFL-CIO president in more than a hundred years.

The new AFL-CIO president was John Sweeney, former president of the Service Employees International Union (SEIU). Richard Trumka, the militant leader of the United Mine Workers, won the post of secretary-treasurer. Sweeney and Trumka were joined by Linda Chavez-Thompson, a Chicano unionist from Texas, as executive vice president. Under Sweeney's leadership the SEIU had recruited a multiracial organizing corps of hundreds, some with New Left backgrounds. The union had spent a sizable proportion of its dues to successfully organize thousands of janitors, health care workers, and public employees. SEIU organizers sometimes deployed the tactics of the civil rights movement—sit-ins, civil disobedience, and public marches—to organize low-wage African Americans, Asians, and Latinos who were so heavily concentrated in fast-growing service jobs.

Sweeney and his allies began to revitalize the AFL-CIO. Top AFL-CIO leaders were suddenly on television, at rallies, and on the picket

"Queremos Justicia! We Want Justice!"

In this article for a labor newsletter, Marcy Rein, communications coordinator for Service Employees International Union [SEIU] Local 1877 during a strike by janitors in northern California, describes the "rolling strike" strategy used to win higher wages for the union's membership.

"In the beginning the [janitorial] contractors said, 'I'm the boss, you do what I say,'" recalls Reyna Alferez of Service Employees Local 1877's bargaining committee. Softly she continues, "I told them, 'You pay a little to us and you take a lot from us. You have Volvos and BMW's. Who makes the money to buy them?'

"The employers said we're paying just a little because those people are just minority people. We got mad, and we understood that when we want something, we have to fight for it."

And fight they did. Local 1877 blindsided the contractors with a month-long rolling strike in June. The bosses never knew where trouble would visit next or how long it would stay. . . .

Local 1877 represents 5,000 janitors in four Northern California counties: Alameda, Contra Costa, San Mateo, and Santa Clara. More than 80 percent are Latino, most of the rest are African American and Asian. Under the old contract, two-thirds earned less than the federal poverty wage—$7.28 per hour for a family of four.

The janitors work for building maintenance companies, which in turn are hired by commercial real estate, high-tech, and other firms. Many of them are household names like Hewlett-Packard, Chevron, and AT&T. On the pit end of the income gap, they typify the new workforce in Silicon Valley where nearly 40 percent of the jobs are subcontracted.

Justice for Janitors [the SEIU campaign] rolled into the Valley in 1991 with an organizing drive at . . . the contractor serving Apple Computer. Over the next five years, Local 1877 organized three-fourths of the janitors in the area. . . .

Four months of strike preparation began in February with the selection of bargaining committee members and worksite organizers. These members were charged with informing and mobilizing others in their buildings.

At a special convention . . . , some 700 janitors set their contract goals: one master agreement, wages above poverty level, family health insurance, and protections for immigrant workers.

Then they hit the streets, demonstrating at work, marching on San Jose Airport, and doing civil disobedience in Oakland and Palo Alto. Each action sent the same emphatic message: "Queremos justicia! We want justice!"

Meanwhile bargaining was getting nowhere. . . . A few people were fired. Two got anonymous death threats, accompanied by warnings to "stop that shit with the union."

Faced with this intimidation and a pitiful contract offer, members voted June 1 to strike.

Local 1877 organizers decided on the "rolling strike" to maximize disruption for the contractors—making it harder to hire permanent replacements—and minimize hardship for members who, living paycheck to paycheck, couldn't weather a continuous strike.

In the first week, workers struck in a different county each night, taking out three to five work sites. But in the second week the strike overran the organizers' careful plans. Workers hit in every county every night, walking out and staying out. Altogether about 70 sites were struck. . . .

Strike committees ran the strike day by day in many places. "Good people came forward who'd never done anything like strike before" said Eugenia Gutierrez, a contract enforcement rep in Oakland. "And mostly it was women who took leadership."

As in other . . . campaigns, community and labor supporters bolstered the strike. Teamsters, communications workers, and construction workers honored picket lines. . . .

Supporters joined the public actions that whirled on at a pace of two to three a week, marching and leafleting, holding a trash-in and a candlelight vigil. They helped take the janitors' case to the public and to the contractors' client companies—and built up a $40,000 strike fund.

After four weeks, the contractors gave in to most of the union's demands.

The new master contract, approved 6-1, brings all members above the current poverty wage. Annual increases average four percent. Members on the bottom of the scale get 5.5 percent, and everyone stays ahead of inflation. . . .

Source: Marcy Rein, "Aggressive Tactics Help Janitors Clean Up on Contract," *Labor Notes,* September 1996.

lines. They reached out to feminists, civil rights leaders, ecologists, left-wing academics, and liberal clergy in an effort to build a pro-union coalition. Thousands of students were recruited for a high-profile "union summer" organizing experience, even as the AFL-CIO put pressure on its affiliates to double and triple their organizing budgets. "Labor must organize without the law," asserted the new AFL-CIO president, "so that we can later organize under the law." Sweeney and his allies recruited scores of energetic labor activists and replaced aging Cold Warriors in the AFL-CIO's International Affairs Department with individuals who had long defended left-wing unionists in South Africa and Central America. It had taken a quarter-century, but the "Sixties" generation was finally making its voice heard at the union movement's leadership level.

The International Brotherhood of Teamsters, the nation's largest union, underwent a remarkable transformation during these years. For decades the top leadership of the Teamsters had been synonymous with corruption and criminality. The most famous American union leader in popular memory was Jimmy Hoffa, Teamster president from 1957 to 1971. Hoffa's 1975 murder, just as he sought to make a comeback, remained unsolved. But at the beginning of the century's last decade the Teamsters were home to one of the most vigorous reform movements in American labor, the Teamsters for a Democratic Union (TDU). In a federally supervised election in 1991, TDU helped to elevate Ron Carey, a local union leader from Queens (New York City), and his rank-and-file reform slate to top union posts. Carey and other reformers battled old-guard unionists to democratize and energize the Teamsters. Their efforts paid off in new organizing drives and the spectacular strike victory of 185,000 Teamsters against the United Parcel Service in August 1997. The first successful nationwide strike in nearly two decades, the UPS strike won widespread public support for labor's demand that UPS upgrade thousands of low-wage, part-time jobs to permanent, full-time positions. "The rank and file felt like, yes, we do make a difference," said Barb Joyce, a Des Moines truck driver. "The day after the strike when we went back to work everybody on the road was waving and blowing kisses to us."

Carey's success was short-lived. In 1996 he had won a bitter reelection contest against James P. Hoffa, son of the legendary Teamster leader. Relying on Washington consultants, Carey had used union funds illegally to bolster his campaign. When this money-laundering scheme became known, the federal judge who supervised Teamster affairs overturned the election and threw Carey out of the union. James P. Hoffa, who was allied with many old-guard Teamsters, then won the 1998 rematch against a candidate fielded by TDU and other union militants.

Carey's fall hurt the entire labor movement, but it did not prevent the unions from demonstrating a new strength in politics. Like their predecessors, the new labor leaders supported the Democrats, but they mobilized union money and people in a more energetic and independent fashion. In 1996 labor spearheaded a successful effort to win from the Republican-dominated Congress the first minimum wage increase in half a decade, after which union voters played a disproportionately heavy role in returning President Clinton to the White House during the November elections. Just a year later, the AFL-CIO's new capacity to mobilize political support became even clearer when the unions helped to convince Congress—including 80 percent of all House Democrats—to reject President Clinton's request for "fast-track" authority that would have made it easier to expand the NAFTA accords. There followed by an enormous mobilizing effort in California, where the unions and their liberal allies turned back right-wing Proposition 226, which would have curbed labor's capacity to raise and spend the money needed for effective political action. And in 1998 labor again demonstrated a newfound sense of political power when unionists turned out in large numbers to hand the GOP a stinging setback in the off-year elections.

Historically low levels of unemployment in the last half of the 1990s raised wages, emboldened workers, and brightened chances for a union revival. By the end of the decade the official joblessness rate stood just above 4 percent, the lowest level in three decades. Low-paid service workers, especially Hispanics and African Americans, who had not shared in the 1980s boom, now began to find jobs at wages that were rising smartly for the first time in a generation. Full employment, sustained for several years, had a radically beneficial impact on the lives of the poorest Americans. Faced with a labor shortage, companies began to offer jobs to people described as unemployable just a few years before. In the cities, crime began to fall, the drug culture to dissipate, and young black men to find steady employment. And as fear of job loss declined, working Americans could once again begin to seek a collective solution to their problems. Union-organizing efforts found a more favorable reception and campaigns to institute citywide

Seattle, November 1999. When a march of trade unionists protesting against the World Trade Organization arrived in downtown Seattle, many labor activists joined youth and environmental protesters who were already blocking access to the WTO meeting. Visible among the banners and placards carried by demonstrators were those of the International Longshore and Warehouse Union, which shut down all Pacific coast ports for a day.

Source: David Bacon, November 30, 1999.

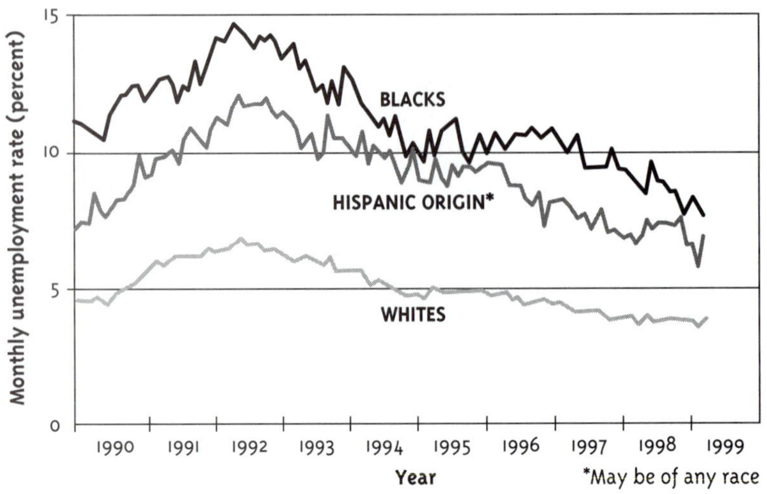

Declining Unemployment During the economic boom that began in 1991, African-American and Hispanic workers were able to participate in the growing job market (as evidenced by their unemployment rates), a benefit that largely eluded both groups during the previous expansion in the 1980s.

Source: *New York Times,* 5/8/99.

"living wages" (sufficient income to put workers above the poverty line) proliferated across the country.

By the end of the 1990s, the American labor movement stood once again, in fact and in the public imagination, on the left side of American politics. For the first time since the 1940s, the unions maintained a firm alliance with most other liberals. This was graphically demonstrated at the Seattle meeting of the World Trade Organization in November 1999. There, unionists and ecological activists mobilized high-profile marches and demonstrations demanding that the WTO and other trade organizations link international commerce to the enforcement of a set of worldwide labor and environmental standards. A protest banner summed up the new alliance: "Teamsters and Turtles: Together at Last!" This unlikely alliance continued into the following spring when in April 2000 ecology and trade union activists again took to the streets — this time in Washington, DC — to protest the World Bank and the International Monetary Fund's policies on Third World debt relief. By the dawn of the twenty-first century, the unions had shed much of the parochial, self-interested reputation that had for so long limited their political and social appeal.

On Trial: Gender, Race, and National Identity

The 1990s were a decade of high-profile investigations, hearings, and trials in which the new politics of race, gender, and American identity were played out before a media-savvy audience of millions. The courtroom and the hearing room now served as a site of furious contention. These televised spectacles were not, in fact, well suited to resolving the nation's deep-seated cultural and social divisions. But a fascinated citizenry focused its gaze on these events because no new election and no new statute could fully represent the complicated and contradictory values Americans brought to their understanding of race, sex, and nationhood.

President Bush's decision to nominate Clarence Thomas to fill the vacant Supreme Court seat of civil rights pioneer Thurgood Marshall in 1991 would have been controversial in any event. Thomas had been born in poverty, but the Yale-educated black conservative had criticized civil rights leaders and had helped undermine affirmative action litigation as chairman of the Equal Employment Opportunity Commission (EEOC) during the early years of the Reagan administration. Republicans therefore backed Thomas, while leaders of the civil rights community, who wanted to keep an African-American on the Court, were split.

Thomas's confirmation battle before the Senate Judiciary Committee became red hot in October 1991 after Anita Hill, a black law professor who had been an aide to Thomas at the EEOC, testified that the nominee had frequently made lurid remarks to her and repeatedly pressured her for dates. Feminists and liberals hostile to the Thomas nomination immediately championed Hill's charges. The nominee charged that his accusers were turning the confirmation proceedings into a "high-tech lynching." The nation watched in stunned amazement as a panel of white male senators subjected Hill's motives and veracity to fierce personal attack.

The Senate confirmed Thomas by a vote of fifty-two to forty-eight, but the battle cast a long shadow. First, post-1960s black conservatism no long seemed an oxymoron; among African-American writers and intellectuals, Thomas symbolized the emergence of an articulate, conservative black minority who challenged civil rights liberalism. Second, the Thomas–Hill confrontation before an all-male committee put the issue of sexual harassment and its meaning at the forefront of public debate. In 1992 the EEOC recorded a 50-percent jump in official complaints on the issue; that same year, female candidates ran for Senate and House seats in record numbers.

Television played a key role in two additional racial spectacles of the early 1990s. On the evening of March 3, 1991, a black motorist, Rodney King, became a symbol of white racism and police brutality when a nearby resident captured on videotape the beating he suffered at the hands of four Los Angeles policemen. Millions saw King, who was lying on the ground, take fifty-odd blows from club, foot, and flashlight. Sympathy for King turned to violent outrage in April 1992 when a white suburban jury acquitted his police assailants. Black and Latino rioters burned hundreds of houses and stores in the South Central section of Los Angeles, particularly those occupied by Korean immigrant shopkeepers.

Digital Manipulation. The avalanche of news coverage of the O. J. Simpson case provoked criticism of the press's preoccupation with celebrity and sensation. The case also sparked controversy over the news media's manipulation of visual information, abetted by the new tool of digital imaging. The June 27, 1994, cover of *Time* magazine featured Simpson's police "mugshot." The *Time* picture seemed unremarkable until it was compared to the same week's cover of *Newsweek,* which also displayed the police photograph. In contrast to *Newsweek's* unretouched cover (shown here), *Time* had digitally darkened Simpson's face to lend the image greater drama and, some commentators suggested, menace.

Source: Los Angeles Police Department/*Newsweek,* June 27, 1994. Used by permission.

The police and National Guard were called in, and fifty-three people were killed and thousands injured. Property damage amounted to a billion dollars, making the riot the most costly in U.S. history.

The King beating and the riot heightened the wall of mutual distrust that had long existed between blacks and Los Angeles police. This tension became a key issue two years later, when police arrested the former football star and sports commentator O. J. Simpson after the stabbing murder of his ex-wife Nicole and her friend Ronald Goldman, both of whom were white. Simpson, who was light-skinned, rich, and articulate, had earned the confidence of corporate advertisers and become famous as a TV personality and pitchman. His trial, which saturated the airwaves and dominated everyday conversation for nine months in 1995, proved an international media extravaganza. Cable News Network (CNN) offered 631 hours of direct televised coverage, which increased its ratings and revenues by close to 50 percent.

Simpson's expensive, high-powered defense team exploited the racial dimensions of the Los Angeles trial. They charged the detectives who investigated the murder with racism and portrayed their client as the victim of a biased system of justice. Although much evidence indicated that Simpson had been an abusive and violent husband, opinion was racially polarized by the trial. Sixty percent of all African Americans thought Simpson innocent, while 75 percent of whites believed him guilty. In October 1995 a jury of ten women and two men—nine blacks, two whites, and one Hispanic—took less than four hours to acquit him of all criminal charges. Although a lawsuit by families of the two murder victims eventually forced Simpson to pay millions in civil damages, his acquittal in 1995 demonstrated how pervasive were the racial constructions that framed a divergent social and legal reality for Americans, white and black.

The success of the 1996 "Million-Man March" seemed to confirm the continuing centrality of race—as opposed to class, or politics, or gender—as a defining identity for huge numbers of African Americans.

Male Bonding. A Promise Keepers gathering in July 1995 attracted 64,000 men to the Kingdome stadium in Seattle, Washington.

Source: Jim Levitt / Impact Visuals.

Answering the call of the Black Muslim leader Louis Farrakhan, hundreds of thousands of African-American men assembled peacefully on the Washington Mall to affirm their solidarity and dignity. Leaders of the march, the largest convocation of African Americans since the 1963 March on Washington headed by Dr. Martin Luther King, made no demands on the government but implored black men to reclaim the moral and economic leadership of the black community and black family. Indeed, the self-affirming, religious quality of the gathering paralleled that of the predominantly white male Promise Keepers, an evangelical Protestant movement that filled scores of football stadiums to preach the return of male authority and responsibility within the Christian family.

The problematic relationship between intensely held religious belief and the claims of the U.S. nation-state stretch back to the origins of the republic. The antebellum era had spawned numerous colonies and communities seeking to build a spiritual and political life counterpoised to the corruption of secular society. In 1979 this impulse had propelled more than a thousand Americans, many African American, to follow the Reverend Jim Jones from California to an agricultural colony in Guyana. There internal division, followed by scrutiny from U.S. officials, generated panic, strife, and a mass suicide that claimed more than 900 lives.

A tragedy of similar character unfolded near Waco, Texas, early in 1993 when the U.S. Bureau of Alcohol, Tobacco, and Firearms (ATF) raided the compound occupied by a Christian cult, the Branch Davidians. Led by their charismatic leader, David Koresh, the Davidians fought and killed four ATF agents. After a fifty-one-day standoff, Attorney General Janet Reno approved a new assault. But instead of a firefight, government agents triggered a massive fire and suicide that killed eighty-six in the compound, including twenty-five children.

For many on the extreme Right, the fiasco at Waco transformed Koresh into a martyr who had defended both gun ownership and Christian separatism. An anti-Semitic, antiblack militia movement intensely hostile to the authority of the federal government emerged in some economically hard-pressed rural areas. The nation became acutely aware of such widespread sentiment on April 19, 1995, precisely two years after the Waco tragedy, when Timothy McVeigh and Terry Nichols, who had contact with right-wing militias, exploded a fertilizer truck bomb in front of the Alfred P. Murrah Federal Building in Oklahoma City. The bomb blew off the entire front of the nine-story structure, killing 168 people. It was the worst terrorist attack ever on U.S. soil. In the aftermath of the bombing, President Clinton pushed through Congress new anti-terrorism measures, including some restrictions on civil liberties.

Instruction Manual. A novel called *The Turner Diaries* was reputed to be the inspiration for the Oklahoma City bombing. Written by American Nazi Andrew Macdonald in 1978 and widely distributed via mail order and sales at gunshows, the book depicted in gruesome detail a white supremacist insurrection against the U.S. government—including the bombing of federal buildings in Washington, D.C., and Houston—and the extermination of the nation's Jews and people of color.

Source: Barricade Books, Inc.

The Impeachment and Trial of a President

The U.S. Constitution provides for the removal of a sitting president if the House of Representatives, by a majority vote, impeaches (charges) and the Senate, by a two-thirds vote, convicts the president of "high crimes and misdemeanors." Three presidents have faced such a quasi-judicial drama. In 1867 the politics of Reconstruction stood at the heart of Andrew Johnson's Senate trial; in 1974 Richard Nixon resigned when the House seemed certain to impeach him for abuse of presidential power as a consequence of his involvement in the Watergate burglary; and in December 1998 the House impeached Bill Clinton on charges of perjury and obstruction of justice. In contrast to Andrew Johnson's trial and Richard Nixon's forced resignation, the constitutional crisis that enveloped Clinton hinged not on his public statecraft but on his character and the

Assassin Fantasies. In an effort to undermine Clinton's credibility, some critics indulged in outlandish attacks against the administration, including charges of conspiracy and assassination. The 1993 death of Deputy White House Counsel Vincent Foster in Fort Marcy Park, Virginia, for example, was ruled a suicide by independent counsel Robert Fiske, but the tabloid press and right-wing print and Internet publications almost immediately began issuing reports of an official coverup to suppress evidence of foul play deriving from Foster's knowledge about Whitewater.

Source: London *Sunday Telegraph,* October 23, 1995. Used by permission.

consequences of his personal conduct. But in an era when sexual conduct and social attitudes had become thoroughly politicized, that was enough.

To conservatives, President Clinton was an intensely polarizing figure. He had appropriated many Republican issues, such as a balanced budget, welfare reform, and tough-on-crime measures to expand the death penalty and put more police on the street. At the same time, Clinton seemed to embody the social and cultural values of the 1960s, including an unconstrained sexuality and freewheeling capacity to spin the truth in his personal and business affairs. Though he had been elected president twice, a substantial minority of Americans had never considered Clinton a truly legitimate occupant of the White House.

Clinton's legal and political troubles began in 1994, when Attorney General Reno appointed an independent counsel, Robert Fiske, to investigate questionable Arkansas real estate investments made in 1978 by Bill and Hillary Clinton in the Whitewater Development Corporation. Although several of the president's associates were eventually jailed in connection with their Whitewater land dealings, Clinton and his wife never faced criminal charges. However, the lengthy Whitewater investigation was transmuted four years later by Kenneth Starr, an aggressive conservative former judge who had replaced Fiske as independent counsel, into a probe of Clinton's sexual conduct and the truthfulness of his testimony on this subject.

In 1995 and 1996, President Clinton had an affair with Monica Lewinsky, a twenty-two-year-old White House intern. This episodic sexual relationship was not illegal, but lying about it under oath, or attempting to convince others to do so, would have constituted perjury and obstruction of justice. Clinton may well have done so, when Lewinsky and he gave depositions in a sexual harassment suit filed against the president filed by Paula Jones, who had worked as a state clerk when Clinton was governor of Arkansas. Clinton damaged his credibility when in January 1998 he publicly denied having had sex with Lewinsky, then six months later admitted to an "inappropriate relationship" with Lewinsky before a grand jury.

The furor over the Lewinsky affair revealed that the nation was deeply divided in what many came to see as a renewal of the culture wars that had been so characteristic of public debate in the late 1980s and early 1990s. To those who sought the president's impeachment and removal from office, Clinton's mendacity about the affair spoke for itself. His recklessness had shamed the nation, subverted its legal institutions, and proven him unfit for office. Clinton seemed to embody all that conservative moralists found intolerable in contemporary American life. Representative Tom DeLay of Texas, one of the most militant of the conservative Republicans, thought the impeachment fight "a debate about relativism versus absolute truth." House Judiciary Committee chairman Henry Hyde wondered if, "after this culture war is over that we are engaged in, an America will survive that's worth fighting to defend."

Clinton's supporters did not defend his sexual escapades or the lies he told about them. But they thought impeachment and removal from office a punishment disproportionate to his transgressions. They drew a sharp line between his personal conduct and his role as an effective political leader. Moreover, to many Clinton partisans, Kenneth Starr's massive, intrusive investigative effort was, in the words of Hillary Clinton, part of "a vast right-wing conspiracy" that represented an attempt by the Republican Right to persecute Clinton and "criminalize" normal political debate.

Nearly two-thirds of all Americans solidly backed Clinton's continuation in the White House, even as they repudiated his private conduct. The president's handsome approval ratings were bolstered by steady economic growth, low unemployment, and Clinton's popularity as a defender of Social Security, public education, and racial reconciliation. African Americans, white women, and liberal Democrats were especially fervent in their support, in part because they found nothing particularly dreadful in lying about extramarital relationships and in part because of the prominent role played by conservative white southerners in the impeachment investigation. Most Americans were offended by Kenneth

Starr's exposure of the most intimate details of the Clinton–Lewinsky relationship; indeed, by late 1998 the Clinton impeachment drama held less public interest than had the O. J. Simpson trial three years before. Therefore Clinton partisans were elated when the Democrats recaptured the California statehouse and gained five congressional seats during the 1998 midterm elections, a remarkable showing for the party that held the White House. Taking responsibility for the GOP debacle, Newt Gingrich resigned both his Speakership and his seat in the House.

In spite of the Democrats' gains in 1998, conservative Republicans still controlled both houses of Congress, and they doggedly persisted in their effort to oust the president. The House Judiciary Committee approved four articles of impeachment on December 11, 1998; one week later the full House of Representatives, by a narrow partisan majority, impeached Clinton on charges of perjury and obstruction of justice. But the House impeachment managers could not convince two-thirds of the Senate to follow suit. After weeks of argument and debate, the Senate acquitted the president on February 12, 1999. Several moderate Republicans joined a solid Democratic minority on the vote. For conservative Republicans, the abortive prosecution of the president constituted a massive miscalculation and a sharp political setback. Some Christian conservatives even speculated that the Senate vote, combined with Clinton's remarkably high poll numbers, proved that no "moral majority" existed, that they had lost the culture wars.

At the Dawn of a New Century

The year 2000 has a numerical uniqueness, but it is meaningless as a guide to our history. For historical purposes the twentieth century actually began with World War I and ended in 1991, with the final collapse of the Soviet Union. War, revolution, economic turbulence, and an intense conflict of ideologies wracked that seventy-seven-year "century." In the United States this short century gave those with economic power and cultural authority a commanding hand. A dangerous world put a premium on the nation's military might, a strong central government, and ideological cohesion. This was an era in which the power of the presidency waxed and American patriotism held a coercive edge.

That century ended in the early 1990s, when upheavals in central Europe, Russia, South Africa, and Asia demonstrated that the democratic idea remains a powerful and contagious impulse. A generation from now, historians may well argue that the twenty-first century had already begun in the 1990s. The most obvious characteristic of the new era is the unprecedented freedom with which capital now flows from one continent to another. In Europe, a single currency, the euro, is obliterating ancient borders; in North America, a new free-trade regime had inexorably linked the fortunes of the Anglo North with the Latin South. But this freewheeling global capitalism has also undermined the nation-state, proletarianized hundreds of millions of agricultural workers, and awakened a sometimes violent politics of ethnic and religious identity.

How will this sea change in the international order resonate in the United States, where political stalemate and economic inequality have put popular social movements, especially the labor movement, on the defensive for more than a generation? History offers no clear blueprint, but it does suggest that fundamental change most frequently comes in sudden and dramatic fashion. The liberation of African Americans came in two great forward leaps: the first during and immediately following the Civil War; the second, a hundred years later, in the civil rights revolution of the 1950s and 1960s. Likewise, American women twice thrust onto the national agenda issues involving their own political and social liberation: first during the decades before World War I, and then half a century later in an even more profound exploration of their personal and political consciousness. Latino, Asian, Indian, and gay Americans have fought their own unfinished battles, often in the wake of the vanguard struggle waged by African Americans. And finally, the growth of American citizenship — for women, people of color, and all those who trade their labor for their bread — cannot be divorced from the activism of the working class itself. American workers have repeatedly discovered their voice and their power in a series of unexpectedly popular insurgencies that have invigorated the republic over the course of the last two centuries.

We cannot foretell the future. But we can be certain that in a globally integrated workplace, where men and women must still labor for their livelihoods, people who see their identity as workers will play a central role in shaping the new world. From Seattle to Ciudad Juarez, they have begun to make clear that the interests of American working people and that of world capitalism do not necessarily coincide. In new immigrant communities on the East and West Coasts, in the old factory towns in the Midwest, in urban ghettos and suburban officeparks, the working class, in all its twenty-first century diversity, is certain to press forward its claim to dignity, security, and social justice. And in the struggle, working people will have once again built a new America.

Believe It or Not. At the close of the twentieth century, 93 percent of the U.S. population professed to believe in angels, 49 percent were sure that the federal government was hiding information about the existence of unidentified flying objects, and 25 percent thought they could communicate with the dead. Many Americans chose mystical options over the grimmer aspects of contemporary life; but popular interest in the fantastic also signaled a love of creative fabrication dating back into U.S. history (linking, for example, the contemporary antics of the more outrageous tabloid press with the mid-nineteenth-century showmanship of P. T. Barnum).

Source: *Weekly World News,* August 13, 1991. Used by permission.

The Years in Review

1980

- Striking Polish workers organize Solidarity, which challenges Communist rule.

1981

- IBM licenses DOS operating system—owned by a small Seattle company called Microsoft—for its line of personal computers.

1988

- Soviet leader Mikhail Gorbachev introduces *perestroika* and *glasnost* reforms. Three years later the Communist party collapses.
- Republican vice president George Bush defeats Michael Dukakis for presidency.
- Computer "worm" crashes thousands of computers in a few hours and brings existence of nationwide Internet to national attention.

1989

- Germans pour through the Berlin Wall, signaling the end of Communism in Eastern Europe.
- Chinese regime crushes student demonstration in Beijing's Tiananmen Square.
- United Mine Workers wage an eleven-month siege of the Pittston Coal Company.

1990

- President Bush breaks his "no new taxes" pledge.

1991

- Operation Desert Storm: U.S. forces launch a massive air assault against Iraq in response to its invasion of Kuwait.
- Senate confirms nomination of Clarence Thomas to Supreme Court despite a former aide's sexual harassment charges.
- Four Los Angeles policemen beat motorist Rodney King; their acquittal in April 1992 leads to riots in South Central Los Angeles.

1992

- Arkansas governor Bill Clinton, Democrat, defeats President Bush and third-party candidate Ross Perot to become president.
- Number of women jumps from twenty-eight to forty-seven in the House of Representatives and from two to six in the Senate.
- National debt hits $3 trillion; it has more than quadrupled since 1981.

- Mall of America — the world's largest mall, with 400 stores — opens in Bloomington, Minnesota.

1993

- Congress enacts employer-friendly NAFTA legislation.
- Clinton unveils a complex, but universal health care plan. Congress rejects it a year later.
- Eighty-six members of Branch Davidian cult die in fire and suicide when federal agents assault their Waco, Texas, headquarters.

1994

- U.S. troops intervene in Haiti in an effort to restore democracy.
- Israeli Prime Minister Itzak Rabin and Palestinian leader Yasir Arafat agree to limited Palestinian self-rule.
- Nelson Mandela elected President of South Africa in nation's first multiracial elections.
- Republicans debut their Contract with America, which calls for reductions in federal social spending and taxes; they capture control of both the House and Senate for the first time in forty years.
- California voters approve Proposition 187 denying illegal aliens access to educational and health services.
- Ex-football star O. J. Simpson is arrested for the murder of his wife after a ninety-minute chase that is watched by millions on television; trial the following year ends in acquittal.
- Attorney General Janet Reno appoints an independent counsel to investigate President Clinton's questionable real estate investments in the 1980s — known as Whitewater.
- Baseball players strike over salary caps; season is canceled; no World Series for first time in ninety years.

1995

- Reformer John Sweeney elected AFL-CIO president.
- The Internet becomes part of everyday life with the growing popularity of the World Wide Web.
- Timothy McVeigh and Terry Nichols explode a truck bomb in front of the Murrah Federal Building in Oklahoma City, killing 169 people.
- President Clinton has a sexual affair with White House intern Monica Lewinsky; when news of the affair surfaces in 1998, he initially denies it.

1996

- President Clinton signs into law a major revision of the welfare law that ends sixty-year commitment to poor families with dependent children.

- California voters approve the California Civil Rights Initiative, which bans affirmative action at the University of California and in state agencies.
- President Clinton reelected, easily defeating Republican Bob Dole and third-party candidate Ross Perot.

1997

- 185,000 Teamsters wage a successful strike against the United Parcel Service, the first successful nationwide strike in nearly two decades.

1998

- Economic growth and new tax revenues combine to turn the federal budget deficit into a surplus for the first time in years.

1999

- The Senate acquits Clinton in second impeachment trial of a president in the nation's history.
- Number of telephone area codes doubles in 1990s as use of fax machines, modems, and cell phones explodes.

2000

- Threat of a "Y2K" international computer disaster dissipates on New Year's Day when few computer glitches actually occur worldwide.
- Al Gore wins popular vote for Presidency but loses to Republican George W. Bush in Electoral College after highly contested vote in Flordia is resolved when the U.S. Supreme Court halts the recount.

Suggested Readings

Barber, Benjamin R., *Jihad vs. McWorld: How Globalism and Tribalism are Re-Shaping the World* (1996).

Beschloss, Michael R., and Strobe Talbott, *At the Highest Levels: The Inside Story of the End of the Cold War* (1993).

Burkett, Elinor, *The Gravest Show on Earth: America in the Age of AIDS* (1996).

Dionne, E. J., Jr., *They Only Look Dead: Why Progressives Will Dominate the Next Political Era* (1997).

Galbraith, James K., *Created Unequal: The Crisis in American Pay* (1998).

Gibson, James, *Warrior Dreams: Violence and Manhood in Post-Vietnam America* (1994).

Henwood, Doug, *Wall Street: How It Works and for Whom* (1997).

Hochschild, Arlie Russell, *The Time Bind: When Work Becomes Home and Home Becomes Work* (1997).

Kuttner, Robert, *Everything for Sale: The Virtues and Limits of Markets* (1999).

Lester, Richard K., *The Productive Edge: How U.S. Industries Are Pointing the Way to a New Era of Economic Growth* (1998).

Levy, Steven, *Hackers: Heroes of the Computer Revolution* (1994).

Manes, Steven, and Paul Andrews, *Gates: How Microsoft's Mogul Reinvented an Industry—And Made Himself the Richest Man in America* (1994).

Maraniss, David, *The First in His Class: The Biography of Bill Clinton* (1996).

Meeropol, Michael, *Surrender: How the Clinton Administration Completed the Reagan Revolution* (1998).

Moody, Kim, *Workers in a Lean World: Unions in the International Economy* (1997).

Mort, Jo-Ann, ed., *Not Your Father's Union Movement: Inside the AFL-CIO* (1998).

Ortega, Bob, *In Sam We Trust: The Untold Story of Sam Walton and How Wal-Mart Is Devouring America* (1998).

Powell, Colin L.(with Joseph E. Persico), *My American Journey* (1995).

Schiller, Dan, *Digital Capitalism: Networking the Global Market System* (1999).

Schrag, Peter, *Paradise Lost: California's Experience, America's Future* (1999).

Skocpol, Theda, *Boomerang: Clinton's Health Security Effort and the Turn Against Government in U.S. Politics* (1996).

Tillman, Ray M., and Michael S. Cummings, eds., *The Transformation of U.S. Unions: Voices, Visions, and Strategies from the Grassroots* (1999).

Vanderbilt, Tom, *The Sneaker Book: Anatomy of an Industry and an Icon* (1998).

Woodward, Bob, *The Agenda: Inside the Clinton White House* (1995).

And on the World Wide Web

- Jerry Goldman, *Oyez, Oyez, Oyez: U.S. Supreme Court Multimedia Database* (http://oyez.nwu.edu/)

Appendix

Constitution of the United States of America

Note: The following text is a transcription of the Constitution in its original form.

We the People of the United States, in Order to form a more perfect Union, establish Justice, insure domestic Tranquility, provide for the common defense, promote the general Welfare, and secure the Blessings of Liberty to ourselves and our Posterity, do ordain and establish this Constitution for the United States of America.

Article I

Section 1

All legislative Powers herein granted shall be vested in a Congress of the United States, which shall consist of a Senate and House of Representatives.

Section 2

The House of Representatives shall be composed of Members chosen every second Year by the People of the several States, and the Electors in each State shall have the Qualifications requisite for Electors of the most numerous Branch of the State Legislature.

No Person shall be a Representative who shall not have attained to the Age of twenty five Years, and been seven Years a Citizen of the United States, and who shall not, when elected, be an Inhabitant of that State in which he shall be chosen.

Representatives and direct Taxes shall be apportioned among the several States which may be included within this Union, according to their respective Numbers, which shall be determined by adding to the whole Number of free Persons, including those bound to Service for a Term of Years, and excluding Indians not taxed, three fifths of all other Persons. The actual Enumeration shall be made within three Years after the first Meeting of the Congress of the United States, and within every subsequent Term of ten Years, in such Manner as they shall by Law direct. The Number of Representatives shall not exceed one for every thirty Thousand, but each State shall have at Least one Representative; and until such enumeration shall be made, the State of New Hampshire shall be entitled to chuse three, Massachusetts eight, Rhode-Island and Providence Plantations one, Connecticut five, New-York six, New Jersey four, Pennsylvania eight, Delaware one, Maryland six, Virginia ten, North Carolina five, South Carolina five, and Georgia three.

When vacancies happen in the Representation from any State, the Executive Authority thereof shall issue Writs of Election to fill such Vacancies.

The House of Representatives shall chuse their Speaker and other Officers; and shall have the sole Power of Impeachment.

Section 3

The Senate of the United States shall be composed of two Senators from each State, chosen by the Legislature thereof for six Years; and each Senator shall have one Vote.

Immediately after they shall be assembled in Consequence of the first Election, they shall be divided as equally as may be into three Classes. The Seats of the Senators of the first Class shall be vacated at the Expiration of the second Year, of the second Class at the

Expiration of the fourth Year, and of the third Class at the Expiration of the sixth Year, so that one third may be chosen every second Year; and if Vacancies happen by Resignation, or otherwise, during the Recess of the Legislature of any State, the Executive thereof may make temporary Appointments until the next Meeting of the Legislature, which shall then fill such Vacancies.

No Person shall be a Senator who shall not have attained to the Age of thirty Years, and been nine Years a Citizen of the United States, and who shall not, when elected, be an Inhabitant of that State for which he shall be chosen.

The Vice President of the United States shall be President of the Senate, but shall have no Vote, unless they be equally divided.

The Senate shall chuse their other Officers, and also a President pro tempore, in the Absence of the Vice President, or when he shall exercise the Office of President of the United States.

The Senate shall have the sole Power to try all Impeachments. When sitting for that Purpose, they shall be on Oath or Affirmation. When the President of the United States is tried, the Chief Justice shall preside: And no Person shall be convicted without the Concurrence of two thirds of the Members present.

Judgment in Cases of Impeachment shall not extend further than to removal from Office, and disqualification to hold and enjoy any Office of honor, Trust or Profit under the United States: but the Party convicted shall nevertheless be liable and subject to Indictment, Trial, Judgment and Punishment, according to Law.

Section 4

The Times, Places and Manner of holding Elections for Senators and Representatives, shall be prescribed in each State by the Legislature thereof; but the Congress may at any time by Law make or alter such Regulations, except as to the Places of chusing Senators.

The Congress shall assemble at least once in every Year, and such Meeting shall be on the first Monday in December, unless they shall by Law appoint a different Day.

Section 5

Each House shall be the Judge of the Elections, Returns and Qualifications of its own Members, and a Majority of each shall constitute a Quorum to do Business; but a smaller Number may adjourn from day to day, and may be authorized to compel the Attendance of absent Members, in such Manner, and under such Penalties as each House may provide.

Each House may determine the Rules of its Proceedings, punish its Members for disorderly Behaviour, and, with the Concurrence of two thirds, expel a Member.

Each House shall keep a Journal of its Proceedings, and from time to time publish the same, excepting such Parts as may in their Judgment require Secrecy; and the Yeas and Nays of the Members of either House on any question shall, at the Desire of one fifth of those Present, be entered on the Journal.

Neither House, during the Session of Congress, shall, without the Consent of the other, adjourn for more than three days, nor to any other Place than that in which the two Houses shall be sitting.

Section 6

The Senators and Representatives shall receive a Compensation for their Services, to be ascertained by Law, and paid out of the Treasury of the United States. They shall in all Cases, except Treason, Felony and Breach of the Peace, be privileged from Arrest during their Attendance at the Session of their respective Houses, and in going to and returning from the same; and for any Speech or Debate in either House, they shall not be questioned in any other Place.

No Senator or Representative shall, during the Time for which he was elected, be appointed to any civil Office under the Authority of the United States, which shall have been created, or the Emoluments whereof shall have been encreased during such time; and no Person holding any Office under the United States, shall be a Member of either House during his Continuance in Office.

Section 7

All Bills for raising Revenue shall originate in the House of Representatives; but the Senate may propose or concur with Amendments as on other Bills.

Every Bill which shall have passed the House of Representatives and the Senate, shall, before it become a Law, be presented to the President of the United States: If he approve he shall sign it, but if not he shall return it, with his Objections to that House in which it shall have originated, who shall enter the Objections at large on their Journal, and proceed to reconsider it. If after such Reconsideration two thirds of that House shall agree to pass the Bill, it shall be sent, together with the Objections, to the other House, by which it shall likewise be reconsidered, and if approved by two thirds of that House, it shall become a Law. But in all such Cases the Votes of both Houses shall be determined by yeas and Nays, and the Names of the Persons voting for and against the Bill shall be entered on the Journal of each House respectively. If any Bill shall not be returned by the President within ten Days (Sundays excepted) after it shall have been presented to him, the Same shall be a Law, in like Manner as if he had signed it, unless the Congress by their Adjournment prevent its Return, in which Case it shall not be a Law.

Every Order, Resolution, or Vote to which the Concurrence of the Senate and House of Representatives may be necessary (except on a question of Adjournment) shall be presented to the President of the United States; and before the Same shall take Effect, shall be approved by him, or being disapproved by him, shall be repassed by two thirds of the Senate and House of Representatives, according to the Rules and Limitations prescribed in the Case of a Bill.

Section 8

The Congress shall have Power To lay and collect Taxes, Duties, Imposts and Excises, to pay the Debts and provide for the common Defence and general Welfare of the United States; but all Duties, Imposts and Excises shall be uniform throughout the United States;

To borrow Money on the credit of the United States;

To regulate Commerce with foreign Nations, and among the several States, and with the Indian Tribes;

To establish an uniform Rule of Naturalization, and uniform Laws on the subject of Bankruptcies throughout the United States;

To coin Money, regulate the Value thereof, and of foreign Coin, and fix the Standard of Weights and Measures;

To provide for the Punishment of counterfeiting the Securities and current Coin of the United States;

To establish Post Offices and post Roads;

To promote the Progress of Science and useful Arts, by securing for limited Times to Authors and Inventors the exclusive Right to their respective Writings and Discoveries;

To constitute Tribunals inferior to the supreme Court;

To define and punish Piracies and Felonies committed on the high Seas, and Offences against the Law of Nations;

To declare War, grant Letters of Marque and Reprisal, and make Rules concerning Captures on Land and Water;

To raise and support Armies, but no Appropriation of Money to that Use shall be for a longer Term than two Years;

To provide and maintain a Navy;

To make Rules for the Government and Regulation of the land and naval Forces;

To provide for calling forth the Militia to execute the Laws of the Union, suppress Insurrections and repel Invasions;

To provide for organizing, arming, and disciplining, the Militia, and for governing such Part of them as may be employed in the Service of the United States, reserving to the States respectively, the Appointment of the Officers, and the Authority of training the Militia according to the discipline prescribed by Congress;

To exercise exclusive Legislation in all Cases whatsoever, over such District (not exceeding ten Miles square) as may, by Cession of particular States, and the Acceptance of Congress, become the Seat of the Government of the United States, and to exercise like Authority over all Places purchased by the Consent of the Legislature of the State in which the Same shall be, for the Erection of Forts, Magazines, Arsenals, dock-Yards, and other needful Buildings;—And

To make all Laws which shall be necessary and proper for carrying into Execution the foregoing Powers, and all other Powers vested by this Constitution in the Government of the United States, or in any Department or Officer thereof.

Section 9

The Migration or Importation of such Persons as any of the States now existing shall think proper to admit, shall not be prohibited by the Congress prior to the Year one thousand eight hundred and eight, but a Tax or duty may be imposed on such Importation, not exceeding ten dollars for each Person.

The Privilege of the Writ of Habeas Corpus shall not be suspended, unless when in Cases of Rebellion or Invasion the public Safety may require it.

No Bill of Attainder or ex post facto Law shall be passed.

No Capitation, or other direct, Tax shall be laid, unless in Proportion to the Census or enumeration herein before directed to be taken.

No Tax or Duty shall be laid on Articles exported from any State.

No Preference shall be given by any Regulation of Commerce or Revenue to the Ports of one State over those of another; nor shall Vessels bound to, or from, one State, be obliged to enter, clear, or pay Duties in another.

No Money shall be drawn from the Treasury, but in Consequence of Appropriations made by Law; and a regular Statement and Account of the Receipts and Expenditures of all public Money shall be published from time to time.

No Title of Nobility shall be granted by the United States: And no Person holding any Office of Profit or Trust under them, shall, without the Consent of the Congress, accept of any present, Emolument, Office, or Title, of any kind whatever, from any King, Prince, or foreign State.

Section 10

No State shall enter into any Treaty, Alliance, or Confederation; grant Letters of Marque and Reprisal; coin Money; emit Bills of Credit; make any Thing but gold and silver Coin a Tender in Payment of Debts; pass any Bill of Attainder, ex post facto Law, or Law impairing the Obligation of Contracts, or grant any Title of Nobility.

No State shall, without the Consent of the Congress, lay any Imposts or Duties on Imports or Exports, except what may be absolutely necessary for executing it's inspection Laws: and the net Produce of all Duties and Imposts, laid by any State on Imports or Exports, shall be for the Use of the Treasury of the United States; and all such Laws shall be subject to the Revision and Controul of the Congress.

No State shall, without the Consent of Congress, lay any Duty of Tonnage, keep Troops, or Ships of War in time of Peace, enter into any Agreement or Compact with another State, or with a foreign Power, or engage in War, unless actually invaded, or in such imminent Danger as will not admit of delay.

Article II

Section 1

The executive Power shall be vested in a President of the United States of America. He shall hold his Office during the Term of four Years, and, together with the Vice President, chosen for the same Term, be elected, as follows:

Each State shall appoint, in such Manner as the Legislature thereof may direct, a Number of Electors, equal to the whole Number of Senators and Representatives to which the State may be entitled in the Congress: but no Senator or Representative, or Person holding an Office of Trust or Profit under the United States, shall be appointed an Elector.

The Electors shall meet in their respective States, and vote by Ballot for two Persons, of whom one at least shall not be an Inhabitant of the same State with themselves. And they shall make a List of all the Persons voted for, and of the Number of Votes for each; which List they shall sign and certify, and transmit sealed to the Seat of the Government of the United States, directed to the President of the Senate. The President of the Senate shall, in the Presence of the Senate and House of Representatives, open all the Certificates, and the Votes shall then be counted. The Person having the greatest Number of Votes shall be the President, if such Number be a Majority of the whole Number of Electors appointed; and if there be more than one who have such Majority, and have an equal Number of Votes, then the House of Representatives shall immediately chuse by Ballot one of them for President; and if no Person have a Majority, then from the five highest on the List the said House shall in like Manner chuse the President. But in chusing the President, the Votes shall be taken by States, the Representation from each State having one Vote; A quorum for this purpose shall consist of a Member or Members from two thirds of the States, and a Majority of all the States shall be necessary to a Choice. In every Case, after the Choice of the President, the Person having the greatest Number of Votes of the Electors shall be the Vice President. But if there should remain two or more who have equal Votes, the Senate shall chuse from them by Ballot the Vice President.

The Congress may determine the Time of chusing the Electors, and the Day on which they shall give their Votes; which Day shall be the same throughout the United States.

No Person except a natural born Citizen, or a Citizen of the United States, at the time of the Adoption of this Constitution, shall be eligible to the Office of President; neither shall any Person be eligible to that Office who shall not have attained to the Age of thirty five Years, and been fourteen Years a Resident within the United States.

In Case of the Removal of the President from Office, or of his Death, Resignation, or Inability to discharge the Powers and Duties of the said Office, the Same shall devolve on the Vice President, and the Congress may by Law provide for the Case of Removal, Death, Resignation or Inability, both of the President and Vice President, declaring what Officer shall then act as President, and such Officer shall act accordingly, until the Disability be removed, or a President shall be elected.

The President shall, at stated Times, receive for his Services, a Compensation, which shall neither be increased nor diminished during the Period for which he shall have been elected, and he shall not receive within that Period any other Emolument from the United States, or any of them.

Before he enter on the Execution of his Office, he shall take the following Oath or Affirmation: —"I do solemnly swear (or affirm) that I will faithfully execute the Office of President of the United States, and will to the best of my Ability, preserve, protect and defend the Constitution of the United States."

Section 2

The President shall be Commander in Chief of the Army and Navy of the United States, and of the Militia of the several States, when called into the actual Service of the United States; he may require the Opinion, in writing, of the principal Officer in each of the executive Departments, upon any Subject relating to the Duties of their respective Offices, and he shall have Power to grant Reprieves and Pardons for Offences against the United States, except in Cases of Impeachment.

He shall have Power, by and with the Advice and Consent of the Senate, to make Treaties, provided two thirds of the Senators present concur; and he shall nominate, and by and with the Advice and Consent of the Senate, shall appoint Ambassadors, other public Ministers and Consuls, Judges of the supreme Court, and all other Officers of the United States, whose Appointments are not herein otherwise provided for, and which shall be established by Law: but the Congress may by Law vest the Appointment of such inferior Officers, as they think proper, in the President alone, in the Courts of Law, or in the Heads of Departments.

The President shall have Power to fill up all Vacancies that may happen during the Recess of the Senate, by granting Commissions which shall expire at the End of their next Session.

Section 3

He shall from time to time give to the Congress Information of the State of the Union, and recommend to their Consideration such Measures as he shall judge necessary and expedient; he may, on extraordinary Occasions, convene both Houses, or either of them, and in Case of Disagreement between them, with Respect to the Time of Adjournment, he may adjourn them to such Time as he shall think proper; he shall receive Ambassadors and other public Ministers; he shall take Care that the Laws be faithfully executed, and shall Commission all the Officers of the United States.

Section 4

The President, Vice President and all civil Officers of the United States, shall be removed from Office on Impeachment for, and Conviction of, Treason, Bribery, or other high Crimes and Misdemeanors.

Article III

Section 1

The judicial Power of the United States shall be vested in one supreme Court, and in such inferior Courts as the Congress may from time to time ordain and establish. The Judges, both of the supreme and inferior Courts, shall hold their Offices during good Behaviour, and shall, at stated Times, receive for their Services a Compensation, which shall not be diminished during their Continuance in Office.

Section 2

The judicial Power shall extend to all Cases, in Law and Equity, arising under this Constitution, the Laws of the United States, and Treaties made, or which shall be made, under their Authority;—to all Cases affecting Ambassadors, other public Ministers and Consuls;—to all Cases of admiralty and maritime Jurisdiction;—to Controversies to which the United States shall be a Party;—to Controversies between two or more States;—between a State and Citizens of another State;—between Citizens of different States;—between Citizens of the same State claiming Lands under Grants of different States, and between a State, or the Citizens thereof, and foreign States, Citizens or Subjects.

In all Cases affecting Ambassadors, other public Ministers and Consuls, and those in which a State shall be Party, the supreme Court shall have original Jurisdiction. In all the other Cases before mentioned, the supreme Court shall have appellate Jurisdiction, both as to Law and Fact, with such Exceptions, and under such Regulations as the Congress shall make.

The Trial of all Crimes, except in Cases of Impeachment, shall be by Jury; and such Trial shall be held in the State where the said Crimes shall have been committed; but when not committed within any State, the Trial shall be at such Place or Places as the Congress may by Law have directed.

Section 3

Treason against the United States, shall consist only in levying War against them, or in adhering to their Enemies, giving them Aid and Comfort. No Person shall be convicted of Treason unless on the Testimony of two Witnesses to the same overt Act, or on Confession in open Court.

The Congress shall have Power to declare the Punishment of Treason, but no Attainder of Treason shall work Corruption of Blood, or Forfeiture except during the Life of the Person attainted.

Article IV

Section 1

Full Faith and Credit shall be given in each State to the public Acts, Records, and judicial Proceedings of every other State. And the Congress may by general Laws prescribe the Manner in which such Acts, Records and Proceedings shall be proved, and the Effect thereof.

Section 2

The Citizens of each State shall be entitled to all Privileges and Immunities of Citizens in the several States.

A Person charged in any State with Treason, Felony, or other Crime, who shall flee from Justice, and be found in another State, shall on Demand of the executive Authority of the State from which he fled, be delivered up, to be removed to the State having Jurisdiction of the Crime.

No Person held to Service or Labour in one State, under the Laws thereof, escaping into another, shall, in Consequence of any Law or Regulation therein, be discharged from such Service or Labour, but shall be delivered up on Claim of the Party to whom such Service or Labour may be due.

Section 3

New States may be admitted by the Congress into this Union; but no new State shall be formed or erected within the Jurisdiction of any other State; nor any State be formed by the Junction of two or more States, or Parts of States, without the Consent of the Legislatures of the States concerned as well as of the Congress.

The Congress shall have Power to dispose of and make all needful Rules and Regulations respecting the Territory or other Property belonging to the United States; and nothing in this Constitution shall be so construed as to Prejudice any Claims of the United States, or of any particular State.

Section 4

The United States shall guarantee to every State in this Union a Republican Form of Government, and shall protect each of them against Invasion; and on Application of the Legislature, or of the Executive (when the Legislature cannot be convened), against domestic Violence.

Article V

The Congress, whenever two thirds of both Houses shall deem it necessary, shall propose Amendments to this Constitution, or, on the Application of the Legislatures of two thirds of the several States, shall call a Convention for proposing Amendments, which, in either Case, shall be valid to all Intents and Purposes, as Part of this Constitution, when ratified by the Legislatures of three fourths of the several States, or by Conventions in three fourths thereof, as the one or the other Mode of Ratification may be proposed by the Congress; Provided that no Amendment which may be made prior to the Year One thousand eight hundred and eight shall in any Manner affect the first and fourth Clauses in the Ninth Section of the first Article; and that no State, without its Consent, shall be deprived of its equal Suffrage in the Senate.

Article VI

All Debts contracted and Engagements entered into, before the Adoption of this Constitution, shall be as valid against the United States under this Constitution, as under the Confederation.

This Constitution, and the Laws of the United States which shall be made in Pursuance thereof; and all Treaties made, or which shall be made, under the Authority of the United States, shall be the supreme Law of the Land; and the Judges in every State shall be bound thereby, any Thing in the Constitution or Laws of any State to the Contrary notwithstanding.

The Senators and Representatives before mentioned, and the Members of the several State Legislatures, and all executive and judicial Officers, both of the United States and of the several States, shall be bound by Oath or Affirmation, to support this Constitution; but no religious Test shall ever be required as a Qualification to any Office or public Trust under the United States.

Article VII

The Ratification of the Conventions of nine States, shall be sufficient for the Establishment of this Constitution between the States so ratifying the Same.

The Word, "the," being interlined between the seventh and eighth Lines of the first Page, the Word "Thirty" being partly written on an Erazure in the fifteenth Line of the first Page, The Words "is tried" being interlined between the thirty second and thirty third Lines of the first Page and the Word "the" being interlined between the forty third and forty fourth Lines of the second Page.

Attest William Jackson Secretary

Done in Convention by the Unanimous Consent of the States present the Seventeenth Day of September in the Year of our Lord one thousand seven hundred and Eighty seven and of the Independence of the United States of America the Twelfth In witness whereof We have hereunto subscribed our Names,

G°. Washington
Presidt and deputy from Virginia

Delaware
Geo: Read
Gunning Bedford jun
John Dickinson
Richard Bassett
Jaco: Broom

Maryland
James McHenry
Dan of St Thos. Jenifer
Danl. Carroll

Virginia
John Blair—
James Madison Jr.

North Carolina
Wm. Blount
Richd. Dobbs Spaight
Hu Williamson

South Carolina
J. Rutledge
Charles Cotesworth Pinckney
Charles Pinckney
Pierce Butler

Georgia
William Few
Abr Baldwin

New Hampshire
John Langdon
Nicholas Gilman

Massachusetts
Nathaniel Gorham
Rufus King

Connecticut
Wm. Saml. Johnson
Roger Sherman

New York
Alexander Hamilton

New Jersey
Wil: Livingston
David Brearley
Wm. Paterson
Jona: Dayton

Pennsylvania
B Franklin
Thomas Mifflin
Robt. Morris
Geo. Clymer
Thos. FitzSimons
Jared Ingersoll
James Wilson
Gouv Morris

The Preamble to the Bill of Rights

Congress of the United States
begun and held at the City of New-York, on
Wednesday the fourth of March, one thousand seven
hundred and eighty nine.

The Conventions of a number of the States, having at the time of their adopting the Constitution, expressed a desire, in order to prevent misconstruction or abuse of its powers, that further declaratory and restrictive clauses should be added: And as extending the ground

---

Note: The capitalization and punctuation in this version is from the enrolled original of the Joint Resolution of Congress proposing the *Bill of Rights,* which is on permanent display in the Rotunda of the National Archives Building, Washington, D.C.

of public confidence in the Government, will best ensure the beneficent ends of its institution.

Resolved by the Senate and House of Representatives of the United States of America, in Congress assembled, two thirds of both Houses concurring, that the following Articles be proposed to the Legislatures of the several States as amendments to the Constitution of the United States, all, or any of which articles, when ratified by three fourths of the said Legislatures, to be valid to all intents and purposes, as part of the said Constitution; viz.

Articles in addition to, and Amendment of the Constitution of the United States of America, proposed by Congress and ratified by the Legislatures of the several States, pursuant to the fifth Article of the original Constitution.

The First 10 Amendments to the Constitution as Ratified by the States

Amendment I

Congress shall make no law respecting an establishment of religion, or prohibiting the free exercise thereof; or abridging the freedom of speech, or of the press; or the right of the people peaceably to assemble, and to petition the Government for a redress of grievances.

Amendment II

A well regulated Militia, being necessary to the security of a free State, the right of the people to keep and bear Arms, shall not be infringed.

Amendment III

No Soldier shall, in time of peace be quartered in any house, without the consent of the Owner, nor in time of war, but in a manner to be prescribed by law.

Amendment IV

The right of the people to be secure in their persons, houses, papers, and effects, against unreasonable searches and seizures, shall not be violated, and no Warrants shall issue, but upon probable cause, supported by Oath or affirmation, and particularly describing the place to be searched, and the persons or things to be seized.

Amendment V

No person shall be held to answer for a capital, or otherwise infamous crime, unless on a presentment or indictment of a Grand Jury, except in cases arising in the land or naval forces, or in the Militia, when in actual service in time of War or public danger; nor shall any person be subject for the same offence to be twice put in jeopardy of life or limb; nor shall be compelled in any criminal case to be a witness against himself, nor be deprived of life, liberty, or property, without due process of law; nor shall private property be taken for public use, without just compensation.

Amendment VI

In all criminal prosecutions, the accused shall enjoy the right to a speedy and public trial, by an impartial jury of the State and district wherein the crime shall have been committed, which district shall have been previously ascertained by law, and to be informed of the nature and cause of the accusation; to be confronted with the witnesses against him; to have compulsory process for obtaining witnesses in his favor, and to have the Assistance of Counsel for his defence.

Amendment VII

In suits at common law, where the value in controversy shall exceed twenty dollars, the right of trial by jury shall be preserved, and no fact tried by a jury, shall be otherwise reexamined in any Court of the United States, than according to the rules of the common law.

Amendment VIII

Excessive bail shall not be required, nor excessive fines imposed, nor cruel and unusual punishments inflicted.

Amendment IX

The enumeration in the Constitution, of certain rights, shall not be construed to deny or disparage others retained by the people.

Amendment X

The powers not delegated to the United States by the Constitution, nor prohibited by it to the States, are reserved to the States respectively, or to the people.

Amendments 11–27 to the Constitution of the United States

Amendment XI

Passed by Congress March 4, 1794. Ratified February 7, 1795.

The Judicial power of the United States shall not be construed to extend to any suit in law or equity, commenced or prosecuted against one of the United States by Citizens of another State, or by Citizens or Subjects of any Foreign State.

Amendment XII

Passed by Congress December 9, 1803. Ratified June 15, 1804.

The Electors shall meet in their respective states and vote by ballot for President and Vice-President, one of whom, at least, shall not be an inhabitant of the same state with themselves; they shall name in their ballots the person voted for as President, and in distinct ballots the person voted for as Vice-President, and they shall make distinct lists of all persons voted for as President, and of all persons voted for as Vice-President, and of the number of votes for each, which lists they shall sign and certify, and transmit sealed to the seat of the government of the United States, directed to the President of the Senate;—the President of the Senate shall, in the presence of the Senate and House of Representatives, open all the certificates and the votes shall then be counted;—The person having the greatest number of votes for President, shall be the President, if such number be a majority of the whole number of Electors appointed; and if no person have such majority, then from the persons having the highest numbers not exceeding three on the list of those voted for as President, the House of Representatives shall choose immediately, by ballot, the President. But in choosing the President, the votes shall be taken by states, the representation from each state having one vote; a quorum for this purpose shall consist of a member or members from two-thirds of the states, and a majority of all the states shall be necessary to a choice. [And if the House of Representatives shall not choose a President whenever the right of choice shall devolve upon them, before the fourth day of March next following, then the Vice-President shall act as President, as in case of the death or other constitutional disability of the President.—]* The person having the greatest number of votes as Vice-President, shall be the Vice-President, if such number be a majority of the whole number of Electors appointed, and if no person have a majority, then from the two highest numbers on the list, the Senate shall choose the Vice-President; a quorum for the purpose shall consist of two-thirds of the whole number of Senators, and a majority of the whole number shall be necessary to a choice. But no person constitutionally ineligible to the office of President shall be eligible to that of Vice-President of the United States.

Amendment XIII

Passed by Congress January 31, 1865. Ratified December 6, 1865.

Section 1

Neither slavery nor involuntary servitude, except as a punishment for crime whereof the party shall have been duly convicted, shall exist within the United States, or any place subject to their jurisdiction.

---

*Superseded by section 3 of the 20th amendment.

Section 2
Congress shall have power to enforce this article by appropriate legislation.

Amendment XIV

Passed by Congress June 13, 1866. Ratified July 9, 1868.

Section 1
All persons born or naturalized in the United States, and subject to the jurisdiction thereof, are citizens of the United States and of the State wherein they reside. No State shall make or enforce any law which shall abridge the privileges or immunities of citizens of the United States; nor shall any State deprive any person of life, liberty, or property, without due process of law; nor deny to any person within its jurisdiction the equal protection of the laws.

Section 2
Representatives shall be apportioned among the several States according to their respective numbers, counting the whole number of persons in each State, excluding Indians not taxed. But when the right to vote at any election for the choice of electors for President and Vice-President of the United States, Representatives in Congress, the Executive and Judicial officers of a State, or the members of the Legislature thereof, is denied to any of the male inhabitants of such State, being twenty-one years of age,* and citizens of the United States, or in any way abridged, except for participation in rebellion, or other crime, the basis of representation therein shall be reduced in the proportion which the number of such male citizens shall bear to the whole number of male citizens twenty-one years of age in such State.

Section 3
No person shall be a Senator or Representative in Congress, or elector of President and Vice-President, or hold any office, civil or military, under the United States, or under any State, who, having previously taken an oath, as a member of Congress, or as an officer of the United States, or as a member of any State legislature, or as an executive or judicial officer of any State, to support the Constitution of the United States, shall have engaged in insurrection or rebellion against the same, or given aid or comfort to the enemies thereof. But Congress may by a vote of two-thirds of each House, remove such disability.

Section 4
The validity of the public debt of the United States, authorized by law, including debts incurred for payment of pensions and bounties for services in suppressing insurrection or rebellion, shall not be questioned. But neither the United States nor any State shall assume or pay any debt or obligation incurred in aid of insurrection or rebellion against the United States, or any claim for the loss or emancipation of any slave; but all such debts, obligations and claims shall be held illegal and void.

Section 5
The Congress shall have the power to enforce, by appropriate legislation, the provisions of this article.

Amendment XV

Passed by Congress February 26, 1869. Ratified February 3, 1870.

Section 1
The right of citizens of the United States to vote shall not be denied or abridged by the United States or by any State on account of race, color, or previous condition of servitude—

Section 2
The Congress shall have the power to enforce this article by appropriate legislation.

*Changed by section 1 of the 26th amendment.

Amendment XVI

Passed by Congress July 2, 1909. Ratified February 3, 1913.

The Congress shall have power to lay and collect taxes on incomes, from whatever source derived, without apportionment among the several States, and without regard to any census or enumeration.

Amendment XVII

Passed by Congress May 13, 1912. Ratified April 8, 1913.

The Senate of the United States shall be composed of two Senators from each State, elected by the people thereof, for six years; and each Senator shall have one vote. The electors in each State shall have the qualifications requisite for electors of the most numerous branch of the State legislatures.

When vacancies happen in the representation of any State in the Senate, the executive authority of such State shall issue writs of election to fill such vacancies: Provided, That the legislature of any State may empower the executive thereof to make temporary appointments until the people fill the vacancies by election as the legislature may direct.

This amendment shall not be so construed as to affect the election or term of any Senator chosen before it becomes valid as part of the Constitution.

Amendment XVIII

Passed by Congress December 18, 1917. Ratified January 16, 1919. Repealed by amendment 21.

Section 1

After one year from the ratification of this article the manufacture, sale, or transportation of intoxicating liquors within, the importation thereof into, or the exportation thereof from the United States and all territory subject to the jurisdiction thereof for beverage purposes is hereby prohibited.

Section 2

The Congress and the several States shall have concurrent power to enforce this article by appropriate legislation.

Section 3

This article shall be inoperative unless it shall have been ratified as an amendment to the Constitution by the legislatures of the several States, as provided in the Constitution, within seven years from the date of the submission hereof to the States by the Congress.

Amendment XIX

Passed by Congress June 4, 1919. Ratified August 18, 1920.

The right of citizens of the United States to vote shall not be denied or abridged by the United States or by any State on account of sex.

Congress shall have power to enforce this article by appropriate legislation.

Amendment XX

Passed by Congress March 2, 1932. Ratified January 23, 1933.

Section 1

The terms of the President and the Vice President shall end at noon on the 20th day of January, and the terms of Senators and Representatives at noon on the 3d day of January, of the years in which such terms would have ended if this article had not been ratified; and the terms of their successors shall then begin.

Section 2

The Congress shall assemble at least once in every year, and such meeting shall begin at noon on the 3d day of January, unless they shall by law appoint a different day.

Section 3

If, at the time fixed for the beginning of the term of the President, the President elect shall have died, the Vice President elect shall become President. If a President shall not have been chosen before the time fixed for the beginning of his term, or if the President elect shall have failed to qualify, then the Vice President elect shall act as President until a President shall have qualified; and the Congress may by law provide for the case wherein neither a President elect nor a Vice President shall have qualified, declaring who shall then act as President, or the manner in which one who is to act shall be selected, and such person shall act accordingly until a President or Vice President shall have qualified.

Section 4

The Congress may by law provide for the case of the death of any of the persons from whom the House of Representatives may choose a President whenever the right of choice shall have devolved upon them, and for the case of the death of any of the persons from whom the Senate may choose a Vice President whenever the right of choice shall have devolved upon them.

Section 5

Sections 1 and 2 shall take effect on the 15th day of October following the ratification of this article.

Section 6

This article shall be inoperative unless it shall have been ratified as an amendment to the Constitution by the legislatures of three-fourths of the several States within seven years from the date of its submission.

Amendment XXI

Passed by Congress February 20, 1933. Ratified December 5, 1933.

Section 1

The eighteenth article of amendment to the Constitution of the United States is hereby repealed.

Section 2

The transportation or importation into any State, Territory, or Possession of the United States for delivery or use therein of intoxicating liquors, in violation of the laws thereof, is hereby prohibited.

Section 3

This article shall be inoperative unless it shall have been ratified as an amendment to the Constitution by conventions in the several States, as provided in the Constitution, within seven years from the date of the submission hereof to the States by the Congress.

Amendment XXII

Passed by Congress March 21, 1947. Ratified February 27, 1951.

Section 1

No person shall be elected to the office of the President more than twice, and no person who has held the office of President, or acted as President, for more than two years of a term to which some other person was elected President shall be elected to the office of President more than once. But this Article shall not apply to any person holding the office of President when this Article was proposed by Congress, and shall not prevent any person who may be holding the office of President, or acting as President, during the term within which this Article becomes operative from holding the office of President or acting as President during the remainder of such term.

Section 2

This article shall be inoperative unless it shall have been ratified as an amendment to the Constitution by the legislatures of three-fourths of the several States within seven years from the date of its submission to the States by the Congress.

Amendment XXIII

Passed by Congress June 16, 1960. Ratified March 29, 1961.

Section 1

The District constituting the seat of Government of the United States shall appoint in such manner as Congress may direct:

A number of electors of President and Vice President equal to the whole number of Senators and Representatives in Congress to which the District would be entitled if it were a State, but in no event more than the least populous State; they shall be in addition to those appointed by the States, but they shall be considered, for the purposes of the election of President and Vice President, to be electors appointed by a State; and they shall meet in the District and perform such duties as provided by the twelfth article of amendment.

Section 2

The Congress shall have power to enforce this article by appropriate legislation.

Amendment XXIV

Passed by Congress August 27, 1962. Ratified January 23, 1964.

Section 1

The right of citizens of the United States to vote in any primary or other election for President or Vice President, for electors for President or Vice President, or for Senator or Representative in Congress, shall not be denied or abridged by the United States or any State by reason of failure to pay poll tax or other tax.

Section 2

The Congress shall have power to enforce this article by appropriate legislation.

Amendment XXV

Passed by Congress July 6, 1965. Ratified February 10, 1967.

Section 1

In case of the removal of the President from office or of his death or resignation, the Vice President shall become President.

Section 2

Whenever there is a vacancy in the office of the Vice President, the President shall nominate a Vice President who shall take office upon confirmation by a majority vote of both Houses of Congress.

Section 3

Whenever the President transmits to the President pro tempore of the Senate and the Speaker of the House of Representatives his written declaration that he is unable to discharge the powers and duties of his office, and until he transmits to them a written declaration to the contrary, such powers and duties shall be discharged by the Vice President as Acting President.

Section 4

Whenever the Vice President and a majority of either the principal officers of the executive departments or of such other body as Congress may by law provide, transmit to the President pro tempore of the Senate and the Speaker of the House of Representatives their written declaration that the President is unable to discharge the powers and duties of his office, the Vice President shall immediately assume the powers and duties of the office as Acting President.

Thereafter, when the President transmits to the President pro tempore of the Senate and the Speaker of the House of Representatives his written declaration that no inability exists, he shall resume the powers and duties of his office unless the Vice President and a majority of either the principal officers of the executive department or of such other body as Congress may by law provide, transmit within four days to the President pro tempore of the Senate and the Speaker of the House of Representatives their written declaration that the President is unable to discharge the powers and duties of his office. Thereupon Congress shall decide the issue, assembling within forty-eight hours for that purpose if not in session. If the Congress, within twenty-one days after receipt of the latter written declaration, or, if Congress is not in session, within twenty-one days after Congress is required to assemble, determines by two-thirds vote of both Houses that the President is unable to discharge the powers and duties of his office, the Vice President shall continue to discharge the same as Acting President; otherwise, the President shall resume the powers and duties of his office.

Amendment XXVI

Passed by Congress March 23, 1971. Ratified July 1, 1971.

Section 1

The right of citizens of the United States, who are eighteen years of age or older, to vote shall not be denied or abridged by the United States or by any State on account of age.

Section 2

The Congress shall have power to enforce this article by appropriate legislation.

Amendment XXVII

Originally proposed Sept. 25, 1789. Ratified May 7, 1992.

No law, varying the compensation for the services of the Senators and Representatives, shall take effect, until an election of representatives shall have intervened.

Population, Labor Force, and Wealth

Population of the United States, 1790–2000

Year	Population	Percentage Increase	Year	Population	Percentage Increase
1790	3,929,214	41.3	1900	75,994,575	20.7
1800	5,308,483	35.1	1910	91,972,266	21.0
1810	7,239,881	36.4	1920	105,710,620	14.9
1820	9,638,453	33.1	1930	122,775,046	16.1
1830	12,866,020	33.5	1940	131,669,275	7.2
1840	17,069,453	32.7	1950	150,697,361	14.5
1850	23,191,876	35.9	1960	179,323,175	19.0
1860	31,443,321	35.6	1970	203,235,298	13.3
1870	39,818,449	26.6	1980	226,545,805	11.5
1880	50,155,783	26.0	1990	248,709,873	9.8
1890	62,947,714	25.5	2000	273,482,000	10.0

Note: These figures largely ignore the Native American population. Census takers never made any effort to count the Native American poplation that lived outside their political jurisdictions and compiled only casual and incomplete enumerations of those living within their jurisdictions until 1890. In that year the federal government attempted a full count of the Indian population: the Census found 125,719 Indians in 1890, compared with only 12,543 in 1870 and 33,985 in 1880.

Source: *Historical Statistics of the United States, Colonial Times to 1970* (1975); *Statistical Abstract of the United States, 1998.*

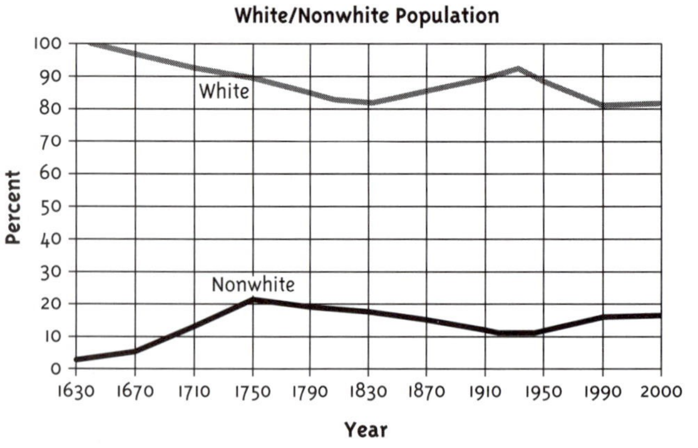

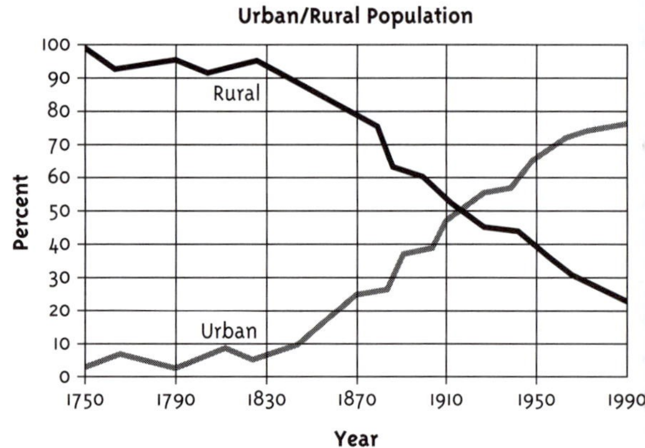

U.S. Population Distribution—1890, Showing States as if Area Were Proportional to Population. Total U.S. population stood at sixty-three million in 1890, but the late-nineteenth-century boom in commerce and manufacturing drew a huge proportion to just a few increasingly urbanized states. With six million citizens, New York was the largest state, closely followed by Pennsylvania, Illinois, Ohio, and Missouri rounded out the top five.

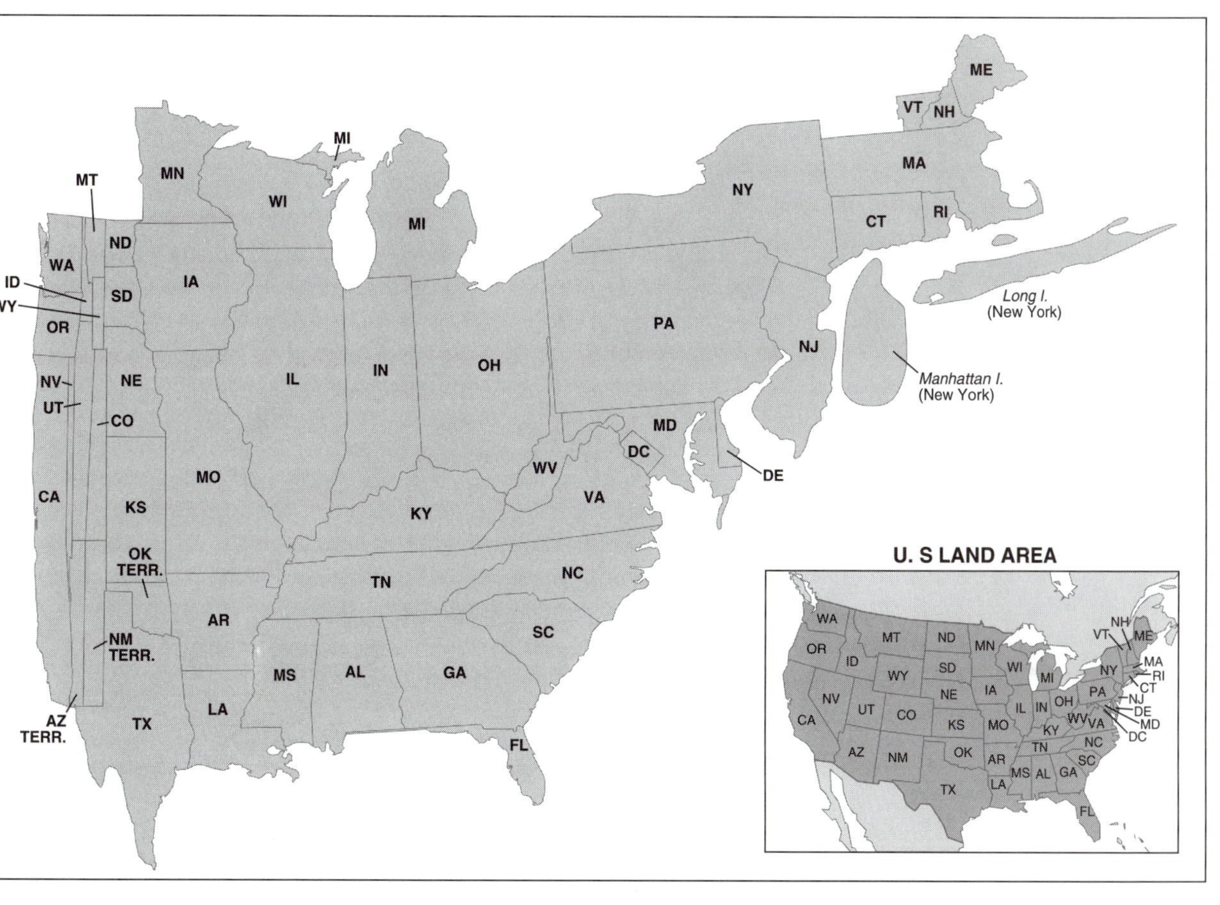

U.S. Population Distribution—1940, Showing States as if Area Were Proportional to Population. Total U.S. population stood at 132 million in 1940, double that of 1890. New York State, with more than half its people concentrated in one great city, accounted for more than 10 percent of the nation's entire population. Pennsylvania was the second largest state with nearly ten million, followed by Illinois, Ohio, California, and Michigan.

U.S. Population Distribution—2000, Showing States as if Area Were Proportional to Population. At the millenium the population stood close to 275 million, which made the United States the world's third most populous nation, after China and India. With 33 million citizens, California far outstripped all other states in population. Texas, the nation's second largest state (20 million), and Florida, the fourth biggest (15 million), anchored the eastern half of the booming Sunbelt. New York State, whose population had barely grown in half a century, now stood as the nation's third largest state.

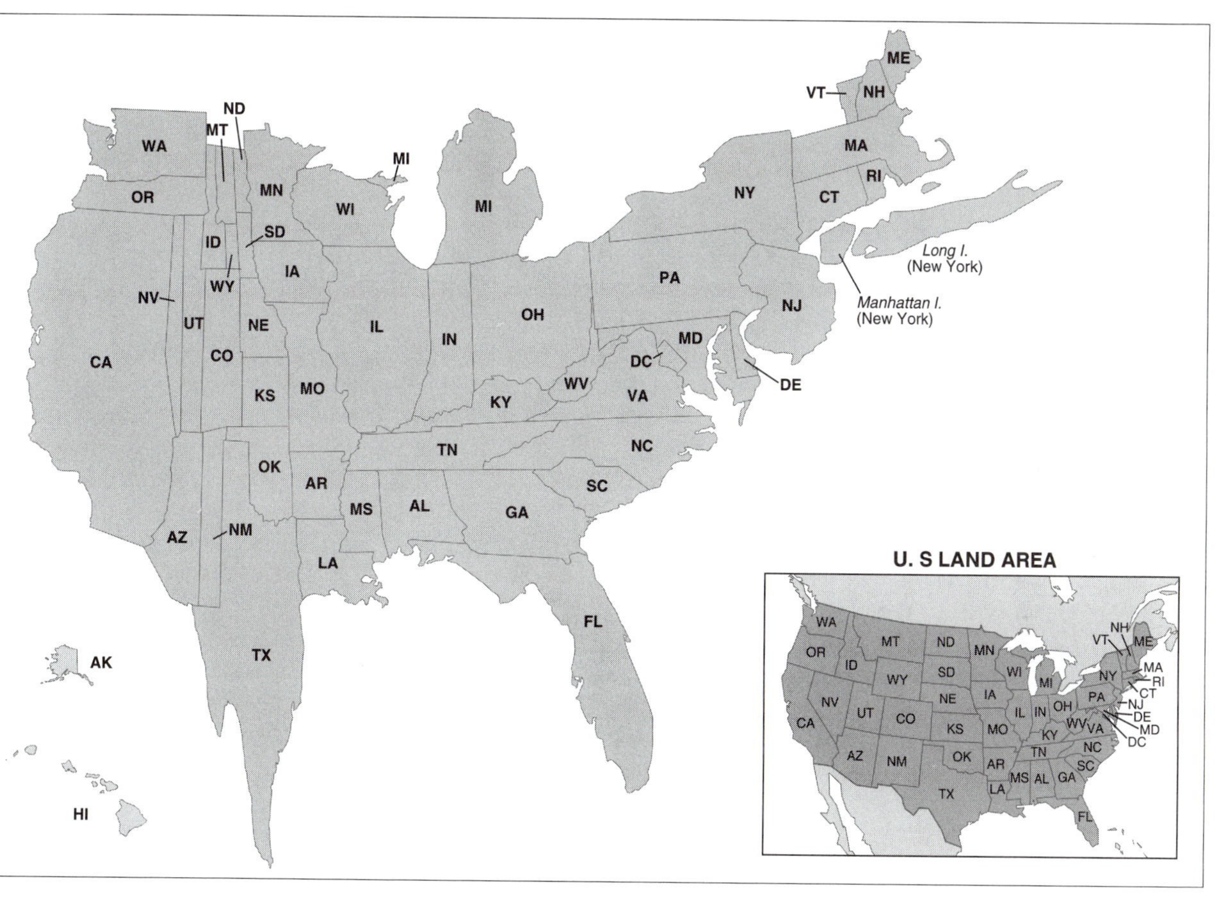

Immigrant Origins of the American Population, 1825–1985

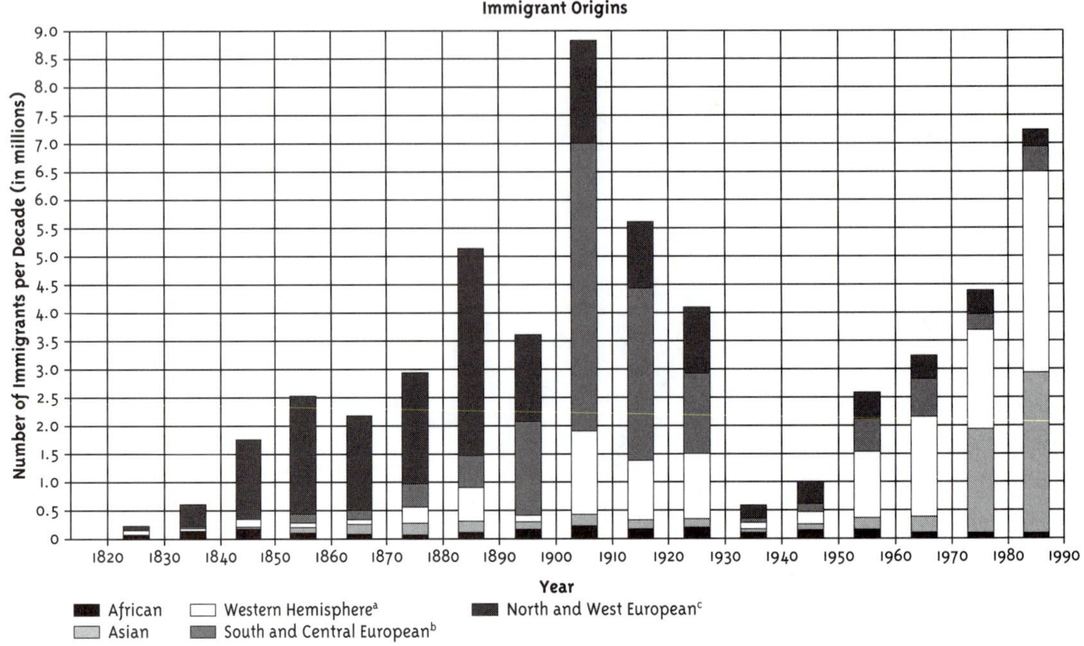

[a]Canada and all countries in South America and Central America.

[b]Italy, Spain, Portugal, Greece, Germany (Austria included, 1938–1945), Poland, Czechoslovakia (since 1920), Yugoslavia (since 1920), Hungary (since 1861), Austria (since 1861, except 1938–1945), former USSR (excludes Asian USSR between 1931 and 1963), Latvia, Estonia, Lithuania, Finland, Romania, Bulgaria, Turkey (in Europe), and other European countries not classified elsewhere.

[c]Great Britain, Ireland, Norway, Sweden, Denmark, Iceland, Netherlands, Belgium, Luxembourg, Switzerland, France.

Source: Stephan Thernstrom, ed., *Harvard Encyclopedia of American Ethnic Groups* (1980), 480; U.S. Bureau of the Census, *Statistical Abstract of the United States, 1991*.

The Labor Force (Thousands of Workers)

Year	Agriculture	Mining	Manufacturing	Construction	Trade	Other	Total
1810	1,950	11	75	—	—	294	2,330
1840	3,570	32	500	290	350	918	5,660
1850	4,520	102	1,200	410	530	1,488	8,250
1860	5,880	176	1,530	520	890	2,114	11,110
1870	6,790	180	2,470	780	1,310	1,400	12,930
1880	8,920	280	3,290	900	1,930	2,070	17,390
1890	9,960	440	4,390	1,510	2,960	4,060	23,320
1900	11,680	637	5,895	1,665	3,970	5,223	29,070
1910	11,770	1,068	8,332	1,949	5,320	9,041	37,480
1920	10,790	1,180	11,190	1.233	5,845	11,372	41,610
1930	10,560	1,009	9,884	1,988	8,122	17,267	48,830
1940	9,575	925	11,309	1,876	9,328	23,277	56,290
1950	7,870	901	15,648	3,029	12,152	25,870	65,470
1960	5,970	709	17,145	3,640	14,051	32,545	74,060
1970	3,463	516	20,746	4,818	15,008	34,127	78,678
1980	3,364	979	21,942	6,215	20,191	46,612	99,303
1990	3,223	724	21,346	7,764	24,622	60,849	117,914
1997	3,399	634	20,835	8,302	26,777	69,611	129,558
1998	3,378	620	20,733	8,518	27,203	71,011	131,463

Source: *Historical Statistics of the United States, Colonial Times to 1970* (1975), 139; *Statistical Abstract of the United States, 1998,* table 675.

Wealth Held by Richest Americans, 1774–1995

Year	Percentage of Total Net Worth Held by Richest 1%
1775	12.6
1861	29.0
1871	27.0
1913	56.4
1924	45.7
1930	44.2
1950	27.1
1962	26.0
1970	31.1
1981	20.5
1982	35.7
1996	40.0

Sources: James L. Huston, *Securing the Fruits of Labor: The American Concept of Wealth Distribution,* 1765–1900 (1998), table 1, p. 84; Edward Wolff, *Top Heavy* (1996), cited in Steve Brouwer, *Sharing the Pie* (1998).

Percentage of Income Received by Richest Americans, 1947–1997

Year	Percentage of Income Received by Richest 20%
1947	43.0
1959	41.1
1969	40.6
1979	41.7
1984	42.9
1988	44.0
1997	47.2

Sources: James L. Huston, *Securing the Fruits of Labor: The American Concept of Wealth Distribution,* 1765–1900 (1998), table 1, p. 84; Lawrence Mishel, Jared Bernstein, John Schmitt, *State of Working America, 1998–99* (1999).

Index

Page numbers in italics refer to illustrations or documents.

Abbott, Lyman, 36
Abortion
  protests over, 704
  right to, feminist battle for, 665
Abraham Lincoln Brigade, 488
Abrams, Elliot, 709
Abstract expressionism, postwar, *547*
Accurso, Carmela, 177
Acheson, Dean, 552, 564, 650
Acquired immune deficiency syndrome (AIDS), 707–708
Adamson Act, 246
Addams, Jane, 151
  Anti-Imperialist League and, 153
  in blocking segregation of Chicago schools, 218
  as garbage inspector, 216
  Hull House and, 213
  "New Nationalism" and, 244
  opposition to WWI, 268
  social activism and, 607
  Women's Trade Union League and, 225
Addiction, drug, in 1980s, 722–723
Advertising, 333–334
  to masses, 179–182
  national, in foreign-language press, 181
Affirmative action programs, 657, 768–769
Afghanistan
  Soviet Union and, 697
Afghanistan, Soviet Union and, 746–747
AFL. *See* American Federation of Labor (AFL)
AFL-CIO
  anti-Wallace activities of, 653
  CIA and, 670
  formation of, 578–579
  Johnson and, 667
  Kennedy and, 667
  revitalization of, in 1990s, 770
  Vietnam War and, 645
African Americans. *See also* Civil rights movement; Racism
  AFL unions and, 158
  amusement parks and, 185
  anti-Communist crusade and, 567
  in armed forces in WWI, 295–296
  baseball leagues and, 188
  Brotherhood of Sleeping Car Porters and, 347
  busing to achieve racial balance and, 701
  Centennial Exposition and, 11–12
  CIO and, 462, 516–517
  civil rights movement for, 515–520, 608–617. *See also* Civil rights movement
  in Clinton cabinet, 759
  as cowboys, 66
  discrimination against, in employment in Great Depression, 375–376
  disfranchising of, 139–141, 237–238
  early 20th century, barriers to participation of, 201
  economic justice and, 460–461
  Eisenhower and, 569
  equal rights struggle of, New Deal and, 459–463
  Farmers' Alliance and, 132
  female
    in civil rights movement, 614–615
    as domestic servants, 81
    garment workers strike and, 226
    in late 19th century, 142
    laundry work and, 82
    settlement houses run by, 213
    in workforce during WWI, 286–287
    in workforce in early 20th century, 196
    in workforce in WWII, 509
  Franklin D. Roosevelt and, 436–437, *438*
  incarceration rate for, 724
  "Jim Crow" laws and, 139–144
  Knights of Labor and, 91–92, 94, 108
  legal spectacles involving, in 1990s, 775–777
  literacy rates for, 190
  managerial/professional jobs closed to, postwar, 591
  middle-class, in early 20th century, choices faced by, 194
  migration of, out of South after WWII, 581–582
  "Million-Man March" and, 776–777
  as miners, 232
  New Deal relief/employment projects and, 437
  New South and, 49–50
  newly emancipated
    churches and, 2
    economic self-sufficiency and, 2
    education and, 2, 7
    expressions of freedom by, 2
    KKK and, 8
    land ownership and, 2, 3, 7
    political activity among, 5–6
    voting by, 6
  in 1920s, 347–353
  Operation Dixie and, 558–559
  politics and, in late 1800's, 103
  post-Civil War labor market and, 33, 34
  in poverty, isolation of, 722
  Progressive Era and, 248
  public recreation and, 168
  Reconstruction and, 2
  rural
    churches and, 83
    consumer economy and, 168
    Southern Tenant Farmers' Union and, 399–400
  seniority system and, 463
  sharecropping and, 51–54
  Social Security Act and, 429
  socializing of, in early 20th century, 192
  southern
    great migration of, to North, 277–282
    libraries and, 191
    movement from rural to urban life during WWII, 516
  in Spanish-American-Cuban War, 151–152
  UMWA and, 108–109
  unemployment among, race riots of 1960s and, 627
  urban, neighborhood cultures of, 77
  vaudeville and, 186–187
  voter registration of, 558, 615–616, 621
  as voters, turnout decline in, Democratic Party and, 699
  Wilson and, 244–245
  in WWII, 501–503
African Blood Brotherhood, 350
Agnew, Spiro, 653–654, 673, 676
Agricultural Adjustment Act (AAA) of 1938, 398–400
  African Americans and, 436
  declared unconstitutional, 475
Agricultural Adjustment Administration, 399
Agricultural Educational Extension Act of 1914, 343

Index

Agricultural Marketing Act of 1929, 382
Agricultural Workers' Organization (AWO), 291
Agriculture. *See also* Farming
in crisis in 1920s, 342–344
depression of 1890's and, 122
drought and, in Great Depression, 376–380
New Deal and, 398–400, 475
parity and, 398–399
population decrease in, after WWII, 581
supports for, in New Deal, 398–402
Aguinaldo, Emilio, 151, 152
Aid to Dependent Children program, 428
Aid to Families with Dependent Children (AFDC), 623, 624, 702
AIDS, 707–708
Air traffic controllers strike (PATCO), 726–727
Alaska, woman suffrage in, 287
Albany (GA), civil rights demonstrations in, 613–614
Alcatraz Island, 661
Alcoholism, crusades against, 87–88
Aldrich, Nelson, 239
Alexander V. Holmes, 656
All in the Family, 672
Allen, Alexander, 517
Allied powers in WWI, *261,* 262
support of, in 1939, 488
Allis-Chalmers strike, 565
Altgeld, John Peter, 100
Amalgamated Association of Iron and Steel Workers, 112, 113
Amalgamated Clothing Workers (ACW), 303
cooperatively owned apartment buildings sponsored by, 327
growth of, 274
industrial unionism and, 433
rebuilding of, National Industrial Recovery Act and, 406
unemployment and, in Great Depression, 371
U.S. participation in war and, 489
Amazon.com, 755
American Association of University Professors (AAUP), 292
American Civil Liberties Union (ACLU), 355–356
American culture
art in, public, New Deal and, 453–454
conflicts among, in 1920s, 353–359
consumer
leisure and, 182–185
new, daily life in, 327–329
in 1920s, 334–338
family-oriented privatization of, postwar, 597–598
movies in, 187, 336–338, 601
music in
counterculture of 1960s and, 646
phonograph records and, 336
rhythm-and-blues, 600
rock-and-roll, 600–601
in 1980s, 733–734
neighborhood, late-19th century, 76–80, 79
political, women's, progressivism and, 216–219
popular, New Deal and, 452–459
radio in, 334–336
rap in, 734
Reaganism and, 732–734
religion in
community and, 82–85
freedpeople and, 2
group tragedies based on, 777–778
labor unions and, 89–90
male groups based on, in 1990s, 776–777
presidential election of 1928 and, 361
suburbs in
development of, 591–595
growth of, in 1920s, 327
individualization of, 593–594
married women and, 594
social-class divisions and, 594–595
television in, 597–598, 665, 672, 733
theater in, 185, 187–188, 457
women and, in 1920s, 341–342
American Dilemma, An (Myrdal), 516
American Expeditionary Forces in WWI, 296
American Farm Bureau Federation, 343
American Federation of Labor (AFL). *See also* AFL-CIO
African Americans in, in WWI, 280
and CIO, 472, 578–579
Columbian Exposition and, 121
craft unions of, 432, 461
industrial unionism and, 446
labor defeats in 1892 and, 114
labor reform and, 227
less-skilled workers and, 158
married women and, in Great Depression, 373
membership decline in, in 1905, 160
in 1920s, 346–347
post-WWI steel strike and, 303
racism and, 109, 159
on railroad ownership, 318
rise of, 106–109
self-help during Great Depression and, 387
Taylorism and, 172
Truman supported by, in 1948, 560
American Federation of State, County, and Municipal Employees (AFSCME)
strike by, in Memphis, 651
Vietnam War and, 671
American Federation of Teachers (AFT), 668, 669–670
American Home Economics Association, 307
American Indian Movement (AIM), 662
American Indians. *See* Indians, American
American Legion, 565
American Liberty League, 415–416
American Medical Association, 561
American Party, 147
"American Plan," 345
American Protective Association (APA), 147–148
American Protective League, 293
American Railway Union (ARU), 127
American Telephone and Telegraph Co. (AT&T)
concentration of productive capacity in, 326
downsizing in, in 1980s, 714
layoffs in, in 1990s, 749
American Woman Suffrage Association, 219
"Americanization" program(s)
company, 173–174
Ford Motor Company, profit-sharing and, 200
Americans for Democratic Action (ADA), 559–560
Americans with Disabilities Act, 687
Ameringer, Oscar, 100–101, *190*
Amnesty, Johnson and, 3–4
Amoskeag Mills, 173, *174*
Amusement parks, 184–185
Anarchists, 228–229
opposition to WWI, 268
Anderson, John, 708
Anderson, Marian, 460
Anderson, Sherwood, 353, 378
Angola revolution, 696
Anthony, Susan B., 11, 219
Anti-Communism
In Cold War, 562–567
homophobia and, 589
"Antifusion" laws, 237
Anti-Imperialist League, 153
Anti-Saloon League, 359
Anti-Semitism
in housing in 1920s, 327
isolationism and, in WWII, 489
KKK and, 356

McCarthyism and, 567
Nazi regime and, 485
Populists and, 148
in U.S. in WWII, 511
A&P. *See* Great Atlantic and Pacific Tea Company (A&P)
Arbuckle, "Fatty," 338
Arbuckle Brothers, 181
Archibald, Katherine, 506
Argonne, battle in, 296
Aristide, Jean Bertrand, 761
Armed forces. *See also* U.S. Army; U.S. Navy
Armijo, Charles, 283
Arms race, 552, 554
Armstrong, Louis, 352
Arnold, Thurmond, 474
Art, public, New Deal and, 453–454
Art Project, Federal, 453–454
Asia
AFL and, 159
anti-immigrant sentiment and, 322
Cold War in, 551–555
Depression in, 483–484
discrimination against, in employment in Great Depression, 374–375
financial crisis in, 762, *763*
immigrants from, in 1970s and 1980s, 715–720
industrialization and, 31
Open Door policy in, 155–156
postwar, American supremacy in, 528
Assembly line, Henry Ford and, 169, 197–198
Associated Farmers, 416, 464
Atlanta (GA)
Booker T. Washington's speech in, 142–143
Union Hall and Library Association of, 89
Atlantic Charter, 488
Atomic bombing of Japan, 526, 528
Austin (MN), Local P-9 strike in, 728
Austria, German annexation of, 486
Austria-Hungary, surrender of, in WWI, 296
Auto Workers' Union, Ford Hunger March and, 391
Automation, working class division and, 596
Automobile(s)
mass production of, 169, 197–200
for masses in 1920s, 329–333
approaches to, 330
financing of, 331
life style and, 331–333
postwar economic boom and, 570–571
Babbs, Jim, on worker rights, 667
Baby boom, 572, *573*
Bakker, Jim, 733
Balkans, assassination in, WWI and, 260–263
Ballinger, Richard, Taft and, 243
Ballot reforms, 237–238
Baltimore and Ohio Railroad, strike at, 13
Baltimore Urban League, African-American employment and, 517
Bankers, American, diplomatic role of, 320
Banking system, national, creation of, 21
Banner coal mine explosion, 227
Barone, Francesco, 31
Barrett, Ethel, 287
Barry, J. B., 131–132
Baruch, Bernard, 273, 541
Baseball as spectator sport, 188
Bass, Sam, 111
Battle of Coral Sea in WWII, 494
Battle of Leyte Gulf in WWII, 525
Battle of Okinawa in WWII, *499*
Battle of Stalingrad in WWII, 495
Battle of the Bulge in WWII, 503, 522
"Battle of the Running Bulls," 443
Battles fought by American troops in WWI, 295–297
Bay of Pigs invasion, 634
Bayonne (NJ), refinery strike in, 290
Beame, Abraham, New York City crisis and, 691–692
Beatles, The, 646
Beatnicks, 598–599
Beecher, Henry Ward, 84
Begin, Menachem, 696
Beijing, Tiananmen Square massacre in, 745
Belgium, German invasion of, 486
Bell, Alexander Graham, 179
Bellamy, Edward, 228
Belmonte, August, National Civic Federation and, 160
Bennett, William, on university curricula, 732
Bentley, Gladys, 353
Bentsen, Lloyd, 746, 760
Berg, Gertrude, 597
Berkeley, Busby, 457, *458*
Berkeley (CA), demonstrations in, in 1960s, 642
Berle, Milton, on movies, 187
Berlin airlift, 550
Berlin Wall
erection of, 634
fall of, 741
Bernstein, Carl, 675
Berrigan, Philip and Daniel, in attacks on draft boards, 643
Berry, Chuck, 600
Bethlehem Steel, resistance of, to unionizing, 465
Bettis, Alexander, 83
Beveridge, Albert J., on overseas expansion, 149, 154
Bezos, Jeff, 755
Billboards, advertising and, 181
Birmingham (AL), civil rights protests in, 616
Bisno, Abraham, 97
Bison, Plains Indians and, 55–56
Black, Hugo, named to U.S. Supreme Court, 464
Black Codes, 4, 7
Black Legion, 472
Black lung disease, 660
Black Muslims, 628
Black Panther party, 630
Black Power, 628–630, 645
Black Star Line, Garvey and, 350
Blaine, James G., 45
Blair, Ezell, in Woolworth lunch counter "sit-in," 612
Blake, Eubie, 352
"Bloody Thursday," 411
Bloom, Allan, 732
Bluestone, Barry, on Reagan era, 712
Boarders as income source, 81–82
Boeing, layoffs in, in 1990s, 749
Boland Amendment, 730
Bolshevik party
postwar strikes and, 303
WWI peace process and, 298–299
Bolshevik Revolution, 306
Bonus March, veterans', 391–392
Bootlegging, Prohibition and, 357–359
Bork Robert, 730, 731
Bosnia, U.S. involvement in, 761–762
Boston (MA)
busing controversy in, 701–702
demonstration of unemployed in, in Great Depression, 388
Bowles, Chester, 531
Boxer Rebellion, 155
Boycotts in labor movement, 90
Boyd, Frederick Sumner, Paterson strike and, 232
Bradley, Omar, on German Army, 523
Brady Bill, 760
Branch Davidian standoff in Waco, 778
Brandeis, Louis, 222, 226
Brando, Marlon, 601
"Bread and butter" wage goals of unions, women and, 158–159
Bretton Woods Conference, 547
Breyer, Stephen, 760
Brezhnev, Leonid, Strategic Arms Limitation Treaty and, 655

Index

Bridges, Harry, 411, 434
British Americans
enclosure conflicts in Texas and, 111
as post-Civil War skilled craftsmen, 32
Britton, Nan, 316
Brophy, John, on UMW rebirth, 406
Brotherhood of Carpenters and Joiners, 107
Brotherhood of Sleeping Car Porters (BSCP)
founding of, 347
March on Washington and, 517
progress made by, 461
Browder, Earl, as presidential candidate, 435
Brown, John, social activism and, 607
Brown, Joseph, 278
Brown lung disease, 660
Brown v. Board of Education, 608
Bryan, William Jennings, 133
defeat of, 242
political climate and, 239
as 1896 presidential candidate, 137
neutrality in WWI and, 266
opposition to WWI, 268
in Scopes trial, 356
Bryant, Anita, homosexuality and, 707
Buchanan, Joseph, 28
Buchanan, Patrick, 700, 758, 769
Buchenwald, 523–524
Buffalo, Plains Indians and, 55–56
"Buffalo soldiers" in Spanish-American-Cuban War, 152
Building Trades Council, founding of, 107
Bulgaria
German invasion of, 486
surrender of, in WWI, 296
Bureaucracies, growth of, industrialization and, 29–30
Burger, Warren, appointed to U.S. Supreme Court, 656
Burma
Japanese seizure of, 493
reclaiming of, from Japan, 525
Burnham, Daniel H., 121
Burns, Arthur F., on inflation in 1970s, 685–686
Bus boycott in Montgomery, 611–612
Bush, George Herbert Walker
background of, 745–746
election of, 746
Gulf War and, 747–748
in 1992 campaign, 759
as presidential candidate, 746
Bush, Prescott, 746
Bush, Vannevar, 527
Business(es)
after 1890's depression, 156–158
American
new shape of, in 1970s, 688–690
WWI and, 265–266
"Americanization" programs of, 173–174
big
business-government relationships and, 157–158
New Deal opposition from, 475
political power of, increased, in 1920s, 316
government mobilization of, in WWI, 273
merger activity and, 157
in 1920s, 318–319
NIRA Section 7a and, 405
overseas expansion of, 149–156
in 1920s, 319–323
Business cycle, economic expansion and, 26–27
Business organization, railroad expansion and, 23
Business unionism, 107–108
Businessmen
backlash of, against labor, 463–464
on democratic power-sharing in businesses, 555–556
Eisenhower and, 568–569
"management security" clause in postwar contracts and, 533
politics and, 43–46
post-WWII, 529–530
Busing, revolt against, 700–703
Butler, Smedley, on military interventions in Central America, 321
Butte (MT), 66
Byrd, Harry F., on resistance to school integration, 609
Byrnes, James F., on diplomatic aspects of atomic bomb, 528

Cagney, James, New Deal and, 457
California
grape growers in, national boycott against, 633
influx into, during WWII, 506
Proposition 13 in, 702
Proposition 226 in, union opposition to, 773
California Civil Rights Initiative, 768
Cambodia, U.S. invasion of, 654
Cambria Steel factory, size of, 156
Camp David accords, 696
Campbell, packaged product development by, 175
Canadians, immigration of, in 1920s, 322–323
Cannery and Agricultural Workers Industrial Union, strikes and, 413
Cannon, Joseph G., 239, 243
Cantor, Eddie, New Deal and, 457
Capitalism
global, 741–782. *See also* Global capitalism
industrial. *See* Industrial capitalism
meaning of democracy and, 68–69
moral, expectations of, in Great Depression, 385–386
welfare
in early 20th century, 172–174
in Great Depression, 385–386
Capone, Al, 358–359
Capra, Frank, 457
Carey, James, 408
Carey, Ron, 772–773
Carmichael, Stokley, 628, 630
Carnegie, Andrew
Anti-Imperialist League and, 153
control over work process and, 43
development of, as capitalist, 39, 41
Gospel of Wealth of, *40,* 41
as philanthropist, 41
philanthropy of, 189
reform agenda and, 211
strikes at Homestead steel mill and, 112
Tuskegee Institute and, 142
Carpenter, R. R. M., 415
Carpenters' Brotherhood, industrial unionism and, 433
"Carpetbaggers," 6
Carson, Rachel, 658
Carswell, G. Harold, 656
Carter, James Earl (Jimmy), 692–695, 709
Carville, James, 759
Casey, William, covert aid to Contras and, 730
Cast-iron stoves, impact of, 81
Castro, Fidel, 634, 747
Catholic Church, American
post-Civil War, 85
transformation of, in 1960s, 647, 649
Catholics
anti-Communist sentiments of, 566–567
nativism and, 147–148
schools of, declining enrollment in, 590–591
Catt, Carrie Chapman, opposition of, to WWI, 268
Cattle ranching in West, 62–64
CCC. *See* Civilian Conservation Corps (CCC)
Censorship, press, during WWI, 292
Centennial Exposition, "other" America and, 10–12
Central Intelligence Agency (CIA), 555
AFL-CIO and, 670

covert aid to Contras and, 730
demonstrations targeting, 643
Central Labor Union (CLU), 89
Central Park, working class and, 191
Central Powers in WWI, *261, 262–263*
Central Trades and Labor Assembly in New Orleans, 92
Chain stores, 182
Chamberlain, Neville, on Munich agreement, 486
Chaney, James, murder of, 619–620
Chaplin, Charlie, 457
Charity Organization Societies, 124
Charles, Ray, 600
Chavez, Cesar, *379,* 633
Chavez-Thompson, Linda, 770
Chew, Lee, 67–68
Chiang Kai-shek, 484, 552
Chicago (IL)
African-American population in, 278
black migration to, 582
demonstrations of unemployed in, in Great Depression, 388
eight-hour day movement in, 98, 100
immigrant work force in, 30–31
post-WWI race riot in, 305
Pullman strike violence in, 128
rapid growth of, 29
SCLC campaign in, 628
tenement workshops in, 35
Workingmen's Exchange in, 86
Chicago Packinghouse Union, 449
Chicanos. *See* Mexican-Americans
Chief Joseph, 55
Child labor, 34–35
banning of, by Fair Labor Standards Act, 429
legislation on, 222–223
Child labor law, first enacted, 246
Children in work force, 34–35
Children's Bureau, federal, 223
Taft and, 242
Childs, Marquis, on middle class in Great Depression, 380
China
civil war in, 552
eastern, Japanese seizure of, 493
invasion of, by Japan, 484
Chinese Americans
discrimination against, in employment in Great Depression, 374–375
hostility towards, in 1880–90s, 67–68
Knights of Labor and, 96
post-Civil War labor market and, 33
western mining and, 66
in WWII, 515
Chinese Exclusion Act, 67, *68*
Knights of Labor and, 96
repealed, 515
Christian socialists, 228
Chrysler Corporation
federal bailout of, 693–694
racial protests at, 518
strikes in, 444
Church(es)
freedpeople and, 2
supporting community life, 82–85
Churchill, Winston
Atlantic Charter and, 488
"Iron Curtain" speech of, 548–549
on post-war America, 545
on post-war Europe, 545–546
at Potsdam, 528
on "second front," 496
on Soviet sphere of influence, 546
at Yalta Conference, 527
CIA. *See* Central Intelligence Agency (CIA)
Cigar Makers' International Union, 106
Cincinnati (OH)
strikes in, 100
union activity in, 88
CIO. *See* Congress of Industrial Organization (CIO)
Citizens' Alliance, Minneapolis strike and, 410
City. *See* Urban areas
City commission, 235
City manager system, 235
Civil Aeronautics Board, abolition of, 693
Civil Rights Act, 1964
literacy tests for voters and, 586
passage of, 619
segregation of public accommodations and, 621
Title VII of, 621, 630–631
women's movement and, 662–663
Civil rights bill of 1866, 4
Civil rights in Truman's 1948 campaign, 560–561
Civil Rights Movement
birth of, 608–612
Black Power in, 628–630
Freedom Rides and, 617
"March on Washington for Jobs and Freedom" in, 616–617
modern, 515–519
race riots in, 626–630
"sit-ins" and, 612–613
unions and, 669
Civil rights revolution in 1960, 541
Civil Service Commission, 45
Civil Works Administration (CWA), 397, 398
women and, 451
Civilian Conservation Corps (CCC), 397, 398
discriminatory policies of, 437
women and, 451
Class(es)
blurring of, in Cold War boom, 575–576
divisions between, suburbs and, 594–595
inequality between, growing, in 1920s, 326
standards of living in early 20th century and, 175–177
wealthy, in Reagan era, 712–713
Class conflict. *See also* Middle class; Working class
in 1870s-1890s, 109–111
in 1893–1904, 161
Great Uprising of 1877 and, 14–15
Pullman strike and, 125–129
Clayton Antitrust Act, 245
Clemenceau, Georges, 264, 299–300
Clemente, Jose, 453
Clerical workers
computerization and, 689
in early 1900s, 194
increase in
post-WWII, 587–588
in 1920s, 324, 340
unionism and, 449–450
women as, 195
increase in, during WWI, 286
Cleveland, Grover, 45, 46, 135, 137, 153
Clifford, Clark, 560, 650
Clinton, Hillary, 759, 764, 779
Clinton, William Jefferson (Bill)
administration of, 759–762
anti-terrorism measures of, 778
background of, 757
challenge of, from Right, 765–769
economy under, views on, *750–751*
election of, 759
health care reform and, 763–765
impeachment hearings on, 778–781
reelection of, 769
sexual misconduct of, 780–781
union support of, 773
Clurman, Harold, Group Theatre and, 457
Cobb, Browne, 52–54
Cobb, Ned, 331, 344, *390*
Coca-Cola, overseas expansion of, 156, 505
Coeur d'Alene (ID), 65
strikes in, 114
Cold War
anti-Communism in, 562–567
arms race in, 552
in Asia, 551–555

Index

beginnings of, 528
boom during, 545–603
classless society and, 575–576
consensus on, disintegration of, 649
cultural impact of popular media in, 597–601
decline in ethnicity, 590–591
division of Europe in, 548–551
Eisenhower and, 568–570
election of 1948 and, 559–562
end of, 742–745
farm losses during, 581–586
labor losses in, 555–559
labor-management accord in, 576–581
naming of, 540–541
origins of, 545–548
postwar economic boom and, 570–575
service sector growth in, 586–590
suburban development in, 591–595
working class splintering in, 596–597
Collective bargaining, Wagner Act and, 432
College/univerisity enrollment, growth of, postwar, 591
Collier, John, New Deal for American Indians and, 404
Collins, William, union prejudice and, 432
Colombia, Panama canal and, 154
Colorado Fuel and Iron Company, open-shop drive and, 232
Colored Farmers' National Alliance, 132
Columbia Mills Company, electricity and, 178
Columbian Exposition, 121
Commission, city, 235
Commission on Industrial Relations, 246
Commissioner system of city government, 235
Committee for Industrial Organization (CIO), 433
Committee on Public Information (CPI), 271–272
Committee to Reelect the President, 674
Communism
European, collapse of, 741, 742–744
movement against, in Cold War, 562–567. *See also* Anti-Communism
Communist party
demonstrations by unemployed organized by, in Great Depression, 388
demonstrations in rural South and, in Great Depression, 389
members of, in union movement, pressure against, 556–557
in 1935, 418–419
in organizing industrial unions, 433–434
Popular Front and, 452–453
presidential candidate of, in 1936, 435
Scottsboro case and, 376
in Soviet Union, collapse of, 744
Community Action Program, 624
Compromise of 1877, 44–45
Computer revolution, 753–754
Comstock, Anthony, 84
Comstock Act, 84
Concentration camps in WWII, 523–524
Congress, U.S.
elections of. *See* Election(s), congressional
lobbying of, big business and, 158
Congress of Industrial Organizations (CIO). *See also* AFL-CIO
and AFL
hostility between, 472
merger of, 578–579
African-American consciousness and, 516–517
anti-Communist tactics of, 566
anti-discrimination policy of, 462
communism and, 483
divisions in, 472
founding of, 433
legacies of, 476–477
Memorial Day Massacre and, 465–466
Operation Dixie and, 558–559
organizational efforts of, 439
Political Action Committee of, 556
post-WWII agenda of, 530
Roosevelt and, 466–467
Truman supported by, in 1948, 560
United Electrical Workers denounced by, 565
U.S. participation in war and, 489
Congress of Racial Equality (CORE), "Freedom Rides" organized by, 613, *614*
Congressional Medal of Honor for Mexican Americans in WWII, 503
Connor, Eugene "Bull," Birmingham protests and, 616
Conscientious objectors to draft in WWII, 511–512
Consciousness-raising (CR) groups for women, 663, *664*
Conservatism in 1920s, 316–317
Conservatives, challenge to Clinton from, 765–769
Constitution, federal, amendments to. *See* specific Amendment, eg. Sixteenth Amendment
Consumer culture
leisure and, 182–185
new, daily life in, 327–329
in 1920s, 334–338
Consumer economy, early 20th century, 168
Consumers, women as, 338–342
Continental Airlines, Frank Lorenzo and, 727
Contract labor system in western agriculture, 66–67
Contras, 730
Control, businessmen seeking, 37–41
Convict labor, 227
Cooke, Jay, & Co., 21, 25
Coolidge, Calvin, 303, 317–319, 344
Coral Sea, Battle of, 494
Corcoran, Thomas, on war and New Deal, 490
Corliss Double Walking-Beam Engine, 10
Corporations
big, reforms and, 242
early 20th century
gender segregation in, 194
growth of, white-collar work explosion and, 192–194
lifelong employment with, 194
mergers of, in 1990s, 752
Corruption
political
in 1920s, 316–317
Watergate and, 674–676
union, McClellan hearings on, 579
Cost-of-living adjustment (COLA) in postwar labor settlements, 576, 577
Cotton Club, Harlem's, 352
Cotton manufacturing, 48–49
Cotton production, 51
Coughlin, Charles E., 417–418, 435
Council of Economic Advisers, 573
Counterculture, 645–649
Catholicism and, 647, 649
environmental movement and, 658
journalism in, 646–647
music in, 646
Court injunctions, 125
Covello, Leonard, 177
Cox, Archibald, 675, 676
Cox, James, 316
Coxey, Jacob S., 124
CPI (Committee on Public Information), 271–272
Craft unions, 75
breach between Knights of Labor and, 106
civil rights and, 669
labor defeats in 1892 and, 114
resurgence of (1897–1904), 158–160
Craft workers in labor pool, 32
Cramer, Charles F., political corruption and, 317

Crawford, Joan, New Deal and, 457
Crazy Horse, murder of, 54
Credit, suburban development and, 592
Creede (CO), 65
Creel, George, 271
Crime, poverty and, 723–724
Cripple Creek (CO), 65–66
Crisco, 167–169
Cronkite, Walter, on Vietnam War, 649
Crop-lien system, 51
Cuba
  CIA-organized invasion of, 634
  revolution in, exile in Miami from, 716
  in Spanish-American-Cuban War, 151
Cuban missile crisis, 634
Cultural reformers, 212
Culture. *See* American culture
Curtiss-Wright plants, size of, 505
Czechoslovakia
  Communist government overthrow in, 742
  German annexation of, 486
Czolgosz, Leon, 239

Daily life
  automobile and, 331–333
  early 20th century, 167–203
    electricity and, 177–178
    entertainment for masses and, 185–188
    Fordism and, 197–200
    indoor plumbing and, 177
    leisure time and, 182–185
    mass marketing and, 179–182
    mass production and, 169–170
    middle-class values and, 192–194
    public recreation and, 182–185
    scientific management and, 170–173
    standards of living and, 175–177
    uplifting masses and, 188–192
    urban landscape and, 200–201
    welfare capitalism and, 172–174
    white-collar work and, 192–194
    women in workforce and, 194–197
  in new consumer culture of 1920s, 327–329
Daley, Richard J., 586, 628, 651
Dance halls, early 20th century, 182–184
Darrow, Clarence, 356
Dartmouth College, murals for, 453
Darwin, Charles, 75, 355–356
Daugherty, Harry, political corruption and, 317
Daughters of the American Revolution (DAR), 149
  racism and, 460
Davey, Martin, 466
Davis, Benjamin, 502
Davis, John W., 319
Davis, Richard L., 108–109
Dawes, Charles, 320
Dawes Act of 1887, 57
Dawes Plan, 320
Dawson, William, 582
Dayton (TN), Scopes trial in, 355–356
D-Day, 522
de Graffenreid, Clare, 49
de Klerk, F. W., 747
De Leon, Daniel, 228
De Priest, Oscar, 350
Deadwood (SD), 66
Dean, James, 601
Debs, Eugene V.
  American Railway Union and, 127, 128–129
  antiwar attitude of, *267*
  on industrial capitalism, 244
  Industrial Workers of the World and, 229
  in 1912 election, 208
  pardoning of, 316
  as presidential candidate, 244, 306
  radicalism of, 288
  social activism and, 607
  as Socialist, 227, 228
  on war, 259
Debski, Joseph, *174*
Debt
  New South farmers and, 51
  Plains farmers and, 61
DeLay, Tom, 780
Democracy, meaning of, capitalism and, 68–69
Democratic National Committee, Watergate offices of, break-in at, 674
Democratic National Convention
  in Chicago, antiwar protest at, 651, *652*
  1964, 620
Democratic Party
  in 1912 election, 208
  African Americans and, 436–437
    after 1896, 141–142
  civil rights and, 561
  fusion of, with Populist Party, 237
  labor reform and, 227
  low voter turn-out and, 699
  southern, KKK and, 8, 9–10
  workingmen and, 104, 105–106
Denmark, German invasion of, 486
Department of Agriculture, photojournalism and, 455
Department of Justice
  American Protective League and, 293
  antiradical activities of, post-WWI, 307
Department stores, women working in, 194–195
Depression
  1870s, 25
    Reconstruction and, 10
  1890s, 122–124
    end of, 156
  Great, 367–421. *See also* Great Depression
Détente, collapse of, 695–698
Detention camps for Japanese Americans, 512–514
Detroit Institute of the Arts, Rivera mural in, 453
Detroit (MI)
  demonstrations of unemployed in, in Great Depression, 388
  government reform in, 236
  joblessness in, in 1930s, 361
  labor movement in, 89
  race riot(s) in, 626–627
    in 1943, 519–520
    black unemployment and, 627
    over housing, 519
  right-conscious activism in, 518
  unemployment in, in Great Depression, 371
Detroit Rifles, 89
Dewey, George, 151
Dewey, John, 454
Dewey, Thomas, 560
DeWitt, John L., 512
Diaz, Porfirio, 282
Diem, Ngo Dinh, 634, 635
Dies, Martin, 472
Disney, Walt, unionism at, 459
Distribution system
  mass, in early 20th century, salesmen and, 194
  new, prosperity and, 167
Dixiecrats, 561
Dodge Revolutionary Union Movement (DRUM), 670
Dole, Robert, 769
Dole, Sanford B., 153
Domestic service, women in, 196
Dorgathen, Matthias, 31
Douglas, William O., 464
Douglas Aircraft, sit-down strike broken at, 464
Douglas Aviation plants, size of, 505
Douglass, Frederick, 12
Dow Chemical Company, demonstrations targeting, 643
Downsizing, corporate, in 1980s, 714
Draft
  peacetime, first, 488
  postwar, 591
  reinstatement of, by Carter, 697

in Vietnam War, 637
evasion of, 643
in WWII
conscientious objectors to, 511–512
egalitarian nature of, 497
Dreier, Mary, 218–219
Drought in farm belt in Great Depression, 376–380
Drucker, Peter, 575
Drug addiction in inner-city neighborhoods in 1980s, 722–723
Drug and Hospital Employees' Union, civil rights struggle and, 631
Du Bois, W. E. B., 144, 585
Du Pont
alternative of, to New Deal vision, 475
downsizing in, in 1980s, 714
overseas expansion of, 156
Dubos, René, 658
Dukakis, Michael J., 746
Duke, James B., 48
Dulles, John Foster, 569
Duniway, Abigail Scott, 219
DuPont, Pierre, 415
Dust Bowl, *377,* 378
Dyer antilynching bill, *348*
Dylan, Bob, 646

Eagleton, Thomas, 673
"Earth Day," 658
East St. Louis (IL), race riot in, 280–281
Easter Rebellion of 1916, 267
Eastern Airlines, Lorenzo and, 727
Eastern Front in WWI, 263
Eastland, James, 518
Eastside/Westside, 622
Economic reformers, 212
Economic self-sufficiency, freedpeople and, 2
Economy
collapse of détente and, 695–698
concentration of, by war mobilization, 504–505
consumer, early 20th century, 168
development of, explosive and unstable, 25–27
forces dominating, 573–574
gender politics and, 703–708
global capitalism and, 749–756
growth and stability of, in 1920s, 324–326
KKK rise in 1920s and, 356–357
labor movement under fire and, 724–728
new immigration in 1970s and 1980s and, 715–720
New Right and, 698–700
new shape of American business and, 688–690
peacetime, conversion to, after WWII, 528–535
postwar boom in, 570–575
end of, 683–688
poverty and, 720–724
Reagan and, 708–715
Reagan reelection and, 728–731
stagflation politics and, 690–695
"throwaway," environmental movement and, 658
Edgefield County (SC), 83
Edison, Thomas A., 177–179
Edison Company, market segmentation and, 181
Education. *See also* Schools
freedpeople and, 2, 7
EEOC. *See* Equal Employment Opportunity Commission (EEOC)
Eighteenth Amendment, 217
passage of, 294
ratification of, 357
Eight-Hour Movement, 75, 97–101
Eisenhower, Dwight David
African Americans and, 569
on atomic bombing of Japan, 527
background of, 568
election of, 568
in European victory, 522–523
on government and religious faith, 591
on school integration, 608–609
El Salvador
civil war in, 730
peace treaty in, 747
Election(s)
congressional
(1866), 5
(1886), 105–106
(1890), 133
(1894), 135–136
(1934), 425
(1938), 468–469, *470*
(1946), 534
(1952), 568
(1964), 620–621
(1980), 709
(1986), 730
(1992), 759
(1994), 759, 767
(1996), 770
(1998), 781
presidential
(1876), 44–45
(1884), 45
(1888), 45–46
(1892), 133–135
(1896), 137–138
political climate of, 239
(1908), 242
(1912), 208, 244
(1916), 269–270
(1920), 306, 316
(1924), 318–319
(1928), 360–361
(1932), 392, 393
(1936), 434–439
(1940), 489
(1948), 559–562
(1952), 568
(1960), 617
(1964), 620–621
(1968), 650, 651–654
(1972), 673–674
(1976), 692
(1980), 708–709
(1984), 728–729
(1988), 746
(1992), 756–759
(1996), 769
Electoral politics, Farmers' Alliance and, 133
Electric Auto-Lite, strike at, 409
Electric streetcars, 178
Electricity
daily life and, 177–179
increased access to, in 1920s, 328
Elijah Muhammad, 628
Ellington, "Duke," 352
Ellis Island immigration depot, 147
Emancipation, meaning of, struggle over, 3
Emergency Banking Act, 396
Emergency Relief Appropriations Act, 426
Emergency work relief programs in Great Depression, 397–398
Employers, immigration restrictions and, 148–149
Employment Act of 1946, passage of, 573
Enclosure conflicts, 110–111
End-Poverty-in-California (EPIC) movement, 418
England. *See* Great Britain
English immigrants. *See also* British Americans
Entente Cordiale, 252
Entertainment for masses, early 20th century, 185–188
Environmental movement, 657–660
Environmental Protection Agency (EPA)
establishment of, 658
in Reagan administration, 710
Equal Employment Opportunity Commission (EEOC), 621, 631, 687, 775

Equal Rights Amendment (ERA), *341*
  controversy over, 705–706
  failure of, in 1920s, 341
ERA. *See* Equal Rights Amendment (ERA)
Espionage Act (1917)
  Debs arrest and, 259
  passage of, 272
Ethnicity
  cultural conflicts and, 353–359
  decline of, in 1950s and 1960s, 590–591
  marketing and, in early 20th century, 168–169
  movies and, 336
  radio broadcasts and, 335–336
Eureka (CA), anti-Chinese mob violence in, 67
Europe
  division of, in Cold War, 548–551
  Great Depression and, 370–371
  pre-WWI, 260–262
  total war in, 263–264
European Theater, WWII
  Soviet Union in, 495
  U. S. in, 495–496
  victory in, 522–525
Evans, Walker, 455
Evers, Medgar, assassination of, 618
Executive Order 8802, 517
Expressionism, Abstract, *547*
Expressway development, human cost of, 595
Extermination by Germans in WWII, 523–524
Exxon, downsizing in, in 1980s, 714

Fahey, James, 498–499
Fair Employment Practices Act, 560
Fair Employment Practices Committee (FEPC)
  creation of, 517
  in Philadelphia transit system dispute, 518
Fair Labor Standards Act (FLSA), 429
Fall, Albert, 317
Falwell, Jerry, 703–704, 706, 733
Family and Medical Leave Act, 687, 760
Family Assistance Plan (FAP), 656–657
"Family wage," union fights for, women and, 158–159
Faneuil Hall, 97–98
Farm Bureau Federation, 561
Farm homes, technologies/utilities in, in 1920s, 328
Farm Security Administration (FSA)
  African Americans and, 437
  photojournalism and, 455
Farmer, James, 613
Farmer-Labor Party, 418
  formation of, 343
Farmers' Alliance
  black farmers and, 132
  electoral politics and, 133
  growth of, 131–132
  People's Party and, 129–135
  political agenda of, 132–133
  women in, 130, *131*
Farming. *See also* Agriculture
  Agricultural Adjustment Act and, 398–400
  automobile ownership and, 331
  crisis in, in 1920s, 342–344
  decline in
    in Cold War, 581–586
    in 1920s, 343
  depression of 1890s and, 122
  drought and, in Great Depression, 376–380
  migrant workers and, 344
  New Deal and, 398–400
  in Plains, 54, 61–62
  protests against land auctions in Great Depression and, 389
  tenant. *See* Sharecropping
  in West, 60–64
Farrakhan, Louis, 628, 776–777
Fascism preceding WWII, 483–486
Father Knows Best, 598
Faubus, Orville, 609
Federal Art Project, 453–454
Federal Aviation Administration (FAA), air traffic controllers strike against, 726–727
Federal budget deficits in Reagan era, 710
  Gramm-Rudman-Hollings Act and, 729
Federal Children's Bureau, 223
  Taft and, 242
Federal Deposit Insurance Corporation, creation of, 396
Federal Emergency Relief Administration (FERA), 397, 398
Federal government
  agricultural support by, in 1920s, 343–344
  business mobilization by, in WWI, 273
  business relationships with, big businesses and, 157–158
  emergency work relief programs of, in Great Depression, 397–398
  industrial mobilization by, economic concentration and, 504–505
  labor conditions and, 245
  response of, to labor disputes in 1880s, 101
  systems of, reform and, 235
  worker protest marches and, 124–125
Federal Housing Administration (FHA)
  restrictive covenants and, 594
  suburban development and, 592
Federal Music Project, 454–455
Federal Reserve Act of 1913, 247, 266
Federal Reserve Board
  stock market crash and, 369
  Volcker on, 694
Federal Reserve System, 246
Federal Theatre Project, 457
  conservative attack on, 472
  investigation of, by HUAC, *470*
Federal Trade Commission, 246
Federal Writers Project, 454
Federation of Organized Trades and Labor Unions, 97
Feminine Mystique, The, 662
Feminism, 216–221
  abortion rights and, 665
  Centennial Exposition and, 11
  Elizabeth Cady Stanton and, 11, 219
  Equal Rights Amendment and, 341
  ERA and, 314, 705–706
  health care and, 665
  Jane Addams and, 151. *See also* Addams, Jane
  Lucy Stone and, 219
  National Woman's Suffrage Association and, 11, 219
  North American Woman Suffrage Association and, 287
  National Organization for Women and, 662–663
  in Progressive Era, 216–217
  rebirth of, in 1960s, 662–667
  Susan B. Anthony and, 11, 219
  union movement in 1930s and, 448–452
  woman suffrage and, 219–221
    in WWI, 287–288
  working class, Women's Trade Union League and, 225–226
  WWI opposition and, 268
Ferdinand, Franz, 260
Ferraro, Geraldine, 729
Field, James G., 135
Fielding, Henry, 519
Fields, W. C., 457
Fifteenth Amendment, 9
Filene, A. Lincoln, 226
Filene, Edward A., 334
Firestone, strike at, women in, 448–449
Fisk, Jim, 37
Fiske, Robert, 779
Fitzgerald, F. Scott, 315, 316
Five-Dollar Day, Ford and, 199, 345
Flanagan, Hallie, 457, *470*

Flint (MI)
consumption in, 334
sit-down strike in, 439–443
Folk, Joseph, reform and, 237
Food Administration, 273
Forbes, Steve, 769
Ford, Edsel, 453
Ford, Gerald, 676, 691
Ford, Henry, 169, 197–200, 330, 348, 361, 391
Ford, Patrick, 94
Ford Hunger March, 391
Ford Motor Company, 197–200
automobile market in 1920s and, 330
black employees of, in 1920s, 348
bomber plant, size of, 505
consumer demand and, 332–333
fascism and, 483
five-dollar day of, 199, 345
foreign "outsourcing" in, 689
racial protests at, 518
sales agencies for, *332*
UAW victory in, 491
workforce size at, 170
Fordism, 197–200
Foreign "outsourcing," 689
Foreign-language press, national advertising and, 181
Foremen, unions and, 445
Forty-hour workweek, Fair Labor Standards Act and, 429
Fossil fuels, industrialization and, 28
442nd Regimental Combat Team, 514
Fourteen Points, 299–300
Fourteen Points peace plan, international conference of women at The Hague and, 268
Fourteenth Amendment, passage of, 5
Fourth of July celebrations, 86–87
Franco-American, packaged product development by, 175
Frankfurter, Felix, 395, 464
Franklin, Aretha, 646
Franklin, Benjamin, 42
Freedmen's Bureau, 2
Black Codes and, 4
"Freedom Rides," 613, *614*
Kennedys and, 617
Freedom Schools, 619
"Free-silver" coinage in Populist program, 136–137
"Free-Speech Movement" (FSM), 642
Freeway development, human cost of, 595
Frick, Henry Clay, 112–113
Friedan, Betty, 589, 662
Fringe benefits, employee, 596–597
Frost, Robert, 607
Fruit and Vegetable Workers' Union, *424–425*
Fulbright, J. William, 555
Fulton (MO), Churchill's "Iron Curtain" speech in, 548–549
Fundamentalism in 1920s, 355–356
Fusion in party politics, 237

Galveston (TX), commissioners system in, 235
Gandhi, Mohandas, 551–552
Gangsters, Prohibition and, 357–359
Garfield, James A., 45
Garment industry
strikes in, 224–226
sweatshop system in, 224
unions in, 226
Garrison, William Lloyd, 607
Garson, Marvin, 645
Garvey, Marcus, 349–350
Gates, Bill, 754–755
"Gay Power," 666
Gay pride, 706–707
Gay vote, 706–707
Gaye, Marvin, 646
Gello, Grace, 337
Gender politics, 703–708
Gender roles, 590
General Electric Company (GE), 157
concentration of productive capacity in, 326
downsizing in, in 1980s, 714
factory size of, 156
foreign investments of, 320
overseas communication and, 320–321
overseas expansion of, 156
Reagan as spokesperson for, 708
wage increases at, 491
welfare cuts by, in Great Depression, 386
worker retention strategy of, in Great Depression, 371
General Managers' Association, Pullman strike and, 128
General Motors Acceptance Corporation, 331
General Motors Corporation (GM)
agreement of, with UAW, 576–577
alternative of, to New Deal vision, 475
CIO and, 433
concentration of productive capacity in, 326
growth of Flint, Michigan and, 330
labor-management accord in, 576
marketing emphasis of, 330, 332
on Office of Price Administration, 531
reshaping of, 689–690
sit-down strike at, 439–443
wage increases at, 491
Wagner Act challenged by, 432
Geoghegan, Thomas, 769–770
George, Henry, 22, 105
George, Walter, 468
Georgia, conflicts over enclosure in, 110
German Democratic Republic (GDR), disintegration of, 742
German-Americans
industrialization and, 31
in post-Civil War Chicago, 76–77
as post-Civil War skill craftsmen, 32
suspicion of, in WWI, 294
in western expansion, 66
Germany
European aggression by, 485–486
Nazism in, 485–486
surrender of
in WWI, 296
in WWII, 525
war declared on U.S. by, 493
Geronimo, surrender of, 55
Ghettos
concentration of poverty in, 722
minority, formation of, lending policies in, 594–595
G.I. Bill, 591
G.I. Bill of Rights, 528
Gibson girls, *195*
Gilded Age, The, 21–72
Gilder, George, 711
Gillette, overseas expansion of, 156
Gingrich, Newt, 765–768
Ginsberg, Allen, 598
Ginsberg, Ruth Bader, 760
Glasnost, 742
Glass, Carter, 140
Glass-Steagall Banking Act of 1933, 396
Global capitalism, 741–782
Bush's "New World Order" and, 745–749
labor movement and, new leadership and new ideas for, 769–774
new economy and, 749–756
racial legal spectacles and, 775–777
Gold Diggers of 1933, 457, *458*
Gold mining, 65
Goldbergs, The, 597
Goldman, Emma, 228–229, 306
Goldmark, Josephine, 222
Goldwater, Barry, 620, 673, 700
Gompers, Samuel, 16
AFL and, 106
Anti-Imperialist League and, 153
business unionism and, 107
on Clayton Antitrust Act, 245

death of, 346
Factory Commission and, 227
Japanese labor and, 159
on labor defeats in 1892, 114
post-WWI steel strike and, 303
Socialists on, 228
Gonzales, Victor, 694
Goodman, Andrew, 619–620
Goodyear Tire and Rubber, 157
Wagner Act challenged by, 432
Gorbachev, Mikhail, 730, 742, 745
Gore, Al, 758–759
Gould, Jay, 37, 45, 48, 91
Grady, Henry, 47
Gramm, Phil, 769
Gramm-Rudman-Hollings Act, 729
Grand Alliance, postwar maneuvering of, 527–528
Grange, 129
Granger, Lester, 517
Grant, Ulysses S., 9
Grapes of Wrath, 378
Grateful Dead, 646
Great Atlantic and Pacific Tea Company (A&P)
foreign expansion of, 320
as grocery chain, 182
mass merchandising by, 181
Great Britain
United States and, cooperation between, in Pacific, 488–489
war on Japan declared by, 493
Great Depression, 367–421
agricultural supports in, 398–400
anti-eviction battles in, 388–389
bank failures in, 393
demonstrations of unemployed in, 388
drought in farm belt and, 376–380
in East Asia, 483–484
ended by WWII, 503
financial rescue and emergency in, 396–398
hard times in, 371–376
Hoover's response to, 380–385
industrial codes in, 400–402
international conflict caused by, 483
international spread of, 369–371
moral capitalism in, 385–386
New Deal and, 392–419. *See also* New Deal
onset of, 368–371
organized labor revival in, 404–407
poor people's movements in, 387–392
psychological toll of, 378, 380
return to land in, 386–387
self-help in, 385–387
overproduction as cause, 326
strikes during, 408–414
"Great Migration," 277–282
Great Society, 621–623
Great Uprising of 1877, 13–15
Greece, civil war in, 549
Greeley, Horace, 29
Green, William, 346–347
Green Corn Rebellion, 271
"Greenbacks," printing of, 21
Grenada, military invasion of, 710
Griffin, Sheila, 715
Griggs v. Duke Power, 656
Guiteau, Charles, 45
Gulf of Tonkin Resolution, 636
repeal of, 654
Gulf War, 747–749
Guthrie, Woody, 372, 455, 646
Guyana, Jones mass suicide in, 777

Haiti
U.S. involvement in, 761
U.S. occupation of, 321
Haldeman, H. R., 674–675
Haley, Alex, 628
Haley, Bill, 601
Hamer, Fannie Lou, 615–616, 620
Hanna, Mark, 154
Harberson, Frederick, 578
Harding, Warren G., 316, 357
Harlan, John Marshall, 139
Harlem Renaissance, 350–353
Harlem's Cotton Club, 352
Harrington, Michael, 622–623
Harrison, Benjamin, 45–46
1892 defeat of, 135
Harrison, Bennett, 712
Harrison, Bessie, 194
Hart, Gary, 729
Hart, Schaffner, and Marx, strike against, 226
Hartley, Fred, 556
Hastings (NE), "movement culture" of populism in, 133
Hate strikes, 518–519
Hawaiian Islands, annexation of, 153
Hay, John, 150, 155–156
Hayden, Tom, 641, 656
Hayes, Rutherford B., 13, 16, 44
Haymarket Square incident, 98, 100
immigrants and, 147
Haynsworth, Clement, 656
Hays, Will, 338
Haywood, William ("Big Bill"), 230, 234
H-bomb development, 552
Head Start program, 623
Health, Education, and Welfare, creation of, 569
Health care
feminist issues in, 665
reform of, Clinton and, 763–765
Hearst, William Randolph, 150
Heinz, H. J.
advertising media and, 181
benefits offered by, 173
marketing campaigns and, 180
packaged product development by, 175
Heller, Walter, 623
Hembree, Diana, *719*
Henry Street Settlement, 214
Hepburn Act, 241
Herrerra, Juan José, 110
Herrod, Charles, 620
Hewitt, Abram, 44–45, 48, 105
High schools, enrollment rise in, postwar, 591
Hill, Anita, 775
Hillman, Sidney, 274, 303, 433, 489–490, 491–492
Hine, Lewis, 223
Hirabayashi v. U.S., 514
Hiroshima, Japan, atomic bombing of, 526
Hispanic Americans. *See also* Mexican-Americans; Puerto Ricans
in Clinton cabinet, 759–760
growth of, in 1960s, 660–661
Hiss, Alger, 562
Hitler, Adolf, 485, 525
Hoffa, James (Jimmy), 579, 772
Hoffa, James P., 772
Hoffman, Abbie, *648, 652*
Holley, Alexander Lyman, 43
Hollywood (CA), unionism in, 459
Home, women working at, 80–82
Home electrification, nationwide, 179
Homelessness in 1980s, 722
Homestead (PA), battles at, 112–114
defeat of workers in, significance of, 161
Homosexuality
anti-Communism and, 589
in armed services, 761
dance halls and, 183–184
New Right and, 707
prohibition and, 353–355
rights consciousness and, 706–707
rights movement and, feminism and, 666–667
WWII and, 501
Honeymooners, The, 597
Hong Kong, Japanese seizure of, 493
Hoover, Herbert
as Food Administration head, 273
in Harding's cabinet, 316
personal background of, 381

as president, election of, 360–361
probusiness ideology of, 318
response of, to Great Depression, 380–385
veterans' Bonus March and, 392
Hopi protests against Peabody Coal Co., 661
Hopkins, Harry, 395–396, 397–398, 425, 426–427
Hormel Meatpacking Company, strikes against, 728
Horton, Willie, 746
Hospital Workers in 1960s, 668–669
Hotel and Restaurant Workers, *580*
Houdini, Harry, 337
House, Edward, 270
House Committee on Un-American Activities (HUAC), *470*, 472
hearings by, 563–564
House Education and Labor Committee in anti-Communist probes, 565
House Rules Committee, attack of, on National Labor Relations Board, 472
Housing
discrimination in, 585
public, failure of, 595
segregated, in North, 595
Houston, Charles, 459–460, 516
Howe, Julia Ward, 86
Howells, William Dean, 12
Hughes, Charles Evans, 269, 319–320, 321
Hughes, Langston, *351*, 352
Hull, Cordell, 489
Hull House, 213
Hull House Woman's Club, 215–216
Humphrey, Hubert H.
in Americans for Democratic Action, 559–560
civil rights in 1948, 561
Mississippi delegation to 1964 Democratic National Convention and, 620
as presidential candidate, 651–652
as vice-president, election of, 620
Wallace, George and, 652–653
Hungary, German invasion of, 486
Hurston, Zora Neale, 352
Hurwitz, Ben, *497*
Hussein, Saddam, 747–748
Hutcheson, William, 433, 446
Hutton, Barbara, Woolworth and, 448
Hyde, Henry, 780

I Am a Fugitive from a Chain Gang, 457, *458*
Iacocca, Lee, 693
Ickes, Harold, 395, 402, 460, 522
ILGWU (International Ladies' Garment Workers Union), 226
Illinois Bureau of Labor, 101
Immigrants. *See also specific group, i.e.* Chinese Americans, Mexican Americans
AFL unions and, 158
"Americanization" programs for, 173–174
in armed forces in WWI, 295
baseball and, 188
children of, in white-collar jobs, 193
differing photographic views of, *212*
early 20th century, barriers to participation of, 201
female
in garment industry sweatshops, 224
in workforce in early 20th century, 196
industrialization and, 30–31
Knights of Labor and, 91–92, 94, 96, 108
liberalized policy on, 622
literacy rates for, 190
as miners, 232
nativism and, 146–149
new, in 1880s-1890s, 144–146
in New South, 50
in 1970 and 1980s, 715–720
politics and, in late 1800's, 103
pre-WWI, political radicalism and, 288–290
Proposition 187 and, 767–768
reformers and, *215*
sentiment against, in 1920s, 321–323
settlement houses and, 213–214
Socialism and, 228
in steel mills, three generations of, *447*
upward mobility of, Prohibition and, 357–359
urban, neighborhood cultures of, 78–80
urban unemployment increase and, 584–585
vaudeville and, 186
war-time labor market and, 276–277
western mining and, 66
in workforce
discrimination against, in Great Depression, 373–375
in WWII, 507
during WWI, suspicion of, 293–294
Immigration, restriction of, nativism and, 146–149
Immigration Act
of 1924, 322
of 1965, 622
Immigration Restriction League, 148
Imperialism, European, U.S. prosperity and, 266–267
Income taxes, federal, 273–274
in Reagan era, 710
revision of, in 1986, 729
Independence Day celebrations, 86–87
Indian Allotment Act of 1887, 57
Indian Reorganization Act of 1934, 404
Indians, American
Centennial Exposition and, 12
New Deal and, 403–404
in 1920s, conflicts over, 359
politics and, in late 1800's, 103
rights movements among, in 1960s, 661–662
in WWII, 503
Indochina, Japanese seizure of, 493
Industrial accidents, 35–37
Industrial armies, 124–125, 161
Industrial capitalism. *See also* Capitalism
progressivism and, 212
work force and, 69, 75–117
Industrial unionism
AFL and, 432, 446
legacies of, 476–477
rise of, 443–448
Industrial Workers of the World (IWW), 199, 229–232
class struggle and, 234
Mexican-Americans in, 285
opposition to WWI, 268–269
radical protests by, during WWI, 290–292
Industrialization
bureaucratic growth and, 29–30
human costs of, 207
immigration and, 30–31
middle class growth and, 29
power sources and, 28
small business ownership and, 27
social impact of, 27–32
social stratification and, 27
urban growth and, 29
Industry(ies)
extractive, 64–68
growth of, Republican Party and, 21
railroad expansion and, 24–25
wartime boom for, 505–507
Inflation
in 1970s, 684
post-WWII, 534
Injunctions, 125
Inland Steel, 465
Insurance
health, industrial conflicts over, 763–764
old-age, 428
International Association of Machinists, growth of, 274
International Brotherhood of Teamsters
in Alliance for Labor Action, 671
growth of, 412
rapid, 446
Hoffa and, corruption and, 579

Mafia influence on, *580*
Minneapolis strike and, 409–410
transformation of, in 1990s, 772
International Business Machines (IBM), 749, 755
International Harvester
Americanization program of, 174, 200
overseas expansion of, 150
International Ladies' Garment Workers' Union (ILGWU), 226
Labor Stage of, 457
rebuilding of, NIRA and, 406
Rose Pesotta in, 407
International Longshoremen and Warehousemen's Union (ILWU), formation of, 412
International Longshoremen's Association (ILA)
Mafia influence on, *580*
San Francisco strike and, 411
International Monetary Fund (IMF), 741
Asian financial crisis and, 762, *763*
International Telephone and Telegraph, overseas communication and, 320–321
International Unemployment Day, 388
Internationalism in WWII, 487–490
Internet, 754–755
Interstate and Defense Highway Program, 575
Interstate Commerce Act of 1887, 24, 46
Interstate Commerce Commission, establishment of, 46
Investment bankers
Civil War and, 21
railroad expansion and, 25
IQ tests in army in WWI, segregation and, 295–296
Iran
hostage crisis in, 697
illegal arms sales to, 730
revolution in, 696–697
Iran-Contra affair, 730
Iraq, war with, 747–749
Irish Americans
as domestic servants, 81
enclosure conflicts in Texas and, 111
industrialization and, 31
Knights of Labor and, 94
post-Civil War labor market and, 33
"Iron Curtain" speech, 548–549
Irwin, Clarence, 407–408
Islam, Nation of, 628
Isolationism in WWII, 486–487, 489
Italo-American Building and Loan Association in Great Depression, 386
Italy, Benito Mussolini in, 484–485
Ivory Soap
advertising of, 180
Crisco and, 167
Iwo Jima, U.S. conquest of, 525
IWW. *See* Industrial Workers of the World (IWW)

J. Edgar Thompson Steelworks, 43
Jackson, Henry, 574, 698
Jackson, Jesse, 728–729
Jackson, Mahalia, 582
Jackson, Michael, 733
Jackson State University, antiwar demonstration at, 654
James, Jesse, 111
Japan
atomic bombs dropped on, 526
expansion of, 483–484
offensive of, in Pacific, 493–494
surrender of, in WWII, 525–528
war declared on, by U.S. and Great Britain, 493
Japanese Americans
AFL and, 159
internment of, U.S. Supreme Court on, 514–515
U.S. treatment of, in WWII, 512–515
western agriculture and, 66
Jaworski, Leon, 676
Jazz, emergence of, 352
Jazz Age, 315
Jefferson, Pete, 694–695
Jeffrey, Millie, 511
Jehovah's Witnesses in WWII, 511–512
Jews
anti-Communist crusade and, 567
Eastern European, as immigrants, 144
prejudice against in U.S. in WWII, 511
"Jim Crow" laws, 139–144
Job Corps, 623
Job segregation by gender, 588
Joblessness. *See* Unemployment
Jobs, Steve, 755
Jobs program, expanded, 425–427
John Birch Society, 673
Johnson, Andrew, 3–5, 8
Johnson, Glenora, 442
Johnson, Hugh, 401
Johnson, Jack, 186
Johnson, Lyndon Baines
AFL-CIO and, 667
election of, 620
"Great Society" of, 541, 621–622
Gulf of Tonkin Resolution and, 636
liberal agenda of, 618, 619–622
school aid bill of, 622
Vietnam policy of, Tet Offensive and, 649
"War on Poverty" of, 619
Johnson-Reed Act (1924), 322
Jolson, Al, 353
Jones, Paula, 780
Jonestown mass suicide, 777
Joyce, Barb, 772
Judiciary, business power and, 46
Juvenile delinquency, 511, 599–601

Kansas, 133
Keith, Benjamin Franklin, 186
Kelley, Florence, 127, 129, 221, 222
Kellogg-Briand Pact of 1928, 320
Kellor, Frances, 219
Kennan, George F., 548, 745
Kennedy, John Fitzgerald
AFL-CIO and, 667
in anti-Communist probes, 565
assassination of, 618–619
on civil rights issues, 617
Cuban missile crisis and, 634
desegregation bill and, 618
election of, 617
inauguration of, 607
motivation of, in Vietnam conflict, 635–636
as Senator, Hoffa and, 579
War of Poverty of, 622–625
Kennedy, Robert
assassination of, 651
FBI wiretaps on civil rights movement and, 617
as presidential candidate in 1968, 650
as Senator, Hoffa and, 579
Kent State University, antiwar demonstration at, 654
Kerouac, Jack, 598
Kerr-McGee, 659–660
Keynes, John Maynard, 473, 573, 690
Khomeini, Ayatollah Ruhollah, 697
King, Martin Luther, Jr.
assassination of, 651
in Birmingham civil rights protests, 616
"I have a dream" speech of, 617
in Montgomery bus boycott, 611
SCLC campaign in Chicago and, 628
King, Rodney, 775–776
Kirkland, Lane, 770
Kirkpatrick, Jeane, 709
Kissinger, Henry, 655, 695
Knights of Labor, 75, 90–103
AFL and, 106–107
breach between craft unions and, 106
in Brooklyn, NY, 92
child labor and, 222
decline of, 101–103
defeats suffered by, significance of, 161
eight-hour movement and, 97–101
equality and, 91–96

growth of, 91, *93*
importance of, 97
membership composition of, in 1880s and 1890s, 108
origins of, 90–91
patronage and, 106
producing classes and, 96
reading rooms of, 89
services provided by, 97
temperance efforts of, 87
White Caps and, 111
Knox, Frank, 490
Koch, Edward, 706–707
Korean War, 554–555
armistice in, 568
Korematsu v. U.S., 514
Koresh, David, 778
Kosovo, U.S. involvement in, 762
Kovacs, Janos, 146
Ku Klux Klan Act, 9
Ku Klux Klan (KKK)
murder of civil rights workers by, 619–620
origins of, 8, 9
post-WWI resurgence of, 305
President Grant and, 9
rise of
in late 1930s, 472
in 1920s, 356–357
Kuwait, Iraqi invasion of, 747–748

La Follette, Phil, 419
La Follette, Robert
labor reform and, 221
opposition to WWI, 268
as presidential candidate, 318–319
farmer support of, 344
reform and, 237
on Roosevelt, 242
La Follette, Robert M., Jr., 419
Labor. *See also* Workforce
anti-Communism polarizing, 565
attack on, in 1938, 471–472
backlash against, New Deal and, 463–467
child, 34–35
banning of, by Fair Labor Standards Act, 429
legislation on, 222–223
convict, 227
in democratization of America, 425–479
Great Uprising of, of 1877, 13–15
immigrant, 30–31, 32
losses of, during Cold War, 555–559
and management, accord between, in late 1940s, 576
in New Left, 641–642
organized. *See also* Union(s)
decline of, in 1920s, 345–347
revival of, in Great Depression, 404–407
problems of, during WWII, 520–522
railroad system and, 22
Sherman Antitrust Act and, 158
wartime gains for, 274–276
Wilson and, 245–246
Labor movement
African Americans and, 279–280
anti-Communism polarizing, 565
beginnings of, 88–90
business, 107–108
civil rights and, 669
Clinton support by, 773
corruption of, 579–581
craft unions in, 75
breach between Knights of Labor and, 106
labor defeats in 1892 and, 114
resurgence of (1897–1904), 158–160
decline of, in 1920s, 345–347
environmental movement and, 658–659
Ford Motor Company and, 199
foremen and, 445
garment industry, 226
Great Depression and, 404–407
growth of
1940–1941, 490–491
in late 1930s, 446
Wagner Act and, 431–432
during WWII, 521
in Hollywood, 459
industrial unions in
AFL and, 432, 446
legacies of, 476–477
rise of, 443–448
interracial, 462–463
mass picketing by, 490–491
membership in, in late 1800s, *103*
mortgage underwriting by, 327
National Recovery Administration and, 401–402
in 1980s, 724–728
NIRA Section 7a and, 405–406
Operation Dixie and, 558–559
postwar economic boom and, 573–574
post-war political strategy of, 558
post-WWII agenda of, 530, 532–534
public-sector, growth and impact of, 668
reading rooms of, 191
Reaganomics and, 724
rebellious rank and file in, 667–671
revitalization of, in 1990s, 770–774
seniority system of, African Americans and, 463
Socialists and, 228
strikes by. *See* Strike(s)
Students for a Democratic Society and, 641–642
"sweetheart" deals of, 579, *580*
Taft-Hartley Act and, 556–557
trade, Clinton health care reform and, 765
Truman supported by, in 1948, 560
Vietnam War and, 670–671
women in
new, 448–452
in WWII, 511
women's auxiliaries of, 448–451
WWI and, 274
Labor reform, 221–223
Land ownership
freedpeople and, 2, 3, 7
Plains Indians and, 54–55
Landers, Ann, 715
Landis, Kenesaw Mountain, 338
Landon, Alfred M., 435
Landsdowne, Helen, 168
Lange, Dorothea, 455
Lansing, Robert, 266
Laos
immigrants from, in Wausau, WI, 718
pro-Western government of, collapse of, 634
Larsen, Nella, 352
Las Gorras Blancas, 110–111
Lathrop, Julia, 223
Latin America
economic expansion in, 154–155
raw material exploitation in, in 1920s, 321
Lawrence, David, 574
Lawrence (MA), textile strike in, 230–231
Leadville (CO), 65
League of Nations, 301
America and, 319
Germany's withdrawal from, 485
World Court of, U.S. and, 486
Leahy, William, 527
Lear, Norman, 672
Lease, Mary Elizabeth, 130, *131*
Legislation
child labor, 222–223
racial, 139–144
Leisure time in early 20th century, 182
Lemke, William, 435
Lemlich, Clara, 224, *225*
Lend-Lease program, 488
Lenin, V. I., 288, 298–299
Lesbianism. *See also* Homosexuality
WWII and, 501, 509
Lester, Richard, 579

Levitt, William, 592, 593, 594
Levittowns, 592, 593
Lewinsky, Monica, 780
Lewis, John L., 669
  health and pension fund for UMW and, 596
  industrial unionism and, 433
  Little Steel formula and, 521–522
  as Nashville sit-in leader, 612
  on Roosevelt's repudiation of steel workers, 467
  support of, for Roosevelt in 1936, 434–435
  UMW rebirth and, 406
  on William Green, 346
  Willkie endorsed by, 489
Lewis, Sinclair, 353, 457
Leyte Gulf, Battle of, 525
Liberty Bonds in WWII, 504
Liberty League, Landon and, 435
Libraries, public, working class and, 189–191
Life of Riley, The, 597, 598
Life style. *See* Daily life
Liliuokalani (Queen), 153
Lincoln Brigade, 488
Lindbergh, Charles A., 489
Lippman, Walter, 545
Literacy rates, early 20th century, 189–190
Literacy requirements for voting, 237–238
Lithuanian Dollar Savings in Great Depression, 386
Little Ceasar, 457
Little Richard, 600–601
Little Rock (AR), school desegregation confrontation in, 609
Lloyd, Henry Demarest, 137
Loans, low-interest, suburban development and, 592
Lobbying, big business and, 158
Local reform politics, 234–237
Lochner v. New York, 222
Locke, Alain, 350, 352
Lockheed Corporation, federal help for, 693
Lodge, Henry Cabot, 140
Loew, Marcus, 187–188
London, Meyer, 290
Long, Huey, 416–417, 435
Longworth, Alice Roosevelt, 316, 317
Looking Backward (Bellamy), 228
López, Damacio, 63–64
Lorenzo, Frank, 727
Loriks, Emil, 389
Los Angeles (CA)
  Latino immigrants in, 715–716
  race riots in, 520
Los Angeles County, Mexican immigrants in, 584
Los Angeles Police Department (LAPD)
  O. J. Simpson trial and, 776
  Rodney King beating and, 776
  Watts riots and, 627
Louis, Joe, 582
Lovett, Robert, 554
Loyal (Union) Leagues, 5–6
Luce, Henry, 547
Ludlow (CO), strike/massacre at, 232–234
Lumber industry
  in Pacific Northwest, 65
  White Caps and, 111
Luscomb, Florence, 449–450
Lusitania affair, 266
Lynch, Peter, 713
Lynchings
  increase in, in Great Depression, 375
  late 19th century, 141–142
Lynd, Robert and Helen, 327–328, 328–329, 334

MacArthur, Douglas
  in Korean War, 554
  in Pacific campaign, 495
  veterans' Bonus March and, 392
MacMahon, Douglas Lincoln, 408
Macune, Charles, 130, 132–133, 134
Madonna, 733
Mafia influence on unions, *580*
Mailer, Norman, 598
Mail-order houses, turnover and, 181
Malaya, Japanese seizure of, 493
Malcolm X, 628, *629, 631*
Malkiel, Theresa, 225–226
Management
  and labor, accord between, in late 1940s, 576
  scientific, 170–173
Management systems, new, 41–43
Manchuria, invasion of, by Japan, 484
Mandela, Nelson, 747
Manhattan Project, 526–527
Manufacturers, market control efforts by, 38
Manufacturing
  assembly line and, 198
  in 1920s, shifts in, 323–324
  women in, in early 20th century, 195
Mao Zedong, 484
Marathon Oil, USX Corp. and, 724
March on Washington, 517
"March on Washington for Jobs and Freedom," 616–617
Marketing
  early 20th century, ethnicity and, 168–169
  market segmentation in, 181
  to masses, 179–182
Marshall, George, 550
Marshall, Thurgood, 459–460, 516, 608
Marshall Plan, 550
Martin, John J., 305
Marx Brothers, 457
Marxism, 227–228
Maryland State Employment Service, discrimination by, 517
Mass culture. *See* American culture
Mass media, New Deal and, 452–459
Mass merchandising, 181
Mass production, 169–170
  Taylorism and, 171–172
Masses
  autos for, in 1920s, 329–333
  entertainment for, in early 20th century, 185–188
  marketing to
    advertising media development and, 180–181
    early 20th century daily life and, 179–182
  uplifting, in early 20th century, 188–192
Mathews, Mary, 82
McCain, Franklin, 612
McCarthy, Eugene, 650
McCarthy, Joseph, 541, 564–567, 568
McCarthy, Patrick Henry, 107, 108
McCarthyism, 541
  decline in, 568–570
McClellan, John, 579
McCloy, John J., 488
McCormick, Cyrus, 43
McCormick Harvesting Machine Company/McCormick Reaper Works
  eight-hour day protest at, 98
  technology in strike prevention at, 43
  workforce size at, 170
McDonald, Leonidies, 466
McDonald's, work opportunities at, 720, *721*
McFadden, Don, 505
McFarlane, Robert, 730
McGlynn, Father Edward, 105
McGovern, George, 673
McKee Rocks (PA), steelworker strike in, 230
McKinley, William, 137, 142, 239
McNary-Haugen bill, 343–344
McNeil, Joe, 612
McNeill, George, 97
McPherson, Aimee Semple, 355
McVeigh, Timothy, 778
Meany, George, 579, 669, 670
Meat Inspection Act, 241
Media, mass, New Deal and, 452–459

Mediation of disputes, National Civic Federation and, 160
Medicaid, 621–622
Medicare, 621
Mellon, Andrew, 316, 318, 361, 368
Memorial Day Massacre, 465–466
Mencken, H. L., 353
Merchandising, mass, turnover and, 181
Meredith, James, 617
Mergers, 157
  in 1990s, 752
Metal mining and smelting, 65
Mexican Americans
  discrimination against, in employment in Great Depression, 373–374
  enclosure conflicts and, 110–111
  as farm laborers, UFW grape boycott and, 631–633
  growth of, in 1960s, 660–661
  influx of, during WWI, 282–286
  language barriers to jobs and, 585
  as migrant workers in 1920s, 344
  migration of, to Los Angeles County, 584
  post-Civil War labor market and, 33
  race riots against, 520
  school protests by, 661
  strikes by, in California commercial agriculture, 412–413
  western agriculture and, 66
  western boom of 1870s and, 63–64
  western mining and, 65, 66
  in WWII, 503
Mexican Revolution, 282–283
Mexico
  economic bailout of, 762
  immigration from, in 1920s, 322
Miami (FL), immigrant population of, in 1980s, 716–717
Michel, Robert, 767
Michigan, influx into, during WWII, 506
Microsoft, 754–755
Middle class
  antiwar movement based in, 643
  in early 20th century
    socializing of, 191–192
    values of, 192–194
  in Great Depression, 380
  progressivism and, 210–211
  in Reagan era, 713–714
Middle East, détente and, 696
Midwifery in 1920s, 340–341
Migrant laborers, UFW grape boycott and, 633
Militancy of labor movement, 668–671
Militarism preceding WWII, 483–486
Military buildup during WWI, 269
Military establishment
  peacetime, postwar economic boom and, 574–575
  spending on, in 1970s, economic problems from, 686–687
Milk, Harvey, 707
Milken, Michael, 713
"Million-Man March," 776–777
Mills, C. Wright, 587
Mills, Florence, 352
Milosevic, Slobodan, 762
Milwaukee (WI), demonstrations of unemployed in, in Great Depression, 388
Mine, Mill, and Smelter Workers' Union, United Steel Workers and, 559
Mine Safety and Health Administration, 660
Minh, Ho Chi, 551, 634, 636
Mining
  decline in, in 1920s, 346
  metal, 65
  Mine Safety and Health Administration and, 660
  working conditions in, 35–36
Minneapolis (MN), strike in (1934), 409–411, 412
Mississippi, Freedom Schools in, 619
Mississippi Freedom Democratic Party (MFDP) at 1964 Democratic National Convention, 620
Mitchell, Charles E., 324
Mitchell, John, 152
Model T Ford, standardization and, 197–198
Molotov, Vyacheslav, 496
Mondale, Walter, 729
"Monetarist" policies, Volcker's, 694
Monroe Doctrine, Roosevelt Corollary to, 154
Montgomery, Robert, 457
Montgomery (AL)
  bus boycott in, 611–612
  civil rights movement born in, 609
Montgomery Ward
  foreign expansion of, 320
  growth of, 157
  turnover and, 181
Moore, Dave, 391
Moral capitalism, expectations of, in Great Depression, 385–386
Moral Majority, 703
  disbanding of, 733
Morgan, J. P.
  coal strike in 1902 and, 240
  monetary crisis of 1893 and, 137
  National Civic Federation and, 160
  U.S. Steel creation by, 157
  WWI orders for American goods and, 265
Morgenthau, Henry, Jr., 415
Mortimer, Wyndham, 407
Moscone, George, 706–707, 707
"Mothers on the March" (MOM), *705*
"Motor-Voter" Bill, 760
"Movement culture" of populism, 133
Movies
  daily life and, 187
  mass culture and, 336–338
  postwar, cultural impact of, 601
Moynihan, Daniel Patrick, 657
"Muckrakers," 210
Muller v. Oregon, 222
Muncie (IN), 177
Munich agreement, 486
Municipal housekeeping in Progressive Era, 213–216
Murphy, Frank, 385, 441, 442, 515
Murray, Charles, 711
Murray, Philip
  anti-discrimination policy of, 462
  on classless society, 575
  on industry councils, 530
  on National Defense Mediation Board, 491
  on post-WWII strikes, 532
  Roosevelt and, 466–467
  on U.S. participation in war, 489
Music
  counterculture of 1960s and, 646
  in 1980s, 733–734
  rhythm-and-blues, 600
  rock-and-roll, cultural impact of, 600–601
Music Project, Federal, 454–455
Music Television (MTV), 733–734
Mussolini, Benito, 484–485
My Lai massacre, 638, 640
Myrdal, Gunnar, 516

NAACP. *See* National Association for the Advancement of Colored People (NAACP)
Nagasaki, Japan, atomic bombing of, 526
NAM. *See* National Association of Manufacturers (NAM)
Namibia, independence of, 747
Nation of Islam, 628
National American Woman Suffrage Association (NAWSA), 219
  opposition to WWI, 268
National Association for the Advancement of Colored People (NAACP), 144
  army during WWI and, 295
  in civil rights leadership, 609
  educational segregation and, 459–460
  founding of, 238

growth of
in 1920s, 349
during WWII, 516
Roosevelt and, 436–437
Scottsboro case and, 376
union movement and, 461
National Association of Manufacturers (NAM), 160, 555
Landon and, 435
National Association of Real Estate Boards, 561
National Biscuit Company, advertising of, 181
National Brotherhood Workers of America, 280
National Child Labor Committee, 223
National Civic Federation (NCF), 160, 275
National Consumers' League (NCL), women's working conditions and, 222
National Defense Mediation Board, 491
North American Aviation strike and, 492
National Economic Council, 760
National Housing Act of 1949, 562
National Industrial Recovery Act (NIRA), 398, 401–402
Section 7a of, 405–407
striking down of, 431
National Labor Board (NLB), establishment of, 407
National Labor Relations Act, 431–432. *See also* Wagner Act
National Labor Relations Board (NLRB)
attack on, 472
elections of, Taft-Hartley Act and, 557
establishment of, 431–432
reform efforts on, 692
"unfair labor practices" enforcement by, 725
National Liberation Front, 649
National Negro Congress (NNC), 461
National Organization for Women (NOW), 662–663
National politics, reform of, 239–243
National Recovery Administration (NRA), 401–402
criticism of, 415
National Security Council (NSC), 655
covert aid to Contras and, 730
National Socialism, 485
National Welfare Rights Organization (NWRO), 624
National Woman's Party (NWP), 287
National Woman's Suffrage Association, 11, 219
National Youth Administration, 426
Nationalism, pre-WWI, 260, 262
Native Americans. *see* Indians, American
Nativism
immigration restriction and, 146–149
during WWI, 292–294
Navajo
as marine "code talkers," 503
protests against Peabody Coal Co., 661
NAWSA. *See* National American Woman Suffrage Association (NAWSA)
Nazis
attrocities committed by, in WWII, 523–524
and Soviets, nonaggression pact between, 486
Nazism, 485
NCF. *See* National Civic Federation (NCF)
NCL. *See* National Consumers' League (NCL)
Nearing, Scott and Helen, 387
Nebraska
Alliance and 1890 election results in, 133
"movement culture" of populism in, 133
"Negro Removal Act," 436
Nehru, Jawaharlal, 551–552
Neibuhr, Reinhold
on capitalism, 385–386
socialism denounced by, 490
Neighborhoods, late-19th century
culture of, 76–80
rural, importance of, 79
Nelson, Donald, 504
Netherlands, German invasion of, 486
Neutrality Acts, 486–487
Roosevelt and public opinion against, 488
New Almaden Quicksilver Mine, 65
New Deal
first, 392–419
agricultural supports in, 398–400
collapse of, 415–416
financial rescue and emergency in, 396–398
for Indians, 404
industrial codes in, 400–402
new union leaders and, 407–408
organized labor revival and, 404–407
populist critics of, 416–419
Roosevelt's promise of, 392–396
in South, 402–403
strikes during, 408–414
in West, 403–404
second, 425–477
African American struggle for equal rights and, 459–463
African Americans and, 437
Associated Farmers opposition to, 463
backlash against labor and, 463–467
Committee for Industrial Organization and, 432–434
defeat of, in South, 467–469
end of, 490–492
expanded jobs program in, 425–427
Flint sit-down strike and, 439–443
industrial unionism in, 443–448
labor division in, 471–472
legacies of, 476–477
popular culture and, 452–459
public art and, 453–454
right-wing mobilization against, 463–464
Roosevelt landslide and, 434–439
Social Security Act in, 427–429
Wagner Act and, *430,* 431–432
women and, 448–452
suburban development and, 591–592
"New Economic Policy" (NEP), Nixon's, 691
New England Telephone and Telegraph, 373
New Era (1920s), 315–364. *See also* 1920s
"New Freedom," 244–247
New Left
Black Power and, 645
cultural impact of, 645–649
international, 644
in 1960s, 641–645
women's movement of 1960s and, 663
New Mexico, conflicts over enclosure in, 110–111
"New Nationalism," 244
New Right
leaders of, 706
rise of, 698–700
New York and New Jersey Telephone Company, 179
New York (city)
African-American population in, 278
Central Labor Union of, 89, 105
demonstrations of unemployed in, in Great Depression, 388
immigrant population of, in 1990s, 716
indoor plumbing in, in 1908, 177
Police Board of, 240
Puerto Rican migration to, 584
rapid growth of, 29
New York City Police Board, Theodore Roosevelt on, 240
New York Consumers' League, 227
New York Society for the Suppression of Vice, 84
New York's Central Labor Union, 105

Newman, Pauline, 223
Newspapers, "underground," 646
Nez Percé, 55
Niagara Movement, 144
Nicaragua
civil war in, movement against intervention in, 730
Contras in, covert aid to, 730
free elections in, 747
guerrilla movement in, 696
U.S. occupation of, 321
Nichols, Terry, 778
"Nickelodeons," 187
Nimitz, Chester, 495
1920s
advertising in, 333–334
African-American life in, 347–353
agriculture in crisis in, 342–344
autos for masses in, 329–333
business in, 318–319
conservatism in, 316–317
cultural conflicts in, 353–359
customer creation in, 333–334
daily life in new consumer culture of, 327–329
demographic changes in, 323–324
economic growth and instability in, 324–326
Hoover in, 360–361
manufacturing shifts in, 323–324
mass culture in, 334–338
organized labor decline in, 345–347
overseas business expansion in, 319–323
political corruption in, 316–317
stock market crash in, 361
women in, as workers and consumers, 338–42
Nineteenth Amendment, 217
passage of, 288
Nitze, Paul, 554
Nixon, E. D., 611
Nixon, Richard Milhous
administration of, 654–657
in anti-Communist probes, 565
China and, 655
economy and, 691
election of, 653–654
"New Economic Policy" of, 691
as presidential candidate, 651–652
reelection campaign of, 673–674
resignation of, 676
"southern strategy" of, 655
Soviet Union and, 655
as vice-president, election of, 568
Vietnam peace plan of, 654
Watergate and, 674–676
NLRB. *See* National Labor Relations Board (NLRB)
Nobel Peace Prize for Sadat and Begin, 696
Noble and Holy Order of the Knights of Labor, 90–97. *See also* Knights of Labor
Non-Partisan League, 343
Noriega, Manuel, 747
Normandy (France), invasion of, 522
Norris, George, 268
North, civil rights improvements in, in WWII, 518
North, Oliver, 730
North American Aviation, strike broken at, 491–492
North American Free Trade Agreement (NAFTA), 758, 762
North American Woman Suffrage Association (NAWSA), 287
North Atlantic Treaty Organization (NATO), creation of, 550–551
North Carolina, Farmers' Alliance in, 131–132
Northern Pacific Railroad
Jay Cooke & Co. and, 25
married women in, in Great Depression, 373
Northern Securities Company, prosecution of, 240
Northerners, Reconstruction and, 8
Norway, German invasion of, 486
Nowicki, Stella, 449
NSC-68, 554
Nuclear arms race, 552, 554
Nuclear "brinksmanship," 569–570
Nuclear power, protests against, 687–688
Nursing, women in, 196

Occupational Safety and Health Act (OSHA)
attempts to undermine, 660
passage of, 659
Occupational Safety and Health Administration (OSHA) in Reagan administration, 710
O'Connor, Sandra Day, 730
Odets, Clifford, 457
Office of Economic Opportunity (OEO), 624
abolition of, 656
Office of Price Administration (OPA), 504
post-WWII fate of, 531
Oglala Sioux protest at Wounded Knee, *661*, 662
Oil, Chemical, and Atomic Workers' Union (OCAW), 659
Oil embargo/shortage, 684–685
Okinawa
Battle of, *499*
U.S. conquest of, 525
Oklahoma City Federal Building bombing, 778
Old-age insurance, 428
Olin Corporation, safety issues at, 659
Oliver, Alphonse, 278
Olmsted, Frederick Law, 191
Olney, Richard C., 125, 128
Olson, Culbert, 464
Olympic Games, 1980 Summer, boycott of, 697
Omaha (NE), People's Party convention in, 133–134
"Open Door" policy, 155–156
"Open shop"
drive for
in 1920s, 345
in Progressive Era, 232
National Association of Manufacturers and, 160
"Operation Bootstrap," 582–584
Operation Dixie, 558–559
Organization of Petroleum Exporting Countries (OPEC), 684
Oswald, Lee Harvey, 618–619
Other America, The, 622–623
Outcault, Richard, 150
"Outsourcing," foreign, 689
Overproduction preceding Great Depression, 326
Overseas expansion, 149–156
Oxnard (CA), farm labor strike in, AFL and, 159

Pacific, U.S. and British cooperation in, 488–489
Pacific Theater, WWII
Japan offensive in, 493–494
U.S. strategies in, 494–495
Packinghouse Workers' Union, Vietnam War and, 671
Pahlavi, Shah Reza, 696–697
Palestinian "homeland," Carter and, 696
Palmer, A. Mitchell, 306–307
Pan-Africanism, 349–351
Panama, U.S. intervention in, 747
Panama Canal, building of, 154
Parent-Teachers Association (PTA), 307
Paris, Treaty of, 152
Parker, Alton B., 241
Parks, Larry, 563
Parks, Rosa, 609–611
Parsons, Albert, 98, 100
Pasquinelli, Bruno, 694
Paterson (NJ), silk workers' strike in, 231–232
Patronage, Knights of Labor and, 106
Patrons of Husbandry, 129
Patterson, John, 235
Paul, Alice, 287, *289*

Payne-Aldrich Tariff, 243
Peabody Coal Company, American Indian protests against, 661
Peace treaty, Versailles, 300–301
Pearl Harbor, attack on, 493
Pendergast, Tom, 524
Pendleton Civil Service Act, 45, 46
Pennsylvania Railroad
- Andrew Carnegie and, 39
- strike at, 13–14

People's (Populist) Party
- decline of, 138
- defeats suffered by, significance of, 161
- Farmers' Alliance and, 129–135
- first convention of, 133–134
- fusion of, with Democratic Party, 237
- platform of, 133–134
- White Caps and, 111

Perestroika, 742
Perkins, Frances, 227, 395, 427, 448, 451
Perot, Ross, 758, 759
Pershing, John Joseph, 296
Persian Gulf War, 747–749
Pesotta, Rose, 407
Peyton Place, 590
Philadelphia (PA)
- Centennial Exposition in, 10–12
- rapid growth of, 29

"Philadelphia Plan," 657
Philanthropy
- libraries and, 189–191
- parks and, 191

Philippines
- acquisition of, 152
- Japanese seizure of, 493
- reconquest of, from Japan, 525
- in Spanish-American-Cuban War, 151

Phonograph records, mass culture and, 336
Photojournalism, New Deal and, 455
Picketing, mass, by unions, 490–491
Pillsbury, packaged product development by, 175
Pinchot, Gifford, 243
Pingree, Hazen, 236
Pittsburgh (PA)
- unemployment in, in Great Depression, 371
- Voters' League of, reform and, *236*

Plains
- agricultural expansion in, 54
- life on, 61–62

Plains Indians
- assimilation attempts and, 56–59
- buffalo slaughter and, 55–56
- white settlers and, 54–55

Plantation system, black landownership and, 3
Platt Amendment of 1901, 154
Playboy magazine, 589–590
Plessy, Homer, 139
Plessy v. Ferguson, 139, 459
Pluralism
- in American life in 1960s, 660–662
- in WWII, limits of, 511–515

Podhoretz, Norman, 598–599
Poland
- partition of, by Germany, 486
- Solidarity in, 742

Police forces, brutality of, 585
Political Action Committee of CIO, 556
Political activity, freedpeople and, 5–6
Political polarization in sixties, 671–672
Political power
- of big business, increased, in 1920s, 316
- labor defeats in 1892 and, 114

Political radicalism during WWI, 288–292
Political reformers, 212
Politics
- businessmen and, 43–46
- corruption in, in 1920s, 316–317
- electoral, Farmers' Alliance and, 133
- gender, 703–708
- reform of
  - local/state, 234–237
  - national, 239–243
- stagflation, 690–695
- workingman and, 103–106

Polk, Leonidas, 133
Pollock, Jackson, *547*
Popular Front, 452–453
- attack on, 472

Populism, "movement culture" of, 133
Populist Party. *See* People's (Populist) Party
Port Huron Statement of SDS, 1962, 641
Porter, Lavinia, 62
Postal employees, militancy of, 668
Potsdam, Germany, meeting in, 528
Poverty, increase in, in 1980s, 720–724
Powderly, Terence V., 87, 91, 94–95
Powell, Adam Clayton, Jr., 460–461
Power
- political. *See also* Political power
- sources of, industrialization and, 28

"Prague Spring," 644
Prentis, H.W., 555
Presley, Elvis, 600
Press censorship during WWI, 292
Prinčip, Gavrilo, 260
Prisons as growth industry, 724
Procter and Gamble Company (P&G)
- advertising by, 180
- Crisco introduction by, daily life and, 167
- packaged product development by, 175

Production
- mass, 169–170
- system of, new, prosperity and, 167

Professional Air Traffic Controllers Organization (PATCO), Reagan and, 726–727
Profit-sharing plan, Ford and, 199–200
Progressive Era, 207–251
- anarchists in, 228–229
- factory reform in, 221–223
- garment industry and, 224–227
- high point of, 243–247
- labor conditions and, 221–223
- local/state reform politics and, 234–237
- Marxists in, 227–228
- militant communities in, 229–234
- modern state and, 247–248
- municipal housekeeping in, 213–216
- national political reform and, 239–243
- political participation and, 237–239
- social settlements in, 213–216
- Socialists in, 227–228
- spelling reform and, 209–212
- woman suffrage and, 219–221
- women's political culture in, 216–219
- working women's activism in, 224–227

Progressive Party
- labor reform and, 221
- new, formation of, 559
- in 1912 election, 208
- revival of, in 1935, 419
- Roosevelt in, 244
- Wilson and, 269–270

Progressivism, 208–209
Prohibition, 294
- conflicts over, 357–359
- homosexuality and, 353–355
- presidential election of 1928 and, 360–361
- repeal of, 397

Promise Keepers, 777
Proposition 13, 702
Proposition 187, 767, *768*
Proposition 226, union opposition to, 773
Protestantism, post-Civil War, 82–85
Pruette, Lorine, 338
Public Enemy, 457
Public housing, failure of, 595
Public ownership of public utilities, 235
Public utilities, public ownership of, 235
Public Works Administration (PWA), 402–403
- African Americans and, 437
- women and, 451

Puerto Ricans
- language barriers to jobs and, 585

migration of, to mainland cities, 582–584
Young Lords and, 661
Puerto Rico, acquisition of, 152
Pulitzer, Joseph, 150
Pullman, George, 127, 129
Pullman (IL), depression of 1890s and, 125–127
Pullman Palace Car Company
Brotherhood of Sleeping Car Porters and, 347
strike against, 125–129
defeat of, significance of, 161
government reaction to, 128–129
magnitude of, 127–128
rise of People's Party and, 129
Pure Food and Drug Act, 241
Puyallup tribe protests, 661
PWA. *See* Public Works Administration (PWA)
Pyle, Ernie, 497–498

Qaddafi, Muammar, 747
Quaker, packaged product development by, 175
Quartermaster Corps, African Americans in, 501
Quayle, J. Danforth, 746
Quill, Mike, 434
Quota Act of 1921, 322

Race riots, post-WWI, 305
Racial discrimination, postwar arrivals in cities and, 585
Racial legislation, 139–144
Racial violence
urban, in 1960s, 626–630
in WWII, 519–520
Racism. *See also* Civil rights movement; Racial violence
AFL and, 109, 159
Centennial Exposition and, 11–12
in Depression, 373–375
in employment
in early 1900s, 194
in New South, 49–50
in 1920s, 348
in federal service in early 1900s, 244–245
Ford Motor Company and, 200
"Great Migration" and, 279–281
in housing, 519
in housing in 1920s, 327
during Jim Crow era, 139–144
KKK and, 8–9, 315, 356
in labor movement in 1880s, 92, 94, 96
in military in WWI, 295–296
in 1920s, immigration restrictions and, 322
post-WWI, 305
in public entertainment in early 1990s, 185, 186, 188
rise of, in late 19th century, 140–142
suburban development and, 594–595
Radical Reconstruction, 5–7
Radical Republicans, Black Codes and, 4
Radicalism, political
in Great Depression, 387–391
repression of, after WWI, 306–307
during WWI, 288–292
Radio, mass culture and, 334–336
Railroad Safety Appliance Act, 36
Railroads
cattle ranching and, 63
depression of 1890's and, 122
economic opportunities provided by, 64
expansion of, industrial impact of, 24–25
hijackings of, by protesting workers, 125
market control efforts by, 37
New South and, 48, 50
political ties to, 104
price declines and, 26–27
Pullman strike and, 125–129
strikes and (1877), 13–14
time zones and, 24
track gauge standardization for, 23
transcontinental system of, 22–25
unionization of, 274
western farming costs and, 61
western settlement and, 60–61
White Caps and, 111
working conditions on, 36
Rainbow Coalition, 729
Ranching in West, 62–64
Randolph, A. Philip, 347, 461–462
armed forces desegregation and, 560–561
Drug and Hospital Employees' Union strike and, *631*
George Meany and, 669
March on Washington and, 517
"March on Washington for Jobs and Freedom" and, 616–617
Rankin, Jeannette, 219, 271
Rap, 734
Raskob, John J., 415
Ray, James Earl, 651
Reagan, Ronald
administration of, 709–711
air traffic controllers strike and, 726–727
background of, 708
as conservative icon, 673
election of, 709
foreign policy problems of, 729–730
legacy of, 734–735
reelection of, 728–729
regional economic booms and, 711–715
Reaganomics, 710–711
problems with, 729
regional booms and, 711–715
unions and, 724
Recession
Ford and, 691
in 1990, 749
"Roosevelt," 473–475
Reconstruction, 1–10
African Americans in, 2
end of, 7–10
presidential, critics and, 3–5
Radical, 5–7
Reconstruction Act, passage of, 5–6
Reconstruction Finance Corporation (RFC), 382–383
Records, phonograph, mass culture and, 336
Recreation, public
African Americans and, 168
in early 20th century, 182
rural Americans and, 168
Redding, Otis, 646
Reese, James, 659
Reform(s)
ballot, 237–238
factory, 221–223
local, 234–237
spelling, 209–212
state, 234–237
Reformer(s)
cultural, 212
economic, 212
factory, 221–223
immigrants and, *215*
political, 212
sanitation, 215–216
social, 212
urban, socialists compared with, 235
Wilson as, 244–247
women, political influence of, 238–239
Rehnquist, William, 700, 730–731
Reich, Robert, 760, 770
Rein, Marcy, *771*
Relief program, national, launching of, 397
Religion
community and, 82–85
freedpeople and, 2
group tragedies based on, 777–778
labor unions and, 89–90

male groups based on, in 1990s, 776–777
presidential election of 1928 and, 361
Reno, Janet, 759, 778, 779
Republic Aviation, anti-Communist tactics of, 565
Republic Steel
massacre at, 465–466
resistance of, to unionizing, 465
Wagner Act challenged by, 432
Republican Party
African Americans and, after 1896, 140
Black Codes and, 4
black political participation and, 6–7
challenge to Clinton from, 765–769
collapse of, in South, 44
in 1894 congressional election, 136
immigration restrictions and, 148
industrial growth and, 21
in 1912 election, 208
Radical Republicans and, 4
workingmen and, 104, 106
Reservation policy, 55
Resettlement Administration, 400, 426
Resolution Trust Company, 731
Restrictive covenants, FHA and, 594
"Restrictive covenants" in suburbs in 1920s, 327
Retailing, new kinds of, in early 20th century, 181
Reuther, Walter
Alliance for Labor Action and, 671
in Americans for Democratic Action, 559–560
Communist-backed opponents denounced by, 566
as labor leader, 434
Mississippi delegation to 1964 Democratic National Convention and, 620
post-WWII agenda of, 530
Revenue Act of 1932, 382–383
Revenue Acts of 1916/1917, 273–274
Reynolds, Malvina, 593
Reynolds Tobacco Company, unionization of, 558
Rhodesia, revolution in, 696
Rhythm-and-blues, 600
Richmond, David, 612
Richmond and West Point Terminal Company, 48
Riesman, David, 593
Right-wing mobilization against New Deal, 463–464
Rio Pact, 555
Riots, race, post-WWI, 305
Rivera, Diego, 453
Rivers, L. Mendel, 574
Robertson, Pat, 703–704, 733
Robinson, Bill, 352
Robinson, Jackie, 586
Robots, fictionalization of, in 1950s, *569*
Rochester (NH), labor ticket in 1886 elections in, 105
Rock Springs (WY), anti-Chinese violence in, 67
Rock-and-roll, cultural impact of, 600–601
Rockefeller, John D., 38–39, 43, 75, 232
Rockefeller Center, murals for, 453
Roe v. Wade, 656, 665
antiabortion protests over, 704
Roebuck, Alvah C., 181
Rogers, Nancy, 587
Rolling Stones, 646
"Rolling strike" strategy, *771*
Romania
Communist dictatorship overthrow in, 742–743
German invasion of, 486
Roosevelt, Eleanor, 393
in Americans for Democratic Action, 559–560
letters to, *394*
as political activist, 451
Roosevelt's "black cabinet" and, 460
women's movement of 1960s and, 662
Roosevelt, Franklin Delano (FDR)
African-American voters and, 436–437, *438*
Atlantic Charter and, 488
background on, 393
"black cabinet" of, 460
CIO and, 466–467
complementary initiatives of, in 1938, 473–474
court-packing plan of, 464
death of, 524
election of, 393
fireside chats of, 395
foreign aggression condemned by, 486
on foreign markets, 483
genocide and, 524
landslide victory of, 434–439
in mobilization of industry for war, 504
Neutrality Acts and, 488
New Deal of, 392–477. *See also* New Deal
organized labor revival and, 406
political transformation under, 476
recession associated with, 473–475
reelection of, in 1940, 489
"second bill of rights" of, 528
on Social Security Act, 428
on Soviet sphere of influence, 546
textile strike and, 414
Tuskegee Airmen established by, 502
on use of National Guard/army to evict strikers, 442
Wagner Act signed by, 432
woman appointees of, 451
on WPA wages, 426
at Yalta Conference, 527
Roosevelt, Theodore
background of, for reform, 239–240
as "Cyclone Assemblyman," 240
Latin America and, 154
national forest system, 240, *241*
in 1912 election, 208
as president, 240–242
as Progressive Party nominee, 244
progressivism and, 209
in Spanish-American-Cuban War, 151
spelling reform and, 210–211, 212
as "Trustbuster," 240
as vice-president, 239
wartime nativism and, 294
Roosevelt Corollary to Monroe Doctrine, 154
Rosenberg, Julius and Ethel, 567
Rothstein, Arthur, 455
"Rough Riders" in Spanish-American-Cuban War, 151
Rubin, Jerry, *652,* 656
Rubin, Robert, 760, 762
Ruby, Jack, 619
Ruffing, Bob, 501
Rural Americans
increase in, in Great Depression, 386–387
public recreation and, 168
Rural Electrification Administration, 402
Russian Revolution, 298–299
"Rustbelt," 694
Ruth, Babe, 337

Sacco, Nicola, 308
Sadat, Anwar, 696
St. Louis (MO), reform in, 236–237
Saint-Gaudens, Augustus, 121
Salesmen, mass-distribution system and, 194
Saloons
crusades against, 87–88
in working class culture, 85–88
Salvation Army, 84
San Francisco (CA)
1934 general strike in, *410,* 411–412, 464
building tradesmen and, 107
gay scene in, 707
Harvey Milk assassination in, 707
Sandino, Augusto, 696
Sandoz, Mari, 62
Sanger, Margaret, 231
Sanitation reformers, 215–216

Sante Fe Railroad, White Caps and, 111
Saroyan, William, 457
Savings and loan scandal, 731
Savio, Mario, 642
"Scalawags," 6
Scalia, Antonin, 731
Schecter v. United States, 419
Schlafly, Phyllis, 700, 706
Schlesinger, Arthur, 676
Schools
  failure to integrate after *Brown* case, 608–609
  freedpeople and, 2, 7
  Ocean Hill-Brownsville fight in 1968 and, 670
  racial balance in, busing to achieve, 701
Schumpeter, Joseph, 689
Schurz, Carl, 57
Schwerner, Michael, 619–620
Scientific management, 170–173
  Ford and, 198
  skilled workers and, 172
Scopes, John T., 356
Scopes trial, 355–356
Scots immigrants. *See also* British Americans
Scott, Thomas A., 39
Scottsboro case, 375–376
Screen Actors Guild, building of, 457
Seaman's Act of 1915, 246
Sears, Richard, 181
Sears, Roebuck and Co.
  growth of, 157
  layoffs in, in 1990s, 749
  manufacturing plants of, 182
  turnover and, 181
Seattle General Strike, 301–302
Seattle (WA), protests against World Trade Organization in, *773,* 774
Secondary labor market
  growth of, flight from farming and, 581
  women in, 589
Securities Acts of 1933 and 1934, 396–397
Securities and Exchange Commission, establishment of, 397
Sedition Act (1918), 272
Segregation
  Brown v. Board of Education and, 608
  de facto, 139
  de jure, beginnings of, 139
  in federal service in early 1900s, 244–245
  George Wallace and, 652–653
  Jim Crow laws and, 140
  Orville Faubus and, 609
  of troops in WWI, 295–296
Selassie, Haile, 484–485
Selective Service System, 504
  in Vietnam War, 637
Self-employment, industrialization and, 27
Semiskilled workers
  assembly line work and, 199
  immigrants in 1880s-1890s as, 144–146
  Taylorism and, 172
Senate Foreign Relations Committee, 555
"Separate but equal," 139
Serbia, 761–762
  WWI and, 260
Sergeant York, 490
Service Employees International Union (SEIU), 770, *771*
Service sector growth after WWII, 586–590
  influx of women into workforce and, 588
Servicemen's Readjustment Act, 591
Settlement houses in Progressive Era, 213–216
Seventeenth Amendment, 237
Sewing machine, impact of, 81
Sexual harassment
  Thomas confirmation battle and, 775
  in workplace in early 1900s, 197
Shakespeare, Federal Theatre Project and, 457
"Share Our Wealth Plan," 417
Sharecroppers' Union (SCU), 389, *390*
Sharecropping
  Agricultural Adjustment Act and, 399–400
  black agricultural labor and, 7
  economic dependence and, 51–54
Shaw, Irwin, 457
Sheppard-Towner Maternity and Infancy Protection Act of 1921, 341
Sherman Antitrust Act (1890), 46, 158
  first use of, 240
Sherrod, Charles, 614–615
Sherwood, William, 564
Shop stewards, 445
Sierra Club, transformation of, 658
Silent Spring, 658
Silicon Valley, 756
Silkwood, Karen, 659–660
Silver as exchange medium, 136–137
Silver mining, 65
Simon, Kate, 337
Simpson, O. J., 776
Simpson, "Sockless" Jerry, 130
Sinclair, Upton, 210, 418
Singer Sewing Machine Company
  overseas expansion of, 150
  production for military, 686–687
Sioux Rebellion, 54
Siqueiros, David Alvara, 453
Sirhan Sirhan, 651
Sirica, John, 674–675
Sissle, Noble, 352
Sit-down strike(s)
  at Firestone, *434*
  in Flint, 439–443
  U.S. Supreme Court on, 490
"Sit-ins" in civil rights movement, 612–613
Sitting Bull
  death of, 59
  on white settlers, 54–55
Sixteenth Amendment
  federal income tax and, 273–274
  ratification of, 242
Sixties, 606–676
  antiwar movement in, 640–645
  Black Power in, 628–630
  civil rights movement in, 608–617. *See also* Civil Rights Movement
  counterculture in, 645–649. *See also* Counterculture
  environmental movement in, 657–660
  Kennedy administration in, 617–618
  labor movement in, 667–671
  liberal programs in, 618–622
  New Left in, 641–645
  pluralism in American life and, 660–662
  political polarization in, 671–674
  race riots in, 626–630
  rights consciousness in workplace in, 630–633
  Vietnam War in, 633–645. *See also* Vietnam War
  War on Poverty in, 622–625
  women's movement in, 662–667
Skilled workers
  AFL and, 106–107
  early 20th century, standard of living of, 176–177
  Homestead incident and, 112–114
  industrial growth at turn of century and, 158, 160
  Knights of Labor and, 89, 91, 105
  late-19th-century, status of, 32–33
  post-WWI steel strike and, 305
  Republican Party and, in 1896 elections, 138
  scientific management and, 172
  in Silicon Valley, 756
  Taylorism and, 172
  UMWA and, 108–109
  wage trends in 1920s for, 325
Sloan, Alfred P., Jr., 330, 331, 415, 439, 530

Small business ownership, industrialization and, 27
Smith, Alfred E., 227, 319, 360, 381, 415
Smith, Ellison DuRant ("Cotton Ed"), 322, 468
Smith, Frank, 303
Smith, George A., 123
Smith, Howard, 472
Smith, Jess W., 317
Smith, Willie "The Lion," 387
Smith-Connally War Labor Disputes Act, 522
Smoot-Hawley Tariff, 370
Social Conservation and Domestic Allotment Act, 475
Social Darwinism, 75
  acquisitive individualism versus, 161
  public assistance and, 124
Social reformers, 212
Social Security Act, 427–429
  coverage broadened under, 569
  racial coding in, 429
  tax increase and, Roosevelt Recession and, 473
  women and, 451
Social settlements in Progressive Era, 213–216
Social stratification, industrialization and, 27
Socialism, National, 485. *See also* Nazism
Socialist Labor Party, 228
Socialists, 227–228
  demonstrations by unemployed organized by, in Great Depression, 388
  demonstrations in rural South and, in Great Depression, 389
  gains by, during WWI, 269
  local/state victories by (1910–11), 234
  Mexican-Americans in, 285
  in 1912 election, 208
  opposition to WWI, 268
  in organizing industrial unions, 433–434
  Southern Tenant Farmers' Union and, 400
  urban reformers compared with, 235
Sod house, *62*
Sojourner Truth housing project, 519
Solidarity in Poland, 742
Somalia, U.S. involvement in, 761
Somervell, Brehon, 505
South
  Democratic Party in
    in 1948 election, 561
    racism and, in early 1900s, 141–142
  farmer displacement in, after WWII, 581–582
  14th Amendment and, 5
  Goldwater vote and, 620
  independent white farmers in, struggle for economic self-sufficiency by, 110
  migration of African Americans out of, in WWI, 277–278
  minimum wage influenced by, 429
  New Deal in, 402–403
    defeat of, 467–469
  New South, 47–50
  Operation Dixie and, 558–559
  power of, in U.S. Congress, 437
    in 1948, 561
    in 1930s, 437
  rural
    communist/socialist demonstrations in, in Great Depression, 389
    exodus from, during WWII, 506
  Sunbelt in
    business relocation to, 688–689
    cities in, growth of, 725
South Africa, liberation of, 747
South Carolina, martial law in, 9
Southeast Asia Treaty Organization, 555
Southern Christian Leadership Conference (SCLC)
  in Birmingham civil rights protests, 616
  Chicago campaign of, 628
"Southern Manifesto," 609
Southern Tenant Farmers' Union (STFU), 399–400
Southwestern Railroad, union victory over, 91
Soviet Union
  Afghanistan invasion by, 697
  Afghanistan withdrawal and, 746–747
  breakup of, *743,* 744
  collapse of, 742
  Cuban missile crisis and, 634
  espionage activities involving, 562, 567
  in European Theater, 495
  German invasion of, 486
  Kennan on, 548, 745
  and Nazis, nonaggression pact between, 486
  postwar relationship with, atomic bomb and, 528
  post-WWII sphere of influence on, 546
Spain, Francisco Franco in, 485
Spanish-American-Cuban War, 149–152
Sparkman, John, 568
Sparks-Harrell Company, 63
Spelling reform, 209–212
Spelling Reform Association, 210
Spider-Web Chart, 307
Spies, August, 98, 100
Spock, Benjamin, 656
Spoils system, 44
Sports, spectator, 188
Sputnik, 569
Stagflation, 685
  politics and, 690–695
Stalin, Joseph
  death of, 568
  nonaggression pact with, broken by Hitler, 486
  in post-war Soviet Union, 546
  at Potsdam, 528
  at Yalta Conference, 527
Stalingrad, Battle of, 495
Standard Oil
  agitation against, 158
  alternative of, to New Deal vision, 475
  breakup of, 240
  market control strategies of, 38–39
  Missouri prosecution of, 237
  overseas expansion of, 156
  public criticism of, in early 20th century, 207
Standard(s) of living
  early 20th century, 175–177
  in 1920s, 325–326
  rise in
    in late 1990s, 773, *774*
    in 1940s and 1950s, 572
    in WWII, 506–507
Stanton, Elizabeth Cady, 11, 219
Starr, Kenneth, 779–781
State reform politics, 234–237
States Rights party, formation of, 561
Staunton (VA), government reform in, 235
Steel industry
  Carnegie and, 39, 41
  Homestead battles and, 112–113
  industrial unionism in, 444–445
  plant closures in, in 1980s, 683, 694–695, 724
  strikes in
    1946, 532
    post-WWI, 303–305
  unionization of
    African Americans and, 462
    resistance of, 465–466
Steel Workers Organizing Committee (SWOC), 445
  African Americans and, 462
  mass picket lines deployed by, 465
  wage increases negotiated by, 573–574
Steelworkers' Union, immigrant family and, *447*
Steffens, Lincoln, progressivism and, 210

Steinbeck, John, 378, 455
Stephens, Uriah, 90–91
Stevens, John L., 153
Stevens, Thaddeus, 4–5
Stevenson, Adlai, 562, 568
Stewart, Jimmy, 457
Stimson, Henry, 489, 490
Stirling, Mary, 94–95
Stock market crash
  1929, 361. *See also* Great Depression
  1987, 731
Stokes, Carl, 700
Stokes, Thomas, 392
Stone, Lucy, 219
Stonewall Inn Riot, 666, *667*
Stoves, cast-iron, impact of, 81
Strasberg, Lee, 457
Strategic Arms Limitation Treaty (SALT), 655, 695
Streetcars, electric, 178
Strike(s)
  coal miners, in 1943, 521–522
  in 1892, failure of, 114
  farm labor, in 1903, AFL and, 159
  in garment industry, 224–226
  in Great Depression, 408–414
  hate, 518–519
  at Homestead, PA, steel mill, 112–114
  Industrial Workers of the World and, during WWI, 291–292
  labor, unsuccessful, Knights of Labor and, 101–102
  Ludlow, 232–234
  in Minneapolis (1934), 409–411
  postwar wave of, 531–533
  post-WWI, 301–305
  railroad (1877), 13–14
  Reagan administration and, 726–727
  rolling, *771*
  sit-down
    at Firestone, *434*
    in Flint, 439–443
    U.S. Supreme Court on, 490
  sympathy, 108
  textile, in Lawrence, Massachusetts, 230–231
  in Toledo (1934), 409
  wildcat, 521, 578
  during WWI, 275
Strong, Josiah, 83
Student Nonviolent Coordinating Committee (SNCC), organization of, 612–613
Students for a Democratic Society (SDS), 641–643, 645
Suburbs
  development of, 591–595
  growth of, in 1920s, 327
  individualization of, 593–594
  married women and, 594
  social-class divisions and, 594–595
Sudentenland, German annexation of, 486
Suffrage
  restrictions on, 237–238
  woman, 219–221, 287–288
Sugar industry, Hawaiian annexation and, 153
Sullivan, John L., 186
Sumner, Charles, Black Codes and, 4
Sunbelt
  business relocation to, 688–689
  cities in, growth of, 725
Sunday, William Ashley, *355*
Sung, Kim Il, 554
Sununu, John, 757
Superhighway development, human cost of, 595
Supreme Court, U.S.
  child labor laws and, 223
  Clinton appointment to, 760
  injunctions against strikes and unions and, 129
  on Japanese American internment, 514–515
  labor reform and, 221–222
  packing of, Roosevelt's plan for, 464
  Reagan appointments to, 730–731
  on sit-down strikes, 490
  Standard Oil breakup and, 240
  Thomas appointed to, 775
Swaggart, Jimmy, 733
Swann v. Charlotte-Mecklenburg Board of Education, 656
Sweatshop system in garment industry, 224
Sweeney, John, 770
Swinton, John, 103–104
Systematic management, 41–43
Szumilyas, Steve, 683

Taft, Robert, 556, *557*
Taft, William Howard, 208, 242–243
Taft-Hartley Act, 556–557
Takoma (WA), anti-Chinese mob violence in, 67
Talmadge, Gene, 558
Tammany Hall
  1886 elections and, 106
  Factory Commission and, 227
  workingmen and, 104
Tarbell, Ida, 210, 240
Tax(es)
  income, federal, 273–274
    in Reagan era, 710
    revision of, in 1986, 729
  revolt against, 702–703
Taylor, Frederick Winslow, 170
Taylor, Myron, 444–445
Taylor, Nelson A., 324
"Taylorism," 170–173
  Ford and, 198
Teamsters. *See* International Brotherhood of Teamsters
Teamsters for a Democratic Union (TDU), 772
"Teapot Dome" scandal, 317
Telephone, 179
Television
  cultural impact of, 597–598
  feminist challenge to, 665
  in late 1980s, 733
  political polarization in 1960s and, 672
Teller Amendment, 151
Temporary National Economic Committee, 474
Tenant farmer. *See* Sharecropping
Tennessee Valley Authority (TVA), 402, *403*
  discriminatory policies of, 436
Terrorism, domestic, 778
Terry, Peggy, 506
Tet Offensive, *635,* 649–650
Texas, enclosure conflicts in, 111
Texas Alliance, 131
Textile manufacturing
  New South and, 48–49
  OSHA and, 660
  strikes in 1934 and, 413–414
Theater
  renaissance of, in New Deal, 457
  turn of century, 185, 187–188
Thomas, Clarence, 775
Thornburgh, Richard, 764
Three Mile Island, 688
Thurmond, Strom, 561
Tiananmen Square massacre, 745
Tilden, Samuel J., 44
Time zones, railroads and, 24
Title VII of 1964 Civil Rights Act, 621
  employment discrimination and, 630–631
Tobacco, New South and, 48
Tobin, Daniel, 432, 446
Toledo (OH), strike in (1934), 409, 412
Toomer, Jean, 352
Townsend, Francis, 418, 428, 435
Transit, urban, electric-powered, 178
Transport Workers' Union, anti-Communist purges in, 567
Treaty of Detroit, 577–578
Treaty of Paris, 152
Treaty of Versailles, repudiation of
  by Germany, 485
  by Italy, 484
Triangle Shirtwaist Company, fire at, 207
Triple Alliance, 252

Triple Entente, 252
Troops, American, in WWI, 295–297
Truman, Harry S.
  atomic bombing of Japan and, 526, 527
  background of, 524
  becomes president, 524
  defense spending and, 554–555
  end of WWII and, 524–525
  H-bomb development and, 552
  Korean War and, 554–555
  on post-war wages and prices, 532
  at Potsdam, 528
  reelection of, 561
  on Soviet sphere of influence, 546
  on Soviet Union, 548
  unions and, 534
Truman Doctrine, 549–550
Trumka, Richard, 770
Trump, Donald, 713
Turkey, surrender of, in WWI, 296
Turner, Bog Joe, 600
Turner, William, 79–80
Turnover, mass merchandising and, 181
Tuskegee Airmen, 502
Tuskegee Institute, founding of, 142
TVA. *See* Tennessee Valley Authority (TVA)
Twain, Mark, 75, 153
Typewriter, workplace changes and, 30
Tyson, Laura, 760

UAW. *See* United Automobile Workers (UAW)
UFO sightings, *549*
UMWA. *See* United Mine Workers of America (UMWA)
Underwood Tariff, 266
Unemployed Citizens' League, 387
Unemployed Councils, anti-eviction battles of, in Great Depression, 388–389
Unemployment
  black, race riots of 1960s and, 627
  in early 1930s, 368, 371–375
  female, in Great Depression, 372–373
  high, in 1980s, 694
  low, in late 1990s, 773
  marches against, in Great Depression, 387–388, 391–392
  in 1920s, 325
  in WWII, 505
Union(s). *See* Labor movement
Union Hall and Library Association, 89
Union (Loyal) Leagues, 5–6
Union Pacific Railroad
  Omaha politics and, 104
  union victory over, 91
Union party, formation of, 435
United Automobile Workers (UAW)
  agreement of, with General Motors, 576–577
  in Alliance for Labor Action, 671
  anti-Communist tactics of, 566
  anti-Wallace activities of, 653
  black activists and, 670
  Flint sit-down strike and, 440–443
  Japanese auto sales and, 724–725
  "March on Washington for Jobs and Freedom" and, 616–617
  pulled out of AFL-CIO, 671
  Reuther as head of, post-WWII agenda of, 530
  Students for a Democratic Society and, 641–642
  Vietnam War and, 671
  wage increases negotiated by, 573–574
  on Wagner Act, *430*
  women's demands and, 511
    victory of, in Ford Motor Company, 491
    wage increase an North American Aviation and, 492
United Automobile Workers' Union, creation of, 412
United Button, 157
United Electrical Workers
  anti-Communist purges in, 567
  denounced for Communist activities, 565
  James Carey, first president of, 408
  racial protest in North Canton, Ohio and, 519
United Farm Workers (UFW)
  national grape boycott by, 633
  in 1960s, 668–669
United Fruit Company, overseas expansion of, 156
United Labor Party in 1886 elections, 105
United Mine Workers of America (UMWA), 108–109, 770
  coal strike in 1902 and, Roosevelt and, 240
  health and pension fund for, 596
  health care benefits and pension rights and, 763–764
  industrial unionism and, 433
  Little Steel formula and, 521–522
    coal industry nationalization and, 303
  Mexican-Americans in, 285
  organizational strategy of, 232
  rebirth of, New Deal and, 405–406
  strike of, in 1922, 346
United Nations, Red China kept out of, 552
United Office and Professional Workers' Union, 449–450
United Parcel Service (UPS), strike victory against, 772
United States Steel Corporation
  CIO and, 433
  creation of, 157
  General Motors capitulation and, 444–445
  labor-management accord in, 576
  public criticism of, in early 20th century, 207
  shift work at, 170
  transformed to USX Corp., job losses and, 724
  union militants and, 448
  wage cut in, in Great Depression, 382
  wage increases at, 491
United Steel Workers (USW)
  Mine, Mill, and Smelter Workers' Union and, 559
  U.S. Steel-USX Corp. transformation and, 724
United Textile Workers' Union (UTW), textile strikes of 1934 and, 414
United We Stand, 758
Universal Negro Improvement Association (UNIA), 349–350
University of California at Berkeley, demonstrations at, in 1960s, 642
Unskilled workers
  assembly line work and, 199
  Democratic Party and, in 1896 elections, 138
  early 20th-century, standard of living of, 176
  immigrants in 1880s-1890s as, 144–146
  Knights of Labor and, 89, 91, 108
  late-19th century, working conditions of, 33
  Taylorism and, 172
  UMWA and, 108–109
  wage trends in 1920s for, 325
Uprising of the Twenty Thousand, 225
Uptown Chamber of Commerce, hiring of African Americans and, 461
Upward Bound, 623
Urban areas
  landscape of, early 20th century, 200–201
  racial violence in, in 1960s, 626–630
  "red-lining" in, 594
Urban League, union movement and, 461
Urban reformers, socialists compared with, 235
Urban transit, electric-powered, 178
Urban industrial life, emergence of, 27–32
U.S. Army, African Americans in, in WWII, 501

U.S. Bureau of Alcohol, Tobacco, and Firearms (ATF) in Waco standoff, 778
U.S. Bureau of Indian Affairs, 404
  destruction of village life and, 57–58
U.S. Bureau of Labor Statistics, 106
U.S. Bureau of Mines, 227
U.S. Chamber of Commerce, Landon and, 435
U.S. Civil Service Commission, Theodore Roosevelt on, 240
U.S. foreign policy
  League of Nations and, 319
  Marshall Plan in, 550
  neutrality in WWI in, 264–266
U.S. Leather, 157
U.S. military
  atomic bombing of Japan by, 526
    diplomatic aspects of, 528
  business interest in WWI, 264–266
  in European Theater in WWII, 495–496
  Great Britain and, cooperation between, in Pacific in WWII, 488–489
  involvement of, in WWI, debate over, 266–269
  in Pacific Theater in WWII, 493–495
  war declared on, by Germany, 493
  war on Japan declared by, 493
U.S. Navy, African Americans in, in WWII, 501
U.S.S. Maine, explosion aboard, 151
USX Corporation, formation of, 724
Utilities, public, public ownership of, 235

Valenti, Adriana, 191
Valentino, Rudolph, 337
Van Dusen, Larry, 378, 380
Vandenberg, Arthur, 549
Vanderbilt, Cornelius, 37
Vanzetti, Bartolomeo, 308
Vasquez, Carlos, 661
Vassar College's Experimental Theatre, 457
Vaudeville, 185–187
Versailles peace treaty, 300–301
Vertical integration, 38
  Andrew Carnegie and, 39
Veterans Administration, suburban development and, 592
Veterans' Bonus March, 391–392
Victory gardens in WWII, 504
Vietnam War, 633–645
  antiwar movement and, 640–645
  diplomatic reversals leading up to, 634
  escalation of, 636–640
  increasing confusion in, 638, 640
  international opposition to, 644
  military strategy in, 637–638
  morality of, debate on, 642–643
  My Lai massacre in, 638, 640
  New Left and, 641–645
  1968 and, 649–654
  rank-and-file workers and, 672
  road to, 633–636
  Tet Offensive in, *635*
  troop morale problems in, 644
  unions and, 670–671
  withdrawal from, 655
Viguerie, Richard, 700
Villa, Francisco "Pancho," 282–283
Violence against African Americans in late 19th century, 141–142
VISTA (Volunteers in Service to America), 623
Volcker, Paul, 694
Volunteers in Service to America (VISTA), 623
Vorse, Mary Heaton, 290
Voters' League of Pittsburgh, reform and, *236*
Voting
  decline in, from 1968 to 1988, 698–699
  by freedmen, 6
    return to conservative rule and, 8
  literacy requirements for, 237–238
  registration for, among blacks
    in 1940s, 558
    in 1960s, 615–616, 621
  in South, limited access to, 468
  by women in 1920s, 341
  by working class, reformers and, 235, 237–239
Voting Rights Act of 1965, 621

Waco (TX), Branch Davidian standoff in, 778
Wage(s), 33–34
  for child labor, 35
  Chrysler bailout and, 693–694
  cost-of-living adjustment and, 576–578
  cutting of, in 1980s, 725–726
  "family," union fights for, women and, 158–159
  fight over, during GM strike, 441
  gender disparity in, in early 1900s, 194–195
  in Great Depression, 386, 404–414
  Great uprising of 1877 and, 13
  inequity of, in 1920s, 325
  minimum, first, 429
  minimum, national, Fair Labor Standards Act and, 429
  in 1980s, 725–726
  post-Civil War, factors determining, 33–34
  post-WWII, 573–574
  "real"
    in Great Depression, 368
    in 1970s-1980s, 684
    post-Civil War, 34
    in WWII, 506–507
  southern, minimum wage and, 429
  WPA, 426
Wage-Earners' Suffrage League, 287
Wagner, Robert, 431, 474
  Factory Commission and, 227
Wagner Act, 431–432, 556
  UAW leaflet on, *430*
Wagner-Steagull Housing Act, 474–475
Waite, Davis, 134
Wald, Lillian D., 214, 223, 225
Walesa, Lech, 742
Wall Street crash of 1929, 367–368. *See also* Great Depression
Wallace, George, 652–653, 673
Wallace, Henry A., 395, 400, 524, 559–560
Wallace, Henry C., 318
Wal-Mart, 690
Walsh, Frank P., 246, 275
Walton, Sam, 690
Wanamaker, John, 46
War Industries Board, 273
War Labor Board, 275
  WWI, 275
  WWII, 504
    end to racial wage differentials ordered by, 516
    "equal pay for equal work" and, 510
    maintenance of union membership policy of, 521
War Manpower Commission, 504
  in Philadelphia transit system dispute, 518
  recruitment of women by, 507–508
War on Poverty, 619, 622–625
  structural changes in economy and, 625
War Production Board, 504
Warner, Charles Dudley, 75
Warren, Earl, 608, 619
Warsaw Pact, 551
Washington, Booker T., 142–144, 152
Washington, D.C., March on (1941), 517
Washington, D.C., March on (1963), 616–617
Washington Commonwealth Federation, 418
Washington Conference of 1921, 320
Watergate crisis, 674–676
Waters, Ethel, 352
Waters, Muddy, 600
Watson, Tom, 137, 139, 268
Watt, James, 710

Watts, race riots in, unemployment and, 627
Wausau (WI), Asian immigrants in, 718
Weathermen, 645
Weaver, James B., 134–135
Wehr Steel Foundry, strike to oust African-American coworkers in, 375
Weimar Republic, instability of, 485
Welfare
  Reaganomics and, 711
  recipients of, changing mood of, in 1960s, 624–625
  reform of, Clinton and, 767
Welfare capitalism
  in early 20th century, 172–174
  in Great Depression, 385–386
  National Civic Federation and, 160
Wells-Barnett, Ida B., 142, *143,* 218
Welsh immigrants. *See also* British Americans
West
  boom-and-bust industrial capitalism in, 65
  farming and ranching in, 60–64
  mining towns in, 65–66
  New Deal in, 403–404
  New Deal setback in, 468
  towns in, churches and, 83
  WWII and, 505
West, Mae, 354, 457
West Coast Defense Command on Japanese Americans in WWII, 512
Western Electric, overseas communication and, 320–321
Western Federation of Miners (WFM), 229–230
  Mexican-Americans in, 285
Western Front in WWI, 263
Westinghouse Electric Corporation, worker retention strategy of, in Great Depression, 371
WFM (Western Federation of Miners), 229–230
Wheat production in Plains, 61
"Whip Inflation Now" campaign, 691
White, Dan, 707
White, Harry Dexter, 562
White, William Allen, 46
White Caps, 110–111
White Citizens' Councils, 609
White City (Chicago), 121–122
White Motor Company, union leadership at, 407
White-collar workers
  "downsizing" and, 714, 749
  in early 1900s, 176–177, 192–194
  in 1980s-1990s, 720
  post-WWII increase in, 587
  Reagan revolution and, 713
  wage trends in 1920s for, 325
Whitewater investigation, 779
Whitman, Walt, 75
Wildcat strikes, 521, 578
Will, George
  in New Right, 700
  in Reagan era, 732
Willard, Frances E., 130
Willkie, Wendell, 489
Wilson, Charles E., 505, 569, 576–577
Wilson, William Julius, 722
Wilson, Woodrow
  on corporate capitalism, 208
  election of, 244
  federal income tax and, 273–274
  Fourteen Points of, 299–300
  government's economic role and, 246–247
  as invalid, 301
  labor and, 246–247
  Latin America and, 282
  League of Nations and, 301
  neutrality in WWI and, 264–266
  peacemaking efforts of, 269–270
  progressivism and, 209
  reelection of, 269–270
  reform agenda of, 244–247
  on union movement, 276
  vacillation of, on WWI, 269–271
  woman suffrage movement and, 287–288
  WWI peace plan of, 299–300
Wisconsin Steel, 683
Wobblies. *See* Industrial Workers of the World (IWW)
Wofford, Harris, 764
Wolfe, Tom, 713
Woman suffrage, 219–221
  WWI and, 287–288
Woman's Christian Temperance Union (WCTU), 87–88
  black women in, 217, 218
Women
  AFL unions and, 158–159
  black. *See* African Americans, female
  Centennial Exposition and, 11
  in Clinton cabinet, 759–760
  in Congress, increase in, 759
  consumer economy and, 168
  as consumers in 1920s, 338–342
  in domestic service, 196
  in early 20th century
    barriers to participation of, 201
    white-collar jobs for, 194
    working, 194–197
  "family wage" and, 158–159
  in Farmers' Alliance, 130, *131*
  as homesteaders, 62
  Knights of Labor and, 94–96
  married, suburbs and, 594
  New Deal and, 448–452
  in new unions, 448–452
  in nursing, 196
  political culture of, progressivism and, 216–219
  politics and, in late 1800s, 103
  in post-Civil War work force, 33, 34
  progressivism and, 209, 248
  protests of, against food prices, 290, *291*
  as reformers, communities of, 218–219
  rights movement by, in 1960s-1970s, 662–667
    reaction against, 672–673
  saloons and, 86
  in secondary labor market, 589
  settlement houses run by, 213–216
  temperance activities of, 87–88
  in unions in WWII, 511
  vaudeville and, 186
  in western mining towns, 66
  in workforce, *588*
    discrimination against, in Great Depression, 372–373
    middle- and working-class, 714
    in 1920s, 338–342
      cultural significance of, 341–342
      job types for, 340–341
      legal consequences of, 341
    during WWI, 286–288
    in WWII, 507–511
  working at home, 80–82
  working-class, woman suffrage and, 219–220
Women's Emergency Brigade, 442
Women's Equity Action League, 664–665
Women's liberation movement, 662–667
  reaction against, 672–673
Women's Peace Party, 268
Women's Political Council, *610*
Women's Trade Union League (WTUL)
  garment workers strike and, 225–226
  woman suffrage and, 220
Wood, Robert, 489
Woodstock rock festival, 657
Woodward, Bob, 675
Woodward, Charlotte, 288
Woolworth
  foreign expansion of, 320
  lunch counter "sit-in" at, 612
  mass merchandising by, 181
  sit down strike at, 449
Work, Hubert, 359
Work relief programs, emergency, in Great Depression, 397–398

Index

Working class
antiwar sentiment in, counteracting, 293
assembly line work and, 198–200
children in, 34–35
convicts in, 227
cultural lives of, efforts to uplift, 189
early 20th century
barriers to participation of, 201
women in, 194–197
empowerment of, impact of, 446–449
farm labor, UFW grape boycott and, 631–633
fringe benefits for, working class division and, 596
immigrants in, 30–31, 32
industrial capitalism and, 69, 75–117
mass production and, 170
in mining, exploitation of, 65
in New South, 49–50
1920s celebrities from, 337
political power of, reformers and, 235, 237–239
politics and, 103–106
productivity of, management control of, 41–43
progressive legislation and, 248
in progressive reform struggles, 247
protest marches by
in 1894, 124–125
in 1930s, 387–392
during WWI, 288–292
radicalization of, 644
remaking of, 32–35
rights consciousness in, 630–633
in 1970s, 687
semiskilled, Taylorism and, 172
skilled, 32–33
scientific management and, 172
Taylorism and, 172
splintering of, 596–597
standards of living among, in early 20th century, 176–177
suburbs and, post-WWII, 593–594
teenagers in, in 1970s and 1980s, 714–715
trade unions emerge out of, 88–90
unskilled, 33
Taylorism and, 172
upsurge of, 1933–34, 405
urban
consumer economy and, 168
neighborhood cultures of, 76–80
as voters, reformers and, 235, 237–239
wages for, 33–34
wartime gains for, 274–276
in western mining towns, diversity of, 66–68
white-collar
layoffs of, in 1980s, 714
middle-class values and, 192–194
women in, 34, *588*
in 1920s, 338–342
during WWI, 286–288
in WWII, 507–511
Workingmen's Party in 1886 elections, 105
Works Progress Administration (WPA), 426–427
African Americans and, 437
Federal Art Project of, 453–454
Federal Music Project of, 454–455
Federal Theatre Project of, 457
Federal Writers Project of, 454
layoffs by, Roosevelt Recession and, 473
photojournalism and, 455
women and, 451
World Trade Organization (WTO), protests against, *773, 774*
World War I (WWI), 259–309
American business and, 264–266
American involvement in, debate over, 266–269
American neutrality in, 264–266
American troops in, 295–297
battles fought by American troops in, 295–297
Congressional declaration of war in, 271
great migration and, 276–282
labor gains during, 274–276
mobilizing home front ion, 271–274
nativism and, 292–294
peace treaty for, 300–301
political radicalism and, 288–292
race riots after, 305
red scare after, 305–308
repression and, 292–294
Russian Revolution and, 298–299
southern border tension and, 282–286
strikes after, 301–305
as total war, 263–264
working-class protest during, 288–292
World War II (WWII), 483–537
aerial bombardment of German industry in, 496
African Americans in, 501–503
American Indians in, 503
civil rights movement in, origins of, 515–520
Depression ended by, 503
economic boom after, 570–575
in Europe, 495–496
fascism preceding, 483–486
Germany's surrender in, 525
homosexuality and, 501
industrial boom during, 505–507
internationalism and, 487–490
isolationism and, 486–487, 489
Japan's surrender in, 525–528
labor policy in, 520–522
life in armed forces in, 496–503
Mexican Americans in, 503
militarism preceding, 483–486
mobilizing home front in, 503–505
in Pacific, 493–495
pluralism in, limits of, 511–515
progressive redistribution of American wealth and, 507
return to peacetime economy after, 528–535
"second front" in, 495–496
victory in Europe, 522–525
West and, 505
women in workforce, 507–511
World Wide Web, 754–755
Wounded Knee (SD)
massacre at, 59, *60*
Oglala Sioux protest at, *661,* 662
Wovoka, 58–59
Wozniak, Steve, 755
WPA. *See* Works Progress (Projects) Administration (WPA)
Writers Project, Federal, 454
WTUL. *See* Women's Trade Union League (WTUL)
Wyatt, Jane, 598

XIT Ranch, 63

Yalta Conference, 527
"Yellow-dog" contracts, 346
Yeltsin, Boris, 744
Yippies, *648*
in Democratic National Convention protest, *652*
Young, Andrew, 692
Young, Coleman, 567, 700
Young, Robert, 598
Young Americans for Freedom, 673
Young Lords, 661
Young Men's Christian Association (YMCA), 84
Youngstown Sheet and Tube Company, 276–277, 407
resistance of, to unionizing, 465

Zedong, Mao, 551
Zimbabwe, 696
Zimmermann, Arthur, 270